GUIDE TO BRITAIN'S
BEST HOTELS

Passport's

GUIDE TO BRITAIN'S
BEST HOTELS

Including Scotland, Wales, & the Channel Islands

EDITED BY
Patricia Yates

PASSPORT BOOKS
a division of *NTC Publishing Group*
Lincolnwood, Illinois USA

This edition first published in 1997 by Passport Books,
a division of NTC Publishing Group, 4255 West Touhy Avenue,
Lincolnwood (Chicago), Illinois 60646-1975 USA.

Published in association with
Which? Ltd., 2 Marylebone Road,
London NW1 4DF
Great Britain

Cover illustration by Dick Vine

Base mapping © Map Marketing Ltd.
European Map Graphics 1997
Map information © Which? Ltd., 1997

ISBN 0-8442-4871-1
Library of Congress Catalog Card Number on file

Photoset by Tradespools Ltd, Frome, Somerset
Printed and bound in Great Britain by
Clays Ltd, St Ives plc, Bungay, Suffolk

Passport's Guide to Britain's Best
Hotels (The Which? Hotel Guide)

Contents

Introduction

Welcome to the seventh *Which? Hotel Guide,* packed with hotels that we are delighted to recommend, where old favourites rub shoulders with new stars and good B&Bs shine alongside the best of Britain's country-house hotels. With our customary energy and enthusiasm we have scoured the country, checking that the hotels that appeared in previous editions are living up to their capabilities and not resting on their laurels, and searching out new establishments, perhaps with the help of readers' recommendations. For this is a hotel guide set apart from all the others. The *Guide* is published by Consumers' Association, has its own team of independent inspectors and is written by consumers for consumers. There are no hidden deals with hotels or hoteliers, hoteliers do not pay for their entries, nor do they see them before publication. The *Guide*'s independence means that we can give a fair and accurate description of hotels that we recommend – and point out some of the hiccups that should be sorted out.

Choosing a good hotel – like playing the lottery?

In its report, *Hotels: The Consumer View* (published in November 1995), the Department of National Heritage (DNH) found that more consumers would like to stay at independently run accommodation if they could be assured of standards: leisure travellers in particular like to choose their accommodation on the basis of 'a reliable (preferably independent) description of the character of the establishment.' Well, here is their answer. To help consumers pick out the places that we recommend and avoid the risk of a disappointing stay, we have decided that main entries in this edition of *The Which? Hotel Guide* will be allowed to mention this fact in brochures and advertisements for the first time ever. We will send hoteliers an official sticker to display, which will be clearly dated, and valid for the life of this *Guide*.

The DNH and the tourist boards have been very busy this year trying to address the problems of high levels of consumer dissatisfaction with some of Britain's budget accommodation and the need to make the Crown grading system for hotels more indicative of quality and therefore more informative to consumers. In writing this introduction it is saddening to be unable to report a happy conclusion to the current review of the Crown grading system. This review seems to have been going on for ever, with leaks suggesting that securing agreement between the English, Welsh and Scottish tourist boards to ensure a nationwide hotel grading system has proved more difficult than anyone had envisaged. There are hopes that a new scheme will be up and running for the 1997 season, but at present they look like high hopes indeed. In the meantime, hoteliers are forced to pay to join the discredited Crown scheme if they wish to be promoted in the tourist boards' brochures. Not surprisingly, many of the good and popular places are withdrawing from the scheme, leaving tourist boards supplying consumers with an incomplete listing. This is a great shame, and no advertisement for British tourism.

What consumers want: it's official

The DNH is to be commended, though, for the amount of work it has done in looking at what consumers want from hotels and then putting this research to practical use by assessing how well a group of 70 small hotels met these standards in a benchmarking exercise. The common standards that consumers felt must be present were found to be (in order of importance):

* high standards of cleanliness throughout the accommodation
* attentive and efficient staff
* a high-quality and well-maintained bathroom with good fittings
* a high-quality bed, mattress and fittings
* a quiet bedroom with no disturbances
* an attractive and pleasant bedroom
* lighting in the room and at the bedside good enough to read by
* a well-furnished bedroom: mirror, chairs, etc.
* prompt and efficient check-in/out
* an efficient and easy booking service.

No surprises there – but the hotels' performance was very uneven, with wide variations in standards between the hotels and with the weakest ratings on overall standards of cleanliness and quality of bathrooms – two of the consumers' top three requirements. Impossible, surely? Well, just look at the horrors from this year's postbag to us.

* 'The shower was so clogged up that about three streams of water came out which were either freezing or boiling – literally, you couldn't even get wet!' *Gloucestershire hotel*
* 'There was hair and other residue on the floor, dust on the ledges.' *Northamptonshire hotel*
* 'When you stood on it, the shower sagged underfoot. More water came out of the screws to the flexible pipe than from the spray.' *Staffordshire hotel*
* 'There was considerable mildew in the shower-room – and lots at the bottom of the shower.' *Oxfordshire hotel*
* 'My husband found evidence that the room was not cleaned properly – a toenail in the carpet. The cheapest fittings had been used throughout, with an untrimmed piece of spare carpet sufficing as a bathmat.' *Cornish hotel*
* 'The bath had to be set running at least two hours before breakfast to enable the trickle to provide some semblance of adequate bath water.' *Shropshire hotel*

Personally, I rather treasure the moment of handing over a pair of men's red underpants found under the bed at one particularly supercilious establishment. And our inspectors too weigh in with stories of hairs in the bed and the bath and rings around the bath that you can feel once you're in. 'Usually occurs in places that don't provide bubblebath,' commented one disgusted inspector. 'I don't mind not having foam but I wish they would make sure that they clean the bath properly.'

The star horror story has to go to one inspector who found herself covered in what looked suspiciously like flea bites after sleeping at one expensive establishment. The managerial response to her embarrassed complaint was to say that they would need a signed doctor's note before they would consider a discount on the bill.

The DNH suggests po-facedly that one of the main reasons for the disappointing performance was the failure to introduce standard procedures – or even a simple checklist for the staff at many establishments. While I'm not a great lover of procedure manuals (except as cures for insomnia) even a short list for chambermaids should surely include '*clean the bath*'. I liked the attitude of one hotelier when I asked how she kept standards up. 'I nag,' she said, 'and neither my husband nor I are afraid of emptying the ashtrays.'

'*I like people who look you in the eye and smile*'

One of the stars of the government benchmarking system was the Seaview Hotel on the Isle of Wight. I know how popular it is with readers, but I had never stayed there myself, so, full of curiosity, I nipped over for a weekend break. I came away thinking how much Nicola and Nick Hayward deserved that top rating, and what a pleasure it is to find a hotel where good service is part of the staff mentality, not just with the front of house staff but everyone we met. They all had the knack of anticipating what customers might like as well as responding to requests – and gave the impression they were enjoying themselves while they were at it. I had given them a good test by taking along my 4- and 2-year-old boys and unfortunately by having an accident with a bottle of shampoo on the bed cover (about which I am still crimson-faced) – and the stay was pure pleasure, relaxed and relaxing.

How do they do it? First of all, they clearly have a very hands-on managerial style. Nick is on reception taking people to their rooms and carrying bags (gold star!) and offering helpful advice to first-timers. Nicola greets diners and takes orders, and they both muck in serving on busy Saturday nights. Speaking on the phone to Nicola some weeks later (and, no, I hadn't been rumbled), I was curious to know whether the successful formula was training or picking the right people. And of course it's clearly both. 'I reckon you can tell a lot at interview,' commented Nicola. 'I like people who look you in the eye and smile. You've got to take on staff who are going to enjoy looking after people. We see many applicants with marvellous qualifications but they don't enjoy fussing over people and aren't going to get pleasure out of the job.' Nicola also comments that if you take pride in your professionalism there is no need for the pretentiousness that many hoteliers hide behind. And that professionalism enables the Haywards to entertain all comers of whatever age, however dressed, and to create a relaxing hotel where people are clearly enjoying themselves.

'*Breakfast? You've missed it*'

I might also commend to hoteliers the Haywards' relaxed attitude over breakfast: 'It doesn't matter if you're a few minutes late,' we were told on arrival. Contrast that with (horrors) the man who scraped into breakfast five minutes late on the day the clocks went back. 'I'm not a hotelier,' he writes, but what is supposed to happen is this: you smile politely at the customer and say, "I'm sorry, but we really have passed the deadline for hot food. Would you like coffee or tea with some cereal or toast? How about some fruit?" And so on.

'What happened was that a waitress showed up at the table and said we were late and we could have some coffee in the lounge. I got up and said she was absolutely right, and, duly put in our place in front of the guests, we filed out. We hadn't got far before the owner was shouting after us telling us that we were late and he didn't expect anyone would stay in bed so long, especially on the clocks-back night/morning, but he had decided to let us sleep rather than call and remind us about breakfast. I kept saying he was absolutely right. I expect you remember the expression "the hotelier is always right". I have never packed so fast in my life – and I pack a lot.'

To cap that unnecessary encounter, here is a story from a couple who stayed for dinner at a different establishment. 'We asked for duck and requested that the duck be cooked pink. The exact reply was a sarcastic "Does duck come any other way?" followed by "I wouldn't presume to tell the chef how to cook."

'In the British tradition we sat uncomfortably through the meal. The duck, incidentally, was not pink when it arrived, but we made no comment. I noted that we were not singled out for contempt as the owner never smiled and was curt to almost every table during the evening. We did ask one member of her staff if she was rude to her employees as well and the reply was that "it was usually just customers but sometimes staff, depending on her mood".'

Which perhaps leads one to the conclusion that it is not just the staff of hotels who need to be 'people people', but there are some hoteliers who could have done with psychometric testing before making their career choice.

It's good to talk

It's clear that many hoteliers manage to rule themselves out of the running by their attitude even before you have arrived. As well as clear information, clearly imparted, consumers are naturally trying to get a feel of the hotel's character when they first contact the hotel. One reader wishing to book a stay for his parents wrote to tell us of his experience. 'Whilst explaining the reason for my wanting to book the visit (my parents had stayed here for their honeymoon 37 years ago), I was told by the owner: "There is no need to get pally, just tell me what you want." She then proceeded to tell me how tough times were and how if I wasn't going to book a whole weekend all-inclusive, then there was absolutely nothing she could do for me. Unacceptable behaviour for anyone, for someone in the service industry unbelievably inept behaviour, but for someone who professes to run a friendly hotel – beyond belief.'

Need I add that no booking was made? The same was the case with another reader whose husband smokes. 'I asked if smoking was allowed in the bedrooms (which according to the tariff it is) and was subjected to a Spanish inquisition regarding the exact number of cigarettes smoked, the anti-social behaviour of it and how much we smelt – at which point I put the phone down. I was most upset by the personal comments made (I don't even smoke myself).'

And you would be surprised at the number of letters we get from readers who think that they are being quoted per room – and then discover that it is per person when the bill arrives (or even realised that they never asked, and were never told, a price). (Just a reminder – all the prices quoted in our *Guide* are per room.) Or from readers who turn up at hotels to find that the hotel was expecting them on a different date. In fact, one couple found this a positive blessing. Their arrival was spoilt by the 'somewhat supercilious young man who appeared and regarded our car and possibly us to boot with an air that *if* we had been in a Rolls, he would actually have tried a smile of welcome...But we were *not* and he did *not*... we would *not* go there again.' And presumably the hotel thinks that the young man is meeting and greeting, rather than visibly working out whether guests can afford to stay there.

Dressing for the occasion

An indignant phone call from one of the *Guide* inspectors started a lively discussion in our office about dress codes and their enforcement. Arriving besuited and briefcased during the cocktail hour for his anonymous stay at a Scottish hotel, he popped his head round the door of the lounge to see residents gathering, casually dressed, some in rugby shirts. Nipping up to his room to do the five-minute change perfected by any aspiring hotel inspector he re-entered the lounge in fresh shirt and a smart pair of jeans (no patches or punk accoutrements.) 'Oh, we don't allow jeans in the dining-room,' boomed mine hostess, balancing the drinks tray and wasting no time on pleasantries or discretion. Somewhat pink-faced (even hotel inspectors have feelings), our man asked why rugby shirts were permitted. 'Oh, no problem with those – they've got collars.'

Whatever the hotel's policy, is this any way to treat a guest, or indeed a fellow human being? As you can imagine, dinner (in an acceptable outfit) was not the most enjoyable of occasions. Women have a clear advantage here. I have never yet been socially shrivelled for not turning up with a jacket, tie, shirt with a collar, and even meeting the sartorial codes of pubs round our London offices – 'no bare chests or vests' – has not proved too taxing.

My first question to hoteliers would be: is a dress code really necessary? Can't you trust your guests to rise to the occasion and wear something appropriate? Eating in a room with men without jackets (or even ties) does not give me the horrors – and if for five days a week you are in the same uniform – pin-striped suit, white shirt and tie – a weekend away means a chance to relax in dress style, too. Hotels which apply no dress code don't seem to upset the more traditionally attired and have a certain relaxed air that I enjoy.

If hoteliers think that guests will resort to anarchy if allowed to choose their own clothes, perhaps they could at least let male guests know what they are in for at the time of booking. 'I'd just like to fit in,' commented one probably typical mild-mannered male. 'Even if the hotel overlooks the fact that I haven't got a jacket, I am going to feel uncomfortable as the odd one out in the restaurant.'

Hoteliers could of course do what some of the larger London hotels do and provide an array of ghastly kipper ties and six 36-inch-chest jackets with genuine '70s lapels for the incorrectly attired. One colleague told the tale of her well-built male friend suffering through a lunch in his borrowed jacket and finally losing his cool when he found it was so tight that he couldn't actually bend his elbows to cut his meat. Calling the waiter over, he asked if he could remove the monstrosity now that he was sitting down. 'Absolutely not, sir.' The hotel might think they had won, but I would guess our miserable diner stood out far more than if he had just been allowed to slip in wearing his own clothes.

One plea to the starchiest of hoteliers: if you have a rigid dress policy, rigidly enforced, spare a thought for the reluctant code breaker. If the preferred option for enforcement is public humiliation, perhaps prison-governing would be a better career choice than hotel-keeping. For my own part, I find hotel dress codes anachronistic and arrogant and would do away with the lot of them.

Cancellations and deposits

One of the running sores among readers' letters is the issue of cancellation charges and lost deposits. A fairly typical story concerned one reader who booked a special weekend away for her parents' wedding anniversary giving a credit card number as guarantee of the booking. A whole six weeks beforehand, one parent became ill and they had to cancel the booking with the promise that they would try to rearrange the weekend when in better health.They were amazed when the hotelier said that naturally they would lose their deposit and she hoped they were insured.

What the hotelier did is perfectly legal. In fact, hoteliers can do more than simply keep the deposit. If you make a booking you have entered into a contract with the hotelier. If you then decide to break that contract, although the hotelier must try to re-let your rooms, if he (or she) cannot he can demand that you make good the lost profit, which may be a high proportion of the room rate. And if he has your credit card number he can do this without your prior agreement.

You can see the hoteliers' side. They are trying to run a business on narrow margins and a couple of no-shows can wipe out the weekend's profits. So while we would hope that hoteliers would show a little humanity – after all, that might be good for business too – consumers need to understand that we have obligations as well as rights in our dealings with hoteliers. (You can find more about your rights and responsibilities in hotels on page 16.)

Money, money, money

Perhaps the most unwelcome surprise to cross our desks in the past year has been the Alton Towers Hotel booking conditions. The hotel requires a ten per cent deposit on booking and payment no later than 30 days before guests arrive at the hotel. Now this may be common practice if you're booking a package holiday, but Alton Towers is a newcomer in the hotel business. In these days when credit cards are commonly used to guarantee bookings, payment *in full* so far in advance looks like a good way of improving the cash flow – and can that be necessary when charging around £100 a room? Our lawyers also raised their eyebrows at the cancellation terms. Just look at this: 'However, if you cancel within 30 days of your scheduled arrival date (or simply fail to arrive) and we are unable to re-let the accommodation booked by you, we reserve the right (in our absolute discretion) to retain any deposit paid by you and charge you the balance of the total cost of the booked stay. If you have used a credit card to make your booking, this balance will be debited against such a card.' That looks to us like rather more than the loss of profit to which the hotel is entitled. We think this clause simply would not stand up in court – and have written to the Alton Towers Hotel to point this out.

News for disabled guests

At the back of the book (on page 659) we have listed hotels which say their rooms and facilities are suitable for wheelchair users. As we went to press there was much debate about the new Disability Discrimination Act and the effect that will have on hoteliers. What is clear is that by the end of this year (1996) hotels that offer an inferior level of service to disabled customers will be breaking the law – so, for example, a hotelier will not be able to sit someone with a facial disfigurement out of view of the rest of the guests, or serve dinner only in the bedroom to a guest who has difficulty eating (unless, of course, this is what the guest wishes). Hoteliers will be legally liable for the attitude of their staff. In the longer term – and the debate is of course how long this will take and how expensive it will be – hotels will need to provide equipment and remove physical obstructions (such as widening entrance doors) to enable disabled people to use the hotel.

Perhaps a salutary point for us all is made in a Mencap report which found that 16 per cent of its members said they had suffered discrimination while on holiday, particularly from other non-disabled holidaymakers.

Competition results

Last year's competition for accounts of good and bad service in hotels was encouraging in that we received far more tales of smiling service than sneering disdain. Many thanks to all of you who wrote to us.

The first prize of £50 goes to Barry Coleman of Daventry for his tale of woe about how he was treated when late for breakfast (see 'Breakfast? You've missed it' above).

The five runners up who each receive £10 are Ann Evans of Oxford, who wrote to praise the staff of a Bath hotel during a convalescent visit; Maggie Jackson of Croydon, whose hotelier in Cornwall rang the newsagent at 10pm to place an order for her favourite newspaper; Lesley Clare of Gullane, who had nothing but praise for the restaurant staff of a Yorkshire hotel; Ian MacBey of London SW6, whose Jersey hotel kept the dining-room open for him when he arrived late, and parked the car and took his bags to his room while he dined; and Sally Kibble of Ipswich, whose London hotel rang to say that they had given her room to someone else as she had failed to give them her credit card number.

And finally

We do urge readers to write in with their reports on hotels in the *Guide*, whether good or bad. We do read and acknowledge every letter and they highlight areas that we need to check during our inspections as well as feed into entries in the next edition. There are report forms at the back of the book that can be sent Freepost, or for those who are linked to the Internet just send us an e-mail ("guidereports@which.co.uk"). You don't need to write pages – just a few short paragraphs will be of help.

We welcome all readers' recommendations, and while we see no point in lowering our standards to include establishments that are simply 'the best available' – inevitably, we get complaints from readers who have trusted our judgement – but recommendations that plug a gap on our maps are doubly welcome. So if you are outraged that there are no main entries in the *Guide* for Liverpool, Cambridge or Aberdeen, for example, and have managed to find somewhere that fits the bill, let us know.

Thank you to all our many correspondents over the year – your letters prove that the art of storytelling is not dead. Thanks too to Michael Diffley, who has survived his baptism of fire running the *Guide* database with humour intact.

Patricia Yates
Editor

Patricia Yates.

County hotels of the year

Here is our pick of hotels for this edition. They are not necessarily the most sumptuous or the most expensive in the book – in some cases, far from it – but they are all offer individuality, comfort, a warm welcome and something just a little bit unusual.

London

London	Basil Street Hotel, SW3

England

Bath & N.E. Somerset	Sydney Gardens, Bath
Berkshire	Royal Oak, Yattendon
Buckinghamshire	Angel Inn, Long Crendon
Cheshire	Frogg Manor, Broxton
Cornwall	Danescombe Valley Hotel, Calstock
Cumbria	Lindeth Fell, Bowness-on-Windermere
Derbyshire	Callow Hall, Ashbourne
Devon	Buckland-Tout-Saints, Kingsbridge
Dorset	Stock Hill House, Gillingham
East Sussex	Stone House, Rushlake Green
Essex	Maison Talbooth, Dedham
Gloucestershire	Cotswold Cottage, Bledington
	New Inn, Coln St Aldwyns
Hampshire	Wykeham Arms, Winchester
Hereford & Worcester	Glewstone Court, Glewstone
Hertfordshire	Tewin Bury Farm, Welwyn Garden City
Kent	Romney Bay House, Littlestone-on-Sea
Lancashire	Inn at Whitewell, Whitewell
Leicestershire	Hambleton Hall, Hambleton
Lincolnshire	Guy Wells, Whaplode
Northamptonshire	Maltings, Aldwincle

Northumberland	Treetops, East Ord
North Yorkshire	Foresters, Carlton-in-Coverdale
	Lastingham Grange, Lastingham
Shropshire	Severn Lodge, Ironbridge
Somerset	Ashwick House, Dulverton
Staffordshire	Old Beams, Waterhouses
Suffolk	Angel Inn, Stoke-by-Nayland
	Theberton Grange, Theberton
Surrey	Langshott Manor, Horley
Warwickshire	Pear Tree Cottage, Wilmcote
West Midlands	Jonathans' Hotel, Oldbury
West Yorkshire	Haley's, Leeds
Wiltshire	Bradford Old Windmill, Bradford-on-Avon

Scotland

Aberdeenshire	Old Manse of Marnoch, Marnoch
Argyll & Bute	Manor House, Oban
Dumfries & Galloway	Balcary Bay Hotel, Auchencairn
Glasgow	Malmaison, Glasgow
Highland	Altnaharrie Inn, Ullapool
	Ardsheal House, Kentallen
	Forss House, Thurso
	Tigh an Eilean, Shieldaig
Stirling	Inversnaid Lodge, Inversnaid

Wales

Caernarfonshire & Merionethshire	Penhelig Arms Hotel, Aberdovey
Pembrokeshire	Penally Abbey, Penally
Powys	Carlton House, Llanwrtyd Wells
	Ffaldau Country House, Llandegley

Your rights in hotels

A few days away at a hotel is a special treat for many of us, so we don't want anything to spoil it. And when we're travelling on business we don't want any hotel hassles that might distract us. But sometimes things do go wrong, and the hotel doesn't live up to expectations.

Below we set out your rights in dealing with hotels and answer some of the questions regularly asked by our readers. This should help you put things straight on the spot, but if it doesn't, we suggest ways to go about claiming your rights.

When I arrived at the city-centre hotel where I'd booked a weekend break I was told that they had made a mistake and the hotel was full. Owing to a popular conference, the only room I could find was in a more expensive hotel at the other side of town, so I'm out of pocket. What are my rights?

The hotel accepted your booking and was obliged to keep a room available for you. It is in breach of contract and liable to compensate you for additional expenses arising out of that breach – the difference in cost between what you were expecting to pay and what you ended up having to pay, plus any travelling expenses. Write to the manager explaining what happened, and enclose copies of receipts for your additional expenditure. (See also points 1–5 on page 18.)

After booking I found that I had to cancel. I immediately wrote to advise the owners, but they refuse to return my deposit, and say they expect me to pay additional compensation.

When you book a room and the hoteliers accept your booking you enter into a binding contract with them – they undertake to provide the required accommodation and meals for the specified dates at the agreed price, and you commit yourself to paying their charges. If you later cancel or fail to turn up, the hotel may be entitled to keep your deposit to defray administrative expenses, although it should be possible to challenge this if the deposited amount is a very high proportion of the total cost.

If a hotelier is unable to re-let the room you have booked – and he or she must try to do so – he or she can demand from you the loss of profit caused by your cancellation, which can be a substantial proportion of the total price. It's important to give as much notice as possible if you have to cancel: this increases the chances of your room being re-let. If after cancelling you find that the full amount has been charged to your credit card you should raise the matter with your credit card issuer, who will ask the hotel whether the room was re-let, and to justify the charge made.

When I phoned to book a room the receptionist asked for my credit card number. I offered to send a deposit by cheque instead, but the receptionist insisted on taking the number.

Hotels have increasingly adopted this practice to protect themselves against loss when guests fail to turn up. It's reasonable for hotels to request a deposit, and where time permits a cheque should be acceptable.

After a long drive I stopped off at a hotel and asked for a room for the night. Although the hotel was clearly not full the owners refused to give me a room. Can they do this?

Hotels and inns are not allowed to refuse requests for food and shelter providing accommodation is available and the guest is sober, decently dressed and able to pay. If you meet these requirements and are turned away by a hotel with a vacancy you are entitled to sue for damages. If proprietors want to be able to turn away casual business, or are fussy about the sort of people they want to stay in their establishment, they are likely to call it 'guesthouse' or 'private hotel'. In any event, it's illegal to exclude anyone on the grounds of race or sex.

When I called to book they told me I would need to pay extra if I wanted to pay by credit card. Is this legal?

Yes. Dual pricing was legalised early in 1991 and some hoteliers have elected to charge guests who pay by credit card extra to recover the commission payable to the card company. You can challenge this if you're not told when you book, or if it's not indicated on the tariff displayed in reception.

I arrived at a hotel in winter and found I was the only guest. Both my bedroom and the public rooms were distinctly chilly. I was uncomfortable throughout my stay and asked the management to turn up the heating, but things didn't improve.

It's an implied term of the contract between you and the hotel that the accommodation will be of reasonable standard, so it should be maintained at a reasonable temperature. You can claim compensation or seek a reduction of the bill. You were right to complain at the time. You are under a duty to 'mitigate your loss' – to keep your claim to a minimum. The most obvious way of doing this is to complain on the spot and give the management a chance to put things right.

I was very unhappy when I was shown to my room. It hadn't been vacuumed, the wastebins were full, the towels hadn't been changed and I found dog hairs in the bed.

You are entitled to a reasonable standard of accommodation having regard to the price paid. But no hotel, however cheap, should be dirty or unsafe. Ask for things to be put right, and if they're not, ask for a reduction of the bill.

While I was in bed a section of the ceiling caved in. I was injured, but I could have been killed.

Under the Occupiers' Liability Act hotel owners are responsible for the physical safety of their guests. You have a claim for compensation, and would be wise to seek legal advice to have it properly assessed.

The hotel brochure promised floodlit tennis courts. When we arrived the lawns had been neglected and the nets were down. We couldn't play.

A hotel must provide advertised facilities. If it doesn't you can claim compensation, or ask for an appropriate deduction from your bill in respect of the disappointment suffered. You might also want trading standards officers to consider bringing a case against the hotel under the Trade Descriptions Act.

While I was staying at a hotel my video camera was stolen from my room.

Hotel owners owe you a duty of care and must look after your property while it is on their premises. They are liable for any loss and damage as long as it wasn't your own fault – you would be unlikely to succeed if you left it clearly visible in a ground-floor room with the door and window unlocked. However, under the Hotel Proprietors Act, providing hotel owners display a notice at reception, they can limit their liability to £50 per item or £100 in total. They can't rely on this limit if the loss was caused by negligence of their staff, although you will have to prove this.

My car was broken into while parked in the hotel car park. I want compensation.

The Hotel Proprietors Act doesn't cover cars. Your claim is unlikely to succeed.

My dinner was inedible. Do I have to pay for it?

The Supply of Goods and Services Act obliges hotels to prepare food with reasonable skill and care. The common law in Scotland imposes similar duties. If food is inedible, you should tell the waiter and ask for a replacement dish. If things aren't put right you can ask for a reduction of the billed amount. If you pay in full, possibly to avoid an unpleasant scene, write a note at the time saying that you are doing so under protest and are 'reserving your rights'. This means that you retain your right to claim compensation later.

Asserting your rights

1 Always complain at the time if you're unhappy. It's by the far the best way, and necessary to discharge your obligation to mitigate your loss.

2 If you reach deadlock you can deduct a sum from the bill in recognition of the deficient service received. Remember that the hotel might try to exercise its rights of 'lien' by refusing to release your luggage until the bill is paid. It's probably easier to pay in full, but give written notice that you are paying under protest and are reserving your rights to claim compensation through the courts.

3 Legal advice is available from a number of sources. Citizens Advice Bureaux, Law Centres and Consumer Advice Centres give free advice on consumer disputes. In certain cases your Local Trading Standards Department might be able to help. If instructing a solicitor be sure to sort out the cost implications at the outset. Or you can write to Consumers' Association's Which? Personal Service, Castlemead, Gascoyne Way, Hertford SG14 1LH, who, for a small fee, may be able to help you.

4 Once you know where you stand, write to the hotel setting out your claim.

5 If this fails to get things sorted out and you feel that you have a strong case, you can sue for sums of up to £3,000 under the small claims procedure in the county court. In the sheriff court in Scotland the limit is £1,000. You shouldn't need a solicitor.

LONDON

THE CLIVEDEN TOWN HOUSE

LONDON SW3

Abbey Court

20 Pembridge Gardens, London W2 4DU
TEL: 0171-221 7518   FAX: 0171-792 0858

Up-market small hotel near popular tourist sights and parks.

In a quiet side-street off busy Notting Hill Gate, Abbey Court is a rather grand Victorian town house with a smart white frontage and beautifully kept bedrooms. A neat gravel terrace at the front of the house with a bay tree and leafy window boxes is an indication of the standards inside. The bedrooms are all individually furnished, and after refurbishment in 1996 are now smart as well as comfortable. All immaculately kept, they range from the simplicity of Room 16, a plain single with a cane bedstead and light neutral décor, to the luxury of Room 11, which has a four-poster bed, dark antiques and a well-lit marble bathroom. Every room has fresh flowers, mineral water, plenty of goodies in the bathroom and a complimentary morning paper. Rooms at the top are the most characterful of the standard rooms thanks to their sloping ceilings and views over the rooftops, while those on the first and second floors at the front are the brightest. Breakfast is served in your room or in the conservatory – an attractive place for dawdling while looking out on a small garden. You can have afternoon tea here too, or snacks (from 11am to 11pm) including soups, sandwiches and simple main courses such as chicken in a mustard sauce with rice.

◑ Open all year   ⏁ Nearest tube station is Notting Hill Gate (Central, District and Circle lines). On-street parking difficult; public car park nearby   ⛜ 6 single, 6 twin/double, 7 double, 3 four-poster; family rooms available; all with bathroom/WC exc 1 single with shower/WC; TV, room service, hair-dryer, trouser press, direct-dial telephone ; no tea/coffee-making facilities in rooms   ⌀ Bar/conservatory, garden; conference facilities (max 10 people residential/non-residential) ; babysitting   ⅊ No wheelchair access   ● No dogs; no smoking in some bedrooms   ▭ Access, Amex, Delta, Diners, Switch, Visa   ⌹ Single £88, single occupancy of twin/double £110 to £118, twin/double £130 to £145, four-poster £175, family room from £156; deposit required. Continental B in room £7; (prices valid till Apr 1997)

Academy Hotel

21 Gower Street, London WC1E 6HG
TEL: 0171-631 4115   FAX: 0171-636 3442

Modern, well-equipped rooms and friendly service in centrally located hotel within walking distance of Oxford Street.

New to the *Guide* last year, the Academy has nearly doubled in size since its inclusion, taking over two more Georgian town houses to add to the three which formed the original hotel. The new rooms have luxurious marble bathrooms and air-conditioning and are decorated in the same style – light flowery fabrics, cream walls and dark reproduction furniture. Clean and neat, most of the rooms have plenty of space, though none has a particularly inspiring outlook: Gower Street to the front is a busy through-route (though double glazing keeps noise at bay), while at the back the gardens are as yet mostly undeveloped. However, the one walled garden which has received attention is lovely, with colourful hanging baskets and leafy creepers, and makes a useful extension to the lounge in summer. Downstairs, the restaurant has an Art Deco feel, with peacock-green tub chairs on a parquet floor and partly panelled walls. The menu is quite short but good value, with plenty of fresh fish and vegetarian dishes alongside traditional roast chicken and lamb with rosemary.

◑ Open all year ⚡ Nearest tube station is Goodge Street (Northern line). On-street parking (metered) ⊨ 12 single, 6 twin, 22 double, 8 suites; some with bathroom/WC, most with shower/WC; TV, room service, direct-dial telephone; hair-dryer and trouser press in some rooms ⚋ Restaurant, bar, lounge, library, conservatory, garden; air-conditioning in some public areas and some bedrooms; conference facilities (max 20 people residential/non-residential); early suppers for children; babysitting, baby-listening ♿ No wheelchair access ● No dogs ☐ Access, Amex, Delta, Diners, Switch, Visa ⑤ Single £90, single occupancy of twin/double £100, twin/double £115 to £130, suite £160; deposit required. Continental B £7, cooked B £9; set L £15, D £17. Special breaks available

The Ascott

49 Hill Street, London W1X 7FQ
TEL: 0171-499 6868   FAX: 0171-499 0705

Exclusive and stylish fully serviced apartments at a price.

Purpose-built in the 1920s as a block of serviced apartments, the Ascott still operates on similar principles. In the past, according to today's brochure, 'the better-off Mayfair bachelor chose an apartment where he had nothing to do except clean his teeth'. These days, executives on a working holiday can leave the laundry and tidying up to someone else, and head off to the gym, or make use of their apartment's CD or video player, telephone or fax machine. One of a chain of six properties throughout the world, the Ascott was only recently taken over and refurbished, opening at the beginning of 1995. Consequently, everything feels brand new and is well maintained. Original Art Deco features have been kept, such as beautiful curved doors and wood panelling, while practical facilities and modern luxuries have been added. In the summer you have the option of taking breakfast in a neat courtyard garden, as well as ordering room service or cooking for yourself in your suite. Apartments at the top of the building overlook neighbouring rooftops and miss out on the leafy views.

◑ Open all year ⚡ Nearest tube station is Marble Arch (Central line). On-street parking (metered) ⊨ 56 suites; all with bathroom/WC; TV, hair-dryer, direct-dial telephone, CD player, VCR ⚋ Bar, lounge, TV room, garden; air-conditioning in all rooms; conference facilities (max 16 people residential/non-residential); gym, sauna, solarium, steam room; babysitting, games ♿ No wheelchair access ● No dogs ☐ Access, Amex, Delta, Diners, Switch, Visa ⑤ Suite £175 to £493; deposit required. Special breaks available

---

See the inside front cover for a brief explanation of how to use the Guide.

Aster House

3 Sumner Place, London SW7 3EE
TEL: 0171-581 5888 FAX: 0171-584 4925

*Family-run B&B in central London, with adequate rooms and a
lovely garden.*

The exterior of Aster House is striking and stands out from the other houses in
the street for its exceptionally leafy frontage, where potted bay trees stand on
smart black and white tiles, and window boxes tumble with ivy. The Carapiet
family are obviously keen on plants; indeed, their garden at the back of the house
– next to Christie's auction rooms – is an award winner. The first-floor
conservatory/breakfast-room continues the theme and is especially lovely in
summer, when the doors are open and the flowers are in full bloom. Comfortable
sofas make it a relaxing place to read the papers or have afternoon tea. Breakfast
is continental-style only and is served from a buffet. The bedrooms are mostly a
good size with light, plain furnishings and small old-fashioned bathrooms,
some of which could do with a little attention. All have basic rather than
generous facilities. You can make tea and coffee on the landing, though it's much
nicer to go down to the conservatory or the garden, where you can admire the
statues and greenery while you linger. Prices don't vary according to the
standard of the room, so the larger, smarter ones are better value for money. One
disappointed guest who wrote to us thought her room was poor value with a
gloomy atmosphere. More reports, please.

◑ Open all year ⊿ Nearest tube station is South Kensington (Piccadilly, Circle and
District lines). On-street parking (metered); public car park nearby ⊨ 2 single, 5
twin, 4 double, 1 four-poster; 3 with bathroom/WC, most with shower/WC; TV,
mini-bar, direct-dial telephone; hair-dryer on request ⌀ Lounge, conservatory,
garden ᕯ No wheelchair access ⊖ No children under 12; no dogs; no smoking
▭ Access, Amex, Diners, Switch, Visa £ Single £70, single occupancy of
twin/double £90, twin/double £111, four-poster £118; deposit required

Basil Street Hotel

Basil Street, London SW3 1AH
TEL: 0171-581 3311 FAX: 0171-581 3693

*A family-run hotel with a long tradition, comfortable rooms and a
superb location in the heart of Knightsbridge.*

Three senior managers at the Basil Street Hotel have more than 100 years' service
between them, and many more of the staff have each worked here for several
decades. Built in 1910 by the Taylor family, by whom it is still run, the hotel has a
happy, informal atmosphere and a dislike of pretension that sets it apart from
some other up-market hotels in central London. The public rooms are elegant,
stuffed full of antiques and interesting bits and pieces collected from the family's
travels, and above all relaxing. The large first-floor lounge, built over the original
Knightsbridge underground station, has sunny yellow walls, rugs on a parquet
floor and bright red curtains and cushions, which make it a cheerful place to have

your afternoon tea. A pianist entertains diners in the restaurant, where the table d'hôte menu is very reasonably priced. Each of the bedrooms is individually kitted out, some with dark antiques and faded flowery fabrics, others with bold colour schemes and recently installed air-conditioning. Bathrooms vary from smart, marble and indulgent to old-fashioned, but not all rooms are *en suite*. Staff are more than willing to help you find the room that suits your taste and pocket. One facility we applaud is the ironing room on each long corridor.

○ Open all year   Nearest tube station is Knightsbridge (Piccadilly line). On-street parking (metered); public car park nearby   42 single, 25 twin, 22 double, 4 family rooms; most with bathroom/WC; TV, room service, hair-dryer, direct-dial telephone; no tea/coffee-making facilities in rooms   Restaurant, lounge; air-conditioning in some bedrooms; conference facilities (max 90 people incl up to 20 residential) ; early suppers for children ; babysitting   No wheelchair access ● No dogs in public rooms ⊟ Access, Amex, Diners, Switch, Visa   Single £70 to £130, single occupancy of twin/double £165, twin/double £110 to £185, family room £260; deposit required. Set L £8.50 to £16.50, D £17 to £22; (prices valid till Mar 1997) . Special breaks available

The Beaufort

33 Beaufort Gardens, London SW3 1PP
TEL: 0171-584 5252   FAX: 0171-589 2834

Beautifully kept, small hotel in cul-de-sac off busy Knightsbridge shopping street.

In a surprisingly quiet row of smart white town houses, the Beaufort is one of the most peaceful small hotels in central London. The exterior is immaculately maintained, with bountiful window boxes and a discreet brass sign; the atmosphere inside is as relaxed as that of a country house. Deep, comfortable sofas in the stylish reception/lounge, with its collection of bright floral watercolours, are made more homely by the presence of the hotel's cat, Harry. Cream teas are served here to tired shoppers, and you can help yourself to drinks, including free champagne. Fresh flower arrangements and baskets of fruit add to the luxury of the bedrooms, which are priced according to their facilities. Rooms at the front tend to be lighter and have leafier outlooks, while all have rich co-ordinated fabrics, mellow colour schemes and generous amounts of goodies in fully tiled bathrooms. There is no dining-room so breakfast is served in your bedroom or downstairs in the lounge; in either case service by the young staff is down-to-earth and cheerful.

○ Open all year   Nearest tube station is Knightsbridge (Piccadilly line). On-street parking (metered)   3 single, 6 twin, 12 double, 7 suites; all with bathroom/WC exc singles with shower/WC; TV, room service, hair-dryer, direct-dial telephone, radio, VCR; tea/coffee-making facilities and trouser press on request   Lounge; air-conditioning in all rooms; toys, games, babysitting, baby-listening   No wheelchair access ● No dogs ⊟ Access, Amex, Diners, Switch, Visa   Single £129 to £153, single occupancy of twin/double £176 to £253, twin/double £176 to £253, suite £282; deposit required. Continental B £6.50

Bedknobs [see map 3]

58 Glengarry Road, East Dulwich, London SE22 8QD
TEL: 0181-299 2004   FAX: 0181-693 5611

A well-equipped, family-run guesthouse in a quiet residential street, 30 minutes from central London.

With one of the best-kept frontages in this quiet south-London street, Bedknobs is actually two houses, with the breakfast/sitting-room and three bedrooms situated in the Jenkins' family home at Number 58, and several more bedrooms next door. Gill Jenkins is fond of Victoriana, and every inch of antique pine is covered with interesting knick-knacks. At breakfast, guests sit around one large table crowded with craft-shop crockery, treats such as home-made marmalade, and a generous supply of cereals and toast. A cooked breakfast costs extra. The pick of the bedrooms in the main house is the triple-bedded Big Blue Room, with its co-ordinated blue décor and a cast-iron fireplace. One reader was rather troubled by noise – you might prefer one of the rooms next door, as they benefit from a quieter setting. The Green Room on the first floor, which overlooks the garden, is possibly the most peaceful. Here, old pine furnishings, simple fabrics and a smart, white bathroom hidden behind a curtain constitute a comfortable, well-equipped room. Be warned that this is a low-key, family operation, and that the hotel doesn't take credit cards.

◑ Open all year   ⏢ Glengarry Road is opposite Dulwich Hospital in East Dulwich.
On-street parking   ⏢ 2 single, 1 twin, 2 double, 1 family room; some in annexe; 1 with bathroom/WC; TV, hair-dryer   ⌀ Dining-room ; toys, baby-sitting   ⏢ No wheelchair access   ● No dogs; no smoking   ⏢ None accepted   £ Single £29, single occupancy of twin/double £40, twin/double £45 to £55, family room from £60; deposit required. Cooked B £3; (prices valid till May 1997)

Blakes Hotel

33 Roland Gardens, London SW7 3PF
TEL: 0171-370 6701   FAX: 0171-373 0442

Plush, extravagant rooms at a price, in a small hotel much visited by the rich and famous.

A stay at Blakes Hotel does not come cheap, but for most guests that is the last consideration. The hotel prides itself on guarding its guests from the paparazzi, which gives you some idea of the company you will keep if you stay here. The brochure describes the hotel as a 'personal statement about what design can achieve'; translated to the bedrooms that means that colour schemes are dramatic – black and mustard in one room, cardinal red in another – fabric has been bought in by the acre, and the stimulation of your senses is given higher priority than mundane concerns such as where to put your suitcase. Perhaps the most romantic is the four-poster wedding suite, described accurately as 'white on white on white on white'. For down-to-earth guests and business people, faxes, phones and other modern paraphernalia are in there somewhere, but they're well hidden. Even the food is designer – Anouska Hempel, in fact. Should you ever come out of your room, you will find that the basement restaurant serves innovative dishes such as inkfish risotto as well as things you recognise like rack of lamb with rosemary and mint. The staff are cheerful and attentive.

● Open all year ⚡ Nearest tube station is Gloucester Road (Piccadilly, District and Circle lines). On-street parking (metered) ⤶ 14 single, 3 twin, 19 double, 7 four-poster, 9 suites; all with bathroom/WC exc 4 singles with shower/WC; TV, 24-hour room service, hair-dryer, mini-bar, direct-dial telephone; no tea/coffee-making facilities in rooms ✧ Restaurant, bar, lounge, garden; air-conditioning in restaurant and some bedrooms; conference facilities (max 20 people residential/non-residential) ; early suppers for children ; babysitting ౬ No wheelchair access ● No dogs ☐ Access, Amex, Diners, Switch, Visa £ Single £135, single occupancy of twin/double £175, twin/double £175 to £320, four-poster £320, suite £500 to £875; deposit required. Continental B £14, cooked B £17; alc L £40, D £60 . Special breaks available

---

Bryanston Court

56–60 Great Cumberland Place, London W1H 8DD
TEL: 0171-262 3141   FAX: 0171-262 7248

No-frills family-run hotel in central London, with straightforward rooms and willing staff.

On a busy through-route just north of Marble Arch, Bryanston Court is noticeable for its bright blue canopies and leafy window boxes. Inside, standards aren't quite so high, but if you're looking for an inexpensive night's stay in a central location then you're in the right place. Downstairs, a lounge with studded leather sofas is rather uninspiring but functional; likewise the bar, where flexible service provides drinks and sandwiches late into the night. The bedrooms are unfussy and modern with light furnishings and muted fabrics, but showing one or two signs of age. Our inspector found the tiny shower room in her single room rather cramped but otherwise clean and reasonably well maintained. In the spacious dining-room in the basement, an adequate but unspectacular breakfast is served, and there are plenty of staff on hand to guarantee swift service. Refreshingly, on departure, the bill is what you would expect, with no added extras.

● Open all year ⚡ Nearest tube station is Marble Arch (Central line). On-street parking (metered); public car park nearby ⤶ 19 single, 24 twin, 7 double, 4 family rooms; some with bathroom/WC, most with shower/WC; TV, limited room service, hair-dryer, direct-dial telephone ✧ Dining-room, bar, lounge; conference facilities (max 12 people residential/non-residential) ౬ Wheelchair access to hotel (2 steps) and restaurant, 2 ground-floor bedrooms ● No dogs ☐ Access, Amex, Diners, Switch, Visa £ Single £73, twin/double £90, family room from £105, deposit required. Cooked B £6

The text of entries is based on unsolicited reports sent in by readers and backed up by inspections. The factual details are from questionnaires the Guide *sends to all hotels that feature in the book.*

Cannizaro House [see map 3]

Westside, Wimbledon Common, London SW19 4UE
TEL: 0181-879 1464   FAX: 0181-879 7338

Grand country house 30 minutes from central London, with leafy views and helpful service.

Look out from any room of Cannizaro House and you're confronted with a leafy green view. Unusually peaceful for London, the hotel is sandwiched between Wimbledon Common on the one side and Cannizaro Park on the other. Inside it has the feel of a grand country house, with swags of heavy fabric hanging at large windows, glass chandeliers beneath decoratively painted ceilings and fires roaring in marble fireplaces. From its smart Georgian frontage you wouldn't realise that the house dates back to several different eras. Its chequered history includes being a venue for non-stop partying by the rich and famous, and, in the 1950s, an old folks' home. The bedrooms are all comfortable and well equipped, with their own individual décor and smart marble bathrooms. Those in the older part of the house are bigger, and the most open views are over traffic-free Cannizaro Park, rather than over the common, which has roads cutting through it. Dress is formal in the restaurant – where fresh flowers adorn every table – though the service is unstuffy throughout the hotel.

◗ Open all year   ⬚ From A3 turn south on to A219 towards Wimbledon; after about 1½ miles turn right into Cannizaro Road; second right is Westside and hotel is 50 yards on left. Private car park   ⤏ 15 twin, 24 double, 4 four-poster, 3 suites; all with bathroom/WC; TV, room service, hair-dryer, trouser press, direct-dial telephone   ⌀ Restaurant, bar, lounge, garden; conference facilities (max 100 people incl up to 46 residential)   ⓬ Wheelchair access to hotel, restaurant and WC (unisex), 4 ground-floor bedrooms   ● No children under 8; no dogs; no smoking in some bedrooms   ⬚ Access, Amex, Delta, Diners, Switch, Visa   ⌂ Single occupancy of twin/double £125 to £150, twin/double £145 to £200, four-poster £315, suite £375; deposit required. Continental B £8.50, cooked B £11.50; set L, D £17 to £26; (1996 prices) . Special breaks available

The Capital

22 Basil Street, London SW3 1AT
TEL: 0171-589 5171   FAX: 0171-225 0011

Pricey but luxurious hotel in the heart of Knightsbridge.

The Capital is the rather swish big sister of L'Hotel a few doors away (see entry). Less than a minute's walk from Harrods, yet in the relative peace and quiet of a residential street, it occupies a much-sought-after location in this popular part of London. Uniformed staff meet you at the door and usher you into a plush interior, where lots of attention has been given to acquiring furniture by the best cabinet-makers, paintings by renowned artists, and colours and fabric combinations by a top interior designer. The result is lavish and something of a showpiece. Well-heeled shoppers take a break to come here for lunch and are treated in the rather austere restaurant to attentive service and excellent food, which varies from imaginative canapés through to, perhaps, lobster with ginger, sugarsnap peas and caviare. Afternoon tea in the smart lounge, with its deep-green walls and bright red cushions, is also a popular event. The bedrooms, all individually designed, have good facilities and housekeeping is impeccable.

---

❶ Open all year ⤢ Nearest tube station is Knightsbridge (Piccadilly line). Private car park (£20 per night); on-street parking (metered) ⤚ 12 single, 12 twin, 16 double, 8 suites; all with bathroom/WC; TV, room service, hair-dryer, mini-bar, trouser press, direct-dial telephone; no tea/coffee-making facilities in rooms ✅ Restaurant, bar, lounge; air-conditioning in all rooms; conference facilities (max 24 people residential/non-residential) ; babysitting, cots ♿ Wheelchair access to hotel (3 steps), restaurant, lift to bedrooms ⬤ No dogs ⊟ Access, Amex, Delta, Diners, Switch, Visa £ Single £196, single occupancy of twin/double £196, twin/double £231 to £294, suite £341; deposit required. Continental B £10.50, cooked B £14.50; set L £25, D £55/75; alc D £75 . Special breaks available

---

Cliveden Town House ☆

26 Cadogan Gardens, London SW3 2RP
TEL: 0171-730 6466   FAX: 0171-730 0236

Elegant hotel with quiet, clubby atmosphere and cheerful, friendly staff.

This hotel, formerly the Draycott, and illustrated on page 19, has changed hands since last year and is now run by the same people who manage Cliveden House, a plush hotel in the Thames Valley. In keeping with the luxury of Cliveden, this good-looking red-brick house has been completely refurbished and the result is a very comfortable mix of smart urban fabrics in restful colours and country touches such as wellies and a worn leather armchair near the entrance. The bedrooms are all different in style and size and are named after notable characters from the theatre world. Noel Coward, a small single, has the feel of a ship's cabin; Ellen Terry has deep pink walls smothered in photographs and prints. All are extremely well equipped, with CD and video players, and larger rooms have touch-button log-effect gas fires. There's no restaurant (though there are plenty of eating places nearby), but members of staff will cheerfully bring snacks such as foie gras and crab sandwiches to your room.

---

❶ Open all year ⤢ Nearest tube station is Sloane Square (District and Circle lines). Parking difficult ⤚ 6 single, 15 twin/double, 4 suites; all with bathroom/WC; TV, room service, hair-dryer, mini-bar, direct-dial telephone, fax, CD player, VCR; no tea/coffee-making facilities in rooms ✅ Lounge, library; air-conditioning in all rooms; conference facilities (max 8 people residential/non-residential) ; early suppers for children ; babysitting ♿ No wheelchair access ⬤ None ⊟ Access, Diners, Switch, Visa £ Single £123, single occupancy of twin/double from £229, twin/double from £229, suite £364; deposit required. Continental B £9.50, cooked B £15

Prices are quoted per room *rather than* per person.

Concorde Hotel

50 Great Cumberland Place, London W1H 7FD
TEL: 0171-402 6169   FAX: 0171-724 1184

Basic accommodation in well-established B&B near Oxford Street shops.

Owned by the same people who own Bryanston Court (see entry) just along the street, the Concorde Hotel is run by different staff and has a warmer, more personal atmosphere. In other respects it's very similar, offering simple functional rooms decorated in muted blues and pinks with not much space but adequate facilities, including a kettle to make tea, a hair-dryer by the mirror, and a small tiled bathroom. Housekeeping standards are high, which goes some way towards compensating for the lack of character. There's no restaurant for evening meals, but continental breakfast is included in the room rate and is served buffet-style in the well-lit basement, where dried-flower arrangements stand on immaculate white tablecloths and give the room a fresh spring-like feel. Afternoon tea is served in the lounge by the receptionist-cum-waiter. With warm orangey-coloured walls, an open fire and papers on sticks it's a pleasant enough place to sit.

○ Closed Chr & New Year   ⤢ Nearest tube station is Marble Arch (Central line). On-street parking (metered); public car park nearby   ⤟ 10 single, 12 twin, 3 double, 3 family rooms; some with bathroom/WC, most with shower/WC; TV, limited room service, hair-dryer, direct-dial telephone   ⊘ Dining-room, bar, lounge
♿ Wheelchair access to hotel (2 steps) and restaurant, 2 ground-floor bedrooms
● No dogs   ▭ Access, Amex, Diners, Switch, Visa   £ Single £65, twin/double £75, family room from £85; deposit required. Cooked B £6

The Connaught

Carlos Place, London W1Y 6AL
TEL: 0171-499 7070   FAX: 0171-495 3262

Formal, classically English hotel with traditional rooms, good food and superb service.

This good-looking red-brick building was built at the end of the nineteenth century to provide luxury without any razzle-dazzle for visitors to London. Its success has become legendary, and the hotel remains little changed since those early days. From the grand mahogany staircase – cared for by a French-polisher who is now in his eighties – to the pampering marble bathrooms, everything at the Connaught is built to last. The hotel prides itself on quality rather than fashion. Everyone dresses the part: staff wear uniforms according to their role, while guests are required to wear a jacket and tie in both the mahogany-panelled restaurant, where the vast menu includes traditional English cooking along with classic French dishes, and the Georgian-style Grill Room, which shares the same menu but adds a less expensive table d'hôte choice. While the bedrooms are elegantly grand, and include three bells to ring should you need a maid, valet or waiter, the present hasn't been completely ignored, and business people have access to faxes, phones and office services.

◑ Open all year ⧄ Nearest tube station is Green Park (Piccadilly, Victoria and Jubilee lines). Public car park nearby ⫪ 30 single, 36 twin/double, 24 suites; family rooms available; all with bathroom/WC; TV, room service, hair-dryer, direct-dial telephone ; no tea/coffee-making facilities in rooms ⦸ 2 restaurants, bar, 2 lounges, 2 private dining-rooms; air-conditioning in all bedrooms, restaurants, bar; conference facilities (max 16 people residential/non-residential); babysitting, cots ♿ Wheelchair access to hotel (ramp), restaurant and WC (M,F), lift to bedrooms ● No dogs ▭ Access, Amex, Diners, Switch, Visa £ Single £233, single occupancy of twin/double £311, twin/double £311 to £335, family room from £380, suite from £582; deposit required. Continental B £14; set L £25/30, D £35/55; alc L £52, D £55 (1996 prices)

Covent Garden Hotel ☆

10 Monmouth Street, London WC2H 9HB
TEL: 0171-806 1000 FAX: 0171-806 1100

Stylish hotel in the hubbub of Covent Garden.

From the black-and-white arty photographs in the brochure to the thoughtful design of each room, everything in the recently opened Covent Garden Hotel oozes style. Antiques, hand-embroidered fabrics and courageous combinations of colours make the rooms luxurious as well as fascinating. And it's not all show – up-to-date facilities like voice-mail telephones and fax machines are in every room should you need them. This is the fourth in the group of London hotels owned by Kit Kemp and she has added a personal touch to this latest addition by naming some of the public rooms after her three children. Bar and Brasserie Max is a continental-style marble-and-chrome bar serving well-priced light meals such as penne pasta with wild mushroom sauce, or lentil soup; Café Min is a tiny room with just a handful of tables; and Tiffany's Library is plush, with vibrant fabrics and deep, comfortable sofas. Smart uniformed staff are friendly and helpful, and as you'd expect, room service continues throughout the night.

◑ Open all year ⧄ Near Leicester Square and Covent Garden tube stations (Piccadilly and Northern lines). Public car park nearby ⫪ 8 single, 26 twin/double, 10 double, 3 four-poster, 3 suites; all with bathroom/WC; TV, 24-hour room service, hair-dryer, mini-bar, direct-dial telephone, CD player; no tea/coffee making facilities in rooms ⦸ Restaurant, bar, lounge, library; gym ; early suppers for children ♿ Wheelchair access to hotel (1 step) and restaurant, lift to bedrooms ● Dogs by arrangement ▭ Access, Amex, Visa £ Single £176, single occupancy of twin/double £206 to £229, twin/double £206 to £229, four-poster £206 to £229, suite £306 to £411; deposit required. Continental B £11, cooked B £14

If you make a booking using a credit card and find after cancelling that the full amount has been charged to your card, raise the matter with your credit card company. It will ask the hotelier to confirm whether the room was re–let, and to justify the charge made.

Cranley Gardens Hotel

8 Cranley Gardens, London SW7 3DB
TEL: 0171-373 3232   FAX: 0171-373 7944

Family-run hotel with good service, well-placed for visiting London's sights.

A new entry in last year's *Guide*, Cranley Gardens continues to impress. Converted from four Georgian town houses, the hotel is much larger than it looks from the outside. The 85 bedrooms are light and modern, with bamboo-style furniture, built-in desks and dressing tables, and generally plenty of space. The well-maintained bathrooms are simple and in some cases not very big, but are spotlessly clean. If yours is a shower room you don't have to wander far to find a public bathroom shared by only a few rooms. The staff, under the management of the Kular family, are both efficient and approachable, though breakfast – in the basement restaurant – can find them fully stretched. Lots of effort has been made to brighten up what might otherwise be a gloomy room, and it works. Tall plants, fresh flowers and sunny yellow walls make it a cheerful place to start the day. Snacks and sandwiches are served at any time in the bar or in your room.

◗ Open all year   ⬚ Near South Kensington and Gloucester Road tube stations (Piccadilly, District and Circle lines). On-street parking (metered)   ⬳ 15 single, 39 twin, 20 double, 11 family rooms; most with bathroom/WC, some with shower/WC; TV, room service, hair-dryer, direct-dial telephone ; mini-bar and trouser press in some rooms; no tea/coffee-making facilities in rooms   ⬥ Restaurant, bar, lounge   ⬚ No wheelchair access   ● No smoking in some public rooms   ⬚ Access, Amex, Delta, Diners, Switch, Visa   £ Single £69, single occupancy of twin/double £79, twin/double £99, family room £118; deposit required. Cooked B £5.50

Dorset Square Hotel

39-40 Dorset Square, London NW1 6QN
TEL: 0171-723 7874   FAX: 0171-724 3328

A luxurious, small hotel with rich furnishings near to Regent's Park.

Just off the busy Marylebone Road, Dorset Square is made up of smart Regency terraces set around two acres of lawns and trees. Double glazing blocks out any street noise, making this a peaceful place in which to stay. Inside, the hotel is lavishly furnished with rich fabrics and antiques collected by the owner, Kit Kemp, for her four London hotels. The bedrooms are all different, and some can be rather small – opt for one overlooking the square. Along with a well-equipped bathroom featuring chrome fittings and plenty of goodies, each room has a helpful folder advising you on everything, from nearby eating places to jogging routes in Regent's Park. The young staff are courteous and friendly; one reader wrote to say that they were among the most pleasant he had met anywhere, but then went on to complain about the surcharges which appeared on his bill. We found room service prompt and efficient, although there is a 10 per cent cover charge each time you order. The same cover charge applies to the restaurant, where the surroundings are characterful. Called the Potting Shed, it's as far removed from the streets of London as you can get: terracotta pots are stacked up against one wall, while a wooden wheelbarrow and other paraphernalia hang against another.

◑ Open all year; restaurant closed Sat ⏀ Nearest tube station is Baker Street (Circle, Jubilee, Metropolitan and Bakerloo lines). On-street parking (metered); public car park nearby ⛛ 6 single, 10 twin, 19 double, 1 four-poster, 1 suite; all with bathroom/WC exc 3 singles with shower/WC; TV, room service, hair-dryer, mini-bar, direct-dial telephone ✅ Restaurant, bar, lounge; air-conditioning in most bedrooms and all public areas; conference facilities (max 8 people residential/non-residential) ; early suppers for children ; baby-sitting ♿ No wheelchair access ● No dogs ▭ Access, Amex, Switch, Visa £ Single £112, twin/double £135 to £182, four-poster and suite £200; deposit required. Continental B £10, cooked B £14; set L £12; alc L, D £25 . Special breaks available

---

Durley House

115 Sloane Street, London SW1X 9PJ
TEL: 0171-235 5537 FAX: 0171-259 6977

Pricey but luxurious all-suite hotel with attentive service.

On a wide, busy road through Knightsbridge, Durley House is one of four hotels owned by Kit Kemp, all of which notable for their lavish interior design. Promoting itself as a place for people who think the hustle and bustle of hotel lobbies and lounges belongs only in 1940s films, this hotel offers suites rather than bedrooms and is ideal if you're looking for privacy. An efficient young staff provides 24-hour room service – including toasted sandwiches, salads and light meals – though each of the suites has its own kitchen if you prefer to cater for yourself. Breakfast is brought to your room or is served in the drawing-room downstairs, where there's an open fire in winter. The grandest of the suites is perhaps Piano, with its dark oil paintings, acres of fabric and of course a grand piano in the plush gold sitting-room. The Park Suite is equally huge and has a more masculine feel with smart tartan armchairs, dark antiques and piles of games and newspapers. Cadogan Park just across the road makes a pleasant place for a stroll.

◑ Open all year ⏀ Nearest tube station is Sloane Square (District and Circle lines). On-street parking (metered) ⛛ 11 suites; all with bathroom/WC; TV, room service, hair-dryer, mini-bar, trouser press, direct-dial telephone ✅ Lounge, garden; tennis; early suppers for children ♿ No wheelchair access ● Dogs by arrangement ▭ Access, Amex, Delta, Switch, Visa £ Suite £229 to £382; deposit required. Continental B £8.50, cooked B £12.50

Durrants Hotel

George Street, London W1H 6BJ
TEL: 0171-935 8131 FAX: 0171-487 3510

Traditional, family-run hotel in the centre of London with nearly 100 well-equipped rooms.

At the eastern end of George Street, near to dozens of interesting bookshops and cafés and only a short walk from Oxford Street, Durrants is a well-established hotel occupying a smart yellow-brick terrace of Georgian town houses. Opened 200 years ago, the hotel has been in the hands of the Miller family since 1921 – and they know a thing or two about tradition. Uniformed staff are both courteous and approachable. The restaurant, where the menu favours game and the good old English roast, is wood-panelled with studded leather seats and dark oil paintings, while a number of smaller public rooms offer you the chance to escape from the bustle if you want to. The George Bar has an open fire, and pistols and hunting scenes on the wall; the equally cosy Pump Room wasn't open to women at one time, owing to the potentially offensive nature of the paintings of nude figures. The Reverend Canon Barry obviously wasn't bothered by them in September 1890: he stayed long enough to clock up quite a bill, which is now framed and on view. The bedrooms vary in size and style but are mostly spacious and well equipped, with dark furniture, light modern fabrics and marble and chrome bathrooms. Rooms at the back tend to be quieter.

● Open all year   ☒ Nearest tube station is Marble Arch (Central line). On-street parking (metered); public car park nearby   ⇌ 15 single, 41 twin, 31 double, 3 family rooms, 3 suites; most with bathroom/WC, some with shower/WC; TV, room service, hair-dryer, direct-dial telephone ; mini-bar and trouser press in some rooms; no tea/coffee-making facilities in rooms   ✅ Restaurant, bar, 4 lounges, air-conditioning in some bedrooms; conference facilities (max 80 people residential/non-residential); early suppers for children ; babysitting   ♿ Wheelchair access to hotel (2 steps) and restaurant, 7 ground-floor bedrooms   ● No dogs   ▭ Access, Amex, Switch, Visa   £ Single £90, single occupancy of twin/double £108, twin/double £108, family room £155, suite £220; deposit required. Continental B £6.50, cooked B £9.50; set L, D £17; alc L, D £25

Egerton House

17–19 Egerton Terrace, London SW3 2BX
TEL: 0171-589 2412   FAX: 0171-584 6540

Luxury town house with unstuffy service in the heart of Knightsbridge.

This six-storey red-brick building was once a youth hostel, a fact the hotel perhaps wouldn't want to be reminded of as it strives to provide a luxurious setting in which your every need is waited on. Today, Egerton House feels like a traditional country house, with lovely antique furnishings in polished wood and ageing leather set against light walls and swathes of rich fabrics. Fresh flower arrangements are an indication of the high standards of housekeeping, while an open fire, honesty bar and (complimentary) newspapers contribute to an informal, homely feel. There is waiter service in the basement breakfast-room, which has a sprig of flowers on each table and pretty, wild-flower crockery, but 24-hour room service is on call if you prefer to stay upstairs. The 28 bedrooms are beautifully furnished with more antiques, while the marble bathrooms, with smart brass fittings, are kitted out with generous supplies of toiletries. An information folder is thoughtfully provided, giving details of local restaurants and a good idea of walking distances. Rooms at the back of the hotel have the advantage of looking out over neatly mown lawns rather than over the street.

◑ Open all year ⊿ Near South Kensington and Knightsbridge tube stations (Piccadilly, District and Circle lines). Private car park (£18 for 24 hours); on-street parking (metered) ⊨→ 10 single, 4 twin, 12 double, 1 four-poster, 1 suite; all with bathroom/WC; TV, 24-hour room service, hair-dryer, mini-bar, direct-dial telephone; no tea/coffee-making facilities in rooms ⊘ Dining-room, bar, lounge: air-conditioning in all rooms ; early suppers for children ; babysitting ⅄ No wheelchair access ● No dogs; no smoking in dining-room ⊟ Access, Amex, Diners, Visa £ Single £147, single occupancy of twin/double £182 to £200, twin/double £182 to £200, four-poster £223, suite £294; deposit required. Continental B £9.50, cooked B £14

Five Sumner Place

5 Sumner Place, London SW7 3EE
TEL: 0171-584 7586   FAX: 0171-823 9962

Immaculate B&B with a leafy conservatory and a friendly welcome.

Just off the Old Brompton Road, within walking distance of good shopping, restaurants and some of London's major museums, Sumner Place is an ideal base for tourists. Number Five is one of a terrace of good-looking white buildings in this quiet residential street, several of which are B&Bs labelled with discreet brass signs. We found the housekeeping immaculate, and the rather plain but comfortable bedrooms, with their dark reproduction furniture and striped or flowery modern fabrics, well equipped with plenty of goodies. Rooms at the back are definitely quieter; our favourite was Room Two, a basement room but not at all gloomy, with plenty of space and the added bonus of a bath rather than a shower. Breakfast is served buffet-style in the blue and white conservatory, spilling out into a small garden in the summer. It is a lovely place either to linger in while you plan your day or to return to for afternoon tea.

◑ Open all year ⊿ Nearest tube station is South Kensington (District, Circle and Piccadilly lines). On-street parking (metered) ⊨→ 3 single, 5 twin, 5 double; most with bathroom/WC, some with shower/WC; TV, room service, hair-dryer, trouser press, direct-dial telephone; tea/coffee-making facilities and mini-bar on request ⊘ Conservatory, garden ⅄ No wheelchair access ● No children under 7; no dogs; no smoking in public rooms and some bedrooms ⊟ Access, Amex, Visa £ Single £79 to £85, single occupancy of twin/double £99 to £110, twin/double £110 to £120; deposit required

---

If you have a small appetite, or just aren't feeling hungry, check if you can be given a reduction if you don't want the full menu. At some hotels you could easily end up paying £30 for one course and a coffee.

Don't expect to turn up at a small hotel assuming that a room will be available. It's always best to telephone in advance.

47 Warwick Gardens

47 Warwick Gardens, London W14 8PL
TEL: 0171-603 7614 (AND FAX)

Bed and breakfast in a beautifully kept family home in a smart residential area of west London.

Just off the busy Kensington High Street, and a long stone's throw from the peace and quiet of Holland Park, Warwick Gardens is a rather grand residential street of white, four-storey houses with smart black railings and steps leading up to the front door. Nanette Stylianou has been running Number 47 as a B&B and family home for seven years, and guests keep returning for the sociable atmosphere as much as for the comfortable rooms. They will also be aware of the one house rule: bookings have to be made in advance and must be for a minimum of two nights. Breakfast is served around a highly polished mahogany table in the elegant dining-room. Nanette chats and offers advice as she treats guests to a continental array of brioche, croissants and cinnamon whirls, or stokes them up for a day's sightseeing with a full English breakfast. Afterwards, you can sit and plan your day in the restful sitting-room (which is open to guests only in the morning), with its muted blue and pink fabrics and French-style sofas. The three bedrooms are in the basement, but they are not at all gloomy. Two are large, with light, modern décor and doors leading out on to a small patio garden full of ivy and terracotta pots, while the third is smaller.

◑ Open all year ⏹ Nearest tube station is Earls Court (District and Piccadilly lines). Private car park (£6 per day); on-street parking at night ⏣ 1 twin, 2 double; all with bathroom/WC; TV, hair-dryer ⏥ Dining-room, sitting-room, garden ⏦ No wheelchair access ● No children under 12; no dogs; no smoking ⏢ None accepted ⏣ Single occupancy of twin/double £50, twin/double £75; deposit required

---

La Gaffe

107–111 Heath Street, London NW3 6SS
TEL: 0171-435 8965   FAX: 0171-794 7592

Comfortable small hotel in Hampstead village, with friendly hosts and popular Italian restaurant.

Right at the top of the hill leading down to Hampstead's trendy High Street, La Gaffe is more obvious as a restaurant than as a hotel. Surprisingly perhaps for London, the building was originally a shepherd's cottage. Although vast Hampstead Heath is only a few minutes' walk away, the days when sheep roamed the area are long gone, and La Gaffe's flamboyant sign and neat canopies are much more typical of this fashionable residential area. The restaurant – predominantly Italian, with a menu that changes frequently – has been run by Bernardo and Androulla Stella for 34 years: 'We might not be the best hotel and restaurant in the world,' Bernardo says cheerfully, but we should win awards for stamina.' The fact is that La Gaffe is an excellent example of its type. The bedrooms are simple and well kept with neat, basic shower-rooms, and though they're not very big, pretty flowery fabrics give them a lift. If you prefer a bath

35

you need to go along the corridor to one of the shared bathrooms. Some of the rooms have been refurbished recently, while those at the back are wonderfully peaceful. Afternoon tea is served in a small, leafy roof-garden and guests can have breakfast in the rather arty coffee bar, busy with local people.

◐ Open all year ⤷ Nearest tube station is Hampstead (Northern line). Private car park (limited); on-street parking ⤶ 5 single, 4 twin, 3 double, 4 four-poster, 2 family rooms; all with shower/WC exc 3 four-posters with bathroom/WC; TV, hair-dryer, direct-dial telephone ⊘ Restaurant, bar, roof-garden; conference facilities (max 30 people incl up to 22 residential); early suppers for children ⅙ No wheelchair access ⊖ No dogs; no smoking in bedrooms and some public rooms ▭ Access, Amex, Diners, Visa 🖃 Single £45, single occupancy of twin/double £55, twin/double £70, four-poster £95, family room £95; deposit required. Cooked B £3.50; alc L, D £16

The Gore

189 Queen's Gate, London SW7 5EX
TEL: 0171-584 6601   FAX: 0171-589 8127

Fun hotel with a nostalgic Victorian theme, close to central London's parks and museums.

This hotel is stuck in a time-warp and proud to be there. Preserving the décor it might have had when it first opened in 1892, the Gore is stuffed full of potted palms and Victorian antiques ranging from beds to carpets to commodes. The dark cream walls are covered in over 4,000 original paintings and sketches. Although the hotel is eccentric and designed to be fun, there is no skimping on creature comforts. As the brochure says, 'by special request, hot water is now conveyed to guests' bathrooms by way of an efficient plumbing system.' Bathrooms in fact have all sorts of quirky features, including throne lavatories and massive brass shower heads, although some bedrooms have shower-rooms only. Bedrooms vary enormously: opt for a corner room with extra windows if you think the Victorian gloom will get you down. For the theatrically inclined, the by-now-famous Venus Room swims in heavy gold fabrics and has an ornate, gilded bed carved with serpents and an eagle. More down-to-earth, colonial-style Bistrot 190 on the ground floor, with its wooden floor, marble-topped tables, candelabra-wielding statues and overhead fan, has a superb atmosphere at any time of day. It serves generous portions of well-priced dishes such as rump of lamb with vegetable and almond couscous; steaks; salads; and an exceptional range of fish, to guests and passers-by.

◐ Closed 25 & 26 Dec ⤷ Nearest tube station is Gloucester Road (Piccadilly, Circle and District lines). On-street parking (metered); public car park nearby ⤶ 24 single, 5 twin, 15 double, 4 four-poster, 6 suites; most with bathroom/WC, some with shower/WC; TV, room service, hair-dryer, mini-bar, direct-dial telephone; no tea/coffee-making facilities in rooms ⊘ 2 restaurants, bar, lounge ⅙ No wheelchair access ⊖ None ▭ Access, Amex, Diners, Switch, Visa 🖃 Single £111, single occupancy of twin/double £124, twin/double £156, four-poster £170, suite £220; deposit required. Continental B £6.50, cooked B £9.50; alc L £25, D £30; bistro meals available

The Goring

Beeston Place, London SW1W 0JW
TEL: 0171-396 9000   FAX: 0171-834 4393

Grand, traditional, family-run hotel half-way between Victoria station and Buckingham Palace.

'When your name is above the door you try that much harder' is the family motto of the Goring family, who have been managing this hotel since O.R. Goring had it built in 1910. It seems to work – the atmosphere is happy, with loyal good-humoured staff, many of whom have been here for decades. Perhaps because this rather grand brick building was specifically designed as a hotel and hasn't been converted from something else, the public rooms work well. A vast marble-floored lobby with a bustling city-hotel feel leads into the traditional Garden Lounge, where comfortable sofas are arranged around log fires or picture windows overlooking lawns and formal borders. Whoever designed the restaurant was blessed with foresight: it is big enough to accommodate the large number of people who eat here. It is especially busy at lunchtime, when it is a popular venue for huddles of business executives tucking in to game and English roasts. The bedrooms too are a good size, and half of them have double glazing and air-conditioning. One attractive feature is that even the singles have the same excellent facilities as the superior rooms. The rooms with balconies overlooking the garden are particularly lovely. The rich fabrics, antique furniture and mellow colour schemes are what you'd expect in such traditional surroundings, as is the luxury of the grand marble bathrooms in a hotel which boasts that it was the first in the world to offer private bathrooms and central heating to each of its cosseted guests.

◖ Open all year   ⚡ Nearest tube station is Victoria (Victoria, Circle and District lines). Private car park (£17.50 for 24 hours), on-street parking (metered)   ⟻ 21 single, 11 twin, 40 double, 4 suites; all with bathroom/WC; TV, 24-hour room service, hair-dryer, direct-dial telephone   ✓ Restaurant, bar, 2 lounges, garden; air-conditioning in some bedrooms and one public room; conference facilities (max 52 people residential/non-residential)   ⅃ Wheelchair access to hotel (ramp), restaurant and WC (unisex); lift to bedrooms   ● No dogs   ▭ Access, Amex, Diners, Switch, Visa   £ Single £135 to £170, single occupancy of twin/double £170, twin/double £170 to £212, suite £276 to £306; deposit required. Continental B £10, cooked B £13.50; set L £20/24, D £30 . Special breaks available

---

Green Park Hotel

Half Moon Street, London W1Y 8BP
TEL: 0171-629 7522   FAX: 0171-491 8971

Efficiently run, mostly business-oriented hotel in central London.

In a relatively quiet side-street not far from the busy stream of traffic along Piccadilly, the Green Park Hotel is modern and comfortable. It is a sound choice if you're looking for a good-sized bedroom in a fairly large hotel without having to pay premium rates. Fourteen Georgian town houses have been linked together to make up the 160 or so rooms. A programme of refurbishment is gradually being carried out, starting on the upper floors, so ask for a room at the top if you want immaculate modern décor and a smart new bathroom. The other rooms are equally well equipped – with satellite television channels, and tea and coffee facilities as well as 24-hour room service – but some can look a bit tired, and the bathrooms are old-fashioned. Executive rooms have extras such as bathrobes and Jacuzzi baths. Downstairs, the hotel has a busy feel, with plenty of people having tea and scones in the open-plan lounge and bar area in the afternoons. In the evenings, smartly turned-out staff in the large Claude Monet restaurant, with its French impressionist prints and tall potted palms, cope with groups of business people as well as individuals.

◑ Open all year   ☒ Nearest tube station is Green Park (Piccadilly, Victoria and Jubilee lines). On-street parking (metered); public car park nearby   🛏 44 single, 40 twin, 67 double, 1 four-poster, 3 family rooms, 6 suites; all with bathroom/WC; TV, 24-hour room service, hair-dryer, trouser press, direct-dial telephone   ⌘ Restaurant, bar/lounge, 2 conservatories; air-conditioning in public areas and conference rooms; conference facilities (max 100 people residential/non-residential) ; babysitting   ᕕ No wheelchair access   ● No dogs; no smoking in some bedrooms   ▭ Access, Amex, Diners, Visa   £ Single £125, single occupancy of twin/double £150, twin/double £150, four-poster £180, family room £170, suite £190; deposit required. Continental B £9, cooked B £11; alc L, D £20 . Special breaks available

---

Halkin Hotel

5–6 Halkin Street, London SW1X 7DJ
TEL: 0171-333 1000   FAX: 0171-333 1100

Extremely smart, modern, Italian-designed hotel, well suited to business executives.

Close to the walls of Buckingham Palace, just a short walk from Victoria station, this unusual hotel is a run-of-the-mill mock-Georgian house on the outside, but an extraordinary model of interior design within. Ultra-modern and minimalist, the hotel has open spaces with only marble floors, blue leather tub chairs and weeping figs to occupy them. Its guests are mostly businessmen, waited on by male staff in dark Armani suits (the owners have a part-share in the Armani company). In the restaurant, the menu offers elegant Italian dishes with long names and plenty of luxury ingredients, such as 'scallop of salmon cooked in clay, served with squid ink farfalle with peas, spring onions and celery sauce'. Service is formal though not unfriendly. Rooms vary from standard doubles to two-bedroom suites, but are all a good size and are similar in décor. Wood-panelled walls and plain sleek furnishings in cream and black make a restful backdrop to modern facilities such as VCRs and fax machines, and there are lots of switches and buttons to play with, to alter the temperature or lock the door by remote control.

Report forms are at the back of the Guide; write a letter or e-mail us if you prefer. Our e-mail address is: "guidereports@which.co.uk".

◑ Open all year; restaurant closed 25 & 26 Dec, and Good Friday ☑ Nearest tube station is Victoria (District, Circle and Victoria lines). On-street parking (metered) 🛏 30 twin/double, 11 suites; family rooms available all with bathroom/WC; TV, 24-hour room service, hair-dryer, mini-bar, direct-dial telephone, radio, VCR; no tea/coffee-making facilities in rooms ✔ Restaurant, bar, lounge, business-room, private dining-room; air-conditioning in all rooms; conference facilities (max 45 people incl up to 41 residential) ; early suppers for children ; toys, babysitting, baby-listening, cots, highchairs ♿ No wheelchair access ● No dogs; no pipes or cigars in restaurant, no smoking in some bedrooms ▭ Access, Amex, Diners, Switch, Visa ⟨£⟩ Single occupancy of twin/double £259 to £323, twin/double £259 to £558, suite £411 to £558; deposit required. Continental B £10.50, cooked B £14.50; set L £18; alc L, D £50; (1996 prices) . Special breaks available

Hazlitt's

6 Frith Street, London W1V 5TZ
TEL: 0171-434 1771   FAX: 0171-439 1524

Characterful small hotel with friendly staff, in the heart of London's Theatreland.

Although the blue plaque outside Number Six Frith Street announces that the eighteenth-century essayist William Hazlitt once lived here, it seems that he was not the only noteworthy resident. All sorts of intriguing people lend their names to the bedrooms of this beautifully kept hotel, which is furnished as a Georgian house might once have been. Three town houses joined together make space enough for 23 rooms, which range from a simple single called Mrs Newdigate (after the landlady famed for keeping Hazlitt's corpse under the bed so that she could re-let the room) to Baron Willoughby, with its leather sofa in front of a grand marble fireplace, which is the only suite. Despite some four-poster and half-tester beds, and masses of other antiques, none of the rooms is particularly luxurious, though they are stylish; most of the old-fashioned bathrooms are a good size. Mary Barker, a quiet room at the back with a large airy bathroom, is one of our favourites. An indulgent, freshly baked continental breakfast is brought up to your room and the porter is always happy to nip out to one of the nearby cafés to fetch you a snack at other times.

◑ Closed 24 to 27 Dec ☑ Nearest tube station is Leicester Square (Piccadilly and Northern lines). Public car park nearby 🛏 5 single, 1 twin, 8 double, 8 four-poster, 1 suite; all with bathroom/WC exc 1 single with shower/WC; TV, hair-dryer, direct-dial telephone; no tea/coffee-making facilities in rooms ✔ Lounge ♿ No wheelchair access ● Dogs by arrangement ▭ Access, Amex, Delta, Diners, Switch, Visa ⟨£⟩ Single £127, twin/double £162, suite £217; deposit required. Continental B £6.50 (prices valid till Mar 1997)

L'Hotel

28 Basil Street, London SW3 1AS
TEL: 0171-589 6286   FAX: 0171-225 0011

Up-market B&B in a quiet residential street behind Harrods.

Basil Street is made up of smart red-brick apartment blocks, and is much sought after for its proximity to top London shops as well as parks, museums and restaurants. Staying at L'Hotel is a relatively inexpensive way to base yourself in the area, (although it is not exactly cheap). Having been completely revamped since last year, the bedrooms now have a cool colonial feel, with neutral fabrics, wooden bedsteads and louvre shutters. The well-equipped bathrooms are half-marble and half-tiled. Rooms at the front have the edge for size. You can have breakfast in your room, or downstairs in the Metro café, where predominantly French staff serve light meals all day to residents as well as to anyone else who happens to drop in. At night, the reception is shared with L'Hotel's sister establishment, the Capital (see entry).

◗ Open all year; restaurant closed Sun eve (Piccadilly line). On-street parking (metered) bathroom/WC; TV, limited room service, mini-bar, direct-dial telephone ✓ Restaurant, bar (both air-conditioned) ; early suppers for children ⬚ Wheelchair access to hotel (3 steps), 1 ground-floor bedroom ● No dogs in public rooms ▭ Access, Amex, Diners, Switch, Visa £ Single occupancy of twin £145, twin £145, suite £165; deposit required. Alc L, D £17.50 ⤵ Nearest tube station is Knightsbridge 🛏 11 twin, 1 suite; all with

The Leonard ☆

15 Seymour Street, London W1H 5AA
TEL: 0171-935 2010   FAX: 0171-935 6700

Luxury suites and outstanding service abound at this recently opened hotel in a convenient central location.

'I had a most enjoyable time staying at this beautifully decorated and homely town house hotel. The standard of service was outstanding' – this was the verdict of one reader after his stay at the Leonard. Another wrote to say that in his opinion it is the best town house in central London. This is high praise indeed, in an area in which there are quite a number of luxury hotels. Most of the rooms are suites, and you certainly get your fair share of grandeur – a state of affairs far removed from the times when the building was a nurses' home. The sitting area in Room 11 is big enough to host a ball, while Room 22 has a full-sized kitchen, which includes a dishwasher and washing machine. Mod cons such as video recorders and CD players are well hidden behind the antiques and rich fabrics, and at a first glance it would be easy to miss some of the thoughtful design points, such as the heated mirrors which don't mist up in the large, and very indulgent, bathrooms. From your room you can order anything you like at any time, but there is also a small bar downstairs, where straightforward snacks such as salmon fish cakes or BLT sandwiches will bring you back to earth.

All entries in the Guide are rewritten every year, not least because standards fluctuate. Don't trust an out-of-date Guide.

◐ Open all year 🔁 Nearest tube station is Marble Arch (Central line). Public car park nearby 🛏 2 single, 3 twin/double, 1 four-poster, 20 suites; all with bathroom/WC exc singles with shower/WC; TV, room service, hair-dryer, mini-bar, direct-dial telephone, CD player, VCR; tea/coffee-making facilities on request 🍴 Restaurant, bar, lounge, drying-room; air-conditioning in all rooms; conference facilities (max 30 people incl up to 15 residential); gym ; early suppers for children ; toys, baby-sitting, baby-listening ♿ Wheelchair access to hotel (2 steps), restaurant (ramp), 1 ground-floor bedroom specially equipped for disabled people ● No dogs ▭ Access, Amex, Delta, Diners, Switch, Visa £ Single £120, twin/double from £160, four-poster £180, suite from £220; deposit required. Continental B £8.50, cooked B £12.50 . Special breaks available

London Outpost ☆

69 Cadogan Gardens, London SW3 2RB
TEL: 0171-589 7333   FAX: 0171-581 4958

A small hotel with smart rooms, impeccable service and the atmosphere of a gentleman's club.

This hotel has changed its name since last year's *Guide* (when it was known as the Fenja) and is under new ownership. Now an outpost to the recently formed Carnegie Club at Skibo Castle in Scotland – a luxurious sanctuary for fishing, hunting and primarily golf – this hotel keeps the quiet atmosphere of a gentlemen's club, though it is not in the least bit stuffy. One delighted guest wrote to say that the reception staff were without fault: 'They were very polite and also amusing – a rare thing these days, when it seems that hotel staff often seem to take themselves rather seriously.... Room service was efficient and prompt, the breakfast a case of "your wish is our command".' Ticking clocks, polished antiques and dark masculine furnishings in the sitting-room and library set the tone for the 11 bedrooms, which are luxurious without being fussy. Named after writers and artists who once lived in this leafy area of central London, the rooms are mostly large with excellent facilities, including air-conditioning, gas-flame fires and smart bathrooms with power showers. There is no restaurant but you can have light snacks at any time.

◐ Open all year 🔁 Nearest tube station is Sloane Square (District and Circle lines). On-street parking (metered) 🛏 6 twin, 4 double, 1 four-poster; all with bathroom/WC; TV, room service, hair-dryer, mini-bar, trouser press, direct-dial telephone 🍴 Lounge, library, conservatory, games room, garden; air-conditioning in all rooms; conference facilities (max 10 people residential/non-residential) ♿ No wheelchair access ● No dogs; no smoking in bedrooms ▭ Access, Amex, Delta, Diners, Switch, Visa £ Twin/double £176 to £235, four-poster £276; deposit required. Continental B £9.50, cooked B £15

It is always worth enquiring about the availability of special breaks or weekend prices. The prices we quote are the standard rates for one night – most hotels offer reduced rates for longer stays.

The Montcalm

Great Cumberland Place, London W1A 2LF
TEL: 0171-402 4288   FAX: 0171-724 9180

Smart and exceptionally well-run hotel in a quiet location in the centre of London.

In a grand sweeping crescent of Georgian town houses a few minutes' walk from Marble Arch, the Montcalm was once the rather elegant home of an eighteenth-century general renowned for his style and generous hospitality. It's a good background for any hotel, and the current owners, Japan Air Lines, have made the most of it. The bedrooms are luxurious without being fussy – custom-made maplewood furniture and generous goodies in plush marble bathrooms are standard, along with power showers, bathrobes, air-conditioning and impeccable housekeeping. Many of the staff have worked here for years. The style of the rooms varies, with standard rooms on the fifth floor having a cottagey feel and executive rooms tending to be smarter and larger. The Montcalm also pays attention to unusual demands, providing a non-allergenic bedroom, where the windows are sealed and dust and fibres are kept to a minimum, as well as shower toilets in the lobby, which are preferred by some Japanese guests. Service throughout is both courteous and good-humoured, not least in the restaurant, where a predominantly modern British menu includes dishes such as scallops and orange salad with honey, pan-fried duck with black pudding, and rabbit braised in cider. In the spacious open-plan lobby, with its comfortable sofas and jade-green armchairs, afternoon tea is a popular event, and the cocktail bar is open 24 hours.

◗ Open all year; restaurant closed Sun eve   ↗ Nearest tube station is Marble Arch (Central line). Private car park (£25 for 24 hours); on-street parking (metered)   ⊨ 45 single, 46 twin, 15 double, 14 suites; all with bathroom/WC; TV, 24-hour room service, hair-dryer, mini-bar, direct-dial telephone, fax ; tea/coffee-making facilities on request, trouser press in some rooms   ✓ Restaurant, bar, lounge; air-conditioning in all rooms; conference facilities (max 80 people incl up to 50 residential) ; early suppers for children ; babysitting   ⅋ No wheelchair access   ● No dogs; no smoking in some public rooms and some bedrooms   ⊟ Access, Amex, Diners, Visa   £ Single from £217, single occupancy of twin/double from £241, twin/double from £241, suite from £294; deposit required. Continental B £10.50, cooked B £14.50; set L £25, D £27 . Special breaks available

---

Morgan House ☆

120 Ebury Street, London SW1W 9QQ
TEL: 0171-730 2384   FAX: 0171-730 8442

Good-value rooms in an immaculate, modern B&B close to Victoria station.

Morgan House is the latest venture of Ian Berry and Rachel Joplin, who also own and run Woodville House, just down the road (see entry). Opened at the beginning of 1996, Morgan House is brighter and more modern than its sister hotel, but shares the same philosophy of friendly service and simple rooms with good facilities. Each floor contains three rooms which share a shower-room, although a few of the rooms (which are more expensive) have their own *en-suite* shower. The higher-up rooms at the back of the house have interesting views over the roof tops of Belgravia. The décor is stylish, and typically features light colours and iron or rattan bedsteads. There is a separate shared kitchen, complete with drink-making and ironing facilities. The breakfast room in the basement is a cheerful place in which to linger, with its bright David Hockney prints and sunny yellow walls. Breakfast duty falls to Ian, who serves up the same generous array of cooked dishes, cereals and home-made muesli that guests enjoy at Woodville House. Plans are afoot to start work on the garden, after which the hotel would be a near-perfect base for sightseers on a budget.

◖ Open all year   ⧖ Nearest tube station is Victoria (Victoria, Circle & District lines). On-street parking at night and weekends; public car park nearby   ⤙ 2 single, 3 twin, 3 double, 3 family rooms; 3 with shower/WC; TV, hair-dryer   ⊘ Dining-room, drying-room, library, garden; toys   ♿ No wheelchair access   ⬤ No dogs; no smoking in public rooms   ▭ Access, Visa   £ Single £39, single occupancy of twin/double £45 to £65, twin/double £58 to £75, family room £68 to £98; deposit required

---

Number Sixteen

16 Sumner Place, London SW7 3EG
TEL: 0171-589 5232   FAX: 0171-584 8615

Mid-sized B&B with a rather grand country-house feel, in an ideal location for tourists.

A few yards from the trendy part of the Old Brompton Road, with its patisseries and interior design shops, Number Sixteen is one of three small hotels in Sumner Place recommended in this *Guide*. A number of major museums are only a short walk away, and the hotel is a beautifully kept house in which the bedrooms are characterful and generally a good size. Given names instead of numbers, the rooms are decorated in traditional style with good-quality fabrics, antiques and padded headboards, in restful blues, yellows and greens. Though they all have the same facilities, including fluffy bathrobes, one or two stand out from the rest: 'London' on the ground floor has the biggest bathroom of the standard rooms, while 'Tapestry', a luxury double, has a rich autumnal décor and is peacefully situated at the back of the house. A generous continental breakfast, with porridge and eggs as well as croissants and fruit juice, is included in the price of the room, and if you're not leaving straightaway, hang around for morning coffee in the lounge.

◖ Open all year   ⧖ Nearest tube station is South Kensington (Piccadilly, District and Circle lines). On-street parking (metered)   ⤙ 9 single, 24 twin/double, 3 suites; most with bathroom/WC, some with shower/WC; TV, hair-dryer, mini-bar, direct-dial telephone ; no tea/coffee-making facilities in rooms   ⊘ Bar, lounge, library, conservatory, garden   ♿ No wheelchair access   ⬤ No children under 8; no dogs   ▭ Access, Amex, Diners, Switch, Visa   £ Single £80 to £105, single occupancy of twin/double £140 to £170, twin/double £140 to £170, suite £180; deposit required. Cooked B £8; (prices valid till Mar 1997) . Special breaks available

Park Lane Hotel

Piccadilly, London W1Y 8BX
TEL: 0171-499 6321   FAX: 0171-499 1965

Grand old hotel with impeccable service and beautiful Art Deco ballroom – a landmark in London.

If you're keen on BBC costume dramas, then the chances are you've already seen the inside of the Park Lane Hotel. The three-storey, 11,000-square-feet Art Deco ballroom is perhaps the hotel's greatest treasure and favoured by swish functions and television crews alike. Beyond are lounges and garden rooms, bars and restaurants, where extremely professional staff, unfazed by the size of the enterprise, keep the whole thing moving like clockwork. Like other grand hotels, Park Lane is continually undergoing refurbishment, and many of the spacious bedrooms are now light and modern with beige or light green décor, or have a bold combination of rich yellows and reds. In all cases the original 1920s features have been kept – Art Deco marble bathrooms have gleaming chrome fittings, and in some rooms *chinoiserie* furnishings are intact. Thanks to the triple glazing, all the rooms are quiet, but those overlooking the garden have a better and leafier outlook. Sheraton Hotels took over the Park Lane in April 1996 promising no major changes... watch this space.

◑ Open all year   ◪ Nearest tube station is Green Park (Piccadilly, Victoria and Jubilee lines). Private car park (£26 for 24 hours)   ⊨ 50 single, 221 twin/double, 40 suites; all with bathroom/WC; TV, room service, hair-dryer, mini-bar, direct-dial telephone ; tea/coffee-making facilities and trouser press on request   ⬦ 2 restaurants, bar, lounge; air-conditioning in public areas and some bedrooms; conference facilities (max 550 people incl up to 311 residential); gym, solarium ; early suppers for children   ᕕ Wheelchair access to hotel (1 step), 4 bedrooms specially equipped for disabled people, lift to rooms   ● Dogs by arrangement; no smoking in some bedrooms   ▭ Access, Amex, Delta, Diners, Switch, Visa   £ Single £200, twin/double £217, suite £270; deposit required. Continental B £11, cooked B £14; set L £21, D £25; alc L, D £35; brasserie meals available

Pelham Hotel

15 Cromwell Place, London SW7 2LA
TEL: 0171-589 8288   FAX: 0171-584 8444

Extreme luxury in a small hotel frequented by the rich and famous, with prices to suit.

Fifty yards from South Kensington tube station, in the thick of west London shopping and museums, the Pelham is a wonderland of extravagant and luxurious interior design. Ticking grandfather clocks, oil portraits, gilt mirrors and rich fabrics combine with bowls of red apples, fragrant flower arrangements and beeswax candles to create a designer world in which every last ornament has been carefully chosen. And it's not just a showpiece. One reader wrote to report that the staff were very helpful, and there is 24-hour room service as well as fax and other office services behind the scenes. The 41 bedrooms range from grand suites with decorated ceilings, chandeliers and lace-edged bed linen to small doubles with acres of fabric but not much room around the bed – one American couple wrote to say that while they loved the location they thought their very small room overpriced. All the rooms have smart marble bathrooms, which are immaculately maintained. Downstairs, Kemps restaurant has a cheerful, informal feel with blue and yellow checks, and bright blue glasses on the tables. A short, modern menu including poached chicken with ginger and bean shoots is good value; note, however, that a 10 per cent service charge is added to your bill.

◖ Open all year; restaurant closed Sat eve & Sun ⬃ Nearest tube station is South Kensington (Piccadilly, District and Circle lines). On-street parking (metered) ⊨ 7 single, 20 twin, 12 double, 2 suites; family rooms available; all with bathroom/WC; TV, 24-hour room service, hair-dryer, mini-bar, direct-dial telephone; trouser press in some rooms ⊘ Restaurant, bar, 2 lounges; air-conditioning in all rooms; conference facilities (max 11 people residential/non-residential) ; early suppers for children
⩇ No wheelchair access ● Dogs by arrangement; no smoking in some public rooms and some bedrooms ⊟ Access, Amex, Delta, Switch, Visa ⊞ Single £141, single occupancy of twin/double £170 to £217, twin/double £170 to £217, suite £264 to £335; deposit required. Continental B £9.50, cooked B £12.50; set L £11, D £12.50 to £15.50

Pembridge Court

34 Pembridge Gardens, London W2 4DX
TEL: 0171-229 9977 FAX: 0171-727 4982

Small family-run hotel with happy atmosphere in a lively area of west London.

Pembridge Court has changed hands over the past year, though the new owners have guaranteed not to alter a thing. And a good job too, because as it is, this little hotel is almost perfect. Most of the cheerful staff have been here for years and are tirelessly friendly and helpful. With the famous tourist sights of Portobello market and Kensington Palace only a five-minute walk away, you can busy yourself all day without going far, and then come back for afternoon tea in the stylish modern lounge with its games, newspapers, tourist guides, and wallpaper designed by a previous guest. Caps restaurant and bar in the basement is a cosy place in the evenings with its exposed brick walls and collection of school caps spanning hundreds of years. The menu is short but varied, ranging from crispy bacon and avocado salad to sweet-and-sour king prawns with rice. Prices for the bedrooms vary according to the size of the room. We were asked not to mention the 'Last Resort' – a single officially kept for emergencies only, but the favourite of many returning guests – but thought it so characterful and such good value that it deserves recommending. Nearly all of the 20 bedrooms are deluxe rooms, thoughtfully kitted out and with plenty of toiletries in good-sized bathrooms. 'Spencer' and 'Churchill', named after the two hotel cats, are perhaps the quietest as they're at the back and have two sets of doors separating them from the rest of the hotel.

◐ Open all year ⊿ Nearest tube station is Notting Hill Gate (Central, District and Circle lines). On-street parking (metered) 🛏 19 twin/double, 1 four-poster; family rooms available; all with bathroom/WC; TV, room service, hair-dryer, trouser press, direct-dial telephone ; no tea/coffee-making facilities in bedrooms ✓ Restaurant, bar, lounge; air-conditioning in public rooms; conference facilities (max 16 people residential/non-residential); early suppers for children ; baby-listening ⅃ No wheelchair access ● No dogs in public rooms ▭ Access, Amex, Diners, Visa £ Single occupancy of twin/double £100 to £125, twin/double £120 to £160, four-poster £155, family room £160 to £165; deposit required. Alc D £15; snack meals available . Special breaks available

Pippa Pop-ins [see map 3]

430 Fulham Road, London SW6 1DU
TEL: 0171-385 2457/8   FAX: 0171-385 5706

An overnight nursery for children aged between 2 and 12, with lots of activities.

Clowns clamber all over the windows, and the coats in the hall have name tags – not the sort of thing you'd usually expect to find in a hotel, but this one is for the under-12s only. A nursery school in the daytime, Pippa Pop-ins is a good-looking, west London town house which takes up to ten overnight guests. All the staff are trained nannies and have a happy attitude towards their job. Activities include cookery, singing, playing with the resident rabbits in the small garden, and painting (of which the mass of children's artwork that lines the walls is testimony). The house is designed to appeal to children, from the bright-yellow exterior paintwork to the themed bedrooms. The Pink Room, with its dozens of soft bunnies and white, wooden beds, is usually the favourite of the older children; youngsters might prefer the Safari Room, with its toy lions, monkeys, hippos and elephants. Even the bathrooms are themed, although last year's clowns have now been replaced with galleons and pirates. Typically, the guests are children whose parents are staying elsewhere in London and will be out late, although there is a daily school-run too. Like any adult hotel, Pippa Pop-ins is open for 24 hours a day, seven days a week, but children may stay up to a maximum of four nights only.

◐ Closed Chr & Easter ⊿ Nearest tube station is Fulham Broadway (District line). On-street parking 🛏 2 bedrooms; 2 public bathrooms; room service, mini-bar with treats for children ✓ Dining-room, milk bar, lounge, drying-room, garden ; early suppers for children ; toys, playrooms, baby-sitting, baby-listening, excursion activities for children ⅃ No wheelchair access ● No children under 2; no dogs ▭ Amex, Visa £ Per child £40 (rate inc dinner); deposit required . Special breaks available

The Guide is totally independent, accepts no free hospitality, and survives on the number of copies sold each year.

The Portobello

22 Stanley Gardens, London W11 2NG
TEL: 0171-727 2777   FAX: 0171-792 9641

Comfortable hotel in quiet residential street, with warm welcome and one or two eccentricities.

A one-minute walk from the arty Portobello street market, this hotel attracts artists and musicians among its guests. It's easy to feel at home with the Bohemian décor and laid-back atmosphere, in particular perhaps because the staff are friendly and flexible – breakfast is served until 11.30am and the restaurant is open 24 hours. One reader praised the courteous service, but was disappointed with his room, which he called 'well *passé*'. One or two of the bedrooms are definitely off-beat and whether or not you like yours may be down to how much you enjoy something different. Room 16, for example, has a circular bed – London's first, it is claimed – and a bath in the bedroom, while Room 22 has a bathing machine with numerous levers as well as taps. Since last year some refurbishment has been carried out and the good-value singles in the attic now have a restful sand-coloured Moroccan theme. Away from the bedrooms, the lounge, with its deep sofas, complimentary daily papers and leafy outlook on to the garden, is a lovely place to while away your time; while the bar and restaurant in the basement are light and modern, serving snacks such as smoked salmon with lemon and juniper berries, provençal fish stew and solid English favourites such as steak and kidney pudding.

◑ Closed 23 Dec to 2 Jan   ⊿ Nearest tube station is Notting Hill Gate (Central, District and Circle lines). On-street parking (metered)   ⤙ 5 single, 2 twin, 9 double, 3 four-poster, 3 suites; some with bathroom/WC, most with shower/WC; TV, room service, hair-dryer, mini-bar, trouser press, direct-dial telephone   ⌀ Restaurant, bar, lounge, drying-room, garden; air-conditioning on top floor; conference facilities (max 20 people residential/non-residential); early suppers for children   ㋛ No wheelchair access   ● No dogs in public rooms   ▭ Access, Amex, Delta, Diners, Switch, Visa   £ Single £80 to £90, single occupancy of twin/double £100, twin/double £140, four-poster £150, suite £190; deposit required. Alc L £15, D £20

Sandringham Hotel

3 Holford Road, London NW3 1AD
TEL: 0171-435 1569   FAX: 0171-431 5932

Smart rooms in a small hotel a few yards from Hampstead Heath, in a quiet residential area.

A new entry in the *Guide* last year, the Sandringham Hotel has boomed over the past 12 months. American ex-pats Michael and Jill von Grey bought the tall red-brick house in 1993, completely gutting it and transforming it into an elegant small hotel. There's no formal reception area, but the lounge, with its unfussy blue and fawn furnishings and elegant marble fireplace, is an impressive introduction, and the welcome is friendly. One guest we overheard was delighted with her room and with the enthusiastic room service, which made no fuss about bringing her tea in bed even at 3am. The bedrooms and well-equipped bathrooms are designed by Jill and are all different – ranging from Room 12's iron bed and colonial cream linen furnishings to Room 9's rich modern fabrics, deep red carpet and sofa bed in a small lounge. The rooms vary greatly in size and are priced accordingly. The ground-floor Garden Room, with leafy views, is the largest and perhaps the most peaceful. Breakfast is an extravagant affair with pancakes, eggs Benedict, French toast and bread baked on the premises, to name but a few items, while in the evenings there's a predominantly Italian room-service menu if you don't fancy one of the local restaurants.

◑ Open all year ⊿ Nearest tube station is Hampstead (Northern line). Private car park 🖛 5 single, 4 twin, 6 double, 2 suites; most with bathroom/WC, some with shower/WC; TV, room service, hair-dryer, direct-dial telephone ✧ Restaurant, lounge, garden; conference facilities (max 25 people incl up to 17 residential); early suppers for children ⅊ No wheelchair access ● No children under 7; no dogs; no smoking in bedrooms ▭ Access, Amex, Delta, Switch, Visa £ Single £65 to £85, single occupancy of twin/double £80 to £95, twin/double £90 to £130, suite £140; deposit required. Cooked B £4.50; alc D £15

The Savoy

Strand, London WC2R 0EU
TEL: 0171-836 4343 FAX: 0171-240 6040

The grande dame of London hotels, with good food and excellent service.

Probably the most famous of the capital's grand hotels, the Savoy opened its doors to a great fanfare in 1889, luring famous people such as Lillie Langtry and the Prince of Wales in its first few months just to set the standard. More than a hundred years later, it has become one of the city's landmarks. You don't need to be royalty, or even famous, to enjoy the hotel's bustling atmosphere: plenty of people from all walks of life pop in for tea in the cavernous Thames Foyer with its marble pillars and numerous chandeliers. It's a sign of the hotel staff's genuine hospitality that they treat once-in-a-lifetime guests with the same polite good humour as they do celebrities. If you are here on a once-only visit opt for a room with a river view. Some of the rooms follow the Art Deco style the hotel established after refurbishment in the 1920s, while others are more traditional, with pale colour schemes and ornate plasterwork. As you would expect, facilities are excellent: everything you need by way of toiletries is there in indulgent marble bathrooms, and as an extra treat the bedsheets are pure linen. A recent innovation means that fit or merely keen guests can now work out in the fitness gallery or laze about beside the covered, rooftop swimming-pool.

Many hotels offer special rates for stays of a few nights or more. It is worth enquiring when you book.

◐ Open all year; 2 restaurants closed Sat L and Sun ⬀ Near Charing Cross and Embankment tube stations (Jubilee, Bakerloo, Circle, District and Northern lines). Private car park (£22 per night); on-street parking (metered) ⟻ 46 single, 98 twin/double, 8 family rooms, 50 suites; all with bathroom/WC; TV, 24-hour room service, hair-dryer, mini-bar, trouser press, direct-dial telephone ; no tea/coffee-making facilities in rooms ⟡ 3 restaurants, bar, lounge, reading room; air-conditioning in all rooms; conference facilities (max 500 people incl up to 100 residential); gym, sauna, solarium, heated indoor swimming-pool ; early suppers for children ; babysitting ♿ Wheelchair access to hotel (1 ramp), restaurant, WC (M,F), 7 rooms specially equipped for disabled people ● No dogs ▭ Access, Amex, Delta, Diners, Switch, Visa £ Single £229, single occupancy of twin/double £282, twin/double £311, family room £358, suite £382 to £881; deposit required. Continental B £12.50, cooked B £16.50; set L £27.50, D £33 to £39.50; alc L, D £40 . Special breaks available

Searcy's Roof Garden Bedrooms

30 Pavilion Road, London SW1X 0HJ
TEL: 0171-584 4921 FAX: 0171-823 8694

Good-value accommodation but no extra services at this block of rooms in central London.

Searcy's Roof Garden is in an excellent location for people visiting London for almost any reason. In a quiet side-street (although the peace is occasionally disturbed by the Household Cavalry clattering past) and close to shops, tourist sights, theatres and restaurants, it couldn't be better situated for those who like to be out all day and don't mind missing out on the feel of a more conventional hotel. There are no public rooms here. After pressing a buzzer and speaking through an intercom you're left to find your own way up in the lift to the small reception area and your room. Well-equipped and beautifully kitted out with dark reproduction furniture, light flowery fabrics and pretty wallpaper, the rooms are a good size, leaving plenty of space for a small table for continental breakfast. Bathrooms tend to be luxurious with proper cast-iron baths, brass or chrome fittings, and plenty of towels on a heated rail. There's no room service, but you can make use of a fully fitted kitchen off one of the landings.

◐ Closed 25 Dec ⬀ Nearest tube station is Knightsbridge (Piccadilly line). Public car park nearby ⟻ 3 single, 5 twin, 4 double, 1 suite; some in annexe; all with bathroom/WC; TV, hair-dryer, direct-dial telephone ⟡ Rooftop garden ♿ No wheelchair access ● No dogs ▭ Access, Amex, Delta, Switch, Visa £ Single £84, single occupancy of twin/double £93, twin/double £119, suite £146; deposit required

Thanet Hotel ☆

8 Bedford Place, London WC1B 5JA
TEL: 0171-636 2869 FAX: 0171-323 6676

Simple, good-sized rooms and generous breakfasts at this inexpensive B&B in central London.

'At only £85 for a family of four, and only a block away from the British Museum, we weren't expecting much,' wrote one reader who was pleasantly surprised by the Thanet Hotel: 'We got a fair-sized room, and the biggest breakfast with the most variety of offerings of our entire trip.' This four-storey brick town house is on a busy London street, so you might want to ask for a room at the back, though traffic is much lighter at night. Beyond that, drawbacks are few. The 14 bedrooms are immaculately kept, with light veneered furniture and flowery fabrics. Some have high ceilings and decorative fireplaces but mostly they are functional rather than grand. Room 5 is a good option for its balcony overlooking the garden, as is Room 9, which brings you eye-to-eye with the top of a huge horse chestnut tree, though the shower room is small. High housekeeping standards extend to the breakfast room, where dried flowers decorate the tables and complement pretty wildflower crockery. Toast and fresh coffee, as well as the Thanet Grill cooked breakfast, are served from behind a bar.

◑ Open all year 🚇 Near Russell Square and Holborn tube stations (Piccadilly and Central lines). On-street parking (metered) 🛏 5 single, 4 twin, 5 double; family rooms available all with shower/WC; TV, hair-dryer, direct-dial telephone; iron on request 🍽 Dining-room, lounge ♿ No wheelchair access ⊖ No dogs; no smoking in dining-room 💳 Access, Amex, Delta, Switch, Visa 💷 Single £54, single occupancy of twin/double £69, twin/double £69, family room £90; deposit required

---

Tophams Belgravia

28 Ebury Street, London SW1W 0LU
TEL: 0171-730 8147   FAX: 0171-823 5966

Old-fashioned hotel with attentive service and a happy atmosphere.

At the end of a busy one-way street, a few minutes' walk from Victoria station, Tophams is one of those well-established hotels that seem to tick along effortlessly, but actually put a lot of work into making their guests feel comfortable. Opened over 60 years ago, it's now run by the third generation of Tophams, and long-serving staff welcome familiar guests by name, remembering their likes and dislikes. In the basement is the rather gloomy Ebury Club bar, which is shared with club members, but there are plenty of other places to retreat to, and the spacious ground-floor restaurant is popular at lunchtime with couples quietly discussing how to spend the afternoon. One option is to have tea in the pretty floral lounge, an elegant and peaceful room well away from the bustle of the street outside.

Tophams' programme of refurbishment means that most of the bedrooms have recently been spruced up, with all but the attic rooms complete. The next stage of the programme is to fit out the last of the bedrooms with *en-suite* bathrooms. At the moment, bathrobes are provided for the quick dash along the landing from the good-sized old-fashioned single rooms in the attic, but if you don't mind that, these rooms are very good value for money. Antiques set against traditional muted colour schemes characterise the larger rooms on the lower floors. All are spotlessly clean, and sensibly laid out, for example with power points next to the mirror.

◑ Closed Chr & New Year; restaurant closed Sun eve 🚇 Nearest tube station is Victoria (Victoria, District and Circle lines). On-street parking (metered) 🛏 14 single, 10 twin, 14 double, 1 four-poster, 1 family room; most with bathroom/WC, 2 with shower/WC; TV, limited room service, hair-dryer, direct-dial telephone
✔ Restaurant, bar, lounge; conference facilities (max 28 people residential/non-residential) ; early suppers for children ♿ No wheelchair access ⊖ No dogs
▭ Access, Amex, Diners, Switch, Visa £ Single £70 to £100, single occupancy of twin/double £95 to £115, twin/double £95 to £115, four-poster £135, family room £150; deposit required. Set L £10; alc D £20

Windermere Hotel

142–144 Warwick Way, London SW1V 4JE
TEL: 0171-834 5163   FAX: 0171-630 8831

Small, family-run hotel near Victoria station, with good-value rooms and friendly informal service.

The streets around Victoria station make a pretty good base for budget visitors to London. With the tube only a few minutes' walk away and the surrounding streets packed with eating places in all styles and price brackets, the Windermere is in an ideal location. It is at the quiet end of Warwick Way, where buses and coaches are forbidden, so it doesn't suffer too much from traffic noise, though light sleepers should ask for a room on the top floor.

None of the 23 rooms is particularly large – some are little bigger than the bed – but all are well maintained and spotlessly clean, with light-blue and fawn décor, which helps to alleviate the sense of being cramped. If lack of space bothers you, opt for Rooms 11 or 21, which are corner rooms enjoying more light than most, or Room 31, which is a characterful attic room with high windows and views over neighbouring rooftops. Bathrooms and shower-rooms tend to be a decent size, and again housekeeping standards are high. Guests who wish to have an early start can have a light snack, otherwise a full English breakfast in the basement restaurant will set you up for the day. If you prefer not to go out at night, you can choose from an inexpensive menu, which includes roast chicken and chips, poached salmon, and various pasta dishes.

◑ Open all year 🚇 Nearest tube station is Victoria (District, Circle and Victoria lines). Public car park nearby 🛏 3 single, 5 twin, 12 double, 3 family rooms; some with bathroom/WC, most with shower/WC; TV, room service, hair-dryer, direct-dial telephone; trouser press in some rooms ✔ Restaurant, lounge ; early suppers for children ; toys, highchairs, cots ♿ No wheelchair access ⊖ No dogs; no smoking in public rooms ▭ Access, Amex, Delta, Switch, Visa £ Single £34 to £57, single occupancy of twin/double £42 to £66, twin/double £48 to £86, family room £69 to £97; deposit required. Set D £10.50; alc D £12

It is always worth enquiring about the availability of special breaks or weekend prices. The prices we quote are the standard rates for one night – most hotels offer reduced rates for longer stays.

Woodville House

£

107 Ebury Street, London SW1W 9QU
TEL: 0171-730 1048 FAX: 0171-730 2574

Simple, friendly B&B with good facilities, near Victoria station.

Ian Berry and Rachel Joplin have found a niche in the hotel market and get on with the job without any fuss. The 12 bedrooms are inexpensive, modern and clean, although – not unexpectedly, given the prices – not very big. They share basic but clean bathrooms on each of the landings, and guests have the use of a kitchen with a fridge, tea and coffee facilities, and an iron. There is no lounge, but the small walled garden is very pretty in summer and makes a lovely place to have tea at the end of a day spent tramping around the sights. Room 4, with its original fireplace and lacy coronet over the bed, is a quiet room overlooking the garden, while the two basement family rooms are light and relatively large, and are very good value for money. One has teddies to go with its bunk beds, while the other has a separate area for the children to sleep in. At breakfast, Rachel will give you all the help you need with planning your day, and a cheerful atmosphere prevails as she serves a 'no-restrictions' breakfast of anything you fancy, including home-made muesli and fresh coffee. She and Ian Berry also run Morgan House (see entry).

◑ Open all year ↗ Nearest tube station is Victoria (Victoria, District and Circle lines). On-street parking at night; public car parks nearby 🛏 4 single, 3 twin, 3 double, 2 family rooms; TV, hair-dryer; no tea/coffee-making facilities in rooms
✓ Dining-room, drying-room, library, garden, kitchenette; air-conditioning in double rooms and dining-room; toys, games, babysitting ♿ No wheelchair access ⊖ No dogs; no smoking in public rooms ▭ Access, Switch, Visa £ Single £34 to £38, twin/double £52 to £56, family room £75 to £85; deposit required

ENGLAND

THRUXTED OAST

CHARTHAM

Uplands Hotel

Victoria Road, Aldeburgh IP15 5DX
TEL: (01728) 452420   FAX: (01728) 454872

Unpretentious, friendly family-owned hotel run with courtesy and charm.

The crest of St Bartholomew's Hospital features on the sign of Uplands: this was Elizabeth Garrett Anderson's family home before she became Britain's first female surgeon to be accepted by Barts. Although the unassuming Regency building sits on the main road into Aldeburgh, once you're inside there's a feeling of old-fashioned gentility that fits in well with the atmosphere of the town itself. The most impressive room is the dining-room, with a coffered plaster ceiling, stone fireplace and deep red carpet. Menus stick to traditional favourites, perhaps baked gammon steak with mustard and cider, or grilled salmon with hollandaise sauce. The lounge is a pleasant place to unwind; one wall is taken up with casements of china above an unusual curved grate containing blue and white Delft tiles. This and the adjoining bar both have french windows opening on to the narrow conservatory at the back – a real sun-trap even when the sea breezes are stiff. The walled garden beyond is surprisingly large and lovingly maintained, with plenty of shrubs and perennials to add interest to the large expanse of lawn. The garden rooms, housed in chalet-style blocks added in 1970, look dated but are of a good size; bedrooms in the house have more character but are just as straightforwardly furnished. Room 1, with double aspect, twin beds and more Delft tiles in what remains of the bathroom fireplace, is probably the nicest.

◑ Closed Chr ⊿ Opposite parish church on main road into Aldeburgh (A1094). Private car park ⮡ 4 single, 9 twin, 5 double, 2 family rooms; some in annexe; most with bathroom/WC, 1 with shower/WC; TV, room service, direct-dial telephone; hair-dryer on request ✅ Dining-room, bar, lounge, TV room, conservatory, garden; conference facilities (max 10 people residential/non-residential) ♿ Wheelchair access to hotel (1 step), restaurant and WC (M,F), 8 ground-floor bedrooms incl 1 specially equipped for disabled people ⊖ No dogs; no smoking in bedrooms or in dining-room ▭ Access, Amex, Delta, Diners, Visa £ Single £35 to £45, single occupancy of twin/double £45, twin/double £63, family room from £75; deposit required. Set D £14.50; alc D £15; (1996 prices). Special breaks available

Ettington Park

Alderminster, Stratford-upon-Avon CV37 8BS
TEL: (01789) 450123   FAX: (01789) 450472

Imposing Victorian Gothic mansion turned into a business-oriented country-house hotel.

Besides the fact that it has good conference and leisure facilities and 40 acres of grounds, the main reason why Ettington Park appears in the *Guide* is that you might think it fun to stay somewhere of such monstrous proportions. With its towers, slate roofs, gargoyles and friezes, it resembles a cross between a mid-sized French château and an ecclesiastical edifice. Inside, stuccoed columns and an ornate wrought-iron staircase embellish the hall, stained glass ornaments the enormous library/bar, and the lounge is the size of a ballroom. You can sleep surrounded by equal magnificence if you're willing to pay for a suite. Otherwise, you may find yourself in a standard room in the new wing – bright, stylish and comfortable but forgettable. Despite the official prices shown below, you may be able to clinch a double room for about £115 a night if the hotel's not busy. The restaurant's menu may irritate: a set-price dinner with rather ordinary choices is livened up by a dozen more exciting 'Specialities of Ettington', all priced as supplements. A fastidious American correspondent had several complaints to make about the service and housekeeping on a recent stay here. More reports, please.

◐ Open all year ⏿ 5 miles south of Stratford-upon-Avon off A3400 just outside Alderminster. Private car park ⇌ 7 twin, 32 double, 2 four-poster, 5 family rooms, 2 suites; all with bathroom/WC; TV, room service, hair-dryer, trouser press, direct-dial telephone ✓ Restaurant, bar, lounge, conservatory, garden; conference facilities (max 80 people incl up to 48 residential); fishing, sauna, solarium, heated indoor swimming-pool, tennis, croquet, clay-pigeon shooting, archery; early suppers for children; baby-listening ♿ Wheelchair access to hotel, restaurant, WC (unisex), 1 bedroom specially equipped for disabled people ● Dogs in bedrooms by arrangement; no smoking in restaurant ▤ Access, Amex, Delta, Diners, Switch, Visa £ Single occupancy of twin/double £115, twin/double from £165, four-poster £300, family room £210, suite £300; deposit required. Set L £10, D £29.50; alc D £32 (1996 prices)

ALDWINCLE Northamptonshire   map 6

The Maltings

Main Street, Aldwincle, Oundle NN14 3EP
TEL: (01832) 720233   FAX: (01832) 720326

Luxury and privacy in a B&B dating from the 1600s.

It's hard to imagine a more comfortable B&B than this. Guests are primarily accommodated in a beautiful conversion of an outhouse granary. Amid much golden pine, downstairs is a plush guests' sitting-room, equipped with TV, lots of local literature and up-market teas, fresh milk and a tub of biscuits. French windows open on to an immaculately maintained garden. Upstairs are two very fetching bedrooms, kitted out with fresh flowers, pillows for headboards and patchwork quilts. Bathrobes are provided to allow you to traverse the few feet to each room's large and luxurious bathroom in modesty. Umbrellas are at the ready to give cover for the trip of a few yards across to the Faulkners' house. If you're on your own you'll be invited to breakfast *en famille* round the kitchen table; relaxed and gregarious Margaret and Nigel Faulkner are good company. Otherwise, you'll probably be treated with a bit more formality in the smart dining-room. There's a further bedroom in the main house, with an equally smashing bathroom. But romantics should note that all accommodation takes the form of twin-bedded rooms.

◑ Closed Chr ◩ Enter village from A605, telephone box on right; Maltings is 150m further along on right. Private car park 🛏 3 twin; all with bathroom/WC; hair-dryer; radio ✧ Dining-room, 2 lounges, drying-room, garden; croquet ♿ No wheelchair access ⊖ No children under 10; no dogs; no smoking ▭ Access, Visa £ Single occupancy of twin £33 to £35, twin £45 to £47; deposit required. Special breaks available

---

ALSTONEFIELD Staffordshire map 5

Stanshope Hall

Stanshope, Ashbourne DE6 2AD
TEL: (01335) 310278 FAX: (01335) 310470

An up-market guesthouse full of surprises, in excellent Peak District walking country; bargain rates for single occupancy.

Stanshope Hall surveys the stone-walled high ground between the Manifold and Dove valleys; fine walks in all directions start at the front door. As befits its hardy location, the sixteenth-to eighteenth-century house appears rather forbidding, making the joyful interior all the more unexpected. *Trompe-l'oeil* paintings cover the walls and ceilings in virtually every room; in the instantly relaxing lounge, for example, you're engulfed by pastoral scenes and a picture-perfect sky, while the ceiling of the elegant, library-like dining-room has been painted to match the pattern of the carpet. The largest, priciest bedroom, which has a king-sized bed and a sofa, features classical pillars flanking the windows and Italianate scenes around a Victorian bath. Yet Stanshope Hall offers more than just visual gimmicks: Naomi Chambers and Nicholas Lourie, both working professionals, have also created a tasteful, casual, family home. Dinner, served at 7pm for 7.30pm, is quite an affair: it begins with home-made nibbles, and then proceeds through three courses, with a choice being offered at each stage (expect the likes of roasts and Bakewell tart), before finishing with home-made chocolates.

◑ Closed 25 & 26 Dec ◩ From Ashbourne, take the A515 to Buxton. Turn left to Thorpe, Ilam and Dovedale. At the Ilam memorial, turn right (signposted Alstonefield). Stanshope is 3 miles from Ilam on the road to Alstonefield. Private car park 🛏 1 twin, 2 double; all with bathroom/WC; TV, hair-dryer, direct-dial telephone ✧ Dining-room, lounge, garden; early suppers for children; baby-listening ♿ No wheelchair access ⊖ No children in dining-room eves; no dogs; no smoking in bedrooms ▭ None accepted £ Single occupancy of twin/double £20 to £32, twin/double £40 to £64; deposit required. Set D £18. Special breaks available

---

It is always worth enquiring about the availability of special breaks or weekend prices. The prices we quote are the standard rates for one night – most hotels offer reduced rates for longer stays.

ALTON Staffordshire   map 5

Alton Towers Hotel ☆

Alton ST10 4DB
TEL: (0990) 204060   FAX: (01538) 704657

Family-oriented hotel within the grounds of Alton Towers, worth considering only if you're visiting the theme park.

Owned by the park, this brand-new complex is just a mono-rail trip away from the rides. The hotel is intended to be fun for all the family, with characters such as an eccentric botanist snooping around and rooms decked out in one of two themes: exploring and horticulture. A combined galleon, helicopter and hot-air balloon contraption rising up through a smart atrium exemplifies the explorer theme. The rather lacklustre indoor pool sports a pirate motif, continued in Explorer bedrooms with skull and crossbones lamps as well as décor depicting the early days of flight. Garden bedrooms, with trellis wallpaper and watering-can lamps, flesh out the horticultural theme, continued in the Secret Garden Restaurant with its fake twittering birds and foliage. The food is quite good. Dinners and self-service breakfasts are basically whatever you want: burgers, pasta, roasts and stir-fries in the evening; croissants, cold meats, lots of fruit plus traditional fry-ups in the morning.

Standard bedrooms are big and comfortable and can accommodate two adults and two children (ask for an Explorer room: they're more fun and have bunk beds). However, with open-plan public areas and no quiet corners, the hotel can soon feel exhausting. Rates are by no means cheap, but become better value if you take a package including entry to the park. Hotel guests have exclusive use of Nemesis (the park's most popular ride) at a specific time of the day. We are simply stunned by the payment terms – the full cost of your stay has to be paid at least 30 days before the date you are due at the hotel. Our inspector stayed soon after the hotel opened in March 1996. The reservations system was appalling, as at times was the service. Were these just teething problems? Reports please.

◑ Open all year   ⊿ Situated midway between Stoke-on-Trent and Derby; theme park is clearly signposted from all motorway exits. Private car park   ⊨ 11 twin, 162 family rooms, 2 suites; all with bathroom/WC; TV, room service, hair-dryer
✧ Restaurant, 2 bars, 2 lounges, TV room, drying-rooms, games rooms, garden; conference facilities (max 150 people non-residential/residential); sauna, solarium, heated indoor swimming-pool; toys, babysitting, baby-listening, outdoor games, children's entertainers   ⅙ Wheelchair access to hotel, restaurant, WC (M,F), 9 bedrooms specially equipped for disabled people   ● No dogs; no smoking in bedrooms   ▭ Access, Amex, Delta, Switch, Visa   £ Single occupancy of twin/double £69 to £79, twin/double £90 to £100, family room from £100, suite £200; deposit required. Set D £18.50; alc L £6.50, D from £16 (prices valid till Jan 1997). Special breaks available

---

☆ *A star next to the hotel's name indicates that the establishment is new to the* Guide *this year.*

Chapel House

Kirkstone Road, Ambleside LA22 9DZ
TEL: (01539) 433143

Converted sixteenth-century cottages in the oldest part of Ambleside.

Just up from the house on the bridge, postcard icon of the village, as the road
fractures into several little lanes, is Chapel House. It's a quiet spot with views
across the town and up Rydal, and the dry-stone grey house with its small porch
is typical of this, the oldest part of the village. Its exact links to the church
opposite are obscure, but the house is known to date back at least to the sixteenth
century. Duncan Hamer's cooking, backed up with friendly thoughtful service,
is what draws many people to it. The menu is a no-choice four-course affair, but
when our inspector mentioned an allergy to an ingredient in the soup, a tasty
leek and potato alternative was knocked up in no time. The main course was
fillet of chicken in mushroom sauce with roast potatoes and ratatouille, and was
followed by a light and frothy fruit meringue. After dinner, coffee is served in the
cordial environment of the lounge, and Duncan and Sandra often join in for a
natter. Bedrooms may come as a bit of a disappointment – smallish with quite
basic furnishings. The bathroom on the top floor is shared by several bedrooms
so there's a bit of a log-jam before breakfast.

◑ Closed Jan & Feb; limited opening Nov & Dec   ⤷ From M6 Junction 36 to
Ambleside on A591; pass through village and turn right into Smithy Brow leading to
Kirkstone Road. On-street parking   ⤷ 2 single, 2 twin, 5 double, 1 family room; 4
with shower/WC; hair-dryer; radio   ⊘ Dining-room, bar, lounge, drying-room; early
suppers for children   ⅙ No wheelchair access   ● No dogs; no smoking in
bedrooms or dining-room   ▭ None accepted   £ Single £33 to £40, single
occupancy of twin/double £50 to £53, twin/double £66 to £85, family room £97 to £135
(rates inc dinner); deposit required. Set D £16.50

Drunken Duck Inn

Barngates, Ambleside LA22 0NG
TEL: (01539) 436347   FAX: (01539) 436781

*Characterful country inn providing food and accommodation a cut
above the usual standard.*

This old inn may be buried up in the fells off the main trail between Ambleside
and Hawkshead, but such is its worthy reputation for good ale, tasty food and
comfortable accommodation that you'll rarely find the assortment of small,
woody and crooked snugs empty. Foxes, badgers and stoats snarl down at you
from the rough plaster walls, while several dozen whisky bottles and even more
little ducks wink back from behind the bar. A plaque on the wall relates the
highly apocryphal Victorian tale of how the inn's eponymous ducks lapped up
some spilt ale, slept off the effects, and woke up plucked and ready for the pot.
The pub does a roaring trade in food selected from the blackboard – hearty and
interesting dishes like vegetable and hazelnut soup, wild boar steak, beef in

Drunken Duck Ale, or pork and apples in cider. In addition to the dining areas in the bar, there is a small, smart dining-room with wheel-back chairs and a quieter atmosphere, where residents will find themselves taking breakfast. Bedrooms are certainly a cut above the usual standard of pub accommodation, with a selection of antiques and some lavish touches in the bathrooms, though the pub's popularity means you should be prepared for a little noise from downstairs if you retire before the bar shuts.

◖ Closed 25 Dec eve ⤢ About 2½ miles out of Ambleside on B5286 to Hawkshead turn right; Drunken Duck Inn is signposted. Private car park ⌁ 1 twin, 7 double, 1 four-poster; 1 in annexe; all with bathroom/WC exc 1 double with shower/WC; TV, hair-dryer, direct-dial telephone ✧ 3 dining-rooms, bar, lounge, drying-room, garden; fishing, clay-pigeon shooting; early suppers for children ♿ Wheelchair access to hotel (1 step), restaurant and WC (M,F), 1 ground-floor bedroom ⊝ Dogs allowed in bedrooms by arrangement; no smoking in one public room ▭ Access, Amex, Delta, Switch, Visa £ Single occupancy of twin/double £50, twin/double £65 to £69, four-poster £79; deposit required. Alc L £6, D £6.50. Special breaks available

Rothay Manor

Rothay Bridge, Ambleside LA22 0EH
TEL: (01539) 433605   FAX: (01539) 433607

Stylish and genteel family-owned country-house hotel close to the centre of the town.

Rothay is surrounded by landscaped grounds fringed with silver birch, magnolia and conifers, though it has had the slight misfortune of being overtaken, from the outside at least, by the twentieth century: Ambleside's infuriating one-way system describes a loop around this island of tranquillity. The Nixon family has been successfully fending off the unsightly aspects of progress for 30 years now, and an air of timeless elegance hangs about this graceful Regency building with its peaceful lounges and plush dining-rooms. The bedrooms are all individually decorated in a pleasant, unflamboyant fashion, while some may boast a splendid fireplace (Room 1), or a carving of an oak-leaf cluster above the bed (Room 10). Those at the front have balconies, those at the side are slightly quieter, and the ground-floor room has been adapted for wheelchair users. One of the suites in the annexe is also suitable for disabled people.

With 27 consecutive years' inclusion, the restaurant is one of the longest-standing entries in *The Good Food Guide,* and on a dinner menu from which you can choose between two and five courses you should find the imaginative (such as corn and wild rice soup with spicy sausage) as well as the more traditional (baked pork fillet stuffed with sage and onion). Gardening, painting, antique-collecting and music courses are run at various times at the hotel.

We mention those hotels that don't accept dogs; guide dogs, however, are almost always an exception. Telephone ahead to make sure.

◑ Closed 3 Jan to 9 Feb ⬀ On A593 south-west of Ambleside towards Coniston. Private car park ⬄ 2 single, 3 twin, 5 double, 5 family rooms, 3 suites; some in annexe all with bathroom/WC; TV, room service, hair-dryer, direct-dial telephone
⌀ Restaurant, dining-room, bar, 2 lounges, garden; air-conditioning in restaurant, dining-room and 1 lounge; conference facilities (max 25 people incl up to 18 residential); early suppers for children; baby-listening, cots, high chairs
♿ Wheelchair access to hotel (1 step), restaurant and WC (unisex), 2 bedrooms specially equipped for disabled people ● Very young children discouraged from restaurant eves; no dogs; no smoking in restaurant, dining-room and 1 lounge ▭
Access, Amex, Diners, Switch, Visa £ Single £78, single occupancy of twin/double £88, twin/double £118, family room from £118, suite from £165; deposit required. Set L £14, D £24 to £30. Special breaks available

Wateredge Hotel

Borrans Road, Ambleside LA22 0EP
TEL: (01539) 432332 FAX: (01539) 431878

Family-owned lakeside hotel, providing smart and relaxing surroundings in a popular location.

Steamer trips, rowing boats and greedy swans and geese on one side of the fence; afternoon tea on the lawn, a private jetty and picture windows overlooking the lake on the other: Wateredge manages to be something of a quiet haven while being right in the thick of lakeside tourist activity. The buildings too exhibit something of a dual personality. The front of the hotel was originally two seventeenth-century fishermen's cottages; the bar is tucked into a woody nook and you dine off oak tables in a dining-room thick with gnarled beams. Two Victorian lounges offer somewhere more intimate for afternoon tea or after-dinner coffee if you don't fancy the expansive conservatory-like main lounge with its arched picture windows overlooking the lake. Bedrooms tend towards being smart in an unassuming way, leaving Windermere to provide the spectacle, though rooms without a view are rather bland. Dinners have the traditional Lakeland multiplicity of courses, with up to six on offer and a choice at each. Our inspector enjoyed garlic mushrooms à la grecque, pea and mint soup, turbot in champagne cream sauce, and a white and dark chocolate terrine, before a rather uninspiring cheeseboard. No quibbles about the friendly, efficient service, though.

◑ Closed mid-Dec to early Feb ⬀ 1 mile south of Ambleside on A591 at Waterhead, adjacent to steamer pier. Private car park ⬄ 3 single, 6 twin, 9 double, 5 suites; some in annexe most with bathroom/WC, some with shower/WC; TV, limited room service, hair-dryer, direct-dial telephone ⌀ Dining-room, bar, 3 lounges, TV room, drying-room, garden; partial air-conditioning in dining-room; fishing, rowing; early suppers for children ♿ No wheelchair access ● No children under 7; no dogs in public rooms and in bedrooms by arrangement ▭ Access, Amex, Delta, Switch, Visa £ Single £59 to £73, single occupancy of twin/double from £72, twin/double £102 to £150, suite £138 to £166 (rates inc dinner); deposit required. Set D £28; (prices valid till Sep 1996). Special breaks available

---

APPLETHWAITE Cumbria map 10

Underscar Manor

Applethwaite, Nr Keswick CA12 4PH
TEL: (01768) 775000   FAX: (01768) 774904

Immaculately turned out country-house hotel with outstanding views of Derwentwater.

The Victorian magnate who built Underscar picked his spot to perfection: it is sheltered in the natural folds of the lower slopes of Skiddaw facing south and has a quite outstanding view of Derwentwater stretching down into Borrowdale. The main lounge and, more particularly, the master bedroom (Room 3), share this view, which can make the other ordinarily pleasing outlooks – acres of landscaped lawns, a walled garden and thick woodland – humble fare by comparison. The view is not the only striking feature: Underscar was built of Lakeland stone, but in Italianate style, with a square tower, rounded arches and shallow-pitched roofs with deep, overhanging eaves. Rich, bold colour schemes, period furnishings and lavish finishing touches such as garlands of dried fruits, nuts and flowers are the work of Pauline and Derek Harrison, while Pauline's brother, Robert Thornton, runs the kitchen, providing inventive menus and plenty of variety: English lobster in a crispy yeast batter with green-pea hummus, followed by lamb served with chorizo sausage, spiced casserole and cannellini beans, for instance. Over breakfast, you may be entertained by the local red squirrels, who are enticed to the house for their daily ration of hazelnuts.

◑ Open all year   ⤒ Leave M6 at Junction 40 and take A66 to Keswick for 17 miles; at large roundabout take third exit and turn immediately right to Underscar; entrance is ½ mile on right. Private car park   ⤶ 11 double; all with bathroom/WC; TV, limited room service, hair-dryer, direct-dial telephone   ✥ 2 restaurants, 2 lounges, drying-room, conservatory, garden; conference facilities (max 20 people incl up to 11 residential);   ⅙ No wheelchair access   ● No children under 12; no dogs; no smoking in restaurants   ▭ Access, Amex, Switch, Visa   £ Single occupancy of twin/double £85 to £125, twin/double £150 to £250; deposit required. Set L £18.50, D £29.50; alc L £18.50, D £36.50. Special breaks available

---

APULDRAM West Sussex map 3

Crouchers Bottom

Birdham Road, Apuldram, Chichester PO20 7EH
TEL: (01243) 784995   FAX: (01243) 539797

Spotless, modern rooms feature in a down-to-earth small hotel.

Close to Chichester harbour, and just a couple of miles from the town centre, Drew and Lesley Wilson run their simple, but immaculately kept, small hotel in a relaxed and unfussy way. As you head out towards Selsey Bill, you'll see a cluster of 'Croucher' properties along the A286 as this area was once the Croucher family's farm; the fields still surround this red-brick farmhouse. The bedrooms, in the converted coach house to the rear of the house, are simply and spotlessly decorated in light, pastel shades and are furnished in modern pine. In the main house, the homely and comfortable lounge features a squidgy leather sofa in which to relax and pleasant, oak-block floors. Evening meals, prepared by the Wilsons' son, Gavin, are taken in the conservatory, which looks out over the small, neat garden and duck pond. The short menu tends to offer uncomplicated dishes such as goats' cheese in roasted red pepper, beef carbonade, or poussin with wild mushrooms.

◗ Open all year ☑ Crouchers Bottom is 2 miles south of Chichester on the A286, just after the Black Horse pub, on the opposite side of road. Private car park 🖚 3 twin, 6 double; family rooms available; all in annexe; all with bathroom/WC; TV, room service, hair-dryer, direct-dial telephone ✅ Dining-room/conservatory, lounge, garden; early suppers for children; baby-listening ♿ Wheelchair access to hotel, restaurant, 7 ground-floor bedrooms, 2 specially equipped for disabled people ⊖ No dogs in public rooms; smoking in lounge only ▭ Access, Amex, Delta, Visa
£ Single occupancy of twin/double £45 to £59, twin/double £65 to £85, family room from £85; deposit required. Set D £18.50. Special breaks available

---

Amerdale House

Arncliffe, Littondale, Skipton BD23 5QE
TEL: (01756) 770250 (AND FAX)

Small country-house hotel with good food and vast views of the Dales.

In a superbly peaceful setting in the Yorkshire Dales National Park, where you're more likely to get stuck in a sheep jam than to meet another car, Amerdale House is a well-established small hotel with lovely views along Littondale. The nearby village of Arncliffe was once suggested as a location for Emerdale Farm, but the locals soon put paid to that idea, valuing their peace and quiet over any profit fame might bring. We get many letters praising Paula and Nigel Crapper's warm welcome, attentive service and good food. One reader in particular liked the way Nigel combines unusual ingredients in his cooking, though you'll also find traditional dishes such as roast leg of Dales lamb with rosemary, or baked fillet of salmon with hollandaise sauce. Puddings, including home-made ice-cream, are reliably good. Most of the 11 bedrooms are comfortably kitted out with light flowery fabrics and with oak furniture made by a local craftsman. Some have shower-rooms only, while all have generous goodies including treats like sugared almonds and shortbread. Littondale, with its black leaded fireplace, was one of our favourites, for although it is the smallest room, it has lots of character as well as the best views along the valley.

All rooms have tea/coffee-making facilities unless we specify to the contrary.

○ Closed mid-Nov to mid-Mar ⬚ On edge of village of Arncliffe, 7 miles north of Grassington. Private car park ⬚ 3 twin, 5 double, 1 four-poster, 2 family rooms; 1 in annexe; most with bathroom/WC, some with shower/WC; TV, room service, hair-dryer; trouser press in some rooms ✓ Dining-room, bar, lounge, drying-room, library, garden; early suppers for children ♿ No wheelchair access ● No dogs; no smoking in dining-room or library ▭ Access, Visa £ Single occupancy of twin/double £65 to £70, twin/double £109 to £119, four-poster/family room £115 to £119 (rates incl dinner). Set D £25. Special breaks available

---

ARRATHORNE North Yorkshire   map 9

Elmfield Country House

Arrathorne, Bedale DL8 1NE
TEL: (01677) 450558   FAX: (01677) 450557

Bright-as-a-button guesthouse in a peaceful rural location.

You may find quite a contrast between the exterior and the interior of Arrathorne House. The L-shaped greyish-brown building that greets you may lower the spirits, in spite of the pretty garden with a goldfish pond and a waterfall. However, the inside, not to mention the genuine warmth of Jim and Edith Lillie's welcome, soon cheers you up again. The Lillies have been in charge for over nine years now but there still seems to be a spanking newness about everything from the plush burgundy seats in the lounge/bar area to the *en suite* facilities in the bedrooms. The conservatory has bright cane and cushion chairs, and while mum and dad are relaxing with a cup of tea and taking in the extensive countryside views, children can nip off to the games room to shoot pool or throw a few darts. The dining-room is very simple, in white with pale green trim, but is decorated with paintings of country scenes from a gallery in Bedale – you can buy one if it takes your fancy. English country cooking – what Edith even calls 'plain' – is the order of the day: mushroom soup, roast beef, Yorkshire pud and two veg, then a home-made sweet might make up the three courses. Bedrooms are neat and pretty and include a four-poster room and two which have been adapted for wheelchair users.

○ Open all year ⬚ From A1 take A684 through Bedale and on to Patrick Brompton; after village turn right at first crossroads; Elmfield is 1½ miles on right. Private car park ⬚ 3 twin, 3 double, 1 four-poster, 2 family rooms; some with bathroom/WC, most with shower/WC; TV, hair-dryer, direct-dial telephone; iron on request ✓ Dining-room, bar, lounge, conservatory, games room, garden; conference facilities (max 50 people incl up to 9 residential); solarium ♿ Wheelchair access to hotel, restaurant, WC (unisex), 2 ground-floor bedrooms specially equipped for disabled people ● No dogs; smoking in some public areas and some bedrooms ▭ Access, Visa £ Single occupancy of twin/double £30, twin/double £41, four-poster £45, family room from £41; deposit required. Set D £11.50. Special breaks available

---

   This denotes that the hotel is in an exceptionally peaceful situation where you can be assured of a restful stay.

ASHBOURNE **Derbyshire** map 5

Callow Hall

Mappleton Road, Ashbourne DE6 2AA
TEL: (01335) 343403   FAX: (01335) 343624

All you could ask from a well-established country-house hotel, run with a lightness of touch.

The setting for this great, creeper-covered, heavy-gabled Victorian mansion is superb: it's only a five-minute drive from Ashbourne, but tucked away in its own 44 acres of Derbyshire countryside. The house's sternness softens inside, though studded chairs, leather sofas, brass chandeliers, tapestries and gilt mirrors maintain a resolutely traditional and old-fashioned feel. The bar displays advertisements from the 1920s for the Spencer family enterprise, which has been feeding locals since the eighteenth century. The cooking is still much admired, not only for its home baking, smoking and curing, but also for its restrained but interesting modern English cuisine. Save room at dinner for a comprehensive breakfast, which includes porridge, kippers, smoked haddock and Derbyshire oatcakes. While heaping praise on the food, one reporter found fault with a rather small bedroom. If size is important, pay a little more for a large room at the front of the house, typically furnished with antiques, draped beds and maybe even a sofa. Smaller rooms in the rear wing are cosier and in a cottagey, piney style. Bathrooms throughout are excellent.

◑ Closed 25 & 26 Dec, and 1 week in Feb   ↗ Follow A515 through Ashbourne towards Buxton; turn left at Bowling Green pub, then first right into Mappleton Road; entrance is on right after hump-backed bridge. Private car park   ⬅ 4 twin, 9 double, 1 four-poster, 1 family room, 1 suite; all with bathroom/WC; TV, room service, hair-dryer, trouser press, direct-dial telephone   ✓ Restaurant, bar, lounge, drying-room, garden; conference facilities (max 40 people incl up to 16 residential); fishing; early suppers for children; baby-listening   ♿ Wheelchair access to hotel (note: 4 steps), restaurant, 1 bedroom specially equipped for disabled people   ● Dogs in bedrooms by arrangement; no smoking in restaurant   ⬜ Access, Amex, Diners, Switch, Visa   ⬜ Single occupancy of twin/double £65 to £85, twin/double £95 to £120, four-poster £120, family room £120, suite £140; deposit required. Set L £15.50, D £30; alc D £26. Special breaks available

---

ASHBURTON **Devon** map 1

Holne Chase

Princetown Road, Ashburton TQ13 7NS
TEL: (01364) 631471   FAX: (01364) 631453

Attractive gabled country-house hotel in extensive grounds close to Buckfast Abbey.

A break in the woodland around Buckfast Abbey reveals Holne Chase, a fine white four-gabled country house looking out over beautifully kept lawns. The hotel's public rooms line up along the front of the house to take advantage of the views over the 30 acres of grounds including a stretch of the River Dart suitable for fly fishing. One of these perfectly poised rooms is the restaurant, where four-course dinner menus offer a choice of three adventurous starters, main courses and desserts; you might choose minestrone of scallops with garlic and saffron, followed by poached fillet of beef on a nest of onion purée with a casserole of snails, shallots and bacon lardons, rounded off by iced rhubarb parfait with almond tuiles and rhubarb compote. Afterwards diners can retire to a comfortable lounge, a bar or a more intimate library. The spacious bedrooms mix the old and new to pleasing effect. One ground-floor room is suitable for guests with limited mobility; another has a door straight into the grounds – ideal for dog owners. Two of the suites have four-posters.

◐ Open all year ↗ Take Ashburton exit off A38; follow signs to Two Bridges for 3 miles. Private car park ⌂ 1 single, 16 twin/double, 4 suites; family rooms available; some in annexe; all with bathroom/WC exc single with shower/WC; TV, room service, hair-dryer, direct-dial telephone; mini-bar and trouser press in some rooms
⊘ Restaurant, private dining-room, bar, lounge, drying-room, library, garden; conference facilities (max 30 people incl up to 21 residential); fishing, putting, croquet; early suppers for children; toys, playroom, babysitting, baby-listening, outdoor games
⅄ Wheelchair access to hotel, restaurant and WC (M,F), 1 ground-floor bedroom specially equipped for disabled people ● No children in restaurant eves, no smoking in restaurant ⊟ Access, Amex, Diners, Switch, Visa £ Single £50, single occupancy of twin/double £65, twin/double £100 to £110, family room/suite £140; deposit required. Cooked B £4.50; set L £16, D £25; alc L £27.50, D £30 (1996 prices). Special breaks available

---

ASHTON KEYNES Wiltshire map 2

Two Cove House

Ashton Keynes, Swindon SN6 6NS
TEL: (01285) 861221 (AND FAX)

Accommodating hosts at a historic family home in a pretty Cotswold village.

Major and Mrs Hartland found a fitting place to set up home, after returning from more exotic parts nearly 30 years ago. Their Cotswold-stone manor has its own military history to complement the Major's collection of old swords and regimental uniforms – during the Civil War a belligerent Roundhead killed his Royalist brother in it, and, centuries later, it was requisitioned by American troops. Though long retired from service (if you discount the years welcoming guests), Major Hartland is still eager to put his organisational skills to the test over in the briefing room, a small study/sitting-room with a TV, stacks of local information, including pub menus and videos of the area, and a large framed map, all designed to help visitors make the most of their stay. But that's where the regimental associations end. Otherwise the house is very much the pleasant, traditional family home, with an assortment of antiques and heirlooms, family portraits and photographs, an elegant drawing-room, and comfortable bedrooms with either brass or wooden beds, cheerful colours and appealing watercolours. Dinner is served round a long, polished table, to the accompaniment of a ticking grandfather clock, and might feature spiced chicken and apricot casserole, or salmon steaks with watercress sauce, rounded off with a traditional home-made dessert – pavlova, chocolate mousse, or rhubarb and orange pudding.

◑ Closed Chr ☷ Turn west off A419 Swindon to Cirencester road towards Ashton Keynes; at White Hart turn left and 100 yards on, turn left. Private car park ⟞ 2 twin, 1 double; family room available; twins with bathroom/WC, double with shower/WC; hair-dryer on request ⊘ Dining-room, lounge, TV room, drying-room, garden; early suppers for children ♿ No wheelchair access ● Dogs in bedrooms by arrangement; no smoking in dining-room ▭ None accepted £ Single occupancy of twin/double £27 to £35, twin/double £46 to £48, family room £58; deposit required. Set D £17

ASHWATER **Devon**   map 1

Blagdon Manor Country Hotel

Ashwater EX21 5DF
TEL: (01409) 211224 FAX: (01409) 211634

Colourful country-house hotel in quiet corner of Devon.

Returning to England after many years in Hong Kong, Tim and Gill Cassey took on a crumbling farmhouse and turned it into Blagdon Manor. A photograph album discreetly placed in the lounge illustrates the transformation. There are still pointers to what went before: the curious contraption filling an alcove in the billiard room is an old scald creamery, a device in which a fire was lit at the bottom and milk placed in two bowls in the top. Another corner of the room houses a small bar, where guests join the Casseys for pre-dinner drinks. Dinner is taken at one sitting, with everyone seated round a long table. When we inspected, a warm Mediterranean quiche was followed by Scotch salmon with a curry and lime vinaigrette and then a plate of hot fudge brownies in chocolate sauce that would have defeated even the heftiest appetite. Breakfast was similarly substantial, with the full fry-up including kidneys and black pudding, but scrambled eggs with salmon made a welcome alternative. Bedrooms here are extravagantly decorated. In Room Three, for example, large blue irises flow off the walls and on to the curtains and headboard; the bedcover and lampshades are all in vivid green. For comfort these rooms would be hard to beat: a jug of fresh milk comes with a lacy cover; a wicker basket offers a choice of teas; the mirror has lots of light; a complimentary glass of sherry stands waiting.

◑ Closed Chr ☷ Leave Launceston on A388 Holsworthy Road; pass first sign to Ashwater; turn right at second sign, then first right signposted Blagdon; entrance on right. Private car park ⟞ 2 twin, 4 double, 1 four-poster; all with bathroom/WC; TV, hair-dryer, trouser press ⊘ Dining-room, bar, lounge, library, games room, garden; conference facilities (max 14 people incl up to 7 residential); fishing, golf, croquet ♿ No wheelchair access ● No children; no dogs; smoking in bar and library only ▭ Access, Amex, Delta, Switch, Visa £ Single occupancy of twin/double £40 to £45, twin/double £80 to £90, four-poster £80 to £90; deposit required. Set D £18. Special breaks available

ASKRIGG **North Yorkshire**   map 8

King's Arms Hotel

Market Place, Askrigg, Leyburn DL8 3HQ
TEL: (01969) 650258   FAX: (01969) 650635

An old coaching inn with characterful bars; the epitome of the village pub.

Cosy bars with inglenook fireplaces, oak settles and hunting prints; seen it all before? In this case, you probably have, especially if you were a fan of the BBC's *All Creatures Great and Small*, in which the King's Arms featured as the Drovers' Arms. It is easy to see why it was chosen, because it is the quintessential rural pub, with three charming bars that retain antique features which seem to belong to another age, such as a wig cupboard and pub games like shove-ha'penny. There's another side to the King's Arms too, however, as the rest of the hotel aspires to the country house rather than the village inn. The restaurant, with its wood panelling and horse paintings, reflects the house's origin as a manor house owned by a racehorse trainer. A typical menu might include fillet of turbot, crowned with a Scottish salmon mousseline and pink peppercorns. Silks Grill, which continues the racing theme with jockeys' silks on the walls, serves large portions of plainer fare. The bedrooms vary quite a bit in size; some have half-tester beds, and there are a couple of cosy attic rooms. Two of the rooms face the street, but the traffic noise is light.

◑ Open all year   ⊡ ½ mile off A684 Sedbergh to Leeming Bar (A1) road, between Aysgarth and Bainbridge. Private car park   ⊨ 1 twin, 7 double, 1 four-poster, 1 family room, 1 suite; most with bathroom/WC, 3 with shower/WC; TV, limited room service, hair-dryer, direct-dial telephone   ⊘ 2 restaurants, 3 bars, lounge, drying-room; conference facilities (max 40 people incl up to 11 residential); early suppers for children; baby-listening   ⅋ No wheelchair access   ⊜ No children under 12 in restaurants; dogs in bedrooms by arrangement; no smoking in some bedrooms   ⊡ Access, Amex, Delta, Switch, Visa   £⨀ Single occupancy of twin/double £45 to £50, twin/double £75 to £89, four-poster/family room £85 to £89, suite £100 to £108; deposit required. Set L £12.50, D £25 (prices valid till Apr 1997). Special breaks available

---

ASPLEY GUISE **Bedfordshire**   map 6

Moore Place Hotel

The Square, Aspley Guise, Nr Milton Keynes MK17 8DW
TEL: (01908) 282000   FAX: (01908) 281888

A beautiful Georgian town house with a modern interior and good food.

At the centre of a good-looking little village not far from Woburn Abbey, Moore Place is tall, red brick and Georgian – a smart family house in its day. Guests park round the back and enter the hotel by crossing a modern terrace, edged by coniferous shrubs and an ornamental waterfall, which is prettily lit at night. The hotel's housekeeping is immaculate, and the large public rooms are modern and light. The conservatory restaurant – in which the service is efficient – is predominantly decorated in pink, and has long windows. A typical evening meal might include a Caesar salad (freshly prepared at your table), roast duck with cherry and kirsch sauce, and a fruits-of-the-forest crumble served with clotted cream. Most of the bedrooms are in a new block that is linked to the reception by means of a glass walkway, while a few are divided between the main house and a cottage along the drive. All are furnished to a high standard and feature co-ordinated modern fabrics and generous amounts of toiletries in the smart bathrooms. Those in the main block can be rather gloomy, so it's worth paying the small supplement for an 'executive' room in the old house, where the high ceilings and large windows add extra character.

◑ Open all year ◩ The hotel is in the centre of Aspley Guise on the left-hand side. Private car park ⟼ 9 single, 9 twin, 35 double, 1 suite; some in annexe; all with bathroom/WC; TV, room service, hair-dryer, trouser press, direct-dial telephone ✓ Restaurant/conservatory, bar, lounge, garden, conference room (air-conditioned); conference facilities (max 50 people residential/non-residential); early suppers for children; baby-sitting ᕂ Wheelchair access to hotel, restaurant, WC (unisex), 2 ground-floor bedrooms ● None ▭ Access, Amex, Delta, Diners, Switch, Visa £ Single from £68, single occupancy of twin/double £78, twin/double from £90, suite £175; deposit required. Set L, D £17 (prices valid till Apr 1997). Special breaks available

---

ASTON CLINTON Buckinghamshire   map 3

Bell Inn

Aston Clinton, Aylesbury HP22 5HP
TEL: (01296) 630252   FAX: (01296) 631250

Good-value rooms in lovely old inn with pricey, though renowned, French-style restaurant.

From the outside, this smart red-brick house may look like a family home, until you notice the stableyard across the lane and realise it has been an inn for over 300 years. The Bell is a family business which puts most of its energy into the excellent restaurant, where local duck has a menu all to itself. In winter this might include lobster and crayfish, followed by roast Aylesbury duck with périgourdine sauce, then Grand Marnier soufflé. After dinner you can retreat to one of the comfortable sofas in the lounge, where the walls are decorated with framed labels from vintage wines, or opt for the more rustic smokers' bar with its flagstone floor, wooden settles around a log fire and collections of bell-shaped coloured glass. One reader reported that the staff and service at this hotel are very good, very helpful and attentive,' but went on to say that she couldn't sleep owing to traffic noise. Rooms in the converted stables across the yard are much quieter than those in the main house. Most are a good size and have a mix of antiques and old-fashioned furnishings in a French country style, and those which have recently been refurbished have smart modern bathrooms. The best open out on to pretty terraces or the geometric rose garden.

◑ Open all year ⤢ In Aston Clinton village, off A41 between Tring and Aylesbury. Private car park ⤢ 10 twin, 3 double, 2 four-poster, 5 suites; some in annexe; all with bathroom/WC; TV, 24-hour room service, hair-dryer, direct-dial telephone ✅ Restaurant, bar, lounge, garden; conference facilities (max 40 people incl up to 20 residential); croquet; early suppers for children; babysitting, baby-listening ♿ Wheelchair access to hotel (1 step), restaurant and WC (M,F), 8 ground-floor bedrooms (note: in cobbled yard) ● No dogs in public rooms; no smoking in restaurant ☐ Access, Amex, Delta, Switch, Visa £ Single occupancy of twin/double £50, twin/double £50 to £70, four-poster £70, suite £75 to £85; deposit required. Continental B £5, cooked B £8; set L £16, D £18/£39; alc D £33. Special breaks available

---

AWRE Gloucestershire   map 2

Old Vicarage

Awre, Newnham GL14 1EL
TEL: (01594) 510282

Cosy and relaxing retreat close to the River Severn and the Forest of Dean.

The old red phone box by Awre's village pub is the landmark you'll need to find your way to May and Nick Bull's substantial but secluded listed Georgian vicarage a short walk from the Severn Estuary; fork left and take the first on the right, and you're there. Once you've negotiated the driveway and passed the greenhouses, plus the chickens and ducks that have free run of the place, you could be forgiven for thinking you've wandered on to the set of *The Good Life*, as the three generations who call this old vicarage home are committed to self-sufficiency in a big way. Mrs Bull senior presides over the grounds, lovingly cultivating herb and kitchen gardens, leaving May and Nick to oversee the house and kitchen respectively. Even the fuel that feeds the blazing fire in the refreshingly unpretentious drawing-room is 'home-grown', hewn from Nick's coal mine! Among the pleasing jumble of local books, jigsaws, Bull family embroideries and collages, relics from service in Singapore and an old chapel harmonium, you'll find the sort of sturdy, comfy furniture that's scattered throughout the house. Décor is unmodish, and a little tired in the bedrooms, but a smattering of antiques and the genuine warmth of the hosts make this unimportant. There are grand views from the agreeable dining-room, where the fruits of the garden are augmented by prime local produce; perhaps garlic mushrooms garnished with fresh parsley served with chunky bread, followed by local wild venison cooked in red wine with sage and thyme, then apricot, orange and banana crumble, and cheese.

◑ Closed Chr; dining-room closed weekday eves during school terms ⤢ 2 miles west of A48 between Newnham and Blakeney; on edge of village of Awre. Private car park ⤢ 1 twin, 3 double; 1 double with shower/WC; limited room service; hair-dryer on request ✅ Dining-room, lounge, study, garden; early suppers for children; toys, baby-listening, high chairs ♿ No wheelchair access ● No dogs; no smoking in bedrooms or dining-room ☐ None accepted £ Single occupancy of twin/double £18 to £20, twin/double £35 to £39; deposit required. Set D £14.50

AYLESBURY **Buckinghamshire**   map 3

Hartwell House

Oxford Road, Aylesbury HP17 8NL
TEL: (01296) 747444   FAX: (01296) 747450

Luxurious stately-home hotel with beautiful grounds and formal hospitality.

Until the twentieth century took its toll, Hartwell House had been home to kings and princes for almost 1,000 years – William the Conqueror's son lived here, as did Richard the Lionheart's successor. Today it is an imposing, mostly eighteenth-century stately home with a vast park through which marked walks wind. From the Great Hall, with its huge fire, ornate baroque ceiling and dark antiques, to the hushed atmosphere of the pale drawing-room, the interior is impressive. Too impressive for some – the statues on each newel post of the dramatic Gothic staircase were apparently removed when Louis XVIII's queen lived here because they spooked her after a drink or two. The bedrooms too are lavish and have lovely views over the park. First-floor rooms are the grandest, with high ceilings and carved fireplaces, while the second-floor rooms in the attic are smart, with lovely cushioned window seats and smaller but equally luxurious bathrooms. Service throughout the hotel is impeccable and formal, you won't be hurried in the non-smoking restaurant, where tall windows look out over a newly created pond. A typical evening meal here might include game consommé flavoured with apple brandy, roast rack of lamb with ratatouille, and a range of wonderful traditional puddings of which you can try two or three if you like.

◖ Open all year   ⇗ In Aylesbury take A418 towards Oxford; Hartwell House is 2 miles along this road on right. Private car park   ⇖ 6 single, 23 twin/double, 5 four-poster, 13 suites; some in annexe; all with bathroom/WC; TV, room service, hair-dryer, trouser press, direct-dial telephone; tea/coffee-making facilities and mini-bar in annexe rooms   ⌁ 2 restaurants, bar, 4 lounges, 2 drying-rooms, library, garden; air-conditioning in spa and some bedrooms; conference facilities (max 80 people incl up to 40 residential); fishing, gym, sauna, solarium, heated indoor swimming-pool, tennis, health spa, croquet; early suppers for children
♿ Wheelchair access to hotel (ramp) restaurant, WC unisex), 10 ground-floor bedrooms, 1 specially equipped for disabled people   ● No children under 8; dogs in annexe bedrooms only; no smoking in some bedrooms   ⊟ Access, Amex, Delta, Switch, Visa   £ Single £105, single occupancy of twin/double £130, twin/double £160, four-poster £220, suite from £260; deposit required. Continental B £9.50, cooked B £13.50; set L £18.50 to £25, D £40; alc L, D £40; buttery meals also available. Special breaks available

---

 Denotes somewhere you can rely on a good meal – either the hotel features in the 1997 edition of our sister publication, **The Good Food Guide,** *or our inspectors thought the cooking impressive, whether particularly competent home cooking or more lavish cuisine.*

Haigs Hotel

273 Kenilworth Road, Balsall Common CV7 7EL
TEL: (01676) 533004   FAX: (01676) 535132

A modest, commercial hotel, worth considering for its good food and enthusiastic hosts.

Although this unmemorable house from the 1920s changed hands at the end of 1994, it remains in the *Guide*, not least because of the high-quality English and French cuisine that continues to be served under the chef, Paul Hartup. The inexpensive table d'hôte menu offers such uncomplicated dishes as soufflés and lamb cooked with garlic and rosemary, followed by bread-and-butter pudding or home-made ice-cream. Alternatively, you might try something more ambitious from the à la carte selection, for example, poached ballottine of guinea-fowl with a truffle mousseline, served with a Madeira sauce. The keen new owners, Hester and Alan Harris, have renamed the restaurant 'Poppy's', and matching red flowers cover the walls prettily; the other public rooms are far less appealing. Hester has been hard at work refurbishing some of the more presentable bedrooms, making the curtains and headboards herself and supervising the installation of new bathrooms. The majority are singles (Number 12 is the biggest) suitable for business people: the NEC is just a few miles down the road. Avoid the rooms which face the busy adjacent A road.

○ Closed 26 Dec to 3 Jan; restaurant closed Sun   ⬈ On A452, 6 miles south of Junction 4 of the M6, 4 miles north of Kenilworth. Private car park   ⬅ 8 single, 5 twin, 1 double; 2 with bathroom/WC, most with shower/WC; TV, room service, hair-dryer, trouser press, direct-dial telephone   ✓ Restaurant, bar, lounge, TV room, garden; conference facilities (max 20 people incl up to 14 residential); early suppers for children, toys   ♿ Wheelchair access to hotel, restaurant, 2 ground-floor bedrooms
● No dogs in public rooms; no smoking in restaurant   ▭ Access, Switch, Visa
£: Single £35 to £53, single occupancy of twin/double £53 to £58, twin/double £53 to £68. Set D £17, Sun L £12; alc D £27.50

Sloop Inn

Bantham, Kingsbridge TQ7 3AJ
TEL: (01548) 560489/560215   FAX: (01548) 561940

Frenetically popular pub-hotel with plain bedrooms just minutes from the sea.

At busy times of the week the sprawling bars of the Sloop Inn will be heaving with drinkers and diners, whose cars will be blocking the road outside. Once inside you can easily see the attraction. The Sloop Inn dates back to the sixteenth century and has the flagstone floors and beamed ceilings to prove it. Its history, too, is suitably studded with tales of smugglers and wreckers. The popular bar menu features staples like scampi and chips, topped up with a selection of daily specials. Unfortunately, the bedrooms lack the character of the bars, and furnishings seem to be fairly flimsy. Given that there is no lounge, this is not the ideal place for couples in search of privacy. On the other hand, with a surfing beach just a short walk downhill, guests are unlikely to spend much time indoors. The Sloop Inn is also perfectly positioned on the south-west coastal path, within easy reach of pretty Hope Cove.

◑ Open all year ▨ At mini-roundabout near Churchstow on A379 take Bantham road and follow for 3 miles. Private car park ⤒ 2 twin, 3 double; family rooms available; all with bathroom/WC; TV, hair-dryer ⬥ Restaurant, bar ⟋ No wheelchair access ● No pipes or cigars in bar or restaurant ▭ Delta, Switch £ Single occupancy of twin/double £27 to £29, twin/double £56 to £58, family room from £70; deposit required. Alc L, D £11

BAPCHILD Kent　　　　　　　　　　　　　　map 3

Hempstead House

London Road, Bapchild, Sittingbourne ME9 9PP
TEL: (01795) 428020 (AND FAX)

Large Victorian house with good food and friendly hosts.

Mandy and Henry Holdstock maintain consistently high standards in this large red-brick Victorian house with an immaculate garden and outdoor swimming-pool. Hempstead House is a very homely sort of a place, with two sitting-rooms. One, the Snug, is certainly cosy, with its wood-panelled window seat surrounded by full-length heavy curtains, a low, comfy sofa and chairs, and lots of family photos. The dining-room is slightly more formal, with white and pink striped walls and long floral curtains; here you might sample such delights as seafood mousse, then pheasant with a gin and juniper berry sauce, followed by mincemeat meringue flan. Dinner is quite a sociable affair with all the guests seated around the large polished mahogany table. Afternoon tea can be taken in the very bright and airy conservatory, with its white muslin drapes and views to the gardens and surrounding countryside. The top floor of the house and an adjoining annexe house the guest bedrooms, all prettily decorated and of a good size. Bathrooms too are spacious and well stocked with lots of goodies.

◑ Open all year ▨ On A2, 1½ miles east of Sittingbourne. Private car park ⤒ 1 twin, 5 double, 1 family room; some in annexe; all with bathroom/WC; TV, room service, hair-dryer, direct-dial telephone, clock radio ⬥ Dining-room, 2 lounges, TV room, drying-room, library, conservatory, garden; conference facilities (max 20 people incl up to 7 residential); heated outdoor swimming-pool, croquet; early suppers for children; toys, playroom, baby-listening, outdoor games ⟋ No wheelchair access ● No dogs in dining-room; no smoking in bedrooms ▭ Access, Amex, Delta, Diners, Switch, Visa £ Single occupancy of twin/double £59, twin/double £62 to £69, family room £69 to £89. Set L, D £19.50; alc L, D £27.50

Use the index at the back of the book if you know the name of a hotel but are unsure about its precise location.

BARWICK Somerset   map 2

Little Barwick House

Barwick, Yeovil BA22 9TD
TEL: (01935) 423902   FAX: (01935) 420908

---

*Off-the-beaten-track restaurant-with-rooms in stately eighteenth-
century dower house.*

With its grand steps leading up to the front door, Little Barwick House is a
Georgian mansion in miniature with its face turned away from the road to look
out over an untamed garden dominated by a sweeping cedar. In what is really a
restaurant-with-rooms, the graceful dining-room with its coral-coloured walls
takes pride of place at the front, where diners can best appreciate the views.
Veronica Colley's four-course dinner menus are mildly adventurous without
being too way out: Popeye' pancake with spinach and cream cheese might be
followed by a chicken tikka salad and pear and almond tart. Afterwards, guests
can retire to a more homely bar-lounge scattered with souvenirs of a recent
family expedition to India. The half-dozen bedrooms boast cheerful modern
décor, although some are rather small and lack baths. A satisfied guest who has
been coming back for years commented that the Colleys run Little Barwick as a
true family business where individual requirements, say for early breakfast, are
accommodated without fuss.

◑ Closed Chr & New Year   ⤤ From Yeovil take A37 towards Dorchester; after 1 mile
turn left at Red House pub; house is ¼ mile on left. Private car park   ⇤ 2 twin, 4
double; all with bathroom/WC exc 2 doubles with shower/WC; TV, direct-dial
telephone; hair-dryer and trouser press on request   ✅ Restaurant (air-conditioned),
bar, lounge, garden; conference facilities (max 20 people non-residential)   ♿ No
wheelchair access   ● No dogs in public rooms; no smoking in restaurant   ⊟
Access, Amex, Delta, Switch, Visa   £ Single occupancy of twin/double £49,
twin/double £78; deposit required. Set D £19 to £25. Special breaks available

---

BASLOW Derbyshire   map 8

Cavendish Hotel

Baslow DE45 1SP
TEL: (01246) 582311   FAX: (01246) 582312

---

*Good food and much art in a traditional country-house hotel on the
edge of the Chatsworth estate.*

The Duke of Devonshire's coat of arms patterns the carpets of the Cavendish, for
he owns this straggle of stone buildings which have grown considerably from an
original 200-year-old inn. Every room overlooks the rolling fields of the duke's
estate. The best of the modish, classy bedrooms are corner rooms, with double
views. In handsome public areas furnished with polished antiques, one's
attention is as likely to be drawn to the cornucopia of paintings and prints, the
formidable collection of the long-time manager Eric Marsh. Dining is praise-
worthy both for the quality of Nick Buckingham's food and also for its flexibility.
In the main restaurant you can wade through four courses of classic but creative

cuisine: venison might be garnished with red onion marmalade, and plaice with banana, and tuna might be served with a spiced pear salad, for example. However, some criticism came from one guest for 'nightmare restaurant pricing' with lots of supplements. The more laid-back conservatory-style Garden Room is open 11am to 11pm for late breakfasts, designer sandwiches, afternoon teas and more down-to-earth full meals. Nick is confident enough of his skills to have a table for two set up in his kitchen.

◑ Open all year ⚡ On A619 in Baslow. Private car park 🛏 10 twin, 10 double, 2 four-poster, 1 family room, 1 suite; all with bathroom/WC; TV, room service, hair-dryer, mini-bar, trouser press, direct-dial telephone ⚶ 2 restaurants, bar, lounge, conservatory, garden; air-conditioning in suite; conference facilities (max 16 people residential/non-residential); fishing; early suppers for children; babysitting, baby-listening, high chairs ♿ No wheelchair access ⊖ No dogs; no smoking in main restaurant and 2 bedrooms ▭ Access, Amex, Delta, Diners, Switch, Visa 💷 Single occupancy of twin/double £79 to £94, twin/double £99 to £114, four-poster £114, family room £114, suite £135. Continental B £5, cooked B £9; set L, D £25 to £33; café meals available; (prices valid till Apr 1997). Special breaks available

---

Fischer's Baslow Hall

Calver Road, Baslow DE45 1RR
TEL: (01246) 583259 FAX: (01246) 583818

An exuberantly furnished Edwardian hall that has become a foodies' mecca.

The basis for the success of Max and Susan Fischer's restaurant-with-rooms is that Max's food is quite outstanding. He turns top-class ingredients, from local organic beef to venison from the neighbouring Chatsworth estate, into sophisticated but unfussy and wonderfully presented creations. Experiencing his cuisine in all its glory is a fairly formal and pricey affair, but Café Max, a separate room, offers a more relaxed and cheaper way to savour dishes such as pig's trotter in red wine sauce. At breakfast, you can look forward to brioche and croissants from the hotel's own bakery and freshly squeezed orange juice. The vivid, rich drapes, wallcoverings and soft furnishings that characterise the public rooms set the tone for the six bedrooms too. These continue the kitchen's high standards, though some are on the small side. All come with bathrobes, fresh fruit and local mineral water. Haddon is the most memorable, for its superb antique bath and shower.

◑ Closed 25 & 26 Dec ⚡ Baslow Hall is on right as you leave Baslow village on A623 Stockport road. Private car park 🛏 1 twin, 3 double, 1 four-poster, 1 suite; all with bathroom/WC exc 1 double with shower/WC; TV, room service, hair-dryer, direct-dial telephone; no tea/coffee-making facilities in rooms ⚶ 3 dining-rooms, bar/lounge, garden; conference facilities (max 40 people incl up to 6 residential); early suppers for children; baby-listening, cots, high chairs ♿ No wheelchair access ⊖ No children under 12 in dining-rooms after 7pm; no dogs; no smoking in dining-rooms ▭ Access, Amex, Diners, Switch, Visa 💷 Single occupancy of twin/double £75 to £90, twin/double £95 to £120, four-poster £120, suite £120; deposit required. Cooked B £7.50; set L £16.50/19.50, D £38.50; café meals available. Special breaks available

Pheasant Inn

Bassenthwaite Lake, Cockermouth CA13 9YE
TEL: (01768) 776234   FAX: (01768) 776002

Comfortable rooms in a country inn with bags of character.

Life at the Pheasant Inn runs at an apparently easy pace, appropriate for a seventeenth-century inn that now finds itself set back from the new course of the A66. Deer, red squirrels and foxes (the prey of the local hunt) inhabit the woodland behind the hotel; well-fed and well-looked-after residents inhabit the black-beamed rooms within. The modest proportions of the whitewashed inn demonstrate a Tardis-like effect once inside, with its thick stone walls enclosing two cottagey residents' lounges, a long dining-room, a snug bar stained and polished the colour of nicotine, and a parquet-floored pub lounge spread with oriental rugs. Seventeen rooms are also tucked beneath the mossy slate roof, and while they are generally modest in size, none is claustro-phobically small. Furnishings have been kept simple and unobtrusive, with the odd antique, a bit of pine or a display of bird prints lending the character. The attractive bathroom in Room 5 and the vaulted ceiling in the small but cosy Room 17 caught our inspector's eye. Local flavours feature strongly on a menu offering plenty of choice, such as Silloth shrimps with tagliatelle, or pheasant in black cherry, elderflower wine, juniper and cream; and the breakfast menu includes grilled local rainbow trout.

◑ Closed 24 & 25 Dec   ⊿ Just off A66, 7 miles west of Keswick on west side of Bassenthwaite Lake. Private car park   ↤ 5 single, 15 twin/double; some in annexe; all with bathroom/WC exc 2 with shower/WC; hair-dryer   ⊘ Dining-room, bar, 3 lounges, drying-room, garden; early suppers for children   ♿ Wheelchair access to hotel, restaurant and WC (M,F), 3 ground-floor bedrooms   ● No dogs in bedrooms (kennels available); no smoking in dining-room & 1 lounge   ▱ Access, Visa
£ Single £58 to £60, single occupancy of twin/double £65 to £70, twin/double £72 to £94; deposit required. Set L £12, D £19.50. Special breaks available

---

Riggs Cottage

Routenbeck, Bassenthwaite Lake, Cockermouth CA13 9YN
TEL: (01768) 776580 (AND FAX)

A super little B&B tucked away in a quiet corner of the Lake District.

Brevity must have been the soul of the Norse language, as 'riggs' apparently means 'dwelling on the side of a hill'. In order to reach Riggs Cottage, you drive uphill off the main road for a mile or so, and then plunge down again along a bumpy, private track to a clutch of houses which, although they are within sight of civilisation, are tucked well away from it. Riggs Cottage is the whitewashed, slate-roofed house beside the ancient stone barn and the flourishing flower garden.

When we inspected, we found Hazel Wilkinson recovering from a bout of flu, but she seemed more concerned about taking care of us than about her own comfort. The cottage is small – a sort of three-up, one-down. Lots of stripped pine and flowery-patterned fabrics abound in the bedrooms. The family room has a platform under the rafters where the children can sleep, and shares a bathroom with the 'straightforward' double. A tiny room, with a bed tucked under a gnarled beam, is available, if needed, for younger guests. Downstairs, the sitting-room features comfy sofas around an enormous fireplace on one side, and an oval table next to a pine dresser displaying Hazel's hand-painted plates on the other. This is all highly conducive to chewing the fat over drinks in front of the log fire, or over the table during Hazel's four-course, traditional dinners.

◑ Open all year ⤢ From the A66 Keswick to Cockermouth road, follow the signs to Wythop Mill. Riggs Cottage is signposted on the right, 1 mile after the Pheasant Inn; cottage on left-hand side. Private car park ⟻ 1 twin, 1 double, 1 family room; family room with shower/WC ⊘ Dining-room, lounge, TV room, drying-room, garden; bowls; baby-sitting, baby-listening ⟽ No wheelchair access ● No children under 5; no dogs; no smoking ⊟ None accepted £ Single occupancy of twin/double £30, twin/double £38 to £50, family room £50; deposit required. Set D £13; packed lunches available. Special breaks available

---

BATH Bath & N.E. Somerset   map 2

Cheriton House   ℒ

9 Upper Oldfield Park, Bath BA2 3JX
TEL: (01225) 429862   FAX: (01225) 428403

Unfussy Victorian B&B with friendly new hosts and splendid views.

John Chiles and Iris Wroe-Parker, the new owners of this comfortable Victorian semi, seem to have adapted well – despite taking over during the 1995 heatwave, and being new to the business. The house has appealing original features and simple décor, although it's likely that the new owners will bring a more contemporary style to the current rather demure Victoriana. Pine furnishings and soft shades are the norm in most rooms, which vary in size, but John and Iris have given a whimsical touch to Room 6 (yellow and white striped duvets, bright flowers, butterflies and dragonflies stencilled on white walls) and a floral flourish to Room 8, both up in the eaves. The vast bay windows of Room 3 and the pretty breakfast-room have splendid views of the city. Further changes are planned, so more reports, please.

◑ Open all year ⤢ ½ mile south of Bath, just off A367 Wells Road. Private car park ⟻ 3 twin, 6 double; family room available; 2 with bathroom/WC, 7 with shower/WC; TV; limited room service; clock radio; hair-dryer and iron on request ⊘ Dining-room, lounge, drying-room, garden; conference facilities (max 12 people incl up to 9 residential) ⟽ No wheelchair access ● Children by arrangement; no dogs; no smoking in public rooms and some bedrooms ⊟ Access, Amex, Visa £ Single occupancy of twin/double £32 to £38, twin/double £45 to £56, family room from £63; deposit required. Special breaks available

---

Reports are welcome on any hotel, whether or not it is in the Guide.

Fountain House

9–11 Fountain Buildings, Lansdown Road, Bath BA1 5DV
TEL: (01225) 338622   FAX: (01225) 445855

All the benefits of a private apartment, with hotel service, in a smart period mansion.

If you value your privacy (or prefer to keep your sociability for members of your own party) this innovative concept in hotel accommodation is for you. A conversion of a honey-coloured Georgian mansion with all the usual period features, the Fountain House has 13 serviced suites, with one, two or three bedrooms, lounge, kitchenette and well-equipped bathroom. The receptionist or chirpy caretaker shows you your suite and explains the house rules; after that you're left with your own private apartment within easy walking distance of all the main sites. Service is a phone call away, and each morning a maid ensures that the housekeeping is immaculate. Guests have their own key, breakfasts (fresh fruit, orange juice, ham, cheese, bread and milk) and newspapers are delivered in a wicker shopping basket, and there's a laundry in the basement. Standard suites are plain but smart, with blue and pink upholstery and beige carpets. Those at the front have views over the rooftops, and morning traffic is not particularly intrusive. For a little more luxury, go for the Huntingdon Suite, with its bed on an upstairs gallery and period cornices, or the Venetian Suite, where plaster garlands decorate Palladian style arches.

● Open all year   ⚏ Take A36 until you reach T-junction with A4; turn right, and, at second major set of traffic lights, turn right again into Lansdown Road; Fountain House is 50 yards on right. Private car park   ⊫ 13 suites; family rooms available; all with bathroom/WC; TV, room service, hair-dryer, mini-bar, direct-dial telephone   ⌀ Babysitting   ⅙ No wheelchair access   ● None   ▭ Access, Amex, Delta, Diners, Switch, Visa   £ Suite £92 to £250; deposit required

---

Haydon House

9 Bloomfield Park, Bath BA2 2BY
TEL: (01225) 444919/427351 (AND FAX)

Affable hosts at a smart B&B with wonderful gardens.

Gordon Ashman-Marr claims to have taught his wife, Magdalene, everything he knows about interior design. She agrees – pointing out that it took only 20 seconds – and there's clearly a feminine touch (though nothing too frilly or floral) in the immaculate co-ordination at this smart Edwardian B&B. The five bedrooms are decorated according to their names – strawberry, gooseberry, elderberry, blueberry and mulberry – and everything matches perfectly, right down to the fluffy bathrobes. Thoughtful extras include hot-water bottles and pot-pourri sachets in the wardrobes. From the front rooms, Royal and Lansdown Crescents are just visible; those to the rear overlook Magdalene's lush, colourful gardens. The wonderful lawns and terrace, with hanging flower baskets, also form a backdrop to the elegant lounge. Guests seeking a quieter corner can wander over to the study; it is here that Gordon, using organisational skills gleaned from 42 years in the Navy, takes care of bookings. He can send visitors personalised directions to the house from virtually anywhere in the country. A collection of prints of old ships hangs in the peach-coloured dining-room, where breakfasts – often sociable, prolonged affairs – are served at a long, communal table.

◑ Open all year 🔁 From Bath centre follow signs for A367 Exeter road and up Wells road for ½ mile; at end of a short dual carriageway, fork right into Bloomfield Road and second right into Bloomfield Park. On-street parking 🛏 1 twin, 2 double, 1 four-poster, 1 family room; all with bathroom/WC exc doubles with shower/WC; TV, hair-dryer, direct-dial phone; trouser press on request ⊘ Dining-room, lounge, study, garden ♿ No wheelchair access ● Children by arrangement only; no dogs; no smoking ▭ Access, Amex, Delta, Visa £ Single occupancy of twin/double £45 to £55, twin/double £60 to £75, four-poster £70 to £75, family room £75 to £95; deposit required. Special breaks available

---

Holly Lodge

8 Upper Oldfield Park, Bath BA2 3JZ
TEL: (01225) 424042 FAX: (01225) 481138

Terraced gardens and good views in a stylish and spotless Victorian guesthouse.

George Hall's double-fronted Victorian house is grander than others in this leafy avenue of B&Bs. The main entrance, reached up a short flight of stone stairs, faces away from the road, with views over the gardens and city. Interior décor is lavish – particularly in the lounge, with its crystal chandelier, china trinkets, sparkling polished antiques and rich drapes. Aided by friendly, professional staff, George runs the place with a cheerful spirit; he admits to having neglected the garden slightly, but visitors are unlikely to be disappointed by the terraces of lawns, shrubs, flower borders and the odd classical statue, and the balustraded stairs leading down to a small summer house. Bedrooms share the same deft co-ordination as public rooms, whether they have light contemporary furnishings, four-posters or polished antiques. Colour schemes tend to be soft pinks, yellows and greens; an exception is the front-facing four-poster with its unusual turquoise bed inscribed with hieroglyphics. All have excellent tiled bathrooms.

◑ Open all year 🔁 ½ mile south-west of Bath city centre, off A367 Wells Road. Private car park 🛏 1 single, 2 twin, 2 double, 2 four-poster; all with bathroom/WC exc single with shower/WC; TV, room service, hair-dryer, trouser press, direct-dial telephone ⊘ Dining-room, lounge, conservatory, garden; baby-listening ♿ No wheelchair access ● No dogs; no smoking ▭ Access, Amex, Diners, Visa £ Single £46 to £48, single occupancy of twin/double £48 to £55, twin/double £75 to £85, four-poster £85; deposit required. Special breaks available

---

Where we know an establishment accepts credit cards, we list them. There may be a surcharge if you pay by credit card. It is always best to check when booking whether the card you want to use is acceptable.

Meadowland

36 Bloomfield Park, Bath BA2 2BX
TEL: (01225) 311079   FAX: (01452) 304507

Pleasant, welcoming and immaculately kept B&B in a secluded spot above the city.

Catherine Andrew's neat, white 1930s villa perhaps doesn't share the architectural distinction of some of the B&Bs in this quiet, leafy suburban area on the southern slopes of Bath. But, screened from the road by mature gardens which include cherry trees and magnolias, it has the advantage of added seclusion and a very warm welcome from Mrs Andrew and Charlie, the King Charles Spaniel. One recent visitor wrote that 'although it was not my first choice, had I known the quality of service at this establishment, it would have been top of my list.' Inside, everything is as spruce and immaculate as out. Breakfasts were described by one reader as 'a culinary delight'. Much thought and creativity has gone into bedroom décor, all elegant but not too flouncy, with frilled pelmets and pleated lampshades. Bathrooms are prettily tiled with excellent showers. Two overlook the mature gardens; the large double at the back has a view of the city.

● Open all year   ⤢ Take A367 towards Exeter up Wells Road; fork right at end of dual carriageway into Bloomfield Road; then second right into Bloomfield Park; hotel is on right. Private car park   ⊨ 1 twin, 2 double; 2 with bathroom/WC, 1 double with shower/WC; TV, hair-dryer, trouser press   ⊘ Dining-room, lounge, garden   ৬ No wheelchair access   ● No children under 10; no dogs; no smoking   ▭ Access, Visa   £ Single occupancy of twin/double £45 to £48; twin/double £58 to £62; deposit required. Special breaks available

Paradise House

88 Holloway, Bath BA2 4PX
TEL: (01225) 317723   FAX: (01225) 482005

An up-market B&B in a beautiful house and with a lovely location.

'The name says it all, truly sublime!', wrote an enthusiastic recent guest. Closer to the centre of Bath than many B&Bs, and situated in a quiet cul-de-sac, this attractive, honey-coloured, part-Georgian, part-Victorian house certainly has much to commend it, including arched windows; a classical pediment over the door; lots of surrounding greenery; an elegant sitting-room whose high, arching patio doors open on to a walled garden (a suntrap in summer); and an expansive city panorama. A homely selection of books, games and soft, pink-and-green sofas counteract the grander features of the sitting-room, such as Liberty fabrics and wallpaper and polished antiques. The deep-red, olive and cream colour scheme is echoed in the small and pretty breakfast-room through the archway, which features lace coverlets and a parquet floor. The bedrooms vary in size, but all are generally light and airy and are decorated in soft colour schemes; Room 6 has a wonderful view. Paradise House's downside is that, in the words of one reader, owners Janet and David Cutting run it 'more like a hotel than a B&B': they're happy to give advice if asked, but those visitors (including our inspector) who expect a warm, family-style welcome and lots of chit-chat may be disappointed.

○ Closed Chr ⤴ Follow A36 Bristol road into Bath. Take A367 Exeter road up hill; Holloway is the third turning on left. Then take the left fork downhill, into the cul-de-sac. Private car park ⊨⊣ 4 twin, 3 double, 1 family room; 4 bathroom/WC, 4 with shower/WC; TV, room service, hair-dryer, direct-dial telephone, clock radio
⌇ Dining-room, lounge, drying-room conservatory, garden; croquet; baby-listening
♿ No wheelchair access ⬤ No dogs; no smoking in bedrooms ▭ Access, Amex, Visa £ Single occupancy of twin/double £40 to £54, twin/double £69 to £72, family room £79 to £82; deposit required. Special breaks available

Queensberry Hotel

Olive Tree, Russel Street, Bath BA1 2QF
TEL: (01225) 447928 FAX: (01225) 446065

Striking contemporary décor in an elegant, Georgian terrace housing one of Bath's top restaurants.

In accordance with Bath's strict preservation rules, Stephen and Penny Ross's four-storey Georgian town house has a plain if elegant façade, with just a smart little portico and a few bright flower baskets to distinguish it from others. While maintaining a healthy respect for tradition and period detail, the interior is more contemporary. The Olive Tree restaurant – surprisingly light despite its basement location, thanks to the white floor tiles and pale terracotta colour-washed walls – mixes English cooking with a dash of Mediterranean colour. Service was a little complacent when we inspected. Those on weekend breaks may be frustrated by the lack of a set-price menu on Saturday and Sunday nights.

Upstairs there's more mixing of traditional and modern style. Bronze statuettes set off the original cornices and fireplace in the soft blue and yellow drawing-room, with comfortable seating by the fire for after-dinner coffee. Bedrooms tend to be decorated in soft colours with no skimping on fabrics. The best rooms are at the back, overlooking the lovely walled courtyard shrouded by greenery. Low-ceilinged attic rooms can feel claustrophobic; high-ceilinged rooms with original cornices and fireplaces are the ones to go for.

○ Closed Chr ⤴ In city centre just north of Assembly Rooms. Private car park
⊨⊣ 22 twin/double; all with bathroom/WC exc 1 with shower/WC; TV, 24-hour room service, hair-dryer, direct-dial telephone; no tea/coffee-making facilities in rooms
⌇ Restaurant (air-conditioned), bar, lounge, garden; conference facilities (max 12 people residential/non-residential); early suppers for children; babysitting, baby-listening ♿ No wheelchair access ⬤ No dogs; no smoking in restaurant
▭ Access, Delta, Switch, Visa £ Single occupancy of twin/double £75 to £89, twin/double £75 to £175; deposit required. Cooked B £7.50; set L £10.50/£12.50, D £19; alc L £25, D £28. Special breaks available

Report forms are at the back of the Guide; *write a letter or e-mail us if you prefer. Our e-mail address is: "guidereports@which.co.uk".*

Royal Crescent

15–16 Royal Crescent, Bath BA1 2LS
TEL: (01225) 739955   FAX: (01225) 339401

Peaceful walled gardens, stylish period décor and good food in an unbeatable setting.

A uniformed porter and flower baskets by the door alert guests to the discreet entrance of this elegant, historic hotel. The dignified façade bears nothing to detract from the perfect symmetry of John Wood's curving masterpiece, the Royal Crescent. The entrance also conceals the hotel's size. The main house – the period features of which include ornate plasterwork and panelling, marble fireplaces, crystal chandeliers and gilt-framed oils in the smart but welcoming drawing-room – eventually opens out on to spruce lawns and flower borders, separating it from the cream-coloured Dower House and Palladian-style Garden Villa. The restrictions of preservation orders mean that suites in the main house are like ballrooms, with high ceilings, chandeliers, stucco and cornices. Standard rooms have plenty of style too, with rich fabrics and fine antiques. Over in the Dower House and Garden Villa, bedroom décor is more contemporary, with chintzy fabrics, soft lighting and fresh colours. The restaurant is especially lovely for afternoon tea and dining on summer evenings. A typical menu may feature pigeon and foie gras salad or sea-fish chowder, followed by salmon with leeks in a light Ricard cream or lamb with wood-mushroom mousse in a lentil gravy.

○ Open all year ⊡ In city centre. Private car park ⟞ 1 single, 11 twin, 16 double, 3 four-poster, 15 suites; family rooms available; some in annexe all with bathroom/WC; TV, room service, hair-dryer, trouser press, direct-dial telephone; tea/coffee-making facilities and mini-bar on request ⧄ Restaurant, bar, 3 lounges, conservatory, garden; air-conditioning in top-floor bedrooms and meeting rooms; conference facilities (max 70 people incl up to 46 residential); heated outdoor swimming-pool, croquet; early suppers for children; toys, babysitting, baby-listening ♿ No wheelchair access ● No dogs in public rooms; no smoking in restaurant ▭ Access, Amex, Diners, Switch, Visa £ Single £105, single occupancy of twin/double £120, twin/double £165, four-poster £205, family room £295, suite from £295; deposit required. Continental B £9.50, cooked B £12.50; set L £18.50, D £35; alc L £20, D £45. Special breaks available

---

Sydney Gardens

Sydney Road, Bath BA2 6NT
TEL: (01225) 464818 (AND FAX)

Unusual Victorian house with amiable hosts just a short walk through the park from the city centre.

The house Diane and Stanley Smithson chose for their comfortable, friendly B&B business suits them exactly. The golden-stone Victorian building, surrounded by shrubs, flower borders and the odd classical statue, has some unusual Italianate features – ornate stone balconies, circular windows and a peaked spire. Stanley's abstract paintings of Italian *palazzi* hang throughout the house, blending in with other *objets d'art* and some attractive antiques. The cat prints and doorstops are in honour of the Smithson's other love, resident cats Ivan and Pushkin, who spend much of their time curled up by the fire. Bedrooms are varied, but pine furnishings and soft colour schemes tend to be the norm. 'Room 7' with lace draped over the bed, is the favourite of honeymooners and has good views over the garden and city. Breakfasts are traditional and served in unlimited quantities (though Stanley remembers only one guest taking up his offer of a second cooked breakfast!). For evening dining, the Smithsons keep a stock of local restaurant menus; they have also devised a few touring routes to encourage visitors to stray a little from the standard tourist trails.

◑ Closed Chr and Jan ↗ On A36 ring road in Bath near Holburne Museum. Private car park ▭ 3 twin, 3 double; family room available; all with bathroom/WC; TV, hair-dryer, direct-dial telephone ⊘ Dining-room, lounge, garden ⅋ No wheelchair access ⊜ No children under 4; no dogs in public rooms; no smoking ▭ Access, Amex, Switch, Visa £ Single occupancy of twin/double £49 to £59, twin/double £59 to £69, family room from £89; deposit required

---

BATHFORD Bath & N.E. Somerset   map 2

Eagle House

23 Church Street, Bathford, Bath BA1 7RS
TEL: (01225) 859946 (AND FAX)

Magnificent Georgian house in a conservation area close to Bath.

John and Rosamund Napier's house in the pretty conservation village of Bathford was once a reform school, but nowadays welcomes visitors more likely to appreciate the splendid architecture of John Wood the Elder. Partly hidden behind a stone wall, the house's golden façade is discreet (preservation rules prevent signs); its perfect symmetry is best appreciated from the rear, where one-and-a-half acres of terraced gardens, including a tennis court, open to expansive views across the valley. Despite the grand proportions and an impressive stone-flagged entrance hall with magnificent curving staircase, the Napiers have created an unintimidating ambience, with few frills and flounces, where guest can relax. The best place for this is the superb polygonal drawing-room, with garden views, pale yellow walls, soft blue upholstery and marble fireplace; brochures containing local information, and a selection of CDs and cassettes, complement the fine surroundings. Continental breakfasts (or full English on request, at a small additional charge) are served at flexible times in a cheerful yellow room, and include fresh home-baked croissants. The best bedrooms – larger and with the most attractive outlook – are at the back of the house, but all are a good size, with bright colour schemes and a mix of antique and modern furnishings. Two rooms in the pretty cottage annexe at the bottom of the garden share an unusual octagonal sitting-room and a small kitchen, provided with all necessary provisions for breakfast.

◑ Closed 20 to 30 Dec ⧖ Leave A4 ¼ mile east of Batheaston on A363 to Bradford-on-Avon; after 150 yards fork left up Bathford Hill; after 300 yards turn first right into Church Street; Eagle House is 200 yards on right. Private car park ⏢ 1 single, 2 twin, 3 double, 1 family room, 1 suite; 2 in annexe; most with bathroom/WC exc single with shower/WC; TV, room service, hair-dryer, direct-dial telephone ⊘ Dining-room, lounge, drying-room, garden; conference facilities (max 20 people incl up to 16 residential); tennis, croquet; babysitting, baby-listening, outdoor games ♿ No wheelchair access ● Dogs in dining-room if other guests consent ▭ Visa
£ Single £35 to £41, single occupancy of twin/double £42 to £52, twin/double £44 to £68, family room £56 to £68, suite £75 to £90; deposit required. Cooked B £3. Special breaks available

Old School House

Church Street, Bathford, Bath BA1 7RR
TEL: (01225) 859593 FAX: (01225) 859590

Victorian guesthouse with affable and accommodating hosts and easy access to Bath city centre.

The Old School House has a central position in this quiet village of pretty Bath-stone houses – not surprisingly, because for 140 years, until 1970, it served as the village school. Twenty years later Sonia and Rodney Stone opened the house as a smart, but warm and friendly B&B. The house was built in the year of Queen Victoria's accession to the throne but has sympathetic modern extensions including a conservatory jutting out into the small walled garden at the back; unusually, visitors enter directly into the main lounge. Little evidence of the house's former life remains – benches have been replaced by leather chesterfields clustered around the stone fireplace, and functional shelving by polished antiques stacked with china. There's certainly nothing stern about the ambience: quirky, homely touches including knitted tea-cosies and a selection of Toby jugs, plenty of tourist information and above all the Stones' exemplary hospitality give it a relaxed feel. Tea and cakes are served in the plant-filled conservatory on arrival, and breakfasts are excellent, with a huge variety of cereals, yoghurts, fruits and cooked dishes to choose from. Two of the bedrooms are on the ground floor and therefore ideal for less mobile people; all are prettily decorated in soft colours, with modern pine furnishings, broderie-anglaise-trimmed duvet covers and frilled curtains. As we went to press, the Stones were thinking about putting the B & B up for sale.

◑ Open all year ⧖ Leave A4 at junction with A363 to Bradford-on-Avon; after 100 yards fork left in front of Crown pub; after 200 yards turn right into Church Street; the Old School is 300 yards further on just past church. Private car park ⏢ 2 twin, 2 double; all with bathroom/WC; TV, hair-dryer, trouser press, direct-dial telephone ⊘ Dining-room/lounge, bar, conservatory, garden ♿ Wheelchair access to hotel and dining-room, 2 ground-floor bedrooms ● Children in dining-room by arrangement; no dogs; no smoking ▭ Access, Visa £ Single occupancy of twin/double £45 to £50, twin/double £65 to £70; deposit required. Set D £21.50. Special breaks available

BATTLE **East Sussex**   map 3

Powdermills

Powdermill Lane, Battle TN33 0SP
TEL: (01424) 775511   FAX: (01424) 774540

An easy-going and popular country house with an interesting past.

Powdermills derives its name from the gunpowder industry, which flourished here until the end of the nineteenth century and helped Britain to some of its most famous historic victories. Remnants of the past still dot the landscape, such as the 30-foot-high chimney, which was part of the drying-room for the powder, and the 7-acre lake, now stocked with carp and surrounded by abundant wildfowl. Julie and Douglas Cowpland's house is a whitewashed Georgian building, clad with a tangled knots of wistaria, with a modern extension and separate, recently completed, barn-style pavilion. The older section of the house, in which much use is made of antique furniture and gilt mirrors, is definitely the most attractive. The grand Georgian library (in which snacks are served) features a Victorian mahogany table and Chippendale chairs, while the pale-lemon music room is home to a harp and grand piano. The bedrooms in this part of the house are crammed with antiques and include real gems, such as the magnificent Wellington Suite.

The Orangery restaurant is a light and airy atrium-style room, with a marble floor and wicker chairs, in which you can choose from creative dishes that include crab-and-mango salad with a vanilla dressing, seared pigeon breasts with bubble and squeak, or couscous and vegetable strudel.

◑ Open all year; restaurant closed Sun eve in winter   ◢ Powdermill Lane leads off the A21, opposite Battle railway station. Private car park   ⤙ 7 twin, 21 double, 2 four-poster, 5 suites; some in annexe; all with bathroom/WC; TV, room service, hair-dryer, trouser press, direct-dial telephone; mini-bar in some rooms; tea/coffee-making facilities on request   ⌗ 2 restaurants, bar, 2 lounges, TV room, drying-room, library, garden; conference facilities (max 250 people incl up to 30 residential); fishing, unheated outdoor swimming-pool; early suppers for children; baby-listening   ♿ Wheelchair access to hotel (1 step), restaurant, WC (unisex), 4 ground-floor bedrooms, 1 specially equipped for disabled people   ● No children in restaurants eves; no smoking in bedrooms   ⊟ Access, Amex, Diners, Switch, Visa   £ Single occupancy of twin/double £49, twin/double £75 to £95, four-poster £85, suite £120 to £155; deposit required. Set L £14.50, D £18.50; alc D £23. Special breaks available

---

BEAMINSTER **Dorset**   map 2

Bridge House Hotel

3 Prout Bridge, Beaminster DT8 3AY
TEL: (01308) 862200   FAX: (01308) 863700

An appealing and historic small hotel with good, uncomplicated food.

A short walk downhill from the main square of this pretty rural village, Peter Pinkster's small hotel is a curious historical amalgam. The oldest parts were probably a thirteenth-century priest's house, and the mullioned windows (all of different sizes, some at different levels) are Tudor, but otherwise the house is predominantly Georgian – apart from the 1991 extension, housing five new bedrooms. The different architectural periods, however, form a harmonious whole, with plenty of ancient features: an Adam fireplace with pewter mouldings in the restaurant; Georgian panelling in the small, cosy sitting-room, with its bright soft sofas, logs stacked by the fire and some vivid modern paintings mixed with more traditional prints; and even a resident ghost. Bedrooms vary from cottage-style decorations – with pine furniture and jaunty colours, particularly those in the converted coach house – to grander rooms with original features, like the large Georgian Room with cornices and high ceilings.

Served in the long, low, pink restaurant or in the conservatory, which juts out into the immaculate walled gardens, the uncomplicated menus may feature duck breast with cassis, venison braised in red wine, or hare with a port-and-shallot sauce. Peter and the house manager, Jan, are friendly and chatty front-of-house hosts.

○ Open all year 🚫 The hotel is in the centre of Beaminster, down the hill from town square. Private car park 🛏 1 single, 4 twin, 8 double; family room available; some in annexe; all with bathroom/WC exc single with shower/WC; TV, room service, direct-dial telephone; hair-dryer on request ✓ Restaurant, bar, lounge, drying-room, conservatory, garden; conference facilities (max 16 people incl up to 13 residential); early suppers for children; baby-sitting ♿ No wheelchair access ● No dogs in public rooms; dogs in bedrooms by arrangement ☐ Access, Amex, Delta, Diners, Switch, Visa £ Single £48 to £53, single occupancy of twin/double £48 to £70, twin/double £51 to £99, family room £79 to £88; deposit required. Set L £12 to £14, D £17 to £19; light lunches available. Special breaks available

---

BEAULIEU Hampshire   map 2

Montagu Arms

Palace Lane, Beaulieu SO42 7ZL
TEL: (01590) 612324   FAX: (01590) 612188

A stylish village inn set in the heart of the New Forest.

Beaulieu is a tiny village in the centre of the New Forest and comes complete with lake, resident swans and ducks, characterful houses and cattle grids. Its hostelry, the Montagu Arms, became an inn following the dissolution of the monasteries – it had originally been built to house the monks from the nearby abbey. Although much of the building has been rebuilt since then, the sombre reception area reflects the initial purpose of the hotel. The lounge has lots of comfortable sofas and a loudly ticking grandfather clock, and the air of quiet sophistication continues through into the bar/library. French windows in the restaurant open out on to a pretty garden, where a wonderful bronze sculpted fountain of elegant arum lilies by Guiseppe Lunt steals the show. The menu puts up a good fight, though, with choices like breast of squab pigeon served on a casserole of herb-scented barley with a rich red wine vinaigrette, or warm tart of seafood with French lettuce and a salmon caviar dressing. All bread is baked on the premises, and service is attentive and formal. Bedrooms are decorated in antique country style with sprigged wallpaper, are named after trees and vary in size from adequate to spacious.

◑ Open all year ⊉ In Beaulieu village. Private car park ⤶ 4 single, 3 twin, 10 double, 4 four-poster, 3 suites; most with bathroom/WC; TV, room service, hair-dryer, trouser press, direct-dial telephone; no tea/coffee-making facilities in rooms
✅ Restaurant, bar/library, lounge, conservatory, garden; conference facilities (max 50 people incl up to 24 residential); early suppers for children; babysitting, baby-listening
🕭 No wheelchair access ● No children under 5 in restaurant eves; no dogs in public rooms; no smoking in restaurant ☐ Access, Amex, Delta, Diners, Switch, Visa 🄴 Single £70, single occupancy of twin/double £76, twin/double £99 to £120, four-poster £140 to £150, suite £176 to £186; deposit required. Set L £17, D £20/24; alc D £31.50 (1996 prices); light lunches available. Special breaks available

---

BEERCROCOMBE Somerset   map 2

Frog Street Farm

Beercrombe, Taunton TA3 6AF
TEL: (01823) 480430

Attractive farmhouse B&B hidden in deepest Somerset.

Frog Street Farm takes its name not from the frogs which undoubtedly lurk in the farmyard, but from the old Saxon word for a meeting place. The farmhouse is a graceful grey-stone longhouse dating back to the fifteenth century. It's still attached to a working farm which has a herd of prize Friesians, but inside the rooms are far from workaday. A small porch opens straight on to a delightful dining-room with exposed stone walls and flagstone floors. Here Veronica Cole serves up good solid farm cooking that makes much use of home-grown ingredients; there's no licence so you'll need to bring your chosen tipple. A comfortable lounge with inglenook fireplace lurks behind a Jacobean screen and manages to offer quiet corners for reading despite its size. Not quiet enough for you? Then try the second, smaller version on the other side of the screen. One of the lounges serves as a TV room. Upstairs, the bedrooms have light, bright décor. There may be only three of them, but they are thoroughly versatile and a family suite complete with lounge can easily be arranged.

◑ Closed Nov to Mar ⊉ Leave M5 at Junction 25 and take the Chard/Ilminster road (A358); at Hatch Beauchamp by Hatch Inn take Station Road for 1 mile. Private car park ⤶ 3 double; 2 with bathroom/WC, 1 with shower/WC; hair-dryer
✅ Restaurant, 3 lounges, drying-room, garden; heated outdoor swimming-pool
🕭 No wheelchair access ● No children under 11; no dogs; no smoking ☐ None accepted 🄴 Double £50 to £54. Set D £16. Special breaks available

---

Prices are what you can expect to pay in 1997, except where specified to the contrary. Many hoteliers tell us that these prices can be regarded only as approximations.

BENENDEN Kent   map 3

Crit Hall

Cranbrook Road, Benenden, Cranbrook TN17 4EU
TEL: (01580) 240609   FAX: (01580) 241743

A smart Georgian country house with considerate and friendly hosts.

Sue and John Bruder say their aim is that 'from the moment you enter our drive and *pull* our front doorbell, you will feel a warm welcome' – and judging by our readers' letters this year they are succeeding. 'Helpful without being pushy,' they praise; 'they really do deserve a medal.' Crit Hall, with its ivy-clad red-and-grey-brick walls and well-kept garden is surrounded by miles of open countryside, which can be seen to good effect from most of the rooms. The stylish dining-room, with its yellow and green walls, many pictures and antique furniture, is described by one reader as being 'like a Noel Coward theatre set'. Here the Bruders serve set dinners which might include salmon pâté with hot buttered toast, rack of herb-encrusted pork with roast vegetables, and Seville orange tart. Breakfast is served in the kitchen, with its flagstone floors and pine tables, and dried hops hanging from the beams. Bold colours and fabrics are used in most of the rooms, particularly the stylish bedrooms. The large double bedroom with its gold bedspread, red and gold canopy, and red and gold star curtains is furnished with antiques such as a Gothic reading stand and antique pine dressing table. 'Excellent in every way,' one report concluded.

◐ Closed mid-Dec to mid-Jan; restaurant closed Sun eve   ⊠ Take B2086 west from centre of Benenden, Crit Hall is 1 mile on left. Private car park   ⊯ 2 twin, 1 double; 2 with bathroom/WC, 1 with shower/WC; TV, hair-dryer   ✧ Dining-room, lounge, conservatory, garden   ⅙ No wheelchair access   ● No children under 10; no dogs; no smoking   ▭ Access, Delta, Switch, Visa   £ Single occupancy of twin/double £35, twin/double £50 to £52; deposit required. Set D £18.50. Special breaks available

---

BEPTON West Sussex   map 3

Park House

Bepton, Midhurst GU29 0JB
TEL: (01730) 812880   FAX: (01730) 815643

A traditional private country hotel with plenty of attractions nearby.

The peaceful rural backdrop and eclectic mix of guests are what give this traditional country-house hotel its peculiar complexion. Thespians drifting out from the Chichester Festival Theatre, polo types down for Cowdray Park, punters from Goodwood racecourse, golfers and hunters all meet in the small bar, the walls of which are covered in memorabilia and photographs of their better-known colleagues. The house has been run as a hotel by the O'Brien family for almost 50 years, so they know well what their guests come for – the relaxing atmosphere of a private residence with efficient service. And where better to start to wind down than the elegant drawing-room, which has comfy old sofas you simply disappear into, shelves of books and soothing pale lemon walls. Outside, a delightful wistaria-covered terrace makes a fine setting for *al fresco* dining in summer, and the more energetic are well provided for with a croquet lawn, swimming-pool and grass tennis courts. Bedrooms are all individually decorated but are generally largish and furnished with a pleasing mix of antique and modern items and the odd high bed or *chaise-longue*.

◑ Open all year ⚡ Take B2226 from Midhurst; hotel is 2½ miles on left. Private car park 🚗 1 single, 6 twin, 4 double; family room available; some in annexe; all with bathroom/WC; TV, room service, hair-dryer, trouser press, direct-dial telephone, clock radio ✥ Dining-room, bar, lounge, TV room, drying-room, garden; conference facilities (max 40 people incl up to 11 residential); heated outdoor swimming-pool, tennis, pitch and putt, croquet; early suppers for children ♿ Wheelchair access to hotel (1 step), restaurant and WC (unisex), 1 bedroom specially equipped for disabled people ● None ▭ Access, Amex, Delta, Switch, Visa [£] Single £48 to £60, single occupancy of twin/double £48 to £60, twin/double £95 to £120. Set L £10/£15, D £15 to £20. Special breaks available

---

Little Hodgeham

Smarden Road, Bethersden, Ashford TN26 3HE
TEL: (01233) 850323

An enchanted, rose-covered cottage with an accomplished and entertaining host.

Erica Wallace has single-handedly turned the derelict Tudor cottage she bought into an enchanted dwelling, the like of which is usually found only between the pages of a story book. It has roses climbing the walls, and small leaded windows; the spell remains unbroken once Erica welcomes you inside her cottage. The small, elegant dining-room is where guests sit around the single polished yew table and are presented with one of her set dinners – a sociable affair which might include a hot seafood starter in a creamy dill sauce, followed by chicken suprême and upside-down apple tart, all served on antique Crown Derby china. The sitting-room leads through to the 'Wallace Collection' – a room of family memorabilia – and on to the small conservatory, the roof of which is canopied by jasmine and clematis. Upstairs, the bedrooms are all stylish and comfortable: the Blue Room is very fresh and bright with a bathroom which looks out over the colourful garden, with its pond and an arbour that is floodlit at night. The entrancing four-poster room has pink floral hand-starched pillow-slips, canopy and curtains, and a platform reached by a small staircase where there are another two beds. The four-poster bed was designed and built by Erica herself: she started with two Georgian mahogany bedposts and built the rest of it around them.

The text of entries is based on unsolicited reports sent in by readers and backed up by inspections. The factual details are from questionnaires the Guide *sends to all hotels that feature in the book.*

◑ Closed 1 Sep to mid-Mar ⊿ 10 miles west of Ashford on the A28 Bethersden road; turn right at the Bull pub and go towards Smarden for 2 miles; the house is on the right. Private car park ⊨→ 1 twin, 1 double, 1 four-poster; hair-dryer
⌁ Dining-room, lounge, TV room, drying-room, conservatory, garden; unheated outdoor swimming-pool; early suppers for children ⅙ No wheelchair access ● Children by arrangement only and not allowed in dining-room eves; dogs in barn only; no smoking in dining-room ⬚ None accepted £ Single occupancy of twin/double £59, twin/double £105, four-poster £105 (rates incl dinner); deposit required. Special breaks available

---

BIBURY Gloucestershire map 2

Bibury Court

Bibury, Nr Cirencester GL7 5NT
TEL: (01285) 740337/740324 FAX: (01285) 740660

The flavour of Old England at an unassuming Jacobean manor in a glorious setting.

Even in an area as replete with pleasing landscapes as the Cotswolds, the cluster of golden-stone buildings that makes up the village of Bibury is something of a jewel. Bibury Court proudly flaunts the date 1633 on the escutcheon that crowns the doorway, but parts of it date back to Tudor times. Over the years the rather grand Jacobean house has offered hospitality to Charles II and the Prince Regent, before finally opening its doors to the hoi polloi when it became a country-house hotel almost 30 years ago. A legal dispute about its ownership in Victorian times is said to have inspired the interminable case of Jarndyce *vs* Jarndyce in Dickens' *Bleak House* – not an epithet that the house itself would share. A nosy pheasant called Eric may well escort you from the car park to the door, and once inside you'll find yourself amid a world of flagstones, bristling antlers, panelled walls, plaster ceilings and ticking grandfather clocks – all the icons of the traditional English country house, with comfy chairs in soothing florals or manly stripes to curl up in. The Art Nouveau maidens that adorn the astonishing metallic wallcovering in the bar are survivors from the house's last remodelling in 1922, and add a touch of the Bridesheads. Much of the bedroom furnishings are of the same vintage, giving the spacious rooms a comfortably well-worn and unmodish feel. These days the main restaurant is aiming at a brasserie-style service, though the menu still revolves around classic fare: perhaps cream of courgette and tarragon soup, followed by tenderloin of pork with garlic and grain mustard, then chocolate roulade with strawberries.

◑ Closed 21 to 31 Dec ⊿ Behind church in Bibury, next to river. Private car park
⊨→ 2 single, 10 twin/double, 6 four-poster, 1 suite; family room available; all with bathroom/WC; TV, room service, hair-dryer, direct-dial telephone ⌁ 2 restaurants, bar, lounge, TV room, drying-room, library, conservatory, games room, garden; conference facilities (max 20 people non-residential/residential); fishing, croquet, clay-pigeon shooting, putting, snooker; early suppers for children ⅙ No wheelchair access ● None ⬚ Access, Amex, Diners, Switch, Visa £ Single £55, single occupancy of twin/double £64, twin/double £78 to £82, four-poster £82, family room £100, suite £105; deposit required. Cooked B £5; alc D £21.50; light lunches available (1996 prices). Special breaks available

The Swan

Bibury, Nr Cirencester GL7 5NW
TEL: (01285) 740695 FAX: (01285) 740473

Swanky hotel in a stunning spot on the banks of the River Coln.

The creeper-drenched exterior and plain Cotswold-stone façade look as if they've come straight from the pages of an Olde English pub manual. So it's hats off to owners of the Swan for defying convention and modelling the interior in a confident, modern way, ebulliently teaming antiques and twentieth-century collectables with contemporary fabrics and *fin-de-siècle* glitz. You'll find a sprinkling of *chinoiserie* as well as Staffordshire figures in the pretty parlour, where non-smoking guests can roast chestnuts or loaf on overstuffed sofas on long winter nights; plus chintzy floral armchairs in the cool-blue writing-room, which once housed the village post office. The delightful pieces of Clarice Cliff and classy Charles Rennie Mackintosh reproductions which dot the corridors and foyer pay homage to the Swan's between-the-wars heyday, when it was a favoured rendezvous of the bright young things who motored out to this famous Gloucestershire beauty spot. All the signs suggest that the hotel is entering a new golden age. The irreproachably tasteful bedrooms are spacious and are furnished in styles from French château to Victorian extravagance and Edwardian elegance. Even the individually designed bathrooms are gloriously hedonistic.

Diners who choose the formality of the rich burgundy and gold Cygnet Restaurant might feast on gravad lax with a blue cheese dressing, followed by breast of chicken topped by an artichoke and wild mushroom mousse, and tarte Tatin with vanilla ice-cream. The glossily modern Jankowski's Brasserie offers lighter fare from baguettes to pasta and simple classics like steak or trout.

◐ Open all year ▨ In Bibury on B4425 between Burford and Cirencester. Private car park ↳ 1 single, 5 twin, 8 double, 3 four-poster, 1 family room; all with bathroom/WC exc 1 double with shower/WC; TV, room service, hair-dryer, trouser press, direct-dial telephone, radio; tea/coffee on request ⊘ 2 restaurants, bar, 2 lounges, garden; conference facilities (max 10 people residential/non-residential); fishing; early suppers for children; baby-listening ら Wheelchair access to hotel, restaurant and WC (unisex), lift to bedrooms ◓ Dogs and smoking in some public rooms only ▭ Access, Amex, Delta, Visa £ Single £86 to £97, single occupancy of twin/double £97 to £107, twin/double £115 to £140, four-poster £175 to £190, family room £230 to £260; deposit required. Set D £21.50, Sun L £16; alc D £30.50; brasserie meals available. Special breaks available

---

Burgh Island

Bigbury-on-Sea TQ7 4AU
TEL: (01548) 810514 FAX: (01548) 810243

A wonderful Art Deco period-piece, bringing the 'racy' days of the 1930s back to life on a secluded islet.

Burgh Island is a delicious one-off, its uniqueness accentuated by the fact that at high tide it is cut off from the mainland. Even the method of approach is novel: a giant sea-tractor trundles through the waves to deposit you at the foot of the drive. Wealthy Midlands industrialist Archibald Nettlefold commissioned Matthew Dawson to design Burgh Island in 1929, and it quickly became a refuge for high society: famous guests included Noel Coward, Edward, Prince of Wales, Mrs Simpson, and Agatha Christie. Locals looked on bemused, and muttered about 'racy' goings-on. What Beatrice and Tony Porter have done in restoring the hotel is little short of a miracle. Ten years ago, the stained-glass Peacock Dome lay shattered, and much of the furniture had been burnt. Now, however, Burgh Island, with its parquet floors, etched mirrors and period furniture, is splendidly restored. The Porters have scoured the country for period furniture; at the last count they had 63 Lloyd Loom chairs. Guests are encouraged to get into the spirit of things by dressing for dinner, and there are plans to restore the diving platform in the Maiden's Pool behind the hotel, where dances used to be held. All the rooms are suites, with period details like bells beside the baths with which to summon the maid. But the mod cons haven't been forgotten: the original central heating works again, and there are televisions in the bedrooms. Cocktails with appropriate names are served in the Palm Court to the soothing sounds of Al Bowley and Jessie Matthews.

◗ Closed weekdays in Jan and Feb ⬈ Follow the signs to Bigbury-on-Sea. At St Ann's Chapel call the hotel from a phone box. Do not drive across the beach to the island. Private car park ⌸ 15 suites; all with bathroom/WC exc 1 with shower/WC; TV, room service, hair-dryer, direct-dial telephone; tea/coffee-making facilities on request ✇ 2 restaurants, bar, 2 lounges, drying-room, conservatory, games room, garden; conference facilities (max 80 people incl up to 15 residential); fishing, gym, sauna, solarium, unheated outdoor swimming-pool, tennis, snooker; early suppers for children; baby-listening ᕃ No wheelchair access ● No dogs ▭ Amex, Delta, Diners, Switch, Visa £ Suite £198 (rates incl dinner); deposit required. Set L £18 to £22.50, D £32. Special breaks available

---

BILLESLEY Warwickshire   map 5

Billesley Manor

Billesley, Alcester, Nr Stratford-upon-Avon B49 6NF
TEL: (01789) 279955   FAX: (01789) 764145

A grand country-house hotel near Stratford – worth considering if you've got plenty of money to spend.

The owners, Queens Moat Houses, call Billesley Manor a conference and leisure hotel. Yet despite its conversion into a large, corporate hotel set tranquilly in 11 acres of games-oriented grounds, the character of this memorable Elizabethan house still wins through. Externally, fantastic topiaries almost conceal a new wing sympathetically added to the impressive, multi-gabled building. Within, in spite of the coats of armour, reproduction Tudor portraits and much contract furniture, the public rooms, such as the enormous, galleried bar and the oak-panelled restaurants, are still quite splendid. In the lounge you'll find copies of Shakespeare's works; the bard may have used the Manor's library, and possibly even wrote *As You Like It* here. Many bedrooms in the original building are grand affairs, sometimes boasting panelling and antiques. Most of the standard rooms are located in the new wing, and are less characterful but still very plush. However, the weekday rates are very high – even for these – and the weekend-break prices offer a reduction of only around 15 per cent. Sadly, the Manor's highly regarded chef, Mark Naylor, has left; reports, please, on newcomer Roger Barstow.

● Open all year 🗷 Just off the A46, 3 miles west of Stratford-upon-Avon. Private car park 🛌 1 single, 13 twin, 22 double, 3 four-poster, 2 suites; family rooms available; some in annexe; all with bathroom/WC; TV, room service, hair-dryer, trouser press, direct-dial telephone; no tea/coffee-making facilities in rooms ✅ 2 restaurants, bar, lounge, 2 libraries, garden; conference facilities (max 100 people incl up to 41 residential); heated indoor swimming-pool, tennis, croquet, pitch and putt; baby-sitting, baby-listening ♿ No wheelchair access ● No dogs; no smoking in restaurants and some bedrooms ▭ Access, Amex, Delta, Diners, Switch, Visa £ Single £105, single occupancy of twin/double £125, twin/double £152, four-poster £170 to £190, family room £190 to £215, suite £190 to £215; deposit required. Continental B £7, cooked B £9.50; set L £10 to £15, D £29.50; alc L, D from £33.50; (1996 prices). Special breaks available

---

BILLINGSHURST West Sussex   map 3

Old Wharf

Wharf Farm, Newbridge, Billingshurst RH14 0JG
TEL: (01403) 784096 (AND FAX)

A welcoming canal-side B&B well off the beaten track.

The Old Wharf is a converted canal-side warehouse, now the charming home of David and Moira Mitchell. Herons, kingfishers, swans and even otters can all be seen in this impossibly idyllic hideaway. Inside, a rustic galleried staircase is dominated by the original hoist-wheel of ancient timber, and leads to the four daintily decorated bedrooms named after the soothing pastel shades they are painted in – Primrose, Pink, Peach and Blue. Views over the canal and meadows beyond enhance the sense of remoteness from the bustle of city life. On the ground floor a cosy lounge opens through french windows to the canal for lazy walks in the company of Max and Merlin, the resident collies.

You can start the day with a real farmhouse breakfast including local free-range eggs, or take the healthy option of organic fruit with cereal or special-recipe muesli in the pleasantly rustic breakfast-room overlooking the walled garden and patio.

● Closed 2 weeks over Chr & New Year 🗷 Head west from Billingshurst on A272 for 2 miles; house is on left-hand side, by banks of canal, just after river bridge. Private car park 🛌 3 twin, 1 suite; all with bathroom/WC; TV, clock radio ✅ Dining-room, lounge, garden; fishing ♿ No wheelchair access ● No children under 12; no dogs; no smoking ▭ Access, Amex, Visa £ Single occupancy of twin £40, twin £50, suite £60; deposit required

BIRCH VALE **Derbyshire**   map 8

Waltzing Weasel

New Mills Road, Birch Vale SK12 5BT
TEL: (01663) 743402 (AND FAX)

A winning combination of atmospheric village pub, recommended restaurant and classy bedrooms.

Although the High Peak uplands provide admirable views, there are more scenic Peak District locations in the *Guide*, and the Waltzing Weasel sits alongside a main road. However, few places in the region offer such good-quality sustenance and accommodation. A local clientele and requisite old-inn accoutrements – venerable settles and dressers, open fires, prints of hunting and cricket scenes – imbue the bar with much vitality and character. Fruit machines and Muzak are noticeably absent, while fresh flowers and convivial publican Michael Atkinson are conspicuously present. Outstanding bar food amounts to a seductive hot-and-cold carvery at lunch time, and dishes such as crayfish tails, lobster salad, duck-and-cherry pie and chocolate whisky cake in the evening. The fare, essentially stout English cooking, overlaps on to the two- or three-course table d'hôte menus in the refined restaurant, which is characterised by classical music, soothing burgundy walls, candelabra and even a tapestry on one wall. Hunger pangs at breakfast can be sated by baked ham and Arbroath smokies. In the smart bedrooms, you'll enjoy the views, antique beds and swish bathrooms with brass fittings. Room 6 is the most luxurious, boasting a fine half-tester.

◑ Open all year ⤴ ½ mile west of Hayfield on the A6015. Private car park
⇤ 1 single, 2 twin, 5 double; all with bathroom/WC exc single with shower/WC; TV, hair-dryer, trouser press, direct-dial telephone ✦ Restaurant, bar, garden; air-conditioning in restaurant and bar; fishing, tennis; early suppers for children
♿ Wheelchair access to hotel (3 steps) and restaurant, 2 ground-floor bedrooms
● No children under 7 ▭ Access, Amex, Delta, Switch, Visa £ Single £45, single occupancy of twin/double £66, twin/double £79; deposit required. Set D £19.50 to £23.50; bar meals available. Special breaks available

---

BIRMINGHAM **West Midlands**   map 5

Copperfield House Hotel

60 Upland Road, Selly Park, Birmingham B29 7JS
TEL: 0121-472 8344   FAX: 0121-415 5655

A modest, peaceful, family-run hotel about 2½ miles from the city centre.

In an up-market, tree-lined suburb, this handsome, red-brick, mid-Victorian residence is probably as quiet as any hotel you'll find in the Birmingham area. Given its proximity to the Pebble Mill TV studios, you may see a famous actor or two over your bowl of cereal. However, Jenny and John Bodycote don't reserve their keen and friendly hospitality for the stars alone.

The best bedrooms are on the ground floor, while the attic rooms are spacious and peaceful but a steep climb away. If you want decent pine furniture, and new tiles and shower units in the bathrooms, make sure you're put in one of the recently refurbished rooms rather than in a room that has yet to undergo an overhaul. John and Jenny's daughter Louise, who is a trained cook, is responsible for the food. It's given more prominence than is usual for a small, city hotel and is served in a fresh dining-room sporting bentwood chairs and Impressionist prints. Keenly priced dinners stick to mainly tried-and-tested home-made dishes, such as melon and Parma ham, baked sole with tartare sauce, and cheesecakes and crumbles.

◐ Open all year; restaurant closed Sun ⤢ Leave M6 at Junction 6, travel on A38 through city centre; at second set of lights turn left (Priory); at next set of lights turn right (A441). The third road on the right is Upland Road. Private car park ⤶ 5 single, 4 twin, 7 double, 1 family room; most with bathroom/WC, 3 with shower/WC; TV, room service, hair-dryer ✅ Dining-room, bar/lounge, drying-room, garden; conference facilities (max 15 people residential/non-residential); early suppers for children ♿ No wheelchair access ⬤ No dogs in public rooms; smoking in bar/lounge and bedrooms only ⊡ Access, Amex, Delta, Switch, Visa £ Single/single occupancy of twin/double £40 to £50, twin/double £50 to £70, family room £60 to £70; deposit required. Set D £17 (prices valid till Dec 1996)

Swallow Hotel

12 Hagley Road, Five Ways, Birmingham B16 8SJ
TEL: 0121-452 1144   FAX: 0121-456 3442

If money is no object, this is place to stay in Birmingham.

One spin of the Swallow Hotel's revolving doors whisks you from the humdrum world of Birmingham's Five Ways roundabout to a ritzy world in which Edwardian elegance is the avowed aim. Concierges in tail coats patrol a marble-and-chandeliered foyer; scones and cakes appear in the plush lounge at teatime; malts line the mobile-phone-free bar; and the pool, in what was the car park of this former office block, assumes the stunning form of Egyptian baths. If you want to impress a client, the flashy fare in the expansive, muralled Sir Edward Elgar Restaurant should do the trick. The less formal Langtry's, which is beautifully styled as an Edwardian conservatory, including statuary and Lloyd Loom furniture, specialises in traditional English dishes.

'When we're not too busy you might get a room for around £100,' says a member of the Swallow's top-notch staff. Otherwise, you'll have to pay considerably more if you want to savour the hotel's seriously luxurious but restrained accommodation: three phones (one by the toilet), a mini-bar containing fresh milk, and expert insulation from any traffic noise are all part of the standard deal.

Many hotels offer special rates for stays of a few nights or more. It is worth enquiring when you book.

◗ Open all year 🛏 Near the centre of Birmingham at Five Ways, where the A456 crosses the A4540. Private car park 🛏 14 single, 38 twin, 42 double, 4 suites; all with bathroom/WC; TV, 24-hour room service, mini-bar, trouser press, direct-dial telephone; hair-dryer in some rooms ✅ 2 restaurants, bar, lounge, library, air-conditioning in all rooms; conference facilities (max 30 people residential/non-residential); gym, solarium, heated indoor swimming-pool, steam room, spa; early suppers for children; baby-sitting, baby-listening ♿ No wheelchair access ● No dogs in public rooms; no smoking in some bedrooms ☐ Access, Amex, Delta, Diners, Switch, Visa £ Single £130, single occupancy of twin/double £140, twin/double £150, suite £299; deposit required. Set L from £17.50, D from £25; alc L, D £37.50 (prices valid till Sept 1996). Special breaks available

---

BISHOP'S TAWTON Devon   map 1

Halmpstone Manor

Bishop's Tawton, Barnstaple EX32 0EA
TEL: (01271) 830321 FAX: (01271) 830826

Luxurious, secluded farmhouse hotel with marvellous views.

Halmpstone Manor is a working arable farm buried deep in the Devon countryside. Finding it can be tricky but as soon as you spot the honey-gold stone house and the glorious, flower-filled garden you know you've hit the jackpot. It may have only five rooms, but each of them is a gem, individually decorated and furnished and equipped with all the 'extras' – bath robes, sherry decanters, spring water, fresh fruit, flowers and chocolates – that mark a luxury hotel. Perhaps the finest are the two suites, Mule and Chichester, with their big four-poster beds, but light sleepers might prefer Hawkey, which has a separate entrance round the back. Downstairs, the house has two contrasting faces. To the left of the hall is a light, bright lounge with big windows and lots of comfortable armchairs, to the right a darker wood-panelled dining-room with a big log fire set in a marble fireplace. Between the two, the hall doubles as a well-stocked bar and there's a wooden settle with wings to shelter its occupants from any draughts. Jane Stanbury's five-course dinner menus put quality before fanciness; typically you might be served a prawn salad, with crab soufflé to follow, then breast of chicken filled with smoked salmon mousse, and a selection of cheeses and sweets to finish.

◗ Closed Nov & Jan 🛏 In Bishop's Tawton turn left opposite BP petrol station; follow road for 2 miles, then turn right at Halmpstone Manor sign; hotel is on left. Private car park 🛏 3 twin/double, 2 four-poster; 3 with bathroom/WC, 2 with shower/WC; TV, room service, hair-dryer, trouser press, direct-dial telephone ✅ Dining-room, bar, lounge, garden ♿ No wheelchair access ● No children under 12; no smoking in bedrooms ☐ Access, Amex, Diners, Visa £ Single occupancy of twin/double £70, twin/double £100, four-poster £130; deposit required. Set L, D £25. Special breaks available

---

All entries in the Guide *are rewritten every year, not least because standards fluctuate. Don't trust an out-of-date* Guide.

Hotel Bambi

27 Bright Street, Blackpool FY4 1BS
TEL: (01253) 343756 (AND FAX)

Great-value small family hotel in quiet street close to seafront and tramway.

Christine Watkin has been welcoming guests to her small hotel, away from Blackpool's brasher areas, for 17 years but still manages to make everyone feel as if they were her first-ever guest. Externally, the Bambi isn't much to write home about, a large picture window, shade and fascia slicing across the ground floor of a bay-windowed, terraced Victorian house. Inside, the décor is comfortable without being at all flashy; some will think it slightly old-fashioned. You can have dinner in a dining-room which opens off the back of the lounge, and Christine is solicitous of people's food fads, even at breakfast. Upstairs, the bedrooms are simple but smart, with low lighting and good showers...no standing in a cold trickle here. The hotel's twee name immediately suggests that families will be welcome and, sure enough, a stock of toys stands waiting. Photos in the hall recall Blackpool in its Victorian heyday, the beach all but invisible beneath the bodies. With space for only two cars, parking could be a headache, especially during the last two weeks in July, when half of Glasgow descends on the town.

◐ Closed Dec & Jan ⤢ Close to the Promenade and South Pier. Private car park; on-street parking ⤙ 1 twin, 2 double, 2 family rooms; 1 with bathroom/WC, most with shower/WC; TV ⚘ Dining-room, lounge; toys ♿ No wheelchair access ● No dogs ▤ Access, Amex, Delta, Diners, Visa £ Single occupancy of twin/double £18, twin/double £35, family room from £39; deposit required. Set D £6

Blackwell Grange

Blackwell, Shipston on Stour CV36 4PF
TEL: (01608) 682357 (AND FAX)

Very comfortable and characterful farmhouse accommodation in an off-the-beaten-track north Cotswolds village.

Liz Vernon Miller was out in the fields tending her lambs when our inspector called this year: proof of the fact that this is a fully operational sheep farm. Her early-seventeenth-century home stands at the back of a courtyard of old thatched and slate-roofed agricultural buildings, and the wind carries the sound of bleatings to the front door. Although its name may not hint at it, the farmhouse is very elegant, with antiques complementing the beamed and flagstoned rooms. A big inglenook fireplace dominates the dining-room, where you may eat separately or communally. Liz sometimes serves her well-regarded dinners – perhaps watercress mousse, roast pheasant and lemon soufflé (bring your own wine) – in front of the log fire in the very cosy sitting-room.

Large, stylish bedrooms, decked out with more handsome old furniture and armchairs, and containing giant, smart bathrooms, are located upstairs amid low ceilings and creaking floors. A ground-floor bedroom in the annexe is equipped for disabled people.

◗ Closed Jan 🅿 Take A3400 towards Oxford from Stratford-upon-Avon; after 5 miles turn right by the church in Newbold on Stour; in Blackwell, fork right. Private car park 🛏 1 single, 1 twin, 1 double, 1 twin/double; 1 in annexe; all with bathroom/WC exc 1 with shower/WC; TV in single; hair-dryer on request ✓ Dining-room, lounge, garden ♿ Wheelchair access to hotel (1 step) and dining-room, 2 bedrooms specially equipped for disabled people ● No children under 13 in main house; no dogs; no smoking ▭ Access, Amex, Delta, Visa £ Single £25 to £27, single occupancy of twin/double £28, twin/double £50; deposit required. Set D (by arrangement only) £11.50/£16. Special breaks available

---

BLAKENEY Norfolk   map 6

White Horse Hotel ℒ

4 High Street, Blakeney, Holt NR25 7AL
TEL: (01263) 740574 FAX: (01263) 741303

A very friendly pub with comfortable, straightforward bedrooms, catering for both locals and visitors.

The heavily silted creek of Blakeney fails to deter the small band of determined crab-fishers on sunny summer afternoons. Sue Catt describes how the locals catch dabs by shuffling barefoot in the water and detecting the fish with their feet. However it is caught, much of this local produce ends up on the restaurant menu, perhaps in the form of deep-fried crab and ginger parcels with a spring onion and chilli salsa, or chargrilled calamari with saffron and truffle *jus*. Sue and her partner, Daniel Rees, are keen to promote the cooking of chef Raymond Maddox, but realise that local views on price and value for money may be slightly at odds with Raymond's London background ('We fall between many stools here'). Perhaps as a result, the bar menu sticks to tried-and-tested favourites such as fish and chips or crab or prawn salad. A secluded, newly paved courtyard at the back provides a bit of peace from the traffic in the narrow street. Look out for the carved horse's head above the arch – it was won by Daniel in a bet. Bar aficionados have a choice between the main split-level bar that runs the length of the building, with a brick fireplace, low red ceiling and paintings of local scenes, and the plum-coloured Gallery Room overlooking the front. The restaurant has more modish touches, with rich, rose-coloured swags and a deep aquamarine carpet. The best bedroom looks out over the harbour: large and airy, it has pine furniture, striped duvets and a Victorian-tiled bathroom. Other rooms are smaller, but in a similar style.

◗ Open all year 🅿 On the High Street in Blakeney. Private car park 🛏 2 single, 1 twin, 4 double, 2 family rooms; all with bathroom/WC exc 1 single with shower/WC; TV, hair-dryer, clock radio ✓ Restaurant, 2 bars, garden; early suppers for children ♿ No wheelchair access ● No dogs ▭ Access, Amex, Delta, Switch, Visa £ Single £30, single occupancy of twin/double £45, twin/double £60, family room £75; deposit required. Alc L £10, D £15; bar meals available. Special breaks available

BLANCHLAND **Northumberland** map 10

Lord Crewe Arms

Blanchland, Nr Consett DH8 9SP
TEL: (01434) 675251 FAX: (01434) 675337

*Ex-monastery building rich in history with plush bedrooms and a
300-year-old resident.*

With its off-the-beaten-track North Pennine location, Blanchland is the kind of
place that people stumble upon by chance. It shouldn't be. The place is suffused
with history – the layout is little changed in almost a millennium. It's essentially
an eighteenth-century model village built on the exact plan, and using many of
the ruins, of a twelfth-century monastery. At its heart is the Lord Crewe Arms,
the former abbots' lodging quarters. The hotel's most renowned feature is
something you may prefer to avoid. It's not the Hilyard Room complete with
priest hole nor the cosy, vaulted Crypt Bar, but the ghost of Dorothy Forster,
one-time occupant and heroine of the 1715 Jacobite rebellion. Her portrait looks
down benignly on guests enjoying fine dinners such as king prawns, turkey
broth and monkfish sauté with smoked bacon in a Calvados cream sauce.
Simpler fare is available in the bar. Bedrooms come in a variety of shapes and
sizes: the Bamburgh Room with its mullioned windows and view over the
walled gardens is, by all accounts, one of Dorothy's favourite haunts; the
Radcliffe Room, with four-poster bed and oak beams, is in the crenellated tower,
while the Honeymoon Suite (Room 13!) has a spa bath and Art Nouveau tiling.
When you finally turn in for the night you will find that your bed has been turned
down. But by whom?

◖ Open all year   ⊠ On B6306, 10 miles south of Hexham. On-street parking
⨼ 4 twin, 12 double, 1 four-poster, 3 family rooms, some in annexe; most with
bathroom/WC, 2 with shower/WC; TV, room service, hair-dryer, trouser press,
direct-dial telephone; iron on request   ⊘ Restaurant, bar, 3 lounges, drying-room,
study, garden; conference facilities (max 20 people residential/non-residential); baby-
listening   ⅙ No wheelchair access   ● No dogs in public rooms   ▭ Access,
Amex, Diners, Switch, Visa   £ Single occupancy of twin/double from £75,
twin/double from £105, four-poster from £105, family room from £105; deposit
required. Set L £14; alc D £27; bar meals available. Special breaks available

---

BLEDINGTON **Gloucestershire** map 5

Cotswold Cottage

Chapel Street, Bledington OX7 6XA
TEL: (01608) 658996 (AND FAX)

*High-quality rooms at a delightful B&B in an unspoilt Cotswold
village.*

With Kingham's main-line station only a mile away, it is just about possible to
commute to London from Bledington, which is in the Cotswolds on the
Oxfordshire/Gloucestershire border. However, with a working farmyard
opposite, Janet Weir's eighteenth-century cottage and barn conversion in a

village famous for its stream and ducks is a world away from metropolitan concerns. A modern annexe in the garden has the effect of creating a little courtyard where an old well and colourful hanging baskets contribute to the rustic idyll. When it comes to interior design Janet has developed a modern cottagey style that highlights the classic features like the sturdy ceiling beams without succumbing to the gloomy clutter that too often passes for period charm. Everything is bright and shiny, with the plain walls and polished table of the breakfast-room set off by conventional pieces, like wall-mounted plates, and unexpected ones like the Russian dolls on the antique sideboard. A miniature Charlie Chaplin figure presides over the small sitting area at the top of the stairs leading to the main-house bedrooms, and there are plans to create a new downstairs sitting-room later in the year. The large bedrooms are attractively furnished with pine or pretty stencilled furniture and cheerful floral drapes. Bathrooms are smarter than you expect in a modestly priced B&B. Romance seekers might prefer the annexe room's grand four-poster, with *en suite* shower.

◖ Closed Chr 🔃 In Bledington take the no through road opposite shop/post office; cottage is on right-hand side. Private car park 🛏️ 2 double, 1 four-poster; 1 in annexe; doubles with bathroom/WC, four-poster with shower/WC; TV, hair-dryer, clock radio; trouser press in 1 room ⌖ Dining-room ♿ No wheelchair access ● No children under 16; no dogs; no smoking ▭ None accepted £ Single occupancy of twin/double £35, twin/double £48 to £52, four-poster £48 to £52; deposit required

---

BLOCKLEY Gloucestershire   map 5

Crown Inn

High Street, Blockley, Nr Moreton-in-Marsh GL56 9EX
TEL: (01386) 700245   FAX: (01386) 700247

Cheerful village pub in a classic honey-coloured village.

The hordes that descend on nearby Stow, Chipping Campden and Broadway are mercifully absent from Blockley though the village boasts the same mellow Cotswold stone and golden ashlar that make those honeypots a joy to behold. You know this is a genuine locals' pub when you see the sprawling dogs nonchalantly lolling at their owners' feet, implacably opposed to yielding an inch of their territory. The bars themselves, with their wooden settles, captain's chairs and photographs of Old Gloucestershire, are at the core of the place, and, perhaps surprisingly, sell champagne by the glass as well as hand-pumped ales. For a quieter time, escape to the cosy, beamed residents' lounge with its floral sofas and leather button-backs, plus a good range of games and books. You can dine in varying degrees of formality, from the formal Coach House Restaurant, ennobled by a spiral staircase, to the simpler brasserie or one of the bars. There's a modern slant to the food: perhaps sliced smoked duck on a salad of asparagus and baby sweetcorn, followed by roast wing of skate on a bed of peppered spinach served with black butter, then sticky toffee pudding. Or opt for something more traditional like the home-made hand-raised venison and pigeon pie in the bar. Bedrooms vary in style and size, with a scattering of antiques and décor running the gamut from bold masculine stripes and plaids to pastels and chintzes. Four have four-posters.

◗ Open all year ⤢ Off the main A44 Oxford to Evesham road, 1 mile from Moreton-in-Marsh. Private car park ⤶ 5 twin, 11 double, 4 four-poster, 1 suite; family rooms available; some in annexe; TV, room service, hair-dryer, direct-dial telephone; trouser press in some rooms ⬦ 2 restaurants, bar, lounge, library, garden; conference facilities (max 40 people incl up to 21 residential); babysitting ⴴ No wheelchair access ◖ None ⊟ Access, Amex, Diners, Visa £ Single occupancy of twin/double £60, twin/double £84, four-poster £110, family room from £96, suite £120; deposit required. Alc L £20, D £25. Special breaks available

---

BOLTON ABBEY North Yorkshire   map 8

Devonshire Arms

Bolton Abbey, Nr Skipton BD23 6AJ
TEL: (01756) 710441   FAX: (01756) 710564

A luxury hotel with a sense of tradition, modern facilities and great attention to detail.

In the years since the A59 was rerouted to bypass the Devonshire Arms, things have quietened down a little. The passing traffic now mainly consists of families on their way to picnic by the River Wharfe on the Bolton Abbey estate, so crossing the road from this sixteenth-century coaching inn to reach its impressive sporting facilities in the converted barn isn't as perilous as it might once have been. The estate has been in the Duke of Devonshire's family since 1753, and the hotel has been operating in its current form since the early 1980s; it is the way in which a sense of tradition is blended with up-to-date facilities that most impresses.

Much of the hotel is furnished with antiques and paintings from Chatsworth, and is thus predictably refined: large portraits of various Cavendish family members watch over the hushed lounges, where newspapers are read by crackling fires and the air is scented by bunches of fresh flowers. For a more informal atmosphere visit the Duke's bar, which is stuffed with all sorts of unusual sporting bric-à-brac, and serves a variety of beers. Chef Andrew Nicholson offers interesting interpretations of British cuisine in the elegant restaurant, such as roasted calf's liver in a puff-pastry case, or black pudding and caramelised onions with morel-mushroom sauce.

The bedrooms (such as Shepherd) in the old wing may have a fairly obtrusive theme, or may just be smart and well co-ordinated. Those in the River Wharfe wing are a little smaller, but equally pretty. One bookworm reader was delighted to find 'excellent reading lights and a thoughtful selection of recent books'.

If you have a small appetite, or just aren't feeling hungry, check if you can be given a reduction if you don't want the full menu. At some hotels you could easily end up paying £30 for one course and a coffee.

◐ Open all year　🅉　The Devonshire Arms is at the junction of the A59 and B6160, 5 miles north-west of Ilkley. Private car park　🛏　18 twin, 10 double, 10 four-poster, 3 suites; all with bathroom/WC; TV, room service, hair-dryer, trouser press, direct-dial telephone, iron　🍴　Restaurant, 2 bars, 2 lounges, TV room, drying-room, conservatory, garden; air-conditioning in 2 suites and conference room; conference facilities (max 150 people incl up to 41 residential); fishing, gym, sauna, solarium, heated indoor swimming-pool, tennis, croquet, putting, falconry; early suppers for children; baby-sitting, baby-listening, cots, high chairs　♿　Wheelchair access to hotel, restaurant, WC (M,F), 16 ground-floor bedrooms, 2 specially equipped for disabled people　● No children under 12 in restaurant; no smoking in restaurant and some bedrooms　🖵　Access, Amex, Diners, Switch, Visa　£　Single occupancy of twin/double from £100, twin/double £140, four-poster £165, suite £250; deposit required. Set L £19, D £32.50. Special breaks available

---

See the inside front cover for a brief explanation of how to use the Guide.

 This denotes that the hotel is in an exceptionally peaceful situation where you can be assured of a restful stay.

 This denotes that you can get a twin or double room for £60 or less per night inclusive of breakfast.

The Guide *office can quickly spot when a hotelier is encouraging customers to write a letter recommending inclusion – and, sadly, several hotels have been doing this in 1996. Such reports do not further a hotel's cause.*

If you make a booking using a credit card and find after cancelling that the full amount has been charged to your card, raise the matter with your credit card company. It will ask the hotelier to confirm whether the room was re-let, and to justify the charge made.

Fitz Manor

Bomere Heath, Shrewsbury SY4 3AS
TEL: (01743) 850295

Convivial hosts at a half-timbered fifteenth-century manor house with splendid gardens.

Retreats don't come much more peaceful and civilised than Fitz Manor, Dawn and Neil Baly's rambling house in the Severn Valley. The face the house shows the world, with weathered straps and peeling paintwork, is not perhaps its best, but having withstood the elements for half a millennium it's entitled to look a little careworn. The interior is an unalloyed delight for anyone with an ounce of soul: a riot of beams, panelling and antiques, tinged with a lived-in feel that means that you never forget that this is a family home. Autumnal colour schemes predominate in the two sitting-rooms, where the odd Dralon buttonback counterpoints the prevailing grandeur. Of the three bedrooms the huge twin in striking racing green is the most memorable, with lovely antique beds. The two public bathrooms are dated but adequate. A typical dinner (eaten with the Balys unless guests request otherwise) is likely to kick off with a soup or pâté, followed by fish, chicken or a traditional roast, a pudding such as apple and blackberry crumble, and cheese. Eaten in the grand setting of the vast dining-room with its portrait-laden aquamarine walls, dinner can't help but feel like something of an occasion. Even after 500 years the house can take the odd innovation, and the recent arrival of a snooker table seems to have met with guests' approval. For those not anxious to revisit a mis-spent youth there are extensive grounds to explore, including a garden ablaze with over 3,000 wallflowers, a croquet lawn and even a large swimming-pool.

◑ Open all year   ⊿ Take A5 to Montford Bridge, just north-west of Shrewsbury; then A4380 to Forton and Fitz; turn off after 1 mile; the manor's drive is 1 mile further on. Private car park   ⌂ 1 single, 2 twin; room service, hair-dryer, trouser press, radio ⌖ Dining-room, 2 lounges, games room, garden; fishing, heated outdoor swimming-pool, croquet, snooker   ♿ No wheelchair access   ● Dogs and smoking by arrangement   ▭ None accepted   £ Single £20 to £25, twin/double £40 to £50; deposit required. Set D £12.50

The Millstream

Bosham, Chichester PO18 8HL
TEL: (01243) 573234   FAX: (01243) 573459

A friendly and welcoming hotel in a historic and picturesque sailing village.

The Millstream is an eighteenth-century hotel which combines the elegance of a small country house with the cosy character and charm of a malthouse cottage. Nestling in the heart of the pretty quayside village of Bosham close to Chichester harbour, it provides a tranquil retreat for both tourists and 'yachties'. Spacious open-plan public rooms are fresh and stylish with beautiful flower displays, and the small lemon-yellow brick bar opens through french doors on to well-tended lawns and gardens, popular for an *al fresco* lunch. Bedrooms are either upstairs or in the modern extension, and all are comfy and individually decorated with pretty, well co-ordinated colours. Downstairs in the lounge, snug armchairs in the bay windows overlooking the millstream are an ideal spot to mull over the menu for dinner, which is served in the formal yet light and summery restaurant. Dishes might include game terrine with plum and apricot compote, followed by venison fillet with roast quail and a port and orange sauce, and a delicious choice of home-made desserts.

◐ Open all year ⊿ From Chichester take A259 to Bosham; turn left at Bosham roundabout and follow signs to church/quay. Private car park ⊨ 5 single, 9 twin, 13 double, 1 four-poster, 1 suite; family rooms available; some in annexe; all with bathroom/WC; TV, room service, hair-dryer, trouser press, direct-dial telephone
✓ Restaurant, bar, lounge, garden; air-conditioning in restaurant, lounge and some bedrooms; conference facilities (max 35 people incl up to 29 residential); early suppers for children ఉ Wheelchair access to hotel (1 step) and restaurant, 4 ground-floor bedrooms ● No dogs in public rooms ⊐ Access, Amex, Diners, Switch, Visa
£ Single £65, single occupancy of twin/double £75, twin/double £105, four-poster £117, family room £105, suite £117; deposit required. Set L £13, D £18 (prices valid till May 1997). Special breaks available

---

BOTALLACK Cornwall   map 1

Manor Farm

Botallack, St Just, Penzance TR19 7QG
TEL: (01736) 788525

Home-from-home stone farmhouse with walled garden offering B&B, near Land's End.

Manor Farm is a dreamy and comfortable stone farmhouse minutes from the sea in a remote area rich in reminders of the old tin trade. Joyce Cargeeg has a flair for picking interesting pieces of furniture. In the hall you'll have trouble squeezing past a wooden Swiss bench with fine bear-head finials, and breakfast is served off a magnificent wooden table originally from Africa. Past guests allowed their youngsters to pick out the inlaid foot from one of a pair of fighting cocks adorning a screen, but last year the fortuitous discovery of a door leading out of the back of the breakfast room made it possible for Joyce to create a tiny study for smokers and to give the screen a safe haven at the same time. Upstairs there are just three bedrooms, two of them *en suite*, with idiosyncratic furnishings; the bedhead in Fiona's Room is made from a fifteenth-century hope chest while the gilt mirror over the sink in Rachel's Room is fantastically exuberant. Joyce serves only breakfast, but a choice of 13 different items is guaranteed to set you up for the rest of the day.

◑ Open all year 🚉 Follow B3306 to north of St Just and fork left towards the coast; pass Queen's Arms on right and Manor Farm is straight ahead at next junction. Private car park 🛏 1 twin, 1 double, 1 four-poster; double with bathroom/WC, 2 with shower/WC; TV, hair-dryer ✥ Dining-room, lounge, study, garden, reading-room ♿ No wheelchair access ● No dogs; smoking in study only 🚭 None accepted £ Single occupancy of twin/double £30, twin/double £44, four-poster £44; deposit required

---

BOTTOMHOUSE **Staffordshire**   map 5

Pethills Bank Cottage

Bottomhouse, Nr Leek ST13 7PF
TEL: (01538) 304277 /304255   FAX: (01538) 304575

A B&B supervised by an extraordinarily enthusiastic host, with outstanding bedrooms and in a winning rural spot.

Chatty and maternal Yvonne Martin evidently adores looking after visitors in her low-slung, eighteenth-century, former farmhouse. In splendid and elevated isolation just beyond the southern fringes of the Peak District, her home cowers from the elements behind thick hedges and stone walls. Yet inside all is pleasantly cosy, with beams, exposed walls and cottagey furnishings. Yvonne's *pièces de résistance* are her bedrooms, lovingly furnished in carefully designed fabrics. The downstairs Garden Room is the largest, and has its own patio. Upstairs, Cottage and Dale feature skylight windows and corner baths. Some of the fanciest of hotels cannot match their wealth of extras: to those listed below, add a profusion of fresh flowers, hot-water bottles and sweets, hand lotions, and even anti-perspirant in the bathrooms.

   Yvonne provides evening meals only two or three times a week, and then only with advance notice. If the super spreads at breakfast time are anything to go by, dinners such as salmon mousse, trout in puff pastry, and trifle are worth applying for.

◑ Closed Chr 🚉 Close to A523, 5 miles south-east of Leek. Turn into lane opposite the Little Chef restaurant and follow signs for ½ mile. Private car park 🛏 1 twin, 1 double, 1 suite; 2 with bathroom/WC, suite with shower/WC; TV, hair-dryer, iron ✥ Dining-room, lounge, garden ♿ No wheelchair access ● No children under 5; no dogs; no smoking 🚭 None accepted £ Single occupancy of twin/double £31 to £33, twin/double £37 to £42, suite £39 to £45; deposit required. Set D £18. Special breaks available

---

BOUGHTON LEES **Kent**   map 3

Eastwell Manor

Eastwell Park, Boughton Lees, Ashford TN25 4HR
TEL: (01233) 219955   FAX: (01233) 635530

Imposing manor house offering luxurious rooms and excellent food.

Eastwell Manor, with its creeper-clad grey-stone walls, turrets and a gated entrance which leads into an eerily silent stone courtyard, looks as if it has been standing for hundreds of years, yet it has an air of newness to it, which is explained by the fact that the old manor house was torn down and then rebuilt in 1926. It is still undeniably impressive, has 62 acres of immaculate grounds and is a place to stay if you want to feel pampered. The dining-room, with its heavy oak doors and panelling, is a formal setting in which to sample the extensive seasonal menu, which might include shredded salt cod and crab with caviar, avocado and curry oil, then loin of hare with celeriac, beetroot and a juniper sauce, and finally blueberry tart with lemon-grass ice-cream.

The lounge is also quite formal, with carved wood panelling and lots of red leather chesterfield sofas and a resident cat called Hugo. The bedrooms, named after historical figures, many of whom have a connection with the house, are elegantly furnished with antiques; bathrooms have parquet floors. Every room comes complete with a life-size fluffy toy cat – and if you put the cat out at night it serves as a 'do not disturb' sign for the staff. Eastwell Manor is under new management but is still a family-owned hotel, now in the hands of Turrloo Parrett and family. More reports, please.

◑ Open all year   ⚡ Take A251 north from Ashford; hotel is on left-hand side just beyond sign for Boughton Aluph. Private car park   🛏 17 twin/double, 1 four-poster, 5 suites; all with bathroom/WC; TV, room service, hair-dryer, trouser press, direct-dial telephone   ✅ Restaurant, bar, lounge, games room, garden; conference facilities (max 100 people incl up to 23 residential); tennis, snooker, pitch and putt; early suppers for children   ♿ Wheelchair access to hotel (1 step) and restaurant (3 steps), 1 ground-floor bedroom   ⬤ No dogs or smoking in restaurant; no smoking in some bedrooms   ▭ Access, Amex, Delta, Diners, Switch, Visa   £ Single occupancy of twin/double £115 to £150, twin/double £145 to £180, four-poster £165, suite £225 to £255; deposit required. Set L £19.50, D £29.50; alc L, D £36.50 (1996 prices). Special breaks available

---

BOUGHTON MONCHELSEA Kent   map 3

Tanyard

Wierton Hill, Boughton Monchelsea, Maidstone ME17 4JT
TEL: (01622) 744705   FAX: (01622) 741998

Stylishly furnished medieval house in stunning surroundings.

Tanyard is set in ten acres of immaculately kept landscaped gardens, and beyond that all you can see is the beautiful countryside of the Kentish Weald with a few other houses dotted around. The house itself is a half-timbered, crooked little place with bags of character. The oldest part of the house, which is now the restaurant, dates from 1350 and with its flagstone floors, stone walls, beams and blue and white colour scheme it is a stylish and slightly formal setting in which to enjoy one of Jan Davies' dinners. The menu might include wild mushroom and herb crêpes, then rack of lamb with a mint and redcurrant sauce, followed by sticky toffee pudding – a house speciality. The comfortable sitting-room, like the rest of the house, is furnished with antiques and lots of unusual bits, like the onyx chess set from Mexico and the wooden carved panels on the wall which came from the sides of a baby's cot Jan picked up in Mombasa on her travels as a stewardess. Once you've navigated the crooked wooden stairs you'll find that the bedrooms are equally stylish. With their leaded windows and beamed, sloping ceilings there is little to choose between them in that they are all full of character and of a high standard. However, the rooms do vary in size – with the Pink Room and the Suite in the eaves of the house being the most spacious.

◑ Closed 2 weeks Chr & New Year ⤭ From B2163 at Boughton Monchelsea turn down Park Lane, opposite Cock pub; take first right down Wierton Lane and fork right – Tanyard is on left at bottom of hill. Private car park 🛏 1 single, 2 twin, 2 double, 1 suite; all with bathroom/WC exc 1 double with shower/WC; TV, limited room service, hair-dryer, direct-dial telephone ⌀ Restaurant, bar, lounge, garden; early suppers for children ♿ No wheelchair access ⬤ No children under 6; no dogs; no smoking in some public rooms ▭ Access, Amex, Delta, Diners, Switch, Visa £ Single £60, single occupancy of twin/double £75 to £80, twin/double £90 to £95, suite £125; deposit required. Set L £20, D £25 (prices valid till May 1997)

BOUGHTON STREET Kent   map 3

Garden Hotel

167–169 The Street, Boughton under Blean,
Boughton Street, Faversham ME13 9BH
TEL: (01227) 751411   FAX: (01227) 751801

Comfortable and unpretentious family-run hotel in bustling Kent village.

The Garden Hotel has been many things in its past, from a soup kitchen during the Second World War to the village school canteen and, more recently, an antique shop. The white Grade-II listed building retains the large shop-window frontage, but nowadays instead of being prime selling space it is a comfortable lounge and reception area overflowing with plants and comfy sofas in floral fabrics. The bright and airy conservatory restaurant with its central wooden pergola covered in trailing plants and views to the garden is a relaxing place to have dinner – which might include smoked chicken and asparagus with a walnut dressing, salmon steak with a creamed spinach sauce and potato crust, followed by duo of chocolate dessert with home-made ice-cream. The bedrooms are mostly of a good size with white wooden half-panelled walls and pine furniture. The bathrooms, some of which are rather small and functional, are spotless. One reader found the hotel 'rather noisy'; indeed, some rooms do suffer slightly from noise from the A2, which runs behind the hotel, and also from the quite busy main street at the front.

◑ Open all year; restaurant closed Sun eve ⤭ Leave M2 for A2 Dover/Canterbury road; turn left 50 yards after roundabout, signposted Dunkirk/Boughton; left at T-junction into village; hotel is on right-hand side. Private car park 🛏 1 single, 7 twin, 2 double; family rooms available; all with bathroom/WC; TV, room service, hair-dryer, trouser press, direct-dial telephone ⌀ 2 restaurants, bar, lounge, garden; air-conditioning in all public rooms; conference facilities (max 35 people incl up to 10 residential); early suppers for children; baby-listening, cot, high chairs ♿ No wheelchair access ⬤ No dogs; no smoking in bedrooms ▭ Access, Amex, Delta, Switch, Visa £ Single £60, single occupancy of twin/double £60, twin/double £80, family room £85; deposit required. Set L £12.50, D £18.50; alc L, D £20. Special breaks available

Bourne Eau House

30 South Street, Bourne PE10 9LY
TEL: (01778) 423621

Some socialising is de rigueur *in this superbly furnished old home.*

A historic house in historic surroundings, Dawn and George Bishop's home is separated from a twelfth-century abbey by the Bourne Eau stream and faces the site of Hereward the Wake's castle, now just grassy mounds. To enhance the building's various periods of development, its rooms – the flagstoned and inglenooked Elizabethan dining-room, Jacobean music-room, Georgian drawing-room, Victorian-styled library – have been beautifully furnished with period antiques. A similar effect is achieved in the striking bedrooms, the most atmospheric of which is the Jacobean Room, with an old, carved-oak double bed and fine bathroom. Bourne Eau House is a member of the Wolsey Lodge chain, the ethos of which is summed up thus by the Bishops: 'We welcome guests as friends to our home... and they all dine together in a convivial dinner-party atmosphere.' The hosts normally socialise for pre-prandial drinks and coffee, but otherwise leave diners alone to tuck in to Dawn's commended four-course dinners. Wine is included in the dinner price.

◖ Closed Chr & Easter; restaurant closed Sun eve ⚡ The concealed entrance to the house is on the A15 directly opposite the cenotaph in Bourne's Memorial Gardens. Private car park ⬅ 2 twin, 1 double; 2 with bathroom/WC, 1 twin with shower/WC; TV, room service, hair-dryer, direct-dial telephone ⊘ Dining-room, lounge, drying-room, library, garden, music-room; early suppers for children; toys, babysitting, baby-listening, outdoor games ♿ No wheelchair access ⊖ No dogs; no smoking ▭ None accepted £ Single occupancy of twin/double £30 to £35, twin/double £60 to £65. Set D £18 to £20

Carlton Hotel

East Overcliff, Bournemouth BH1 3DN
TEL: (01202) 552011   FAX: (01202) 299573

Smart, modern chic mixed with old-fashioned seaside charm on the clifftop.

The Carlton manages to combine the slick efficiency of a business-orientated hotel with the easy-going cheerfulness of a good, old-fashioned seaside one. Its position (just a short walk from the town centre), the lift to the beach and the leisure facilities (which include a sauna and gym) make it well suited to both. And leisure visitors need not be put off by the daily room rates: weekend and short-break rates are good value. The hotel's typically Edwardian façade is rather plain, but the interior – full of mirrored panelling, polished metal, sparkling chandeliers and rich upholstery – is quite the opposite. The salon, restaurant and cocktail bar all have picture windows, through which the sea is just visible, over the wall beyond the swimming-pool and flower borders. The restaurant is smart, bright and elegant. Daily menus are lengthy, with several fish and meat choices (traditional bases but with some rich sauces) beside a vegetarian option. The salon, which extends into an orangery, is more traditional with green leather chairs, but it is the clubby cocktail bar, with its curving benches and leather burgundy upholstery, which best evokes the spirit of a more sedate age of seaside holidays. Bedrooms are extremely well co-ordinated, in contrasting colours, such as yellow and green, or pink and blue. No two are alike, but all have good-quality modern furniture.

◗ Open all year ⤷ In Bournemouth follow signs to East Cliff. Private car park ⤷ 6 single, 44 twin, 13 double, 7 suites; all with bathroom/WC; TV, 24-hour room service, direct-dial telephone; hair-dryer and trouser press in most rooms; mini-bar on request ✅ Restaurant (air-conditioned), bar, 2 lounges, library, conservatory, games room, garden; conference facilities (max 150 people incl up to 70 residential); gym, sauna, solarium, heated swimming-pool, snooker; early suppers for children; babysitting, baby-listening, games ♿ No wheelchair access ● No children under 7 in restaurant eves; no dogs in public rooms; no smoking in restaurant and some bedrooms ▭ Access, Amex, Delta, Diners, Switch, Visa £ Single £95, single occupancy of twin/double £115, twin/double £130, suite £170; deposit required. Set L £15, D £23.50. Special breaks available

---

Langtry Manor

26 Derby Road, Bournemouth BH1 3QB
TEL: (01202) 553887   FAX: (01202) 290115

An unusual hotel with a romantic past in a quiet area close to the seafront.

A minstrels' gallery, a bed slept in by a king, and a heart-shaped spa bath are just some of the surprises at this comfortable hotel. On a broad, leafy avenue a short drive from the town centre but close to the seafront, the part red brick, part half-timbered house looks unassuming. But its name indicates that this particular hotel – built in 1877 by the Prince of Wales (later to become Edward VII) for his mistress Lillie Langtry – is a little different from others in the neighbourhood. The lovers' initials are carved above the fireplace in the dining-room, which rises to fill two floors and is decorated in regal tones of deep red and gold. Waitresses in black and white period dress serve well-presented but not-too-adventurous food. Our inspector had delicious Stilton and Guinness croquettes followed by sole with grilled banana. For those who really want to indulge, a six-course Edwardian banquet (period dress optional) is held every Saturday night. One of the grandest bedrooms, the King's suite, with its vaulted roof supported by dark beams, an immense fireplace and imposing carved four-poster, is undisputedly masculine. Other bedrooms, like the Langtry Suite, are full of feminine flounces – rich floral drapes and soft shades.

◑ Open all year 🔁 Turn off the A338 at the railway station, continue over the next roundabout, then left into Knyveton Road. The hotel is at the end, at the junction with Derby Road. Private car park 🛏 8 twin, 5 double, 8 four-poster, 1 family room, 3 suites; some in annexe; most with bathroom/WC, 1 with shower/WC; TV; room service, hair-dryer, mini-bar, direct-dial telephone; radio ✅ Dining-room, bar, 2 lounges, conservatory, garden; conference facilities (max 100 people incl up to 25 residential); early suppers for children ♿ Wheelchair access to hotel and restaurant (1 step), WC (unisex), 3 ground-floor bedrooms ⊜ No children under 7 in restaurant eves; no dogs in public rooms; no smoking in restaurant and some bedrooms ▭ Access, Amex, Diners, Switch, Visa £ Single occupancy of twin/double £60, twin/double from £80, four-poster from £100, family room from £140, suite from £140; deposit required. Set D £20. Special breaks available

---

BOURTON-ON-THE-WATER Gloucestershire   map 5

Coombe House

Rissington Road, Bourton-on-the-Water GL54 2DT
TEL: (01451) 821966   FAX: (01451) 810477

Comfortable B&B in a prime tourist spot, but the house rules may not suit everyone.

In an area stuffed with picture-postcard tourist-traps, Bourton-on-the-Water is as great a magnet to daytrippers as any. Coombe House, the unremarkable but creeper-clad detached home of Diana and Graham Ellis, is an agreeable base from which to explore the Windrush Valley, the wider Cotswolds and beyond. Guests can expect high standards of comfort and cleanliness at modest cost, and the Ellises are happy to share their local knowledge to help visitors make the most of their stay; you're likely to encounter the sort of friendliness that's hard to find in a more formal hotel. The downside is that this remains very much the Ellises' home, so guests don't really have the run of the place, or, as the brochure warns, 'the tourist board rating does not denote unlimited house access, and no keys are given out'. Those accustomed to slipping back for an afternoon nap, beware. On the plus side, there's a sunny front garden as well as a neat lounge in soothing pastels with comfy floral armchairs in which to unwind. You'll find proper napkins neatly rolled into rings lining the pine tables in the bright, cheerful breakfast-room. Soft colours predominate in the simply decorated bedrooms, which boast a smattering of antiques, as well the odd homely item, like Dralon headboards, or cane bedside tables.

◑ Closed 24, 25 & 31 Dec 🔁 300 yards past Birdland in Bourton-on-the-Water, on left. Private car park 🛏 2 twin, 5 double; family rooms available; 4 with bathroom/WC, 3 with shower/WC; TV; hair-dryer on request ✅ Dining-room, lounge, garden ♿ No wheelchair access ⊜ No dogs; no smoking ▭ Amex, Visa £ Single occupancy of twin/double £40, twin/double £54 to £66, family room from £66; deposit required. Special breaks available

---

Please let us know if an establishment has changed hands.

BOVEY TRACEY **Devon** map 1

Edgemoor

Haytor Road, Bovey Tracey TQ13 9LE
TEL: (01626) 832466   FAX: (01626) 834760

Comfortable converted old schoolhouse on the edge of Dartmoor.

Edgemoor's Victorian schoolhouse origins are most apparent in the huge lounge with pitched roof and unexpected wooden gallery at the back, but five unusually versatile new bedrooms have recently been created out of old classrooms in the Woodland Wing. Proprietor Rod Day designed them as motel-style rooms, accessible from inside the main hotel or from the car park. All five are spacious and modern, with power showers and large-screen televisions; Willhays and Wistmans have a connecting door so they can serve as a family suite, while Merrivale offers disabled access. Inside the main building the bedrooms are just as comfortable, but the decoration is more fussy. The restaurant has gracefully swagged curtains and pictures by local artists on the walls. Dinner menus are rich in choice, whether your taste is for meat, fish or something vegetarian. A typical meal might start with twice-baked cheese soufflé and move on to chicken suprême stuffed with spinach and ham. On sunny days you can take tea in the pretty front garden although a passing road robs the setting of peace and quiet.

○ Open all year 🔁 Turn off A38 on to A382 Bovey Tracey road; turn left at second roundabout towards Widecombe; after ½ mile fork left and hotel is ½ mile along this road. Private car park 🛏 3 single, 3 twin, 8 double, 2 four-poster, 1 family room; some in annexe; most with bathroom/WC, some with shower/WC; TV, room service, hair-dryer, trouser press, direct-dial telephone ⌀ Restaurant, 2 bars, lounge, 2 gardens; conference facilities (max 50 people incl up to 17 residential); early suppers for children; baby-listening ♿ Wheelchair access to hotel, 7 ground-floor bedrooms, 1 room specially equipped for disabled people (note: access to main hotel via a gravel drive) ● No children under 8 in restaurant eves; no dogs in some public rooms; no smoking in restaurant and some bedrooms ☐ Access, Amex, Delta, Diners, Switch, Visa £ Single £43 to £50, single occupancy of twin/double £49 to £60, twin/double £75 to £89, four-poster £83 to £100, family room from £83; deposit required. Set L £12.50 to £15, D £17 to £19.50; bar meals available. Special breaks available

---

BOWNESS-ON-WINDERMERE **Cumbria** map 8

Lindeth Fell

Lyth Valley Road, Bowness-on-Windermere
LA23 3JP
TEL: (01539) 443286   FAX: (01539) 447455

Caring and friendly country house with lake views and glorious gardens.

The brochure describes Lindeth Fell as 'pleasantly aloof' from the busy village of Bowness. But don't be misled by the 'aloof'. The stone and whitewashed Edwardian country house overlooking Lake Windermere may have all the trappings of grandeur – magnificent gardens ablaze with rhododendron and azalea blooms through spring and summer, nutty oak panelling, Adam fireplaces and moulded ceilings – but has none of the stuffy pretensions. And that is down to Pat and Diana Kennedy, who run the show more along the lines of a house party than of a hotel. As one reader put it, 'The service was excellent and the whole atmosphere is caring and friendly.' Praise was also forthcoming for the 'spacious and very comfortable rooms and imaginative food, well prepared and presented'. Dinner is a set menu but there's a choice of where to eat: the elegant 'old' dining-room or the new extension with its picture windows exploiting the view. The cooking is largely traditional, featuring roasts and fresh local ingredients, and brown sugar meringues are a particular favourite for dessert. Diana has planned, but not interior-designed, the bedrooms, which means they are full of thoughtful touches and feel more comfortably homely than swanky. Most have lake views, and master bedrooms – Tarn Howes, Windermere and Grasmere – justify their 'premium' rates in a sensibly priced tariff. Free fishing is offered on local waters, but not in the hotel's own tarn, where the mirror carp are virtually family friends.

◑ Closed 11 Nov to 15 Mar ⚹ 1 mile south of Bowness on A5074. Private car park ⊨ 2 single, 5 twin, 5 double, 2 family rooms; some with bathroom/WC, most with shower/WC; TV, room service, hair-dryer, direct-dial telephone; trouser press on request ⚹ 2 dining-rooms, 3 lounges, drying-room, garden; fishing, tennis, pitch and putt, croquet; early suppers for children ⅋ Wheelchair access to hotel (ramp), restaurant and WC (unisex), 1 bedroom specially equipped for disabled people ● No children under 7; no dogs; smoking in one public room only ⊟ Access, Visa £ Single £45, single occupancy of twin/double £70 to £90, twin/double £90 to £102, family room from £90; deposit required. Set D £19, Sun L £10 (prices valid till Apr 1997)

Linthwaite House

Crook Road, Bowness-on-Windermere LA23 3JA
TEL: (01539) 488600   FAX: (01539) 488601

Polished and friendly Edwardian country-house hotel overlooking Windermere.

Linthwaite House is a grand Edwardian affair of multiple gables, Lakeland stone and black timbering, with a verandah to take advantage of its splendid setting above Lake Windermere. Amid the landscaped grounds of clipped evergreens and rhododendrons there's space for those gentle outdoor pursuits of putting and croquet, even fly-fishing for brown trout in a private tarn. Plush furnishings, deep red carpets and an abundance of amusing bric-à-brac reinforce the clubby period feel inside. Gladstone bags, bottles of port and bound volumes ring the dining-room, ale jugs line the mantelpiece in the bar and wicker chairs, tapestry armchairs and weeping figs fill the spacious sitting-room. No two bedrooms are alike – they vary in size, shape and outlook – though all are indulgently supplied with bathrobes, herb teas and satellite television among the goodies. Those overlooking the lake command a premium rate; the attractive gardens and surrounding woodland are the compensation for the others.

Dinners are highly flavoursome four-course affairs where you might find chicken liver parfait served with Cumberland sauce and brioche, followed by escalope of salmon with black ink pasta and saffron sauce. But given that it costs nearly £30 a head, the supplements for certain dishes seem niggardly.

◗ Open all year ⓩ On B5284 from Kendal, 1 mile past Windermere golf club. Private car park ⏡ 1 single, 4 twin, 9 double, 3 four-poster, 1 suite; all with bathroom/WC; TV, room service, hair-dryer, trouser press, direct-dial telephone, radio ⌖ Restaurant, bar, lounge, drying-room, conservatory, garden; conference facilities (max 20 people incl up to 18 residential); fishing, croquet, putting green; early suppers for children ♿ Wheelchair access to hotel (1 step), restaurant and WC (M,F), 5 ground-floor bedrooms ● No children under 7 in restaurant eves; no dogs; no smoking in some bedrooms ▭ Access, Amex, Delta, Switch, Visa £ Single £90 to £100, twin/double £100 to £130, four-poster £120 to £170, suite £140 to £195; deposit required. Set D £29.50; alc L £10. Special breaks available

---

BRADFIELD COMBUST Suffolk   map 6

Bradfield House ☆

Bradfield Combust, Bury St Edmunds IP30 0LR
TEL: (01284) 386301   FAX: (01284) 386177

Small but smart family-run restaurant with rooms offering good-value breaks.

The name of the village has its roots in fourteenth-century riots and arson, but Bradfield House is an altogether more civilised place. It's very much a family concern, with Douglas Green in charge of the kitchen, and his sister Moya taking care of publicity and marketing. The pink half-timbered building stands just off the A134, with attractive gardens, including a summer house, behind. The interior feels quite modern, with good use of strong colour contrasts and paint effects tempered by careful lighting. Downstairs, there is a straightforward four-square layout, with the breakfast room opposite the reception at the front, and the restaurant and lounge at the back, overlooking the gardens. Upstairs, the nicest bedroom, Room 3, is at the back, with a bay window, wooden four-poster bed and good-sized bathroom. The dinner menu is priced according to the number of courses, which are largely based on classic combinations like roulade of smoked salmon and watercress with quail's egg salad, or steamed halibut with chive and tomato beurre blanc. Desserts span the globe, from Grandma Green's steamed syrup pudding to dark chocolate cup with chestnut and Amaretto cream. 'We would certainly be happy to go back,' reported one satisfied visitor.

◗ Open all year; restaurant closed Sun eve & Mon ⓩ Just off A134 between Bury St Edmunds and Sudbury. Private car park ⏡ 1 single, 1 twin, 2 four-poster; all with bathroom/WC exc single with shower/WC; TV, room service, hair-dryer, direct-dial telephone ⌖ Restaurant, dining-room, bar, lounge, conservatory, garden; early suppers for children ♿ No wheelchair access ● Children by arrangement only; no dogs in public rooms; no smoking in bedrooms or restaurant ▭ Access, Delta, Diners, Switch, Visa £ Single £45, single occupancy of twin £55, twin £65, four-poster £80; deposit required. Set L £10.50, D £15.50 to £19.50. Special breaks available

BRADFORD West Yorkshire map 8

Restaurant Nineteen

North Park Road, Heaton, Bradford BD9 4NT
TEL: (01274) 492559 FAX: (01274) 483827

*Lavishly furnished restaurant-with-rooms in the suburbs of
Bradford.*

This nineteenth-century terraced villa, overlooking Lister Park, looks pretty
ordinary from the outside but is a real treat on the inside. Guests are given a
courteous welcome and are settled in the elegant blue and yellow drawing-room
where they can dawdle in luxury while choosing from the three- and four-course
set menus. Stephen Smith's cooking is superb – as well as being good value for
money. A typical three-course dinner, with lots of option at each course, might
include ragoût of veal kidneys with mushrooms, fillet of sea bass with a chive
fishcake and langoustine sauce, and one of a range of wonderful puddings such
as rhubarb and ginger crème brûlée, chocolate and Tia Maria ice-cream trifle, or
raspberry and redcurrant tartlet. Spread through two open-plan rooms, with a
warm glow from orangey coloured walls, the restaurant is a lovely place to take
your time over your meal, and service is friendly and unhurried. Housekeeping
is immaculate in the four good-sized bedrooms. Well equipped and furnished
with antiques, they're stylish as well as comfortable, with homely touches such
as books and radios, and smart bathrooms.

○ Closed 1 week Chr, 2 weeks Sept; restaurant closed Sun & Mon eves 🔁 Follow
A650 Manningham Lane to north of Bradford; North Park Road is a left turning just
before Bradford Grammar School. Private car park 🛏 2 twin, 2 double; 3 with
bathroom/WC, 1 with shower/WC; TV, room service, hair-dryer, trouser press,
direct-dial telephone, radio; no tea/coffee-making facilities in rooms ✓ Restaurant,
lounge, garden ♿ No wheelchair access ● No children under 8; no dogs
☐ Access, Amex, Switch, Visa £ Single occupancy of twin/double £70,
twin/double £85. Cooked B £7.50; set D £28

Victoria Hotel

1 Bridge Street, Bradford BD1 1JX
TEL: (01274) 728706 FAX: (01274) 736358

*A grand Victorian hotel at the heart of the city that has been given a
thoroughly modern makeover.*

If the 'designer hotel' turns out to be a phenomenon rather than fad, then
Jonathan Wix will be regarded as one of its pioneers. After the success of 42 The
Calls (see entry) in Leeds, Jonathan took on the Victoria, and imposing his
personal vision on this late-Victorian leviathan posed both new problems and
offered new opportunities. In a sense, one characteristic is common to both
buildings: space – there's lots of it. When the Victoria was built in 1875, it was
the pride of the city, and expressed the commercial confidence of its time in its
grand proportions. This is obviously good news as far as the bedrooms are
concerned, but it can make the public areas seem a little cool and impersonal.

The bedrooms are priced according to size and facilities, though all feature TVs and stereos, as well as Jonathan Wix's trademark: chic minimalism and a fondness for two-tone colour schemes, such as black and grey or burgundy and cream. Weekend rates are virtually unbeatable. Unless you're a budding Lowry, you won't find the views of the bus depot inspiring, but at least the triple-glazing cuts out most of the city noise.

The brasserie has a good selection of Anglo-Asian dishes, as well as such hardy annuals as Cajun chicken and boeuf bourguignon, and you can warm yourself up with a drink in the Pie-eyed Parrot pub – a spacious affair with wooden floorboards and film prints on the walls.

◐ Open all year ☒ From the M62/M606 follow signs to city centre. Hotel is opposite the metro interchange station. Private car park ⮞ 30 twin, 30 double, 3 suites; family rooms available; all with bathroom/WC; TV, room service, hair-dryer, trouser press, direct-dial telephone, radio, cassette and CD player, VCR ✓ Restaurant, dining-room, bar, lounge; conference facilities (max 185 incl up to 63 residential); gym, sauna, solarium; early suppers for children ♿ Wheelchair access to hotel (ramp), restaurant, WC (M,F), lift to bedrooms, 1 specially equipped for disabled people ● No dogs in public rooms; no smoking in some bedrooms ☐ Access, Amex, Delta, Diners, Switch, Visa £ Single occupancy of twin/double and twin/double £35 to £89, family room £65 to £99, suite £99; deposit required. Continental B £7, cooked B £10; set L, D £8 to £10; alc L, D £20. Special breaks available

---

BRADFORD-ON-AVON Wiltshire   map 2

Bradford Old Windmill

4 Masons Lane, Bradford-on-Avon BA15 1QN
TEL: (01225) 866842 FAX: (01225) 866648

COUNTY HOTEL OF THE YEAR

Quirky, appealing accommodation with sumptuous vegetarian feasts.

Bradford's only windmill may have lost its sails, but otherwise this local landmark is perfectly preserved. Inside, the irregularly shaped rooms, wooden beams and spiral staircase are a constant reminder of its utilitarian origins and give the small hotel a very special character, which is enhanced by the imaginative design skills and eclectic furnishings of proprietors Peter and Priscilla Roberts. The Roberts are inveterate travellers and mementos from overseas – musical instruments, mobiles, statuettes – fill the rooms. Priscilla also draws on her travels to create delicious vegetarian meals: perhaps Mexican, Caribbean or Indonesian (her latest discovery) in the form of gado-gado (stir-fried vegetables) followed by fried rice with spiced cabbage and coconut milk. Carnivores are catered for at breakfast time, but are more likely to be tempted by 'Priscilla's passionate pancakes' – Staffordshire oatcakes with sheep's milk yoghurt, peach, passion fruit and maple syrup. Meals are communal, taken at a long pine table. Bedrooms are unusual too: Great Spur, the largest, has a round king-size bed to match its circular shape and a wicker chair swinging from the beams; smaller Damsel has a water bed; Wallower has a minstrels' gallery (useful for a child's bed); and Fantail has a lovely old walnut bed. But you can best appreciate the building in the circular lounge with its low-beamed ceiling, open fire, stripped-pine furnishings and views over the garden and valley.

○ Closed Dec to Feb; dining-room closed Tue, Wed, Fri and Sun eves ⌷ In Bradford-on-Avon on the A363, find the Castle pub; go down the hill towards the town centre; after 75 yards turn left into a gravelled private drive immediately before the first roadside house (no sign on road). Private car park ⌷ 1 single, 1 twin, 2 double; family room available; 2 with bathroom/WC, 2 with shower/WC; TV, hair-dryer, clock radio ⌹ Dining-room, lounge, drying-room, garden; games ⌷ No wheelchair access ● No children under 6; no dogs; no smoking ⌷ Access, Amex, Visa ⌷ Single £45 to £55, single occupancy of twin/double £55 to £65, twin/double £55 to £75, family room from £74; deposit required. Set D £18

Priory Steps

Newtown, Bradford-on-Avon BA15 1NQ
TEL: (01225) 862230   FAX: (01225) 866248

Lovely views and gardens feature at a smart but unstuffy Wolsey Lodge.

Diana and Carey Chapman have put their own distinctive stamp on this conversion of six seventeenth-century weavers' cottages. The five bedrooms are imaginatively decorated in bright colours, pretty fabrics and floral runners, and are furnished with fine antiques. The English Room (a lovely, sunny, corner room with twin oak beds and striped wallpaper) and the smaller Flower Room, which have both been recently redecorated, are particularly spruce and fresh. The bathrooms – also newly refurbished – are excellent. The house's best features, however, are possibly the gardens and views. From the road, Priory Steps appears to be two storeys high; to the rear, it drops one storey, and opens on to a delightful walled garden which features bright flowerpots and borders, and which then falls away in terraces towards the valley. The elegant dining-room, in which Diana serves a blend of English and Continental cuisine (such as chicken breasts in orange juice with shallots and horseradish, or maybe plaice wrapped in cabbage leaves) has patio doors, while the clubby lounge, with its leather sofas and tempting array of books, is lightened by large, garden-facing windows.

○ Open all year ⌷ Newtown is a left-hand turning, 200 yards to the north of the town centre, off the A363, signposted Bath. Private car park ⌷ 2 twin, 2 double, 1 suite; all with bathroom/WC; TV, hair-dryer ⌹ Dining-room, lounge, library, garden ⌷ No wheelchair access ● No children; no dogs; smoking in library only ⌷ Access, Visa ⌷ Single occupancy of twin/double £45 to £48, twin/double £58 to £64, suite £58 to £64; deposit required. Set D £17

Where we know an establishment accepts credit cards, we list them. There may be a surcharge if you pay by credit card. It is always best to check when booking whether the card you want to use is acceptable.

Woolley Grange

Woolley Green, Bradford-on-Avon BA15 1TX
TEL: (01225) 864705   FAX: (01225) 864059

Good food and fun for adults and children are on offer at a Jacobean country manor.

Heather and Nigel Chapman have four children of their own, as well as two springer spaniels, so they could hardly have created the sort of country-house atmosphere at their Jacobean manor house in which children and dogs are frowned upon. Instead, they've created a relaxing, unstuffy environment, in which children are as well catered for as their parents. For the younger ones, there's the Woolley Bear's Den (a haven of toys and games supervised by qualified nannies between 10am and 6pm), a climbing frame, a sandpit, bicycles, table tennis and a special dining area for those who don't want to join Mum and Dad in the main restaurant. Kids' delicacies such as sausages and mash, hamburgers and toad-in-the-hole are served here. For grown-ups, there's the security of knowing that your children are being well cared for, tennis, swimming, badminton, snooker and feasts – either in the restaurant or in the airy, less formal conservatory. The food is no less yummy than the children's: perhaps duckling with mango and a chilli-and-citrus sauce, or pork with black pudding, sage and apples. The bedrooms are also arranged with families in mind: many have space for cots and zed-beds, a number interconnect, and some even have gas-fuelled coal fires. Despite its family focus and lived-in air, Woolley Grange also boasts all the traditional features and character of a country house, including antique furnishings, wood panelling, open fires, plenty of soft seating, and lots of reading material. The bedrooms are smartly furnished with period carved or brass beds, patchwork quilts and Victorian bathroom fittings.

◑ Open all year ↗ Woolley Grange is on the B3105, 1 mile north-east of Bradford-on-Avon. Private car park ⌂ 1 single, 18 double, 3 suites; family rooms available; some in annexe; most with bathroom/WC, 3 with shower/WC; TV, room service, hair-dryer, direct-dial telephone; tea/coffee-making facilities on request ✣ 2 restaurants, 4 lounges, games room, garden; conference facilities (max 40 people incl up to 22 residential); heated outdoor swimming-pool, tennis, putting, croquet, badminton; early suppers for children; toys, playrooms, baby-sitting, baby-listening, cots ⌂ No wheelchair access ● No smoking or dogs in restaurants ▭ Access, Delta, Switch, Visa £ Single £85, single occupancy of twin/double from £90, twin/double from £99, family room from £145, suite from £155. Set D £29; light meals available. Special breaks available

---

BRAITHWAITE **Cumbria**   map 10

Ivy House Hotel

Braithwaite, Keswick CA12 5SY
TEL: (01768) 778338   FAX: (01768) 778113

A friendly, family-run hotel, in a quiet village close to Keswick.

The ivy may have disappeared from the walls of this substantial, seventeenth-century house, but its loss has been compensated for with plenty of green paint, making it easy to spot in the centre of the village. A lusher shade of green has been used in the bar, while the gallery-style, first-floor dining-room is decorated in a rather swanky, dark hue, with 'shiny paper on the ceiling looking like Christmas wrapping paper,' in the view of one correspondent, who, after a ten-year gap between visits, found that 'all the eccentricity had been retained, and plenty of charm had been added'. He went on to commend the service: 'warm, friendly and concerned. We felt completely relaxed'.

Compliments on the good-value food have been received too, and a typical four-course dinner might start with something international, like Thai pork satay with peanut sauce, before moving on to a distinctly meaty English main course, such as rack of lamb with redcurrant-and-thyme gravy. The large breakfasts have been commended, with only one quibble: the individually wrapped butter portions seem out of character.

The bedrooms range from compact to generous, and are furnished in an attractive, homely style, mixing antiques with plainer, modern fittings. Room 5 remains a favourite on account of its unusual four-poster bed.

◑ Closed Jan   ⤢ In Braithwaite turn left after the Royal Oak pub. Private car park ⤶ 2 single, 2 twin, 6 double, 2 four-poster; most with bathroom/WC, some with shower/WC; TV, hair-dryer, direct-dial telephone   ✅ Dining-room, bar, lounge, drying-room; early suppers for children; baby-listening   ⅙ No wheelchair access ● No smoking in dining-room; dogs by arrangement only   ☐ Access, Amex, Delta, Diners, Switch, Visa   £ Single £30, single occupancy of twin/double £40, twin/double £60, four-poster £66; deposit required. Set D £19. Special breaks available

---

BRAMPTON Cumbria   map 10

Farlam Hall

Brampton CA8 2NG
TEL: (01697) 746234   FAX: (01697) 746683

Luxurious country-house hotel with lovely grounds and links with George Stephenson and his Rocket.

Set in six acres of landscaped grounds, Farlam Hall is a beautifully maintained nineteenth-century mansion with sixteenth-century bits, partially obscured by ivy. Inside, the Quinion and Stevenson families have concentrated on bringing out the Victorian flavour, with appropriate furnishings and wallpaper even in the bedrooms, which boast fine desks and dressers. Framed with heavy gold and blue curtains, the elegant restaurant has a stylish plaster ceiling. Four-course dinner menus offer a choice of three starters and main courses, two of them playing safe, the third pushing the culinary boat out a bit further; you could, for example, choose fresh spinach with nutmeg and cream in a filo basket with poached egg and hollandaise sauce, to be followed by piccata milanese, slices of pork coated with egg and cheese on a bed of spaghetti with tomato and wine sauce. Even the dessert menu proffers some unexpected options: prune meringue pie, and ginger and advocaat syllabub. Should your party number 13, a large Victorian doll in a linen shift will be provided to make up the numbers. The 12 bedrooms are very different in style and shape; one of the most inviting is the ground-floor Garden Room, with an antique four-poster and a window seat overlooking the garden where George Stephenson's prototype steam engine, the Rocket, spent some time before being donated to the Science Museum by Farlam's then owners. One annexe room, the Hayloft, comes complete with fridge, kettle and Jacuzzi.

○ Closed 24 to 30 Dec ⚐ On A689, 2 miles south-east of Brampton; not in Farlam village. Private car park ⚏ 5 twin, 6 double, 1 four-poster; 1 in annexe; all with bathroom/WC; TV, room service, hair-dryer, trouser press, direct-dial phone; no tea/coffee-making facilities in rooms ⚙ Restaurant, 2 lounges, garden; conference facilities (max 20 people incl up to 12 residential); early suppers for children ♿ Wheelchair access to hotel (1 step), restaurant, 2 ground-floor bedrooms ● No children under 5 ▭ Access, Amex, Switch, Visa £ Single occupancy of twin/double £105 to £120, twin/double £190 to £220, four-poster £220 (rates incl dinner). Set D £28.50. Special breaks available

---

BRANSCOMBE Devon map 2

The Bulstone

Higher Bulstone, Branscombe EX12 3BL
TEL: (01297) 680446 (AND FAX)

Family-focused hotel in quiet, rural surroundings.

Judith and Kevin Monaghan have recently taken over the Bulstone, a hotel with a long history of providing a holiday refuge for young families. Everything here has been chosen on the assumption that it could come in contact with questing fingers; kettles are on lofty perches and the décor is simple and easily repairable. The six en-suite family units have slightly more modern pine furnishings, but in general the rooms here are much of a muchness, designed to accommodate at least two adults and two children. Indeed, room prices assume this, with supplements charged for a third child sharing. In the dining-room, breakfast is served to all the family together, but children are served high tea in the late afternoon, leaving the room free for their parents to dine in peace later on. Menus are pretty straightforward, although the odd vegetable korma puts in an appearance. There is a fair-sized children's playroom, and a parents' kitchen with fridge, iron, bottle steriliser, microwave, etc. Adults can retreat to a sun lounge at the front of the house or to a cosy, child-free lounge with log fire and soft, chintzy armchairs. The one television lurks in a curiously impersonal room which could do with more pictures on the walls. 'It's mainly used by dads to watch sport,' says Kevin.

○ Open all year ⚐ On A3052 at Branscombe Cross junction take turning for the Bulstone, 1 mile away; ignore all other Branscombe turnings. Private car park ⚏ 1 twin, 1 double, 4 family rooms, 6 suites; suites with bathroom/WC; hair-dryer ⚙ Dining-room, bar, lounge, TV room, drying-room, conservatory, garden; conference facilities (max 30 people incl up to 12 residential); early suppers for children; playroom, babysitting, baby-listening, cots, high chairs ♿ No wheelchair access ● No children in dining-room eves; no dogs; smoking in lounge only, and no smoking at all from 1997 ▭ None accepted £ Single occupancy of twin/double £26 to £32, twin/double £38 to £42, family room £42 to £52, suite from £61; deposit required. Set D £14. Special breaks available

The Look Out

Branscombe EX12 3DP
TEL: (01297) 680262   FAX: (01297) 680272

Cluster of stone cottages knocked into a single, small hotel alone on a cliffhead.

You drive through a shallow ford and past a small shop to reach the road to the Look Out, standing all alone on a headland above pretty Lyme Bay. The hotel was once a group of six coastguards' cottages which let Customs and Excise officers keep an eye on comings and goings in the secluded bay. In the 1950s Peter Leach bought the cottages, knocking them together so neatly that it would take a skilled architectural sleuth to make out the joins. The front door opens straight into a lounge which manages to look both grand and cottagey at the same time, its flagstoned floor so well polished you can almost see your face in it. At one end, twin fireplaces stand at a 90-degree angle to each other; at the other a church-style wooden screen separates the dining area from the lounge. Unless you arrive on a Monday night you can tuck into a three-course dinner featuring such exotic temptations as duck and green peppercorn terrine with tomato and onion relish, and pheasant with wild mushroom and port wine velouté. On Mondays soup and sandwiches can be provided. At first glance the bar is conspicuous by its absence, but the doors of a massive wooden sideboard soon swing open to reveal the hidden bottles. Upstairs, the bedrooms are reasonably spacious and furnished with discretion and lots of dried flowers; all the windows are double-glazed, a wise precaution given the pane-rattlingly exposed position. One room has private access up steps from the back garden, perfect for dog owners. The garden itself is pleasantly secluded, with plentiful sun loungers for those days when the wind is not howling.

◑ Closed Chr; restaurant closed Mon eve   ⤷ Take road in Branscombe to beach; drive through shallow ford; continue straight ahead and up hillside driveway to hotel. Private car park   ⤶ 5 twin/double; family rooms available; 3 with bathroom/WC, 2 with shower/WC; TV, hair-dryer, mini-bar, direct-dial telephone   ⌗ Restaurant, lounge, garden   ♿ No wheelchair access   ● No children under 8; no dogs in public rooms; smoking discouraged in bedrooms   ▭ None accepted   £ Single occupancy of twin/double £48 to £58, twin/double £82 to £89, family room from £97; deposit required. Alc D £21 (1996 prices). Special breaks available

---

BRAY Berkshire   map 3

Monkey Island Hotel

Old Mill Lane, Bray SL6 2EE
TEL: (01628) 23400   FAX: (01628) 778188

Smart Georgian buildings on a small island in the Thames, with restful views from the bedrooms and a formal restaurant.

Peacocks pipe you aboard as you walk across the narrow metal gangway to reach Monkey Island. Built by the third Duke of Marlborough in 1738 to amuse his friends, the two smart white buildings which make up the hotel have been receiving guests ever since. The 25 bedrooms are in the Temple, along with a light and sunny breakfast-room. All the rooms look out over the grounds and the river (which is not surprising, because the island is not very wide), are smartly decorated with rich fabrics and boast well-kept, modern bathrooms. Rooms 11 and 12 are worth a little extra if you like the idea of your own small terrace. A hundred yards away, the Pavilion – formerly the Duke's fishing lodge – houses the restaurant and bar, which features a bizarre, painted ceiling on which monkeys dressed as country gentlemen play out rural pursuits. With its high-domed ceiling, well-spaced tables and leafy outlook, the restaurant is a formal room, and you are expected to dress up for dinner. The menu might include such dishes as a goats' cheese and bacon soufflé, grilled escalope of salmon, and poached pear in puff pastry or treacle sponge and custard. Alternatively, snacks are served in the Terrace Bar.

◑ Closed 26 Dec to 15 Jan ⤢ Hotel is signposted in Bray village. Private car park
⨺ 2 single, 12 twin, 8 double, 1 family room, 2 suites; all with bathroom/WC exc 1 single with shower/WC; TV, room service, hair-dryer, mini-bar, trouser press, direct-dial telephone ✅ Restaurant, dining-room, bar, lounge, garden; conference facilities (max 150 people incl up to 25 residential); fishing, croquet, boating, laser clay-pigeon shooting; early suppers for children ♿ No wheelchair access ● No dogs
☐ Access, Amex, Delta, Diners, Switch, Visa £ Single from £90, single occupancy of twin/double from £95, twin/double from £110, family room from £125, suite from £150; deposit required. Continental B £7, cooked B £11; set L £20, D £27; alc L £22, D £29; (prices valid till Dec 1996). Special breaks available

---

BRIGHTON East Sussex   map 3

The Dove ☆

18 Regency Square, Brighton BN1 2FG
TEL: (01273) 779222   FAX: (01273) 746912

A stylish B&B with thoughtful and attentive hosts.

The Dove shares the same Regency Square location as its neighbour Topps (see entry). Any external resemblance imposed by conservation rules ends at the bright blue front door. Clean white walls and a minimalist, continental eye for décor give the Dove an unusually airy and uncluttered feel for a small seaside hotel. Peter and Deborah Kalinke are attentive to the needs of their guests, and children are especially welcome. Each room is differently presented, although the motif throughout is lightness enhanced by crisp cotton linen, white muslin or bold prints framing the windows, a selective choice of tasteful modern prints on the walls, and characterful items of old furniture. Some rooms are small, and certainly live in the shade of the stars of the show, such as Room 3, a huge front-facing treat with high ceilings and full-length sash windows opening on to the canopied wrought ironwork around the balcony. Attic rooms, although charming, are reached via a precipitous stairway which is not for the elderly or inebriated. Excessive competition on the restaurant front nearby means that evening meals are cooked to order only, from fresh local produce bought in just for you.

○ Open all year ☑ On west side of Regency Square, opposite West Pier. On-street parking (metered), public car park nearby ⊨ 3 single, 2 twin, 4 double, 1 family room; half with bathroom/WC, half with shower/WC; TV, room service, direct-dial telephone; hair-dryer and trouser press on request ✓ Dining-room, lounge; conference facilities (max 10 people residential); early suppers for children; toys, babysitting, baby-listening ⅙ No wheelchair access ● No dogs; no smoking in public rooms ▢ Access, Amex, Delta, Diners, Switch, Visa £ Single £28 to £35, single occupancy of twin/double £35 to £58, twin/double £45 to £68, family room £65 to £88; deposit required. Set L £8, D £14. Special breaks available

Topps Hotel

17 Regency Square, Brighton BN1 2FG
TEL: (01273) 729334 FAX: (01273) 203679

A well-kept hotel in a classic square close to the sea.

Regency Square is a short walk along the coast road from the hustle of touristy Brighton, yet seems worlds apart with its refined town houses and dignified view of the tumbledown West Pier. The interior of Topps Hotel is what you expect from the outside – immaculate, calm and spacious. The complicated room-numbering system is explained by the fact that Topps is in fact two houses, so Room 167 is Room 7 in House 16. Paul and Pauline (hence the double 'p' in Topps) Collins are gracious hosts, providing a warm welcome. The décor is coffee and cream throughout, and the bedrooms are all a good size with plenty of furniture; some have walk-in wardrobes and huge bathrooms. Fluffy bathrobes, ironing boards, razors and cotton buds are among the luxuries provided, earning Paul and Pauline a deserved reputation for attentive service and a good eye for detail. The restaurant downstairs has plenty of wines on display and a short but varied menu including seafood tart, pork tenderloin stuffed with apricots and a vegetarian choice. Topps may not be a particularly cheap option but you can expect quality and a peaceful stay. At the time of our inspection the Collinses had put the hotel up for sale.

○ Open all year; restaurant closed Sun to Tue eves and in Jan ☑ In Regency Square, opposite West Pier. On-street parking (metered), public car park opposite ⊨ 2 single, 3 twin, 8 double, 2 four-poster; family rooms available; all with bathroom/WC; TV, room service, hair-dryer, mini-bar, trouser press, direct-dial telephone ✓ Restaurant, lounge ⅙ No wheelchair access ● No dogs; no smoking in public rooms ▢ Access, Amex, Delta, Diners, Switch, Visa £ Single £45, single occupancy of twin/double £59 to £99, twin/double £79 to £99, four-poster £109, family room from £99; deposit required. Set D £20/23. Special breaks available

The 1998 Guide *will be published in the autumn of 1997. Reports on hotels are welcome at any time of the year, but are extremely valuable in the spring. Send them to* The Which? Hotel Guide, FREEPOST, 2 Marylebone Road, London NW1 1YN. *No stamp is needed if reports are posted in the UK. Our e-mail address is: "guidereports@which.co.uk".*

BRIMFIELD Hereford & Worcester   map 5

Poppies at the Roebuck

Brimfield, Ludlow SY8 4NE
TEL: (01584) 711230   FAX: (01584) 711654

An excellent restaurant in a traditional, rural pub with neat, modern rooms.

Situated bang in the centre of the village Poppies at the Roebuck's neat, white frontage appears deceptively unexceptional among the brick and stone cottages that make up Brimfield. Once inside, however, you're in an award-winning environment, which is a real treat. Poppies restaurant is perhaps the major attraction for the crowds of people who return again and again to sample Carole Evans' cooking. She's well established now in her empire, and provides an interesting menu that is loyal to the region, including dishes such as rabbit terrine with rhubarb chutney, roast fillet of Herefordshire beef, and farmhouse cheeses such as Hereford hop, Shropshire blue and Cerney ash pyramid. The menu in the cosy bar, with its dark-wood panelling and eclectic memorabilia left behind by local people, is just as imaginative. The three bedrooms are of a good size and are well co-ordinated, with pretty floral prints and plain walls. The nice touches include very generous amounts of home-made cake and biscuits, coffee and fresh milk.

◑ Closed 25 & 26 Dec; restaurant closed Sun and Mon   ⤧ In the village of Brimfield. Private car park   ⨺ 1 twin, 2 double; twin with bathroom/WC, doubles with shower/WC; TV, room service, hair-dryer, trouser press, direct-dial telephone ⌖ Restaurant, bar, lounge   ♿ No wheelchair access   ● No dogs in public rooms   ▭ Access, Delta, Switch, Visa   £ Single occupancy of twin/double £45, twin/double £60; deposit required. Set L, D £16 to £20; bar meals available

---

BRISTOL Bristol   map 2

Berkeley Square Hotel

15 Berkeley Square, Clifton, Bristol BS8 1HB
TEL: 0117-925 4000   FAX: 0117-925 2970

Comfortable town house hotel handy for Bristol University, business guests and weekend breaks.

Berkeley Square is definitely one of the most salubrious parts of the city, and the hotel's handsome Georgian façade leads to expectations of something very grand. In fact, the interior is smaller and more modern, though smart and comfortable (if just a little institutional) and very welcoming, thanks to the cheerful, helpful staff. For relaxation, there's a small lounge on the ground floor, but given its size, viewers may well prefer their bedrooms. More sociable guests stray to the basement Cocktail Bar, hung with trendy prints, and open all day for a drink, light meal or sandwich, and afternoon tea. Otherwise, the hotel is best suited for those with other fish to fry at night, although Nightingale's restaurant, decked out in smart burgundy and cream tones, has some tempting options with

Cajun and Creole influences – chicken stuffed with banana and bacon on salsa, swordfish with almonds and cream, steak with peppercorn sauce. Named after prominent Bristolians, including Billy Butlin and W.G. Grace, the bedrooms have been kitted out primarily with comfort and convenience in mind. All the essentials (hair-dryer, trouser press, and often a writing desk) are there, plus a few thoughtful extras such as sherry decanters and bowls of fruit.

◑ Open all year; restaurant closed Sun eve ⬕ Turn left at top of Park Street into Berkeley Avenue leading into Berkeley Square. Private car park ⏻ 25 single, 6 twin, 10 double, 1 suite; all with bathroom/WC exc 3 single with shower/WC; TV, room service, hair-dryer, trouser press, direct-dial telephone ✓ Restaurant, bar; conference facilities (max 30 people residential/non-residential); early suppers for children; baby-listening ♿ No wheelchair access ● Dogs in bedrooms by arrangement; no smoking in some bedrooms ▭ Access, Amex, Delta, Diners, Switch, Visa ▦ Single £49 to £78, single occupancy of twin/double £59 to £85, twin/double £80 to £102, suite £95 to £115; deposit required. Alc L, D £20; light meals available. Special breaks available

---

Downlands Guesthouse

33 Henleaze Gardens, Bristol BS9 4HH
TEL: 0117-962 1639 (AND FAX)

Well-priced, comfortable family guesthouse close to Durdham Downs.

In a residential, tree-lined street on the edge of Durdham Downs and a couple of miles from the city centre, Ulla and Peter Newham's Victorian semi makes a pleasant home-from-home for business guests and parents visiting offspring at the nearby university. It has been open as a B&B for nearly 15 years, but is still very much a family home. The bedrooms are comfortable, well co-ordinated in restful pinks, greens and blues, and of varying sizes (those on the second floor have sloping ceilings). Some have patchwork quilts hand-sewn by Ulla. But it's the communal family areas – full of interesting bits and pieces, plants, books and assorted works of art, giving a slightly Bohemian touch – which have the most character. Guests are welcome to use the family lounge, where classical music provides a gentle background; in summer, the patio doors may be thrown open to the small, paved garden hung with honeysuckle, clematis and ivy. Breakfasts are taken in a cheerful green and pink room, with china displayed on a built-in dresser.

◑ Open all year ⬕ From city centre head towards Westbury on Trym; Henleaze Gardens is 2 miles on right. On-street parking ⏻ 2 single, 3 twin, 3 double; TV, hair-dryer ✓ Dining-room, lounge ♿ No wheelchair access ● No dogs or smoking in public rooms ▭ Access, Visa ▦ Single £25 to £36, single occupancy of twin/double £29 to £36, twin/double £42 to £46; deposit required

---

The Guide is totally independent, accepts no free hospitality, and survives on the number of copies sold each year.

BROAD CAMPDEN **Gloucestershire**   map 5

Malt House

Broad Campden, Nr Chipping Campden GL55 6UU
TEL: (01386) 840295   FAX: (01386) 841334

Delightfully quaint Cotswold cottage with wonderful garden.

Take a deep breath. Country cottages don't come much more idyllic than Jean and Nick Brown's seventeenth-century affair in this small hamlet a mile away from the bustle of Chipping Campden. It's not just the mellow stone, leaded windows and creeper cladding, nor the proximity to the village church; add lavender bushes, the stream that winds through the old cherry orchard, sheep-studded hills and a splendid rear garden that includes a croquet lawn and you're pretty close to the specification of the perfect country bolt-hole. Even the road that sweeps close by the front windows has the decency to be fairly quiet.

The interior is no anti-climax. Light floods into the residents' lounge from leaded windows on three sides, illuminating a charming room complete with beams, decorative stencilling and antiques. There's a good selection of books, guides and maps to hand to help you plan your stay. The bedrooms are appositely cottagey, without being twee, and team good old furniture with restful pastels and floral fabrics. Plans are afoot to change the dining-room, but for the moment it's a characterful room dominated by a huge inglenook fireplace and a long, polished table. Food, prepared by the Browns' son Julian, is imaginative and accomplished; perhaps warm pigeon breast salad with truffle oil, roasted black pudding and cassis dressing, followed by tournedos of Scottish beef with herb dressing and spinach, and lemon posset.

○ Closed 25 Dec; restaurant closed Mon eve   ⊠ 1 mile from Chipping Campden, signposted from B4081; on left, 500 yards beyond Bakers Arms pub. Private car park ⊨ 1 single, 3 twin, 3 double, 1 four-poster; family rooms available; all with bathroom/WC; TV, hair-dryer, clock radio; trouser press in some rooms ⊘ Dining-room, 2 lounges, drying-room, garden; conference facilities (max 10 people incl up to 8 residential); croquet; early suppers for children & No wheelchair access ● No children under 10 in dining-room eves; no dogs or smoking in public rooms ▭ Access, Amex, Switch, Visa £ Single £50 to £70, single occupancy of twin/double £50 to £70, twin/double £83 to £90, four-poster £83 to £90, family room £90 to £98; deposit required. Set D £22.50 to £25.50. Special breaks available

BROADWAY **Hereford & Worcester**   map 5

Collin House

Collin Lane, Broadway WR12 7PB
TEL: (01386) 858354

Relaxing country retreat with good food and a cosy bar.

The detached late-sixteenth-century house was built, like so many in these parts, by a wealthy wool merchant, in the glowing golden stone that gives the area its character. The interior wears its age well, with the combination of flagstones and beams conferring a measure of rustic charm that is unexpected given the size of the place. The heart of things is the cosy bar, with rugs over bare boards, a huge slate fireplace and a medley of chairs from chintzy florals to a chesterfield and dignified old wooden settles. This is the place to peruse the menu and wine list, or to choose a bar supper from the tempting offerings listed on the blackboard. On chilly nights another fire blazes in the small sitting-room across the passageway. It's a homely place, and houses the hotel's only permanent television and a range of board games. Staffordshire figures add a dash of period flavour. There is more of it in the dining-room, with beams and leaded, mullioned windows, which are romantic in candlelight. Food here is nostalgically English; perhaps Stilton and walnut soufflé with a watercress sauce, followed by a lightly cooked breast of wood pigeon with a wild berry and gin sauce, and Bramley apple and clove pie with custard.

Bedrooms combine old and new, sometimes pine, furniture to pleasing effect. There's no overarching style, and some pieces look comfortably worn-in, but owner John Mills is an agreeable host, and something of a raconteur, especially on the works of art scattered around the hotel.

◑ Closed 24 to 29 Dec ⬈ 1 mile north-west of Broadway off A44. Turn right at Collin Lane and house is 300 yards on right. Private car park ⊨ 1 single, 3 twin, 1 double, 2 four-poster; most with bathroom/WC, 1 with shower/WC; room service, hair-dryer; TV on request ⊘ Restaurant, bar, lounge, garden; conference facilities (max 12 people non-residential/residential); unheated outdoor swimming-pool, croquet; early suppers for children ɔ̆ No wheelchair access ● Children under 7 by arrangement only; no dogs ⊟ Access, Visa ⌷ Single £45, single occupancy of twin/double £65, twin/double £87, four-poster £97; deposit required. Set L £16, D £16 to £24; bar meals available. Special breaks available

---

Dormy House

Willersey Hill, Broadway WR12 7LF
TEL: (01386) 852711 FAX: (01386) 858636

Slick hybrid of old and new with excellent leisure facilities.

Its situation, on a hillside high above the village, means that Dormy House escapes the throng of daytrippers who swell the streets of Broadway. The original seventeenth-century farmhouse shares the same honeyed tones as the houses that line the village's much-visited High Street, and the recently added low-slung complex of outbuildings that contains many of the bedrooms favours the same golden stone. The creeper-clad façade looks suitably venerable, and contrasts starkly with the modern minimalism of the rear-facing reception area. Stylistically the hotel oscillates between these two moods, with state-of-the art leisure facilities on the one hand, and a central core happy to flaunt its flagged floors, exposed stonework, and beams, notably in the agreeable cocktail bar. Food is modern and well designed; perhaps tian of Cornish white crabmeat with freshwater crayfish and a cucumber and yoghurt sauce, followed by grilled supreme of chicken served on a galette potato with a green lentil and thyme sauce, and iced pistachio nougat served with a summer berry compote. Service is careful and attentive. The comfortable bedrooms team antiques, including some spectacular carved headboards, with modern chintzy fabrics.

◐ Closed 25 & 26 Dec ⤢ Just off A44 at sign marked Saintbury/Picnic area; 1 mile from Broadway village centre. Private car park ⬅️ 7 single, 14 twin, 22 double, 3 four-poster, 3 suites; all with bathroom/WC exc 1 single with shower/WC; TV, room service, hair-dryer, trouser press, direct-dial telephone, clock radio; mini-bar in some rooms ✅ Restaurant, 3 bars, 2 lounges, games rooms, garden, conference suite (air-conditioned); conference facilities (max 200 people incl up to 49 residential); gym, sauna, croquet, putting green; early suppers for children; babysitting, baby-listening, cots, high chairs ♿ No wheelchair access ⚫ Children discouraged from restaurant eves; no dogs in public rooms and some bedrooms ▭ Access, Amex, Delta, Diners, Switch, Visa £ Single £63 to £83, single occupancy of twin/double £83, twin/double £125, four-poster £150, suite £160; deposit required. Set L £17.50, D £27.50; alc D £30.50. Special breaks available

Lygon Arms

High Street, Broadway WR12 7DU
TEL: (01386) 852255   FAX: (01386) 858611

Beautiful sixteenth-century inn on the high street of one of the prettiest Cotswold villages.

The Lygon Arms has welcomed many illustrious guests in its long history, most notably both Charles I and Oliver Cromwell, and many of its stylish rooms have been named after such visitors. It maintains the high standards for which it is renowned, and its owners, Savoy Group, have added on modern amenities, such as the Country Club – which has a Grecian-style indoor pool with a slide-back roof – without any of the sense of history being lost. The bedrooms are all smart and very comfortable, but for the rooms with most character those in the original building cannot be beaten. The Great Bedchamber, with its beamed ceiling and bed which dates from 1620, is certainly an impressive room. The service in the hotel is top-notch, and even runs to providing room-service trays for guests' dogs. Dinner for human guests is served in the Great Hall, with its seventeenth-century minstrels' gallery, barrel-vaulted ceiling and panelled walls. It is a formal setting in which to enjoy such delights as Scottish oak-smoked salmon and capers, followed by noisette and mignon of Cotswold lamb with paloise sauce and artichokes, perhaps finishing with almond tulip with raspberry compote and pink champagne ice-cream.

◐ Open all year ⤢ On main street in centre of Broadway. Private car park ⬅️ 3 single, 8 twin, 43 double, 6 four-poster, 5 suites; family rooms available; all with bathroom/WC; TV, room service, hair-dryer, trouser press, direct-dial telephone; no tea/coffee-making facilities in rooms ✅ Restaurant, 2 bars, 5 lounges, TV room, drying-room, games room, garden; conference facilities (max 80 people incl up to 65 residential); gym, sauna, solarium, heated indoor swimming-pool, tennis, croquet, billiards, steam room, spa; early suppers for children; baby-listening ♿ Wheelchair access to hotel, restaurant, WC (M,F), 5 ground-floor bedrooms ⚫ No children under 5 in restaurant eves; no dogs in public rooms ▭ Access, Amex, Diners, Visa £ Single £95, single occupancy of twin/double £122, twin/double £147, four-poster £195, family room £255, suite £225; deposit required. Cooked B £9; set L £22, D £34; alc L £27, D £35 (prices valid till Dec 1996). Special breaks available

College House

Chapel Street, Broadwell, Moreton-in-Marsh GL56 0TW
TEL: (01451) 832351

*Top marks for this some-time academic retreat in a pretty
Gloucestershire village.*

'Absolutely super...the whole house has a lovely welcoming feel,' reported one
reader after a stay at Sybil Gisby's seventeenth-century house in the spruce
Cotswold village of Broadwell. There is no sign to indicate that it is a
guesthouse, just the name of the house etched on an inset panel, so you could
easily sweep past the restrained, creeper-clad, mellow-stoned building. The
name reflects the houses's history as an Oxford don's bequest to his seat of
learning, but there's nothing dustily donnish or cluttered about the place.
Instead, Sybil has adopted a virtually open-plan layout for the public areas, and
this sense of space sets off the flag-stoned floors, heavy beams and sturdy walls to
great effect. The interior design is a happy marriage of old and new, finding room
both for horse brasses and modish stencils, with lots of books on subjects of local
interest and plenty of comfy chairs in which to read them. The same arty,
uncluttered style prevails in the dining-room, where, with 24 hours' notice,
Sybil (a former restaurateur) is happy to serve dinner, perhaps smoked salmon
and avocado bake, followed by Forester's chicken with seasonal vegetables, and
citron tart.

The three bedrooms are attractively furnished and tastefully decorated, and
priced individually according to size. Bathrooms are equally attractive; the one
in the premier yellow room is particularly luxurious. Ask to see the priest's hole,
now prettified with a fetching orange-tree stencil.

◗ Closed 24 to 27 Dec; restaurant closed Sun eve   ⬀ North of Stow-on-the-Wold,
turn off A429 to Broadwell; at Broadwell village green follow signposts to Evenlode;
College House is located on Chapel Street. Private car park   ⊨ 3 double; 2 with
bathroom/WC; TV, hair-dryer, clock radio   ✓ Dining-room, lounge, garden   ♿ No
wheelchair access   ⬟ No children under 16; no dogs; no smoking in bedrooms
▭ None accepted   £ Single occupancy of twin/double £40 to £57, twin/double £45
to £62. Set D £16.50

Grove House

Bromsberrow Heath, Ledbury HR8 1PE
TEL: (01531) 650584

Imposing public rooms in a Wolsey Lodge of character.

On a Sunday morning, as people in Bromsberrow Heath tends their garden in a
scene of rural timelessness, it's hard to believe that the tiny hamlet is a couple of
minutes' drive from the traffic roar of the M50, making it ideally placed for
antique-hunting forays into Ross-on-Wye or Tewkesbury. Judging by the
delightful furnishings at Grove House, Ellen and Michael Ross have themselves

made a few expeditions from the listed fifteenth-century home. Some 13 acres of garden and fields surround the plain, wistaria-clad house, and the Rosses are currently extending the top terrace area to the rear. There's direct access to this part of the house via a flight of stairs from the lovely (upstairs) drawing-room, a light, civilised space with creamy sofas, ornate plasterwork, and walls graced by some fine landscapes and a couple of Russell Flints, as well as family polo photographs. You can brush up your knowledge of the rules of polo or other interests such as garden design by browsing through the good selection of books. The panelled dining-room is rather grand, and a fun collection of hip flasks and cigarette cases seems to have escaped the attentions of the health police. Dinner, served to guests seated together at one table in time-honoured Wolsey Lodge-style, is classic dinner-party fare: perhaps cream of carrot soup, followed by scallops, roast duck, and open strawberry tart. The three bedrooms (two of which house four-posters), combine a generous dash of antiques and lots of cosseting extras with lived-in, unco-ordinated décor.

◑ Closed Chr & 1 Jan   ⤢ In Bromsberrow Heath turn right by post office and go up the hill. Grove House is on the right. Private car park   ⇨ 1 twin, 2 four-poster; all with bathroom/WC; TV, hair-dryer   ✓ Dining-room, lounge, garden; unheated outdoor swimming-pool, tennis; early suppers for children   ♿ No wheelchair access
● Children discouraged from dining-room eves; no dogs; no smoking in bedrooms
▭ None accepted   £ Single occupancy of twin/double £47, twin/double £64, four-poster £64. Set D £20

BROMSGROVE Hereford & Worcester   map 5

Grafton Manor

Grafton Lane, Bromsgrove B61 7HA
TEL: (01527) 579007   FAX: (01527) 575221

Elegant red-brick manor house set in beautiful grounds.

Commissioned by the Earl of Shrewsbury in 1567 and rebuilt in the eighteenth century after a fire, Grafton Manor is now run as a hotel by the resident Morris family. Amid the tranquil grounds, consisting of six acres of well-tended gardens including a water garden and lake, a large formal herb garden laid out in the shape of a chessboard and even a chapel, it is easy to forget that the busy M5 runs very close by. Inside, the eighteenth-century dining-room is the place to sample one of the dinners cooked by chef and family member Simon Morris, which might include pumpkin and nutmeg soup, guinea-fowl poached with calvados and apples served with a pot of quince jelly, followed by crème brûlée served with a damask rose sorbet. There is also an excellent vegetarian menu. The bedrooms are all comfortable and traditionally decorated.

Don't expect to turn up at a small hotel assuming that a room will be available. It's always best to telephone in advance.

◑ Open all year � Leave M5 at Junction 5 and travel north on A38 towards Bromsgrove; then take B4091; Grafton Lane is on left. Private car park ⊨ 1 single, 2 twin, 3 double, 1 four-poster, 2 suites; all with bathroom/WC; TV, room service, hair-dryer, trouser press, direct-dial telephone; no tea/coffee-making facilities in rooms ✅ Dining-room, bar, library, garden; conference room (air-conditioned); conference facilities (max 12 people incl up to 9 residential); fishing; early suppers for children ♿ No wheelchair access ⊖ No dogs; no smoking in dining-room or library ▭ Access, Amex, Diners, Switch, Visa £ Single £85, single occupancy of twin/double £95, twin/double £105, four-poster £125, suite £150; deposit required. Set L £20.50, D £31.50. Special breaks available

---

BROXTED Essex   map 3

Whitehall

Church End, Broxted CM6 2BZ
TEL: (01279) 850603 FAX: (01279) 850385

Sympathetically extended Elizabethan manor run with personal touch, popular with business conferences.

'The luxury hotel at Stansted Airport' trumpets the brochure. It therefore comes as a welcome surprise to find that you have to wend along country lanes to Whitehall, with only the occasional aircraft passing overhead to disturb the peace. The heart of the complex is an attractive Elizabethan manor backed by appealing gardens with truncated yews and formal lawns; to this has been added a new wing (spot the join) and a converted barn. Décor is of the comfortable country-house variety, all pale pastels and mufflingly thick carpets, which add comfort and fortunately do little to detract from the character of the crooked half-timbering, leaded panes and exposed brickwork. The *pièce de résistance* is the main restaurant, with a splendid array of exposed timbers, some of which have been cleverly used to frame a modern mural of the house. The smart à la carte menu features dishes like hot spinach soufflé with herb sauce or sauté monkfish and scallops with basil, saffron and pasta; a cheaper chef's selection has been added, intended to compete with local pubs, offering choices such as deep-fried mushrooms with garlic dip or fillet of plaice with tomato and basil. Bedrooms, named after prime ministers or Cambridge colleges, maintain the style and standard, with individual touches like a print of the eponymous college in Pembroke.

◑ Closed 26 to 31 Dec ⊡ In Broxted village. Private car park ⊨ 6 twin, 19 double; family rooms available; all with bathroom/WC; TV, room service, hair-dryer, trouser press, direct-dial telephone ✅ 3 restaurants, 2 bars, 2 lounges, garden; conference facilities (max 100 people incl up to 25 residential); unheated outdoor swimming-pool, tennis, clay-pigeon shooting; early suppers for children ♿ Wheelchair access to hotel (2 steps), restaurant, WC (M,F), 9 ground-floor bedrooms ⊖ No dogs ▭ Access, Amex, Delta, Diners, Switch, Visa £ Single occupancy of twin/double £80, twin/double £110 to £140, family room £155; deposit required. Set L, D £13.50 to £16.50; alc D £27.50. Special breaks available

Broxton Hall

Whitchurch Road, Broxton, Chester CH3 9JS
TEL: (01829) 782321   FAX: (01829) 782330

A relaxing, convivial country house liberally endowed with splendid antiques.

Continuing to run Broxton Hall as a country-house hotel was not foremost in Rosemary and George Hadley's plans when they first moved to this luxuriantly half-timbered Tudor house eight years ago. However, popular demand for George's easy, convivial hospitality, while being surrounded by fine antiques (courtesy of the family business, now based in nearby Chester), rather took the decision out of their hands.

The initial impression is of abundant half-timbering and leaded lights, followed by wood panelling, dark portraits and a vast, open fireplace – once you've squeezed past the heavy oak table in the small entrance hall. The lounge features winged-back armchairs around an open fire, and parlour palms perch between the tables in the cocktail bar. White damask, polished silverware and dining by candlelight are standard in the restaurant, where the country-house menu is influenced by the Hadleys' enthusiasm for the south of France. Typical dishes include fish soup with aïoli croûtons, rack of lamb with blackcurrant sauce, crêpes with apple and cinnamon, and bread-and-butter pudding.

In comparison with the splendour downstairs, some of the bedrooms may feel a little underdressed, but this is certainly not true of the four-poster room, which is dominated by a magnificent carved-oak bed that was once owned by the judge who condemned Charles I to death.

◑ Closed 25, 26 Dec & 1 Jan ⊿ 8 miles from Chester on A41 towards Whitchurch. Situated at Broxton roundabout on the left. Private car park ⊨ 2 single, 3 twin, 5 double, 1 four-poster; all with bathroom/WC; TV, room service, hair-dryer, trouser press, direct-dial telephone, clock radio ⊘ Restaurant, bar, lounge, TV room, drying-room, conservatory, garden; conference facilities (max 20 people incl up to 11 residential); early suppers for children; toys, baby-listening ⅙ No wheelchair access ● None ▭ Access, Amex, Diners, Switch, Visa £ Single £60, single occupancy of twin/double £65, twin/double £70 to £80, four-poster £105; deposit required. Set L £14, D £25; alc L £18, D £30. Special breaks available

---

Frogg Manor

Nantwich Road, Fullers Moor, Broxton, Chester CH3 9JH
TEL: (01829) 782280/782629   FAX: (01829) 782238

Small country house with a hugely successful blend of comfort, style and idiosyncrasy.

'My favourite hotel by a wide margin. Mr Sykes may be regarded by some as "off-the-wall", but really it is his influence and style that make this hotel special.' 'As an ex-hotel manager and head chef at a variety of hotels both large and small (and a nit-picking perfectionist!), I was knocked out by the place. It's definitely a one-off and we loved it.' 'Refreshingly individual. From John Sykes', aka Chief Frog's, warm welcome you know this is going to be an overnight stay that will be remembered.'

Tributes to Frogg Manor have rolled in, indicating that the invention and imagination of John Sykes, the workaholic, perfectionist proprietor, has struck just the right chord. Drive up to this long, whitewashed Georgian house just off the main road – keeping a watchful eye for migratory frogs – and you find Al Bowley (or his ilk) drifting mellifluously through the doorway, and John Sykes close at hand brandishing a paintbrush, pen or paring knife. Repair to the residents' lounge and you'll find refined elegance and an abundance of glass frogs, pot frogs, china frogs, frogs in hats, and stuffed-toy frogs. Press on to the restaurant and it's silver cutlery, white linen, glass chandeliers, and an ancient Chinese wistaria wrapped around the conservatory. John's cooking is character-istically inventive, and among several choices you might find Brie baked in filo pastry and served with Greek yoghurt and fresh lime juice, followed by local chicken with Danish ham and green lentils, cream of English mustard and a hint of rosemary.

The six bedrooms range from the compact Sherlock Holmes to king-sized Wellington, with its chintz-canopied central bed and secret doorway, but all are immaculate and amusing, with Bakelite telephones, valve radios, biscuits, bathrobes, toy frogs, shoe-cleaning kits and patent medicines. A not-so-small fortune has been invested in luxurious mattresses, 'as the bed is one of the principal reasons you are going to a hotel!'.

◑ Open all year 🔁 From Chester head south on A41; turn left on A534 towards Nantwich; Frogg Manor is 1 mile on right. Private car park 🛏 5 double, 1 four-poster; 4 with bathroom/WC, 2 with shower/WC; TV, room service, hair-dryer, trouser press, direct-dial telephone; iron on request ✅ Restaurant, dining-room, bar, lounge, drying-room, conservatory, garden; conference facilities (max 25 people incl up to 6 residential); tennis; early suppers for children ♿ No wheelchair access ● No dogs in public rooms ▭ Access, Amex, Delta, Diners, Switch, Visa £ Single occupancy of twin/double £45 to £95, twin/double £55 to £115, four-poster £100 to £115. Continental B £4.50, cooked B £7.50; set L £15, D £25. Special breaks available

---

BUCKLAND Gloucestershire   map 5

Buckland Manor

Buckland, Nr Broadway WR12 7LY
TEL: (01386) 852626   FAX: (01386) 853557

A luxurious country manor-house hotel with high standards.

Buckland Manor is a grand country hotel with a long history of which it is justifiably proud. In a peaceful and sleepy hamlet of honey-coloured stone cottages, overlooked by the adjacent thirteenth-century St Michael's church, and in its own immaculately tended 10 acres of grounds, Buckland Manor's setting is certainly idyllic. The interior of the hotel is rather plush, and includes a lounge that has oak panelling and parquet floors, a bright and sunny morning-room with an open fire and views of the grounds, as well as an elegant dining-room – all overflowing with antiques. Formal dress is required at dinner, and the à la carte menu offers dishes such as oak-smoked Scottish salmon and Cornish crab terrine, marinated and roasted rack of English lamb with a garlic-and-herb crust, and a passion-fruit soufflé served with its own sorbet. The bedrooms also offer a taste of luxury: the Summer Room is a bright and airy double, decorated in pink and turquoise with period furniture and a view of the garden, while at the top of the range is the Delany Suite – a suite of rooms with a four-poster bed and a wardrobe so big that you could get lost in it.

◑ Open all year   🔁 From Broadway, take the A46/B4632 towards Cheltenham. Buckland Manor is off to the left after 2 miles. Private car park   🛏 5 twin, 5 double, 3 four-poster, 1 family room; all with bathroom/WC; TV, room service, hair-dryer, direct-dial telephone; trouser press on request   ✅ Dining-room, 2 lounges, drying-room, garden; heated outdoor swimming-pool, tennis, putting green, croquet ⅙ No wheelchair access   ⊖ No children under 12; no dogs   ⬚ Amex, Diners, Visa   £ Single occupancy of twin/double £160 to £275, twin/double £170 to £285, four-poster £285 to £325, family room £285; deposit required. Set L £28.50; alc D £40 (prices valid till Jan 1997). Special breaks available

---

BUCKNELL Shropshire   map 7

Bucknell House

Bucknell SY7 0AD
TEL: (01547) 530248

Affordable B&B accommodation in a Georgian vicarage on the cusp of three counties.

Part of the fun in exploring this area comes from the constant guess-work as to which country you're in, as the Anglo-Welsh border runs its ragged path, looping unpredictably'twixt the *Land of my Fathers* and the *Land of Hope and Glory*. Brenda Davies' Georgian vicarage, agreeably relaxing behind the classical grace of its white portico, is firmly on the English side of Offa's Dyke. However, Brenda, a fund of local information, will happily point out the views of Shropshire, Herefordshire and Radnorshire (she doesn't have truck with the new-fangled county names) from upstairs. The house has a big two-sectioned drawing-room, with conservative décor, well-polished furniture and sofas in autumnal shades. Swag and tail drapes and an Adam-style fireplace add a touch of class, and an old chapel organ and an upright piano await the attention of those who can tinkle the ivories.

The well-equipped bedrooms couple pleasant antique pieces with more prosaic items. Colour schemes are traditional and easy on the eye. Perhaps the nicest, the twin/family room, was once Brenda's son's room, and the now-married thirtysomething's school photos still proudly line the walls. Breakfast is served in the elegant dining-room, where the places are set on crisp white linen complemented by napkin rings and flowers on the table; collections of silverware and wall-mounted plates add the personal touch.

Reports are welcome on any hotel, whether or not it is in the Guide.

◑ Closed Dec & Jan   ⤴ Follow A4113 Ludlow to Knighton road, then B4367 towards Craven Arms; house is on fringe of Bucknell. Private car park   ⬅ 1 twin, 2 double; family room available; TV, radio   ⊘ Dining-room, lounge, garden; fishing, tennis   ⎔ No wheelchair access   ● No children under 12; no dogs in dining-room   ⊡ None accepted   £ Single occupancy of twin/double £23, twin/double £37. Special breaks available

---

BURBAGE Wiltshire   map 2

Old Vicarage   ℒ

Burbage, Marlborough SN8 3AG
TEL: (01672) 810495   FAX: (01672) 810663

A comfortable former vicarage full of Victoriana with enthusiastic hosts, some quirky touches and lovely gardens.

Jane Cornelius and her husband have a love for their smart, Victorian house, which they like to pass on. 'We hope visitors will appreciate the setting and ambience, not just come to get a bed,' they say. Not that those who hide away upstairs miss out on style or comfort, for the bedrooms have an attractive mix of modern and antique furnishings and lots of extras, including bathrobes, magazines, truffles, fruit and a variety of teas. The bathrooms come as a surprise – the house previously belonged to the manager of a local tile company, who decked out the twin room's bathroom in stunning bright-yellow tiles, and the double room's in elaborate blue and grey. He also filled the walls of this unusual, high-ceilinged room (it occupies one of the house's peaked gables) with a bright, theatrical mural of Lake Garda. Downstairs, the décor and furnishings are more in keeping with the house's period features, although brightly painted doors and the abundance of flowers and plants mix freshness and originality with the rich fabrics and polished antiques. Jane's showpiece, however, is her garden, which she restored from a complete wilderness. She's still working on her Victorian rose garden, but there's much else to admire in the two acres of lawns, borders and shrubbery.

◑ Closed Chr & New Year   ⤴ From Burbage High Street turn east into Taskers Lane; take the third turning on the right into Eastcourt; Old Vicarage is on the left. Private car park   ⬅ 1 single, 1 twin, 1 double; all with bathroom/WC; room service, hair-dryer; TV and telephone on request   ⊘ Dining-room, lounge, drying-room, garden   ⎔ No wheelchair access   ● No children; dogs in bedrooms by arrangement; no smoking   ⊡ Access, Visa   £ Single £35, single occupancy of twin/double £40, twin/double £60; deposit required

---

BURFORD Oxfordshire   map 2

Andrews Hotel

High Street, Burford OX18 4QA
TEL: (01993) 823151   FAX: (01993) 823240

Good-value accommodation at the centre of a tourist honeypot.

Right in the thick of things on the busy High Street, Andrews doubles as a successful tea-shop and has a bustling atmosphere at any time of day. It's a good-looking building, golden Cotswold stone at the bottom and half-timbered in black and white at the top, and is immaculately maintained, with tubs and hanging baskets tumbling with flowers. Of the five four-poster bedrooms, Room 8 is the grandest, and it has a large fully tiled bathroom with a Mediterranean feel and a Victorian free-standing bath. Room 1, with no bath but a small shower-room, is the quietest, being away from the road. All rooms are characterful, with dark beams and smart furnishings, and are well equipped. The hotel doesn't serve dinners, but tea downstairs is quite an event, and well worth a stop even if you're not staying – a mouth-watering display of cakes will tempt the figure-conscious. One reader wrote in to say: 'The welcome was warm, but the best thing was that having missed breakfast we were offered whatever we wanted to eat before we checked out. A rare thing nowadays.'

◗ Closed 24 to 26 Dec ◪ Half-way along Burford High Street. On-street parking ⍟ 1 twin, 1 double, 5 four-poster; 5 with bathroom/WC, 2 four-posters with shower/WC; TV; hair-dryer in some rooms; no tea/coffee-making facilities in rooms ⍟ Dining-room, 2 lounges ⅙ No wheelchair access ● No dogs; smoking in lounges only ⛶ Access, Delta, Switch, Visa £ Single occupancy of twin/double £55, twin/double £75, four-poster £95. Special breaks available

---

Bay Tree Hotel

12-14 Sheep Street, Burford OX18 4LW
TEL: (01993) 822791   FAX: (01993) 823008

Historic inn of great character with luxurious rooms and unstuffy service.

Built by a prominent Elizabethan politician in days when money was no object, the Bay Tree is a wonderful example of sixteenth-century architecture. Stone mullioned windows surrounded by creepers on the outside and ornately carved fireplaces and flagstone floors on the inside give the place its character. The bar, where snacks include duck terrine and home-made soup, has a country pub feel; the lounge, with comfortable armchairs and logs piled high, is small and cosy enough to be your own sitting-room. Though the restaurant is large, it is very popular with locals coming to dine, so you need to give notice if you're staying in to eat. Scattered around the hotel is a fascinating collection of samplers, some left over from the days when this was a finishing school. It's fun to read the earnest embroidered messages – such as: 'This is my work my friends may see, and when I am dead may think of me, Elizabeth Crane aged 12' – as you wind your way through the corridors to your room. Most of the bedrooms are in the main house, and these have the edge for creaking-floor character, though all are luxurious with plenty of space and smart well-equipped bathrooms. Nine rooms in a cottage across the yard are equally comfortable, and four ground-floor annexe rooms, though slightly plainer, have the advantage of overlooking the pretty walled garden.

○ Open all year ⤢ Just off High Street in Burford. Private car park ⨼ 2 single, 7 twin, 9 double, 3 four-poster, 2 suites; family rooms available; some in annexe; all with bathroom/WC; TV, room service, hair-dryer, direct-dial telephone ✓ Restaurant, bar, lounge, library, conservatory, garden; conference facilities (max 35 people incl up to 23 residential); croquet; early suppers for children; baby-listening ♿ No wheelchair access ● No dogs or smoking in restaurant; dogs in some bedrooms only ▭ Access, Amex, Delta, Diners, Switch, Visa £ Single £60, single occupancy of twin/double £80, twin/double £110, four-poster £155, family room/suite £195; deposit required. Set L £13, Sun L £14, D £20; alc D £22.50; bar meals available (1996 prices). Special breaks available

Lamb Inn

Sheep Street, Burford OX18 4LR
TEL: (01993) 823155 FAX: (01993) 822228

An up-market, historic inn – a luxury option in a busy tourist area.

High-backed settles placed either side of a log fire, faded rugs on a flagstone floor, and wood smoke hanging in the air are a good introduction as you step through the door of this old inn. The calm, rather genteel, atmosphere is a welcome contrast to the hustle and bustle of the heart of the village, a few minutes' walk away. Service at the Lamb Inn has had 500 years in which to develop to its existing high standards, and the current owners definitely make the most of their inheritance. On the outside, the hotel is a gabled, stone building, with creepers and roses growing around the windows; on the inside, it is a stylish and comfortable inn, which hasn't lost its rustic touches. The bedrooms vary in size, although not in price, which makes the bigger rooms better value than the others. They're all very comfortable, and are smartly furnished with heavy fabrics and a mix of antiques; the bathrooms are plush. Guests tend to dress for dinner in the medieval-feel dining-room, in which the meals are pricey but excellent, and the staff are helpful and unstuffy. A typical three-course dinner might include sauté button mushrooms and prawns in a garlic cream sauce, followed by poached fillets of local trout with hazelnuts and orange, and then a platter of English cheeses. As one reader commented, 'Another good pick from the book, a lovely old inn and good food'.

○ Closed 25 & 26 Dec ⤢ Just off the High Strret in Burford. Private car park ⨼ 3 twin, 11 double, 1 four-poster; all with bathroom/WC exc 1 double with shower/WC; TV, room service, hair-dryer, direct-dial telephone; no tea/coffee-making facilities in rooms ✓ Dining-room, bar, 3 lounges, library, garden; early suppers for children ♿ No wheelchair access ● No dogs or smoking in dining-room ▭ Access, Switch, Visa £ Single occupancy of twin/double £58 to £75, twin/double/four-poster £90 to £100; deposit required. Set D £24, Sun L £17.50; bar lunches available (prices valid till Nov 1996). Special breaks available

Hotels in our Visitors' Book *towards the end of the* Guide *are additional hotels that may be worth a visit. Reports on these hotels are welcome.*

Burland Farm

Wrexham Road, Burland, Nr Nantwich CW5 8ND
TEL: (01270) 524210   FAX: (01270) 524419

A small, family-run farmhouse B&B with countrified, comfortable bedrooms.

Burland looks every inch the traditional Cheshire dairy farm, with a courtyard enclosed by pleasingly tumbledown, red-brick outbuildings, and a pretty farmhouse with honeycomb windows that are concealed behind the blooms of a climbing hydrangea for most of the summer. A waft of 'country air' may remind you that this is very much a working farm – some of the milk produced here is used in the farm's frozen-yoghurt business.

Two rooms, a double and a twin with brass bedsteads, were available at the time of our spring inspection, both fresh and unfussy, furnished with antique dressers and wardrobes, and decorated in plain colours and country prints. A four-poster (being made by a local woodturner) is promised for the double room.

Comfy floral sofas, an open coal fire and plenty of family photographs should draw guests towards the attractive sitting-room, while breakfasts are served around the large, oak table in the dining-room. Fruits of the season, porridge, or some unusual extras like American muffins, might form part of Sandra Allwood's hearty farmhouse breakfasts.

◑ Closed Chr & New Year   ⊿ 3 miles west of Nantwich on A534, 1 mile on the Wrexham side of Burland canal bridge. Private car park   1 twin, 2 double; 2 with bathroom/WC, 1 double with shower/WC; TV, hair-dryer   ⌀ Dining-room, lounge, library, garden; conference facilities (max 12 people incl up to 3 residential); croquet   ♿ No wheelchair access   ● No children under 10; no dogs in dining-room   ⊟ None accepted   £ Single occupancy of twin/double £20 to £25, twin/double £40 to £50

Use the maps at the back of the Guide *to pinpoint hotels in a particular area.*

🍲 *Denotes somewhere you can rely on a good meal – either the hotel features in the 1997 edition of our sister publication,* The Good Food Guide, *or our inspectors thought the cooking impressive, whether particularly competent home cooking or more lavish cuisine.*

Use the index at the back of the book if you know the name of a hotel but are unsure about its precise location.

Hoste Arms

The Green, Burnham Market, Nr Kings Lynn PE31 8HD
TEL: (01328) 738777   FAX: (01328) 730103

A characterful inn run with passion and commitment in an attractive coastal village.

Paul Whittome used to be a potato merchant before turning his enthusiasm and energy towards the hotel trade – you feel that his is the sort of passion that could have persuaded everyone to consume tubers for breakfast, lunch and dinner had he been so minded. He took over the seventeenth-century Hoste Arms in 1989, but describes it, perhaps a touch disingenuously, as 'still very much a fishermen's inn'. Not that your average fisherman wouldn't enjoy a pint of real ale in the snug bar, with its beams and deep-red walls, or a cup of freshly brewed coffee (free to residents) in the newer, airier conservatory at the back. Or perhaps he could sample some of his catch in the smart restaurant, dining on dishes such as grilled scallops and deep-fried oysters with squid-ink pasta and champagne sauce, or roasted fillet of brill on a bed of braised red cabbage. The bedrooms are decked out in smart, co-ordinated fabrics, and the walls are sometimes stripped back to the original flint (Room 10), or offer a hand-painted, four-poster bed (Room 17). There's also an art gallery, featuring works by local East Anglians. Those who – for some peculiar reason known only to themselves – wish to get away from here can even book a holiday through Paul's wife, Jeanne, who runs a small travel agency next to the gallery.

○ Open all year   ⊋ In Burnham Market, overlooking village green. Private car park   ⊢⊣ 4 twin, 12 double, 4 four-poster, 1 family room; some in annexe; most with bathroom/WC, some with shower/WC; room service, hair-dryer, trouser press, direct-dial telephone   ✓ Restaurant, bar, conservatory, garden; conference facilities (max 30 people incl up to 21 residential); early suppers for children; baby-listening   ও Wheelchair access to hotel (1 step), restaurant and WC (unisex), 5 ground-floor bedrooms, 1 specially equipped for disabled people   ⊖ No children in restaurant eves   ▭ Access, Amex, Switch, Visa   £ Single occupancy of twin/double £60, twin/double £84 to £96, four-poster £108, family room from £153; deposit required. Set D £20.50/24; alc D £24; bar meals available (prices valid till May 1997). Special breaks available

Ounce House

Northgate Street, Bury St Edmunds IP33 1HP
TEL: (01284) 761779   FAX: (01284) 768315

Spotlessly smart town-house accommodation in a gracious family home.

Jenny and Simon Pott have been living it up over the past year: in his post as President of the Royal Institute of Chartered Surveyors, Simon has been jetting all over the world, and Jenny has taken the opportunity to join him whenever she can. Back in Bury St Edmunds, however, their elegant Victorian town house seems to have suffered little from their absence: there are fresh flowers everywhere; the swagged curtains at the windows are as carefully draped as ever; the antiques in the dining-room and ornately carved wooden mantelpiece in the drawing-room gleam with polish; while the endearing little library – the only room in the house that even hints at its previous incarnation as a nursery school – is still a relaxing place in which to watch the fish exploring the outer limits of their tank. The bedrooms are spotless; the most popular, justifiably, is Barclay – a huge, yellow room at the back, with a coronet drape above the bed and an *en suite* bathroom, with a separate bath and shower cabinet situated down a couple of steps. Jenny offers evening meals only by arrangement; breakfast is a communal affair in the dining-room, overlooking the secluded walled garden behind.

◑ Open all year ⤴ Leave A14 at second Bury St Edmunds exit and head towards town centre. Take the left turn at the first roundabout into Northgate Street. Private car park ⏚ 1 single, 2 twin, 1 double; all with bathroom/WC exc single with shower/WC; TV, room service, hair-dryer, trouser press, direct-dial telephone, radio ⌘ Dining-room, bar/library, lounge, study, garden; conference facilities (max 12 people incl up to 4 residential); early suppers for children; toys, baby-sitting ઙ No wheelchair access ● No dogs; smoking in bar/library only ⊟ Access, Switch, Visa £ Single £35 to £40, single occupancy of twin/double £40 to £50, twin/double £60 to £75. Set D £18 to £20. Special breaks available

Ravenwood Hall

Rougham, Bury St Edmunds IP30 9JA
TEL: (01359) 270345   FAX: (01359) 270788

A country hotel with a very personal feel and atmospheric dining.

Ravenwood Hall is the home of Craig Jarvis, and feels very much like it: as well as seeing his face (together with his loving Labrador) beaming out at you from the hotel's brochure, you may also come across a photo in your room of man and dog frolicking on the beach. The attractive tile-hung main building is set in seven acres of grounds (featuring a pony paddock and goats by the car park), which shield it from the nearby A14. Inside, it becomes clear that Mr Jarvis has a passion both for country pursuits and for all things equine: stuffed birds and fish, pairs of antlers, hunting horns and racing prints adorn the walls. Draw back the tantalising set of curtains over the vast fireplace in the bar for a glimpse of some wall paintings that were uncovered during restoration (a photo album kept at the entrance to the restaurant tells the full story). You can eat in the bar, choosing from a wide selection of dishes chalked on to the various blackboards, or head for the restaurant, which also retains such Tudor features as a vast inglenook and sixteenth-century beams. Extra atmosphere is provided in the evening by real candles burning in the sconces. The food can be excellent, but is irritatingly inconsistent in small details: when we inspected, a main course of duck with cranberry sauce was very good, but the fruit salad that followed was disappointing. Similarly, the kedgeree at breakfast was extremely tasty, but the toast was burnt. The bedrooms in the main house have plenty of characterful touches, like half-testers of 'princess-and-the-pea' proportions; go for these rather than those in the mews, which are smaller and blander.

○ Open all year ▢ Ravenwood Hall is 3 miles east of Bury St Edmunds, just off the A14. Private car park ⬌ 2 twin, 11 double, 1 four-poster; some in annexe; all with bathroom/WC; TV, room service, hair-dryer, direct-dial telephone ⌀ Restaurant, bar, lounge, garden; conference facilities (max 200 people incl up to 14 residential); heated outdoor swimming-pool, tennis, clay-pigeon shooting, croquet; early suppers for children; baby-listening ⅄ Wheelchair access to hotel (1 step), restaurant, WC (unisex), 5 ground-floor bedrooms ⊜ Dogs in bar and bedrooms only; smoking in bar only ☐ Access, Amex, Delta, Diners, Switch, Visa ⸬ Single occupancy of twin/double £59 to £87, twin/double £77 to £97, four-poster £97; deposit required. Set L, D £17; alc L, D £23; bar meals available (1996 prices). Special breaks available

Twelve Angel Hill

12 Angel Hill, Bury St Edmunds IP33 1UZ
TEL: (01284) 704088   FAX: (01284) 725549

A highly regarded B&B where service and attention to detail are second to none.

'The most wonderful B&B I have stayed at . . . I am originally from Bury and this has become my vacation home every time I come home', writes an enthusiastic expatriate now based in the United States. Other reports, too, testify to the continuing excellence of Bernie and John Clarke's elegant but relaxed Georgian establishment right in the heart of town. If you follow the instructions in the *Guide*, you'll arrive at the back and will enter the stone-flagged hall, hung with Victorian portraits and Pre-Raphaelite prints, through the pretty, paved garden. Strong colours and robust designs are evident throughout the house, from the Zoffany birds-of-paradise wallpaper in the breakfast room, to the poppy fabric of the suite in the lounge. The bar, which is painted deep-red with one panelled wall, caters for the comfort of both animals and humans, featuring a Knole sofa for the house's dog and cat, and a fabric chesterfield for visitors ('though most people don't mind, and are quite happy to cuddle up with the cat', says Bernie). The bedrooms are named after wines, the *grands crus* being Claret (which has a four-poster, a bay-window seat and a smart shower room) and Chablis (a huge room at the front, with plenty of room for a small sofa and chairs). Breakfast is 'silver service'. 'Most highly recommended' seems to be the general verdict.

○ Closed Jan ▢ Follow the A14 to the Bury St Edmunds ring road, and take the second exit (Bury St Edmunds central). Follow the road to the next roundabout and take the left exit (Northgate Street). Turn right into Looms Lane; after 50 yards, turn left under archway. Private car park ⬌ 1 single, 1 twin, 2 double, 1 four-poster, 1 suite; 2 with bathroom/WC, 4 with shower/WC; TV, hair-dryer, trouser press, direct-dial telephone, clock radio ⌀ Dining-room, bar, lounge, garden, meeting-room ⅄ No wheelchair access ⊜ No children under 16; no dogs; no smoking ☐ Access, Amex, Diners, Visa ⸬ Single £45, single occupancy of twin/double £55, twin/double £65, four-poster £75, suite £75; deposit required (prices valid till Feb 1997). Special breaks available

Bridge Hotel

Buttermere CA13 9UZ
TEL: (01768) 770252 (AND FAX)

*A friendly and informal hotel for which the surrounding
countryside provides the inspiration.*

All the roads to Buttermere enjoy some of the Lakes' most outstanding scenery, whether you come over the Honister Pass, the Newlands Pass or alongside Crummock Water. Buttermere village lies sandwiched between two lakes in plum walking territory, and the Bridge Hotel has been providing hospitality to hikers for over 250 years.

Inside the hotel, there is something of a division of styles. The public bar – all black beams, brass-topped tables and beers in which you could stand a spoon – is thoroughly traditional. In contrast, the subdued ambience of the residents' lounge is rather genteel, while the dining-room is soothing and elegant. As you might expect, the fare is hearty, with five courses available should you have worked up a sufficient appetite and not over-indulged in the complimentary afternoon tea.

Despite the illustrious list of past guests – including A.J.P. Taylor, Wainwright and Thomas Carlyle – the bedrooms are uninspiring (unless you pay a supplement for a four-poster). Although they are in good condition and generally fine in terms of size, the colour schemes and mundane fitted furnishings are rather bland.

○ Open all year ⊠ In Buttermere village. Private car park ⤙ 2 single, 7 twin, 11 double, 2 four-poster; all with bathroom/WC; room service, hair-dryer, direct-dial telephone ✓ Dining-room, bar, lounge, drying-room; conference facilities (max 25 people incl up to 22 residential); early suppers for children ㋴ No wheelchair access ● No dogs in public rooms; no smoking in lounge ▭ Access, Delta, Switch, Visa £ Single £42 to £56, single occupancy of twin/double £63 to £84, twin/double £84 to £112, four-poster £96 to £124; deposit required. Set D £19. Special breaks available

Pickett Howe

Buttermere Valley CA13 9UY
TEL: (01900) 85444 FAX: (01900) 85209

A Lakeland retreat with bags of character and attentive hosts.

'What a wonderful experience this was. House-party style! David and Dani Edwards are charming, and the food incredible', so reads one ringing endorsement that we have received. On arrival at Pickett Howe, a whitewashed, stone longhouse situated deep in the Lake District's finest scenery, you'll be greeted by Dani or David and welcomed into the flagstoned sitting-room for tea loaf and Cumberland rum butter; there'll be a log fire burning in the ancient hearth if it's chilly outside.

The five-course dinners are sociable affairs, served in the snug dining-room amid candlelight and to the accompaniment of chamber music. The emphasis is on using local produce and there is a cosmopolitan feel to Dani's recipes. Although she cooks for a maximum of only four groups, a choice is offered for most courses, including creative vegetarian dishes. Repairing to the fireside with a malt whisky or local bottled beer from the Jacobean carved cabinet is one option after dinner, or you could indulge in some quiet reflection or digest a supply of local guide books in the reading-room upstairs.

The four bedrooms are full of character and offer some unexpected luxury, such as iron-and-brass bedsteads and whirlpool baths in Georgian, Statesman's and 1730, or beams and exposed stone in Rafters. The breakfasts share the dinner menus' inventiveness.

◐ Closed Nov to Mar ⯎ From Keswick take the B5292 to Lorton, and then the B5289 towards Buttermere. After 2 miles turn left and Pickett Howe's entrance is almost 1 mile further, on the right. Private car park ⯈ 1 twin, 3 double; 3 with bathroom/WC, 1 double with shower/WC; TV, hair-dryer, direct-dial telephone, radio ⬦ Dining-room, lounge, drying-room, library, garden ⅛ No wheelchair access ● No children under 10; no dogs; no smoking ▭ Access, Visa £ Single occupancy of twin/double £60, twin/double £72; deposit required. Set D £21

CALDBECK Cumbria   map 10

Parkend Restaurant

Parkend, Caldbeck, Nr Wigton CA7 8HH
TEL: (01697) 478494

A peaceful setting in which to enjoy hearty fare and comfortable rooms.

Sheep wander without a care in the lane outside this tranquil, seventeenth-century, whitewashed cottage, set among the gentler, northern hills of the Lake District. Making good use of skills gained from their former careers as a cookery teacher and a banker, Carol and Phil Cornes run their restaurant-with-rooms in a friendly, down-to-earth style, with Carol cooking the food. Inside, the dark, low beams and exposed stone walls echo the hearty country solidity of Carol's culinary delights. As you sit on the church-pew benches in the bar, looking over the menu, note the stone cattle stall which remains as a memento of Parkend's origins as a stable for a nearby farm. In the interconnecting restaurant rooms, a cast-iron, wood-burning stove keeps the Lakeland chills at bay while diners tackle a steak served with Dijon-mustard sauce, or duckling cooked in a Grand Marnier and orange sauce. Anyone with an appetite hearty enough to take on the mixed grill – a Rabelaisian platter of sirloin steak, lamb and bacon chops, Cumberland sausage, black pudding, tomatoes, mushrooms and eggs – will achieve celebrity status in the Parkend book of records. The bedrooms are decorated in a light and simple mixture of pink and olive green, and are furnished with modern pine furniture, all fully in keeping with the hayloft feel of the upper floor.

◑ Closed 5 to 31 Jan ⚡ Parkend is on the B5299, 1½ miles west of Caldbeck. Private car park 🛏 3 twin/double; family rooms available; all with bathroom/WC; TV, hair-dryer ✣ Restaurant, bar, lounge, garden; early suppers for children; baby-listening ♿ No wheelchair access ● No dogs in public rooms; no smoking in restaurant ▭ Access, Amex, Delta, Diners, Visa £ Single occupancy of twin/double £32, twin/double £48, family room from £53; deposit required. Set L £8/9; alc D £15. Special breaks available

---

CALNE Wiltshire   map 2

Chilvester Hill House

Calne SN11 0LP
TEL: (01249) 813981/815785   FAX: (01249) 814217

Well-proportioned Victorian country manor with extremely affable and accommodating hosts.

Having spent much of their lives abroad, Gill and John Dilley learnt through experience what hotel guests expect, and since returning to England have established a comfortable and extremely welcoming Wolsey Lodge in their Victorian country manor. John still has a full-time doctor's consultancy so Gill does most of the work in the house. She is happy to adapt to visitors' requests: breakfast is 'what you like when you like', and special dietary requirements, likes and dislikes are no problem for the daily-changing dinner menus, using home or locally grown vegetables. There's a clear feminine touch to design, too, particularly in the spacious bedrooms (Pink, Blue and Green), which have floral paper, thick carpets and thoughtful extras like fresh milk, mineral water and detergent. Elegant antiques and the ordered clutter of a family home blend together downstairs. The immaculate drawing-room and dining-room are quite grand, while the sitting-room has a more lived-in feel, with a piano which guests are welcome to play (if they ask Gill nicely!).

◑ Closed 1 week in spring or autumn ⚡ 1 mile from Calne on A4 towards Chippenham. Take a right turn marked Bremhill and Ratford and immediately turn right again through gateposts. Private car park 🛏 3 twin/double; family room available; all with bathroom/WC; TV, limited room service; hair-dryer available on request ✣ Dining-room, lounge, TV room, garden; conference facilities (max 10 people incl up to 3 residential) ♿ No wheelchair access ● No children under 12; no dogs; no smoking in dining-room ▭ Access, Amex, Diners, Visa £ Single occupancy of twin/double £40 to £50, twin/double £60 to £75, family room from £81; deposit required. Set D £18 to £22

The 1998 Guide *will be published in the autumn of 1997. Reports on hotels are welcome at any time of the year, but are extremely valuable in the spring. Send them to* The Which? Hotel Guide, FREEPOST, 2 Marylebone Road, London NW1 1YN. *No stamp is needed if reports are posted in the UK. Our e-mail address is:* "guidereports@which.co.uk".

CALSTOCK **Cornwall**   map 1

Danescombe Valley Hotel

Lower Kelly, Calstock PL18 9RY
TEL: (01822) 832414   FAX: (01822) 832446

Perfect tranquillity in a distinguished Georgian house close to Cotehele Gardens.

Below Cotehele House, the River Tamar executes a sweeping turn across the flood-plain, offering perfect views of Danescombe Valley Hotel standing alone like a seafront Regency villa at the end of a riverside lane. From the balcony of the house the views are just as mesmerising; if you're lucky a cormorant will be fishing beneath your window. Anna and Martin Smith keep the outside world at bay by refusing to install televisions or radios. However, just to prove they're no Luddites they already have their own Internet page (http:// www.danescombe.com/~lower/dvi), which allows potential guests to call up images of peace and mouth-watering menus; a typical no-choice meal might start with goats' cheese and pine-nut tart, move on to baked chicken breast stuffed with mushrooms and bacon, and round off with a pancake filled with custard and Cointreau. Martin Smith prides himself on his cheeseboard, which usually features a dozen West Country varieties. The dining-room and lounge are both chock-a-block with bright modern paintings by local artist Mary Martin and others.

All the bedrooms are spacious, and Rooms 1 and 5 have baths standing in the centre of big bathrooms. First-floor rooms monopolise the balcony but the views are still good from higher up. Furnishings and fabrics are a fine blend of old and new; there are books and magazines everywhere (even in the bathrooms). Pretty new bedroom rugs are souvenirs of the Smiths' recent trip to Nepal, but on the whole this is somewhere to come back to in confidence that all will be as before.

◑ Closed Nov to Mar   ⤴ ½ mile west of Calstock village along river road. Private car park   🚗 2 twin, 3 double; all with bathroom/WC; limited room service, hair-dryer; no tea/coffee-making facilities in rooms   ⊘ Dining-room, bar, lounge, drying-room, garden   ⚹ No wheelchair access   ⬤ No children under 12; no dogs; no smoking in dining-room   ⊟ Access, Amex, Delta, Diners, Switch, Visa   ⬚ Twin/double £125; deposit required. Set D £30

CAMPSEA ASHE **Suffolk**   map 6

Old Rectory

Campsea Ashe, Nr Woodbridge IP13 0PU
TEL: (01728) 746524 (AND FAX)

Comfortable Wolsey Lodge where good food and a laid-back approach keep people coming back for more.

A couple who come here every year to celebrate the wife's birthday cite the peace and tranquillity of its location, the friendly, relaxed atmosphere and the excellent wine list as the main reasons for their regular returns. Although they had some minor quibbles this year about the rather brusque initial greeting from the waitress ('it improved later') and the plumbing (the inefficiency of the flush in their toilet 'would not have amused Queen Victoria') they still said 'we have no hesitation in recommending [the hotel's] continued inclusion.' Stewart Bassett's unpretentious Georgian rectory certainly feels tranquil, with birds nesting in the ivy and the sound of cooing pigeons floating over from the nearby church. The comfortable drawing-room contains an assortment of seating to pander to most tastes, and dinners take the form of a no-choice set three-course menu, decided in consultation with guests (maybe lemon sole with crab mousse and white wine sauce, then roast rack of lamb with redcurrant sauce, followed by hot ginger and pear upside-down pudding). Unlike at other Wolsey Lodges you're not expected to share a table, and the smart conservatory has plenty of wicker chairs and pine tables to cater for non-resident diners as well as staying guests. Bedrooms, like the rest of the house, are fitted out with the needs of guests, rather than the self-expression of interior designers, in mind; the Garden Room, with its Victorian Gothic detail, is probably the most stylish.

○ Closed Chr; restaurant closed Sun eve ⊿ In Campsea Ashe village. Private car park ⊨ 1 single, 2 twin, 5 double, 1 four-poster; all with bathroom/WC ⊘ Restaurant/conservatory, dining-room, bar, lounge, TV room, garden; conference facilities (max 16 people incl up to 9 residential); early suppers for children ⅃ No wheelchair access ● No dogs in public rooms and some bedrooms; no smoking ⊟ Access, Amex, Diners, Visa £ Single £35, twin/double £50, four-poster £60; deposit required. Set D £16 (1996 prices). Special breaks available

CARBIS BAY Cornwall map 1

Boskerris Hotel

Boskerris Road, Carbis Bay, St Ives TR26 2NQ
TEL: (01736) 795295 FAX: (01736) 798632

Family holiday base overlooking the sea and convenient for St Ives.

Traffic congestion being what it is, Carbis Bay offers a relaxing, wider-street alternative to St Ives. Boskerris House is in a quiet side-street with sweeping views over the sea. Over the last year, Marie Monk and her son Spencer have refurbished many of the bedrooms, installing double glazing and inset ceiling lights, changing the wallpaper, modernising the fabrics and even adding panels to old wardrobe doors to make them more interesting. The effects are very pleasing and the gold-standard rooms are these new ones. Other bedrooms are still comfortable, and all the bathrooms have windows, which spare guests from noisy ventilators. The lounge and dining-room both have sea views, the one drawback being the ugly flat roof immediately in front. There are lots of board games piled up in the lounge for rainy days, and a small games room in a shed in the car park. Unpretentious dinner menus change daily on a fortnightly cycle: sensible soups, steak and kidney pie, and bread-and-butter pudding are staples.

◗ Closed Nov to Easter ☒ Take St Ives exit at roundabout on A30; Boskerris Road is third turning on right in Carbis Bay. Private car park ⛐ 2 single, 4 twin, 9 double, 4 family rooms; all exc singles with bathroom/WC; TV, room service, direct-dial telephone; hair-dryer on request ✅ Restaurant, bar, 3 lounges, TV room, drying-room, games room, garden; putting green, heated outdoor swimming-pool; early suppers for children; toys, baby-listening ♿ Wheelchair access to hotel (3 steps) and restaurant, 2 ground-floor bedrooms ⬤ No dogs in public rooms; no smoking in restaurant ▭ Access, Amex, Diners, Switch, Visa £ Single £32 to £36, single occupancy of twin/double £39 to £46, twin/double £72 to £83, family room from £72; deposit required. Set D £17.50; bar lunches available. Special breaks available

---

CAREY Hereford & Worcester map 5

Cottage of Content

Carey, Hereford HR2 6NG
TEL: (01432) 840242 FAX: (01432) 840208

Interesting country pub in a charming Herefordshire backwater.

As you drive along the winding road that leads to Carey you somehow expect to see Joe Grundy leading his dairy herd to the milking shed, or Phil Archer at the wheel of his tractor. Even the Bull, Ambridge's famous watering-hole, would defer in the charm stakes to the Cottage of Content, a curious hybrid of rustic hostelry and roses-around-the-door country abode. Approaching from the direction of Ross-on-Wye you'll see the most emphatically cottage-style part first, and it may take a glance at the traditional, sun-bleached pub sign to convince you that this really is an inn. Once inside you'll find all the classic country-pub paraphernalia: rustic chairs, wheel-back chairs and time-worn trestle tables, pewter tankards, lots of pendant copper and hops hanging over the bar, and even a couple of dogs, Shadow and Storm. Wander through to the restaurant section and you'll see beams, strapping on the walls, chintzy drapes and an assortment of fish prints. Food is imaginative – perhaps wild tiger prawns in garlic butter, followed by roast duck in a blueberry and red wine sauce, and locally made damson and sloe-gin ice cream.

The simple bedrooms are bursting with character, boasting a medley of beams, crooked walls and exposed stone, cheerful floral soft furnishings and assorted good old furniture.

◗ Closed 25 Dec ☒ Turn off A49 towards Hoarwithy; pub is 1½ miles from Hoarwithy village. Private car park ⛐ 4 double; all with bathroom/WC; TV ✅ Restaurant, 2 bars, garden ♿ No wheelchair access ⬤ None ▭ Access, Amex, Switch, Visa £ Single occupancy of double £35, double £48; deposit required. Alc L, D £13. Special breaks available

---

CARLISLE Cumbria map 10

The Beeches

Wood Street, Carlisle CA1 2SF
TEL: (01228) 511962

Inviting Georgian B&B in unexpected conservation area.

After going past an off-licence and a chip shop, it's quite a surprise to turn down Wood Street and discover a delightful vista of white, pink and green cottages, wrought-iron lamp-posts and a red-brick church. The pretty, pink Beeches wears its date (1767) with pride above the front door and it is no surprise to discover that it was once a farmhouse even though it's now just a mile from Carlisle city centre. Across the threshold you step into a thoroughly feminine environment, with lots of pretty lace, china plates on the wall, and candles on the dining tables. The ubiquitous Laura Ashley fabrics and wallpapers are more than just proprietorial whim: Heather Kilpatrick actually works for the company. With only three bedrooms, the Kilpatricks like to treat their guests like friends and there's only one breakfast table, to encourage intimacy. None of the bedrooms is *en suite*, but they're all extremely comfortable, with rag-rolled walls, magazines piled up on blanket boxes, and curtains tied back with ribbon. Prior notice is required for dinner.

◑ Open all year　⬕ Leave M6 at Junction 43 for A69 to Carlisle; after 1 mile, turn left into Victoria Road (with the Esso station to your right); at top of hill turn sharp left into Wood Street. Private car park　⬔ 2 twin, 1 double; TV, hair-dryer, trouser press ⬗ Dining-room, garden　♿ No wheelchair access　⬤ No dogs; no smoking in public rooms　▭ None accepted　£ Single occupancy of twin/double £20 to £25, twin/double £32 to £38; deposit required. Special breaks available

---

CARLTON-IN-COVERDALE **North Yorkshire**　　　　　map 8

Foresters Arms ☆

Carlton-in-Coverdale,
Nr Leyburn DL8 4BB
TEL: (01969) 640272 (AND FAX)

COUNTY HOTEL OF THE YEAR

Traditional Dales pub with cottage-style rooms and adventurous cuisine.

If you get the chance, approach the Foresters the long way around, coming from Kettlewell along the twisting road that skirts Great Whernside and runs the length of Coverdale, passing through some wild and wonderful scenery. The long drive enhances the agreeable sense of Carlton's remoteness and the pleasure of arriving at this lovely seventeenth-century pub. The bars are everything you would expect with flagstoned floors, beamed ceilings and open fires and the place has the feel of a real local – in fact, if you call in on a Tuesday night in winter you may find yourself caught up in the passion of the Upper Wensleydale Darts League.

But it's the food that will really stay in your memory. From a long and adventurous menu our inspector enjoyed a boneless quail with wild mushroom pâté, followed by a fillet of sea-bream with scallops in garlic cream. Whether you eat in the bar or in the restaurant, with its low-beamed ceiling and powder-pink walls, the service is calm, unhurried and knowledgeable. There are three bright cottage-style bedrooms with pine furniture and combinations of yellows and blues in the décor. Fresh fruit is supplied but toiletries are minimal. Two of the rooms have the view towards the back where you might see lambs leaping over the Viking burial mound.

◑ Open all year; restaurant closed Sun & Mon eves ⤢ Off A684, 5 miles south-west of Leyburn. Private car park ⨼ 1 twin, 2 double; twin with bathroom/WC, doubles with shower/WC; TV, room service, hair-dryer ✅ Restaurant, 2 bars, drying-room; early suppers for children ⬥ No wheelchair access ● Dogs in bar and 1 bedroom only ▭ Access, Delta, Switch, Visa £ Single occupancy of twin/double £30, twin/double £55; deposit required. Alc L, D £19; light lunches available. Special breaks available

---

CARTMEL **Cumbria** map 8

Aynsome Manor

Cartmel, Nr Grange-over-Sands LA11 6HH
TEL: (01539) 536653 FAX: (01539) 536016

Old manor house with period features, fine food and friendly, professional service.

Antony Varley arrived at Aynsome Manor in 1981 'to take life a little more quietly'. Sixteen years later he may now get the chance, as his son Christopher and daughter-in-law Andrea are in charge, ensuring the hotel runs as smoothly and as individually as always. A veteran of many visits writes, 'Over the years my wife and I have always been impressed by the sheer professionalism and I am happy to report this continues to be the case. Personal idiosyncrasies – like blankets instead of duvets, Tio Pepe in the downstairs lounge at 6.30pm – were dealt with as a matter of course and without asking.' This manor house in the midst of the south Lakes farming country goes back to 1750, and the dark-grey rendering and stone porch can have quite a forbidding look, an impression immediately dispelled as you settle down by the Adam fireplace in the spacious residents' lounge. The dining-room has perhaps the best-preserved original features, with panelled walls, a coffered ceiling and tongue-and-ball mouldings. 'The food was of the high quality, and the host was always on hand to select an appropriate wine from the cellars,' wrote one impressed guest, while another 'had gravad lax and beef Wellington followed by a good lemon mousse. We thought it excellent and could not fault either the quality of the food or the service.' Bedrooms are pleasantly understated with some interesting features, such as the massive A-frame timbers in Room 12A, the old 'wig room', the oak four-poster in Room 8, and the *en suite* bathroom hewn from the thick stone walls of Room 3.

◑ Closed 2 to 25 Jan ⤢ ½ mile before Cartmel village on road south from A590. Private car park ⨼ 5 twin, 6 double, 1 four-poster; family rooms available; some in annexe; all with bathroom/WC exc 1 twin with shower/WC; TV, limited room service, direct-dial telephone, clock radio ✅ Dining-room, bar, 2 lounges, drying-room, garden; early suppers for children; baby-listening ⬥ No wheelchair access ● No children under 5 in dining-room eves; no dogs in public rooms; no smoking in dining-room ▭ Access, Amex, Delta, Switch, Visa £ Single occupancy of twin/double £50 to £60, twin/double £86 to £104, four-poster £86 to £104 (rates incl dinner); deposit required. Set L £11.50, D £16.50. Special breaks available

Uplands

Haggs Lane, Cartmel, Nr Grange-over-Sands LA11 6HD
TEL: (01539) 536248   FAX: (01539) 536848

Small country-house hotel offering excellent food and stylish modern décor.

The Uplands sign hanging in the lane a little way out of the village proclaims 'in the Miller Howe manner', flagging up the hotel's pedigree. Tom and Diana Peter have been running their small country house for a dozen years now and have fine reputations in their own right. While the smart, contemporary furnishings in subtle pale shades that predominate throughout the house make for relaxing and comfortable surroundings, it is Tom's cooking that is the major attraction. Guests gather for aperitifs among the Impressionist prints in the lounge before moving through to dinner; the table in the window overlooks the Leven estuary. Tom was one of John Tovey's head chefs at Miller Howe for 12 years, as aficionados may detect in the inventive combinations of flavours and the extravagant vegetable dishes. You might find main courses such as saddle of hare in Madeira sauce or duckling with honey and Calvados accompanied by carrots with coriander, leeks with almonds and beetroot with lime. The five bedrooms are adequate rather than generous for size, but individual and all bright and cheerful with lots of fresh white woodwork and plain walls showing off prints of country scenes.

◑ Closed Jan & Feb; restaurant closed Mon eve   ⤢ From Cartmel village with Pig and Whistle pub on right, turn immediately left up Haggs Lane; hotel is 1 mile up this road on left. Private car park   ⬕ 3 twin, 2 double; 2 with bathroom/WC, most with shower/WC; TV, room service, hair-dryer   ⊘ Restaurant, lounge, drying-room, garden   ⅋ No wheelchair access   ● No children under 8; no dogs in public rooms; no smoking in restaurant   ▭ Access, Amex, Delta, Visa   £ Single occupancy of twin/double £68 to £78, twin/double £96 to £136 (rates incl dinner). Set L £14.50, D £26. Special breaks available

---

CARTMEL FELL Cumbria   map 8

Lightwood Country Guesthouse

Cartmel Fell, Nr Bowland Bridge, Grange-over-Sands LA11 6NP
TEL: (01539) 531454

Homely farm guesthouse in the fells near Windermere.

When Evelyn Cervetti gives directions to the secluded stone farmhouse she runs with husband Fideo, she sends you the long way round: it's easier to find approaching from the west, among the sheep-farming fells above the Lyth Valley. But the real bonus of this route is the magnificent view back over the lake as you climb up from the southern reaches of Windermere. Fideo's latest exploits involve dismantling an old barn, having already converted one shippen (where hay was stored), shifting several tons of stone in the process. The four rooms in the shippen have been fitted with lots of pine and have cream-painted rough plaster walls. Those in the farmhouse are cosy with a more cottagey feel, and are now all *en suite* thanks to Fideo's handiwork. On one side the views are of up-and-down fields framed by dry-stone walls, on the other is a pretty landscaped garden with a pond. In the sitting-room, the alcove cupboard beside the wood-burning stove overflows with books and games, while a little conservatory at the back is like a tropical rainforest sprouting from makeshift pots. Dinners feature lots of roasts and casseroles in Evelyn's quite traditional repertoire.

◗ Closed Chr ⊅ 2 miles from A592 between Fell Foot Park and Bowland Bridge. Private car park ⊫ 2 twin, 3 double, 3 family rooms; some in annexe; most with bathroom/WC, 2 with shower/WC; room service; TV in some rooms; hair-dryer on request ⌘ Dining-room, lounge, drying-room, conservatory, garden ♿ No wheelchair access ● No dogs; smoking in lounge only ▭ Switch, Visa £ Single occupancy of twin/double £25 to £30, twin/double £46 to £50, family room £55 to £60; deposit required. Set D £14. Special breaks available

---

CASTLE ASHBY Northamptonshire map 5

Falcon Hotel

Castle Ashby, Northampton NN7 1LF
TEL: (01604) 696200   FAX: (01604) 696673

A stylish hotel constructed around a sixteenth-century inn.

The Falcon Hotel is a visual feast, thanks to proprietor Jo Watson's professional expertise in interior design. She has coupled traditional, old-inn elements such as beams, exposed stone walls and flagstones (best evidenced in the Cellar Bar) with features such as stencilled walls, glasses coloured to match the wallpaper in the restaurant, and maybe a single large candle burning in a sitting area. Bedrooms exhibit the same flair. Those in the main building are antiquey; the majority, in annexe cottages 75 yards down the road, employ tartan, ribbon and rich floral patterns, as well as smart pine units, whose painted knobs co-ordinate with the rooms' scheme. Flashes of primary colour appear in bathrooms, along with magnifying mirrors and bathrobes. All bedrooms are priced the same, so ask for a big one; some are singularly small.

The hotel's quality extends into its good, rich, modern English cuisine; the fixed-price menu offers a generous number of choices (including vegetarian options), and is competitively priced. The enterprising Watsons also offer a wide range of special breaks, although you may prefer just to potter around the handsome, sleepy village – part of the Marquess of Northampton's estate.

◗ Open all year ⊅ Leave A428 Northampton-Bedford Road at the signpost to Castle Ashby. Private car park ⊫ 4 single, 4 twin, 8 double; most in annexe; all with bathroom/WC exc 1 single with shower/WC; TV, room service, hair-dryer, trouser press, direct-dial telephone ⌘ Restaurant, 2 bars, lounge, garden; conference facilities (max 20 people incl up to 16 residential); early suppers for children ♿ Wheelchair access to hotel, restaurant, WC (M,F), 5 ground-floor bedrooms, 1 specially equipped for disabled people ● No children in restaurant after 8pm; no dogs in restaurant ▭ Access, Amex, Delta, Switch, Visa £ Single £63, single occupancy of twin/double £63, twin/double £75; deposit required. Set L, D £19.50; alc L, D £23 (1996 prices). Special breaks available

CASTLE CARY **Somerset**   map 2

Bond's

Ansford, Castle Cary BA7 7JP
TEL: (01963) 350464 (AND FAX)

Highly imaginative cooking at a smart Georgian town house.

Kevin and Yvonne Bond see food as the great strength of their small hotel and
restaurant, and their devotion to quality and originality is rare. The red-brick
Georgian house, facing the main road to the front and with views over pastures
and hills to the rear, contains seven neat bedrooms, all of different size and
design, and priced accordingly. Downstairs, sofas and chairs are clustered on
opposite sides of the fireplace and grandfather clock in the smart salon-cum-bar.
Across the entrance hall, the dining-room is fresher and lighter, decorated in
light green and salmon shades, and generally plain – presumably to allow the
food to take centre-stage. Menus feature so many mouthwatering combinations
that it's hard to make a choice – and equally hard to believe that Yvonne has no
formal training. Wok-fried chicken livers and bacon served with green leaves
and orange and mint vinaigrette may be followed by monkfish with lime and
coconut cream, or coriander and walnut-crusted roast rabbit, finished off with a
deliciously revitalised old favourite – rice pudding caramelised with mango. The
vegetables are also prepared with creative flair: tomatoes stuffed with walnut
purée, carrots with fresh coriander. Service is efficient and welcoming, if on the
formal side.

◑ Closed Chr ⬚ On A371, 400 yards from Castle Cary station. Private car park
⬚ 2 twin, 5 double; all with bathroom/WC exc 1 double with shower/WC; TV, room
service, hair-dryer, trouser press, direct-dial telephone ⬚ Restaurant, bar, lounge,
garden; early suppers for children; baby-listening ⬚ No wheelchair access ◐ No
children under 8 exc babies; no dogs ⬚ Access, Visa £ Single occupancy of
twin/double £38 to £51, twin/double £60 to £80; deposit required. Set D £12.50; alc D
£20; light lunches available (1996 prices). Special breaks available

---

CASTLE COMBE **Wiltshire**   map 2

Manor House Hotel

Castle Combe, Chippenham SN14 7HR
TEL: (01249) 782206 FAX: (01249) 782159

*Formal but friendly luxury, peaceful grounds and lavish bedrooms
in one of England's prettiest villages.*

With rows of honey-coloured Cotswold-stone cottages, Castle Combe has claims
to being England's prettiest village. The Jacobean Manor House is at its heart,
although the curving drive, immaculate striped lawns and 26 acres of surrounding parkland, golf course and gardens provide seclusion from the crowds.
Like the village, the gracious building has much traditional charm – inglenook
fireplaces, dark panelling, elaborate cornices, iron and crystal chandeliers,
leather chesterfields – but guests are as likely to be drawn by modern comforts.
Top bedrooms are as luxurious as they come and even the 'paupers' staying in

the hotel's private row of cottages or the former stables do well, although furnishings are more standardised. There's a choice of rooms for relaxation – the elegant fresh, yellow and blue drawing-room, the more clubby Shakespeare room, or the small, flagstoned conservatory, which catches the morning sun. The restaurant (in an unobtrusive extension, with suitably baronial features) offers an expensive à la carte mix of classical and nouvelle. More affordable 'seasonal selections' might include smoked turbot with foie gras and butter sauce, or crispy duck confit with garlic hash and pea purée. Despite the expense (and apparent formality), service is unpompous, friendly and welcoming.

● Open all year   ⚡ From Chippenham take the A420 towards Bristol; fork left on to the B4039 to Castle Combe. Private car park   ⤶ 1 twin, 21 twin/double, 9 double, 7 four-poster, 2 suites, 1 cottage; family rooms available; some in annexe; all with bathroom/WC; TV, 24-hour room service, hair-dryer, direct-dial phone; tea/coffee-making facilities and mini-bar in some rooms   ✓ Restaurant, bar, 3 lounges, library, conservatory, games room, garden; conference facilities (max 60 people incl up to 41 residential); fishing, golf, heated outdoor swimming-pool, tennis; early suppers for children; babysitting, baby-listening   ♿ Wheelchair access to hotel, restaurant, WC (unisex), 2 ground-floor bedrooms   ● No dogs; no smoking   ▭ Access, Amex, Diners, Switch, Visa   £ Single occupancy of twin/double from £100, twin/double from £100, four-poster from £190, family room from £190, suite from £235, cottage £350; deposit required. Continental B £9, cooked B £11; set L £17/19, D £35; alc D £44. Special breaks available

---

Chadlington House

Chapel Road, Chadlington OX7 3LZ
TEL: (01608) 676437   FAX: (01608) 676503

Small country hotel with large old-fashioned rooms and highly regarded hospitality.

Rita and Peter Oxford have had more experience than most in the hotel business, and try as they might to go into retirement, they're still going strong. Little has changed at Chadlington House in over 20 years. The Oxfords have managed their mock Tudor manor house with notable enthusiasm, prompting readers to report on their helpfulness and tireless commitment to their guests. The bedrooms are constantly being improved with the Oxfords doing much of the work themselves. All rooms are now *en suite*, though some have small shower rooms only. With their pale muted décor and mix of modern and old-fashioned furniture, the three at the front are the best choice as they're the largest and have views over the Evenlode valley. Some rooms now sport patchwork quilts after recent refurbishment, and all have lots of goodies and have been well thought through, so the hair-dryer is next to the mirror and the towels are soft. With its picture windows, old-fashioned chairs and well-spaced square tables, the dining-room has something of a seaside guesthouse feel to it and people tend to chat with other tables over breakfast. Evening meals of straightforward English cooking are served on request.

◑ Closed Jan & Feb ⊿ Chadlington is 2 miles south of Chipping Norton. Private car park ⊫→ 2 single, 2 twin, 5 double, 1 four-poster; family room available; most with bathroom/WC, some with shower/WC; TV, hair-dryer, direct-dial telephone
⌧ Dining-room, bar, lounge, drying-room, garden; early suppers for children ﴾ No wheelchair access ● No dogs in public rooms; no smoking ▭ Access, Visa
£ Single £30 to £35, single occupancy of twin/double £35 to £40, twin/double £45 to £50, four-poster £55 to £60, family room from £60; deposit required. Special breaks available

---

CHAGFORD Devon   map 1

Easton Court Hotel

Easton Cross, Chagford TQ13 8JL
TEL: (01647) 433469 (AND FAX)

Pretty thatched cottage with secluded garden which inspired Evelyn Waugh.

Evelyn Waugh was staying at Easton Court when he wrote *Brideshead Revisited*, and Patrick Leigh-Fermor also took refuge here to work on *The Traveller's Tree*, neither of which seems a surprise once you've stepped inside this inspirational partially fifteenth-century thatched cottage. Gordon and Judy Parker are new owners and have been busily refurbishing it to emphasise its cottagey aspects; the dining-room now has beautifully polished floorboards and several of the bedrooms have been redecorated, with the baths given tongue and groove side panelling. The lounge remains much as it was, with a huge stone fireplace, exposed stone walls and low ceiling beams. Waugh's imagination was sparked off by the bar, which is similarly unchanged, but there are plans to open what was once the library as a second sitting-room. Probably the finest bedroom is Room 4 with a four-poster bed, exposed stone walls and views over the adjoining rabbit-filled fields. In keeping with Easton Court's character, four-course dinners stick to the fairly traditional: perhaps gateau of melon with citrus sauce, a mushroom soup laced with sherry, roast rack of lamb in rosemary and redcurrant *jus*, and grilled bananas in toffee sauce.

◑ Closed Jan ⊿ From A30 take A382 exit at Whiddon Down; follow signs to Moretonhampstead; hotel is 3 miles along this road on left-hand side. Private car park
⊫→ 2 twin, 4 double, 2 four-poster; most with bathroom/WC, 2 with shower/WC; TV, direct-dial telephone; hair-dryer on request ⌧ Dining-room, bar, lounge, library, garden ﴾ Wheelchair access to hotel (1 step) and restaurant, 2 ground-floor bedrooms ● No children under 12; no dogs in public rooms; no smoking in some public rooms ▭ Access, Amex, Switch, Visa £ Single occupancy of twin/double £40 to £48, twin/double £80 to £96, four-poster £86 to £102; deposit required. Set D £22 (prices valid till Jan 1997). Special breaks available

---

Many hotels put up their tariffs in the spring. You are advised to confirm prices when you book.

Mill End

Sandy Park, Chagford TQ13 8JN
TEL: (01647) 432282   FAX: (01647) 433106

Inviting whitewashed old millhouse, close to the National Trust's Castle Drogo estate.

'A surplus of charm' is how one satisfied guest summed up a stay at Mill End, going on to praise owner Mr Craddock for 'delightful and informative conversation concerning the surrounding area and the whole of England ...language, cultures and history!' Once you've heard Mr Craddock's discourse on the striking heraldic shield above the fireplace in the lounge you understand exactly what was meant; the shield used to hang in Bideford Town Hall and he has analysed its design to suggest it may date back to the reign of James II. The lounge is big and bright with lots of chintzy chairs, but should it not match your mood, you can retreat to one of several smaller public rooms, each with its own character. The bedrooms are also individual; those in the original building having the most character, although those in the newer annexe have the bonus of french windows opening directly on to a garden patio. Dinners in the curvy restaurant manage pleasingly adventurous innovations without losing sight of popular favourites; you could, for example, start with a kipper, potato, whisky and bacon pâté, and move on to noisette of English lamb, finishing off with Kentucky chocolate pie. Many of Mill End's guests come for the fishing on the River Teign, which flows through the well-kept grounds, but the hotel makes just as good a base for those who want to walk or visit local National Trust properties.

○ Closed 6 to 16 Dec and 6 to 16 Jan   ⬚ Turn south from A30 at Whiddon Down taking A382 signposted Moretonhampstead. Private car park   ⬚ 2 single, 3 twin, 10 double, 2 family rooms; some in annexe; all with bathroom/WC; TV, room service, hair-dryer, direct-dial telephone   ⬚ Restaurant, bar, lounge, TV room; fishing; early suppers for children; baby-listening   ⬚ No wheelchair access   ● No dogs in public rooms; no smoking in restaurant   ⬚ Amex, Delta, Diners, Switch, Visa   £ Single £35, single occupancy of twin/double £50, twin/double £80, family room £80; deposit required. Set L £14.50; alc D from £14.50. Special breaks available

---

CHARINGWORTH Gloucestershire   map 5

Charingworth Manor

Charingworth, Nr Chipping Campden GL55 6NS
TEL: (01386) 593555   FAX: (01386) 593353

Striking combination of grand, medieval character and end-of-millennium leisure facilities.

When a hotel's brochure features an Ordnance Survey grid reference for helicopter pilots, you know you're talking serious money. Despite its proximity to the honey-pot village of Chipping Campden, Charingworth Manor is not the easiest place to find, so even those who arrive by more prosaic means might find the information useful. The creeper-draped fourteenth-century house flaunts all the insignia of its age – golden ashlar façade, painted beams, leaded windows – all set amid attractive grounds, but combines these with glitzy leisure facilities, including a tempting classical-style swimming-pool.

There's a choice of restful sitting-rooms, one of which retains the chevron-emblazoned beams which are believed to date back to 1316. There's no bar, as the hotel likes to emphasise the country-house and personal-service elements. The restaurant basks in a soft pink glow, and features mullioned windows and the odd beam to testify to its age. The three-course set dinner bears a hefty price tag (stray on to à la carte territory and you'll have to dig even deeper) but the ambitious food is generally acclaimed; perhaps rabbit and potato rillette flavoured with fresh herbs, followed by grilled red snapper on a bed of mixed leaves with a caper and almond beurre noisette, and iced strawberry parfait.

Bedrooms are spacious and tastefully furnished with a sprinkling of antiques and carefully co-ordinated fabrics. As you might expect, those in the old house have more authentic character, but there's a special frisson to be derived from knowing that the stylish courtyard rooms were once the manor's pigsty!

◑ Open all year ⤷ Turn off A429 on to B4035 towards Chipping Campden. Hotel is 3 miles on the right. Private car park ⤶ 21 twin/double, 2 four-poster, 3 suites; all with bathroom/WC; TV, room service, hair-dryer, trouser press, direct-dial telephone; no tea/coffee-making facilities in rooms ⚟ Restaurant, 3 lounges, games room, garden; conference facilities (max 34 people incl up to 26 residential); sauna, solarium, heated indoor swimming-pool, tennis, steam room; early suppers for children; babysitting, baby-listening ♿ No wheelchair access ● Dogs by arrangement only ▭ Access, Amex, Delta, Diners, Switch, Visa £ Single occupancy of twin/double from £95, twin/double from £132, four-poster £222, suite £239; deposit required. Set L from £16, D from £32.50. Special breaks available

---

CHARTHAM Kent   map 3

Thruxted Oast

Mystole, Chartham, Nr Canterbury CT4 7BX
TEL: (01227) 730080

Stylishly converted oast house with luxurious rooms and thoughtful, friendly hosts.

When you first see Thruxted Oast it's difficult to imagine how it looked in 1986 when Tim and Hilary Derouet bought it as a five-bay, 90-ft-long, disused oast house and barn. Nowadays it is a comfortable family home where guests are made to feel very welcome indeed. Breakfast is served in the farmhouse-style kitchen around a well-scrubbed pine table, and might feature freshly laid eggs from the Derouets' hens and perhaps some home-grown rhubarb. The bedrooms all have stripped pine furniture, locally made patchwork quilts and lots of thoughtful touches such as hand cream, shoe polish, hot-water bottles, detergent and even disposable toilet seat covers – not that you'd ever need them, as the whole house is spotlessly clean. Chaucer's Room, a large twin, has excellent views to the well-tended garden and the fields beyond, and a large collection of antique bottles and jars which Hilary collects on regular forays to car boot sales. A framed poem in the room reads – 'We're glad to have you as our guest and hope you have a good night's rest. Tomorrow you again may roam, but while you're here just feel at home', and the Derouets certainly do go out of their way to make sure that this is the case.

○ Open all year ⚡ From Canterbury take A28 Ashford road; after crossing bypass, turn left into St Nicholas Road; continue for 2 miles until crossroads; continue straight on – house is near bottom of hill, on right. Private car park 🚗 3 twin; all with shower/WC; TV, hair-dryer, direct-dial telephone ✓ Lounge, drying-room, garden; croquet ⅙ No wheelchair access ● No children under 8; no dogs; no smoking in bedrooms ☐ Access, Amex, Diners, Visa £ Single occupancy of twin £68, twin £78; deposit required

---

CHEDDLETON Staffordshire | map 5

Choir Cottage & Choir House

Ostlers Lane, Cheddleton, Nr Leek ST13 7HS
TEL: (01538) 360561

B&B provided in two feminine, four-poster bedrooms in a tiny old cottage.

Two bedrooms alone take up the whole of the diminutive Choir Cottage, a 350-year-old dwelling once used as a resting place by ostlers. Each has its own front door, as well as lattice windows, beams and a four-poster bed. The fussy décor takes the form of frilly drapes and dainty floral patterns. The Pine Room can be used as family accommodation, while the Rose Room has french windows that open on to a private patio. Owners Elaine and William Sutcliffe live next door in Choir House, an undistinguished though sprucely kept modern building, where guests can relax in a well-furnished lounge and dine in a pretty conservatory. Charging an extra £2.50 for a cooked full English breakfast is a strange practice for such a small establishment. Straightforward three-course dinners are also offered, served usually at around 7pm, with a choice at each stage; bring your own wine.

○ Closed 25 Dec ⚡ In Cheddleton turn off A520 opposite Red Lion Inn into Hollow Lane, then turn left (200 yards after the church) into Ostlers Lane. The cottage is on the right, halfway up the hill. Private car park 🚗 2 four-poster; family room available; 1 with bathroom/WC, 1 with shower/WC; TV, room service, hair-dryer, direct-dial telephone telephone, clock radio ✓ Dining-room, lounge, conservatory, garden ⅙ No wheelchair access ● No children under 5; no dogs; no smoking in bedrooms ☐ None accepted £ Single occupancy of four-poster £30, four-poster £45, family room from £57; deposit required. Cooked B £2.50, set D £15; packed lunches available. Special breaks available

---

CHEDINGTON Dorset | map 2

Chedington Court

Chedington, Beaminster DT8 3HY
TEL: (01935) 891265 FAX: (01935) 891442

Unassuming country manor with wonderful views and large rooms.

Hilary and Philip Chapman's mock-Jacobean country manor has a glorious hilltop setting amidst 100 acres of gardens tumbling down in terraces towards the plain, each tier becoming wilder, and hiding duck ponds, a grotto and a maze of paths and stairways; it also has a quiet, unassuming charm. The interior has none of the carefully manicured tweeness found in many country houses, although there are plenty of fine antiques and traditional trappings – a stone fireplace in the panelled library, rugs over the bare floor and an iron chandelier in the baronial entrance hall. There's a sense of tradition among staff, too; the Chapmans have been here over 20 years, and some of the staff are almost as long-serving. The large, comfortable bedrooms vary. Four-Poster has a dark, intricately carved bed, Rhododendron is a huge twin with lace coverlets and fresh pink and green colours, whilst Dorset, with similar colours and wonderful views from the bay window, was the original master bedroom and is probably the nicest. Dinner menus change daily, featuring perhaps rack of lamb with red pepper confit or monkfish with cumin and lime, and are served either in the restaurant or terracotta-tiled conservatory.

◑ Closed Jan ⊅ Just off A356 Crewkerne to Dorchester road; 4½ miles south-east of Crewkerne at Winyard's Gap. Private car park ⤶ 4 twin, 4 double, 1 four-poster, 1 family room; all with bathroom/WC exc 1 single with shower/WC; TV, room service, hair-dryer, direct-dial telephone, radio; trouser press on request ⊘ Restaurant, bar, lounge, drying-room, library, conservatory, games room, garden; conference facilities (max 30 people incl up to 10 residential); golf, croquet, snooker; early suppers for children; babysitting, baby-listening ♿ No wheelchair access ● No children under 9 in restaurant eves; no dogs in public rooms ⊟ Access, Amex, Visa
£ Single occupancy of twin/double £55 to £88, twin/double £89 to £135, four-poster £135, family room £141; deposit required. Set D £27.50. Special breaks available

---

CHELTENHAM Gloucestershire   map 5

Cleeve Hill Hotel

Cleeve Hill, Cheltenham GL52 3PR
TEL: (01242) 672052

A stylish B&B with thoughtful and welcoming hosts.

As the name suggests, Cleeve Hill Hotel occupies an upland spot, and from this elevated position the hotel – particularly the front and the rear-facing bedrooms – boasts excellent views of the Malvern hills and Cleeve Common. The spacious and bright lounge area, decorated in pastel pinks and greens with several sofas and easy chairs, is very comfortable. Breakfast is served in the conservatory – and what a breakfast it is! There is a buffet of cereals, a large selection of prepared fresh fruit and a choice of fruit juices. As you savour this light breakfast, you can order a cooked breakfast to follow. Marian and John Enstone's attention to detail is outstanding, and they offer a choice of milk, from full fat to skimmed, with your morning tea or coffee. Sophie, the family dog (a white fluffy Bichon Frise, who looks so much like a lamb that even the sheep in the fields behind the house get confused), is so well trained that she will not set foot inside the conservatory, even when offered the odd sausage by well-meaning guests! The bedrooms are large and very stylishly decorated – Room 5, for example, has a sitting area with a deep-blue sofa and a couple of steps leading up to the bedroom.

◑ Closed Chr & New Year ⬚ The hotel is situated between Prestbury and Winchcombe on the B4632, 2½ miles from Cheltenham. Private car park ⬚ 1 single, 1 twin, 5 double, 1 family room, 1 suite; most with bathroom/WC, some with shower/WC; TV, room service, hair-dryer, direct-dial telephone; trouser press on request ⬗ Dining-room/conservatory, bar, lounge, drying-room, garden ⬚ No wheelchair access ● No children under 8; no dogs; no smoking ⬚ Access, Amex, Delta, Visa £ Single £45, single occupancy of twin/double £50 to £60, twin/double £60 to £75, family room £75 to £85, suite £75; deposit required. Special breaks available

Hotel on the Park

Evesham Road, Cheltenham GL52 2AH
TEL: (01242) 518898 FAX: (01242) 511526

Regency elegance in a tasteful house well positioned for savouring the spa town's considerable delights.

It's only fitting that a Regency town house as characteristically white as the Hotel on the Park should be the domain of a cat called Ebony. The classical grace exemplified by the Ionic columns of the portico is sustained in the reception lobby with its checkerboard floor and ticking grandfather clock. A large bronze of a steeplechaser in the restful bar and drawing-room celebrates one of Cheltenham's most famous diversions. Here guests enjoy pre-dinner drinks, perched on floral chairs in delicate pastels. The deliciously symmetrical library is more formal, and reveres the age of reason with pedimented bookshelves and dark buttonback seating.

Ornate polychrome plasterwork cornices join traditional Regency stripes on the drapes and chairs in the light and graceful restaurant which overlooks Pittville Park. A couple of dishes of the day give additional options to those not seduced by the seasonal menus: perhaps cappuccino of mushroom and madeira with celeriac beignets, home-made herbal sorbet, followed by loin of venison with pear and cider risotto, and hot banana and bitter chocolate soufflé.

Bedrooms are well equipped and irreproachably stylish in a designer-nostalgic way, using rich, heavy fabrics to set off well-chosen, antique and other furnishings. The superior rooms, like Joseph Pitt, are worth the supplement they command. For a real splurge try the top-of-the-range Duke of Wellington Room.

◑ Open all year ⬚ Opposite Pittville Park approximately 1 mile from centre. Private car park ⬚ 4 twin, 6 double, 1 four-poster, 1 suite; all with bathroom/WC; TV, room service, hair-dryer, direct-dial telephone ⬗ Restaurant, bar, lounge, library, garden; conference facilities (max 20 people incl up to 12 residential); early suppers for children; baby-listening ⬚ No wheelchair access ● No children under 8; no dogs in public rooms ⬚ Access, Amex, Diners, Visa £ Single occupancy of twin/double £75, twin/double £90 to £110, four-poster £150, suite £120; deposit required. Continental B £6, cooked B £8.50; set L £15, D £21.50; alc L, D £25. Special breaks available

All rooms have tea/coffee-making facilities unless we specify to the contrary.

Lypiatt House

Lypiatt Road, Cheltenham GL50 2QW
TEL: (01242) 224994   FAX: (01242) 224996

A gracious Victorian villa with a laid-back approach and close to all amenities.

As you turn into the gravel drive in the stylish area of Montpellier, you'll see this imposing cream-coloured villa with its triple arched windows tucked away in its own grounds. If you like to be left to your own devices this is the perfect place to stay, because on our visit, after the warm and friendly welcome from Jane Medforth, she preferred to stay in the background and let us make her home our own. There is an immediate feeling of grandeur as you step into the lounge, which is reflected in the luxurious and uncluttered furniture, and enhanced by the high ceilings. Yet the burning log fire and Charlie, the purring cat, add a warm and homely touch. If you would like dinner you need to arrange this on booking, but there is a wide variety of restaurants and pubs a short walk away and an honesty bar is available in the adjoining colonial-style conservatory. The spacious and comfortable bedrooms are furnished in warm pastel colours that mix well with the pine furniture and livened up by colourful patchwork quilts.

○ Open all year ▣ On A40 from London; 3 miles from M5 Junction 11. Private car park ⌷ 2 single, 3 twin, 5 double; all with bathroom/WC exc 1 double with shower/WC; TV, room service, direct-dial telephone, radio ⊘ Dining-room, bar, lounge, drying-room, conservatory, garden; conference facilities (max 26 people incl up to 10 residential); early suppers for children ♿ No wheelchair access ● No dogs ▭ Access, Amex, Visa £ Single £48, single occupancy of twin/double £50, twin/double £65 to £68. Set D £18.50. Special breaks available

---

CHESTER Cheshire   map 7

Castle House

23 Castle Street, Chester CH1 2DS
TEL: (01244) 350354 (AND FAX)

A comfortable B&B off the main roads in the city centre.

To find a coat of arms sculpted in plaster, old timbers and a stone fireplace at the top of the stairs in Castle House is something of a surprise, given its elegant, orderly exterior and its situation on one of the city centre's quieter backstreets close to the River Dee. However, Coyle Marl will be happy to explain that the house actually dates back to the mid-sixteenth century, and that the Georgian front was added only during 'modernisation' carried out in the 1720s.

The little Elizabethan heart of the house serves as a sitting-room and breakfast-room, while small sections of the original timber framing occasionally appear in the five tidy, compact and homely bedrooms that combine some older touches with functional modern furnishings. The two singles share a bathroom just across the corridor. If a little short on space, Castle House is certainly not claustrophobic, and offers good value and friendly accommodation in a historic city.

◑ Open all year ◪ Castle House is adjacent to the police headquarters and racecourse in Chester. On-street parking 🛏 2 single, 1 twin, 1 double, 1 family room; 3 with shower/WC; TV ✓ Dining-room, drying-room, garden; toys, babysitting, baby-listening ♿ No wheelchair access ⊖ No dogs or smoking in public rooms ▭ Access, Visa £ Single £21, single occupancy of twin/double £32, twin/double £42, family room from £48; deposit required. Special breaks available

Green Bough Hotel

£

60 Hoole Road, Chester CH2 3NL
TEL: (01244) 326241 FAX: (01244) 326265

Frills and Victoriana feature in a good-value hotel on the busy outskirts of the city.

Hoole Road is one of Chester's main, arterial, suburban roads, and is lined with big Victorian guesthouses. Green Bough – which is about a mile from the city centre and not very far from the M53 – makes a good-value base, and is also somewhere where you can leave the car while you take the bus into town in order to explore Chester without experiencing its notorious parking problems.

In keeping with the late-Victorian style of the two neighbouring villas, Doreen and David Castle have furnished a 'parlour' (or lounge) with deep-red chesterfield sofas, a magnificent, carved-oak fireplace and a wind-up, working gramophone; and a moody, dark, half-panelled bar with wing-backed armchairs. The bedrooms seem subdued in comparison, although most feature good antique beds and some period furniture among the lacy frills, coronets and plain or flowery wallpaper. The rooms in the annexe are equally comfortable, if slightly plainer.

At the time of our spring inspection, Green Bough offered B&B only; the arrival of a new chef was imminent, however, and David is promising a return to traditional, home-cooked dinners.

◑ Closed Chr & New Year ◪ Leave M53 at Junction 12 and follow A56 into Chester. Green Bough is ½ mile from motorway on the right-hand side. Private car park 🛏 2 single, 1 twin, 12 double, 1 four-poster, 3 family rooms, 1 suite; some in annexe; most with bathroom/WC, some with shower/WC; TV, room service, hair-dryer, direct-dial telephone, clock radio ✓ Dining-room, bar, lounge, TV room; baby-listening ♿ No wheelchair access ⊖ No dogs in public rooms; no smoking in dining-room ▭ Access, Amex, Delta, Switch, Visa £ Single £38 to £39, single occupancy of twin/double £37 to £44, twin/double £52 to £58, four-poster £58, family room £60 to £65, suite £62 to £66; deposit required. Set D £13. Special breaks available

Redland Hotel

64 Hough Green, Chester CH4 8JY
TEL: (01244) 671024 FAX: (01244) 681309

A flamboyant, Victorian-Gothic B&B guesthouse, conveniently situated for the city.

The Victorian builders of the Redland Hotel were clearly enthusiastic about the Gothic revival, and Teresa White, the ebullient, imaginative owner, has certainly gone overboard on Victoriana. The combined result is tremendous fun, and the hotel boasts turrets, pointed arches, ribbed vaulting and stained glass. Aspidistras thrive in the powder-blue lounge, the breakfast-room is oak panelled, half timbered, and features a medieval stone fireplace, while a crusader figure in chain-mail guards the honesty bar in the entrance hall.

Teresa, acting on a tip-off or two from her various sources, has unearthed such treasures as the carved oak four-poster from Perth Castle (now in the Jacobean Room) and the converted gas mantles from a Glasgow tenement (in the Victorian Room), from antique auctions, flea markets and junk shops around the country. And if it can't be found, Teresa will design and commission it, as she did the stained-glass panels in the Regency Room. Some of the rooms are less splendid, but are still furnished with plenty of carefully selected antiques.

Having read this description, you might be expecting the hotel to be a castle on a remote hill; the Redland is actually a detached suburban house on an unexceptional road that is prone to rush-hour traffic. There is nothing unexceptional about the building or the hospitality, however.

◑ Open all year ⤢ On A5104, 1 mile from the city centre. Private car park ⤙ 2 single, 2 twin, 5 double, 3 four-poster; most with bathroom/WC, 4 with shower/WC; TV, hair-dryer, direct-dial telephone ✅ Dining-room, lounge; sauna, solarium No wheelchair access ● No dogs; no smoking in dining-room and some bedrooms ⛶ Amex, Visa £ Single and single occupancy of twin/double £45, twin/double £55 to £65, four-poster £70 to £75; deposit required

---

CHESTER-LE-STREET Co Durham   map 10

Lumley Castle

Chester-le-Street DH3 4NX
TEL: 0191-389 1111   FAX: 0191-387 1437

A fourteenth-century castle with exquisite rooms and courteous, costumed staff.

As you are constantly reminded on a visit to Lumley Castle, this is 'no ordinary hotel', although you're likely to have come to this conclusion long before you arrive. The great, turreted, medieval castle stands foursquare on a hilltop outside the town, inviting awed glances from miles around. Every effort has been made to create a sense of entering a different time, although exactly what time is can vary according to where you find yourself in the hotel. The dimly lit library, with its floor-to-ceiling bookcases and dark-red colour scheme, has the feel of an eighteenth-century club, while an evening in the Baron's Hall, with its stone floor and magnificent stone fireplace, evokes Elizabethan times – a feeling that is compounded by the costumed staff serving you 'fyshe with potato' and 'checkyn in mead', to the accompaniment of troubadours singing ballads in the minstrels' gallery. With its statues, stone columns, vaulted ceiling, and main courses featuring such dishes as pan-fried Dover sole or tenderloin of pork, the main restaurant's atmosphere is a little more rarefied.

The bedrooms have both courtyard and castle locations, and within the castle they are divided into rooms and 'feature' rooms. All are plush and furnished with antiques and fine drapes, but the feature rooms offer something unusual – maybe a bath in the bedroom itself, or a 20-foot-long four-poster bed.

○ Closed 25, 26 Dec & 1 Jan   🡵 Leave A1(M) at exit for Chester-le-Street, and follow A167 south for 3 miles. Private car park   🛏 8 single, 14 twin, 31 double, 6 four-poster, 2 family rooms, 1 suite; all with bathroom/WC; TV, room service, hair-dryer, trouser press, direct-dial telephone   ✅ Restaurant, 2 bars, lounge, library, games room, garden, banquet hall; conference facilities (max 150 people incl up to 62 residential); putting green, croquet, snooker; early suppers for children; babysitting, baby-listening   ♿ No wheelchair access   ● No children in the banquet hall; no dogs   🔲 Access, Amex, Delta, Diners, Switch, Visa   £ Single and single occupancy of twin/double from £83, twin/double from £100, four-poster £135 to £145, family room from £100, suite £180; deposit required. Set L £13.50, D £21; alc D £26.50. Special breaks available

---

CHILGROVE West Sussex

map 3

Forge Cottage ☆

Chilgrove, Nr Chichester PO18 9HX
TEL: (01243) 535333   FAX: (01243) 535363

A designer B&B in a tranquil Sussex hamlet.

Tucked among the fields and hills of the idyllic Chilgrove Valley, this seventeenth-century flint-walled cottage has been restored and tastefully extended to create a cosy and romantic retreat. Owner Neil Rusbridger is a partner and chef in the adjacent White Horse Inn, so top-quality cuisine is on the doorstep (see *The Good Food Guide 1997*). It is clear that the keen eye for presentation and detail which Neil applies to his culinary creations carries over into the stylish décor, which at Forge Cottage blends modern touches effortlessly with traditional elements. Low-slung warped beams abound, and sloping floors and narrow stairs as steep as a ladder add tremendous character. Bright, cheerful tones combined with good-quality modern furniture enhance the light and space in the snug little rooms upstairs, and in Mereden you can relax in the bath while enjoying the views. Wildham has its own entrance from the garden and is the most romantic room, with beamed ceilings and an old bread-oven. The breakfast-room is dominated by a huge navy-blue Aga range in the massively timbered fireplace, and is a delightful place to kick off the day with a spread of local sausages and free-range eggs, bacon from the Chilgrove smokery and home-made yoghurts and jams.

☆ *A star next to the hotel's name indicates that the establishment is new to the* Guide *this year.*

◑ Closed last week Oct and 1-2 weeks Feb; restaurant closed Sun eve & Mon ◪ On B2141 between Chichester and Petersfield, next to White Horse Inn. Private car park 🛏 1 single, 3 twin/double, 1 suite; all with bathroom/WC exc single with shower/WC; TV, room service, hair-dryer, direct-dial telephone; no tea/coffee-making facilities in rooms ⊘ Dining-room, garden; conference facilities (max 10 people incl up to 5 residential); croquet ⴲ Wheelchair access to hotel (1 step), 2 ground-floor bedrooms, 1 specially equipped for disabled people ● No children under 16; no dogs in public rooms and in bedrooms by arrangement only; no smoking in bedrooms ▭ Access, Amex, Delta, Diners, Switch, Visa £ Single £30 to £35, single occupancy of twin/double £50 to £55, twin/double £70 to £79, suite £95 to £120; deposit required. Set L £17.50, D £23; alc L £22.50, D £25. Special breaks available

---

CHIPPERFIELD Hertfordshire   map 3

Two Brewers

The Common, Chipperfield, Kings Langley WD4 9BS
TEL: (01923) 265266   FAX: (01923) 261884

Popular ancient inn with busy atmosphere and lovely outlook.

Along with its history – prize boxers used to train here for bare-knuckle fights – the location of the Two Brewers is its main attraction. Right on the edge of the village common, the black and white creeper-covered building with its smart picket fence is in a peaceful position and makes a good launch-pad for gentle walks. On your return you can have lunch or tea in the busy hotel lounge. With its rich yellow walls, window seats and comfortable armchairs, it is a cosy room in which to while away an hour or two. The bar has slightly less character but is equally popular with local people popping in for snacks. The restaurant, where window tables overlooking the common are the most sought after, is a more formal room, though it is light, with pretty trellis wallpaper. A typical lunch might include melon with raspberry sauce, casserole of chicken, ham and mushroom, followed by sticky toffee pudding. The bedrooms are something of a let-down in comparison with the public rooms. In a modern extension block, linked to the main house by a glass corridor, they look out over the car park. Opt for one of the corner rooms – these are the brightest.

◑ Open all year ◪ Leave M25 at Junction 20 and follow A4251 to Kings Langley; take second left after Rose & Crown pub, continue 2 miles then turn left by Royal Oak pub; Inn is 100 yards on the right. Private car park 🛏 13 twin, 7 double, 4 family rooms; all with bathroom/WC; TV, room service, hair-dryer, trouser press, direct-dial telephone ⊘ Restaurant, bar, lounge, garden; conference facilities (max 20 people residential/non-residential); early suppers for children; baby-listening ⴲ Wheelchair access to hotel (1 step) and restaurant, 10 ground-floor bedrooms ● Dogs in bedrooms at £10 per stay; no smoking in restaurant and some bedrooms ▭ Access, Amex, Delta, Diners, Switch, Visa £ Single occupancy of twin/double £85, twin/double £90, family room £90; deposit required. Continental B £6.50, cooked B £9; set L £12/13, Sun L £15, D £17/19; bar meals available (1996 prices). Special breaks available

---

See the inside front cover for a brief explanation of how to use the Guide.

CHIPPING CAMPDEN Gloucestershire   map 5

Cotswold House

The Square, Chipping Campden GL55 6AN
TEL: (01386) 840330   FAX: (01386) 840310

New owners but same high standards at an elegant town-house hotel.

Chipping Campden's High Street, an essay in golden stone, is one of England's most delectable. The mellow ashlar frontage of Cotswold House echoes the general mood, but the pillars of the portico fail to prepare you for the splendours that lie within this austere seventeenth-century building. Venture into the hallway and you encounter a sweeping, delicately elegant staircase framed by an archway of Doric columns. This sets the scene for the gracious sitting-rooms, where chairs in bold plaids and lush florals complement plain walls. New owner Christopher Forbes is especially proud of the ingenious drinks cabinet, a splendid piece of furniture he brought back from the Far East, which obviates the need for a bar. The Garden Room Restaurant is the hotel's venue for fine dining, and boasts a wonderful plaster ceiling, crisply laid tables, plus a grand piano, played regularly by the resident pianist. As its name suggests, it overlooks a large, intricate and perfectly kept garden. Food is imaginative: perhaps a tartlet of buttered spinach, veal kidneys and artichokes, followed by red and grey mullet and black bream, pan-fried with chilli, ginger and coriander with a timbale of wild rice, followed by hot chocolate soufflé pudding with pistachio ice-cream. The Forbes Brasserie, a cheerfully modern yet beamed room, offers less formal fare.

The bedrooms are individually designed with lush fabrics and furnishings of a high order. All show imagination and flair, from the masculine Military Room to the bright English Room with its brass bed and wartime wireless.

○ Closed 24 to 26 Dec   🅿 On the High Street in Chipping Campden. Private car park ⊨ 3 single, 5 twin, 6 double, 1 four-poster; all with bathroom/WC exc 1 single with shower/WC; TV, room service, hair-dryer, trouser press, direct-dial telephone, radio; no tea/coffee-making facilities in rooms   ✇ 2 restaurants, 2 lounges, drying-room, garden; conference facilities (max 30 people incl up to 15 residential); croquet; early suppers for children   ⅙ No wheelchair access   ● No dogs; no smoking in 1 restaurant and discouraged in bedrooms   ⊟ Access, Amex, Delta, Diners, Switch, Visa   £ Single £70 to £80, single occupancy of twin/double £85 to £95, twin/double £100 to £140, four-poster £160; deposit required. Set D £17.50, Sun L £16; alc D £20; brasserie meals available. Special breaks available

---

CHITTLEHAMHOLT Devon   map 1

Highbullen

Chittlehamholt, Umberleigh EX37 9HD
TEL: (01769) 540561   FAX: (01769) 540492

Victorian mansion with minimalist service at heart of expanding leisure complex in countryside.

For sports-lovers Highbullen has everything...indoor and outdoor pools, indoor and outdoor tennis courts, a golf course, a squash court, even a croquet lawn. First stop inside the house should therefore be the Viewing Tower, from where you can look down and work out what's where. Downstairs, a tiled hall leads to a gracious lounge with lovely views through its bay window, then to a smaller library where you can easily imagine the gentlemen retiring with port and cigars, and finally to a billiards room for those too-wet-to-venture-outside days. There's also a pleasant add-on conservatory-style dining-room upstairs. In winter, however, dinner is served in a windowless basement with low ceilings, which our inspector found depressing, although the many repeat diners seemed unworried by it. One reader described Highbullen as 'a gem...the sort of hotel to recommend, without reservation'. However, the hands-off approach to service which the writer interpreted as pleasing informality could very easily strike others as offhand. Given that there is no real reception, every transaction with staff seems to involve descending to the bar, ringing a bell and waiting. At breakfast guests even have to serve their own tea from the buffet, rather than having teapots delivered to the table. Our usual advice is to go for the rooms in the main house, most of them huge and furnished in comfortable antique style with samples of owner Pam Neil's embroidery collection on the walls. However, if travelling alone and offered poky Room 11, opt instead for a pleasantly modern annexe room.

◐ Open all year ⟋ Turn off B3226 (from South Molton) to Chittlehamholt; hotel is ½ mile beyond the village on the left. Private car park ⟋ 1 single, 36 twin/double; some in annexe; all with bathroom/WC; TV, room service, hair-dryer, direct-dial telephone, radio ✦ Restaurant, dining-room/conservatory, bar, 2 lounges, drying-room, library, 2 games rooms, garden; conference facilities (max 20 people non-residential/residential); fishing, golf, gym, sauna, solarium, 2 swimming-pools, tennis, squash, snooker, croquet, table tennis, indoor putting ⑆ No wheelchair access ● No children under 8; no dogs; no smoking in restaurant ▭ Access, Delta, Switch, Visa £ Single £60 to £80, single occupancy of twin/double £60 to £80, twin/double £105 to £160 (rates incl dinner). Set D £18.50; bar lunches available. Special breaks available

---

CLANFIELD Oxfordshire   map 2

Plough at Clanfield

Bourton Road, Clanfield OX18 2RB
TEL: (01367) 810222   FAX: (01367) 810596

Former Elizabethan manor house, now an up-market inn, at centre of Cotswold village.

The Plough looks nothing like the pub you might be expecting from the name of this hotel. But once you realise that the fancy gables, stone-mullioned windows and tall chimneys were built as a manor house for a wealthy sixteenth-century gentleman, everything makes sense. The lounge is now the focal point of the hotel. With its comfortable old sofas, leather fireside armchairs and cushioned window seats looking out over lawns, it's a cosy room in which you could happily while away the morning with a book or one of the newspapers the hotel provides. Bar snacks include interesting choices such as fricassee of pasta with smoked bacon, mushrooms and basil. Similar high standards are maintained in the restaurant, which is popular with well-heeled local business people at lunch time. White table linen, silver cutlery and candlelight reflected in the highly polished glasses make evening meals an elegant affair where service is unpretentious and friendly. The hotel was taken over by new owners at the beginning of 1996; they plan to double the number of bedrooms from six to 12 by building an extension at the back of the house. When we visited, this work hadn't been carried out, though the six existing bedrooms – named after wild flowers – had been spruced up, some with new patchwork quilts to add to their smart modern décor.

◐ Closed 27 to 29 Dec ↗ At the junction of A4095 and A4020 at the edge of Clanfield. Private car park ⇐ 1 single, 4 double, 1 four-poster; all with bathroom/WC exc 2 doubles with shower/WC; TV, room service, hair-dryer, trouser press, direct-dial telephone ✧ Restaurant, bar, lounge, 2 gardens; conference facilities (max 8 people incl up to 7 residential) ⅋ No wheelchair access ● No children under 12; no dogs in bedrooms ▭ Access, Amex, Delta, Diners, Switch, Visa £ Single £65 to £75, single occupancy of twin/double £65 to £75, twin/double £85 to £95, four-poster £95 to £110; deposit required. Set L £17.50, D £28.50; bar meals available. Special breaks available

---

CLAPPERSGATE Cumbria   map 8

Grey Friar Lodge

Clappersgate, Ambleside LA22 9NE
TEL: (01539) 433158 (AND FAX)

Home comforts, great views and eclectic curios in a friendly, unpretentious guesthouse.

Sheila and Tony Sutton's handsome dark-grey Lakeland-stone guesthouse is awash with exotic and incongruous bric-à-brac, and that's only the stuff that made it out of the boxes when they moved here a dozen years ago. Sheila's mum's wedding-present dinner service, along with several other sets of china, adorns the plate shelf around the dining-room; you'll meet a stuffed turtle on the stairs and a sawfish's mandible in the hallway. Personalised cartoons by the late Lakeland artist Wilkie hang in the busily Victorian sitting-room, while next door you can lounge inside among aspidistras or outside on a patio that catches the sun all day (should it shine!).

Bedrooms are of a simple style, in light, fresh colours, some with coronet beds and pine furnishings, all with home-made cake and biscuits, and bags of fluffy towels in the bathrooms. Room 3 is the pick, not so much for the four-poster as for the view of the river wending its way down the Brathay Valley. Rooms 5 and 8 also have the valley views. Sheila does the cooking, preparing honest-to-goodness English food with a bit of flair, such as cod and prawn pancake, pork, pear and red wine cobbler, and sticky toffee pudding before the cheeseboard and coffee with home-made chocolates. Sheila and Tony's natural exuberance is infectious, so first-name terms are assured, probably before you've unpacked.

◑ Closed Nov to Feb 🔁 On A593, 1½ miles west of Ambleside. Private car park ⊨⊷ 2 twin, 5 double, 1 four-poster; 6 with bathroom/WC, 2 doubles with shower/WC; TV, hair-dryer, clock radio ⊘ Dining-room, 2 lounges, drying-room, garden ⅋ No wheelchair access ● No children under 10; no dogs; smoking in 1 lounge only 🗔 None accepted ⎡£⎤ Single occupancy of twin/double £28 to £30, twin/double £50 to £56, four-poster £56 to £62; deposit required. Set D £15.50. Special breaks available

---

CLEARWELL Gloucestershire   map 2

Tudor Farmhouse

Clearwell, Nr Coleford GL16 8JS
TEL: (01594) 833046   FAX: (01594) 837093

Stylish bedrooms and bags of character at a converted Tudor farmhouse with medieval antecedents.

The childhood reminiscences of the late Dennis Potter have helped to reacquaint the public with the attractions of the Forest of Dean, an area of ancient forest set high in the hills between the Rivers Severn and Wye. Clearwell, a small village dominated by a ramparted castle and right at the Forest's edge, is a good base not only for exploring the Forest, but for planning expeditions across the border to Monmouth, or having a flutter at the Chepstow races. Deborah and Richard Fletcher's small hotel, a cluster of roseate stone buildings next to a village pub, boasts – despite its name – thirteenth-century origins. Its interior successfully straddles the claims of old and new. Visitors are asked to enter from the rear, where bright soft furnishings in modern prints lend a cheerful feel to the light conservatory. Tradition reasserts itself in the restaurant, where the ceiling beams and mixture of wood panelling and exposed stone walls, plus leaded windows, testify to the house's antiquity. Diners can choose from a standard menu offering perhaps asparagus flan, cheese and avocado crêpes and dessert, or go for options from the grill menu, including standards like fillet steak, Dover sole or lamb cutlets.

There are bedrooms both in the main house (reached via a venerable oak spiral staircase) and in a Garden extension, where there's a Japanese spin on the décor. The rooms are uniformly comfortable and well equipped, with a sprinkling of antiques and modern art.

◑ Closed 24 to 30 Dec; restaurant closed Sun eve 🔁 3 miles off A466 between Chepstow and Monmouth. Private car park ⊨⊷ 2 single, 1 twin, 4 double, 2 four-poster, 3 family rooms, 1 suite; some in annexe; most with bathroom/WC, some with shower/WC; TV, hair-dryer, direct-dial telephone ⊘ Restaurant, bar, lounge, drying-room, conservatory, garden; conference facilities (max 12 people non-residential/residential); early suppers for children; babysitting, baby-listening ⅋ No wheelchair access ● No children in restaurant after 7.30pm; no dogs in public rooms and some bedrooms; no smoking in restaurant and some bedrooms 🗔 Access, Amex, Delta, Switch, Visa ⎡£⎤ Single £45, single occupancy of twin/double £45, twin/double £55, four-poster £65, family room £65, suite £75; deposit required. Set D £17.50 (1996 prices). Special breaks available

Bailiffscourt

Climping BN17 5RW
TEL: (01903) 723511 FAX: (01903) 723107

A 'medieval' country hotel which is really a magnificent deception.

It is with a sense of amazement that you approach this medieval hamlet nestling a mere pike's throw from the sea. Surely a relic of such antiquity could not be so well preserved? Give yourself a pat on the back for spotting this masterpiece of architectural deceit. Apart from the Norman chapel, this is a rich man's caprice, built by the late Lord Moyne of the Guinness family under the guidance of antiquarians and historians given free rein and a blank cheque. But it's not that simple. This is, paradoxically, a 'genuine fake', as all the Gothic mullioned windows, rough-hewn stones, monumental arches, doorways and beams are real – painstakingly salvaged from derelict fifteenth- and sixteenth-century structures around the country. The result is convincing enough as you gaze up at moulded oak ceilings and walk the creaking floors of the public areas grouped around a sheltered courtyard. Grand four-poster suites are spectacular without exception – Baylies has a ceiling the timbers of which resemble the hull of the Mary Rose soaring up to the height of a chapel, and twin baths like sarcophagi. More down-to-earth accommodation is to be found in the Coach House and Thatched House sections, but all rooms share the same style. An elegant dining-room serves rich fare including roast guinea-fowl with vanilla onions and thyme gravy or a bourride of seafood with aïoli and garlic croûtes followed perhaps by hot walnut tart or mille-feuille of plums with a mascarpone sabayon.

○ Open all year ⊿ In Climping, just off A259, 4 miles south of Arundel. Private car park ⊨ 1 single, 5 twin, 10 double, 10 four-poster, 1 suite; most in annexes; all with bathroom/WC; TV, room service, hair-dryer, direct-dial telephone; trouser press in some rooms ⊘ Dining-room, bar, 3 lounges, garden; conference facilities (max 50 people incl up to 27 residential); unheated outdoor swimming-pool, tennis, croquet; early suppers for children; babysitting, baby-listening ♿ No wheelchair access ● No dogs in dining-room or bar; no smoking in dining-room ⊡ Access, Amex, Diners, Switch, Visa £ Single £95, single occupancy of twin/double £95, twin/double £125, four-poster £155, suite £250; deposit required. Set L £18, D £30; bar lunches available. Special breaks available

White Hart

Market End, Coggeshall, Colchester CO6 1NH
TEL: (01376) 561654 FAX: (01376) 561789

Attractive old inn that combines English tradition with Italian overtones.

The history of the White Hart is about as solidly English as you can get: the principal meeting place for local and visiting tradesmen and cloth merchants in the fifteenth century, and the only staging post between Colchester and

Braintree in the nineteenth century. Inside, the oldest room, dating from 1420 and part of the original guildhall, is the first-floor residents' lounge, with a delightfully asymmetrical brick chimney breast and exposed chestnut beams. Downstairs, the beams are lower (and younger) but equally characterful in the split-level restaurant, adorned with stuffed fish and arrangements of fresh and dried flowers. A glance at the menu, however, transports you to a different country altogether: fresh pasta, risotto and the wine list all reflect the tastes of proprietor Mario Casella's Italian homeland (though having lived in the area for over 28 years, he almost qualifies as a local). Traditionalists may prefer to retreat to the cocktail bar, where a *tranche* of bar favourites like scampi and french fries or steak and kidney pie are supplemented with daily fishy specials like grilled sea bass or swordfish. Bedrooms are very smart, and make judicious use of strong colours and boldly patterned fabrics. Service is helpful, but be sure to notify them about what time you intend to arrive, as the reception desk closes down in the afternoon.

◑ Open all year; restaurant closed Sun eve 🔁 From A12 follow signs through Kelvedon and then take B1024 to Coggeshall. Private car park 🛏 2 single, 16 twin/double; family rooms available; most with bathroom/WC, some with shower/WC; TV, limited room service, hair-dryer, trouser press, direct-dial telephone ✅ Restaurant, bar, lounge, garden; conference facilities (max 25 people incl up to 18 residential) ♿ No wheelchair access ● No dogs ▭ Access, Amex, Delta, Switch, Visa ⌷£⌷ Single £55 to £67, single occupancy of twin/double £60 to £74, twin/double £87 to £97, family room from £102; deposit required. Set Sun L £15; alc L, D £25; bar meals available. Special breaks available

---

COLERNE Wiltshire   map 2

Lucknam Park

Colerne, Nr Chippenham SN14 8AZ
TEL: (01225) 742777   FAX: (01225) 743536

De-luxe country manor with opulent rooms in 500 acres of parkland.

A mile-long beech-lined drive leads to the stately façade of this sumptuous and imposing Georgian manor, with portico and pillars providing a more flamboyant Palladian flourish. Surrounded by acre upon acre of parkland and gardens (suggested walking routes are provided), and with good leisure facilities, the hotel may tempt visitors to ignore the no less magnificent attractions of Bath, just six miles away. The individually styled bedrooms also provide plenty to massage the senses. Top-of-the-range suites have log fires, antique four-posters and *chaises-longues*; all have ritzy marble bathrooms, silver carafes with water from the Lucknam spa, opulent drapes and fresh flowers. The choice of places – and plumped-up cushions – to enjoy afternoon tea, the newspaper, or just the surroundings, is endless, from the wood-panelled library with shelves of leather-bound books to the more feminine lemon-yellow drawing-room, full of antiques and oil portraits, and plenty of uniformed staff on hand to attend to your every need. Despite all this – and the racehorses trotting round the paddocks and the limos parked outside – Lucknam's opulence is never overstated. The restaurant, in particular, has a slightly old-fashioned Victorian air; food is creative, modern English.

◗ Open all year ⏀ Approximately ¼ mile from the crossroads for Colerne. Private car park ⏋ 1 single, 11 twin, 18 double, 1 four-poster, 11 suites; some in annexe; all with bathroom/WC; TV, room service, hair-dryer, direct-dial telephone
⍟ Restaurant, 2 lounges, library, games rooms, garden; conference facilities (max 100 people incl up to 42 residential); gym, sauna, solarium, heated indoor swimming-pool, tennis, putting green, clay-pigeon shooting, croquet, snooker; early suppers for children; babysitting, baby-listening ♿ Wheelchair access to hotel (1 step), restaurant, WC (unisex), 16 ground-floor bedrooms ⬤ No children under 12 in restaurant eves; no dogs; no smoking in restaurant or bedrooms ▭ Access, Amex, Delta, Diners, Switch, Visa ⌸ Single £120, single occupancy of twin/double £150, twin/double £170 to £230, four-poster £230, suite £340 to £550; deposit required. Cooked B £6.50; set L £24.50, D £42.50 (prices valid till Mar 1997). Special breaks available

---

COLN ST ALDWYNS Gloucestershire   map 2

New Inn ☆

Coln St Aldwyns, Nr Cirencester GL7 5AN
TEL: (01285) 750651 FAX: (01285) 750657

Sixteenth-century coaching inn with rustic character and a dash of panache.

Brian Evans has had a varied career, latterly in electronic publishing. This refugee from the metropolis is now firmly at the helm of the now eccentrically named New Inn, a creeper-clad sixteenth-century coaching stop in the sleepy Cotswold village of Coln St Aldwyns, a short drive from Bibury. As the brochure puts it, 'The New Inn was old when Wren built St Paul's'. A central fireplace divides the space in the Courtyard Bar, a picture-postcard country pub with *de rigueur* beams draped with dried hops, and stone walls bedecked with swords, pistols, horse brasses, sepia photos and old coaching prints. The food served here is noticeably imaginative: perhaps salad of duck confit and duck livers, followed by rabbit casserole with mustard and coriander, and rhubarb crumble with ginger anglaise.

Things move up a notch in the candle-lit but rustic restaurant, where an inglenook fireplace extends a warm glow, and copper warming pans, flagstones and Van Gogh chairs sustain the country feel. Here you can kick off with pan-fried John Dory and a bouillabaisse *jus*, and follow it up by roast breast of chicken with basil, olives and tomatoes, and poached pear with honey and stem ginger ice-cream. Each of the 11 bedrooms was individually devised by Brian's wife Sandra-Anne, an interior designer. All are well equipped and team cheerful, often chintzy, soft furnishings with decent (but not necessarily antique) furniture, often set off by beams. The four-poster and half-tester rooms stand out from a strong field.

○ Open all year ⤧ Between Bibury (B4425) and Fairford (A417); 8 miles east of Cirencester. Private car park ⮡ 1 single, 2 twin, 7 double, 1 four-poster; family room available; some in annexe; most with bathroom/WC, 2 with shower/WC; TV, limited room service, hair-dryer, trouser press, direct-dial telephone ⌑ Restaurant, bar, lounge; conference facilities (max 22 people incl up to 11 residential); early suppers for children ♿ No wheelchair access ● No children under 10 in restaurant eves; no smoking in restaurant or bedrooms; dogs in bar only ⊟ Access, Amex, Switch, Visa £ Single £55, single occupancy of twin/double £65, twin/double £79, four-poster £79, family room £95; deposit required. Set D £22.50, Sun L £14.50; bar meals available (prices valid till Apr 1997). Special breaks available

---

COLYFORD Devon   map 2

Swallows Eaves

Colyford, Colyton EX13 6QJ
TEL: (01297) 553184 (AND FAX)

Comfortable small hotel in quiet village within easy reach of brasher Devon resorts.

The 'swallow eaves' which gave this hotel its name jut up perkily from the tiled roof of the well-maintained 1920s house with a neat garden. A period-piece fireplace with brown glazed tiles adorns the dining-room, where guests can peruse the menu on sofas grouped at one end around a table bearing a bowl of sugared almonds to assist in the selection of starter and dessert. A typical meal might start with creamy watercress soup and croûtons, with lemon sole to follow, and hot date and orange pudding with the happily inevitable Devonian clotted cream to finish. 'We stayed for a fortnight,' reported one satisfied customer, 'and dinners were such we never thought to eat out.' Upstairs, the bedrooms are cosy without being flashy. Some of the most interesting are up in the eaves, with sloping ceilings, skylights and pastel-coloured walls. More praise came in this year for 'Jon and Jane Beck's happy and cheerful personalities' – this and the good food led our correspondents to describe the hotel as 'an ideal set-up'.

○ Closed Dec & Jan ⤧ On A3052 Lyme Regis to Sidmouth Road; in centre of village. Private car park ⮡ 4 twin, 4 double; 6 with bathroom/WC, 2 with shower/WC; TV, room service, hair-dryer ⌑ Dining-room, lounge, garden ♿ No wheelchair access ● No children under 14; no dogs; no smoking in dining-room and most bedrooms ⊟ Delta, Switch, Visa £ Single occupancy of twin/double £39 to £47, twin/double £59 to £74. Set D £18. Special breaks available

---

CORELEY Shropshire   map 5

Corndene

Coreley, Ludlow SY8 3AW
TEL: (01584) 890324

Friendly hosts offer simple accommodation in a remote spot a short drive from Ludlow.

Despite its relative proximity to Ludlow, Clare and David Currant's eighteenth-century former rectory is off the beaten track – and then some. The winding A4117 holds the promise of remoteness, and the private track that wends down to Corndene, with its two acres of garden and woodland, certainly delivers. Creepers add a touch of lushness to the two-storey red-brick house, and the welcome afforded by the dogs Sophie and Jesse confirms that this is very much a low-key family affair. Flagstones and rugs and an antique writing desk hint at the house's age. Elsewhere the décor is more functional, with beige walls, and chairs and sofas in heathery tones in the spacious and uncluttered sitting-room, where the log fire adds a dash of cosiness and a good range of paperbacks is on hand to curl up with. Carpet tiles run through this room and the cheerful dining-room, where blue and white gingham tablecloths, pine ladderback chairs and wall-mounted plates give a farmhouse-kitchen feel. The wildlife photographs are by Clare's father, and guests who share the dry sense of humour will particularly enjoy the picture of gannets in such a setting. Food is traditional English home-cooking. 'I daren't take shepherd's pie off the menu', sighs Clare, who might also offer pork and prunes, and a damson mousse featuring fruit from Corndene's trees, plus cheese and biscuits to round things off.

All three bedrooms are fully wheelchair-accessible, with drive-in shower rooms. They are bright and homely with emulsioned wood-chip and floral vinyl wall-covering; suitably rustic pine furnishings feature in Oak and Ash.

◐ Closed Dec to Feb 🔁 1 mile south of A4117 crossing Clee Hill Common. Private car park 🛏 3 twin; family rooms available; all with shower/WC ✓ Dining-room, lounge, drying-room, garden; croquet; early suppers for children; toys, babysitting, baby-listening ♿ Wheelchair access to hotel and dining-room, all bedrooms specially equipped for disabled people ● No dogs; no smoking ⬜ None accepted ⓔ Single occupancy of twin/double £22 to £24, twin/double £38 to £42; deposit required. Set D £10. Special breaks available

---

CORSE LAWN Gloucestershire map 5

Corse Lawn House

Corse Lawn, Gloucester GL19 4LZ
TEL: (01452) 780771   FAX: (01452) 780840

Country-house hotel in elegant Queen Anne building with friendly and welcoming hosts.

Set back from the road and in its own 12 acres of grounds, Corse Lawn House makes a fine first impression as you approach along the short private road. Inside the house an air of formality pervades the public rooms: the drawing-room with cool grey sofas and black wicker-backed chairs; starched white linen tablecloths and napkins in the dining-room. The menu in the restaurant changes daily; a typical offering from the table d'hôte menu might be vichyssoise soup followed by best end of lamb with red wine and aubergine gâteau, rounded off with the strawberry collection of shortcake, soufflé and sorbet. The Bistro bar has a more relaxed atmosphere and friendly staff.

Many of the bedrooms have splendid views and are a good size – the best of these is Hasfield (named, as are most of the rooms, after a local village), which boasts views on three sides, including the ornamental duck pond, which was originally a coach wash (a pool into which you could drive and turn a stage and four horses). This is the kind of hotel where many guests make return visits, but a letter from one reader who has been returning to Corse Lawn House for ten years notes that, 'although it still provides a wonderfully calm and relaxing break,' in his opinion, standards have slipped, 'slightly but noticeably' during the recession.

◑ Open all year ⊿ 5 miles south-west of Tewkesbury on B4211. Private car park ⤶ 7 twin, 8 double, 2 four-poster, 2 suites; all with bathroom/WC; TV, room service, hair-dryer, trouser press, direct-dial telephone ✧ 3 restaurants, bar, 2 lounges, TV room, drying-room, garden; conference facilities (max 35 people incl up to 19 residential); heated outdoor swimming-pool, tennis, croquet; early suppers for children; cots, high chairs ⅃ Wheelchair access to hotel, restaurant and WC (M,F), 5 ground-floor bedrooms ● No dogs or smoking in restaurant ⊟ Access, Amex, Diners, Visa £ Single occupancy of twin/double £73, twin/double £100, four-poster £110, suite £125; deposit required. Set L £15/£17, D £24.50; alc L, D £30; bistro meals available. Special breaks available

---

COVENTRY West Midlands   map 5

Crest Guesthouse

39 Friars Road, Coventry CV1 2LJ
TEL: (01203) 227822   FAX: (01203) 227244

A natty little B&B in the centre of Coventry.

Turn-of-the-century, cream and blue Crest Guesthouse is much the most enticing establishment on this cul-de-sac wedged between Coventry's ring road and a multi-storey car park. The railway station and the city's pedestrian precincts are just a few hundred yards away. Furnished with patterned carpets, whirled glass panels on the stairs, a log-effect fire in the front room, and net curtains and humble pine units in the bedrooms, Peggy Harvey's B&B is entirely without airs. Yet it's meticulously maintained, notably with flower arrangements, and much care has gone into making the bedrooms as comfortable as space allows. The two twins have *en suite* facilities, with good modern shower units, while the two singles share a bathroom and a separate lavatory. Peggy doesn't officially do evening meals, but since she's such a warm, accommodating hostess it's no surprise to learn she sometimes offers single female guests what she and her husband are having if they don't fancy going out.

◑ Closed 25 & 26 Dec ⊿ Turn off inner ring-road at Junction 5; follow city-centre signs; continue past first set of traffic lights and turn left immediately. Private car park ⤶ 2 single, 2 twin; twins with shower/WC; TV, hair-dryer ✧ Dining-room, lounge, garden; baby-listening ⅃ No wheelchair access ● No dogs in public rooms and in bedrooms by arrangement only; no smoking ⊟ None accepted £ Single £22 to £25, single occupancy of twin £28 to £30, twin £40 to £45; deposit required

---

Prices are quoted per room *rather than* per person.

COWAN BRIDGE Lancashire   map 8

Hipping Hall

Cowan Bridge, Kirkby Lonsdale LA6 2JJ
TEL: (01524) 271187
FAX: (01524) 272452

*A delightful, small, stone country house, whose hosts create a
dinner-party atmosphere.*

Hipping Hall is a seventeenth-century house that is closely surrounded by stone
outbuildings arranged around a stone-flagged courtyard. A few ducks waddle
around the old wash house, which was built over a tiny stream, and a thick beech
hedge blocks out the noise of the traffic speeding along the A65.

Jocelyn Ruffle and Ian Bryant aim for an informal atmosphere, far removed
from hotel stuffiness, and many a reticent soul has been won over by the
convivial air of the timbered stone hall, with its wood-burning stove, single long
table, gallery and grand piano. Jos's skilful, five-course set menu has a broad
appeal, and might comprise home-cured gravad lax, mushroom soup, poached
breast of guinea-fowl with quince, a runny chocolate soufflé and northern
cheeses, all accompanied by a selection of wines specially chosen by Ian to
complement the various courses. Should you be feeling less gregarious first
thing in the morning, there are separate tables in the breakfast-room, which will
enable you to be alone with the newspaper, your full English breakfast and toast
and marmalade.

The bedrooms combine antique furniture with stylish, contemporary colour
schemes, while the two cottages across the courtyard are decorated in
modern-rustic style, featuring lots of pine and spiral iron staircases.

◑ Closed Dec to Feb ⬰ On A65, 8½ miles east of M6 (Junction 36), 2 miles east of
Kirkby Lonsdale. Private car park ⤺ 2 twin, 3 double, 2 suites; suites in annexe; all
with bathroom/WC exc 1 double with shower/WC; TV, hair-dryer, direct-dial
telephone ⧪ 2 dining-rooms, bar, lounge, drying-room, conservatory, garden;
conference facilities (max 20 people incl up to 7 residential); croquet ⅙ No
wheelchair access ● No children under 12; no dogs or smoking in public rooms
▭ Access, Amex, Visa £ Single occupancy of twin/double £67, twin/double £84,
suite £94; deposit required. Set D £22. Special breaks available

---

CRACKINGTON HAVEN Cornwall   map 1

Manor Farm

Crackington Haven EX23 0JU
TEL: (01840) 230304

An immaculate rural hideaway, ideal for house parties.

Part-stone, part-white washed, the Manor Farm is an idyllic farmhouse,
without the slightest hint of mud to mar its flagstoned floors. The
breakfast-room, with its inglenook fireplace with inset bread and salt ovens and
beamed ceilings, oozes seventeenth-century character, while the long, thin
dining-room, with its polished dining-table which seats eight, is more elegant

than cosy. Diners eat together at a single sitting, making the Manor Farm especially suitable for groups of people who know each other well. There's no choice as to what's served, but Muriel Knight's cooking goes down well with most guests and is pleasantly inventive...walnut savoury pie followed, perhaps, by pheasant casserole. Guests are encouraged to join the Knights for pre-prandial drinks, and there's an honesty bar for carousing later. Most bedrooms have lovely views over neatly kept lawns and flowerbeds to the moors beyond. Some are small, but make up for their lack of space with attractive furnishings such as big brass beds. The lack of phones and televisions in the bedrooms adds to the sense that the stresses of everyday life have been left far behind.

◑ Closed 25 Dec ⬕ From A39 take B3263 towards Crackington Haven. At the seafront, turn inland, ignoring High Cliff Road. After 1 mile turn left into Church Park Road, then first right. Private car park 🛏 2 twin, 3 double; 3 with bathroom/WC, 2 with shower/WC; hair-dryer on request ✅ Dining-room, bar, 2 lounges, TV room, games room, garden ♿ No wheelchair access ⊖ No children; no dogs; no smoking ▭ None accepted £ Single occupancy of twin/double £30 to £35, twin/double £60 to £70; deposit required. Set D £15

CRANBROOK Kent   map 3

Hancocks Farmhouse

Tilsden Lane, Cranbrook TN17 3PH
TEL: (01580) 714645

Sixteenth-century farmhouse with high standards in idyllic setting.

If you want to be woken by the sound of a cockerel crowing, this is the place for you. Hancocks Farmhouse, a half-timbered Grade II listed building with a country-cottage-style garden and surrounded by acres of farmland, is a peaceful retreat for those wishing to escape the hustle and bustle of urban life. Bridget and Robin Oaten welcome you into their stylish home ('the finest B&B I've ever stayed in', according to one reader) with great enthusiasm. Readers also like the Oatens' relaxed style: 'we and the other guests were made to feel we could lounge indoors for as long as we liked'. Warmed by the cast-iron stove in the huge brick inglenook fireplace, guests can choose to sit at separate tables or together for one of the Oatens' set dinners – which might include smoked salmon parcels, lamb ragoût, and chocolate and coffee roulade – described as 'absolutely marvellous' by one correspondent. The bedrooms are all very pretty and comfortable and have fruit, sweets and a decanter of madeira provided. The bright and sunny Garden Room downstairs has an outside door (which makes it ideal for people with dogs). Upstairs, there is a four-poster room with wooden floorboards and a private bathroom across the corridor, and a suite of rooms with a lovely sitting-room which has great views over the surrounding countryside.

  This denotes that you can get a twin or double room for £60 or less per night inclusive of breakfast.

◑ Open all year; restaurant closed Sun eve ⤢ From Cranbrook take Tenterden road past windmill on left; take right fork signposted Benenden; Hancocks is up first farm track on left, adjacent to farm cottages. Private car park ⤒ 1 twin, 1 four-poster, 1 suite; 2 with bathroom/WC, twin with shower/WC; TV, limited room service, hair-dryer; tea/coffee-making facilities on request; trouser press available ⊘ Dining-room, lounge, garden ⅊ No wheelchair access ⊖ No children under 9; no dogs in public rooms and some bedrooms; no smoking ⊡ None accepted £ Single occupancy of twin/double £30 to £35, twin/double £50 to £60, four-poster/suite £54 to £60; deposit required. Set D £19/20

Old Cloth Hall

Cranbrook TN17 3NR
TEL: (01580) 712220 (AND FAX)

Attractive, half-timbered manor house in peaceful surroundings.

Old Cloth Hall is a bit off the beaten track and a little difficult to find – however, Elizabeth I managed it and was entertained for lunch. Guests arriving in the present day find that they too receive a warm welcome – from Katherine Morgan, whose home it is now. With its beautifully landscaped gardens full of rhododendrons and azaleas in spring, a tennis court and outdoor swimming-pool, Old Cloth Hall is a relaxing place to stay. The elegant wood-panelled dining-room, which has a large mahogany table around which all the guests (and often Katherine too) sit down together to a delicious set dinner, is the scene of many a sociable evening, as is often the case in a Wolsey Lodge house. You can linger over your coffee in the large, comfortable drawing-room with its oak beams and panelling and huge open fire; when you return to your bedroom you are likely to find that Katherine has popped in to turn down the beds and maybe slip a hot-water bottle in if the night is cold. The bedrooms themselves are very comfortable – the large four-poster room upstairs with its peach floral patterned bedding and enormous *en suite* bathroom is perhaps the most romantic.

◑ Closed Chr ⤢ 1 mile out of Cranbrook on Golford road to Tenterden; turn right just before cemetery. Private car park ⤒ 1 twin, 1 double, 1 four-poster; 2 with bathroom/WC, twin with shower/WC; TV, hair-dryer, trouser press; tea/coffee on request ⊘ Dining-room, lounge, garden; unheated outdoor swimming-pool, tennis, croquet; early suppers for children ⅊ No wheelchair access ⊖ No dogs; smoking discouraged in bedrooms ⊡ None accepted £ Single occupancy of twin/double £45 to £55, twin/double £65 to £85, four-poster £90 to £95; deposit required. Set D £20/£22

CRANFORD Northamptonshire
map 6

Dairy Farm

Cranford, Kettering NN14 4AQ
TEL: (01536) 330273

Beamy and creaky old farmhouse B&B in a pretty village.

This deep-gabled, thatched early-seventeenth-century manor house stands in a most picturesque setting. A disused Norman church, fine Georgian mansion, medieval dovecote and sheep-filled meadows – part of the farm's 350 acres – surround it. Inside, it feels like a long-established family home, which it is: John Clarke has lived here for over 40 years. On display in the hall, the roomy, homely sitting-room and the dining-room are antique dressers and ceremonial swords and muskets. John's wife Audrey prepares traditional three-course dinners on request: perhaps asparagus soup, lamb chops and a choice of desserts such as treacle pudding or rhubarb crumble. Alternatively, you could stroll down to the pub a couple of hundred yards down the road. Chunky Victorian pieces and simple modern units furnish the bedrooms. The best is the large four-poster room. Candlewick bedspreads set the tone in the other, considerably more modest, rooms: one requires a trip down the corridor to its own bathroom.

◑ Closed 25 Dec to 1 Jan ⟱ Leave A14 at sign for Cranford; from the High Street take Grafton Road; turn right into St Andrew's Lane; Dairy Farm is at the end. Private car park ⊨ 1 twin, 1 double, 1 four-poster; family rooms available; all with bathroom/WC; TV, room service, hair-dryer ✧ Dining-room, lounge, garden; conference facilities (max 20 people incl up to 5 residential); croquet; early suppers for children; babysitting ♿ Wheelchair access to hotel (1 step) and dining-room (2 steps), 1 ground-floor bedroom ● No dogs in public rooms and in annexe by arrangement; no smoking ▭ None accepted £ Single occupancy of twin/double £22 to £30, twin/double £44 to £60, four-poster £60, family room from £50; deposit required. Set D £12.50

CREWKERNE Somerset   map 2

Broadview

43 East Street, Crewkerne TA18 7AG
TEL: (01460) 73424 (AND FAX)

Homely small-town hotel with attractive gardens.

Broadview is the sort of family-run hotel which sets great store by comfort – you know you'll be made welcome as soon as you see the brollies waiting in the car park lest you should arrive in the middle of a shower. Gillian and Robert Swann moved to Crewkerne from Scotland, bringing a dog, cat and plum-headed parakeet. Robert has since landscaped the gardens so that they look inviting even in the depths of winter. Rooms come thoughtfully equipped: fresh milk and biscuits to go with a choice of teas; plentiful toiletries; and lots of sightseeing information are welcome extras. The décor will be too fussy for some tastes; others will love the collection of plates and porcelain figures to examine while they're dining. Food is tasty and filling. When we inspected, a thick onion soup was served with tasty bread, the fish came with plentiful vegetables, and the French pancake with sugar and lemon made a very satisfying finish. There's no choice, so vegetarians should announce themselves when booking. The small lounge looks on to a miniature waterwheel, the conservatory out across Crewkerne.

○ Open all year ⚡ From A303 take A356 Crewkerne Road; when in Crewkerne take Yeovil Road out, hotel is 200 yards on left. Private car park 🛏 2 twin, 1 double; twins with bathroom/WC, double with shower/WC; TV, hair-dryer ⚿ Dining-room, lounge, conservatory, garden ♿ No wheelchair access ● No dogs in public rooms and in bedrooms by arrangement; no smoking ▭ Access, Delta, Visa 💷 Single occupancy of twin/double £25 to £35, twin/double £46 to £54; deposit required. Set D £12.50

CROOKHAM Northumberland   map 10

Coach House at Crookham

Crookham, Cornhill-on-Tweed TD12 4TD
TEL: (01890) 820293 FAX: (01890) 820284

A cheerful farmhouse with a convivial atmosphere and an attentive hostess.

Lynne Anderson's enthusiasm for her guests and attention to their needs never seem to flag, prompting a long letter of commendation from one couple, who enjoyed the fact that you can be as private or as sociable as you like, without feeling self-conscious. Although the bedrooms are pleasant enough, with their plain, wood-chip walls and simple furnishings, it is the smaller details that guests remember, such as filter coffee and fresh milk rather than sachets and fiddly plastic cartons, fresh flowers and crisp bed linen. There is also wheelchair access to six bedrooms, three of which have bathrooms specially converted to accommodate them.

Lynne's dinners feature fresh and local produce, and the fruit and vegetables come from the garden of this seventeenth-century farmhouse. One reader managed to find the dinners both 'home style' and 'quirky', but praised the panache with which they were served and the 'general desire to make sure that everyone is satisfied'.

The Coach House stands just outside the village of Crookham on the A697, but the passing traffic is light, and most of the bedrooms are set well back from the road.

○ Closed mid-Nov to mid-Mar ⚡ On A697, 3½ miles south of Cornhill-on-Tweed. Private car park 🛏 2 single, 5 twin, 2 double; most with bathroom/WC; TV in some rooms ⚿ Dining-room, lounge, TV room, library, garden ♿ Wheelchair access to hotel, dining-room and WC (unisex), 6 ground-floor bedrooms, 3 specially equipped for disabled people ● No dogs in public rooms; no smoking in dining-room ▭ Access, Amex, Visa 💷 Single and single occupancy of twin/double £21 to £34, twin/double £42 to £68; deposit required. Set D £15.50. Special breaks available

---

If you make a booking using a credit card and find after cancelling that the full amount has been charged to your card, raise the matter with your credit card company. It will ask the hotelier to confirm whether the room was re-let, and to justify the charge made.

CROSTHWAITE Cumbria map 8

Crosthwaite House

Crosthwaite, Nr Kendal LA8 8BP
TEL: (01539) 568264

---

*A delightful country guesthouse with friendly hosts in a picturesque
Lake District backwater.*

Crosthwaite is, as one delighted reader reported, 'so close to all the touristy areas
and yet it felt so remote'. Windermere is only a few miles to the west, while
Kendal and the M6 are easily accessible to the east, yet the Lyth valley, in which
Crosthwaite lies, is a relatively undiscovered corner of the Lake District. It's
known for its damson trees (which, should you visit in spring, are covered in
white blossoms) by the aficionados of the area.

Marnie and Robin Dawson are now into their second decade at Crosthwaite
House – an elegant, three-storey, square Georgian house close to the village
church – and are accomplished hosts: 'they were always around to give advice
and check everything was OK. As they were so relaxed and informal, so were
we,' said a guest. Marnie's four-course dinners come recommended, as do the
cooked breakfasts – the scrambled eggs are apparently 'much talked about'.

The bedrooms are simply and tastefully furnished, and are of comfortable
sizes, although the small *en suite* shower-rooms feel as though they were
squeezed in. Ask for a room at the front of the house as these overlook the
pastoral scene across the valley.

◑ Closed mid-Nov to mid-March ⇗ Leave M6 at Junction 36 and take A590 (signed
Barrow). Turn right on to A5074 (signed Bowness and Windermere). Turn right after
passing the Lyth Valley Hotel, continue to a T-junction, turn left; hotel is on the right.
Private car park ⬅ 1 single, 2 twin, 3 double; all with shower/WC; TV
⌖ Dining-room, lounge; early suppers for children; baby-listening ⅋ No wheelchair
access ● No dogs or smoking in public rooms ▭ Amex £ Single and single
occupancy of twin/double £22, twin/double £44. Set D £12

CROYDE Devon map 1

Whiteleaf at Croyde

Croyde, Nr Braunton EX33 1PN
TEL: (01271) 890266

---

*Peaceful small hotel with excellent reputation for food, in holiday
area but away from beaches.*

As the front door opens and a glorious smell of fresh cooking wafts from the
kitchen you'll know that Flo and David Wallington have still not managed to
deliver on their oft-repeated threat to retire. While they wait they haven't been
resting on their laurels. The sitting-room with its little sun lounge jutting out
may be unchanged, but the dining-room furniture has been rearranged and two
of the bedrooms have been given a connecting door so they can serve as a family
suite. The other two rooms are neat and welcoming, with books for bedtime

reading and bowls of pot pourri. Although furnishings are fairly simple, Room 2 has a lovely Indonesian picture above the bed, a reminder, like other souvenirs in the lounge, of the Wallingtons' years in the Far East. But life at Whiteleaf really does centre on the kitchen. When we inspected, David had just returned from a bread-making course in Cumbria. Despite all his years in the business he still reckoned he'd picked up a trick or two and claims his loaves are now rising higher than ever before. His dinner menus feature occasional exotic concoctions like crab-and prawn-stuffed local rock salmon en croûte in a yellow pepper and ginger sauce, but those with simpler tastes will be reassured to find staples like steak and kidney pie putting in an appearance too.

Closed Dec & Jan, 1 week Mar, 2 weeks May, July, Oct; restaurant closed Mon to Wed eves, Jul & Aug. Off B3231 Braunton to Croyde; situated at entrance to village. Private car park. 1 twin, 2 double, 1 family room; all with bathroom/WC; TV, hair-dryer, mini-bar, direct-dial telephone, clock radio. Dining-room, lounge, garden; baby-listening. No wheelchair access. No dogs in public rooms; no smoking in dining-room. Access, Switch, Visa. Single occupancy of twin/double £35, twin/double £50 to £54, family room £85; deposit required. Set D £19.50/21. Special breaks available

CRUDWELL Wiltshire map 2

Crudwell Court Hotel

Crudwell, Malmesbury SN16 9EP
TEL: (01666) 577194 FAX: (01666) 577853

Good food at a rambling country rectory with lovely walled gardens.

'We will definitely go back.' This seems to be the unanimous verdict of recent visitors to Nick Bristow and Iain Maclaren's rambling, seventeenth-century rectory. The feature most singled out for praise was the 'fabulous food' – perhaps warm pigeon, bacon and pine-kernel salad, followed by venison with leeks and juniper-berry sauce, roast pheasant with wild mushrooms, or duck with Madeira and shallot sauce – served up in the fresh, airy restaurant with wall panelling, rattan chairs, crisp, white linen, garden views and a pleasing informality.

Culinary pleasures aside, it's the relaxed, easy-going ambience and the uncluttered, unflashy décor that make this country house a little different – even 'slightly eccentric' in the words of one reader – although the partly creeper-clad stone façade and surviving period features are traditional enough. The high-ceilinged lounges, with seats ranged beneath the tall, garden-facing windows, are spacious and light, decorated in soft yellow and peachy tones, with plain upholstery, more chintzy curtains and plenty of floor space. One reader's second-floor attic room was 'enormous'; even the smallest bedroom is of a good size. The bedrooms' colour schemes are pale but warm, and the fabrics are floral. Some have fireplaces and old beams, and there are particularly lovely garden views through small, gabled windows, from the top floor.

◑ Open all year ◿ On A429, 3 miles north of Malmesbury. Private car park 🛏 1 single, 1 twin, 13 twin/double; family rooms available; all with bathroom/WC; TV, limited room service, direct-dial telephone ✓ Restaurant, 2 lounges, 2 conservatories, garden; conference facilities (max 40 people incl up to 15 residential); heated outdoor swimming-pool, croquet; early suppers for children; baby-listening, high chairs ♿ No wheelchair access ● No dogs in public rooms; no smoking in restaurant ▭ Access, Amex, Delta, Diners, Switch, Visa £ Single £50, single occupancy of twin/double £60, twin/double £88, family room £134. Set L from £7.50, D from £19.50. Special breaks available

---

CUCKFIELD West Sussex   map 3

Ockenden Manor

Ockenden Lane, Cuckfield RH17 5LD
TEL: (01444) 416111   FAX: (01444) 415549

An opulent country manor with fabulous views and first-rate service.

Tucked away in a leafy lane at the heart of picture-postcard Cuckfield, Ockenden Manor has impressive wrought-iron gates and massive stone walls which seem cut off from modern times. The original manor was burnt down in 1608 but was soon rebuilt with the wealth of the Burrell family and stayed with them until 1876, sprouting extensions in Victorian times and also more recently. The interior is classy, stylish and decked out with imposing pieces of antique furniture. The dark and clubby residents' bar has unusual fluted mahogany panels above the grand fireplace, while a trio of vintage ports stands ready on the side. Among the restaurant's dark oak panels the Burrell family's coat of arms presides over diners who might try a bisque of Chichester crab with Cornish mussels or perhaps a haunch of Ashdown venison pan-fried with port and walnuts from the excellent table d'hôte menu. The bedrooms also bear the Burrell stamp, being named after family members, and all are individually styled. Luke has a splendid double aspect over the gardens and unusual hand-painted furniture; Charlotte has green and cream hues, antique urns and a luxurious bathroom to spread out in; Master, however, is the grandest.

◑ Open all year ◿ In centre of Cuckfield. Private car park 🛏 1 single, 4 twin, 12 double, 3 four-poster, 2 suites; all with bathroom/WC; TV, limited room service, hair-dryer, trouser press, direct-dial telephone ✓ Restaurant, bar, lounge, conservatory, garden; conference facilities (max 50 people incl up to 22 residential); babysitting, baby-listening ♿ No wheelchair access ● No dogs ▭ Access, Amex, Delta, Switch, Visa £ Single £85, single occupancy of twin/double £85 to £110, twin/double £150, four-poster £180, suite £205; deposit required. Cooked B £5; set L £15.50/18.50, D £29.50/32.50. Special breaks available

---

 Denotes somewhere you can rely on a good meal – either the hotel features in the 1997 edition of our sister publication, The Good Food Guide, *or our inspectors thought the cooking impressive, whether particularly competent home cooking or more lavish cuisine.*

DEDHAM Essex map 6

Dedham Hall

Brook Street, Dedham CO7 6AD
TEL: (01206) 323027   FAX: (01206) 323293

Charmingly unstuffy family house secluded from the tourist traffic of Dedham, serving good food.

The six acres of grounds, glorious in spring when the daffodils and magnolia are out, screen the Sartons' house from the much-visited High Street, providing a quiet oasis in a very popular village. Wendy Sarton was doing her best to catch up on some gardening at the front when our inspector called, while the builders were busy landscaping the back ('the geese and chickens will soon roughen the edges'). How she finds the time is anyone's guess, for as well as cooking in the popular Fountain House Restaurant, Wendy also runs art and painting courses – fittingly enough, for this is Constable country, after all. The house bursts with art samples from previous tutors, ranging from watercolours to Chinese brush painting, and books. A rather confusing layout is the result of a fifteenth-century cottage that, Topsy-like, has just 'growed', but the overall feel is of a comfortable, well-lived-in house, with pink walls throughout, buttonback or pine headboards in the bedrooms and light, fresh fabrics. The restaurant, overlooking the garden, also feels relaxed; the weekly changing menu features good, honest cooking like avocado with smoked mackerel mousse, breaded pork fillet with fresh tomato sauce, and baked trout with green peppercorn sauce. In addition to the main rooms, ten annexe rooms are available for painting holidays.

◑ Open all year; restaurant closed Sun in winter   ⇗ From A12 follow signs into Dedham; hotel is at end of High Street on the left. Private car park   ⤷ 1 single, 2 twin, 2 double, 1 family room; 4 with bathroom/WC, 2 with shower/WC; TV, room service, hair-dryer   ⊘ Restaurant, dining-room, 2 bars, lounge, TV room, garden; early suppers for children   ⅙ No wheelchair access   ● No dogs; no smoking in some public rooms   ▭ Access, Delta, Switch, Visa   £ Single £34, single occupancy of twin/double £38, twin/double £47 to £57, family room from £67. Set L £16.50, D £18.50

Maison Talbooth

Stratford Road, Dedham CO7 6HN
TEL: (01206) 322367   FAX: (01206) 322752

Smart and very comfortable rooms in Victorian country house with well-established sister restaurant just down the road.

If you're searching for a sophisticated country house in the heart of Constable country, look no further. Over 26 years ago the Milsom family started offering accommodation in this pink Victorian rectory to provide diners at their successful restaurant, Le Talbooth, with equally stylish rooms. They've succeeded admirably. Principal suite Keats is big enough to hold a small tea dance in, while its newly refurbished bathroom is the ultimate in opulence, all pillars and mirrors surrounding a vast circular whirlpool bath. Standard rooms like Masefield, though smaller, are still luxurious, with canopy drapes and birds-of-paradise paper. The drawing-room is more understated, a large airy room overlooking the gardens and filled with a good mix of antiques and seating, oil paintings and fresh flowers. Although the restaurant is down the road (a courtesy car is provided), the smell of freshly baked shortbread wafting through the house as you arrive in the afternoon stimulates the appetite and is a welcoming touch. Otherwise, hold your horses to do justice to creations such as layered Cromer crab with mange-tout, pan-fried tiger prawns and balsamic vinaigrette, or breast of duck with home-made duck sausage and braised cabbage on a citrus sauce.

---

❶ Open all year ◪ A12 towards Ipswich; take left exit to Dedham; turn right over A12 flyover; hotel is 600 yards on right. Private car park ⊨ 2 twin, 7 double, 1 suite; all with bathroom/WC; TV, room service, hair-dryer, mini-bar, direct-dial telephone; trouser press on request ⊘ Restaurant, bar, lounge, garden; conference facilities (max 30 people incl up to 10 residential); croquet; early suppers for children; babysitting ৬ No wheelchair access ● No dogs; no smoking in public rooms ▭ Access, Amex, Delta, Switch, Visa £ Single occupancy of twin/double £85 to £120, twin/double/suite £125 to £160; deposit required. Cooked B £7.50; set L, D £21; alc L, D £25. Special breaks available

---

DENT Cumbria   map 8

Stone Close

Main Street, Dent, Sedbergh LA10 5QL
TEL: (01539) 625231

Great-value, simple, cottagey rooms above a superior Dales tearoom.

A teashop-with-rooms might be one way in which to describe Stone Close, but it wouldn't do justice to this charming cottage in a delightful village. Located some way between the big-name locations of the Yorkshire Dales and the Lake District, and reached by winding, up-and-down lanes that cannot be navigated with a caravan in tow, Dent is a relatively undiscovered joy. You'll find Stone Close – a couple of combined, whitewashed farmers' cottages – just at the point at which the narrow 'main street' breaks into cobbles, before it weaves around a couple of pubs and through the little village.

  Stone Close is first and foremost a teashop, but a superior one, serving exclusively home-made cooking using largely organic and wholefood ingredients. This has its advantages come breakfast time, when potato cakes, freshly squeezed juices and all sorts of dried fruits make the morning menu more imaginative than most. Situated above the flagstoned floors, pine tables and iron ranges of the ground floor, the three bedrooms are cottagey in style, and, since this is a seventeenth-century building, they are understandably modest in size (particularly Room 1).

---

❶ Closed Jan & Feb ◪ On the cobbled main street next to the car park. Public car park nearby ⊨ 1 single, 1 twin, 1 family room; radio; hair-dryer on request ⊘ 2 dining-rooms; early suppers for children ৬ No wheelchair access ● No smoking ▭ None accepted £ Single and single occupancy of twin/double £18, twin/double £31, family room £33 to £38; deposit required. Alc L £8.50

DISS Norfolk   map 6

Salisbury House

84 Victoria Road, Diss IP22 3JG
TEL: (01379) 644738 (AND FAX)

Smart and friendly restaurant with rooms, with consistently high standards of food and welcome.

'A real find,' purred a contented reader's report on Sue and Barry Davies' sturdy Victorian establishment in this market town. The location, it must be admitted, is not ideal – just off the busy main road running through the town – but the gardens behind the hotel provide a surprisingly peaceful respite. The building was originally a mill house, and you can see the sail-less remains of the eight-sailed Barton Mill beyond the back garden. Inside, the public rooms play up to their Victorian proportions, with a burgundy colour scheme in the front lounge and William Morris-patterned paper at the rear. There's also a choice of restaurants. In the cheery yellow bistro – a new enterprise since our last entry – you can pick and mix from a selection that includes dishes such as fillets of monkfish with lime vinaigrette, aubergine and almond tortillas with Mexican red sauce, and pear mousse with blackcurrant sauce. There are only three bedrooms: four-poster fans will head for the converted stable, where the bed canopy is suspended from the ceiling, but the two rooms in the house have also been well thought out – the Cane Room, with a Victorian brass bed and *en suite* whirlpool bath, is probably the nicer.

◑ Closed 1 week Chr, 2 weeks summer; restaurants closed Sun & Mon ⬈ ¼ mile from Diss town centre, heading east on the A1066 (Victoria Road). Private car park ⬐ 2 double, 1 four-poster; 1 in annexe 2 with bathroom/WC, 1 with shower/WC; TV, room service, hair-dryer, mini-bar ⊘ 2 restaurants, 2 lounges, conservatory, garden; conference facilities (max 20 people incl up to 3 residential); croquet; early suppers for children; baby-listening ⅙ No wheelchair access ⬤ No dogs; no smoking in bedrooms ▭ Access, Visa £ Single occupancy of twin/double £39 to £50, twin/double £59 to £70, four-poster £66; deposit required. Cooked B £3.50; set L, D £25; bistro meals available. Special breaks available

---

DITTISHAM Devon   map 1

Fingals

Old Coombe, Dittisham, Dartmouth TQ6 0JA
TEL: (01803) 722398   FAX: (01803) 722401

Laid-back, arty rural retreat with big swimming-pool in grounds.

Sunday mornings at Fingals find newspapers spread across the tables and hot buttered croissants and coffee at the ready. You enter the house straight into the bar, which is as it should be in a place so easy-going. All the other public rooms open off a low-ceilinged dining-room, where guests eat together unless they particularly crave the privacy of the separate breakfast-room. Most nights of the week four-course dinner menus offer three choices of main course, but on

Sunday and Monday a simpler roast or barbecue is substituted. The wood-panelled lounge comes well-stocked with books and magazines; television has been banished to a separate room where a pile of videos includes children's favourites. Paintings hang everywhere; those of the Taj Mahal and Venice in the dining-room were done by Andras Kaldor, the artist responsible for the mural overlooking the covered pool outside. The pool is a particular delight, surrounded by plants and ceramics; the roof slides back to let in the sun on hot days. Bedrooms at Fingals favour mix-and-match style, with big, comfy wooden beds and distinctive but never flashy colour schemes; a self-catering barn reached along a walkway is especially inviting. With a sauna and Jacuzzi, and a tennis court, croquet lawn and snooker table, there's always plenty to do. If the isolation gets too much, you can even slip away down river to Dartmouth.

◖ Closed 1 Jan to Easter   ↗ From Dittisham take road to Totnes; after 1 mile turn left up second lane; follow signs to Fingals. Private car park   ⊨ 2 twin, 7 double, 1 four-poster; family room available; all with bathroom/WC; room service, direct-dial telephone; TV in some rooms   ⊘ Dining-room, bar, lounge, TV room, drying-room, library, conservatory, games room, garden; conference facilities (max 10 people residential); sauna, solarium, heated indoor swimming-pool, tennis, croquet, snooker, table tennis; early suppers for children   ও No wheelchair access   ● No dogs in public rooms   ☐ Access, Amex, Switch, Visa   £ Single occupancy of twin/double £40 to £60, twin/double £60 to £80, four-poster £75 to £95, family room £105 to £135; deposit required. Set D £25. Special breaks available

---

                                                    map 1

Nobody Inn

Doddiscombsleigh, Nr Exeter EX6 7PS
TEL: (01647) 252394   FAX: (01647) 252978

Oak-beamed inn offering extensive choice of food, wine and whisky in a quiet corner of Dartmoor.

How the Nobody Inn came about its curious name is the sort of topic to exercise the brains and imaginations of those arriving here to sample a wine list that runs to 700-plus vintages and a whisky list strayed from the Highlands, with more than 200 choices on offer. For those in search of the quintessential English inn, the Nobody, with its low beams, inglenook fireplaces and myriad brasses, should fit the bill nicely. Guests can opt to stay in one of the four rooms above the pub, which ooze character (but could also soak up noise), or in the three larger, quieter rooms in Town Barton, a Georgian annexe 150 yards away. Dinner is served in a restaurant that flows out into the back of the bar; popular dishes include chicken and oyster or wild boar casserole, while the cheeseboard offers a chance to sample all sorts of Devon delicacies that still don't make it to supermarket shelves. Breakfast is also served in the restaurant, although Town Bartoners have cereals provided in their rooms in case they don't fancy even a short pre-breakfast stroll.

◑ Closed 25, 26 Dec pm; restaurant closed Sun & Mon eves　⤳ Leave A38 at Devon & Exeter racecourse (signposted Dunchideock); follow signs to Nobody Inn for 3 miles. Private car park　⭲ 1 single, 2 twin, 4 double; some in annexe; 3 with bathroom/WC, most with shower/WC; TV, direct-dial telephone; hair-dryer on request; mini-bar in some rooms　⌖ Restaurant, bar; conference facilities (max 25 people incl up to 7 residential)　⮑ No wheelchair access　● No children under 14; no dogs; no smoking in restaurant　▭ Access, Amex, Delta, Switch, Visa　£ Single £23 to £35, single occupancy of twin/double £35, twin/double £48 to £59; deposit required. Cooked B £3 supplement in annexe rooms; alc D £14; bar meals available (prices valid till Sept 1997). Special breaks available

---

DORCHESTER Dorset　　　　　　　　　　　　　　　　　　　map 2

Casterbridge Hotel

49 High East Street, Dorchester DT1 1HU
TEL: (01305) 264043　FAX: (01305) 260884

An elegant Georgian town house with excellent breakfasts.

The neat façade of Rita and Stuart Turner's three-storey Georgian town house sets the tone for the interior: welcoming, immaculately kept and elegant in a sober, understated way. Yet beyond this simplicity are many features to set this small hotel apart from others. Between the main house and the modern annexe, part of the courtyard has been glassed over to form an unusual conservatory extension, with walls of unplastered stone, bright garden furniture, and an abundance of plants and mock classical statues. Breakfasts – served here or in the smart dining-room, with sparkling polished floors and tables – are impressive; choices include fruit (fresh and dry), yoghurts, juices, cereals, porridge, eggs 'anyway you please', kipper, haddock, muffins, croissants – or alternatively a continental breakfast brought to your room. Bedrooms vary in size and aspect, but all combine style and comfort. Some are cottagey with pine furniture, others more contemporary. The Turners are mindful of the needs of business visitors – many rooms have writing desks and trouser presses – but there's also plenty round about to keep holiday-makers occupied.

◑ Closed 25 & 26 Dec　⤳ 100 yards east of town centre. Private car park　⭲ 5 single, 3 twin, 5 double, 1 four-poster, 1 family room; some in annexe; most with bathroom/WC, some with shower/WC; TV, room service, hair-dryer, direct-dial telephone; trouser press in most rooms　⌖ Restaurant, bar, lounge, library, conservatory, garden; conference facilities (max 12 people residential); early suppers for children; baby-listening　⮑ Wheelchair access to hotel (2 ramps) and restaurant, 3 ground-floor bedrooms　● No dogs; no smoking in most bedrooms　▭ Access, Amex, Delta, Diners, Switch, Visa　£ Single £32 to £36, single occupancy of twin/double £38 to £45, twin/double £55 to £60, four-poster £65 to £70, family room £60 to £65; deposit required. Special breaks available

---

The text of entries is based on unsolicited reports sent in by readers and backed up by inspections. The factual details are from questionnaires the Guide *sends to all hotels that feature in the book.*

George Hotel

High Street, Dorchester OX10 7HH
TEL: (01865) 340404   FAX: (01865) 341620

*Good-value accommodation in a black and white inn at the centre of
an attractive Oxfordshire village.*

On the high street of a small village, the buildings of which represent a variety of
different eras, the George Hotel is a much-modified fifteenth-century coaching
inn right opposite the medieval abbey. Inside, there's a comfortable mix of
styles, from the mock-rustic restaurant with its tapestry-backed chairs and
exposed brick walls, to the gloomy but genuinely ancient Potboy bar, where
locals and guests happily mix, choosing their food from a blackboard menu and
toasting their toes in front of the log fire. Standard pub fare here includes black
pudding, ploughman's and hot puddings, while the restaurant is more exotic,
with perhaps a savoury pear starter, roast quail for main course, and iced fruit
parfait to follow.

Most of the bedrooms are arranged around the stable yard. Some are newly
refurbished and have smart modern furnishings and power showers, while
others are comfortable and old-fashioned. Rooms Two and Four, both twin
rooms, are the largest and have a lovely outlook over the abbey – light sleepers
might like to opt for a room at the back as the clock strikes every quarter of an
hour.

◑ Open all year   ⤢ Situated off A4074, Oxford to Henley road. Private car park
🛏 4 single, 5 twin, 7 double, 2 four-poster; family room available; some in annexe; all
with bathroom/WC; TV, room service, hair-dryer, direct-dial telephone
🍴 Restaurant, bar, lounge, garden; conference facilities (max 40 people incl up to 18
residential); baby-listening   ⅃ No wheelchair access   ● No dogs in public rooms
▭ Access, Amex, Diners, Switch, Visa   £ Single £53, twin/double £65, four-poster
£75, family room £85; deposit required. Set L £15, D £18; bar meals available (1996
prices). Special breaks available

Ashwick House

Dulverton TA22 9QD
TEL: (01398) 323868 (AND FAX)

*Wonderful isolated Edwardian country-house hotel with good food
and innumerable welcoming touches.*

Ashwick House stands in splendid isolation in the middle of Exmoor. Step
inside and it's hard to believe that the Great Hall, with its soaring windows,
stencilled beams and deep-red sofas set before a roaring log fire, was serving as a
sheep barn as recently as the 1970s. Upstairs, owner Richard Sherwood has
thought of everything. A collection of 'Teach Yourself Russian' tapes waiting to
be borrowed on the landing is typical of his attention to detail; 'I noticed that
more of my guests were visiting the ex-Soviet Republics and thought they might

like to make a start at learning the language,' he explained. On arrival you'll be served tea and scones in one of the huge bedrooms with crown canopy beds, comfortable chairs and plentiful cupboard space. If you're lucky you'll be able to watch some of the rabbits, foxes, badgers, pheasants and even occasional red deer which stroll across the lawn in the evening to drink at the lake. If not, there's still plenty to keep you occupied, with Scrabble sets, videos, cassettes to help you identify local birdsong, magazines and much, much more. Indeed it would be like giving away the ending of a good detective story to reveal all the many surprises that make Ashwick House such a joy. Bathrooms come equipped with American 'tell your weight' machines. Try them before dinner and then resist the temptation to step on again or they'll announce the embarrassing consequences of a dinner which might start with carrot and orange soup and move on to fresh fillet of salmon with rich vermouth sauce, rounding off with a diet-busting chocolate hazelnut truffle slice.

○ Open all year ⊿ At post office in Dulverton take B3223 signposted Exford and Lynton; drive over moor; cross 2 cattle grids and take a left turn to Ashwick House. Private car park ⤷ 2 twin, 4 double; all with bathroom/WC; TV, room service, hair-dryer, trouser press, direct-dial telephone, clock radio; mini-bar in some rooms ✢ Restaurant, lounge, drying-room, library, garden; conference facilities (max 12 people incl up to 6 residential); solarium; early suppers for children ⅊ No wheelchair access ● No children under 8; no dogs; no smoking in restaurant or library ▭ None accepted ⅊ Single occupancy of twin/double £57, twin/double £95 to £97; deposit required. Set D £22, Sun L £14.50. Special breaks available

---

Carnarvon Arms

Dulverton TA22 9AE
TEL: (01398) 323302   FAX: (01398) 324022

A huntin', shootin' and fishin' hotel which welcomes walkers and National Trust garden-lovers too.

Dulverton Station may have been consigned to history, but the hotel built for its passengers by the fourth Earl of Carnarvon in 1874 goes from strength to strength. In this particular corner of Exmoor it's hardly surprising to find that riding to hounds is a primary interest of guests, and the hall is decorated with antlers, trophies and cartoons of the hunt. For those with tamer interests, a stock of leaflets promotes the many attractions within walking or driving reach of the hotel. The two ground-floor lounges are very different, in keeping with the changing moods of the moor: the main lounge is wood-panelled, with comfy chairs grouped for conversation, a roaring fire and plenty of magazines; the second is a light, airy room, perfect for soaking up the sun. Red-carpeted stairs lead down from the lounge to a dining-room dominated by an alcove full of wine; menus are heavy with roasts and steaks. A rolling programme of refurbishment means that some rooms are always more newly decorated than others, but each is slightly different and many have pleasant views; Room 14 offers a grandstand view of the West Somerset Polo Club in action. There are no tea and coffee-making facilities in the rooms because proprietor Toni Jones believes that people go to hotels to escape from doing things for themselves. On the way out, don't miss the original Victorian bells once used for summoning the servants in the hall.

◑ Open all year ☑ On edge of Brushford village, 1½ miles from Dulverton. Private car park ⮌ 4 single, 6 twin, 12 double, 1 family room, 1 suite; all with bathroom/WC exc 1 single with shower/WC; TV, room service, direct-dial telephone; tea/coffee-making facilities and hair-dryer on request ✔ Dining-room, bar, 2 lounges, drying-room, library, games room, garden; conference facilities (max 180 people incl up to 24 residential); fishing, outdoor heated swimming-pool, tennis, croquet; early suppers for children; baby-listening ♿ Wheelchair access to hotel (2 ramps), restaurant, WC (M), 2 ground-floor bedrooms ● No smoking in some public rooms ▭ Access, Amex, Switch, Visa ₤ Single £45, single occupancy of twin/double £90, twin/double £90, family room £90, suite £100; deposit required. Continental B £7, cooked B £11, set L £11.50, D £23.50; bar meals available (1996 prices). Special breaks available

---

DURHAM Co Durham   map 10

Georgian Town House

10 Crossgate, Durham DH1 4PS
TEL: 0191-386 8070

A small, Georgian house with unusual decorative features close to the historic town centre.

While the 'Edwardian semi' or the '1920s bungalow' wouldn't really work as the name of a hotel or guesthouse, there's something simple and alluring about a place called the 'Georgian Town House'. Don't be taken in by the plainness of the nomenclature, however, as Jane and Robert Weil's home is hardly an archetype. The green tree that is stencilled on the white façade lends a clue to the riot of stencilling and other internal decorative effects that give the house its character and charm. Walls, corridors, bedrooms, public areas – little has escaped the owners' urge to add a bush or tree here, or the moon and the stars there. Overall, the result is refreshing, and distracts your attention from the rather parsimonious dimensions of the rooms.

The residents' lounge is something of an exception to the general decorative rule: with its smart, striped sofa, straight-backed chairs and stone lion by the fire, it seems to aspire to a more traditional idiom – perhaps the stately home that is depicted in miniature on the mantelpiece is the room's alter ego. One reader complained about being expected to take a room shortly after it had been decorated, when the smell of paint was still strong.

◑ Closed mid-Dec to early Jan ☑ From A1(M) take A690 to the city; follow signs to Crook and Newcastle; at 3rd roundabout turn left. On-street parking ⮌ 2 twin, 3 double, 1 family room; all with bathroom/WC; TV; hair-dryer on request ✔ Dining-room/conservatory, lounge, garden; ♿ No wheelchair access ● No dogs; no smoking in bedrooms ▭ None accepted ₤ Single occupancy of twin/double £38 to £40, twin/double £50 to £55, family room £55 to £60; deposit required

---

Don't forget that other hotels worth considering are listed in our Visitors' Book.

Grinkle Park

Easington, Saltburn-by-the-Sea TS13 4UB
TEL: (01287) 640515   FAX: (01287) 641278

A Victorian country house, designed by Alfred Waterhouse, in a peaceful, rural setting.

Situated in a tranquil spot a couple of miles away from the nearest village, Grinkle Park may be an option for those who want to tour the moors and visit the coast, but who then wish to retreat to a place of absolute calm. Set in 35 acres of gardens, its isolation and, indeed, the building itself – a pleasing jumble of pointed eaves, gables and a turreted tower – are the hotel's strongest selling points. Inside, however, things don't really live up to the rich promise of the exterior, and although there is plenty of space and natural light, the decorative styling tends towards the bland, while the public areas seem curiously soulless.

With its pale-green colour scheme, the Camellia Room has the feel of a conservatory and is used for light lunches, while the main meals are served in the restaurant, which is simply decorated and features large windows that look out on to the lawn. A typical choice on the à la carte menu might be sauté scallops of monkfish with prawns, served with a white-wine and shellfish sauce. The bedrooms are more notable for their absolute quiet than for any flourishes in design, and many have lovely views towards the lake.

○ Open all year   ⤢ Off A171 Guisborough to Whitby road, 9 miles from Guisborough. Private car park   🛏 5 single, 6 twin, 7 double, 2 four-poster; family rooms available all with bathroom/WC exc 3 singles with shower/WC; TV, limited room service, trouser press, direct-dial telephone, clock radio; hair-dryers in some rooms   ⌁ 2 restaurants, bar, 2 lounges, drying-room, conservatory, games room, garden; conference facilities (max 150 people incl up to 20 residential); tennis, croquet, snooker; early suppers for children; baby-listening   ⅗ No wheelchair access   ● No dogs in public rooms; dogs in bedrooms at £4.50 per night, free kennels   ▭ Access, Amex, Diners, Visa   ⊡ Single/single occupancy of twin/double £45 to £65, twin/double £70 to £80, four-poster £70 to £85, family room from £84; deposit required. Set L £9.50/11.50, D £16.50; alc D £24. Special breaks available

---

Lower Pitt

East Buckland, Barnstaple EX32 0TD
TEL: (01598) 760243 (AND FAX)

Tranquil farmhouse restaurant-with-rooms in depths of Devon countryside.

With its glistening white farmhouse and courtyard with old milk churns and ploughs dotted about, Lower Pitt is the farmyard of popular imagination, and its remote setting ensures you feel the peace and quiet working its way under your skin even as you're parking. Suzanne and Jerome Lyons will be waiting to offer a warm welcome; on a cool day a cheering fire will be lit in the big fireplace dominating their lounge/bar. The focal point of Lower Pitt is a long, thin dining-room, split up by discreet partitions for privacy. From the plant-filled conservatory at the end, diners can watch finches and tits fighting for space on a string of nuts. The à la carte menus offer plenty of choice, and alongside the more usual dishes come less expected ones: the Thai stir fry has been winning friends for many years now. Upstairs, the three small but comfortable bedrooms come with fresh flowers and bottled Dartmoor water but without televisions. Having noticed a growing number of enthusiastic walkers heading their way, the Lyons are now trying to fit their own circuit of the south-west coastal footpath around the cooking and housekeeping, so they are in a better position to advise their guests.

◖ Open all year   ↗ 3 miles north of A361, signposted East and West Buckland; hotel is around corner from church. Private car park   ⊨ 1 twin, 2 double; twin with bathroom/WC, doubles with shower/WC; hair-dryer; TV in one bedroom   ⊘ 2 dining-rooms, bar/lounge, conservatory, garden   ♿ No wheelchair access   ● No children under 12; no dogs; no smoking in bedrooms or dining-room   ▭ Access, Amex, Switch, Visa   £ Single occupancy of twin/double £35, twin/double £60; deposit required. Alc D £25. Special breaks available

---

EAST GRINSTEAD West Sussex   map 3

Gravetye Manor

Vowels Lane, East Grinstead RH19 4LJ
TEL: (01342) 810567   FAX: (01342) 810080

An aristocratic country manor, with excellent food, in a peaceful setting.

The imposing manor house, built of honey-coloured stone and embraced by a thick cladding of ivy and climbing roses, finally comes into sight at the end of a winding track through thickly forested land. Restfulness is guaranteed here, in the bosom of the West Sussex countryside, and was clearly a key factor in the siting of Gravetye Manor when Richard Infield built it for his bride, Katharine Compton, in 1598. Their initials are still to be seen, carved in stone above the entrance door from the formal garden, and their portraits are carved in oak in the master bedroom, Ash. Tranquil years passed by at the manor (ruffled only by a period of use as a smugglers' hide-out), until the great gardener William Robinson took up residence and created one of England's finest 'natural' gardens. Inside, his hand can be seen in the acres of oak panels taken from the estate, the deep-yellow ceilings, the magnificently carved chimney pieces, and in the air of understated refinement which pervades the house like the sweet smell of the wood smoke that emanates from the sizzling log fires in the blackened hearths. Creaky leather armchairs and polished antiques tempt you to soak up the clubby atmosphere with port and cigars in the front lounge. Chef Mark Raffan's menu offers delicacies such as pike sausage with braised fennel, chargrilled fillets of red mullet, or Gressingham duck in liquorice-flavoured sauce, with a wine list equal to the challenge. The bedrooms, which are named after trees, are individually shaped and styled as a result of the nature of the building, but are all spacious and furnished in the elegant style that one would expect.

◐ Open all year   ☒ Off B2028; after Turners Hill fork left, then turn left at Gravetye sign. Private car park ⊑→ 1 single, 12 twin, 4 double, 1 four-poster; all with bathroom/WC; TV, room service, hair-dryer, trouser press, direct-dial telephone, radio ⍋ 2 restaurants, bar, 3 lounges, garden, air-conditioning in 1 lounge; conference facilities (max 14 people residential/non-residential); fishing, croquet; baby-sitting, baby-listening   ᕃ No wheelchair access ● No children under 7 exc babes in arms; no dogs; no smoking in 1 restaurant ⊟ Access, Visa £ Single £123, twin/double £165 to £247, four-poster £24; deposit required. Continental B £12, cooked B £16.50; set L £26 to £35, D £35; alc L £47

EAST KNOYLE Wiltshire   map 2

Milton Farm

East Knoyle, Salisbury SP3 6BG
TEL: (01747) 830247

Friendly, family farmhouse with pretty rooms and lots of original features.

Flagstones, wood beams and a narrow oak staircase have all been carefully restored in this lovely Queen Anne farmhouse of uneven grey stone, white pointed-arch windows and tall chimneys. They're used to most creative effective in the pretty, cottage-style twin bedroom decorated in soft green and yellow tones. The double room across the landing is more floral and flouncy, with a canopy above the bed. Both are a good size and well maintained. Downstairs, the lounge and dining-room have unplastered stone walls, open log fires and flowers, both fresh and dried. Janice Hyde, the ebullient hostess, no longer does dinners, except on request, freeing up more time to help on the family's 300-acre mixed farm and run her other business, importing pottery from Portugal. Anyone tempted by the display of colourful ceramics in the hallway should wander across the shady, gravelled courtyard; her small shop is in the thatched cottage opposite.

◐ Closed Dec to Feb   ☒ Turn off A350 just north of East Knoyle for the hamlet of Milton. Private car park ⊑→ 1 twin, 1 double; double with bathroom/WC, twin with shower/WC; TV ⍋ Dining-room, garden; heated outdoor swimming-pool; early suppers for children   ᕃ No wheelchair access ● No dogs ⊟ None accepted £ Twin/double £40 to £49; deposit required

Swainscombe

The Green, East Knoyle, Salisbury SP3 6BN
TEL: (01747) 830224 (AND FAX)

Welcoming hosts and much-praised food at an archetypal thatched cottage in the country.

Joy and Rex Orman's seventeenth-century thatched house has well-kept lawns and views over verdant countryside. The cottage was once two smaller dwellings, but the halves have been joined so seamlessly that few visitors would realise it, were it not for the rather curious arrangement of the bedrooms. Two rooms, a bathroom and a small seating area with a TV on the landing fill the east 'wing'; up the other stairway, in the west 'wing', are two singles and a four-poster. The house's interior has all the requisite period features – beams, inglenook fireplaces, sloping ceilings – plus plenty of antiques, but its character is more the result of over 25 years of family residence than any pre-planned design. It is neat and spotless, espousing no particular style, though very comfortable; bedrooms, for example, have electric blankets, fine linen, large bath-towels and a good set of toiletries.

The dining-room, however, has a definite period atmosphere. Joy has built up quite a reputation for her cooking (comments in her visitors' book claim it's 'better than Claridges') and candlelit dinners eaten round a communal, polished table are quite an occasion. Main courses might be chicken breast in brandy and orange sauce, lemon sole with grapes and white wine sauce or lamb with orange and redcurrants. Joy prefers a large party at mealtimes, so singles and couples will be encouraged to try the pub across the road, but won't miss out on the hearty breakfasts – bacon, sausage, the full works in fact, all cooked up on the Aga.

◑ Closed 25 & 26 Dec　☒ Turn off A350 in East Knoyle at post office; continue up Wise Lane and over crossroads to hamlet (The Green); turn right at red telephone box; Swainscombe is 30 yards on right. Private car park　⊫→ 2 single, 1 twin, 1 double, 1 four-poster, 1 suite; all with bathroom/WC exc singles with shower/WC; TV, room service, hair-dryer; tea/coffee on request　⊘ Dining-room, lounge, TV room, garden; early suppers for children　⅋ No wheelchair access　● No children under 5; no dogs; no smoking　⊏ None accepted　£ Single £23 to £25, single occupancy of twin/double £25, twin/double £40, four-poster £45, suite £40 to £45; deposit required. Set D £15.50. Special breaks available

---

EASTON GREY Wiltshire　　　　　　　　　　　　　　　　map 2

Whatley Manor

Easton Grey, Malmesbury SN16 0RB
TEL: (01666) 822888　FAX: (01666) 826120

Extensive leisure and conference facilities and good-value breaks at a rambling country manor.

Much of Whatley Manor was built by a wealthy sportsman in the 1920s, so it's appropriate that many of today's visitors come for the sport and leisure facilities – tennis, croquet, swimming. The creeper-clad manor, with a courtyard of outbuildings, formal gardens and extensive lawns dropping towards the River Avon, is Jacobean in origin, but most of what you see today as you wind down the conifer-lined drive dates from the overhaul early this century. The interior, with a scattering of fine antiques, is smart, if a little formidable, despite the best efforts of the owners to soften the vast rooms with comfy seating, wall lighting and fresh flowers. The dark panelled drawing-room is huge, with a stone fireplace as centrepiece and various clusters of chairs around low tables. With cane chairs and rows of books, the cocktail bar is cosier, while the peachy dining-room is a suitably grand, though rather formal, setting for enjoying dishes such as guinea-fowl with sage, grapefruit, limes and stem ginger or beef fillet pan-fried with Stilton, cider and garlic sauce. One correspondent, here for a big boys' weekend, commended the management for showing flexibility when half the party failed to make Sunday breakfast! Bedrooms come in a variety of sizes and styles. Those in the main house are large, and generally have antique furnishings, chintzy fabrics, and pastel shades of apricot or pink. Rooms in the annexe are cheaper and have less character, but are very comfortable.

○ Open all year ↗ On B4040, 3 miles west of Malmesbury. Private car park ⊨ 9 twin, 17 double, 1 four-poster, 2 family rooms; some in annexe; all with bathroom/WC; TV, hair-dryer, direct-dial telephone; room service in main house ✧ Dining-room, bar, 2 lounges, library, games room, garden; conference facilities (max 30 people incl up to 29 residential); fishing, sauna, solarium, heated outdoor swimming-pool, tennis, croquet; early suppers for children; babysitting, baby-listening ♿ Wheelchair access to hotel (3 steps), restaurant and WC (unisex), 14 ground-floor bedrooms ● No dogs in public rooms ▭ Access, Amex, Delta, Visa £ Single occupancy of twin/double £70 to £80, twin/double £82 to £114, four-poster £114, family room £82 to £114. Set L £14.50, D £28. Special breaks available

---

EAST ORD Northumberland   map 10

Tree Tops ☆

Village Green, East Ord,
Berwick-upon-Tweed TD15 2NS
TEL: (01289) 330679

A homely guesthouse with gregarious hosts and a colourful garden a stone's throw from Berwick.

Tree Tops is an unassuming 1920s bungalow set just off the broad village green and seems oddly named until you get better acquainted. The colourful window boxes and hanging baskets give you a clue, but it's only when John and Elizabeth Nicholls bring you out to the summer house for complimentary tea and home-made scones on your arrival that its hidden beauty starts to unfold. The neat croquet lawn leads down through a shrubbery into a small pocket of woodland filled with bluebells, daffodils and purslane, below which a stream gently gurgles; so whether you like your nature wild or tamed there's something here for you. The house too is deceptive – stretching a good way back from the road, it's much more spacious inside than you would expect. The sitting-room looks out on to the garden and is packed with tourist information about the historic walled town of Berwick, a mile or so away, as well as folders painstakingly prepared by John packed with suggestions for itineraries both in Northumbria and north of the border. John's Scottish roots are never far from the surface but are given full expression on Border Night, when he serves traditional Scottish and Borders dishes to the background of piped music while wearing his clan regalia. Needless to say, a good selection of single malts is available. Otherwise, dinners may be based on more familiar recipes like chicken chasseur. The small wine list is good value, with several decent bottles for around £6. The two bedrooms have pine and wicker furniture and matching bed covers and curtains and are exceedingly peaceful.

◑ Closed 1 Nov to 31 Mar; restaurant closed Mon, Wed & Fri eves Turn right at East Ord green at mini crossroads; take second right into hotel. Private car park 1 twin, 1 double; double with bathroom/WC, twin with shower/WC; TV, hair-dryer, clock radio Dining-room, lounge, garden; croquet No wheelchair access No children; no dogs; no smoking None accepted Single occupancy of twin/double £35, twin/double £48; deposit required. Set D £15. Special breaks available

EAST PORTLEMOUTH Devon map 1

Gara Rock

East Portlemouth, Salcombe TQ8 8PH
TEL: (01548) 842342 FAX: (01548) 843033

Child-friendly hotel with self-catering facilities on clifftop overlooking National Trust property.

Despite its off-the-beaten-track location, the Gara Rock is first and foremost a family-holiday complex, where simply furnished rooms and a wide range of entertainment (clowns, magic and regular children's parties) cater for a clientele of children, whose parents will no doubt relish the footpaths running across the adjacent National Trust clifftop countryside. Approaching from these same footpaths, the hotel looks like the attractive group of nineteenth-century cottages it once was. Unfortunately the main entrance and reception area are typical of 1960s architecture. With no other eating places in the vicinity, the hotel's cheerful pine-floored dining-rooms and inviting bar do their best to cater for every eventuality from brunch breakfasts through picnic lunches to fondue parties. There's also a handy 'Shop at the Top' for when you find you've forgotten the toothpaste. The bedrooms in the main house boast sea views and smartish décor. Gara Rock also has 22 self-catering suites; those in the neighbouring blocks cost less but lack the character of those in the main house. Note that usually bookings are taken only for stays of three days or more.

◑ Closed Nov to Easter At Frogmore turn right; go over bridge and follow signs for East Portlemouth and Gara Rock. Private car park 1 single, 5 twin, 4 double; most with bathroom/WC, some with shower/WC; TV 2 restaurants, bar, 3 lounges, TV room, drying-room, conservatory, games room, garden; conference facilities (max 100 people incl up to 10 residential); fishing, gym, heated swimming-pool, tennis; early suppers for children; toys, playrooms, babysitting, baby-listening, outdoor games Wheelchair access to hotel (2 steps), restaurant, 10 ground-floor bedrooms None Access, Switch, Visa Single £28 to £40, twin/double £66 to £90; deposit required. Alc D £10; bar meals available (prices valid till Oct 1996). Special breaks available

Prices are what you can expect to pay in 1997, except where specified to the contrary. Many hoteliers tell us that these prices can be regarded only as approximations.

EDITH WESTON **Leicestershire**   map 6

Normanton Park

Rutland Water South Shore, Edith Weston, Oakham LE15 8RP
TEL: (01780) 720315   FAX: (01780) 721086

A multi-purpose lakeside hotel catering well for day-trippers and those staying for business and pleasure.

Normanton Park has a lot going for it even before you step through its doors. It stands 50 yards from scenic Rutland Water, England's second-largest reservoir; in view, a lonesome neo-classical church occupies a tiny promontory. Moreover, the hotel building itself is rather striking: a fine Georgian stable block, once part of the estate of the demolished Normanton Park manor house. Inside, the hotel lives up to good first impressions. Public rooms each have a well-defined, singular style. For example, the formal Orangery Restaurant, where the menu includes local produce such as venison, pheasant and Rutland Water trout, complements its lake views with classical *trompe l'oeil*. By contrast, the vaulted Sailing Bar, with canvas sails strung out across the rafters, is in effect a stylish pub open to all-comers. The best bedrooms, in a new extension, come with swish modern furnishings including a plump sofa-bed or armchair, and capitalise on the lake views too. Rooms round the courtyard have undeniably bright and cheery design schemes, but for some the words 'shoe' and 'box' come to mind. Staff, as at Normanton Park's sister hotel Barnsdale Lodge (see under Oakham), are perky and youthful.

◑ Open all year   ⊿ Take turning off A606 signposted Edith Weston/Rutland Water. Private car park   ⤶ 1 single, 5 twin, 10 double, 2 four-poster, 5 family rooms; some in annexe; all with bathroom/WC; TV, room service, hair-dryer, trouser press, direct-dial telephone, clock radio, iron   ⌘ 4 restaurants, 2 bars, lounge, drying-room, garden; conference facilities (max 100 people incl up to 23 residential); fishing, clay-pigeon shooting, archery, quad bikes; early suppers for children; babysitting, baby-listening   ঙ Wheelchair access to hotel (1 ramp), restaurant and WC (unisex), 8 ground-floor bedrooms   ● No dogs in restaurants; dogs in bedrooms £10 surcharge   ⌷ Access, Delta, Switch, Visa   £ Single £50, single occupancy of twin/double £50, twin/double £70, four-poster £80, family room £80. Set Sun L £14; alc L, D £23.50. Special breaks available

---

ELY **Cambridgeshire**   map 6

Black Hostelry

The College, Cathedral Close, Ely CB7 4DL
TEL: (01353) 662612   FAX: (01353) 665658

A rare opportunity to savour some historical, ecclesiastical atmosphere, at a very reasonable price.

It isn't very often that you get the chance to stay in a canon's house, particularly one with so much history attached. The Greens have been offering B&B accommodation in this former Benedictine infirmary for 15 years now. Walking through the apartment, the largest of the two spaces on offer, is like a potted guide to 1,000 years of English architecture: stone Norman arches, a Tudor fireplace and Georgian panelling all feature in the sitting-room, where breakfast is served. The bedroom has views over the garden and a small bathroom, though the toilet is on the floor below, tucked into a space beneath the stairs that was once the entrance to the kitchen. The other room, decked out in pink, has plenty of space for relaxing, but an added bonus is the chance to take breakfast in the medieval undercroft, from the original dean-and-chapter table that is stained with centuries' worth of ink and sealing wax. With a house that has such a wealth of venerable history, the Greens don't try to compete: furnishings are straightforward but comfortable, and the atmosphere is that of a private house rather than a hotel.

○ Open all year ⟶ In centre of Ely, within the Cathedral close. Private car park ⟶ 2 double; both with bathroom/shower/WC; TV, hair-dryer, direct-dial telephone ♿ No wheelchair access ⬜ None accepted £ Single occupancy of double £49, double £49; deposit required

---

ETCHINGHAM East Sussex map 3

King John's Lodge ☆

Sheepstreet Lane, Etchingham TN19 7AZ
TEL: (01580) 819232 FAX: (01580) 819562

A great-value, historic country house with fantastic gardens.

Even at first glance, the stone walls, mullioned, leaded windows and fish-scale cascade of tiles decorating the façade of this wonderful rural hideaway clearly have a tale to tell. Mainly Jacobean, but with Elizabethan and Victorian additions, Jill and Richard Cunningham's family home reputedly served as a prison to King John of France, who was held here by the Black Prince in the fourteenth century. The Cunninghams are rightly proud of their historic home, and take great pleasure in sharing its quirks and secrets with guests. The dining-room, where the huge fireplace has been worn away by centuries of knives being sharpened on its stones, is the most perfect venue for a romantic, candlelit dinner: a meal here is a real event. Elsewhere, the heavily beamed rooms, inglenook fireplaces and oil paintings are softened by squidgy sofas and a lived-in atmosphere. The bedrooms are named and decorated according to the era to which they belong, the grandest being Jacobean, which is very roomy and boasts an unusual front-window bay, along with its full complement of massive beams and stone fireplace. For lovers of horticulture, a relaxing stroll around the lily ponds and rose walks of the wild garden, before emerging into the secret garden, is another magical experience to savour.

○ Closed Chr & New Year ⟶ Just off A265, 7 miles north of Battle. Private car park ⟶ 1 twin, 2 double, 1 family room; 3 with bathroom/WC, 1 double with shower/WC; hair-dryer on request ✓ Dining-room, lounge, TV room, garden; heated outdoor swimming-pool, tennis, croquet, pool ♿ No wheelchair access ● No dogs; no smoking in bedrooms ⬜ None accepted £ Single occupancy of twin/double £30 to £35, twin/double £50 to £55, family room from £50; deposit required. Set D £17.50

EVERSHOT Dorset   map 2

Summer Lodge

Summer Lane, Evershot, Nr Dorchester DT2 0JR
TEL: (01935) 83424   FAX: (01935) 83005

A cheerful and relaxing country house with good food and gardens.

Summer Lodge lives up to its name. A friendly young staff; wonderful gardens, which include a small pool and shady rose arbour; bright country-house décor, mixing modern paintings and chintzy fabrics with antique tables and chests; and flowers, flowers everywhere. All these could turn even the bleakest rainy day into a cheering, relaxing experience. The elegant, whitewashed Georgian villa strikes just the right balance between efficiency and informality, traditional and contemporary elegance. Through french windows, the colourful lawns can be enjoyed from the bright, fresh dining-room, while you feast on veal rump with calf's kidney, asparagus, Madeira and truffle sauce, honey-roasted Gressingham duck or grilled Dover sole with chive butter. Coffee or afternoon tea (which is included in the daily rate) can be taken beside the log fire in the classically styled drawing-room. Most bedrooms overlook the garden or village rooftops and fields; ground-floor rooms in the coach-house annexe have french doors and small patios. Décor and furnishings tend to be smart and light, with wicker furniture and soft shades; the master bedroom has bolder colour schemes while annexe rooms are more chintzy. Standards of housekeeping are immaculate.

◐ Open all year   ☒ 1 mile from A37, mid-way between Dorchester and Yeovil; entrance to hotel is in Summer Lane. Private car park   🛏 3 single, 14 twin/double; some in annexe; all with bathroom/WC; TV, room service, hair-dryer, direct-dial telephone, radio   ✣ Dining-room, bar, 2 lounges, garden; conference facilities (max 20 people incl up to 17 residential); heated outdoor swimming-pool, tennis, croquet; early suppers for children   ♿ Wheelchair access to hotel, restaurant and WC (M,F), 3 ground-floor bedrooms, 1 specially equipped for disabled people   ● No dogs in public rooms; no smoking in dining-room   ▭ Access, Amex, Delta, Diners, Switch, Visa   £ Single £105, single occupancy of twin/double £135 to £225, twin/double £135 to £225; deposit required. Set L £10, D £32.50; alc L £20 (1996 prices). Special breaks available

---

EVESHAM Hereford & Worcester   map 5

Evesham Hotel

Coopers Lane, Off Waterside, Evesham WR11 6DA
TEL: (01386) 765566   FAX: (01386) 765443

Joyfully eccentric, exuberantly idiosyncratic hotel with a big heart – and a grown-up attitude to the needs of children.

John and Sue Jenkinson's *joie de vivre* is so infectious that hitherto sensible and sober-minded guests instantly succumb. How else do you explain the (tasteful) display of hunks that adorns the ladies' loo, the donation of assorted women in response to reports of the *deshabillées* maidens who disport themselves beside the

Dennis the Menace clock in the gents'? There's a Tudor farmhouse lurking behind the business-like, white-rendered Georgian exterior of the large building close to the Avon, but the Jenkinsons make light of the house's antiquity, concentrating instead on ministering to the needs of today's guests. The public rooms have a rambling quality, with assorted seating areas and toy-filled corridors leading to the grander Cedar Restaurant, where ornate plasterwork, a chandelier, elegant chairs and swag and tail drapes suggest that dining, at least, is taken seriously. The menu (and wine list) notes provide another platform for John's quirky sense of humour, but diners are likely to pronounce themselves well pleased with offerings such as bouillabaisse, walnut lamb cutlets, and toasted hazelnut ice-cream. Vegetarians get more than the usual grudging nod, and there's a simple grill menu for calorie-counters. Youngsters have a decent choice, from cheese on toast and fish fingers to pasta, on the early supper menu. The refurbished bedrooms with their classy colour schemes have the edge on those awaiting the upgrade. All feature lots of extras.

Baywatch fans will be pleased to know that Coco, the hotel's famous stuffed gorilla, is now kitted out as a lifeguard and presides over the indoor pool (and general fun emporium).

◖ Closed 25 & 26 Dec ▨ Coopers Lane is off Waterside (A44) which runs along the River Avon in Evesham. Private car park ⛬ 6 single, 11 twin, 22 double, 1 family room; most with bathroom/WC, 3 with shower/WC; TV, room service, hair-dryer, direct-dial telephone; ironing facilities available, fridges in some rooms
✧ Restaurant, bar, lounge, 2 drying-rooms, garden; air-conditioning in conference room; conference facilities (max 12 people non-residential/residential); heated indoor swimming-pool, croquet, putting, table tennis; early suppers for children; toys, playrooms, babysitting, baby-listening, outdoor games ⅁ No wheelchair access
● No dogs in public rooms; no cigars or pipes in restaurant; no smoking in some bedrooms ▭ Access, Amex, Delta, Diners, Switch, Visa £ Single £57 to £58, single occupancy of twin/double £63 to £64, twin/double £86 to £88, family room £110; deposit required. Alc L £19.50, D £20. Special breaks available

---

EXETER Devon   map 1

Southgate Hotel

Southernhay East, Exeter EX1 1QF
TEL: (01392) 412812 FAX: (01392) 413549

Large city-centre hotel with ample parking, designed along Prince-Charles-school-of-architecture lines.

What was once the Forte Crest Hotel has now been renamed and added to the Forte portfolio of 'Heritage' hotels despite the fact that it's a mere seven years old. Still, in a move that would find favour with Prince Charles, it was designed to mimic Exeter's remaining Georgian buildings, albeit on a scale (110 bedrooms) no Georgian would recognise. The focal point of the ground floor is a large, low-ceilinged bar/lounge where meals are available, sometimes to the background tinkling of a pianist. A conservatory lounge to one side comes into its own in summer when a television is installed and strawberries and cream made available for Wimbledon-watching. The rest of the ground floor is swallowed up by the Clubhouse Restaurant, a sprawling dining-room with ivy-coloured walls and tartan-backed chairs which divides into a variety of different semi-private dining areas. Set three-course dinner menus serve up fairly predictable dishes but remember to offer vegetarians a choice too. Upstairs, the premium rooms overlook the Cathedral, and light sleepers might worry about the clanging of bells. All the rooms are smart, modern and routinely equipped with 'extras' (trouser presses, 18-channel satellite television, security keys, individual temperature controls). A few have been equipped to appeal to women in particular, with fresh flowers and extra toiletries; if that appeals, ask for one when making a booking. With Exeter as traffic-choked as any British city, it's comforting to see such a large parking lot beside the hotel.

● Open all year 🗷 In city centre. Private car park 🛏 46 twin, 53 double, 5 family rooms, 6 suites; all with bathroom/WC; TV, room service, hair-dryer, mini-bar, trouser press, direct-dial telephone ⌖ Restaurant, bar, 3 lounges, conservatory; air-conditioning in public rooms; conference facilities (max 150 people incl up to 110 residential); gym, sauna, solarium, heated indoor swimming-pool; early suppers for children; babysitting, baby-listening ⚲ Wheelchair access to hotel, restaurant, WC (unisex), 5 bedrooms specially equipped for disabled people ● No dogs in public rooms ☐ Access, Amex, Diners, Switch, Visa £ Single occupancy of twin/double £69 to £90, twin/double £69 to £90, family room £69 to £90, suite £94 to £115; deposit required. Continental B £8, cooked B £11; set L £12.50, D £20; alc L £15, D £25; bar meals available. Special breaks available

---

EYTON Hereford & Worcester   map 5

Marsh Country Hotel

Eyton, Leominster HR6 0AG
TEL: (01568) 613952

Medieval majesty tempered by modern comforts, plus pleasant food and a glorious garden.

When we inspected, Jacqueline and Martin Gilleland were doing their bit for the local community by opening their gates under the National Gardens Scheme. Locals were quick to praise the Gillelands for their enterprise in rescuing the derelict fourteenth-century half-timbered house, while gardening buffs and naturalists clustered around the herbaceous borders and reed beds respectively. At the core of the house is a grand medieval hall, complete with flagstoned floor, exposed wall-timbers and hammer-beamed ceiling. Country-house-style soft furnishings in modish florals humanise the space, and banish any notions of blustery breezes blasting down the centuries. Pink and white candy-stripe chairs and floral drapes, plus a wood-burning stove, help to make the bar, where there's a good range of guidebooks and tourist information, a cosier spot. Light from windows on three sides pours into the dining-room, an elegantly cheerful room in shades of lemon and yellow. The food is highly regarded; perhaps pasta with crab and bacon, followed by roast Herefordshire duck breast with duck and mushroom filo parcels, and pineapple and mango upside-down pudding.

The pretty bedrooms adopt superior chintzy soft furnishings and restful pastels to set off the coronet canopies that crown the beds.

◑ Closed 4 to 31 Jan ↗ 2 miles north-west of Leominster; turn right on to B4361 to Richards Castle; turn left after 1 mile (signposted Eyton and Lucton) and continue to common. Private car park ⬏ 1 twin, 2 double; all with bathroom/WC; TV, room service, hair-dryer, direct-dial telephone; no tea/coffee-making facilities in rooms ⚇ Dining-room, bar, lounge, garden ♿ No wheelchair access ⬤ No children under 8; no dogs; no smoking in bedrooms or dining-room ▭ Access, Amex, Delta, Diners, Switch, Visa £ Single occupancy of twin/double £80, twin/double £112; deposit required. Set D £22.50, Sun L £20 (prices valid till Mar 1997). Special breaks available

---

Penmere Manor

Mongleath Road, Falmouth TR11 4PN
TEL: (01326) 211411   FAX: (01326) 317588

Large hotel with indoor pool and extensive grounds on the outskirts of Falmouth.

Don't be put off by the approach to Penmere Manor which drags you through Falmouth's unscenic industrial outskirts. As soon as you turn into the drive you come face to face with a swish hotel which boasts its own indoor swimming-pool, sauna, solarium and snooker room. The surrounding gardens beckon immediately, and hotel corridors are lined with photographs and descriptions of other Cornish gardens; in spring Penmere offers Cornish Garden Weekend Breaks with visits to gardens in the company of botany expert Michael Leech. The best bedrooms in the Garden Wing are extremely well equipped. It's also good to report that some of the standard single rooms have double beds and space to swing a cat. Menus in the restaurant mix familiar English dishes like roast leg of lamb with rosemary with more imaginative twirls like spinach carbonara. The bar also serves a selection of tasty snacks like pork satay with hoi sin sauce, and a choice of ciabatta sandwiches and filled jacket potatoes. Anyone who over-indulges can always work off the excess calories on a 'trim trail' through the grounds afterwards.

◑ Closed 24 to 27 Dec ↗ Take A39 towards Falmouth; turn right at Hillhead roundabout; turn left after 1 mile into Mongleath Road. Private car park ⬏ 9 single, 7 twin, 7 double, 15 family rooms; most with bathroom/WC, some with shower/WC; TV, room service, hair-dryer, direct-dial telephone; mini-bar and trouser press in some rooms ⚇ Restaurant, 2 bars, 3 lounges, library, games room, garden, air-conditioning in some public rooms and most family rooms; conference facilities (max 80 people incl up to 38 residential); gym, sauna, solarium, 2 swimming-pools, croquet, fitness trail, boules; early suppers for children; baby-listening ♿ Wheelchair access to hotel (1 step), restaurant, WC (unisex), 14 ground-floor bedrooms ⬤ No dogs in public rooms; no smoking in restaurant and some bedrooms ▭ Access, Amex, Delta, Diners, Switch, Visa £ Single £57, single occupancy of twin/double £68, twin/double £83, family room £105; deposit required. Set L £5, D £19; alc D £10; bar meals available (prices valid till May 1997). Special breaks available

FARNHAM **Dorset** map 2

Museum Hotel

Farnham, Blandford Forum DT11 8DE
TEL: (01725) 516261

Village pub mixing tradition with good food and smart bedrooms.

Farnham is a pretty, peaceful village with rows of neat thatched cottages. The Museum Hotel, a red-brick Victorian house with bright flower borders, is at its centre, both geographically and socially, and has all the features of the traditional village pub – an affable landlord in John Barnes, an extensive menu and two bars. But it also has a dash of urban style, most noticeable in the modern prints lining the corridors (potential purchasers should consult Lizzie, John's wife) and the imaginative options on the menu. Meals are served in the atmospheric Cooper's bar, a narrow, low-ceilinged room with an inglenook fireplace, in the oldest part of the house (which dates from Cromwellian times), or alternatively in the small, pastel-pink restaurant. Locals sup in the Wood-land's bar, a good old-fashioned public bar with stags' heads and antlers on the walls and a large billiard table. It's back to the more contemporary for the conservatory, where breakfast is served, an airy room with lots of plants facing towards the car park. The smart, neat bedrooms are in the restored stable block; all have pretty pine furnishings and soft colour schemes. Bathrooms are a good size, attractive and well equipped.

◑ Closed 25 Dec ◪ Off A354, 18 miles west of Salisbury. Private car park ⬛ 3 twin/double, 1 four-poster; all in annexe; all with bathroom/WC; TV, limited room service, mini-bar, direct-dial telephone ✓ Restaurant, 2 bars, conservatory, games room, garden; conference facilities (max 20 people non-residential); early suppers for children ♿ Wheelchair access to hotel (1 step) and restaurant, 4 ground-floor bedrooms ● No dogs ⬜ Access, Delta, Switch, Visa £ Single £35 to £40, single occupancy of twin/double £35 to £40, twin/double £50 to £60, four-poster £65 to £75; deposit required. Alc L £12.50, D £15; bar meals available

---

FERSFIELD **Norfolk** map 6

The Strenneth

Airfield Road, Fersfield, Diss IP22 2BP
TEL: (01379) 688182 FAX: (01379) 688260

Friendly warmth and home comforts in a peaceful corner of Norfolk.

Ken and Brenda Webb, who have been running their guesthouse for over ten years now, ambitiously added more rooms in a 'courtyard annexe' to their seventeenth-century farmhouse when they moved in. The features of the original building are seen to best effect in the dining-room, with its chairs invitingly drawn up around the cosy inglenook fireplace and the low beams and timbers set off by shiny horse brasses, an alcove of books and cheerful family paraphernalia; next door, the non-smoking lounge contains a doll collection that belongs to the Webbs' daughter. Unfortunately, evening meals are no longer served, but a selection of menus from local pubs is available, and the Webbs are happy to make reservations and book taxis. To compensate, breakfasts have expanded, including delights such as scrambled eggs with smoked salmon. Bedrooms, like the buildings, mix old and new and vary in size and facilities. Some have shower and toilet facilities; others feature corner baths large enough for a luxurious wallow.

○ Open all year ⚐ Off A1066 near South Lopham, 3 miles west of Diss. Private car park ⮡ 1 single, 2 twin, 3 double, 1 four-poster; some in annexe; 4 with bathroom/WC, 3 with shower/WC; TV ✧ Dining-room, lounge, garden ♿ No wheelchair access ⚫ No dogs in public rooms; no smoking in public rooms and some bedrooms ☐ Access, Amex, Diners, Visa £ Single £25, single occupancy of twin/double from £25, twin/double from £36, four-poster £58; deposit required. Special breaks available

---

FILEY North Yorkshire   map 9

Downcliffe House ☆

The Beach, Filey YO14 9LA
TEL: (01723) 513310   FAX: (01723) 516141

Recently renovated beach-front hotel with smart bedrooms and a welcoming, family-run atmosphere.

This neat honey-coloured Victorian building has an enviable location just across the road from Filey's seemingly endless beach. It was built in 1860 as the private residence of John Unett, who was responsible for designing much of nineteenth-century Filey. Elise Garland has run the hotel for over 20 years, but in 1994 she and husband David set about a complete renovation and redecoration pro-gramme. The result is a smart hotel which retains the atmosphere of a family guesthouse. The bedrooms are stylish, co-ordinated and well equipped, and each has an uninterrupted view of the sea. The bar/lounge has pink walls and green horseshoe seating, and serves Tetley and Eden on draught. The restaurant is spacious, with pink striped walls and large plants. Dinner may consist of garlic mushrooms followed by julienne of chicken; the wine list, though small, is varied and good value. Both public rooms enjoy the sea view but if you need the sea air as well you can enjoy your drinks on the flower-filled patio on fine days.

○ Closed Jan ⚐ On sea-front in Filey. Private car park ⮡ 1 single, 1 twin, 6 double, 2 family rooms; 8 with bathroom/WC, 2 with shower/WC; TV, room service, hair-dryer, direct-dial telephone; trouser press in some rooms ✧ Restaurant, bar/lounge; conference facilities (max 15 people incl up to 10 residential); early suppers for children; baby-listening ♿ No wheelchair access ⚫ No children under 5; no dogs; no smoking in restaurant ☐ Access, Delta, Visa £ Single £30 to £35, single occupancy of twin/double £40 to £60, twin/double £60 to £70, family room £75 to £85; deposit required. Set L £8, D £12; alc D £15; light meals available. Special breaks available

---

☆ *A star next to the hotel's name indicates that the establishment is new to the* Guide *this year.*

Manor House

Flamborough, Bridlington YO15 1PD
TEL: (01262) 850943 (AND FAX)

Stylish Georgian farmhouse B&B furnished with some striking antiques.

It was quite by chance that Lesley Berry decided to revive the ancient art of gansey knitting. Making these patterned fishermen's sweaters (the name is thought to be a corruption of 'guernsey') was a thriving cottage industry in the days when the likes of Staithes, Robin Hood's Bay and Runswick Bay were prosperous fishing villages. Being an antique dealer and making knitwear in her spare time, Lesley put up a sign at the Manor House saying 'antiques sweaters' and it was only when somebody tried to purchase an 'antique sweater' that Lesley thought about the possibilities. Incredibly, there was a lady in the village who had committed many of the patterns to memory and so the revival began. The sign is still there, and now you really can buy an 'antique sweater' in the little shop in front of this old Georgian farmhouse.

Lesley's other interest is evident throughout the house; the finest piece has to be the Portuguese rosewood bed dating from the seventeenth century or even earlier. The second bedroom has a Victorian brass bed. The sitting-room is dark green and jade with rug-covered polished wood floors and cream sofas. Dinner, Wolsey Lodge style, is by prior arrangement.

◑ Closed Chr ☒ From Bridlington B1255 to Flamborough; pass church on right; hotel is on next corner (Lighthouse Road/Tower Street). Private car park 🛏 1 double, 1 four-poster; family room available; both with bathroom/WC; TV, limited room service, hair-dryer ⊘ Dining-room, lounge, library, garden; croquet; early suppers for children; babysitting ⅙ No wheelchair access ● No children under 8; no dogs; no smoking in bedrooms and in public rooms only if other guests consent ▭ Access, Amex, Visa £ Single occupancy of double £37, double £58, four-poster £68, family room £74; deposit required. Set D £19.50

Griffin Inn

Fletching, Nr Uckfield TN22 3SS
TEL: (01825) 722890   FAX: (01825) 722810

Wonderful food and rooms with character are on offer in a classic, sixteenth-century inn.

Fletching is a charming, unspoilt Sussex village, in which the Griffin Inn blends harmoniously with the mixture of red-brick and half-timbered façades. Local life has centred on the inn for 400 years, and the local folklore abounds with stories of an old tunnel leading to the nearby Norman church and then on to Piltdown. These days the Pullan family runs the Griffin as a bustling pub, with a restaurant providing food which is a step up from the traditional pub grub. The place gets really hectic, particularly at weekends, so arrive early if you want to sit down. The inventive chef tempts you with dishes prepared with local Sussex produce, such as seared scallops and squid with a shallot and sorrel dressing, or maybe a brochette of marinated lamb, followed by old favourites from the dessert world. From the large rear garden, the views over the South Downs form a perfect backdrop to the frequent *al fresco* barbecues and themed events which maintain the vibrant atmosphere. The watchword in most of the bedrooms is 'duck', since the low, crazily warped timbers make it highly probable that you will bump your head; three of the four rooms offer four-posters and have bags of character. Fletching is the most spacious, and features a magnificent open fireplace.

◑ Closed 25 Dec; restaurant closed Sun eve ⤢ Take A22 south from East Grinstead, and take the right-hand turning to Fletching at Nutley. Private car park ⤙ 1 twin, 3 four-poster; family room available; 1 four-poster with bathroom/WC, 3 with shower/WC; TV, limited room service; hair-dryer on request ✓ Restaurants, 2 bars, drying-room, garden; conference facilities (max 25 people incl up to 4 residential); early suppers for children ⅋ No wheelchair access ● No dogs in restaurant or bedrooms; no smoking in bedrooms ▭ Access, Amex, Delta, Switch, Visa £ Twin £50 to £60, four-poster £55 to £75; deposit required. Alc L, D £16; bar meals available. Special breaks available

---

FORD Wiltshire   map 2

White Hart

Ford, Nr Chippenham SN14 8RP
TEL: (01249) 782213   FAX: (01249) 783075

Popular and traditional riverside lunch spot with comfortable accommodation.

This coaching inn built in 1553 by the River Bybrook has all the features of a traditional pub – log-burning stoves, exposed stone, hunting prints and a pair of antlers – and a couple of quirky touches: peacocks in the garden and fantails cooing by their dovecote home above the entrance. Set mid-way between Bath and Chippenham, and with plenty of seating both inside and out, the creeper-clad building is a popular lunch spot. Staff informed us that what appeared to us to be a busy Monday lunchtime was 'dead'; on average they serve about 80 lunches each day. Lengthy menus with a few daily specials are served in a large, light, uncluttered room, and include everything from up-market bistro fare (duck with caramelised apples and orange and brandy sauce) to traditional roasts and bar snacks (macaroni cheese, chicken cordon bleu with sauté potatoes). The smaller, low-ceilinged bar stocks a range of real ales. Bedrooms are spick-and-span with pine furnishings, floral curtains, woven bedspreads and neutral paintwork. Most are in the converted stable block across the road, but the three above the pub have more character; Room 10, with a brass bed and yellow walls, is the most attractive.

See the inside front cover for a brief explanation of how to use the Guide.

○ Open all year ⊠ Between Bath and Chippenham on A420. Private car park
⊨→ 2 twin, 4 double, 4 four-poster, 1 family room; most in annexe; all with
bathroom/WC; TV, room service, trouser press, direct-dial telephone ⊘ Restaurant,
bar, garden; conference facilities (max 14 people incl up to 11 residential); fishing,
outdoor swimming-pool; early suppers for children ⅋ Wheelchair access to hotel
and restaurant, 4 ground-floor bedrooms ● No children in restaurant eves
⊟ Access, Amex, Delta, Diners, Switch, Visa £ Single occupancy of twin/double
£45, twin/double £65, four-poster £65; deposit required. Alc L £10, D £17.50; bar meals
available. Special breaks available

FOWEY Cornwall   map 1

Marina Hotel

The Esplanade, Fowey PL23 1HY
TEL: (01726) 833315   FAX: (01726) 832779

---

*Holiday hotel with superb food and friendly service backing on to the
Fowey estuary.*

Whether by night or by day the views from the bedroom windows at the back of
the Marina Hotel are magnetic. There's always something happening on the
Fowey estuary: huge cargo ships ferrying china clay up and down, smaller
pleasure craft whipping past, seagulls dipping and screeching. Only four of the
bedrooms don't share the views and it's well worth paying the supplement to
feast your eyes. The same views are available to diners in an unexceptional
restaurant where quite exceptional food is served. On the night we inspected, a
delectable crab parcel was followed with a filling mussel chowder with crab
dumplings and a beautifully presented plate of John Dory. No doubt the desserts
were just as delicious but our inspector was too sated to try any. Conversation
flowed easily in the lounge/bar, presided over with aplomb by Carol and John
Roberts...it's hard to believe they're newcomers to the hotel trade. The one snag
is one that plagues Fowey as a whole: the narrow streets leave no space for
parking so guests must leave their bags at the door and drive to the main car park,
a good five minutes' walk away up steep steps. Although a courtesy minibus
ferries guests and luggage back to their cars, not everyone will be happy to leave
their vehicle so far away.

○ Closed Jan and Feb ⊠ On marina in Fowey. Public car park ⊨→ 5 twin, 6
double; all with bathroom/WC exc 2 doubles with shower/WC; TV, room service,
hair-dryer, direct-dial telephone ⊘ Restaurant, lounge/bar, garden; fishing, sailing;
early suppers for children; baby-listening ⅋ No wheelchair access ● No smoking
or dogs in restaurant ⊟ Access, Delta, Switch, Visa £ Single occupancy of
twin/double £39 to £51, twin/double £52 to £88; deposit required. Set D £16; alc D £19.
Special breaks available

---

*Where we know an establishment accepts credit cards, we list them. There
may be a surcharge if you pay by credit card. It is always best to check
when booking whether the card you want to use is acceptable.*

FRAMPTON Dorset   map 2

Hyde Farm House

Dorchester Road, Frampton, Nr Dorchester DT2 9NG
TEL: (01300) 320272

A peaceful setting, extensive grounds and extremely friendly hosts at a stylish house.

'The civilised atmosphere enveloped us at once,' wrote a recent visitor, enthused by 'the pleasure of waking up to see the green Dorset hills and revel in the friendly peace of the countryside.' The flower baskets in the rough, paved yard and the red-brick façade of John Saunders' and Jan Faye-Schjoll's stylish house are attractive enough, but it's the back of the house and the gardens that are special. A conservatory, where meals are served, juts out into the centre of the paved terrace, and extends, gallery-like, down one side of the house. Inside the conservatory, soft-cushioned garden chairs and tables mix with the abundant foliage beneath the chintzy roof blinds; below, the gardens – with their stone urns, statues, immaculate lawns and wilder, wooded sections – fall away in tiers towards a stream.

   The two twin bedrooms – one with white, wicker furniture and chintzy curtains, the other with pink and blue coronet drapes and matching curtains – share this view, while the double has a side-garden view. The public rooms are just as smart, characterised by rich, deep-coloured fabrics and upholstery, polished wood, and John's collection of Clarice Cliff pottery and Staffordshire figures. The meals are generously portioned; spring-time menus featured spinach and feta cheese rolled in filo pastry, salmon in dill sauce, and stir-fried pork with peppers and paprika. Our correspondent thoroughly enjoyed his wok-steamed chicken with mushrooms and cream.

◐ Closed Chr ⤢ On the left-hand side of A356 through Frampton to Maiden Newton. Private car park ⇥ 2 twin, 1 double; all with bathroom/WC; hair-dryer ⬥ Dining-room/conservatory, TV room, drying-room, study, garden; fishing ♿ No wheelchair access ● No children under 13; no dogs; no smoking ☐ None accepted £ Single occupancy of twin/double £28, twin/double £55. Set D £15

FRANT East Sussex   map 3

Old Parsonage ☆

Church Lane, Frant, Nr Tunbridge Wells TN3 9DX
TEL: (01892) 750773 (AND FAX)

A large, well-restored rectory with lots of character in a peaceful village.

Set right next to the church in the small, pretty village of Frant, the Old Parsonage was built in 1820 by Lord Abergavenny for his son who was the parish priest. Nowadays it is occupied by Mary and Tony Dakin, the first non-clerics to live here, who have carefully restored it to its former glory. The Old Parsonage is a huge white-painted house with grey window shutters, a

Victorian conservatory and stone urns full of flowers at both the entrance and on the large west-facing balustraded terrace at the rear. The spacious and bright sitting-room with its peach and cream sofas, sparkling chandelier and antique furniture looks out on to the terrace, the three acres of well-kept garden and Eridge Park in the distance. As you go through the hallway and up the stairs do not miss the collection of large black and white photos on the walls. All taken and developed by Tony himself, they are an excellent series of portraits of local people – a fortune-teller, a dentist, a grave-digger and the local Lord of the Manor among others. There is not much to choose between the bedrooms as all are stylishly decorated and furnished, but perhaps the large four-poster room is the most romantic with its pink and grey canopied bed, pink Chinese rug, overflowing bookcase and a large *en suite* bathroom.

◑ Open all year ⊿ From Tunbridge Wells, take A267 south for 2 miles to Frant; take first left into Church Lane. Private car park ⊨ 1 twin, 1 double, 2 four-poster; 2 with bathroom/WC, 2 with shower/WC; TV, hair-dryer, clock radio ✅ Dining-room, lounge, drying-room, conservatory, garden; conference facilities (max 14 people incl up to 4 residential); croquet; babysitting ♿ No wheelchair access ⊜ No dogs in public rooms; smoking in conservatory only ▢ Access, Visa £ Single occupancy of twin/double £39 to £49, twin/double/four-poster £59 to £64; deposit required. Set D £16.50. Special breaks available

---

GATESHEAD Tyne & Wear

map 10

Eslington Villa

8 Station Road, Low Fell, Gateshead NE9 6DR
TEL: 0191-487 6017   FAX: 0191-420 0667

Small, suburban hotel with good modern British cooking.

In a suburban area on the outskirts of Gateshead, the Eslington Villa offers a comfortable low-key environment ideal for the business traveller looking for a high standard of cuisine and something a little more personal than the typical business hotel might offer. It sits right above the Team Valley industrial estate and is also only a short distance from the giant shopping mecca that is the Metro Centre. The public areas are quiet and unexciting. There is a small residents' bar, a lounge with floral sofas, and a restaurant in a conservatory which gives you the full benefit of the industrial landscape.

What sets Eslington apart is the standard of its cooking: British, but with a distinctly modern outlook and presentation, and a good deal of choice too. A two- or three-course table d'hôte menu operates from Monday to Friday only but there is also an à la carte menu offering starters like grilled Scottish scallops with a mango and red onion salsa and main courses such as roasted pheasant on a bed of braised cabbage with smoked bacon. The bedrooms have a combination of old dark wood furnishings and white wicker seating. Sycamore, in the older part of the house, is the largest – a well co-ordinated four-poster room with a front view.

◑ Closed public holidays; restaurant closed Sun eve ⚡ From Durham Road take turning into Belle Vue Bank; turn left at end, then second right and veer right up hill. Private car park ⬅ 1 single, 2 twin, 7 double, 2 four-poster; family rooms available; some in annexe; all with bathroom/WC exc single with shower/WC; TV, room service, hair-dryer, trouser press, direct-dial telephone ⚒ Restaurant/conservatory, bar, lounge, garden; conference facilities (max 30 people incl up to 12 residential); early suppers for children ♿ Wheelchair access to hotel (2 steps), restaurant, WC (unisex), 3 ground-floor bedrooms ◓ No dogs in public rooms; no smoking in restaurant ⬚ Access, Amex, Delta, Switch, Visa £ Single/single occupancy of twin/double £45 to £55, twin/double £50 to £65, four-poster/family room £55 to £65. Set L £16, D £22; alc L £25, D £28. Special breaks available

---

GILLAN Cornwall   map 1

Tregildry Hotel

Gillan, Manaccan, Helston TR12 6HG
TEL: (01326) 231378   FAX: (01326) 231561

Small hotel with panoramic views over the Helford under promising new ownership.

Huw and Lynne Phillips used to run a hotel in the Lake District, and since taking over the Tregildry, in the depths of the Lizard peninsula, they have moved fast to stamp their own style on the premises. Curvaceous Indonesian rattan chairs now adorn the Herra Restaurant, and the main lounge has been completely refurnished with big, squashy, inviting settees. The sea can be glimpsed only at an oblique angle but the views across a field of daffodils are still glorious. For the time being a second lounge clings to its sixties-style seating, but not, one suspects, for much longer. Upstairs, you can pick out Lynne's modernising touches at a glance, although the rooms are pretty in a light, cottagey way rather than being conspicuously 'designed'. The views are real winners: Room 3, in particular, has windows framing a picture-postcard setting of the village of St Anthony; Room 1 sweeps its gaze over Gillan creek, the Helford River and the sea. Three-course dinner menus concentrate on mainstream ingredients given a novel twist: mushroom soup flavoured with sherry, suprême of chicken filled with mango and banana. A thoroughly promising venture. Reports, please.

◑ Closed mid-Nov to mid-Mar ⚡ Take A3083 Lizard Road from Helston; take first left for St Keverne and follow signs to Manaccan and Gillan. Private car park ⬅ 4 twin, 4 double, 2 family rooms; all with bathroom/WC exc 1 double with shower/WC; TV, direct-dial telephone ⚒ Restaurant, bar, 2 lounges, TV room, garden; conference facilities (max 20 people incl up to 10 residential); early suppers for children ♿ No wheelchair access ◓ No children under 8 in restaurant eves; no dogs in public rooms; smoking in bar and lounge only ⬚ Access, Delta, Switch, Visa £ Single occupancy of twin/double £65 to £70, twin/double £100 to £110, family room £125 to £135 (rates incl dinner); deposit required. Set D £19.50. Special breaks available

---

 This denotes that the hotel is in an exceptionally peaceful situation where you can be assured of a restful stay.

GILLINGHAM Dorset map 2

Stock Hill House

COUNTY
HOTEL
OF THE
YEAR

Stock Hill, Gillingham SP8 5NR
TEL: (01747) 823626   FAX: (01747) 825628

A warm welcome and delicious food in a wonderful, eclectic Victorian mansion.

During this year's visit to Stock Hill House, we met a couple on their twentieth or so stay. For them, winding down the beech-lined drive towards the creeper-clad Victorian house is like returning home. Another regular visitor, commenting on recent changes, wrote that 'certain aspects, including the food, the impeccable service and the genuine warmth of the welcome, would be difficult to improve.' The enthusiasm and care with which Peter and Nita Hauser run their small country-house hotel is certainly exemplary, and despite their many satisfied customers they are constantly looking to refurbish and improve. Over the last year, they have converted the stable house (formerly a little used indoor pool) to provide three brand new bedrooms, all bright and airy with a contemporary design. For those who prefer to stay in the main house, bedrooms here are equally appealing, with beautiful antique beds and rich fabrics. Elsewhere in the house, tradition, in the form of log fires, chandeliers and oil paintings, blends perfectly with the unusual and quirky (sculpted cherubs, sphinx candlesticks, Venetian painted wood furniture) to set the house's style: slightly eccentric but always comfortable and never intimidating.

Peter, who has been a chef 'all my life', combines influences from his native Austria with traditional local fare. Spring favourites included monkfish tail rolled in black pepper with mustard-seed sauce, Hungarian paprika chicken with spätzli (Austrian pasta), and calf's liver dipped in egg and breadcrumbs with a celery rémoulade – a healthy version of a schnitzel.

◑ Open all year   ⤢ On B3081, 1½ miles west of Gillingham, 3 miles south of A303. Private car park   ⤙ 1 single, 4 twin, 3 double, 1 four-poster, 1 family room; some in annexe; all with bathroom/WC; TV, room service, hair-dryer, trouser press, direct-dial telephone; tea/coffee-making facilities on request   ✣ 2 restaurants, bar, 2 lounges, garden; conference facilities (max 12 people incl up to 10 residential); fishing, sauna, tennis, croquet, putting; early suppers for children   ♿ Wheelchair access to hotel and restaurant, 3 ground-floor bedrooms   ♠ No children under 6; no dogs; no smoking in restaurants and discouraged in bedrooms   ▭ Access, Amex, Diners, Visa   £ Single £105 to £145, single occupancy of twin/double £145 to £160, twin/double/four-poster £230 to £280 (rates incl dinner); deposit required. Set L £19.50, D from £28. Special breaks available

---

Please let us know if an establishment has changed hands.

The Guide *is totally independent, accepts no free hospitality, and survives on the number of copies sold each year.*

Old Guildhall

Mill Street, Gislingham, Nr Eye IP23 8JT
TEL: (01379) 783361

Charming thatched cottage offering warm welcome from owners and their canine companions.

Gislingham has a thatched house or two among its newer developments, but the Old Guildhall is hard to beat for period charm. A large evergreen hedge shields the Suffolk-pink cottage from village activity, but an attractive large back garden and the attentions of Holly or Bella, the two house labradors who try to cajole you into playing ball, provide enough distractions. Ethel and Ray Tranter's welcome is just as warm, if more subtle – even after 32 years in the hospitality trade their enthusiasm is undimmed. 'We love it,' says Ray. 'Many of our guests are now good friends and come back every year.' The interior is just what you would expect: a beamy lounge with chintzy armchairs and brick fireplaces (well-used in winter), horse brasses and plate collections on the walls, and pottery knick-knacks (including a model of the Old Guildhall itself, made by a guest). There's a small bar tucked beside the passage to the dining-room, where Ethel serves up traditional roasts and puddings on chunky wooden tables. More plates decorate the walls of the three bedrooms, reached via a sturdy spiral staircase. Although the ceilings gradually get lower as you proceed along the landing, this doesn't stop Room 3, at the end, being a favourite, thanks to its double aspect over the back garden and side. If you don't have a view of the garden from your room, you can sit in the small landing gallery instead.

◑ Closed Jan ⬀ In centre of Gislingham, opposite the village school. Private car park 🛏 2 twin, 1 double; all with bathroom/WC; TV; hair-dryer on request ✧ Dining-room, bar, lounge, garden ᝣ No wheelchair access ● No dogs in public rooms; no smoking ▭ None accepted £ Single occupancy of twin/double £35, twin/double £50; deposit required. Set D £10. Special breaks available

---

Many hotels put up their tariffs in the spring. You are advised to confirm prices when you book.

The 1998 Guide *will be published in the autumn of 1997. Reports on hotels are welcome at any time of the year, but are extremely valuable in the spring. Send them to* The Which? Hotel Guide, FREEPOST, 2 Marylebone Road, London NW1 1YN. *No stamp is needed if reports are posted in the UK. Our e-mail address is:* "guidereports@which.co.uk".

No 3

3 Magdalene Street, Glastonbury BA6 9EW
TEL: (01458) 832129

*Smart Georgian house close to Glastonbury Abbey, offering
aromatherapy and other stress-relieving therapies.*

Glastonbury may be a small town but as you approach No 3 country-style from
the back, where there's a small car park and a garden, it is a relief to escape from
the bustle of tourists. There are two bedrooms in the main house, where the
Tynans' interest in all things Indian is visible in distinctive bedcovers and
curtains. A neo-Georgian building houses three more bedrooms across the car
park, one of them featuring two wonderful brass Damascene lamps. All the
bedrooms are spotless, stylish and spacious, mostly with crown canopy beds
and inviting windowed bathrooms. Ann Tynan offers aromatherapy and
massage from the house. As she points out, people are sometimes wary of the
intimacy involved in aromatherapy, so a stay at No 3 offers the ideal opportunity
to dip a toe into the water of unaccustomed pleasures. Fresh from this luxury you
will then need to venture into town for an evening meal.

◑ Closed Nov to Mar ⊿ Adjoining Glastonbury Abbey. Private car park 🛏 2
twin, 2 double, 1 family room; some in annexe; all with bathroom/WC; TV, room service,
direct-dial telephone; hair-dryer on request ✅ Dining-room, lounge, garden ♿ No
wheelchair access ⊖ No dogs; no smoking in dining-room and some bedrooms
▤ Access, Visa £ Single occupancy of twin/double £50, twin/double £65, family
room £75; deposit required. Cooked B £5.50

---

*It is always worth enquiring about the availability of special breaks or
weekend prices. The prices we quote are the standard rates for one night –
most hotels offer reduced rates for longer stays.*

*The Guide office can quickly spot when a hotelier is encouraging
customers to write a letter recommending inclusion – and, sadly, several
hotels have been doing this in 1996. Such reports do not further a hotel's
cause.*

Glewstone Court

Glewstone, Nr Ross-on-Wye HR9 6AW
TEL: (01989) 770367   FAX: (01989) 770282

Thumbs-up for this refreshingly unstuffy country-house hotel.

'Excellent accommodation. Large, comfortable room and warm bathroom with white towelling robes provided,' reported one correspondent who enjoyed an 'excellent New Year's package' and commended the good atmosphere at the hotel. Our inspection confirmed that while Bill Reeve-Tucker runs a tight ship, he seems to have the happy knack of putting guests, whether residents or bar-lunchers, instantly at ease. The house, Georgian with Victorian add-ons, plays its part, with grounds encompassing fruit orchards, a croquet lawn and a semi-recumbent cedar of Lebanon. It's the interior, however, that imbues the place with its special character, generously sprinkled with fascinating pieces of ephemera, from framed collections of cigarette cards to nostalgic photographs of the Roaring Twenties, to the Victoria and Albert screen near the entrance. Light panelling adds elegance to the Victorian bar/lounge where diners peruse the menus amid a collection of ceramic frogs. Bookworms might prefer the older area where rugs cover the boards, and assorted volumes on gardening and biographies compete with copies of *Country Life* and *Harpers* stuffed into wicker baskets. Stencilling and other paint effects add an imaginative touch, both in public areas, such as the slightly decadent bistro, and in the bedrooms.

A diverse array of artworks, from Victorian sentiment to a poster for the New Orleans Mardi Gras, lines the apricot walls of the Georgian Restaurant. Here you might dine on carrot and coriander soup, followed by sorbet and truffled chicken breast wrapped in Parma ham with a vermouth cream, and treacle and walnut tart. Bedrooms combine attractive and individualised décor with their share of antiques, and unconventional hospitality trays featuring novelty teapots.

◑ Closed 25 to 27 Dec   ⊿ Glewstone is off A40 between Ross-on-Wye and Monmouth. Private car park   ⤶ 1 single, 4 double, 2 four-poster; family rooms available; all with bathroom/WC exc 2 doubles with shower/WC; TV, room service, hair-dryer, direct-dial telephone   ✦ Restaurant, dining-room, bar, 2 lounges, garden; conference facilities (max 20 people incl up to 7 residential); croquet; early suppers for children; babysitting, baby-listening   ⅋ No wheelchair access   ● No dogs in restaurant   ▭ Access, Amex, Delta, Switch, Visa   £ Single £40, single occupancy of twin/double £50, twin/double £80, four-poster £94, family room from £95; deposit required. Set D £23, Sun L £13; bistro meals available (prices valid till Apr 1997). Special breaks available

---

If you make a booking using a credit card and find after cancelling that the full amount has been charged to your card, raise the matter with your credit card company. It will ask the hotelier to confirm whether the room was re-let, and to justify the charge made.

GLOSSOP **Derbyshire**   map 8

Wind in the Willows

Derbyshire Level, Glossop SK13 9PT
TEL: (01457) 868001   FAX: (01457) 853354

An intimate, well-run Victorian country house on the Peak District border.

Just a few minutes from the centre of the old cotton town of Glossop, this early-Victorian house stands surveying the National Park's lush green fields and stone walls from within five acres of grounds that include the requisite willow tree. Victoriana and family photos and games make public areas such as the drawing-room and oak-panelled study both elegant yet homely. The same could be said of the pleasing no-choice dinners, served to residents only. Classical dishes, such as smoked salmon and scrambled egg, steak pie, roast lamb, raspberry tartlets and bread and butter pudding, feature strongly. Bedrooms in the original part of the house show off more fine antiques, particularly the superior rooms called Erika Louise (with a half-tester and a period free-standing bath) and Lucy Anne. By contrast, the four bedrooms in a recent extension exhibit modern country-house furnishings and rich fabrics. All are personalised by plenty of literature, and good facilities that extend to the likes of sewing kits. The domestic touches which so characterise the hotel stem from the careful stewardship of owner Anne Marsh and her convivial son, Peter.

○ Closed Chr   ⟲   1 mile east of Glossop centre turn down road opposite Royal Oak pub; hotel is 400 yards down on right. Private car park   ⊨   3 twin, 8 double, 1 four-poster; some in annexe; some with bathroom/WC, some with shower/WC; TV, room service, hair-dryer, trouser press, direct-dial telephone   ✓ Dining-room, bar/lounge, study, conservatory, garden; conference facilities (max 16 people incl up to 12 residential); early suppers for children   ⅙   No wheelchair access   ● No children under 10; no dogs in public rooms and in bedrooms by arrangement   ⊟ Access, Amex, Diners, Switch, Visa   £ Single occupancy of twin/double £59 to £75, twin/double £69 to £95, four-poster £95; deposit required. Set D £18.50

GOATHLAND **North Yorkshire**   map 9

Mallyan Spout ☆

Goathland, Whitby YO22 5AN
TEL: (01947) 896486   FAX: (01947) 896327

A traditional Yorkshire hotel whose characterful, ivy-covered building dominates the picturesque village green.

This ivy-covered, stone building, and the nearby waterfall after which it was named, were probably just as significant village landmarks as the endearing little train station until *Heartbeat* came along and turned this sleepy village into a tourist hot spot. The hotel itself has admirably resisted the temptation to exploit its proximity to Nick Berry's beat, since Judith and Peter Heslop, who have managed the hotel since the 1970s, know full well that it was doing good business long before the TV phenomenon came along, and will continue to do so for long after. It retains its pleasantly old-fashioned feel in the public areas, where hunting pictures adorn the bar's walls, or Winston Churchill peers down from above the fireplace in one of the lounges. The bedrooms come in all shapes and sizes, and most have a cottagey feel. The best are the newest rooms, 11 and 23, which are spacious, well co-ordinated, and boast glorious views.

The bar's snack menu, which offers children's portions, includes cod from Whitby or local lamb, while in the more elegant surroundings of the restaurant you can opt for a three- or four-course dinner – perhaps quail's egg and prawn mayonnaise for starters, and then grilled monkfish wrapped in Cumbrian ham. Although the menus have a set price, many of the main courses come with hefty supplements.

◗ Open all year ⊿ Off A169 Pickering to Whitby Road. Private car park ⊨ 2 single, 4 twin/double, 14 double, 4 four-poster; family room and suites available; all with bathroom/WC exc 1 double with shower/WC; TV, room service, hair-dryer, trouser press, direct-dial telephone; tea/coffee-making facilities on request ✓ Restaurant, bar, 3 lounges, drying-room, garden; conference facilities (max 48 people incl up to 24 residential); early suppers for children 𝆕 Wheelchair access to hotel (1 step), restaurant and WC (unisex), 2 ground-floor bedrooms ● No children under 6 in restaurant eves ☐ Access, Amex, Diners, Switch, Visa ⊡ Single/single occupancy of twin/double £50 to £65, twin/double £70 to £130, four-poster £80, family room £90, suite £130; deposit required. Set L £13.50, D £19.50; bar meals available. Special breaks available

---

Goldhill Mill

Golden Green, Tonbridge TN11 0BA
TEL: (01732) 851626 FAX: (01732) 851881

A luxuriously restored mill-house set in beautiful countryside with exceptionally considerate hosts.

Goldhill Mill was a working water-mill until 1918. Nowadays the water wheel turns only in the morning for the benefit of guests, who can watch the machinery behind the glass casing in the kitchen while tucking into a lavish breakfast. Despite being only 3 miles from Tonbridge, Goldhill Mill is in an extremely peaceful location and is surrounded by 20 acres of its own grounds. The River Bourne runs past the house (and turns the water wheel), and the Millpool Room, with its pretty floral patterned wallpaper and bedding and sloping white-painted beamed ceiling, is best placed to appreciate this as it overlooks the river. This room also has the most elaborate bathroom, with an enormous double Jacuzzi bath and *trompe l'oeil* wall paintings. The other two bedrooms, the very sunny South Room with its Louis XV bed, *chaise-longue* and large bathroom, and the four-poster room, full of antique furniture and a smaller bathroom, are just as lovely. Shirley and Vernon Cole are very friendly and thoughtful hosts – rooms are well stocked with lots of little extras like cotton wool, clothes brushes and luxurious toiletries, and a list of personally recommended local pubs and restaurants can be produced in a flash.

◗ Closed 25 & 26 Dec; 1 July to 31 Aug ⬛ Take A26 (Hadlow Road) out of Tonbridge towards Maidstone; turn right into Elm Lane towards Golden Green; Goldhill Mill is about 1 mile down on the left. Private car park ⬛ 2 double, 1 four-poster; all with bathroom/WC; TV, limited room service, hair-dryer, trouser press, direct-dial telephone ⬙ Dining-room, TV room, drying-room, garden; tennis ⬛ No wheelchair access ⬛ No children under 12; no dogs; no smoking ⬛ Access, Visa ⬛ Single occupancy of twin/double £50 to £65, twin/double £75, four-poster £70; deposit required. Special breaks available

---

GOUDHURST Kent   map 3

Star & Eagle

High Street, Goudhurst TN17 1AL
TEL: (01580) 211512 FAX: (01580)211416

Lively, friendly country pub with plain and traditional rooms.

From its elevated position overlooking the main street running through Goudhurst and also the church and its graveyard next door, the Star & Eagle certainly seems to be a popular haunt for locals. The traditional bar with its bay windows, beamed ceiling, horse brasses and lanterns hanging above the bar, serves solid pub food, such as scampi and chips or a ploughman's lunch. The split-level restaurant, which has larger tables and tapestry chairs, is also popular in the evenings and serves dishes such as roast rack of lamb or butterfly trout fillets. It also has a very good vegetarian menu. (Any item from the menu can be ordered to eat in the bar or the restaurant.) As you go up the wooden stairs under the curved, beamed ceiling towards the guest rooms, you begin to appreciate the age of the pub; it was established as an inn in 1600. Leading off narrow corridors are the bedrooms, mostly of a good size and comfortable with plain, no-frills bathrooms. Room 5 is a particularly big room with a four poster bed and period furniture, while some of the rear-facing rooms have excellent views of the surrounding countryside. One or two of the rooms could do with a bit of redecoration.

◗ Open all year ⬛ Goudhurst is 2 miles off A21, on A262. Private car park ⬛ 1 single, 4 twin, 5 double, 1 four-poster; most with bathroom/WC; TV, hair-dryer, trouser press, direct-dial telephone ⬙ Restaurant, bar, lounge, garden; conference facilities (max 25 people incl up to 11 residential); toys, cot, high chairs ⬛ No wheelchair access ⬛ No dogs; no smoking in bedrooms ⬛ Access, Amex, Switch, Visa ⬛ Single/ single occupancy of twin/double £35, twin/double £53, four-poster £70. Alc L, D £12.50; bar meals available

---

GRANGE-IN-BORROWDALE Cumbria   map 10

Borrowdale Gates

Grange-in-Borrowdale, Keswick CA12 5UQ
TEL: (01768) 777204 FAX: (01768) 777254

Timeless family hotel in a superb valley in the heart of the Lake District.

Practicality must have been the watchword of the architects who have added over the years to Borrowdale Gates. For while the Victorian house is now a labyrinth of annexes and additions, the design allows maximum appreciation from inside its magnificent setting. The grassy valley floor runs away to the north, on to Derwentwater, while all around steep fellsides enclose the grey-stone village of Grange with its double-humpback bridge over a shallow river. Picture windows run the length of an expansive restaurant and lounge area, looking out over fields of sheep penned in by dry-stone walls. Subdued décor, space enough for privacy and a request for jacket and tie at dinner instill an air of timeless gentility and propriety, but don't mistake this for stuffiness. Christine Parkinson may well discuss the menu with you, making helpful suggestions about special dishes and accompanying wines, while you sit with an aperitif. Meanwhile, Terry Parkinson, the chef/patron, is busy to good effect in the kitchen. Our inspector's spring meal consisted of a mild-flavoured and light haddock fishcake with mustard sauce followed by perfectly cooked hake on a bed of blackened shallots. Only a rather ordinary cheeseboard proved disappointing. Bedrooms are off an initially confusing series of corridors, and are designed quite functionally with fitted furniture and pleasant, if uninspiring, decoration, but lack nothing in comfort and most, particularly those at the back, have fine views.

Closed 2 to 30 Jan and 8 to 18 Dec ⚡ From Keswick follow B5289 towards Borrowdale for 4 miles; turn right over double-humpback bridge signposted Grange; hotel is on right. Private car park 4 single, 7 twin, 9 double, 2 family rooms; most with bathroom/WC, 3 with shower/WC; TV, direct-dial telephone radio; hair-dryer and trouser press in some rooms ⚬ Restaurant, bar, 3 lounges, drying-room; early suppers for children ♿ Wheelchair access to hotel (1 step) and restaurant, 6 ground-floor bedrooms ● No children under 7 in restaurant eves; no dogs; no smoking in restaurant ☐ Access, Amex, Delta, Switch, Visa £ Single £55 to £73, single occupancy of twin/double £83, twin/double £105 to £140, family room from £120 (rates incl dinner); deposit required. Set D £23.50, Sun L £13.50; light lunches available. Special breaks available

GRANGE-OVER-SANDS Cumbria map 8

Graythwaite Manor

Fernhill Road, Grange-over-Sands LA11 7JE
TEL: (01539) 532001 FAX: (01539) 535549

Family-run, old-fashioned hotel in a timeless seaside resort.

Like Grange itself, this creeper-clad Edwardian country house seems to have seen the years pass by with little effect, and that must be largely due to the continuity of ownership by the Blakemore family since 1937. The hallways, bars and lounges retain some splendid features, like plasterwork friezes, oak panelling and neo-classical overmantels, and the leaded windows at the front overlook Morecambe Bay, across Graythwaite's renowned gardens. The ravages of time have been less kind to some of the bedrooms, where woolly bedspreads and fitted furnishings are looking dated. Other bedrooms may have a smattering of antiques and mullioned windows; all are generous for space and most have splendid views of the Bay. Room 21 has french doors that open on to a front patio, while Room 11, with a double aspect, was Violet Carson's (Ena Sharples in *Coronation Street*) favourite on her regular visits. Reports sing high praise for the helpful staff, the relaxing and peaceful atmosphere, and the good-value food. Dinner is a six-course affair, with plenty of choice over starters and main dishes, and may include favourites such as smoked fish roulade encased in smoked salmon, deep-fried Brie with pineapple and pink pepper sauce, and roast Gressingham duckling with orange sauce.

◑ Closed 4 to 19 Jan ⤾ Follow main road through Grange-over-Sands; Fernhill Road is opposite fire station. Private car park ⤙ 5 single, 11 twin, 4 double, 1 family room, 1 suite; all with bathroom/WC exc 2 doubles with shower/WC; TV, room service, hair-dryer, direct-dial telephone ✓ Restaurant, bar, 2 lounges, conservatory/games room, garden; conference facilities (max 30 people incl up to 22 residential); tennis, snooker, putting green; early suppers for children; baby-listening, cots
 ⅋ Wheelchair access to hotel and restaurant, 5 ground-floor bedrooms ● No dogs; no smoking in restaurant and 1 lounge ▭ Access, Amex, Delta, Visa
£ Single from £45, twin/double from £80, family room/suite from £90; deposit required. Set L £11.50, D £18; bar lunches available. Special breaks available

---

GRASMERE Cumbria   map 8

White Moss House

Rydal Water, Grasmere LA22 9SE
TEL: (01539) 435295   FAX: (01539) 435516

Exceptional food and attractive rooms are offered in a guesthouse with a Wordsworth link.

If the Wordsworth connection (he once owned the house, and composed poetry in the porch) is not sufficient to draw you to this Lakeland stone guesthouse engulfed in ivy, then Peter Dixon's cooking should do the trick. Peter prepares some of the most highly rated food in the Lake District – an area that offers some pretty stiff competition. Fresh, lightly cooked, local produce is the general principle; more specifically, on a five-course set menu you might find courgette and chervil soup, a salad of chicken smoked with oak and bracken, suckling pig baked with rosemary and bay (and crackling), and then a choice of desserts.

A sample of the extensive wine list fills the fireplace in the dining-room, while the lounge has plenty of easy chairs and, should the weather turn inclement, a useful assortment of books and games. Elsewhere, there is the fine half-panelling to admire, or the famous Twyford's Victorian loo, which was photographed by Lucinda Lambton for her book. The upstairs bedrooms are very pretty, featuring plenty of floral designs and fine antiques; the cupboard-like bathrooms, however, are overly snug. Number 3 – perhaps the largest – would be our choice. Thickly planted rhododendrons and holly around the front garden screen off the sight, if not the sound, of the main road to Windermere, although the traffic quietens down during the evening.

Reports are welcome on any hotel, whether or not it is in the Guide.

◐ Closed Dec, Jan & Feb; restaurant closed Sun ⏎ On A591 at the northern end of Rydal Water, halfway between Ambleside and Grasmere. Private car park ⤙ 3 twin, 2 double, 2 four-poster; 2 in annexe; all with bathroom/WC; TV, room service, hair-dryer, trouser press, direct-dial telephone; no tea/coffee-making facilities in rooms ⊘ Dining-room, lounge, drying-room, garden; fishing ⅄ No wheelchair access ● No children under 5; no dogs; no smoking in dining-room ⊟ Access, Visa £ Single occupancy of twin/double £65 to £85, twin/double/four-poster £120 to £175 (rates incl dinner); deposit required. Set D £27.50. Special breaks available

---

GRASSINGTON North Yorkshire   map 8

Ashfield House

Grassington, Skipton BD23 5AE
TEL: (01756) 752584 (AND FAX)

A small, welcoming guesthouse in the centre of a picture-book Dales village.

The best time in which to appreciate the lovely cobbled square and winding lanes of one of the Dales' loveliest villages is in the early evening, when the teashops and car park have emptied, and the day-trippers have tripped off home. Ashfield House is set a little way back from the square, and although the two-storey, ivy-covered stone cottage looks thoroughly rustic, the interior has been styled using some modern decorative techniques which enhance the original features of the house. Thus the main lounge has an exposed stone wall and a wooden crossbeam, but also features colourful, modern sofas, and bright-orange, rag-rolled walls that are covered with vivid, modernist prints. The dining-room is plainer, and dinners tend to be traditional affairs, with main courses such as roast lamb. The small wine list is cheap and varied, but at the time of our inspection included no half-bottles. The bedrooms are simply decorated, with pale colour schemes and pine furniture; those overlooking the rear garden are particularly peaceful.

◐ Closed Jan to early Feb ⏎ 50 yards from Grassington village square. Private car park ⤙ 3 twin, 4 double; 1 double with bathroom/WC, 6 with shower/WC; TV; hair-dryer on request ⊘ Dining-room, 2 lounges, drying-room, garden ⅄ No wheelchair access ● No children under 5; no dogs; no smoking ⊟ Access, Visa £ Single occupancy of twin/double £25 to £39, twin/double £49 to £57; deposit required. Set D £12.50 to £14.50. Special breaks available

---

GREAT DUNMOW Essex   map 3

The Starr

Market Place, Great Dunmow CM6 1AX
TEL: (01371) 874321   FAX: (01371) 876337

An excellent restaurant with smart rooms in an unspoilt market town.

The road narrows from the market square as it leads past this 400-year-old coaching inn – a dignified black and white building with bedrooms in the converted stables behind. Handily located for visitors to the US air-base and for Stansted pilots alike, the restaurant has an excellent reputation for its food, which derives inspiration from varied sources and features dishes such as fresh tuna grilled with a tempura of vegetables and chilli, tomato and spring-onion dressing, or venison faggots with braised cabbage and field mushrooms. Such indulgence takes place in the fresh, pale-green restaurant at the back of the building; there's also a darker, cosier, beamed bar at the front for pre- and post-prandial imbibing. The weatherboarded stables – complete with clock tower and weather vane – house the eight bedrooms, which, at these prices, are more than simply rooms in which to sleep off the effects of dinner. The superior Pine Room has furniture made from the eponymous wood, a large corner bath with gold-plated taps, and double basins; others, like the Blue Room, are still quite spacious, with pretty blue and white drapes above the bed. The service is young and friendly.

◑ Closed 1st week in Jan; restaurant closed Sun ⊅ In centre of Great Dunmow's market place. Private car park ⇥ 1 twin, 6 double, 1 four-poster; all in annexe; all with bathroom/WC; TV, hair-dryer, direct-dial telephone ⌀ Restaurant, bar; conference facilities (max 36 people incl up to 8 residential); early suppers for children ♿ No wheelchair access ● ▭ Access, Amex, Delta, Switch, Visa £ Single/single occupancy of twin/double £58, twin/double £90, four-poster £108; deposit required. Set L £23, D £23/35; alc L £25. Special breaks available

---

GREAT LONGSTONE Derbyshire map 8

Croft Country House

Great Longstone, Nr Bakewell DE45 1TF
TEL: (01629) 640278

A Victorian country house with a difference in a Peak District village.

The talking-point of Robert Allan and Lynne Macaskill's hotel, secluded in three acres of part-rambling, part-formal gardens, is its huge galleried central hall with a lantern ceiling. Created by a Victorian engineer, its inspiration was apparently an Italian courtyard. The result as seen today is a splendid parquet-floored, pink-coloured, skylit space, furnished with antiques and hung with period watercolours. A cosier bar and sitting-room opening on to a wistaria-draped verandah provide alternative seating areas. The nine bedrooms that lead off the hall's galleried landing are furnished sometimes in pine, sometimes with Victorian pieces and marble fireplaces. On arrival you may be equally taken by the pot of tea and decanter of sherry to welcome you. Visitors are also impressed by the immaculate housekeeping standards achieved by the hands-on owners. At the same time, the rather restrictive dining arrangements may not suit all. The largely traditional dinners are adjudged tasty but begin promptly at 7.30pm. They run to four courses, with a soup or sorbet course and a set main dish such as chicken Mornay served between a choice of starters and puddings.

◐ Closed 2 Jan to 6 Feb   ⚡ From Bakewell take A6 Buxton road and turn right on to A6020; after 1 mile turn left towards Great Longstone; hotel entrance is on right in village. Private car park   🛏 1 single, 2 twin, 6 double; most with bathroom/WC, some with shower/WC; TV, room service   ✅ Restaurant, bar, 2 lounges, drying-room, garden; conference facilities (max 25 people incl up to 9 residential); croquet, pitch and putt; early suppers for children   ♿ Wheelchair access to hotel (2 steps), restaurant and WC (unisex), lift to bedrooms, 1 specially equipped for disabled people   ● No dogs; no smoking in restaurant   ⬜ Access, Visa   £ Single £60, single occupancy of twin/double £75, twin/double £98; deposit required. Set D £21.50

GREAT MALVERN Hereford & Worcester   map 5

Red Gate

32 Avenue Road, Great Malvern WR14 3BJ
TEL: (01684) 565013 (AND FAX)

Friendly and attentive hosts in a red-brick Victorian B&B.

The plus-point of this Victorian house on a leafy, residential street in the suburbs is the warmth of the welcome extended by Barbara and Richard Rowan. They are keen to make everyone feel at home and the house certainly has an atmosphere in which guests feel at ease and relaxed. The guests' lounge (which leads out into the rear garden) has a lovely carved wooden fireplace and plenty of books to browse through on a rainy day or to read in the evening, while the dining-room, with its prints of old Malvern lining the walls, is where guests enjoy their cooked-to-order breakfasts. The seven bedrooms are individually decorated and vary in size, but all are very tidy and smart. Décor ranges from heavy floral patterned drapes, bedspreads and wallpaper to cottage-style roses.

◐ Closed Chr, New Year and 2 weeks Apr   ⚡ Close to Great Malvern station and Malvern Girls' College; 10 minutes' walk from town centre. Private car park   🛏 1 single, 2 twin, 4 double; 4 with bathroom/WC, 3 with shower/WC; TV, room service; hair-dryer on request   ✅ Dining-room, lounge, drying-room, garden   ♿ No wheelchair access   ● No children under 8; no dogs; no smoking in bedrooms or dining-room   ⬜ Access, Visa   £ Single £25 to £28, twin/double £45 to £50; deposit required. Special breaks available

---

GREAT MILTON Oxfordshire   map 2

Le Manoir aux Quat' Saisons

Church Road, Great Milton, Oxford OX44 7PD
TEL: (01844) 278881   FAX: (01844) 278847

Luxurious rooms and a world-renowned restaurant – excellence at a price.

With a ratio of 103 staff to a maximum of 38 overnight guests, it's no surprise to discover that Le Manoir achieves the excellence it aims for. Headed by the world-renowned chef Raymond Blanc, the fifteenth-century golden-stone hotel is focused around its restaurant, and people come from all over the world to experience the eight-dish *menu gourmand*. Among this year's plans is a project to expand M. Blanc's cookery school and to add a spa complex so that all your senses, not just your taste buds, can be pampered. Public rooms have a sumptuous country-house feel with log fires, fresh flowers and lots of sunny yellow. Some of the bedrooms are taking on a theme as they're refurbished. Mermaid Rose is the latest addition, with smart gold and green fabrics, and a spiral staircase leading up to a lavish bathroom in which *trompe l'oeil* mermaids swim around a pair of Victorian baths standing side-by-side under an ephemeral canopy. A Venetian room is under discussion. Fruit, fresh flowers and luxury bathrobes are standard to every room, but the garden rooms, doors opening on to their own terraces, perhaps have the edge in summer.

◑ Open all year ⤢ Off A329, signposted 'Great Milton Manor'. Private car park
🛏 10 twin/double, 2 four-poster, 7 suites; all with bathroom/WC; TV, room service, hair-dryer, trouser press, direct-dial telephone; no tea/coffee-making facilities in rooms ⌘ 3 restaurants, 2 lounges, garden; conference facilities (max 36 people incl up to 19 residential); heated outdoor swimming-pool, tennis, croquet; early suppers for children; toys ⅙ No wheelchair access ● No dogs ⌐ Access, Amex, Delta, Diners, Switch, Visa ⌑ Twin/double £185 to £285, suite £345 to £395; deposit required. Continental B £9.50, cooked B £14.50; set L, D £29.50/69; alc L, D £65. Special breaks available

---

GREAT SNORING Norfolk   map 6

Old Rectory

Great Snoring, Nr Fakenham NR21 0HP
TEL: (01328) 820597   FAX: (01328) 820048

Secluded, peaceful accommodation in fascinating Elizabethan manor house.

It's not until the end of the drive, which curves round to the entrance of the house opposite the church, that you get a good look at the rectory's Tudor architecture – mullioned windows, hexagonal towers and terracotta friezes of heads thought to represent sixteenth-century members of the Shelton family, whose seat this was. Victorian extensions and development have disturbed the original layout somewhat, but in keeping with the house's history the interior is very English, relaxed and understated. Rosamund Scoles lets its features speak for themselves. The strangely shaped dining-room (the whole building was originally hexagonal) contains a ticking longcase clock and a carved Elizabethan-style dresser displaying figurines. The living-room is bolder, with deep rose-red paper up to the neat egg-and-dart moulding, and plenty of comfortable seating. Bedrooms vary in shape and colour too, mixing ancient and modern furniture, and have unpretentious but practical bathrooms. English tradition also reigns over the menus, which might start with home-made soup or quail's egg salad, followed by a roast or a fish dish; vegetarians are also catered for.

Report forms are at the back of the Guide*; write a letter or e-mail us if you prefer. Our e-mail address is: "guidereports@which.co.uk".*

◑ Closed 24 to 27 Dec ⤢ Great Snoring is 3 miles north-east of Fakenham; hotel is behind church on Barsham Road. Private car park ⤶ 3 twin, 3 double; all with bathroom/WC; TV, room service, direct-dial telephone; hair-dryer on request; no tea/coffee-making facilities in rooms ⚹ Dining-room, lounge, garden; conference facilities (max 12 people incl up to 6 residential); early suppers for children ♿ No wheelchair access ● Children by arrangement only; no dogs; no smoking in dining-room ▭ Access, Amex, Delta, Diners, Switch, Visa £ Single occupancy of twin/double £68, twin/double £91. Set D £22

GRIMSTON Norfolk   map 6

Congham Hall

Grimston, Nr King's Lynn PE32 1AH
TEL: (01485) 600250   FAX: (01485) 601191

Smart country house with excellent service and scrupulous attention to detail.

'I arrived and parked in their car park, listening to the radio...After ten minutes a worried receptionist came out of her office – "I saw you through the window and wondered if you were OK". Of course I was, but that reflected the general standard of service.' That satisfied reader left a generous tip, having had his room upgraded without asking, and having enjoyed an excellent meal. The smart white Georgian manor sits just outside Grimston in 40 acres of gardens and parkland, the pride and joy of Christine and Trevor Forecast. Those of a horticultural bent can take a wander round the herb garden to inspect over 500 varieties; for the more active, the hotel has its own cricket pitch in addition to the more usual tennis courts and pool. Inside, strong colours, good-quality fabrics and furnishings, including a smattering of antiques, and plenty of fresh flowers and home-made potpourris abound. Bedrooms range from the massive Garden Suite on the ground floor to the smaller standard room, which still has space for a couple of wicker chairs and dressing table. Much more is being made this year of the Orangery Restaurant, which lives up to its name in colour and style. Here the menu might offer dishes like poached oysters in tarragon and shallot tortellini with mushroom and champagne velouté, and roast-lamb steak with pumpkin risotto, roast aubergine and spiced hummus.

◑ Open all year ⤢ Turn off A148 towards Grimston; hotel is 2½ miles further on on the left. Private car park ⤶ 1 single, 7 twin, 3 double, 1 four-poster, 2 suites; all with bathroom/WC exc single with shower/WC; TV, room service, hair-dryer, direct-dial telephone, radio; trouser press in some rooms; tea/coffee-making facilities on request ⚹ 2 restaurants, bar, lounge, drying-room, garden; conference facilities (max 18 people incl up to 14 residential); heated outdoor swimming-pool, tennis, croquet, cricket ♿ No wheelchair access ● No children under 12; no dogs; no smoking in 1 restaurant and discouraged in bedrooms ▭ Access, Amex, Diners, Visa £ Single £69, single occupancy of twin/double £79, twin/double £105, four-poster £135, suite £170; deposit required. Set D £20 to £35; light lunches available (prices valid till Apr 1997). Special breaks available

GRITTLETON Wiltshire   map 2

Church House

Grittleton, Nr Chippenham SN14 6AP
TEL: (01249) 782562   FAX: (01249) 782546

Smart, family home in a Georgian rectory with good meals and a warm welcome.

With steps up to the door and pillars either side, Anna and Michael Moore's sturdy Georgian rectory is grander than the church next door. Sandwiched between churchyard and the village pub, the concealed gravel driveway curls round a well-tended lawn to reach the imposing three-storey house. Behind, 11 acres of grounds include a walled garden in the process of renovation, extensive lawns, and strutting territory for Anna's green Javanese peafowl, besides free-range hens (which provide the eggs for your breakfast) straying from next door. Inside, accumulated mementos from 30 years of family life here combine with a love of art: Michael's mother was a painter, and oils, pencil studies and watercolours fill the walls of the pale-yellow drawing-room and deep-red dining-room. Dinners are communal, eaten round a long polished table, and may feature ham with gingered melon or peaches in Stilton sauce, followed by salmon with orange and thyme dressing, or chicken 'on horseback' with orange mashed potatoes. Bedrooms, reached via a beautiful curving staircase, are less grand but comfortable; bathroom facilities may be hidden behind wooden screens. By the time of publication, a *trompe l'oeil* mural brightening the indoor pool in the former stables should be complete.

◑ Open all year ⊿ Between church and pub in Grittleton. Private car park ⇗ 2 twin, 1 double, 1 family room; all with bathroom/WC exc double with shower/WC; TV, hair-dryer ⌀ Dining-room, lounge, music room; conference facilities (max 12 people incl up to 4 residential); heated indoor swimming-pool, croquet ও No wheelchair access ● No children under 12 exc babes in arms; no dogs; smoking allowed only if other guests consent ⌷ None accepted £ Single occupancy of twin/double £33, twin/double £55, family room £75; deposit required. Set D £15.50; packed lunches available. Special breaks available

GUILDFORD Surrey   map 3

Angel Hotel

91 High Street, Guildford GU1 3DP
TEL: (01483) 564555   FAX: (01483) 33770

A smartly maintained old coaching-inn in the town centre.

The Angel is located on a semi-pedestrianised road bang in the centre of busy Guildford, and yet inside all is hushed and plush historic grandeur. Not to say that this old black and white coaching-inn is particularly big – despite the recent addition of ten new bedrooms, it maintains a cosy, rather gentlemen's-club atmosphere. The galleried lounge area has exposed beams, low ceilings and a huge fireplace, and in the 'library' bar very realistic fake books line the walls – a tongue-in-cheek touch in an otherwise traditional and immaculate refurbishment. Downstairs, in the crypt-like Undercroft Restaurant with its stone arches and hanging tapestries the serious tone is continued, and tales of the thirteenth-century secret passageway from the Angel to the castle in Guildford will keep you entertained before dinner. The up-market English menu may include dishes like oxtail consommé 'laced with shavings of truffle and artichoke', followed by lobster and basil ravioli 'embraced with langoustine tails and veiled with a luxuriant lobster and brandy sauce'. The bedrooms in the old part of the hotel are in keeping with the style of the public rooms, with huge beds and draped half-testers, and are well decorated in flowery pinks, blues and greens. The new bedrooms are approached through a corridor flanking the outside of the house, and lack the individuality of the others although they are just as luxurious. However, what you lose in character you make up for in facilities, as power showers have been installed in the extravagant bathrooms.

○ Open all year ⤴ Follow signs to town centre; hotel is half-way up High Street (closed to vehicles 11am to 4pm). On-street parking eves 🛏 5 twin, 6 double, 10 suites; some in annexe; all with bathroom/WC; TV, room service, hair-dryer, direct-dial telephone; no tea/coffee-making facilities in rooms ✍ Restaurant, bar, lounge, drying-room, library; conference facilities (max 40 people incl up to 20 residential); early suppers for children; babysitting, baby-listening 🚶 Wheelchair access to hotel, lift to bedrooms, 1 specially equipped for disabled people ● No dogs in public rooms 🗂 Access, Amex, Delta, Diners, Switch, Visa 💷 Single occupancy of twin/double £135, twin/double £135, suite £150 to £200; deposit required. Continental B £6.50, cooked B £8.50; set L £15, D £18.50; alc D £29. Special breaks available

HADLEY WOOD Hertfordshire

map 3

West Lodge Park

Cockfosters Road, Hadley Wood EN4 0PY
TEL: 0181-440 8311   FAX: 0181-449 3698

Luxurious rooms in a country-house hotel at the centre of a large park.

Exactly 12 miles from Piccadilly Circus, according to the brochure, West Lodge Park is a good-looking country house set in 34 acres of parkland. It was built as a hunting lodge for royalty, who had hunted here since Henry IV's time – Elizabeth I came here to hunt deer 'with a retinue of 12 ladies in white satin...and 20 yeomen clad in green.' Today, you're more likely to see a fleet of wedding cars crossing the park. The management does a good job in keeping standards high and the atmosphere informal. One reader wrote: 'An excellent experience. The room was spacious, colour co-ordinated, with outstanding facilities...All in all, I was impressed.' Each room has its own character – some pretty, some more masculine – and all are well equipped. If anything, corner rooms are the best for their double-aspect views. A ticking grandfather clock, comfortable sofas and a well-stoked log fire make the lounge a relaxed place in which to spend your time, while the conservatory restaurant is at its best in summer, when the tables can spill out on to a leafy terrace. The extensive dinner menu might include smoked salmon with shallots, capers and salad, breast of Barbary duck with caramelised pears, lemon tart with plum sauce, and a vast choice of locally made ice-cream.

◑ Open all year ⤣ Exit M25 at Junction 24, follow signs to Cockfosters. Hotel is first turning on the left, ½ mile down the road. Private car park ⤒ 13 single, 8 twin, 20 double, 4 four-poster; family rooms and suites available; some in annexe; all with bathroom/WC; TV, room service, hair-dryer, trouser press, direct-dial telephone; mini-bar in 2 rooms ⦸ Restaurant, bar, lounge, conservatory, garden, air-conditioning in private dining-rooms; putting green, croquet, fitness trail, clay-pigeon shooting, archery; conference facilities (max 80 people incl up to 30 residential); early suppers for children; toys, baby-listening ⧘ Wheelchair access to hotel (2 steps), restaurant and WC (unisex), 1 bedroom specially equipped for disabled people, lift to bedrooms ⬤ No dogs; no smoking in restaurant and some bedrooms ⊟ Access, Amex, Delta, Switch, Visa £⧛ Single £73, single occupancy of twin/double £90, twin/double £105, four-poster £155, family room £155, suite £155 to £177; deposit required. Continental B £7.50, cooked B £9.50; set L £20, D £22.50 (prices valid till Sept 1996). Special breaks available

---

HALIFAX **West Yorkshire**   map 8

Holdsworth House

Holdsworth, Halifax HX2 9TG
TEL: (01422) 240024   FAX: (01422) 245174

A grand, Jacobean manor house offering period charm and adventurous cooking.

The less said about the approach to Holdsworth House, the better (but just for the record, it's on the outskirts of Halifax, along a dreary road lined with small industrial estates and sombre, terraced houses). The next disappointment occurs on your arrival at the hotel itself: this Grade II listed manor house is a beautiful example of Jacobean architecture, but you drive into a car park that is located at the building's rather anonymous rear. From there on, however – as you wander through the charming, period-style lounges with their wooden floors, mullioned windows, and doughty, antique sideboards – things pick up. And there's nothing to stop you from wandering to the neat lawns at the front of the house, in order to admire its venerable façade.

The pick of the public areas has to be the panelled dining-room – a classic of its kind – in which gilt-framed portraits hang below the beamed ceiling on dark, panelled walls, and guests dine at polished wooden tables on elaborately carved chairs. Dinners may typically begin with a dish of queen scallops marinated with cumin, shallow fried and served with a sauce gribiche; the main course might be steamed Cornish lemon sole filled with a lobster mousse and accompanied by sauté langoustines.

There are a number of four-posters and half-testers in the bedrooms, and the furnishings range from plain, pine tables to heavy, antique chests of drawers. Many of the rooms feature sloping ceilings with skylights.

◑ Closed Chr to New Year ▨ From Halifax, take A629 towards Keighley. After 1½ miles, turn right into Shay Lane (signposted Holmfield). The house is 1 mile further up, on the right. Private car park ⌐ 18 single, 3 twin, 13 double, 1 four-poster, 5 suites; family room available; all with bathroom/WC; TV, room service, hair-dryer, direct-dial telephone; mini-bar in some rooms ⌘ Dining-room, 2 bars, 2 lounges, garden; conference facilities (max 150 people incl up to 40 residential); early suppers for children; baby-sitting, baby-listening ♿ Wheelchair access to hotel (1 step), restaurant and WC (unisex), 20 ground-floor bedrooms, 2 rooms specially equipped for disabled people ● No dogs in public rooms ▭ Access, Amex, Delta, Diners, Switch, Visa £ Single £55 to £73, single occupancy of twin/double £60 to £80, twin/double/four-poster/family room £75 to £90, suite £90 to £110; deposit required. Cooked B £6.50; set L £12.50, D £19.50; alc L £20, D £25. Special breaks available

---

HAMBLETON Leicestershire   map 6

Hambleton Hall

Hambleton, Oakham LE15 8TH
TEL: (01572) 756991 FAX: (01572) 724721

 COUNTY HOTEL OF THE YEAR

One of Britain's top-flight country-house hotels.

It's hard not to gush about Stefa and Tim Hart's sumptuous, long-established hotel. The house's position is magical: ensconced by mature cedars in an elevated position on a peninsula poking into Rutland Water. The great, Victorian pile may be no great beauty in itself, but it has been furnished with much élan, and comes across as being surprisingly intimate. The public rooms convey an impression of classical elegance, and include the requisite fires roaring within exquisite marble fireplaces in winter, while opulent fabrics and magnificent flower displays feature everywhere. Like the super, zestful staff, the atmosphere is formal, but without any hint of reverential stuffiness. The most imaginative interior design appears in the highly individual bedrooms. Qazvin, for example, boasts hand-painted, seventeenth-century Persian panels. If money's no object, ask for Fern, which has stencilled walls and a large bay window through which to survey the lake. Much cheaper rooms, such as Lake, also look over the water. The least expensive rooms still boast features such as grand half-tester beds and slick bathrooms.

Hambleton Hall has long been famous for its food. Chef Aaron Patterson's elaborate seasonal creations may include langoustine ravioli in a Pernod and orange sauce, or honey-roasted duck in a jasmine-tea sauce. You can savour his cuisine, without breaking the bank, by sticking to a three-course, no-choice menu.

 Denotes somewhere you can rely on a good meal – either the hotel features in the 1997 edition of our sister publication, The Good Food Guide, *or our inspectors thought the cooking impressive, whether particularly competent home cooking or more lavish cuisine.*

○ Open all year 🄩 3 miles east of Oakham, on a peninsula which juts into Rutland Water. Private car park ⭰ 10 twin, 4 double, 1 four-poster; all with bathroom/WC; TV, room service, hair-dryer, direct-dial telephone, radio; no tea/coffee-making facilities in rooms ⌀ 3 restaurants, bar, lounge; conference facilities (max 40 people incl up to 15 residential); heated outdoor swimming-pool, tennis; early suppers for children; baby-sitting, baby-listening ⅍ Wheelchair access to hotel (ramp), restaurant and WC (unisex), lift to bedrooms ● No dogs in public rooms and in bedrooms by arrangement ▭ Access, Amex, Delta, Diners, Switch, Visa £ Single occupancy of twin/double £110 to £125, twin/double £150 to £275, four-poster £180; deposit required. Cooked B £12; set L £14.50 to £29.50, D £35; alc L, D £50 (prices valid till Mar 1997). Special breaks available

---

HAMPTON COURT Surrey

map 3

Mitre Hotel

Hampton Court Road, Hampton Court KT8 9BN
TEL: 0181-979 9988 FAX: 0181-979 9777

A comfortable riverside hotel close to Hampton Court Palace.

There is an underground passageway that links the Mitre Hotel with Hampton Court Palace; it is closed off now, of course, but its existence serves as a reminder of the excesses of the 'Merry Monarch'. Charles II had the Mitre built to serve as an overspill when the bedrooms at the palace filled up, and when one sees the vastness of the palace, one wonders how much the 36 bedrooms in this cosy hotel helped his hospitality problem. It may be that the guests preferred the hotel's peaceful river aspect, with its boats and overhanging trees. Such tranquillity, best viewed from the restaurant – which features a large rotunda – or from the bar which opens out on to a small terrace and jetty, is in stark contrast to the roar of traffic on the other side of the hotel. The bedrooms that face the palace have to contend with the road – so it's best to ask for one at the back – but they are all comfortable and spacious, and feature reproduction walnut furniture and ruffled pelmets over the beds. The décor is in pink or blue, with floral drapes and prints of Tudors and Stuarts lining the walls. The menu offers a choice of à la carte or business lunches, with such dishes as a warm salad of chicken livers and bacon, flavoured with balsamic vinegar, perhaps followed by roasted cod with cabbage, shiitake mushrooms and herbs. .

○ Open all year 🄩 Opposite Hampton Court Palace and next to the bridge. Private car park ⭰ 19 twin, 11 double, 6 suites; family rooms available; all with bathroom/WC; TV, room service, hair-dryer, trouser press, direct-dial telephone ⌀ Restaurant, bar, 2 lounges; conference facilities (max 110 people incl up to 36 residential); early suppers for children; babysitting, baby-listening, cots, high chairs ⅍ No wheelchair access ● No dogs in public rooms ▭ Access, Amex, Delta, Diners, Switch, Visa £ Single occupancy of twin/double £65 to £75, twin/double £105 to £140, family room from £105 , suite £115 to £210; deposit required. Continental B £7, cooked B £9; set L £12, alc L, D £20 (prices valid till Apr 1997). Special breaks available

HAMSTERLEY FOREST Co Durham   map 10

Grove House

Hamsterley Forest, Bishop Auckland DL13 3NL
TEL: (01388) 488203   FAX: (01388) 606306

A small, family-run guesthouse situated in the woods, boasting superb hospitality.

Perhaps the main attraction of Grove House is its superbly secluded location: although only 20 minutes from the city of Durham, it has a fairy-tale setting at the end of a 3-mile-long forest road and, apart from the 5,000 acres of trees, it is surrounded by sheltered flower gardens that include a suntrap terrace. Named the County Hotel of the Year in last year's *Guide*, Helene and Russell Close's family home was once an aristocrat's shooting lodge, and the long, beamed sitting-room – with its open fire and photographs and trophies from the family's riding exploits – is still a lovely place in which to put up your feet after a hard day's activity in the open air. One reader wrote to praise the relaxed atmosphere, adding: 'It was like staying in a country house with friends. The owners were very friendly and helpful, and the bedrooms charming. We had to share the sitting-room with the family, but they are fun.' The three modern bedrooms, with their light colour schemes, co-ordinated floral fabrics and neat bathrooms, all have leafy outlooks. If you're here to walk, Helene is happy to provide you with a packed lunch, while her three-course set dinners are a treat in the evening, and often feature game from the forest.

◐ Closed Chr & New Year   ⓩ North of West Auckland off A68. Follow signs to Hamsterley Forest; at Bedburn fork left – hotel is situated 3 miles inside the forest on a tarmac road. Private car park   ⌂ 2 twin, 1 double; 2 with bathroom/WC, 1 with shower/WC; hair-dryer   ✅ Dining-room, lounge, garden; conference facilities (max 15 people incl up to 3 residential); early suppers for children   ♿ No wheelchair access   ⬤ No children under 8; no dogs; no smoking   ▭ None accepted   £ Single occupancy of twin/double £24 to £27, twin/double £48 to £53; deposit required. Set D £13.50; packed lunches available. Special breaks available

---

HANLEY CASTLE Hereford & Worcester   map 5

Old Parsonage Farm

Hanley Castle, Worcester WR8 0BU
TEL: (01684) 310124

Red-brick farmhouse with friendly hosts and an emphasis on wine-tasting.

Ann and Tony Addison didn't set out with the intention of running a guesthouse – in fact, Old Parsonage Farm is a little unusual on that front as the Addisons do not really encourage passing trade, preferring instead to have as their guests like-minded people who have come to enjoy an evening of good food, lively conversation and fine wines, then stay over. Tony is by trade an importer of fine wines from around the world, and proffers a list of about 100 of his selections at dinner. The couple started out offering wine-tastings and then wine breaks 12 years ago, and the business has snowballed from there. The emphasis is very firmly upon the social aspect of the evening, with none of the three bedrooms having televisions (but there is a TV in the sitting-room downstairs for those suffering withdrawal symptoms). The bright and sunny lounge, known to the family as the 'quiet room', is comfy, and has views out to the nearby Malverns. The simple and neat bedrooms are all a good size.

◖ Open all year ⚡ Take B4211 out of Upton-upon-Severn for 2 miles towards Worcester; turn left on to B4209; the farm is 200 yards on right. Private car park ⤙ 1 twin, 2 double; all with bathroom/WC; limited room service, hair-dryer; no tea/coffee-making facilities in rooms ✧ Dining-room, lounge, TV room, drying-room, library, garden ⚹ No wheelchair access ● No children under 12; no dogs; no smoking in bedrooms ⊟ None accepted £ Single occupancy of twin/double £27 to £30, twin/double £44 to £49; deposit required. Set D £15. Special breaks available

---

HAROME North Yorkshire   map 9

Pheasant Hotel

Harome, Helmsley YO6 5JG
TEL: (01439) 771241   FAX: (01439) 771744

An easy-going country house in a quiet village close to the Yorkshire Moors.

Everything about the Pheasant seems designed to soothe. The bedrooms are reasonably spacious, decorated in muted tones, such as cream, beige and pale green, and feature simple botanical prints. A complimentary glass of sherry, books (although disappointingly, there were mostly hotel guides in our inspector's room) and bathrobes are provided to make you feel at home. The large lounge, which was once a blacksmith's cottage, overlooks the duck pond, and has plenty of low-slung, floral-print sofas into which to sink, while country-life magazines are scattered around and prints of rural scenes hang on the walls. In contrast to the drama of the Yorkshire Dales or the melancholy of the Moors, even the surrounding countryside, which is flattish with gentle folds, is in on the soothing act. Given the laid-back, country-house feel, and the relative lack of business custom, it comes as something of a surprise to find a heated indoor swimming-pool.

The atmosphere in the Sinnington Bar has a hint of the traditional pub – including a decent pint of Theakston's, wooden beams and a real fire – but there's something about the ordered arrangement of the trestle tables and wooden chairs that gives it a slight feeling of the classroom. Tricia Binks' dinners eschew adventure in favour of the wholesome and filling: duck pâté with orange may be followed, for example, with crab salad and then Scottish salmon. The service is youthful and enthusiastic, but apart from at meal times, the staff can seem a little detached.

We mention those hotels that don't accept dogs; guide dogs, however, are almost always an exception. Telephone ahead to make sure.

⬤ Closed Chr, Jan and Feb ⤴ Leave Helmsley on A170 towards Scarborough. After ¼ mile, turn right for Harome. Hotel near village church. Private car park ⤙ 2 single, 6 twin, 4 double, 3 suites; suites in annexe; all with bathroom/WC; TV, room service, hair-dryer, direct-dial telephone ✅ Dining-room, bar, lounge, drying-room, garden; conference facilities (max 20 people incl up to 15 residential); heated indoor swimming-pool ⅃ Wheelchair access to hotel, dining-room and WC (M,F), 1 bedroom specially equipped for disabled people ⬤ No children under 10; no dogs in public rooms and in bedrooms by arrangement; no smoking in dining-room ▭ None accepted ⓔ Single £52 to £60, twin/double £104 to £120, suite £104 to £124 (rates incl dinner); deposit required. Set D £20 (prices valid till May 1997). Special breaks available

---

White House

10 Park Parade, Harrogate HG1 5AH
TEL: (01423) 501388   FAX: (01423) 527973

Elegant yet homely Italianate villa overlooking Harrogate's vast expanse of green.

Anyone familiar with the film *A Private Function*, that gentle send-up of Yorkshire one-upmanship, will understand the desirability of a place 'on the parade'. In the case of the White House, it's not just the address but its position overlooking the Stray which must make it the envy of the town's hoteliers. Add to that the gracious Italianate façade, with its triple-arched windows beneath sea-shell lunettes, and you have an establishment very much in keeping with the town's spirit of refinement. The house was built in 1836 as a private residence for the Mayor of Harrogate on the design of a Venetian villa, but the current owner, Jennie Forster, is at pains to point out that it is now very much a family home. Guests choose between the sitting-room and library, both of which overlook the Stray, in which to unwind before heading for the elegant dining-room. Beneath the ornate stuccoed ceiling you can enjoy starters like goat's cheese and herb soufflé and main courses like medallions of venison with an orange and gin sauce. Bedrooms are individually designed, often with brightly coloured floral fabrics and swagged curtains. Front rooms like Harriet, with its half-tester bed, get lots of natural light. One couple, however, were disappointed by a lack of attention to detail: teabags not replenished, a newspaper charged for that had failed to turn up, only two hangers in the wardrobe.

⬤ Open all year ⤴ Off A59; telephone for directions. On-street parking ⤙ 2 single, 3 twin, 4 double, 1 four-poster; all with bathroom/WC exc 1 single with shower/WC; TV, limited room service, direct-dial phone; hair-dryer on request ✅ Restaurant, bar/lounge, library, garden; conference facilities (max 40 people incl up to 10 residential); early suppers for children; toys, babysitting, baby-listening ⅃ No wheelchair access ⬤ No dogs; no smoking in bedrooms or restaurant ▭ Access, Amex, Delta, Diners, Switch, Visa ⓔ Single £55 to £89, single occupancy of twin/double £75 to £110, twin/double £85 to £122, four-poster £95 to £128; deposit required. Set L £15, D (two-course, no-choice) £13; alc D £24 (1996 prices). Special breaks available

Bolebroke Watermill

Edenbridge Road, Hartfield TN7 4JP
TEL: (01892) 770425 (AND FAX)

An ancient watermill in unspoilt idyllic surroundings.

All that marks the bumpy track leading to this delightful old mill and cluster of barns is a hand-painted B&B sign, so keep your eyes peeled. The scene nestling around the mill pond with its willows, ducks and geese is one of pure romantic seclusion. First mentioned in the Domesday Book in 1086, and a working corn-mill until 1948, Bolebroke has been converted by David and Christine Cooper into wonderfully characterful and quirky rooms shared between the white weather-boarded Mill and the black Elizabethan Miller's Barn. Huge cog-wheels, millstones and grain hoppers are preserved in the cosy lounge, as well as all sorts of unusual knick-knacks. Steep rustic ladders lead up to Pond and Meadow, dinky rooms bursting with character, both with bathrooms built into ancient grain-storage chambers – it's an adventure to go to the loo, but not suitable for the unsteady. Access to the red-brick house for Christine's award-winning breakfasts is via a trapdoor in the floor. Expect the likes of herb-stuffed mushrooms or toast baskets with bacon and chives rather than your average fry-up in the morning. Over in the barn, the three rooms are more spacious and rather easier to get to. Upstairs, past the moose's head, Honey-mooners' Hayloft and Dovesnest both have rustic four-posters, while Burrow beneath benefits from high ceilings and a profusion of exposed beams.

◑ Closed Chr ▨ Take A264 from East Grinstead towards Tunbridge Wells for 6 miles; at crossroads turn right to Hartfield on B2026 for 1 mile; turn left into unmade lane just past Perryhill Nursery and follow signs. Private car park ▭ 1 twin, 2 double, 2 four-poster; some in annexe; all with bathroom/WC; TV, hair-dryer, radio ⚜ 2 dining-rooms, 2 lounges, garden ⅁ No wheelchair access ● No children under 7; no dogs; no smoking ▭ Access, Amex, Visa £ Single occupancy of twin/double £50, twin/double £55, four-poster £72; deposit required

---

Mill at Harvington

Anchor Lane, Harvington, Evesham WR11 5NR
TEL: (01386) 870688 (AND FAX)

Neat conversion of a riverside mill offering good food and riparian relaxation at a reasonable price.

The non-designer signs that steer you through the pretty thatches of Harvington village towards the river and the Mill offer a clue to the unpretentious nature of the place. There's a Georgian formality to the red-brick house on the banks of the Avon, but overall the place seems to revel in the simplicity of its symmetry. Unlike most in this neck of the woods, the interior makes light of its antiquity, so the beams and other features, like the old ovens which have survived the quarter-millennium since the place began life as a malting mill, are never allowed to dominate. Pastels predominate in both public and bedroom areas, creating a lightness of touch that surprises in a building with an industrial past. A red and green colour scheme and stencilled walls distinguish the sitting-room, from which there is direct access to the river and eight acres of garden and wooded parkland. The same straightforward approach characterises the menu, where jargon-free notes seem genuinely designed to help the diner's choice, rather than to boost the chef's ego. Food is well executed but unflashy; perhaps salad of pigeon breast followed by halibut with lime and ginger butter. Bedrooms feature pastel or floral soft furnishings, decent polished wooden furniture and a range of reading material to while away the hours when the sun has set on the lovely river views.

● Closed 24 to 29 Dec ⬕ Turn south off B439 opposite Harvington village, down Anchor Lane; hotel driveway is 600 yards on left. Private car park ⬅ 3 twin, 12 double; all with bathroom/WC; TV, room service, hair-dryer, direct-dial telephone; trouser press on request ⬥ Restaurant, lounge, garden; conference facilities (max 20 people incl up to 15 residential); fishing, heated outdoor swimming-pool, tennis, croquet; early suppers for children; baby-listening ♿ No wheelchair access ● Children under 10 by arrangement; no dogs; no smoking in restaurant ▭ Access, Amex, Delta, Diners, Switch, Visa £ Single occupancy of twin/double £58, twin/double £90. Set L £14.50; alc D £25. Special breaks available

---

The Pier at Harwich

The Quay, Harwich CO12 3HH
TEL: (01255) 241212 FAX: (01255) 551922

A good seafood restaurant with handy rooms for early-morning travellers or late-night revellers.

It has to be said that the sea views from the Pier are not the most romantic – to be sure, there are fishing boats and excursion ferries, but these tend to be dominated by the cranes and derricks of the industrial wharves further along the quay. The smart, blue-painted Victorian building feels a little out of place among such workaday activity, but it's certainly the place to go for fresh seafood. A strong nautical theme runs throughout the Pier, with murals of underwater scenes featuring in the bar, and of clippers and paddle steamers in the two restaurants. Of the latter, the Ha'penny Pier on the ground floor – which is aimed at informal family eating – provides expertly battered fish and chips, as well as local crab, prawns or chicken served with a mild curry mayonnaise or, for those who prefer turf to surf, sirloin steak and beef-tomato sandwiches. On the first floor, the more formal Pier, which is adorned with ships' wheels and bells, offers more sophisticated versions of similar themes – perhaps a terrine of local crab with lemon mayonnaise, or baked fillet of cod with tapénade, roasted cauliflower and basil oil. The bedrooms are more modest than those of their sister establishment, Maison Talbooth in Dedham (see entry), but then so are the prices. Rooms 1 and 3 feature plenty of space and face the front, giving excellent views of modern maritime operations.

◗ Closed 24 to 26 Dec ⊠ On the quay, at the end of A120. Private car park ⊨ 2 twin/double, 4 double; family rooms available; all with bathroom/WC; TV, room service, direct-dial telephone; hair-dryer on request ⌀ 2 restaurants (1 air-conditioned), bar; conference facilities (max 50 people incl up to 6 residential); early suppers for children ⅙ No wheelchair access ● No dogs ⊟ Access, Amex, Delta, Diners, Switch, Visa £ Single occupancy of twin/double from £48, twin/double from £65, family room £85; deposit required. Cooked B £4; set L £13.50; alc L, D from £20; bar meals available. Special breaks available

---

HASSOP Derbyshire   map 9

Hassop Hall

Hassop, Nr Bakewell DE45 1NS
TEL: (01629) 640488   FAX: (01629) 640577

A grand, pleasantly old-fashioned and magnificently sited country house.

With a history dating back to the Domesday Book, it's appropriate that Hassop Hall should ignore most contemporary country-house-hotel fashions and mores. Thomas Chapman, convivial hands-on owner since 1975, persists with quaint traditions such as bringing breakfasts to bedrooms on trolleys. Lunch and dinner menus, featuring prawn cocktail, mushroom vol-au-vents, a 'cold table of honey-baked ham', bread-and-butter pudding and the like, look as if they're from a previous culinary era. A noticeable paucity of modern touches also characterises the public rooms – from the pillared and chandeliered dining-room to the snug, panelled bar with the ancient settles and heraldic symbols associated with Hassop's long past painted on its ceiling. The shuttered bedrooms, which may be large, very large or larger still, and which are furnished in a mix of antique and cane, look pleasingly dated. The largest of them boasts fluted pillars and a freestanding Victorian bath. Yet the image of the hotel which is likely to remain with you the longest is of the mansion itself – a wave of bay windows, balustraded roofs and soaring chimneys lording it over the rolling meadows, mature trees and little lake of its old estate.

◗ Closed Chr; restaurant closed Sun eve ⊠ 2 miles north of Bakewell on B6001. Private car park ⊨ 2 twin, 5 double, 2 twin/double, 2 four-poster, 2 family rooms, 1 suite; all with bathroom/WC; TV, room service, hair-dryer, direct-dial telephone, radio ⌀ 3 restaurants, bar, lounge, garden; conference facilities (max 60 people incl up to 14 residential); tennis, croquet; early suppers for children; baby-sitting ⅙ Wheelchair access to hotel (2 steps), restaurant and WC (M,F), lift to bedrooms ● No dogs in public rooms and in bedrooms by arrangement only; no smoking in some public rooms ⊟ Access, Amex, Delta, Diners, Switch, Visa £ Single occupancy of twin/double £65 to £109, twin/double £79 to £119, four-poster £79 to £119, family room from £109; deposit required. Continental B £6, cooked B £9; set L £14 to £18, D £25 to £28 (prices valid till Apr 1997). Special breaks available

---

All rooms have tea/coffee-making facilities unless we specify to the contrary.

HATCH BEAUCHAMP **Somerset**   map 2

Farthings

Hatch Beauchamp, Taunton TA3 6SG
TEL: (01823) 480664   FAX: (01823) 481118

Stylish Georgian hotel with Oriental touches within easy reach of Taunton.

Farthings is an elegant Georgian villa complete with wrought-iron verandah that wouldn't look out of place in Cheltenham. Here, however, it can spread out in three acres of grounds with a pretty walled garden to one side and views over the local cricket pitch at the front. Inside, the picture of Singapore above the lounge fireplace is a clue to the source of most of the fabrics and furnishings. Marie and David Barker spent 18 years in the Far East before moving to Somerset and they brought with them souvenirs ranging from notepaper holders to teapots, from rattan chairs to lampstands, with which to decorate their new home. Even one of the cats came with them from Singapore, its tail docked Chinese-style to ward off bad luck. The individually decorated bedrooms are all named after trees. The staff are proudest of Rowan, the honeymoon suite, with a canopied bed built into the rafters, but our inspector was especially taken with Bay, a big room with a bay window and a spiral staircase winding up to a bathroom in what was once a loft. Dinner menus favour British dishes like pigeon and guinea-fowl. Saturday nights are gourmet nights; arrange in advance if you want a vegetarian meal.

◑ Open all year ⊿ Off A358, 5 miles south of Taunton. Private car park 🛏 4 twin, 5 double; family rooms and suites available; all with bathroom/WC exc 1 twin with shower/WC; TV, room service, hair-dryer, direct-dial telephone ⊘ Restaurant, bar, 2 lounges, drying-room, library, garden; conference facilities (max 13 people incl up to 9 residential); croquet; early suppers for children ⅙ No wheelchair access ● No children under 7 in restaurant after 7pm; no dogs in public rooms; smoking in bar and 1 lounge only ▭ Access, Amex, Delta, Diners, Switch, Visa £ Single occupancy of twin/double £49 to £55, twin/double £55 to £65, family room/suite £65 to £80; deposit required. Set L £15, D £20; alc L from £12, D £18. Special breaks available

---

HATHERLEIGH **Devon**   map 1

George Hotel

Market Street, Hatherleigh EX20 3JN
TEL: (01837) 810454   FAX: (01837) 810901

Atmospheric fifteenth-century inn in quiet town centre.

'The sort of hotel that one usually sees only in films,' was how one guest described the George, a picturesque thatched coaching-inn perched midway up Hatherleigh hill. Step inside and the spell isn't broken. The reception is in a small, cosy bar with a huge inglenook fireplace so inviting that the hotel cat often curls up in a bread oven cut into the top corner of the fireplace. On market days this room used to double as a hairdresser's-cum-courthouse and the window in the panelled screen dividing it from the dining-room was to enable farmers to watch mares foaling outside. These days, guests can dine in style in the long, thin restaurant or choose from an extensive bar menu boasting such unexpected delicacies as Sri Lankan curry alongside the more usual grills and fish. A small upstairs lounge provides a quiet retreat for when the pub is busy. Low-ceilinged, narrow corridors link bedrooms which are inevitably small but sometimes manage to squeeze in four-poster beds. Two cheaper rooms lack *en suite* facilities, but in any case the bill was judged very reasonable by a reader who dubbed this 'a real gem of a hotel.'

◑ Open all year; restaurant closed Sun eve   ⤢ In centre of Hatherleigh, 6 miles from Okehampton on A386. Private car park   ⤙ 1 single, 3 twin, 2 double, 3 four-poster; family rooms available; 6 with bathroom/WC, 3 with shower/WC; TV, room service, direct-dial telephone; hair-dryer on request   ✅ Restaurant, bar, lounge, drying-room, games room, garden; conference facilities (max 40 people incl up to 9 residential); heated outdoor swimming-pool; early suppers for children; babysitting, baby-listening   ♿ No wheelchair access   ⬤ No children in restaurant after 8pm; no dogs or smoking in restaurant   ▭ Access, Amex, Visa   £ Single £29, single occupancy of twin/double £29 to £48, twin/double £50 to £70, four-poster £80, family room £82. Set D £14; alc D £18; bar meals available. Special breaks available

---

HATTON Warwickshire

map 5

Northleigh House

Five Ways Road, Hatton, Warwick CV35 7HZ
TEL: (01926) 484203   FAX: (01926) 484006

Plenty of comfort and jollity in a rural Warwickshire B&B.

Turn-of-the-century Northleigh House looks rather ordinary at first glance, but everything about this B&B is exemplary. Top of the bill is its owner, Sylvia Fenwick, who is caring and chatty, with a sense of fun. Her bedrooms are carefully stylised, their furnishings, decorations and bric-à-brac fleshing out their titles, namely Gold, Victoria, Chinese, and so forth. The Blue Room is the best and the priciest, with a king-sized bed, a sitting area and a further fold-out bed. All have hidden fridges, a splendid complement of teas and coffees, and good bathrooms. In the smart dining-room, communal eating fits in with the friendly spirit of the place, but there are separate tables too for those feeling less sociable. Breakfasts are much praised, not least because you are served essentially whenever you want, and each table has its own toaster. Sylvia will arrange a 'visiting chef' (a friend) to prepare dinners for four or more. Otherwise, she'll be more than happy to rustle up a salad or omelette on a supper tray.

◑ Closed mid-Dec to end Jan   ⤢ 5 miles north-west of Warwick on the A4177 is the Five Ways roundabout. Take the Five Ways Road to the south-west (signposted Shrewley) – it is ½ mile to Northleigh House. Private car park   ⤙ 1 single, 1 twin, 5 double; 3 with bathroom/WC, 4 with shower/WC; TV, hair-dryer   ✅ Dining-room, lounge, drying-room, garden   ♿ No wheelchair access   ⬤ No dogs in public rooms; no smoking   ▭ Access, Visa   £ Single £30, single occupancy of twin/double £30 to £38, twin/double £38 to £55. Set D £14.50

HAWKRIDGE **Somerset**   map 1

Tarr Steps Hotel

Hawkridge, Nr Dulverton TA22 9PY
TEL: (01643) 851293   FAX: (01643) 851218

*Small country-house hotel immediately beside prehistoric clapper
bridge with views.*

Having just taken over the Tarr Steps Hotel, Sue and Sean Blackmore have given
it a complete face-lift to restore it to a standard appropriate to a building in such
an exquisite setting. A new-look dining-room now has lovely floral wallpaper
and curtains framing an array of round, wooden tables, each bearing a vase of
flowers; a magnificent marble fireplace and fine pine dresser provide suitable
focal points at each end. Four-course dinner menus don't stray too far from the
traditional. At the back of the house the lounge has squashy, comfortable-
looking chairs that invite you to sink into them after a lengthy walk, and fox
heads and deer antlers adorn the small front bar. Upstairs, the front bedrooms
have the finest views. A couple of single rooms at the back are down a few steps
and currently look out on a bank of rhododendrons, soon to be cleared. Room 12
has a small verandah and Room 14 (a quirk of the numbering system given there
are only 13 bedrooms) a four-poster, but perhaps the nicest is Room 19, with a
sweeping bay window. There's one ground-floor bedroom with a four-poster
bed that is accessible to wheelchairs. Reports please.

◑ Open all year   ⌇ From B3222 on entering Dulverton follow signs to Hawkridge
(not to Tarr Steps). Go through village following signs to hotel. Private car park   ⌂ 3
single, 4 twin, 4 double, 2 four-poster; 2 in annexe; all with bathroom/WC; room service;
hair-dryer on request   ✓ 2 dining-rooms, bar, lounge, drying-room, garden;
conference facilities (max 30 people incl up to 13 residential); fishing, clay-pigeon and
rough shooting; early suppers for children   ♿ Wheelchair access to hotel, restaurant
and WC (M,F), 1 ground-floor bedroom   ● No dogs in some public rooms
▭ Access, Delta, Switch, Visa   £ Single £35 to £46, single occupancy of
twin/double £45 to £51, twin/double/four-poster £80 to £90; deposit required. Set L
from £10, D from £21.50; light meals available (prices valid till Mar 1997). Special breaks
available

HAWKSHEAD **Cumbria**   map 8

Highfield House

Hawkshead Hill, Nr Ambleside LA22 0PN
TEL: (01539) 436344   FAX: (01539) 436793

*Smart and unpretentious small hotel, ideal base for a walking
holiday.*

Pauline and Jim Bennett's Victorian Lakeland stone house stands above
Hawkshead, and from its elevated position you have a good view of the southern
lakes' highest peaks, including Helvellyn should you be scanning the horizon on
a clear day. Framed photographs of dramatic local scenery jolt the senses in what
is otherwise easy-on-the-eye décor in an unstuffy household. One reader

encapsulates the feel succinctly: 'A well-decorated hotel with a warm and friendly atmosphere. Suitable for a long stay. A very welcoming lounge with a good supply of books and maps which the owners were happy to loan for a day trip. The overall atmosphere was very friendly with good facilities for walkers. Breakfast hours were very flexible (up till 10am).' The four-course dinner should be just the ticket after a day on the fells. Cooking is fairly traditional, with an exotic touch here and there, such as curried prawn cocktail with crisp poppadums to start, beef Stroganov to follow and a steamed sticky pudding to finish. Bedrooms are all comfortable and individually decorated in subdued colour schemes; Room 1 is the pick for its double aspect views of the surrounding mountains.

● Closed Chr & Jan 🔁 1 mile north of Hawkshead on B5285 Coniston road. Private car park 🛏️ 2 single, 3 twin, 6 double; family rooms available; all with bathroom/WC exc 2 doubles with shower/WC; TV, hair-dryer, clock radio ✓ Restaurant, bar, lounge, drying-room, garden; early suppers for children; baby-listening, cots, high chairs ♿ No wheelchair access ⊝ No dogs in public rooms; no smoking in restaurant ▭ Access, Delta, Visa £ Single £37, single occupancy of twin/double £47, twin/double £70; deposit required. Set D £17; light lunches available. Special breaks available

---

Ivy House

𝒧

Main Street, Hawkshead, Nr Ambleside LA22 0NS
TEL: (01539) 436204

Very friendly family guesthouse in the centre of this honey-pot village.

Look for an ivy-coloured house, rather than one covered with ivy, and you'll have no trouble finding David and Jane Vaughan's Georgian town house in the centre of the village. It's a beautifully proportioned building inside and out, particularly notable for the curving staircase at the end of the hall. Off to one side, the TV-free sitting-room lends itself to convivial evenings on the loose-covered floral sofas – often drawn up around the log fire should there be a nip in the air. Across the hall, the fine china displayed on the walls and wheel-back chairs lend a refined, tea-room elegance to the dining-room. Cooking is quite traditional too: good and homely four-course set menus with plenty of roasts and casseroles, drawn up after Jane or David have asked your preferences. Bedrooms are divided between the main house and a conversion just across the driveway. Things have been kept quite simple, with a photograph or two of the local scenery hung over the white wood-chip, cheery floral fabrics and a mix of new pine and built-in furniture. There's nothing second-best about the annexe rooms, though those in the main house have the edge for character.

● Closed Nov to Mar 🔁 In centre of Hawkshead village. Private car park 🛏️ 2 twin, 7 double, 2 family rooms; some in annexe; most with bathroom/WC, some with shower/WC; hair-dryer; TV in annexe rooms ✓ Dining-room, lounge, TV room, drying-room; early suppers for children ♿ No wheelchair access ⊝ No dogs in public rooms; smoking in lounge only ▭ None accepted £ Single occupancy of twin/double £27 to £29, twin/double £54 to £58, family room from £64; deposit required. Set D £11. Special breaks available

Queen's Head

Main Street, Hawkshead, Nr Ambleside LA22 0NS
TEL: (01539) 436271   FAX: (01539) 436722

Characterful rooms and good grub at a traditional inn in the middle of the village.

Tony Merrick is certainly in the thick of things in Hawkshead, chair of the village Traders' Association and owner of the old inn at the centre of Hawkshead's warren-like cobbled lanes of stone cottages, shops and galleries thriving on the Beatrix Potter and Wordsworth associations. As it was built in the sixteenth century, creaky floorboards, black beams and small showers *en suite* are de rigueur for the bedrooms above the inn, but banish all fears of horrible modern boxes if you are offered a room in the annexe. Brown Cow Cottage (the annexe was itself once an inn) has three splendid rooms – a four-poster, a pretty double and Room 1 – all thick stone walls, gnarled beams, rough plastered walls and a little private garden. Guests have no private lounge, but fans of traditional pubs (blackened timbers, horse brasses, toby jugs and such) will be in clover with the Queen's Head bar. A cosmopolitan menu (Cumberland sausage to Szechuan chicken, smoked salmon to seafood risotto) is served in both the bar and the wood-panelled dining-room.

● Open all year   ▣ In centre of Hawkshead village. Public car park nearby
⊨ 8 double, 2 four-posters, 2 family rooms, 1 suite; some in annexe; some with bathroom/WC, most with shower/WC; TV, room service, hair-dryer, direct-dial telephone, radio   ⊘ Dining-room, bar; early suppers for children; baby-listening
⅊ Wheelchair access to hotel (2 steps), dining-room and WC (M,F), 1 ground-floor bedroom   ● Dogs in annexe rooms only   ▭ Access, Delta, Diners, Switch, Visa
£ Single occupancy of twin/double £35 to £45, twin/double £48 to £60, four-poster £66 to £70, family room from £68, suite £60 to £65; deposit required. Alc L, D from £10; bar meals available (prices valid till Mar 1997). Special breaks available

---

Hole Farm

Dimples Lane, Haworth BD22 8QS
TEL: (01535) 644755

Comfortable rooms and warm hospitality in characterful old farmhouse on a working farm.

Just outside the tourist honey-pot of Haworth, which attracts thousands of summer visitors tracking down the one-time home of the Brontë sisters, Hole Farm is a 300-year-old stone farmhouse with views over the moors. Beamed ceilings, wood-panelled walls and the narrow staircase give the house a characterful historic feel which, combined with the friendliness and generosity of Janet Milner and her family, makes it a lovely place to stay. The bedrooms are old-fashioned and very comfortable, with flowery wallpaper, pictures of moorland scenery and a good collection of books on Yorkshire, especially Haworth and the Brontës. An annexe room across the yard offers more space, but not such a good view down the valley. Janet is happy to chat and give you information while she serves a cooked breakfast that would set anyone up for a hard day's sightseeing. Home-cured bacon and free-range sausages and eggs are straight from the farm, while the more health-conscious can choose from fruit, cereals, yoghurt and cheese as well as a selection of croissants and toast.

◑ Open all year ⤤ In Haworth follow signs for Brontë Museum past the Sun pub on left; take first left and immediately turn left again, then follow sign to Hole Farm. Private car park ⤐ 1 twin, 1 double; 1 in annexe; both with shower/WC; TV, hair-dryer ⌇ Lounge, drying-room, garden ⟲ No wheelchair access ● No children under 12; no dogs; no smoking ▭ None accepted ⌷ Single occupancy of twin/double £25, twin/double £36; deposit required

---

Weavers

15 West Lane, Haworth BD22 8DU
TEL: (01535) 643822   FAX: (01535) 644832

A characterful restaurant-with-rooms at the centre of Brontë country.

This popular establishment couldn't be closer to the heart of the village, which can be something of a mixed blessing. Although you won't have to walk very far to the Parsonage or the countless souvenir shops which line the handsome, cobbled street, in busy periods it can feel as if you are living in a Brontë theme park rather than in a living community.

The Weavers building is a conversion of a group of traditional weavers' cottages, and inside, a number of touches, including the bobbins, perns and sundry other weaving implements which hang from the ceiling around the bar area, suggest a link with its origins. When it comes to their cooking, Jane and Colin Rushworth are comfortable with the description of 'honest northern', but this may imply a plainness which is far off the mark, as a taste of their pan-fried calf's liver in a gin-and-lime sauce would prove. A good-value, fixed-price menu operates at 'early doors' times (last orders are at 7.15pm). With their unusual antique bed frames, old-fashioned easy chairs, and maybe a carved wooden chandelier, the bedrooms have a period feel.

◑ Closed 3 weeks Chr; restaurant closed Sun and Mon ⤤ In Haworth follow the signs to the Brontë Parsonage Museum. Public car park nearby ⤐ 2 single, 1 twin, 1 double; all with bathroom/WC; TV, limited room service, hair-dryer, trouser press, direct-dial telephone ⌇ Restaurant (air-conditioned), bar, lounge; early suppers for children ⟲ No wheelchair access ● No children under 5; no dogs; no smoking in restaurant ▭ Access, Amex, Delta, Diners, Switch, Visa ⌷ Single £50, single occupancy of twin/double £60, twin/double £70; deposit required. Set D £12.50, Sun L £12.50; alc D £20

Prices are what you can expect to pay in 1997, except where specified to the contrary. Many hoteliers tell us that these prices can be regarded only as approximations.

HAYFIELD Derbyshire map 8

Bridge End

7 Church Street, Hayfield SK12 5JE
TEL: (01663) 747321   FAX: (01663) 742121

A sophisticated bistro with simple bedrooms in stone Victorian cottages on the high street of a rugged Peak District village.

The ensemble of tasters from the pudding menu of this deceptively simple-looking restaurant should be the highlight (and bargain) of your stay. Plank floors, plain pine tables, exposed beams and brick walls belie cuisine which is inventive and well presented, particularly in the realms of starters and desserts. A wood-pigeon salad served with apple, bacon, spinach and hazelnut oil, and a ginger pudding, made with ginger wine and served with brandy sauce, were particularly highly rated on a recent inspection. The same, however, could not be said for the tacky pop-music accompaniment, which seemed entirely out of place. Owner Barbara Tier is a friendly, informal hostess, and her waitresses are positively chummy. The four bedrooms, furnished in pine, would perhaps benefit from being invested with a bit more character, and their electric lavatories make a ghastly whirring noise every time they are flushed. Barbara is very relaxed about when to serve breakfast, and may suggest local walking options.

◑ Open all year; restaurant closed Sun and Mon   ⤢ Opposite the church in the middle of Hayfield village. Private car park   ⤶ 1 twin, 3 double; all with bathroom/WC; TV, direct-dial telephone; hair-dryer and trouser press on request
⌖ Restaurant; early suppers for children; baby-sitting, baby-listening   ㅤ No wheelchair access   ● No dogs in public rooms and in bedrooms by arrangement; no smoking in bedrooms   ▭ Access, Amex, Diners, Visa   £ Single occupancy of twin/double £30, twin/double £45; deposit required. Alc D £20.50

HAYTOR Devon map 1

Bel Alp House

Haytor, Nr Bovey Tracey TQ13 9XX
TEL: (01364) 661217   FAX: (01364) 661292

An elegant Edwardian house with panoramic views in a dip on Dartmoor.

Completely concealed from the road above it, Bel Alp House, an elegant Edwardian building with crisp white walls and unusual, rounded doorways, runs along an escarpment so positioned as to offer sweeping views over the rose bushes to Dartmoor beyond. The views are best appreciated from the upstairs bedrooms, some the size of small apartments, and all immaculately decorated with great swathes of curtains and bedcoverings. Two still have original baths, standing in marble saucers to catch the water from any overflow. The views are just as good from the dining-room below, where most tables are arrayed along the window to take advantage of them. Choiceless four-course dinner menus play it fairly safe, although the Curnocks always keep a few alternatives, including something for vegetarians, in reserve. On a typical evening you might be served tomato soup with herbs, then Brixham scallops en cocotte and honey-roast fillet of Deben duckling, with strawberries and cream to finish. Afterwards you can choose between a comfortable small lounge, with log fire and corner bar, and a larger version, adorned with paintings by James Curnock and James Jackson Curnock, ancestors of Roger Curnock, the present owner.

◑ Closed Dec to Feb ⬈ 2½ miles west of Bovey Tracey the B3387 Haytor Road. Private car park 🛏 5 twin, 4 double; all with bathroom/WC exc 1 double with shower/WC; TV, room service, hair-dryer, direct-dial telephone ✧ Dining-room, bar, 2 lounges, drying-room, games room, garden; early suppers for children ♿ Wheelchair access to hotel (3 steps), restaurant and WC (M,F), 2 ground-floor bedrooms ● No dogs in public rooms; no smoking in dining-room ▭ Access, Switch, Visa £ Single occupancy of twin/double £78 to £87, twin/double £120 to £156; deposit required. Set D £30

Hotels in our Visitors' Book *towards the end of the* Guide *are additional hotels that may be worth a visit. Reports on these hotels are welcome.*

Use the index at the back of the book if you know the name of a hotel but are unsure about its precise location.

Many hotels offer special rates for stays of a few nights or more. It is worth enquiring when you book.

The Guide *is totally independent, accepts no free hospitality, and survives on the number of copies sold each year.*

Don't expect to turn up at a small hotel assuming that a room will be available. It's always best to telephone in advance.

Use the maps at the back of the Guide *to pinpoint hotels in a particular area.*

Red Lion

Hart Street/River Side, Henley-on-Thames RG9 2AR
TEL: (01491) 572161   FAX: (01491) 410039

Traditional family-run inn in Henley town centre, overlooking the river.

The Red Lion has a prime riverside position in Henley overlooking the finishing line of the Henley regatta. In keeping with its surroundings, its sixteenth-century red-brick frontage is smartly kept, with a Union Flag run up the flagpole and neatly trimmed wistaria growing up the walls. Inside, it is old-fashioned and traditional. In the sunny yellow breakfast-room, the crockery is stamped with the hotel's logo, and uniformed waitresses bring tea in a silver pot that you need a cloth to handle. The bar, with its stone floor and plain furnishings, is rather gloomy in comparison. In the Regatta Restaurant, which faces the river, you can choose from a predominantly traditional dinner menu including dishes such as Scotch broth, baked Dover sole, and fillet of pork with baby onions and prunes. Some of the bedrooms have recently been refurbished and these are certainly the ones to go for, especially if they have the added benefit of a river view. With a mix of antique and reproduction furniture, bedrooms generally have plenty of space, and are plainly but solidly furnished with modern, immaculately kept bathrooms.

◑ Open all year   ◪ Beside Henley Bridge. Private car park   ⊨ 5 single, 10 twin, 8 double, 2 four-poster, 1 family room; most with bathroom/WC; TV, room service, hair-dryer, direct-dial telephone; trouser press in some rooms   ⌘ Restaurant, dining-room, bar, lounge, drying-room; conference facilities (max 80 people incl up to 26 residential); early suppers for children; baby-sitting, baby-listening   ჱ No wheelchair access   ◓ No dogs   ▭ Access, Amex, Delta, Switch, Visa   ⒠ Single £49 to £79, single occupancy of twin/double £93, twin/double £99, four-poster £115, family room £125; deposit required. Continental B £6, cooked B £9; set L £13, D £17.50. Special breaks available

---

Hall House

Broadoak End, Off Bramfield Road, Hertford SG14 2JA
TEL: (01992) 582807 (AND FAX)

Well-equipped rooms in a modern family house with generous hosts.

The last building on a private lane just a few miles out of Hertford town centre, the Hall House is the beautifully kept home of the Whitings. Continue along the lane, and you'll come to a 50-acre country park where nature walks are well marked out – guests are welcome to take along the family dog, who's always a willing companion. With just three bedrooms, the Hall House is the sort of place where guests tend to mix together, sharing one table for dinner in the modern dining-room, or chatting over coffee in the large sitting-room, with its restful blue and cream décor. Dinner tends to be at a set time after consultation with guests each morning. Two of the bedrooms are in a garden annexe, and are of a reasonable size, with their large windows making the most of the leafy outlook. Each has a shower-room which, though small, has plenty of toiletries and other goodies. The third room, in the main house, is a little bit bigger, and has the advantage of a large private bathroom with a sunken bath and every facility that you could think of, including exercise bikes. Tired business people are sometimes treated to a complimentary gin and tonic in order to make their wallowing that bit more luxurious.

◑ Closed Chr   ⊿ On A119 Hertford to Stevenage road, pass Hertford North station; turn left into Bramfield Road. After ½ mile turn right into Broadoak End, via a private lane between the Broad Oak Manor nursing home signs. Private car park   ⊑ 3 double; 1 with bathroom/WC, 2 with shower/WC; 2 in annexe; TV, hair-dryer, trouser press   ✧ Dining-room, lounge, conservatory, garden;   ໄ No wheelchair access ● No children under 14; no smoking   ⊟ Access, Visa   £ Single occupancy of double £48, double £65; deposit required. Set D £20

HEXHAM Northumberland   map 10

East Peterelfield Farm

Hexham NE46 2JT
TEL: (01434) 607209   FAX: (01434) 601753

A remote farmhouse offering fine food, peace and quiet, and genuine northern hospitality.

The seventeenth-century farmhouse is off a long, bumpy, unmade road, deep in the heart of the gently undulating countryside around Hexham. 'The view is the house,' says Sue Carr with admirable modesty. The chintzy lounge and open-plan kitchen-cum-breakfast-room certainly have panoramic views, but Sue's eye for pleasing colour schemes and her confident cooking should not be overlooked. Dinners were praised by one reader as being 'inventive and plentiful'. A typical meal might be asparagus soup served with home-made bread, followed by salmon with a herb sauce, rounded off with chocolate-mousse cake.

The bedrooms feature lacy canopies, dark-wood furniture, and Victorian prints, and both the doubles have brass beds; the larger of the doubles also boasts creamy wood-panelled walls and a spacious bathroom. Two suites were being created from the old garage at the time of our inspection. Although the activities of the working stud-farm must be demanding, Sue still finds the time to be a charming hostess. One couple, who arrived on a cold February day, were immediately revived with some complimentary tea and home-made biscuits by the fire, and this pampering continued on subsequent afternoons. 'Charming hostess, success deserved,' they applauded.

Where we know an establishment accepts credit cards, we list them. There may be a surcharge if you pay by credit card. It is always best to check when booking whether the card you want to use is acceptable.

◑ Open all year ⤤ From the main street in Hexham, take road towards Whitley Chapel for 2 miles. After the crossroads, take the right turning for East and West Peterelfield farms. Private car park ⌕ 2 twin, 2 double; family room available; 2 with bathroom/WC; TV, hair-dryer ⌀ Dining-room, lounge, garden; early suppers for children ⌂ No wheelchair access ⬤ No dogs; no smoking in bedrooms ▭ None accepted £ Single occupancy of twin/double £35, twin/double £48 to £54, family room £80. Set D £17

Middlemarch

Hencotes, Hexham NE46 2EB
TEL: (01434) 605003

Immaculately kept B&B near the Northumberland National Park.

Bang in the middle of the pretty market town of Hexham, Eileen Elliot's neat B&B overlooks the gardens of Hexham Abbey. A couple of miles from Hadrian's Wall, it makes a good base for walkers heading for the National Park, especially as Eileen's breakfasts would keep a whole army on the move. She cooks local bacon and free-range eggs on the Aga while chatting to guests around the table in the huge family kitchen, which, with its plates on the dresser, and rows of home-made jam, is the hub of the household. Elsewhere in this beautifully kept Georgian house, you can browse through books and leaflets on local sights in the restful green sitting-room, or take your morning coffee into the walled garden, where there's a sunny terrace, and unusual animal sculptures hiding in the undergrowth. The bedrooms have plenty of space, with high ceilings, rag-rolled walls and pretty Victorian-style furnishings. Those at the front overlooking the road don't really suffer traffic noise because it's quiet at night, but you might opt for a room at the back anyway for a leafy view of the Abbey gardens.

◑ Open all year ⤤ From Hexham Abbey take Beaumont Street to Hencotes; house is next to St Mary's RC church. Private car park ⌕ 2 twin, 1 double, 1 four-poster; family room available; 2 with shower/WC; TV, hair-dryer ⌀ Dining-room, lounge, drying-room, garden ⌂ No wheelchair access ⬤ No children under 10; small dogs only, in bedrooms by arrangement; no smoking ▭ None accepted £ Single occupancy of twin/double £26 to £30, twin/double £42 to £44, four-poster £50, family room £42; deposit required

---

HIGH BUSTON Northumberland   map 10

High Buston Hall

High Buston, Alnmouth NE66 3QH
TEL: (01665) 830341 (AND FAX)

Gracious listed Georgian house in a peaceful village with views of the Northumbrian coastline.

It would be hard to find a better base for touring the fascinating coastline of Northumbria than High Buston Hall. The Grade-II listed Georgian house has been restored with the flair you would expect from an English Heritage architect and with its elevated position offers the bonus of sea views. John Williams hasn't stopped at the main house, though. The ongoing programme of refurbishment continues to sweep through the estate, providing stylish self-catering accommodation in a variety of cottages, farm buildings and towers. The key to the main house lies in its simplicity: the desire to pad out the gracious Georgian dimensions with 'characterful' bric-à-brac is entirely absent. Instead you will find one or two robust antique pieces and comfortable, unobtrusive seating with the rich drapes or deep-coloured walls adding touches of elegance. Dinners are taken communally at the polished oak dining-table and may start with cream of asparagus soup with home-made bread, followed by salmon parcels, local beef or something a little spicier like vegetable chilli. The bedrooms are also spacious with handsome antique wardrobes and chests of drawers and patchwork quilts. The largest room, the four-poster room, has rugs on wooden floorboards and like the neighbouring double, views towards the sea.

◑ Closed Chr & New Year; dining-room closed Sun eve   🔁 Just off A1068 between Warkworth and Alnmouth; first house on right in High Buston. Private car park 🔙 2 double, 1 four-poster; doubles with bathroom/WC, four-poster with shower/WC; TV, hair-dryer   𝒱 Dining-room, lounge, drying-room, garden; conference facilities (max 10 people incl up to 3 residential); early suppers for children   🔥 No wheelchair access   ● No dogs; no smoking   🔲 None accepted   £ Single occupancy of twin/double £33 to £45, twin/double/four-poster £50 to £65; deposit required. Set D £22.50. Special breaks available

---

HIGHER BURWARDSLEY Cheshire   map 7

Pheasant Inn

Higher Burwardsley CH3 9PF
TEL: (01829) 770434   FAX: (01829) 771097

A splendid, no-nonsense, country inn boasting good food and some high-quality accommodation.

The Highland cattle grazing in the fields around this old inn would be chewing a little less contentedly if they could read the menu in the bar or see the hairy pelts and long horns of their ancestors scattered around the walls or on the floors of the rooms. The award-winning cattle (rosettes proliferate like bunting in the Highland Room) are David Greenhaugh's pride and joy, along with the Pheasant itself, which has a magnificent hillside setting overlooking the Cheshire plain – on a clear day you can see Liverpool and the Mersey, Chester and the Welsh hills in the distance.

The Pheasant is a country pub that offers good beer and food, as well as comfortable accommodation, in traditional surroundings. Everything is exactly in line with David's unpretentious approach, including the food: wholesome home cooking using fresh ingredients, such as fish from the Liverpool market, beef from the fields outside, 'and plenty of gin in the gravad lax'. You can eat either among the timbers and stuffed wildlife in the bar, or while admiring the view from the flagstoned conservatory. The bedrooms are divided between the inn itself (characterful, a bit crooked and homely), the main converted barn (modern-rustic style, with fitted hotel-standard furnishings) or – our choice – the new barn conversion, in which Tabley boasts a spa bath and a private stone terrace next to a dovecote, while Tatton has an oak half-tester bed, exposed stonework, and a former prize-winner for a hearth rug.

○ Open all year; restaurant closed 25 Dec ⚡ From A41 follow signs to Tattenhall, then Burwardsley. Bear left at post office; inn at the top of the hill on the left. Private car park ⟻ 2 twin, 6 double, 1 four-poster, 1 family room; most in annexe; all with bathroom/WC; TV, hair-dryer, direct-dial telephone, radio; trouser press in some rooms ✦ Restaurant/conservatory, bar, garden; conference facilities (max 40 people incl up to 10 residential); early suppers for children; toys, baby-listening, high chairs ♿ No wheelchair access ● No dogs in public rooms and in bedrooms by arrangement only; no smoking in some bedrooms ▭ Access, Amex, Diners, Visa £ Single occupancy of twin/double £40 to £45, twin/double £70 to £80, four-poster/family room £80; deposit required. Set Sun L £10.50, Sat D £14.50; bar meals available. Special breaks available

---

HILLTOP Shropshire   map 5

Wenlock Edge Inn ☆

Hilltop, Wenlock Edge, Nr Much Wenlock TF13 6DJ
TEL: (01746) 785678   FAX: (01746) 785285

Friendly pub with good food close to a famous beauty spot.

'So often hotels in fine settings do not measure up to their ambience, and so it is a particular pleasure to report on one that does,' wrote one correspondent singing the praises of the Waring family's roadside hotel. From the outside, there's nothing special about the well-kept, golden-stone building which lies beside the B4371 Much Wenlock to Church Stretton road, but its position on the fringe of one of the highest points of Wenlock Edge, a vast escarpment enclosing areas of equatorial coral reef, helps ensure its popularity. The rest is down to the sterling efforts of the Warings, in providing both a convivial atmosphere and the sort of hearty pub fare that folk will drive from the other end of Shropshire to enjoy. The cosy bar is the heart of the place, and its exposed walls, low beams, trestle tables and wheelback chairs conform to the country-pub standard. Guests can eat here or in the small, neat dining-room, where diners perch on pews from the Manor Road Methodist Chapel in Blackpool. It's a friendly sort of place, so solo diners may find regulars asking to double up at busy times, and it is impossible to take offence. An inspection meal of mushrooms in cream, garlic and sherry, followed by a delicious shortcrust venison pie with scallop potatoes and good, chunky vegetables, then treacle tart with ice-cream proved impressive. One guest warmly applauded the simple fare, and went on to commend the hotel for getting the basics right in the simple but cosy bedrooms too.

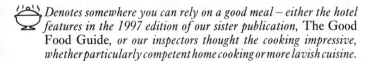

Denotes somewhere you can rely on a good meal – either the hotel features in the 1997 edition of our sister publication, The Good Food Guide, *or our inspectors thought the cooking impressive, whether particularly competent home cooking or more lavish cuisine.*

● Closed Chr   ⤢ 4½ miles south of Much Wenlock on B4371. Private car park
⊨ 1 twin, 3 double; 1 in annexe; all with shower/WC; TV, hair-dryer
✓ Dining-room, bar, lounge   ♿ Wheelchair access to hotel (2 steps) and restaurant,
1 ground-floor bedroom   ● No children under 8; dogs in bar and 1 bedroom only; no
smoking in dining-room   ▭ Access, Amex, Delta, Switch, Visa   £ Single
occupancy of twin/double £45 to £50, twin/double £60 to £70; deposit required. Alc L
£9, D £13.50. Special breaks available

HINTLESHAM **Suffolk**   map 6

Hintlesham Hall

Hintlesham, Ipswich IP8 3NS
TEL: (01473) 652268   FAX: (01473) 652463

*A top-of-the-range country-house hotel that combines
professionalism with welcoming friendliness.*

Boasting 150 acres of land, a championship golf course and a helipad on the front
lawn, Hintlesham Hall certainly has all the trappings of a first-rate
country-house hotel. Yet not everything is always as it seems: the stately,
peach-coloured Georgian façade envelops an Elizabethan core, while the
bedrooms, some of which are named after fabrics or interior designers, may also
get their names from more down-to-earth sources (Canary, for example, is
derived from the colour of Norwich City Football Club's strip – general manager
Tim Sunderland is an avid fan). In fact, the variety of sizes and prices of
bedrooms seems designed to confuse; the cheapest option of a small double
offers exactly what it says, and it's better to trade up to a good-sized double. The
principal doubles and large principal doubles are very plush, decorated with
oodles of fabric and featuring timbered walls or ceilings. If expense is no object,
you can choose between the ultra-modern Cherry Orchard Suite, with its
galleried bedroom, or the more traditional Braganza Suite, which has a stunning
plasterwork ceiling and a bathroom overlooking the garden.

Of the smart public rooms, the most impressive is the Salon – a wonderful,
double-height restaurant, panelled in a delicate mauve colour, with an
imposing, pedimented entrance. It provides a suitably august setting for a menu
that encompasses dishes such as a pressed duck, shallot and lentil terrine lined
with Parma ham, which is served with a toasted herb brioche, or grilled suprême
of cod with roasted vegetables and rosemary juices. 'We do not make a service
charge, because at Hintlesham Hall service is our pleasure,' proclaims the menu.
Other hotels please take note.

The 1998 Guide *will be published in the autumn of 1997. Reports on
hotels are welcome at any time of the year, but are extremely valuable in
the spring. Send them to* The Which? Hotel Guide, FREEPOST, 2
Marylebone Road, London NW1 1YN. *No stamp is needed if reports
are posted in the UK. Our e-mail address is:
"guidereports@which.co.uk".*

◑ Open all year ⊿ In Hintlesham, 4 miles west of Ipswich on A1071 towards Sudbury. Private car park ⊨ 8 twin, 19 double, 2 four-poster, 4 suites; all with bathroom/WC; TV, room service, hair-dryer, mini-bar, direct-dial telephone ⊗ 2 restaurants, 2 bars, 4 lounges, library, games room, garden; conference facilities (max 80 people incl up to 33 residential); fishing, golf, gym, sauna/solarium, heated outdoor swimming-pool, tennis, snooker; early suppers for children; baby-sitting, baby-listening ⅙ No wheelchair access ● No children under 10 in restaurant eves; no dogs in public rooms; no smoking in restaurants ⊟ Access, Amex, Diners, Switch, Visa £ Single occupancy of twin/double £89, twin/double £110, four-poster £200, suite £225. Cooked B £6.50; set L £19.50, D £25; alc L, D from £35. Special breaks available

---

HINTON CHARTERHOUSE Bath & N. E. Somerset   map 2

Green Lane House

Hinton Charterhouse, Nr Bath BA3 6BL
TEL: (01225) 723631 FAX: (01225) 723773

A small, very comfortable B&B with relaxed, amiable hosts, in a peaceful village close to Bath.

Two things make Christopher and Juliet Davies' small, informal B&B a little unusual. First is the 'security guard' Dessie, a huge white Pyrenean mountain dog, who bounds around in the (unfortunately now grassless) walled garden, and second the quirky collection of mementos from 30 years of living overseas, which Dessie may be called on to guard: an ebony elephant and rhinos, Egyptian papyrus prints, tribal statues and an ostrich egg. These give a touch of the exotic to the Davies's otherwise traditional 1725 cottage (actually an amalgam of three knocked into one), which, with its soft floral upholstery and curtains and open fires, has a quaint, endearing country charm. The bedrooms are in pairs at opposite ends of the building; one twin and double, decorated in pinks, greens and yellows, share a bathroom; the other twin and double, with a predominance of pink, have *en suite* facilities. There are two pubs in the village serving dinner, and copies of the menus can be seen in the lounge.

◑ Open all year ⊿ From Bath take B3110 towards Frome; in Hinton Charterhouse turn left after Rose & Crown Inn into Green Lane. On-street parking ⊨ 2 twin, 2 double; 2 with shower/WC; ⊗ Dining-room, lounge; babysitting, baby-listening ⅙ No wheelchair access ● Dogs in bedrooms by arrangement only; no smoking in public rooms ⊟ Access, Amex, Visa £ Single occupancy of twin/double £24 to £37, twin/double £36 to £49; deposit required. Special breaks available

---

Homewood Park

Hinton Charterhouse, Bath BA3 6BB
TEL: (01225) 723731 FAX: (01225) 723820

An imaginatively decorated and informal country house with lovely gardens, just outside Bath.

'The décor was outstanding, the food excellent, the staff pleasant and helpful but not intrusive, the gardens lovely,' wrote two recent guests at Sara and Frank Gueuning's small Georgian country manor. Refreshingly, the Gueunings don't court the business market, which accounts for a small proportion of customers, but this doesn't prevent them from moving with the times. When we visited, an open-air pool was due to open, and four new suites were being built (one will be a showcase for Marks & Spencer's new interior-design department) in an unobtrusive rear extension which doesn't detract from the many-gabled, creeper-clad house's gracious façade, or the immaculate lawns. The drawing-room was being given a new look with a window seat in the vast bay window, golden walls and bright, floral curtains. The elegant main restaurant, featuring gilt-framed oil paintings and a log fire remains the same, but the chef has changed. Gary Jones, formerly of Le Manoir aux Quat' Saisons (Great Milton) has stoked things up a bit, and a typical menu might start with hot foie gras, followed by chicken roasted on pancetta with morels, asparagus, spiced-pea pudding and served with a Madeira-scented *jus*, and rounded off with mille-feuille of rhubarb with a sorbet, berries and vanilla custard. We hope that this kind of dessert will have ironed out the complaints about the 'heavy puddings' that we received from one visitor last year. There are no complaints about the 'lovely' rooms, however, which are priced according to size and outlook, and are imaginatively co-ordinated, often decorated in bold colours and with rich fabrics draped above the beds.

◖ Open all year ◪ 6 miles south-east of Bath on A36 to Warminster. Private car park ⌸ 15 twin/double, 4 suites; all with bathroom/WC; TV, room service, hair-dryer, direct-dial telephone; no tea/coffee-making facilities in rooms ✅ 3 restaurants, bar, 2 lounges, library, garden; conference facilities (max 40 people incl up to 19 residential); heated outdoor swimming-pool, tennis, croquet; early suppers for children; baby-sitting, baby-listening ⚿ Wheelchair access to hotel, restaurant and WC (unisex), 2 ground-floor bedrooms, 1 specially equipped for disabled people
● No dogs ▢ Access, Amex, Delta, Diners, Switch, Visa ⚿ Single occupancy of twin/double £90 to £160, twin/double £98 to £170, suite £210; deposit required. Set L £17.50, D £32.50; alc L £35, D £37

HOLDENBY Northamptonshire   map 5

Lynton House

Holdenby NN6 8DJ
TEL: (01604) 770777 (AND FAX)

A country setting for a creative, predominantly Italian restaurant-with-rooms.

Though not far from Northampton's outskirts, this handsome red-brick Victorian rectory occupies a thoroughly rural spot. It's owned by Carol and Carlo Bertozzi, who have been engrossed in the hotel trade for over three decades. Engaging Carlo hails from a town near the gastronomic capital of Bologna, but it is, in fact, Carol who is responsible for the highly regarded cooking. Her creations range from traditional Italian – such as ham and melon or carpaccio – to inventive Italian dishes with British influences and ingredients: how about home-made pasta stuffed with game and poultry, smoked eel in a pesto sauce, or apple pie topped with ricotta? Carlo's paintings of Italian landscapes decorate the elegantly proportioned dining-room and the more humble bar, but otherwise the environment is that of a modest Victorian country house. A pair of conservatories, one a dining-room extension used for breakfasts, make the most of the trim garden and the house's elevated position.

A rather grand, red-carpeted staircase leading to the bedrooms promises more than they can deliver. While entirely satisfactory, they're rather dated, and all have showers only in their ample bathrooms. For their views, Rooms 3 and 4 are the pick of the bunch.

◖ Closed Sun, public holidays and Chr ⤬ To the east of Holdenby on the East Haddon to Church Brampton road. Private car park ⤙ 2 single, 1 twin, 2 double, 1 suite; all with shower/WC; TV, room service, hair-dryer, trouser press, direct-dial telephone ⌀ 2 dining-rooms, bar, lounge, 2 conservatories, garden; conference facilities (max 20 people non-residential); early suppers for children ⅊ No wheelchair access ◗ No children under 6; no dogs; no smoking in some bedrooms and 1 dining-room; no pipes or cigars ▭ Access, Amex, Visa £ Single £49, twin/double £55, suite £70; deposit required. Cooked B £7.50; set L £13.50 to £18.50, D £22.50

HOLMESFIELD Derbyshire

map 9

Horsleygate Hall ☆

Horsleygate Lane, Holmesfield, Nr Chesterfield S18 5WD
TEL: 0114-289 0333

B&B in a handsome, tastefully furnished family home.

Margaret Ford's half-Georgian, half-Victorian house is secreted down a back lane on the Peak District's rural eastern fringes. Country life impinges all around the property: chickens and geese waddle about the pleasantly ramshackle outhouses and horses exercise in an adjacent paddock; rockeries, ponds, an enormous vegetable plot and daffodil-spattered lawns characterise a two-acre garden that is Margaret's pride and joy. Her home is good-looking and devoid of pretension. Rugs on flagstones, pine doors, a number of striking fireplaces and unflashy family antiques set the style. Downstairs, there's a breakfast-room (kippers and Derbyshire oatcakes may be on offer) and a very inviting sitting-room, but you may well end up setting the world to right with Margaret in front of her kitchen Aga. Upstairs, the three bedrooms are very comfortable and appealing, flushed with blue and pink colour schemes, and antique and pine fittings intermingle with loose-covered armchairs and plenty of homely touches.

◖ Closed Chr ⤬ Off B6051 from Chesterfield. Private car park ⤙ 1 twin, 1 double, 1 family room; 1 with bathroom/WC ⌀ Lounge, garden ⅊ No wheelchair access ◗ No children under 5; no dogs; no smoking ▭ None accepted £ Single occupancy of twin/double £21 to £23, twin/double £37 to £42, family room from £37; deposit required. (Prices valid till Apr 1997)

HOPESAY Shropshire map 5

Old Rectory

Hopesay, Craven Arms SY7 8HD
TEL: (01588) 660245

Welcoming hosts offer restful accommodation in a former rectory with beautiful garden.

Georgian clergymen weren't exactly miserly when it came to putting a roof over their heads, and we know from Trollope that the Victorians were no more abstemious. Roma and Michael Villar's house, Georgian with later additions, is no exception to the rule, boasting spacious rooms with lofty ceilings. If you're lucky enough to arrive on a fine day, you may decide to dally in the lovely garden, distracted only by the chorus of birdsong punctuated on the quarter-hour by the bells of the adjacent twelfth-century church of St Mary. Autumnal shades predominate in the drawing-room, an elegant room distinguished by landscapes, antiques and a baby-grand piano. It's an agreeable place to gather for a pre-dinner drink, but the Villars have plans to revamp the room, eliminating what they see as intrusive non-period features. Antiques sustain the period feel in the formal dining-room, where guests gather round an oak refectory table, and enjoy fine views over the National Trust's Hopesay Hill. The food is accomplished dinner-party fare: perhaps smoked trout mousse followed by lamb noisette in tarragon sauce and rhubarb crumble. Bedrooms are spacious, and team tastefully apposite décor with antique furniture. They're generously equipped.

◑ Closed Chr ⤱ Leave A49 at Craven Arms and take B4368 towards Clun; at Aston-on-Clun turn right over humpbacked bridge; Hopesay is 1½ miles from bridge and house is on left-hand side. Private car park ⨏ 1 twin, 1 double, 1 suite; all with bathroom/WC; TV, radio; hair-dryer on request ⊘ Dining-room, lounge, drying-room, garden ໒ No wheelchair access ● No children under 12; no dogs; no smoking ⊟ None accepted £ Single occupancy of twin/double £32, twin/double/suite £64; deposit required. Set D £18

HOPTON CASTLE Shropshire map 5

Park Cottage

Hopton Castle, Craven Arms SY7 0QF
TEL: (01547) 530351

Rustic charm at modest prices at this half-timbered house in a sleepy backwater.

Southern Shropshire is a surprisingly undiscovered area of rolling hills and sheep-studded fields dotted with the remnants of border conflict between the English and the Welsh, not least the Norman keep which gave its name to this isolated village. These days any sort of conflict seems unthinkable at this small but spruce house in an emphatically tranquil spot. The conservatory which overlooks the small, colourful sun-trap garden adds elegance to John and

Josephine Gardner's home, with white wrought-iron garden furniture, trellised panels and stacks of seed trays adding an *al fresco* feel. The spacious lounge is conservatively decorated in autumnal colours with predominantly cottagey furniture and floral drapes and border; a plate shelf displaying china confirms the rustic feel. The centuries roll back in the dining-room, where leaded windows, Jacobean panelling and fireplace breathe antiquity. Food is hearty and wholesome: perhaps mushrooms with cream and port, followed by braised local pheasant with cider and calvados, and home-made pudding. The bedrooms are simple and uncluttered, with the odd antique, plus floral bedding and drapes.

○ Open all year ☑ At Knighton, turn on to B4367 towards Hopton Heath, from where Hopton Castle is signposted. When in village, take a left turning to Bedstone Road. Private car park ⊨ 1 twin, 1 double; twin with bathroom/WC, double with shower/WC; TV, limited room service; no tea/coffee-making facilities in rooms ⌀ 2 dining-rooms, lounge, conservatory, garden ♿ No wheelchair access ● No children under 7; no dogs; no smoking ▭ None accepted £ Single occupancy of twin/double £30, twin/double £47; deposit required. Set D £16.50

HORLEY Surrey — map 3

Langshott Manor

COUNTY HOTEL OF THE YEAR

Langshott, Horley RH6 9LN
TEL: (01293) 786680   FAX: (01293) 783905

A wonderful, family-run Elizabethan manor house with characterful bedrooms, handy for Gatwick Airport.

This timber-framed, red-brick, sixteenth-century hotel is reached along a short lane leading out of Horley, and the landscaped gardens and surrounding trees give it a peaceful, rural atmosphere. The Nobles run it as a family concern, and they have focused on retaining the original character of the house, while at the same time providing luxury accommodation. Crossing the threshold is like walking back in time: the stained-glass windows, creaky floors and wood-panelled walls greet you like an old friend. The place has a sophisticated (but not stifling) English charm; rugs are strewn over the floor, and there are flowers everywhere. The morning-room is low beamed, with plenty of cosy sofas from which to choose, while St Peter's Room, with its huge, oval dining-table, creates a banqueting spectacle when lit up with candles for the evening meal. The up-market menu offers traditional English dishes such as sorrel soup, followed, perhaps, by spring lamb with braised fennel (but don't toss the bones over your shoulder).

The bedrooms have bags of character, and come in all shapes and sizes, according to their location in the hotel. The Nursery in the eaves, for example, has stained-glass windows and a cavernous bathroom with a freestanding bath, while the Cook's Room downstairs has a ceiling so low in parts that you have to stoop. All are spotlessly clean and decorated in bold and tasteful country styles.

◑ Closed Chr & New Year ⤢ From A23 Horley Chequers roundabout, take Ladbroke Road to Langshott; hotel about 1 mile up on the right. Private car park ⤙ 5 twin/double, 3 double; family room available; most with bathroom/WC, some with shower/WC; TV, room service, hair-dryer, direct-dial telephone ⌀ 2 dining-rooms, bar, lounge, library, garden; conference facilities (max 12 people incl up to 8 residential); croquet; early suppers for children ⅘ Wheelchair access to hotel (1 step), restaurant and WC (unisex), 1 bedroom specially equipped for disabled people ● No children under 10; no dogs; no smoking in some public rooms and in bedrooms ⊟ Access, Amex, Diners, Visa ⌞£⌟ Single occupancy of twin/double £95, twin/double from £118, family room from £133; deposit required. Set L £22.50, D £26.50 (1996 prices). Special breaks available

---

HORNDON ON THE HILL Essex   map 3

Bell Inn & Hill House

High Road, Horndon on the Hill SS17 8LD
TEL: (01375) 673154 FAX: (01375) 361611

Historic inn offering good food and wine as well as good-value accommodation.

A blue plaque on the outside of the Bell Inn records that one Thomas Higbed was burned at the stake for his Protestant faith in 1555 in the courtyard. You need have no similar fears today: the inn, under the management of Christine and John Vereker, accords visitors of any faith a warm welcome. The atmosphere plays up to the inn's history: the bar has wooden settles on stone flags, old photos on the walls, and hot-cross buns nailed to the beams (a 90-year-old tradition). The suites are also named after historical characters – Anne Boleyn has a half-tester and large Chinese rug, while Lady Hamilton's bathroom, so to speak, is a splendid affair, containing a huge claw-foot bath. Hill House, a couple of doors along, under the same ownership, is a couple of hundred years younger than the Bell, with its own elegant dining-room, though the food comes from the same kitchen. Rooms here are cheaper and less imaginative, except for the Captain's Cabin in the converted stable block, where the bed is perched aloft a gallery reached by a wooden ladder. This room is not recommended if you've been indulging in some of the very reasonably priced wines to accompany the eclectic dishes chalked up on the blackboard, which may offer combinations such as fillet of lamb with haggis, preserved garlic and thyme, or cod wrapped in Parma ham with mushy peas and red-wine gravy.

◑ Open all year; restaurant closed Mon to Thur, Sun ⤢ From M25 Junction 30 follow A13 to Grays and then B1007. Follow the signs to Horndon on the Hill. Private car park ⤙ 3 twin, 7 double, 4 suites; family room available; some in annexe; all with bathroom/WC exc 1 double with shower/WC; TV, room service, hair-dryer, trouser press, direct-dial telephone ⌀ Restaurant, bar; conference facilities (max 24 people incl up to 14 residential); ⅘ No wheelchair access ● No dogs in public rooms; no dogs or smoking in some bedrooms ⊟ Access, Amex, Delta, Switch, Visa ⌞£⌟ Single occupancy of twin/double £45 to £60, twin/double £45 to £60, family room £55, suite £60. Continental B £3.50, cooked B £6; alc D £20

HORTON **Dorset**   map 2

Northill House

Horton, Wimborne BH21 7HL
TEL: (01258) 840407

Homely cooking and considerate hosts at a peaceful Victorian farmhouse.

Joy and Courtney Garnsworthy's Victorian farmhouse stands amid pastures at the end of a long, narrow drive, and the only noise, apart from birds, is likely to come from the jumble of (still working) farm buildings behind. The grand red-brick house, with crown and shield embossed above the door and a lovely blue and terracotta mosaic in the hallway, was once part of Lord Shaftesbury's estate, and regularly receives guests coming to hunt at nearby Cranborne Chase. Most of the clientele, however, are in search of gentler country pursuits. The calm, accommodating Garnsworthys cater for all, although the menus, featuring traditional fare such as soups, terrines, roasts, casseroles and, usually, a choice of one hot and three cold puddings, are perhaps aimed at the quieter, older crowd. Bookcases, soft chairs and a log fire make the lounge a homely, relaxing place, while the dining-room extends into a lovely plant-filled conservatory jutting out into the part-wild, part-tended gardens. Bedrooms in the main house, with pine and rattan furnishings and soft pastel shades, have the most character; peachy Room 2, a large twin, has a lovely view of the surrounding hills. 'Cottage' rooms, with outside access and more floral prints, tend to be smaller, although the largest has been fitted out for disabled visitors.

◗ Closed 20 Dec to 15 Feb ◿ 6 miles north of Wimborne on B3078; half-way between Horton Inn and village. Private car park ⌂ 4 twin, 4 double, 1 family room; some in annexe; 7 with bathroom/WC, 2 with shower/WC; TV, direct-dial telephone, clock radio ⌗ Dining-room/conservatory, bar, lounge, drying-room, garden ⌖ Wheelchair access to hotel (1 ramp), restaurant and WC (unisex), 4 ground-floor bedrooms, 1 specially equipped for disabled people ● No children under 8; no dogs; no smoking in dining-room ▭ Access, Amex, Visa £ Single occupancy of twin/double £39, twin/double £68, family room from £102; deposit required. Set D £14; bar lunches available. Special breaks available

---

HOVINGHAM **North Yorkshire**   map 9

Worsley Arms

Hovingham, Nr York YO6 4LA
TEL: (01653) 628234 FAX: (01653) 628130

Old coaching-inn on the village green with a country-house hotel ambience.

The process of change and upgrading continues at the Worsley Arms even if that means some breaks from tradition. The hotel was built by Sir William Worsley in 1841 and has been run by the family until this year: since our last inspection, Euan Rodger, who was the manager, has become the proprietor and is now responsible for operations. One of his first moves was to bring in Andrew Jones from Bilborough Manor as head chef. Dinner may now start with chicken liver parfait served with orange salad, toasted brioche and truffle, to be followed by a main course such as chargrilled tuna with chargrilled vegetables and a citrus olive oil dressing.

Although built as a coaching-inn, the Worsley Arms has long been closer to country-house hotel than village pub and any last vestiges of the inn atmosphere have disappeared with the conversion of the Cricketers pub into a bar and bistro. The décor may look similar – cricket bats and photos of matches on the walls – but the emphasis is now firmly on the food and you might 'open the innings' with tagliatelle or rabbit, hare and chicken terrine. Steady progress is being made in the bedrooms too, brightening things up with light, plain colours. More reports please.

◑ Open all year 🔁 On B1257 in central Hovingham, opposite the village green. Private car park 🚗 2 single, 1 twin, 8 double, 8 twin/double; some in annexe; all with bathroom/WC; TV, room service, direct-dial telephone ✓ 2 restaurants, bar, 2 lounges, garden; conference facilities (max 60 people incl up to 19 residential); tennis, shooting, squash; early suppers for children; babysitting, baby-listening, cots ♿ No wheelchair access ⊖ No dogs in public rooms 🗔 Access, Amex, Delta, Switch, Visa £ Single £55, single occupancy of twin/double £75, twin/double £75; deposit required. Set L £15, D £23.50; bistro meals available. Special breaks available

---

HUDDERSFIELD **West Yorkshire**   map 9

Lodge Hotel

48 Birkby Lodge Road, Birkby, Huddersfield HD2 2BG
TEL: (01484) 431001 FAX: (01484) 421590

Small hotel conveniently placed for the M62 with Art Nouveau styling and imaginative cooking.

The rather sober, blackened and creeper-covered exterior doesn't really prepare you for the highly individual, even idiosyncratic, features inside. The front door, with its striking stained-glass and pewter panels, is the first real clue. Public rooms are lifted above the ordinary by unusual panelling, ornate plasterwork and distinctive ceilings, as in the lounge, where narrow beams with cream and gold panels catch the eye. Dinners too give the hotel an advantage over other small, suburban hotels. Proprietors Garry and Kevin Birley are assisted in the kitchen by Richard Hanson, and together they have built up a reputation for delivering imaginative cooking, throwing a variety of culinary traditions into the melting pot. So you may have a starter which combines Whitby crab and clams with linguine, and a main course like tournedos with polenta and salsa verde on a rich Madeira sauce. The pick of the bedrooms is Room 8, the honeymoon choice – a spacious four-poster room with antique furniture and a grand bay window overlooking the garden.

Many hotels put up their tariffs in the spring. You are advised to confirm prices when you book.

❍ Closed 25 to 27 Dec; restaurant closed Sun eve ⏀ Take A629 to Huddersfield; turn left down Birkby Road at first set of traffic lights; first right into Birkby Lodge Road; hotel is 100 yards on left. Private car park 🛏 3 single, 4 twin, 3 double, 1 four-poster; family room available; all with bathroom/WC exc 2 singles with shower/WC; TV, room service, hair-dryer, direct-dial telephone ✓ Restaurant, bar, lounge, drying-room, library, garden; conference facilities (max 60 people incl up to 11 residential); early suppers for children; baby-listening ♿ No wheelchair access ● No children under 10 in restaurant eves; dogs in some bedrooms only; no smoking in bedrooms or restaurant ▭ Access, Amex, Visa ⊡ Single £55, single occupancy of twin/double £55, twin/double £65, four-poster £75, family room £95; deposit required. Set L £14, D £23 (prices valid till Jan 1997). Special breaks available

---

HUNGERFORD Berkshire   map 2

Marshgate Cottage Hotel

Marsh Lane, Hungerford RG17 0QX
TEL: (01488) 682307   FAX: (01488) 685475

A small, inexpensive hotel with simple rooms, in a quiet rural setting.

Mind the ducks on your approach to Marshgate Cottage as you drive along the rough track from the outskirts of Hungerford: they'll waddle about – ducklings in tow – quite oblivious to the danger of cars. The hotel is a one-storey red-brick building, named after the white thatched cottage to which it is joined, as well as the marshy meadows which it overlooks. The owner, Mike Walker, is happy to direct you on walks, one of the nicest of which is to cross the nearest field and follow the canal towpath into the centre of the attractive old market town of Hungerford. The six ground-floor bedrooms are arranged around a small brick courtyard, and are modern and simple, with light, flowery fabrics and pine furniture. The four-poster room is the biggest, with its own little sitting-room. All have small shower-rooms with plenty of goodies – for a little more luxury you have to trot along the corridor to the smart public bathroom with its huge corner bath. All the bedrooms, except for Room 7, which faces the car-parking area, have lovely views over the fields. Evening meals are by arrangement only, though there's a good choice of eating places in the town.

❍ Closed Chr to New Year; dining-room closed Sun eve ⏀ From Hungerford High Street turn at railway bridge into Church Street. After ½ mile, cross over stream and right immediately into Marsh Lane. Private car park 🛏 2 twin, 1 double, 1 four-poster, 2 family rooms; all with shower/WC; TV, room service, direct-dial telephone; hair-dryer and trouser press on request ✓ Dining-room, bar, lounge, garden; conference facilities (max 20 people incl up to 6 residential); early suppers for children ♿ No wheelchair access ● No smoking in some bedrooms ▭ Access, Amex, Visa ⊡ Single occupancy of twin/double £36, twin/double £49, four-poster £55, family room £56 to £66; deposit required. Set D £11.50; alc D £15. Special breaks available

---

 This denotes that you can get a twin or double room for £60 or less per night inclusive of breakfast.

Hunstrete House

Hunstrete, Chelwood BS18 4NS
TEL: (01761) 490490   FAX: (01761) 490732

A peaceful and intimate country house in a lovely setting in 90 acres of grounds.

The driveway rises gently towards the honey-coloured stone façade of Hunstrete House, which is set amidst 90 acres of grounds, including a deer park and a traditional kitchen garden, giving way to pleasantly undulating pasture land. The setting aside, perhaps the most appealing feature of this relaxing, unstuffy country house is its courtyard. The hotel is clustered around a pretty patio, furnished with wooden tables and chairs, and boasting abundant flowers and foliage in ornamented terracotta pots. The bedrooms, whether in the main house or the courtyard extension, are named after birds, and graded according to size and outlook. With two bathrooms and an elaborate, antique four-poster, the top of the range is Dove. The best of the standard rooms is Owl – a smart, bright-blue and yellow room, with a window seat and a view over the car park. The various interlocking drawing-rooms are on a more intimate scale than in similar establishments, although there are still plenty of fine antiques, crystal chandeliers, and flowers from the gardens in summer. The restaurant, with patio doors leading to the courtyard, is an appropriately grand setting for dishes such as sauté calf's liver with rosemary and onion purée, served with calvados sauce, or red mullet with a confit of fennel and white wine and mushroom velouté. One regular, however, was dismayed by the poor service in the restaurant on a recent visit (although the food was good) – more reports, please.

◑ Open all year ⊿ Take A39 through Marksbury on to A368; turn off to Hunstrete village; hotel is 30 yards on left. Private car park ⮞ 1 single, 15 twin/double, 4 double, 1 four-poster, 2 suites; all with bathroom/WC; TV, 24-hour room service, hair-dryer, trouser press, direct-dial telephone; no tea/coffee-making facilities in rooms all with bathroom/WC ✧ Restaurant, bar, lounge, library, garden, 3 conference rooms (1 air-conditioned), conference facilities (max 50 people incl up to 23 residential); heated outdoor swimming-pool, tennis, croquet, archery, clay-pigeon shooting; early suppers for children; baby-listening ﴾ No wheelchair access ● No dogs in public rooms and in bedrooms by arrangement; no smoking in restaurant ⊡ Access, Amex, Delta, Diners, Switch, Visa £ Single/single occupancy of twin/double £125, twin/double £160 to £180, four-poster £160, suite £250; deposit required. Set L £17.50, Sun L £19.50, D £29.50. Special breaks available

---

If you make a booking using a credit card and find after cancelling that the full amount has been charged to your card, raise the matter with your credit card company. It will ask the hotelier to confirm whether the room was re-let, and to justify the charge made.

map 1

Huntsham Court

Huntsham, Nr Tiverton EX16 7NA
TEL: (01398) 361365   FAX: (01398) 361456

A Victorian castle in the Devon countryside offering the perfect setting for house parties.

'Nothing's changed,' hostess Andrea Bolwig laughed, and for once this came as music to the ears, because Huntsham Court's greatest charm lies in its predictability. Externally reminiscent of a medieval castle, Huntsham somehow sends the imagination into overdrive: as you cross the threshold, you half expect to hear doors banging, see lightning flashing and witness Frankenstein stepping into the hall. In reality, of course, you're more likely to bump into one of the other regulars down for a weekend of laid-back hedonism.

Everything at Huntsham Court is on a monumental scale. In Beethoven, the grandest of all the rooms, you'll have not one, but two, freestanding baths to soak in; in Brahms you can hear an organ recital while you bathe; in Handel you can polish up your arpeggios on the piano by the bed. 'Even my room, in what used to be the servants' quarters, had its own sitting-room,' said one contented guest, who added, 'but there's always somewhere to sneak away to if you want a bit of privacy.'

Andrea and Mogens Bolwig specialise in running weekend house parties, and their dining-table comfortably seats 28 for the five-course dinners which evolve out of discussions of individual likes and dislikes. Should you not make it to bed until the wee hours (and one guest commented that the hall and 10,000 records were highly conducive to dancing ...'I didn't get to bed until four'), breakfast in bed is available right through till noon.

◑ Open all year   ⛿ Leave M5 at Junction 27 to Sampford Peverell, turn right after bridge and follow signs to Uplowman and then to Huntsham. Private car park   🛏 2 twin, 8 double, 1 four-poster, 3 family rooms; all with bathroom/WC; hair-dryer, radio; no tea/coffee-making facilities in rooms   ✓ Dining-room, bar, lounge, TV room, drying-room, library, games room, garden; conference facilities (max 100 people incl up to 14 residential); gym, sauna, tennis, croquet, snooker, table tennis; early suppers for children; baby-sitting   ⅙ No wheelchair access   ● Dogs by arrangement
⊟ Access, Delta, Visa   £ Single occupancy of twin/double £85, twin/double £125, four-poster £125, family room £135; deposit required. Set D £35. Special breaks available

map 3

Ye Olde Bell

High Street, Hurley, Nr Maidenhead SL6 5LX
TEL: (01628) 825881   FAX: (01628) 825939

A popular ancient inn on a quiet lane, with a mix of traditional and modern rooms.

Not on a high street at all, but on a quiet lane leading down to the river, Ye Olde Bell has changed hands frequently over the past few years, and has grown away from the monastery guesthouse that it once was, to become a bustling, split-site hotel run by the Jarvis chain. If you're looking for historic charm, you'll find it in the bar, where leather horse tack hangs from the beams, and you can choose between rustic chairs and cushioned window seats. Bar snacks, including salmon fillet or steak and mushrooms, are served here or in the lounge, with its textured white walls, copper bed-warmer, and horse brasses around the fireplace. The restaurant is a grander, oak-panelled room, with leaded windows overlooking the terrace and the gardens. There's a busy, rather than formal, atmosphere here, as locals dine alongside guests, choosing from a menu which includes Parma ham served with fresh figs, beef in a peppercorn sauce, and puddings from the trolley. The bedrooms are split between four different sites. Those in the main building and in the malthouse have more character than the small, plain rooms in the lodge and the light, modern rooms in the converted barn, both of which adjoin the car park across the road.

◗ Open all year ⚡ Take A4130 towards Hurley and Henley, turn right into Hurley village. Hotel is on the right. Private car park ⨱ 33 twin/double, 2 four-poster, 1 suite; most in annexe; some with bathroom/WC, some with shower/WC; TV, room service, hair-dryer, mini-bar, trouser press, direct-dial telephone ✓ Restaurant, bar, lounge, garden; conference facilities (max 140 people incl up to 20 residential); croquet; baby-listening ⅙ No wheelchair access ● No dogs in public rooms; no smoking in some bedrooms ▭ Access, Amex, Diners, Switch, Visa £ Single occupancy of twin/double £105, twin/double £115, four-poster £135, suite £150; deposit required. Continental B £7.50, cooked B £9.50; set L £16, D £19.50; alc L, D from £21.50; bar meals available (prices valid till Dec 1996). Special breaks available

---

HURSTBOURNE TARRANT Hampshire   map 2

Esseborne Manor

Hurstbourne Tarrant, Andover SP11 0ER
TEL: (01264) 736444   FAX: (01264) 736725

A small, friendly country house with a family atmosphere and good food.

This four-square, cream-painted late-Victorian country hotel greets you with a sense of unassuming gentility. It stands on the top of a rise in the rolling Hampshire countryside, and feels remarkably isolated despite its proximity to the road to Andover. The hotel's new owner, Ian Hamilton, is enthusiastic and unpretentious, rather like the house itself. The blue and yellow theme of the lounge, with its deep sofas and resident stuffed clown, follows through into the restaurant, where it is highlighted with pink linen and heavy drapes. Here you might sample dishes such as pan-fried fillet of skate on a bed of potatoes and red peppers with capers and Parma ham, followed by hot home-made pancakes stuffed with banana and rum and topped with butterscotch ice-cream. The pick of the bedrooms is Madingley, done out in golden tones with a four-poster bed dripping with raw silk. The bedrooms in the stable block do not have the character of those in the main house, but are just as spacious and well equipped.

◑ Open all year ⊿ On A343 between Newbury and Andover; 2 miles north of Hurstbourne Tarrant. Private car park ⟶ 4 twin, 5 double, 1 four-poster; family rooms available; some in annexe; all with bathroom/WC; TV, room service, hair-dryer, trouser press, direct-dial telephone ⊘ Dining-room, bar, lounge, garden; conference facilities (max 12 people incl up to 10 residential); tennis, croquet ⅋ No wheelchair access ● No children under 7; no dogs ⊟ Access, Amex, Delta, Diners, Switch, Visa ⟨£⟩ Single occupancy of twin/double £84, twin/double £95 to £112, four-poster £135, family room £135; deposit required. Set L £12/15, D £14/18; alc L, D £20. Special breaks available

---

HUXLEY Cheshire　　　　　　　　　　　　　　　　　　　　　　　map 7

Higher Huxley Hall

Red Lane, Huxley, Chester CH3 9BZ
TEL: (01829) 781484 FAX: (01829) 781142

An elegant family house run as a Wolsey Lodge, set in quiet, dairy-farming countryside.

The whitewashed and Georgian-style windows take centuries off the appearance of the Marks' family home. Its long history becomes much more apparent at the foot of the magnificent carved wooden Elizabethan staircase in the entrance lounge, and the origins of parts of the manor house have been traced back to before the thirteenth century. The house is situated just outside the village of Huxley, and is surrounded by open Cheshire dairy farmland, some of which belongs to Higher Huxley Hall. Jeremy concentrates on the farm, while Pauline runs the house as a Wolsey Lodge.

Dinners are taken in a light and elegant room, around a long, central table, and beneath a pastel portrait of Jeremy's parents. Pauline's set four-course menus (plus cheese and biscuits) run along quite traditional lines, and might include such dishes as venison served in red wine, or pork fillet in cream-and-sherry sauce, for the main course, with rhubarb pie or lemon soufflé possibly featuring as dessert.

There's plenty of opportunity to wonder at the craftsmanship of the staircase, since the three bedrooms are located at the top of the house. Antique bedsteads have been installed beneath the gnarled timbers of the gables, and each room features a drawer packed full with everything that you might need, from cotton wool to Alka Seltzer.

◑ Open all year ⊿ 7 miles south-east of Chester. Private car park ⟶ 1 twin, 1 double, 1 family room; double with bathroom/WC, 2 with shower/WC; TV, hair-dryer, direct-dial telephone; iron on request ⊘ Dining-room, lounge, conservatory, garden; fishing, heated indoor swimming-pool, croquet; toys, baby-listening, outdoor games ⅋ No wheelchair access ● No children in dining-room eves; no dogs; no smoking ⊟ Access, Visa ⟨£⟩ Single occupancy of twin/double £35 to £40, twin/double £65 to £70, family room £70 to £80; deposit required. Set D £20. Special breaks available

---

Prices are quoted per room *rather than* per person.

Manor House Farm

Ingleby Greenhow, Nr Great Ayton TS9 6RB
TEL: (01642) 722384

Comfortable rooms and sociable hosts feature in an eighteenth-century farmhouse on the edge of the Yorkshire moors.

You are almost guaranteed not to be the only guests at Margaret and Martin Bloom's farm. Apart from their own unusual rare-breed collection of sheep, goats, rheas, peacocks, and even a wallaby, the Blooms are often visited by deer and waterfowl, which make themselves at home in the 300-year-old pond. You could use the farmhouse as a launch pad for walks over the moors, or you could simply potter about in the local woods (you're welcome to bring your own horse). Inside, the white-painted, spacious-feeling bedrooms are comfortable and immaculately kept, and feature sachets of potpourri on your pillow and lacy curtains. Although only one has an *en suite* bathroom, the other two each have a private bathroom – boasting a large sunken or corner bath – along the corridor. After dinner, Martin and Margaret join their guests in the sitting-room, where a wood-burning stove and wall full of books create a cosy atmosphere. In the morning, Martin is back on duty, giving guided tours of the farm and the animals.

◑ Closed Chr ⤢ In Great Broughton turn at village hall to Ingleby Greenhow. Entrance signposted opposite the church. Private car park ⛥ 2 twin, 1 double; all with bathroom/WC; room service, radio ✧ Dining-room, lounge, library, garden; fishing ♿ No wheelchair access ● No children under 12; no dogs; no smoking ▭ Access, Delta, Switch, Visa £ Single occupancy of twin/double from £40, twin/double £73 to £82 (rates incl dinner); deposit required

Belstead Brook Hotel

Belstead Road, Ipswich IP2 9HB
TEL: (01473) 684241   FAX: (01473) 681249

Business hotel with expanding leisure facilities, run with zestful enthusiasm.

Although the hotel boasts nine acres of grounds, their location, amid a strange mix of modern suburbs and country lanes, hardly plays to their strengths. The attractive red-brick façade, largely dating from the sixteenth century, hides a wing of modern bedrooms and, when we inspected, a considerable amount of building work as the construction of a new reception area, banqueting room and leisure club was in progress. All this activity, however, was causing surprisingly little disruption to the rest of the hotel: ruched nets in the lounge screened out the construction work, and the carved Danish kings on the wooden fireplace in the cosy panelled bar retained their air of smug tranquillity. Olaf and Ulf make another appearance in the stained-glass of the former library, now one of three interlocking dining-rooms, with lighter white-painted panelling. An excellent range of menus includes vegetarian, gluten-free and diabetic choices as well as table d'hôte and à la carte. One couple on a special break, however, thought that though the dinner on one night was excellent, standards dropped on the other two nights of their stay when large parties were also dining there – it is hoped that the new banqueting room should take care of this in future. Bedrooms are fairly uniform in style and standard, though general manager Patrick Mauser, a veritable whirlwind of energy, has introduced various shades of difference: executive rooms may have half-tester beds or whirlpool baths, 'ladies' rooms' have security chains, net curtains and make-up remover pads, and rooms suitable for disabled visitors have low spy-holes in the door and useful supports.

◑ Open all year ⤢ 1½ miles south of Ipswich railway station. Private car park
⇥ 16 single, 16 twin, 40 double, 2 family rooms, 2 suites; all with bathroom/WC exc 8 singles with shower/WC; TV, room service, hair-dryer, mini-bar, trouser press, direct-dial telephone ⧳ Restaurant, bar, lounge, garden; conference facilities (max 200 people incl up to 76 residential); gym, sauna, solarium, heated indoor swimming-pool, croquet; early suppers for children; toys, babysitting, baby-listening, outdoor games ♿ Wheelchair access to hotel, restaurant and WC (unisex), 23 ground-floor bedrooms, 2 specially equipped for disabled people ● No dogs in public rooms; no smoking in some bedrooms ▭ Access, Amex, Diners, Switch, Visa ▣ Single/single occupancy of twin/double £72, twin/double £72 to £82, family room £82, suite £115; deposit required. Continental B £7, cooked B £9; set L, D £19.50; alc L, D £30. Special breaks available

---

IRONBRIDGE Shropshire   map 5

Library House

11 Severn Bank, Ironbridge, Telford TF8 7AN
TEL: (01952) 432299   FAX: (01952) 433967

Modest but comfortable B&B run with vigour by friendly hosts with a sunny disposition.

That the front room of Chris and George Maddocks' guesthouse was, until 1960, the village library, suggests that the funding of public libraries has been miserly for longer than most of us are inclined to remember. The room encapsulates the spirit of the house: small in scale, but irreproachably neat and well-cared-for. The trim exterior of the Georgian building sets the tone, so it's hardly surprising that at the time of our inspection George was half-way up a ladder washing down the paintwork of this spruce, flower-bedecked house a two-minute walk from the famous iron bridge across the gorge. The Maddocks obviously revel in things industrial, so the walls in the autumnal-toned lounge not given over to books bristle with Lowry prints as well as strikingly stylish modern monochrome studies by a local photographer. Guests take breakfast in the cosy quarry-tiled farmhouse-style kitchen (complete with Welsh dresser and lots of antique pine), which was the doctor's surgery in another of the house's previous incarnations. Bedrooms have fresh décor in pretty colour schemes, but tend to be small, not to say cramped. Wren, the smallest of all and often let as a single, has the advantage of a little terrace which leads up to the small secluded garden.

Chris and George obviously love their business, proudly stapling the many thank-you notes received into a visitors' book full of glowing testimonials.

◗ Closed 24 to 26 Dec 🔁 In Ironbridge town centre 60 yards from bridge. Public car park 🅿️ 2 twin, 1 double, 1 family room; 1 with bathroom/WC, 3 with shower/WC; TV, hair-dryer, trouser press ✅ Lounge, TV room, library, garden ♿ No wheelchair access ● No children under 12; no dogs in public rooms; no smoking 🍽 None accepted £ Single occupancy of twin/double £38, twin/double £48, family room from £60; deposit required

---

Severn Lodge

New Road, Ironbridge, Telford TF8 7AS
TEL: (01952) 432148 (AND FAX)

Civilised hosts offer superior B&B accommodation in a gracious house convenient for the gorge.

An elevated position simultaneously confers upon Severn Lodge excellent views of the gorge and a welcome remove from the hordes of day-trippers who throng to the bridge and its associated museums. It's hard to see how things can get much better at this price, but when our inspector called, Nita and Alan Reed, not content to rest on their laurels, were designing an ornamental pool to set off the charming terraced garden of their gracious red-brick Georgian house. The house itself is a box of delights, with tasteful interior design in stylish colours enlivened by interesting personal pieces, like the hallway's illustrated Chinese horoscopes that the well-travelled Reeds brought back from Thailand. There's a restrained formality to the elegant dining-room, where classic burgundy Regency stripes are set off by framed embroideries and silk paintings mostly done by family members or friends. The little-used guest sitting-room is a low-key affair; it has a television, but you might prefer to retreat to the sofa in the grand entrance hall to browse through a guide or other book from the well-stocked shelves. Bedrooms are distinctly up-market, imaginatively furnished and decorated to a standard worthy of a country-house hotel at more than twice the price. Torches are provided to help guests who use the shortcut via the garden to the gorge, and the shops and eateries that line it, after dark.

◗ Closed Chr & New Year 🔁 With bridge on your left, New Road is right turn immediately before Malthouse restaurant. Private car park 🅿️ 1 twin, 2 double; 2 with bathroom/WC, twin with shower/WC; TV, hair-dryer ✅ 2 dining-rooms, lounge, TV room, drying-room, garden ♿ No wheelchair access ● No children under 12; no dogs; no smoking 🍽 None accepted £ Single occupancy of twin/double £38, twin/double £48; deposit required

---

The text of entries is based on unsolicited reports sent in by readers and backed up by inspections. The factual details are from questionnaires the Guide *sends to all hotels that feature in the book.*

Park Farmhouse

Melbourne Road, Isley Walton, Derby DE74 2RN
TEL: (01332) 862409   FAX: (01332) 862364

A seventeenth-century farmhouse turned into a rustic, laid-back small hotel.

John and Linda Shields' enterprise offers various kinds of facilities, including a caravan park and giant eighteenth-century barn used for all sorts of knees-ups. Gradual expansion and growing sophistication since they opened in 1984 have brought two new bedrooms to the hotel this year. Across the scruffy courtyard and adjacent to the barn, they are the best on offer, featuring vaulted ceilings, beams and smart modern pine furniture; one is simply enormous. Other rooms, dotted around the former farmhouse, may have anything from refined soft furnishings to unadorned wood-chip wallpaper. The roar of big engines from Donington Park racetrack, a mere five-minute walk away, often reverberates around the courtyard. More atmospheric than the bedrooms are the beamed bar and wood-panelled and tiled dining-room, with chunky pine tables and a log fire. For evening meals, termed 'farmhouse suppers', residents and their guests select traditional dishes like whitebait, lasagne, steak and kidney pudding and spotted dick with custard from a short à la carte menu and a blackboard of specials.

◗ Closed Chr ⤢ On A453 at Isley Walton, take the Melbourne turning; hotel is ½ mile on right. Private car park ⤝ 3 twin, 7 double, 1 family room; some in annexe; most with bathroom/WC, some with shower/WC; TV, limited room service, hair-dryer, trouser press, direct-dial telephone, iron ⌘ Dining-room, bar, lounge, library, garden; conference facilities (max 15 people incl up to 11 residential); early suppers for children; baby-listening ᶑ Wheelchair access to hotel (1 step) and restaurant, 2 ground-floor bedrooms, 1 specially equipped for disabled people ● No dogs in public rooms; no smoking in dining-room and 2 bedrooms ▭ Access, Amex, Diners, Visa £ Single occupancy of twin/double £41 to £45, twin/double £55 to £65, family room £75 to £85; deposit required. Alc D £13 (1996 prices)

Upper Court

Kemerton, Tewkesbury GL20 7HY
TEL: (01386) 725351   FAX: (01386) 725472

Mixed reports on this imposing Georgian manor on the edge of the Cotswolds.

This year correspondents are fiercely divided over the merits of a stay at Bill and Diana Herford's grand and imposing Cotswold-stone manor house in a picture-postcard village near Tewkesbury. 'Could not have been more pleasant,' enthused one guest, praising the rooms, 'wonderful dinner' and friendly hosts. None can gainsay the majesty of the building with its imposing courtyard archway, nor the splendour of its lake, grounds and surrounding countryside.

Even the correspondent who left disappointed had good things to say about the tennis court and outdoor swimming-pool. His view that 'we felt more like an unfortunate necessity than welcome guests,' and feeling that the house 'has seen better days' is in marked contrast to another visitor's conclusion that, 'We were made to feel extremely welcome and comfortable and will definitely be returning.' In truth the house remains an (undoubtedly posh) family home, so the décor reflects family tastes and whims, never conforming to the carefully co-ordinated design agenda of the average hotel. Proportions dictate that these are not the sort of rooms to get an annual makeover, and in true 'to the manor born' tradition the gracious drawing-room has changed little since 1760, while the French silk curtains may well be older than the average guest. Paintings line the walls and set off the polished table of the dining-room, where guests eat communally on dinner-party fare: perhaps orange, coriander and carrot soup, followed by Herefordshire lamb and crème caramel. The Herfords also dabble in antiques, so you'll find stock pieces scattered around the house, adding to the charm of the exuberantly, if occasionally chaotically, designed bedrooms. Upper Court has self-catering cottages, some of which are now used as hotel rooms.

◑ Closed Chr ⬚ From Cheltenham travel north on the A435/B4079. 1 mile after the A438 crossroads, turn right to Kemerton. Turn off the main road at the war memorial. Private car park ⬚ 6 twin, 4 double, 5 four-poster, 1 suite; family rooms available; some in annexe; most with bathroom/WC, some with shower/WC; TV, hair-dryer; direct-dial telephone in some rooms ⬚ Dining-room, 2 lounges, drying-room, library, conservatory, games room, garden; conference facilities (max 30 people incl up to 16 residential); fishing, heated outdoor swimming-pool, tennis, boating; baby-listening ⬚ Wheelchair access to hotel (1 ramp), restaurant and WC (M,F), 2 ground-floor bedrooms specially equipped for disabled people ● Dogs in 1 bedroom only ⬚ Access, Visa ⬚ Single occupancy of twin/double £50 to £65, twin/double £75 to £95, four-poster £95, family room from £100, suite £115; deposit required. Set D £27; breakfast incl in room prices (£8.50 for those in cottages). Special breaks available

KENILWORTH Warwickshire

map 5

Castle Laurels

22 Castle Road, Kenilworth CV8 1NG
TEL: (01926) 856179   FAX: (01926) 854954

Meticulously maintained and competitively priced small hotel a stone's throw from Kenilworth Castle.

The *Guide* inspectors keep on handing out laurels for the neatness and quality of the housekeeping of this good-looking Victorian house. The hallway's tiles, bannisters and panelling are always gleaming, the spruce little dining-room's tables are well polished and the sitting-room is full of healthy plants and shiny drinks coasters on side-tables. Sue and Joe Glover's uniformed staff, polite almost to the point of formality, add a touch of dignity to the establishment. Bedrooms are as fresh and orderly as the rest of the house leads you to expect, and some contain a few modest antiques. Their main drawback is that they all have just shower rooms, some of which are cramped. When choosing, try to avoid the few small rooms, and note that those at the front enjoy views of the moody red sandstone ruins of Kenilworth Castle in winter, when the trees are leafless, but suffer from some traffic noise – unlike those at the rear. The town's pubs and restaurants lie within easy walking distance, or you can eat in on home-made fare such as prawn cocktail, chilli con carne and fruit crumble.

◑ Closed last 2 weeks Dec; restaurant closed Fri to Sun eves ⤢ On A452 almost opposite entrance to Kenilworth Castle. Private car park ⤶ 3 single, 3 twin, 5 double, 1 family room; all with shower/WC; TV, hair-dryer, direct-dial telephone ⊘ Dining-room, lounge; early suppers for children ⟁ No wheelchair access ● No dogs; no smoking ▭ Access, Visa £ Single £31, single occupancy of twin/double £38, twin/double £50, family room £62. Alc D £12.50 (prices valid till Feb 1997)

KESWICK Cumbria   map 10

Craglands ☆

Penrith Road, Keswick CA12 4LJ
TEL: (01768) 774406

A warm welcome and wonderful home-cooking are offered near the heart of Keswick.

Attention to detail along with a truly friendly reception are the features that help to raise Craglands above the multitude of small hotels in this popular base for exploring the surrounding fells. When our inspectors visited Wendy Dolton's immaculately kept B&B, home-made cakes and shortbread appeared in a flash in the front lounge, and Wendy cheerfully agreed to prepare dinner for them with minimal notice. One of the main approaches to Keswick runs by outside, but noise is not a problem, and the town centre is a mere ten-minute stroll away, along the peaceful, leafy path of a disused railway line. The elevated position of this whitewashed Victorian house provides all the rooms with a view over the fells, looking towards Grisedale Pike at the front and Latrigg at the rear. The recently refurbished bedrooms are individually styled in warm colours and feature good-quality, wooden furniture, while the bathrooms are kitted out with a comprehensive variety of toiletries. Wendy's cuisine is spot-on – we tucked into a rich Stilton soufflé; smoked salmon cooked in sour cream and chives, served on a feather-light potato pancake; beautifully presented lamb chops in herb crusts with a port-and-redcurrant sauce; and finished with sticky-toffee pudding. You are welcome to bring your own tipple to wash it all down.

◑ Closed Chr & weekends Jan to Mar ⤢ At the foot of Chestnut Hill in Keswick. Private car park ⤶ 1 single, 1 twin, 3 double; 2 with bathroom/WC, doubles with shower/WC; TV, hair-dryer, clock radio ⊘ Restaurant, lounge, drying-room; early suppers for children ⟁ No wheelchair access ● No children under 8; no dogs; no smoking ▭ None accepted £ Single/single occupancy of twin/double £25, twin/double £40 to £50; deposit required. Set D £17. Special breaks available

---

Don't forget that other hotels worth considering are listed in our Visitors' Book.

Dale Head Hall

Thirlmere, Keswick CA12 4TN
FREEPHONE: (0800) 454166   FAX: (01768) 771070

A secluded, characterful, small country house run with style and good humour.

A narrow, private drive through a corridor of rhododendrons and mossy stone walls takes you off one of the Lake District's busiest roads to a secluded spot on the forested inner slopes enclosing Thirlmere. The house that overlooks the water dates from the eighteenth century at the front, and is Elizabethan behind, and has an interesting dual personality inside. The bar and lounge on the lake side are graceful and spacious, while the low-ceiling, black beams and whitewashed walls of the restaurant at the back make it more intimate and cosy. 'You should feel comfortable, relaxed, when you come to eat here,' says the larger-than-life Hans Bonkenburg, who runs Dale Head Hall with his wife, Caroline. And some fine, country-house cooking – along the lines of Angus beef stuffed with Stilton and baby leeks, or pears poached in Sauternes and wrapped in sugar-coated puff pastry – should do the trick.

The bedrooms are divided along historic lines; the six in the 'modern' part at the front are in demand for their views, and the three at the back (particularly Room 6) are popular for the character of their timbers and panelling.

○ Open all year   ⊘ Midway between Keswick and Grasmere on A591, at the end of a long private drive on the shore of Lake Thirlmere. Private car park ⊨ 2 twin, 4 double, 1 four-poster, 1 family room, 1 suite; 7 with bathroom/WC, 2 with shower/WC; room service, hair-dryer, direct-dial telephone   ⊘ Restaurant, bar, lounge, drying-room, garden; fishing, tennis; early suppers for children; baby-listening   ⅙ No wheelchair access   ● No children under 10 in restaurant eves; no dogs; no smoking in bedrooms   ▭ Access, Amex, Delta, Switch, Visa   ⅙ Single occupancy of twin/double £72 to £87, twin/double £94 to £138, four-poster £104 to £148, family room £94 to £138, suite £114 to £158; deposit required. Set D £24.50. Special breaks available

The Grange

Manor Brow, Keswick CA12 4BA
TEL: (01768) 772500

Comfortable, relaxing surroundings feature at a very pleasant guesthouse on the leafy outskirts of Keswick.

Jane and Duncan Miller are fiercely proud of their smart, Lakeland-stone, Victorian house – with good reason – and as experienced, perceptive hosts, they ensure that things run smoothly and according to all preferences and predilections. As one reader puts it: 'The welcome is genuine; standards of cleanliness, of provisions, service of cuisine is very high – in fact, everything is done with pride and the desire to ensure your stay is as you would want it to be. The service and friendliness is unobtrusive; Jane and Duncan's reward is in seeing the pleasure the guests derive from being there.'

The food continues to please too, with the set menus offering unusual and interesting dishes while appealing to all tastes; watercress and pear soup, for instance, might be followed by breast of guinea-fowl or fillet of salmon, and then a hot traditional pudding or lighter chilled dessert. After dinner, the spacious main sitting-room, with its fine original plasterwork might appeal, or you could repair to the restyled, pub-like bar, where minerals glisten in the stonework of the fireplace.

The bedrooms vary in size and décor, ranging from the modern and unfussy to the more cottagey (those up in the gables), while the *en suite* bathrooms tend to be on the small side. Room 5, with its double aspect and polished-wood half-tester, is particularly nice.

◖ Closed mid-Nov to mid-Mar ⟋ Take A591 from Keswick towards Windermere for ½ mile. Take the first right; hotel is 200 yards on the right. Private car park ⟋ 3 twin, 7 double; 5 with bathroom/WC, 5 with shower/WC; TV, room service, hair-dryer, direct-dial telephone ✧ Dining-room, bar, 2 lounges, drying-room, garden ౬ No wheelchair access ● No children under 7; no dogs; no smoking in bedrooms ⊟ Access, Visa £ Single occupancy of twin/double £56 to £63, twin/double £92 to £105 (rates incl dinner); deposit required. Set D £19. Special breaks available

---

Swinside Lodge

Newlands, Keswick CA12 5UE
TEL: (01768) 772948 (AND FAX)

A stylish Victorian house in an idyllic countryside setting.

Although only a few miles outside Keswick and a short stroll from the shores of Derwentwater, Swinside Lodge feels a million miles away from the more commercialised parts of the Lake District. Tucked away at the foot of Cat Bells, which presents hardy guests with the opportunity for a vigorous pre-breakfast walk, the hotel enjoys a setting of perfect views and tranquillity. Neatly kept gardens frame an elegant Victorian family house which Graham Taylor has furnished with taste and comfortable style. The small reception area leads through to a choice of smart, but still intimate, lounges where antique furniture and Japanese silk prints form a fine back-drop for a pre-dinner sherry – one guest remarked that you cannot fail to get talking to the other residents, many of whom are on a return visit and full of praise for the comfort and conviviality they find here. Bedrooms are named after trees and all are furnished and decorated to a high standard mainly in pastel tones. Beech is a spacious and light room from which a bay window looks over the lovely copper beech at the front of the house, and Lilac, painted in cool cream and green, has a double aspect with views to Causey Pike and Skiddaw. The dining-room is equally refined and the five-course dinners created from local produce are much praised by guests. The menu might feature pan-fried loin of lamb with a shallot tartlet and rosemary sauce, followed by fresh fruit salad in a brandy-snap basket.

◑ Closed Dec to mid-Feb exc Chr ⇗ From Keswick take A66 towards Cockermouth and turn left at Portinscale; follow road towards Grange for 2 miles; ignore signs to Swinside and Newlands Valley. Private car park ⇥ 2 twin, 5 double; most with bathroom/WC, 1 with shower/WC; TV, hair-dryer ✅ Dining-room, 3 lounges, drying-room, garden ♿ No wheelchair access ● No dogs; no smoking ⌺ None accepted £ Single occupancy of twin/double £35 to £52, twin/double £60 to £100; deposit required. Set D £25 to £29. Special breaks available

---

KETTLEWELL North Yorkshire map 8

Langcliffe Country Guesthouse ☆

Kettlewell, Skipton BD23 5RJ
TEL: (01756) 760243

Homely guesthouse with cottage-style bedrooms and great views down Wharfedale.

The Dales village of Kettlewell attracts large numbers of visitors, many of whom are attracted by the great walking opportunities the area offers. In Langcliffe Country Guesthouse you can be close to the centre of the village, with its rows of converted lead miners' cottages and characterful pubs, yet enjoy perfect tranquillity. The solid stone building is a few hundred yards along a no through road and offers fantastic views up the ridges behind or down the broad expanse of the Wharfedale valley, all dry-stone walls and pocket-sized enclosures. The views make the house, and given that the conservatory really gets the best of them, Richard and Jane Elliot show good sense in serving all the meals here. A typical dinner menu would include starters like garlic mushrooms with crusty bread, followed by a fish pie with large prawns and salmon in a creamy sauce with a Parmesan pastry crust. The Elliots have used the knowledge gained from having previously run a pub to put together a small, unpretentious wine list with low mark-ups. There are other clues to their former careers dotted around the house like the framed 1930s certificate from the Bushmills Distillery that Richard brought with him to add to the homely lounge. Bedrooms have a cottagey feel with pale yellows and pinks and pine furniture. Room 6 is adapted for wheelchair users and rooms 2 and 3 have the best valley views.

◑ Open all year ⇗ Kettlewell is on B6160 6 miles north of Grassington; take road opposite King's Head pub which says 'Access only'; hotel is 500 yards down on right. Private car park ⇥ 3 twin, 3 double; family room available; all with bathroom/WC; TV, room service, direct-dial telephone; hair-dryer on request ✅ Restaurant, lounge, conservatory, garden; early suppers for children ♿ Wheelchair access to hotel (ramp), restaurant, 1 ground-floor bedroom specially equipped for disabled people ● No dogs or smoking in public rooms ⌺ Access, Visa £ Single occupancy of twin/double £25 to £37, twin/double £50 to £56; deposit required. Set D £15. Special breaks available

---

This denotes that the hotel is in an exceptionally peaceful situation where you can be assured of a restful stay.

KILVE Somerset   map 2

Meadow House

Sea Lane, Kilve TA5 1EG
TEL: (01278) 741546   FAX: (01278) 741663

Attractive, secluded Georgian house in lovely gardens just minutes from the sea.

Garden-lovers will adore Kilve House, a fine, mainly Georgian, house down a secluded lane leading to the sea. The elegant lounge and dining-room are both sited to scoop views of the garden, as are several of the bedrooms, which are furnished with a pleasing mix of old and new; Room 1 has a bed so lofty a step is provided to help you up, while Room 4 has an Edwardian dressing table of such complexity that even owner Judith Wyer-Roberts calls it startling. Bathrooms, with cruelty-free toiletries, favour pine and porcelain. Dinner menus offer a choice of starters and main courses and follow a seasonal pattern as far as possible; you might perhaps choose lobster soup and follow up with pork with apple and onion. Afterwards there's a cosy smoking-room in which to take coffee. Your nights are unlikely to be disturbed by anything more than the odd owl hoot, but even more peace can be had in the converted outhouses which, with their own bathrooms and sitting-rooms, represent excellent value for money. 'We found the atmosphere very relaxing,' confirmed one reader, 'and return whenever possible.'

◑ Open all year   ⤢ Take A39 from Bridgwater; in Kilve turn right just before Hood Arms pub into Sea Lane; hotel ½ mile on left. Private car park   🛏 2 twin/double, 4 double, 4 suites; family rooms available; some in annexe; all with bathroom/WC exc 2 suites with shower/WC; TV, room service, hair-dryer, direct-dial telephone; iron on request   ✓ Dining-room, lounge, drying-room, study, conservatory, garden; conference facilities (max 20 people incl up to 10 residential); croquet; early suppers for children; baby-listening   ♿ No wheelchair access   ● No dogs in public rooms and most bedrooms; smoking in study and some bedrooms only   ▭ Access, Amex, Delta, Diners, Switch, Visa   £ Single occupancy of twin/double £55, twin/double £75 to £95, family room from £80, suite from £80; deposit required. Set D £23.50. Special breaks available

---

KINGHAM Oxfordshire   map 5

Mill House

Kingham OX7 6UH
TEL: (01608) 658188   FAX: (01608) 658492

A business hotel in quiet countryside with reasonable weekend packages.

Mill House is chiefly a business hotel with good-value room rates at the weekend. In flat open countryside on the edge of the Cotswolds, the building dates back to the eleventh century, when it was a thriving flour mill. Apart from a well-restored proving-oven, there's very little evidence now of its long history. Since the 1970s the house has been greatly extended and today's well-run hotel dwarfs the original building which makes up the lobby and the bar. The bedrooms are all a good size with light modern fabrics. What they lack in character they make up for in facilities including smart bathrooms with every goody you could think up. Morley Street and Adlestrop were our favourites for the views over the grounds and down to the millstream. The lounge and bar are comfortable if not imaginatively furnished, while the restaurant has more atmosphere, especially when the candles are lit at dinner. The fixed-price menus offer up to eight choices per course, from cream of vegetable soup or fennel mousse for starters to pan-fried lamb's liver or monkfish for main course.

◖ Open all year ⤢ South of Kingham village; just off B4450 between Chipping Norton and Stow-on-the-Wold. Private car park ⨼ 6 twin, 7 twin/double, 8 double, 1 four-poster, 1 family room; some in annexe; all with bathroom/WC; TV, room service, hair-dryer, direct-dial telephone ✓ Restaurant, bar, lounge, drying-room, garden; conference facilities (max 70 people incl up to 23 residential); fishing, golf; early suppers for children ♿ Wheelchair access to hotel and restaurant, 6 ground-floor bedrooms ⊖ No children under 5; no dogs in public rooms; no smoking in restaurant ▭ Access, Amex, Diners, Switch, Visa £ Single occupancy of twin/double £55 to £65, twin/double £90 to £110, four-poster £110, family room £110; deposit required. Set L £13, D £20; alc L £16.50, D £25. Special breaks available

---

KINGSBRIDGE Devon   map 1

Buckland-Tout-Saints Hotel

Goveton, Kingsbridge TQ7 2DS
TEL: (01548) 853055 FAX: (01548) 856261

Fine Queen Anne house in extensive grounds with good food and excellent service.

Buckland-Tout-Saints sounds as if it should be a converted monastery but in fact its extraordinary name is a corruption of the Norman-French *tout-sain*, meaning all-healing, after a particular healing plant. From the outside, this late seventeenth-century building is distinguished by its solid squareness. Inside, however, bedrooms come in some unexpected shapes and sizes. In Hill, for example, a roof-supporting pillar provides an unusual television table, while a stair with an iron handrail leads up to a pleasantly spacious bathroom. In the main wood-panelled restaurant the only people looking unamused are the man and woman whose portraits hang on either side of the fireplace, faces carefully averted from a third picture of a young girl lying naked on a bed between them. Dinner here is served with great gusto, prepared under head chef Richard Cranfield. The menu might include ceviche, then poached fillet of English lamb in its own juices, finished off by chocolate truffle torte with home-made honeycomb ice-cream. In the lounge the huge log fire, the table set with family photo albums and the piano in the corner with music opened at a Grade 5 piece add just the right dash of informality to what might otherwise be a slightly intimidating room. Under John and Tove Taylor's meticulous supervision, service at Buckland-Tout-Saints is impeccable. Passing reference to plans for the following day led to the appearance of an appropriate guidebook alongside the newspaper at the breakfast table. You would travel a long way to top that.

◑ Open all year ⤢ 2 miles north of Kingsbridge on A381; hotel sign to Buckland-Tout-Saints through village of Goveton. Private car park ⤷ 3 twin, 6 double, 1 four-poster, 3 suites; all with bathroom/WC; TV, room service, hair-dryer, trouser press, direct-dial telephone, radio; no tea/coffee-making facilities in rooms ⊘ 2 restaurants, bar, lounge, drying-room, garden; conference facilities (max 20 people incl up to 13 residential); putting green, croquet; early suppers for children; cots, high chairs ♿ No wheelchair access ⬤ No smoking in restaurants ▭ Access, Amex, Delta, Diners, Switch, Visa £ Single occupancy of twin/double £60 to £80, twin/double £120 to £160, four-poster £140 to £180, suite £160 to £200; deposit required. Set L £14.50, D £27.50. Special breaks available

---

KINGSTON BAGPUIZE Oxfordshire   map 2

Fallowfields

Kingston Bagpuize, Nr Abingdon OX13 5BH
TEL: (01865) 820416 FAX: (01865) 821275

Large, stylish bedrooms in a country house with good home-cooking.

After a successful first three years of running their family home as a small hotel and restaurant, Peta and Anthony Lloyd are continuing to make improvements and there are no signs of their enthusiasm flagging. One reader wrote to recommend the 'splendid attention to detail; the proprietors are so helpful, friendly and thoughtful.' The red-brick, mostly Victorian house – though parts of it date back nearly 400 years – has only three bedrooms for guests. They're all large and elegantly furnished, and, thanks to the high ceilings and huge, arched windows, feel airy and light. Each has its own, good-sized bathroom. The rest of the house is occupied by the Lloyds' own family, although it's big enough to allow everyone to co-exist quite happily. The family cat might even join you in the sunny, south-facing sitting-room, with its classic pink and green furnishings and collections of china and coloured glass. Dinner is served in Fallowfields' two dining-rooms, both open to non-residents, and often fully booked with local people returning for Peta Lloyd's home-cooking. Four-course evening meals come at a fixed price and are served at a set time. The choices typically include fresh crab with ginger, lime and chilli; pork fillet stuffed with prunes and marinated in Madeira; and a vast choice of home-made puddings. One report told us that 'Anthony's special cheeses were a real treat.' While Peta manages the cooking, Anthony is in charge of growing organic vegetables, with a particular emphasis on flavour. Don't be surprised to find a white, 'ivory egg' tomato on your breakfast plate – it is guaranteed to have infinitely more flavour than its shop-bought counterparts.

◑ Open all year; dining-rooms closed Sun ⤢ On main road at south end of Kingston Bagpuize. Private car park ⤷ 1 double, 2 four-poster; all with bathroom/WC; TV, room service, hair-dryer, trouser press, direct-dial telephone ⊘ 2 dining-rooms, lounge, garden; conference facilities (max 20 people incl up to 3 residential); heated outdoor swimming-pool, tennis, croquet ♿ No wheelchair access ⬤ No children under 10; no dogs in public rooms; no smoking in bedrooms ▭ Amex, Visa £ Twin/double £79, four-poster £89; deposit required. Set D £22.50 (1996 prices)

Dundas Arms

53 Station Road, Kintbury RG17 9UT
TEL: (01488) 658263   FAX: (01488) 658568

Large, modern rooms in this waterside pub, with the emphasis on the restaurant.

This year, David Dalzell-Piper is celebrating 30 years of running the Dundas Arms. Little has changed in recent years: it's still run as a restaurant-with-rooms, with the food being its chief attraction. People come from a quite a distance to linger over lunch in the plain, French-*auberge*-style restaurant, with its bench seats, dark-green walls and assortment of paintings and sketches on a wildlife theme. The short menu here might include potted duck with prune chutney, breasts of wild pigeon with a shallot and balsamic-vinegar sauce, or a grilled sirloin steak, while there's a simpler menu of first-rate snacks in the pub-style bar. In either place, there's generally a chatty, low-key atmosphere, helped along by wine from a vast cellar, or real ale. The five bedrooms are in a converted stable block at the side of the eighteenth-century house. All are on the ground floor and have doors opening out on to a small terrace on the river bank. The rooms are of a good size, and the furnishings are comfortable, if somewhat dated; the small bathrooms are old-fashioned, but spotlessly clean.

◑ Closed Chr to New Year; restaurant closed Sun and Mon   🔁 As you drive into Kintbury off A4, first building on left after canal. Private car park 🅿️ 2 twin, 3 double; all with bathroom/WC; TV, limited room service, direct-dial telephone; hair-dryer on request   ⚡ Restaurant, bar, garden; early suppers for children   ♿ No wheelchair access   ● No dogs in public rooms and in bedrooms by arrangement only
▢ Access, Amex, Delta, Switch, Visa   £ Single occupancy of twin/double £55, twin/double £65; deposit required. Set L £19.50; alc D £24.50; bar meals available

---

The Courtyard

5 Fairbank, Kirkby Lonsdale, Carnforth LA6 2AZ
TEL: (01524) 271613

Stately Georgian town house in walled garden.

This B&B takes its name from a pretty flagstoned courtyard concealed behind an arch next door to the Fleece Inn. Built in 1811 to house a Westmorland MP while a more substantial mansion was being constructed, it's a grand town house with impressive hall and portrait-lined staircase. Yet with only four bedrooms, it is still a homely place where you sit down to breakfast round a single table with whoever else happens to be staying. Only one of the spacious bedrooms has its own bathroom, so that may be the one to plump for, but the others are attractively, if simply, decorated. The big, comfortable lounge on the first floor offers a television and music centre, and views over the walled garden. Owner Gill Grey doesn't serve dinner but will be happy to advise on restaurants in the town centre, a short walk away.

◐ Open all year ⤓ From market square exit via New Road; then first right downhill; left at bottom of hill; house is on right-hand side of left-hand bend. Private car park ⨄ 1 single, 1 twin, 1 four-poster, 1 suite; suite with bathroom/WC; TV, hair-dryer, trouser press ⌗ Restaurant, lounge, drying-room, garden ⅙ No wheelchair access ⊜ No children under 10; no dogs; no smoking ⊟ None accepted £ Single £20 to £22, single occupancy of twin £20 to £22, twin £40 to £42, four-poster £45, suite £45; deposit required

---

KNUTSFORD Cheshire   map 8

Belle Epoque

60 King Street, Knutsford WA16 0NG
TEL: (01565) 633060   FAX: (01565) 634150

A flamboyant restaurant-with-rooms in the town centre; some rooms are more showy than others.

The larger-than-life brass lady clutching a massive bouquet of dried flowers is 'Delilah'. She is the centrepiece of Belle Epoque's deliciously swanky restaurant – a flamboyant affair featuring deep-blue drapes and walls, Art Nouveau prints, white damask table linen and silver cutlery – in whose secluded alcoves many a whispered proposal has been accepted. If you don't feel in the mood for such chichi surroundings, you could choose the brighter, but similarly Gallic, café that is situated behind the bow window which overlooks Knutsford's narrow, olde-worlde main street. The menu is an eclectic affair offering a variety of possibilities, from Bury black pudding to Worcestershire snails, or chargrilled tuna steak with a red-pepper coulis to fish and 'proper' chips.

Two of Belle Epoque's bedrooms could be described in similar terms to the restaurant: Rooms 6 and 7 have been lavishly designed, with dark-blue, rag-rolled walls and splendid Victorian/Edwardian-style bathrooms. Room 3 features burnt-orange, striped wallpaper and an antique bedstead, but elsewhere the accommodation is more humble, with wood-chip walls, small *en suite* bathrooms, and mock-rococo bedroom suites.

◐ Closed Sat, Sun & bank holidays; restaurant closed Sun ⤓ 2 miles from Junction 19 of M6, in the centre of Knutsford. On-street parking ⨄ 1 single, 2 twin, 4 double; all with bathroom/WC; TV ⌗ Restaurant, bar, garden; conference facilities (max 50 people incl up to 7 residential) ⅙ No wheelchair access ⊜ No children under 14; no dogs ⊟ Access, Amex, Delta, Diners, Switch, Visa £ Single/single occupancy of twin/double £40, twin/double £50. Cooked B £4; set L £9.50; alc L £14, D £18. Special breaks available

---

Longview Hotel

51 & 55 Manchester Road, Knutsford WA16 0LX
TEL: (01565) 632119   FAX: (01565) 652402

A home-from-home guesthouse with comfortable rooms and charming hosts.

Behind its late-Victorian front, the Longview Hotel, situated on a busy commuter road near the centre of Knutsford, offers a series of very pleasant discoveries to the uninitiated: a cosy, brick-walled, basement bar with its *Punch* prints and comfortably worn armchairs; thoughtful touches like hot-water bottles and sewing kits in the homely bedrooms; and inventive and imaginative food served in the busy Victorian-style restaurant. Chef James Falconer Flint has devised a menu with prices to suit different pockets, although from the detailed descriptions you'd be hard pushed to see why some of the 'standard' dishes don't qualify as 'premium' or 'connoisseur's choice'. Slot the following into the above categories if you can: pigs' trotters stuffed with pine nuts and pork forcemeat; a brace of pigeons' breasts served with crushed-juniper, bacon and venison sausage; or fillet steak with chasseur sauce. And, given a little notice, James is more than amenable to any special requests.

Such is the enthusiasm with which the hotel is run, that it also comes as something of a surprise to learn that Pauline and Stephen West are into their twentieth year at Longview. Their amiability and easy-going approach go a long way towards explaining the hotel's appeal.

◑ Closed 24 Dec to 6 Jan; restaurant closed Sun ◪ Leave M6 at Junction 19 and take A556 towards Chester/Northwich to traffic lights; turn left to Knutsford. At the roundabout, turn left; hotel is 200 yards on the right. Private car park 🛏 6 single, 5 twin, 11 double, 1 family room; all with bathroom/WC; TV, room service, hair-dryer, trouser press, direct-dial telephone ✓ Restaurant, bar, lounge, drying-room; conference facilities (max 16 people residential/non-residential); early suppers for children; toys ♿ No wheelchair access ● No dogs in public rooms; no smoking in restaurant ▭ Access, Amex, Diners, Visa £ Single £37 to £65, single occupancy of twin/double £48 to £65, twin/double £58 to £83, family room from £68; deposit required. Alc D £16.50; light lunches available. Special breaks available

LACOCK Wiltshire map 2

At the Sign of the Angel

Church Street, Lacock, Nr Chippenham SN15 2LB
TEL: (01249) 730230 FAX: (01249) 730527

Bags of character and atmosphere in a perfectly preserved, historic village.

With its row upon row of beautifully preserved cottages – some half-timbered, some of golden stone – Lacock is the perfect example of an English country village. The National Trust has owned the village since 1944, which is fortunate for the Levis family, who have held the lease of this historic inn since 1953, as it relieves them of the financial burden of caring for the building's more delicate features: some of them, such as wood beams, stone fireplaces, flagstones and horse-hair plasterwork, could be up to four centuries old. The interlocking dining-rooms are plainly furnished with wooden tables and benches. The menus have a traditional focus, and include dishes such as wild-boar sausages with Cumberland sauce, pan-fried lambs' kidneys in Madeira, or a pan-fried fillet of beef with peppercorn sauce. Upstairs, a cosier, wood-panelled lounge is the central point from which crooked corridors lead to atmospheric bedrooms, through doorways apparently designed for midgets (by twentieth-century standards). Furnishings – dark, carved beds and chests – fit the period.

◑ Closed 23 to 31 Dec ⌷ Lacock is signposted to the left 3 miles south of Chippenham on A350. On-street parking ⌷⌷⌷ 1 twin, 4 double, 1 four-poster; all with bathroom/WC; TV, limited room service, hair-dryer, direct-dial telephone ⊘ 3 dining-rooms, lounge, garden ⌷⌷ Wheelchair access to hotel, restaurant and WC (unisex), 1 ground-floor bedroom ● No dogs in public rooms ▭ Access, Amex, Delta, Switch, Visa ⌷£⌷ Single occupancy of twin/double £55 to £75, twin/double/four-poster £75 to £93; deposit required. Alc L £15, D £16.50. Special breaks available

---

LANCASTER Lancashire   map 8

Edenbreck House

Sunnyside Lane, Lancaster LA1 5ED
TEL: (01524) 32464

Comfortable, slightly eccentric B&B in a secluded garden near the city centre.

You'll find Margaret and Barrie Houghton's guesthouse tucked away down a short private drive in the nineteenth-century back-streets of Lancaster. Edenbreck, with its double gables and bay windows, looks in keeping with its not-too-near neighbours, but seems to be in pristine condition. Which it is, having been built only a dozen years ago to the Houghton's Victorian-style requirements, right down to the tiled fireplaces with iron grates. Samplers, a profusion of pressed flowers and lacy table cloths complete the period picture. Those with a taste for extravagance will love the master bedroom. A modern four-poster rests on a two-step dais, and behind the glass double doors stands a big Jacuzzi bath on a central pedestal. The four other rooms are less dramatic, but have individual attractions: a dark antique bedroom suite in the Victorian room, or a view of the Lancaster's distinctive folly from the Monument room, for instance. Breakfast is served under the mock-timbering of the large dining-room; before retiring, tick your requirements on the menu in your room and hang it outside on the doorknob.

◑ Open all year ⌷ Turn off A6 towards Castle station; fourth left is Ashfield Avenue which becomes Sunnyside Lane. Private car park ⌷⌷⌷ 2 twin, 2 double, 1 four-poster; all with bathroom/WC; TV, hair-dryer ⊘ Dining-room, lounge, TV room ⌷⌷ No wheelchair access ● No dogs or smoking in public rooms ▭ None accepted ⌷£⌷ Single occupancy of twin/double £30, twin/double £40, four-poster £50

LANGAR Nottinghamshire   map 5

Langar Hall

Langar, Nottingham NG13 9HG
TEL: (01949) 860559   FAX: (01949) 861045

Individual, personable country-house hotel in the gentle Vale of Belvoir countryside.

When Radio 4's *Test Match Special* team is commentating from Trent Bridge, you may hear the experts singing the praises of this honey-coloured house built in 1835. Back in the 1930s cricketers themselves would be entertained here by the present owner's father. Such continuity, coupled with the house's intimate scale and the cultured hospitality offered by Imogen Skirving, invests the hotel with much of the atmosphere of a private house. Its furnishings contribute to the effect too: a great collector, Imogen has decked out the Hall from top to bottom with a plethora of rugs, paintings, prints, fine furniture and chandeliers. The grandest room is the pillared and statue'd main restaurant, the setting for accomplished British food that caters for both adventurous and conservative palates. Spring menus offered black pudding ravioli with mushy peas, or pigeon and foie gras terrine as starters, but came back down to earth with treacle tart and custard or Stilton for dessert (the cheese is made just a mile away). Bedrooms are as characterful as their names suggest, such as Bohemia (where Imogen's husband used to paint), the Barristers (resembling an old-fashioned lawyer's office) and Desert Orchid (in the stable annexe).

● Closed 25 to 27 Dec ☒ Signposted off A46 mid-way between Leicester and Newark, and off A52 mid-way between Grantham and Nottingham; hotel is behind church in Langar. Private car park ⌂ 1 single, 2 twin, 7 double, 1 four-poster, 1 suite; 1 in annexe; all with bathroom/WC; TV, room service, hair-dryer, direct-dial telephone; trouser press on request ✓ Restaurant, lounge, TV room, drying-room, library, garden; conference facilities (max 20 people incl up to 10 residential); fishing, croquet; early suppers for children; babysitting, baby-listening & No wheelchair access ● Dogs by arrangement; smoking in 1 public room only ☐ Access, Amex, Diners, Visa £ Single £50 to £60, single occupancy of twin/double £65 to £85, twin/double £75 to £115, four-poster £135, suite £135; deposit required. Set L £14.50, D £15; alc L £22.50, D £25. Special breaks available

---

LANGHO Lancashire   map 8

Northcote Manor

Northcote Road, Langho, Blackburn BB6 8BE
TEL: (01254) 240555   FAX: (01254) 246568

Informal yet impeccably run country house with a top-class restaurant.

You can't help thinking that Northcote Manor deserves a long rhodo-dendron-lined private drive through acres of parkland. As it is, the red-brick Victorian house stands proud alongside a busy roundabout in rural Lancashire – not exactly spectacular surroundings, but pleasant enough and well-connected for exploring the Ribble Valley, or for pressing on north or south after a very fine dinner and a highly comfortable night's sleep. Most bedrooms are on the generous side, with space for armchairs as well as antique beds and some huge pieces of period furniture. Room 4 boasts an Art Nouveau wardrobe, Room 6 has an original Victorian bathroom with swirling blue tiles and a full-length mirror, while the Doris Suite has a four-poster draped in chintz and a walk-in shower that blasts jets of water in ten different directions (not for the faint-hearted first thing in the morning). Downstairs, things are much in keeping with the Victorian period: open fires, plenty of nutty oak panelling and chesterfields and button-back armchairs in the sitting-room; the restaurant is an exercise in understated elegance and appropriately overlooks the walled herb garden. Co-proprietor Nigel Haworth continues to collect plaudits for his innovative and expert cooking with a particular emphasis on local ingredients. From one spring menu you could choose to start with Bury black pudding with buttered pink trout or a Lancashire cheese soufflé, then move further afield for glazed Orkney scallops with chive mash or smoked breast of Goosnargh duckling with tempura.

◑ Open all year   ⤴ Leave M6 at Junction 31 and take A59 towards Clitheroe for 9½ miles; hotel is on left-hand side. Private car park   ⇑ 5 twin/double, 8 double, 1 suite; 3 with bathroom/WC, most with shower/WC; TV, room service, hair-dryer, trouser press, direct-dial telephone   ✓ Restaurant, private dining-room, bar, 2 lounges, garden; conference facilities (max 14 people residential); early suppers for children; baby-listening   ♿ Wheelchair access to hotel (2 ramps), restaurant and WC (M,F), 4 ground-floor bedrooms, 1 specially equipped for disabled people   ⬤ No dogs ▭ Access, Amex, Delta, Diners, Switch, Visa   £ Single occupancy of twin/double £75 to £85, twin/double £95 to £110, suite £110 to £130; deposit required. Set L £15, D £35; alc L, D £40. Special breaks available

---

LANGLEY MARSH Somerset   map 2

Langley House Hotel

Langley Marsh, Wiveliscombe TA4 2UF
TEL: (01984) 623318   FAX: (01984) 624573

Lovingly decorated small hotel with good food and pretty gardens.

It would be easy to drive straight past the Langley House Hotel but for the golden grasshopper, previously of Martin's Bank, jutting out above the back door; Anne and Peter Wilson found it in an outhouse and decided that it would make a perfect signpost. Inside, every inch of the house reveals their eye for possibilities. The bedrooms are all individually decorated with bold, inviting colour and lots of ingenuity; none of them is huge, although the corners have been so artfully co-opted to provide wardrobe and dressing-table space that you hardly notice. Perhaps the best is Friendly Hall, which boasts a four-poster, but even the one single room is pleasantly cottagey, with stencilling on its sloping ceiling. Downstairs, the lounge is painted a deep coral, while a second sitting-room beyond is decorated in bright yellow and blue. The restaurant is quieter, its fawn-coloured walls stencilled with flowers to match the swags of dried flowers above the fireplace. Four-course dinners are of the no-choice variety, so vegetarians need to say so when booking. Typically, a meal might start with a two-tone bavarois of sweet peppers with a tomato coulis, and follow with a serving of sea bass and then of lamb. For dessert there's a choice of sticky sweets or local cheese served with home-made bread. And then there's the garden...pretty and peaceful with a rivulet running through it.

See the inside front cover for a brief explanation of how to use the Guide.

◑ Open all year ⤷ From Taunton B3227 head for Wiveliscombe town centre. Turn right (signposted Langley Marsh); hotel is ½ mile out of town on the right-hand side. Private car park ⤷ 1 single, 2 twin, 3 double, 1 four-poster, 1 family room; all with bathroom/WC exc 1 double with shower/WC; TV, room service, hair-dryer, direct-dial telephone ⌘ Restaurant, bar, 2 lounges, drying-room, conservatory, garden; conference facilities (max 16 people incl up to 8 residential); croquet; early suppers for children; toys, babysitting, baby-listening, outdoor games, high chairs, cots ⎱ No wheelchair access ● No children under 7 in restaurant eves; no dogs in public rooms; no smoking in restaurant and some bedrooms ⊟ Access, Amex, Visa ⒠ Single £65 to £69, single occupancy of twin/double £69 to £73, twin/double £83 to £86, four-poster £103 to £115, family room £128 to £140; deposit required. Set D £25.50 to £29.50 (prices valid till Apr 1997). Special breaks available

---

LASTINGHAM North Yorkshire   map 9

Lastingham Grange

Lastingham, York YO6 6TH
TEL: (01751) 417345/417402

Country-house comforts and total tranquillity in a converted farmhouse.

In the delightfully peaceful village of Lastingham, just around the corner from St Mary's church and its famous crypt, is Lastingham Grange, once lauded as 'the most peaceful hotel in Britain'. The village sees little traffic and being along a no-through road enhances the hotel's sense of remoteness. Originally a farmhouse dating back to the seventeenth century, the building was converted into a country-house hotel in the 1920s and has been in the Wood family since the Second World War. A reassuring sense of tradition pervades the house without any of the stuffiness that can sometimes go with it. The lounge and dining-room are bright and spacious, furnished with antiques and unusual touches like a cabinet containing a collection of miniature ethnic figures. Both overlook the terrace (where teas and light lunches might be served in summer) and the thoughtfully laid out gardens, which conceal a children's play area and where you might bump into canine double-act Basil and Charley. All except one of the bedrooms share this view and an undramatic flowery décor. Dinner menus offer a good choice of main courses such as baked halibut with Pernod hollandaise and ragoût of kidneys in red wine.

◑ Closed Dec to Feb ⤷ 2 miles east of Kirkbymoorside on A170; turn left (north) through Appleton-le-Moors to Lastingham. Private car park ⤷ 2 single, 7 twin, 3 double; family rooms available; all with bathroom/WC; TV, room service, hair-dryer, trouser press, direct-dial telephone, radio ⌘ Dining-room, lounge, drying-room; early suppers for children; baby-listening, outdoor games ⎱ No wheelchair access ● No dogs in public rooms; no smoking in dining-room ⊟ None accepted ⒠ Single £65 to £71, single occupancy of twin/double £65 to £71, twin/double £120 to £131, family room £120 to £131. Set L £15, D £25.50; (prices valid till Mar 1997). Special breaks available

Angel Hotel

Market Place, Lavenham, Sudbury CO10 9QZ
TEL: (01787) 247388 FAX: (01787) 248344

A charming English inn in a charming English village, with very friendly service.

Lavenham claims to be the finest medieval town in England, and has 300 listed buildings. At its heart, on the attractive Market Place, stands the Angel Hotel, licensed since 1420, though its exterior hints at a Georgian remodelling. Inside, however, many of the earlier nooks and crannies remain, and the space around the bar is divided up by half-timbered walls and partitions, conjuring up an intimate feel, and allowing non-smokers to dodge one of the more traditional aspects of pub life if they so wish. Watercolours, old photos of the inn in earlier incarnations, and prints of birds and animals hang on the walls; a carved wooden angel adorns the fireplace. Residents also have the option of the first-floor lounge, whose fine plaster ceiling dates from the sixteenth century. Food is a cut above the average pub grub: typical dishes might be a hot Suffolk cheese and ham pie, or pork casserole with apricot and walnuts, and can be eaten at one of the assorted scrubbed pine tables inside, or in the garden tucked away behind when weather permits. Service is solicitous, as is Guinness, the black and white cat, who looks on hopefully. Bedrooms are straightforward, comfortable and neatly furnished, with rattan bedheads and plain duvets; beams or half-timbered walls add character.

◑ Closed 25 & 26 Dec   ⚡ In Market Place, off the High Street. Private car park   🛏 1 twin, 6 double, 1 family room; 3 with bathroom/WC, 5 with shower/WC; TV, room service, hair-dryer, direct-dial telephone   ✓ Restaurant, bar, lounge, drying-room, garden; early suppers for children; toys, baby-listening, high chair   ♿ Wheelchair access to hotel (1 step) and restaurant, 1 ground-floor bedroom   ● Dogs allowed in bar and in bedrooms by arrangement only   ▭ Access, Amex, Delta, Switch, Visa   £ Single occupancy of twin/double £38 to £48, twin/double £50 to £60, family room £60 to £70; deposit required. Alc L £10, D £15. Special breaks available

Great House

Market Place, Lavenham CO10 9QZ
TEL: (01787) 247431 FAX: (01787) 248007

Smart oasis of Gallic charm and rusticity in the centre of a classic English village.

The façade looks archetypally English: smart, white Georgian proportions, sash windows framed in dark green, and window boxes bursting with colour. The interior, however, dates from some three to four hundred years earlier than the Georgian period, with creaky wooden floors, low ceilings and enough strange angles and bumps to render plumb lines redundant. To these attractive features Martine and Regis Crepy have added a little touch from across the Channel, starting with the Napoleonic cut-out figure that greets you as you enter, and continuing with an eclectic mix of antiques and curios, crooning *chanteuses* during Saturday lunch, and a menu featuring French classics such as onion soup, moules marinière and tournedos Rossini (though there is the occasional nod to Italy, too, with items like melon with Parma ham and tiramisù creeping in). The restaurant is a delightful place in which to do the food justice, with crisp, white linen and the glow from the fire in the vast inglenook lighting up the rosy walls. Alternatively, for summer suppers, there's a lovely little secluded courtyard at the back filled with flowers and foliage. There are only four rooms – more like suites, really, most with separate sitting areas – furnished in a similarly appealingly mix-and-match style to the rest of the building, with faded rugs, antique beds and unusual fire screens. The pick of the bunch is Room 4, right at the top, which has two bedrooms separated by a lounge.

◐ Open all year; restaurant closed Sun eve and Mon ☒ In Lavenham's Market Place. Public car park nearby ⊨ 2 twin, 2 double; family rooms and suites available; 3 with bathroom/WC, 1 with shower/WC; TV, room service, hair-dryer, direct-dial telephone ⊘ Restaurant, bar, lounge, garden; conference facilities (max 10 people incl up to 4 residential); early suppers for children; toys, baby-listening, outdoor games, cots, high chairs ⅙ No wheelchair access ● No dogs in public rooms; smoking discouraged in public rooms ▭ Access, Amex, Delta, Visa £ Single occupancy of twin/double £40 to £50, twin/double £50 to £78, family room £60 to £88, suite £50 to £78; deposit required. Set L £10/13, Sun L £17, D £17, alc D £25; light lunches available. Special breaks available

---

The Swan

High Street, Lavenham, Sudbury CO10 9QA
TEL: (01787) 247477   FAX: (01787) 248286

A wonderful medieval landmark, sympathetically restored and extended.

The Swan makes the most of its venerable history – which dates back over 500 years – but then in Lavenham, crooked half-timbering and creaky wooden floors are not so unusual. Situated in a busy corner of this touristy village, the hotel was luring in a fair bit of passing trade for lunch when we inspected on a sunny bank-holiday Monday. The public rooms include a series of interlocking lounges – decorated in deep greens and reds, featuring Chinese lamps, and hung with brass and copper artefacts and modern tapestries – and a cosy bar, which contains memorabilia of the air crews that were stationed in the village during the Second World War. On pleasant days there's also a small garden behind the Swan, in which the white garden furniture is set off by terraces of shrubs and spring daffodils. For more formal occasions, the restaurant offers set-price menus, including dishes such as cream of asparagus soup, braised lamb shank served with vegetables and rosemary, and sticky-toffee pudding. The bar meals are much more limited, but the service – even under pressure – is courteous and helpful. As you would expect in a chain hotel (formerly owned by Forte Heritage – now Granada), the bedrooms are uniform in both style and standard of furnishings, although they vary in size, depending on what the joinery allows. Similarly, some bathrooms may be ingeniously squeezed in beneath the eaves.

○ Open all year 🔼 In centre of Lavenham, on A1141. Private car park 🛏 7 single, 12 twin, 22 double, 3 four-poster, 2 suites; all with bathroom/WC; TV, room service, hair-dryer, trouser press, direct-dial telephone ⊘ Restaurant, 2 bars, 5 lounges, garden; conference facilities (max 50 people incl up to 46 residential); early suppers for children; babysitting, baby-listening ♿ No wheelchair access ● No dogs in restaurant or bars; no smoking in restaurant ▭ Access, Amex, Delta, Diners, Switch, Visa £ Single £75, single occupancy of twin/double £90, twin/double £120, four-poster £140, suite £145; deposit required. Continental B £8, cooked B £10; set L £16, D £25; alc L £25, D £35; bar meals available. Special breaks available

---

LEAMINGTON SPA Warwickshire   map 5

The Lansdowne

87 Clarendon Street, Leamington Spa CV32 4PF
TEL: (01926) 450505   FAX: (01926) 421313

A dainty, long-established, town-house hotel in the centre of Leamington Spa.

Though the sign by the reception desk says 'one nice person and one old grouch live here,' both owners – Gillian and David Allen – are likely to be most welcoming. They have been fine-tuning their hospitality at their Regency town house for some 18 years now. Behind the green, creepered façade lie a profusion of flowers, a smart, black and white tiled hall, and handsome fireplaces, button-back and period furnishings in the quaint bar and sitting-room. By comparison, the small restaurant comes across as a bit guesthousey. The keenly priced menus, which change daily, contain crudités, interesting soups, Aberdeen Angus steaks, fish dishes such as brill baked in puff pastry, and puddings such as apple flan and cheese platters. Coffee, served with home-made petits fours, rounds off the proceedings.

Smart pine furnishings typify the fetching bedrooms. A few have no *en suite* facilities, and this is reflected in their low rates. Light sleepers should ask for a room at the rear: the hotel stands at a busy junction.

○ Open all year 🔼 In Leamington Spa town centre, at the junction of Warwick Street and Clarendon Street. Private car park 🛏 7 single, 4 twin, 3 double, 1 family room; some with bathroom/WC, most with shower/WC; TV, hair-dryer, direct-dial telephone, clock radio ⊘ Restaurant, bar, lounge, garden; early suppers for children ♿ No wheelchair access ● No children under 5; no dogs; no smoking in restaurant ▭ Access, Delta, Visa £ Single £30 to £50, single occupancy of twin/double £35 to £55, twin/double £40 to £62, family room from £50; deposit required. Set D £15/18; alc D £22. Special breaks available

York House   𝓛

9 York Road, Leamington Spa CV31 3PR
TEL: (01926) 424671   FAX: (01926) 832272

An establishment somewhere between a simple, unassuming hotel and an up-market guesthouse, in a pleasant corner of Leamington Spa.

Sue and Robert Davis' house is one of a curved row of rather fine, three-storey, red-brick, Victorian residences that lines this quiet avenue alongside Leamington's Pump Room Gardens; the town's high street is a three-minute walk away. Inside, the building is cosily atmospheric, and its age is complemented by the décor and furnishings, such as rather grand fireplaces, thickly floral-patterned walls, deep-red carpeted corridors, tasselled curtains and a *chaise-longue* in the lounge; family portraits make the dining-room more homely. The Davises play down their food, but Sue will prepare either traditional three-course meals, or the equivalent of a bar meal – perhaps a gammon steak or lasagne. There's a good choice at breakfast, but the packaged jams let the side down. The bedrooms are decorated in unco-ordinated, modern, chintzy and pine-furnished styles. You can stay here inexpensively if you opt for a room without *en suite* facilities.

◖ Closed 23 to 31 Dec   ☑ From main parade in Leamington Spa turn right into Dormer Place, left into Dale Street, then left into York Road. Private car park   🛏 2 single, 4 twin, 2 double; family rooms available; 3 with bathroom/WC, 2 with shower/WC TV, room service, hair-dryer, direct-dial telephone   ✔ Dining-room, lounge; early suppers for children; toys, baby-sitting   ♿ No wheelchair access ● Dogs and smoking in lounge and some bedrooms   ▭ Access, Amex, Visa £ Single £18 to £23, single occupancy of twin/double £23 to £35, twin/double £30 to £50, family room from £55; deposit required. Set D £12.50; alc D £20. Special breaks available

---

LECK **Lancashire**   map 8

Cobwebs

Leck, Cowan Bridge LA6 2HZ
TEL: (01524) 272141 (AND FAX)

Small but luxuriously appointed Victorian villa with lovely views.

From the outside Cobwebs Country House may look like an unexceptional three-storey stone house, but inside Paul Kelly and Yvonne Thompson have turned it into a luxury country retreat with the emphasis on a personal welcome; guests' names appear on the doors of their rooms and welcome notes are laid on the beds. Despite the quirky name you need have no fear of shabby house-keeping here. The spotless bedrooms are decorated in a thoroughly feminine style some will find fussy, with crown canopies above the beds, floral wallpaper and lots of watercolours. The bathrooms are more low-key, the country views delightful. Yvonne takes charge of the cooking while Paul advises on wines, a theme picked up throughout the house, with maps of the great wine regions on the dining-room walls and wine reference books in the sitting-room. Among the many highlights of dinner at Cobwebs are Yvonne's double-flavour soups, accomplished by pouring from two ladles simultaneously, and a cheeseboard which showcases local specialities. Behind the house fields fall away to countryside described by John Ruskin as a 'priceless possession'; ask in reception for details of an eight-mile walk along the Leck Beck and past a salmon jump.

◑ Closed Jan to mid-Mar; dining-room closed Sun eve   ⤳ Leave M6 at Junction 36 and take A65 to Cowan Bridge; turn left for Leck; hotel is 200 yards on left. Private car park   ⤸ 2 twin, 3 double; 3 with bathroom/WC, 2 with shower/WC; TV, room service, hair-dryer, direct-dial telephone   ⊘ Dining-room, bar, lounge, drying-room, conservatory, games room, garden; snooker   ⅍ No wheelchair access   ● No children under 12; no dogs; no smoking in dining-room   ▭ Access, Visa   £ Single occupancy of twin/double £45, twin/double £60; deposit required. Set D £28. Special breaks available

---

LEDBURY Hereford & Worcester   map 5

Hope End

Hope End, Ledbury HR8 1JQ
TEL: (01531) 633613   FAX: (01531) 636366

Acclaimed food in a house with literary associations deep in the Herefordshire countryside.

Before they were the Barretts of Wimpole Street they were the Barretts of Hope End, and it was here, decades before her marriage to Robert Browning, that Elizabeth wrote her first verses. The present creeper-clad red-brick house with its surviving Turkish-style minarets retains the air of a lost domain, and chef-patronne Patricia Hegarty is very much its queen; her portrait hangs over the stairs, a homage to her culinary reputation. The public rooms hardly suggest the starving writer's garret of legend, but neither do they suggest the opulence of today's typical country-house hotel. Instead you'll find three light sitting-rooms furnished in a fairly homely way and dotted with antique chests and ceiling beams which add character to a stark modern style. Bedrooms are generally spacious and team pine with some rather battered pieces. The new Room 3, with its striped sofa, agreeable furniture and smart bathroom, bodes well for the future. Straightforward English food is served in a simple dining-room: perhaps celery, lentil and tomato soup, followed by venison medallions with Madeira gravy and pine-nuts, then baked custard with caramel sauce and praline. Hope End leaves correspondents divided. One described the house and gardens as 'faultless', and the Hegartys as 'friendly'. Another found it 'thoroughly disappointing': 'too expensive for the degree of comfort given' was his caustic conclusion. More reports, please.

◑ Closed mid-Dec to end Jan   ⤳ 2 miles north of Ledbury, just beyond Wellington Heath. Private car park   ⤸ 3 twin, 5 double; some in annexe; all with bathroom/WC; limited room service, hair-dryer, direct-dial telephone   ⊘ Dining-room, 3 lounges, library, garden; conference facilities (max 8 people residential)   ⅍ No wheelchair access   ● No children under 12; no dogs; no smoking in dining-room   ▭ Access, Delta, Switch, Visa   £ Single occupancy of twin/double £85 to £108, twin/double £120 to £140; deposit required. Set D £30. Special breaks available

---

All entries in the Guide *are rewritten every year, not least because standards fluctuate. Don't trust an out-of-date* Guide.

42 The Calls

42 The Calls, Leeds LS2 7EW
TEL: 0113-244 0099   FAX: 0113-234 4100

Ultra-smart waterfront hotel with top-notch facilities and unobtrusive service.

While developers were fantasising about transforming the seedy, run-down riverside streets just south of Leeds city centre into a twenty-first century housing and leisure zone, Jonathan Wix just jumped in and got it started. If you need any testimony to the minor miracle that has been worked here, have a look at the photos in reception of the three adjacent eighteenth- and nineteenth-century mill buildings which have been converted into one of Britain's slickest hotels. Several years on, the regeneration of the area is almost complete and the recent opening of the Armouries Museum has provided another welcome boost.

The hotel has clearly been designed with one eye on the business community and the rooms have a high level of facilities; while not everybody will want to use their desks, the CD and cassette players, satellite TVs and mini-bars will meet with universal approval. The styling is contemporary, with lots of greys and matt blacks and modern prints but, where possible, the Victorian architectural features have been left in place – so you may find an old hoist, once used for pulling grain up from the water, hanging from your ceiling. Many of the rooms have grand views along the waterfront. The hotel doesn't have its own restaurant but has a standing arrangement with many of the city's eateries (including the chic Brasserie 44 next door and the more up-market Pool Court at 42 round the corner, for which prices are quoted below) so that you can eat out and have the bill charged to your room. Public space is limited to a small bar area and the reception, both of which have amusing coffee tables and abstract art but a slightly clinical atmosphere.

Attention to guests' needs is very much a feature at the hotel and little touches like the valet parking service will be appreciated – especially if you've just negotiated the city's notorious one-way systems.

◐ Closed Chr; restaurant closed Sun eve and Bank Hols   ⊿ In centre of Leeds; opposite Tetleys Brewery Wharf on river. Private car park ⊫ 7 single, 25 twin/double, 6 double, 3 suites; all with bathroom/WC; TV, room service, hair-dryer, mini-bar, trouser press, direct-dial telephone; CD player   ⊘ Dining-room, bar, lounge; air-conditioning in public rooms; conference facilities (max 55 people incl up to 41 residential); early suppers for children; toys, babysitting, baby-listening, cots   ⅖ Wheelchair access to hotel, restaurant and WC (unisex), lift to 1 bedroom specially equipped for disabled people ● Dogs in bedrooms by arrangement; no smoking in some bedrooms ☐ Access, Amex, Delta, Diners, Switch, Visa £ Single £65 to £95, single occupancy of twin/double £65 to £140, twin/double £65 to £145, suite £110 to £220; deposit required. Continental B £7, cooked B £11.50; set L £12.50/17, D £23.50 to £37.50; alc L, D £32.50; brasserie meals available. Special breaks available

---

Reports are welcome on any hotel, whether or not it is in the Guide.

Haley's

COUNTY HOTEL OF THE YEAR

Shire Oak Road, Headingley, Leeds LS6 2DE
TEL: 0113-278 4446   FAX: 0113-275 3342

An elegant and welcoming hotel-cum-restaurant in a leafy and lively suburb.

For many, the word Headingley conjures up images of cricket, but it is Leeds University rather than the cricket ground which lends the area its true character. The large student population gives Headingley a youthful feeling, while the leafy lanes and imposing Victorian mansions add the impression of an affluent village. One such house is Haley's – an unusual, turreted building tucked away in quiet road.

Haley's public areas are relaxing and, with their plush drapes and ornate fireplaces, quietly elegant, while the bedrooms are neat and well equipped, furnished with one eye firmly on the needs of the business traveller and boasting smart bathrooms. The four turret rooms, with their large, curving windows, are more spacious and light, but are otherwise similar in style.

One area in which the hotel has really earned its spurs is in its cooking. Chef Jon Vennell changes his menu monthly, but is happy to cook a dish in a different style if you're not tempted by creations like chargrilled breast of Barbary duck served with a shallot confit and crisp celeriac in a pool of port sauce. Sticky toffee pudding or home-made ice-cream might follow. One reader praised the warm welcome and young, enthusiastic staff who were on hand to help with advice and bandages for a badly sprained ankle.

◗ Closed 26 to 30 Dec ⊿ Just off A660 Leeds to Otley road, between the Yorkshire and Midland banks in Headingley. Private car park ⊑ 8 single, 4 twin, 10 double; family room and suite available; all with bathroom/WC; TV, room service, hair-dryer, trouser press, direct-dial telephone, iron ⊘ Restaurant (air-conditioned), bar/lounge, library; conference facilities (max 30 people incl up to 22 residential); early suppers for children; baby-listening, cot, high chair ⅙ No wheelchair access ● No dogs; no smoking in restaurant ▭ Access, Amex, Diners, Switch, Visa £ Single £55 to £95, single occupancy of twin/double £75 to £102, twin/double £75 to £112, family room/suite £150 to £185; deposit required. Set Sun L £14.50; alc L from £11.50, D from £23. Special breaks available

---

LEINTWARDINE Hereford & Worcester   map 5

Upper Buckton Farm

Leintwardine, Craven Arms SY7 0JU
TEL: (01547) 540634

Smashing value and good food at a graceful Georgian home on a working farm.

At the time of our inspection the Lloyd family was celebrating a new addition: Hamish, the black labrador. Although he was keen to make our inspector's acquaintance, he was pipped at the post by Yvonne's son who, on seeing the car, ran over to open the heavy farmyard gate. As farmhouses go, this generously proportioned, whitewashed Georgian example tends towards the grand, with a pleasant verandah from which guests can enjoy panoramic views over fields, hills and the mill-stream. Rooms are bright and sunny, with a generous sprinkling of antiques and lots of prints and watercolours to hold your interest, plus a good selection of books, maps and guides to help visitors get the most from their trip to this area. A wood-burning stove, plus an array of ornaments and pictures and a pretty floral display, make the pinkish sitting-room cosy. Things move up a notch in the dining-room, where gleaming polished tables and tied-back drapes lend an air of formal elegance. Correspondents down the years have been impressed by Yvonne Lloyd's well-judged dinners: perhaps chicken liver pâté, followed by grilled salmon steaks with fresh asparagus and hollandaise sauce, then ginger pavlova with strawberries and cheese and biscuits. The bright bedrooms have fine views as well as decent furniture and cheerful soft furnishings.

◑ Open all year ⧖ Take A4113 from Ludlow towards Knighton; turn right at Walford for Buckton; second farm on left. Private car park ⟻ 2 twin, 2 double; all with bathroom/WC; room service, hair-dryer; no tea/coffee-making facilities in rooms ⍢ Dining-room, lounge, drying-room, games room, garden; fishing, croquet, table tennis, snooker; early suppers for children ⅙ No wheelchair access ● No children under 5; no dogs; no smoking ⊟ None accepted £ Single £35, twin/double £50; deposit required. Set D £16

Lewtrenchard Manor

Lewdown, Okehampton EX20 4PN
TEL: (01566) 783256 FAX: (01566) 783332

An intriguing, seventeenth-century country-house hotel redeveloped by hymn-writer Sabine Baring-Gould.

Even the experts are baffled by Lewtrenchard Manor, which is an extraordinary mishmash of authentic seventeenth-century architecture and Victorian additions, mainly made by the hymn-writer Reverend Sabine Baring-Gould of 'Onward Christian Soldiers' fame. He was certainly responsible for the circular dovecote and tower house, and for the statue of the gooseman in the fountain facing the porch – a copy of a larger version in Nuremberg. Baring-Gould also discovered the lavish plaster ceiling that now adorns the Long Gallery, and had it transported from Exeter to Lewtrenchard in a farm cart. Not surprisingly, then, his portrait takes pride of place at the top of the main staircase.

Sue and James Murray have restored the house, and have made the most of features such as the stone-mullioned windows, panelled walls, plastered fireplaces, and even a gold-leather frieze, while also introducing modern fabrics and wallpapers to brighten the rooms that might otherwise have seemed dark. All the bedrooms are individually decorated, and each has something to commend it: the stained-glass panels illustrating Aesop's fables in Hornsea; the plaster angel holding a crescent moon in Lyndhurst; the huge Jacobean four-poster in Melton; and the door leading to the garden in Sandown. The public rooms are equally splendid, with panels of heraldic glass in the hall and paintings of the virtues in a small restaurant. The dinner menus are mouth-wateringly rich: you could, for example, choose terrine of duck with wild mushrooms and a blackberry coulis, followed by a steamed fillet of turbot with crab mousse and a red-pepper coulis, and then a gratin of oranges with a Grand Marnier sabayon. James Murray's South African roots explain a wine list that is particularly strong on South African vintages. Guests with mobility problems will be pleased to learn that the back stairs now have a chair lift.

○ Open all year **☒** Take old A30 to Lewdown, then take road signposted Lewtrenchard. Private car park **⊨** 3 twin, 2 double, 2 four-poster, 1 suite; all with bathroom/WC; TV, room service, hair-dryer, direct-dial telephone **⊘** 2 restaurants, bar, 2 lounges, garden, ballroom; conference facilities (max 60 people incl up to 8 residential); fishing, croquet, clay-pigeon shooting; early suppers for children **ᕕ** Wheelchair access to hotel (1 step), restaurant and WC (unisex), lift to bedrooms **●** Children by arrangement only; no children under 8 in restaurants eves; no dogs in public rooms; no smoking in restaurants **▭** Access, Amex, Delta, Diners, Switch, Visa **£** Single £75, single occupancy of twin/double £75, twin/double £90 to £100, four-poster £111 to £130, suite £119 to £140; deposit required. Set L £16, D £28. Special breaks available

---

LEWES East Sussex   map 3

Millers

ℒ

134 High Street, Lewes BN7 1XS
TEL: (01273) 475631   FAX: (01273) 486226

An off-beat B&B with a cottagey feel and charming hosts.

Once you have overcome the quaint, but frustratingly haphazard, numbering system along Lewes' picturesque St Anne's Hill, the dove-grey façade of Millers gives no hint of the exceptional individuality of the sixteenth-century, timber-framed, house that it conceals. An excellent base for exploring Sussex's historic county town, the guesthouse derives its name from the succession of millers who sold their produce from the front, roadside, room. This is now the guests' lounge and dining-room, and is decorated in the style of a farmhouse kitchen, featuring a huge, walk-in, stone fireplace, and a monumental pine dresser that is weighed down with a mountain of fascinating *objets*. When we arrived, Tony Tammar was playing the old carved harmonium (which provides another surface for the accumulation of antiques). Breakfast taken here – in the company of the three resident cats – is typical of the care which Tony and Teré take of their guests, and features plenty of fresh orange juice, good wholemeal toast, and a filling cooked platter. The two bedrooms are roomy and boast huge, mahogany four-posters, as well as some fascinating curios.

○ Closed 5 Nov, and 20 Dec to 5 Jan **☒** In centre of Lewes. On-street parking **⊨** 2 four-poster; 1 with bathroom/WC, 1 with shower/WC; TV; hair-dryer on request **⊘** Dining-room, lounge, garden **ᕕ** No wheelchair access **●** No children; no dogs; no smoking **▭** None accepted **£** Single occupancy of four-poster £44, four-poster £49. Special breaks available

Park Gate House ☆

Constable Burton, Leyburn DL8 5RG
TEL: (01677) 450466

Small, rustic B&B well placed for touring the Dales.

A Canadian visitor to England wrote to extol the virtues of Park Gate House in Lower Wensleydale, calling it 'a beautiful and welcoming retreat for travellers in the Dales.' The name of this stone-built 1750s cottage comes solely from its proximity to the gardens and parkland of the Constable Burton estate rather than any previous function as a gatehouse. Geoff and Sandra Thornber have gradually been refurbishing the house to bring out its country-cottage character with pine furniture and pretty floral patterns in the bedrooms. At the time of inspection only two of the four rooms were *en suite*, though one of the doubles was about to be upgraded. Being right on the A684 is a mixed blessing: the road interrupts views into the gardens opposite and there's some traffic noise, but it makes access to the Dales and historic towns like Richmond easy. The guests' lounge is cosy and rustic with exposed stonework, low oak crossbeams and an inglenook fireplace; there's a good supply of maps and books on the area. Telly addicts won't take long to find the TV discreetly hidden in a corner cupboard.

◗ Closed 24 to 26 Dec ⊿ Between Bedale and Leyburn on A684, opposite entrance to Constable Burton Hall. Private car park ⊫ 1 twin, 3 double; 1 in annexe; 1 with bathroom/WC, 3 with shower/WC; TV, hair-dryer ⊘ Dining-room, lounge, garden ⅋ No wheelchair access ● No children under 12; no dogs; no smoking ▭ None accepted £ Single occupancy of twin/double £30 to £35, twin/double £40 to £50; deposit required

---

Arundell Arms

Lifton PL16 0AA
TEL: (01566) 784666   FAX: (01566) 784494

Historic roadside inn with comfortable rooms and a strong fishing tradition.

As soon as you spot Horace, a prize catch of 1942, installed in a glass case on the reception wall, you realise how much pride the Arundell Arms takes in its long fishing tradition. The nearby River Tamar and its tributaries are the cause, of course, and the hotel has fishing rights over 20 miles. Even if you've never fished before it doesn't matter since the hotel offers courses to suit even a complete beginner. The building itself has an intriguing history. What is now an elegantly furnished restaurant was once the village assembly rooms, while the bar used to be a courtroom and the conference rooms a school. The garden even accommodates one of only two original cockpits left in the country, albeit pressed into service as a tackle shop. Joining these disparate areas is a long, inviting lounge with armchairs and settees strewn across a slate floor and piles of magazines – mainly on shooting and fishing – ready to hand. Front bedrooms are double-glazed, although noise is hardly a problem now that the A30 siphons traffic safely past Lifton. Most have been refurbished to pair modern fabrics and wallpapers with older wooden furniture. Those in the new wing are more of a piece, with prettily tiled bathrooms. Chef Philip Burgess has won considerable praise for menus which mix interesting starters like saffron risotto with leeks, Parmesan and artichokes, with traditional sirloins (from an organic butcher) and lamb cutlets.

◑ Closed Chr 🅩 Just off A30 in Lifton. Private car park 🛌 10 single, 11 twin, 8 double; some in annexe; most with bathroom/WC, some with shower/WC; TV, room service, hair-dryer, direct-dial telephone, radio ✅ 2 restaurants, 2 bars, lounge, drying-room, games room, garden; conference facilities (max 100 people incl up to 29 residential); fishing, golf; early suppers for children; baby-listening, high chairs, cots ♿ No wheelchair access ● No dogs or smoking in restaurants ▭ Access, Amex, Diners, Switch, Visa £ Single £64, single occupancy of twin/double £74, twin/double £101; deposit required. Set L £17.50/32, D £26/32. Special breaks available

---

LINCOLN Lincolnshire   map 9

D'Isney Place Hotel

Eastgate, Lincoln LN2 4AA
TEL: (01522) 538881 FAX: (01522) 511321

An up-market B&B in old uphill Lincoln, but you may feel cramped if you're staying for some time.

There's nothing Mickey Mouse about D'Isney Place, a Georgian house with Victorian extensions situated yards from the magnificent cathedral – the city's premier sight. However, although you can relax in the large, peaceful garden in fine weather, there are no public rooms whatsoever, and breakfast is the only meal on offer – of necessity served in the bedrooms. As a result, it is important that these are comfortable and attractive. They generally are, and feature handsome fireplaces, stencilled walls, a mix of antique and modern limed furniture, bathrobes and fresh milk on tea trays. The standard rooms can be on the small side, however, so you may want to consider a larger, de luxe room, with the added boon of a spa bath and maybe an antique bed.

◑ Open all year 🅩 On the Eastgate, approximately 100 yards from the cathedral. Private car park 🛌 1 single, 3 twin, 12 double, 1 four-poster; suites and family rooms available; most with bathroom/WC, some with shower/WC; TV, direct-dial telephone; hair-dryer and trouser press in some rooms ✅ Drying-room, garden; babysitting, baby-listening ♿ No wheelchair access ● None ▭ Access, Amex, Delta, Diners, Switch, Visa £ Single/single occupancy of twin/double £53, twin/double £66, four-poster £86, family room £76, suite £86; deposit required. Special breaks available

---

It is always worth enquiring about the availability of special breaks or weekend prices. The prices we quote are the standard rates for one night – most hotels offer reduced rates for longer stays.

Harrow Inn

Little Bedwyn, Marlborough SN8 3JP
TEL: (01672) 870871

Victorian inn in a peaceful village with cheerful rooms and imaginative bar food.

Just past the little bridge crossing the Kennet and Avon Canal (a favourite route of walkers and cyclists), a sign advertising lunches and teas directs visitors to this popular inn in a village. The red-brick Victorian façade, chequered with grey flint and brightened by a few flower boxes, is relatively plain but appealing, setting the tone for an unfussy, uncluttered interior. Three interlocking rooms, painted in deep red, occupy the ground floor, with a log burning fire at the centre. At the front of the inn, the lightest and most attractive has stripped floorboards, a clutter of spice jars on the mantelpiece and a cheerful mural of a barge and steam train. Elsewhere there are soft green carpets, old maps and prints, and a large ship's wheel. Daily changing menus are chalked up on a blackboard framed by grapevine stencils; the extensive list ranges from traditional to up-market international. Sunday lunchtime, for example, offered the ubiquitous roast beef and Yorkshire pudding, and smoked salmon, but also scallops and duckling. The three bedrooms display a true zest for colour; sunny yellow, deep pink or green hues with bold printed duvet covers. The pine furnishings are simple and pretty.

🌒 Open all year; restaurant closed Sun eve & Mon   ⤢ Little Bedwyn is signposted from Marlborough. On-street parking   🛏 1 single, 1 twin, 1 double; all with bathroom/WC; TV, hair-dryer, trouser press   🍴 Restaurant, bar, lounge, drying-room, garden; early suppers for children   ⅗ No wheelchair access   ⬤ No dogs; no smoking in restaurant   🔲 Access, Delta, Switch, Visa   £ Single £25, twin/double £45 to £50; deposit required. Alc L £7.50, D £12.50

Elmdon Lee

Littlebury Green, Nr Saffron Walden CB11 4XB
TEL: (01763) 838237 (AND FAX)

Welcoming, smart but unfussy family farmhouse providing home comforts at a cheerful price.

Elmdon Lee has been owned by the Duke family for 70 years; the 900 acres of farmland is still worked by Robert, while his mother, Diana, divides her time between providing accommodation in the substantial Georgian house and running a crafts shop in one of the farm buildings. This is not one of those 'duck or grouse' low-beamed establishments: the vast dining-room, with wooden floor, polished antique sideboard and table, and oil portrait of Diana's mother-in-law's grandfather gazing down, could almost double as a small ballroom. A single diner here would feel lonesome indeed, but with more guests, the Wolsey Lodge approach of seating everyone around the same table perks up the atmosphere no end. Diana's main sources of inspiration are Delia Smith and Gary Rhodes, and a typical dinner might start with smoked duck breast with pink grapefruit, followed by salmon with watercress sauce, then coffee and amaretti cream. The green breakfast-room is cosier: here a vast inglenook takes pride of place (this was originally the kitchen, with a large range). Upstairs, the twin bedroom above the dining-room takes the honours for light and space, but the other three, including the single, are all of reasonable size.

○ Closed Chr 🛇 On outskirts of Littlebury Green between B1383 and B1039 west of Saffron Walden. Private car park 🛏 1 single, 2 twin, 1 double; all with bathroom/WC; TV, hair-dryer ⊘ 2 dining-rooms, lounge, garden; conference facilities (max 12 people incl up to 4 residential) 🦽 No wheelchair access ● No children; no dogs ▭ Delta, Diners, Visa £ Single/single occupancy of twin/double £30, twin/double £55 to £60; deposit required. Set D £16.50

LITTLE PETHERICK Cornwall

map 1

Molesworth Manor

Little Petherick, Wadebridge PL27 7QT
TEL: (01841) 540292

Elegant, rural B&B with welcoming hosts, convenient for Padstow.

A spiralling drive conceals Molesworth Manor from the passing gaze. From the outside it looks exactly what it is: a sprawling, seventeenth-century rectory which was taken over and drastically altered by Sir Hugh Molesworth in the nineteenth century. Inside, however, there's not a trace of clerical austerity. The genial hosts, Peter Pearce and Heather Clarke, have a great eye for furnishings. Ask the story behind any individual bed or sideboard and you will learn that they discovered it in a pub or were offered it by friends whose house it had outgrown. The stairwell is dominated by tall windows incorporating the Molesworth coat of arms in stained-glass; the lower part was concealed behind wood until Heather and Peter were creating their breakfast conservatory and suddenly glass glinted through. The newel posts, also boasting the Molesworth arms, were another great discovery. Each bedroom has a distinct personality: Her Ladyship's has a fine brass Victorian half-tester bed and a side window overlooking what was once a private bridge; His Lordship's has a handsome freestanding bath. Don't miss the period details...gas lamps re-fitted for electricity, old-fashioned wooden ventilation panels and a row of servants' bells in the hall. Peter and Heather don't serve dinner, although there's a dining-room for guests who want to bring in food from outside.

 This denotes that you can get a twin or double room for £60 or less per night inclusive of breakfast.

◑ *Closed Nov, Chr & 1 Jan* ⤢ On A389 from Wadebridge to Padstow. Through St Issey and Little Petherick, manor is 200 yards up the hill on the right. Private car park ⤺ 1 single, 1 twin, 7 double, 1 family room; most with bathroom/WC, 3 with shower/WC; tea/coffee-making facilities and hair-dryer on request ⚉ 2 dining-rooms, 2 lounges, TV room, drying-room, library, conservatory, garden ♿ No wheelchair access ● No dogs; no smoking ▭ None accepted £ Single £19, single occupancy of twin/double £20 to £33, twin/double £31 to £49, family room £53 (prices valid till May 1997)

LITTLE SINGLETON **Lancashire**   map 8

Mains Hall

Mains Lane, Little Singleton, Nr Blackpool FY6 7LE
TEL: (01253) 885130   FAX: (01253) 894132

A historic hall, serving as a secluded country-house hotel, on the banks of the River Wyre.

Since it was built in 1536, Mains Hall has had something of colourful history. Its origins as a monastery explain the existence of the numerous priest-holes and secret passageways hidden beneath the floorboards and behind the dark-oak panelling, and such devices may also have come in useful when the Prince Regent was wooing Maria Fitzherbert on the premises. Today, those of similarly romantic intentions should request Room 2, with its Elizabethan panelling and four-poster, although the *en suite* shower is a tad dated and dull. Of the other rooms – all individual in style – the best are Room 9, which has an antique half-tester and a patchwork quilt, and Room 8, with its antique brass bedstead and a Victorian bathroom lined with tulip-patterned tiles.

In the 1930s, a previous owner had a brainstorm and painted all the panelling white; thankfully it has since been painstakingly restored, and carved faces again peer out from the pillars in the entrance hall, while one of the restaurants features moody, blackened beams. The menu is similarly imposing, and features dishes such as a farmhouse-style pork-and-chicken terrine set in a pool of rosemary jelly, French Maigret duck roasted with wild herbs and served with a red- and blackcurrant sauce, followed by a dark-chocolate marquise laced with rum and sultanas.

◑ Open all year ⤢ From Junction 3 on the M55, follow signs to Fleetwood (A585) for 5 miles. Ignore signs to Singleton; Mains Hall is ½ mile past second set of traffic lights on the right. Private car park ⤺ 4 twin, 3 double, 3 four-poster; 5 with bathroom/WC, 5 with shower/WC; TV, room service, hair-dryer, trouser press, direct-dial telephone ⚉ 2 restaurants, bar, library, conservatory, garden; conference facilities (max 60 people incl up to 10 residential); early suppers for children ♿ No wheelchair access ● No dogs in public rooms; no smoking in bedrooms ▭ Access, Amex, Diners, Visa £ Single occupancy of twin/double £40 to £70, twin/double £50 to £90, four-poster £100; deposit required. Set L £15, D £20; alc D £30. Special breaks available

---

Use the index at the back of the book if you know the name of a hotel but are unsure about its precise location.

LITTLESTONE-ON-SEA Kent   map 3

Romney Bay House ☆

Coast Road, Littlestone-on-Sea, New Romney TN28 8QY
TEL: (01797) 364747   FAX: (01797) 367156

Stylish guesthouse in spectacular coastal location.

Romney Bay House has an illustrious past – designed by Sir Clough
Williams-Ellis (creator of the Italianate Portmeirion in North Wales), built for
Hedda Hopper, the American actress and journalist, in the 1920s, and venue for
parties frequented by Noel Coward. It is now a stylish yet relaxed guesthouse
run by Jennifer and Helmut Görlich. The white painted house with its red-tiled
roof stands at the windswept end of a private road on a stretch of coastline facing
the English Channel. To the rear of the house are two golf courses and in the
grounds there is a tennis court and croquet lawn (and Tom, a pot-bellied pig who
lives in the garden shed). Inside the house, the bright and airy dining-room with
its blue gingham tablecloths, wicker chairs and cream-coloured walls is lovely
for breakfast, while in the evenings the tables are laid more formally for one of
Jenny's set dinners. One reader wrote and said, 'Jenny is an excellent cook – the
four-course dinner was superb and there was a very good, selective wine list.'
The drawing-room with its open fire, comfy sofas and antique furniture is a good
place for relaxing, as is the look-out room – which as its name suggests looks out
over the sea and even has an antique naval telescope. The seven bedrooms are all
very comfortable and are decorated to a similarly high standard, although some
rooms are rather small.

◑ Closed Chr   ⊅ From New Romney head for Littlestone; pass Romney Hythe mini-
railway station; at sea turn left and follow signs for hotel. Private car park   ⊫ 1
single, 1 twin, 3 double, 2 four-poster; 2 with bathroom/WC, 5 with shower/WC; TV,
room service, hair-dryer, clock radio   ✅ Restaurant, dining-room, bar, lounge, library,
garden; conference facilities (max 12 people incl up to 7 residential); fishing, golf,
tennis, croquet, clay-pigeon shooting, boules   ♿ No wheelchair access   ● No
children under 14; no dogs; smoking in lounge and bar only   ⊡ Access, Diners, Visa
£ Single £40, single occupancy of twin/double £45 to £75, twin/double £65 to £80,
four-poster £75 to £95; deposit required. Set D £25; light lunches available (prices valid
till Apr 1997)

LITTLE WALSINGHAM Norfolk   map 6

Old Bakehouse

33 High Street, Little Walsingham NR22 6BZ
TEL: (01328) 820454 (AND FAX)

---

*Excellent restaurant with straightforward rooms in an attractive
pilgrimage village.*

In the eleventh century Lady Richeldis de Faverches had a vision of the
Annunciation here; Little Walsingham has been a busy pilgrimage site ever
since. The Old Bakehouse, despite its position on the narrow High Street,
provides a quiet haven from the throngs of ecumenical visitors. The building has

had a varied history: half of the high-ceilinged, beamed restaurant, now decked with pink cloths and hung with brass rubbings, once formed part of Gurneys Bank (owned by one of the five Quaker families who went on to found Barclays). Behind, the smaller, older, breakfast-room still contains the bakery ovens, though they haven't been used now for 25 years. Chris and Helen Padley's more modern kitchen continues to produce excellent food that finds favour with locals and visitors alike: maybe crab pastries served with anchovy sauce, followed by breast of Barbary duck finished with honey-and-ginger glaze, and then summer pudding. In the basement, the old corn store is now a cool bar hung with bird prints (both the Padleys are keen bird-watchers). There are only three bedrooms; with pine furniture, simple white woven or patchwork bedspreads, and well-thumbed collections of paperbacks, they provide straightforward, unfussy comfort. 'We know our clients, and we cater for their tastes,' says Chris. 'If the guidebooks like what we're doing, that's a bonus.' All we can say is – keep up the good work.

◑ Closed 1 week June and Nov, 2 weeks Jan/Feb, restaurant closed Sun & Mon (to non-residents), and Tue Nov to Easter **⤴** In centre of Little Walsingham. On-street parking **⤙** 1 twin, 2 double; 1 with shower/WC; TV, hair-dryer **⟡** 2 restaurants, bar/lounge **⟐** No wheelchair access **●** No small children; no dogs in public rooms and in bedrooms by arrangement; smoking in bar only **⬜** Access, Delta, Switch, Visa **£** Single occupancy of twin/double £23 to £26, twin/double £36 to £42; deposit required. Set D £13, Sun L £12; alc D £30

LLANFAIR WATERDINE Shropshire

map 5

Monaughty Poeth

Llanfair Waterdine LD7 1TT
TEL: (01547) 528348

Friendly farmhouse where comfort is elevated over style.

On the table of the hall in Jocelyn William's Victorian farmhouse you'll find copies of her illustrated book for children, *Bobsy Bunny and the Birds*. Few locations can be more auspicious for a teller of tales than this village amidst glorious frontier country with its Welsh name and (current) English allegiance, the inheritor of centuries of national conflicts and rivalries and the legends they produce. The sign for the border is visible as you leave the house, and much of the farmland is on the Welsh side. The house shows its red-brick Victorian face to the world, but it stands on the site of a twelfth-century monastery farm – the 'monaughty' of the title, put to the flame in a border skirmish. Its only remnant, a sturdy chimney breast, runs along the wall of one of the two letting bedrooms. These are cottagey in style, with lots of florals, and pine, bamboo or old-fashioned furniture, plus a decent selection of books. The sitting-room is a light, bright room with blue tied-back drapes, and sky-blue walls to set off a homely display of china. The pink breakfast-room is cheerful and finds room for a dresser bedecked with decorative plates, as well as a piano laden with family photographs. Views over wooded hillsides, sheep-studded fields and the Teme Valley are delightful.

○ Closed mid-Nov to mid-Feb ⤢ Monaughty Poeth is 3 miles from Knighton on A4355. Private car park 🛏 2 twin/double; family room available; TV ✓ Dining-room, lounge, garden ♿ No wheelchair access ● No children under 7; dogs in public rooms if other guests consent ▭ None accepted £ Single occupancy of twin/double £18, twin/double £36. Special breaks available

---

LONG CRENDON Buckinghamshire   map 3

Angel Inn ☆

Bicester Road, Long Crendon,
Aylesbury HP18 9EE
TEL: (01844) 208268
FAX: (01844) 238569

Characterful restaurant-with-rooms with busy, informal atmosphere.

From the outside, this converted sixteenth-century inn wouldn't stop you in your tracks. But once you are settled indoors, it's the sort of place you could dawdle in for hours. Primarily a restaurant-with-rooms, the Angel doesn't pretend to be a luxury hotel. The reception area has a rustic feel and doubles as a lounge, with old sofas in front of a log-burning stove, and fresh flowers arranged in a champagne bucket on an ancient wooden chest. The owner and chef, Mark Jones, is quick to point out that sometimes meals can go on into the early hours and as the bedrooms are above the restaurant, you'd be better off staying up and joining in. It's no wonder people linger at the table as the food and hospitality are superb – and staff are good-humoured even when busy. Breakfast, in front of a fire in the beamed, dark green dining-room, or in the sunny front-room, with its scrubbed tables and high-backed settles, includes kidneys and black pudding as well as kippers and smoked haddock. Dinner is served in any one of the small rooms leading from the bar area – the most interesting dining-seats are those fashioned from old wooden church pews. Fish is delivered to the Angel Inn three times weekly from Scotland, Cornwall or Billingsgate and this is reflected in the extensive daily blackboard specials which cover every type of fish. You could start with a warm scallop and bacon salad, and move on to pan-fried skate with a gherkin and caper butter. Puddings are homemade – strawberry and almond meringue with strawberries and cream was crunchy, chewy and light. While the bedrooms are simple they are stylish and comfortable, with walls painted in strong colours, smart white bathrooms and few frills.

○ Open all year; restaurant closed Sun eve ⤢ 1 mile north of Thame on B4011; in centre of village. Private car park 🛏 2 double, 1 four-poster; 1 with bathroom/WC, 2 with shower/WC; TV, room service, direct-dial telephone ✓ 3 restaurants, bar, conservatory, terrace ♿ No wheelchair access ● No dogs ▭ Access, Delta, Switch, Visa £ Single occupancy of twin/double £40, twin/double £50. Cooked B £5.50; alc L, D £17

Hotels in our Visitors' Book *towards the end of the* Guide *are additional hotels that may be worth a visit. Reports on these hotels are welcome.*

Linden Hall

Longhorsley, Morpeth NE65 8XF
TEL: (01670) 516611   FAX: (01670) 788544

An up-market country-house hotel with its own health spa and golf course.

With its Tuscan portico, this ivy-covered, Georgian building has all the authority and dignity that you would expect of a house that was built for the first president of the Newcastle Mechanics Institute. Charles William Bigge – a friend and contemporary of Rocket creator, George Stephenson – was clearly a man who liked to get involved, since he was a partner in a merchant bank, a sheriff of Northumberland, the leader of the local Liberal Party, a mayor of Morpeth, the founder of the Newcastle Literary and Philosophical Society, and so on.

After many subsequent owners, Linden Hall has evolved into a traditional country-house hotel and health spa, and although it manifestly combines these two functions with great success, Callers-Pegasus Travel Service – which now owns the estate – is not resting on its laurels. At the time of our inspection, the creation of a golf course (scheduled to open in May 1997) was well under way, as were plans to transform the village-inn ambience of the pub into a more up-market restaurant and bar. The main public areas – elegant, high-ceilinged spaces featuring a mixture of antique and reproduction furniture – seem oblivious to the passing of time, however. Keep an eye out for the superb, French 'mystery-lady timepiece' that was first seen at the Paris Exhibition of 1878. The bedrooms in the two newer wings are bright, smart and well equipped, while those in the main house offer more period styling. Whether you need a manicure, pedicure, facial – or just a good, old-fashioned swim – such first-class facilities are also on hand.

◑ Open all year   ⤢ Off A697, 1 mile north of Longhorsley. Private car park
⊨ 2 single, 40 twin/double, 5 four-poster, 3 suites; family rooms available; all with bathroom/WC; TV, room service, hair-dryer, trouser press, direct-dial telephone
⍫ 2 restaurants, 2 bars, 2 lounges, library, conservatory, games room, garden; conference facilities (max 300 people incl up to 50 residential); golf, gym, sauna/solarium, heated indoor swimming-pool, tennis, croquet, clay-pigeon shooting, archery, snooker; early suppers for children; babysitting, baby-listening
ふ Wheelchair access to hotel (note: 6 steps), restaurant and WC (M,F), 15 ground-floor bedrooms, 1 specially equipped for disabled people   ● No dogs in public rooms; no smoking in restaurants   ⊟ Access, Amex, Delta, Diners, Switch, Visa   £ Single £98 to £110, twin/double/four-poster/family room £125 to £195, suite £195; deposit required. Set D £25; alc L £15.50, D £25. Special breaks available

---

If you make a booking using a credit card and find after cancelling that the full amount has been charged to your card, raise the matter with your credit card company. It will ask the hotelier to confirm whether the room was re-let, and to justify the charge made.

LONG MELFORD **Suffolk** map 6

Black Lion Hotel/Countrymen Restaurant

The Green, Long Melford CO10 9DN
TEL: (01787) 312356   FAX: (01787) 374557

*An exemplary restaurant and rooms, run with dedication and
enthusiasm.*

First came the Countrymen restaurant; building on its success, Janet and
Stephen Errington decided to expand, bought a seventeenth-century
coaching-inn on a corner of the Green, and added nine rooms to their bow, so to
speak. It also gave them the chance to experiment with different decorative
techniques – ragging and colour-washing feature throughout – as well as the
space in which to display their collections of plates (in the restaurant) and toby
jugs (in the bar). Variety is also the spice of life when it comes to Stephen's
menus: in the main restaurant you can choose from four set-price menus, or pick
and mix from the à la carte – a fairly traditional selection that might include a
smoked-salmon roulade and grilled rump steak served in a blue-cheese sauce. In
the past year, the Erringtons have also started offering informal options in the
bistro/wine bar, a pleasant room overlooking the Green, where you can order a
plate of pasta or a main course such as lamb's liver with mashed potato. Equal
thought and effort have gone into the bedrooms; the top of the range is the Green
Room, which has a half-tester bed and a separate sitting-room, featuring more
antiques. Many of the other rooms also boast four-poster or antique beds, pine
furniture, and stencilling in the bathrooms.

◑ Open all year; restaurant closed Sun   ⬀ On the village green, 2 miles north of
Sudbury on A134. On-street parking   ⮎ 2 twin, 4 double, 2 four-posters, 1 suite;
family rooms available; all with bathroom/WC; TV, hair-dryer, direct-dial telephone;
mini-bar in some rooms; trouser-press on request   ✓ 2 restaurants, bar, lounge,
garden; conference facilities (max 10 people residential/non-residential); early suppers
for children; toys, baby-listening, outdoor games   ㅤ No wheelchair access   ⊖ No
dogs in public rooms   ▭ Access, Amex, Delta, Switch, Visa   £ Single occupancy
of twin/double £50 to £60, twin/double £70 to £80, four-poster £80, family room from
£70, suite £90; deposit required. Set L, D from £14; alc L, D £20; bistro meals available.
Special breaks available

LONGNOR **Shropshire** map 5

Moat House

Longnor, Shrewsbury SY5 7PP
TEL: (01743) 718434 (AND FAX)

*Friendly hosts and medieval splendour in a peaceful Shropshire
backwater.*

The name might lead you to expect a chain hotel; chain-mail would be more
apposite. As the lord of a moated fifteenth-century half-timbered house in a
wonderfully tranquil village, Peter Richards seems an unlikely warrior.
Regimental prints, the large artillery shell by the door, and wife Margaret's

assertion that 'I was a TA widow' suggest otherwise. The evidence indicates that down the years the house has seen the odd bit of knightly, perhaps even kingly, derring-do. Sharp-eyed visitors to the upstairs grand hammer-beamed dining-hall will notice pictures of a pair of English Royals, and enquiries as to their significance are just the excuse Peter needs to show the carved wooden masks that line one wall, and to explain that the missing face is believed to be that of Henry VI. A Jacobean chest and wonderful carved chairs add to the noble period flavour. Dinner can be provided if requested in advance; perhaps smoked trout, followed by lamb Shrewsbury, apple and raspberry fool, a cheeseboard, and fruit. There are more venerable antiques in the large beamed sitting-room, although the electric fire and modern seating make it surprisingly cosy. Compared with the public areas the bedrooms are compact, but they're bright and comfortable, with chintzy soft furnishings.

◑ Closed Nov to Mar; dining-room closed Thur eve ⊠ Go through village past school and shop; turn left into lane signposted 'No Through Road'; where lane turns left, Moat House is straight ahead. Private car park ⊭ 1 twin, 1 double; twin with bathroom/WC, double with shower/WC; TV, hair-dryer ✓ Dining-room, lounge, garden ♿ No wheelchair access ● No children; no dogs; no smoking in bedrooms and in public rooms if other guests consent ☐ Access, Amex, Switch, Visa ⊡ Single occupancy of twin/double £40, twin/double £70; deposit required. Set D £20

LORTON Cumbria   map 10

New House Farm

Lorton, Cockermouth CA13 9UU
TEL: (01900) 85404 (AND FAX)

An inviting family farm guesthouse with bags of character.

New House Farm has occupied the spot where Lorton Vale spreads into an idyllic, grassy plain, sandwiched between the Lorton and Mosser Fells, for 300 years. Within, Hazel and John Hatch's whitewashed farmhouse is appropriately rustic – low ceilings thickly encrusted with timbers, burnished flagstones and exposed stone walls – but features some bold and vibrant touches. Pheasant feathers sprout from the fireplace in the hallway (betraying John's sporting inclinations), the dining-room is decorated in brilliant, flamingo pink, and a bright-red chesterfield sofa glows in the radiant sitting-room.

The house's old-world character has been enhanced in the three bedrooms by means of lots of stripped pine, bright, flowery fabrics, wildlife prints and silk flowers. Whiteside shares the lush pink of the dining-room, while Low Fell and Swinside are decorated in more tranquil shades.

Hazel cooks four-course meals along traditional lines that are strong on local ingredients – even something that John has hooked or shot. Depending on the season and a successful day, dinner might be salmon or roast pheasant, followed by a hearty pudding such as spotted dick or suet pudding, with a selection of local cheeses to round things off.

○ Open all year ⤤ On B5289 between Lorton and Loweswater, 6 miles south of Cockermouth. Private car park ⌁ 3 twin/double; 2 with bathroom/WC, 1 with shower/WC; hair-dryer ⍋ Dining-room, sitting-room, garden ⛿ No wheelchair access ● No children under 12; no dogs in public rooms; no smoking ▭ None accepted £ Single occupancy of twin/double £35 to £40, twin/double £60 to £70; deposit required. Set D £18 to £20. Special breaks available

---

LOWER BEEDING West Sussex   map 3

South Lodge

Brighton Road, Lower Beeding RH13 6PS
TEL: (01403) 891711 FAX: (01403) 891766

An imposing mansion with fine views and landscaped grounds.

Once the home of Victorian gentleman-explorer and botanist Frederick Ducane Godman, this grand house has commanding views over the South Downs from its elevated position set in acres of gardens. Frederick's ample fortune from the family involvement in Whitbread & Co allowed him to wander the globe in search of rare plants and artefacts which once formed a world-class collection. Inside, the oak-panelled walls and large marble fireplaces create a clubby atmosphere which is still redolent of the Victorian gentleman, although an abundance of fresh-flower arrangements and plush pink and cream rugs on the oak-block floors help to soften the effect. A softly ticking grandfather clock sets the scene for a sophisticated dinner of, perhaps, faggots of foie gras and rabbit, galantine of English duck, or lightly grilled brill with a bouillabaisse sauce. With the exception of the whimsically named Ronnie Corbett, the rooms in the old part of the house are spacious and kitted out in solid traditional style, with perhaps King George winning out thanks to the superb view over the Downs and an opulent marble and oak bathroom.

○ Open all year ⤤ On A281 at Lower Beeding, just south of Horsham. Private car park ⌁ 2 single, 9 twin, 22 double, 2 four-poster, 4 suites; family rooms available; all with bathroom/WC; TV, 24-hour room service, hair-dryer, direct-dial telephone; no tea/coffee-making facilities in rooms ⍋ Restaurant, bar, lounge, games room, garden; conference facilities (max 85 people incl up to 39 residential); tennis, croquet, putting, archery, clay-pigeon shooting, snooker; early suppers for children; babysitting, baby-listening ⛿ Wheelchair access to hotel (1 step), restaurant and WC (unisex), 9 ground-floor bedrooms, 1 specially equipped for disabled people ● No dogs; no smoking in restaurant ▭ Access, Amex, Delta, Diners, Switch, Visa £ Single from £110, single occupancy of twin/double from £135, twin/double from £135, four-poster from £175, family room/suite from £205; deposit required. Continental B £8, cooked B £10; set L £18.50, Sun L £21, D £25; alc D £38. Special breaks available

---

 This denotes that the hotel is in an exceptionally peaceful situation where you can be assured of a restful stay.

Lower Slaughter Manor

Lower Slaughter GL54 2HP
TEL: (01451) 820456　FAX: (01451) 822150

Accomplished food at a top-hole country-house hotel in one of the Cotswold's prettiest villages.

Lower Slaughter is one of those Cotswold villages that makes the heart sing, with its almost absurd prettiness, a knot of houses in glowing mellow stone through which the Slaughter Brook runs wide as it courses below a series of tiny bridges. Today's manor was largely rebuilt in 1658, but there's been a manor on the site since before the Norman Conquest, remaining in the family of the High Sheriff of Gloucestershire for over three and a half centuries. The owners celebrate the history of tradition of the house, and the well-drilled staff help guests appreciate its elegance and grace, without a trace of stuffy formality. The public areas are smart and tasteful, decorated in a dignified style that emphasises the delightful proportions of the rooms, and the splendour of the ornate plasterwork. This is at its finest in the restful drawing-room and gracious dining-room. In the latter, guests can dine from chef Alan Dann's menu, which finds room for both the innovative and the classical; perhaps button ravioli of chicken liver flavoured with tarragon, followed by Dover sole and hot pear soufflé served with its purée flavoured with cinnamon. The spacious, well-planned bedrooms are attractively furnished in appropriate country-house style, matching polished antiques with sumptuous fabrics. Bathrooms are luxurious.

Leisure facilities include a heated indoor swimming-pool and an all-weather tennis court, if you can resist the lure of the garden and the glories of the surrounding countryside. 'A bit "upper crust" on first appearances but friendly beneath that...Room and service high standard,' was one correspondent's satisfied verdict.

◖ Closed 2 to 9 Jan　↗ Off A429 towards 'The Slaughters'; hotel is on right-hand side of lane approaching village centre. Private car park　🛏 10 twin/double, 2 four-poster, 2 suites; some in annexe; all with bathroom/WC; TV, room service, hair-dryer, trouser press, direct-dial telephone; no tea/coffee-making facilities in rooms　✓ Dining-room, 3 lounges, library, garden; conference facilities (max 30 people incl up to 14 residential); sauna, heated indoor swimming-pool, tennis, croquet, putting green　&. No wheelchair access　● No children under 10; no dogs; no smoking in dining-room　⊟ Access, Amex, Delta, Switch, Visa　£ Single occupancy of twin/double £115 to £190, twin/double £130 to £205, four-poster £240, suite £260; deposit required. Set L £13/19, D £32.50. Special breaks available

---

Prices are what you can expect to pay in 1997, except where specified to the contrary. Many hoteliers tell us that these prices can be regarded only as approximations.

LOWESTOFT Suffolk map 6

Ivy House Farm ☆

Ivy Lane, Oulton Broad, Lowestoft NR33 8HY
TEL: (01502) 501353/588144   FAX: (01502) 501539

Attractive restaurant in newly converted barn with very comfortable rooms.

The Sterrys have had their work cut out over the last year, going from three rooms in the farmhouse offered on a B&B basis to full-blown restaurant with 44 covers and an additional nine bedrooms, some of them in converted out-buildings. Not to mention the flock of rare-breed sheep that graze the 40 acres of marshland, plus 'a menagerie of various chickens, ducks and turkeys,' as Caroline Sterry describes them. The car park still feels very new, as the shrubs planted in the raised beds will take time to mature, but elsewhere the conversions have worked well. At the heart of the complex, the Crooked Barn Restaurant exposes its high raftered ceilings and half-timbered and brickwork walls to great effect, set off by straightforward wooden floors and white cloths. The ambitious table d'hôte menu offers almost as many choices as the à la carte, in the vein of sauté fillets of mackerel on a bed of stewed leeks and caramelised onions, or saddle of venison en croûte with glazed beetroot and redcurrant sauce and crispy straw potatoes. For pre- or post-dinner drinks, there's the option of a small conservatory or more traditional sitting-room. The surrounding courtyard rooms, converted from further outbuildings, have plenty of space and are individually furnished in smart fabrics. Some, like Beech, are specially adapted for disabled visitors. The original bedrooms in the farmhouse are also still available, more old-fashioned and slightly cheaper because of the walk across the garden to breakfast.

◗ Open all year ⤤ From A146 (Norwich to Lowestoft Road), turn into Ivy Lane (beside Esso petrol garage) and drive over small railway bridge. Private car park ⤶ 3 twin, 8 double, 1 family room, some in annexe; all with bathroom/WC; TV, room service, hair-dryer, direct-dial telephone ✓ Restaurant, bar, 2 lounges, conservatory, garden ♿ Wheelchair access to hotel, restaurant and WC (M,F), 11 ground-floor bedrooms, 2 specially equipped for disabled people ⦾ No smoking in bedrooms; no dogs in some public rooms ▭ Access, Amex, Delta, Switch, Visa £ Single occupancy of twin/double £69, twin/double £89, family room £99; deposit required. Set L £15, D £20; alc L £20.50, D £22 (1996 prices). Special breaks available

---

LOXLEY Warwickshire map 5

Loxley Farm

Loxley, Warwick CV35 9JN
TEL: (01789) 840265

A romantic B&B in a quiet village four miles away from Stratford.

The Hortons' fourteenth-century home is the classic English cottage: black-timbered and creamy walled, with peek-a-boo windows peering out of the thatch and roses round the door. It's initially disappointing to discover that you probably won't be staying here, but worry not: the two main letting rooms (an unadvertised third in the main house is sometimes also used) occupy the almost-as-lovely Shieling, a seventeenth-century thatched and timbered bungalow in the picturesque garden. Unsociable types will relish being able to come and go as they please without bumping into their hosts. Both bedrooms employ pine furnishings to give a pretty and rustic but unfussy effect, and have interesting corner baths. They're separated from each other by a little, vaulted sitting-room and a useful kitchenette, stocked with fresh milk, jars of coffee, mugs and teapots. At breakfast – eaten round one big table – you'll get to glimpse the lovely interior of the main house, with its flagstone floors, low beams and shiny antiques. In the evening, the village pub – a five-minute walk away – serves good food.

◑ Closed Chr   ◿ Turn off the A422 at the signpost for Loxley. Go through the village and turn left at the bottom of the hill; Loxley Farm is the third on the right. Private car park   ⊨ 2 double; both in annexe; both with bathroom/WC; TV, hair-dryer   ⊗ Lounge, garden; croquet, badminton, bowling; cot   ♿ No wheelchair access   ● No dogs or smoking in public rooms   ▭ None accepted   £ Single occupancy of double £30 to £32, double £44 to £46

LYDFORD Devon   map 1

Castle Inn   𝓛

Lydford, Okehampton EX20 4BH
TEL: (01822) 820241/820242   FAX: (01822) 820454

An atmospheric inn offering lively menus beside the Norman castle in Dartmoor village.

The Castle Inn is not just right beside the ruined Norman castle which gave it its name, but is also painted a bright, unmissable pink. This is a real step-back-in-time place, and the pub itself is stone-walled, wood-beamed and usually packed with enthusiastic locals. A cosy snug, screened off from the corridor with huge wooden settles, is deservedly popular with younger visitors. At the back, the Forester's Restaurant is similarly traditional, its beams hung with ornamental plates. During the ongoing building of a new wing, the log fire must remain unlit, but that's a minor inconvenience. Mo and Clive Walker offer an unexpectedly lively table d'hôte menu, with a choice of starters like wild-boar pâté rubbing shoulders with main-course dishes like Provençale chicken with olives, herbs and tomatoes or spiced casserole of venison with a hint of herbs. The equally promising à la carte menu features desserts like lemon, wine and brandy syllabub, and apricot and pistachio rolls. Afterwards, there's a choice of ports to go with a local cheeseboard. Upstairs, wonky corridors link up small bedrooms, which are perfectly comfortable unless you have trouble sleeping on a slight slant.

Report forms are at the back of the Guide; *write a letter or e-mail us if you prefer. Our e-mail address is: "guidereports@which.co.uk".*

◑ *Closed 25 Dec* ↗ Next to Lydford castle and opposite the public car park. Private car park ⟜ 1 single, 2 twin, 4 double, 1 four-poster; family rooms available; 5 with bathroom/WC, 3 with shower/WC; TV, room service ⚡ Restaurant, bar, drying-room, garden; early suppers for children ♿ No wheelchair access ● No children under 7 in restaurant eves; no dogs in restaurant ▭ Access, Amex, Delta, Diners, Switch, Visa £ Single/single occupancy of twin/double £29 to £39, twin/double £44 to £55, four-poster £59, family room from £75; deposit required. Set D £16; alc D £20; bar meals available (prices valid till Apr 1997). Special breaks available

---

LYME REGIS Dorset map 2

Alexandra Hotel

Pound Street, Lyme Regis DT7 3HZ
TEL: (01297) 442010 FAX: (01297) 443229

Excellent service at a reassuringly old-fashioned seaside hotel.

The Alexandra is one of those pleasant, unassuming hotels which captures perfectly the spirit of a bygone age when seaside resorts were eminently genteel and calming places. Forming an L-shape round immaculate lawns on the cliff edge, the traditional, whitewashed villa also has magnificent views of Lyme's main attractions: the sea and the Cobb. Despite the hotel's old-fashioned seaside charm, little needs updating in the standards of service and maintenance. The welcome is warm and friendly, and housekeeping is excellent; bedroom curtains are drawn and lights switched on during dinner, beds are made while guests breakfast. The dining-room is smart and elegant, the conservatory alongside is a lovely sunny room, with light garden furniture and lots of plants, whilst the lounge is more cluttered and homely. Bedrooms, in contrast, are surprisingly modern with bright colour schemes and cheerful fabrics, all perfectly co-ordinated. Menus don't stray far from tradition (turkey escalope with pistachio, ginger and soya sauce, and scallops with Cointreau and orange cream were the most adventurous items on offer when we visited) but there's plenty of choice and the food is tasty and well presented.

◑ Closed mid-Dec to mid-Jan ↗ Head up main street of town (Broad Street) away from sea; take left fork into Pound Street by cinema. Private car park ⟜ 2 single, 6 twin, 11 double, 8 family rooms; most with bathroom/WC, some with shower/WC; TV, room service, hair-dryer, direct-dial telephone, radio; trouser press on request ⚡ Dining-room, bar, lounge, drying-room, conservatory, garden; conference facilities (max 30 people incl up to 27 residential); early suppers for children; babysitting, baby-listening, cots, high chairs ♿ Wheelchair access to hotel (3 steps), 3 ground-floor bedrooms ● No dogs in public rooms ▭ Access, Amex, Diners, Switch, Visa £ Single £35 to £45, single occupancy of twin/double £35 to £93, twin/double £45 to £98, family room £90 to £108; deposit required. Set L £10.50, Sun L £12.50, D £18.50; alc L £19.50, D £23.50; bar meals available (1996 prices). Special breaks available

---

Many hotels put up their tariffs in the spring. You are advised to confirm prices when you book.

LYMINGTON **Hampshire** map 2

Gordleton Mill Hotel

Silver Street, Hordle, Lymington SO41 6DJ
TEL: (01590) 682219 FAX: (01590) 683073

A small, sophisticated old watermill with a cosmopolitan approach and excellent restaurant.

Set in rolling countryside just north of the fishing town of Lymington, and surrounded by the New Forest, Gordleton Mill is up-market enough for the most refined of tastes and friendly enough for those requiring a relaxing break. The seventeenth-century creeper-clad watermill has been modernised with flair in stylish peach and white, with the restaurant in particular having been given the full Provençale treatment – the white beamed ceiling, back-to-plaster walls and wonderful aspect over the mill-stream make for a bright and sophisticated atmosphere. Outside, the terrace provides the ideal place to drink the complimentary half-bottle of champagne offered to guests on arrival, watch the sun set over the lily pond and anticipate the food being prepared by chef Toby Hill. His French cuisine is delicate and beautifully presented; among the choices you may find a terrine of poached pork knuckle layered with nuts and fresh herbs, served with a balsamic and hazelnut dressing and salad leaves, or pan-fried fillets of red mullet with a black-olive-scented sauce. The bedrooms, done out in pretty florals, are small but luxurious and inviting, with extras like fresh fruit and fluffy bathrobes. Six of the seven rather glamorous marble bathrooms are fitted with whirlpool baths.

Closed 2 weeks Nov; restaurant closed Sun eve and Mon. On A337 just before Lymington pass under railway bridge, go straight across at mini roundabout and take first turning on right into Sway Road, becoming Silver Street; hotel is 1½ miles on right. Private car park. 4 twin, 2 double, 1 suite; all with bathroom/WC; TV, room service, hair-dryer, direct-dial telephone. Restaurant (air-conditioned), 2 lounges, library, conservatory, garden; conference facilities (max 18 people incl up to 7 residential); fishing; early suppers for children. No wheelchair access. No children under 7; small dogs only and not in public rooms; smoking in 1 lounge and some bedrooms only. Access, Amex, Delta, Diners, Switch, Visa. Single occupancy of twin/double £97, twin/double £116 to £123, suite £129 to £136; deposit required. Set D £36 to £40; alc L £26, D £36. Special breaks available

LYNDHURST **Hampshire** map 2

Parkhill Hotel

Beaulieu Road, Lyndhurst SO43 7FZ
TEL: (01703) 282944 FAX: (01703) 283268

A wonderfully secluded country house with relaxed family atmosphere surrounded by New Forest ponies.

You have to drive slowly on the approach to Parkhill. There are ponies everywhere, and in spring the foals are testing their long legs across the roads and in and out of the trees. At night deer visit the grounds of the hotel, and all day the lawns are patrolled by the resident ducks. If you are really stealthy you may spot a badger. The building itself is a large cream-painted Georgian family home with a colonnaded porch flanked by cupid statues. As one reader summed up, 'Managerial style was relaxed and pleasant and there was a good atmosphere – the staff seemed contented.' All the rooms have wonderful views; the library is a perfect place to write a letter while looking out at the cedars. If you feel like being slightly more energetic, there's a giant chess set on the terrace. The spacious restaurant is partly housed in the old conservatory, and here you may try a duet of quail with chicken liver, garlic and mustard farci with a rosemary *jus*, or sample a delicacy from the separate and extensive vegetarian menu, while feasting your eyes on the illuminated lake outside. The most expensive bedrooms are called 'feature rooms' because of their views, and are worth paying extra for, but all the bedrooms are large, rather chintzy and comfortable.

○ Open all year ⊿ From Lyndhurst take B3056 to Beaulieu; Parkhill is about 1 mile on right. Private car park ⊨ 6 twin/double, 7 double, 2 four-poster, 4 suites; family rooms available; some in annexe; all with bathroom/WC; TV, room service, hair-dryer, trouser press, direct-dial telephone; iron in some rooms ⊘ Restaurant, bar, lounge, library, conservatory, garden; conference facilities (max 60 people incl up to 19 residential); fishing, heated outdoor swimming-pool, putting green, croquet; early suppers for children; babysitting, baby-listening ⅄ No wheelchair access ● Dogs in annexe bedrooms only; no smoking in restaurant ▭ Access, Amex, Delta, Diners, Switch, Visa £ Single occupancy of twin/double £60 to £81, twin/double £98 to £142, four-poster £142, family room £142, suite £108 to £152; deposit required. Set L £16.50, D £27.50; alc L from £11.50, D from £21.50. Special breaks available

---

LYNMOUTH Devon map 1

Rising Sun Hotel

Harbourside, Lynmouth EX35 6EQ
TEL: (01598) 753223   FAX: (01598) 753480

Partially thatched, partially medieval, pub-hotel in a lovely harbourside setting.

On a sunny day the Rising Sun is almost absurdly picturesque. Lynmouth has grown up around this hotel, which started life in the fourteenth century and has managed to hold on to its prime waterside setting. Over the years, however, extra bits have been added on, and the hotel now runs up the hill, with separate front doors leading into groups of rooms as if they were individual houses. Inevitably, given the age of the building, some of the rooms are quite small, and creaky floorboards can be irritating. On the other hand, if you value character above space, all the comforts are here; there's even a cottage-suite where the poet Shelley honeymooned in 1812. In the evening, the candlelit dining-room, with its panelled walls, orchids on the table and huge mirror, is simply magical. There's no set menu and our inspector felt that prices on the à la carte menu added up rather alarmingly. However, the scallops and sea bass in a raspberry sauce were delicious, and the cheeseboard sported a fine West Country selection. Although there's a small lounge, many guests will prefer to spend their evenings in the popular bar. In summer months, parking is likely to be rather a problem, best solved by stopping briefly at the hotel to leave your bags before proceeding to the car park, a few minutes' walk round the corner.

○ Open all year ⊅ Next to harbour in Lynmouth. On-street parking ⏎ 1 single, 2 twin, 9 double, 3 four-poster, 1 suite; some in annexe; some with bathroom/WC, most with shower/WC; TV, room service, direct-dial telephone; hair-dryer on request
✥ Dining-room, bar, lounge, drying-room, garden; fishing; early suppers for children
⅍ No wheelchair access ● No children under 7; dogs in bar only; no smoking in dining-room and some bedrooms ⊏ Access, Amex, Delta, Diners, Switch, Visa
£ Single £45, single occupancy of twin/double £60, twin/double from £79, four-poster £99, suite £130; deposit required. Alc L, D from £21.50. Special breaks available

---

LYNTON Devon   map 1

Bear Hotel

Lydiate Lane, Lynton EX35 6AJ
TEL: (01598) 753391

A partly Georgian town house in a quiet back street, where the style sometimes descends into the twee.

Much praise is heaped by readers this year on the former Waterloo House, where an attractive, three-storey Victorian bay wing has been added on to the more sedate, now listed, Georgian house. Inside there are two lounges: one, for non-smokers, is clean and bright and dotted with teddy bears (one of the reasons for the hotel's change of name – Sheila Mountis has a thing about them); the other, for smokers, is darker and furnished with gilded mirrors and lamps. Sheila brought many of the furnishings with her when she moved from London, and one of the most striking pieces is the huge, carved sideboard that dominates a dining-room, which is prettily dressed up in pink and white. No matter what your dietary requirements, Sheila will be happy to adapt the menu to them, and she has a fine list of nut-free dishes to hand. Upstairs, the bedrooms also bear the imprint of her handiwork, with subtly marbled walls and not-so-subtly streaked ones. Perhaps the nicest are Room 6 – a family room able to accommodate up to five people in three fairly separate areas – and Room 5, which is tucked under the eaves. The corridor bookshelves offer a wide range of reading matter: everything from poetry to Margaret Thatcher's autobiography. A reader commented that the 'staff and owners are helpful beyond the call of duty,' and that 'the food is of excellent quality.'

○ Closed for owner's holidays ⊅ Take turning opposite Lynton Town Hall. Turn left at the end of the road; hotel is on the right. Private car park ⏎ 2 single, 3 twin, 3 double, 1 four-poster, 3 suites; family room available; some with bathroom/WC, some with shower/WC; TV, limited room service; hair-dryer on request ✥ Dining-room, 2 lounges, TV room, drying-room; early suppers for children; baby-listening ⅍ No wheelchair access ● No dogs in dining-room; no smoking in 1 lounge and some bedrooms ⊏ None accepted £ Single £20 to £27, single occupancy of twin/double from £25, twin/double £40 to £54, four-poster £48, family room from £40, suite £54; deposit required. Set D £12.50. Special breaks available

Highcliffe House ☆

Sinai Hill, Lynton EX35 6AR
TEL: (01598) 752235 (AND FAX)

Spectacularly sited Victorian hotel, newly refurbished, with promising menus.

Steven Phillips and John Bishop have recently taken over Highcliffe House, which must boast one of the finest settings in central Lynton, with panoramic views of the sea framed by the Canterbury Cliffs. Almost their first act was to construct a proper drive with parking and turning space to save guests what used to be a long hike up from town. With a velvet-padded window seat wrapping round the bay window, the spacious lounge takes full advantage of the views, as does the smaller lounge in a conservatory beyond the dining-room. Classical music plays at meal times in an elegant dining-room which features an elaborate tiled fireplace and some of Steven and John's antique collection. Food here has already received very favourable reviews, hardly surprisingly when one table d'hôte menu kicks off with Gordon's gin tomato soup. In refurbishing the hotel Steven and John have tried to recapture its Victorian ambience; once-hidden fireplaces have been uncovered again and furnishings tend to be antique rather than modern. The bedrooms all have *en suite* facilities and lots of extras like complimentary sherry and toffees. More reports, please.

◑ Open all year   ⤢ Take A39 through Lynmouth; at top of hill fork right; turn left at public car park; go up Sinai Hill, hotel is on left-hand side. Private car park   ⊫ 2 twin, 6 double, 1 four-poster; all with bathroom/WC; TV, room service, hair-dryer
✧ Dining-room, lounge, conservatory, garden; horse-riding   ⅋ No wheelchair access   ● No children; no dogs; no smoking   ▭ Access, Delta, Switch, Visa
⌸ Single occupancy of twin/double £50, twin/double £70, four-poster £70. Set D £18.50. Special breaks available

---

Valley House

Lynbridge Road, Lynton EX35 6BD
TEL: (01598) 752285

Homely, small hotel with stunning views across the Lyn Valley.

You need a nifty way with the first gear to negotiate the drive up to Valley House, but after that (and Russell and Joan Herbert are emphatic that they haven't lost any guests), a much gentler path through vegetation luxurious enough to be from a tropical hill-station leads to the front door. Inevitably, the best rooms here boast spectacular views, and Rooms 2 and 4 have wide balconies on which to sit and soak up birdsong and the sounds of a nearby waterfall. Should you be feeling more energetic, several footpaths pass the house and Russell and Joan will be happy to advise. Their lounge is comfortable and homely rather than smart, but that's likely to be just what you want at the end of a hard day's trekking in the hills. After a fortuitous meeting with a woman who had worked as a nanny at Valley House in its previous existence, the Herberts have returned the two upper floors to their original condition, with six *en suite* rooms (confusingly numbered 2 to 7) instead of the ten they inherited five years ago.

Room 7 is especially attractive, with roundels of glass in the windows and a newer skylight to let in more sun, but Room 5 has an interesting layout, with twin beds under the eaves and a bathroom with fine views round the corner. In what is a nice touch, guests can choose between a full table d'hôte menu with traditional dishes like pork with apples and cider, and a lighter evening meal of, say, chilli con carne or lasagne.

○ Open all year ☑ On B3234 Lynmouth to Barnstaple road at top of Lynmouth Hill. Private car park ⟶ 1 twin, 1 twin/double, 4 double; family room available; 2 with bathroom/WC, 4 with shower/WC; TV; hair-dryer on request ✓ Dining-room, bar, lounge, conservatory, garden; early suppers for children 𝄐 No wheelchair access ● No children under 9; no dogs in dining-room and in bedrooms by arrangement only; no smoking ☐ Access, Amex, Delta, Switch, Visa £ Single occupancy of twin/double £18 to £30, twin/double £36 to £60, family room from £54; deposit required. Set D £10/15. Special breaks available

---

MADELEY Shropshire map 5

Madeley Court Hotel

Castlefields Way, Madeley, Telford TF7 5DW
TEL: (01952) 680068 FAX: (01952) 684275

Modern facilities feature in an evocative sixteenth-century manor house that is handy for the Ironbridge museums.

When our inspector called, maidens and swains dressed in Elizabethan costume (members of a period music society) were milling around the golden courtyard of Madeley Court, a Salopian manor house situated incongruously close to Telford new town. It's hard to think of a more fitting setting for the Tudor garb of the musicians than this grand house, with its impressive, arched gateway, coats of arms and leaded windows. The Muzak and pastel shades of the modern contract furnishings jar a little in the vaulted reception area, but for the most part the decoration of the public areas is in keeping with the antiquity of the house. Panelling and stone fireplaces add distinction to a couple of cosy seating areas, but the highlight is the Priory Restaurant – formerly the manor's great hall – in which a medieval painting crowns the inglenook, and suspended, iron-hoop lamp fittings create an atmospheric glimmer. The cuisine is modern and imaginative, and a typical menu might include a shredded roast-goose and apple salad, followed by braised leg of lamb glazed with honey and served with a tropical salsa, and finally a hot flambé of mixed berries. Less formal fare is served in the brasserie in the undercroft.

Anyone with a romantic soul will prefer to climb the creaking, wooden spiral staircase to reach one of the beamed, antique-dotted bedrooms in the original house to strolling to one of the bright and comfortable, but essentially characterless, rooms in the newer extensions.

Please let us know if an establishment has changed hands.

○ Open all year ⊿ On B4373, off A4169, 2 miles from M54. Private car park

⊨ 8 single, 8 twin, 28 double, 2 four-poster, 1 family room; all with bathroom/WC exc 1 single with shower/WC; TV, room service, hair-dryer, trouser press, direct-dial telephone ⊘ 2 restaurants, 2 bars, 3 lounges, conservatory, garden; conference facilities (max 200 people incl up to 47 residential); early suppers for children; babysitting, baby-listening ⅙ Wheelchair access to hotel, restaurant and WC (unisex), 23 ground-floor bedrooms, 2 specially equipped for disabled people ⊖ No dogs in public rooms and in bedrooms by arrangement only; no smoking in 1 restaurant and some bedrooms ▭ Access, Amex, Delta, Diners, Switch, Visa

£ Single/single occupancy of twin/double £85, twin/double £95, four-poster £110, family room from £105; deposit required. Continental B £6, cooked B £8; set L £9, Sun L £9.50; alc L, D £25; brasserie meals available. Special breaks available

---

MALMESBURY Wiltshire   map 2

Old Bell

Abbey Row, Malmesbury SN16 0AG
TEL: (01666) 822344   FAX: (01666) 825145

A medieval ambience which will delight grown-ups, and child-friendly attractions too.

One of the brains behind this newly restored town-centre inn is Nigel Chapman, of Woolley Grange, Bradford-on-Avon (see entry). Nigel brought his child-friendly policies with him, so, like its sister hotel, the Old Bell has a 'den' in which parents can leave their offspring with a qualified nanny for the day; cots and extra beds which are provided at no extra charge; and menus for kids. But with smaller gardens and a fine sense of history, it's more the grown-up attractions that make it special. Founded in 1220 by the Abbot of Malmesbury in order to house visitors to the neighbouring library, it has claims to be the oldest hotel in the country. Despite the Edwardian additions, many features remain from the Abbot's time – carved-stone window surrounds and the canopied fireplace in the Great Hall, for example – but though traditional in style, the furnishings and décor are very much of the latest quality and comfort. Two lounges – one decorated in soft pastels with books and a piano, the other with deep red leather chesterfields – provide space in which to relax, while the elegant restaurant, with two Gothic fireplaces, polished Regency chairs, blue drapes and carpet and neutral-coloured walls, is a fine setting in which to indulge in duckling with braised lentils, cider and thyme, or a rib of beef with shallots and red-wine sauce. The bedrooms may have patchwork quilts, brass or carved-wooden antique beds, and Victorian-style bath fittings. The wistaria-and ivy-clad hotel could not be more central: the abbey is just across the square. From the gardens there are views over the Avon valley.

Where we know an establishment accepts credit cards, we list them. There may be a surcharge if you pay by credit card. It is always best to check when booking whether the card you want to use is acceptable.

◑ *Open all year* ⏎ In centre of Malmesbury, adjacent to the abbey. Private car park ⤶ 3 single, 3 twin, 21 double, 1 four-poster, 2 suites; family room available; some in annexe; most with bathroom/WC, 3 with shower/WC; TV, room service, hair-dryer, direct-dial telephone ✓ Restaurant, bar, 2 lounges, TV room, library, garden; conference facilities (max 35 people incl up to 30 residential); early suppers for children; playroom, baby-sitting, baby-listening, cots, high chairs ♿ Wheelchair access to hotel (1 step) and restaurant, 7 ground-floor bedrooms ● None ▭ Access, Amex, Delta, Diners, Switch, Visa £ Single £60 to £70, single occupancy of twin/double £70 to £95, twin/double £85 to £130, four-poster £125, family room £180, suite £150; deposit required. Set L £15, D £18.50; alc D £24 (1996 prices). Special breaks available

---

MALTON North Yorkshire
map 9

Newstead Grange ☆

Beverley Road, Norton-on-Derwent, Malton YO17 9PJ
TEL: (01653) 692502   FAX: (01653) 696951

An elegant country house, surrounded by pretty gardens, run with warmth.

Pat Williams' own watercolours, which feature on the walls throughout the house, add a nice personal touch to this elegant Georgian house. You'll have to keep your eyes peeled if you want to find it in the first place, however, as Pat and her husband, Paul, like to create the sense of entertaining friends in a country home rather than running a hotel, and consequently eschew anything more than a tiny plaque with which to draw attention to Newstead Grange.

There are lots of period flourishes in the house, as well as many original features, such as the shutters in a lounge, which have been carefully restored. The generous dimensions mean that there are two spacious lounges, one of which serves as the 'getting-to-know-everybody' room, and the other for post-prandial cordiality. In the dining-room in between, guests can enjoy table d'hôte dinners, which may include crème vichyssoise and roast leg of lamb. The 2½ acres of grounds which surround the house provide not only an oasis of peace among the chestnut and copper-beech trees, but also many of the fruit and vegetables for Pat's kitchen.

The bedrooms feature a variety of lovely antique pieces, from Belgian oak wardrobes to Art Nouveau dressers. Swagged curtains, mahogany half-tester beds and (in some bathrooms) Victorian ceramic suites, complete the picture.

◑ Closed 18 Nov to 13 Feb ⏎ From Malton follow signs to Beverley; hotel is on B1248, ½ mile beyond last houses on left and at junction with Settrington Road. Private car park ⤶ 4 twin, 4 double; 5 with bathroom/WC, 3 with shower/WC; TV, hair-dryer ✓ Dining-room, 2 lounges, garden; conference facilities (max 15 people incl up to 8 residential) ♿ No wheelchair access ● No children under 10; no dogs; no smoking ▭ Access, Visa £ Single occupancy of twin/double £40 to £45, twin/double £62 to £76; deposit required. Set D £16. Special breaks available

---

Prices are quoted per room *rather than* per person.

MALVERN WELLS Hereford & Worcester map 5

Cottage in the Wood

Holywell Road, Malvern WR14 4LG
TEL: (01684) 575859 FAX: (01684) 560662

A family-run country-house hotel with spectacular views, situated on the slopes of the Malvern Hills.

The name of this hotel conjures up an image of a small, whitewashed cottage, surrounded by woodland. Well, the Cottage in the Wood is certainly surrounded by woodland (7 acres in its own grounds alone, and then that of the Malvern Hills beyond), but a small cottage it is not. The hotel comprises three buildings: the main Georgian dower house; the Coach House; and Beech Cottage; and in recent months the Pattin family, which owns and runs the hotel, has carried out some pretty extensive refurbishment. Sue and John Pattin designed the restaurant around their collection of Indian pictures, and the result is a striking room, decorated in greens and pale golds, and filled with light by the full-length, Georgian windows. Their son, Dominic, is the sous chef, and guests can sample such dishes as fresh mackerel croquettes, then lamb and feta parcels, followed by a rum-and-banana trifle. This is very much a family-run hotel (Dominic's wife, Romy, is the housekeeper, and his sister, Maria, the general manager), thus adding to the level of service, which has been commended by several readers. One correspondent writes, 'We arrived after an epic drive through blizzards to a warm welcome and smoked salmon sarnies at 11 o'clock on a Friday night – it gives you a warm glow to have this kind of attention.' The bedrooms (spread across the three buildings), vary in size, but are well maintained and stylishly decorated, although one reader felt that they were 'probably crammed with too much stuff – remove the trouser presses and they would seem much more comfortable.' Almost all of them boast magnificent views.

Open all year | 3 miles south of Great Malvern off A449. Private car park | 4 twin, 13 double, 3 four-poster; most in annexe; all with bathroom/WC; TV, limited room service, hair-dryer, direct-dial telephone; trouser press in some rooms | Restaurant (air-conditioned), bar, lounge, garden; conference facilities (max 14 residential/non-residential); early suppers for children; baby-listening | No wheelchair access | No dogs in public rooms and some bedrooms; no smoking in restaurant | Access, Amex, Delta, Switch, Visa | Single occupancy of twin/double £68 to £74, twin/double £89 to £115, four-poster £115 to £135; deposit required. Set L £10, Sun L £13; alc L, D £25; light meals available (1996 prices). Special breaks available

The Old Vicarage

Hanley Road, Malvern Wells WR14 4PH
TEL: (01684) 572585

A Victorian vicarage in a quiet, residential area on the slopes of the Malvern Hills.

Several years ago, the clergy deserted the Old Vicarage for somewhere more modern, and the Gorvins moved in to run the place as a B&B in 1986. Built in 1860, the large, solid house still retains a clerical feel with its stone Gothic entrance arch and cruciform windows, and this quiet and dignified air is today cultivated by Michael Gorvin. The large lounge, which features a pretty bay window with views over the garden, is an unfussy room containing lots of book-crammed shelves. In the traditional dining-room – another room boasting a view of the garden – guests can enjoy the help-yourself buffet, as well as a cooked breakfast, or sometimes an evening meal (by prior arrangement only), which might consist of a cream of celeriac soup, followed by fresh salmon flavoured with coriander and served with a tomato sauce.

The bedrooms are all of a decent size and, despite being decorated in the Victorian style, are free of fussy details. Rooms 4 and 5, both of which look out on to the rear garden, are very quiet and peaceful. As in the public rooms downstairs, there are plenty of paperbacks to be found, just in case you find yourself short of a book at bedtime.

◑ Open all year; dining-room closed Sun　🔁 From A449, take B4209 Hanley Road to Upton-on-Severn. Hotel is close to Three Counties Agricultural Showground. Private car park　🛏 2 twin, 3 double, 1 family room; 3 with bathroom/WC, 3 with shower/WC; TV, room service; hair-dryer on request　✅ Dining-room, bar/lounge, drying-room, garden; early suppers for children; babysitting　🦽 Wheelchair access to hotel (1 ramp) and dining-room, 1 ground-floor bedroom　● No dogs or smoking in public rooms　🚭 None accepted　💷 Single occupancy of twin/double £28 to £32, twin/double £44 to £46, family room £52 to £56. Set D £14. Special breaks available

---

MANCHESTER Greater Manchester　　　　　　　　　map 8

Etrop Grange

Thorley Lane, Manchester Airport, Manchester M90 4EG
TEL: 0161-499 0500　FAX: 0161-499 0790

An airport hotel geared for business travellers but with individual style.

With jets soaring overhead and traffic thundering past outside, this hotel would seem to have little in its favour. But if you are looking for somewhere highly convenient for the airport and the motorways, and with more character than the average overnight rest-stop, Etrop Grange is the place. The original farmhouse about which the hotel has grown was built in 1760, and the recent extensions done in sympathetic Georgian style are blending in nicely as the bricks and gardens mature. Original features and reproduction furnishings have been combined throughout the inter-connecting public areas that flow from a parlour-like lounge through an Edwardian bar area to a smart restaurant broadening into a conservatory. Light meals and snacks are available all day to a background of piped classical tunes, while a more elaborate dinner menu, strong on fish courses, is served in the evening. Antique beds and Edwardian styling make the bedrooms something more than just a box for the night, and the original 1920s tiling in the bathroom of Room 15 is a treat. All looked in order at the time of our spring inspections, though we have received criticisms of the housekeeping from one reader. More reports, please.

◗ Open all year ⊠ Leave M56 at Junction 5, follow signs for Terminal 2 up slip road. Take first left, then left again into Thorley Lane. Private car park 🚗 2 single, 4 twin, 25 double, 6 four-poster, 2 suites; all with bathroom/WC; TV, room service, hair-dryer, mini-bar, trouser press, direct-dial telephone ✧ Restaurant, bar, lounge, library, conservatory, garden; conference facilities (max 85 people incl up to 39 residential); early suppers for children ও No wheelchair access ● None ⌷ Access, Amex, Delta, Diners, Switch, Visa ⟨£⟩ Single/single occupancy of twin/double £65 to £99, twin/double £65 to £104, four-poster £90 to £115, suite £100 to £140; deposit required. Continental B £7, cooked B £9.50; set L £13, D £22.50; light meals available (1996 prices). Special breaks available

Holiday Inn Crowne Plaza

Peter Street, Manchester M60 2DS
TEL: 0161-236 3333   FAX: 0161-932 4100

A grand old hotel brought up right to date, in the heart of the city.

During the turn-of-the-century heyday of the railways, the trains of the Midland Railway Company pulled into Central Station and the wealthy passengers were disgorged through the station's tunnel into the Midland Hotel, built in 1903, and intended to be 'the finest hotel in the world.' Today, however, the Central Station is the G-Mex Centre, and the Midland Hotel carries a rather unwieldy prefix – that of the Holiday Inn Crowne Plaza. The gargantuan red-brick and granite exterior, plastered with balustrades, balconies, carvings and mascots, has survived the years intact, while the interior has suffered mixed fortunes. The entrance atrium's décor is all luminous creams and reds, while the Wyvern Bar is an informal barn of a room, serving brasserie-style meals in front of satellite television. Elsewhere, there is a gloriously rococo French restaurant, and a carvery restaurant with its original fancy plasterwork.

Some of the marble panelling survives on the walls of the wide, vaulted corridors and the tunnel that connected the hotel with the station is to be restored to its former glory – part of an ongoing process of sympathetic renovation. The bedrooms run the gamut from modest single to hexagonal-shaped suite, expensive to hugely extravagant, and show all the hallmarks of an impersonal interior-design programme (including swagged curtains and swathes of bold colours), as well as a nod towards the building's history in the form of framed architectural drawings.

The 1998 Guide *will be published in the autumn of 1997. Reports on hotels are welcome at any time of the year, but are extremely valuable in the spring. Send them to* The Which? Hotel Guide, FREEPOST, 2 Marylebone Road, London NW1 1YN. *No stamp is needed if reports are posted in the UK. Our e-mail address is:* "guidereports@which.co.uk".

◖ *Open all year* 🅿 In city centre, just north of Oxford Road and adjacent to the G-Mex Centre. Public car park nearby 🚗 83 single, 60 twin, 146 double, 14 suites; family rooms available; all with bathroom/WC; TV, 24-hour room service, hair-dryer, mini-bar, trouser press, direct-dial telephone ⌀ 3 restaurants, 2 bars, lounge; air-conditioning in all rooms; conference facilities (max 700 people incl up to 303 residential); gym, sauna, solarium, heated indoor swimming-pool, squash court; early suppers for children; babysitting ♿ Wheelchair access to hotel (1 ramp), restaurant and WC (unisex), lift to bedrooms, 1 specially equipped for disabled people ● No dogs; no smoking in some bedrooms ▭ Access, Amex, Delta, Diners, Switch, Visa £ Single/single occupancy of twin/double £120, twin/double £120, family room £140, suite £180 to £399; deposit required. Continental B £10, cooked B £11.50; set D £32.50; alc D £35; light meals available (1996 prices). Special breaks available

Victoria & Albert Hotel

Water Street, Manchester M3 4JQ
TEL: 0161-832 1188   FAX: 0161-834 2484

Luxury city-centre themed hotel in an exceptional warehouse conversion.

Take two derelict and bombed-out riverside warehouses in a run-down inner-city industrial area, lavish millions renovating to an exceptionally high standard, add a generous helping of staff and garnish with icons of popular culture. The result is the Victoria & Albert Hotel, a huge spruced-up red-brick monolith filled with brightly painted girders, natural timbers and polished glass: it's part hotel, part showcase for the achievements of Granada Television. You can buy the latest news from the 'What the Papers Say' shop, drink in Dr Watson's Edwardian gentlemen's club and dine with Sherlock Holmes' diagnostic experiments bubbling away in the background or in Café Maigret, under the gaze of Michael Gambon as the French detective. The bedrooms are of the highest order too, combining modern styling with the original brick and iron fabric of the building, and all are named after a past Granada production with the appropriate stills and programme bumph framed on the walls. Twenty-five more rooms were under construction, in a seamless addition, at the time of our spring inspection, and if you still crave more TV history, the Granada Studios Tour is just across the street.

◖ Open all year 🅿 In city centre beside River Irwell and Granada Studios. Private car park 🚗 22 twin, 126 double, 8 suites; family rooms available; all with bathroom/WC; TV, room service, hair-dryer, mini-bar, trouser press, direct-dial telephone ⌀ 2 dining-rooms, 2 bars, lounge, conservatory, games room, garden; air-conditioning in all rooms; conference facilities (max 350 people incl up to 156 residential); gym, sauna, solarium, snooker; babysitting ♿ Wheelchair access to hotel, restaurant and WC (unisex), lift to 2 bedrooms specially equipped for disabled people ● No dogs ▭ Access, Amex, Diners, Visa £ Single occupancy of twin/double £135, twin/double/family room £135, suite from £250; deposit required. Continental B £10.50, cooked B £13.50; set L £18; alc L £30, D £35. Special breaks available

Goldstone Hall

Market Drayton TF9 2NA
TEL: (01630) 661202   FAX: (01630) 661585

A cheerful country hotel with jolly, imaginative hosts.

Although we've racked our brains, we can't think of another hotel in the *Guide* which can boast South American-style garden sculptures gracing its lawns. On first impressions, you'd never expect such an innovation from Goldstone Hall either – a rambling, but modest, red-brick building situated in a tiny village near Market Drayton – which only goes to prove that you should never judge a book by its cover. In fact, the sculptures are displayed as part of a Visual Arts Trust touring exhibition, the sort of esoteric event (such as Clive of India banquets and Russian folk-music nights) that makes Helen Ward and John Cushing's enterprise so different from the average rural hotel. The décor is generally conventional, and guests have a choice of where to unwind: in the large bar, in a panelled lounge, or in the bright and airy Green Room, in which antique pieces rub shoulders with homelier furnishings. A *trompe l'oeil* balustrade and classical urn add an unusual touch to the conservatory. The cuisine encompasses both classical and innovative dishes, so you might opt for moules marinière, followed by a fillet of beef wrapped in smoked bacon topped with an Irish-stout glaze and served with crisp leeks, and finally a crème brûlée.

The bedrooms are individually decorated; some, such as the pretty, stencilled Westcott, feature modish effects, while others, such as Ellerton, may have simple, wood-chip wallpaper, but compensate for this by means of fine antiques and attractive soft furnishings.

○ Open all year ⊿ Off A41 at Hinstock, follow sign to Goldstone. Turn right in village to hotel. Private car park ⤙ 2 twin, 5 double, 1 four-poster; family room available; all with bathroom/WC; TV, room service, hair-dryer, direct-dial telephone, radio; no tea/coffee-making facilities in rooms ⊘ Restaurant, bar, 3 lounges, conservatory, games room, garden; conference facilities (max 50 people incl up to 8 residential); billiards; early suppers for children ⅙ No wheelchair access ● No dogs; smoking discouraged ▭ Access, Amex, Delta, Diners, Switch, Visa £ Single occupancy of twin/double £60, twin/double £84, four-poster £94, family room from £84. Set Sun L £16.50; alc D £25. Special breaks available

Hob Green

Markington, Harrogate HG3 3PJ
TEL: (01423) 771589   FAX: (01423) 771589

Subdued elegance in a country-house hotel with 800 acres of award-winning gardens.

The slightly elevated position of Hob Green, at the end of a long driveway a mile outside the village of Markington, affords spectacular and peaceful views of the 800 acres of gently undulating countryside. The public rooms benefit from this but have other attractions besides. The drawing-room has some fine marquetry cabinets and yellow flower-pattern wallpaper which is outshone only by the real thing: eye-catching arrangements of fresh flowers around the room. A second, slightly more sober, sitting-room, though equally peaceful, has large oil portraits and soothing autumnal colours. The dining-room is an area of subdued elegance in which to enjoy dependable British cooking. Scotch salmon, fillet of trout, fillets of steak or medallions of venison might provide the basis of the main course.

Given the restrained elegance of the rest of the house, the bedrooms come as something of a disappointment though at the time of inspection some redecoration was planned. Room 1 is a superior twin with beige carpets and solid dark-wood furniture; Room 10 is a standard double with a predominance of blues. In most cases, the peace and quiet and lovely views redeem any shortfalls in design.

◑ Open all year ⚡ Turn off A61 Harrogate to Ripon road at Wormald Green and continue towards Markington; Hob Green is 1 mile through village. Private car park
⊨ 3 single, 4 twin, 3 double, 1 four-poster, 1 suite; all with bathroom/WC; TV, room service, hair-dryer, mini-bar, direct-dial telephone; trouser press on request
⊘ Dining-room, 2 lounges, conservatory, garden; conference facilities (max 12 people non-residential/residential); croquet; early suppers for children   ⅚ No wheelchair access ● No dogs in public rooms ⬚ Access, Amex, Diners, Visa £ Single £70, single occupancy of twin/double £80, twin/double £85 to £95, four-poster £102, suite £115; deposit required. Set Sun L £12; alc D £22 (prices valid till Mar 1997). Special breaks available

---

MARLOW BOTTOM Buckinghamshire   map 3

Holly Tree House

Burford Close, Marlow Bottom, Marlow SL7 3NF
TEL: (01628) 891110   FAX: (01628) 481278

Immaculate modern B&B with very well-equipped rooms, a few minutes' drive from the motorway.

After a day's work and perhaps a tedious drive, Holly Tree House is a business person's idea of a real treat, so they tell us, and you will be made equally welcome at the weekend by owners Tina and Mike Le Clercq. On the edge of a modern housing estate which makes up most of Marlow Bottom – a mile north of its more historic neighbour, Marlow – the house is on high ground overlooking rooftops. Inside, light modern rooms are beautifully kept with plenty of thought for guests' comfort. The five bedrooms vary in size – three of them have large bathrooms with corner baths. All are decorated in pastel colours and furnished with modern pine furniture, and have every facility you can think of from shoe-cleaning kits and irons to television guides. At breakfast in the dining-room, with its stone fireplace and orange pine tables, you can help yourself to a newspaper, and afterwards, if you have time to linger, the conservatory/lounge makes a sunny place to have your coffee.

◐ Open all year ⊠ 1½ miles north-west of Marlow, just off A4155. Private car park
🛏 1 single, 3 double, 1 four-poster; all with bathroom/WC; TV, hair-dryer, trouser
press, direct-dial telephone, radio, iron ⊘ Dining-room, conservatory/lounge,
garden; conference facilities (max 9 people incl up to 5 residential); heated outdoor
swimming-pool; toys ♿ No wheelchair access ● Dogs in bedrooms by
arrangement ▭ Access, Amex, Visa £ Single £58, single occupancy of
twin/double £63, twin/double £63 to £68, four-poster £69

MARTINHOE Devon   map 1

Old Rectory

Martinhoe, Parracombe, Barnstaple EX31 4QT
TEL: (01598) 763368 FAX: (01598) 763567

Welcoming Georgian house in Exmoor hamlet.

Since taking over the cream and stone Georgian rectory in tiny Martinhoe, John
and Suzanne Bradbury have been updating its unflashy carpets and furnishings,
with more than a little help from son Daniel, a cabinet-maker whose pine fittings
now brighten up the best bedrooms and decorate the dining-room. Here
Suzanne dishes up what she describes as home-made fare with the emphasis on
good soups. Dinners offer four courses with only limited choices but have drawn
praise from past visitors. After dinner guests can relax in the Vineyard
Conservatory, where a 250-year-old vine spreads its branches above them. The
Old Rectory stands in three acres of attractive grounds with a stream running
through them. Guests have commented on the homely atmosphere and the
warmth of the Bradburys' welcome – and the excellent attention to detail: beds
turned down at nights, immaculate bathrooms and fresh flowers in the
bedrooms.

◐ Closed Nov to Easter ⊠ Martinhoe is off A39, between Parracombe and Lynton.
Private car park 🛏 4 twin, 3 double, 1 suite; 6 with bathroom/WC, 2 with
shower/WC; TV, hair-dryer ⊘ Dining-room, 2 lounges, conservatory, garden
♿ Wheelchair access to hotel (2 steps) and dining-room, 2 ground-floor bedrooms
● No children under 14; no dogs; no smoking ▭ None accepted £ Single
occupancy of twin/double £65, twin/double £105 to £115, suite £130 (rates incl dinner);
deposit required. Set D £22 (prices valid till Apr 1997)

MARYPORT Cumbria   map 10

The Retreat

Birkby, Maryport CA15 6RG
TEL: (01900) 814056

A Victorian restaurant-with-rooms in a pocket-sized village
en route to the Lakes.

'An excellent place to have oneself spoilt by the host food-wise, drink-wise and
comfort-wise,' is how two satisfied guests summed up the Retreat, once the
country refuge of a Victorian sea captain, now a cosy restaurant-with-rooms. Ali
and Rudi Geissler originally bought the house as a family home, opening a

restaurant on the ground floor in 1985, and then adding three bedrooms so that diners need not worry about driving home after their meal. Captain Joseph Cubertson obviously had an eye for wood, hence the presence in the Retreat of several fine doors made of Honduran mahogany, and a framed letter in reception which discusses the mid-nineteenth-century trade in ebony from the Congo. The Geisslers have inherited his tastes, and the bedrooms also boast some fine, heavy, wood furniture, most notably Room 1 – a huge, alluring room featuring lots of pictures in big gilt frames. The polished timber tables in the restaurant echo the wooden theme. Rudi's four-course menus offer plenty of choice (unless you're a vegetarian) but few surprises; a typical meal might consist of melon served in sherry, followed by garlic mushrooms, then grilled lamb chops with mint jelly, and a sticky toffee pudding to finish. After dinner, you can relax in a lounge which leads through to a bar with panelled walls and a marble fireplace. The reception area is dominated by a grandfather clock which brings out the curiosity in guests: 'they do like to open it up and poke their heads in,' laughs Rudi.

◑ Closed 24 & 25 Dec   ◰ 2 miles north of Maryport, just off A596. Private car park ⊢ 3 twin/double; all with shower/WC; TV, room service, hair-dryer   ✅ Restaurant, bar, lounge, garden   ♿ No wheelchair access   ● No dogs; no smoking in restaurant   ▭ Access, Delta, Visa   £ Single occupancy of twin/double £34, twin/double £47; deposit required. Set D £18; alc L from £4.50, D from £7.50. Special breaks available

---

MASHAM North Yorkshire   map 8

King's Head

Market Place, Masham HG4 4EF
TEL: (01765) 689295   FAX: (01765) 689070

A grand old pub which is the focal point of this friendly market town.

The King's Head pub dominates the large, handsome square at the centre of this small market town, on the periphery of the Dales, which is famous for its breweries. Both Theakstons and its younger offspring, Black Sheep, have interesting visitor centres within easy walking distance of the King's Head, and there is a small craft village just behind the pub, where you can appreciate the glassblower's art, among other things. The bedrooms – furnished with varnished-pine dressing tables, decorated in plain colour schemes, and maybe featuring a fruit print or two – are nothing to get excited about, but are comfortable. The bathrooms are spacious, but on our inspection the provision of toiletries was niggardly.

Most people seem to opt for the informality of the bar, with its lively mixture of local farm folk and tourists, where they can enjoy decent pub grub such as farmhouse pâté and toast or Cumberland sausages, washed down with a dream of a pint of real ale. One regular visitor reported that the bar can be too crowded on occasions, so if you prefer a quieter setting for dinner, then there is a slightly more formal restaurant, featuring alcove seating and 'friendly and helpful service', according to readers.

◑ Open all year ⊿ In Masham's market square. On-street parking ⊨ᵣ 2 single, 1 twin, 6 double, 1 four-poster; 8 with bathroom/WC, 2 with shower/WC; TV, hair-dryer, trouser press, direct-dial telephone ⌁ Restaurant, bar, lounge, garden; conference facilities (max 40 people incl up to 10 residential) ⅙ No wheelchair access ● No dogs ☐ Access, Amex, Delta, Diners, Switch, Visa £ Single £39, single occupancy of twin/double £45, twin/double £58, four-poster £65. Bar meals available. Special breaks available

---

MATLOCK Derbyshire   map 5

Riber Hall

Riber, Matlock DE4 5JU
TEL: (01629) 582795   FAX: (01629) 580475

An intimate, historic retreat hidden away on the edge of the Peak District.

Attention all honeymooners! This Elizabethan country-house hotel, situated far from, and high above, the crowds of tourists in Matlock and Matlock Bath in the valley below, has some of the most romantic bedrooms around. Located in the old stable block, all sport antique beds, nine of which are four-posters. Moreover, five, which cost a little extra, feature bathrooms equipped with whirlpool baths. Beams, mullioned windows and heavy old wooden furniture complete the beguiling picture, and also essentially provide the ambience of the manor itself. A fire crackles within an awesome Jacobean fireplace in one of the sitting-rooms, while polished tables laid with cut-glass and candelabra create a suitably refined atmosphere for a restaurant with such a good reputation. Vegetarians have a whole menu to themselves, but they'll be missing out on such creations as boudin blanc (white sausage flavoured with foie gras and truffles) and roast duck with caramelised shallots and roasted garlic. Lovebirds should not miss the opportunity to whisper sweet nothings to each other in the lovely walled garden, which is bedecked with floral archways.

◑ Open all year ⊿ 1 mile off A615; in Tansley turn left at the Murco filling station into Alders Lane and follow road to the hotel. Private car park ⊨ᵣ 2 double, 9 four-poster; all in annexe; all with bathroom/WC; TV, room service, hair-dryer, mini-bar, trouser press, direct-dial telephone, radio ⌁ 2 restaurants, bar, 2 lounges, conservatory, garden; conference facilities (max 20 people incl up to 11 residential); tennis, croquet; early suppers for children ⅙ No wheelchair access ● No children under 10; no dogs in public rooms; no smoking in some public rooms and bedrooms ☐ Access, Amex, Delta, Diners, Switch, Visa £ Single occupancy of twin/double £85 to £99, twin/double £105, four-poster £105 to £150; deposit required. Cooked B £8; set L £12/15; alc D £27.50. Special breaks available

---

If you have a small appetite, or just aren't feeling hungry, check if you can be given a reduction if you don't want the full menu. At some hotels you could easily end up paying £30 for one course and a coffee.

The Guide *is totally independent, accepts no free hospitality, and survives on the number of copies sold each year.*

MATLOCK BATH **Derbyshire** map 5

Hodgkinson's Hotel

150 South Parade, Matlock Bath DE4 3NR
TEL: (01629) 582170   FAX: (01629) 584891

Much Victoriana in this exotically furnished small hotel.

Nothing could be further removed in tone from this rather recherché establishment than the surrounding fish-and-chip shops and amusement arcades of the trippers' spa town of Matlock Bath. Malcolm Archer and Nigel Shelley's tall, narrow Georgian house serves as a treasure trove of mainly Victorian and often environmentally unsound oddments. Fox furs, leopard-skin hand-mitts, riding whips, pith helmets, sepia portraits and even a miniature ivory temple appear amid gold-painted tables and tasselled lamps in the lounge and the tiny restaurant. Fun, often rather grand, bedrooms are showcases of period details and furniture, too. Light sleepers and bath-lovers should note that all but the small Room 2 look on to the main road, and all have showers only. Tea drinkers would be better served with UHT milk at least, rather than dried milk sachets on bedroom trays.

Rather flamboyantly formal service and operatic music determine the mood for four-course table d'hôte dinners. Malcolm and Nigel's food is interesting but can be very rich, particularly when it comes to the dessert trolley. Dishes such as a bacon-wrapped baked avocado stuffed with a cheese-and-herb pâté, and lamb in a hone- and-lavender sauce are over-complicated; stick to less elaborate options. You can smarten up for dinner with a short back and sides or a perm: Malcolm has a hairdressing salon on the first floor.

○ Open all year ◪ In the centre of Matlock Bath, on A6 Derby to Manchester road. Private car park ⌐ 1 single, 6 double; all with shower/WC; TV, room service, direct-dial telephone; ✓ Restaurant, bar, lounge, drying-room, garden ও No wheelchair access ● No dogs in public rooms ⊡ Access, Amex, Delta, Switch, Visa £ Single £30, single occupancy of twin/double £40 to £60, twin/double £50 to £90; deposit required. Set D £19.50 to £24.50. Special breaks available

---

MAWNAN SMITH **Cornwall** map 1

Budock Vean Hotel

Mawnan Smith, Nr Falmouth TR11 5LG
TEL: (01326) 250288   FAX: (01326) 250892

Popular golfing hotel on a palatial scale.

For enthusiastic golfers, Budock Vean, with its 9/18-hole course laid out in spectacular grounds stretching away to the Helford River, must be the next thing to heaven. With a round completed, they can relax in a lovely indoor swimming-pool with a conical glass roof and a vast log fire beside it. Any lingering excess energy can be worked off simply by walking through the telescoping (and curiously soulless) lounges back to reception, and then up the stairs to the bedrooms. These vary considerably, depending on how recently they have been refurbished. The nicest are those on the second floor, which have been given more substantial furniture and redecorated with delicately striped wallpaper. In a hotel built to monumental proportions, Room 10 is particularly enormous, with its own sitting-room and a dressing area big enough to accommodate a cot. Many of the rooms have separate bathrooms and lavatories, and most have fine views over the golf course. The wood-panelled restaurant is hung with small heraldic shields, which don't do much to cheer it up. However, readers have thoroughly enjoyed dinners chosen from menus which tend to stick to the familiar: roasts, casseroles and a choice of fish dishes. Afternoon teas are served in the cosiest of the lounges under the watchful eyes of assorted hunting trophies. As happened last year, the staff here have come in for particular praise, and a reader wrote to say that after a happy stay they would be joining the contingent of Budock regulars.

◗ Closed 3 Jan to 12 Feb ⬀ Travelling south, fork right at the Red Lion in Mawnan Smith; hotel is on the left. Private car park ⬐ 6 single, 23 twin, 18 double, 1 four-poster, 4 family rooms, 3 suites; all with bathroom/shower/WC; TV, room service, hair-dryer, direct-dial telephone ✓ Restaurant, 2 bars, 3 lounges, TV room, drying-room, conservatory, games room, garden; conference facilities (max 100 people incl up to 55 residential); fishing, golf, heated indoor swimming-pool, tennis, putting green, snooker, table tennis, clay-pigeon shooting, croquet, archery, riding; early suppers for children; playroom, toys, baby-listening ♿ No wheelchair access ● No children under 7 in restaurant eves; no dogs in public rooms; no smoking in restaurant ▭ Access, Delta, Diners, Switch, Visa £ Single £38 to £75, single occupancy of twin/double £58 to £95, twin/double £76 to £150, four-poster £76 to £150, family room £76 to £150, suite £92 to £166 (rates incl dinner); deposit required. Set D £18.50; alc D £25 (1996 prices). Special breaks available

---

Meudon Hotel

Mawnan Smith, Nr Falmouth TR11 5HT
TEL: (01326) 250541 FAX: (01326) 250543

A comfortable, well-run hotel, with a hidden gem of a garden.

In a county famed for its gorgeous gardens, Meudon somehow manages to keep one all to itself. In the restaurant a vibrant red and white colour scheme can't hope to compete with what's on view through the picture windows: soaring magnolia trees, flower-heavy rhododendron and azalea bushes, and huge Australian tree ferns. A vine creeps across the glass roof, and guests dine immediately beneath it. During the day, flower-lovers can get their fix in a long gallery linking up the two wings of the house and lined with garden-facing chairs. Although it's hard to imagine now, Meudon was once a private house: one lounge was a bedroom and the neat bar, up a few steps to one side, a dressing-room-cum-bathroom. Owner Harry Pilgrim does not rest on his laurels, even after a 30-year tenure, and is always on the look out for ways in which to make life more comfortable for his guests. Spacious suites have recently been created by combining several smaller rooms, and many bathrooms now boast bidets. A lift is also in the offing. Nor has the lengthy dinner menu stood still. Those on low-fat diets will be pleased to learn that they can now sample ostrich steak here. Best of all, the brutalist wall overlooking the car park on which we once commented has now disappeared beneath much more appealing rustic tiles and a Virginia creeper.

◐ Closed Nov to Feb **↗** Travelling south, fork left at the Red Lion in Mawnan Smith; hotel is on the right. Private car park **�** 2 single, 26 twin/double, 1 family room, 2 suites; all with bathroom/WC exc singles; TV, room service, hair-dryer, direct-dial telephone; trouser press in some rooms **✓** Restaurant, bar, 3 lounges, games room, garden; conference facilities (max 60 people incl up to 31 residential); golf, billiards; early suppers for children; baby-listening **占** No wheelchair access **●** No dogs in public rooms **▭** Access, Amex, Delta, Diners, Switch, Visa **£** Single £50, single occupancy of twin/double £75, twin/double £126, family room £190, suite £190; deposit required. Set D £25, Sun L £15; light lunches available. Special breaks available

---

MAXSTOKE **Warwickshire**   map 5

Old Rectory

Church Lane, Maxstoke, Nr Coleshill B46 2QW
TEL: (01675) 462248   FAX: (01675) 481615   *ℒ*

A completely relaxed B&B, popular with business people going to the NEC, a ten-minute drive away.

Judy Page entered the B&B business by accident a few years ago, when a local friend had overbooked her B&B and asked Judy to put up a few guests for the night. From such modest beginnings, Judy has reached the dizzy heights of being a 1996 *Guide*'s hotel of the year: a well-justified accolade, according to one reader, who found her friendly ways and the very relaxed atmosphere at the Old Rectory just right. The Pages' handsome Victorian rectory is set in five acres of grounds that originally belonged to an Augustinian priory; substantial monastic remnants still stand, and there are fish ponds, a mill stream and meadows to explore. With its high-ceilinged rooms, wide corridors and a few chunky Victorian antiques, the house has a certain dignity but, more importantly, it really feels like an informal family home, with maybe a dog to greet you and baby toys scattered over the sitting-room floor. Judy will prepare whatever her guests want for dinner (possibly a roast, a pasta, or just a salad), on request. Two of the three bedrooms are very large and sport sofas; smart, modern shower units have been, or are being, installed in all. The nearby M6 is really only an audible presence if the wind is blowing in the wrong direction, or when the trees are leafless, claims Judy.

◐ Closed 2 weeks over Chr **↗** Leave M42 at Junction 6. Follow A45 south for 2 miles. Turn left by Little Chef restaurant and continue for 3 miles to a T-junction. Turn left; entrance is at a bend at the bottom of the hill through a gateway to the left. Private car park **⟞** 1 twin, 1 double, 1 family room; single with bathroom/WC, 2 with shower/WC; TV, hair-dryer **✓** Dining-room, lounge, garden **占** No wheelchair access **●** No dogs in public rooms; smoking in lounge only **▭** None accepted **£** Single occupancy of twin/double £29, twin/double £46, family room £65; deposit required. Set D £18

MELDRETH **Cambridgeshire**   map 6

Chiswick House

Meldreth, Royston SG8 6LZ
TEL: (01763) 260242

A B&B full of historical character and curiosity, with charming,
chatty hosts.

Bernice and John Elbourn have lived here for 17 years, but the house was bought
by John's grandmother in 1898 (and her ghost has reputedly been seen around).
If you're susceptible to other-worldly visits, then Chiswick House is exactly the
sort of place that you'd expect to be haunted. It's a half-timbered, fourteenth-
century house, upgraded in Tudor times when the fireplaces and chimneys were
added, and was used as a hunting lodge by James I (his royal crest is above the
fireplace in the drawing-room). The Jacobean panelling in the dining-room
complements the dining chairs that were bought by Bernice's father at auction
when she was 16, as well as the barley-twist and leather Knole-type chairs and
sofa that were designed to be deep enough to accommodate a Victorian bustle.
The bedrooms in the main house are small but suitably characterful: an old wig
room has been converted into an *en suite* shower-room, while the large twin on
the ground floor is panelled, and has doors that open on to the garden. The
bedrooms in the converted stable block are more spacious and very light, and
feature high ceilings and pine furniture; the shower-rooms are lit by means of
Velux windows. On fine days, breakfast can be taken in the modern conservatory overlooking the garden; the Elbourns were in the process of replacing the
pond with a summer house when we inspected.

◐ Open all year ⤴ In Meldreth village, 1 mile west of the A10, 8 miles south of
Cambridge. Private car park ⤚ 2 twin, 4 double; some in annexe; 1 with
bathroom/WC, 5 with shower/WC; hair-dryer; TV on request ⊘ Dining-room, lounge,
drying-room, conservatory, garden; babysitting, cot, high chair ⅋ Wheelchair
access to hotel (2 steps) and dining-room, 4 ground-floor bedrooms ● No dogs in
public rooms; no smoking ⊡ None accepted £ Single occupancy of twin/double
£33, twin/double £40; deposit required

MELKSHAM **Wiltshire**   map 2

Sandridge Park

Melksham SN12 7QU
TEL: (01225) 706897   FAX: (01225) 702838

An elegant and tranquil family home in beautiful countryside.

The driveway leading to Sandridge Park curves round a gently rising hillock.
Annette and Andrew Hoogeweegen's handsome Victorian villa of soft Bath
sandstone sits atop the mound, with magnificent views extending over
Salisbury Plain. Surrounded by 30 acres of parks and gardens, which contain
mature cedars and chestnuts, badgers, deer and a croquet lawn, the house has an
illustrious past: it was home to Eisenhower (and his troops) during the Second
World War. The Hoogeweegens, however, found it in a derelict state, and it took

them nearly four years to set it right. Now, the house mixes the trappings of grandeur – immense high-ceilinged rooms, chandeliers, vast bay windows, marble fireplaces – with an easy-going lived-in feel. Annette serves four-course communal dinners by candlelight round the polished oval table, using home-grown vegetables and herbs; in summer guests may dine on the lawn. The three bedrooms are bright and contemporary, and the large bathrooms come equipped with fluffy robes and an excellent selection of toiletries. The smaller lemon-yellow double to the rear has a lovely view over the plain.

◑ Closed Chr   **⚄** From Melksham take A3102 towards Calne; hotel is 2 miles along this road on left. Private car park   **🛏** 1 twin, 2 double; all with bathroom/WC; TV, trouser press; hair-dryer on request   **✓** Dining-room, lounge, TV room, drying-room, garden; conference facilities (max 12 people non-residential)   **🚫** No wheelchair access   **⚫** No children under 16; no dogs; no smoking   **☐** Visa   **£** Single occupancy of twin/double £40, twin/double £80; deposit required. Set D £20

Shurnhold House

Shurnhold, Melksham SN12 8DG
TEL: (01225) 790555   FAX: (01225) 793147

Well-maintained, unfussy rooms in a lovely Jacobean house.

Hidden from the main Melksham to Bath road by a thick wall of tall trees, this mellow, golden-stone Jacobean house, with mullioned, leaded windows framed by clinging creepers, stands in 1½ acres of semi-formal gardens. The interior of Sue Mead's smart B&B reflects its exterior. The furnishings are simple and neat, turning one's attention to the house's own features – stone fireplaces, flagstone floors, oak beams and window seats – and giving it an uncluttered character. One of the small lounges has soft green and red seating arranged around the open fire and plenty of books to read; the more sociably inclined might congregate in the bar (the B&B has a resident's licence); while the pretty pink and green breakfast-room has simple, straight-backed wooden chairs. There is a good choice of bedrooms, all decorated in the same straightforward manner, and all with excellent, large bathrooms. The larger first-floor rooms have a touch of romance – four-posters, lace drapes and coverlets – while the smaller attic doubles boast bolder fabrics and a more contemporary style.

◑ Open all year   **⚄** Set back off main A365 to Bath road. Private car park   **🛏** 1 twin, 3 double, 2 four-poster, 2 family rooms, 1 suite; all with bathroom/WC; TV, room service, hair-dryer, trouser press, direct-dial telephone   **✓** Dining-room, bar, 2 lounges, garden; croquet; babysitting, baby-listening   **🚫** No wheelchair access   **⚫** No dogs in public rooms; smoking in bar/lounge only   **☐** Access, Visa   **£** Single occupancy of twin/double £48 to £50, twin/double £68 to £78, four-poster £78, family room/suite £88 to £98; deposit required. Continental B £2, cooked B £4.50

Prices are what you can expect to pay in 1997, except where specified to the contrary. Many hoteliers tell us that these prices can be regarded only as approximations.

Toxique

187 Woodrow Road, Melksham SN12 7AY
TEL: (01225) 702129

Combination of startlingly original décor and imaginative food.

Toxique describes itself as 'an ideal place' for 'the more adventurous' and, certainly, lovers of the conventional may find this highly original restaurant-with-rooms a little overwhelming. The traditional stone façade and well-tended front gardens of Helen Bartlett's and Peter Jewkes' converted farmhouse on the outskirts of Melksham does nothing to prepare visitors; but step inside and you'll find stripped floorboards coated with dark varnish, pine cones hanging from the midnight-blue ceiling, and chairs draped with mulberry, purple and terracotta colours. Bedrooms are no less striking. The Colonial Suite (light parquet floor, wicker chairs and table, muslin draped over the bed) and Oriental Suite (carved wood imported from India and the Far East, bright wall hangings) are predominantly white, with a minimalism in design which doesn't detract from their originality. In contrast, the Desert Suite (striking turquoise and yellow, with rich velvet draped tent-like over the bed) and Rococo Suite (the largest, most luxurious, with deep-red walls, and deep-green drapes cascading over the corners of the four-poster) couldn't be more flamboyant. Menus display equal creativity and exotic influences, such as tiger prawn kebab with tabbouleh and Thai dressing, confit of duck's leg in filo pastry, fresh tuna with bitter leaves, and potato salad with orange, ginger and coriander dressing.

◑ Open all year ⤢ Take Calne Road at Melksham centre mini-roundabout; turn left into Forest Road and Toxique is on left. Private car park ⬄ 3 double, 1 four-poster; all with bathroom/WC; room service; TV in 1 room; hair-dryer on request ✇ 2 restaurants, lounge, garden; early suppers for children Ġ No wheelchair access ◔ No dogs; no smoking in restaurants and discouraged in bedrooms ☐ Access, Amex, Delta, Diners, Switch, Visa £ Single occupancy of twin/double £95, twin/double/four-poster £145 (rates incl dinner); deposit required. Set L £16/19, D £29.50. Special breaks available

---

Chetcombe House Hotel

Road, Mere BA12 6AZ
TEL: (01747) 860219   FAX: (01747) 860111

An exceptionally friendly and accommodating small hotel in a convenient location.

'My sister and I are delighted they decided not to sell,' wrote a recent guest at Colin and Sue Ross's hotel. The Rosses did consider moving on, but instead decided to expand the catering side of their business, so that travellers can continue to enjoy the hotel's quiet, unassuming charms as a base from which to explore the area, or as a stopover *en route* to or from the West Country; the hotel is just off the A303. Traffic noise can be intrusive in the front two bedrooms, despite the double glazing, but otherwise the hotel is a haven of peace. The lounge, with soft chairs gathered round a log-burning stove, plenty of plants and local information, looks through patio doors over well-tended gardens and fields; the cottage-style dining-room is also light and airy. Upstairs is likewise immaculate. The bedrooms are pretty, neat and very light, with pine or rattan furniture and soft pastel decoration. Dinners are prepared using home-grown or local produce when possible; a thick, home-made soup may be followed by duck with orange and ginger, roast chicken with lime and fennel, or Hungarian pork casserole. But it's the hosts who make the hotel exceptional: 'they were *so* nice', continues our reader, 'my overnight stay was as peaceful as could be.'

◑ Open all year   ⤢ Just off A303, before reaching Mere (from the east). Private car park ⮞ 1 single, 1 twin, 2 double, 1 family room; 2 with bathroom/WC, 3 with shower/WC; TV; hair-dryer on request ⌀ Dining-room, bar, lounge, garden; early suppers for children ♿ No wheelchair access ⬤ No dogs in public rooms; no smoking ▭ Access, Amex, Visa £ Single £29, single occupancy of twin/double £33, twin/double £50, family room £66; deposit required. Set D from £13.50. Special breaks available

---

MERIDEN West Midlands   map 5

Forest of Arden

Maxstoke Lane, Meriden, Nr Coventry CV7 7HR
TEL: (01676) 522335 FAX: (01676) 523711

A large conference hotel and country club with two 18-hole golf courses.

Taken over by the Marriott group in early 1996, the Forest of Arden is best known for its championship golf course, where the English Open has been held in recent years. The vast estate offers plenty of other outdoor pursuits besides golf, and the actively inclined can also use the excellent indoor leisure facilities centred round a tropical-style landscaped pool. On weekdays, the hotel's 14 conference rooms become its focus. Then, it may be difficult to escape from mobile phones and laptops in the public areas, which are stylish in a trendily rustic Mediterranean way with terracotta tiling, whitewashed and rugged walls and exposed wood. The main restaurant offers refreshingly unfancy cuisine, such as rack of lamb, steak and kidney pudding and a double-baked cheese soufflé. The hotel possesses no fewer than 155 bedrooms, each furnished in uneventful country-house style; another 60 are due to be opened by March 1997. All are well equipped, but particularly so the executive rooms, which boast king-size beds and mini-bars. Rates fluctuate wildly according to occupancy levels, from around £85 up to £140 for a standard room and the hotel suggests you phone for a price quote.

The text of entries is based on unsolicited reports sent in by readers and backed up by inspections. The factual details are from questionnaires the Guide *sends to all hotels that feature in the book.*

◗ *Open all year* ◰ Leave M42 at Junction 6 and take A45 to Coventry; go straight over flyover; after mile turn left into Shepherds Lane and continue 1½ miles. Private car park ⇌ 76 twin, 77 double, 2 suites; family rooms available all with bathroom/WC; TV, 24-hour room service, hair-dryer, trouser press, direct-dial telephone; mini-bar in some rooms ✓ 2 restaurants, 4 bars, lounge, TV room, games room, garden; air-conditioning in all public areas; conference facilities (max 500 people incl up to 155 residential); fishing, golf, gym, sauna, solarium, heated indoor swimming-pool, tennis, snooker, croquet, dance studio, health/beauty treatments; babysitting, baby-listening & Wheelchair access to hotel, restaurant and WC (M,F), 48 ground-floor bedrooms, 2 specially equipped for disabled people ⬤ No dogs; no smoking in main restaurant and some bedrooms ⊟ Access, Amex, Delta, Diners, Visa £ Single occupancy of twin/double £95, twin/double/family room £95, suite £200; deposit required. Continental B £9, cooked B £11; set L £16.50, D £21 (prices valid till Mar 1997). Special breaks available

---

MIDDLE CHINNOCK Somerset map 2

Chinnock House

Middle Chinnock, Crewkerne TA18 7PN
TEL: (01935) 881229

A tastefully decorated Georgian house with a walled garden, in a minuscule village.

The tiny village of Middle Chinnock seems an unlikely setting for an outsized, nineteenth-century cast of the Venus de Milo but, strangely enough, that is exactly what you will find standing at the foot of the stairs of Charmian and Guy Smith's lovely, late-Georgian house. This one wild touch aside, everything else in Chinnock House is discreetly interesting, including the old kilims on the floor, the framed maps that decorate the breakfast-room's walls and the reproduction eighteenth-century baby's crib in Room 3. There are only three bedrooms in the house itself – and one of these is relatively small – but a fourth room in the coach house outside features a small downstairs kitchen in which guests can make breakfast if they prefer to eat alone; 'we usually let it to people who're staying for three days or so,' commented Guy. The dinner menus evolve from discussion with the guests, and often feature vegetables from the Smiths' two-acre garden. On the whole, however, the garden is more of a pretty, ornamental area, which is occasionally open to the public through the National Gardens Scheme. There's a swimming-pool at the back, which must be a delight in summer, when the only disturbance is likely to come from the birds.

◗ Open all year ◰ Next to rectory, opposite Middle Chinnock church. Private car park ⇌ 3 twin, 2 double; 1 in annexe; all with bathroom/WC; hair-dryer, radio; tea/coffee-making facilities and trouser press on request ✓ Dining-room, lounge, drying-room, conservatory, garden; heated outdoor swimming-pool; early suppers for children; babysitting, cot & No wheelchair access ⬤ No dogs; no smoking in bedrooms ⊟ None accepted £ Single occupancy of twin/double £25, twin/double £50; deposit required. Set D £20

Greystones

Market Place, Middleham DL8 4NR
TEL: (01969) 622016

A homely guesthouse with neat rooms and good, traditional dinners.

If you find that large, rambling, country houses can be a bit impersonal at times, you might be tempted by the little Georgian house which is Greystones. With just four rooms, you're guaranteed a friendly reception and a homely atmosphere during your stay. It's also a good base for touring the area, with Wensleydale and Coverdale being equally accessible. The neat dining-room is decorated with old pencil drawings, while the book-filled lounge features family photos, a green-leather, button-back sofa and a log fire; both look out on to the lovely, cobbled square, and you can witness the early-morning procession of racehorses on their way from stable to moor. The bedrooms are pretty, and boast either pale-pink or blue colour schemes, pine furniture, and the occasional teddy bear. If you like a bit of space in which to spread out, ask for the family room.

Frances Greenwood changes her menu daily, and the guesthouse's relatively small scale means that she can cater for guests' preferences and special needs. A typical dinner may include a warm salad of chicken livers with mushrooms and bacon, followed by a fillet of Whitby salmon served with a lemon-and-chive sauce.

◑ Closed Dec & Jan (open New Year) ⊡ In centre of Middleham. On-street parking ⟻ 1 twin, 2 double, 1 family room; 1 with bathroom/WC, 3 with shower/WC; room service, hair-dryer, radio ⊘ Dining-room, lounge, drying-room; early suppers for children; babysitting, baby-listening ⅋ No wheelchair access ● No dogs in public rooms; smoking in lounge only ⊟ None accepted £ Single occupancy of twin/double £40, twin/double £55 to £60, family room £70 to £80; deposit required. Set D £15. Special breaks available

---

Miller's House

Market Place, Middleham DL8 4NR
TEL: (01969) 622630 FAX: (01969) 623570

A welcoming small hotel, offering some imaginatively themed weekend breaks.

Even Oscar, the family cat, seems to have been trained in the art of greeting, and hurries down the drive to meet guests; he likes to set the tone for the kind of welcome for which the Miller's House is famed. A New Zealand couple singled it out for praise: 'We were made most welcome by Judith and Crossley Sunderland and their friendly staff.'

The quietly elegant Georgian house is set back just a little from the main square, and while the bar area may seem a little gloomy, the conservatory – in which breakfast is served – looks out on to a small, enclosed garden, which is a real suntrap on a summer's day. The smart restaurant, with its deep, pink carpet and striped wallpaper, is the venue for such exotic-sounding dinners as ostrich fillet with oyster mushrooms and Madeira sauce, or traditional dishes such as breast of duck with redcurrant sauce. 'The food and its presentation surpassed expectations raised by the interesting menu, and the recommended wines were superb,' reports one correspondent. Indeed, wine is something close to the Sunderlands' hearts, and they offer special wine-tasting weekends throughout the year.

◗ Closed Jan ⬛ Set back off the small market square in Middleham. Private car park 🛏 1 single, 3 twin, 2 double, 1 four-poster; all with bathroom/WC; TV, room service, hair-dryer, direct-dial telephone, radio ✅ Restaurant, bar/lounge, drying-room, conservatory, garden; conference facilities (max 24 people incl up to 7 residential) ♿ No wheelchair access ● No children under 10; no dogs; no smoking in restaurant or conservatory ▭ Access, Switch, Visa £ Single £37, twin/double £73, four-poster £88; deposit required. Set D £19.50. Special breaks available

---

Waterford House

Kirkgate, Middleham, Leyburn DL8 4PG
TEL: (01969) 622090   FAX: (01969) 624020

An antique-filled restaurant-with-rooms overlooking the village square.

At Waterford House, Everyl Maddell tempts you to leave behind the world of restless cares and pass away the time engaged in the idle pleasures of good eating and conversation. In the small main restaurant, the tables are huddled together, and every inch of the surrounding walls and sideboards is covered with prints, paintings and *objets d'art*. It is an ideal place to indulge in merry meetings or weighty arguments over Everyl's memorable dinners, in which roast Barbary duck cooked with apricots, figs and plums may follow baked scallops served with prawns and smoked bacon, with a lemon-treacle or chocolate-and-pear tart to follow if you still have room. The house now also hosts grander occasions than mere evening dinners, as it now holds a civil-wedding licence.

Like the other public rooms, the lounge boasts an equally dense provision of ornaments (as well as a baby-grand piano,) but it lacks natural light. An alternative seating area was being developed at the time of our inspection: a paved and flower-filled yard at the rear of the house, where guests will be able to take tea on fair days.

The bedrooms are all spacious, and each features sloping floors, old beams and a distinctive style. Most overlook the front of the house, but there is not a great deal of traffic and little other than the rhythmic, early-morning clopping of thoroughbred hooves to disturb the gentle peace.

 Denotes somewhere you can rely on a good meal – either the hotel features in the 1997 edition of our sister publication, The Good Food Guide, *or our inspectors thought the cooking impressive, whether particularly competent home cooking or more lavish cuisine.*

○ *Open all year* ▣ Just off Market Square in centre of Middleham. Private car park ⊭ 1 twin, 2 double, 1 four-poster, 1 family room; all with bathroom/WC exc four-poster with shower/WC; TV, room service, hair-dryer, radio ⌑ 2 restaurants, 2 bar/lounges, drying-room, garden; conference facilities (max 15 people incl up to 5 residential); early suppers for children; toys, babysitting, baby-listening, cot ⅙ No wheelchair access ● No dogs in public rooms; smoking in 1 bar/lounge only ▭ Access, Delta, Diners, Visa £ Single occupancy of twin/double £40 to £50, twin/double £60 to £70, four-poster £70 to £75, family room £80 to £90. Set L £15.50, D £17.50 to £19.50; alc L £21.50, D £22.50 (1996 prices). Special breaks available

---

MIDHURST West Sussex   map 3

Angel Hotel

North Street, Midhurst GU29 9DN
TEL: (01730) 812421 FAX: (01730) 815928

An impeccably furnished, historic coaching-inn, run with flair.

The Georgian frontage of the Angel Hotel overlooks the main thoroughfare of this bustling, old market town, where it has been a hub of social life since the fifteenth century. In the 1880s, H G Wells was apprenticed to a local chemist, and he lodged at the inn, mentioning it in three of his books – a blue plaque is on its way! When our inspector arrived, the owner, Peter Crawford-Rolt, was elbow deep in the innards of a vacuum cleaner, and it's precisely this hands-on, energetic attitude which makes the hotel a success. Food is certainly a main focus of the Angel, ranging from the simple fare that is served in the fifteenth-century bar, through to that of the brasserie (which is furnished in light pine and pale yellows), in which a varied and adventurous menu – prepared from fresh ingredients – offers such choices as seared tuna loin served with a Thai noodle salad and a red-chilli pickle; roast saddle of rabbit; or penne with wild mushrooms and a Parmesan cream sauce. The more formal and elegant Cowdray Room serves similar fare, but its beefed-up prices reflect the grander setting.

Tudor beams add character to many of the bedrooms, which are generally airy and spacious, and are fitted out with taste and plenty of antique furniture. Room 22 gets the gold star for its gorgeous, double-aspect view over the eerie ruins of Cowdray Castle and the medieval meadows beyond the garden.

○ Open all year ▣ On Midhurst High Street (North Street) going south on A286. Private car park ⊭ 3 single, 9 twin, 10 double, 1 four-poster, 1 family room, 1 suite; some in annexe; all with bathroom/WC exc 2 singles with shower/WC; TV, room service, hair-dryer, direct-dial telephone; tea/coffee-making facilities on request ⌑ 2 restaurants, bar, 2 lounges, garden; conference facilities (max 60 people incl up to 25 residential); early suppers for children; babysitting, baby-listening, high chairs ⅙ Wheelchair access to hotel, restaurants and WC (unisex), 2 ground-floor bedrooms, 1 specially equipped for disabled people ● No dogs ▭ Access, Amex, Delta, Diners, Switch, Visa £ Single/single occupancy of twin/double from £75, twin/double from £80, four-poster from £130, family room/suite from £140; deposit required. Set L £10/15; alc L £25, D £30; bar and brasserie meals available. Special breaks available

Spread Eagle

South Street, Midhurst GU29 9NH
TEL: (01730) 816911   FAX: (01730) 815668

An ancient and characterful inn in the town centre.

Set amid rows of sagging, half-timbered and Georgian, red-brick houses, the Spread Eagle boasts an amazing amalgam of architectural styles. The hotel was once two separate buildings (which are now fused together in the red-brick hall, where 1430 meets 1620), and it creaks underfoot like the medieval ships' timbers which form its ancient skeleton. Flemish stained-glass windows dating from 1625, Tudor bread ovens, a wig closet and a gently ticking grandfather clock (originally intended for Kaiser Wilhelm) all play their part in this cast of antiquity.

At the heart of the restaurant, the smoke-blackened, inglenook fireplace – which is festooned with gleaming copper pans – is witness to some pretty serious culinary endeavours, in the form of such dishes as a terrine of hare and wild duck, sauté calf's liver served with wild mushrooms (the chef's speciality), or sauté monkfish presented on a bed of creamed fennel with smoked bacon. Finish with a dark-chocolate marquise and coconut cream, if you dare. The residents' lounge is the place in which to take a leisurely *digestif*, and boasts the oldest medieval beam in the house, which looms above crazily inclined floors and walls, plush sofas and an antique clavichord. The bedrooms vary in style and ambience, but are all comfortable and well furnished. Some are situated in a separate annexe overlooking the courtyard, whereas others (such as the more pricey four-poster suites) look on to the street through leaded windows.

● Open all year   ⚡ In Midhurst on A272. Private car park   🛏 4 single, 12 twin/double, 19 double, 5 four-poster, 1 suite; family rooms available; some in annexe; all with bathroom/WC exc 4 doubles with shower/WC; TV, room service, hair-dryer, direct-dial telephone   ⊘ Restaurant, bar, lounge, garden; conference facilities (max 60 people incl up to 41 residential); early suppers for children; babysitting, baby-listening   ♿ No wheelchair access   ● No dogs in public rooms; no smoking in restaurant   ▭ Access, Amex, Delta, Diners, Switch, Visa   £ Single £75, single occupancy of twin/double from £79, twin/double from £92, four-poster from £175, family room from £115, suite from £175; deposit required. Cooked B £4; set L £16.50, D £26. Special breaks available

---

MILDENHALL Suffolk   map 6

Riverside Hotel

Mill Street, Mildenhall, Bury St Edmunds IP28 7DP
TEL: (01638) 717274   FAX: (01638) 715997

A neat, traditional hotel with waterside restaurant (nearly).

The Riverside Hotel's location alone would make it popular with Americans visiting relatives at the local air base, but the place has a reliable, traditional feel, combined with attentive service that more than justifies the choice. The stolid, red-brick Georgian exterior reveals a smart blue lobby with a splendid wooden staircase that was designed by Sir Christopher Wren, according to Keith

Lardner, one of the proprietors. At the back, the modern restaurant extension has huge glass walls, allowing you a full view of the terrace, croquet lawn and, if you were to stand on the table, the river beyond. The pleasant, peach-coloured Terrace Bar next door has the same views, but feels more institutional, with its bookshelves crammed with condensed classics. Bedrooms vary in size and outlook. Those on the top floor are due for redecoration and feel slightly dated, though they have all the standard facilities. We would agree with the reader who recommends a bedroom overlooking the garden on the first floor – 'the first blush of spring gave us a taste of what was to come in the garden.' The food generally sticks to tried-and-trusted favourites: main courses might include a mixed grill, baked salmon with hollandaise sauce, or steak pie. Service, under the watchful eye of the Lardners and the Childs, is first rate.

◑ Open all year ⤢ Take A1101 to Mildenhall; at the mini roundabout turn left; hotel is the last building on the left leaving town. Private car park ⭲ 3 single, 5 twin, 7 double, 1 four-poster, 4 family rooms; some in annexe; some with bathroom/WC, some with shower/WC; TV, room service, hair dryer, trouser press, direct-dial telephone, radio ⌀ Restaurant, 2 bars, lounge, drying-room, garden; conference facilities (max 100 people incl up to 20 residential); fishing; early suppers for children; baby-listening ⅋ No wheelchair access ● No dogs in some public rooms ▭ Access, Amex, Delta, Diners, Switch, Visa £ Single £53, single occupancy of twin/double £62, twin/double £82, four-poster £94, family room £82; deposit required. Set L £17, D £18; alc D from £20; light meals available. Special breaks available

---

Periton Park Hotel

Middlecombe, Minehead TA24 8SW
TEL: (01643) 706885 (AND FAX)

Peaceful inland country-house haven above the coastal madness.

When ex-King Constantine of Greece visited this solid Victorian house he brought his own butler, but there's no need of that nowadays since host Richard Hunt performs the role to perfection, dispensing pre-dinner drinks in the elegant lounge before escorting you to the panelled billiards room turned dining-room with prints of the Quorn Hunt on the wall. Three-course dinner menus come with plenty of choice and may in any case be topped up with 'specials' if Angela Hunt is feeling particularly enthusiastic; a typical meal might start with a Stilton, watercress and walnut terrine and move on to Exmoor venison. The bedrooms, some with big bay windows, are all individually furnished and have such hot water that a sign warns you to beware. The bathroom of Room 6 even retains its original Victorian fittings, including a graceful claw-foot bathtub. The one ground-floor bedroom has french windows so that dogs can be let out straight into the garden. Its door is wide enough to admit a wheelchair too.

All rooms have tea/coffee-making facilities unless we specify to the contrary.

◑ *Closed Jan* ⊉ On the south side of A39 Minehead to Porlock road. Private car park ⟞⟶ 5 twin/double, 3 double; all with bathroom/WC exc 1 double with shower/WC; TV, room service, hair-dryer, direct-dial telephone ⟡ 2 restaurants, lounge, drying-room, garden; conference facilities (max 24 people incl up to 8 residential); croquet, riding; early suppers for children ⟓ Wheelchair access to hotel (2 steps) and restaurant, 1 ground-floor bedroom specially equipped for disabled people ● No children under 12; no dogs in public rooms and most bedrooms; no smoking in restaurants and some bedrooms ⊟ Access, Amex, Diners, Switch, Visa £̲ Single occupancy of twin/double £60 to £66, twin/double £80 to £92; deposit required. Set D £21.50 (1996 prices). Special breaks available

---

MITHIAN Cornwall   map 1

Rose-in-Vale

Mithian, St Agnes TR5 0QD
TEL: (01872) 552202   FAX: (01872) 552700

Small but expanding Georgian hotel with pretty gardens, convenient for Perranporth.

The Cornish tin-mining industry may be no more, but reminders of it still litter the landscape, and Rose-in-Vale started life as the much smaller home of an eighteenth-century tin-mine captain; his bedroom is one of the best rooms that Vanda and Tony Arthur now let to guests. As you approach their house, you catch tantalising glimpses of the stream, duck pond and woodlands that make the 11 acres of grounds such a pleasure. There's also a heated outdoor pool tucked away to the side, for those days when even strolling amid the roses is too much effort. What seems from the outside to be a standard Georgian house has grown and changed in order to accommodate its expanding clientele, and the dining-room has migrated into a long, thin, side extension with views over the garden. The bedrooms above share the views, and boast the most modern décor. A further extension at the back has three ground-floor rooms, one of them adapted for disabled guests.

◑ Closed Jan & Feb ⊉ Signposted off B3284. Private car park ⟞⟶ 2 single, 7 twin, 8 double, 2 suites; family rooms available; all with bathroom/WC; TV, room service, hair-dryer, direct-dial telephone, radio ⟡ Dining-room, bar, lounge, TV room, library, games room, garden; conference facilities (max 50 people incl up to 19 residential); solarium, heated outdoor swimming-pool, croquet, badminton; early suppers for children; babysitting, baby-listening ⟓ Wheelchair access to hotel, dining-room and WC (M,F), 3 ground-floor bedrooms, 1 specially equipped for disabled people ● No children under 7 in dining-room eves; no dogs in public rooms; no smoking in dining-room ⊟ Access, Amex, Diners, Visa £̲ Single £43, single occupancy of twin/double £60 to £73, twin/double £75 to £91, family room from £75, suite £105 to £113; deposit required. Set L £10, D £19; alc D £22.50; bar lunches available (1996 prices). Special breaks available

---

Don't forget that other hotels worth considering are listed in our Visitors' Book.

MOBBERLEY Cheshire   map 8

Laburnum Cottage Guest House

Knutsford Road, Mobberley WA16 7PU
TEL: (01565) 872464 (AND FAX)

A pretty guesthouse with gregarious hosts in rural Cheshire,
convenient for the airport.

'Tea on the lawn, antique-filled rooms, log fire, croquet on the lawn, prize-winning garden, chauffeur-driven car available' – the description in the brochure might lead you to expect a grand country house. In fact, Laburnum Cottage is a small guesthouse with grand designs. Lots of floral fabrics and Shirley Foxwell's collections of china plates and figurines create a cottagey feel within this modern, detached house. Breakfasts are taken around a single table beside the wooden staircase, and an alternative to the sitting-room and its comfy armchairs is the conservatory – filled with geraniums and spider plants – which overlooks a delightful, lawned garden, bursting with colour throughout the summer.

The five bedrooms in the house are modest in size and homely, and are decorated in matching chintz fabrics and scented with lavender, while the small, *en suite* bathrooms are provided with all sorts of goodies. Manchester Airport is only 15 minutes away, making the offer of long-term parking attractive, and Malcolm Collinge will often be on hand to provide lifts.

◑ Open all year ⤢ On B5085, 1½ miles from Knutsford town centre. Private car park �└ 2 single, 2 twin, 1 double; 1 with bathroom/WC, 2 with shower/WC; TV, hair-dryer, radio ✣ Dining-room, lounge, drying-room, conservatory, garden; conference facilities (max 15 people incl up to 5 residential); croquet ⅙ No wheelchair access ● Children by arrangement only; no dogs; no smoking ⊟ None accepted £ Single £29 to £38, single occupancy of twin/double £35 to £40, twin/double £40 to £48; deposit required

---

MOLLINGTON Cheshire   map 7

Crabwall Manor

Parkgate Road, Mollington, Chester CH1 6NE
TEL: (01244) 851666   FAX: (01244) 851400

Large business-cum-conference hotel with good food and wine,
convenient for Chester.

Crabwall Manor is an architectural potpourri, its battlemented red-brick façade a seventeenth-century addition to an older farmhouse, the east and west wings and clocktower tacked on in the 1980s, a conservatory restaurant added in 1990. Even the cobblestones outside the front door have a history; owner Carl Lewis spotted them when Dock Road in Liverpool was being re-laid, and bought them on the spot. With 48 rooms, Crabwall Manor can hardly hope to feel as cosy as smaller hotels, although it tries hard, with individually decorated bedrooms and features like a bar made out of an old pulpit and the surrounds of an old organ.

The à la carte menu offers bags of choice, with tempting starters like warm lamb mousseline with sage sauce, and pea soup garnished with cod brandade. Main courses like sauté roast sea scallops with deep-fried leeks and liquorice sauce sound equally mouth-watering, although with nothing under £14.50 they're hardly budget-priced. The suites to go for, with fireplaces and lavish antique furnishings, are in the older part of the building; some even overlook the crenellations. Bedrooms in the modern extensions are comfortable but in the rather characterless way of city-centre chain hotels.

◐ Open all year ⤵ Go to end of M56 (ignore signs for Chester); turn first left on to A5117 signposted Queensferry & North Wales; take first left on to A540; hotel is 2 miles along on right. Private car park ⤙ 42 double, 1 four-poster, 5 suites; all with bathroom/WC; TV, room service, hair-dryer, trouser press, direct-dial telephone; tea/coffee-making facilities on request ✦ Restaurant, bar, 2 lounges, games room, garden; air-conditioning in restaurant & conference suites; conference facilities (max 100 people incl up to 48 residential); croquet, snooker, clay-pigeon shooting, archery, falconry; early suppers for children; babysitting, baby-listening ♿ Wheelchair access to hotel (2 steps), restaurant and WC (M,F), 18 ground-floor bedrooms ● No dogs ▭ Access, Amex, Delta, Diners, Switch, Visa £ Single occupancy of twin/double £99, twin/double £130, four-poster/suite from £140; deposit required. Continental B £5.50, cooked B £8.50; alc L, D £32.50 (1996 prices). Special breaks available

---

MONKTON COMBE Bath & N. E. Somerset   map 2

Combe Grove Manor

Brassknocker Hill, Monkton Combe, Bath BA2 7HS
TEL: (01225) 834644 FAX: (01225) 834961

Glorious views and good leisure facilities at a much-expanded country manor.

Combe Grove Manor is built on a scenic terrace high above the Limpley Stoke Valley, with a glorious panorama over hills and woodland, two miniature cricket greens and a viaduct. Over two centuries ago, a visitor to this golden-stone Georgian house with Italianate features described it as 'the most delightful situation in the vicinity of Bath.' The view – best enjoyed from the restaurant and the original curving vestibule, reached via an imposing flight of stairs – remains the same, but nowadays the focus of activity is away from the valley. The approach road winds through the hotel's 82 acres of woods and parkland, arriving at a cluster of buildings. Modern additions house the manor's extensive conference and sports facilities (all free to guests), which make this a popular business venue – although the leisure facilities, coupled with a crèche and discounted weekend tariffs, are an inducement for families. The hotel's smart and immaculately co-ordinated country-house style doesn't entirely manage to avoid the business-hotel impersonality, and though there's plenty of soft seating and rich fabrics, visitors are unlikely to feel tempted to linger too long in the three inter-connecting lounges. The Manor Vaults Bistro, with classical style frescoes, is a fun alternative to the formal restaurant where uniformed staff serve rich, creamy dishes from silver-domed casings. Bedrooms are split between the main house and the garden annexe; many, even the cheaper ones in the annexe, have valley views.

○ Open all year ⊠ 2 miles south-east of Bath city centre, just off A36. Private car park ⤶ 25 twin, 11 double, 2 four-poster, 2 suites; family rooms available; most in annexe; all with bathroom/WC; TV, room service, hair-dryer, mini-bar, direct-dial telephone ⌀ Restaurant, bar, lounge, library, garden; conference facilities (max 80 people incl up to 40 residential); golf, gym, sauna, solarium, heated indoor and outdoor swimming-pools, tennis, croquet, volleyball, aerobics, jogging trail, horse-riding; early suppers for children; babysitting, baby-listening, crèche ᕱ No wheelchair access ● No children under 7 in restaurant eves; no dogs ⊟ Access, Amex, Delta, Switch, Visa £ Single occupancy of twin/double £98, twin/double from £98, four-poster £180, family room £125, suite from £198; deposit required. Cooked B £6.50; set L £16.50, D £19.50; bistro meals available (1996 prices). Special breaks available

Monkshill

Shaft Road, Monkton Combe, Bath BA2 7HL
TEL: (01225) 833028 (AND FAX)

Smart, family B&B with lovely gardens and valley views.

If you're enticed by the location and views of Combe Grove Manor (see entry), but are looking for comforts on a smaller, more intimate, scale, Catherine and Michael Westlake's friendly Edwardian B&B makes an attractive alternative. Reached via a winding, narrow lane, the creeper-clad house stands on the crest of a hill above the village, with views plunging to the Avon valley below, and is surrounded by 1½ acres of neat terraced gardens with low stone walls, paths and stairways, fruit trees, tumbling aubretia and a graceful acer. The interior is smart, with lots of polished antiques and good-quality fabrics, but photographs and pictures by the Westlakes' artist daughter add the individual touches of a family home. Signs of musical leanings in the family are visible too: a grand piano in the lounge – a comfortable but elegant room, with cream and blue damask chesterfields and an armoire stacked with china – and another piano and a cello in the dining-room, where guests eat round a communal polished table. Bedrooms are pretty and well maintained, with cream carpets, brass beds, Austrian blinds and soft chairs; the twin has the best views.

○ Closed Chr ⊠ Head south from Bath on B3062; at top of hill turn left into North Road, then right into Shaft Road; Monkshill is on right. Private car park ⤶ 1 twin, 2 double; doubles with bathroom/WC, twin with shower/WC; TV ⌀ Dining-room, lounge, conservatory, garden; croquet ᕱ No wheelchair access ● No dogs; no smoking ⊟ Access, Visa £ Single occupancy of twin/double £35 to £45, twin/double £50 to £65

Many hotels offer special rates for stays of a few nights or more. It is worth enquiring when you book.

All entries in the Guide *are rewritten every year, not least because standards fluctuate. Don't trust an out-of-date* Guide.

MONTACUTE **Somerset** map 2

Milk House

The Borough, Montacute TA15 6XB
TEL: (01935) 823823

*Small Ham-stone restaurant-with-rooms forming a charming group
with other houses opposite the gates to Montacute House.*

What could be better, after exploring Montacute House, than to cross over the
main village square to stay in a honey-coloured-stone house that played a
blink-and-you'll-miss-it cameo role in Emma Thompson's *Sense and Sensibility*?
Ask Lee Dufton, once an actress herself, and she'll happily explain how the
square was adapted to recreate a Hollywood vision of eighteenth-century
England. Indeed, Lee is a great raconteur, as well as being the eye (and hand)
behind the delicate painting of honeysuckle and roses that adorns the cupboards
in the Chinese Room. Another bedroom, named the Persian Room after its
carpet, boasts a huge wooden bed and an inviting bathroom with a window. In
the fifteenth century, the Milk House was two small cottages which later became
a house with stables; milk was sold from the stables, hence the name. Walk
though to the plant-filled summer dining-room, and some of the alterations
become apparent: there's a well in the middle of the room and you sit looking at
stone-mullioned windows that once faced outwards but are now part of an
internal wall. In winter, dinner is served in a second dining-room, hung with
striking modern paintings. Wherever you eat, the food, chosen from an
imaginative menu, will be delicious: creamed walnut soup could, for example,
be followed by a herb-coated guinea-fowl in its own juice, with a French
toffee-apple tart to finish.

◖ Closed Chr & 1 month in late summer; restaurant closed Sun to Tue ⬚ In village
square opposite entrance to Montacute House. On-street parking ⬚ 1 twin, 2
double; all with bathroom/WC; hair-dryer ⬚ 2 dining-rooms, lounge, TV room,
conservatory, garden ⬚ No wheelchair access ● No children under 8; no dogs;
smoking in TV room only ⬚ Access, Delta, Visa ⬚ Single occupancy of
twin/double £40, twin/double £48; deposit required. Cooked B £5; set D £15 to £24,
Sun L £14.50; alc D from £15. Special breaks available

MORSTON **Norfolk** map 6

Morston Hall Hotel

Morston, Holt NR25 7AA
TEL: (01263) 741041   FAX: (01263) 740419

*A first-class small hotel that serves excellent food and strives
constantly to maintain and improve standards.*

'Informal yet professional, with no airs and graces,' is how Galton Blackiston
sums up the aim of his small country hotel on the picturesque north Norfolk
coastal road, and the balance certainly seems to be pitched at a level that draws
people back time and time again. The traditional flint-and-brick exterior dates

back to Jacobean times, but the interior is spacious, smart and unfussy, with kilim-print sofas and chairs, Chinese rugs on the flagstone floors, and attractive arrangements of fresh flowers. The modern conservatory, overlooking the gardens, is a pleasant place in which to enjoy pre-dinner drinks on summer evenings, as well as the afternoon cream tea that is included on arrival as part of the good-value, three-night breaks. A new arrival in the kitchen, Danny Smith from Le Gavroche, has taken some of the pressure off Galton. This will, it is hoped, help to solve the gripe that we had last year about the stinginess over extra toast and bread rolls. The no-choice set menu, however, will continue; an early-April menu included panzanella on toasted ciabatta with Parmesan; deep-fried cod in beer batter and a dill and lemon beurre blanc; roast loin of venison on buttery mashed potato with game *jus*, cabbage, carrots and fried baby onions; and then cheese, or rhubarb and strawberry crème brûlée with a champagne sorbet. Bedrooms, named after local villages, are of equal quality and are exceedingly comfortable: for spaciousness (two double beds) and some eye-opening bathroom tiles (left over from the previous proprietor, who was a goldsmith), go for Sandringham.

◐ Closed Jan to mid-Feb ☑ On main A149 coastal road, 2 miles west of Blakeney. Private car park 🛏 1 twin, 5 double; all with shower/WC; TV, room service, hair-dryer, direct-dial telephone, radio ✦ Restaurant, 2 lounges, conservatory, garden; early suppers for children; toys, baby-listening, cots, high chairs ♿ No wheelchair access ● No dogs in public rooms; no smoking in restaurant ▭ Amex, Delta, Switch, Visa £ Single occupancy of twin/double £80 to £120, twin/double £150 to £170 (rates incl dinner). Set L £15, D £26 (1996 prices). Special breaks available

---

MOSEDALE Cumbria   map 10

Mosedale House

Mosedale, Mungrisdale, Nr Penrith CA11 0XQ
TEL: (01768) 779371

Victorian farm guesthouse at the base of Skiddaw, with thoughtful hosts.

The photograph album on the lounge coffee table has been much thumbed by guests marvelling at the conversion of this Victorian stone farmhouse. Colin and Leslie Smith arrived at this remote spot by a deep cleft into the eastern side of Skiddaw in 1983, and they haven't rested on their laurels yet: their latest ventures include improving the access for those less able to get about to the surrounding woodland and to the donkeys, sheep and chickens that have free rein in the fields to the front of the house. The rustic features of the house have been brought to the fore, with exposed stone walls and beams much in evidence, and modern comforts introduced. The food too has broad appeal, with perhaps parsnip and apple soup being followed by chicken in white wine, then sticky toffee pudding or elderflower sorbet with home-baked shortbread. Little plaques depicting farm animals identify the bedrooms, which maintain the theme of smart, unfussy modern fixtures being sympathetically incorporated into the stone and timber structure. The Hayloft suite has a little sitting-room and kitchenette, while the downstairs twin room has been adapted for disabled visitors.

◗ Closed Chr　☑ Turn off A66 for Mungrisdale and Caldbeck; hotel is 3½ miles on left. Private car park　◪ 1 single, 2 twin, 3 double; family room and suite available; all with shower/WC exc single; TV, hair-dryer　✅ Dining-room, lounge, drying-room, garden; early suppers for children　♿ Wheelchair access to hotel and dining-room, 1 ground-floor bedroom specially equipped for disabled people　● No dogs in dining-room; no smoking　▱ None accepted　£ Single from £20, single occupancy of twin/double from £25, twin/double from £42, family room from £56, suite from £52; deposit required. Set D £12; packed lunches available. Special breaks available

---

MOTCOMBE Dorset　　　　　　　　　　　　　　　　　　map 2

Coppleridge Inn

Motcombe, Shaftesbury SP7 9HW
TEL: (01747) 851980　FAX: (01747) 851858

An expanding eighteenth-century farm with lots of facilities and attractive bedrooms.

This former farm is turning into quite a little business empire. A hairdressing salon has been added to the existing facilities, which include a conference-cum-function room in the clapboard tithe barn, tennis courts, a cricket pitch and even a skittle alley. Surrounded by pastures and undulating hills (Shaftesbury is just visible in the distance), it's still a peaceful place – unless you arrive with the lunch-time crowds or there happens to be a function in progress. Nor has the conservatory extension spoilt the appeal of the main, eighteenth-century, grey-stone house with its latticed portico. Inside, old farming implements, hunting memorabilia, stuffed birds and other rustic mementoes combine with the typical trappings of country-cottage chic – stripped-pine furniture and light, fresh colours. The bar is neat; daily menus, chalked on the blackboard, include pancakes, ploughman's and game, together with international options like chicken korma. There's also an excellent-value bistro menu (three courses for £10), with main courses such as pasta or fish pie, served in the bar or in the more formal restaurant, with a full à la carte service. The former stables and dairy, set round a pretty grass courtyard, have been converted into good-sized, chintzy bedrooms with pine furniture, and full-length windows overlooking the fields and tennis courts.

◗ Open all year　☑ At northern end of Motcombe, 2 miles from Shaftesbury. Private car park　◪ 4 twin, 4 double, 2 family rooms; some in annexe; all with bathroom/shower/WC; TV, room service, hair-dryer, mini-bar, direct-dial telephone
✅ Restaurant, bar, lounge, conservatory, games room, garden; conference facilities (max 60 people incl up to 10 residential); fishing, tennis, clay-pigeon shooting, cricket, pool; early suppers for children; toys, playroom, babysitting, baby-listening, outdoor games　♿ Wheelchair access to hotel and restaurant, 10 bedrooms specially equipped for disabled people　● No dogs in restaurant　▱ Access, Amex, Visa
£ Single occupancy of twin/double £40, twin/double £70, family room from £75; deposit required. Alc L, D £15; bar and bistro meals available. Special breaks available

MOULSFORD **Oxfordshire** map 2

Beetle & Wedge

Ferry Lane, Moulsford OX10 9JF
TEL: (01491) 651381   FAX: (01491) 651376

*Good-looking small hotel on the banks of the river, with
country-house feel and choice of restaurants.*

The Beetle & Wedge is one of very few hotels that is actually on the banks of the
River Thames. The hotel is made up of two lovely old buildings, one the rather
grand former home of Jerome K Jerome, and the other a converted boathouse,
once the ferry crossing point. The lounge, with its light panelled walls, log fire
and pile of board games, has the genteel atmosphere of an English country
house. Breakfast is served in the conservatory restaurant with sprigs of fresh
flowers on the tables; it's particularly pretty in summer, when the gardens
leading down to the river are at their best. You can eat here in the evening too, or
less formally in the boathouse restaurant, which can get very busy. One reader
wrote to praise everything about the hotel, saying, 'Above all the staff were
efficient, relaxed and friendly...the next morning we vacated our room but
returned for lunch – some comment – excellent food and service.' Most of the
bedrooms are in the main house with the remainder in a cottage next door, and
all but one overlook the river. Light muted colours and solid antiques
characterise the bedrooms, which have plenty of space and are immaculately
kept.

◑ Open all year; restaurant closed Mon & Tue eves   ↗ In Moulsford turn towards
river via Ferry Lane. Private car park   ⊨ 9 double, 1 four-poster; some in annexe; all
with bathroom/WC; TV, hair-dryer, trouser press, direct-dial telephone; trouser press on
request   ⊘ 2 restaurants, bar, lounge, conservatory, garden; early suppers for
children; toys, babysitting, baby-listening   ⅋ Wheelchair access to hotel, restaurant
and WC (unisex), 2 ground-floor bedrooms   ● No dogs; no smoking in bedrooms
▭ Access, Amex, Diners, Switch, Visa   £ Single occupancy of twin/double £80 to
£95, twin/double/four-poster £80 to £95. Set L £27.50, D £35. Special breaks
available

MULLION **Cornwall** map 1

Polurrian Hotel

Mullion, Helston TR12 7EN
TEL: (01326) 240421   FAX: (01326) 240083

A big, family-oriented hotel overlooking the sea and coastal footpath.

After a few unsettled years, the Polurrian is benefiting from new owner Barry
Adams' whirlwind efforts to update both the public areas and the bedrooms. The
lounge, which boasts lovely sea views, remains much the same, but the
restaurant has been re-carpeted and has been supplied with so many pictures to
hang on the walls that some are still waiting to find homes. The best tables are at
the far end, with sweeping views that encompass St Michael's Mount. The
four-course dinner menus offer a sensible choice of main courses that recognises

the dainty appetites of the weight-conscious, tempting dieters with pickles, ham and salad; the ravenous are offered dishes such as braised breast of guinea-fowl, and a selection of cheeses. High tea is provided for children between 5 and 6pm in the Marconi Lounge (and there is praise for the staff from guests for 'managing to stay cheerful amidst the din'), after which the room reverts to its daytime role as a small and dark alternative lounge. All the bedrooms on the second floor – and half of those on the first – have been refurbished with modern furnishings and fabrics, and feature plentiful stencilling. The older rooms are adequate and comfortable, but will strike some as being old-fashioned. With a purpose-built leisure centre housed in its own building, as well as a tennis court, snooker room and children's play area, there's more than enough to keep the whole family occupied. As one reader concluded, the Polurrian strikes 'exactly the right balance between fun for the children and luxury for us.'

◑ Closed 6 Jan to 7 Feb ⊠ Opposite cricket field in Mullion. Private car park
⤶ 1 single, 4 twin, 14 twin/double, 12 double, 3 four-poster, 4 family rooms, 1 suite; all with bathroom/WC; TV, room service, hair-dryer, direct-dial telephone
✐ Restaurant, bar, 3 lounges, TV room, 2 games rooms, garden; gym, sauna, solarium, outdoor and heated indoor swimming-pools, tennis, snooker, squash, putting green; early suppers for children; toys, playrooms, babysitting, baby-listening, outdoor games, crèche ᕯ Wheelchair access to hotel, restaurant and WC (M,F), 8 ground-floor bedrooms, 1 specially equipped for disabled people ● No children under 7 in restaurant eves; no dogs in public rooms and some bedrooms; no smoking in some public rooms and some bedrooms ⊟ Access, Amex, Diners, Switch, Visa
£ Single/single occupancy of twin/double £45 to £76, twin/double £90 to £152, four-poster £100 to £172, family room from £100, suite £120 to £192 (rates incl dinner); deposit required. Set Sun L £8.50, D £18; light meals available. Special breaks available

---

MUNGRISDALE Cumbria
map 10

Mill Hotel

Mungrisdale, Nr Penrith CA11 0XR
TEL: (01768) 779659 FAX: (01768) 779155

Excellent food, quiet Cumbrian hamlet and relaxing, unpretentious surroundings.

'Only ten hours to go until dinner,' one guest remarked to our incognito inspector over breakfast – such anticipation is praise indeed for Eleanor Quinlan's cooking, and was found to be fully justified. Smoked trout with mustard mayonnaise was followed by a tasty carrot and coriander soup (served with home-baked raisin and soda breads), then roast quails with sour cherry sauce. Richard Quinlan is the consummate host, taking orders, delivering dishes, creating sculptures on the candelabra as the candles burn down and easing the conversation along. 'He knows – or gets to know – his guests in a very unobtrusive way and can catalyse conversation, but there is no pressure on anyone to socialise,' writes one guest so delighted by the Mill as to stay longer than planned. A walk may be tempting after dinner, or you can opt for coffee in the cosy beamed sitting-room with log fire. And if you want quiet contemplation rather than conversation, there's a small reading-room with material on the local flora and fauna. Bedrooms are homely and comfortable, if unspectacular, with multiple patterns of wallpaper and humble furnishings, and you can be lulled to sleep by the brook babbling below (occasionally accompanied by the plumbing).

◑ Closed Nov to Feb ⤵ 2 miles north of A66, midway between Penrith and Keswick. Private car park ⤶ 4 twin, 5 double; 6 with bathroom/WC, 1 with shower/WC; TV, room service, hair-dryer ⊘ Restaurant, 3 lounges, drying-room, conservatory, garden; fishing; early suppers for children; babysitting, baby-listening ⅗ No wheelchair access ● No dogs in public rooms; no smoking in restaurant ▭ None accepted £ Single occupancy of twin/double £25 to £37, twin/double £50 to £70; deposit required. Set D £22.50. Special breaks available

---

MYTHOLMROYD West Yorkshire   map 8

Redacre Mill

Mytholmroyd, Hebden Bridge HX7 5DQ
TEL: (01422) 885563 (AND FAX)

Characterful rooms and friendly hosts are features of this former mill on the banks of a canal.

Situated halfway between Halifax and Burnley, and a couple of miles from the well-trodden Pennine Way, Redacre Mill makes a good base if you're exploring Calderdale's industrial heritage, or if you're hardy enough to be fond of walking on the windswept moors. Judith and John Clegg have created their unpretentious guesthouse from a former Victorian cotton mill, and they've been careful to keep some of its unusual historical details: alongside the light, modern décor and cottagey fabrics in your bedroom, you might also find winding gear hanging from the ceiling, or the varnished wood cladding that once added a bit of luxury to the mill manager's office. The bedrooms are fairly simple, but very well kept, and the small, modern bathrooms are provided with plenty of goodies. Choose a room overlooking the canal if you fancy watching the boats going by in the summer. You can do the same from the neatly maintained garden, or from the comfortable lounge, which boasts floor-to-ceiling patio doors and plenty of books (which you're encouraged to browse through). Dinner is a straightforward affair, featuring generous portions and a choice of starters and puddings. A typical meal might include cream of chicken soup, followed by a marinaded leg of lamb flavoured with herbs and red wine, and finally fresh peaches in brandy.

◑ Closed Chr & New Year, and weekends in winter ⤵ In Mytholmroyd turn right after fire station; cross humpback bridge, and take first right. Private car park ⤶ 2 twin, 3 double; 2 with bathroom/WC, 3 with shower/WC; TV, room service, hair-dryer ⊘ Dining-room, lounge, garden; early suppers for children; babysitting, cots, high chairs ⅗ No wheelchair access ● No dogs; no smoking ▭ Access, Visa £ Single occupancy of twin/double £33 to £38, twin/double £48 to £55; deposit required. Set D £12.50. Special breaks available

Buckle Yeat

Near Sawrey, Ambleside LA22 0LF
TEL: (01539) 436538/436446   FAX: (01539) 436446

An attractive, old cottage offering B&B in a busy tourist village.

With her eye for beauty, Beatrix Potter illustrated *The tale of Tom Kitten* and *The tale of the pie and the patty pan* with drawings of Buckle Yeat, and Helen Kirby's little whitewashed cottage, draped in creepers and with dangling flower baskets throughout the summer, still presents an idyllic picture. The sitting-room – part flagstoned, with a low, beamed ceiling and a grandfather clock ticking away the seconds in the corner – maintains the atmosphere. Breakfasts are taken in the adjoining, spacious, converted barn, which also serves as a souvenir shop and tearoom during the day. Creamy-coloured, flowery fabrics and Laura Ashley wallpaper enhance the cottage-like feel in the spick-and-span, potpourri-scented bedrooms. The rooms in the barn conversion are more spacious, but although a little smaller, those in the cottage have greater character.

◑ Open all year ⤢ In centre of Near Sawrey village. Private car park 🛏 1 single, 2 twin, 4 double; family room available; some in annexe; 4 with bathroom/WC, 3 with shower/WC; TV, hair-dryer ✦ Dining-room, lounge, TV room, garden ⟨ No wheelchair access ● No dogs in public rooms; no smoking in dining-room ▭ Access, Amex, Delta, Switch, Visa £ Single £20 to £23, single occupancy of twin/double £30 to £35, twin/double £40 to £45, family room £50 to £55; deposit required

Ees Wyke

Near Sawrey, Ambleside LA22 0JZ
TEL: (01539) 436393 (AND FAX)

A winning combination of good food, ebullient hosts and lake views.

Even trouble with the drains on a wet bank holiday couldn't disturb Margaret Williams' ebullient disposition. When our inspector arrived unannounced, workmen were busy removing the evidence of their handiwork from the usually flawless views across the fields to Esthwaite Water; a man from the council was waiting impatiently to see some plans; and a pan full of chicken thighs was approaching a critical stage in its preparation by John Williams. And Margaret and John sailed through all this activity with the humour and equanimity that is the hallmark of their friendly Georgian country house. While Margaret is sparking pre-dinner conversation and tickling funny bones among the guests in one of the two elegant and colourful lounges, John will be grilling goat's cheese, crisping the duck, and preparing a suprême of pheasant or a highly distinguished smoked-haddock rarebit. Reports continue to sing the praises of his 'delicious five-course meals.'

The bedrooms, named after their colour schemes, are generally of a good size (although the bathrooms are compact) and are smartly decorated, with those on the top floor sporting sloping roofs and blackened rafter beams. Green boasts a splendid, carved, Victorian bedstead, Blue and Sunshine have double-aspect views, while from Lilac you can stare down the dale while soaking in the bathtub.

◗ Closed Jan & Feb ⬈ On edge of village. Private car park 🛏 3 twin, 5 double; 2 with bathroom/WC, 6 with shower/WC; TV, hair-dryer ⚘ Restaurant, 2 lounges, drying-room, garden ♿ No wheelchair access ● No children under 8 in restaurant eves; no dogs in public rooms ▭ Amex £ Single occupancy of twin/double £42 to £52, twin/double £84. Set D £12. Special breaks available

---

NEEDHAM MARKET Suffolk   map 6

Pipps Ford

Needham Market, Ipswich IP6 8LJ
TEL: (01449) 760208   FAX: (01449) 760561

Excellent food and stylish bedrooms, but some niggles over details.

The location of this attractive, half-timbered, sixteenth-century farmhouse is more peaceful than you might expect, since it is but a bollard's throw from the A14; however, the trees in the hollow in which it sits seem to blot out most of the traffic noise. Raewyn Hackett-Jones has put a lot of thought and effort into making the rooms stylish, with home-made patchwork quilts and stencilled walls in the bedrooms, and appealing arrangements of antiques and china throughout the house. There are grumbles, however, which seem to centre on function rather than form: one reader complained about poor housekeeping standards and a lack of hot water, while our inspector found that although the temperature of the water was fine, the lack of pressure resulted in a shivery dribble (a problem apparently shared by others, it was revealed at the breakfast table). Our inspector's room in the converted stables was also rather chilly as the storage heaters had been turned off, although an electric heater was willingly produced. The food, however, really hits the spot: an April dinner offered a choice of four or five starters, such as garlic prawns or melon sorbet, the set main course was loin of pork with a Madeira and mushroom sauce, and the excellent desserts included summer pudding and treacle tart. Breakfast, too, is very good, and, like dinner, is eaten communally around the single dining-table. The service is very friendly and helpful, although a clearer indication of where to park, and a slightly earlier greeting would be appreciated. More reports, please.

◗ Closed mid-Dec to mid-Jan; dining-room closed Sun eve ⬈ Follow private road off roundabout where A140 joins A14. Private car park 🛏 3 twin, 3 double, 1 four-poster; some in annexe; all with bathroom/WC; hair-dryer ⚘ Dining-room, 3 lounges, TV room, conservatory, garden; conference facilities (max 25 people incl up to 7 residential); fishing, tennis, croquet; early suppers for children ♿ Wheelchair access to hotel (1 step) and dining-room, 4 ground-floor bedrooms, 1 specially equipped for disabled people ● No children under 5; no dogs; no smoking in dining-room or bedrooms ▭ None accepted £ Single occupancy of twin/double £33 to £38, twin/double £45 to £61, four-poster £65; deposit required. Set D £16 to £18.50. Special breaks available

NETHERFIELD **East Sussex**   map 3

Netherfield Place

Netherfield, Battle TN33 9PP
TEL: (01424) 774455   FAX: (01424) 774024

A stylish country retreat with impressive cuisine and excellent service.

High standards are the keynote in this Georgian-style country house set in 30 acres of beautifully landscaped gardens and woodland. Battle, the epicentre of 1066 heritage country, is a mere four miles away, and the knighted families who fought in the Battle of Hastings are honoured here in the names of the tasteful and immaculately decorated bedrooms. The resident proprietors Michael and Helen Collier take a keen 'hands-on' approach to running their hotel and impeccable service is assured from their friendly young staff. Public rooms are comfortable and elegant areas in which to wind down before dining in the Californian-redwood-panelled restaurant, where you might be tempted by a wild mushroom ravioli, collops of monkfish on stir-fried vegetables with tapénade, or venison sausages with braised red cabbage. Of the plush bedrooms, perhaps Pomeroy has the edge thanks to excellent views over the gardens, although Montgomery with its stripped wood panels or Mandeville, another huge room with canopied bed and panelled window bays, are strong contenders. Michael Collier describes the constant process of refurbishment as a 'Forth Bridge' undertaking.

◑ Closed Chr & New Year   ▨ Take A2100 north from Battle for 1 mile; take right-hand turn towards Netherfield; hotel is 2 miles on left. Private car park   ⟻ 4 single, 4 twin, 5 double, 1 four-poster; family rooms available; all with bathroom/WC; TV, room service, hair-dryer, direct-dial telephone; no tea/coffee-making facilities in rooms   ⊗ Restaurant, bar, lounge, TV room, drying-room, conservatory, garden; conference facilities (max 80 people incl up to 14 residential); tennis, croquet, putting green; early suppers for children; toys, babysitting, baby-listening, outdoor games   ♿ No wheelchair access   ● No children in restaurant eves; no dogs in public rooms   ▭ Access, Amex, Diners, Visa   £ Single £60, single occupancy of twin/double £75, twin/double £105, four-poster £140, family room £210. Set L £11.50, D £24.50; alc L, D £28. Special breaks available

---

NETTLETON **Wiltshire**   map 2

Fosse Farmhouse

Nettleton Shrub, Nettleton, Nr Chippenham SN14 7NJ
TEL: (01249) 782286   FAX: (01249) 783066

A curious but successful combination of English style and French rusticism in an isolated spot.

An isolated farmhouse is not the most obvious place in which to set up a mini business empire, but that of former antique dealer Caron Cooper seems to be thriving. The main house – once an abandoned wreck – now contains a restaurant and bedrooms, the former stables a teashop-cum-breakfast room and a few further bedrooms, while Caron still trades in antique knick-knacks in a small outbuilding, as the rocking horse outside and price tags in unexpected places show. The interior décor combines French rustic influences and English country style with her love of the antique and quirky. The breakfast-room, with its cheery red and white checked tablecloths, maintains the original stable's cobbled floor and hay racks. The sitting-room is full of clutter, such as pine shelves stacked with china and a child's cradle full of bric-à-brac, but the restaurant, with its lace curtains, stone fireplace and pine dresser, is more in step with country tradition. Caron's menus are simple but imaginative, and she also prepares vegetarian and vegan options. The bedrooms are certainly individual: pastel-pink cherubs float on the Pink Room's new wallpaper, and wood panelling from a local pub has been used in the bathroom. The bedrooms above the stables are on the small side. One reader questioned the hotel's value for money, and it's true that the prices seem to be more appropriate to a country house than a farmhouse.

◑ Open all year ⤧ From M4 take B4039 to village of The Gib, then first left; hotel is 1 mile further on the right. Private car park ⤆ 1 single, 1 twin, 4 double; family room available; some in annexe; 2 with bathroom/WC, 4 with shower/WC; TV, room service, hair-dryer, clock radio ✧ Restaurant, lounge, garden; conference facilities (max 15 people incl up to 6 residential); early suppers for children; toys, outdoor games, high chairs ⅄ No wheelchair access ● No dogs in public rooms and in bedrooms by arrangement only; no smoking in restaurant ☐ Access, Amex, Delta, Visa £ Single £45 to £58, single occupancy of twin/double £65 to £72, twin/double £80 to £120, family room £110 to £130; deposit required. Set Sun L £18, D £24. Special breaks available

---

NEWCASTLE UPON TYNE **Tyne & Wear**   map 10

The Copthorne

The Close, Quayside, Newcastle upon Tyne NE1 3RT
TEL: 0191-222 0333   FAX: 0191-230 1111

A pricey business hotel, situated near to the station, featuring extensive views over the Tyne.

No one should have reason to complain about this large, mainly business-oriented hotel. Purpose-built to make the most of its setting, the hotel boasts 150 or so bedrooms, each of which has a river view (which is restful for its guests, if a little ugly from the outside). The public rooms are huge and stylish: the atrium foyer, with its marble floor and leather seating, includes a glass wall, through which you can watch the activity on the river, while the sunny yellow restaurant continues the fluvial theme with a large model of a sailing boat. For dinner, you have a choice between the traditional food (such as fish and chips or rib of beef) of the informal Boaters bar, or the extensive menu of Le Rivage, in which the reasonably priced meat dishes are served with rich sauces; a caviare starter will, however, set you back more than £50. The bedrooms – some of which have balconies – are of a good size, and feature plain, Art-Deco-style furnishings, along with well-equipped bathrooms.

◑ Open all year ⤧ From A695, follow signs for Newcastle city centre, then take
B1600 Quayside road. At traffic lights, take right fork down the hill and round corner to
left. Hotel is on right. Private car park ⤶ 24 twin, 122 double, 10 suites; all with
bathroom/WC; TV, room service, hair-dryer, mini-bar, trouser press, direct-dial
telephone ⌮ 2 restaurants, 2 bars, lounge; air-conditioning in all rooms; conference
facilities (max 220 people incl up to 156 residential); gym, sauna, solarium, heated
indoor swimming-pool; babysitting ♿ Wheelchair access to hotel, restaurant and
WC (unisex), lift to 1 bedroom specially equipped for disabled people ● No dogs in
public rooms ▭ Access, Amex, Delta, Diners, Switch, Visa £ Single occupancy of
twin/double £115, twin/double £128, suite from £160. Continental B £10, cooked B
£11; set L £13, D £16.50; bar meals available. Special breaks available

---

NEW MILTON Hampshire   map 2

Chewton Glen

Christchurch Road, New Milton BH25 6QS
TEL: (01425) 275341 FAX: (01425) 272310

*A luxurious country-club retreat with extensive leisure facilities and
prices to match.*

Approached along an immaculate drive, Chewton Glen is a sprawling,
red-brick, Palladian building, flying a flag, albeit with an unpretentious air: all
suggestive of an up-market retreat. Nestling in 70 acres of parkland, the hotel is
lavish in every respect, from its grand public rooms, huge golf course and leisure
complex, to its princely price bracket. The energetic can make use of the health
club, which offers every imaginable sporting activity, but if you prefer
relaxation, after your massage you can walk down to the sea along the 20-minute
footpath known as 'Chewton Bunny'. The indoor swimming-pool – built along
classical lines, with *trompe-l'oeil* wall paintings that conjure up images of a
Roman bathhouse – is particularly impressive. The attentive staff foster a relaxed
atmosphere, and the hotel manages to be simultaneously luxurious and
sophisticated, without being stiff and ostentatious. The conservatory restaurant
is splendid, and has lovely views of the grounds. The dishes on offer may include
a double-baked Emmental soufflé, followed by a mousseline of cauliflower and
flat mushrooms served on a bed of mixed-leaf salad, accompanied by a wine
chosen from a list of 400 bottles.

The bedrooms range from extravagant, two-storeyed apartments with private
gardens in the converted coach house, to smaller, but equally well-decorated,
rooms in the main house.

---

*Use the index at the back of the book if you know the name of a hotel but
are unsure about its precise location.*

Report forms are at the back of the Guide; *write a letter or e-mail us if
you prefer. Our e-mail address is: "guidereports@which.co.uk".*

◑ Open all year 🔁 From A35 turn off towards Walkford and Highcliffe (do not follow the New Milton signs). Drive through Walkford and take the fourth left turning (Chewton Farm Road). Entrance on right. Private car park 🔚 37 twin/double, 18 suites; some in annexe; all with bathroom/WC; TV, room service, hair-dryer, trouser press, direct-dial telephone ✅ 3 restaurants, bar, 3 lounges, games room, garden; air-conditioning in conference/banqueting suite and 4 suites; conference facilities (max 110 people incl up to 53 residential); golf, gym, sauna, solarium, outdoor and heated indoor swimming-pools, tennis, croquet ♿ Wheelchair access to hotel, restaurants and WC (unisex), 11 ground-floor bedrooms, 6 specially equipped for disabled people ● No children under 7; no dogs; no smoking in restaurants ⬜ Access, Amex, Diners, Switch, Visa £ Single occupancy of twin/double £195, twin/double £195, suite £395; deposit required. Continental B £9.50, cooked B £16; set L £18.50 to £23.50, D £42 (prices valid till Apr 1997). Special breaks available

---

NEWQUAY **Cornwall**   map 1

Headland Hotel

Fistral Beach, Newquay TR7 1EW
TEL: (01637) 872211   FAX: (01637) 872212

A large, professionally run, family-oriented hotel, situated on the headland overlooking a prime surfing beach.

At first glance, the Headland Hotel looks like a large Victorian hospital, but this huge, red-brick structure was always intended to be a hotel, hence its splendid position looking down on to Fistral Beach, where the world surfing championships take place each summer. The Headland Hotel makes every effort to ensure that its guests rarely need to venture far from its environs, boasting tennis courts, indoor and outdoor swimming-pools, a surfing school on the beach, and separate rooms designed for the entertainment of both young children and their teenage brothers and sisters. Guests can even fly over the hotel in a hot-air balloon (weather permitting). The scale of the public areas is appropriate to the hotel's size; the restaurant, in particular, is huge, and is designed to enable as many guests as possible to land a window table, but there's also a less formal coffee shop, as well as a smaller lounge area, to which you can retreat. The daily-changing dinner menu offers a choice of five fairly traditional starters and main courses. The bedrooms vary enormously in size and décor. The four-bedded Room 103, in which the Prince and Princess of Wales stayed in 1909, looks fairly humble nowadays, but Room 130 – a few doors away – boasts a half-tester bed and a two-piece suite that is angled to take advantage of the sea views.

Prices are quoted per room *rather than* per person.

Use the maps at the back of the Guide *to pinpoint hotels in a particular area.*

◗ *Closed Chr & first 3 weeks in Jan* ↗ On approaching Newquay by A30, follow signs to Fistral Beach. Private car park ⇤ 8 single, 12 twin, 20 double, 1 four-poster, 44 family rooms, 14 family suites, 1 suite; all with bathroom/WC exc 1 double with shower/WC; TV, room service, direct-dial telephone; hair-dryer on request ⌀ 2 restaurants, bar, 5 lounges, TV room, study, conservatory, 2 games rooms, garden; conference facilities (max 250 people incl up to 100 residential); fishing, golf, sauna/solarium, outdoor and heated indoor swimming-pools, tennis, hot-air ballooning, putting green, croquet, surfing; early suppers for children; toys, playrooms, babysitting, baby-listening, outdoor games ♿ Wheelchair access to hotel (ramp), restaurant and WC (unisex), lift to bedrooms ⬤ No children in restaurant eves; no smoking in restaurant ▭ Access, Amex, Delta, Diners, Switch, Visa £ Single from £42, single occupancy of twin/double from £45, twin/double from £84, four-poster from £94, family room from £105, suite from £124; deposit required. Cooked B £3; set D £17.50; alc D from £19.50; light lunches available. Special breaks available

---

NIDD North Yorkshire   map 9

Nidd Hall

Nidd, Harrogate HG3 3BN
TEL: (01423) 771598   FAX: (01423) 770931

A sumptuous country house, rich in architectural interest, set in wonderfully peaceful grounds.

If part of the pleasure of staying in country hotels is to enjoy buildings designed in a haughtier age, Nidd Hall will not disappoint. The seemingly endless, tree-lined drive fosters a sense of anticipation, although the rather sombre Georgian exterior of the building gives little away. The entrance hall – a grandiose, domed space, with pale-lemon walls laced with intricate plasterwork, marble statues set into alcoves and a skylight that floods the area with light – really sets the tone for the rest of the house. Beyond this is a hallway whose marble columns support elaborate, wrought-iron balustrades, and whose doorways are topped with detailed entablatures. Through one such set of doors lies the elegant drawing-room, with its polished wooden floor and bright-golden drapes; delicate plasterwork covers the ceiling, and monumental fireplaces stand at each end, like Roman triumphal arches. The walls of the dining-room are hung with large, dignified oil portraits, and the windows overlook the grounds. A la carte menus combine the local – such as loin of Nidderdale lamb en croûte – with more Gallic flavours, for example, provençale pancakes or tuna niçoise.

The bedrooms are predictably plush, and feature swagged curtains, marble fireplaces and coronet-crowned beds; many have grand views across the gardens and lake. The courtyard rooms, situated beneath the clock tower, are equally stylish, with candy-striped walls and floral fabrics.

We mention those hotels that don't accept dogs; guide dogs, however, are almost always an exception. Telephone ahead to make sure.

◑ *Open all year* 🔁 5 miles north of Harrogate, just off A61 Ripon road. Private car park 🛏 3 single, 12 twin, 37 double, 3 four-poster, 4 suites; some in annexe; all with bathroom/WC; TV, room service, hair-dryer, mini-bar, trouser press, direct-dial telephone ✅ Dining-room, bar, lounge, library, games room, garden conference facilities (max 250 people incl up to 59 residential); fishing, gym, sauna, solarium, heated indoor swimming-pool, tennis, croquet, squash, boating; early suppers for children; playrooms, babysitting, baby-listening, crèche, outdoor games 🦽 Wheelchair access to hotel (1 step), dining-room and WC (M,F), 8 ground-floor bedrooms ● No dogs 🔲 Access, Amex, Delta, Diners, Switch, Visa £ Single £95, single occupancy of twin/double £110, twin/double £120, four-poster £150, suite £195 to £230. Set Sun L £13.50; alc L, D £21. Special breaks available

---

NORTHAMPTON Northamptonshire   map 5

Swallow Hotel

Eagle Drive, Northampton NN4 7HW
TEL: (01604) 768700   FAX: (01604) 769011

A slick, modern, business hotel on Northampton's outskirts.

A humdrum location – on a nexus of ring roads 3 miles from Northampton's centre – and an instantly forgettable low-rise, red-brick, exterior conceal this hotel's stylishness. Marble in the lobby, striking abstract art on stark white walls, and sophisticated spot-lighting everywhere make a refreshing change from the traditional country-house decoration so prevalent in many smart business hotels. A fake citrus tree enlivens the cocktail lounge, while the leisure centre focuses on an inviting, tear-shaped pool. Both restaurants are fetching, too: Spires, serving English and French cuisine, occupies an octagonal conservatory, where spires are etched on to the glass; while classical busts and mosaics ennoble La Fontana, where you can dine on Italian fare. The imaginatively co-ordinated décor in the bedrooms is equally arresting: the blue rooms look the best. Expect good facilities, such as power-showers, ironing equipment and fresh milk in the fridges. The pricier executive rooms offer more space, but no other advantages. With a dedicated conference centre, you'll have the company of many suited guests at this Swallow hotel. However, it does offer good-value, two-night leisure breaks, which, if begun on a Friday, include Sunday night for free.

◑ Open all year 🔁 3 miles from Junction 15 of M1. Private car park 🛏 30 twin, 90 double; family rooms and suites available; all with bathroom/WC; TV, room service, hair-dryer, mini-bar, trouser press, direct-dial telephone, iron ✅ 2 restaurants, bar, lounge; air-conditioning in all public areas; conference facilities (max 220 people incl up to 120 residential); gym, sauna, solarium, heated indoor swimming-pool; early suppers for children; babysitting, baby-listening 🦽 Wheelchair access to hotel, restaurant and WC (unisex), 50 ground-floor bedrooms, 2 specially equipped for disabled people ● No smoking in some bedrooms 🔲 Access, Amex, Delta, Diners, Switch, Visa £ Single occupancy of twin/double £95, twin/double £105, family room from £105, suite £130; deposit required. Set L £13.50, D £19. Special breaks available

---

See the inside front cover for a brief explanation of how to use the Guide.

Blackaller Hotel

North Bovey, Nr Moretonhampstead, Newton Abbot TQ13 8QY
TEL: (01647) 440322 (AND FAX)

A gem of a converted woollen mill overlooking a stream in a picture-postcard Dartmoor village.

It would be hard to imagine a prettier setting than Blackaller's. A whitewashed, seventeenth-century, former woollen mill, it looks straight over a lawn set with benches to a small stream lined with blackallers – the local name for black alders. In the yard at the back there are usually a couple of Jacob sheep; come in spring, and you'll see their lambs there too. Peter Hunt and Hazel Phillips have aimed to maintain a farmhouse feeling inside, so reception is in a flagstone-floored room with a big log fire. Hazel describes the dining-room beyond as being 'higgledy-piggledy', but the mix of tables and chairs actually works extremely well. Across the hall, the sitting-room is used to host slide shows and talks about local walking tours. Upstairs, the bedrooms are decorated in a fresh, cottagey style, with lacy covers on the beds and new showers added to all the baths. Four-course dinners give a new look to traditional ingredients: tomato ice-cream with avocado mayonnaise is one possible starter, and pot-roasted, boned quail with a mushroom-and-spinach stuffing in a red-wine sauce a likely main course. Ducks' breasts sometimes come marinated in the hotel's own honey, because on top of running the hotel, Hazel Phillips somehow finds the energy to tend 20 beehives.

◑ Closed Jan & Feb   ⊉ On North Bovey road (B3212). Private car park   ⌸ 1 single, 1 twin, 3 double; 1 in annexe; all with bathroom/WC; TV, room service, hair-dryer   ⊘ Dining-room, bar, lounge, drying-room, garden; conference facilities (max 20 people incl up to 5 residential); fishing; early suppers for children; babysitting   ♿ No wheelchair access   ⊜ No children under 12 in dining room; no dogs in public rooms; smoking in bar only   🗀 None accepted   ₤ Single £29 to £31, single occupancy of twin/double £45, twin/double £70 to £72; deposit required. Set D £19.50 (1996 prices). Special breaks available

---

Brookdale House

North Huish, South Brent TQ10 9NR
TEL: (01548) 821661   FAX: (01548) 821606

An elegant rural retreat with spacious rooms and Victorian landscaping.

Brookdale House, with its triple gables, crenellations and grotesque heads above the porch, is the sort of Victorian rectory modern vicars can only dream about. Since taking over two years ago, Gill and Michael Mikkelsen have transformed the hotel, ripping out the dark-wooden panelling and replacing it with a marvellous array of paintings (the best of them by Russian artists) and prints culled from auctions. The house's structure needed a lot of work, but, fortunately, pleasing features such as the grapevine cornice around the ceiling in one lounge were salvageable. One of the bedrooms now has a patch of wall exposed to reveal the signature of a painter working on it in 1889, while a bathroom retains a brass gadget for measuring the level of water in the tank; in a previous age, when it fell too low, the butler was sent out to the well to fetch more water. The bedrooms, named after flowers, are spacious and enticing; Crocus, boasting an original fireplace, is especially attractive. Two more rooms are in a separate building behind the house. Michael Mikkelsen is Danish, which explains the Scandinavian bias to the 'in addition' list of starters, which tops up the otherwise fairly conventional three-course dinner menus. The Mikkelsens are welcoming hosts who like to greet their guests at the door. Although a stream running through the garden was due to be fenced in when we inspected, they feel that it renders Brookdale House unsuitable for young children.

○ Open all year ⤢ From A38 take South Brent exit, follow signs to Avonwick. Turn right opposite Avon Inn, then take first left. Continue to top of hill and turn right. At bottom of hill turn right. Private car park ⌸ 2 twin, 6 double; some in annexe; all with bathroom/WC; TV, room service, hair-dryer, trouser press, direct-dial telephone ⬦ 2 restaurants, 2 lounges, garden; conference facilities (max 40 people incl up to 8 residential); early suppers for children ⅄ No wheelchair access ● Children by arrangement only; no dogs in public rooms and some bedrooms; no smoking in some bedrooms ☐ Access, Amex, Switch, Visa £ Single occupancy of twin/double £45 to £55, twin/double £60 to £90; deposit required. Set L £9.50, D £16/19

NORTH NEWINGTON **Oxfordshire** map 5

La Madonette Guesthouse

North Newington, Banbury OX15 6AA
TEL: (01295) 730212 FAX: (01295) 730363

Comfortable old-fashioned rooms in secluded former mill.

A quick hop from the M40 motorway, yet half a mile away from its nearest neighbours, La Madonette is a popular mid-week choice for business people wanting B&B away from the expense and anonymity of bigger and smarter business hotels. The house dates back to the seventeenth century and has leaded stone-mullioned windows. It was once a mill which began life pulping paper and ended up mashing bones! Its current owner, Patti Ritter, will tell you the full story as she shows you to your room. You can choose from one of five large and comfortably furnished bedrooms in the main house or opt for one of the three one-bedroomed cottages (if they have not been let on a self-catering basis) overlooking the millstream. The rooms have pretty well everything you need from soap and shampoos to a telephone, and though they're all of a similar old-fashioned character they differ in the size of their bathrooms. Room 6 has a small shower-room, two others have enormous bathrooms with corner baths. The small lounge doubles as a bar and is likely to be a sociable place as people return from the dining-room where dinner is by arrangement only. You can expect straightforward home cooking including dishes such as chicken with tarragon and lots of fresh vegetables and fruit.

◑ Open all year ⏚ From Banbury Cross turn right on to B4035 for 2½ miles; turn right for North Newington. Private car park ⏗ 1 twin, 3 double, 1 four-poster; family rooms available; 2 with bathroom/WC, 3 with shower/WC; room service, hair-dryer, direct-dial telephone; TV in most rooms ⏀ Dining-room, lounge/bar, garden; conference facilities (max 15 people incl up to 5 residential); unheated outdoor swimming-pool; baby-listening ⏓ No wheelchair access ● No dogs ☐ Access, Switch, Visa £ Single occupancy of twin/double £32, twin/double £48, four-poster £60, family room £58

NORTH WHEATLEY Nottinghamshire　　　　　　　　map 9

Old Plough

Top Street, North Wheatley, Retford DN22 9DB
TEL: (01427) 880916

A gracefully furnished home with indulgent bedrooms and tasty, communally served meals.

Pauline and Ted Pasley call their good-looking, Grade II-listed, Victorian building, which was once the local pub, a country guesthouse. Appealing period features, such as pine fireplaces and stuccoed ceilings in the drawing-room and dining-room, enriched by smart antiques, set the tone. All three swish bedrooms have interesting beds: there is a canopied brass bed in a small double, coroneted singles in a twin, and a four-poster. They're also well stocked with extras, including bathrobes, fruit, sherry and mineral water. North Wheatley is a quiet village renowned for its strawberries, some of which find their way on to the Old Plough's single, well-polished breakfast table in summer. Pauline's praised traditional dinners are without choice, except for puddings, and there is a selection of wines. She might try to tempt you with broccoli and watercress soup; chicken breast with spinach stuffing, wrapped in bacon; gooseberry crumble; cheese and biscuits; and home-made sweets with coffee. Many of the guests here are business people, but for those on holiday, bikes, on which to explore the surrounding countryside, are laid on *gratis*.

◑ Open all year ⏚ On A620 between Retford and Gainsborough, 200 yards from Wheatley church. Private car park ⏗ 1 twin, 1 double, 1 four-poster; 2 with bathroom/WC, double with shower/WC; TV, hair-dryer ⏀ Dining-room, lounge, drying-room, garden; conference facilities (max 12 people non-residential) ⏓ No wheelchair access ● No children under 15; no dogs; no smoking in bedrooms ☐ None accepted £ Single occupancy of twin/double £28, twin/double/ four-poster £55; deposit required. Set D £13.50

NORTON Shropshire　　　　　　　　map 5

Hundred House Hotel

Bridgnorth Road, Norton, Telford TF11 9EE
TEL: (01952) 730353 FAX: (01952) 730355

Bags of character and delightful bedrooms are offered at this bustling, roadside inn.

Although the volume of vehicles in its car park at lunchtime testifies to its popularity, when seen from the road there's little to distinguish the Hundred House Hotel from the scores of similar, red-brick hostelries that are dotted along the trunk roads of England. At its core, the hotel remains fundamentally a pub, so it's ironic that on entering reception you are steered through doors (just two examples of the fine, Art Nouveau glass that you'll see scattered about the place) that were scavenged from a temperance hall. The bar areas have been deftly divided into many sections, thus ensuring that a cosy atmosphere prevails.The Phillips family has struck on a simple, but effective, decorative ploy: hops, herbs and dried flowers – like a bizarre cross between bridal bouquets and Christmas decorations – cascading in exuberant bunches from the beams of the ceiling. A wood-burning stove, curving settles, spindle-back chairs and a smattering of copper and brass artefacts complete the rustic scene. Food – which transcends normal pub-grub, with dishes such as a casserole of venison served with herb-flavoured macaroni and beetroot marmalade – is served throughout the bars, and one section (complete with an old kitchen range) is designated a brasserie. There's a more formal dining-room, too, featuring old panelling and Tiffany lamps, in which you might dine on a chicken and cream-cheese terrine accompanied by grape chutney and toast, followed by a tuna fillet served with mange-tout and salsa verde, and finally fresh pineapple with caramel-and-hazelnut ice-cream.

The bedrooms are whimsical and delightful, and may include crooked beams, antique furnishings and pretty, pastel, patchwork quilts. There's a puckish air to the little swings that grace four of the rooms, conjuring up the magical world of Shakespeare's Forest of Arden.

● Open all year ▣ On A442 in Norton, midway between Telford and Bridgnorth. Private car park ⬅ 1 single, 2 twin, 3 double, 4 family rooms; all with bathroom/WC; TV, room service, hair-dryer, direct-dial telephone ✓ Dining-room, bar, lounge, garden; conference facilities (max 30 people incl up to 10 residential); early suppers for children; baby-listening ♿ No wheelchair access ● No dogs in public rooms and in bedrooms by arrangement only; no smoking in some bedrooms ▭ Access, Amex, Delta, Switch, Visa £ Single £59, single occupancy of twin/double £65, twin/double £79 to £90, family room £90; deposit required. Set Sun L £15; alc L, D from £22.50; bar meals available. Special breaks available

---

NORWICH Norfolk map 6

By Appointment ☆

25-29 St Georges Street, Norwich NR3 1AB
TEL: (01603) 630730

Flamboyant intimacy at this characterful, fifteenth-century merchant's house.

Tim Brown and Robert Culyer (not to mention Tuppence, the cat) are gradually expanding their empire: having started off with just a single house containing their restaurant, they have now swallowed up the adjacent buildings (in order to branch out into selling antiques), thereby also increasing the number of bedrooms from one to four. As we went to press, building work on the three additional bedrooms was still in progress, but the bones were in place, and roll-top baths were standing ready in the bathrooms. With its sloping, wood-panelled ceiling and cushioned window seat, the one bedroom that was in use when we inspected – situated right at the top of the original house, and crammed with antique goodies and vases full of ostrich feathers – offers a charmingly over-the-top experience. Expect more of the same when the others are completed. The restaurant downstairs, whose interlocking dining-rooms are painted deep green and dazzling yellow, and which is dotted with elegant flower arrangements, statuettes and plant-filled jardinières, is equally flamboyant. The menus (which are chalked on blackboards) often offer new twists on old favourites, such as a smoked-chicken terrine accompanied by a gooseberry vinaigrette, baked fillet of cod cooked in a herb crust and served with a lemon, garlic and vodka sauce, or a Jamaican banana and pecan-nut crumble. The lounge also doubles as an antique shop – it is therefore a veritable Aladdin's cave, and invites exploration.

◑ Open all year; restaurant closed Sun & Mon   ⊿ On junction of St Georges Street and Colegate. Private car park   ⤙ 1 single, 1 twin, 2 double; all with bathroom/WC; TV, hair-dryer; trouser press in some rooms   ⍻ Restaurant, lounge; early suppers for children   ⅊ No wheelchair access   ● No children under 12; no dogs; no smoking in some public rooms and some bedrooms   ▭ Access, Delta, Switch, Visa
£ Single £65; twin/double £85; deposit required. Alc D £25

NOTTINGHAM Nottinghamshire   map 5

Rutland Square Hotel

St James's Street, Nottingham NG1 6FJ
TEL: 0115-941 1114   FAX: 0115-941 0014

A reasonably priced hotel in Nottingham's city centre.

The Rutland Square Hotel makes much of its central location, just 150 yards from the entrance to Nottingham Castle. However, when we inspected, a new office block was being erected directly opposite, and a building site was marring this handsome, red-brick, warehouse conversion. The rather impressive marble, pillared lobby, with statues painted intriguingly on to the lift doors, suggests that the hotel is swankier than it actually is. Beyond the lobby lies an imaginatively arranged, sky-lit lounge and restaurant. The prices for table d'hôte meals of uncomplicated fare such as roasts, steaks and crumbles seem very reasonable, but the city must have more appealing places in which to dine. The bedrooms are cheerfully furnished in limed fittings. The hotel must possess one of the highest proportions of single rooms anywhere, and many are quite small; if you're on your own, it's worth paying just a few pounds more for a 'mini double' (which also offer cramped, but cheap, accommodation for two). Most guests stay here while on business: the hotel has a conference centre in a separate block. Prices therefore plummet on Friday, Saturday and Sunday nights – especially for occupancy of the singles and mini doubles.

◑ Open all year 🔁 Near Nottingham Castle. Private car park ⬛ 73 single, 9 twin, 20 double, 2 four-poster, 1 suite; family rooms available; all with bathroom/WC; TV, room service, hair-dryer, direct-dial telephone ✅ Restaurant (air-conditioned), 2 bars, lounge; conference facilities (max 340 people incl up to 105 residential); baby-listening ♿ Wheelchair access to hotel, restaurant and WC (unisex), lift to 2 bedrooms specially equipped for disabled people ● No dogs in public rooms ▭ Access, Amex, Delta, Diners, Switch, Visa £ Single £32 to £58, mini double £38 to £60, single occupancy of twin/double £54 to £65, twin/double £54 to £65, four-poster £98, family room £100 to £120, suite £132; deposit required. Continental B £3.50, cooked B £8; set L £7, D £12; alc L, D £13.50. Special breaks available

---

NUNNINGTON North Yorkshire map 9

Ryedale Lodge

Station Road, Nunnington, Nr Helmsley YO6 5XB
TEL: (01439) 748246 FAX: (01653) 694633

A peaceful converted railway station, with an emphasis on fine cooking.

Ryedale Lodge is situated in a peaceful rural area, about one mile from the National Trust's Nunnington Hall. The dark, stone building, which has lost its symmetry through its various extensions, gives little indication to the outsider of its previous life as the village's railway station. If you look a little closer, however, you may pick out the form of the railway track in the long, narrow garden, or notice the remains of a platform beyond the conservatory. The lounge's exposed stone wall shows the limit of the original building, and two lovely French tapestries of wine-pressing scenes (the originals are in the Louvre) help to soften the décor. There's a hint of France in the dining-room too, where the walls feature champagne posters and labels. Janet Laird's four-course dinners may start with queen scallops with bacon and white-wine sauce, and include main courses such as roast Lonsdale duckling with an orange-and-cranberry sauce. One reader concluded that 'the food and the excellent service are the mainstays here.'

The pretty bedrooms are named after their dominant colour, and although 'Apricot', 'Blue' and 'Pink' follow this theme, 'Brown' is more raspberry-hued, while 'Peacock' – despite being the largest – is not as extravagantly plumed as the name suggests.

◑ Open all year 🔁 1 mile west of Nunnington village, towards Helmsley. Private car park ⬛ 2 twin, 5 double; all with bathroom/WC; TV, room service, hair-dryer, mini-bar, trouser press, direct-dial telephone ✅ Dining-room, bar, lounge, drying-room, conservatory, garden; early suppers for children; babysitting, baby-listening ♿ Wheelchair access to hotel, restaurant and WC (M,F), 1 ground-floor bedroom specially equipped for disabled people ● No dogs; no smoking in dining-room ▭ Access, Delta, Switch, Visa £ Single occupancy of twin/double £43 to £48, twin/double £75 to £79; deposit required. Set D £27. Special breaks available

Barnsdale Lodge

The Avenue, Rutland Water, Oakham LE15 8RP
TEL: (01572) 724678   FAX: (01572) 724961

Visually fun and bustling hotel complex.

Something catches your eye wherever you look in this much-expanded
seventeenth-century farmhouse. Stone pigs appear in its gravel courtyard. Putti
and a teasing painting of English high society inhabit the grandest of the three
individually contrived dining-rooms, each professedly in Edwardian style.
Ducks, teddies, tea cosies, old-fashioned hats and even a kitchen range crop up
in the corridors and cosy bar areas; watering cans hang from the rafters in the
adjacent cheery conservatory. A smattering of interesting antiques, such as a
double-ended *chaise-longue* and marble-topped dressers, contribute to the appeal
of the smart bedrooms. Those in the new block, with distant views of Rutland
Water, cost extra, but they are the most comfortable. The Lodge thrives at
mealtimes, with a team of well-trained staff in black and white pinafores fussing
over residents and much local trade. The expansive buttery/bar menu offers
paella, baked local trout, pork, sage and apricot sausages and even desserts for
diabetics, while the restaurant menu offering 'Edwardian country farmhouse
fare' includes beef layered with wild mushrooms and foie gras in a truffle sauce.

◑ Open all year   ⊠ On A606, 2 miles east of Oakham. Private car park   ⊭ 8
single, 7 twin, 10 double, 2 four-poster, 2 family rooms; some in annexe; most with
bathroom/WC, singles with shower/WC; TV, room service, hair-dryer, trouser press,
direct-dial telephone, iron   ⊘ 3 restaurants, bar, lounge, conservatory, garden;
conference facilities (max 330 people incl up to 29 residential); fishing, golf, clay-pigeon
shooting; early suppers for children; baby-listening   ⅙ Wheelchair access to hotel (1
step), restaurant and WC (unisex), 2 ground-floor bedrooms specially equipped for
disabled people   ● Dogs by arrangement only; no smoking in some rooms
⊟ Access, Delta, Switch, Visa   £ Single/single occupancy of twin/double from £50,
twin/double from £70, four-poster from £80, family room from £95; deposit required.
Set Sun L £14; alc L, D £21; bar meals available. Special breaks available

---

George Hotel

100 High Street, Odiham, Basingstoke RG25 1LP
TEL: (01256) 702081   FAX: (01256) 704213

A village inn with comfortable rooms and lots of stories to tell.

As soon as you walk through the doors of this busy inn, you know that you're in
for a historical adventure. Apart from its Georgian façade, the building is over
450 years old, and is low ceilinged and oak beamed inside. The dark-wood walls
are about 2 feet thick and, because they were not cured before installation, have
dried out over the centuries to give the house its 'bent' and characterful style.
Wherever you choose to sit, there is always something interesting to look at: the
original wattle-and-daub walls in the lounge; the photographs of old Odiham

in the typical pub bar; or the tombstone that dates from 1639 and the Roundhead helmet in the Cromwell Restaurant, which also boasts a wonderful, flagstoned floor. The menu specialises in seafood and features such interesting preparations as grilled sea bass with red cabbage and beurre blanc, or escalopes of brill served with courgettes and fresh coriander. The bedrooms are divided between the main house and the converted outbuildings, and all are simply, but comfortably, furnished. The best is the four-postered Room 1, beneath whose plasterwork Elizabethan wall paintings (reputedly depicting Chaucer's poem *The Parlement of Foules*) have been discovered.

◑ Closed Chr; restaurant closed Sun eve ⬛ In centre of Odiham village. Private car park ⬚ 6 single, 2 twin, 8 double, 2 four-poster; family room available; some in annexe; all with bathroom/WC; TV, room service, hair-dryer, direct-dial telephone ⬦ Restaurant, bar (partly air-conditioned), lounge, garden; conference facilities (max 12 people residential/non-residential); early suppers for children ♿ No wheelchair access ⬤ No dogs in public rooms; no smoking in some bedrooms ▭ Access, Amex, Delta, Diners, Switch, Visa £ Single/single occupancy of twin/double £45 to £65, twin/double £75, four-poster £90, family room from £80; deposit required. Set Sun L £14; alc L, D £22; bar meals available (1996 prices). Special breaks available

---

OLDBURY West Midlands   map 5

Jonathans' Hotel

16-26 Wolverhampton Road, Oldbury, Warley B68 0LH
TEL: 0121-429 3757   FAX: 0121-434 3107

COUNTY HOTEL OF THE YEAR

One of Britain's most peculiar hotels – little less than a miniature Victorian/Edwardian theme park.

Such is the scale and complexity of this labyrinthine enterprise that to embark on this 'exciting journey into Victorian Britain' visitors are equipped with a map. Here's a Black Country pub that time forgot, there a whole street of Edwardian shop windows, an Edwardian kitchen, and cosy 'Withdrawing Rooms' full of antique clutter. If you're lucky, you might find the Fishmarket, a galleried café. Or you may come across the new Boulton Watt Bistro, which serves modern cuisine amid shocking purple and yellow décor that features Kandinsky and Hopper prints. At Jonathans' Original Restaurant, you're again surrounded by Victoriana and are served traditional English dishes.

Lace curtains, old-fashioned stuffed toys and tiny sitting-rooms with wing chairs, period books and china set around period fireplaces ensure that the hugely atmospheric bedrooms continue the theme of this Victorian fantasy land. At the same time, the two proprietorial Jonathans (Baker and Bedford) have not overlooked the essentials of a quality hotel: for example, bathrooms are first rate and the staff very perky. Their establishment needs to be something special to compensate for its unlovely location on a busy roundabout five miles west of Birmingham city centre, and it is.

Reports are welcome on any hotel, whether or not it is in the Guide.

◐ Open all year; restaurant closed Sun eve ⤢ At junction of A456 and A4123 towards Birmingham. Private car park ⇤ 8 single, 4 twin, 8 double, 2 four-poster, 11 suites; family rooms available; all with bathroom/WC; TV, room service, hair-dryer, direct-dial telephone, iron ⊘ 2 restaurants, 4 bars, 2 lounges, library, 2 conservatories; conference facilities (max 80 people incl up to 33 residential); early suppers for children; babysitting 🐦 No wheelchair access ● No dogs in public rooms ☐ Access, Amex, Delta, Diners, Switch, Visa £ Single/single occupancy of twin/double £69, twin/double/four-poster £80 to £118, family room £118, suite £89 to £150; deposit required. Set L £5 to £15, D £24.50; alc L, D £30. Special breaks available

---

OXFORD Oxfordshire   map 2

Cotswold House

363 Banbury Road, Oxford OX2 7PL
TEL: (01865) 310558 (AND FAX)

Good-value accommodation in modern family house in the north Oxford suburbs.

In an area where good-quality but inexpensive accommodation is hard to find, Cotswold House solves many travellers' problems. This modern family house in yellow Cotswold stone, window boxes spilling over with pretty flowers in summer, is on a busy main road in the suburbs of north Oxford, but is surprisingly quiet inside owing to its double-glazing. There's parking too, which is a bonus for Oxford. Jim and Anne O'Kane are a friendly, approachable couple whose housekeeping is immaculate. The breakfast-room with its plain wooden tables and off-white walls is simple and modern; while the sitting-room, with its green leather suite and flower arrangements, gives you plenty of space to meet fellow guests or sit and plan your day. The seven bedrooms vary from small singles to large family rooms, and all are similar in their light fresh décor and flowery fabrics. Facilities are excellent with lots of goodies and even a fridge in your room, though there are no baths save for one public bathroom. If you're a very light sleeper you might prefer a room at the back.

◐ Closed Chr ⤢ 2 miles north of Oxford city centre on A4260 Banbury Road. Private car park ⇤ 2 single, 1 twin, 2 double, 2 family rooms; all with shower/WC; TV, hair-dryer, fridge ⊘ Dining-room, lounge 🐦 No wheelchair access ● No children under 5; no dogs; no smoking ☐ None accepted £ Single £37 to £39, single occupancy of twin/double £50, twin/double £54 to £56; deposit required

Old Parsonage Hotel

1 Banbury Road, Oxford OX2 6NN
TEL: (01865) 310210   FAX: (01865) 311262

Small luxurious rooms in a busy city-centre hotel with a long tradition.

Originally run by nuns for the 'poor and infirm', the Old Parsonage has moved well away from its humble roots. Squeezed behind St Giles' church, between two busy main roads leading into Oxford's city centre, the two-storey gabled building is easy to miss at first glance. Parking is tricky too unless you arrive early. Inside, the hotel is a mix of modern and traditional décor. In the lobby an ancient stone fireplace contrasts with the marble floor, small Manhattan-style bar, and waiters in long butcher's aprons. Food is served from here to people in the lounge, who eat at low tables from sofas or leather dining-chairs. You can choose from a menu with a good variety of light dishes, particularly fish, including salmon cakes with lemon mayonnaise, tuna steak with avocado and tomato salsa, and warm salad of monkfish, scallops and prawns. There's no formal restaurant at the Old Parsonage, so if this arrangement doesn't suit, you could eat at Browns across the road, owned by the same company, and have the meal charged to your hotel bill. By fitting 30 bedrooms into the building, the hotel has achieved something of a miracle, and some of them are rather small. But with pretty colour schemes, stylish fabrics and good-sized marble bathrooms they're luxurious for their size. The best of them – about half – overlook or open out on to a courtyard at the back of the church.

◐ Closed 25 & 26 Dec ⬀ In centre of Oxford, at north end of St Giles Street. Private car park ⬏ 1 single, 6 twin, 19 double, 4 suites; all with bathroom/WC; TV, 24-hour room service, hair-dryer, mini-bar, direct-dial telephone; trouser press in some rooms; no tea/coffee-making facilities in rooms ✓ Restaurant/bar (air-conditioned), lounge, garden; babysitting, baby-listening ૐ No wheelchair access ● Dogs in bedrooms by arrangement ▭ Access, Amex, Diners, Switch, Visa £ Single/single occupancy of twin/double £120, twin/double £155, suite £195; deposit required. Alc L £18.50, D £22.50. Special breaks available

---

Randolph Hotel

Beaumont Street, Oxford OX1 2LN
TEL: (01865) 247481   FAX: (01865) 791678

Large Victorian city-centre hotel, very much a part of the tradition of Oxford.

Built in 1864 to play host to well-heeled visitors to Oxford, the Randolph is an increasingly rare phenomenon in the hotel world. Its Victorian Gothic façade is something of a landmark in the centre of the city, and being taken to tea here by your parents is a long-standing student tradition. Despite the grand entrance, uniformed concierge, ornate plasterwork ceilings and references everywhere to the Oxford colleges, the Randolph is not a stuffy place. American tourists and university dons happily mix with people just popping in for tea in the drawing-room, or morning coffee in front of the log fire in the lounge. The restaurant is a formal room decorated with the heraldic badges of the colleges, and guests are expected to dress for dinner. You can opt instead for the bistro in the basement, a former student drinking den but now a modern wine bar under the vaults, with live music at the weekend. The bedrooms are smart and traditional with heavy fabrics and good-sized bathrooms. There's double glazing throughout, though rooms overlooking the Ashmolean Museum can be slightly quieter. Parking around the city is difficult so you're better off leaving your car in the hotel garage and taking advantage of the hotel's newest service, a rickshaw.

◑ Open all year ⊡ In centre of Oxford, opposite Ashmolean Museum. Private car park (£9 for 24 hours) ⊭ 43 single, 20 twin, 39 double, 1 four-poster, 8 suites; all with bathroom/WC; TV, room service, hair-dryer, trouser press, direct-dial telephone; mini-bar in some rooms ⊗ 2 restaurants, bar, 2 lounges; air-conditioning in 2 public rooms; conference facilities (max 300 people incl up to 111 residential); early suppers for children; babysitting, baby-listening ♿ Wheelchair access to hotel (1 ramp), restaurant and WC (M,F), lift to 1 bedroom specially equipped for disabled people ● No dogs in public rooms; no smoking in some bedrooms ☐ Access, Amex, Delta, Diners, Switch, Visa £ Single £125, single occupancy of twin/double £140, twin/double £150, suite £225 to £380; deposit required. Continental B £9.50, cooked B £13; set L £17.50, D £25 to £29.50; bar meals available. Special breaks available

---

OXHILL Warwickshire   map 5

Nolands Farm

Oxhill, Nr Warwick CV35 0RJ
TEL: (01926) 640309   FAX: (01926) 641662

Good-value accommodation is offered on a working, arable farm.

In order to enjoy Nolands Farm, you need to be willing to fit in with the ways of Sue Hutsby and her husband, Robin, a down-to-earth farmer who likes to speak his mind. And prepare for an agricultural atmosphere – evidenced not only in the surrounding sweeping fields, but also in the bales of hay that are piled high in the courtyard; you may even have to reach your bedroom by means of an alley leading past a corrugated shed. Over the 20 years that they've been taking guests, the Hutsbys have adapted and built a collection of red-brick outbuildings to accommodate their guests. The focal point is a lovely dining-room – decorated with glazed, tiled floors and pine beams – off which lies a very inviting conservatory sitting-room, which overlooks the garden and duck pond. The milk for breakfast can be unpasteurised if you wish, and Sue will serve three-course, traditional dinners if asked: perhaps something like garlic mushrooms, venison in a red-wine sauce, and apple crumble. The layout of the bedrooms means that you can come and go as you please. While essentially simple and rustic, the rooms have plenty of good features, such as wicker or wing chairs, smart shower-rooms and pretty patchwork quilts; two even have four-posters.

◑ Closed Dec & New Year; dining-room closed Sun & Mon eve ⊡ 8 miles from Stratford-upon-Avon, just off the A422. Private car park ⊭ 1 single, 1 twin, 3 double, 2 four-poster, 1 family room; some in annexe; 2 with bathroom/WC, 6 with shower/WC; TV, clock radio; hair-dryer in some rooms ⊗ Dining-room, bar, lounge, drying-room, conservatory, garden; fishing, clay-pigeon shooting ♿ No wheelchair access ● No children under 7; no dogs; no smoking in dining-room ☐ Access, Delta, Visa £ Single £25, single occupancy of twin/double £30, twin/double £36 to £40, four-poster £40 to £44, family room £54 to £60; deposit required. Alc D £18. Special breaks available

PADSTOW Cornwall map 1

Seafood Restaurant and St Petroc's House

Riverside, Padstow PL28 8BY
TEL: (01841) 532700/532485   FAX: (01841) 532942/533344

A justly famous seafood restaurant-with-rooms and small hotel-cum-bistro.

Since Rick Stein was granted his own BBC fish-cookery show, the fame of Padstow's Seafood Restaurant has spread, and the few lovely rooms above have had to be supplemented by more in nearby St Petroc's Hotel. If you want to eat in the restaurant, you will certainly need to book, but if you stay on a Sunday (when the restaurant is closed) it's no hardship to dine in St Petroc's Bistro instead. Both restaurants are stylishly decorated, and feature colourful, modern paintings on the walls. Not surprisingly, both the table d'hôte and à la carte menus of the Seafood Restaurant are dominated by fish, although steak usually appears for the benefit of anyone who hasn't cottoned on to the restaurant's speciality. You can also eat fish in the bistro, but there's more of a choice of alternatives. On the night of our inspection, the shrimp won ton, served with a chilli jam, were a delight, as was the salmon and salad, as well as the light, palate-cleansing lemon-and-cinnamon tart. In whichever building you stay, the bedrooms are all furnished with large beds and chairs, and are decorated in lots of striking fabrics and colours. Sadly, however, single travellers might find themselves shoehorned into a tiny room, in which no amount of attractive bathroom tiling can compensate for the absence of space – even for a bedside table. The Steins' colonisation of Padstow continues: in Middle Street you'll find an espresso bar and delicatessen (as well as a few more bedrooms), all of which are under their ownership.

◑ Closed 21 to 28 Dec; restaurant closed Sun eve ☒ Seafood Restaurant is on quayside in Padstow; St Petroc's is just above Strand. Private car park (for St Petroc's) ⟞ 1 single, 2 twin, 15 double, 2 four-poster, 1 family room; some in annexe; all with bathroom/WC; TV, room service, hair-dryer, direct-dial telephone; mini-bar in some rooms; no tea/coffee-making facilities in rooms ⌀ 2 restaurants (1 air-conditioned), bar, lounge, conservatory, garden; early suppers for children; babysitting, cots ⅄ No wheelchair access ● No children under 5 in restaurant eves ▭ Access, Delta, Switch, Visa £ Single £30, single occupancy of twin/double £41, twin/double £62, four-poster £75, family room £100; deposit required. Set L £21.50, D £29.50; alc L £30, D £40; bistro meals available. Special breaks available

---

PALGRAVE Norfolk map 6

Malt House

Denmark Hill, Palgrave, Nr Diss IP22 1AE
TEL: (01379) 642107   FAX: (01379) 640315

Excellent down-to-earth hospitality from well-travelled hosts.

From the outside it's a scene of bucolic Englishness: a tidy seventeenth-century house overlooking the village duck-pond, surrounded by an acre of lovingly tended gardens. Inside, however, Phil and Marj Morgan's guest-house is a shrine to the time they have spent abroad, mainly the 27 or so years in Hong Kong. Chinese lions support the coffee table in the lounge, the breakfast-room contains elaborate Oriental sideboards bearing small Chinese figurines, and rugs and hangings from the Far East adorn the walls throughout the house. The bedrooms are a good size and comfortable, if not quite as elaborate in terms of furnishings, with plenty of extra and unexpected touches, like torches, hairspray and deodorant. Evening meals are traditional English and largely based on seasonal produce from the walled Victorian kitchen garden. The menu might offer tomato and basil soup to start with, followed by roast beef and Yorkshire puddings, then red berry pavlova or apple pie. Fresh fruit is also in plentiful supply at breakfast. Phil is more than happy to give fellow horticultural enthusiasts a tour of the garden – his latest passion is the new pond.

◑ Closed 20 Dec to 3 Jan ⬚ Off A143 on village green in Palgrave behind church. Private car park ⊫ 1 twin, 2 double; all with bathroom/WC; TV, radio; hair-dryer on request ✔ Dining-room, lounge, study, garden; early suppers for children ♿ No wheelchair access ⊖ No children under 2; no dogs; no smoking ▭ Access, Diners, Visa £ Single occupancy of twin/double £30, twin/double £60; deposit required. Set D £20

PARRACOMBE Devon   map 1

Heddon's Gate Hotel

Heddon's Mouth, Parracombe, Barnstaple EX31 4PZ
TEL: (01598) 763313   FAX: (01598) 763363

A sprawling Victorian hotel hidden away in a beautiful National Trust valley.

Splendidly positioned in the isolated, woody Heddon valley, Heddon's Gate was originally built as a hunting lodge in 1890, but has experienced many changes of owner since then. The surrounding estate now belongs to the National Trust – hence the dearth of prominent, directional signs to the hotel. The various owners have all left their mark, and the big picture windows (that the Victorians couldn't have envisaged) now make it possible to appreciate the views from both the lounge and dining-room. Fresh from overseeing the repainting of the façade at the time of our inspection, Bob Deville and Heather Hurrell have recently been refurbishing the inside of the house, and the lounge now features restful, fern-coloured walls that are adorned with tapestries (copies of eighteenth-century French originals) depicting the four seasons. 'Wonderful, top-class meal,' wrote a guest regarding the food that is served in the sweeping dining-room on the opposite side of the house. Bob Deville describes his cooking as being 'modern English with a Mediterranean bias', but points out that there's usually an old-fashioned British pudding – such as a pineapple upside-down cake – on the menu. Every year someone writes in praise of the afternoon tea, and this year was no exception: 'a real bonus', wrote the same, satisfied guest. The bedrooms at Heddon's Gate all boast individual identities and wonderful views, but they're comfortable rather than flashy. The Master

Room, with its solid, wooden half-tester bed and new power-shower (a welcome addition), is probably the nicest.

○ Closed early Nov to late Mar/Easter ⇗ From A39, 4 miles west of Lynton, take road signposted 'Martinhoe and Woody Bay'. Take next left. Carry straight on at next crossroads and down steep hill; hotel drive is on right. Private car park 🛏 1 single, 3 twin, 5 double, 1 four-poster, 4 suites; some in annexe; all with bathroom/WC exc 1 single with shower/WC; TV, hair-dryer, direct-dial telephone ⚅ Dining-room, bar, lounge, library, garden; croquet ♿ Wheelchair access to hotel (1 step), dining-room and WC (M,F), 3 ground-floor bedrooms ● No children in dining-room eves; no dogs in dining-room and in bedrooms by arrangement only; no smoking in dining-room ▭ Access, Amex, Visa £ Single £50 to £58, single occupancy of twin/double £66 to £78, twin/double/four-poster £95 to £129, suite £110 to £135 (rates incl dinner); deposit required. Set D £25. Special breaks available

---

PAULERSPURY Northamptonshire   map 5

Vine House

100 High Street, Paulerspury, Nr Towcester NN12 7NA
TEL: (01327) 811267   FAX: (01327) 811309

A husband-and-wife teams operates this accomplished yet easy-going restaurant with spruce bedrooms.

In the heart of a peaceful village, Marcus and Julie Springett's cottagey seventeenth-century limestone house is known primarily for the quality of its food. Surrounded by beams, crisp linen and ruched curtains, you can savour Marcus's imaginative concoctions – maybe wild rabbit and venison pâté, wood pigeon with bubble and squeak, bacon and truffles, and Bramley apple and plum mousse with marinated plums. Three-course table d'hôte menus (more expensive on Fridays and Saturdays) offer four choices at each stage. Kick off and finish with home-made lemonade and ginger beer (aimed at drivers), canapés and petits fours, served amid racks of wine, cook books, coal fires (in winter) and plump soft furnishings in the cosy and homely sitting-room and bar. Bedrooms amount to considerably more than afterthoughts. Fussy but pretty, they feature such treats as brass and antique walnut beds, along with drapes and more beams. However, they are small, and all but one have diminutive shower-rooms.

○ Closed 24 Dec to 8 Jan; restaurant closed Sun ⇗ Just off A5 in village of Paulerspury, 2 miles south of Towcester. Private car park 🛏 1 single, 2 twin, 2 double, 1 four-poster; 1 double with bathroom/WC, 5 with shower/WC; TV, direct-dial telephone ⚅ Restaurant, bar, lounge, garden; conference facilities (max 12 people incl up to 6 residential); early suppers for children ♿ No wheelchair access ● No dogs ▭ Access, Visa £ Single £39, twin/double £61, four-poster £61. Set L £14, D £21.50

Hotels in our Visitors' Book *towards the end of the* Guide *are additional hotels that may be worth a visit. Reports on these hotels are welcome.*

PELYNT Cornwall   map 1

Jubilee Inn

Pelynt, Nr Looe PL13 2JZ
TEL: (01503) 220312   FAX: (01503) 220920

A pub-hotel handy for Polperro and Looe which plays its royalist theme quietly.

A row of columns capped with crowns heralds the Jubilee Inn, a part-sixteenth-century building featuring an attractive, modern spiral staircase encased in a glass tower that was designed by the Cornish artist Stuart Armfield. In the various bars you can amuse yourself by inspecting the assorted images of Queen Victoria that proliferate in the pictures, on the porcelain, and on a tea service that hangs from the beams; there are an increasing number of images of the present queen, too, thus keeping the royalist theme up to date. Some of the bedrooms suffer from rather frumpy décor, but others are impressive – especially the big family room. A tiled Victorian fireplace makes a fine feature alongside the antique furnishings in Room 4, although the turquoise bathroom suite is now somewhat dated. Another room boasts a four-poster bed and exposed stone walls, as well as a refurbished bathroom. Guests can eat either in the Albert Bar, or – more formally – in the pretty restaurant, which features whitewashed walls, polished wooden tables, and a fine brass hood over the fireplace. An extensive menu offers everything from roasts to pasta, but the emphasis is on local seafood.

◑ Open all year   ⤢ In Pelynt village, 4 miles north of Looe. Private car park ⬆ 1 twin, 5 double, 1 four-poster, 2 family rooms; 7 with bathroom/WC, 1 with shower/WC; TV, room service, hair-dryer, direct-dial telephone   ⌀ Restaurant, bar, lounge, games room, garden; early suppers for children; baby-listening, outdoor games   ⅙ No wheelchair access   ♠ None   ⊟ Access, Switch, Visa   £ Single occupancy of twin/double £33 to £35, twin/double £56 to £60, four-poster £65, family room from £70 to £75; deposit required. Set Sun L £7.50/9.50; alc L, D £18; bar meals available. Special breaks available

---

PENRITH Cumbria   map 10

North Lakes Hotel

Ullswater Road, Penrith CA11 8QT
TEL: (01768) 868111   FAX: (01768) 868291

A good business hotel with attractions for leisure travellers; convenient if unappealing location beside the motorway.

To describe the outside of this modern hotel as unprepossessing would be an understatement – fortunately it has a number of other attractions. As the name suggests, it's convenient for the northern Lake District; being virtually on the motorway makes it a handy stopping point; and for a smart business hotel it has a lot of character. The entrance hallway is an imposing space of hefty timbers, Lakeland stone and a log fire surrounded by tapestry-covered sofas. Off on all sides are various lounges, bars or restaurants in similarly new-rustic vein –

timber ceilings, floorboards, flagstones and exposed stone. The idea is that you can eat whatever you want – a sandwich, a bar snack or a full-blown restaurant dinner – pretty much throughout the day. The leisure club boasts a full range of torture implements, and a recent addition is a games room, with a 60-foot Scalextric track and Sega Mega Drive games for the children – if you can prise the controls away from the men in suits! Bedrooms are of the purpose-built, modest-sized boxy shapes associated with new hotels, but have all the swish furnishings and facilities deemed necessary to pamper the business traveller.

◑ Open all year ⤢ Leave M6 at Junction 40; hotel is located just off the roundabout, first right, off Ullswater Road. Private car park ⤙ 40 twin, 11 double, 2 four-poster, 20 family rooms, 11 suites; all with bathroom/WC; TV, room service, hair-dryer, trouser press, direct-dial telephone ⌀ Restaurant, 5 bars, 2 lounges, TV room, drying-room, games room, cinema; conference facilities (max 200 people incl up to 84 residential); gym, sauna, solarium, swimming-pool, squash; early suppers for children
&. Wheelchair access to hotel, restaurant and WC (M,F), 22 ground-floor bedrooms, 2 specially equipped for disabled people ● No smoking in some bedrooms
▭ Access, Amex, Delta, Diners, Switch, Visa ⟨£⟩ Single occupancy of twin/double £92, twin/double £114, four-poster £134, family room £114 to £126, suite £134; deposit required. Set L £10, D £18; light meals available. Special breaks available

---

PENZANCE Cornwall   map 1

Abbey Hotel

Abbey Street, Penzance TR18 4AR
TEL: (01736) 66906   FAX: (01736) 51163

A striking Gothic house, boasting stylish interior design, situated at the top of the slipway leading to Penzance harbour.

Since the streets of Penzance are more like alleyways, you may have difficulty negotiating your way into the small car park that is concealed behind the Abbey Hotel's startling blue façade. Once this manoeuvre has been achieved, however, it's a joy to find everything so spacious inside the hotel. The décor makes you appreciate the full potential of colour: everything is brightly painted, and yet the strong colours blend perfectly with the mainly antique furnishings. The lounge is the inviting heart of the house, and features three chintzy sofas arranged around a big log fire, croquet mallets ranged behind the sofa, and a Buddha gazing down on the writing desk; one end of the room consists of a solid wall of books. No two bedrooms are alike. Room 8 (in the eaves) boasts a blue and yellow fretwork pattern criss-crossing the walls of the bedroom and bathroom; a porcelain parrot that serves as a table lamp; and a dressing table in the bathroom, from which you can admire the views of the town's domed Lloyds Bank building. In Room 6, across the corridor, a coolie hat hangs over the bed, and a false bookcase leads to the bathroom. The corridor and stairwell provide hanging space for the big, modern paintings that are executed in many different styles. The three-course dinner menus offer limited choice; when we inspected, the tagliatelle was tasty – if cooked well past the *al dente* stage – but the plum, pear and strawberry water-ice was delectable. In the morning, the breakfast arrangements fell apart: there was no menu, and no butter for the toast, which grew cold while the butter was being fetched.

◗ Closed Chr ⏏ On entering Penzance take sea-front road. After 300 yards, just before bridge, turn right. After 10 yards, turn left and drive up slipway; hotel is at top. Private car park ⏎ 2 single, 2 twin, 2 double, 1 suite; family room available; 3 with bathroom/WC, 4 with shower/WC; TV, limited room service ⏀ Dining-room, lounge, garden; early suppers for children; babysitting, baby-listening ♿ No wheelchair access ● No dogs in public rooms ▭ Access, Amex, Delta, Visa £ Single £65, single occupancy of twin/double £85 to £125, twin/double £90 to £125, family room from £100, suite from £130; deposit required. Set D £17.50/23.50. Special breaks available

---

PETERSTOW Hereford & Worcester   map 5

Peterstow Country House

Peterstow, Ross-on-Wye HR9 6LB
TEL: (01989) 562826 FAX: (01989) 567264

A former rectory that has been given a new lease of life as an unpretentious country house, handy for Ross-on-Wye.

The serene, doll's-house-style façade of this clotted-cream-painted house epitomises Georgian order; pass within, however, and the flagstoned floor confirms that the house is older. In fact, for centuries it served as the rectory of the adjacent church of St Peter, the last in a long line of chapels that have been calling the faithful to prayer since before the Norman Conquest. A lingering respect for erstwhile ecclesiastical concerns about the effects of the demon drink may explain why the bar is cunningly disguised as an old-fashioned pharmacy – this is a fun place, in which Mike Denne might prescribe a dram of Glenfiddich rather than a shot of cod-liver oil to cure your ailments. When we inspected, his wife, Jeanne, was dispensing sympathy (along with glasses of hangover preparations) to wedding guests. Lots of personal collections – novelty teapots, framed cigarette cards, Russian dolls – add character to an interior that otherwise largely adheres to the traditional country-house mould. A log fire burns in the airy lounge, while swagged drapes, polished tables, and an assortment of prints complement the elegance of the pink restaurant. The cuisine is English with Continental overtones, and you might opt for a cappuccino of woodland mushrooms, followed by a grilled fillet of sea bass, accompanied by fresh pasta, baby fennel and sauce vierge, and finally tarte Tatin, served with cinnamon ice-cream and sauce anglaise. An international menu is served in the Cedar Bistro, a converted coach house.

The bedrooms are light and spacious, and may feature canopied or half-tester beds; as well as the usual, country-house-type antiques, you may also find the odd piece of church furniture (rescued from a deconsecrated chapel) helping to keep the hotel's clerical connection alive.

If you make a booking using a credit card and find after cancelling that the full amount has been charged to your card, raise the matter with your credit card company. It will ask the hotelier to confirm whether the room was re-let, and to justify the charge made.

◖ Closed 1 to 15 Jan ⬈ 3 miles from Ross-on-Wye off A49 to Hereford. Private car park 🛏 1 single, 3 twin, 5 double; family rooms available; some with bathroom/WC, most with shower/WC; TV, room service, hair-dryer, direct-dial telephone; trouser press in some rooms ⌀ Restaurant, bar, lounge, garden; conference facilities (max 10 people incl up to 9 residential); fishing, clay-pigeon shooting; early suppers for children ♿ Wheelchair access to hotel, restaurant and WC (M,F), 1 ground-floor bedroom ● No children under 7; no dogs; no smoking in restaurant ▭ Access, Amex, Delta, Diners, Switch, Visa ▣ Single/single occupancy of twin/double from £43, twin/double £55 to £99, family room £148; deposit required. Set L £14, D £26.50; bistro meals available. Special breaks available

 This denotes that the hotel is in an exceptionally peaceful situation where you can be assured of a restful stay.

 This denotes that you can get a twin or double room for £60 or less per night inclusive of breakfast.

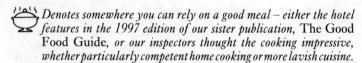 *Denotes somewhere you can rely on a good meal – either the hotel features in the 1997 edition of our sister publication,* The Good Food Guide, *or our inspectors thought the cooking impressive, whether particularly competent home cooking or more lavish cuisine.*

The 1998 Guide will be published in the autumn of 1997. Reports on hotels are welcome at any time of the year, but are extremely valuable in the spring. Send them to The Which? Hotel Guide, FREEPOST, 2 Marylebone Road, London NW1 1YN. *No stamp is needed if reports are posted in the UK. Our e-mail address is: "guidereports@which.co.uk".*

The Guide *office can quickly spot when a hotelier is encouraging customers to write a letter recommending inclusion – and, sadly, several hotels have been doing this in 1996. Such reports do not further a hotel's cause.*

POOLE Dorset map 2

Mansion House

Thames Street, Poole BH15 1JN
TEL: (01202) 685666   FAX: (01202) 665709

A grand old Georgian house with spacious rooms and a clubby atmosphere.

The Mansion House boasts of 'the most elegant staircase to any hotel in Dorset'. The *faux* marble pillars framing the iron balustrade and sweeping stairway certainly provide an impressive entrance to this grand red-brick Georgian house, built for the Lesters, the fishing merchants who brought prosperity to Poole. The grandeur continues inside – original cornices and panelling, marble fireplaces, crystal chandeliers, gilt-framed mirrors and oils fill the lounges and function rooms – but the hotel retains an informal, clubby atmosphere, not surprisingly because the Mansion House is actually a dining club. It's the sort of place where you either feel you instantly belong, or feel distinctly 'not in the club'. Two readers' letters reflect this dichotomy: one has nothing but praise for the 'unremitting enthusiasm' of staff, the 'well presented' food and 'extensive, fairly priced' wine list (in his words, 'the excellence continues'), while another found staff 'cool and offhand' and the food 'rather pretentious'. The spacious bedrooms, on the other hand, shouldn't disappoint. Each is imaginatively decorated along a given theme – pastel pinks and greens with white furniture in Indian Summer, rich prints of deep blue and gold in Gothic – but in a subtle and unobtrusive way.

◑ Open all year; restaurant closed Sun eve   ⤢ From A31 approaching Poole, follow signs to Channel Ferry; at lifting bridge turn left on to Poole Quay; take first road on left (Thames Street); hotel is on corner. Private car park   ⊨ 9 single, 6 twin, 13 double; family rooms and suite available; all with bathroom/WC; TV, 24-hour room service, hair-dryer, trouser press, direct-dial telephone   ⌁ Restaurant (air-conditioned), bistro, 2 bars, lounge; conference facilities (max 40 people incl up to 20 residential); early suppers for children   ⅃ No wheelchair access   ● No children under 5 in restaurant eves; dogs in bedrooms by arrangement   ▭ Access, Amex, Diners, Switch, Visa   £ Single £52 to £77, single occupancy of twin/double £77 to £83, twin/double/family room £85 to £122, suite £130 to £150; deposit required. Set L £10/11.50, D £19.50/22.50; bistro meals available. Special breaks available

PORLOCK Somerset map 1

Oaks Hotel

Porlock TA24 8ES
TEL: (01643) 862265 (AND FAX)

An extremely comfortable small hotel, situated on a bluff above Porlock village.

Meticulously stripped woodwork, pretty, tiled fireplaces and tastefully co-ordinated, modern fabrics combine to give the Oaks – an Edwardian hotel perched on a hill above Porlock village – the appearance of being a carefully restored, family home. From the outside, there's little to indicate the specialness of the hotel but, as you settle into your room with your complimentary glass of sherry, you'll quickly realise that nothing has been left to chance. Although the bedrooms, for example, initially look like particularly smart, extremely spotless versions of those at home, you'll soon discover that all the extras that are usually provided by much bigger hotels are discreetly scattered around them. The restaurant, which is located at the back of the house, features wrap-around picture windows that enable diners to enjoy the splendid views fully. A grandfather clock in the corner of the room announces the set meal times; there's no choice of main course, but Anne Riley welcomes special requests. Our inspector especially enjoyed a pear and watercress soup, followed by a smoked-haddock mousse, and she loved the home-made chocolates – one was in the shape of a mouse, and another (appropriately enough) was formed like an acorn. A demurely decorated downstairs lounge houses a barometer to help you to assess whether it will be a moor-walking day or not. Whatever the weather, you need to take care when leaving – there's a nasty blind bend at the end of the drive.

◑ Closed Jan & Feb ↗ On A39, west of Minehead, on left before you enter Porlock village. Private car park ⊫ 3 twin, 7 double; all with bathroom/WC; TV, room service, hair-dryer, direct-dial telephone ✅ Restaurant, bar, 2 lounges, drying-room, garden; early suppers for children ♿ No wheelchair access ● No children under 8; no dogs in public rooms; no smoking in some public rooms or bedrooms
▢ Access, Amex, Delta, Diners, Switch, Visa £ Single occupancy of twin/double £50, twin/double £80; deposit required. Set D £24. Special breaks available

---

PORT ISAAC Cornwall   map 1

Slipway Hotel

Harbour Front, Port Isaac PL29 3RH
TEL: (01208) 880264 (AND FAX)

An intriguing old fish restaurant-with-rooms, situated at the heart of an idyllic fishing village.

That the Slipway's restaurant is approached from the ground floor, while the hotel part is accessible by means of a flight of steps running up the side of the building, is a clear indication of the owners' priorities. This is primarily a restaurant-with-rooms, in which fish (hardly surprisingly, given the location) looms large on the menu. Indeed, the restaurant manages to sneak up on to the first floor, too, where there's also a small, rather basic, TV lounge for residents. The bedrooms are quite simple, and several are uncomfortably small, but if you land a room at the front, the views can make up for the lack of space. Room 3 features an interesting cupboard, made out of driftwood by Napoleonic prisoners of war. Situated right at the heart of Port Isaac, facing the lifeboat station and harbour, the Slipway actually started life as a group of sixteenth-century cottages, before becoming a ship's chandler's base. Its position, while attractive to look at, brings its own problems: driving in Port Isaac is tricky at the best of times, and is diabolical in summer, so competition for parking places is likely to be intense.

◗ Closed Jan to Mar ⚡ At bottom of hill, in centre of village opposite harbour entrance. Public car park nearby ⊨ 2 single, 2 twin, 5 double, 1 family room; 5 with shower/WC; limited room service, direct-dial telephone; hair-dryer on request
⚄ Restaurant, bar, lounge/TV room; early suppers for children ♿ No wheelchair access ● No dogs in public rooms; dogs in bedrooms at £3.50 per night
▭ Access, Amex, Delta, Switch, Visa £ Single £19 to £24, single occupancy of twin/double £30 to £50, twin/double £38 to £64, family room £75 to £100; deposit required. Alc L £7, D £29.50. Special breaks available

---

PORTLOE Cornwall   map 1

The Lugger

Portloe, Nr Truro TR2 5RD
TEL: (01872) 501322 FAX: (01872) 501691

A picturesque pub-hotel with a smuggling history, situated on the coastal footpath.

This whitewashed hotel boasts a prime position: above the slipway leading down to the rocky cove, with the south-west coastal path passing its door. Indeed, its setting is so picturesque that it has even been reproduced in a diorama in the lounge. Inevitably, the best seats in the restaurant, which offer the wildest views, are located at the front of the hotel, but the tables along one side still look out over the fishing boats and lobster pots. It would be surprising if fish didn't feature prominently on the set four-course and à la carte menus, but several dishes combine fish and meat: Cornish carpetbagger, for example, is a fillet steak stuffed with oyster flesh and served with an oyster, whisky and cream sauce. More unusually, you can tuck into ostrich steak here, and vegetarians are well catered for (although £16 seems exorbitant for a vegetable lasagne). The Lugger actually consists of two separate buildings: one dating from the seventeenth century, the other from the nineteenth. All the bedrooms in the newer building (including the single) have baths, and sometimes also showers; the beds steal the show, as far as the furnishings are concerned, and include several Victorian brass beds and half-testers. And the smugglers? Well, the nineteenth-century landlord, 'Black' Dunstan, was hanged for the crime in the 1890s.

◗ Closed early Nov to late Feb ⚡ Take B3287 to Tregony, then A3078 St Mawes road. After 2 miles, fork left for Veryan and Portloe, then turn left at T-junction for Portloe. Private car park ⊨ 3 single, 8 twin, 8 double; most with bathroom/WC, some with shower/WC; TV, room service, hair-dryer, mini-bar, direct-dial telephone
⚄ Restaurant, bar, lounge, drying-room, games room; sauna, solarium ♿ No wheelchair access ● No children under 12; no dogs; no smoking in restaurant
▭ Access, Amex, Delta, Diners, Switch, Visa £ Single £57 to £70, single occupancy of twin/double £86 to £105, twin/double £114 to £140; deposit required. Set Sun L £12.50, D £25; alc D £30; bar lunches available (prices valid till Nov 1996). Special breaks available

---

Please let us know if an establishment has changed hands.

PORTSCATHO Cornwall map 1

Roseland House

Rosevine, Portscatho TR2 5EW
TEL: (01872) 580644   FAX: (01872) 580801

A comfortable, secluded hotel with a private beach, situated on the
pretty Roseland peninsula.

A private road runs down to the Roseland House Hotel – an unexciting building
in an exciting setting: standing alone on the edge of a cliff, overlooking a small,
private beach, in a particularly pretty corner of Cornwall. A cluster of Scots pines
(a flash of lightning recently destroyed two of them, but the others still stand
proud) frames the views from one of the lounges and the restaurant. Pre-dinner
drinks are served in a small bar, which opens into the mundanely decorated
restaurant fronted by a conservatory – ask for a table here, if you want to enjoy
the view. One of the two comfortable bedrooms tucked away behind the
conservatory boasts what must be a record five windows, making it a
particularly good choice if you want to gaze out over the sea; Room 2, in the main
part of the house, runs a close second, with three windows, all of them double
glazed. The décor is generally along cottagey lines, featuring peachy walls and
lots of pine and cane furniture. The popular four-course dinner menus rarely
deviate from tried-and-tested favourites. The good-value room prices include
dinner for little more than you'd pay elsewhere for B&B.

◑ Open all year   ⏃ From St Austell, take A390 towards Truro. Just beyond Sticker,
fork left on to B3287 to Tregony. At bottom of hill, turn left on to A3078 St Mawes road.
Pass through Ruan High Lanes, then 2 miles on look for sign to hotel on the right.
Private car park   ⏘ 1 twin, 3 double, 3 family rooms, 3 suites; most with
bathroom/WC, 2 with shower/WC; TV, room service, hair-dryer, direct-dial telephone
⌁ Restaurant, bar, 2 lounges, conservatory, garden; fishing; early suppers for
children; baby-listening   ⅙ No wheelchair access   ● No dogs in public rooms and
some bedrooms; no smoking in some public rooms and bedrooms   ▭ Access, Amex,
Delta, Switch, Visa   £ Single occupancy of twin/double £48 to £72, twin/double £72
to £108, family room from £90, suite from £108 (rates incl dinner); deposit required. Set
L £11, D £17. Special breaks available

POSTBRIDGE Devon map 1

Lydgate House

Postbridge PL20 6TJ
TEL: (01822) 880209   FAX: (01822) 880202

A small, simple hotel situated on a quiet lane, boasting dramatic
views of Dartmoor.

Just beyond the Clapper Bridge, a narrow, rutted lane leads down to Lydgate
House, depositing you in a small car park that overlooks the East Dart river
valley. The same view greets you from the lounge, which is stocked with plenty
of games, cassettes and CDs for whiling away wet days, and binoculars for
homing in on any passing wildlife. The simple dining-room extends

into a plant-filled conservatory, whose walls are lined with photographs of Dartmoor. The three-course dinners offer alternatives of starter, main course and dessert, and a typical meal might start with a lentil soup prepared with coconut, corn and coriander, then progress to lamb braised in white wine and ginger, and end with a hazelnut roulade served with raspberries. The bedrooms are mainly fairly small, but several have had character injected into them by means of stencilling or painting: in Room 3, for example, two bending, Etruscan women with flowing locks appear to pour water into the bath. A split-level, ground-floor room would be ideal for families, and Rooms 3, 5 and 6 boast the best views.

◑ Closed Jan & Feb 🅿 Off B3212 in Postbridge, turn right between humpback bridge and East Dart pub. Private car park ⬕ 1 single, 2 twin, 4 double, 1 family room; 5 with bathroom/WC, 3 with shower/WC; TV, hair-dryer ✧ Dining-room, bar, lounge, drying-room, conservatory, garden; conference facilities (max 8 people residential/non-residential); fishing; early suppers for children ♿ No wheelchair access ● Dogs in lounge if other guests consent; smoking in lounge only and discouraged in bedrooms ▭ Access, Visa ☖ Single £30, single occupancy of twin/double £35, twin/double £49 to £59, family room from £55; deposit required. Set D £15.50 (prices valid till Mar 1997)

POULTON-LE-FYLDE Lancashire

map 8

River House

Skippool Creek, Thornton-le-Fylde, Poulton-le-Fylde FY5 5LF
TEL: (01253) 883497   FAX: (01253) 892083

Highly individual house, host and location.

River House is a very distinctive place – one you are likely either to love to death, or not. Reasons to treasure the place should it be your cup of tea are: Bill Scott's house, Bill Scott's cooking, Bill Scott and Skippool Creek. The creek wriggles into the muddy banks of the River Wyre and is the natural habitat of young and old salts in Wellingtons and scruffy jumpers tending to fishing boats moored at the end of rickety wooden stages. The house is a red-brick mid-eighteenth-century villa standing on the bank where the creek meets the broad expanse of the river. The iron-framed conservatory that overlooks the orchard garden is a relatively new addition; otherwise, little has changed for 40 years or so, and the old armchairs, curling carpets and wooden table tops have become increasing worn-in (or worn-out?). The five bedrooms, each a happy domestic jumble of antiques and oddments, are similarly free of the interior designer's hand. The Pink Room and Chez Martin come with tremendous Victorian hooded baths. The essence of Bill's cooking, a craft learnt on his various wanderings around the world, is having the right ingredients, then not smothering the flavour. Classics like chateaubriand or innovations such as trout in port or with teriyaki sauce, are equally likely to find their way on to the menu, while the ticky-tacky pudding should never be removed. As for Bill himself, the man is the arch raconteur (with a sideline in broadcasting to the people of Lancaster), but with a finely tuned sense of whom to amuse and whom to let lie.

◑ Open all year; restaurant closed Sun eve ⊡ Take A585 towards Fleetwood and follow road through 3 sets of traffic lights; at roundabout take third exit towards Little Thornton; as you leave roundabout Wyre Road is immediately on right; house is at end of this road on left. Private car park ⊨ 2 double, 3 twin/double; all with bathroom/WC exc 1 with shower/WC; TV, room service, hair-dryer, trouser press, direct-dial telephone ✓ Restaurant, bar, lounge, conservatory, garden; croquet; early suppers for children ⅋ No wheelchair access ● No dogs in restaurant ▭ Access, Delta, Switch, Visa £ Single occupancy of twin/double £65, twin/double £80. Set L, D £18.50; alc L, D £38. Special breaks available

---

POWBURN **Northumberland**   map 10

Breamish House Hotel

Powburn, Nr Alnwick NE66 4LL
TEL: (01665) 578266 FAX: (01665) 578500

A restful Georgian house offering fine English cooking and views of the Cheviot Hills.

'Well done, the Johnsons!' concludes one of our positive reports. A couple who stayed for five nights found the room service 'both immaculate and thoughtful throughout our stay,' and were also greatly impressed by the quality and presentation of the food. Another couple concluded: 'the food was first class and the bedrooms kept in immaculate order.'

Doreen and Alan Johnson's home started life as a seventeenth-century farmhouse, and was given its Georgian styling when it was converted into a hunting lodge in the nineteenth century. The public rooms all feature log fires and attractive drapes and pelmets, but with the emphasis on comfort and peace and quiet, the elegance is low key. Dinner is a four-course affair, offering a choice of two main courses, such as seasonal leg of Northumbrian lamb or poached fillet of monkfish with a burnt-orange sauce. The unadorned English cooking relies on fresh local produce, and many of the vegetables come from the hotel's own garden.

The bedrooms are restful, are supplied with fresh flowers and home-made biscuits, and many have wonderful views towards the Cheviot Hills. The two twin rooms in the coach-house annexe are a little more rustic, and feature wooden beams, pine furniture, and bunches of dried flowers.

◑ Closed Jan to mid-Feb ⊡ In centre of Powburn village. Private car park ⊨ 1 single, 5 twin, 5 double; family room available; some in annexe; most with bathroom/WC, 2 with shower/WC; TV, room service, hair-dryer, direct-dial telephone ✓ Restaurant, 2 lounges, drying-room, garden; conference facilities (max 15 people incl up to 11 residential); croquet; early suppers for children ⅋ No wheelchair access ● No children under 12; no dogs in public rooms; no smoking in restaurant ▭ Access, Delta, Switch, Visa £ Single £49 to £56, single occupancy of twin/double £64 to £74, twin/double £78 to £110; deposit required. Set Sun L £13.50, D £23.50 (prices valid till Apr 1997). Special breaks available

---

Prices are quoted per room *rather than* per person.

White House Manor

New Road, Prestbury SK10 4HP
TEL: (01625) 829376   FAX: (01625) 828627

A luxurious hotel boasting individually designed bedrooms and an award-winning, separately located restaurant.

The White House Manor's nine bedrooms offer something to suit almost any taste. Art lovers will appreciate the Studio, whose walls are papered with paintings, while music lovers will enjoy Glyndebourne, which is equipped with its own musical library. The Crystal Room boasts a four-poster bed and a crystal chandelier, while Minerva features a private, Turkish steam room. Campion celebrates Laura Ashley's fabrics, while Earl Grey, with its wide choice of teas and tisanes alongside dressers laden with English bone china, will make a tea-lover of any guest. Even guests of a military bent are catered for, in Trafalgar, whose striking colour scheme of burgundy and gold braid complements a selection of naval mementoes. Because the bedrooms are so interesting, it is perhaps less important that the public areas are spacious, which is just as well, since the cane-furnished conservatory is pretty small. The lack of space also explains why the restaurant is in another building, just 400 yards away. Here guests dine in a delightful plant and flower-filled room, that features more cane and rattan furniture, as well as restful walls that are rag-rolled in lemon and green. It is hard to know where to start with regard to the à la carte menu, which overflows with mouth-watering dishes such as an aromatic mussel stew accompanied by parsley pesto, or tandoori monkfish served with a raita salad and nan bread in miniature. The Simply Ryland's set three-course menu simplifies the choice without forfeiting the originality: you could, for example, start with crab and salmon fritters served with chourchamps sauce(a sort of piquant mayonnaise), then proceed to baked fillet of silver hake in a garlic crumble accompanied by a dill sauce, and finish with spiced-blueberry bread-and-butter pudding with a banana sauce. After a dinner like this, you may be grateful for the opportunity to breakfast in your own room the next morning.

◑ Open all year; restaurant closed Sun eve 🔁 In centre of Prestbury on A538. Private car park 🛏 3 single, 1 twin, 3 double, 2 four-poster; 4 with bathroom/WC, 5 with shower/WC; TV, room service, hair-dryer, mini-bar, trouser press, direct-dial telephone; radio ✅ Restaurant, lounge, drying-room, conservatory, garden; conference facilities (max 80 people incl up to 9 residential); early suppers for children; toys, baby-listening 🚫 Wheelchair access to hotel (1 step) and restaurant, 2 ground-floor bedrooms ● No dogs in public rooms and in bedrooms by arrangement only 🗀 Access, Amex, Delta, Diners, Switch, Visa £ Single £65, single occupancy of twin/double £80, twin/double £95, four-poster £110; deposit required. Continental B £5, cooked B £8.50; set L £12.50, D £14/17; alc L, D £22

It is always worth enquiring about the availability of special breaks or weekend prices. The prices we quote are the standard rates for one night – most hotels offer reduced rates for longer stays.

Quorn Country Hotel

Charnwood House, 66 Leicester Road, Quorn, Nr Loughborough LE12 8BB
TEL: (01509) 415050   FAX: (01509) 415557

A small, smart and keenly run, primarily business hotel.

Despite the pleasant enough gardens running down a river, take the 'country' in the hotel's title with a pinch of salt: it lies in the middle of a suburban village. It mainly occupies a trim, modern brick-and-stone block tacked on to a seventeenth-century building. The adopted tone, of a conventional, restrained country house, is faultlessly comfortable but rather impersonal in the capacious bar and lounge. More spirited are the dining areas, namely the tiny, beamed Shires Restaurant and the jolly, less formal Orangery Brasserie in a ferny conservatory painted with pastoral murals. Shires specialises in complicated English haute cuisine, while the Orangery's menus include simpler offerings such as salads, pastas and grills. The very presentable, standardised and good-sized bedrooms all come with a pair of armchairs and excellent mod cons, such as three phone extensions (including one in the bathroom), and power points and modem sockets by desks. Since the hotel receives much business custom, rates for Friday and Saturday nights are far more competitive than for other nights of the week. As you might expect from an establishment marketed by the Virgin group, the staff are professional and efficient, and the hotel claims to go out of its way to make single women feel at ease.

◑ Open all year   ⊿ On main road in village of Quorn. Private car park   ⊨ 8 twin, 10 double, 2 suites; all with bathroom/WC; TV, room service, hair-dryer, mini-bar, trouser press, direct-dial telephone   ⍁ 2 restaurants, bar, lounge, drying-room, conservatory, garden; air-conditioning in all rooms; conference facilities (max 100 people incl up to 12 residential); fishing; early suppers for children; babysitting, baby-listening   & Wheelchair access to hotel (1 ramp), restaurant and WC (unisex), 9 ground-floor bedrooms, 1 specially equipped for disabled people   ● No dogs in public rooms   ▭ Access, Amex, Diners, Switch, Visa   £ Single occupancy of twin/double £64 to £84, twin/double £76 to £96, suite £105 to £125. Continental B £6, cooked B £9; set L £15, D £19; alc L £26, D £31.50; brasserie meals available. Special breaks available

---

Black Swan

Ravenstonedale, Kirkby Stephen CA17 4NG
TEL: (01539) 623204   FAX: (01539) 623604

An attractive, turn-of-the-century hotel with a pub attached, boasting a brook at the end of the garden.

Perhaps surprisingly, relatively forgotten corners of the Lake District still exist, including the Eden valley. Indeed, Norma and Gordon Stuart at the Black Swan – a solid, multi-gabled, Lakeland-stone building with a beck at the end of the garden – know all about walkers' needs (indeed, their brochure comments that

378

the television is rarely switched on). The Eden and Lune rivers are just a short walk away, and are brimming with trout and salmon (a 22-pounder was landed recently). It's therefore hardly surprising to find both types of fish cropping up regularly on the lunch and dinner menus, although venison, pigeon, quail and more run-of-the-mill meats are always offered as alternatives. The Stuarts also place great stock on their breakfasts, which they regard as being essential in ensuring complete enjoyment of a day in the countryside. The bedrooms, which are available in all shapes and sizes, are smart without being flashy; the three ground-floor rooms would suit guests with mobility problems. A top-notch dining-room features oval tables laid with silverware, crystal and fresh flowers, thus perfectly complementing the oil paintings hanging on the walls. One of the lounges also sports a fine selection of pictures alongside Gordon Stuart's collections of such items as clocks and nineteenth-century ships tickets. A crackling fire greets visitors retreating to one of the cosy bars from the cold outside; its walls are densely covered with old maps (including one giving details of every conceivable fishing opportunity), landscape paintings and stags' heads.

◑ Open all year ☑ Leave M6 at Junction 38 and take A685 towards Brough; Ravenstonedale is 6½ miles further on. Private car park ⊨ 1 single, 6 twin, 9 double; some in annexe; most with bathroom/WC, 2 with shower/WC; TV, limited room service, hair-dryer, direct-dial telephone ✧ 2 dining-rooms, 2 bars, 2 lounges, drying-room, garden; conference facilities (max 25 people incl up to 16 residential); fishing; early suppers for children; baby-listening ⎜ Wheelchair access to hotel, dining-rooms and WC (F), 3 ground-floor bedrooms, 1 specially equipped for disabled people ● No dogs in public rooms; no smoking in dining-rooms ⊟ Access, Amex, Diners, Visa ⬓ Single/single occupancy of twin/double £45; twin/double £65 to £70; deposit required. Set L £10, D £23; alc L £12, D £28. Special breaks available

---

The Fat Lamb

Crossbank, Ravenstonedale, Kirkby Stephen CA17 4LL
TEL: (01539) 623242   FAX: (01539) 623285

An olde-worlde pub-hotel abutting the Crossbank nature reserve and the moors, offering good access for disabled guests.

The Fat Lamb is a long, low-slung, converted farmhouse, featuring a slate roof and a couple of cartwheels propped up against the wall. Completely surrounded by fields and moors, it's a perfect base for walking holidays. The wetlands nature reserve at the back is an additional bonus: Paul Bonsall has worked with the Countryside Commission to turn it into a wildlife haven, in which you might spot up to 80 different types of bird, including snipe and a wide variety of waterfowl. In keeping with its olde-worlde exterior, the Fat Lamb boasts a beamed bar in which brasses hang on either side of the old-fashioned range. The four-course dinner menus offered in the restaurant are more adventurous than you might anticipate, including starters such as grilled banana served with Cumberland sauce, and main courses such as vegetable balti with nan bread. Alternatively, you could try the extensive bar-meals menu, which features some exotic touches alongside standards such as scampi and gammon. The bedrooms are comfortable, although some might find the décor rather old-fashioned.

Guests with disabilities will be pleased to learn that there are four specially adapted ground-floor bedrooms, and that the restaurant is easily accessible, too. The nature reserve also offers wheelchair access to its viewing and picnic areas.

◑ Open all year ⊿ Midway between Sedbergh and Kirkby Stephen, on A683. Private car park ⊫ 1 twin, 7 double, 4 family rooms; all with bathroom/WC; hair-dryer; TV on request ⊘ Restaurant, bar, lounge, TV room, drying-room, garden; conference facilities (max 20 people incl up to 12 residential); early suppers for children; outdoor games ⅋ Wheelchair access to hotel, restaurant and WC (M,F), 5 ground-floor bedrooms, 4 specially equipped for disabled people ● No smoking in restaurant and bedrooms ▭ None accepted £ Single occupancy of twin/double £33, twin/double £56, family room from £62; deposit required. Set L £11.50, D £17; alc L, D £15; bar meals available

---

REDMILE Leicestershire   map 5

Peacock Farm

Redmile NG13 0GQ   𝒫𝓛
TEL: (01949) 842475 FAX: (01949) 843127

Relaxed rural restaurant and B&B, where children will have fun.

During the two decades in which the Need family having been offering B&B, they have cultivated an engagingly informal atmosphere. The needs of children are one of the areas in which they excel, and they supply various animals to befriend, a playroom, bicycles to ride, and a small, outdoor pool. At the heart of their jumble of buildings lies an eighteenth-century former farmhouse. Feathers Restaurant, beamed and decorated with rustic implements, tries to entice all-comers. As well as breakfasts until 11am, tapas, and tea and crumpets, there are good-sounding dinners which specialise in country fare, such as venison steak with crab-apple sauce, rabbit with mustard sauce, and pigeon pie. The better, cottagey bedrooms lie in the main house; some enjoy views of Belvoir Castle, home of the Duke of Rutland, whose coat of arms explains Peacock Farm's name. Others are pine-panelled and occupy a coach-house annexe.

◑ Open all year ⊿ From A1 or A5, follow signs to Belvoir Castle; Redmile is a nearby village. Private car park ⊫ 2 twin, 2 double, 2 family rooms, 2 suites; some in annexe; 1 with bathroom/WC, 7 with shower/WC; TV, hair-dryer ⊘ Restaurant, bar, lounge, TV room, drying-room, conservatory, games room, garden; conference facilities (max 30 people incl up to 8 residential); unheated outdoor swimming-pool, table tennis, snooker; early suppers for children; toys, playrooms, babysitting, baby-listening, outdoor games ⅋ Wheelchair access to hotel and restaurant, 1 bedroom specially equipped for disabled people ● No dogs; no smoking in public rooms ▭ Access, Amex, Diners, Switch, Visa £ Single occupancy of twin/double £32, twin/double £45, family room from £60, suite £75; deposit required. Set L £10.50, D £13.50; alc L, D £15. Special breaks available

---

☆ *A star next to the hotel's name indicates that the establishment is new to the* Guide *this year.*

Arkleside Hotel ☆

Reeth, Nr Richmond DL11 6SG
TEL: (01748) 884200 (AND FAX)

Small, decorous rooms in a hotel with an increasing reputation for informal and attentive service.

The Arkleside's new owners, Dorothy Kendall and Richard Beal, left behind stressful careers in the NHS and BT respectively for a more peaceful existence among the folds and crags of Swaledale – a wise decision, it seems, as their relaxed and friendly approach is widely appreciated: 'The most pleasant hosts we have met in years,' commented one couple. The hotel has been undergoing a gradual redecoration programme over the last few years, resulting in well co-ordinated rooms often with lacy canopies above the beds and patchwork quilts. The rooms are quite small, though, and some of the rather fussy floral designs serve to emphasise this. Dorothy's dinners are four-course affairs with limited choice, and offer reliable, unpretentious versions of standards like duck à l'orange. Before the meal guests tend to congregate in the bar where they might enjoy a pint of draught Theakstons and take in the fine view towards Fremlington Edge. The final word goes to one long-time visitor to Reeth who has followed the fortunes of the Arkleside for over 25 years: 'Under the new owners the hotel has reached a new high in terms of quality of service, delicious food and a pleasant, informal atmosphere.'

◗ Closed Jan ◪ From Richmond follow signs to Reeth; turn right by war memorial; hotel is 100 yards beyond post office. Private car park ⬅ 3 twin, 5 double, 1 suite in annexe; suite with bathroom/WC, rest with shower/WC; TV, hair-dryer clock radio ⌗ Restaurant, bar, lounge, drying-room, garden; conference facilities (max 24 people incl up to 9 residential) ♿ No wheelchair access ● No children under 10; smoking in bar only ⊟ Access, Visa £ Single occupancy of twin/double £35 to £40, twin/double £53 to £59, suite £60 to £75; deposit required. Set D £15.50. Special breaks available

---

Burgoyne Hotel

On the Green, Reeth, Nr Richmond DL11 6SN
TEL: (01748) 884292 (AND FAX)

Neat rooms with lovely views over Swaledale and fine English cooking are features in this village hotel.

Standing at the top of the broad village green – the prime position in Reeth – the Burgoyne Hotel looks down over the handsome, three-storey buildings which enclose the green, and beyond, to Swaledale. Seven of the nine bedrooms benefit from the view south over the valley, and the names of the rooms are evocative of the hotel's location – Muker, Eskeleth, Grinton and Keld, for example. The rooms vary considerably in size and style: Eskeleth is a decent-sized, *en suite* ground-floor twin room, with one exposed stone wall and a door opening out on to the lawn; Keld – the smallest twin – is decorated in subdued golden tones, and its bathroom is located across the corridor. A mixture of antique and reproduction furniture is to be found in the rooms, while gentle, pictorial landscapes provide additional colour.

There are two lounges, to cater for smokers and non-smokers. In the deep-green restaurant a daily changing, five-course dinner might commence with a sauté of chicken livers, grapes and cream, followed by a main-course dish of roast breast of duckling in a black-cherry sauce.

◖ Closed Jan   ⬚ Hotel overlooks the green in Reeth. Private car park   ⊨ 3 twin, 6 double; 2 with bathroom/WC, 7 with shower/WC; TV, limited room service, hair-dryer, trouser press, direct-dial telephone   ✓ Dining-room, 2 lounges, drying-room, garden; early suppers for children; babysitting, baby-listening   ♿ No wheelchair access ● No children in dining-room after 7pm; no smoking in dining-room, 1 lounge or bedrooms; no dogs in dining-room   ▭ Access, Visa   £ Single occupancy of twin/double £58 to £80, twin/double £68 to £90; deposit required. Set D £21 (prices valid till Mar 1997). Special breaks available

---

RENDCOMB Gloucestershire   map 2

Shawswell Country House

Rendcomb, Cirencester GL7 7HD
TEL: (01285) 831779

An outstanding guesthouse situated in a tranquil spot deep in the Gloucestershire countryside.

Wonderful open views over rolling hills and the Churn valley are the reward for those who make the journey from the tiny village of Rendcomb along the no-through road to Shawswell Country House.

The seventeenth-century building is more modest than its name might suggest, but what this delightful guesthouse lacks in designer, off-the-peg, country-house-hotel chic, it more than compensates for in comfort, cosiness and character. The interior is resolutely cottagey, and the period beams and uneven walls are complemented by collections of porcelain and toby jugs, as well as plenty of copper- and brassware. The wood-burning stove makes the inglenook warm and snug, matching the welcome extended by Muriel and David Gomm. These days, only breakfast is served at Shawswell, and it is taken at round tables in the neat breakfast-room, whose spindle-back chairs, exposed stone walls and beams (not to mention the blackened range, Welsh dresser and willow-pattern plates) confirm the guesthouse's rustic credentials.

The bedrooms (which feature the same mixture of beams and antiques, as well as the occasional piece of country pine) are excellent, and represent outstanding value for money. All are well equipped, and include lots of extras such as bottled mineral water and a range of toiletries. There's a grand four-poster, and one room – the most popular, although it faces the back of the house, so missing out on the best of the views – boasts a huge bathroom.

See the inside front cover for a brief explanation of how to use the Guide.

◑ Closed Dec & Jan ⤾ From A435, follow signs to Rendcomb. From village, take 'Shawswell No Through Road' for 1½ miles. Turn left and immediately right at old stone barn. Private car park ⤙ 1 single, 1 twin, 1 twin/double, 2 double, 1 four-poster; all with bathroom/WC exc single with shower/WC; TV, hair-dryer ⍋ Dining-room, lounge, garden ⅙ No wheelchair access ◐ No children under 10; no dogs; smoking in lounge only ☐ None accepted £ Single £30 to £35, single occupancy of twin/double £40 to £45, twin/double £45 to £55, four-poster £55 to £60; deposit required. Special breaks available

---

RHYDYCROESAU Shropshire   map 5

Pen-y-Dyffryn Hall

Rhydycroesau, Nr Oswestry SY10 7DT
TEL: (01691) 653700 (AND FAX)

A friendly, relaxing house situated amid glorious countryside on the Anglo-Welsh Marches.

The hotel's brochure helpfully provides a pronunciation guide for the linguistically challenged, since Rhydycroesau ('Rud-uh-croy-sigh') – a delightful hamlet situated on the banks of the River Cynllaith, 3 miles from Oswestry – straddles the Anglo-Welsh border. Despite its name, Pen-y-Dyffryn (which means 'the head of the valleys') Hall is on the English side of the Marches, and is run by the friendly Audrey and Miles Hunter. Creeper cladding is the only embellishment that the plain, silver-stoned building (a former rectory) boasts, but its setting – against a backdrop of lush greenery – is stunning. The interior has a nostalgic, Victorian/Edwardian focus and, despite the odd example of emulsioned Anaglypta or homely piece of furniture, it is just grand enough to make you feel that coming here is a bit of a treat. The bar's counter was once an old dresser, and the adjacent, cosy, seating area features a wood-burning fire and lots of plants, as well as a range of local books and maps. The restaurant is simple but elegant, and is a fitting venue for the good-value dinners that might include New Orleans devilled crab, cod fillet with a herb crust served with a tomato-and-rosemary sauce, and a home-made pudding accompanied by 'proper' custard. The bedrooms are pleasantly decorated and furnished – particularly the refurbished Terrace Room, with its soothing blue and yellow décor and access to the garden, and the Champagne Room, which boasts a four-poster. 'An overridingly friendly atmosphere, thanks to all the staff,' reported one satisfied guest.

◑ Open all year ⤾ From Oswestry town centre follow signs to Llansilin (B4580); hotel is 3 miles west of Oswestry, on left. Private car park ⤙ 1 single, 3 twin, 3 double, 1 four-poster; family room available; 6 with bathroom/WC, 2 with shower/WC; TV, room service, hair-dryer, trouser press ⍋ Restaurant, bar, 2 lounges, drying-room, garden; conference facilities (max 30 people incl up to 8 residential); fishing; early suppers for children; baby-listening, outdoor games ⅙ Wheelchair access to hotel (2 steps) and restaurant, 1 ground-floor bedroom specially equipped for disabled people ◐ No dogs in public rooms; no smoking in restaurant and 1 lounge ☐ Access, Amex, Delta, Switch, Visa £ Single £40 to £44, single occupancy of twin/double £42 to £47, twin/double £62 to £68, four-poster/family room £76 to £84; deposit required. Set D £15; alc D from £11. Special breaks available

Moortown Lodge

244 Christchurch Road, Ringwood BH24 3AS
TEL: (01425) 471404   FAX: (01425) 476052

A small Georgian family-run hotel with excellent food and a French style.

Jilly and Bob Burrows-Jones' love of France is stamped all over this small hotel, from the emphasis on good eating to the understated décor throughout. Having been built originally as the fishing lodge for the River Avon, it is now unfortunately situated on a small main road out of Ringwood. Once you are inside, however, the calm and simplicity are evident. The lounge, decorated and furnished in muted tones, has fresh flowers and maps of France on the walls. The restaurant is the focal point and is decorated in quiet peach hues with radio memorabilia from Jilly's days as a producer – her vocation has changed radically, as she now does all the cooking herself. Fresh local produce and the personal touch combine to tempt you with specialities such as a floating cheese island, followed by chicken Normandie with caramelised apple, and a choice of tempting home-made puddings. The bedrooms are all named after herbs, so you might find yourself in Coriander, Chervil or Anise, but thankfully they are not decorated accordingly – Coriander is done out prettily in white and pink, and Anise in blue stripes with blue linen on its imposing four-poster. The bedrooms are quite small and simply furnished and most have only a shower-room.

○ Closed 24 Dec to mid-Jan ⊿ 1½ miles south of Ringwood town centre on B3347. Private car park ⟜ 1 single, 2 twin, 2 double, 1 four-poster; family room available; 2 with bathroom/WC, 4 with shower/WC; TV, room service, direct-dial telephone; hair-dryer on request ⊘ Restaurant, bar, lounge; early suppers for children ⅏ No wheelchair access ● No dogs; no smoking in restaurant and some bedrooms ▭ Access, Amex, Visa £ Single £30 to £32, single occupancy of twin/double £35 to £42, twin/double £50 to £65, four-poster £60 to £75, family room £60 to £75; deposit required. Set D £18; alc D £22. Special breaks available

Boar's Head

Ripley, Harrogate HG3 3AY
TEL: (01423) 771888   FAX: (01423) 771509

A grand country house featuring adventurous cooking in a historic little village.

If you like to feel the solidity of English tradition beneath your feet, you couldn't do better than stay at this grand, patrician, country house owned by the Ingilby family, who have lived in Ripley since the Middle Ages. The history of the hotel itself doesn't conform to such straight lines. It served as a coaching-inn for the Leeds-Edinburgh run from the early nineteenth century, but in 1919 Sir William Ingilby, whose sensibilities couldn't quite encompass the Sunday-morning church-to-pub procession, had the inn closed on Sundays. After the landlord left in protest, the village remained dry until Sir Thomas reinstated the tradition of hospitality by opening the house as a hotel in 1990.

The family are also stewards of the neighbouring castle and its lavish estate, designed by Capability Brown. The estate, in fact, provides the backbone of the seasonally changing menu, which features starters like wild-mushroom ravioli with chargrilled chicken livers, and main courses such as baked sea bass with stir-fried sweet-and-sour vegetables.

The bedrooms, which are divided between the main house, the courtyard and the keeper's cottage across the road, range from smart to luxurious, while the drawing-rooms exude an aura of understated elegance.

◑ Open all year ⤢ In village of Ripley, 3 miles north of Harrogate on A61 Harrogate to Ripon Road. Private car park ⊨ 24 twin/double, 1 family room; some in annexe; all with bathroom/WC; TV, room service, hair-dryer, mini-bar, trouser press, direct-dial telephone ⊘ Restaurant, bar, 2 lounges, drying-room, garden; conference facilities (max 80 people incl up to 25 residential); fishing, tennis, clay-pigeon shooting; early suppers for children; babysitting, baby-listening ⅛ Wheelchair access to hotel, restaurant and WC (unisex), 5 ground-floor bedrooms, 1 specially equipped for disabled people ● No dogs in public rooms and most bedrooms; no smoking in 1 lounge and some bedrooms ⊟ Access, Amex, Delta, Diners, Switch, Visa ⟦£⟧ Single occupancy of twin/double £80 to £95, twin/double £95 to £110, family room £130; deposit required. Set L £13.50/17.50, D £25 to £35; bar and bistro meals available. Special breaks available

---

ROGATE West Sussex map 3

Mizzards Farm

Rogate, Petersfield GU31 5HS
TEL: (01730) 821656 FAX: (01730) 821655

A gorgeously grand farmhouse B&B, hidden away in a setting of complete tranquillity.

This imposing stone and red-brick farmhouse, clad in climbing roses, ivy and clematis, nestles at the end of a rutted and overgrown track along the River Rother in the heart of rural Sussex. Harriet Francis is active in local historical restoration, and informed us that this 400-year-old building (which bears a twelfth-century family's name) conceals the ruins of an older structure in the cellar. It is set in a designated area of outstanding natural beauty, and nothing louder than the sound of badgers digging up the lawn or the cries of pheasants and partridges will disturb your morning slumber. You can then take breakfast in the galleried dining-room, which features exposed timbers soaring high above the flagstones to the roof and a huge, walk-in fireplace. How better to start the day than with eggs Reuben (scrambled with smoked salmon), specially ordered Isle of Man kippers, or kedgeree? The whole house is stuffed with the Francis family's furniture, especially the elegant and airy drawing-room, which boasts superb views over the landscaped gardens, pergola and knot garden. The three spacious and light bedrooms share the views and antique furniture. Thanks to the glittery tastes of its previous glam-rock owner, the largest is a showbiz extravaganza, and features a gigantic four-poster bed, a double-sized bath set within caramel marble and mirrored walls, and remote-controlled curtains. Guests are consistently impressed by the owners' helpfulness and knowledge of local attractions.

◑ Closed Chr ⤵ Travel south from the crossroads in Rogate, cross the bridge and take the first road on the right. Private car park ⇌ 1 twin, 1 double, 1 four-poster; all with bathroom/WC; TV, hair-dryer ✦ Dining-room, lounge, drying-room, conservatory, garden; heated indoor swimming-pool, croquet ⅙ No wheelchair access ● No children under 8; no dogs; no smoking ☐ None accepted
£· Single occupancy of twin/double £32 to £38, twin/double £48 to £52, four-poster £58; deposit required

---

ROMALDKIRK Co Durham   map 10

Rose and Crown

Romaldkirk, Barnard Castle DL12 9EB
TEL: (01833) 650213 FAX: (01833) 650828

An old coaching-inn offering well-equipped rooms, good food and excellent service.

'On arrival at the Rose and Crown we were warmly welcomed, and throughout our stay the staff, and particularly the proprietor, Mr Davy, were friendly and helpful' – so reports one reader in praise of Christopher and Alison Davy's eighteenth-century coaching-inn. Situated at the centre of a pretty village, and surrounded by spectacular fells and moorland, the pub is exactly what a village pub ought to be. Outside, the parasol-shaded tables are occupied by locals and resting walkers in summer, while in winter everyone heads for the cosy atmosphere of the main bar, in which copper and brass artefacts reflect the blazing fire, snares and traps decorate the walls, and low beams and a grandfather clock complete the ambience. The bedrooms in the main house, which feature stripped-pine furniture and sunny colour schemes, inevitably suffer some noise from the sociable chat downstairs, so opt for a room in the annexe if you plan to go to bed early. Dinner is another of the hotel's fortes: indeed, the bar food attains the same high standard as that of the restaurant, where a typical evening meal of generous portions might include fresh mussels served in cream and Muscadet, a chargrilled baby spring chicken, followed by a honey-and-whisky ice-cream or a more traditional hot sticky toffee pudding.

◑ Closed 25 & 26 Dec ⤵ In Romaldkirk, 6 miles north-west of Barnard Castle on the B6277. Private car park ⇌ 5 twin, 3 double, 1 four-poster, 1 family room, 2 suites; some in annexe; most with bathroom/WC, 3 with shower/WC; TV, limited room service, direct-dial telephone; trouser press in some rooms; hair-dryer on request
✦ Restaurant, bar, lounge, drying-room; early suppers for children; baby-listening
⅙ Wheelchair access to hotel and restaurant, 5 ground-floor bedrooms ● No dogs in public rooms; no smoking in restaurant ☐ Access, Switch, Visa £· Single occupancy of twin/double £56, twin/double/four-poster £78, family room £90, suite £86; deposit required. Set L £12, D £22.50; bar meals available. Special breaks available

---

Many hotels put up their tariffs in the spring. You are advised to confirm prices when you book.

ROSEDALE ABBEY **North Yorkshire**   map 9

White Horse Farm Hotel ☆

Rosedale Abbey, Pickering YO18 8SE
TEL: (01751) 417239   FAX: (01751) 417781

*A characterful pub-hotel boasting some unusual features, situated in
a sleepy, moorland village.*

You'll want to regain your equilibrium after experiencing the sweeping drive
down the 'Rosedale Chimney' – a scenic 1:3 road that leads you down to this
village from the top of the moors in no time. Be warned, however: if you call
here, you may end up staying longer than you had anticipated.

This characterful pub-hotel was once a seventeenth-century farmhouse, to
which Victorian extensions were later added and, once inside, it's not that
difficult to see which was which. The darkened, crooked, wooden pillars in the
bar tell you that this is part of the original building; its dimensions and beamed
ceiling help to create a cosy atmosphere in which to enjoy such Yorkshire ales as
Theakstons, Tetleys and Black Sheep, or one of the 30 malt whiskies on offer.
The residents' lounge is newer and brighter, and features paintings by local
artists. The wooden, arched alcoves in the restaurant are obviously Victorian,
and, like the misericords hanging on the wall (which give the restaurant its
name), come from a nearby church. The three- and four-course dinner menus
may feature such dishes as roast saddle of lamb or suprême of salmon.

The bedrooms in the main house have wooden beams and solid, dark, wood
furniture; many boast lovely views. The advantage of staying in the annexe is
that you're at a good distance from the busy bar.

◑ Closed 24 & 25 Dec   ⬛ From A170, take turning for Rosedale. Follow signs to
Rosedale Abbey for 7 miles; in village, take first turning on left. Private car park
🛏 3 twin, 11 double, 1 family room; some in annexe; some with bathroom/WC, most
with shower/WC; TV, direct-dial telephone, radio; hair-dryer on request   ⊘
  Restaurant, bar, lounge, drying-room, garden; conference facilities (max 30 people
incl up to 15 residential); baby-listening, cots, high chairs   ⅙   No wheelchair access
● No dogs in restaurant   ▭ Access, Amex, Delta, Switch, Visa   £ Single
occupancy of twin/double £35 to £44, twin/double £60 to £68, family room from £90;
deposit required. Alc Sun L £8, D £17; bar meals available. Special breaks available

---

ROSS-ON-WYE **Hereford & Worcester**   map 5

Upper Pengethley Farm

Ross-on-Wye HR9 6LL
TEL: (01989) 730687 (AND FAX)

*An easy-going farmhouse B&B, featuring pleasant bedrooms and
bags of homely charm.*

If you belong to the Linda Snell school of country life, and believe that farmyards
should be sterile, antiseptic places, stay away: Upper Pengethley Farm is the real
thing, complete with the lowing of cattle, traditional farmyard clutter and a

mud-spattered Landrover parked on a muddy track. The sturdy, red-brick house has the lived-in feel of the family home that it actually is, so you'll find flaking paint on the front door, and a Paddington bear or badminton racket on the old wooden settle in the hallway. Despite the high ceiling and sense of space in the large public room, the big Welsh dresser, wonderful antique sideboard and assortment of hunting, equine and other prints give it a cottagey feel. Guests breakfast around the sort of solid farmhouse table that is piled high with goodies in rural scenes such as those in *The Darling Buds of May*, although the owner, Sue Partridge, is certainly no Ma Larkin. The bedrooms are decorated in strong colours: fuchsia predominates in the ground-floor double room, which is a pretty and civilised bedroom featuring a patchwork quilt on the bed, well-stocked bookshelves, and a bathroom that is big enough to house a lovely Art Nouveau dressing table and still have room to spare. Burgundy prevails in the upstairs room, which also has a small private sitting-room.

◑ Closed Chr ⤢ Just off A49, 4 miles from Ross-on-Wye, next to the Pengethley Manor Hotel and Pengethley Nurseries. Private car park ⬅ 1 twin, 2 double; all with bathroom/WC; TV, hair-dryer ⊘ Dining-room, garden ⅋ No wheelchair access ◔ No smoking; no dogs in public rooms ▭ None accepted £ Single occupancy of twin/double £20, twin/double £35

ROSTHWAITE Cumbria   map 10

Hazel Bank

Rosthwaite, Borrowdale, Keswick CA12 5XB
TEL: (01768) 777248

Very friendly and stylish small country guesthouse in terrific countryside.

Gwen and John Nutall's Lakeland-stone Victorian house sits in a plum position, across a humpbacked bridge and up the bank just outside of the village of Rosthwaite. Gwen and John are into their 17th year at Hazel Bank, but are still enthralled by the surrounding countryside and fiercely proud of their stylish house. Plenty of attention has recently been lavished on the six bedrooms. Gold highlights in the plaster mouldings, swagged curtains and rag-rolled panels have added sophisticated touches to the highly comfortable rooms, and the smart bathrooms (gold taps and marble-effect facings) are brimming with goodies. A skilled decorator's hand has also enhanced the other fine original features of the house, such as the ogee-headed arches along the landing and the plasterwork radiating across the ceiling of the Regency-style sitting-room. Following a snifter from the honesty bar in the hallway, you could sit down to a dinner cooked by John consisting of smoked haunch of venison with salad followed by seared fresh tuna, steamed lemon sole or baked salmon, then steamed marmalade pudding and custard and finally the cheeseboard; in other words, interesting cooking but with broad appeal.

◑ Closed Nov to Mar exc some weekends in Mar & Nov ⤵ From Keswick follow B5289 signposted Borrowdale; just before Rosthwaite village, turn left, crossing the river over the humpbacked bridge. Private car park ⤶ 1 single, 1 twin, 3 double, 1 four-poster; all with bathroom/WC; TV, hair-dryer ⌖ Dining-room, lounge, drying-room, garden ♿ No wheelchair access ● No children under 11; no dogs in public rooms; no smoking ⊟ Access, Switch, Visa £ Single £45, twin/double/four-poster £90 (rates incl dinner); deposit required. Special breaks available

---

RUAN HIGH LANES Cornwall   map 1

Hundred House Hotel

Ruan High Lanes, Nr Truro TR2 5JR
TEL: (01872) 501336   FAX: (01872) 501151

A popular small hotel on the pretty Roseland peninsula, convenient for Truro.

From the outside, Hundred House Hotel is nothing to write home about, partly because a conservatory at the front conceals the older building behind. Inside, however, this is the sort of hotel that attracts plenty of return trade; when we inspected, the lounge and dining-room buzzed with conversation, and one guest commented: 'My wife's idea of hell would be to get here and find the chef's changed.' The food certainly lived up to that introduction. Our inspector thoroughly enjoyed the watercress soup, the salmon steak with suitably crisp vegetables and, best of all, the banana, butterscotch and walnut crumble with clotted cream. The cheeseboard, with a fine array of Cornish cheeses, also tempted. 'A wonderful place to recharge the batteries,' praised one reader. 'I stay alone and never feel left out as it's such a welcoming place.' There's a big, inviting lounge for non-smokers, but most guests seem to gravitate towards the bar. The bedrooms, named after Roseland villages, are pleasingly decorated without being grand. Only minor details let them down ... towels with thin pile, and sachets offering combined shower-gel and shampoo. The name of the hotel derives from the fact that the monthly petty sessions for the 'Hundred of South Powder', an administrative division dating back to the Middle Ages, used to be held in the nineteenth-century Kempe Armes. When the building became a private house at the turn of the century, the name changed to reflect the historic connection.

◑ Closed 1 Nov to 11 Mar ⤵ Take A3078 to St Mawes; hotel is 4 miles beyond Tregony on the right-hand side, just before Ruan High Lanes. Private car park ⤶ 2 single, 4 twin, 4 double; family rooms available; 6 with bathroom/WC, 4 with shower/WC; TV, hair-dryer, direct-dial telephone ⌖ Dining-room, bar, lounge, library, conservatory, garden; early suppers for children; ♿ Wheelchair access to hotel (1 step), dining-room and WC (M,F), 1 ground-floor bedroom ● No dogs in public rooms; no smoking in dining-room or lounge ⊟ Access, Amex, Visa £ Single £36 to £39, twin/double £72 to £77, family room £98 to £103; deposit required. Set D £22.50. Special breaks available

---

Prices are quoted per room *rather than* per person.

RUSHLAKE GREEN East Sussex map 3

Stone House

Rushlake Green, Heathfield TN21 9QJ
TEL: (01435) 830553 FAX: (01435) 830726

A special treat: rural tranquillity with magnificent food.

The twentieth century does not intrude into life at Stone House; the stone walls which screen off this aristocratic family home are just a corner of a 1,000-acre estate, so guests are helpfully provided with a map before setting off for a stroll in order to ensure their eventual return. Peter and Jane Dunn are clearly proud of their home – indeed, a visit here is more an invitation to share a glimpse of their family history than a mere stay at a hotel. The architecturally interesting house has two distinct parts: the Georgian frontage, with imposing wings that flank the entrance hall, and the older fifteenth-century stone manor house. Inside, the gracious drawing-room and library are liberally adorned with antique furniture, rich fabrics, old English china, paintings and embroidery, yet remain relaxed and comfortable settings for afternoon tea or a pre-dinner drink. Upstairs, the two four-poster rooms overlooking the small lake are the grandest and have bathrooms big enough to throw a party in. In the older section the rooms are more modest, but still retain the essential character of the house and are special by any standards. Jane is a Master Chef, and her impeccably presented dishes are served in the intimate dining-room. Our inspectors enjoyed inventive dishes of filo pastry tartlet with artichoke hearts, tomato and quail's eggs and monkfish in lemon and lobster sauce with squid ink pasta, followed by delicious chocolate amaretti torte with kirsch, and home-made brown-bread ice-cream with maple syrup.

◑ Closed 24 Dec to 2 Jan, and 1 to 15 Feb ⌑ From Heathfield take B2096 towards Battle; take fourth turning on right to Rushlake Green. Private car park ⌑ 1 double, 3 twin/double, 2 four-poster, 1 suite; all with bathroom/WC; TV, hair-dryer, direct-dial telephone; hair-dryer in some rooms ⌑ Dining-room, lounge, drying-room, library, games room, garden; conference facilities (max 26 people incl up to 7 residential); snooker, clay-pigeon shooting, croquet, archery ⌑ No wheelchair access ● No children under 9; no dogs in public rooms ⌑ None accepted ⌑ Single occupancy of twin/double £55 to £71, twin/double £98, four-poster/suite £130 to £168. Set L £19, D £26.50

RYE East Sussex map 3

Jeake's House

Mermaid Street, Rye TN31 7ET
TEL: (01797) 222828 FAX: (01797) 222623

Up-market historic B&B run with pride and enthusiasm.

A foundation stone on the high gable proclaims that Samuel Jeake built this fascinating house along Rye's most archetypically charming cobbled lane in 1689. The modest creeper-clad façade hides a deceptively lofty galleried room with a distinctly church-like quality – hardly surprising as it was once a Quaker meeting-house and later a Baptist chapel. Nowadays it is Francis and Jenny Hadfield's breakfast-room, where portraits of their grandparents watch over guests, who start the day accompanied by soothing strains of Bach – all in all, a refined and stylish ambience, which sets the tone for Jeake's House. The designer bedrooms are a real delight, luxuriously furnished with mahogany and brass beds, bold fabrics and a generally Victorian style. It is hard to choose a favourite room, but perhaps the Conrad Aiken suite with its four-poster, exposed beams and panoramic views to the sea and Romney Marsh, or Elder's Attic, reached via a steep staircase, with its rooftop views (which once proved useful to smugglers on the lookout for excise men) along Mermaid Street, have the edge on atmosphere. Downstairs, guests can meet over a drink in the residents' bar, which is a favourite spot for Jenny's brace of Siamese cats, or in the tiny parlour.

◐ Open all year   ⚡ Centrally located in old Rye. On-street parking   🛏 1 single, 1 twin, 6 double, 1 four-poster, 2 family rooms, 1 suite; all with bathroom/WC exc 2 doubles with shower/WC; TV, limited room service, hair-dryer, direct-dial telephone, radio   ⚶ Dining-room, bar, 2 lounges; baby-listening   ♿ No wheelchair access ● No dogs in public rooms; no smoking in dining-room   ▭ Access, Visa   £ Single £23, single occupancy of twin/double £36 to £54, twin/double £41 to £59, four-poster £59, family room £77, suite £82; deposit required. Special breaks available

---

Little Orchard House

West Street, Rye TN31 7ES
TEL: (01797) 223831

A truly individual guesthouse with a lively young owner.

Anyone wanting to photograph England's heritage of classic steep cobbled streets would do well to seek out Little Orchard House. The ancient cobblestones here are so uneven that walking is tricky, and wearing light shoes will ensure a thorough foot massage as you ascend the incline between the ranks of red-brick and half-timbered houses. The tiny frontage of Sara Brinkhurst's house at first appears too small to hide any accommodation within, but such expectations are turned on their head by the maze-like interior. The country-style kitchen opens on to a very large walled garden, where one of Rye's landmarks, a red-brick smugglers' tower, sprouts from a corner of the colourful flower beds. Back inside, Sara's growing collection of teddy bears keeps you company while you relax in the cosy sitting-room, which is positively stuffed with dried flowers, cats in wood and china, and numerous fascinating items amassed on Sara's travels. The light-hearted feel of the house is continued in the bedrooms, which are pleasantly roomy to sprawl in and are all inhabited by a resident teddy. Lloyd George was a friend of the family, and stayed in the room with a Thai horoscope which may or may not describe you in a favourable light. No less delightful are the Garden Room with an oak four-poster built from a storm-felled tree by Sara's joiner husband and the Hayloft, a small split-level room with great character. Readers have praised the fruit bread and croissants served at breakfast.

◐ Open all year 🅿 West Street is off the High Street in Rye. Private car park
🛏 1 twin, 1 double, 1 four-poster; 2 with bathroom/WC, double with shower/WC; TV,
hair-dryer, clock radio ✅ Dining-room, lounge, library, garden ♿ No wheelchair
access ● No children under 12; no dogs; no smoking in bedrooms ▭ Access,
Delta, Visa £ Single occupancy of twin/double £45 to £65, twin/double £60 to £80,
four-poster £70 to £84; deposit required. Special breaks available

Old Vicarage

66 Church Square, Rye TN31 7HF
TEL: (01797) 222119 FAX: (01797) 227466

An exceptionally friendly guesthouse in the centre of Rye's Old Town.

St Mary's church square crowns the ancient town of Rye. The pink-painted
Georgian frontage of the Old Vicarage adds a happy splash of colour to the
weathered stones of the churchyard opposite and the house boasts an interesting
history of its own. This was the original vicarage before the grander premises
across the square acquired that status (see below). At a later date it became home
to Henry James, where he is said to have written *The Spoils of Poynton*
accompanied by 'his fat dog, servants and canary'. Modern visitors will receive a
cheerful welcome from Julia and Paul Masters, as well as a complimentary glass
of sherry in the cosy lounge, and voluminous information about Rye and its
environs to help you fully enjoy your visit here. This is a comfortable, unfussy
family home with bedrooms decorated in bright and fresh fabrics and with
heaps of added character lent by the crazily warped beams. Each room has some
attraction, such as the antique French bed in the garden room or the steeply
angled ceilings in the attic, and views over the patterned tile rooftops of this
picturesque town. Breakfast is a real treat, with a lavish selection of freshly
baked scones, free-range eggs, sausages and smoked bacon from Mr Ashbee, the
award-winning local butcher, Rwandan tea selected by Julia, who was once in
the trade, and home-made jams and marmalade.

◐ Closed Chr 🅿 Enter the Old Town by Landgate Arch to High Street; turn third left
into West Street; by St Mary's Church. Private car park 🛏 1 twin, 2 double, 2
four-poster, 1 family room; family room with bathroom/WC, rest with shower/WC; TV,
hair-dryer; trouser press in most rooms ✅ Dining-room, lounge, study, garden
♿ No wheelchair access ● No children under 8; no smoking in bedrooms
▭ None accepted £ Single occupancy of twin/double £32 to £52, twin/double £34
to £57, four-poster £50 to £59, family room £61 to £72; deposit required. Special breaks
available

Old Vicarage Hotel

15 East Street, Rye TN31 7JY
TEL: (01797) 225131 (AND FAX)

A friendly, family-run hotel, situated in the centre of this old town.

Rye's hotels all claim to have been frequented at some time or another by Henry
James before he took up more permanent residence in Lamb House, and the Old

Vicarage Hotel (like the previous entry) is no exception. What is certain is that this red-brick town house in the heart of Rye's ancient conservation area was built by a prominent wool-stapler at the beginning of the eighteenth century, and was later home to the vicar of St Mary's (until 1976). The land drops away steeply at the rear of the house, providing excellent views from the garden across the River Rother to Romney Marsh. Several of the bedrooms, as well as the Taverner dining-room – which is smartly decorated in midnight blue and features white pillars – are favoured by this impressive and unchanging panorama. The bedrooms are of various sizes and are individually decorated; some boast beds with testers and closing curtains. Visitors have written to praise the friendliness and helpfulness of the owners, Sarah and Bill Foster, as well as the good-value dinner menu, which features such items as crab and salmon fishcakes served with a tomato and sweet-pepper sauce, or trout presented in an orange and ginger sauce, followed, perhaps, by a home-made honey and stem-ginger ice-cream for dessert.

◗ Closed Jan   ⤢ Follow Rye town-centre signs and enter High Street through Landgate Arch. East Street is first turning on right after arch. On-street parking   ⊨ 1 twin, 1 double, 2 four-poster; family room available; all with bathroom/WC; TV, room service, hair-dryer, direct-dial telephone   ✅ Dining-room, bar, conservatory, garden; early suppers for children   ♿ No wheelchair access   ● No dogs in public rooms   ▭ Access, Amex, Visa   £ Twin/double/four-poster £68 to £84, family room from £82; deposit required. Alc D £20. Special breaks available

---

ST ALBANS Hertfordshire   map 3

Sopwell House

Cottonmill Lane, Sopwell, St Albans AL1 2HQ
TEL: (01727) 864477   FAX: (01727) 844741

Large smart rooms and first-rate restaurant in a country-club hotel close to London.

Part-Georgian, part-Victorian, Sopwell House has an unremarkable history, lived in quietly by princes and dukes until it became a hotel in 1969. Now run as a country club as well as a hotel, it's particularly popular with business people making the most of the fitness facilities and the Art-Deco pool. Football teams on their way to Wembley often spend the night here, leaving behind signed shirts which now decorate the corridor linking the informal breakfast- room-cum-health café with the rest of the hotel. The public rooms are smart and clubby, with deep-red fabrics and racing-green leather armchairs in the lounge and bar, while the conservatory restaurant, with its magnolia trees growing in the centre of the room, is lighter and more original. Service here is friendly and unobtrusive, and the food excellent. If you make it past the exotic starters and rich main courses, we can strongly recommend the wild rice pudding with fruit and crème fraîche. The bedrooms mostly overlook other parts of the building with glimpses of the gardens. All have plenty of space, and are very comfortably kitted out with co-ordinated décor and fabrics, smart marble bathrooms and a generous array of goodies.

● Open all year ⊉ Turn off M25 at Junction 21A and follow signs to St Albans; join A414; turn left and follow signs for Sopwell. Private car park ⊨ 12 single, 20 twin, 36 double, 22 four-poster, 2 suites; family rooms available; all with bathroom/WC; TV, room service, hair-dryer, trouser press, direct-dial telephone; mini-bar in suites ⌀ 2 restaurants, 2 bars, 2 lounges, library, conservatory, games room, garden; conference facilities (max 400 people incl up to 92 residential); gym, sauna, solarium, heated indoor swimming-pool, croquet, snooker; early suppers for children; babysitting, baby-listening ♿ No wheelchair access ● None ⊟ Access, Amex, Delta, Diners, Switch, Visa £ Single £70 to £100, single occupancy of twin/double £74 to £109, twin/double £95 to £130, four-poster/family room £106 to £138, suite £150 to £165; deposit required. Continental B £7.50, cooked B £9.50; set L £15/17, D £22/23.50; alc L, D £25; brasserie meals available. Special breaks available

---

ST AUSTELL Cornwall   map 1

Boscundle Manor

Tregrehan, St Austell PL25 3RL
TEL: (01726) 813557 FAX: (01726) 814997

Spa baths abound in this small and pleasing eighteenth-century hotel on the quiet outskirts of St Austell.

Looking at it now, it's hard to imagine that Boscundle Manor was once three houses, owned by a tea-seller, a farmer and the captain of Wheal Eliza. The remains of the mine can still be inspected on the hill beside the house, where there's also a barn which has been converted to accommodate a small gym and an outdoor heated swimming-pool. Inside the house, a long, thin hall turns abruptly right, opening into a welcoming lounge that is warmed by a log fire – the perfect place in which to enjoy a pre-dinner drink. The main dining-room, too, is long and thin, and features cream-coloured walls and comfortable, velvet-padded chairs. A guest who wrote warmly of the house's relaxing atmosphere also commented that the food was 'superbly cooked and presented' by Mary and Andrew Flint, and that the wine list was 'probably the best in Cornwall'. A typical meal might start with salmon mayonnaise, continue with rack of lamb, and wind up with chocolate mousse, and finally a cheeseboard. All the bedrooms are supremely comfortable and well equipped; some even boast phones in their bathrooms (which also feature spa baths, and advice on how to use them without drowning in bubble bath). The best of all is Room 5, which is furnished with enough books to keep an insomniac reading until dawn. In giving Boscundle Manor a resounding thumbs-up, a guest concluded that although the stay wasn't particularly cheap, it was 'worth every penny'.

● Closed end Oct to end Mar ⊉ 2 miles east of St Austell, 200 yards off A390 on road signposted Tregrehan. Private car park ⊨ 2 single, 3 twin, 2 double, 1 family room, 2 suites; some in annexe; all with bathroom/WC exc singles with shower/WC; TV, hair-dryer, mini-bar, trouser press, direct-dial telephone ⌀ 2 dining-rooms, bar, lounge, library, conservatory, games room, garden; golf, gym, heated outdoor swimming-pool, croquet, badminton, snooker; early suppers for children; babysitting, baby-listening ♿ No wheelchair access ● No dogs in public rooms; no smoking in dining-rooms ⊟ Access, Amex, Visa £ Single £60 to £70, single occupancy of twin/double £70 to £80, twin/double £110 to £130, family room £135 to £155, suite £140 to £160; deposit required. Set D £22.50. Special breaks available

ST BLAZEY **Cornwall**   map 1

Nanscawen House

Prideaux Road, St Blazey, Nr Par PL24 2SR
TEL: (01726) 814488 (AND FAX)

*Quietly located, small rural B&B with some enormous rooms and
lovely views.*

As you approach Nanscawen House, scattering rabbits on both sides, you will
see a lovely japonica- and wistaria-draped stone building, once home to the
wealthy Nanscawen family, with a stylish pink extension and breakfast
conservatory added on. The harmonious proportions of the exterior in no way
prepare you for stepping into a hall big enough to welcome an army and a lounge
with space for a convention. In spite of this, Janet and Keith Martin have only
three bedrooms, two of them – Treffry and Prideaux – of conventional size, the
third – Rashleigh – so big that you could practise ballroom dancing in it. All three
rooms, but especially Treffry and Prideaux, are decorated in a very feminine
style, with lots of pink, ribbons and teddies. All have spa baths, with thick
towels and lots of toiletries with which to make the most of them laid out on the
beds. Tucked in the garden, out of sight of the house, are two real luxuries: a
heated outdoor swimming-pool and a Jacuzzi, where you can soak and stargaze
at the same time. The Martins don't serve evening meals but will be happy to
advise on local restaurants.

◑ Closed 25 & 26 Dec ⬕ Travelling south, in St Blazey turn right directly after
railway crossing, opposite garage. Private car park ⤶ 1 twin, 1 double, 1
four-poster; all with bathroom/WC; TV, hair-dryer, direct-dial telephone
✅ Dining-room, lounge, conservatory, garden; heated outdoor swimming-pool
🚫 No wheelchair access ● No children under 12; no dogs; no smoking
▭ Access, Visa £ Single occupancy of twin/double £40 to £58, twin/double £68 to
£78, four-poster £72; deposit required

ST HILARY **Cornwall**   map 1

Ennys

St Hilary, Penzance TR20 9BZ
TEL: (01736) 740262 (AND FAX)

Neat and tidy farmhouse with outdoor pool in remote countryside.

Ennys may be a working farm, but you would never realise that unless you
snooped around at the back. From the front, the farmhouse is an immaculate
stone building draped with wistaria looking out on lovingly cultivated gardens.
The bedrooms take their names from other local farms. Prettiest is Tregembo,
which boasts a Victorian four-poster usually covered by a delicate quilt, a family
heirloom; it has only a shower, but bath-lovers can creep along the corridor to a
sprawling bathroom. The two family suites in the Hayloft and Stable outside
come equipped with fridges, with microwave ovens on standby if needed. The
dining-room is homely rather than grand, although it features a fine fireplace and
plenty of pictures on the walls. Owner Sue White's dinners come with no choice

of main course (though she's happy to handle all dietary requests) but with alternative starters and puddings; you might kick off with vegetable tagliatelle, progress to pan-fried monkfish and finish with home-made lemon ice-cream. One reader who stayed for a few days felt there was too much reliance on pork in various guises in the menu. Breakfasts are a treat, with home-made brioche, croissants and jam to top up the bacon and eggs. 'You can have it in bed, but hardly anyone does,' Sue says. They are probably too keen to be out exploring the surrounding countryside or taking a dip in the (heated) outdoor pool.

◑ Open all year   ⊿ 2 miles east of Marazion on B3280; just before Relubbus turn left into Trewhella Lane. Private car park   ⤙ 1 twin, 1 double, 2 four-poster, 2 suites; family rooms available; some in annexe; 1 with bathroom/WC, most with shower/WC; TV, room service, hair-dryer   ✓ Dining-room, lounge, drying-room, study, games room, garden; conference facilities (max 15 people incl up to 6 residential); outdoor heated swimming-pool, tennis; early suppers for children; baby-listening   ⅃ No wheelchair access   ● No dogs; no smoking in bedrooms   ▭ Access, Delta, Visa £ Single occupancy of twin/double £35, twin/double £45 to £55, four-poster £55, family room/suite from £75; deposit required. Set D £17.50; alc D £22. Special breaks available

---

ST KEYNE **Cornwall** map 1

Well House

St Keyne, Liskeard PL14 4RN
TEL: (01579) 342001   FAX: (01579) 343891

A thoroughly urbane hotel, offering excellent food in a secluded, rural setting.

The Well House hides its light under a bushel, for its conventional Victorian exterior offers little hint of what lies inside. Nick Wainford's partner, Ione Nurdin, has gone to town with the paintbrush, resulting in seven strikingly individual bedrooms that are painted in deep blues, pinks and yellows (even the dried flowers are colour co-ordinated, as one guest pointed out). The furnishings are similarly varied, and include interesting bedheads, and huge wardrobes and dressing tables. Unexpectedly, for such an up-market hotel, there's a capacious family suite tucked away at the top of the house, and another guest was impressed to see how much attention was lavished on a family with young children at breakfast, 'with suggestions about quantities of cereal and offers of porridge'. Orders for dinner are taken in a cosy little bar beside the front door, although there's also an inviting lounge in which a log fire glows. The cuisine attracts regular accolades: this year a happy guest commented that lamb and braised cabbage, which was served with slivers of buttery carrots, tiny florets of cauliflower and broccoli, a few green beans and new potatoes, was 'really pungent and delicious', while the chocolate marquise, accompanied by a coffee-bean sauce, was 'a calorific, potential clot-former, but l don't regret a mouthful!' The cheeseboard, offering a 'bewildering array of English cheeses', and the cooked breakfasts, featuring meaty, succulent sausages, and bacon that was 'just smoky enough', were also much appreciated. Once you've eaten your fill, there are extensive grounds in which you can stroll; Nick Wainford can direct you to the eponymous well. According to legend, whichever partner of a newly-wed couple reached it first could expect to wear the trousers in their marriage.

◗ Open all year　☑ Pass through St Keyne, past church, and take road to St Keyne Well. Hotel is ½ mile from church. Private car park　🛏 2 twin, 5 double, 1 family room; all with bathroom/WC; TV, room service, hair-dryer, trouser press, direct-dial telephone; no tea/coffee-making facilities in rooms　✅ Restaurant, bar, lounge, garden; heated outdoor swimming-pool, tennis; early suppers for children　♿ No wheelchair access　● No children under 8 in restaurant eves　☐ Access, Amex, Delta, Switch, Visa　💷 Single occupancy of twin/double £60, twin/double £72 to £105, family room £105 to £140; deposit required. Cooked B £7.50; set L, D £20 to £29.50. Special breaks available

---

ST MARGARET'S AT CLIFFE Kent　　　　　　　　　　　　map 3

Wallett's Court

West Cliffe, St Margaret's at Cliffe, Dover CT15 6EW
TEL: (01304) 852424　FAX: (01304) 853430

A historic manor house of great character that serves good food, five minutes' drive from Dover.

Surrounded by fields, and located just a quarter of a mile from the cliff tops, Wallett's Court gives the impression of occupying an isolated spot. In fact, since it is only 3 miles from the port of Dover, it makes an excellent place in which to stay if you're planning an early-morning Channel crossing. This Grade-II listed building, which was recorded as 'The Manor of Westcliffe' in the Domesday Book, has been restored by Lea and Chris Oakley, who have maintained the house's historic feel. With its beamed ceiling and comfy sofas, the lounge/bar area is a great place in which to relax and enjoy the views of the surrounding countryside. Dinners are cooked by Chris, and served in the main restaurant, which features a large, brick fireplace. The extensive, seasonal menu might include such dishes as oak-smoked chicken breasts, a venison terrine with Cumberland jelly, jugged hare – or maybe medallions of ostrich – followed by orange syllabub. The bedrooms in the manor house have lots of character; with small bunches of dried red roses and heather decorating the cream muslin canopy of its four-poster bed, Queen Eleanor's is the most romantic. The bedrooms in the converted farm buildings are rather plainer, although still comfortable.

◗ Closed Chr　☑ From M20 or A2 take A258 Dover to Deal road, and first right turning for West Cliffe. Private car park　🛏 2 twin, 6 double, 2 four-poster, 1 family room; most in annexe; all with bathroom/WC; TV, room service, hair-dryer, direct-dial telephone　✅ 3 restaurants, lounge/bar, TV room, conservatory, garden; conference facilities (max 30 people incl up to 11 residential); tennis, clay-pigeon shooting, croquet; early suppers for children; baby-listening　♿ No wheelchair access　● No dogs ☐ Access, Amex, Delta, Diners, Switch, Visa　💷 Single occupancy of twin/double £50, twin/double £60 to £80, four-poster £80, family room £75; deposit required. Set D £23 to £28. Special breaks available

St Martin's

St Martin's TR25 0QW
TEL: (01720) 422092   FAX: (01720) 422298

A relaxed and relaxing family hotel, in which the service is highly praised.

As ever, our favourite hotel in the Scillies has received praise from satisfied guests: 'We have stayed for six consecutive Easters, and the hotel has improved each time we have been there. The staff from top to bottom, so to speak, are very friendly and go out of their way to be so.' Reports also commend St Martin's as being a good place for families to stay, since it is truly happy to cater for all ages – from youngsters to guests in their 80s. The hotel, which is situated next to a sandy beach, is designed to resemble a cluster of cottages. It's an ideal place in which to relax, and you can wander along the island paths and maybe catch a boat to explore the other islands – or, indeed, indulge yourself on the hotel's own yacht, which is crewed by a local skipper. The bedrooms are all bright and nicely decorated, and its goes without saying that it's worth asking for a sea view.

If you're lucky, you might also be able to admire the view from the restaurant, and possibly watch the spectacular sunset while dining on locally caught fish, or perhaps a fricassee of pheasant, wild mushrooms, chicory and thyme charlotte, followed by a honey-nougat glace served with a Melba sauce. The breakfasts and lunches are also well up to standard, and younger guests can be served an early high tea. The owners intend to create more bedrooms and add an outdoor swimming-pool.

◗ Closed Nov to Feb   ⊠ Flights from Bristol, Exeter, Plymouth, St Just; helicopter or boat from Penzance. There are no cars on the Isles of Scilly   ⊨ 16 twin, 2 four-poster, 4 family rooms, 2 suites; all with bathroom/WC; TV, room service, hair-dryer, direct-dial telephone   ⌀ Restaurant, bar, lounge, TV room, games room, garden; conference facilities (max 24 people residential); fishing, heated indoor swimming-pool, yachting, clay-pigeon shooting; early suppers for children; toys, playrooms, babysitting, baby-listening, outdoor games   ᯤ No wheelchair access ● No children under 12 in restaurant eves; no dogs in public rooms; smoking in bar only   ▭ Access, Amex, Delta, Diners, Switch, Visa   £ Single occupancy of twin £50 to £70, twin/four-poster £100 to £140, family room £150 to £220, suite £190 to £260; deposit required. Set D £29.50. Special breaks available

---

Atlantic Hotel

Hugh Town, St Mary's TR21 0PL
TEL: (01720) 422417   FAX: (01720) 423009

A centrally located, harbourside hotel, boasting lovely views.

The Atlantic Hotel is just a couple of minutes' walk away from the quay at St Mary's – the largest of the inhabited Isles of Scilly. It's a rambling old inn that has been nicely modernised without losing its character. The staff are young and friendly, and are happy to help all ages, from the very young to the more mature. The harbour views from the dining-room are among the best in the hotel, and will surely command your attention when you dine from the fairly traditional menu, which will probably include locally caught fish. The light bedrooms are decorated in floral patterns – and, of course, the pick of the rooms boast sea views.

◐ Closed Nov to Feb ✈ Plane, helicopter or boat from Penzance. There are no cars on the Isles of Scilly 🛏 1 single, 10 twin, 12 double, 1 four-poster, family rooms available; all with bathroom/WC exc 1 double with shower/WC; TV, direct-dial telephone; hair-dryer on request ✓ Dining-room, bar, lounge; early suppers for children; baby-listening ♿ No wheelchair access ● No smoking in dining-room ▭ Access, Visa £ Single £69 to £72, single occupancy of twin/double £92 to £96, twin/double £138 to £144, four-poster £146 to £152, family room from £158 (rates incl dinner); deposit required. Set D £19.50

Tregarthen's

Hugh Town, St Mary's TR21 0PP
TEL: (01720) 422540/422960 FAX: (01720) 422089

A hotel whose warm welcome ensures plenty of return visitors.

This is the sort of place to which visitors return year after year – just listen to the conversations in reception about who usually stays here at this time of year. It certainly isn't the swankiest place in which to stay on the Scillies – 'comfortable' is more the adjective that comes to mind – but Tregarthen's good service and pleasant position overlooking the quay make it welcoming and convenient. The bedrooms are similarly homely. Traditional food is served in the restaurant, often featuring a roast, as well as locally caught fish such as grilled Cornish rainbow trout or poached fillet of cod à la dieppoise. The portions are generous, and the display of desserts is very popular with the guests.

◐ Closed last week in Oct to mid-Mar ✈ Plane, helicopter or boat from Penzance. There are no cars on the Isles of Scilly 🛏 5 single, 14 twin, 8 double, 5 family rooms; all with bathroom/WC; TV, room service, hair-dryer, trouser press, direct-dial telephone ✓ Restaurant, bar, lounge, 2 drying-rooms, garden; early suppers for children; baby-listening ♿ No wheelchair access ● No dogs ▭ Access, Amex, Delta, Diners, Switch, Visa £ Single £68 to £78, single occupancy of twin/double £90, twin/double £136 to £156, family room from £141 (rates incl dinner); deposit required. Set L from £9, D £20

Idle Rocks

Harbourside, 1 Tredenham Road, St Mawes TR2 5AN
TEL: (01326) 270771 FAX: (01326) 270062

A comfortable small hotel, looking directly over St Mawes harbour, with some bedrooms located in an inland annexe.

Beneath Idle Rocks, the sea laps against the rocks which gave the hotel its name. The bar and restaurant are filled with appropriately nautical touches: there are model ships in the bar, and the restaurant's painted ships have been incorporated into the wooden partitions that provide semi-private areas within the larger room. Predictably, fish features prominently on the three-course dinner menus, although chicken, beef and lamb are offered as alternatives. The upstairs bedrooms are named after local British birds – they may not be especially large, but are all individually decorated with colourful fabrics; those that lack sea views look out over the Little Percueil estuary. There are four more bedrooms in Bohella House across the road; the reconstruction there was nearing completion when we inspected. Two of the new rooms will feature four-poster beds, and all will boast spa baths. A wrought-iron balcony is also being added to the building. Although these bedrooms will be slightly further from the sea, guests will be only a few steps away from the comfortable lounge in the main hotel. Unfortunately, the hotel has no private parking space, and guests have to use (and pay for) the public car park behind the Rising Sun.

● Open all year ⬀ By harbour in St Mawes. On-street parking, public car park nearby ⤆ 3 single, 4 twin, 11 double, 4 four-poster, 2 family rooms; some in annexe; all with bathroom/WC exc singles with shower/WC; TV, room service, hair-dryer, direct-dial telephone ✓ Restaurant, bar, lounge; conference facilities (max 20 people residential/non-residential); early suppers for children; babysitting, baby-listening ⅼ No wheelchair access ● No smoking in restaurant and 1 lounge ▭ Access, Amex, Delta, Switch, Visa £ Single £30 to £61, single occupancy of twin/double £45 to £92, twin/double £60 to £122, four-poster £60 to £110, family room from £98; deposit required. Set D £22.50 to £25; light meals available (1996 prices). Special breaks available

---

SALCOMBE Devon   map 1

Soar Mill Cove Hotel

Soar Mill Cove, Salcombe TQ7 3DS
TEL: (01548) 561566   FAX: (01548) 561223

A pleasingly furnished and welcoming haven of tranquillity within easy reach of Salcombe.

A narrow road meanders down towards Soar Mill Cove; 'We don't want to make it any wider, because it keeps the coaches at bay,' admits the hotel's owner, Norma Makepeace. This year, she and her husband, Keith, have had the car park moved from the beach at the front to the back of the hotel, in order to make even more of the splendid, rolling views across the daffodil-dotted lawns to the sea. They've also built a wooden chalet to act as a children's playroom; when we inspected, the toys were just being taken out of their boxes. Perhaps the nicest of the bedrooms are the four located in the new wing, whose décor boasts colourful, modern fabrics; also included are inviting armchairs that are angled for you to admire the sea views, and attractively tiled bathrooms. The Makepeaces are particularly proud of their family suites, which feature separate rooms for offspring, complete with fold-down beds and private televisions. A lot of thought goes into making guests feel at home, including jugs of fresh milk instead of UHT cartons, but one guest objected to being subjected to a 'Spanish inquisition' when she asked if smoking was allowed in the bedrooms. Great care also goes into the production of the daily menus, which are presented inside a folder bearing a watercolour image of Soar Mill Cove. The extra information provided regarding the ingredients was always a bonus, but this has become even more reassuring since the beef scare. The delicious-sounding starters include a Cornish Yarg soufflé, or swede and ginger soup, while the main-course section of the menu advises you that such dishes as breast of chicken served with a cider and onion sauce can be provided without the sauce, if you prefer.

◑ Closed Nov to Jan ☑ From A381 Salcombe road, turn right at Malborough and follow signs towards sea and Soar Mill Cove. Private car park ⊨ 6 twin, 7 double, 1 four-poster, 2 family rooms, 3 suites; all with bathroom/WC; TV, room service, hair-dryer, trouser press, direct-dial telephone ✅ 2 restaurants, bar, 2 lounges, drying-room, 2 games rooms, garden; fishing, heated indoor and outdoor swimming-pools, tennis; early suppers for children; toys, playrooms, babysitting, baby-listening, outdoor games ♿ No wheelchair access ● No very young children in restaurant eves; no dogs in public rooms; no smoking in restaurant ▭ Access, Delta, Switch, Visa £ Single occupancy of twin/double £70 to £105, twin/double £124 to £170, four-poster £144 to £170, family room £165 to £212, suite £190 to £240; deposit required. Set D £34; alc L £18; light lunches available. Special breaks available

---

Tides Reach

South Sands, Salcombe TQ8 8LJ
TEL: (01548) 843466   FAX: (01548) 843954

An alluring hotel in a quiet location overlooking the beach.

The road zigzags alarmingly southwards from Salcombe and by the time you reach Tides Reach you've shaken off most of the other traffic. Luckily, once you get there you need not face the road again until it's time to leave, since a regular ferry conveys guests to the town centre in a more relaxing fashion. Water is central to the charm of Tides Reach: not only does the sea lap against the shore just across the road, but there's also a small pond in the sun lounge, a much larger one beside the hotel, and a splendid swimming-pool that is so densely surrounded by greenery that it reminds you of an indoor tropical paradise. Not surprisingly then, most of the bedrooms boast watery views, although the best are the ones whose balconies are angled to catch the sun shining across the sea. The restaurant sweeps round the hotel within a big bay window, offering most diners a sea vista as they eat. The three-course dinners are more adventurous than those of some other seaside hotels, and you could start with a curried-lobster soup, and then move on to the vegetable risotto, or you could play it safer and begin with a smoked-salmon parcel, following it up with a roast. Tides Reach attracts a devoted band of regular guests who have made many friends over the years. One of them sent this ringing endorsement of the hotel: 'One cannot fault the atmosphere and service in any way. Whatever the weather, it just does not matter.'

◑ Closed 20 Dec to 12 Feb 🔁 Take A381 to Salcombe. Turn right in Salcombe at seafront, and follow signs to South Sands. Private car park 🛏 17 twin, 18 double, 3 family rooms; all with bathroom/WC; TV, room service, hair-dryer, direct-dial telephone, radio ✅ Restaurant, bar, 3 lounges, drying-room, games room, garden; gym, sauna, solarium, heated indoor swimming-pool, snooker, squash, water-skiing, windsurfing ♿ No wheelchair access ● No children under 8; no dogs in public rooms; no smoking in restaurant and 1 lounge ▭ Access, Amex, Delta, Diners, Switch, Visa £ Single occupancy of twin/double £57 to £71, twin/double £104 to £140, family room £175 to £221; deposit required. Set D £26; alc D £33.50 (prices valid till Mar 1997). Special breaks available

---

SALTFORD Bath & N. E. Somerset map 2

Brunel's Tunnel House

High Street, Saltford, Bristol BS18 3BQ
TEL: (01225) 873873 FAX: (01225) 874875

A friendly, reassuring hotel with an interesting history.

'As usual, I was very pleased with this little hotel and the owners,' wrote a regular visitor to this Georgian town house, situated just off the busy A4 road linking Bath and Bristol, and owned by Sarah Leighton and her mother, Muriel Mitchell. The handsome, three-storey house, encircled by lawns and flower borders, certainly has a modest charm – and an interesting history, too: in the nineteenth century, its famous owner and resident, the railway pioneer Isambard Kingdom Brunel, ploughed the tracks for the Great Western Railway deep beneath its foundations. Today's visitors could remain oblivious to this interesting fact (fortunately, there's rarely any noise or vibrations), were it not for Sarah's large and illuminating aerial photograph. Sarah collects Brunel memorabilia, including prints of trains, extracts from his diary, and old bills, which are displayed on the landings and in the corridors. But even without this connection, the house still has plenty to recommend it: the high-ceilinged bedrooms are immaculately maintained, and their décor is beautifully co-ordinated; those on the first floor feature fireplaces and window shutters, and many also boast half-tester beds and fine antique furniture. Sarah serves a set, three-course meal, followed by coffee, by prior arrangement.

◑ Closed Chr; dining-room closed Sun 🔁 In centre of Saltford, turn off A4 at Saltford Motor Services into Beech Road. Hotel faces bottom of this road. Private car park 🛏 1 twin, 6 double; 1 with bathroom/WC, 6 with shower/WC; TV, room service, direct-dial telephone; hair-dryer and iron on request ✅ Dining-room, bar/lounge, garden; conference facilities (max 14 people incl up to 7 residential); early suppers for children; toys, baby-listening, cots, high chairs ♿ No wheelchair access ● No dogs; no smoking in dining-room ▭ Access, Amex, Delta, Visa £ Single occupancy of twin/double £42 to £49, twin/double £49 to £57; deposit required. Set D £14. Special breaks available

---

Prices are what you can expect to pay in 1997, except where specified to the contrary. Many hoteliers tell us that these prices can be regarded only as approximations.

SANDIWAY **Cheshire**   map 7

Nunsmere Hall

Tarporley Road, Sandiway, Northwich CW8 2ES
TEL: (01606) 889100   FAX: (01606) 889055

Top-drawer country-house hotel with an excellent restaurant.

Nunsmere Hall was built at the turn of the century, virtually within the compass
of a natural moat – a 60-acre lake that surrounds the hotel on three sides. But the
proximity of such an expanse of water comes as something of a surprise, being
hidden behind borders of birch trees and monumental rhododendrons along the
driveway. More surprises are in store inside the house, which is light and
tranquil with lots of immaculate toffee-coloured woodwork in the galleried
entrance hall. The overall impression throughout the public rooms is of
understated contemporary elegance, with oriental rugs spread over stripped
floorboards, and fine china and exquisite antiques mixing with modern sofas in
the sitting-room. Bedrooms too combine modern comforts with period
furniture. Top-of-the-range rooms boast state-of-the-art showers; while others
may have a corner bath you could swim in. The only surprise with the food
would be if you had a bad meal. Cooking is creative, beautifully presented and of
the highest standard. Our inspector's kaleidoscopic dinner involved vegetable
terrine with a cabbage coulis, and roast duck on a bed of Mediterranean
vegetables surrounded by beetroot juice.

◑ Open all year ⊉ Off A49, 4 miles south-west of Northwich. Private car park
🛏 6 single, 11 twin, 11 double, 3 four-poster, 1 suite; all with bathroom/WC; TV,
room service, hair-dryer, trouser press, direct-dial telephone ✓ Restaurant, bar, 2
lounges, library, games room, garden; air-conditioning in private dining-room;
conference facilities (max 50 people incl up to 32 residential); snooker, croquet,
archery; early suppers for children ⅙ Wheelchair access to hotel (3 steps),
restaurant and WC (unisex), 2 ground-floor bedrooms ● No children under 10 in
restaurant eves; no dogs; no smoking in restaurant ▱ Access, Amex, Diners, Switch,
Visa £ Single £99, single occupancy of twin/double £115, twin/double £130 to £150,
four-poster £200 to £275, suite £275. Continental B £8.50, cooked B £13.50; set L £17;
alc D £30 (1996 prices). Special breaks available

SANDRINGHAM **Norfolk**   map 6

Park House

Sandringham PE35 6EH
TEL: (01485) 543000   FAX: (01485) 540663

*Spacious Victorian manor house on royal estate providing haven of
hospitality for disabled holidaymakers.*

In 1997 Park House will celebrate its tenth anniversary. Originally presented by
the Queen to the Leonard Cheshire Foundation, the hotel is a unique
establishment, providing 24-hour care by qualified and experienced staff for
disabled people on holiday. The proportions of the 1863 building provide plenty
of space for turning wheelchairs, and the large bay windows offer restful

viewing over the well-maintained gardens and lawns outside. Décor remains old-fashioned – despite occupancy rates of over 90 per cent the hotel still runs at a loss – but facilities are first rate, from billiards, darts and skittles in the airy conservatory and games room to the outdoor pool. Special-interest weeks devoted to crafts, health and beauty, music or painting are also offered. Bedrooms cater for various types of disability and may feature overhead hoists or taps controlled by fingertips; able-bodied carers can share a room or opt for a cheaper bedroom in the adjacent coach-house. Dinner menus offer three or four choices at each course and tend to stick to traditional favourites like egg mayonnaise, roast turkey with stuffing and cranberry sauce, and queen of puddings from the sweets trolley.

◐ Open all year ⤢ Turn right (east) off A149, 3 miles north of Knight's Hill roundabout, and follow hotel signs. Private car park ⬅ 8 single, 8 twin; twins with bathroom/WC, singles with shower/WC; TV, direct-dial telephone; hair-dryer on request ⌀ Dining-room, bar, lounge, library, conservatory, games room, garden; conference facilities (max 60 people incl up to 16 residential); heated outdoor swimming-pool, clay-pigeon shooting ♿ Wheelchair access to hotel, restaurant and WC (M,F, unisex), all bedrooms specially equipped for disabled people ● No dogs; smoking in conservatory only ▭ Access, Delta, Visa £ Single £56 to £76, twin £94 to £134 (rates incl dinner); deposit required (1996 prices). Special breaks available

---

SANDWAY Kent map 3

Chilston Park

Sandway, Lenham, Maidstone ME17 2BE
TEL: (01622) 859803   FAX: (01622) 858588

A romantic country-house hotel with luxurious rooms and an unpretentious manner.

Set in acres of beautifully landscaped gardens and parkland, including a lake that you can go punting on, as well as a helicopter landing pad, Chilston Park initially seems an intimidating prospect. Its faded elegance and friendly staff are, however, rather more indicative of the hotel's style, and as soon as you walk into the reception area, with its huge, squashy sofas and candles (250 of which are lit nightly in the hotel), you feel instantly at ease. The elegant drawing-room, featuring lots of comfy sofas and chairs and antique furniture, overlooks the gardens, as does the Orangery – the black and white tiled conservatory in which guests can enjoy afternoon tea. Dinner is served by staff dressed in Edwardian costume, and might include a roasted fillet of grey mullet or a roulade of chicken, followed by a baked chocolate-and-pecan pie served with a vanilla sauce. The bedrooms are reached by means of a magnificent eighteenth-century wooden staircase, which was built around the courtyard of the original fifteenth-century manor house. They are all spacious, and are furnished with period furniture; the Regency Room is particularly large, and boasts an enormous, Jacobean, four-poster bed and a marble fireplace. With its wooden floorboards and rafters, the amazing Tudor Suite runs the full length of the attic. It is often used as a bridal suite after the numerous wedding receptions which are held here and, in view of this, one can't help but be amused by the placing of an antique baby's cradle next to the bridal bed! Chilston Park has changed hands recently, and the new owner, Philip Humphreys, is planning an extension incorporating a new reception area and new bedrooms. More reports, please.

◑ Open all year ⚑ 2 miles south of Lenham, which is on A20 midway between Ashford and Maidstone. Private car park ⊨ 12 twin, 15 double, 7 four-poster, 4 suites; family rooms available; some in annexe; all with bathroom/WC; TV, room service, hair-dryer, direct-dial telephone; trouser press in some rooms ⊘ 2 dining-rooms, bar, drawing-room, conservatory, games room, garden; conference facilities (max 120 people incl up to 38 residential); fishing, tennis, croquet, billiards; early suppers for children ਠ No wheelchair access ● No dogs in public rooms and in bedrooms by arrangement only ⊟ Access, Amex, Delta, Diners, Switch, Visa £ Single occupancy of twin/double £95 to £140, twin/double £110, four-poster £155 to £170, family room £215, suite £160 to £185; deposit required. Set L £17 to £20, D £30 to £36; alc D from £29. Special breaks available

---

SCARBOROUGH North Yorkshire map 9

Interludes ☆

32 Princess Street, Scarborough YO11 1QR
TEL: (01723) 360513 FAX: (01723) 368597

Small, stylish town-centre hotel with highly developed theatrical theme.

As Scarborough celebrates the opening of the Stephen Joseph Theatre enter, stage left, Interludes, a small hotel with a strong theatrical flavour. Ian Grundy and Bob Harris opened the hotel in 1991 and have been wowing the critics since: 'We would have no hesitation in recommending it to our friends – the rooms are delightful and the service of a very high standard,' said one visitor. The theatre-break packages, which include B&B, taxis and theatre tickets, are good value and have proved enormously popular. The plain, mid-Georgian building has been refurbished with great verve throughout – bright modern colour schemes complemented by an impressive collection of historic theatre prints. The bedrooms, named after famous theatres or opera houses, are individually designed with either four-poster or canopied beds, are uniformly peaceful and virtually all have views across the South Bay. The dining-room is small but quietly elegant with meals eaten communally at two polished mahogany tables. Dinners have also drawn plaudits for their use fresh local produce and main courses like baked breast of chicken or Scottish salmon.

◑ Closed for owners' holidays ⚑ Follow tourist signs to harbour; take small road between Newcastle Packet pub and Princess café; Princess Street is second turning on left. On-street parking ⊨ 1 twin, 1 twin/double, 1 double, 2 four-poster; 1 with bathroom/WC, 4 with shower/WC; TV, limited room service, hair-dryer, clock radio; trouser press in most rooms ⊘ Dining-room, bar, lounge; conference facilities (max 10 people incl up to 5 residential) ਠ No wheelchair access ● No children under 16; no dogs; no smoking in bedrooms or dining-room ⊟ Access, Visa £ Single occupancy of twin/double £26 to £30, twin/double £44 to £50, four-poster £50; deposit required. Set D £11.50. Special breaks available

SEATOLLER **Cumbria**   map 10

Seatoller House

Seatoller, Borrowdale, Keswick CA12 5XN
TEL: (01768) 777218

A simple, seventeenth-century hotel, situated at the head of
Borrowdale – perfect for walkers.

With plenty of space around it, the 300-year-old Seatoller House spreads out,
rather than up, offering unimpeded views in all directions of either the garden or
the countryside. Most guests come here in order to explore the countryside, and
the demand for televisions and kettles in the bedrooms is generally disregarded
in favour of the more vital drying- and boot-rooms. The manager, Ann Pepper,
encourages guests to do their own thing, and to get to know their fellow guests at
the same time. There's an honesty bar, where you can also make up your own
picnic lunch, and evening meals are served around two huge tables in the
high-ceilinged dining-room. The no-choice menus are unsurprisingly traditional in flavour: a cheese, cucumber and prawn mousse might be followed by
breast of Gressingham duck, and then a frosted apple pudding. All the bedrooms
have *en suite* facilities, and blend old and new furniture and decorations to give a
pleasing effect; Badger boasts a wonderful wooden fireplace. Downstairs,
there's a piano in the sitting-room, and a library stocked with books to read on
non-walking days.

◑ Closed Nov to Mar; dining-room closed Tue ⬈ 8 miles south of Keswick on
B5289. Private car park ⬏ 3 twin, 1 double, 5 family rooms; 1 in annexe; all with
bathroom/WC; no tea/coffee-making facilities in rooms; hair-dryer on request
⌗ Dining-room, lounge, drying-room, library, garden ♿ No wheelchair access
● No children under 5; no dogs in public rooms; no smoking in bedrooms ▭ None
accepted £ Single occupancy of twin/double £37, twin/double £54, family room
from £70; deposit required. Set D £10; packed lunches available

---

SEATON BURN **Tyne & Wear**   map 10

Horton Grange

Seaton Burn, Newcastle upon Tyne NE13 6BU
TEL: (01661) 860686   FAX: (01661) 860308

A relaxing country-house hotel serving sumptuous dinners in open
countryside not far from the city.

The flat farmland around Seaton Burn could hardly be described as scenic, but
it's quiet enough and convenient for Newcastle and the main traffic arteries. The
exterior is rather severe – blackened Georgian – but the well-tended lawns and
ornamental pond brighten things up. The spacious interiors and unostentatious
décor give the house a calming ambience. That is not to say that is not without
style – there are swagged curtains, ornate, carved-wood fireplaces, bedrooms
with antique furniture, and many other such country-house trappings – but the
muted colour schemes and light, comfy sofas lend the place a soft-focus, dreamy

appeal. Indeed, the pre-Raphaelite prints couldn't have found a more suitable home.

Lazing about in such a restful environment may not be the best way in which to work up the kind of appetite that you'll need to do justice to Stephen Martin's momentous dinners. Six courses (if you include chocolates and coffee) centre on a main course such as honey-roasted breast of duck with apple barrels, caramelised in ginger with a cider sauce. One reader found his meal 'delicious and well presented', but could find little else of a positive nature to say about the service. He reported that his wife had to wait over 1½ hours for her main course, service at breakfast was slow, and that in spite of having arranged a late-evening meal because they were reaching the hotel at 9.30pm, they found that only sandwiches were available. More reports, please.

● Closed 25 & 26 Dec; restaurant closed Sun ⊿ North-bound off A1 western bypass, take A19 exit. At the roundabout, take first exit; after 1 mile turn left (Ponteland and airport). Hotel is 2 miles down the road on the right. Private car park ⊯ 4 single, 5 double; some in annexe; all with shower/WC; TV, room service, hair-dryer, direct-dial telephone, radio; no tea/coffee-making facilities in rooms ⌀ Dining-room, lounge, garden; conference facilities (max 20 people incl up to 9 residential); fishing, clay-pigeon shooting; early suppers for children ⅙ Wheelchair access to hotel (ramp), dining-room, WC (unisex), 4 ground-floor bedrooms ● No dogs ⊡ Access, Amex, Switch, Visa £ Single £59, single occupancy of twin/double £69, twin/double £80. Set L £20, D £32. Special breaks available

---

SEAVIEW Isle of Wight   map 2

Seaview Hotel

High Street, Seaview PO34 5EX
TEL: (01983) 612711   FAX: (01983) 613729

Good service and the buzz of a successful venture are features of this hotel, situated in a sleepy resort.

One of the major laurels that has come the way of Seaview Hotel in the past year is the news that it came top of the government's bench-marking exercise on small hotels. There are all sorts of positive things that one could say about the hotel, but let's start with the service: on our inspection visit, all the staff – from chambermaids and junior waitresses to the owners, Nicky and Nick Hayward, themselves – demonstrated the sort of service that reflects initiative and good manners rather than trained responses. Not surprisingly, the place was buzzing, and the staff gave casually dressed yachties, families with young children, as well as locals on a special night out an equally warm welcome. It is a delight to be able to wear what feels comfortable, and not to have to worry about contravening some stuffy dress code. A guest's letter also praised the care that the hotel lavished on a parent's 80th-birthday celebrations – including taking a last-minute change of date in its stride.

Seaview itself is one of those few delightful, hidden-away places, a seaside resort that consists of little more than a sand-and-shingle beach with a yacht club and a tea-room situated halfway up the high street. The hotel is part of a row of beautiful, double-fronted, bay-view houses, from which chairs and tables spill out into the little front gardens in good weather. The small, traditional restaurant has now been supplemented by another bright, white and blue restaurant for the busier periods; the decoration is stylish, although perhaps a little stark, and it presents quite a contrast to the wooden-floored back bar, cluttered with nautical artefacts, and with walls lined with photographs of ships. The menu might feature knuckle of lamb served with mashed celeriac and potatoes, followed by a pear William sorbet accompanied by crunchy filo pastry and exotic fresh fruit.

The bedrooms are all well furnished, but the nicest are Rooms 15 and 16. Families will want to snap up the second-floor flat, which includes a small bedroom furnished with bunk beds for the children, as well as a lounge and bedroom for their – by now relaxed – parents.

○ Open all year; restaurants closed Sun ⟋ Take B3330 from Ryde and follow signs to Seaview; hotel is on High Street, 25 yards from seafront. Private car park ⤙ 9 twin, 6 double, 1 suite; family rooms available; 1 in annexe; most with bathroom/WC, 2 with shower/WC; TV, room service, direct-dial telephone; no tea/coffee-making facilities in rooms; hair-dryer on request ✅ 2 restaurants (1 air-conditioned), 2 bars, lounge, drying-room, conservatory (air-conditioned); conference facilities (max 40 people incl up to 16 residential); sailing; early suppers for children; toys, babysitting, baby-listening ♿ No wheelchair access ● No children under 5 in restaurant eves; no smoking in 1 lounge & 1 restaurant ⊡ Access, Amex, Diners, Switch, Visa £ Single occupancy of twin/double £45 to £55, twin/double £70 to £75, family room/suite £90 to £95; deposit required. Set Sun L £11; alc L, D from £19. Special breaks available

SEAVINGTON ST MARY Somerset   map 2

The Pheasant

Seavington St Mary, Nr Ilminster TA19 0QH
TEL: (01460) 240502   FAX: (01460) 242388

An immaculately presented pub-hotel with stylish, individually decorated rooms.

Even if you had managed to miss the signboard, you would be able to identify the Pheasant by the row of straw pheasants running along its roof. Inside, the dining-room and lounge/bar are all that you would expect of a thatched farmhouse turned pub: low wooden beams, exposed stone walls and big stone fireplaces. The bedrooms, however, are completely modernised, each of them designed along wholly individual lines: Dorset has a Victorian brass bed, Camelot a four-poster, and Winsham reproduction Chippendale furniture. Although all the rooms in the main building are delightful, the ones in the converted outhouses across the drive are probably the quietest. Several of these have connecting doors which create family suites, while Rooms 6 and 7 are designed to be able to accommodate a party of up to eight. After a glass of sherry in your room, you can proceed to the dining-room, where Jacqueline and Edmondo Paolini's menus display the same imagination as the bedrooms. Among the many delicious-sounding starters you'll find dishes like filo tartlet with double Gloucester and leeks. Main-course choices include plenty of pasta.

◑ Closed 26 Dec to 3 Jan; dining-room closed Sun eve ⚏ From South Petherton roundabout on A303 follow signs to Ilminster local services. Turn left by the Volunteer Inn; hotel is 200 yards on the right. Private car park 🛏➝ 2 single, 4 twin, 3 double, 1 four-poster; family rooms available; some in annexe; all with bathroom/WC; TV, room service, hair-dryer, trouser press, direct-dial telephone ✓ Dining-room, lounge/bar, garden; early suppers for children ⅓ No wheelchair access ● No dogs; smoking in some public rooms and some bedrooms ▭ Access, Amex, Diners, Visa
£· Single £50, single occupancy of twin/double £60, twin/double £90, four-poster £99, family room £120. Alc D £27.50. Special breaks available

---

SEDBUSK North Yorkshire   map 8

Stone House

Sedbusk, Nr Hawes DL8 3PT
TEL: (01969) 667571 FAX: (01969) 667720

A darkly atmospheric turn-of-the-century house with cheerful owners and magnificent views.

The Gothic overtones of its architecture may be suggestive of an earlier era, but Stone House was built in the twentieth century – in 1908, to be precise. The interior décor, with the dark wooden panelling, stone fireplace and leaded windows in the Oak Room lounge, the leather button-back sofas in the bar, and the tall bookcases in the library, create an impression of high seriousness. This impression is soon dispelled, however, by the relaxed and informal approach of the Taplin family, whose collection of thimbles, teapots or Dinky cars you may run into in some corner or other. The atmosphere is indeed convivial, and guests are often to be found enjoying the board games provided in the lounge or the snooker table in the library.

The dining-room also features lots of dark wood, but the daily changing menu is no slave to English tradition, and spicy vegetable curry or Hungarian goulash may appear alongside the roast breast of Nidderdale chicken.

Three of the bedrooms have their own conservatory, three have four-poster beds, and those at the front boast superlative views across Wensleydale.

◑ Closed Jan ⚏ Take Muker road from Hawes for ½ mile; go up steep hill and turn right towards Askrigg. Hotel is on the left. Private car park 🛏➝ 1 single, 7 twin, 8 double, 3 four-poster; family room available; some in annexe; most with bathroom/WC, some with shower/WC; TV, direct-dial telephone ✓ Dining-room, bar, lounge, drying-room, library, games room, garden; conference facilities (max 45 people incl up to 19 residential); tennis, croquet, snooker; early suppers for children; baby-listening
⅓ Wheelchair access to hotel (3 steps) and dining-room, 4 ground-floor bedrooms
● No smoking in dining-room or lounge ▭ Access, Delta, Switch, Visa £· Single £28 to £33, single occupancy of twin/double £28 to £45, twin/double £55 to £65, four-poster/family room £78; deposit required. Set D £16.50. Special breaks available

---

If you make a booking using a credit card and find after cancelling that the full amount has been charged to your card, raise the matter with your credit card company. It will ask the hotelier to confirm whether the room was re-let, and to justify the charge made.

Whitley Hall Hotel

Elliott Lane, Grenoside, Sheffield S30 3NR
TEL: 0114-245 4444   FAX: 0114-245 5414

Peaceful gardens and some pretty bedrooms feature in an Elizabethan hall that is much used for conferences and special occasions.

The phrase 'William Parker made this worke' has a nice, childlike quality to it, and when you realise that in this piece of Elizabethan graffito the 'worke' referred to is Whitley Hall itself, it seems the height of understatement. He can't take all the credit, of course. This once-honey-coloured building, with its courtyard and stepped gables, has been subject to many additions since the 1580s.

The hotel is popular with the Yorkshire business community, so if you stay during the week, be prepared for young thrusters talking into mobile phones – one visitor left with 'the impression that personal visitors weren't the core business'. You could, however, always retreat to the peace of the 30 acres of grounds and discover the lake, with its romantic little boathouse, or bump into one of the peacocks. The bedrooms are neat and well co-ordinated, with the occasional creaky floorboard and paintings by Flint or Sturgeon adding a splash of colour.

There's a weekly changing five-course dinner, and a monthly changing à la carte menu, which may include lamb noisettes, duck satay or Dover sole.

◑ Closed bank holidays   ⚡ Off A61 Sheffield to Barnsley road at Grenoside. Private car park   ⟼ 2 single, 8 twin, 7 double, 1 four-poster; family room and suite available; all with bathroom/WC exc 1 single with shower/WC; TV, room service, trouser press, direct-dial telephone, clock radio; hair-dryer in some rooms   ⚶ Restaurant, 2 bars, lounge, garden; conference facilities (max 75 people incl up to 18 residential); putting green, croquet, clay-pigeon shooting; early suppers for children; babysitting   ♿ No wheelchair access   ● No dogs in public rooms; no smoking in some public rooms and bedrooms   ☐ Access, Amex, Delta, Diners, Switch, Visa   💷 Single/single occupancy of twin/double £52 to £78, twin/double £62 to £93, four-poster £98, family room £93, suite £165. Set L £13.50, D £19.50; alc L, D £30. Special breaks available

---

Fishers Farm

Shefford Woodlands, Hungerford RG17 7AB
TEL: (01488) 648466   FAX: (01488) 648706

Good-value accommodation and home-produced food on a working farm.

Surrounded by 600 acres of its own farmland, Fishers Farm is a peaceful place to break your journey or spend the weekend as it is close to good walking country on the Lambourn Downs. The smart red-brick house and farm buildings are immaculately kept; one recently replaced chimney pot is carved with the current farmer's name, Henry Wilson, and the date, 1980. Inside, the house is comfortably furnished, with armchairs in front of a brick fireplace and logs piled high. There's a tropical indoor swimming-pool with humorous parrot mobiles and Mary Wilson's seedlings sunning themselves in front of french windows. The kitchen, with its low ceilings and beams, has a more traditional farmhouse feel; guests share one large table here for meals. Each of the three bedrooms is large with views over the garden and open fields, and their good-sized private bathrooms are well equipped with toiletries and bath towels. Dinner tends to be served early in winter and late in summer to fit in with farming hours, and is often roast lamb from the farm's own stock along with home-grown vegetables. Puddings are an extravagant treat thanks to Mary's connections with a luxury catering business.

◑ Open all year ⬕ Leave M4 at Junction 14 and take A338 towards Wantage; after mile turn left on B4000; pass Pheasant Inn, and Fishers Farm is first drive on right. Private car park ⇤ 1 twin, 1 double, 1 family room; all with bathroom/WC; tea/coffee and hair-dryer on request ⌁ Dining-room, lounge, drying-room, garden; heated indoor swimming-pool, croquet; early suppers for children; toys, babysitting
 ♿ No wheelchair access ● Dogs in utility room only; smoking in lounge only
▭ None accepted £ Single occupancy of twin/double £30, twin/double £42 to £46, family room £52 to £66; deposit required. Set D £16. Special breaks available

---

SHENINGTON Oxfordshire   map 5

Sugarswell Farm

Shenington, Banbury OX15 6HW
TEL: (01295) 680512 FAX: (01295) 688149

Modern rural farmhouse with huge rooms and cordon bleu cooking – convenient for the NEC and Stratford.

After the short drive from the M40 through cramped picture-book villages of thatch-roofed cottages, Sugarswell Farm looks a bit bleak. On the edge of a plateau that was once the scene of Civil War battles, Sugarswell is a modern farmhouse in local ironstone surrounded by flat fields. Inside, however, things begin to look up. Every room is immaculately kept and stylishly decorated in striking colours. The kingfisher-blue living-room, with its deep sofas, Liberty-print furnishings and plenty of books and games either side of the modern fireplace, is a comfortable room, and large enough for Rosemary Nunneley's house guests to sit together. The bedrooms – mint green, Wedgwood green and salmon pink – are all huge and light with large bathrooms. The green rooms are both at the back of the house and have perhaps the most peaceful views, overlooking the garden and open fields where there's a sweet mineral water well which gives the farm its name. The pink room, the largest of the three, faces the front of the farm and the comings and goings of farm traffic. Dinner is served around one highly polished table in the formal dining-room. A typical evening menu might include Stilton and broccoli soup, roast duck with ginger, and crème brûlée with a fresh strawberry base. With the Warwickshire border just at the end of the driveway, it's a comfortable base for business people going to the NEC and theatregoers alike.

○ Open all year ⬚ From A422 Banbury to Stratford road, drive through Shenington village; after 1 mile turn right at T-junction and right at next crossroads; hotel is 1 mile further on right. Private car park ⬚ 2 twin, 1 double; all with bathroom/WC; hair-dryer ✓ Restaurant, lounge, garden; conference facilities (max 12 people incl up to 3 residential) ᕫ No wheelchair access ● No children under 12; no dogs; no smoking ⬚ None accepted ⬚ Single occupancy of twin/double £30 to £45, twin/double £40 to £60; deposit required. Set L £15, D £17 to £18

SHEPTON MALLET Somerset   map 2

Bowlish House

Wells Road, Shepton Mallet BA4 5JD
TEL: (01749) 342022(AND FAX)

A small restaurant-with-rooms in an elegant Georgian town house.

Inconspicuously situated on the outskirts of Shepton Mallet, Bowlish House is a stately Georgian town house, which contrives to look bigger from the outside than it actually is. Inside, the flagstoned hall is flanked by the comfortable lounge and a small bar which features a painting above the fireplace that has been designed as part of the panelled walls. More paintings appear in the restaurant, which terminates in a conservatory – ideal for summer evenings. Upstairs, the layout of the bedrooms reflects the way in which the walls have been moved around as the house has evolved over the centuries, from a time when the bedrooms ran into each other into today's style, in which they're suitably private. The bedrooms are all individually decorated in a low-key style, the common theme being the panelling that runs around the walls of each. Our favourite room boasts a separate entrance and exit to the bathroom (rather like being on a stage). The floorboards creak underfoot, but since there are only three rooms, this shouldn't be a problem – besides, after a typical dinner of carrot, ginger and chive soup, followed by saddle of lamb and then a sticky toffee pudding, you'll be too sleepy to notice.

○ Closed 1 week in autumn and 1 week in spring ⬚ ¼ mile from centre of Shepton Mallet, on A371 Wells road. Private car park ⬚ 1 twin, 2 double; all with bathroom/WC; TV; hair-dryer on request ✓ Restaurant, bar, lounge, conservatory, garden; conference facilities (max 24 people non-residential); cot ᕫ No wheelchair access ● No dogs in public rooms ⬚ Access, Amex, Visa ⬚ Single occupancy of twin/double £48, twin/double £48; deposit required. Cooked B £3.50; set D £22.50

SHERIFF HUTTON North Yorkshire   map 9

Rangers House

Sheriff Hutton Park, Sheriff Hutton, York YO6 1RH
TEL: (01347) 878397 (AND FAX)

A flexible approach and eclectic taste give this historic house an informal air.

The list of its royal associations may be long (James I's coat of arms is visible above its entrance), but Rangers House wears its pedigree lightly. Built from stone taken from Richard III's castle nearby, in the sixteenth century it served as a stables and brewhouse for the royal hunting lodge. Inside the house, however, Dorianne and Sid Butler foster a relaxed and informal atmosphere and a sense of fun.

The lounge features a parquet floor covered by a large rug, with chairs and sofas huddled together around the fire, and a piano in the corner. A wooden staircase leads up to a gallery furnished with a bookcase and a lovely wooden cot found in a shop in a Sorrento backstreet. The bedrooms are simply furnished, perhaps including a single, marble-topped chest of drawers, but retain many original features, such as mullioned windows and beams in the family room, or an old stove in the small single.

A touch of levity is very noticeable is in the conservatory, which takes the biscuit for recherché bric-à-brac: the wing of a light aircraft is suspended below the ceiling in one corner, an old diving suit hangs in another, while plastic fruit and 1950s seating abound. The Butlers are fairly flexible about dining – dinners are usually served by arrangement, while breakfast can be taken at any time of the day.

○ Open all year ⚡ At southern end of Sheriff Hutton, on a private road leading to Sheriff Hutton Park. Private car park 🛏 1 single, 1 twin, 4 double; family room available; 3 with bathroom/WC, 1 with shower/WC; room service, hair-dryer
⌁ Dining-room, lounge, library, conservatory, garden; early suppers for children; toys, babysitting ⅙ No wheelchair access ● No dogs ☐ None accepted
£ Single £33, single occupancy of twin/double £43 to £45, twin/double £62 to £66, family room £90; deposit required. Set D £23. Special breaks available

---

SHIPHAM Somerset   map 2

Daneswood House

Cuck Hill, Shipham, Nr Winscombe BS25 1RD
TEL: (01934) 843145   FAX: (01934) 843824

Good food and some home-from-home suites in a comfortable house with panoramic views.

Zigzag bends wind up a steep hill to deposit you outside Daneswood House, where a brand-new, lantern-topped, Victorian-conservatory-style entrance was taking shape when we inspected. Another conservatory built on to the other side provides a superb breakfast-room, light and bright in contrast to the deeper, darker feel of the restaurant, with its William Morris-style wallpaper. The finest bedrooms at Daneswood are the three suites added on in the 1980s. For business travellers, these offer a real home from home, with a sitting-cum-working area downstairs and a bedroom upstairs; a reader commented that 'the suite was excellent, with tasteful décor and plenty of space...the perfect place for my boss to stay.' The rooms inside the original house are less homogenous, but what you lose in cohesive design you gain in terms of interest. Room 1, for example, has a sunken bath on a podium and an old Victorian vis-à-vis love seat; Room 8 has a

Queen Anne four-poster bed. Almost all the rooms come equipped with stereos.

Daneswood House has quite a reputation for its food. A typical dinner menu might start with sauté wild mushrooms and continue with the chef's Bismarck steak *en cheval,* winding up with a home-made dessert. A separate menu for vegetarians features starters like sweetcorn-and-egg soup and main courses like red onion en croûte.

○ Open all year; restaurants closed Sun eve 🔃 South of Bristol, 1½ miles off the A38 towards Cheddar. Private car park 🛏 4 twin, 4 double, 1 four-poster, 3 suites; family rooms available; most with bathroom/WC, 2 with shower/WC; TV, room service, hair-dryer, trouser press, direct-dial telephone ✅ 2 restaurants, bar, lounge, drying-room, 2 conservatories, garden; conference facilities (max 20 people incl up to 12 residential); early suppers for children; baby-listening ♿ No wheelchair access ● No dogs in public rooms and in bedrooms by arrangement only; smoking in some public rooms and some bedrooms 🖃 Access, Amex, Delta, Diners, Switch, Visa 💷 Single occupancy of twin/double £60 to £70, twin/double £80, four-poster £95, family room from £118, suite £113; deposit required. Set L, D £18; alc L, D £24. Special breaks available

---

SHIPTON GORGE Dorset
map 2

Innsacre Farmhouse

Shipton Lane, Shipton Gorge, Bridport DT6 4LJ
TEL: (01308) 456137 (AND FAX)

Affable host in a traditional farmhouse with a dash of imaginative colour.

Sydney Davies is keen to show off recent refurbishments at his peaceful seventeenth-century farmhouse, a long, low building surrounded by pastures and hills. The bedroom corridor, which we previously described as 'functional', has been smartened up. A dash of colour has also been added downstairs. The rustic, beamed lounge-cum-bar, with soft seating clustered around the huge stone fireplace, has been brightened with a coat of deep red paint, which sets off the gilt-framed mirror and exposed stone walls perfectly. There's more imaginative use of colour upstairs. Room 2 mixes various shades of blue; Room 3, with shades of green, brown and blue-grey walls, has a more antique feel; the twin has perhaps the most unusual colour scheme – deep-mauve walls with blue and white striped duvet covers. All contrast well with the dark, elegant antique beds and the patches of exposed stone wall. Breakfasts feature local sausages, bacon and fish and are definitely not, stresses Sydney, portion-controlled. He also encourages guests to 'mix and match' and feel free to make special requests.

○ Closed Chr & New Year 🔃 Hotel is signposted from road to Shipton Gorge and Burton Bradstock. Private car park 🛏 1 twin, 3 double; all with bathroom/WC; TV; hair-dryer and iron on request ✅ Dining-room, bar/lounge, drying-room, garden ♿ No wheelchair access ● No children under 9; no smoking in bedrooms 🖃 Access, Delta, Switch, Visa 💷 Twin/double £59 to £66; deposit required

Lamb Inn

High Street, Shipton-under-Wychwood OX7 6DQ
TEL: (01993) 830465   FAX: (01993) 832025

Characterful inn in a quiet Cotswolds village with no-frills rooms and a warm welcome.

As a quiet base from which to embark upon tourist trips around the Cotswolds, the Lamb Inn must take some beating. Set back off the main road which runs through the village, the mellow stone inn has been a hostelry for several hundred years and still keeps much of its country-pub character. The bar, with its wooden floor, beams and exposed stone walls, is the focal point of the inn. Well-heeled locals come to chat or read newspapers on sticks in front of a roaring log fire which also warms the small lounge next door. You can eat here – choosing from lengthy bar or blackboard menus – or in the restaurant, which has dim lighting and a rustic air, but which lacks some of the character of the main bar. At lunch time the chef also serves from a lavish buffet including a leg of ham, whole salmon and salads. The five bedrooms, named after local villages, are simple and immaculate, with light, modern décor and small, neat bathrooms. You can make tea and coffee in your room, though it's likely that you'll be brought a tea tray as part of the Valentas' warm welcome. If you like a window in your bathroom, opt for Swinbrook, though Bruern is our favourite room because of its characterful sloping ceiling and corner position.

○ Open all year ▨ 4 miles north of Burford on A361. Private car park ⊨ 1 twin, 4 double; all with bathroom/WC; TV, room service, hair-dryer, direct-dial telephone ⚡ Restaurant, bar, lounge, garden ♿ No wheelchair access ● No children under 14; no dogs; no smoking in bedrooms or restaurant ▭ Access, Amex, Visa ⊡ Single occupancy of twin/double £58, twin/double £75; deposit required. Set D £21; bar meals available

Shrewley House

Shrewley, Nr Warwick CV35 7AT
TEL: (01926) 842549   FAX: (01926) 842216

A de-luxe B&B in a rural former Georgian farmhouse.

Being virtually equidistant from Stratford, Birmingham and the NEC, the Greens' family home, standing in 1½ acres of lawned gardens, is ideally sited both for business and pleasure. Red-brick Georgian in style yet dating from the sixteenth century, it's one of the classiest of the many B&Bs in the area. By way of example, breakfast tables are laid with Potteries china, bathrooms have heated towel rails and toiletries in bottles rather than sachets, and no fewer than three of the four cosseting, sizeable bedrooms (including the family room) boast a four-poster, in either pine or mahogany. Inspectors single out the Rose Room as their favourite for being the prettiest and the most romantic. Each room also has a tea tray complete with beer, whisky, sherry, biscuits, nuts and fruit juice, all included in the price. Two-bedroomed self-catering cottages converted from a stable block are let on a B&B basis if needed.

◑ Open all year ☒ 5 miles north-west of Warwick on B4439. Private car park
🛏 1 double, 2 four-poster, 1 family room; all with bathroom/WC; TV, room service, hair-dryer, mini-bar, direct-dial telephone; trouser press on request ✅ Dining-room, lounge, drying-room, garden; toys, babysitting, baby-listening ♿ No wheelchair access ● Dogs in bedrooms by arrangement; no smoking ☐ Access, Visa
£ Single occupancy of twin/double £43, twin/double £61, four-poster £67, family room £67 to £102; deposit required

---

SHREWSBURY Shropshire   map 5

Albright Hussey

Ellesmere Road, Shrewsbury SY4 3AF
TEL: (01939) 290571   FAX: (01939) 291143

A merrie-England-style manor house run with Florentine flair, situated close to the historic town of Shrewsbury.

With its proximity to the scene of the Battle of Shrewsbury, where Henry IV defeated Harry Hotspur, and the presence of the black swans which glide around the moat, there's something satisfyingly Shakespearean about Albright Hussey's setting. In fact, the oldest part of the house (which is appropriately half-timbered and decidedly skew-whiff) had been standing for 40 years when the Bard of Stratford bawled his way into the world; the red-brick extension, which must be nearly 400 years old, is a mere stripling in comparison. The house's age is apparent from the interior of what the owners, the Subbiani family from Florence, call 'the historic building', and an autumnally coloured bar features all the leaded windows and beams that you could wish for. Various insignia dating from the age of chivalry survive in the two-sectioned restaurant, in which a coat of arms ennobles the inglenook fireplace, and timbers buttress the ceilings and walls; the large, panelled, Moat Room restaurant comes into its own when things are hectic. The good-value table d'hôte menu is inventive, and you might opt for duck-liver foie gras, followed by a cream of asparagus and toasted-almond soup, then a ragoût of rabbit saddle, and finally a white-chocolate truffle cake.

All the bedrooms are spacious, elegant and very well equipped, and beams abound in those that are located in the old house; antique beds help confer character on those on the 'main' (or modern) building. As you would expect, however, the most memorable are the premier bedrooms in the old section, especially the vast Hussey Suite – which boasts a four-poster spa bath (as well as a mere bed) – and the imaginative Corbett, Regency and Royalist rooms.

The text of entries is based on unsolicited reports sent in by readers and backed up by inspections. The factual details are from questionnaires the Guide *sends to all hotels that feature in the book.*

◑ Open all year ⤢ On A528, 2½ miles north of Shrewsbury town centre. Private car park ⤢ 4 twin, 4 double, 5 four-poster, 1 suite; family rooms available; some in annexe; all with bathroom/WC; TV, room service, hair-dryer, trouser press, direct-dial telephone ✓ 2 restaurants, 2 bars, lounge, conservatory, garden; conference facilities (max 200 people incl up to 14 residential); croquet; early suppers for children ♿ Wheelchair access to hotel, restaurant and WC (unisex), 2 ground-floor bedrooms, 1 specially equipped for disabled people ● No children under 2; no dogs in public rooms and in bedrooms by arrangement only ⊟ Access, Amex, Diners, Switch, Visa £ Single occupancy of twin/double from £60, twin/double from £75, four-poster from £90, family room £150, suite £130; deposit required. Set L £12.50, D £18.50; alc D £28. Special breaks available

The Citadel

Weston-under-Redcastle, Nr Shrewsbury SY4 5JY
TEL: (01630) 685204 (AND FAX)

Smashing views and comfortable rooms are offered in a very distinctive guesthouse.

You shouldn't have any difficulty in identifying the Citadel as you drive through Weston-under-Redcastle: the name so obviously suits the imposing building – complete with turrets and crenellations – that crowns the elevated mound at the village's heart. At the time of our inspection, the Citadel was very much the focus of Weston-under-Redcastle, since its owner, Sylvia Griffiths, was playing host to the village fête, and stalls were cascading amongst the rhododendron and azaleas over the lovely garden lawns. Despite the house's distinctly medieval, fortress-like appearance, it was actually built in the early nineteenth century – as a dower house for the Hill family, whose principal seat was the nearby Hawkstone Hall – and the interior exudes effortless Georgian grace and elegance. Fine plasterwork distinguishes the ceilings of both the hallway and drawing-room, and the latter is a spacious, light room featuring lots of comfy sofas upholstered in delicate, pastel colours, landscape paintings on the walls, and a baby grand piano. There's a more masculine feel to the adjacent snooker room, in which a burgundy-coloured chesterfield and leather button-backs, as well as the hunting scene in which the house is depicted in the background, emphasise the Englishness of the place. The dining-room is appositely grand, and a polished table, bedecked with crystal and silverware, provides the central focus of this stately, salon-like room. Sylvia's dinners have a firmly traditional slant, and a typical meal could include such dishes as smoked haddock and avocado *au gratin*, followed by lamb Shrewsbury, then spiced pears served with a lemon flummery, and finally a cheeseboard. The bedrooms (two of which are located in the turrets) are attractively decorated, furnished with antiques, and offer lots of pampering extras.

◑ Closed Nov to Mar; dining-room closed Sun ⤢ ¼ mile out of village of Weston on road to Hodnet. Private car park ⤢ 1 twin, 2 double; 2 with bathroom/WC, 1 with shower/WC; TV, room service, hair-dryer, trouser press; no tea/coffee-making facilities in rooms ✓ Dining-room, lounge, games room, garden; fishing; snooker ♿ No wheelchair access ● No children; no dogs; no smoking in bedrooms ⊟ None accepted £ Twin/double £65; deposit required. Set D £17.50

The Manse

16 Swan Hill, Shrewsbury SY1 1NL
TEL: (01743) 242659

Impressive B&B in a pretty, historic part of town near to parks and the river.

The ancient centre of Shrewsbury is made up of narrow streets lined with a hotch-potch of good-looking old buildings. The Grade-II listed Manse is one of these, a tall brick Georgian-town house covered with virginia creeper, hydrangea and ivy, squeezed in next to the Congregational church it once served. Inside, Maureen Cox is the softly spoken host, and the house is still very much her family home with photos of the children who've now flown the nest. One bedroom – a very small double – is on the first floor with a private shower-room next door along the landing; the twin bedroom is up another flight of the beautiful eighteenth-century wooden staircase and is larger, with plenty of space to unpack if you're staying a while. The twin shares a bathroom with the family. Both bedrooms are clean and neat and rather old-fashioned, with flowery patchwork fabrics and plain walls. The enormous sitting-room on the first floor, with its antique furniture and cherubs on the ceiling, is a sociable place to mingle. Although you're only a minute's walk from the centre of town, Swan Hill is a relatively peaceful spot with hardly any traffic at night. Many of the guests take picnics in the daytime and walk along the river to the Dingle, a large park just a few minutes away.

◗ Closed Chr & New Year ☑ In Shrewsbury, turn into Swan Hill opposite Kingsland Bridge; the Manse is first on left. Private car park (overnight only), on-street parking 🛏 1 twin, 1 double; double with shower/WC; TV ⊘ Dining-room, lounge ♿ No wheelchair access ● No children under 12; no dogs; no smoking ☐ None accepted 💷 Single occupancy of twin/double £25 to £30, twin/double £34 to £38

SHURDINGTON Gloucestershire map 5

The Greenway

Shurdington, Cheltenham GL51 5UG
TEL: (01242) 862352   FAX: (01242) 862780

Splendid gardens and comfortable rooms in a well-run sixteenth-century manor house.

'A most enjoyable stay,' reported one guest after a visit to David White's impressive venture a short distance from the attractions of Regency Cheltenham. There were still Tudors on the throne when William Lawrence began building the manor house, close to the pre-Roman 'green way' or sheep path that ran to the hills behind, and the pastoral landscape still exerts a strong pull on those who want a retreat from the spa town's bustle: 'We spent most of the time sitting by the sunken pool whilst a fountain played and the water was enjoyed by birds and dragonflies,' confided our correspondent, describing an idyllically lazy weekend. The interior is pleasantly traditional and has many period features, from the grand pedimented fireplace and portraits in the reception hallway, to the leaded windows and panelling of the private dining-room with its Jacobean overmantel and enviable position overlooking the magnificent floodlit gardens. The drawing-room is light and spacious, with green floral print sofas and co-ordinating drapes adding a modern country-house flourish. There are views over the lily pond, and the Cotswolds behind, from the conservatory dining-room, where dinner (described as 'excellent') might involve crab risotto with a saffron fish sauce, followed by roast rack of lamb with dauphinois potatoes and foie gras, and glazed lemon tart with a lime parfait. Bedrooms, whether in the main house or the adjacent converted coach-house, are well equipped, and feature good, sometimes antique furniture and pretty, top-quality fabrics.

◑ Closed 1 week after New Year ↗ 3 miles south-west of Cheltenham town centre, off A46. Private car park ⌗ 2 single, 17 twin/double; some in annexe; all with bathroom/WC; TV, room service, hair-dryer, direct-dial telephone; tea/coffee-making facilities on request ✅ Dining-room/conservatory, bar, lounge, garden; conference facilities (max 35 people incl up to 19 residential); croquet, clay-pigeon shooting ♿ Wheelchair access to hotel (1 step), dining-room and WC (M,F), 4 ground-floor bedrooms, 1 specially equipped for disabled people ⊖ No children under 7; no dogs; no smoking in some bedrooms ⊡ Access, Amex, Diners, Switch, Visa £ Single £88, single occupancy of twin/double £95, twin/double £128 to £180; deposit required. Set L £17, D £28.50 (1996 prices). Special breaks available

---

SIDMOUTH Devon   map 2

Hotel Riviera

The Esplanade, Sidmouth EX10 8AY
TEL: (01395) 515201   FAX: (01395) 577775

Striking sea-front Regency hotel with inviting bedrooms and welcoming staff.

Amid the many hotels and guesthouses lining Sidmouth esplanade, the Riviera stands out not just for its graceful curvy façade but for the loving care with which it is maintained; when we inspected, the white paintwork was glistening from a recent re-touch. Inside, reception keeps a low profile at the back of the lobby, but it's staffed by thoroughly professional personnel whose welcome immediately suggests you'll enjoy your stay. With lots of space to spare, the ground floor boasts a large sea-facing lounge, where cream teas are served, and a smaller Regency Bar decked out in red velvet – cosy or garish depending on your tastes. In the elegant dining-room, five-course dinner menus are a happy blend of the familiar and the unexpected: a chilled fruit juice might be followed, for example, by sweet-potato soup and fricassee of monkfish with a mango and curry sauce, with a pink grapefruit sorbet served between courses. A lift ascends to the three different categories of bedrooms. The category-three suites are the biggest and boast the widest range of extras such as fresh flowers and trouser presses; category-two rooms are still extremely inviting, their décor a restful peachy colour, and with chairs arranged in their bay windows for sea viewing. The smaller category-one rooms, although just as comfortable, lack sea views, and it's really worth paying the extra to take full advantage of the hotel's prime asset.

○ Open all year 🔁 On the sea-front. Private car park 🛏️ 7 single, 12 twin, 6 double, 2 suites; family rooms available; all with bathroom/WC; TV, room service, hair-dryer, mini-bar, trouser press, direct-dial telephone, radio, VCR ✅ Dining-room, 2 bars, lounge, drying-room, conservatory, ballroom, garden; air-conditioning in dining-room and 1 bar; conference facilities (max 90 people incl up to 27 residential); early suppers for children; babysitting, baby-listening 🦽 Wheelchair access to hotel (1 step), dining-room and WC (M,F), lift to 2 bedrooms specially equipped for disabled people ● No dogs in public rooms ▭ Access, Amex, Delta, Diners, Visa
£ Single £62 to £72, twin/double £108 to £128, suite £152 to £172; deposit required. Set L £12.50, D £22; alc L, D £16.50. Special breaks available

---

SIMONSBATH Somerset   map 1

Simonsbath House

Simonsbath, Minehead TA24 7SH
TEL: (01643) 831259   FAX: (01643) 831557

Comfortable country-house hotel in a tiny Exmoor village.

Few villages come smaller than Simonsbath, so Simonsbath House, a two-storey mansion dating back to the seventeenth century, has a dominating presence. A weathervane of a rutting stag pays homage to the importance of the hunting community, but this is not a hotel where you risk confrontation with the head of a small (or large) furry animal over your breakfast. On the contrary, discretion is very much the tone of Simonsbath House, where a wood-panelled library-cum-bar is tucked away at the end of the sunken lounge, and the dining-room lurks in a newer wing behind a huge inglenook fireplace, the date 1654 etched into its lintel. The dining-room's pale mint walls make a pleasing contrast to the wood panelling of the lounge and bar. Four-course dinner menus favour the traditionally British; you might start off with potato and rosemary soup, move on to venison steak in a rich stock, and wind up with an apple and mincemeat crumble. Owners Mike and Sue Burns are nearing the end of a rolling programme of bedroom refurbishment which has seen part of a corridor absorbed into Room 9 to make a bigger bathroom. Many of the bedrooms have breathtaking views out over the moor; Sue says guests in Room 8 are particularly prone to breakfasting in bed to take advantage of the panorama. One reader who asked for a tea-tray rued the lack of a teapot – dunking teabags isn't quite the same, is it?

○ Closed Dec & Jan 🔁 In Simonsbath village, on B3223. Private car park 🛏️ 3 twin, 1 double, 3 four-poster; all with bathroom/WC; TV, room service, hair-dryer, direct-dial telephone; tea/coffee-making facilities on request ✅ Dining-room, bar/library, lounge, drying-room, garden 🦽 No wheelchair access ● No children under 10; no dogs; no smoking in dining-room ▭ Access, Amex, Delta, Diners, Switch, Visa £ Single occupancy of twin/double £46 to £56, twin/double/four-poster £108; deposit required. Set D £22. Special breaks available

---

Don't expect to turn up at a small hotel assuming that a room will be available. It's always best to telephone in advance.

SISSINGHURST Kent   map 3

Sissinghurst Castle Farm

Sissinghurst, Cranbrook TN17 2AB
TEL: (01580) 712885   FAX: (01580) 712601

Victorian farmhouse with welcoming, attentive hosts set in the peaceful grounds of Sissinghurst Gardens.

This red- and grey-brick farmhouse, with its ivy-clad walls and gables, has been lived in by the Stearns family since the 1930s. Now owned by the National Trust but still run as a working farm by James and Pat Stearns, it is a well-sited and good-value base from which to see local sights. The large entrance hall leading to the wooden staircase with its mounted stag's head and large portraits (on permanent loan from the castle as there isn't a wall high enough to accommodate them there) sets the tone for the whole house – that of a relaxed, comfortable and well-loved family home. The bright and airy sitting-room with large wood-panelled windows, fireplace, sofa and bookshelves makes a comfortable place to rest your aching feet after a day exploring Sissinghurst Gardens. The five bedrooms do not all have *en suite* facilities, but the shared bathroom is huge and even has a comfy, over-sized sofa in it. The bedrooms are all very comfortable but do vary in size and décor, which ranges from simple to elaborate. Henrietta, a room decorated by Laura Ashley and used in one of the company's catalogues, was the talk of all the guests when our inspector visited. The dining-room is very much a farmhouse room, with an open fireplace and views to the well-kept garden.

◑ Closed Chr ↗ 1 mile out of Sissinghurst village on A262 towards Biddenden; turn left down lane marked Sissinghurst Castle Gardens; hotel is on right. Private car park ⇌ 5 twin/double; family room available; 1 with bathroom/WC, 1 with shower; TV and hair-dryer in 2 rooms ⊘ Dining-room, lounge, garden; conference facilities (max 25 people incl up to 5 residential); croquet ⅊ No wheelchair access ◆ No children under 5; no dogs; no smoking ▭ None accepted £ Single occupancy of twin/double £20 to £23, twin/double £38 to £50, family room £48 to £56; deposit required. Special breaks available

---

SMARDEN Kent   map 3

The Bell

Bell Lane, Smarden TN27 8PW
TEL: (01233) 770283

A traditional country pub, offering plain, simply furnished bedrooms.

The name 'Smarden' apparently derives from an Anglo-Saxon word meaning a 'fat and wooded place' – which probably isn't how present-day residents would like to describe the village, which has won the best-kept village in Kent title in the past. Situated on the outskirts of Smarden, the Bell (which was built in 1536 and has been a registered hostelry since 1769) is a friendly and popular pub, serving real ales and local wines. With a beer garden at the rear, and three inter-connecting bars featuring inglenook fireplaces, beamed ceilings, dried hops hanging on the walls, and cut-out wooden barrels as seats, it is a relaxed, informal place. The bar meals are reasonably priced, and the daily specials add a bit of variety to the usual pub menu. The plain, but comfortable, bedrooms are reached by means of a black, wrought-iron, spiral staircase positioned outside the pub to the rear. None of the rooms has *en suite* facilities, and share the two shower-rooms. In the corridor you will find a fridge and a toaster – indeed, everything that you will need to prepare yourself a continental breakfast to take back to bed. If you plan to arrive outside pub-opening times, be sure to phone first.

◑ Closed 25 Dec ⬚ In village of Smarden, off B2077 between Charing and Biddenden. Private car park 🛏 3 twin, 1 double; TV ✓ 3 bars, games room, garden; early suppers for children ♿ No wheelchair access ● No smoking in 1 bar ▭ Access, Amex, Delta, Switch, Visa £ Single occupancy of twin/double £20, twin/double £30; deposit required. Bar meals available

---

SOMERTON Somerset   map 2

The Lynch   ℒ

4 Behind Berry, Somerton TA11 7PD
TEL: (01458) 272316   FAX: (01458) 272590

Gracious Georgian house with stable block and lake, offering B&B on edge of small historic town.

As you approach the Lynch, the glass lantern on its roof acts as a handy landmark. Later on you can look down from inside it over the lake, with black swans, pintail ducks and other ornamental waterfowl swimming on it, and on the stable block, which offers self-catering accommodation. The Lynch is a cool white and grey Georgian house where Roy Copeland offers bed and breakfast in five rooms of assorted shapes and sizes; those at the top are slipped in under sky-lit sloping ceilings, while Goldington is large enough for a four-poster bed. Breakfast is served in a big, bright room overlooking the lake, with room at the back set aside as a sitting area to make up for the absence of a proper lounge. In the evening Roy will be happy to advise on places to eat in Somerton, the capital of ancient Wessex.

◑ Closed Chr ⬚ On northern edge of Somerton. Private car park 🛏 2 twin, 2 double, 1 four-poster; family room available; all with bathroom/WC; TV, hair-dryer, direct-dial telephone; tea/coffee-making facilities on request ✓ Dining-room/ lounge ♿ No wheelchair access ● No dogs; no smoking ▭ Access, Amex, Visa £ Single occupancy of twin/double £40 to £45, twin/double £55, four-poster/family room £65; deposit required

---

 This denotes that you can get a twin or double room for £60 or less per night inclusive of breakfast.

Pebbles Guest House ☆

190 Eastern Esplanade, Thorpe Bay, Southend-on-Sea SS1 3AA
TEL: (01702) 582329

Spotless seaside guesthouse bursting with flowers and foliage.

Edna Christian used to be a nurse, but nine years ago she went into the B&B business instead: 'I decided I could carry on doing the same work but get paid more for doing it!' Pebbles sits in the middle of a terrace of Edwardian houses, its neat black and white paving set off in summer by a veritable blaze of flower power, with geraniums seeming to sprout from every nook and cranny and cheerful tubs of bedding standing in the porch. Inside, everything is just as spick-and-span: shiny white venetian blinds shade the window of the dining-room, where breakfast cereals and juice are laid out on the large wooden dresser with jolly ceramics. Edna also serves evening meals on request 'home-made soups, fresh veg, nothing frozen'. Although there's no lounge, a small roof terrace complete with pergola and climbers provides pleasant summer seating. Bedrooms are modern, with built-in pine furniture and neat matching duvets; spotless shower rooms are squeezed into corners. Rooms at the front face the sea, but also the traffic on the busy road, the drone of which double-glazing doesn't quite manage to keep out.

○ Open all year ⊿ On sea-front, 1 mile east of the pier. On-street parking, public car park nearby ⊨ 1 single, 2 twin, 2 double; family room available; all with shower/WC; TV, room service; hair-dryer available on request ✓ Dining-room; early suppers for children ⅙ No wheelchair access ● No dogs; no smoking in public rooms ⊟ None accepted £ Single/single occupancy of twin/double £25, twin/double £40, family room £50; deposit required. Set D £12.50

Marsh Hall

South Molton EX36 3HQ
TEL: (01769) 572666   FAX: (01769) 574230

Large red-brick Victorian hotel with spacious rooms and quiet gardens.

A grand façade added to Marsh Hall in the 1830s conceals the fact that the core of the building is a more humble seventeenth-century farmhouse. In the stairwell, a panel of stained-glass depicts an earlier owner, Francis Germain, as a medieval knight in armour. Marsh Hall's architects believed in the virtues of space. The capacious lounge has been made to look even bigger by the use of pale colours for walls and upholstery. Hugest of the large bedrooms is Room 3, which has more than enough space for a four-poster bed, a *chaise-longue*, two armchairs in a bay window up two steps, and a bathroom enclosed behind an extraordinary curving wall. The more Lilliputian bar has a delightful two-tone marble fireplace. Marsh Hall stands in three acres of land which Tony and Judy Griffiths are slowly revitalising. Near the back door their bird-table has proved a hit with

Loonie, a cock pheasant turned honorary pet. A reader who visited on a particularly chilly night praised the cosiness of the house and service, remarking that, 'the reception was friendly and efficient throughout, though without any of that sense of being obliged to make conversation with hosts that sometimes spoils small hotels.'

◗ Closed 2 to 3 weeks in Feb ⤢ From Junction 27 of M5 take A361 Barnstaple road; at roundabout where South Molton is first signposted, continue on main road for approx 1½ miles; turn right at sign for North Molton; after ¼ mile turn right and right again. Private car park 🛏 1 single, 2 twin, 3 double, 1 four-poster; most with bathroom/WC, 2 with shower/WC; TV, room service, hair-dryer, direct-dial telephone ✅ Restaurant, bar, lounge, drying-room, conservatory, garden; conference facilities (max 20 people incl up to 7 residential) ♿ No wheelchair access ● No children under 12; no dogs; no smoking in restaurant ▭ Access, Amex, Diners, Visa £ Single £43, single occupancy of twin/double £49, twin/double £70, four-poster £88; deposit required. Set D £18.50. Special breaks available

---

Park House

South Molton EX36 3ED
TEL: (01769) 572610

Elegant Victorian house in quiet, rural setting with delightfully varied gardens.

There can't be many hotels that boast a chocolate factory at the end of the drive; stay at Park House and you'll be invited to sample the produce at the end of your evening meal. Park House is also the sort of establishment where there's always something to catch your eye. While you're collecting your key don't forget to inspect the triangular cock-fighting chair in the hall: you put your bird under the seat, your legs through the back and use the dips in the ledge at the top to score. A grand stairway winds up to a landing with a striking Devon and Italian marble arcade; sadly the stained-glass dome over the stairwell was beyond restoration. Bedrooms here are comfortable and tidily furnished without being at all grand. The best look over the gardens which reach their peak in May when the azaleas, rhododendrons and magnolia flower. According to hostess Anne Gornall, three-course dinners in the stylish ivy-green dining-room concentrate on 'unsophisticated' cooking, by which she means beautifully prepared favourites such as roast duckling with apple sauce, rainbow trout à la meunière and plain fillet steak. The large smoking lounge has something of the feel of a colonial gentlemen's club while the smaller non-smoking lounge is more cottagey.

◗ Closed Feb ⤢ Leave M5 at Junction 27 and follow A361 towards Barnstaple for approx 24 miles; after second roundabout take next left (signed Pathfields); hotel is 300 yards on left. Private car park 🛏 3 twin, 4 double, 1 family room; 4 with bathroom/WC, 3 with shower/WC; TV, hair-dryer, direct-dial telephone, clock radio ✅ Dining-room, lounge, bar/lounge, drying-room; fishing, croquet; early suppers for children ♿ No wheelchair access ● No children under 11; dogs in bar/lounge only; smoking in bar/lounge and bedrooms only ▭ Access, Amex, Visa £ Single occupancy of twin/double £45, twin/double £80, family room £110; deposit required. Set D £16; alc L £10. Special breaks available

Whitechapel Manor

South Molton EX36 3EG
TEL: (01769) 573377   FAX: (01769) 573797

Beguiling sixteenth-century stone manor house overlooking terraced gardens in tranquil countryside.

For the first time in 2½ years Pat and John Shapland can sleep easy in the knowledge that a scheme to build 250 timeshare units on their doorstep has been thrown out. The decision is just as well given that a recent Council for the Protection of Rural England report pinpointed the area round South Molton as one of England's few remaining havens of tranquillity. Whitechapel Manor is a place to indulge fantasies of Tudor-style romance. You approach this fine manor house via layers of terraced gardens and fetch up at a creeper-covered porch opening into a hall closed off from the lounge with a seventeenth-century wooden screen. On the far side of the screen, big sofas cluster round a log burner beneath a low plastered ceiling that slopes as crazily as most of the floors and window ledges. Across the hall, a second lounge gives way to a dining-room which has very different atmospheres depending on whether the curtains are drawn or open. A three-course dinner here might kick off with seared scallops on a saffron, onion and chive risotto, and continue with roast quail on white cabbage braised in veal *jus*. The cheeseboard highlights local varieties like Somerset Tornegous or Jersey Blue from Exmoor, and desserts are equally mouth-watering. Bedrooms are not as grand as you might imagine although they're very comfortable and most boast lovely rural views.

◑ Open all year 🔁 Leave M5 at Junction 27 and follow signs to Barnstaple; at second roundabout turn right; hotel is 1 mile down an unmarked track. Private car park 🅿 2 single, 5 twin, 2 double, 1 four-poster; family room available; all with bathroom/WC; TV, room service, hair-dryer, direct-dial telephone; no tea/coffee-making facilities in rooms ✓ Dining-room, bar, 2 lounges, garden; conference facilities (max 40 people incl up to 10 residential); croquet; early suppers for children; babysitting, baby-listening ♿ No wheelchair access ● No children under 7 in dining-room eves; no dogs; no smoking in dining-room 🖃 Access, Amex, Delta, Diners, Switch, Visa 💷 Single £70, single occupancy of twin/double £95, twin/double £110, four-poster £170, family room £170; deposit required. Set L from £19, D £34. Special breaks available

---

SOUTHWOLD Suffolk   map 6

The Crown

High Street, Southwold IP18 6DP
TEL: (01502) 722275   FAX: (01502) 727263

An old posthouse, featuring good-value rooms and a popular restaurant.

Southwold is an Adnams town, and the brewery owns both the Crown and its sophisticated sister, the Swan (see entry), so wine and ale buffs should enjoy themselves here. Dating from about 1750, the Crown is situated in the centre of the town, and boasts an imposing, Georgian façade adorned with neo-classical columns and a flagpole. Inside, you'll find an unfussy hotel, whose antique furniture is offset by a bold use of colour, and which prides itself on its reputation for some of the best food in the area. The sunshine-yellow restaurant is small and busy; the menu changes twice daily, and guests can also dine in the bar, which is dominated by a huge, semi-circular, wooden settle. Delicacies such as pan-fried medallions of venison served with black pudding and a juniper-and-plum sauce, fish and shellfish dishes, and exotic specialities like mahi mahi (a white-fleshed sea fish tasting unexpectedly like trout) bring in the crowds, so make sure that you book a table. Other bonuses include an extensive wine list and a relaxed atmosphere. The saloon bar features wood-panelled walls, a curved, glazed screen, a ship's binnacle and lots of marine paintings – all lending it a nautical feel. The hotel regards itself as a restaurant-with-rooms, but the 12 bedrooms (of which all but three are *en suite*) are perfectly adequate – especially the family room, whose bathroom has entirely sloping ceilings. The bedrooms at the front of the house retain their original beams and character. Tea- and coffee-making facilities have been introduced this year, and a newspaper can be brought to your room in the morning.

◐ Closed 2nd week in Jan ☒ In centre of Southwold. Private car park ⊨ 2 single, 4 twin, 5 double, 1 family room; all with bathroom/WC exc 1 twin with shower/WC; TV, limited room service, hair-dryer, direct-dial telephone ✓ Restaurant (air-conditioned), private dining-room, 2 bars, lounge; conference facilities (max 45 people incl up to 12 residential); early suppers for children; babysitting, cots, high chairs 🕭 No wheelchair access ● Dogs in 1 bar only; no smoking in restaurant ▭ Access, Amex, Delta, Diners, Switch, Visa £ Single £41, single occupancy of twin/double £49, twin/double £63, family room £87. Cooked B £4.50; set L £13/15.50, D £18/20

The Swan

Market Place, Southwold IP18 6EG
TEL: (01502) 722186   FAX: (01502) 724800

The smartest and priciest of the Adnams establishments, right in the heart of Southwold.

The Adnams brewery is at the centre of Southwold, both literally and metaphorically. Its two best-known hotels, the Crown (see entry) and the Swan, screen the brewery off from the High Street and Market Square, and chairman Simon Loftus takes a close personal interest in the hotel side. Most of the antique furniture and local prints in the hotel were bought by him, and a copy of his book on wine is provided in every bedroom in the Swan. The frontage is imposing, with three-storey pairs of long casement windows and a flagpole practically long enough to reach the Blyth. The drawing-room, painted a restful green, overlooks the front, its chintzy armchairs providing a comfortable spot for afternoon tea, while the formal pink dining-room is the setting for fairly classic dishes like Stilton and walnut pâté, grilled Dover sole with hollandaise sauce and asparagus tips, and apple and sultana crumble or crème brûlée. Bedrooms in the main house vary quite a lot in size and outlook, but all have personalised touches, like framed maps or paintings by local artists. Opinion is more mixed about the appeal of the garden rooms, contained in a 1960s extension looking out on to the garden behind. One couple enjoyed the camaraderie: 'We waved to each other from our little terraces and bid each other good evening and good morning with an air of familiarity and community', but another visitor found the room too hot and thought the quality of the furnishings 'dull and poor' (his complaint prompted the offer of a refund or a free two-night stay in the main part of the hotel from Mr Loftus).

◗ Open all year ↗ In Southwold's market square. Private car park ⊨ 6 single, 22 twin, 16 double, 1 four-poster, 1 family room, 2 suites; some in annexe; all with bathroom/WC; TV, limited room service, hair-dryer, direct-dial telephone; trouser press on request; no tea/coffee-making facilities in rooms ✓ Dining-room, bar, lounge, garden; conference facilities (max 40 people residential/non-residential); croquet; early suppers for children ♿ Wheelchair access to hotel, dining-room and WC (unisex), 18 ground-floor bedrooms, 1 specially equipped for disabled people ● No children under 5 in dining-room after 7pm; dogs in annexe rooms only; no smoking in dining-room ▭ Access, Amex, Diners, Switch, Visa £ Single £40 to £69, single occupancy of twin/double £69 to £86, twin/double £84 to £118, four-poster £149, family room/suite £139 to £149; deposit required. Set L £12.50 to £15, Sun L £15 to £17, D £19.50 to £31.50 (prices valid till Apr 1997). Special breaks available

---

SPARSHOLT Hampshire map 2

Lainston House ☆

Sparsholt, Winchester SO21 2LT
TEL: (01962) 863588   FAX: (01962) 776672

A quietly impressive stately home in an idyllic location.

Approached along an avenue of beech trees, Lainston House boasts views away over the Hampshire plain. The drive sweeps round the back of the house past an ancient dovecote and brings you round to the front again, so you immediately have a sense of the peaceful location and wonderful grounds the hotel possesses. Built around 1670 (opinions vary as to the exact date) the house is a balconied red-brick William and Mary manor house and has been refurbished in a dignified country-house style, with lots of wood panelling and antique furniture. The public rooms are light and airy with plenty of space and comfortable furniture. A large bouquet of sunflowers greets you in the reception and the impressive wooden staircase which sweeps upstairs is inlaid with beautiful panels on the landing. The bedrooms in the main house are large and characterful with exposed beams in some, and those in the converted coach yard retain interesting stable-like features; the ones in Chudleigh Court are more standard. Back downstairs, the formal restaurant, with its perfect linen and high-backed chairs, offers such delights as a salad of confit of pheasant with chopped hazelnuts and walnut oil, followed perhaps by pan-fried turbot on a bed of buttered samphire.

☆ *A star next to the hotel's name indicates that the establishment is new to the* Guide *this year.*

◑ Open all year ⊿ 2½ miles from centre of Winchester, just off B3049 (formerly A272) to Stockbridge. Private car park ⟼ 7 single, 11 twin, 15 double, 2 four-poster, 3 suites; family room available; some in annexe; all with bathroom/WC exc 1 single with shower/WC; TV, room service, hair-dryer, direct-dial telephone; no tea/coffee-making facilities in rooms ∜ Restaurant, bar, lounge, drying-room, garden; conference facilities (max 40 people incl up to 38 residential); tennis, putting, croquet, clay-pigeon shooting, archery, snooker; early suppers for children; babysitting, baby-listening, cots, high chairs ⅄ Wheelchair access to hotel, restaurant and WC (unisex), 14 ground-floor bedrooms ● None ▭ Access, Amex, Delta, Diners, Switch, Visa £ Single £95, single occupancy of twin/double £130, twin/double £130 to £225, four-poster £225, family room £185, suite £245; deposit required. Continental B £9, cooked B £11; set L £16.50; alc L £22, D £36. Special breaks available

---

STAMFORD Lincolnshire   map 6

George of Stamford

71 High Street, St Martins, Stamford PE9 2LB
TEL: (01780) 55171 FAX: (01780) 57070
(NUMBERS TO BE PREFIXED BY 7 AFTER JAN 1997)

A large, lively and famous old coaching-inn, serving good, traditional food and outstanding wines.

The sixteenth-century George makes the bold claim to be 'perhaps England's greatest coaching-inn'. If it isn't, it's not far off the mark. It has all the required historical elements, such as royal visitors (including Charles I and William III), a flagstoned hall, beamed bars and an oak-panelled restaurant hung with heraldic banners. At the same time, modern components have been sensitively introduced, and snazzy fabrics and stylish colour schemes are used to good effect in the bedrooms (the courtyard-facing rooms are the most peaceful). Likewise, while the main restaurant is memorable for such time-honoured events as roasts served with much ceremony from silver wagons and the impressive arrival of the heaving dessert and cheese trolleys, the Garden Lounge, which is decked out with exotic foliage, delivers interesting bistro-style fare such as crab pasta. As well as achieving this sensitive balance between old and new, the hotel excels in two further respects: the zestful, unstuffy staff come in for constant praise year after year, and, to quote our sister publication, *The Good Food Guide*, the wines are 'staggeringly good'; many bottles are also very affordable.

◑ Open all year ⊿ In centre of Stamford. Private car park ⟼ 12 single, 9 twin, 22 double, 3 four-poster, 1 suite; most with bathroom/WC, 3 with shower/WC; TV, 24-hour room service, hair-dryer, trouser press, direct-dial telephone; no tea/coffee-making facilities in rooms ∜ 2 restaurants, 2 bars, 2 lounges, garden; conference facilities (max 50 people incl up to 47 residential); croquet; early suppers for children; babysitting, baby-listening ⅄ No wheelchair access ● None ▭ Access, Amex, Delta, Diners, Switch, Visa £ Single £78, single occupancy of twin/double £85, twin/double £105, four-poster £160, suite £125; deposit required. Set L £13.50 to £16.50; alc L, D £32.50; bistro meals available. Special breaks available

STANTON WICK **Bath & N.E. Somerset** map 2

Carpenters Arms

Stanton Wick, Nr Pensford BS18 4BX
TEL: (01761) 490202   FAX: (01761) 490763

A popular local pub combining tradition with a dash of up-market flair.

Situated just off the main road to Bath – though far enough away to escape the traffic – the Carpenters Arms is well placed for passing trade. The crowds filling the bars or enjoying the sunshine on the terrace at weekends are evidence that it has also established quite a reputation locally. Although a dash of urban chic can be detected in the menus and in the chirpy, young staff, there's much here to epitomise the classic English country pub. Converted from a row of miners' cottages, it has all the traditional cottagey features: low ceilings, lots of exposed stone, wood beams, and huge bunches of dried flowers. A series of small through-rooms fills the ground floor, with the main bar and a small lounge with comfy sofas separating the informal Cooper's Parlour (choose from local lamb cutlets with rosemary, chilli con carne or pan-fried liver and bacon with onion gravy) from the smarter restaurant (where the à la carte menu may include chateaubriand, magret duck with a brandied black-cherry sauce, and medallions of monkfish with creamed spinach and nutmeg). The neat, well co-ordinated bedrooms have pine furnishings, pastel shades and floral fabrics, and excellent bathrooms.

◑ Open all year ⚡ Stanton Wick is near the junction of the A37 and the A368. Private car park 🛏 3 twin, 9 double; all with bathroom/WC; TV, room service, hair-dryer, direct-dial telephone; trouser press in some rooms ✓ 2 restaurants, bar, lounge; conference facilities (max 25 people incl up to 12 residential); boules; babysitting, baby-listening ♿ No wheelchair access ● Dogs in bar only; no smoking in bedrooms ⊟ Access, Amex, Delta, Diners, Switch, Visa £ Single occupancy of twin/double £49, twin/double £66. Alc D £20. Special breaks available

---

STAPLEFORD **Leicestershire** map 5

Stapleford Park

Stapleford, Nr Melton Mowbray LE14 2EF
TEL: (01572) 787522   FAX: (01572) 787651

A country-house hotel that manages a refreshing informality.

This enormous stately home, part neo-classical, part Jacobean, stands amid 500 acres of woods and Capability Brown parkland which incorporate stables, a church, a lake and rentable thatched cottages. The rubric below gives an idea of sporting activities available on the estate. With public rooms such as a dining-room of ballroom proportions featuring Grinling Gibbons stucco to boot, you might well expect a rather stuffy, orthodox country house. Not a bit. This iconoclastic vision of the late American restaurant magnate Bob Payton (owner of Chicago Rib Shacks and Pizza Pie Factories) adopts a casual, even jocular tone. Friendly young staff wear Stapleford Park T-shirts, for example, and, amid the tapestries and period portraits in the two imposing halls, a dog sporting a Stars and Stripes neckerchief appears in a *trompe l'oeil* mural. As for bed and board, many of the amazing bedrooms, such as Liberty and Crabtree & Evelyn (which boasts 270 flower paintings on its walls), have been put together by well-known designers. Dinners, chosen from an à la carte menu, range from uncomplicated options such as a Caesar salad and crème brûlée, to fanciful concoctions like crab cake and scallops in a tequila and grapefruit sauce with tortilla strips.

◐ Open all year ⊠ In Stapleford, approx 5 miles east of Melton Mowbray. Private car park ⇤⇥ 40 double, 2 four-poster; family rooms and suites available; some in annexe; all with bathroom/WC; TV, room service, hair-dryer, trouser press, direct-dial telephone; no tea/coffee-making facilities in rooms ✧ 2 dining-rooms, bar, lounge, library, garden; conference facilities (max 300 people incl up to 42 residential); fishing, golf, indoor heated swimming-pool, tennis, clay-pigeon shooting, archery, falconry, croquet; early suppers for children; babysitting, baby-listening ㅤ&. Wheelchair access to hotel (2 steps), dining-rooms and WC (M,F), lift to bedrooms ● No dogs in bedrooms ▭ Access, Amex, Delta, Diners, Visa £ Single occupancy of twin/double £145 to £300, twin/double £145 to £300, four-poster £215 to £255, family room £290 to £500, suite £230 to £300; deposit required. Cooked B £10; set L £15; alc D £30 (1996 prices)

STOKE-BY-NAYLAND Suffolk　　　　　　　　　　　　　　　　　　　map 6

Angel Inn

COUNTY
HOTEL
OF THE
YEAR

Stoke-by-Nayland CO6 4SA
TEL: (01206) 263245　FAX: (01206) 263373

Excellent food and good-value accommodation in the middle of Constable country.

The sleepy village of Stoke-by-Nayland is famous for the 120-foot tower of the local church and the food at the Angel Inn. So popular is the inn with diners, indeed, that it's worth reserving a table in the restaurant if you can't face a wait for a table in the bar. The menu, chalked up on blackboards, changes twice daily, and combinations like roast poussin stuffed with wild rice served with white wine and tarragon sauce, or tartelette of poached pear and ginger with caramel sauce, keep them coming. The main bar provides understated atmospheric surroundings for supping and sampling, eschewing horse-brasses and dried flowers in favour of candles in bottles on the tables and rows of tankards hanging from the sixteenth-century beams. A log fire glows in the brick grate on chilly evenings. There's also a new non-smoking area, with dark-stained tables and chairs and flowery wallpaper. Named after the 52-foot-deep well in one corner of the room, the restaurant opens up into a high-raftered barn of a place, rough brickwork contrasting with deep red on the walls. The food served here is the same as in the bar. The bedrooms are well kept and neatly co-ordinated, a cut above normal pub rooms. Room 6, with timbered walls and ceiling, and facing the back, away from the road, is probably the pick.

Report forms are at the back of the Guide; *write a letter or e-mail us if you prefer. Our e-mail address is: "guidereports@which.co.uk".*

◑ Closed 25 & 26 Dec ⤢ In Stoke-by-Nayland, on B1068. Private car park
⤒ 1 twin, 5 double; 1 in annexe; all with bathroom/WC; TV, room service, hair-dryer, direct-dial telephone ⊘ Restaurant, 2 bars, lounge; early suppers for children
♿ No wheelchair access ● No children under 10; no dogs ⊟ Access, Amex, Delta, Diners, Switch, Visa £ Single occupancy of twin/double £45, twin/double £59. Alc L £11, D £14

Stoke Manor

Stoke on Tern, Market Drayton TF9 2DU
TEL: (01630) 685222   FAX: (01630) 685666

Relaxing accommodation on a working farm in a quiet corner of north-east Shropshire.

If the name suggests something Jacobean, huge inglenooks and priests' holes, you may wonder at the landmark placed to distinguish the right path from the network of lanes and byways that criss-cross a landscape worthy of Housman, and to steer your way to Mike and Julia Thomas's welcoming B&B. The simple plough is, however, an appropriate symbol for this working farm on 259 acres, and agricultural and rustic implements are central to the house's decorative scheme. A Civil War conflagration consumed the original Stoke Manor but today's red-brick Georgian/Victorian hybrid is at the classy end of the farmhouse league, with a portico to add distinction, and an open vista plus a dash of cedar and copper beech trees to gladden the heart. Unusually for a rural B&B, there's a bar in the cellar, where the more gregarious guests gather, leaving the rather plain sitting-room to those content with a crossword or the latest John Grisham. Traditional décor prevails in the autumnally toned breakfast-room, where Civil War musket balls are displayed as a reminder of the Manor's history. The three large bedrooms are comfortably furnished with dark-wood or stripped-pine furniture, and pretty, cottagey soft furnishings. The twin room still features the carefully labelled larder where Julia's Victorian predecessor stashed her home-made preserves on wooden shelves.

◑ Closed Dec ⤢ 5 miles south-west of Market Drayton, midway between A53 and A41 in village of Stoke on Tern. Private car park ⤒ 1 twin, 1 double, 1 family room; all with bathroom/WC; TV, room service, hair-dryer, radio ⊘ Bar, lounge, garden; fishing ♿ No wheelchair access ● No children under 5; no dogs; smoking in bar and lounge only ⊟ None accepted £ Single occupancy of twin/double £25 to £30, twin/double £40 to £45, family room £60 to £68

Chapters

27 High Street, Stokesley, Middlesbrough TS9 5AD
TEL: (01642) 711888   FAX: (01642) 713387

An old coaching-inn offers the buzz of a busy bistro and interesting interior design.

In the 1740s, when the main Newcastle to York route passed through Stokesley, halfway between the two, this old coaching-inn had a virtually captive market. Today, however, the A-roads and motorways have somehow conspired to leave Stokesley off the main tourist trail, so Catherine and Alan Thompson have implemented some highly unusual design ideas in the Georgian building in order to keep it in the traveller's mind long after the chain hotels have faded. The policy is certainly working.

The continuing rise of the bistro means that the earlier division into restaurant and something less formal has fallen by the wayside, and the emphasis is now on creating a lively, informal atmosphere with a varied international menu. Duck breast with a kumquat-and-ginger compote and red-wine sauce, for example, rubs shoulders with paella Valencia and Indonesian chicken satay, while the proximity of the port of Hartlepool explains the strong presence of fresh fish such as sole, sea bass and monkfish.

The surroundings mirror the sense of adventure that informs much of the cooking. Alan took a bit of a risk in handing over his hotel to a bunch of unknown Newcastle art students, but he feels vindicated by the results. Striking murals cover the walls of the bistro, as well as the stairs and corridors and even one or two of the bedrooms. With their plain, dark-wood furniture, light-coloured decorative schemes, and maybe an Edwardian print or two, the other bedrooms are rather more restrained.

◑ Closed 25 Dec & 1 Jan; restaurant closed Sun　🛋 In centre of Stokesley. On-street parking　🛏 3 single, 5 twin, 5 double; all with bathroom/WC exc 1 single with shower/WC; TV, room service, direct-dial telephone; hair-dryer in some rooms and on request　✔ 2 restaurants, 2 bars, lounge, garden; conference facilities (max 30 people incl up to 13 residential); early suppers for children; baby-listening　🔥 No wheelchair access　● No dogs in public rooms　⬜ Access, Amex, Delta, Diners, Switch, Visa　£ Single £37 to £48, single occupancy of twin/double £37 to £50, twin/double £50 to £62; deposit required. Alc L £10, D £20. Special breaks available

---

STON EASTON　Somerset　　　　　　　　　　　　map 2

Ston Easton Park

Ston Easton, Bath BA3 4DF
TEL: (01761) 241631　FAX: (01761) 241377

Luxury living in a splendid Palladian mansion in Humphrey Repton parkland.

For a really special occasion you could hardly do better than go to Ston Easton Park, a magnificent Palladian mansion set in parkland landscaped by Humphrey Repton in 1793. The entrance hall immediately sets the tone for everything that follows, with its flagstoned floors, painting over the fireplace, plaster ceiling and homely wellington boots waiting in the corner. Orders for dinner are taken in the main lounge, a spectacular room with lofty windows and a plaster eagle as the ceiling's centrepiece; the chances are that a fire will be blazing in the hearth with a spaniel stretched out in front of it. The twin dining-rooms beyond are on a more modest scale, although there's nothing modest about the wonderful food: typically, a warm salad of baked goat's cheese with red pesto and tapénade might be followed by a fillet of salmon in filo pastry with a spinach and rocket salad and a choice of hot or cold desserts. All the bedrooms live up to expectations, but the best two must be the Master Bedroom, with a magnificent Chippendale four-poster and multi-angled views of the grounds, and Ludlow, with another four-poster and fire screens. A serving woman, whose portrait can be seen downstairs in the Yellow Dining Room, is said to haunt this latter room. Ask the manager, and he'll show you round the basement with its original kitchen and wine cellar. Indeed, don't be afraid to ask about anything: the masterly service at Ston Easton is designed to make you feel relaxed, despite what could appear to be the daunting grandeur of the surroundings.

◑ Open all year ⤢ Off A37, 11 miles south of Bristol and Bath. Private car park ⊨ 11 twin, 2 double, 6 four-poster, 2 suites; some in annexe; all with bathroom/WC; TV, room service, hair-dryer, direct-dial telephone, clock radio; tea/coffee-making facilities, mini-bars and trouser presses in some rooms ⌗ 2 dining-rooms, 3 lounges, drying-room, library, games room, garden; air-conditioning in suites; conference facilities (max 24 people incl up to 21 residential); golf, tennis, croquet, clay-pigeon shooting, billiards; early suppers for children ⅋ No wheelchair access ⚫ No children under 7 exc babes in arms; no smoking in dining-rooms; kennel for dogs ▭ Access, Amex, Diners, Switch, Visa £ Single occupancy of twin/double £95 to £115, twin/double £145 to £265, four-poster £195 to £320, suite £245 to £265; deposit required. Continental B £8.50, cooked B £12.50; set L £26, D £38; alc D from £40. Special breaks available

---

Stonor Arms

Stonor, Henley-on-Thames RG9 6HE
TEL: (01491) 638866   FAX: (01491) 638863

Large, smart bedrooms and a restaurant with an excellent reputation.

From the outside, the Stonor Arms is very much a country inn; there's a swinging sign on a pole and it's surrounded by fields and woodland. Inside, however, the hotel has a distinctive character of its own which attracts all sorts from walkers to the dressed-up with a sense of occasion. There's a restaurant which extends into two conservatories; if you prefer a pub atmosphere you could eat in the bar, with its deep-red walls, flagstone floors, mix of comfortable armchairs and sofas and oars criss-crossed on the ceiling. Portions are generous wherever you choose and the staff are relaxed and friendly. The ten bedrooms are in a converted barn at the back of the inn. All have plenty of room with a mix of antiques and light modern fabrics, and bathrooms are in smart marble.

 Denotes somewhere you can rely on a good meal – either the hotel features in the 1997 edition of our sister publication, **The Good Food Guide,** *or our inspectors thought the cooking impressive, whether particularly competent home cooking or more lavish cuisine.*

◑ Open all year ⧉ In centre of Stonor village, 4 miles from Henley-on-Thames. Private car park ⧉ 5 twin, 5 twin/double; all with bathroom/WC; TV, room service, hair-dryer, direct-dial telephone ✅ Restaurant, bar, lounge, conservatory, garden; conference facilities (max 12 people incl up to 10 residential); early suppers for children; baby-listening ♿ Wheelchair access to hotel (2 ramps), restaurant and WC (unisex), 6 ground-floor bedrooms, 1 specially equipped for disabled people ● No dogs ⧉ Access, Amex, Delta, Switch, Visa ⟨£⟩ Single occupancy of twin/double £85, twin/double £95; deposit required. Alc L, D £23. Special breaks available

---

STRATFORD-UPON-AVON Warwickshire   map 5

Caterham House Hotel

58/59 Rother Street, Stratford-upon-Avon CV37 6LT
TEL: (01789) 267309   FAX: (01789) 414836

Sophisticated hosts and the atmosphere make this the most beguiling place to stay in Stratford.

It has taken Olive Maury and her jaunty French husband, Dominique, two decades to make their Georgian house the chic establishment that it is today. Situated just on the edge of the old part of Stratford's town centre, it is most creatively furnished. Yellow walls and beautiful white drapes ennoble the breakfast room; the bar sports classical Greek murals, rugs on flagstones and striking leather sofas; and a stencilled wistaria curls over the stairs. Furnished with interesting antiques, the bedrooms are just as stylish. And if you want to impress, choose Room 12 for its rather grand French furniture. If you're an easily disturbed sleeper, ask for a room at the back. And if you're looking for privacy, take one of the two rooms in a cottage 75 yards down the road. Succumbing to late twentieth-century expectations, the Maurys have finally put TVs in some rooms, though they still serve tea unless specifically asked for a self-service tea tray. They are happy to provide pre-theatre snacks as they no longer serve dinners. Their breakfasts are a cut above the average, featuring croissants and interesting fruit concoctions, such as prunes and apricots with cinnamon.

◑ Open all year ⧉ In centre of Stratford, opposite the police station. Private car park ⧉ 5 twin, 8 double, 1 family room; some in annexe; 1 with bathroom/WC, most with shower/WC; room service, hair-dryer; TV in some rooms; no tea/coffee-making facilities in rooms ✅ Dining-room, bar, lounge, drying-room, conservatory; conference facilities (max 30 people incl up to 14 residential) ♿ No wheelchair access ● No dogs in public rooms and in bedrooms by arrangement only ⧉ Access, Visa ⟨£⟩ Single occupancy of twin/double £36 to £58, twin/double £40 to £68, family room £57, annexe room £75 to £95; deposit required (prices valid till Apr 1997)

Victoria Spa Lodge

𝓛

Bishopton Lane, Stratford-upon-Avon CV37 9QY
TEL: (01789) 267985   FAX: (01789) 204728

A high-quality B&B in a fine Victorian house just outside Stratford in the countryside.

The Victoria Spa Lodge's interesting history becomes evident when you look at an evocative print reproduced on its brochure cover, depicting it in its heyday in the last century. The building was once a thriving spa to which Queen Victoria gave her name, and where Princess Vicky, the Queen's eldest daughter, stayed. Now the pump room is a private dwelling, and what was the hotel is divided into two residences. The Tozers' half looks best in the splendid open-plan lounge/breakfast-room, which is flooded with light and rigged out with ornate fireplaces, lacy tablecloths, a sideboard with an array of cut glass and candelabra, and rugs on boarded floors. The bedrooms, generally equipped with very decent dark-wood furnishings, and all fitted with good shower units, are likeable, but can't quite maintain such stylishness. The best-looking bedroom is the blue Room 1, which boasts a classical frieze, while the beamed attic rooms are quaint. You might also want to ask for a room overlooking the Stratford Canal, which runs right alongside the house.

◑ Open all year ⬚ 1½ miles north of Stratford; take Bishopton Lane from the roundabout where A3400 and A46 meet. Private car park ⬚ 1 twin, 3 double, 3 family rooms; all with shower/WC; TV, hair-dryer, clock radio ✔ Dining-room (air-conditioned), lounge (air-conditioned), garden ⬚ No wheelchair access ● No dogs; no smoking ⬚ Access, Visa ⬚ Single occupancy of twin/double £38, twin/double £50; deposit required

---

STRETTON Leicestershire   map 6

Ram Jam Inn

Great North Road, Stretton, Oakham LE15 7QX
TEL: (01780) 410776   FAX: (01780) 410361

A paragon in the field of highway motels and fast-food establishments.

Everyone should visit the Ram Jam Inn just once, if only to understand what they're missing out on whenever they stop off at a motorway service station. The reason for the high standards of this historic hostelry (its wonderful name originates from a brew concocted by an eighteenth-century landlord) is that it is run efficiently by the owner of a nearby top-notch country-house hotel (Hambleton Hall, see entry). Its hub is an open-plan, quarry-tiled dining area. Hardworking chefs in the exposed kitchen and dynamic waiters ensure that dishes appear in next to no time. The food is delicious: simple yet at times creative, in such offerings as carrot and sweet-potato soup, spicy lamb, grilled salmon and local bangers and mash. Punters also eagerly tuck into cream teas, home-made ice-creams, cakes, kiddy food and breakfast fare – the latter off an à la carte menu, served to residents and passing trade alike. Though the inn stands right by the A1, all but one of the bedrooms are as tranquil as could be imagined, looking away from the road over an orchard. Their furnishings – smart pine, modish wicker, cork tiles in capacious bathrooms – would shame many hotels that charge twice the price.

◗ Closed 25 Dec; restaurant closed 31 Dec ⤢ On west side of A1 approx 9 miles north of Stamford. Private car park ⤙ 6 twin, 1 double; family room available; all with bathroom/WC; TV, direct-dial telephone; hair-dryer on request ✓ Restaurant, bar, lounge, garden; conference facilities (max 80 people incl up to 7 residential); early suppers for children ⅙ No wheelchair access ● No dogs in public rooms; no smoking in restaurant ▭ Access, Amex, Diners, Switch, Visa £ Single occupancy of twin/double £41, twin/double £51, family room £65. Cooked B £4.50; set L £8; alc D £17; light meals available

---

STURMINSTER NEWTON Dorset   map 2

Plumber Manor

Sturminster Newton DT10 2AF
TEL: (01258) 472507   FAX: (01258) 473370

Easy-going ancestral country home with emphasis on good food.

The chestnut-lined driveway to the ancestral home of the Prideaux-Brunes sweeps over a trout stream and past a croquet lawn and flower borders to reach the golden stone seventeenth-century house with mullioned windows framed by magnolia and wistaria. Family portraits fill the flagstoned hallway, staircase and gallery, but umbrellas and coats by the doorway, and Bertie the Labrador (father Humphrey sadly had to be put down last year) give it a friendly, family dimension. Despite the smart, historic setting and many heirlooms, the current generation of Prideaux-Brunes run their 'restaurant-with-bedrooms' with easy-going pragmatism, aiming to keep prices 'sensible' without skimping on service or style. Three interlocking restaurant rooms, popular with locals, fill most of the ground floor: a breakfast-room with garden views; a large, central room with bright blue shades setting off gilt-framed mirrors and oils; and a smaller, vaulted room ideal for private dinners. Guests can tuck into guinea-fowl with blackcurrants and cassis, venison with rosemary, redcurrant and chestnut purée or Aylesbury duck with apricot and raspberry coulis. The largest double in the main house, with fireplace, antique furnishings and a grand window and seat below is considered the best, but bedrooms in the converted barn and stable annexes have contemporary furnishings and brighter colour schemes.

◗ Closed Feb ⤢ 2 miles south-west of Sturminster Newton on road to Hazelbury Bryan. Private car park ⤙ 2 single, 6 twin, 8 double; some in annexe; all with bathroom/WC; TV, room service, hair-dryer, direct-dial telephone; trouser press in some rooms ✓ 3 restaurants, bar, lounge, garden; conference facilities (max 12 people residential/non-residential); tennis, croquet; early suppers for children ⅙ Wheelchair access to hotel, restaurants and WC (unisex), 6 ground-floor bedrooms ● Dogs in 2 bedrooms only ▭ Access, Amex, Diners, Switch, Visa £ Single £63 to £85, single occupancy of twin/double from £65, twin/double £90 to £120. Set D £15 to £25, Sun L £17.50. Special breaks available

---

Where we know an establishment accepts credit cards, we list them. There may be a surcharge if you pay by credit card. It is always best to check when booking whether the card you want to use is acceptable.

SUTTON COLDFIELD **West Midlands**   map 5

New Hall

Walmley Road, Sutton Coldfield B76 1QX
TEL: 0121-378 2442   FAX: 0121-378 4637

Reputedly the oldest inhabited moated house in England, New Hall is, surprisingly, a chain-owned country-house hotel.

You don't expect a hotel with 62 bedrooms that is owned by the Thistle group to have a personal feel. That it does – perhaps even more so than many a small, privately owned hotel – is due to the super management of Caroline and Ian Parkes, the spirited, well-trained staff, and their Labrador, Rupert. Moreover, you don't imagine a hotel situated just eight miles from the centre of Birmingham to feel rural. Yet it's set at the end of a long drive, within 26 acres of woodlands and gardens which encompass a trout pool and a nine-hole, par-three, golf course. New Hall itself – all gables, crenellations and turrets dating back some 800 years – is separated from its grounds by a lily-filled moat. Inside, the intimate rooms, not least the romantic restaurant, lined with dark panels and stained-glass etched with coats of arms, are as full of character as you would hope to find in a building whose history runs to an 18-page booklet. Plump soft furnishings and rich fabrics characterise the very appealing, spacious bedrooms. A dozen are dotted round the old part of the house; the rest occupy a vast new wing, but are hardly less characterful. The most publicised room is a ground-floor suite especially created for Pavarotti so that he could reside in splendour without having to negotiate any stairs. A new chef took up the reins in November 1995: more reports, please.

○ Open all year   ☑ North-east of Birmingham on the B4148. Private car park ⊨ 4 single, 16 twin, 33 double, 3 four-poster, 6 suites; all with bathroom/WC; TV, room service, hair-dryer, trouser press, direct-dial telephone   ⊘ Restaurant, bar, lounge, garden; conference facilities (max 45 people incl up to 40 residential); golf, tennis, croquet; early suppers for children; babysitting, baby-listening   ⅙ Wheelchair access to hotel (1 step), restaurant and WC (unisex), 22 ground-floor bedrooms, 1 specially equipped for disabled people   ● No children under 8; no dogs; no smoking in restaurant   ▭ Access, Amex, Diners, Visa   £ Single/single occupancy of twin/double from £100, twin/double from £120, four-poster from £170, suite from £170; deposit required. Continental B £9, cooked B £10.50; set L £16.50/19.50, D £27.50/33. Special breaks available

SWAFFHAM **Norfolk**   map 6

Strattons

Stratton House, 4 Ash Close, Swaffham PE37 7NH
TEL: (01760) 723845   FAX: (01760) 720458

Excellent food, companionable hosts, colourful and stylish rooms – the superlatives go on and on.

The plaudits continue to flood in for Vanessa and Les Scott's eighteenth-century villa, tucked away in a secluded corner off the bustling market square. A typical letter was sent to us by a couple who live only 20 miles down the road but went to stay for a weekend after enjoying a meal there: 'By Sunday midday we did not want to leave...So you don't have to drive 150 miles to feel you are away!' was their conclusion. The Scotts met at art college, and evidence of their artistic leanings are all around, from the murals in the cheerful basement restaurant and the *trompe l'oeil* in one of the drawing-rooms, to the vast collections of paintings, prints and china cats of every size and shape. The bedrooms show an equal love of colour and detail: 'Hand-sewn quilts...beautiful upholstery, peaceful, tasteful colour arrangements ...so many cushions! The bed linen deserves a line all of its own – the freshest and whitest ever,' enthused another fan. Vanessa is in charge of the kitchen, and 'her artistic talents spread across the menu: I had the unusual combination of grilled salmon with rhubarb vinaigrette, which was superb, and her home-made ice-creams leave you wanting more,' sums up one reader, who felt that 'over the weekend we had become part of the Scott family.' All we can say is: keep up the good work!

○ Closed 24 to 26 Dec ⊿ At north end of market place, behind the shop fronts. Private car park ⌂ 1 single, 1 twin, 5 double; family room available; 5 with bathroom/WC, 2 with shower/WC; TV, room service, hair-dryer, direct-dial telephone ⊘ Restaurant, bar, 3 lounges, TV room, drying-room, library, garden; conference facilities (max 20 people incl up to 7 residential); croquet; early suppers for children; toys, babysitting, baby-listening, outdoor games, cots ⅙ No wheelchair access ● Smoking in lounges only ⊟ Access, Visa £ Single/single occupancy of twin/double £58, twin/double £80, family room from £85; deposit required. Set D £24

SWINHOPE Lincolnshire   map 9

Hoe Hill

Swinhope, Nr Binbrook LN3 6HX
TEL: (01472) 398206

High standards and low prices in a Lincolnshire Wolds guesthouse.

Erica Curd's home dates from the late eighteenth century, when it was the warren bailiff's (or rabbit catcher's) cottage. Nowadays, local game or fresh fish from nearby Grimsby features on the menu. That Erica lays on cookery demonstrations from time to time gives you an indication of the quality of her cooking. Her creative dinners, which include a complimentary glass of wine or sherry (guests can also bring their own wine), are absolute bargains. Virtually everything is home-made, including the bread, marmalade and muesli for breakfast, which is served at any reasonable time. Hoe Hill occupies a rural spot, and the french windows in the sitting-room open on to a pretty garden with a croquet lawn and Jacob sheep, while its fetching, cottagey bedrooms enjoy pleasant views across the Wolds. One bedroom, which can operate as a twin or double, is *en suite*, with a fancy bathroom. But if you can bring a dressing-gown, consider staying in one of the other two – since they share a bathroom, their rates are enticingly low.

Prices are quoted per room *rather than* per person.

● Closed Jan to mid-Feb ☑ On B1203 Market Rasen to Grimsby road, 1 mile north of Binbrook. Private car park 🛏 1 twin, 2 double; 1 with bathroom/WC; hair-dryer; trouser press on request ✅ Dining-room, lounge, drying-room, garden; croquet; early suppers for children; toys ♿ No wheelchair access ● No children under 5; no dogs; smoking in lounge only ☐ None accepted £ Single occupancy of twin/double £16 to £25, twin/double £30 to £50; deposit required. Set D £12 (prices valid till Apr 1997). Special breaks available

---

TALLAND Cornwall
map 1

Talland Bay

Talland, Looe PL13 2JB
TEL: (01503) 272667 FAX: (01503) 272940

Immaculate modern bedrooms in an architectural hotch-potch of a building with stunning sea views.

Piecing together which bits of the Talland Bay Hotel came when could take up many hours. Parts of the building probably date back to the sixteenth century, but they were heavily overlaid in the 1930s and 1940s when Lady Cooke added the dining-room and the Moroccan-style tiles around several of the fireplaces. Her son was too busy with his seven wives and fleet of pink Rolls Royces to do much to the house, but in the 1970s another new wing was added to bring the house to its present erratic shape. Since taking over in 1994 Barry and Annie Rosier have been busily updating the bedrooms and most now boast stylish fabrics and interesting bedframes. Rooms 19 and 20 have striking Zoffany wallpaper depicting eighteenth-century rural life in red and green. Room 18 is a single with cast-iron bed which opens straight into the garden. The two lounges and dining-room gaze out over an enticing swimming-pool to the sea. Dinner menus feature some unexpected twists: choices might include medallion of beef fillet on a potato rösti with onion marmalade and marsala wine *jus*, or lemon sole with Thai spices and coconut and coriander sauce. Talland Bay is perfectly placed for walking along the coast to Looe and Polperro and then retreating to tranquillity in the evening.

● Closed Jan ☑ In Looe take road for Polperro for 2 miles until sign for hotel at crossroads; turn left down hill and hotel is on left-hand side. Private car park 🛏 3 single, 8 twin, 3 double, 2 four-poster, 2 family rooms, 1 suite; some in annexe; all with bathroom/WC; TV, room service, hair-dryer, direct-dial telephone; trouser press in some rooms ✅ Dining-room, bar, 2 lounges, games room, garden; conference facilities (max 30 people incl up to 19 residential); sauna, heated outdoor swimming-pool, croquet, putting green; early suppers for children; baby-listening ♿ No wheelchair access ● No children under 5 in dining-room eves; dogs by arrangement and not in public rooms; no smoking in dining-room ☐ Access, Amex, Diners, Switch, Visa £ Single £40 to £74, twin/double £98 to £128, four-poster £108 to £148, family room £96 to £124, suite £88 to £118; deposit required. Set L £12, D £21; alc D £35. Special breaks available

---

 This denotes that the hotel is in an exceptionally peaceful situation where you can be assured of a restful stay.

TARPORLEY Cheshire   map 7

Willington Hall

Willington, Tarporley CW6 0NB
TEL: (01829) 752321   FAX: (01829) 752596

Grand country house with old-fashioned charm.

The glory days of Willington Hall seem long past, but what remains is a grand old country house imbued with a sedate atmosphere offering old-fashioned, unfussy comfort. The Jacobean-style hall remains in the hands of the Tomkinsons (who built it in 1829), a family whose history reads like a ripping yarn of cavalry charges and hunting heroics. A portrait of the present co-owner Richard Tomkinson in his younger hunting days as Master of the Cheshire Hounds hangs in one of the three dining-rooms. Other portraits adorn the adjoining rooms of high ceilings and oak woodwork where the fare is in the appropriate country-house vein of duckling, steaks, salmon and lamb with rich sauces. Lighter food, such as pies, salmon crumble or spinach pancakes is on offer in the two bars – one a green study and the other a lighter drawing-room, both overlooking the 2,000-acre estate of rolling farmland. Bedrooms are quite humbly furnished, given the grandeur of the house, but lack nothing for comfort, though bathrooms would benefit from freshening up. Rooms 1 and 2 are the pick for size and for the best views, particularly the double aspect in Room 1, which takes in both the Picton and Welsh hills.

◑ Closed 25 Dec ⤢ Take A51 towards Chester from Tarporley; turn right at Bull's Head in Clotton; hotel is 1 mile further on left. Private car park ⇢ 2 single, 5 twin, 3 double; family room available; all with bathroom/WC; TV, room service, direct-dial telephone; hair-dryer and iron on request ✧ 3 dining-rooms, 2 bars, lounge, drying-room, garden; conference facilities (max 16 people incl up to 10 residential); tennis; early suppers for children; baby-listening ⅙ No wheelchair access ● No dogs in public rooms ▭ Access, Amex, Diners, Switch, Visa £ Single £40, single occupancy of twin/double £50, twin/double £70, family room from £75. Continental B £4, cooked B £6; set Sun L £13.50; alc L, D £17; bar meals available

---

TAUNTON Somerset   map 2

Castle Hotel

Castle Green, Taunton TA1 1NF
TEL: (01823) 272671   FAX: (01823) 336066

Grand wistaria-draped town-centre hotel with high-class restaurant.

Built right beside the remains of Taunton's Norman castle, the modern Castle Hotel has a lot to live up to – and manages it with style. Size alone makes it stand out amid its rather disappointing surroundings, and when the wistaria is in flower in May the grey-stone walls are prettily softened. Inside, the halls are decked with mock-medieval tapestries but the bedrooms opt for modernity with most of the trappings you would expect, although not anything to drink. The heart of the hotel is very much the restaurant, with its autumnal colouring and grand candelabra. Its reputation runs before it and, on the night we inspected, other diners were as thoroughly impressed by the crab tart as our inspector was by the rhubarb crumble tart with clotted cream. It's probably quibbling to point out that neither the set menu nor the à la carte offered a full vegetarian meal when one had been requested on booking. It was also obvious that some non-gourmet diners were nonplussed by the rather unusual ingredients which dominated the menus; 'couldn't I just have a sirloin?' one was heard to wail. Service here is excellent, discreet but thoroughly welcoming, and despite the building's size there are lots of little nooks and crannies in which to hide away.

◑ Open all year ⤵ In Taunton town centre follow signs for the Castle. Private car park 🚗 12 single, 10 twin, 9 double, 5 suites; all with bathroom/WC; TV, room service, hair-dryer, direct-dial telephone, radio; no tea/coffee-making facilities in rooms ✥ Restaurant, bar, 2 lounges, garden; conference facilities (max 100 people incl up to 36 residential); early suppers for children; babysitting, baby-listening ♿ Wheelchair access to hotel (1 ramp) and restaurant, lift to bedrooms ● Small dogs in bedrooms by arrangement; no smoking in restaurant ▭ Access, Amex, Diners, Switch, Visa £ Single £75, single occupancy of twin/double £87, twin/double £115, suite £185 to £235; deposit required. Set L £8.50 to £18, D £23/28.50; alc L, D £36 (1996 prices). Special breaks available

---

TAVISTOCK Devon

map 1

Horn of Plenty

Gulworthy, Tavistock PL19 8JD
TEL: (01822) 832528 (AND FAX)

Renowned Georgian restaurant-with-rooms in quiet countryside close to Tavistock.

Eating is taken very seriously at the Horn of Plenty, so it comes as no surprise to find that the house itself is almost entirely devoted to the restaurant, with all but one of the bedrooms in the coach-house at the back. Dinner menus are perused in the comfort of a spacious lounge full of the sort of squidgy armchairs and sofas that seduce you into the right mood to enjoy yourself. Depending on the day and date the menu might proffer such temptations as artichoke and pea soup topped with lemon and mint cream, roast loin of lamb coated with garlic, parsley and feta cheese in a Madeira sauce, and lemon and lime mousse cake with strawberry sauce. Horn of Plenty vegetables also come in for particular praise. On Monday nights diners are offered a cheaper 'pot luck' menu. Your choice made, you cross the hall to a long, thin dining-room which, in summer, overlooks the River Tamar; in winter, when the views are concealed, a log fire offers compensation. For once, sleeping in an annexe is no hardship at all, since the coach-house rooms are comfortable, capacious suites with beamed ceilings and french windows opening on to patios beyond.

Many hotels put up their tariffs in the spring. You are advised to confirm prices when you book.

● Closed 25, 26 Dec ⊿ Head west from Tavistock on A390; after 3 miles turn right at Gulworthy Cross and follow signs to hotel. Private car park ⤶ 7 twin/double; most in annexe; 5 with bathroom/WC, 2 with shower/WC; TV, room service, hair-dryer, mini-bar, direct-dial telephone ✓ Restaurant, dining-room, bar, lounge, drying-room, garden; conference facilities (max 14 people incl up to 7 residential); early suppers for children ♿ Wheelchair access to hotel (ramp), restaurant and WC (M,F), 4 ground-floor bedrooms ● No children under 13; no dogs in public rooms; no smoking in restaurant and 2 bedrooms ⊟ Access, Amex, Visa £ Single occupancy of twin/double £63 to £78, twin/double £83 to £98; deposit required. Cooked B £7.50; set L £10.50 to £17.50, D £19.50/28.50. Special breaks available

---

TEFFONT EVIAS Wiltshire   map 2

Howard's House

Teffont Evias, Nr Salisbury SP3 5RJ
TEL: (01722) 716392   FAX: (01722) 716820

A quiet country mansion with good food in the depth of rural Wiltshire.

'This place is above and beyond all expectations. The rooms are lovely, the setting peaceful and quiet, the food outstanding and the owners especially gracious,' wrote a recent enthusiastic guest. It is certainly hard to find fault with this small hotel in a pretty, thatched farming village in the heart of rural Wiltshire. The external architecture is a touch eccentric – the original seventeenth-century house was extended in Victorian times and was given a Swiss-style roof (the owner had just returned from his Grand Tour) – but the interior is perfect. Period features, including beamed ceilings, stone fireplaces and flagstones, blend perfectly with an unostentatious, undemanding, country-house style of demure colour schemes and plain upholstery. Dinner is served in the bright, plant-filled restaurant or, weather permitting, *al fresco* by the small pond and fountain in the pretty gardens. A typical spring menu offered lamb in puff pastry with pistachios and walnuts, scallops with leeks and an orange vinaigrette, and venison with apple chutney, red cabbage and rosemary. The bedrooms are spacious and well styled, with either soft colour schemes or bold, bright tones; nearly all have large bathrooms and good views.

● Open all year ⊿ Turn off B3089 at Black Horse pub in Teffont Magna; hotel is 500 yards on the right. Private car park ⤶ 1 twin, 7 double, 1 family room; all with bathroom/WC; TV, room service, hair-dryer, direct-dial telephone ✓ Restaurant, lounge, garden; conference facilities (max 25 people incl up to 9 residential); early suppers for children; baby-listening ♿ No wheelchair access ● No dogs or smoking in restaurant ⊟ Access, Amex, Delta, Diners, Switch, Visa £ Single/single occupancy of twin/double £75 to £95, twin/double £100 to £125, family room from £125. Set L £18.50, D £25. Special breaks available

---

It is always worth enquiring about the availability of special breaks or weekend prices. The prices we quote are the standard rates for one night – most hotels offer reduced rates for longer stays.

TEIGNMOUTH Devon map 1

Thomas Luny House

Teign Street, Teignmouth TQ14 8EG
TEL: (01626) 772976

Wonderful hideaway Wolsey Lodge, its four rooms bursting with individual character.

The road running down to the Teignmouth Quays looks none too promising, but turn through an arch cut into a white wall and you'll discover Thomas Luny House, a delightful hidey-hole of a Georgian house which was once home to the eponymous marine artist. Since it has only four bedrooms you're bound to feel as if you're staying in somebody's family home, and Alison and John Allan play on that fact by offering Wolsey Lodge arrangements, where guests dine *en famille* around a single table. Informality means that there are no printed menus; what's for dinner is discussed with guests in an inviting double lounge where you can while away the waiting time by inspecting a collection of cuttings about Thomas Luny's life. Typically, dinner might consist of a warm goat's cheese salad with walnut oil dressing, lemon sole with herb-scented sauce, and a pear tart. Upstairs, there's nothing casual about the quality of the rooms, each of them with its own distinctive look and decorated with interesting bits and bobs: a Japanese travelling theatre in the Chinese Room, huge old bathroom scales in Luny, travelling trunks in Bitton and Clairmont. The Allans have created a pretty strip of back garden, complete with patio and (covered) fish pond. Tariffs, inclusive of afternoon and early-morning tea and a newspaper, are a veritable snip.

◗ Closed Jan ⤢ In Teignmouth follow signs to quay, then for Teign Street. Private car park ⤐ 2 twin, 1 double, 1 four-poster; all with bathroom/WC exc double with shower/WC; TV, room service, direct-dial telephone, radio ◈ Dining-room, 2 lounges, garden ⅋ No wheelchair access ● No children under 12; no dogs; no smoking in dining-room ⊟ None accepted £ Single occupancy of twin/double £35, twin/double/four-poster £70. Set D £18.50. Special breaks available

---

TENTERDEN Kent map 3

Brattle House

Watermill Bridges, Tenterden TN30 6UL
TEL: (01580) 763565

Beautiful and stylish B&B with friendly hosts.

Brattle House, surrounded by a large garden and fields of sheep beyond that, makes a relaxing base from which to explore the surrounding countryside. Mo and Alan Rawlinson welcome guests into their home as if they are old friends, and as a consequence many come back year after year just to visit them. The house is stylishly furnished and decorated. From the light sitting-room with its sloping, low-beamed ceiling, comfy sofas and chairs you can admire the view across the garden. The sunny, small conservatory where guests have breakfast overflows with plants. Mo and Alan usually join their guests for dinner in the candlelit dining-room with its polished mahogany table and antique furnishings, and Mo's set dinners might include dishes such as sweet-and-sour cucumber and lamb with apricots and almonds, followed by pears in red wine. Guests are asked to bring their own wine as the Rawlinsons are not licensed to sell it. The bedrooms are all large, beautifully furnished rooms with *en suite* shower facilities; a large bathroom is available for those who would prefer a bath.

❍ Closed Chr ⤢ From Tenterden head towards Hastings on A28; proceed downhill past signpost indicating Cranbrook and widening of A28 at junction with Cranbrook Road (signposted); turn right and continue for approximately ¼ mile; house is on left. Private car park ⟕ 1 twin, 2 double; all with shower/WC; hair-dryer
⟜ Dining-room, lounge, conservatory, garden ♿ No wheelchair access ● No children under 12; no dogs; no smoking ▭ None accepted £ Single occupancy of twin/double £38 to £40, twin/double £50 to £56; deposit required. Set D £17. Special breaks available

---

Little Silver

St Michaels, Tenterden TN30 6SP
TEL: (01233) 850321 FAX: (01233) 850647

A well-maintained and comfortable hotel with very considerate proprietors.

One of Little Silver's claims to fame is that the current Archbishop of Canterbury, George Carey, stayed in the hotel in 1995 – and there is a small brass plaque on the four-poster bedstead to prove it. This 1930s mock-Tudor house has been converted into a comfortable self-styled country-house hotel by its owners, Dorothy Lawson and Rosemary Frith. The large sitting-room, with its oak-beamed ceiling, a fireplace at either end and its mix of flowery upholstered and leather sofas and chairs, has the feel of a lounge in a family home. The spacious conservatory, where breakfast and afternoon tea are served, is very bright and airy, while the more formal dining-room, with the owners' artwork on the walls, has a beautiful rocking horse in one corner as well as several board games. The traditional evening menu is a little pricey and includes family favourites such as prawn cocktail, sirloin steak and a large selection of luxury ice-creams. The bedrooms themselves are of a good size and are all spotlessly clean and well maintained; some have a video recorder and selection of videos in them.

❍ Open all year ⤢ Set back off A28, 1 mile north of Tenterden. Private car park
⟕ 3 twin, 4 double, 3 four-poster; family room available; all with bathroom/WC; TV, room service, hair-dryer, trouser press, direct-dial telephone; VCR in some rooms
⟜ Restaurant, bar, lounge, conservatory, garden; conference facilities (max 150 people incl up to 10 residential); babysitting, baby-listening ♿ Wheelchair access to hotel (1 step), restaurant and WC (unisex), 4 ground-floor bedrooms, 1 specially equipped for disabled people ● Dogs by arrangement and not in public rooms; no smoking in restaurant or conservatory ▭ Access, Amex, Delta, Switch, Visa
£ Single occupancy of twin/double £60, twin/double £85, four-poster £110, family room from £120; deposit required. Set L £15; alc D £24. Special breaks available

Calcot Manor

Tetbury GL8 8YJ
TEL: (01666) 890391   FAX: (01666) 890394

Thumbs-up for this smart but unstuffy (and child-friendly) Cotswold manor house.

'Calcot is a manor house by name, but a farmstead by nature,' says the brochure of the cluster of buildings that make up Richard Ball's hostelry. This might seem unduly modest, given that the 'farmstead' includes a fourteenth-century tithe barn where Cistercian monks once went about their daily chores before vespers! Today's hotel is a combination of the main creeper-clad house (complete with flagstones and logs for the fire stacked high inside the arched doorway) and skilfully converted barns and stables of irreproachably pretty golden Cotswold stone. For the most part the interior conforms to modern country-house hotel style, so you'll find lots of places to unwind on pastel sofas amid floral drapes, plaid accessories and a sprinkling of antiques, plants and lifestyle magazines – but all without a hint of formality or snootiness. The generally laid-back approach to things (commended by one guest), extends to dining arrangements, so guests might choose to feast on minestrone risotto with roasted scallops, followed by whole pan-fried lemon sole, and chocolate marquise with pistachio cream in the bright formal dining-room, or to snack on Caesar salad and pasta in the pubby and cheerfully rustic Gumstool Inn. Staff were praised as helpful (getting a guest's laundry done at no charge, fixing a faulty television control) and professional: 'They actually remember your name very early – most satisfactory,' wrote one correspondent. The only niggles have been over lack of hot water first thing, and occasional dilatory service. Bedrooms are faultlessly equipped, and have modish, carefully co-ordinated soft furnishings and decent furniture.

○ Open all year ☑ 4 miles west of Tetbury on A4135, near intersection with A46. Private car park ↥ 1 double, 14 twin/double, 1 four-poster, 4 family rooms; half in annexe; all with bathroom/WC; TV, room service, hair-dryer, trouser press, direct-dial telephone ⊘ 2 restaurants, 2 bars, 2 lounges, library, garden; conference facilities (max 70 people incl up to 20 residential); heated outdoor swimming-pool, tennis, croquet, archery, clay-pigeon shooting; early suppers for children; toys, babysitting, baby-listening, outdoor games, high chairs ⅙ Wheelchair access to hotel (1 step), restaurants and WC (unisex), 10 ground-floor bedrooms ● No dogs; no smoking in restaurants ▭ Access, Amex, Delta, Diners, Switch, Visa £ Single occupancy of twin/double £75, twin/double £97 to £115, four-poster/family room £135. Cooked B £5; set L £17, D £22; alc D £26; light meals available. Special breaks available

Tavern House

Willesley, Nr Tetbury GL8 8QU
TEL: (01666) 880444   FAX: (01666) 880254

Homely B&B with well-equipped rooms and friendly hosts.

Janet and Tim Tremellen's seventeenth-century home is one tavern that's very definitely not in the town: the one-time staging-post and coaching-inn stands beside the A433 in the village of Willesley, about 4 miles from Tetbury, where the shops proudly display their royal warrants. Although there's a rather grand-looking porched entrance at the front, guests are directed to enter from the rear, the better to appreciate the garden (where Tim was hard at work at the time of our inspection) and the higgledy-piggledy row of slate roofs that are an eloquent testimony of the house's age and an indication of how it has grown and developed down the years. Once inside, there's no doubting the house's antiquity, as you're confronted by a riot of flagstones, beams and exposed stonework, plus suspended brass and copper items, including horse brasses. With all this period charm on tap, the Tremellens have opted to furnish the house in a homely vein, elevating comfort above style. Plates and hunting prints line the walls of the neat, autumnally toned sitting-room, where logs blaze in the slate and stone fireplace, with collections of teddy bears and shells adding a personal touch. Wheelback chairs and gleaming copper by the fireside assist the beamed ceiling and leaded windows in emphasising the rustic elements in the breakfast-room, where haddock and kippers are welcome additions to the usual grill offerings. You'll find the odd Dralon chair and headboard amid the stripped pine, antiques and ceiling beams of the cosy bedrooms. Extras – from trouser presses, to nail brushes and hand-wrapped soaps – abound.

◑ Open all year ⊿ On A433, 1 mile before Westonbirt Arboretum heading towards Cirencester. Private car park 🚗 1 twin, 3 double; all with bathroom/WC; TV, hair-dryer, trouser press, direct-dial telephone ✓ Dining-room, lounge, drying-room, garden ⅙ No wheelchair access ● No children under 10; no dogs; smoking in lounge only ⊡ Access, Visa £ Single occupancy of twin/double £43 to £48, twin/double from £59; deposit required. Special breaks available

---

THEBERTON Suffolk   map 6

Theberton Grange

Theberton, Nr Leiston IP16 4RR
TEL: (01728) 830625 (AND FAX)

COUNTY HOTEL OF THE YEAR

A welcoming country house that strikes exactly the right balance between relaxing informality and professional courtesy.

Dawn and Paul Rosher have been at Theberton Grange for only two years, but they've already expanded the hotel. When we inspected, they had just finished decorating Room 7, up in the eaves on the second floor. The stairs may prove a little tricky for the less mobile, but it's worth the effort when you reach the room, which features a Victorian brass bed with a crisp, white coverlet, and a roll-top, claw-foot Victorian bath in the bathroom. All the other rooms also have interesting antique beds and plenty of space; Room 1 has the added advantage of a double aspect over the gardens. Another innovation is the smart, herringbone-patterned, brick terrace at the back, which looks down over the woodland dell (a mass of snowdrops in early spring) and is a real boon on warm summer evenings (the local ducks obviously think so too – one pair built a nest on it last spring). Of the public rooms, the drawing-room is gloriously light, with windows on three sides, a log fire in the winter, and fresh flowers whatever the season; an honesty bar, or trolley, sits in the corner. The dining-room, on the other side of the house, is slightly darker, but its pale-yellow walls, which are hung with framed maps, add a cheerful touch. Paul's cooking is straightforward: possible dishes include a hot prawn-and-cheese soufflé or garlic mushrooms to start, followed by fresh local fish or Italian lamb casserole, rounded off with lemon tart or chocolate roulade. As a former military man, he likes to get things right – something that the guests certainly acknowledge and appreciate.

◗ Closed Chr 🔀 Go through Theberton on B1122 from Yoxford. On leaving the village turn immediately right at the small crossroads, and then take first left turning. Private car park 🅿 1 single, 1 twin, 5 double; family room available; 5 with bathroom/WC, 2 with shower/WC; TV; hair-dryer on request ◈ Dining-room, lounge, garden; conference facilities (max 15 people incl up to 7 residential) ♿ No wheelchair access ● No children under 7; no dogs or smoking in bedrooms ⊟ Access, Amex, Visa ⌨ Single £35, single occupancy of twin/double £45, twin/double £70, family room £90; deposit required. Set D £17.50 (prices valid till Apr 1997). Special breaks available

---

THIRSK North Yorkshire   map 9

Sheppard's

Front Street, Sowerby, Thirsk YO7 1JF
TEL: (01845) 523655   FAX: (01845) 524720

A popular, informal restaurant, with country-style rooms.

A couple of minutes' drive from the handsome market town of Thirsk, Sheppard's is situated in a pleasant, leafy road opposite the local church. It's made up of farm buildings grouped around a cobbled courtyard, which have gradually been brought into play as the place has undergone expansion from a small B&B in the main farmhouse to an establishment which encompasses a restaurant in the old stable block, a bistro in the granary, and a bar in the building that connects them. The bistro seems to be the heart and soul of the place, and features a polished stone floor, a profusion of plants and dried flowers, and a flood of natural light provided by the atrium-style glass roof in the main area. The weekly changing menu includes starters such as a ballottine of guinea-fowl served with port-wine sauce, and main courses that range from lasagne to pan-fried lamb's liver flamed in marsala. The lounge/bar and main restaurant are equally cosy and rustic, but the small, slightly sombre residents' lounge tends to be forgotten. The bedrooms have a definite country feel, with their pine furniture, dried flowers and the occasional beamed ceiling; Room 11 has a four-poster bed.

 Denotes somewhere you can rely on a good meal – either the hotel features in the 1997 edition of our sister publication, The Good Food Guide, *or our inspectors thought the cooking impressive, whether particularly competent home cooking or more lavish cuisine.*

◑ Open all year   ⤢ ½ mile from Thirsk market square; take Sowerby road from Castle Gate, Thirsk. Private car park   ⤒ 1 twin, 6 double, 1 four-poster; family room available; some in annexe; all with bathroom/WC; TV, room service, hair-dryer, direct-dial telephone, clock radio   ✅ 3 restaurants, bar, bar/lounge, lounge, conservatory; conference facilities (max 50 people incl up to 8 residential)   ♿ No wheelchair access   ⊖ No children under 10; no dogs; no smoking in some bedrooms   ▭ Access, Switch, Visa   £ Single occupancy of twin/double £40 to £62, twin/double £50 to £85, four-poster £90, family room £65 to £95; deposit required. Set Sun L £10.50; alc L £15.50, D £25; bistro meals available

---

THORNBURY South Gloucestershire   map 2

Thornbury Castle

Castle Street, Thornbury, Nr Bristol BS12 1HH
TEL: (01454) 281182   FAX: (01454) 416188

Vineyards, lavish food, modern comforts and bags of atmosphere in a wonderful sixteenth-century setting.

It's not surprising that Thornbury Castle is a popular place for weddings. With crenellated stone walls enclosing its lawns, topiary hedges and vineyard, the sixteenth-century creeper-clad façade, mullioned oriel windows, towers, turrets and battlements – not to mention the suits of armour, tapestries, heraldic shields and oil paintings inside – it oozes history and romance. (The two didn't always go hand in hand, however: Henry VIII stayed here with Anne Boleyn, but had to have the original owner beheaded before getting his hands on the place.) Mixed in with the atmosphere and antiques is plenty of modern comfort and style. Top-of-the-range bedrooms – those in the tower are circular – may have lavish wall hangings over exposed stone, dark carved four-posters with rich drapes and vast Gothic fireplaces. Even standards and singles have drapes over the beds, stone fireplaces, leaded windows, high ceilings and lots of character. All come with sherry, fruit, mineral water, fresh flowers, heated towel rails and good toiletries. For soaking up the atmosphere, choose between the oak-panelled lounge or the smaller library. Refreshingly, despite the venerable setting, the uniformed staff are friendly and not too formal, and the food is adventurous (though with an eye on tradition). Lamb topped with almond and rosemary, and a shallot and Madeira sauce, or duck breast on a piquant plum sauce may be served in the light, hexagonal Tower room, or the more baronial atmosphere of the dark-panelled Oriel room.

◑ Closed 2 days in Jan   ⤢ Entrance to castle is to left of parish church in Thornbury. Private car park   ⤒ 2 single, 4 twin, 3 double, 8 four-poster, 1 suite; all with bathroom/WC; TV, room service, hair-dryer, trouser press, direct-dial telephone; tea/coffee-making facilities on request   ✅ 3 dining-rooms, lounge, library, garden; conference facilities (max 34 people incl up to 18 residential); croquet   ♿ No wheelchair access   ⊖ No children under 12; no dogs; no smoking in dining-rooms   ▭ Access, Amex, Diners, Switch, Visa   £ Single £75 to £95, single occupancy of twin/double £95 to £220, twin/double £95 to £220, four-poster/suite £175 to £210; deposit required. Set L £20.50, D £31. Special breaks available

THORNTON WATLASS North Yorkshire   map 8

Old Rectory

Thornton Watlass, Ripon HG4 4AH
TEL: (01677) 423456 (AND FAX)

B&B with country-house hotel standards and genuinely hospitable hosts.

Though there are parts of the Old Rectory which date back to the fourteenth century, the aspect it presents to the world is considerably less ancient. One half of the frontage is Georgian and the other Victorian, but when the wistaria and climbing rose are in full bloom it's impossible to spot which is which. In fact, it's not easy to spot the house at all if you're a new arrival – the building is set back from the road on the corner of the expansive village green and has no sign to alert you to its existence. Olivia and Richard Farnell are attracted to the whole social side of the business, and their obvious enthusiasm and warm welcome keep their visitors coming back year after year. This is B&B with country-house hotel standards and the small scale of the operation means that the Farnells really can take an interest in their guests from the moment they make a booking, when Olivia will chat to them at length about their likes and dislikes and send a pack of information about the house and the area. The pick of the three bedrooms is the half-tester room or, for the cognoscenti, Baroness Orczy's room, after the author of *The Scarlet Pimpernel* who often slept here. Note that the Old Rectory is run on a B&B basis only, and daytime access to the house is limited.

◑ Closed 1 Nov to Easter   ⤢ In Thornton Watlass, south-west of Bedale. Private car park   🛏 1 twin, 2 double; doubles with bathroom/WC; twin with shower/WC; hair-dryer   ⊘ Dining-room, lounge, drying-room, garden; croquet   ⅙ No wheelchair access   ⬤ No children under 12; no dogs; no smoking   ▭ None accepted   £ Single occupancy of twin/double £50, twin/double £70; deposit required

---

TILSTON Cheshire   map 7

Tilston Lodge ☆

Tilston, Malpas SY14 7DR
TEL: (01829) 250223 (AND FAX)

A beautifully maintained B&B offering imaginative rooms and very thoughtful hosts.

This grand, Victorian country house was built as a gentleman's hunting lodge, but is now more concerned with preserving the animal life than polishing it off. While Kathie Ritchie looks after the house guests, her husband, Neil, tends a small herd of black Hebridean sheep and some rare breeds of poultry in the 16 acres of Cheshire meadows that surround the lodge.

Like the rest of the house, the bedrooms are all beautifully decorated and brimming with thoughtful touches such as home-made biscuits, sewing kits, and a multitude of items for the bathroom to replace the ones you forget or never knew you needed. You'll also find things that you'd only expect in a grand hotel (including bathrobes and decanters of sherry). Riots of stencilled flowers (geraniums in the Rose Room!) cover the cream walls, the beds are spread with crisp, lace-edged linen, and many original features – like the black, iron fireplaces – remain intact.

If the elegant, mosaic-tiled hallway feels rather formal, the huge Summer Room is a complete contrast, and is excellent for children. The parquet floor is covered with baskets of toys, and there are also sofas, books and magazines for the grown-ups, as well as french doors that open out on to the garden. Breakfast is accompanied by the soothing ticking of a grandfather clock, and specialist sausages, black pudding and home-made jams feature on the menu. Tilston Lodge is mainly a B&B, although evening meals can be arranged.

◐ Open all year ⇗ In Tilston village, turn left at the T-junction signposted Malpas; hotel is 200 yards further on, on the right. Private car park ⇥ 1 twin, 1 double, 2 four-poster; family room available; all with bathroom/WC; TV, hair-dryer; trouser press in one room ⌁ Dining-room, lounge, drying-room, garden; croquet; early suppers for children; toys ⅙ No wheelchair access ● No dogs; no smoking ☐ None accepted £ Single occupancy of twin/double £38, twin/double £56, four-poster £64, family room from £70. Set D £22 (1997 prices). Special breaks available

---

Trebrea Lodge

Trenale, Tintagel PL34 0HR
TEL: (01840) 770410   FAX: (01840) 770092

Stately Georgian town house in quiet countryside above Tintagel.

Trebrea Lodge, set high above the village where it can take advantage of the views while escaping the commercialism of Tintagel itself, is an elegant three-storey Georgian house of mellow stone. It contains seven bedrooms, all looking out to the sea and furnished in a variety of styles. Most striking is Room 1 with a massive four-poster bed, probably created out of older pieces of furniture in Victorian times; steps lead to a bathroom whose twin windows take in lovely views of spring daffodils or bluebells. Downstairs a log fire burns in the comfortable bar/lounge, even in summer. In fact it's almost too comfortable in there – Sean Devlin and John Charlick have trouble persuading their guests to venture upstairs, where a much bigger, brighter lounge is poised for sunset spectaculars. Tintagel may long since have forfeited any claim to fishing village status, but fish still takes pride of place on the hand-written dinner menus. The no-choice dinner might feature tuna pâté with Melba toast followed by perch fillet medallions with ginger sauce and Cornish Yarg cheese.

◐ Closed 5 Jan to 10 Feb ⇗ Leave Tintagel on Boscastle road; turn right at modern RC church; turn right at top of lane. Private car park ⇥ 3 twin, 3 double, 1 four-poster; 1 in annexe; 4 with bathroom/WC, 3 with shower/WC; TV, hair-dryer, direct-dial telephone ⌁ Dining-room, bar/lounge, library, garden ⅙ No wheelchair access ● No children under 8; smoking in 1 public room only ☐ Access, Visa £ Single occupancy of twin/double £53 to £58, twin/double £72 to £84, four-poster £84; deposit required. Set D £19.50. Special breaks available

TITCHWELL **Norfolk**   map 6

Titchwell Manor

Titchwell, Nr Brancaster PE31 8BB
TEL: (01485) 210221   FAX: (01485) 210104

Excellently managed hotel with first-class service.

'Hello, you're new here, aren't you?' This congenial enquiry from a lunching diner to one of the waitresses sums up the ambience of this friendly hotel overlooking the marshes, dunes and saltings of this attractive part of the Norfolk coast. Visitors return year after year, certain in the knowledge that they will be well looked after, carefully noting changes in furnishings as well as staff. When our inspector called, another resident was commenting favourably on the pine extension to the bar, which provides more space for lighter lunchtime snacks. The décor of the public rooms and many of the bedrooms sticks to appropriately Victorian colours and style: deep burgundy and green in the lounge, plum and cream in the bar and dining-room, and occasional chintzes. A couple of bedrooms in the annexe take on a more modern aspect, in smart and cheerful yellow and green checks, but maintain their air of informal comfort with teddies on the bed. Food makes good use of local suppliers, with dishes like Brancaster mussels poached in white wine with cream or Cromer crab and prawn salad with new potatoes; there's also a good range of bar food chalked on the blackboard. Service, by smartly dressed staff in tartan waistcoats, is exemplary and well worth coming back for.

◗ Open all year   ⓩ On A149 between Thornham and Brancaster. Private car park
🛏 3 single, 6 twin, 5 double, 1 family room; some in annexe; all with bathroom/WC;
TV, room service, hair-dryer, direct-dial telephone; trouser press in most rooms
✧ 2 dining-rooms, bar, lounge, drying-room, garden; conference facilities (max 25
people incl up to 15 residential); early suppers for children; toys, baby-listening
ふ Wheelchair access to hotel and dining-rooms, 1 ground-floor bedroom specially
equipped for disabled people   ● No dogs in public rooms   ☐ Access, Amex, Delta,
Diners, Switch, Visa   £ Single £30 to £40, single occupancy of twin/double £40 to
£50, twin/double £60 to £80, family room £60 to £80; deposit required. Set L £15, D
£25; light lunches available. Special breaks available

TORQUAY **Devon**   map 1

Mulberry House

1 Scarborough Road, Torquay TQ2 5UJ
TEL: (01803) 213639

*Cosy restaurant-with-rooms which dispels any lingering
Torquay/*Fawlty Towers *associations.*

Externally, Mulberry House looks like just another Torquay end-of-terrace guesthouse, albeit with a glistening, newly painted façade. Inside, however, nothing could be further from ignominious memories of *Fawlty Towers*. For ten years, ex-chemistry teacher Lesley Cooper has been running this delightful little hotel-cum-restaurant where you can tuck into dinners that feature plenty of local vegetables and farm produce. The menus are carefully annotated to indicate low-fat, low-cholesterol and high-fibre dishes. Guests who particularly enjoy their meals can even sign up for demonstration cookery lessons that wind up with a leisurely lunch. The three bedrooms are all light, bright and inviting, with restored fireplaces, pine furnishings and bathrooms equipped with triple jets so you need never stand shivering. One has a bathroom across the corridor – but what a bathroom! – with a big yellow suite, lots of mirrors and plenty of space to exercise off any excess dinnertime calories. With no space in the house for a lounge, the landing has been pressed into service, with a table and chairs and tea- and coffee-making facilities. Bottles of wine stand at the ready for guests who fancy something stronger.

◑ Open all year; restaurant closed Mon & Tue to non-residents ⤢ From middle of Torquay seafront, turn up Belgrave Road; Scarborough Road is first right and Mulberry House is on left at end. On-street parking 🛏 1 twin, 2 double; 1 double with bathroom/WC, 2 with shower/WC; TV, room service, hair-dryer ⚤ Restaurant; early suppers for children; baby-listening ♿ No wheelchair access ● No dogs; no smoking ▭ None accepted £ Single occupancy of twin/double £25 to £35, twin/double £42 to £50. Set L £6 to £8; alc L, D £12.50. Special breaks available

---

TOWERSEY Oxfordshire   map 2

Upper Green Farm

Manor Road, Towersey, Nr Thame OX9 3QR
TEL: (01844) 212496   FAX: (01844) 260399

A beautifully kept, fifteenth-century farmhouse with lovely gardens.

At the edge of an exceptionally peaceful little village with thatched buildings and old brick cobblers' cottages, Upper Green Farm is wonderfully quiet, yet only 5 miles from the motorway. There's little evidence now that this was once a working farm: the yard has been grassed over and is scattered with ornamental stone and flowers. The duck pond and gardens in front of the white thatched farmhouse paint a chocolate-box image, particularly in summer. Low beams and latched doors give the inside great character too. The main sitting-room, with its assortment of comfortable armchairs and sofas and logs crackling away in the fireplace, is a cosy room in winter – if it's wet you can watch videos in another sitting-room across the yard. Eight of the ten bedrooms are in a converted barn. Like those in the main house, all have crisp white sheets and duvet covers, as well as beams, dried flowers and china bits and pieces which underline the cottagey character. Marjorie and Euan Aitken are good-humoured hosts, and both preside over breakfast, at which there's a lavish menu, including free-range eggs, bacon and faggots from the local butcher, local honey and Scottish oatcakes. You'd be forgiven for dawdling a while, as the breakfast-room also has lovely views towards the Chilterns.

Use the index at the back of the book if you know the name of a hotel but are unsure about its precise location.

◑ Closed Chr & New Year 🔃 From the Thame ring-road take the Towersey road. The farm is just past Towersey Manor on the left. Private car park 🛏 1 single, 2 twin, 7 double; most in annexe; 6 with bathroom/WC, 4 with shower/WC; TV, hair-dryer ✅ Dining-room, 2 lounges ♿ Wheelchair access to hotel and dining-room, 4 ground-floor bedrooms, 2 rooms specially equipped for disabled people ● No children under 13; no dogs; no smoking ▭ None accepted £ Single £34, single occupancy of twin/double £30 to £40, twin/double £40 to £55; deposit required

---

TRESCO Isles of Scilly   map 1

Island Hotel

Tresco TR24 0PU
TEL: (01720) 422883   FAX: (01720) 423008

One of the Scilly Isles' institutions, a comfortable base.

This is the *grande dame* of the hotels on the Scilly Isles, and attracts a faithful following. That's not to say that the hotel, with large picture windows making the best of the surrounding beach and gardens, is old-fashioned in style. However, in the restaurant a traditional pecking order determines who gets the coveted window tables. If it's not you, console yourself with an elaborate dinner that might include grilled fillet of local hake with a herb and black olive crust, and baby sweetcorn and mushrooms served with a fresh raspberry dressing, followed by oven-baked pecan pie with fresh strawberries in Grand Marnier. Local shellfish is usually available as an extra, subject to supply and priced according to the daily market. Bedrooms vary enormously in style and size. The best are those in the Flower Wing with secluded patios for relaxing on.

◑ Closed Nov to Feb 🔃 Take helicopter to Tresco from Penzance. There are no cars on the Isles of Scilly 🛏 5 single, 33 twin/double, 2 suites; family rooms available; all with bathroom/WC; TV, room service, hair-dryer, direct-dial telephone; mini-bar in some rooms ✅ Restaurant, bar, lounge, drying-room, library, garden; heated outdoor swimming-pool, tennis, croquet, bowls; early suppers for children; toys, babysitting, baby-listening ♿ Wheelchair access to hotel, restaurant and WC (M,F), 2 ground-floor bedrooms ● No dogs ▭ Access, Amex, Delta, Switch, Visa £ Single £70 to £95, twin/double £140 to £254, family room from £243, suite £200 to £320 (rates incl dinner); deposit required. Set D £30

TROUTBECK Cumbria   map 8

Mortal Man

Troutbeck, Nr Windermere LA23 1PL
TEL: (01539) 433193   FAX: (01539) 431261

Substantial hotel in remote countryside but convenient for Ambleside and Windermere.

The hotel's sign displays the eponymous 'mortal man' replying to the query 'What is it makes thy nose so red?' with the scornful retort, 'Thou silly fool, who look'st so pale, 'tis drinking Sally Birkett's ale.' Guests, too, can down an ale in the hotel's brass-bedecked beamed bar before proceeding through to a restaurant whose picture windows look out on wonderful unspoilt countryside. Five-course dinners are served promptly in a hushed atmosphere. There's plenty of choice, and some imaginative twists like a kiwi-fruit sorbet with diced apple for a second course and smoked ham grilled with mango chutney on toast as an alternative to cheese. Bedrooms are comfortable and well equipped; those on the second floor, for which you pay a little more, are quietest and scoop the best views. A guest who has been returning for 20 years wrote to praise Christopher and Annette Poulsom's welcome and care of their guests, especially appreciated as he was recuperating from illness. The Mortal Man stands just south of the bleak Kirkstone Pass, but within easy reach of bustling Ambleside and Windermere.

○ Closed mid-Nov to mid-Feb ◪ Troutbeck is on A592, 3 miles north of Windermere. Private car park ⊨ 2 single, 6 twin, 4 double; all with bathroom/WC; TV, limited room service, hair-dryer, trouser press, direct-dial phone ✠ Restaurant, bar, lounge, drying-room, garden ⅙ No wheelchair access ● No children under 5; no smoking in restaurant ▭ None accepted £ Single £50 to £55, single occupancy of twin/double £54 to £59, twin/double £100 to £110 (rates incl dinner). Set D £21, Sun L £13. Special breaks available

TROWBRIDGE Wiltshire   map 2

Old Manor

Trowle, Trowbridge BA14 9BL
TEL: (01225) 777393   FAX: (01225) 765443

Very comfortable accommodation and thoughtful hosts in imaginatively converted farm.

It's hard to match the harmonious cluster of farm buildings which make up Diane and Barry Humphreys' small, pleasant hotel on the outskirts of Trowbridge with the 1979 photograph of derelict outbuildings. With the major work long completed, the Humphreys – currently creating a rockery, fish pond and arbour in the front gardens for early evening relaxation – aren't sitting on their laurels. As one reader wrote: 'They obviously spend time thinking about visitors' possible needs,' providing trays of aspirin, plasters and so on in the bathrooms, even sleeping over in each room (a habit we commend to all hoteliers) to check the position of the lighting. Décor is suitably rustic with lots of stripped pine and dried flowers, although the three interlocking lounges in the main Queen Anne farmhouse have smart soft furnishings and antiques to fit the period. Bedrooms come in various shapes and sizes, some in the main house, others – more cottagey in style – in the former stables; the most imaginative are the split-level four-posters with high vaulted ceilings and unplastered walls in a converted barn. The milking parlour is now the restaurant. Menus aim to provide good 'home-from-home cooking' with generous daily specials like Caribbean chicken with pineapple and cream sauce, or peppered chicken with marsala sauce.

🌒 Closed Chr; restaurant closed Sun eve   ↗ On A363, south of Bath, between Bradford-on-Avon and Trowbridge. Private car park 🛏 1 single, 1 twin, 9 double, 3 four-poster; most in annexe; all with bathroom/WC; TV, room service, hair-dryer, direct-dial telephone, clock radio; mini-bar in 2 rooms   ✓ Restaurant, bar, 3 lounges, library, garden; early suppers for children; baby-listening   👌 Wheelchair access to hotel (1 step) and restaurant, 7 ground-floor bedrooms ● No dogs; smoking in lounge and some bedrooms only ☐ Access, Amex, Delta, Diners, Switch, Visa £ Single £49, single occupancy of twin/double £49, twin/double £50 to £66, four-poster £80; deposit required. Set D £15; alc D £21. Special breaks available

---

TRURO Cornwall   map 1

Alverton Manor

Tregolls Road, Truro TR1 1XQ
TEL: (01872) 76633   FAX: (01872) 222989

A majestic pile standing on the hillside above the main St Austell road.

Both the library and Great Hall at Alverton Manor are licensed as venues for civil weddings, so weekends see the midweek business travellers swap places with wedding revellers. Originally built as a Victorian home, Gothic-looking Alverton Manor was taken over in the 1880s by the Bishop of Truro and the Sisters of the Epiphany. Looking at the vibrant colours and materials used to decorate the present-day bedrooms, it's hard to envisage that era, when one wing was simply a corridor, with cell-like rooms opening off it and sinks at each end. The modern bedrooms may have fairly simple furniture, but the variety of colours and acres of fabrics used to decorate them elevate them into luxury cocoons. Those in the newer wing are the smallest, but even the singles are perfectly acceptable. Some are double-glazed to keep traffic noise at bay; Room 21 has four windows in the bathroom alone. One twin room is adapted for disabled visitors. The lounge and restaurant match the elegance of the bedrooms, although their colour schemes are more restrained.

🌒 Open all year   ↗ On A39 (Tregolls Road) from St Austell leading into Truro. Private car park 🛏 6 single, 5 twin, 19 double, 4 suites; all with bathroom/WC; TV, room service, hair-dryer, trouser press, direct-dial telephone   ✓ Restaurant, bar, lounge, drying-room, conservatory, games room, garden; conference facilities (max 220 people incl up to 34 residential); snooker; early suppers for children; babysitting 👌 Wheelchair access to hotel (1 step), restaurant and WC (M,F), 3 ground-floor bedrooms, 1 specially equipped for disabled people ● No dogs or smoking in restaurant ☐ Access, Amex, Delta, Diners, Switch, Visa £ Single £63, single occupancy of twin/double £75, twin/double £99, suite £130; deposit required. Set L £7 to £13, D £19.50; alc D £25. Special breaks available

---

The 1998 Guide *will be published in the autumn of 1997. Reports on hotels are welcome at any time of the year, but are extremely valuable in the spring. Send them to* The Which? Hotel Guide, FREEPOST, 2 Marylebone Road, London NW1 1YN. *No stamp is needed if reports are posted in the UK. Our e-mail address is:* "guidereports@which.co.uk".

Alexander House

East Street, Turners Hill RH10 4QD
TEL: (01342) 714914   FAX: (01342) 717328

Unashamed luxury in a stylish country-house hotel.

The Alexander House estate boasts 135 acres of beautiful Sussex countryside at the edge of Ashdown Forest. The poet Shelley once lived here, and it's hard not to wax lyrical about the unstinting opulence which greets you beyond the monumental honeyed-stone columns flanking the entrance of this imposing red-brick mansion. A pale-gold glow bathes acres of light oak panels, fine antiques and elegantly carved stone fireplaces in the public areas, where sumptuous furniture, grand oil paintings and sparkling crystal chandeliers round off the delightfully sybaritic scene. Only the finest fabrics, oriental rugs and porcelain make their way into Alexander House, and this single-minded pursuit of style characterises the décor in the bedrooms. Although superbly furnished and styled, standard rooms live in the shadow of the unrepentant extravagance of Goodwood, with its wonderful views and fantasy onion-domed gilt four-poster. Classic English and French cuisine is served in the sophisticated restaurant, where you might choose medallions of pork with Roquefort and tarragon mousse or roast breast of guinea-fowl with wild mushrooms and thyme.

○ Open all year ⤢ Off B2110, 4 miles south of East Grinstead. Private car park ⨽ 3 single, 1 twin, 5 double, 2 four-poster, 4 suites; family room available; all with bathroom/WC; TV, room service, hair-dryer, trouser press, direct-dial telephone ⌦ Restaurant, bar, lounge, TV room, library, games room, garden; conference facilities (max 55 people incl up to 15 residential); gym, sauna, solarium, tennis, croquet, clay-pigeon shooting, snooker, clock golf; babysitting, baby-listening ⅙ No wheelchair access ● No children under 7; no dogs ▭ Access, Amex, Diners, Switch, Visa £ Single £95, single occupancy of twin/double £105, twin/double £125, four-poster £195, family room £165, suite £150; deposit required. Set L £19, D £25; alc L, D £37.50 (1996 prices). Special breaks available

Mill House

Cornmill Lane, Tutbury, Burton-on-Trent DE13 9HA
TEL: (01283) 813300/813634

Excellent bedrooms and caring hosts in a stylish Georgian house surrounded by meadows, half a mile from Tutbury.

Elizabeth and James Chapman's home doubles as an up-market B&B. It's somewhat overshadowed by their adjacent mill buildings that have been converted into a sheepskin and women's clothing shop. The mill stream flows alongside, with willows and daffodils covering the banks. Inside, there are just three guest bedrooms, all twins. They stand out for the quality of their furnishings, and for such details as dried-flower arrangements, hand-sewn cushions and plenty of towels. The best bedroom is Vernon, complete with a sitting area and a super bathroom with separate bath and shower. Bibliophiles should consider Moseley, which has a cupboard stuffed full of books. Downstairs, guests are encouraged to use the smart sitting-room only early in the evening. Breakfast is taken round one table in a formal, rather masculine room; Elizabeth's fruit concoctions, such as sliced orange and kiwi-fruit, are popular, but you can order what you want.

◑ Closed 25 & 26 Dec   ⤵ In Tutbury turn into Cornmill Lane by Lloyds Bank. House is ¾ mile on left. Private car park   ⤶ 3 twin; 1 with bathroom/WC, 2 with shower/WC; TV, hair-dryer   ⦸ Dining-room, garden   ⅋ No wheelchair access   ⊖ No dogs; no smoking   ▭ None accepted   ⌷ Single occupancy of twin/double £35, twin/double £40 to £55

UCKFIELD East Sussex   map 3

Hooke Hall

250 High Street, Uckfield TN22 1EN
TEL: (01825) 761578   FAX: (01825) 768025

Stylish and friendly town house with a touch of individuality.

There can't be many places where a life-size tribal carving from the Ivory Coast greets you eye-to-eye in the hallway, so you soon realise that Hooke Hall is not as predictable as the elegant red-brick Queen Anne façade would have you think. Alister and Juliet Percy have achieved a stylish but informal atmosphere in this gracious town house made of ship's timbers which, Juliet swears, move with the wind on a stormy day. Ancestral oils look down from the oak panels in the comfy drawing-room, which does not suffer from noise despite its position overlooking Uckfield's busy High Street. Famous lovers and mistresses give names to the delightful bedrooms, all individually styled with a distinctly feminine touch. Madame de Pompadour is frilly and frivolous with a huge four-poster, Nell Gwynne has cane furniture and sky-blue and gold themes. Top-floor rooms are more orthodox and make a feature of the house's exposed beams. The restaurant, La Scaletta, boasts Italian chefs who specialise in regional Italian cuisine, such as creamy risotto with scallops and wild mushrooms or guinea-fowl breast with rosemary and baked aubergines. One happy customer found 'very friendly staff and some lovely chambermaid ladies who quickly doubled up and down the precipitous backstairs to serve breakfast without complaint even though we were comfortably the last.'

◑ Closed Chr; restaurant closed Sat L & Sun   ⤵ At northern end of High Street in centre of Uckfield. Private car park   ⤶ 3 twin, 4 double, 1 four-poster, 1 family room; all with bathroom/WC; TV, hair-dryer, mini-bar, trouser press, direct-dial telephone   ⦸ Restaurant, lounge; conference facilities (max 20 people incl up to 9 residential)   ⅋ No wheelchair access   ⊖ No children under 12; no dogs; no smoking in restaurant   ▭ Access, Amex, Visa   ⌷ Single £40, single occupancy of twin/double £43, twin/double £60, four-poster £100, family room £95; deposit required. Continental B £5, cooked B £7; set L £9.50; alc L £15, D £20. Special breaks available

Horsted Place

Little Horsted, Uckfield TN22 5TS
TEL: (01825) 750581   FAX: (01825) 750459

An imposing, converted stately home and sporting estate for those with deep pockets.

Keep a look out for lazy rabbits hopping out as you approach this Victorian Gothic mansion along a thickly wooded drive. The soaring turrets and mullioned windows blend well with criss-crossed red and white brickwork and with much of the detail added by Augustus Pugin. The interior pursues the theme with heavy medieval-style furniture and a magnificent, intricately carved main staircase – a real masterpiece which was unfortunately painted at some time in its life. Most of the bedrooms are rather opulent suites, such as the Nevill Suite, the palatial master bedroom which the original owner would not vacate even for a royal visit, or the Tower Suite with private access to the rooftop turrets. Naturally both carry a hefty price tag. The more modest standard rooms are all immaculately decorated and airy. During the week the hotel seems to centre around conferences but is otherwise perfect for golf or stylish dining from the à la carte menu – French with English translations – featuring carré d'agneau or perhaps suprême de pintadeau.

○ Open all year ⊉ 2 miles south of Uckfield on A26. Private car park ⟻ 9 twin, 6 double, 5 suites; some in annexe; most with bathroom/WC; TV, room service, hair-dryer, mini-bar, direct-dial telephone; no tea/coffee-making facilities in rooms ⍋ Restaurant, lounge, library; conference facilities (max 100 people incl up to 20 residential); golf, heated indoor swimming-pool, tennis, croquet; early suppers for children ⑃ Wheelchair access to hotel (1 ramp) and restaurant, 2 ground-floor bedrooms ● No children under 8; dogs in bedrooms only, by arrangement; no smoking in restaurant ▭ Access, Amex, Delta, Diners, Switch, Visa £ Single occupancy of twin/double £90 to £180, twin/double £90 to £180, suite £200 to £250; deposit required. Continental B £8.50, cooked B £11.50; set L £15, D £28.50; alc L £31.50, D £40 (1996 prices). Special breaks available

---

UFFINGTON Oxfordshire   map 2

The Craven

Fernham Road, Uffington SN7 7RD
TEL: (01367) 820449

Stylish rooms in a characterful country cottage with relaxed informal atmosphere.

If an archetypal country cottage is your idea of bliss, this B&B is for you. Carol Wadsworth's white thatched cottage started life as a hostelry over 300 years ago and Carol is proud to tell you that it even gets a mention in *Tom Brown's Schooldays* as a 'low-lying wayside inn'. As you might expect, there are roses growing round the door: in fact, they are so wild at the front that you're asked to go round the back, where Edward the Old English Sheepdog meets you, wagging his tail. A stern command of 'on your mat' is enough if you don't want him to follow you to your room. The cottage has been very stylishly decorated using bold colours to go with lacy bedspreads and embroidered Victorian pillowslips. There are few extras – you'll need to bring your own toiletries – and except in the four-poster bedroom downstairs not much space to spread out. Magnolia, with its brass bed and bright yellow walls, was our favourite, though you should opt for the four-poster if you want a bathroom *en suite* – otherwise you'll have to make the short journey across a narrow, higgledy-piggledy corridor. Meals, by arrangement, are served at a pine table in the L-shaped kitchen where you can chat while your host cooks. Readers have praised the evening meals, which might consist of watercress soup, pork in cider and lots of fresh vegetables.

◖ Open all year   ⤢ On the northern outskirts of Uffington, south-west of Oxford. Private car park   ⤙ 1 single, 2 twin, 3 double, 1 four-poster, 1 family room; 1 in annexe; 3 with bathroom/WC, 1 with shower/WC; room service, hair-dryer; TV in some rooms   ⊘ Lounge, TV room, drying-room, garden; early suppers for children; babysitting   ♿ Wheelchair access to hotel (1 step), 3 ground-floor bedrooms, 1 specially equipped for disabled people   ⬤ No dogs; no smoking in bedrooms   ▭ Access, Amex, Visa   £ Single £28 to £35, single occupancy of twin/double £30 to £38, twin/double £48 to £50, four-poster £58, family room from £55; deposit required. Set D £12.50

ULLINGSWICK Hereford & Worcester   map 5

The Steppes

Ullingswick, Nr Hereford HR1 3JG
TEL: (01432) 820424   FAX: (01432) 820042

Half-timbered sixteenth-century farmhouse in a peaceful spot.

Henry and Tricia Howland have carefully restored their characterful farmhouse to make it the welcoming hotel that it is today. Parts of the building date from the 1380s, but much of the main house is sixteenth and seventeenth century, and the sense of history has been maintained in the hotel's interior. The dining-room, with its tiled floor, stone fireplace and long-case clock, makes for cosy and rustic surroundings in which to enjoy one of Tricia's set dinners – which might be wild boar and juniper berry pâté followed by roast quail stuffed with chicken mousseline, then chocolate truffle cake. Down the narrow stairs you find yourself in what was once the cider cellar, but is now a lovely atmospheric bar with cobbled floors, stone walls and plenty of dried hops. The bedrooms are in the converted outbuildings in a courtyard behind the farmhouse. They have a cottagey feel with stripped wooden doors and dried hops on the beams. Each room also comes complete with a teddy – as in fact does the garden, where there are several unusual stone teddies dotted about keeping a watchful eye on the hotel residents.

If you have a small appetite, or just aren't feeling hungry, check if you can be given a reduction if you don't want the full menu. At some hotels you could easily end up paying £30 for one course and a coffee.

○ Closed Dec & Jan (exc Chr & New Year)　↗ Just off A417 Gloucester to Leominster road. Private car park　🚗 2 twin, 4 double; all in annexe; all with bathroom/WC; TV, room service, hair-dryer, mini-bar, direct-dial telephone, radio　✓ Dining-room, bar, lounge, drying-room, garden　♿ No wheelchair access　● No children under 10; no dogs in public rooms; no smoking in dining-room, bar and 2 bedrooms　▭ Access, Amex, Delta, Switch, Visa　£ Single occupancy of twin/double £50 to £55; twin/double £80 to £90; deposit required. Set D £24. Special breaks available

---

ULLSWATER Cumbria　　　　　　　　　　　　　　　　　　　　map 10

Sharrow Bay

Ullswater, Nr Penrith CA10 2LZ
TEL: (01768) 486301/486483　FAX: (01768) 486349

Epitome of the country-house hotel: relaxed, refined and luxurious.

Sharrow Bay is the quintessential English country-house hotel: a Victorian house on the water's edge, ringed with rhododendrons and with a backdrop of high fells; fussy surroundings of fine china, antiques, watercolours and fresh flowers; proper service that is not obtrusive or obsequious; and sandwiches with the crusts cut off at afternoon tea. It is approaching a half-century since Francis Coulson and Brian Sack first opened the house to guests, and their impeccable standards have never dipped. One couple returning after 25 years had a 'truly memorable experience', which would seem also to apply to their first visit, so clear were their recollections of the 'still gentle and caring atmosphere'. Another devotee wrote to praise the 'exemplary staff' and the 'sense of occasion'. 'It was never less than a wonderful experience.' A rare letter of complaint did speak of 'settees being shoehorned into every possible space', and being 'overwhelmed by assorted knick-knacks', so perhaps the profusion of soft furnishings and *objets d'art* is not to every taste.

Food plays an essential part to any visit, whether it is the 'best-ever breakfasts', the monumental afternoon teas or dinner overlooking Ullswater from the coffered dining-room or the oak-panelled, ornate library. The menu is appropriately busy, with extravagant descriptions and multiple choices, and its richness often defies full appreciation of all five courses. Monkfish, venison, quail, lobster and salmon make frequent appearances, in conjunction with port, brandy, Madeira and red wine, shallots, fruit chutneys and mussels.

Bedrooms divide between the main house and rather superior annexes, including Bank House, a splendid Elizabethan building a further mile along the lakeside. Many rooms have lake views; all are luxuriously furnished in a cosy rather than imposing fashion, with chandeliers, coronets and lavish fabrics combined with pictures and plenty of books and magazines.

Prices are what you can expect to pay in 1997, except where specified to the contrary. Many hoteliers tell us that these prices can be regarded only as approximations.

◑ Closed end Nov to end Feb ⬘ Leave M6 at Junction 40 and follow signs for Ullswater; at Pooley Bridge take a right turn to Howtown; follow this road for 2 miles to the lakeside. Private car park ⬅ 3 single, 4 twin, 11 twin/double, 8 double, 2 suites; most in annexe; all with bathroom/WC exc 1 single with shower/WC; TV, room service, hair-dryer, trouser press, direct-dial telephone; mini-bar in some rooms; no tea/coffee-making facilities in most rooms ✅ 3 dining-rooms, 4 lounges, drying-room, 2 conservatories; air-conditioning in dining-rooms and 5 bedrooms; conference facilities (max 12 people residential/non-residential); fishing ♿ No wheelchair access
⬤ No children under 13; no dogs; no smoking in dining-rooms and discouraged elsewhere ☐ None accepted £ Single £80 to £155, single occupancy of twin/double £105 to £155, twin/double £160 to £320, suite £254 to £320 (rates incl dinner). Set L £27 to £32, D £42 (1996 prices). Special breaks available

---

ULVERSTON Cumbria   map 8

Appletree Holme

Blawith, Nr Ulverston LA12 8EL
TEL: (01229) 885618

A luxurious and characterful old stone farmhouse in a remote spot in the fells.

Take the lane opposite Blawith church, drive through the farmyard, then head off on the rugged track across the fells, and eventually you'll arrive at a clutch of old, stone, lichen-coated buildings, whose windows were built deliberately small to keep out the weather. Shirley and Roy Carlsen used to run one of the north's grandest hotels, but now their attention has been absorbed by one of the smallest and most luxurious. Appletree Holme is not so much a hotel as a remote retreat and sybaritic battery-charger: indeed, life here seems to centre on soaking up fine food and wine and soaking away your worries.

Baths feature prominently: the Blue Room – up among the sloping timbers – for example, boasts an enormous, circular, whirlpool bath. The Down House (once the preserve of the family cow) is now a characterful apartment featuring a private patio garden and a huge double bath set in a stone surround. The Orchard Room has a loo-with-a-view, while the Rose Room has to make do with a mere semi-sunken bath in its private bathroom.

Food is an abiding passion, if not an obsession. Roy likes to engage his guests in discussions over the menu and, according to individual preferences, combines Mediterranean influences (the public rooms are filled with classical statues and artefacts gathered during Roy and Shirley's regular trips to Greece) with the choicest local produce, such as trout from the nearby stream and tarn, mushrooms from the fields, fruit and vegetables from the garden, and cheese or yoghurt from the surrounding farms. Pheasants strut outside the dining-room window in blissful ignorance of the delights within.

All rooms have tea/coffee-making facilities unless we specify to the contrary.

◑ Open all year 🔁 Turn into the lane opposite Blawith church, pass through the farm, and take first right and then first left turning at the sign. Private car park 🛏 1 twin, 3 double; doubles with bathroom/WC, twin with shower/WC; TV, room service, hair-dryer, radio, telephone (not direct-dial) ✅ Dining-room, lounge, drying-room, library, garden ♿ No wheelchair access ➊ Children in dining-room by arrangement only; no dogs; no smoking ▭ Access, Visa 💷 Single occupancy of twin/double £69 to £73, twin/double £118 to £126 (rates incl dinner); deposit required. Set D £23

Bay Horse Inn ☆

Canal Foot, Ulverston LA12 9EL
TEL: (01229) 583972   FAX: (01229) 580502

Old inn offering great food and outstanding views, despite having a factory for a near neighbour.

The Bay Horse must surely have one of the most bizarre locations of all in this book, though its positive points – impeccable service, very good food and splendid views, providing you don't turn round – far outweigh the negative (pedestrian rooms and a chemical plant for a neighbour). The inn sits right on the edge of the Leven Estuary, overlooking the beautifully bleak expanses of sand to the bright lights of Morecambe in the distance. A conservatory grafted on to the front of the pub means you can be mesmerised by the myriad streams that swirl through the sand while waiting between the various courses. Selections are made first over aperitifs in the traditional black-beams-and-horse-brasses bar, then everyone is taken next door in a procession that feels more like being introduced to the Queen than sitting down to your dinner. Apart from some woolly home-made pasta, our inspector thoroughly enjoyed venison medallions in a game sauce and a fine fruit meringue, plus a first-class breakfast. Only the bedrooms are disappointing, but for a lack of character rather than any shortfall in facilities or comfort. John Tovey cookbooks by the bedside point to the pedigree of the inn: John Tovey co-owns it with chef Robert Lyons, who spent many years at Miller Howe (see entry).

◑ Open all year 🔁 From A590 follow signs for Canal Foot on entering Ulverston. Private car park 🛏 4 twin, 3 double; all with bathroom/WC; TV, room service, hair-dryer, trouser press, direct-dial telephone; no tea/coffee-making facilities in rooms ✅ Restaurant/ conservatory (air-conditioned), bar ♿ No wheelchair access ➊ No children under 12; no dogs in public rooms ▭ Access, Amex, Visa 💷 Single occupancy of twin/double £80, twin/double £150 (rates incl dinner); deposit required. Set L £16; alc L, D £22.50 (prices valid till Jan 1997). Special breaks available

---

If you make a booking using a credit card and find after cancelling that the full amount has been charged to your card, raise the matter with your credit card company. It will ask the hotelier to confirm whether the room was re-let, and to justify the charge made.

UPPER SLAUGHTER Gloucestershire map 5

Lords of the Manor

Upper Slaughter, Nr Bourton-on-the-Water, Cheltenham GL54 2JD
TEL: (01451) 820243   FAX: (01451) 820696

Confident country house in one of the Cotswolds' prettiest villages.

It's hard to think of a scene more quintessentially English than the vista with Lords of the Manor at its heart: a gracious seventeenth-century house of golden ashlar and mellow Cotswold stone with leaded, mullioned windows, fronted by an apron of immaculate lawn that tumbles down to the Slaughter Brook, beyond which sheep graze in the surrounding fields. You can hear their bleats counterpointing the birdsong if you take tea on the terrace. The custodians of such an exemplar of the picturesque bear a heavy burden, and the hotels' owners have discharged this by re-opening the original quarry to provide the stone for the recent extension which, as a result, blends well with the original. Once indoors guests can choose between a rather masculine bar and a range of sitting-rooms where chintzy sofas and fine antiques help disguise the occasionally less-than-pristine nature of the décor. The *trompe l'oeil* parterre adds distinction to the bright conservatory, but most of the serious dining takes place in the citron-shaded dining-room. Here guests are treated to an ambitious and well-executed menu; perhaps fish chowder with black rum and chilli sherry, followed by chump of new-season lamb with asparagus, morels, peas and a walnut dressing, then prune and armagnac ice-cream. The bedrooms (three of which have four-posters) are individually styled in plaids, stripes or florals, and feature antiques and extravagant bathrooms. Many have wonderful views.

❍ Open all year   ⬛ The Slaughters lie west of A429 between Stow-on-the-Wold and Bourton-on-the-Water. Private car park   ⬛ 2 single, 10 twin, 12 double, 3 four-poster; all with bathroom/WC; TV, room service, hair-dryer, direct-dial telephone; no tea/coffee-making facilities in rooms   ⬦ Dining-room, bar, lounge, library, conservatory, garden; conference facilities (max 20 people residential/non-residential); fishing, croquet; early suppers for children; babysitting, baby-listening, cots   ⬛ No wheelchair access   ● No dogs   ⬛ Access, Amex, Delta, Diners, Switch, Visa   ⬛ Single £90, single occupancy of twin/double £120, twin/double £120 to £225, four-poster £225; deposit required. Set L £17/20, D £32.50; alc Sun L £22.50, D £36.50. Special breaks available

UPPINGHAM Leicestershire map 5

Lake Isle

16 High Street East, Uppingham LE15 9PZ
TEL: (01572) 822951 (AND FAX)

A former barber's shop turned into a sophisticated yet relaxed restaurant with dainty bedrooms.

The town-centre hotel is named after a Yeats poem which evokes a lovely place – aptly so, for Claire and David Whitfield's establishment is very appealing. It focuses on its restaurant, serving serious, predominantly French, cuisine.

Panelled walls, bare tables, a pine dresser and a fine collection of scales provide the unpretentious background for three- to five-course dinners. Dishes such as quail's eggs wrapped in smoked salmon served with a sundried-tomato hollandaise, and loin of venison served with apple rösti in a damson and juniper sauce hint at the ambitions of David's cuisine. He's equally proud of the 300 or so wines in his cellar; regular 'wine dinners' allow guests to sample four or five bottles at a sitting. The Lake Isle is considerably bigger than it looks from the high street, since much lurks down a back alley in a sizeable Georgian extension and in cottages converted into suites. Bedrooms are stylish in a feminine bed-drape and flouncy-curtain way, and extras, such as a bowl of fruit, sherry and home-made biscuits, are appreciated. Many rooms are incontrovertibly small – Champagne and Dom Pérignon are exceptions – so the graceful residents' lounge comes in handy.

◑ Open all year; restaurant closed Mon L   ⤷ In Uppingham's High Street, reached via Reeves Yard. Take first right turn after hotel into Queen Street, then 2 right turns to the rear of the hotel. Private car park   ⤷ 1 single, 2 twin, 7 double, 2 suites; family rooms available; some in annexe; most with bathroom/WC, 3 with shower/WC; TV, room service, hair-dryer, trouser press, direct-dial telephone   ⊘ Restaurant, bar, lounge, garden; conference facilities (max 10 people residential/non-residential)   ♿ No wheelchair access   ● Smoking discouraged in public rooms   ▭ Access, Amex, Diners, Visa   £ Single £43 to £49, single occupancy of twin/double £43 to £49, twin/double £60 to £74, family room/suite £75 to £79; deposit required. Set D £21.50/24.50, Sun L £9.50/12.50 (prices valid till Apr 1997). Special breaks available

---

VELLOW Somerset   map 2

Curdon Mill

Vellow, Williton TA4 4LS
TEL: (01984) 656522   FAX: (01984) 656197

An enticing converted watermill in pretty grounds with a mill stream, situated deep in the countryside.

Curdon Mill is a three-storey, sandstone building, which might look austere were it not for the soft creeper that covers it, and the pretty gardens that radiate out from it on all sides. At the back, the surroundings get even better, with a shallow stream whose banks are dotted with flowers, and a big, old waterwheel still in place (ask, and it can be made to turn). Inside, the watchword is comfort, and the public areas are decorated in a suitably cottagey style, featuring chintzy armchairs in the lounge, and wooden beams and a huge, old dresser in the first-floor dining-room. None of the six bedrooms is particularly large, but they're all individually decorated and each reflects its contents: the Walnut Room boasts walnut furniture, while the Candy Room is deliciously feminine. Owner Daphne Criddle is in charge of the cooking, which sticks to traditional English ingredients that are in keeping with the rural setting. On a typical Saturday night you might, for example, be offered leek and potato soup and venison braised in red wine, with home-made desserts to follow. There's always at least one main course that is suitable for vegetarians ...perhaps 'nut case', a mixture of nuts and vegetables baked in a pastry case and served with tomato sauce. While you eat, the sound of the mill stream flowing below offers a soothing accompaniment.

◑ Open all year; restaurant closed Sun eve   ↗ Take turning to Vellow off the A358; hotel is 1 mile further on, on the left. Private car park   ⇔ 3 twin, 3 double; 1 with bathroom/WC, 5 with shower/WC; TV, room service, hair-dryer   ⊘ Dining-room, bar, lounge, drying-room, garden; conference facilities (max 60 people incl up to 6 residential); fishing, heated outdoor swimming-pool, tennis, clay-pigeon shooting   ⅙ No wheelchair access   ● No children under 8; kennel for dogs; smoking in lounge only   ⊟ Access, Switch, Visa   £ Single occupancy of twin/double £35 to £45, twin/double £60 to £70; deposit required. Set L £12.50, D £19.50. Special breaks available

---

VENTNOR Isle of Wight   map 2

Hillside

Mitchell Avenue, Ventnor PO38 1DR
TEL: (01983) 852271 (AND FAX)

Friendly family-run hotel in traditional seaside resort with good views over the rooftop down to the sea.

Hillside is close enough to pop into the resort or down to the beach and far enough away to be able to relax. This three-storey thatch and stone hotel is said to be the third oldest building in the town, and was once the home of Victorian poet John Sterling – as well as being visited by Dickens and Thackeray; it is now run by the Hart family as a friendly hotel. Public rooms are informal and comfortable; from the sea-facing conservatory guests may be lucky enough to spot badgers and foxes while relaxing in the cane armchairs. Dinners are served from 7 to 7.30pm and guests are asked to make their choice from the menu at breakfast. They'll often find a roast featured plus proper puddings like jam roly-poly, and, as Brenda herself is a vegetarian, an imaginative vegetarian item or two – all at a very good value £8.50 for four courses plus coffee and mints. Bedrooms are simply but prettily done out and robes are provided in those that are not *en suite* for the dash down the corridor. Dogs are 'made welcome indeed', though not young children.

◑ Open all year   ↗ Just outside Ventnor, off B3327 Newport road. Private car park   ⇔ 1 single, 2 twin, 7 double, 1 family room; 2 with bathroom/WC, most with shower/WC; TV, room service, hair-dryer   ⊘ Dining-room, bar, lounge, drying-room, library, conservatory, garden   ⅙ No wheelchair access   ● No children under 5; no dogs or smoking in public rooms   ⊟ Access, Amex, Visa   £ Single £20 to £23, single occupancy of twin/double £20 to £33, twin/double £39 to £45, family room £58 to £67; deposit required. Set D £8.50. Special breaks available

---

The text of entries is based on unsolicited reports sent in by readers and backed up by inspections. The factual details are from questionnaires the Guide *sends to all hotels that feature in the book.*

Nare Hotel

Carne Beach, Veryan, Nr Truro TR2 5PF
TEL: (01872) 501279   FAX: (01872) 501856

An elegantly decorated and well-run hotel overlooking the isolated, sandy Carne Beach.

Sea views are everything at the Nare Hotel. Whether you're in one of the many lounges, the restaurant, the Gwendra sun lounge, or even in the best bedrooms, your eye is irresistibly drawn towards picture windows offering spectacular views of the secluded Carne Beach, right on the south-west coastal path. Bearing in mind the British climate, the hotel is well stocked with diversions in case it should be too wet or windy to venture outside. However, you could entertain yourself perfectly well just by looking at all the pictures and paintings hanging in the hotel, particularly in the Gwendra Room – a sort of Tate Gallery in miniature. All the bedrooms are immaculate, with welcoming flowers and bowls of fruit. Room 41, a family suite, runs to two sinks in the bathroom and french windows on two sides of the room. Spacious Room 4, on the ground floor, is accessible to wheelchair-users. Particularly popular is Room 26, theoretically a cheaper back bedroom, but with a sofa angled so as to soak up the side sea views. In the cheerful restaurant, five-course dinner menus usually feature lobster and uncomplicated British staples like roast pork with apple sauce, or saddle of lamb. Delicious light meals are also served in the Gwendra Room, and afternoon teas in the lounge.

◑ Closed 3 Jan to 5 Feb   ⬀ 1 mile south-west of Veryan, on Carne Beach. Private car park ⬐ 5 single, 13 twin, 13 double, 3 family rooms, 2 suites; all with bathroom/WC; TV, room service, hair-dryer, direct-dial telephone; trouser press in some rooms   ⌀ Restaurant, 2 bars, 4 lounges, drying-room, conservatory, games room, garden; conference facilities (max 50 people incl up to 36 residential); gym, sauna, solarium, heated outdoor swimming-pool, tennis, billiards; early suppers for children; babysitting, outdoor games   ↻ Wheelchair access to hotel, restaurant and WC (M,F), 5 ground-floor bedrooms, 2 specially equipped for disabled people   ● No children under 7 in restaurant eves; no dogs in public rooms   ⊡ Access, Visa
⌷ Single £53 to £115, twin/double £106 to £198, family room £158 to £248, suite £376 to £388; deposit required. Set L £13, Sun £15, D £28; alc L, D from £33; light meals available. Special breaks available

---

Haycock Hotel

Wansford, Peterborough PE8 6JA
TEL: (01780) 782223   FAX: (01780) 783031

Traditional old buildings offering up-to-date hospitality.

The hotel brochure gives the address as 'Wansford-in-England' after the story depicted on the inn's eighteenth-century sign – ask someone to tell you the tale behind it. The original seventeenth-century coaching-inn in honey-coloured stone sticks largely to traditional style, with oak panelling, exposed stone walls and hunting gear, and contains the main day-rooms as well as the formal barrel-vaulted Tapestry Restaurant. Food is very English, in the vein of quail's eggs and artichoke salad, roast rack of lamb with mint sauce and redcurrant jelly, and puddings from the trolley. The old building also contains some of the bedrooms, including the Gainsborough Room with its oak four-poster, where Queen Victoria stayed as Princess Alexandra Victoria in 1835. Other bedrooms, in the much renovated and expanded outbuildings around a beautiful formal garden, are more uniform but well co-ordinated and comfortable. For large functions and parties, the ballroom has its own private garden, while the completely separate business centre ensures that travellers staying here for pleasure are not disturbed by the rattle and hum of business chat.

○ Open all year ⤢ 8 miles north of Peterborough just off A1. Private car park ⌂ 7 single, 7 twin, 33 double, 3 four-poster, 1 suite; family rooms available; some in annexe; all with bathroom/WC exc 2 singles with shower/WC; TV, room service, hair-dryer, trouser press, direct-dial telephone, iron ⌀ 2 restaurants, bar, lounge, library, conservatory, garden, ballroom; air-conditioned business centre; conference facilities (max 200 people incl up to 51 residential); fishing; early suppers for children; babysitting, baby-listening ♿ Wheelchair access to hotel (2 steps), 1 restaurant and WC (unisex), 14 ground-floor bedrooms, 1 specially equipped for disabled people ● Dogs in bedrooms by arrangement ▭ Access, Amex, Delta, Diners, Switch, Visa £ Single £78, single occupancy of twin/double £82 to £90, twin/double £115 to £125, four-poster £140, family room from £125, suite £175; deposit required. Alc L, D £28 (prices valid till Oct 1996). Special breaks available

---

WAREHAM Dorset   map 2

Priory Hotel

Church Green, Wareham BH20 4ND
TEL: (01929) 551666   FAX: (01929) 554519

Luxurious and historic small hotel in a wonderful riverside location.

Once the priory belonging to the adjoining church, this sixteenth-century hotel now houses worshippers of good food, wine and luxury. Tucked away in a corner of the pretty church green, the hotel's walls conceal 4 acres of wonderful landscaped gardens bound by the River Frome. Inside, historic features – flagstones, mullioned windows, huge stone fireplaces – blend perfectly with rich floral fabrics, velvet, chintz and the rustic touch of dried flowers and copperware to induce an immediate sense of well-being. Dinners can be enjoyed either overlooking the gardens and river, or in the stone-flagged Abbot's Cellar, and are unlikely to disappoint. Springtime menus featured guinea-fowl on creamed Savoy cabbage with Madeira *jus*, roast duck with plum and ginger compote and, more traditionally, grilled Dover sole. Top-of-the-range bedrooms (in the boathouse) have private riverside patios, or small balconies and high vaulted ceilings, and spa baths. Over in the main house, the rooms are smaller and have more atmosphere – attic rooms especially so; all are smart and even the singles have plenty of space and style. Service is just as it should be: friendly but unobtrusive, and not too formal.

● Open all year   ⊿ Leave A351 for Wareham along the North Causeway and enter North Street; turn left past Town Hall and right into Church Street. Private car park
⌂— 3 single, 12 twin/double, 2 four-poster, 2 suites; some in annexe; all with bathroom/WC exc 1 double with shower/WC; TV, room service, hair-dryer, mini-bar, trouser press, direct-dial telephone; tea/coffee-making facilities on request
✓ 2 restaurants, bar, 2 lounges, garden; conference facilities (max 20 people incl up to 19 residential); fishing, croquet ♿ Wheelchair access to hotel, restaurant and WC (unisex), 4 ground-floor bedrooms ● No dogs ▭ Access, Amex, Delta, Diners, Switch, Visa £ Single £70, single occupancy of twin/double £65 to £105, twin/double £80 to £140, four-poster £170, suite £195. Set L £13/15, D £28.50; alc D £35. Special breaks available

---

WARMINSTER Wiltshire   map 2

Bishopstrow House

Warminster BA12 9HH
TEL: (01985) 212312   FAX: (01985) 216769

Extensive leisure facilities and bold décor at an impressive Georgian country house.

Howard Malin, Simon Lowe and Andrew Leeman, the new owners of this impressive Georgian manor (and also of Feathers at Woodstock – see entry) with extensive grounds which include lawn and a private stretch of river (fly fishing possible), have undertaken a major revitalisation since taking over in September 1995. They want their country house to be a little different, a 'country house for the '90s': chintz is out; bold, deep tones are in. This approach is most apparent in the restaurant, where pale colours have been replaced by a deep-red carpet and red and blue checked upholstery. Rich suppers – served here or in the plant-filled conservatory – may feature pork with roast shallots and wild mushrooms, or peppered venison with potato and blueberry sauce. Elsewhere in the house, the trappings of traditional elegance blend with the modern thrust – a selection of oils by lesser French and Russian impressionists, rugs on flagstones, marble fireplaces and open log fires. Bedrooms have also been given a new look, and are likely to have brightly coloured soft seating, deep, rich drapes, fewer florals and more checks and stripes. Also new are the fitness centre and hairdressing salon, complementing the lavish indoor pool and hangar-like indoor tennis court. Unusually, especially for a country-house hotel with a business orientation, children and pets are welcome and there is no dress code (although the manager will probably draw the line at shorts in the restaurant).

The Guide *is totally independent, accepts no free hospitality, and survives on the number of copies sold each year.*

All entries in the Guide *are rewritten every year, not least because standards fluctuate. Don't trust an out-of-date* Guide.

◑ Open all year ⤢ Approaching Warminster on B3414, after a sharp left-hand bend, take a right turn into the hotel's drive. Private car park ⤸ 20 twin/double, 1 four-poster, 3 family rooms, 6 suites; all with bathroom/WC; TV, room service, hair-dryer, direct-dial telephone; trouser press in some rooms; no tea/coffee-making facilities in rooms ✅ Restaurant, bar, lounge, drying-room, library, conservatory, garden; conference facilities (max 60 people incl up to 30 residential); fishing, gym, sauna, solarium, heated indoor swimming-pool, tennis, clay-pigeon shooting, croquet; early suppers for children; babysitting, baby-listening & No wheelchair access ● No dogs in public rooms; no smoking in restaurant ▭ Access, Amex, Diners, Switch, Visa £ Single occupancy of twin/double £75, twin/double £110 to £130, four-poster £145 to £165, family room £110 to £130, suite £195 to £215; deposit required. Set D £26.50; bar meals available. Special breaks available

---

WASDALE HEAD Cumbria   map 8

Wasdale Head Inn

Wasdale Head, Nr Gosforth CA20 1EX
TEL: (01946) 726229   FAX: (01946) 726334

Climbers' refuge in remote, spectacular countryside.

Considering its position, within easy reach of Scafell, Yewbarrow and the Great Gable where British climbing first got into its stride, it's hardly surprising that the Wasdale Head Inn is a long-time climbers' haunt. The residents' bar is hung with photos of famous climbers and stocked with books and magazines on every aspect of climbing, the public bar is hung with ice axes and wooden skis, and Alex, the barman, is well used to detailing every local climbing possibility. There's even a shop for those bits of climbing tackle that somehow got left behind at home. A large wood-panelled restaurant is hung with yet more black and white photos and serves up solid helpings of traditional food like saddle of hare, with alternatives like wild mushroom and pepper pie for vegetarians; some guests order Perrier, thereby wasting the opportunity to sample tap water straight from a spring on Yewbarrow. Upstairs, the bedrooms are simple and functional, lacking the character of the public areas and without fripperies like TV sets. Many climbers prefer to opt for the self-catering apartments, which come equipped with microwaves, dishwashers and televisions; the hardiest of all pitch tents outside.

◑ Closed mid-Nov to 28 Dec ⤢ Follow signs for Wasdale Head from Gosforth or Holmrook off A595. Private car park ⤸ 3 single, 2 twin, 2 double, 2 family rooms; all with bathroom/WC exc 2 singles with shower/WC; hair-dryer, direct-dial telephone; trouser press on request ✅ Restaurant, 2 bars, lounge, drying-room, games room, garden; early suppers for children; baby-listening & No wheelchair access ● No children in restaurant after 8pm; no dogs in public rooms; no smoking in restaurant ▭ Access, Visa £ Single £29, single occupancy of twin/double £34, twin/double £58, family room from £87; deposit required. Alc L, D £16.50; bar meals available (1996 prices)

  This denotes that you can get a twin or double room for £60 or less per night inclusive of breakfast.

WATERHOUSES Staffordshire   map 5

Old Beams

Leek Road, Waterhouses ST10 3HW
TEL: (01538) 308254   FAX: (01538) 308157

One of the best restaurants and the most stylish bedrooms for miles around.

Lorries trundle down the A-road a few feet from the front door of this eighteenth-century building; if you're searching for a rural hideaway, look elsewhere. However, if fine food and pampering bedrooms are high on your list of priorities, read on. Nigel and Ann Wallis' restaurant serves creative, ambitious, beautiful-looking French-based cuisine. Full six-course dinners, including interesting appetisers, a sorbet course and home-made petits fours, plus dishes such as grilled duck with a boudin of foie gras on a Madeira sauce, are pricey. However, from Tuesday to Friday evenings you can dine from a much more limited menu for virtually half the price. It's hard to overestimate the seductiveness of the bedrooms, located across the road in an annexe. Their colour schemes are sophisticated, their soft furnishings and marble bathrooms swanky. Each room is inspired by a local pottery, and tea is brought to the room using the appropriate china. All are double-glazed, but ask for Royal Doulton or Royal Stafford: they overlook a stream and meadows instead of the road.

◗ Open all year; restaurant closed Sat L, Sun eve & Mon   ⊅ On main A523 between Ashbourne and Leek. Private car park   ⟻ 4 double, 1 four-poster; all in annexe; all with bathroom/WC; TV, room service, hair-dryer, direct-dial telephone; no tea/coffee-making facilities in rooms   ⊗ Restaurant, bar, lounge, conservatory, garden; conference facilities (max 12 people incl up to 5 residential); early suppers for children; baby-listening   ⅙ No wheelchair access   ● No dogs; no smoking in restaurant and discouraged in bedrooms   ▭ Access, Amex, Delta, Diners, Switch, Visa   £ Single occupancy of twin/double £60, twin/double £90, four-poster £90. Set L £13/19.50, D £22 to £38

WATERMILLOCK Cumbria   map 10

Old Church Hotel

Old Church Bay, Watermillock, Penrith CA11 0JN
TEL: (01768) 486204   FAX: (01768) 486368

Splendid lakeside position for a fine country house with distinctive décor.

A church used to stand on the water's edge some four or five hundred years ago, but for the last two centuries a solitary, whitewashed country house has occupied the site on the western bank of Ullswater. The front lawn runs down to the lake and a wooden landing stage stretching out into the water; to the rear all is pastoral, with a long private drive keeping the main road at a fair distance. Kevin and Maureen Whitemore's tastes are for distinctive elegance in the country-house tradition: polished antiques, fresh flowers and coal or log fires. The entrance hall, with its carved wooden fireplace and Corinthian columns, is warm deep red, there's rich green in the dining-room overlooking the lake and soothing pink in the sitting-room, including the pink-tinged original glass in the window frames. The harmonious colour schemes affirm that Maureen is a talented interior designer, and her courses combining tuition and accommodation at the hotel are a popular option. Bedrooms, named after local birdlife, have also benefited from Maureen's design skills, with lavish fabrics converted into canopies, coronets and extravagant curtains. Some fine antique pieces complete the stylish picture. Most rooms have fabulous views, though Peregrine Falcon, for its outlook on the lake in two directions, probably has the edge. Dining has become more flexible, with the menu now offering starters, main course and dessert rather than the former five-course extravaganzas, and from the four or five choices you might pick whiskied prawns, then fillets of trout with orange butter sauce and finish with hazelnut parfait with fudge sauce, or the stalwart sticky toffee pudding.

● Closed Nov to Mar; dining-room closed Sun eve �️ 2 miles south of Pooley Bridge just off A592. Private car park 🅿️ 3 twin, 7 double; all with bathroom/WC; TV, room service, hair-dryer ✓ Dining-room, bar, lounge, garden; fishing; early suppers for children; baby-listening, cot, high chair ♿ No wheelchair access ● No young children in dining-room eves; no dogs; no smoking in dining-room ▭ Access, Amex, Visa £ Single £59, single occupancy of twin/double £59 to £99, twin/double £85 to £125. Set D £25. Special breaks available

---

Rampsbeck Hotel

Watermillock, Penrith CA11 0LP
TEL: (01768) 486442 FAX: (01768) 486688

Smooth-running and friendly country house on the shores of Ullswater.

The main sitting-room in the original eighteenth-century part of Rampsbeck sports a beautiful coffered ceiling, a carved marble fireplace and a large bay window overlooking the lake. Across the hall, the wide open spaces of the more recent dining-room have huge picture windows through which to admire the view. The combination of old and new works well, if not seamlessly, in this comfortable and relaxing country house, and where it is a little staid in places, plans are afoot for improvements. Service has come in for particular praise: 'Superb, Mrs Gibbs welcomed us and appeared to be "on duty" from early morning to late at night.' Bedrooms at the front may be boxy but enjoy superb views and have private balconies. Silver Cragg is the pick of these, with an antique half-tester and a whirlpool bath. Ravenoaks next door has a corner bath in an *en suite* you could hold a dance in. Those in the older part are more interesting in shape, and more variable in character. Room 2 would have been the master bedroom and is wood panelled with a four-poster. Lower down the range, furnishings become comparatively plain, and views may be restricted to the topiary hedges or a side-on sighting of the nearby marina. Dinner is four courses of Andrew McGeorge's country-house classics with a modern approach: perhaps fillet of pork wrapped in bacon and served with pimento chutney, followed by grilled wild salmon served with crab cake and salsa. 'Glorious situation, excellent food, comfortable hotel,' concluded one report.

◑ Closed Jan to mid-Feb ⤢ Take A592 to Ullswater; turn right at T-junction at lake's edge; hotel is on left after 1¼ miles. Private car park ⤓ 2 single, 4 twin, 13 double, 1 four-poster, 1 suite; all with bathroom/WC exc 2 with shower/WC; TV, limited room service, hair-dryer, direct-dial telephone; tea/coffee facilities on request
⊘ Dining-room, bar, 2 lounges, garden; conference facilities (max 40 people incl up to 21 residential); croquet; early suppers for children ♿ No wheelchair access
● No children in dining-room eves; no dogs in public rooms and some bedrooms; no smoking in some public rooms and some bedrooms ▭ Access, Visa £ Single £50, single occupancy of twin/double £70 to £110, twin/double £90 to £160, four-poster £130, suite £150; deposit required. Set L £22, D £26 to £36; bar lunches available (prices valid till Jan 1997). Special breaks available

---

WATER YEAT Cumbria   map 8

Water Yeat

Water Yeat, Ulverston LA12 8DJ
TEL: (01229) 885306

Good value and great cooking are offered at this characterful country guesthouse.

Room 3 holds a special place in the affections of Jill and Pierre Labat – they spent their first night at Water Yeat in it, after hearing that it was soon to become their new home. The room is now one of seven guest bedrooms in this seventeenth-century, Lakeland-stone farmhouse situated at the quiet end of Coniston Water. Unsurprisingly, in such an old house, the rooms are on the intimate side, and their old beams, creaky floors and rough-plaster, whitewashed walls lend them bags of character. More modern thoughtful touches include the decanters of bath crystals that are provided to help soothe any aching muscles after the day's activities (mountain bikes are available, and Pierre's minibus will drop keen walkers close to their chosen route).

Pierre's (naturally) French-influenced cooking has inspired appreciative reports. 'Fabulous! The meal I had consisted of braised beef with olives, tomatoes and red wine with *perfect* vegetables, a choice of seven cheeses, all contrasting with one another, followed finally by the most divine chocolate cheesecake – more like a soufflé, as it was served hot.' The following morning's breakfast drew an equally glowing commendation.

◑ Closed Jan; dining-room closed Sun ⤢ On A5084, 7 miles north of Ulverston, on the western side of Coniston Water. Private car park ⤓ 2 single, 2 twin, 2 double, 1 family room; 1 with bathroom/WC, 2 with shower/WC; room service; TV and hair-dryer on request ⊘ Dining-room, lounge, drying-room, garden; early suppers for children ♿ No wheelchair access ● No children under 4; no dogs; no smoking in bedrooms ▭ None accepted £ Single £20 to £22, single occupancy of twin/double £26 to £40, twin/double £39 to £57, family room £55 to £60; deposit required. Set D 16.50. Special breaks available

---

Don't forget that other hotels worth considering are listed in our Visitors' Book.

WATH-IN-NIDDERDALE North Yorkshire map 9

Sportsman's Arms

Wath-in-Nidderdale, Pateley Bridge HG3 5PP
TEL: (01423) 711306   FAX: (01423) 712524

Seventeenth-century pub with good northern cooking in a lovely woodland setting.

'A marvellous place,' said one reader, 'the rooms are fairly priced, the meals are really superb and the location is excellent – well off the beaten track.' Which just about covers everything really. The seventeenth-century pub is found just over a humpbacked bridge crossing the River Nidd in a lovely woodland setting which is popular with walkers and ornithologists who head for the nearby Gouthwaite Reservoir. The residents' lounge and bar/lounge are genial, undramatic spaces with patterned carpets and a variety of seating, though the latter is a little brighter and with its jug-lined beams just shades the other in the atmosphere stakes. There is a low-key bar which has a good lunchtime menu with perhaps Cajun chicken or loin of local pork and seafood selections on the blackboard. Fresh Whitby fish features in the main menu too, although the meat dishes, like best end of Dales lamb, have come in for equal praise. The service is always pleasant and informed. The bedrooms have pale colour schemes, sometimes enlivened by modern techniques like rag-rolling, and light wood furnishings with a few prints of Dales scenes on the walls.

◑ Closed 25 Dec; restaurant closed Sun eve ⊿ In Pateley Bridge follow signs for Ramsgill but turn off at Wath after 2 miles. Private car park ⊯ 2 twin, 5 double; 2 with shower/WC; TV, room service ⊘ Restaurant, bar, 2 lounges, garden; fishing; early suppers for children ⅚ No wheelchair access ● Dogs and smoking in some public rooms only ▭ Access, Switch, Visa £ Single occupancy of twin/double £39 to £42, twin/double £60 to £65; deposit required. Set L £15, D £21.50; alc L £14, D £21.50; bar meals available. Special breaks available

WEEDON Northamptonshire map 5

Crossroads

High Street, Weedon, Northampton NN7 4PX
TEL: (01327) 340354   FAX: (01327) 340849

A chain motel, recommendable for being good value and well run.

This isn't the kind of place you normally find in the *Guide*. Like other members of the Premier Lodge chain, it is marketed first and foremost as a cheap pit-stop with standardised facilities. Moreover, it stands at a busy road junction, and most bedrooms occupy an unprepossessing modern block. Yet the Crossroads has a few pleasant surprises. For example, you'll find that the assistant manageress has been working here for 27 years, and you'll see the front pages of that day's newspapers on display above the gents' urinals. Bedrooms are peaceful and roomy and come with more sophisticated mod cons, such as ironing equipment and baths with showers, than you might expect at their modest price. A number look out over a stream and sheep-dotted pastures. All are priced the same, making the four-poster and family rooms, in which under-16s stay for free, a bargain. Room prices at this hotel, geared primarily towards business people, drop considerably at weekends. A large, late-Victorian-styled pub offers bar food, while a jolly restaurant delivers a rather alarming mix of Indian, Mexican and traditional British dishes.

◖ Open all year ⤢ 4 miles south-east of Daventry at the junction of A5 and A45. Private car park ⤶ 9 single, 14 twin, 16 double, 3 four-poster, 5 family rooms; all with bathroom/WC exc 2 singles; TV, hair-dryer, trouser press, direct-dial telephone, iron ⌁ Restaurant, bar; conference facilities (max 90 people incl up to 44 residential) ⅙ Wheelchair access to hotel, restaurant and WC (unisex), 17 ground-floor bedrooms, 2 rooms specially equipped for disabled people ● No dogs; no smoking in some bedrooms ☐ Access, Amex, Delta, Diners, Switch, Visa £ All rooms £35 to £42; deposit required. Continental B £3.50, cooked B £5; alc L, D £13; bar meals available. Special breaks available

---

WELLAND Hereford & Worcester   map 5

Holdfast Cottage

Welland, Little Malvern WR13 6NA
TEL: (01684) 310288   FAX: (01684) 311117

Pretty country cottage with attentive hosts.

Holdfast Cottage is a long, cream and brown seventeenth-century cottage with a 70-year-old wistaria casually winding itself along the full length of the frontage. Set in peaceful surroundings with views of the Malvern Hills yet within easy reach of the M5, it is a well-placed base from which to explore the area. Several readers' letters we've received this year bear testament to this, and one reader tells us that he 'can commend Holdfast Cottage with unqualified enthusiasm.' Stephen and Jane Knowles lay the emphasis very firmly on friendly and personal attention, and our correspondent confirms that 'the service was exemplary.' The dining-room is in the Victorian extension to the cottage, where Jane serves home-cooked evening meals using fresh herbs from the garden and home-made bread. The set dinner menu – which changes daily – might consist of home-smoked trout and prawn salad with pink peppercorn dressing followed by a rosemary sorbet, then roast breast of duck with a plum sauce, finished off with pears baked in spiced red wine with cinnamon cream. Another reader writes: 'The dinner was the best I've eaten for a long time, I recommend it thoroughly.' The bedrooms, which are named after the Malvern hills, are all prettily decorated in a country-cottage style and have well-equipped bathrooms complete with a toy duck.

◖ Open all year ⤢ On A4104 half-way between Little Malvern and Welland. Private car park ⤶ 1 single, 2 twin, 5 double; family room available; all with bathroom/WC exc single with shower/WC; TV, room service, hair-dryer, direct-dial telephone ⌁ Dining-room, bar, lounge, conservatory, garden; conference facilities (max 8 people residential); croquet; early suppers for children; toys, baby-listening ⅙ No wheelchair access ● Dogs in bedrooms and conservatory only; smoking in bar and conservatory only ☐ Access, Delta, Switch, Visa £ Single £42 to £44, single occupancy of twin/double £50 to £52, twin/double £80 to £82; deposit required. Set D £17 to £18, Sun L £15. Special breaks available

WELLS Somerset   map 2

Swan Hotel

11 Sadler Street, Wells BA5 2RX
TEL: (01749) 678877   FAX: (01749) 677647

Olde-worlde hotel superbly positioned immediately opposite Wells Cathedral.

The Swan Hotel has a thoroughly covetable position immediately opposite the wonderful West Front of Wells Cathedral. The best room in the house has to be Room 40, where a four-poster bed is positioned to look straight out at the cathedral. Sadly, buildings on the other side of the road obscure the view from the lounge and dining-room; perhaps to make up for this the dining-room's walls provide a showcase for a collection of costumes worn by actor Henry Irving. Three-course dinner menus err on the side of caution, with starters like chilled honeydew melon or chef's pâté maison, and a variety of roasts to follow. The Swan is actually bigger than it appears from the outside, and its rambling corridors lead to a variety of styles of bedroom, some of them old and wood-panelled, others recently created out of an adjacent cottage and much more modern in style. This being a hotel that sees a lot of business travellers, there are several inviting single rooms – even one with a four-poster. Once the Wells relief road is completed, some of the traffic that currently thunders along Sadler Street should be siphoned safely away from the hotel.

◗ Open all year   ⊿ In the centre of town, opposite the cathedral. Private car park
🛏 9 single, 10 twin, 11 double, 8 four-poster; family rooms available; most with bathroom/WC, some with shower/WC; TV, room service, direct-dial telephone, clock radio; hair-dryer on request, trouser press in all single rooms   ✇ Dining-room, 2 bars, lounge, TV room, drying-room, garden; conference facilities (max 100 people incl up to 24 residential); squash; early suppers for children; babysitting, baby-listening
  ふ Wheelchair access to hotel, dining-room and WC (M,F), 2 ground-floor bedrooms
● None   ▭ Access, Amex, Delta, Diners, Switch, Visa   £ Single £68, single occupancy of twin/double £73, twin/double £88, four-poster £95, family room £95; deposit required. Set L £12.50, D £16.50. Special breaks available

---

WELWYN GARDEN CITY Hertfordshire   map 3

Tewin Bury Farmhouse

Tewin, Nr Welwyn Garden City AL6 0JB
TEL: (01438) 717793   FAX: (01438) 840440

COUNTY
HOTEL
OF THE
YEAR

A complex of rooms scattered about a working farm, with a popular and lively restaurant.

Every year Tewin Bury Farm seems to change and develop. Thanks to the down-to-earth expertise of Angela and Vaughan Williams and their growing number of staff, a business that started off as a farm shop has become a slickly run hotel and conference centre. Sixteen bedrooms occupy converted barns and chicken sheds and all overlook the comings-and-goings of the farmyard. Six are split-level with small sitting-rooms upstairs, though all have plenty of space and are stylishly furnished in bright spring colours or classy muted fabrics. The modern décor sits well with rustic beams and exposed brick walls, and the rooms are well equipped with good-sized smart bathrooms. Moles, a former tractor shed with a tall ceiling, has perhaps the greatest sense of space, while Hedgehogs, at the end of a block, was our inspector's favourite. Tewin Bury Pie, the hotel's restaurant, is informal, serving up solidly English dishes such as braised rabbit or lamb cutlets, and home-made puddings. A word of warning – at weekends, especially in summer, the farm can be busy with weddings and guests who stay overnight, and is then not for people seeking peace and quiet.

◗ Closed Chr to New Year ⤴ Take B1000 towards Hertford, farmhouse is on left. Private car park ⤴ 1 single, 3 twin, 3 double, 3 four-poster, 6 suites; some in annexe; all with bathroom/WC; TV, room service, hair-dryer, trouser press, direct-dial telephone ✓ Restaurant, bar, lounge, drying-room, garden; conference facilities (max 70 people incl up to 16 residential); fishing, clay-pigeon shooting, table tennis, snooker; early suppers for children; babysitting, baby-listening ⅙ Wheelchair access to hotel, restaurant and WC (unisex), 13 ground-floor bedrooms, 1 specially equipped for disabled people ● No dogs in public rooms ▭ Access, Amex, Delta, Switch, Visa £ Single/single occupancy of twin/double £63, twin/double £63, four-poster/family room/suite £72. Set D £14 to £16; alc L £10

WEM Shropshire   map 5

Soulton Hall

Nr Wem, Shrewsbury SY4 5RS
TEL: (01939) 232786   FAX: (01939) 234097

Homely rooms in a grand historic house on a working farm.

The combination of topiaries, pillared portico, escutcheoned entrance and ponies in the paddock all spell grand, but the minute you enter the door you'll find that there's nothing at all stuffy about the Ashtons, who will welcome you warmly, and do everything possible to arrange a pleasant stay. The house has been in the family for more than a quarter of a millennium, but there's nothing remotely shrine-like or reverential about it, and the plain décor of the public rooms, with their frankly chaotic colour schemes and mixture of antiques and homely pieces, encourages visitors to kick off their shoes and relax. Plates and tankards line the dresser in the sitting-room, while the bar has the sort of garden-style bamboo furniture found in conservatories the length of the kingdom. The grandest public room is the dining-room, where a regal lion is the focus of a carved fireplace, though even here spindle-back chairs confer an unassuming air. Dinner is a hearty business: perhaps home-made farmhouse soup followed by lemon sorbet served with sparkling wine, a curiosity like 'Mrs Fettiplace's mutton pie' (an old English recipe of 1556), then dessert. There's good old furniture in the comfortable but unflashy main-house bedrooms. A more co-ordinated, cottagey approach prevails in the delightful coach-house rooms.

See the inside front cover for a brief explanation of how to use the Guide.

◗ Open all year ☒ 1½ miles east of Wem on B5065. Private car park ⛛ 6 twin/double; family rooms available; some in annexe; all with bathroom/WC; TV, room service, hair-dryer, direct-dial telephone ✅ Dining-room, bar, lounge, drying-room, garden; fishing, archery, clay-pigeon shooting, musket shooting; early suppers for children; babysitting, baby-listening ♿ No wheelchair access ● No dogs in public rooms and in bedrooms by arrangement; smoking in 1 public room only
▭ Access, Amex, Diners, Visa £ Single occupancy of twin/double £32 to £39, twin/double £50 to £63, family room from £62; deposit required. Set D £16.50 to £18. Special breaks available

---

WEOBLEY Hereford & Worcester   map 5

Ye Olde Salutation Inn

Market Pitch, Weobley HR4 8SJ
TEL: (01544) 318443   FAX: (01544) 318216

Film-set rustic pub in a picture-postcard village.

The local tourist board has devised a trail around the picturesque black and white villages of Herefordshire, but it's hard to believe that they can come any prettier or any more special than Weobley, where the plasterwork is milky white and the timber braces bible-black. The Salutation is well named, because you'll instantly greet it as the pub of your dreams – absurdly pretty, with skew-whiff timbers and quaint off-centre walls. Be warned, it's likely to be love at first sight.

As with all the best rural hostelries, the pub is the heart of the enterprise. Don't get tipsy, or the combination of sloping floors, uneven walls and haphazardly angled beams will have you adopting a sailor's gait. The exposed stone has been dressed up in *de rigueur* rustic style, with antlers plus lots of copper, wall-mounted plates and suspended tankards. Drinkers jostle for the settles or spindle-back chairs and can order from a bar menu which offers the likes of prawn and red pepper salad, and roast loin of pork. Things move up a notch in the slightly more formal Oak Room Restaurant, where the tables are set with crisp white linen, and you might choose pan-fried breast of pigeon, fillet of salmon with noodles on a soya and ginger cream, and sticky toffee pudding. Upstairs, the residents' lounge mirrors the quaintness and skewed perspectives of the bar. The bedrooms have bags of character, chintzy décor and a generous sprinkling of antiques.

◗ Closed 25 Dec; restaurant closed Sun eve & Mon ☒ In Weobley village centre at top end of Broad Street. Private car park ⛛ 2 single, 2 twin, 2 double, 1 four-poster; family room available; some in annexe; 3 with bathroom/WC, 4 with shower/WC; TV, hair-dryer, trouser press ✅ Restaurant, 2 bars, lounge, TV room, conservatory; conference facilities (max 20 people non-residential); gym ♿ No wheelchair access ● No children under 14 exc in annexe; dogs in annexe and 1 bar only; no smoking in bedrooms or restaurant ▭ Access, Amex, Delta, Diners, Switch, Visa
£ Single/single occupancy of twin/double £35, twin/double £60, four-poster £65, family room from £86; deposit required. Alc L, D £22; bar meals available. Special breaks available

---

Reports are welcome on any hotel, whether or not it is in the Guide.

WEST BAGBOROUGH Somerset　　　　　　　　　　　　　map 2

Higher House

West Bagborough, Taunton TA4 3EF
TEL: (01823) 432996　FAX: (01823) 433568

---

*A partially seventeenth-century house offering B&B on the fringe of
a Quantocks village.*

'Superb value for money,' is how one reader described a stay at Higher House, a
fine, mullion-windowed stone house dating back to the seventeenth century
which overlooks the vale of Taunton and the Brendon hills; you'll find it just at
the point where West Bagborough fades out into the countryside. With only
three fairly simply furnished bedrooms, Breezie and Martin Eyre run a small
family enterprise which quickly fills up, but the existence of an outdoor, heated
pool suggests the sort of comfort that has brought it such accolades. In theory,
Higher House offers bed and breakfast and self-catering arrangements only, but
the Eyres happily rustle up dinner on request: a satisfied guest praised the
'excellent food...all cooked using fresh local produce.' Those keen on ceramics
will be pleased to note that there's a pottery in the village, just minutes down the
road.

◑ Open all year　⚡ Off A358 from Taunton, Higher House is the last house on the
right before you leave West Bagborough. Private car park ⤙ 2 twin, 1 double;
family room available; all with bathroom/WC; TV, direct-dial telephone
✦ Dining-room, lounge, drying-room, garden; heated outdoor swimming-pool, tennis;
early suppers for children; babysitting　⚲ No wheelchair access　⬤ No dogs; no
smoking　⊟ None accepted　£ Single occupancy of twin/double £25, twin/double
£45; deposit required. Set D from £14.50

WEST BEXINGTON Dorset　　　　　　　　　　　　　　map 2

Manor Hotel

Beach Road, West Bexington, Nr Dorchester DT2 9DF
TEL: (01308) 897616　FAX: (01308) 897035

A cheerful, family-run hotel with sea views and good food.

Jayne and Richard Childs' pretty, light-stone manor, which stands above
terraced gardens on the crest of a hill overlooking Chesil Beach, is run with a
relaxed and informal efficiency. This year, readers were unanimous in their
praise of the staff: 'very good and friendly,' wrote one; 'only too anxious to be
helpful,' wrote another, who was particularly impressed by their flexibility
regarding meal times. Though unassuming in style, the Manor Hotel has some
pretensions: it apparently features in the Domesday Book, while the dark
panelling in the hallway (actually imported from another house in the village),
and the inglenook fireplace in the restaurant, give it a venerable, ancient
atmosphere. Much of the house, however, is more recent, and is decorated in a
more contemporary style than the entrance and restaurant suggest. Prints of
horses and jockeys, riding tackle and horseshoes are evidence of the Childs'
enthusiasm – even the complimentary chocolates are shaped like horses. Other

welcoming extras in the fresh, cheerful bedrooms, which sport antique pine furnishings and bold shades of yellow, pink and blue, include sherry, fruit and a selection of books. Menus offer imaginative variations on traditional fare: steak, kidney, oyster and Guinness pie, or maybe roast partridge with port and grapes.

◐ Open all year ▯ Off B3127 Bridport to Weymouth coastal road. Private car park ⬚ 1 single, 3 twin, 8 double, 1 family room; most with bathroom/WC, some with shower/WC; TV, room service, hair-dryer, direct-dial telephone ✧ Restaurant, bar, 2 lounges, conservatory, garden; conference facilities (max 60 people incl up to 13 residential); early suppers for children; baby-listening, outdoor games ♿ No wheelchair access ● No dogs in bedrooms ▭ Access, Amex, Delta, Diners, Visa £ Single £47 to £51, twin/double £80 to £86, family room from £88; deposit required. Set L £12.50 to £14.50, D £18 to £21. Special breaks available

---

WESTDEAN East Sussex map 3

Old Parsonage

Westdean, Nr Seaford BN25 4AL
TEL: (01323) 870432

A magnificent medieval house in a hidden hamlet.

Enthusiastic visitors to the Old Parsonage seem to run out of superlatives when writing about their experience of this wonderful haven from the hustle and bustle of modern life. The idyllic hamlet of Westdean nestles at the edge of Friston Forest, between the chalk ridges of the South Downs and within walking distance of the Cuckmere Estuary and the chalk cliffs of the Seven Sisters. Built by monks from Wilmington Priory in 1280, its flint walls are now home to Raymond and Angela Woodhams, whose attentiveness and sincere interest in their guests have won comments like: 'A perfect place to spend a weekend of indulgence.' The tremendous character of the house is due to the incredibly well-preserved original features: chalk block walls, warped oak beams and stone fireplaces which create a truly historic atmosphere. The bedrooms all exude enormous character, enhanced by fresh flowers and lovely bathrooms. The Hall and Solar are both reached via stone spiral staircases and have impressive high timbered roofs. Views look over the churchyard to the Norman belltower. Angela's breakfasts, which can be taken in the garden as a special treat, come in for yet more praise – 'leaves no wish unfulfilled,' commented one reader impressed by the array of bacon, eggs, sausage, croissants, toast, home-made jams and honey. 'Don't tell anyone,' chides one correspondent – sorry, but we've given the secret away!

◐ Closed Chr & New Year ▯ Off A259 Brighton to Hastings road, east of Seaford. Private car park ⬚ 1 twin, 1 double, 1 four-poster; 2 with bathroom/WC, twin with shower/WC; hair-dryer ✧ Lounge, library, garden ♿ No wheelchair access ● No children under 12; no dogs; no smoking ▭ None accepted £ Single occupancy of twin/double £35 to £42, twin/double £50 to £60, four-poster £65

WEST DOWN Devon   map 1

Long House

The Square, West Down EX34 8NF
TEL: (01271) 863242 (AND FAX)

Delightful Devon long house at the heart of the small village.

Situated in the centre of West Down, the black and white half-timbered Long House has had a chequered history to match its position at a crossroads. In its time it has served as a smithy and as a post office-cum-shop, and the tea shop which now doubles as the dining-room still has hooks in the ceiling from which produce used to hang. With only four bedrooms, this is a cosy place to stay, and Pauline and Rob Hart look after their guests as the potential friends that many of them become. Pre-dinner drinks are served in a comfortable lounge with a big log fire and lots of newspapers and magazines. Dinners come without choice, thereby removing the need to mull over menus. That's just as well, since it leaves more time to concentrate on a wine list that benefits from Rob's years as a wine dealer. You are likely to be served something like stuffed mushrooms followed by roast duck on a bed of rice, with a traditional English dessert like apple charlotte to finish. You eat to an accompaniment of rousing classical music. The bedrooms are bigger than you might expect, with space for interesting fittings like brass beds. *En suite* facilities come liberally festooned with plants.

◑ Closed Nov to Feb ⓩ ½ mile off the A361 Barnstaple to Ilfracombe road, 4 miles from Woolacombe Bay. On-street parking ⓛ→ 1 twin, 3 double; all with bathroom/WC exc 1 double with shower/WC; TV, limited room service, radio; hair-dryer on request ⓥ Restaurant, dining-room, lounge, drying-room, garden; early suppers for children; toys, baby-listening ⓖ No wheelchair access ⬤ No dogs; smoking discouraged ▭ Access, Visa ⓔ Single occupancy of twin/double £31, twin/double £55; deposit required. Set D £15.50; alc L £7.50. Special breaks available

---

WEST MALLING Kent   map 3

Scott House ☆

37 High Street, West Malling ME19 6QH
TEL: (01732) 841380   FAX: (01732) 870025

A very elegant yet friendly and relaxed B&B in a small historic town.

Scott House is a white Grade-II listed Georgian town house set on the High Street in West Malling, a small bustling town in Kent. From the moment you step inside Margaret and Ernest Smith's antique shop, which is below the guest rooms, you are made to feel very welcome indeed. The elegant drawing-room, with its wooden floorboards, pink Chinese rugs, marble fireplace and antique furnishings miraculously transforms into a perfect setting for breakfast when the specially chosen tables ingeniously unfold into much larger ones. Upstairs is a huge sitting-room with comfy sofas and chairs for the guests to use in the evenings. The bedrooms themselves, of which there are only three, are a little on the small side but don't feel cramped. They are all individually and very stylishly decorated – Room 1 is the larger double room with a yellow floral canopied bed and matching curtains at the two windows. In the corridor outside is a small fridge in the wall stocked with fresh milk and mineral water, and also an illuminated bell to alert Margaret and Ernest should you need help during the night.

◑ Closed Chr   ⊿ West Malling is on A228, ¼ mile from A20 and 1 mile from M20 Junction 4. On-street parking   ⊨ 1 twin, 2 double; all with shower/WC; TV, hair-dryer, trouser press   ⊘ Dining-room, lounge   ⅙ No wheelchair access ● No children under 10; no dogs; no smoking   ⊟ Access, Delta, Switch, Visa ⒠ Single occupancy of twin/double £39, twin/double £49; deposit required

---

WEST PORLOCK Somerset   map 1

Bales Mead

West Porlock TA24 8NX
TEL: (01643) 862565

Immaculate small B&B in a delightful setting close to Porlock Harbour.

Even if you didn't know that Peter Clover was an illustrator, you'd soon guess that someone of artistic disposition lived at Bales Mead when you spotted the lovely stencilling in the bedrooms and in the brand new bathroom with a power shower. Stephen Blue's musical interests are also apparent: in the lounge a grand piano is much more conspicuous than the tiny television set. In fact, one of the nicest things about staying here is feeling that you're staying in someone's lovingly cared-for home. The setting is another huge plus. Bossington and Selworthy, the two main bedrooms, look out on lovely sea views or on a garden backed by hills. A third bedroom can be made available if a party is staying and the guests do not mind sharing a bathroom. All three rooms are individually decorated and the fresh flowers, fruit, sherry and Body Shop toiletries are indicative of the care that goes into making guests welcome. Stephen and Peter don't serve dinner but make up for it with lavish breakfasts that ring the changes through kedgeree, fish-cakes and eggs and bacon to top up fruit compote, fresh fruit salad and pastries. Ten minutes' walk in one direction brings you to Porlock village, ten minutes in the other to the harbour.

◑ Open all year   ⊿ Mid-way between Porlock village and Porlock Weir; follow signs to West Porlock. Private car park   ⊨ 3 double; 1 with bathroom/WC, 1 with shower/WC; TV, hair-dryer, radio   ⊘ Dining-room, lounge, drying-room, garden ⅙ No wheelchair access   ● No children under 14; no dogs; no smoking   ⊟ None accepted   ⒠ Single occupancy of twin/double £35 to £38, twin/double £50; deposit required

---

Many hotels offer special rates for stays of a few nights or more. It is worth enquiring when you book.

Wensleydale Heifer

West Witton, Wensleydale DL8 4LS
TEL: (01969) 622322   FAX: (01969) 624183

A cosy Dales pub with simple rooms but accomplished cooking.

The appearance of this lovely whitewashed inn, situated opposite the green in a quiet Dales village, is deceptive. Looking for all the world like a two-up, two-down cottage, it actually stretches far enough back from the road to encompass a front lounge and snug, a bistro, a restaurant and a back bar. Both lounge and bistro have beamed ceilings and a cosy atmosphere. The restaurant, which features a rather rustic, whitewashed stone wall, is much larger and brighter, and looks out on to the apple trees in the garden. The bar and bistro share the same menu, which includes dishes such as mixed grills, bangers and mash, and one or two more adventurous ideas – broccoli and hazelnut crêpes, for example – while the main dinner menu has been praised as having a 'good choice...excellent quality.'

The bedrooms are simple, with wood-chip walls and basic furniture, and one reader complained of a shower that leaked badly. The Gallops room does have a fine four-poster bed but, by having just one small window, is lacking in natural light. Room 15, in the Old Reading Room across the road, features french windows that open on to the garden.

◑ Open all year ↗ At the west end of the village of West Witton on A684 Leyburn to Hawes road. Private car park ⇱ 4 twin, 7 double, 3 four-poster, 1 family room; some in annexe; most with bathroom/WC, 3 with shower/WC; TV, hair-dryer, direct-dial telephone ✓ 2 restaurants, bar, lounge, garden; early suppers for children; baby-listening ⴺ No wheelchair access ● None ▭ Access, Amex, Delta, Diners, Switch, Visa £ Single occupancy of twin/double £50, twin/double £70, four-poster £80, family room £90; deposit required. Set L £11.50, D £17.50; bistro meals available. Special breaks available

---

Guy Wells

Eastgate, Whaplode, Spalding PE12 6TZ
TEL: (01406) 422239

Flowers are the talking point in this restful, no-smoking guesthouse in the Fens.

Fields and greenhouses filled with daffodils, lilies and tulips surround this creeper-covered Queen Anne farmhouse and its ample garden; Anne and Richard Thompson grow flowers commercially, and Richard is happy to show guests around the farm. Naturally, their home is full of flowers too, and floral fabrics and pictures continue the theme. Just as eye-catching are the displays of fine china in the cosy, beamed sitting-room and dining-room from Anne's grandparents' shop in nearby Spalding. Anne's cooking relies on home-grown vegetables and free-range eggs from their own hens. In order to savour her substantial and good-value dinners and breakfasts, you may have to share a table with other guests. Lacy and candlewick bedspreads, along with a few Victorian antiques, typify the homely, pleasantly old-fashioned bedrooms. Only the largest and most attractive has *en suite* facilities, while the smallest has a half-tester bed. That Guy Wells receives lots of returning visitors bears out the fact that the Thompsons make warm and considerate but unpushy hosts.

◑ Closed Chr ⏻ 2 miles west of Holbeach on A151, the farm is the first house on left in Eastgate Lane in Whaplode. Private car park ⛟ 1 twin, 2 double; family room available; 1 with shower/WC ⌀ Dining-room, lounge, garden ♿ No wheelchair access ⊖ No children under 10; no smoking; no dogs ⊟ None accepted
£ Single occupancy of twin/double £20 to £29, twin/double £34 to £40, family room from £50; deposit required. Set D £10 to £12. Special breaks available

---

WHEDDON CROSS Somerset   map 1

Raleigh Manor

Wheddon Cross, Nr Dunster TA24 7BB
TEL: (01643) 841484

A small, friendly hotel with panoramic views standing isolated in the middle of fields.

Raleigh Manor is so cut off from the road that in order to reach it you must first bump down a farm track and cut across two cattle grids, while lazy sheep look on in bewilderment. Once you get there, you'll find that it looks out over the foothills of the Brendons, and that the only sounds are those of the birds and running water from a nearby stream. The Pipers have been hard at work refurbishing the bedrooms, the best of which, the Squire's Room, boasts a half-tester bed and a big bay window. There's still one small single with a shower, but all the other bedrooms now have baths. Downstairs, the dining-room has swapped places with the lounge – a cosy room focused on a log fire. There's a second lounge – more like a library – at the front of the house, which is piled high with books and games. Jenny Piper has opted for a fairly straightforward set evening meal – perhaps something like home-made leek and Stilton soup, breast of chicken in a cranberry and red-wine sauce, followed by a steamed golden pudding with glacé fruits – but discusses guests' likes and dislikes with them over a welcoming cup of tea on arrival. In the hall, there's a fine, embroidered picture of Raleigh Manor, stitched by Chris Piper's mother Eileen, who also created the roundels and the wall hangings that decorate each of the bedrooms.

◑ Closed mid-Nov to mid-Mar ⏻ Turn left 200 yards north of Wheddon Cross down a private road. Hotel is 800 yards past Watercombe Farm, across the fields. Private car park ⛟ 1 single, 2 twin, 3 double, 1 four-poster; all with bathroom/WC exc single with shower/WC; TV, hair-dryer, radio ⌀ Dining-room, lounge, library, conservatory, garden ♿ No wheelchair access ⊖ No children under 5; no dogs in public rooms; smoking in library only ⊟ Access, Visa £ Single/single occupancy of twin/double £29, twin/double £58, four-poster £70; deposit required. Set D £15.50. Special breaks available

WHIMPLE **Devon**

map 1

Woodhayes

Whimple, Nr Exeter EX5 2TD
TEL: (01404) 822237   FAX: (01404) 822337

Immaculate rural retreat with warm welcome and good food.

As you sweep along the drive leading to Woodhayes you'll set off a tripwire, alerting hostess Katherine Rendle to your imminent arrival and ensuring you won't be left hanging about in the hall. That ready welcome typifies a small hotel which is big on comfort, its bedrooms equipped with soft sofas and armchairs, its bathrooms large enough to linger in. Frank and Katherine Rendle are trained chefs so it's hardly surprising to find that good food plays a crucial role in the welcome, with afternoon tea, cakes and scones included in the room rates. The five-course dinner menus (no choices, but Katherine will check they suit you before serving up) feature dishes like courgette soup with red pepper cream, roast fillet of monkfish niçoise and delicious home-made ice-creams. Even breakfasts are special, with a choice of Indian, Chinese and herbal teas, fresh croissants and even fried bananas. With the exception of the small flagstoned ex-kitchen bar where drinks are served across an old haberdasher's counter in front of a fire, Woodhayes is unusually cohesive, the décor of the lounges, dining-room and bedrooms strong on warm peaches and pinks, flourishing houseplants colonising the hall.

◑ Closed 23 to 26 Dec   ⊿ Turn off A30 Exeter to Honiton road at sign for Whimple; hotel is just before the village. Private car park   ⇨ 3 twin, 3 double; all with bathroom/WC; TV, room service, hair-dryer, direct-dial telephone, radio; tea/coffee on request   ⊘ Dining-room, bar, 2 lounges, garden; early suppers for children   ♿ No wheelchair access   ⚫ No children under 12; no dogs; no smoking in dining-room   ▭ Access, Amex, Delta, Diners, Switch, Visa   £ Single occupancy of twin/double £65, twin/double £95. Set L £17.50, D £27.50. Special breaks available

---

WHITEWELL **Lancashire**

map 8

Inn at Whitewell

Whitewell, Forest of Bowland, Nr Clitheroe BB7 3AT
TEL: (01200) 448222   FAX: (01200) 448298

Idiosyncratic inn, rooms of great character, magnificent setting.

Richard Bowman's highly distinctive hotel is a splendid stone, mullion-windowed inn by a bend in the River Huddle, with a little village green to the front and the shallow waters babbling off down the vale behind. The flagstoned passageways are lined with paintings, prints and cartoons; the woody bars and lounges are the last resting place of assorted wildlife; and huntin', shootin' and fishin' bric-à-brac is tucked away in every available corner and cranny. Six of the 11 rooms look down the river. Stripped pine, Victorian bathrooms, fine art prints and antique furnishings are the general order of things, and some rooms are equipped with top-of-the-range hi-fi equipment, video players (films available at reception), Bakelite telephones and, for a small supplement, can be suffused with the rich smell of peat smoke from an open fireplace. The bathroom in Room 8 is particularly splendid, while Room 11 has perhaps the finest of the river views through its french windows. Mr Bowman's hand is also evident on the paperwork, with illuminating comments made on the well-balanced wine list and menus. In the bar you might find smoked salmon 'as good or better than any you have eaten before' or bangers and champ (mashed potato with spring onions) and cheeses 'made by people in beards and sandals'. Goosnargh duck breast with redcurrant gravy or medium-rare Bowland lamb could feature in the restaurant.

◑ Open all year ▱ Whitewell is 6 miles north-west of Clitheroe. Private car park
⊨ 3 twin, 5 double, 2 four-poster, 1 suite; family rooms available; all with bathroom/WC; TV, room service, direct-dial telephone, radio, cassette player; CD player and VCR in some rooms; hair-dryer/trouser press on request; no tea/coffee-making facilities in rooms ⊘ Restaurant, bar, lounge, drying-room, garden; conference facilities (max 150 people incl up to 11 residential); early suppers for children; babysitting, baby-listening ♿ No wheelchair access ● None
▱ Access, Amex, Diners, Switch, Visa £ Single occupancy of twin/double £49 to £55, twin/double/four-poster £65 to £72, suite £93; deposit required. Alc L £9, D £22; bar meals available (prices valid till mid-1997)

WICKHAM Hampshire

map 2

Old House

The Square, Wickham PO17 5JG
TEL: (01329) 833049   FAX: (01329) 833672

An unfussy village hotel with friendly proprietors and a strong French influence.

Richard and Annie Skipwith run this fine early Georgian hotel in their own particular style. They have chosen a simple and bright provincial French approach for the public rooms, a regional French style for the cuisine and a traditional oak-beamed country influence for the bedrooms. The bar, good for pre-dinner drinks, has a wonderful carved old sideboard which has been customised for serving drinks. However, the restaurant is the focal point of the hotel and is to be found in a converted barn at the rear of the house with french windows opening out on to a small lawned garden. Herbs are grown for the kitchen, which prepares such delicacies as twice-baked soufflé of goat's cheese served on a salad of slices of sun-dried tomatoes, marinated black olives from Nice, baby spinach and corn, and fresh turbot lightly grilled, served with a warm vinaigrette of extra-virgin olive oil, ceps and garden tarragon. Service is friendly, as Richard himself doubles as a waiter in the evenings. The bedrooms are comfortable and flowery with old-fashioned furniture and low ceilings; Room 6 has the edge for character with its sloping roof, exposed beams and bold floral wallpaper.

Please let us know if an establishment has changed hands.

○ Closed 2 weeks Chr, 2 weeks summer, 1 week Easter and bank holidays; restaurant closed Sun eve ⟳ 3 miles north of Fareham at junction of B2177 and A32. Private car park ⟲ 3 single, 3 twin, 5 double, 1 family room; some in annexe; all with bathroom/WC; TV, room service, hair-dryer, trouser press, direct-dial telephone; tea/coffee-making facilities in annexe rooms only ✓ Restaurant, bar, 2 lounges, garden; conference facilities (max 10 people residential/non-residential); early suppers for children; baby-listening ⟳ No wheelchair access ● No dogs
⊟ Access, Amex, Diners, Visa £ Single £70 to £75, twin/double £80 to £90, family room from £85; deposit required. Continental B £6, cooked B £10; set L, D £30. Special breaks available

---

WIDEGATES Cornwall

map 1

Coombe Farm

Widegates, Nr Looe PL13 1QN
TEL: (01503) 240223 FAX: (01503) 240895

Pleasant 1920s house with interesting fittings and comfortable family rooms.

In spring, a double row of daffodils line up like sentinels to welcome you along the drive to Coombe Farm. At the door several dogs and/or cats will probably emerge to add their greeting. Coombe Farm is a thoroughly homely place which nevertheless manages to find space for all sorts of interesting talking points: look out for the cross-written Victorian letter on the stairs and for the salad servers big enough for a giant in Room 8. The bedrooms in the house are simply furnished and come equipped with showers; there's a large communal bathroom for tub devotees. But the nicest room is not in the house at all, but in a separate, three-bedroomed annexe. Also in the grounds is a games room intended for children, 'although the ones who really enjoy it are the oldies,' laughs hostess Sally Low. Her four-course dinners steer clear of the new-fangled in favour of old friends like home-made soups, roasts and filling puddings. Afterwards you can drink your coffee in front of the fire in a lounge overlooked by a dovecote.

○ Closed Nov to Feb ⟳ On B3253, 3½ miles east of Looe and just south of Widegates village. Private car park ⟲ 3 twin, 3 double, 4 family rooms; some in annexe; all with shower/WC; TV, hair-dryer, direct-dial telephone ✓ Dining-room, bar, lounge, games room, garden; outdoor heated swimming-pool, croquet
⟳ Wheelchair access to hotel (1 step) and dining-room, 5 ground-floor bedrooms
● No children under 5; no dogs; no smoking ⊟ Amex, Delta, Diners, Switch, Visa
£ Single occupancy of twin/double £20 to £26, twin/double £40 to £52, family room from £55; deposit required. Set D £14; packed lunches available. Special breaks available

---

Don't expect to turn up at a small hotel assuming that a room will be available. It's always best to telephone in advance.

We mention those hotels that don't accept dogs; guide dogs, however, are almost always an exception. Telephone ahead to make sure.

WILLITON **Somerset**   map 2

White House

11 Long Street, Williton TA4 4QW
TEL: (01984) 632306/632777

*Stylish Georgian villa convenient for Minehead and the Quantocks,
with imaginative menu and wine list.*

You need to keep your eyes peeled to spot the White House as you whip through
Williton, but the palm trees that look as if they've strayed from the Riviera give
the game away. It seems only right, then, that the White House sports shuttered
château-style windows despite its situation right on the A39. Dinner menus,
with three or four choices for each course, also boast a French twist although
standard English favourites like Gressingham duck usually crop up alongside
more unexpected Californian dishes like black-baked chicken with mango salsa
and sweet-potato purée. Commendably, Kay and Dick Smith put as much care
into offering a decent range of house wines as they do into selecting pricier
labels. The recently refurbished bedrooms sport some interesting bedheads and
cane furniture although those at the front will inevitaby suffer some traffic noise,
as will the bar and lounge downstairs. The three rooms in the rear courtyard are
likely to be quieter.

◑ Closed early Nov to mid-May ⬈ On right-hand side on entering Williton from A39
towards Minehead. Private car park ⬳ 4 twin, 8 double; some in annexe; most with
bathroom/WC; TV, hair-dryer, direct-dial telephone ⌀ Restaurant, bar, lounge,
study ♿ No wheelchair access ⊖ No dogs or smoking in restaurant; dogs in
some bedrooms only ▭ None accepted £ Single occupancy of twin/double £32
to £50, twin/double £56 to £84; deposit required. Set D £28. Special breaks available

---

WILMCOTE **Warwickshire**   map 5

Pear Tree Cottage

Church Road, Wilmcote, Stratford-upon-Avon CV37 9UX
TEL: (01789) 205889   FAX: (01789) 262862

*Warwickshire's top B&B is an Elizabethan house that's been in the
same family since 1923.*

The *Guide*'s mailbag confirms Pear Tree Cottage as the area's number one B&B.
The sight of the picturesque, black-timbered building, set in an acre of
well-tended gardens, raises high expectations on arrival. The interior, all beams
and flagstone floors, doesn't disappoint. The Manders have furnished the rooms
with some lovely antiques that include a trio of wonderful collections in the
dining-room – of Staffordshire china, toast racks and egg cups. A number of the
super bedrooms have brass beds. Though some occupy a modern extension,
they're designed with old beams and quarry tiles and generally with such
panache that they're hardly less characterful than those in the old part of the
building. The Rose Room is popular for having its own front door and what is in
effect a private patio.

Pear Tree Cottage's most imaginative features are two small but well-equipped guest kitchens, used by some just to stock cold drinks, but by others for slap-up meals. However, don't forgo the Manders' breakfasts: 'the best I have ever eaten in a restaurant,' judges one eulogistic reader.

◗ Closed Chr to 2 Jan ⟋ 1 mile west of the A3400, 3½ miles north-west of Stratford-upon-Avon. Private car park ⟞⟍ 2 twin, 4 double, 1 family room; some in annexe; 3 with bathroom/WC, 4 with shower/WC; TV, hair-dryer ⊘ Dining-room, lounge, TV room, garden ஂ No wheelchair access ● No children under 3; dogs in annexe rooms only; no smoking in dining-room ⊟ None accepted £ Single occupancy of twin/double £30, twin/double £45, family room £60

WIMBORNE MINSTER Dorset   map 2

Beechleas

17 Poole Road, Wimborne Minster BH21 1QA
TEL: (01202) 841684   FAX: (01202) 849344

A variety of immaculately maintained, comfortable rooms are offered in this smart town house.

Set behind a smart, green fence, this handsome, red-brick, Georgian town house actually faces away from the main road (some traffic noise is audible from the walled garden and the bedrooms at the rear of the house) on to a much quieter side street. The spruce façade is matched by a spotless interior, in which the subtle tones and subdued lighting complement the house's many original features and create a warm ambience. Dinners are served in more contemporary surroundings: a bright, pagoda-style conservatory that juts out into the immaculate walled garden. Using organic ingredients wherever possible, the dishes mix French influences with English tradition, and may include home-made soup or pâté, followed by beef cooked with horseradish and rosemary, lamb served with a redcurrant, red-wine and mint sauce, or salmon with fresh lime and chive butter. The service is friendly and efficient.

There's a good variety of bedrooms, all with spotless, well-equipped bathrooms. The exceptionally high ceilings give the first-floor rooms a light, airy feel, while the attic rooms are cosier and more cottagey. Perhaps the nicest rooms of all are those in the original coach house and the 'lodge' (a recent replica), on opposite corners of the car park; those on the top floor, which have vaulted ceilings and beams, are especially attractive.

◗ Closed 24 Dec to 12 Jan ⟋ Take A31 to Wimborne Minster. At the roundabout, take B3073. At the next roundabout turn left on A349 towards Poole. Beechleas is on the right. Private car park ⟞⟍ 2 twin, 7 double; family rooms available; some in annexe; all with bathroom/WC; TV, room service, hair-dryer, direct-dial telephone; radio; no tea/coffee-making facilities in rooms ⊘ Restaurant, lounge, conservatory, garden; conference facilities (max 12 people incl up to 9 residential); early suppers for children; baby-listening ஂ Wheelchair access to hotel and restaurant, 2 ground-floor bedrooms ● Dogs in bedrooms only, by arrangement; smoking in lounge only ⊟ Access, Amex, Visa £ Single occupancy of twin/double £60 to £80, twin/double £75 to £95, family room from £75. Set D £20. Special breaks available

WINCHCOMBE **Gloucestershire**   map 5

Wesley House ☆

High Street, Winchcombe GL54 5LJ
TEL: (01242) 602366   FAX: (01242) 602405

A small, stylish medieval house with friendly owners.

Wesley House is situated in the small but thriving village of Winchcombe, in which it is well known for the excellent food served in its restaurant. The half-timbered, leaded-window building dates from 1435, and its crookedness bears testament to its age. With its beamed ceiling, log fire and sofas, the small lounge area makes a cosy place in which guests and diners can relax and enjoy a drink while trying to decide which option to choose from the menu. Typical dishes might include a warm scallop mousse served with courgette ribbons and a vermouth sauce, venison with morel mushrooms, followed by a pear and black-cherry charlotte with a calvados sorbet and poached fruit. The five twin/double bedrooms, each named after the fields surrounding Sudeley Castle, are individually decorated; there is also a single room. The front-facing Embury has a low, beamed ceiling and a sloping floor, while Almsbury (at the back) boasts a large double bed and its own balcony, where you can enjoy your breakfast in summer. Matthew Brown and Jonathan Lewis pamper their guests with crisp, beautifully laundered, bed linen and towels, and bowls of fruit are placed along the corridors from which you can help yourself.

◐ Closed 14 Jan to 12 Feb; restaurant closed Sun eve ⬈ On High Street in Winchcombe. On-street parking ⬛➔ 1 single, 2 twin, 3 double; single with bathroom/WC, rest with shower/WC TV, room service, hair-dryer, direct-dial telephone ⌀ Restaurant, bar, lounge, drying-room; early suppers for children; babysitting, baby-listening ⅙ No wheelchair access ● No dogs; no smoking in bedrooms ▭ Access, Amex, Delta, Switch, Visa ⌑£⌑ Single £59, single occupancy of twin/double £64, twin/double £110 (rates incl dinner); deposit required. Set L £14, D £23; alc L £14. Special breaks available

WINCHESTER **Hampshire**   map 2

Hotel du Vin & Bistro

14 Southgate Street, Winchester SO23 9EF
TEL: (01962) 841414   FAX: (01962) 842458

A popular hotel with cosmopolitan style, simple bright furnishings and a superb restaurant.

This beautiful Georgian hotel is in the heart of historic Winchester and has been crisply refurbished with natural materials by the impressive joint skills of Robin Hudson and chef/*sommelier* Gérard Basset. Their approach has been to combine idiosyncratic sophistication with value for money, and it has worked. The hotel has a relaxed buzzy atmosphere, from the lounge with its *trompe l'oeil* wall paintings and sisal flooring to the fine restaurant with round tables on a stripped floor. Here you might sample a wafer-thin-tomato tart with Emmental, grain mustard and rocket, followed by paillard of chicken with sage, Parma ham, buffalo mozzarella and plums. Delicious. The walls are lined with wine-related lithographs and prints, and this theme continues upstairs where each of the large bedrooms has been sponsored and decorated by a renowned wine-house. In the main building, where rooms on the second floor have cathedral views, Courvoisier rubs shoulders with such famous names as Berenger and Renault, while in the recently refurbished garden rooms, Freixenet boasts 'the biggest bath this side of the Dorchester.'

◐ Open all year　☑ In Winchester city centre. Private car park　🛏 19 double; some in annexe; all with bathroom/WC exc 1 with shower/WC; TV, hair-dryer, mini-bar, trouser press, direct-dial telephone　✓ Restaurant, bar, lounge, garden; conference facilities (max 40 people incl up to 19 residential); baby-listening　♿ Wheelchair access to hotel (1 step) and restaurant, 4 ground-floor bedrooms, 1 specially equipped for disabled people　● No dogs　▭ Access, Amex, Delta, Diners, Switch, Visa　💷 Single occupancy of twin/double £69 to £99, twin/double £69 to £99; deposit required. Continental B £4, cooked B £8; alc L, D £25

Wykeham Arms

75 Kingsgate Street, Winchester SO23 9PE
TEL: (01962) 853834　FAX: (01962) 854411

COUNTY
HOTEL
OF THE
YEAR

A hugely characterful inn in the old part of town with an excellent restaurant.

The Wykeham Arms is in a winding back-street behind the cathedral and a stone's throw from the house where Jane Austen died. Always busy, the inn is run by Anne and Graeme Jameson, who seem to have perfected the art of innkeeping. Each area of the restaurant and bar has its own name and particular character, stuffed full of engaging paraphernalia: the 'bishop's bar' comes complete with pews and a mitre; the 'watchmakers' room' used to be a shop; the 'sportsroom' is strewn with old oars, steering wheels and pictures. The food is definitely a cut above standard pub fare: on offer when we visited were starters such as salmon carpaccio with melon and ginger dressing, followed by guinea-fowl slowly cooked in cider and thyme with pearl barley risotto. For dessert you'll have to choose between such tempting delights as tipsy raspberry trifle and apricot and frangipane tart. Upstairs, bedrooms are well equipped and comfortable – Hamilton is done out in rich reds with four-feet-high beds and royal paraphernalia, while Nelson takes a more nautical tack.

◐ Closed 25 Dec　☑ Immediately south of cathedral by Kingsgate at junction of Canon Street and Kingsgate Road. Private car park　🛏 2 twin, 5 double; all with bathroom/WC; TV, hair-dryer, mini-bar, direct-dial telephone, radio　✓ 4 restaurants, 2 bars, drying-room, garden; conference facilities (max 10 people incl up to 7 residential); sauna　♿ No wheelchair access　● No children under 14; no smoking in bedrooms and 3 public rooms　▭ Access, Amex, Delta, Switch, Visa　💷 Single occupancy of twin/double £68, twin/double £78. Alc L £11, D £18

☆　*A star next to the hotel's name indicates that the establishment is new to the* Guide *this year.*

The Archway

13 College Road, Windermere LA23 1BU
TEL: (01539) 445613

Small but perfectly formed guesthouse in the centre but away from the hubbub of Windermere.

Aurea Greenhalgh's small guesthouse is a grey Lakeland-stone town house in the centre of Windermere, close to the tourist trappings but on a quieter side-street. From the front the view is of the Langdales and the Old Man of Coniston, framed by oak and copper beech trees. Since last year's *Guide*, a small single room has been converted into an *en suite* shower/dressing-room, making Laurel, with its hand-made patchwork quilt, pre-Raphaelite prints and front-facing view, the pick of four lovely guest rooms. Clover shares the front view, while Bracken and Number 1, though pleasant enough, are snugger in size and have rather compact shower rooms. Not that these disappoint: 'room comforts so homely and relaxing' are a favourite with one regular guest, who also enthused about the food and the attention. Breakfasts are something of a speciality, with Aurea providing home-made yoghurt and fruit purée, freshly pressed fruit and vegetable juices, and meats from some of the area's premium smokehouses. Organic and wholefood ingredients feature prominently, and an evening menu might find Aurea, after due consultation with her guests, preparing stuffed chicken thighs with pea lentils, or pork and pigeon pie, always followed by a good old-fashioned pudding. The country-style dining-room of stripped-pine tables and dresser stacked with china fits comfortably alongside the verdant foliage and busy fireplace tiles of the Victorian sitting-room.

○ Open all year; restaurant closed Wed & Sun eves   ↗ From Windermere Main Street turn left by Methodist church into College Road. Private car park   ⊨ 2 twin, 2 double; 1 twin with bathroom/WC, 3 with shower/WC; TV, direct-dial telephone; hair-dryer on request   ✓ Dining-room, lounge, garden; early suppers for children   ♿ No wheelchair access   ● No children under 10; no dogs; no smoking   ▭ Access, Amex, Visa   £ Single occupancy of twin/double £22 to £27, twin/double £40 to £54; deposit required. Set D £12.50. Special breaks available

Gilpin Lodge ☆

Crook Road, Nr Windermere LA23 3NE
TEL: (01539) 488818   FAX: (01539) 488058

Excellent, adventurous food at stylish small country house a few miles from Windermere.

'Our food is our obsession!' proclaims the brochure, and while the house itself is certainly stylish, and the bedrooms mightily comfortable, it is the food that should draw you to Gilpin Lodge. Cooking is adventurous, with multifarious combinations of flavours, and wide-ranging choices in a four-course menu. Our spring inspection meal consisted of a powerful and pungent venison and smoked bacon sausage with a spiced red cabbage confit, a mild mousseline of sole and smoked trout and tender roast Goosnargh duckling with caramelised lemon and lime sauce. Breakfast was cooked with equal expertise and served with friendly informality, a little more of which would have been appreciated at dinner. Bedrooms, named after local places, are generally spacious, favour lots of floral fabrics and warm colours and have plush bathrooms.

◗ Open all year   ⬿ Leave M6 at Junction 36; take A590/A591 to roundabout north of Kendal; take B5284 signposted Crook and Hawkshead and continue for 5 miles. Private car park ⬿ 3 twin, 6 double, 4 four-poster; all with bathroom/WC; TV, room service, hair-dryer, mini-bar, trouser press, direct-dial telephone, clock radio
⌗ 3 dining-rooms, 2 lounges, garden; conference facilities (max 25 people incl up to 13 residential); croquet; early suppers for children   ♿ Wheelchair access to hotel (1 step) and restaurant, 4 ground-floor bedrooms specially equipped for disabled people
⬤ No children under 7; no dogs; no smoking in dining-rooms   ▭ Access, Amex, Delta, Diners, Switch, Visa   £ Single occupancy of twin/double £65 to £85, twin/double £80 to £140, four-poster £100 to £140; deposit required. Set D £27.50, Sun L £14; alc L £15. Special breaks available

Holbeck Ghyll

Holbeck Lane, Windermere LA23 1LU
TEL: (01539) 432375   FAX: (01539) 434743

Professionally run stylish country house with great views and fine architectural details.

David and Patricia Nicholson's imposing late-Victorian hunting lodge has provoked some mixed reactions over the past year: praise for the style and the helpful service, but grumbles about the standard of some rooms. As not every window can face westwards for a panoramic view of Windermere, it's inevitable that some rooms will disappoint. And compared with a mullioned-windowed room with a private wooden balcony, like Room 6, a rear-facing room in the gables such as Room 10, despite its tasteful facelift, is going to seem relatively unspectacular. With building work going on at the time of our spring 1996 inspection, more rooms will see improvements, like a private rooftop patio for Room 8, which will give it more than its current oblique view of the distant water. Meanwhile, Rooms 1, 2, 4 and 11 should impress. Stained-glass, ornate plasterwork and gleaming Art Nouveau door handles are some of the striking features of the hallway and lounges, with more of the same in the main oak-panelled restaurant. Two new chefs have joined the team in the kitchen in 1996, working on a quite traditional and complex country-house menu with French influences and an emphasis on good local produce. More reports, please.

ℒ This denotes that you can get a twin or double room for £60 or less per night inclusive of breakfast.

Hotels in our Visitors' Book *towards the end of the* Guide *are additional hotels that may be worth a visit. Reports on these hotels are welcome.*

◑ Open all year ⤢ 3 miles north of Windermere on A591; turn right on to Holbeck Lane after Brockhole Visitors' Centre, hotel is ½ mile on left. Private car park ⇤⤍ 6 twin, 4 double, 1 four-poster, 1 family room, 2 suites; all with bathroom/WC exc 1 double with shower/WC; TV, room service, hair-dryer, trouser press, direct-dial telephone; no tea/coffee-making facilities in rooms ⬗ 2 restaurants, bar, 2 lounges, drying-room, garden; conference facilities (max 35 people incl up to 14 residential); gym, sauna, steam room, tennis, putting green, croquet; early suppers for children; babysitting, baby-listening ♿ No wheelchair access ⚫ No children under 8 in restaurants eves; no dogs in public rooms; no smoking in restaurants ▭ Access, Amex, Diners, Visa £ Single occupancy of twin/double £78 to £88, twin/double £130 to £190, four-poster/family room £140 to £190, suite £160 to £240 (rates incl dinner); deposit required. Set D £27.50/30; alc L £12.50. Special breaks available

Miller Howe

Rayrigg Road, Windermere LA23 1EY
TEL: (01539) 442536   FAX: (01539) 445664

A flamboyant country house famed for its distinctive service and cuisine.

Miller Howe is one of the country's most distinguished hotels and offers glorious views of Lake Windermere, country-house luxury and a famed cuisine. It is run along distinctive lines, and its flamboyant style may not suit all tastes. Most guests will be preoccupied by the food. The performance begins as diners gather in one of the three Edwardian lounges for canapés and a discussion of the evening's set menu (no choice is given except for dessert, although negotiations over an alternative main course are not unknown). There are two restaurants: one is caught in a 1970s split-level time warp, while the other features a *trompe-l'oeil* Tuscan landscape. The Miller Howe manner favours bombarding its guests with textures and tastes, and our spring inspection meal included baked black pudding and onion cake, served with mashed, spiced parsnips and a hazelnut-oil dressing; followed by baby halibut with basil salad and a curried leek and onion purée; and five vegetable dishes that were overpowered by the kidney gravy that accompanied the rack of lamb.

The bedrooms are supremely comfortable, with hi-fi systems, bathrobes and binoculars featuring among the extras; the only quibble we received concerned the vicissitudes of the plumbing – and the lack of a shower. Prices escalate according to the magnificence of the view.

◑ Closed Dec to Feb ⤢ On A592 between Windermere and Bowness. Private car park ⇤⤍ 8 twin, 4 double; all with bathroom/WC; TV, room service, hair-dryer, trouser press, direct-dial telephone, hi-fi; no tea/coffee-making facilities in rooms ⬗ 2 restaurants (1 air-conditioned), 3 lounges, drying-room, conservatory, garden; conference facilities (max 24 people incl up to 12 residential) ♿ No wheelchair access ⚫ No children under 8; no dogs in public rooms; no smoking in restaurants; no pipes or cigars ▭ Access, Amex, Diners, Visa £ Single occupancy of twin/double £95, twin/double £150 to £260 (rates incl dinner); deposit required. Set L £13, D £30. Special breaks available

Winteringham Fields

Silver Street, Winteringham DN15 9PF
TEL: (01724) 733096   FAX: (01724) 733898

Excellent food and comfortable accommodation at a restaurant-with-rooms near the Humber Bridge.

The minute you arrive at Winteringham Fields the young staff whisk away your bags and offer you a welcoming cup of tea. The service at this restaurant-with-rooms – last year's County Hotel of the Year for Humberside – keeps up the same high standards throughout your stay. Annie Schwab looks after front-of-house and the bedrooms in her sixteenth-century home, while her Swiss husband, Germain, does the cooking. Four of the bedrooms are in the main house while another three are in converted stables across the courtyard. With low beams – some originally ships' timbers – and solid antiques, they're spacious, characterful rooms, with good-quality towels and bathrobes, and nice bits and pieces like marble washstands. Lord Fitz Hugh, with its four-poster bed and steps down to the bathroom, is perhaps the grandest. The restaurant is a warren of oak-beamed rooms stuffed full of Victoriana, and the meals include lots of extras like canapés with your pre-dinner drink and tiny cakes and truffles with your coffee. A typical evening meal might include fresh Loch Fyne scallops with dill butter, rolled rack of Lincolnshire lamb with rosemary, and Swiss lemon tart with orange if you can manage it after the dazzling cheese trolley.

◑ Closed 2 weeks Chr, first week Aug & bank holidays; restaurant closed Sun eve
▨ 4 miles west of Humber Bridge, off A1077 in centre of village. Private car park
🛏 2 twin, 3 double, 1 four-poster, 1 suite; some in annexe; most with bathroom/WC, 2 with shower/WC; TV, room service, hair-dryer, direct-dial telephone; no tea/coffee-making facilities in rooms ⊘ 2 restaurants, bar, lounge, conservatory, garden; conference facilities (max 10 people incl up to 7 residential) ♭ No wheelchair access ● No children under 8 exc babes in arms; no dogs or smoking in bedrooms
▭ Access, Amex, Delta, Switch, Visa £ Single occupancy of twin/double £65, twin/double £90, four-poster £100, suite £95. Cooked B £8; set L £14/18.50, D £29/45; alc D £48

Old Vicarage

Church Road, Witherslack LA11 6RS
TEL: (01539) 552381   FAX: (01539) 552373

An informal and individual country-house hotel that is both relaxing and sophisticated.

The Old Vicarage is blissfully free of the stiff formality that is often associated with country-house hotels. The reception-desk and register-type welcome is not the style of the owners, the Reeves and Burrington-Browns, who ensure that the mossy, ivy-clad, rambling stone house provides the atmosphere of a country house party. The surrounding lanes that meander through the wooded countryside make the hotel feel as though it were in a rural backwater, thus adding to the ambience.

The ideal place in which to start to unwind is the 'bar', although it is not really a bar as such, but rather a collection of shelves heaving with malt whiskies. The dining-room (once the vicarage's kitchen) is similarly unconventional, consisting as it does of two intimate, interlinking rooms, with wine bottles stored in the former fireplace. Dinner is a five-course affair, and now offers choices at most stages. Local game, Gressingham duck, Mansergh lamb and Waberthwaite hams feature prominently and, come the season, so do damsons (featuring in ice-cream, gin, or brandy sauces) – Witherslack is famous for them. The bedrooms also demonstrate individuality. Those in the main house, boasting plenty of pine furniture and brass bedsteads, are perhaps more traditional, although Room 5 is unusual in having a bath hidden behind designer curtains. The light garden rooms (you enter them from the orchard garden) are quirkier, while the new – but sympathetically designed – annexes, whose rooms are decorated in a modern, rustic style, is extremely swish. Roe deer, red squirrels, foxes and even badgers are frequently spotted in the surrounding woodland through the patio windows.

◐ Open all year ⤢ Turn off A590 into Witherslack and turn left after the telephone box; hotel is 1 mile further on along this lane, on the left. Private car park ⌲ 4 twin, 9 double, 1 four-poster, 1 family room; some in annexe; most with bathroom/WC, 3 with shower/WC; TV, room service, hair-dryer, direct-dial telephone; CD player and mini-bar in some rooms ✦ Dining-room, 2 lounges, drying-room, garden; conference facilities (max 12 people residential/non-residential); tennis; early suppers for children; cot, high chair ♿ No wheelchair access ◖ No dogs in public rooms; no smoking in dining-room and discouraged in bedrooms ▭ Access, Amex, Delta, Switch, Visa £ Single occupancy of twin/double £59, twin/double £98, four-poster/family room £158; deposit required. Set L £13.50, D £26.50. Special breaks available

---

WITHYPOOL Somerset   map 1

Royal Oak

Withypool TA24 7QP
TEL: (01643) 831506/831507   FAX: (01643) 831659

A village-centre pub-hotel with a strong hunting tradition.

The Royal Oak Inn boasts what must be one of the tiniest reception desks ever, but that's because space has to be found on the ground floor for a public bar, a second bar that doubles as a residents' lounge and a dining-room. In the bars you're thrust straight into the world of the hunt, with stag and fox heads and antlers at every turn. Across the hall, the dining-room, with its deep-blue upholstery and carpets, crisp white linen and flowers on the table, could be in a different building were it not for the wooden beams that provide a linking theme with the bar. Should you feel the need to escape, there's a tiny sitting-room on an upstairs landing, with plants winding up a disused stairwell to meet it. Inevitably, in such an old building, the bedrooms are quite small and the floorboards creaky, but if you relish the occasional awkwardly angled beam you'll love Room 10, where even the bathroom is squeezed in under the eaves. One reader commented about the service at dinner that 'one felt more attention being given to non-residents on some occasions.' But no one could argue with the choice of food available: a table d'hôte menu is supplemented with an à la carte version and the even longer list of bar meals with daily specials chalked up on a board.

◑ Closed 24 to 26 Dec 🔁 In Withypool village. Private car park ⬉ 2 twin, 5 double, 1 four-poster; all with bathroom/WC; TV, room service, hair-dryer, direct-dial telephone ✅ Dining-room, 2 bars, lounge, drying-room; early suppers for children ♿ No wheelchair access ● No children under 10 ⬜ Access, Amex, Diners, Switch, Visa £ Single occupancy of twin/double £45 to £53, twin/double £68 to £76, four-poster £76 to £84; deposit required. Set D £22; alc D £26; bar lunches available. Special breaks available

---

Westerclose Country House

Withypool TA24 7QR
TEL: (01643) 831302 FAX: (01643) 831307

Elegant country-house hotel in a quiet position on the edge of Exmoor village.

Westerclose House started life as a 1920s hunting lodge, but for all that it's less in thrall to the hunting ethos than some other Exmoor hotels: no stags' heads over the fireplace here. As you drive round to the rear car park, you look across a newly constructed traditional Somerset hedge to the moors, a view also available to diners in the elegant restaurant. Three-course dinners come with plenty of choice, or there's a short à la carte menu. A reader thoroughly enjoyed the 'fabulous cream teas' and 'excellent breakfasts' which augment the usual fry-up with stewed fruit and bowls of Greek yoghurt. After dinner there's plenty of choice of somewhere to sit. In the hall a cosy sitting-area is centred around a wood-burner, or you can retreat to a conservatory full of rattan chairs and plants. Sandwiched between them is a small bar, well stocked with books and games, and with footstools on which to rest legs weary from tramping the moors. All the bedrooms are individually decorated and most (but not the singles) overlook the moors. Room 6 is huge, with a four-poster bed and sunken corner bath. Service from Mrs 'Tinker' Foster and her family comes in for particular praise from readers.

◑ Closed Jan to 1 Mar 🔁 Enter Withypool village from Dulverton on B3223. Turn right at the inn and follow hotel signs. Private car park ⬉ 2 single, 4 twin, 3 double, 1 four-poster; family room available; all with bathroom/WC exc 1 single with shower/WC; TV, limited room service; hair-dryer on request ✅ Restaurant, bar, 2 lounges, drying-room, conservatory, garden; early suppers for children; baby-listening ♿ No wheelchair access ● No dogs or smoking in restaurant; smoking discouraged in bedrooms ⬜ Access, Amex, Visa £ Single £29 to £34, single occupancy of twin/double £44 to 49, twin/double £68 to £80, four-poster £85, family room £110; deposit required. Set L £12.50, D £20/22; alc D £16.50; light lunches available. Special breaks available

WOLTERTON Norfolk   map 6

Saracen's Head ☆

Wolterton, Nr Erpingham NR11 7LX
TEL: (01263) 768909

Excellent food and comfortable bedrooms in back lanes of Norfolk.

'Lost!!! in North Norfolk' proclaims the brochure – and they're not kidding. But follow the detailed instructions, and you'll happen upon the smart, red-brick building with secluded courtyard behind, originally based on the plan of a Tuscan farmhouse. The difficulty of finding it, however, does little to deter the crowds who flock here for some excellent country cooking, like Morston mussels in cider and cream, roast Norfolk pheasant with almonds and marsala, and brown bread-and-butter pudding. You can eat in either the snug bars, with their deep-plum walls, wicker chairs and blackboard menus, or the parlour, where cheerful oilcloths cover the tables and a huge 1940 map of the world sprawls across one wall. On summer days, of course, there's also the *al fresco* option. The number of bedrooms is slowly expanding; our inspector's double room, overlooking the courtyard, was comfortable and warm, with tartan print duvet cover and pine furniture. The electric heater and bedside light had thoughtfully been switched on for her late arrival. Another reader, however, complained of a draughty window and shabby bathroom. Service is very willing, if a little slow at times.

◖ Open all year ⬈ 2 miles west of A140; go through Erpingham, continue straight past church; hotel is ½ mile further on right. Private car park ⬏ 1 twin, 3 double; family room available; all with bathroom/WC; TV, room service, hair-dryer ⍩ Restaurant, bar, lounge, garden; conference facilities (max 40 people incl up to 4 residential); early suppers for children ♿ No wheelchair access ● No dogs in public rooms; no smoking in bedrooms ▱ Access, Amex, Visa £ Single occupancy of twin/double £35 to £40, twin/double £50; deposit required. Set L £5; alc L £13, D £15. Special breaks available

---

WOODSTOCK Oxfordshire   map 5

Feathers Hotel

Market Street, Woodstock OX20 1SX
TEL: (01993) 812291   FAX: (01993) 813158

An up-market hotel with smart rooms, a busy restaurant and friendly service, in the centre of an attractive tourist town.

Woodstock tends to get overlooked in favour of its more famous neighbour – Oxford – just 8 miles down the road. But this attractive little market town with an 800-year-old history is more than just a satellite to Oxford: it makes a good base in its own right. The Feathers is right at the heart of the town's daytime activity and is usually busy, with locals dropping in for a long lunch in the smart, wood-panelled restaurant, or for lighter meals in the characterful bar. The restaurant menu typically includes dishes such as baked cheese soufflé, pot-roasted guinea-fowl and fillet of brill, while the salmon fish-cakes in the bar are highly recommended. Because the hotel was converted from four seventeenth-century town houses, the corridors are long and winding, and it can be a job remembering where your room is. At the end of your journey, you're well rewarded with antiques, good-quality fabrics and smart, marble bathrooms. Priced according to size and outlook, the bedrooms vary enormously: Wren, a smallish double room with a heraldic-patterned bedspread and window in the bathroom looking along Market Street, was our favourite.

◑ Open all year 🔁 Centrally located in Woodstock. On-street parking 🛏 6 twin/double, 7 double, 3 suites; all with bathroom/WC; TV, room service, hair-dryer, direct-dial telephone; no tea/coffee-making facilities in rooms ✅ Restaurant (air-conditioned), bar, lounge, study, garden; conference facilities (max 25 people incl up to 16 residential); early suppers for children; baby-listening, high chairs ♿ No wheelchair access ● No smoking in restaurant; no dogs in bar or restaurant ▭ Access, Amex, Diners, Visa £ Single occupancy of twin/double £78 to £98, twin/double £99 to £150, suite £185 to £195. Cooked B £7.50; set L £16.50/21; alc L, D £27.50; bar lunches available. Special breaks available

---

WOOLACOMBE Devon   map 1

Little Beach

The Esplanade, Woolacombe EX34 7DJ
TEL: (01271) 870398

A pleasingly decorated, small seafront hotel overlooking Woolacombe beach.

The sea views from the front of Little Beach are so spectacular that it would be easy to imagine fights breaking out for the one table in the dining-room that hogs them. However, Brian and Nola Welling are old hands at seeing that everyone gets their turn, and besides, the sun lounge offers much more of the same. Dinner menus major on British favourites like braised pork chops, but the more adventurous will be pleased to note that dishes like beef, rolled and stuffed Chinese style, also put in an appearance. Brian Welling is a graduate of the antiques trade, and cherishes a small shop squeezed in alongside a TV room...'handy if you want to catch the news headlines, or if the wife wants an early night,' he explained. For those who'd rather read or write, the main lounge has books and magazines, as well as a fine desk. The most covetable bedrooms are the three at the front, which share a large balcony from which to appreciate the views, but that's not to deny the comfort of those at the back. The chocolate-coloured bathroom suites can be a shock, but others are decorated in a tamer tan or blue.

◑ Closed Nov to Feb 🔁 On the seafront in Woolacombe. Private car park 🛏 2 single, 1 twin, 7 double; 4 with bathroom/WC, 4 with shower/WC; TV, direct-dial telephone; trouser press and hair-dryer on request ✅ Dining-room, bar, 3 lounges, TV room, drying-room, garden ♿ No wheelchair access ● No children under 6; no dogs in public rooms; no smoking in some public rooms and some bedrooms ▭ Access, Visa £ Single/single occupancy of twin/double £28 to £30, twin/double £70 to £74; deposit required. Special breaks available

Watersmeet

Mortehoe, Woolacombe EX34 7EB
TEL: (01271) 870333   FAX: (01271) 870890

A smaller-than-it-looks hotel poised above Woolacombe's beach and rock pools.

Watersmeet Hotel is a long, low, creamy Edwardian building, which appears to spring almost organically from the eastern end of Woolacombe Bay. In recent years, Pat and Brian Wheeldon have been trying to return it to its 1907 prime; the latest round of refurbishment restored the old dining-room to its status as a billiards room, while a local glazier releaded and revived the stunning stained-glass window in the stairwell. What they won't be changing, however, are the extensions that were added in the 1980s to increase the window footage; wherever you're placed for dinner, you're bound to have a wonderful sea view. The lounge, too, makes the most of the views. England being England, it's no good relying on the weather, so Watersmeet is equipped with plenty of books, games and jigsaws. Apart from the new billiards room, there's also a games room, which boasts table-tennis, pool and bar-billiards tables, and is popular with the younger guests. The premier bedrooms are bigger than their standard cousins and boast more extras, but the latter are just as stylishly furnished and decorated. Room 25 is particularly attractive, because it has a side window as well as a main one overlooking the sea. The only disappointment is the small, height-of-season, overflow lunch bar, which has some very 1960s décor.

◑ Closed Dec & Jan   ⊡ From the centre of Woolacombe follow the Esplanade. The hotel is on the left-hand side. Private car park   ⤙ 4 single, 9 twin, 8 double, 1 four-poster, 1 suite; family rooms available; all with bathroom/WC; TV, room service, hair-dryer, direct-dial telephone, clock radio; no tea/coffee-making facilities in rooms   ⊘ Restaurant, 2 bars, lounge, drying-room, games room, garden; conference facilities (max 40 people incl up to 20 residential); heated outdoor swimming-pool, tennis, croquet, pool, billiards; early suppers for children   ᵶ No wheelchair access   ⊖ No children under 8 in restaurant eves; no dogs; no smoking in restaurant   ▭ Access, Visa   £ Single £68 to £90, twin/double £126 to £190, four-poster £136 to £190, family room from £136, suite £140 to £196 (rates incl dinner); deposit required. Set D £25.50; alc D from £16.50; light lunches available (1996 prices). Special breaks available

---

WOOLSTASTON Shropshire   map 5

Rectory Farm

Woolstaston, Church Stretton SY6 6NN
TEL: (01694) 751306

Charming house and friendly hosts offering first-class B&B at bargain rates.

Anyone with an ounce of soul will perk up at the sight of Rectory Farm. Its position just beside Woolstaston's village green means that the landscape suddenly opens up, and the open views across the plain and towards the Wrekin come as a spectacular bonus. Add to this the fact that the house is an idyllic half-timbered specimen dating back to 1620, that the garden is an impeccable assemblage of colour and topiary, and that you can stay here, sharing a double, for £20 a night, and you may well think that you've died and gone to heaven. The sitting-rooms have the beams and exposed stone the exterior seems to promise, and Jeanette and John Davies display enough personal knick-knacks on the lovely old sideboard to reinforce the idea that this remains principally a family home. There are two breakfasting areas, one a galleried affair (complete with grand piano!) where the table has embroidery by Jeanette's mother, the other impressively medieval with a beamed ceiling, Jacobean panelling and illumination denoting the space that once cradled the old bread oven. Breakfasts are both hearty and convivial enough to do justice to the setting. Delightful antiques and chintzy soft furnishings, as well as the odd Dralon chair or headboard, characterise the generously proportioned bedrooms.

◑ Closed mid-Dec to 1 Feb   ⬀ To the right of the village green in Woolstaston. Private car park   ⬱ 2 twin, 1 double; all with bathroom/WC; TV; hair-dryer on request   ⬥ 2 dining-rooms, 3 lounges, TV room, garden   ⬥ No wheelchair access   ⬤ No children under 12; no dogs; no smoking   ⊟ None accepted   ⌹ Single occupancy of twin/double £25, twin/double £40

WOOLSTONE Gloucestershire   map 5

Old Rectory

Woolstone, Nr Cheltenham GL52 4RG
TEL: (01242) 673766

Good-value B&B in very peaceful location.

As you drive along the gravelled entrance to the Old Rectory and come to a halt in front of the main house you can't fail to be impressed by the imposing nineteenth-century building and wonder at what it must have cost the poor rector, who never even got to live here owing to the untimely demise of his wife. The house is flanked by a large and pleasant garden with a white gazebo and plenty of garden furniture for those sunny days when you can sit outside. Inside Susan and Peter Taylor's house are some very interesting pieces of furniture, such as the huge Welsh dresser adorned with Spode china, a cabinet of antique silver and lots of family mementos. The drawing-room, with its wooden floorboards (complete with the old heating grating at their edges), several bookcases and a three-piece suite around an enormous fireplace, is also used by the Taylor family if there are no guests staying. The bedrooms themselves are less striking, with unremarkable furniture and slightly drab décor, although one of the doubles has great views over the Severn Valley and an imposing marble fireplace. The adjacent old coach-house and stables have been converted into self-catering cottages.

Use the maps at the back of the Guide *to pinpoint hotels in a particular area.*

◐ Closed Nov to Mar ⊡ 2 miles north of Bishop's Cleeve turn right to Woolstone; hotel is down first drive on left after church. Private car park ⊫→ 1 twin, 2 double; twin with bathroom/WC, doubles with shower/WC; TV, hair-dryer ⊘ Dining-room, lounge, garden; conference facilities (max 30 people incl up to 3 residential) ♿ Wheelchair access to hotel (3 steps), 1 ground-floor bedroom ● No dogs; no smoking ▭ None accepted £ Single occupancy of twin/double £28, twin/double £40; deposit required

---

WOOLTON HILL Hampshire map 2

Hollington House

Woolton Hill, Newbury RG20 9XR
TEL: (01635) 255100   FAX: (01635) 255075

A grand but friendly country house with an excellent restaurant and luxurious bedrooms.

Hollington House is the kind of hotel which manages to combine grandeur with a homely welcome and comfortable atmosphere. Built at the turn of the century, the creeper-clad golden-stone house is set in 14 acres of woodland gardens landscaped by Gertrude Jekyll. The reception is huge, with dark wood panelling, a minstrels' gallery and, in winter, a roaring open fire. The lounge has inspiring views out over the terrace, woods and pasture, and the deep sofas are the perfect place for relaxing after dinner under the watchful eyes of the original owner, Mrs Eliot Cohen, whose portrait hangs above the fireplace. The current owners, Penny and John Guy, have a strong connection with Australia and this is reflected in the wine list, with its emphasis on quality New World wines, and the menu, which offered kangaroo steak on the day of our visit! More traditional delicacies are a roast breast of Trelough duck with a fricassee of artichoke, perhaps followed by hot raspberry soufflé with a compote of red berries. The bedrooms upstage the restaurant by a narrow margin, though – huge, sumptuous and well equipped. A lovely individual touch is that all the bedspreads are intricately home-made by Penny Guy. Half of the 20 guest rooms have spa baths, and all the bathrooms are particularly luxurious.

◐ Open all year ⊡ From Newbury take A343 towards Andover; follow signs to Hollington Herb Garden. Private car park ⊫→ 1 twin, 15 double, 1 four-poster, 3 suites; family room available; all with bathroom/WC; TV, room service, hair-dryer, trouser press, direct-dial telephone; no tea/coffee-making facilities in rooms ⊘ Restaurant, 2 lounges, drying-room, games room, garden; conference facilities (max 30 people incl up to 20 residential); heated outdoor swimming-pool, tennis, croquet; early suppers for children; toys, babysitting, baby-listening, outdoor games ♿ Wheelchair access to hotel (1 ramp), restaurant and WC (M), lift to bedrooms ● No dogs; no smoking in some bedrooms ▭ Access, Amex, Delta, Diners, Visa £ Single occupancy of twin/double £95, twin/double £135, four-poster £250, family room from £135, suite £350 to £375; deposit required. Set L £14.50/17.50, D £30; alc L, D £35. Special breaks available

---

Many hotels put up their tariffs in the spring. You are advised to confirm prices when you book.

Old Vicarage

Worfield, Nr Bridgnorth WV15 5JZ
TEL: (01746) 716497   FAX: (01746) 716552

Sympathetically run country house wins high marks for food, wine and fulsome hospitality.

As a rule of thumb when searching for an Old Vicarage, keep your eyes peeled for the church spire and steer. It works in Worfield, where the proximity of both church and cricket pitch, twin focuses of village life (at least in *The Archers*!) combine to produce a potent distillation of all that is England. You'll hear birdsong, as well as peals of bells, and the thud of leather on willow, but little else. Typically, this Old Vicarage is an unflashy red-brick affair, flirting with frivolity in the appended conservatory, but otherwise true its to its Edwardian roots. Overlooking the croquet lawn, the said room is a lovely spot for a pre-prandial drink, cheered by its summery blue and yellow furniture. The bar is a colourful retreat (and interesting, too) thanks to the veritable gallery of artworks lining its white Anaglypta walls. Paintings and *objets d'art* are equally prominent in the elegant restaurant, where plates bedeck an Art-Nouveau overmantel, and lamps cast a soft light. The food was described by one reader as 'uniformly good and interesting, without ever being bizarre;' perhaps sweetcorn soup with toasted cheese and onion flutes, followed by roasted fillet of salmon with saffron, caper and orange dressing, and then salad of fresh fruits with orange Curaçao and mango sorbet – plus a completely captivating cheeseboard. The individually designed bedrooms, whether in the main house or converted coach-house, are smart and well equipped, with a range of 'sybaritic delights', including sherry, fresh fruit, fresh milk and sweets. 'The Iles are thoughtful, caring and completely unpretentious hosts who give their guests' comfort priority,' declared one couple who also commended the choice of half-bottles on the extensive wine list.

◑ Closed Chr & New Year   ⃟ Near cricket ground in Worfield. Private car park ⌂ 5 twin, 7 double, 1 four-poster, 1 suite; family room available; some in annexe; all with bathroom/WC exc 1 twin with shower/WC; TV, room service, hair-dryer, mini-bar, trouser press, direct-dial telephone   ✔ Restaurant, bar, lounge, conservatory, garden; conference facilities (max 14 people residential/non-residential); early suppers for children; baby-listening, cot, high chair   ⅙ Wheelchair access to hotel (2 ramps), restaurant and WC (unisex), 2 ground-floor bedrooms specially equipped for disabled people   ● No children under 8 in restaurant eves; no dogs in public rooms; no smoking   ▭ Access, Amex, Diners, Visa   £ Single occupancy of twin/double £69, twin/double £97, four-poster £135, family room £125, suite £135; deposit required. Set L £15.50, D £25/30. Special breaks available

---

 Denotes somewhere you can rely on a good meal – either the hotel features in the 1997 edition of our sister publication, The Good Food Guide, *or our inspectors thought the cooking impressive, whether particularly competent home cooking or more lavish cuisine.*

WYE Kent   map 3

Wife of Bath ☆

4 Upper Bridge Street, Wye, Nr Ashford TN25 5AW
TEL: (01233) 812540/812232   FAX: (01233) 813630

Stylish, homely B&B above a small popular restaurant.

At the Wife of Bath in Wye, Chaucer is still very much alive – both in spirit, as the guest rooms are named after the famous pilgrims, and in body – in the shape of Geoffrey Chaucer, the resident cat. The Wife of Bath, as John Morgan the proprietor is quick to point out, is not so much a hotel as a restaurant-with-rooms. The restaurant is in the main house (which used to be the village doctor's home). The dinner menu might include steamed local asparagus with a black pepper beurre blanc, then sauté breast of pigeon and guinea-fowl with juniper berries and thyme, followed by home-made ice-cream. The guest rooms are an effective blend of old and new, with the Yeoman's room having deep-pink painted walls and ceiling between the beams and rafters and a four-poster bed, fireplace and a good-sized bathroom. The Friar's room is a small single but is equally stylish. Outside, the stables have been converted into two more guest rooms, the bright and sunny Miller's room, with yellow walls and curtains and blue and yellow bedding, and the Knight's room. These two rooms share a small reception/kitchen area with a flagstone floor, where you will find everything you want for a continental breakfast should you wish to get your own; if not you can always join the other guests in the restaurant for a continental or cooked breakfast.

◗ Closed first 2 weeks Sept; restaurant closed Sun & Mon eves   ⤵ Leave M20 at Junction 9 (Ashford); follow signs to Canterbury on A28; after 4 miles turn right to Wye. Private car park   ⤶ 2 twin, 2 double, 1 four-poster; family room available; some in annexe; 3 with bathroom/WC, 2 with shower/WC; TV, room service, hair-dryer, trouser press, direct-dial telephone   ✓ Restaurant, bar, garden; conference facilities (max 10 people incl up to 5 residential)   ♿ Wheelchair access to hotel, restaurant and WC (unisex), 2 ground-floor bedrooms   ● Children discouraged from restaurant eves; no dogs; no smoking in bedrooms   ▭ Access, Delta, Switch, Visa   £ Single occupancy of twin/double £40, twin/double £45 to £50, four-poster £70, family room £55. Cooked B £5; set L £9, D £22; alc L £16

YATTENDON Berkshire   map 2

Royal Oak

The Square, Yattendon, Newbury RG18 0UG
TEL: (01635) 201325   FAX: (01635) 201926

Stylish rooms and good food at the centre of a beautifully kept, traditional English village.

Set in the main square of Yattendon, the Royal Oak is a creeper-covered, red-brick inn which dates back four hundred years. Like the rest of the village (including the telephone box, by special dispensation), the hotel's exterior paintwork is a smart racing green – by order of the Yattendon estate, whose lord of the manor still owns much of the local property. With its wooden floor and tables, the bar has an ancient, rustic atmosphere; for more luxury, head for the stylish lounge, with its log fire, cushioned window seats and loose-covered armchairs. Legend has it that Oliver Cromwell dined at the Royal Oak the night before he faced the Roundheads at the Battle of Newbury. Guests under less pressure can make the most of a fancy menu which includes traditional dishes such as rabbit stew and honey-glazed duck, as well as more unusual options, such as 'daube of beef garniture grand-mère with parsnip purée'. The five bedrooms – three at the front, and two overlooking the walled garden – have undergone more refurbishment since last year. They vary in size, but are all very luxurious and beautifully designed, with plush fabrics and smart, well-equipped bathrooms. Room 2, a pretty, yellow room with dark-wood furniture, is the smallest, though the large window makes up for some of the lack of space.

◗ Open all year; restaurants closed Sun eve   ⃟ In Yattendon village centre. Private car park   ⤙ 1 twin, 3 double, 1 suite; all with bathroom/WC; TV, room service, hair-dryer, trouser press, direct-dial telephone   ⌀ 2 restaurants, bar, lounge, garden; conference facilities (max 40 people incl up to 5 residential); early suppers for children   ♿ No wheelchair access   ⬤ No dogs or smoking in restaurants   ▭ Access, Amex, Delta, Diners, Switch, Visa   ⚟ Single occupancy of twin/double £85 to £90, twin/double £85 to £90, suite £105 to £110; deposit required. Continental B £6.50, cooked B £9.50; alc L £20, D £29

YORK North Yorkshire map 9

Dairy Guesthouse

3 Scarcroft Road, York YO2 1ND
TEL: (01904) 639367

An informal Victorian town house with many original features situated just outside the centre of York.

Things suddenly get busy after 4pm, when guests begin to arrive (check-in is between 4 and 6pm) and are met by Keith Jackman, who tells you where you will find a parking space, runs though a few details about the house (it's non-smoking), takes your order for breakfast, and books you in for one of the two morning sittings. After this brief whirl of activity you're left to your own devices, and can either while away a quiet hour in the internal courtyard or relax in your simple, Victorian-style bedroom.

The building was originally turned into a dairy by the Trapp family, and the 'sound of music' jokes are not as corny as you might think, since Keith still spends much of his spare time playing drums and percussion in the city's music venues. If you're curious enough, you can even borrow one of Keith's tapes and listen to it on the cassette player provided in each bedroom. One reader experienced some difficulty in securing a single room two weeks in advance, but our inspector, also travelling solo and booking a few days in advance, had no such problem.

◐ Closed mid-Dec to end Jan ⤢ On south side of the city wall, off A1036. On-street parking ⤢ 2 twin, 2 double, 1 four-poster; 1 with bathroom/WC, 1 with shower/WC; TV, hair-dryer, CD player ⊘ Dining-room, garden; toys, cots ⅏ No wheelchair access ⊜ No dogs in public rooms; no smoking ▭ None accepted £ Single occupancy of twin/double £25 to £33, twin/double £32 to £42, four-poster £36 to £38

Holmwood House

114 Holgate Road, York YO2 4BB
TEL: (01904) 626183   FAX: (01904) 670899

Suburban B&B under new ownership with pretty bedrooms.

At the time of inspection, newly installed owners Rosie Blanksby and Bill Pitts had hardly had time to stamp their own identity on Holmwood House, so new reports would be welcome. That's not to say that there is a great deal that needs changing. The house has a delightfully light feel, with lots of bright Laura Ashley fabrics and flowery patterns. The bedrooms are all very pretty and have simple dark-wood contract and reproduction furnishings. The building is actually made up of two Victorian terraced houses. As it is on a busy road about half an hour's walk from the centre there is inevitably a fairly constant flow of traffic, but the rear of the hotel, with an extremely handy little car park, overlooks one of the prettiest squares in York. If silence is important to you, get a room at the back of the house.

◐ Open all year ⤢ On A59 York to Harrogate road near city walls and station. Private car park ⤢ 3 twin, 7 double, 2 four-poster; family room available; all with bathroom/WC exc 1 double with shower/WC; TV, hair-dryer, direct-dial telephone ⊘ Dining-room, lounge, garden ⅏ No wheelchair access ⊜ No children under 8; no dogs; no smoking ▭ Access, Amex, Delta, Switch, Visa £ Single occupancy of twin/double £35 to £45, twin/double £50 to £55, four-poster £55 to £65, family room from £65; deposit required. Special breaks available

Middlethorpe Hall

Bishopthorpe Road, York YO2 1QB
TEL: (01904) 641241   FAX: (01904) 620176

A grand and lavishly restored stately home offering friendly service.

Situated on the outskirts of the city of York, and screened from the busy A64 bypass by trees, Middlethorpe Hall stands in its own, vast grounds. Built in 1699, the red-brick house is a grand, symmetrical building. More than a decade ago, it provided a challenging restoration project for Historic House Hotels, which succeeded in turning it into a luxury hotel with an excellent restaurant. From the hall's marble floor and carved staircase to a restaurant's oak panels, the public rooms are impressive, and are decorated in top-quality materials. The deep, comfortable sofas, the books and magazines that are scattered around, as well as the pretty flower arrangements, all ensure that you can relax while admiring the décor; indeed, there's even a discreet notice asking guests not to use mobile phones or laptop computers in the public rooms. In the bedrooms, any indications of being in the 1990s (such as televisions and trouser presses) are hidden away. The muted colour schemes and elegant antiques, along with the Edwardian-style bathrooms, give the rooms a very luxurious, traditional feel. Downstairs, in the main restaurant, the menu is similarly stylishly traditional, offering perhaps smoked salmon to start, roast pork with caramelised apple to follow, and a hot chocolate soufflé or sticky toffee pudding as a finale; the dearer, 'gourmet', fixed-price menu justifies the extra pennies.

◐ Open all year ⚡ 1½ miles south of York, beside York racecourse. Private car park 🛏 4 single, 8 twin, 8 double, 2 four-poster, 8 suites, all with bathroom/WC; family room available; TV, room service, hair-dryer, trouser press, direct-dial telephone; no tea/coffee-making facilities in rooms ⚒ 2 restaurants, 2 bars, lounge, library, garden; conference facilities (max 60 incl up to 30 residential); croquet ♿ No wheelchair access ● No children under 8; no dogs; no smoking in restaurants ▭ Access, Amex, Delta, Switch, Visa £ Single £89, single occupancy of twin/double £108, twin/double £125 to £139, four-poster £185, suite £160 to £199, family room £210; deposit required. Continental B £7.50, cooked B £10.50; set L £12.50, D from £28; alc D £34 (prices valid till Apr 1997)

Mount Royale ☆

The Mount, York YO2 2DA
TEL: (01904) 628856 FAX: (01904) 611171

Family-run hotel with good facilities near York racecourse.

Christine and Richard Oxtoby have owned the Mount Royale since the mid-'60s and have made a great many friends since then. Not all of them are as famous as the showbiz stars and sports personalities whose photos cover the walls of the bar, for whom the proximity of York racecourse is no doubt as much an attraction as the medieval alleyways 15 minutes away. Many will simply be drawn by the friendly, family-run atmosphere and the impressive facilities such as the sauna, sunbed and swimming-pool.

The house is made up of two adjoining William IV houses plus a modern extension and is bulging with antiques, paintings and plants. Paintings of horses and jockeys are probably what you'd expect in the lounge, but pineapple, lemon and orange trees in the conservatory should raise an eyebrow or two. Bedrooms are divided between the main house, where you may find a half-tester or four-poster bed, swagged curtains and ornate plaster ceilings, and the more modern rooms in the new wing which have the benefit of patio doors which open straight on to the delightful landscaped garden.

◐ Open all year ⚡ On A1036 near York racecourse. Private car park 🛏 6 twin, 8 double, 3 four-poster, 6 suites; some in annexe; all with bathroom/WC; TV, room service, hair-dryer, trouser press, direct-dial telephone ⚒ Restaurant, bar, lounge, TV room, games room, garden; conference facilities (max 23 people residential/non-residential); sauna, solarium, heated outdoor swimming-pool, snooker; early suppers for children; babysitting, baby-listening ♿ No wheelchair access ● None ▭ Access, Amex, Diners, Switch, Visa £ Single occupancy of twin/double £70, twin/double £80, four-poster £90, suite £120; deposit required. Alc D £28.50. Special breaks available

SCOTLAND

LESLIE CASTLE

LESLIE

ABERDOUR **Fife**   map 11

Hawkcraig House

Hawkcraig Point, Aberdour KY3 0TZ
TEL: (01383) 860335

A good-value, friendly guesthouse, situated in a charming location.

With its tangle of lobster pots on the wooden jetty, and fine views across the Firth
of Forth to Edinburgh and Arthur's Seat, Elma Barrie's waterfront guesthouse is
well worth the half-hour journey from the capital. Hawkcraig House is a
whitewashed Georgian building with black lintels, and a modern conservatory
attached. Inside, it's a friendly, homely place, featuring family photographs on
the sitting-room's walls, and a ticking grandfather clock in the hall. There's a
smarter sitting-room upstairs, boasting some fine old furniture and good views
of St Columba's Isle. The dining-room is also furnished with antiques, including
chairs, a writing desk and a sideboard, and is home to some well-polished silver,
too; this is the venue for Elma's tasty four-course dinners. There's no licence, so
bring your own wine. The two bedrooms are downstairs, and are decorated in a
simple, comfortable style, featuring old-fashioned furniture and pretty watercolours. The double has recently had an extra window added, which has
improved the lighting and the views.

◑ Closed Nov to mid-Mar   ⊠ Turn off A921 in Easter Aberdour, and follow
Hawkcraig Road to a large car park. Drive through and down the very steep access
road to hotel. Private car park   ⊨ 1 twin, 1 double; double with bathroom/WC, twin
with shower/WC; TV, hair-dryer; tea/coffee on request   ⊘ Dining-room, 2 lounges,
conservatory, garden   ᕃ No wheelchair access   ● No children under 10; no dogs;
no smoking   ▭ None accepted   £ Single occupancy of twin/double £26 to £29,
twin/double £42 to £48. Set D £21

ABERFELDY **Perthshire & Kinross**   map 11

Farleyer House Hotel

Aberfeldy PH15 2JE
TEL: (01887) 820332   FAX: (01887) 829430

---

*A comfortable, hillside hotel situated above the River Strath, which
will appeal to anglers.*

At breakfast on a sunny morning, with the rays of light filtering into the
dining-room, Farleyer House can seem an optimistic sort of place: 'We're due a
run of salmon today'; 'Don't expect us back for dinner – the river is just right.' A
large salmon (preserved in a glass case) scowls down from reception as the
anglers are sent off with flasks of coffee. Set on the hillside above the River
Strath, the white-walled hotel was once a mere sixteenth-century croft that was
later extended as the Menzies clan fortunes improved. A staircase leads up from
reception and the dining-room to a classic, country-house-style drawing-room,
which boasts excellent views across the valley. Next to this you'll find a cosy
library and a less attractive TV room, which is rather redundant since all the
bedrooms have TV sets.

The bedrooms are smart, and are lifted by the occasional piece of antique furniture. Our inspector's room, however – located at the back of the house and above the kitchens – was noisy: it would be better to ask for a front room, all of which enjoy the view across to Ben Vorlich.

For dinner, Farleyer House offers you a choice between the less formal bistro and the smart dining-room, which serves a set four-course menu. The emphasis of the cuisine is on local ingredients, which are cooked with a light touch, thus allowing the flavours to come through. Our inspector enjoyed a starter of grilled wood pigeon accompanied by bacon, which was followed by an excellent haunch of venison served with plum sauce, and finally a strawberry gâteau. One reader (as well as our inspector) felt that the surcharges incurred for such extras as newspapers and phone calls from bedrooms were unwarranted – and this coloured their judgment of the hotel's value for money.

◑ Open all year ⤴ From Aberfeldy take B846 to Kinloch Rannoch through Weem. Hotel is 1 mile down on right. Private car park ⤷ 4 twin, 10 double, 1 family room; some in annexe; most with bathroom/WC, some with shower/WC; TV, hair-dryer, direct-dial telephone; tea/coffee-making facilities in some rooms; limited room service in some rooms ⬥ 2 dining-rooms, bar, lounge, TV room, drying-room, library, garden; conference facilities (max 25 people incl up to 15 residential); fishing, golf, croquet, putting green; early suppers for children; babysitting, baby-listening, outdoor games ♿ Wheelchair access to hotel (2 steps), dining-rooms and WC (unisex), 4 ground-floor bedrooms, 1 specially equipped for disabled people ● Dogs in drying-room only; no smoking in main dining-room ▭ Access, Amex, Delta, Diners, Switch, Visa £ Single occupancy of twin/double £65 to £100, twin/double £80 to £170, family room £80 to £150; deposit required. Set D £32; alc L £21; bistro meals available. Special breaks available

---

Guinach House

By the Birks, Aberfeldy PH15 2ET
TEL: (01887) 820251   FAX: (01887) 829607

An unassuming, family-run hotel, with good food.

A pair of flower-filled stone boots on the doorstep is an indication of what most visitors come here for: walking, because Aberfeldy is well placed for walks through beauty spots such as Glen Lyon or the Birks. This is a family-run hotel, hence the tree house in the garden, the school sporting trophies in the lounge and the fact that Bert MacKay was busy preparing cakes for the local school when we called. The dining-room is smart and homely, and boasts views over the town. The four-course dinners are good value, and offer three or four choices: the starters, for example, might include oak-smoked trout, a ragoût of wild mushrooms, or a soft-poached egg topped with ham and prawns. The main-course selections demonstrate a good range and a liberal use of alcohol in choices such as roast guinea-fowl with a port-wine and bramble sauce, venison in red wine, pork fillet in cider, or grilled lemon sole.

The bedrooms vary in size, and are comfortably traditional in style, with plain, old-fashioned bathrooms.

◑ Closed Chr ⤻ From Aberfeldy take the road to Crieff; hotel is just past the Church of Scotland on the right-hand side. Private car park ⤼ 1 single, 2 twin, 4 double; family rooms available; all with bathroom/WC; TV, hair-dryer ✓ Dining-room, lounge, drying-room, garden ⎨ Wheelchair access to hotel (1 step), dining-room and WC (unisex), 1 ground-floor bedroom ● No dogs in public rooms; no smoking in dining-room ▭ Access, Visa £ Single £28 to £38, single occupancy of twin/double £53, twin/double £55 to £75, family room from £60. Set D £22.50 (prices valid till Apr 1997)

ABOYNE Aberdeenshire   map 11

Hazlehurst Lodge Gallery

Ballater Road, Aboyne AB34 5HY
TEL: (01339) 886921   FAX: (01339) 886660

A stylish, art- and design-conscious restaurant-with-rooms.

It would be easy to drive past Anne and Eddie Strachan's house on the outskirts of Aboyne, but its pink-granite walls, stepped gables and pretty garden reward a closer look. Inside, Hazlehurst Lodge Gallery begins to show real character, bright splashes of colour and mysterious artefacts, along with chiffon drapes and custom-made cherrywood furniture, betraying Anne's enthusiastic interest in Scottish art and design. Situated at the back of the house is an art gallery, in which works by local sculptors, painters and cabinet-makers are displayed; many others can be seen around the house, including a large fertility symbol that often gets mistaken for a model of a whale. The effect is refreshingly different and imaginative – just like Anne's cooking, which blends Scottish, oriental and Belgian traditions (she was once a long-term resident of Brussels). The white bedrooms are modern, and feature cherrywood furniture.

◑ Closed Jan ⤻ On A93, west of centre of Aboyne village. Private car park ⤼ 2 twin/double, 1 double, 1 suite; family room available; suite in annexe; most with bathroom/WC, 1 twin with shower/WC; room service, hair-dryer; TV on request ✓ Restaurant, drying-room, garden; conference facilities (max 12 people incl up to 5 residential); early suppers for children; babysitting ⎨ No wheelchair access ● Dogs by arrangement only; smoking restricted in public rooms ▭ Access, Amex, Diners, Visa £ Single occupancy of twin/double £30 to £45, twin/double £60 to £76, family room £90, suite £110; deposit required. Set D £24. Special breaks available

---

ACHILTIBUIE Highland   map 11

Summer Isles Hotel

Achiltibuie IV26 2YG
TEL: (01854) 622282   FAX: (01854) 622251

Top-notch cooking is offered at this superbly located country-house hotel.

A route encompassing 15 miles of single-track road, skirting three lochs and the sea, brings you to Achiltibuie – a place that remains almost as idyllic and isolated as when Mark Irvine's father came here in the 1960s. Mark and his wife, Gerry, run a sophisticated hotel for guests who want to ramble, fish, or watch birds all day, and then come back, dress for dinner, and eat good, locally produced food. Their management style demonstrates how things should be done: as one report concluded, 'Gerry's insistence on knowing guests by name rather than room number has completely spoiled us – other hotels will never be the same again.' When viewed from the car park at the front, the pebble-dashed building itself – which features picture windows in the lounge and dining-room – appears deceptively ordinary but, as one visitor commented, 'It's a model for what can be achieved with unpromising premises, albeit in beautiful surroundings.'

The main lounge is decorated in a classic, country-house style, and the small bar behind it allows guests to bring their drinks through to enjoy the view across to the Summer Isles. Upstairs, there's another small lounge with an honesty bar, as well as a study which is hung with photographs of the area taken in the hotel's early years. The bedrooms are situated here, and also out in the Verandah – a log-cabin-style annexe that includes a more private suite. All the bedrooms are comfortable and beautifully kept.

Dinners are five-course set meals. The dishes are slanted towards local ingredients, such as scallops, crab or fresh fish. A typical menu begins with gazpacho, followed by warm goat's cheese served on croûtons, fresh scallops on a bed of leeks with basil, vermouth and brandy, and finally a choice from the sweets trolley, or cheeses.

◑ Closed Oct to Easter ⊿ 10 miles north of Ullapool on A835, turn left on to a single-track road leading to Achiltibuie. The village is 15 miles along this road, and the hotel is 1 mile further on, on the left. Private car park ⊨ 1 single, 5 twin, 5 double, 1 suite; most in annexe; all with bathroom/WC; hair-dryer, direct-dial telephone
✧ Dining-room, 2 bars, 2 lounges, drying-room, study; fishing; early suppers for children; babysitting ⅙ No wheelchair access ● No children under 5 in dining-room eves; no dogs in public rooms; smoking discouraged in bedrooms
⊟ None accepted £ Single £48, single occupancy of twin/double £55 to £65, twin/double £70 to £100, suite £130; deposit required. Set D £34; alc L £16.50. Special breaks available

---

ALLOA Clackmannan   map 11

Gean House

Gean Park, Tullibody Road, Alloa FK10 2HS
TEL: (01259) 219275   FAX: (01259) 213827

Country-house sophistication and comfort is offered surprisingly close to Alloa.

As you swing into the drive of Gean House on the outskirts of Alloa, you notice its almost Jacobean look, with its mullioned windows, creeper-clad walls, and tall chimneys glimpsed between the trees. In fact, it was built in 1912 as a wedding gift by a local industrialist who was obviously a romantic at heart. The centrepiece is the Great Hall, which rises through two floors and boasts a vast inglenook fireplace and gallery. In the evening it is lit by a blazing log fire and candles, and guests gather here for drinks before moving across to an elegant, panelled dining-room.

The cuisine is a good mix of both traditional dishes and the more adventurous. The three-course dinner offers four or five choices at each stage: watercress soup served with a poached quail's egg, for example, might be followed by a cutlet of 'Old Berkshire' pork with tarragon mousse and a red-wine sauce. The desserts are firmly traditional, with such delights as bread-and-butter and sticky toffee pudding making regular appearances.

With their smart, classic colour schemes, the bedrooms demonstrate restrained good taste, and also offer some nice touches, such as the original Edwardian bathroom in Ludquharn.

◑ Open all year ⤢ At Alloa town hall roundabout take exit to Tullibody; hotel on left-hand side. Private car park ⌂ 6 twin/double, 1 double; family room available; 5 with bathroom/WC, 2 with shower/WC; TV, room service, hair-dryer, direct-dial telephone; no tea/coffee-making facilities in rooms ⬥ 2 dining-rooms, 2 lounges, drying-room, garden; conference facilities (max 50 people incl up to 7 residential); early suppers for children; baby-listening ⭥ No wheelchair access ● No dogs ▭ Access, Amex, Delta, Diners, Visa £ Single occupancy of twin/double £80, twin/double £120 to £140, family room from £145; deposit required. Set L £15, D £29. Special breaks available

---

ARDUAINE Argyll & Bute   map 11

Loch Melfort Hotel

Arduaine, Oban PA34 4XG
TEL: (01852) 200233   FAX: (01852) 200214

A hotel offering a superb location next to the Arduaine gardens, and boasting a high reputation for its seafood.

Arduaine is one of those little peninsulas that jut out from Scotland's west coast and benefit from the Gulf Stream – an advantage that the Victorian tea-planter James Arthur Campbell recognised when choosing it as site for his gardens. His portrait hangs on the stairs in the main part of the hotel, which has been added to since his day, in the form of a large, double-storey, chalet-style extension that houses most of the bedrooms. The dining-room and lounge-bar, which boast magnificent views south across Asknish Bay, are located in the main building. A pair of tripod-mounted binoculars are on hand for anyone who spots an otter or seal in the sea; the library at the back of the house looks less well used, despite its good collection of books. The food at Loch Melfort has received mixed reports this year and, as its cuisine is seafood oriented, some may find the choice limited. A typical meal might start with a local shellfish bisque, followed by Asknish Bay crab served with mango and melon, then an escalope of Braevallich trout, and finally a walnut-and-toffee tart. 'The seafood buffet on Sunday is not to be missed,' wrote one correspondent. For more informal dining, there's the Scandinavian-style Chartroom Bar, which has a good deal more character than the main dining-room. The bedrooms are divided between the main house (comfortable and well furnished), and the Cedar Wing. The walk around the back of the hotel to the latter is uninspiring (though improvements are in the offing), and one guest found the rooms 'generally a bit run-down,' although another remarked that they were 'ideal for dog-owners.'

○ Closed 5 Jan to end Feb 🔁 Midway between Oban and Loch Gilphead on A816.
Private car park 🛏️ 1 single, 13 twin, 13 double; family rooms and suites available;
most in annexe; all with bathroom/WC exc single with shower/WC; TV, room service,
direct-dial telephone; hair-dryer on request ✓ Dining-room, bar, lounge,
drying-room, library, garden; conference facilities (max 20 residential/non-residential);
early suppers for children; baby-listening ♿ Wheelchair access to hotel (1 step) and
dining-room, 20 ground-floor bedrooms ⊖ No dogs in some bedrooms, no smoking
in dining-room 🗀 Access, Amex, Switch, Visa £: Single/single occupancy of
twin/double £35 to £65, twin/double £70 to £99, suite/family room £83 to £112; deposit
required. Set D £27.50 to £31; bar meals available. Special breaks available

---

ARISAIG Highland   map 11

Arisaig House

Beasdale, By Arisaig PH39 4NR
TEL: (01687) 450622   FAX: (01687) 450626

A fine country-house hotel set in peaceful gardens.

The Gulf Stream is a capricious thing, but it certainly favours the gardens at
Arisaig House: rhododendrons bloom here from January onwards and, by May,
along with the azaleas, they are magnificent. The house itself – a slate-grey
building of plain appearance, built in 1864 but totally refurbished between the
wars – is tucked back from the single-track road. Inside, the décor is that of a
smart country house, enlivened by some colourful Art Deco touches. The
drawing-room is a bright, vaulted space, furnished with floral-print sofas and a
window seat, while the other public rooms, including the lounge, the morning
room and the bar, with its rattan 'mama-san' chairs and view across the rose
garden, continue the style. Of the bedrooms, Linnhe and Shiel boast the
probably finest views, but all are comfortably furnished, featuring the occasional
antique piece and some interesting 1930s-style tiled bathrooms (when these
were first installed, the locals would come just to tour around them). Also
situated on the upper floor is an excellent billiards room.

The new chef, Gary Robinson, uses plenty of local seafood and fish in the
four-course menus. A typical meal might include a sauté of scallops with lime
and soya, then a courgette and artichoke soup, followed by a meunière of
monkfish tail, and finally an orange tart served with a white-chocolate sauce.

○ Closed Nov to Mar 🔁 1 mile past Beasdale railway station on A830 to Mallaig.
Private car park 🛏️ 4 twin, 2 twin/double, 6 double, 2 suites; all with bathroom/WC;
TV, room service, hair-dryer, trouser press, direct-dial telephone; tea/coffee on
request ✓ Dining-room, bar, 3 lounges, drying-room, games room, garden;
conference facilities (max 12 people residential/non-residentiall); croquet, billiards
♿ No wheelchair access ⊖ No children under 10; no dogs; no smoking in
dining-room 🗀 Access, Amex, Switch, Visa £: Single occupancy of twin/double
from £114, twin/double from £168, suite £220; deposit required. Set D £33.50 (1996
prices). Special breaks available

Prices are quoted per room *rather than* per person.

Balcary Bay Hotel

Auchencairn, Nr Castle Douglas DG7 1QZ
TEL: (01556) 640217 FAX: (01556) 640272

A peaceful country-house hotel featuring good views and friendly owners.

Twentieth-century visitors in search of peace and quiet are not the first to seek out the hotel's remote setting on the shore of Balcary Bay: soon after the house was first built in 1625, it saw service as a landing point for smugglers, who packed its cellars to the rafters with contraband shipped over from the Isle of Man. Its exciting past is rather hard to imagine, for nowadays Clare and Graeme Lamb's hotel is a quiet retreat in a quiet corner of Scotland, whose décor shows a delicate, feminine touch. Guests tend to gather in the main lounge or bar before dinner (the residents' lounge lacks the same comfortable atmosphere), before heading through to the classically elegant dining-room. The four-course menus offer a choice at each stage; you might perhaps dine on smoked duck breast or scallops for starters, then celery and Stilton soup, followed by a venison casserole, and rounded off with a cheeseboard. 'The cooking was universally splendid,' reported one satisfied reader 'and Clare is a real spark and clearly sets the general tone of comfort and relaxation.' The bedrooms which have views out to Heston Isle are worth the small extra charge; Room 10 particularly is a bright, large room with a four-poster, situated in a corner. All are decorated in a straightforward, traditional country-house style. 'A splendid example of how good a British hotel can be,' concluded one contented guest.

◑ Closed mid-Nov to Feb ⊅ Off A711 Dumfries to Kirkcudbright road, 2 miles from Auchencairn on the shore road. Private car park ⊫ 3 single, 7 twin, 5 double, 1 four-poster, 1 family room; all with bathroom/WC; TV, room service, hair-dryer, direct-dial telephone; trouser press on request ⊘ Dining-room, bar, 2 lounges, drying-room, conservatory, games room, garden; early suppers for children; babysitting, baby-listening ⅙ No wheelchair access ● No dogs in public rooms; no smoking in some public rooms ⊟ Access, Amex, Delta, Switch, Visa ⒡ Single £52, twin/double £92 to £104, four-poster/family room £104; deposit required. Set D £20.50, Sun L £8.50 (1996 prices). Special breaks available

---

Collin House

Auchencairn, Nr Castle Douglas DG7 1QN
TEL: (01556) 640292 FAX: (01556) 640276

Good cooking and characterful rooms abound at this family-run country house.

The pink walls of Pam Hall and John Wood's house, which is situated on the hillside overlooking Balcary Bay, are easily spotted from the road. Thanks to its elevated position, the views are superb: on a clear day you can see all the way to Skiddaw and the Cumbrian fells from the highest rooms. With its rugs, old furniture and racing memorabilia (Pam's grandfather saddled a record eight winners in a day at Wetherby races), the reception area sets the tone for the rest of Collin House; there's also a smart drawing-room and an elegant dining-room, which is distinguished by its deep-pink walls. John is the chef, and he uses as much local produce as he can, which might result in dishes involving Kirkcudbright scallops, roe deer from the Galloway Forest, or sea trout from the Solway Firth. His puddings are traditional, but often display a flourish: hazelnut meringue combined with fresh raspberries, or Drambuie parfait accompanied by a chocolate sauce, for example. There are always two or three choices for all but the soup course. The bedrooms are named after local hills and beaches, and all feature a nice mixture of old and antique furniture, as well as some individual touches: Screel boasts some fine old Gustavian furniture inherited from the Swedish side of the Hall family, while Old Torr offers fine views and cane chairs in which to sit at the window and enjoy them. 'Absolutely superb,' wrote one visitor, 'a warm, friendly welcome and wonderful food.'

○ Closed Jan & Feb 🗗 ¼ mile east of Auchencairn off A711. Private car park
🛏 2 twin, 4 double; all with bathroom/WC; TV, room service, hair-dryer, direct-dial telephone, clock radio; tea/coffee on request ✓ Dining-room, lounge, drying-room, garden; conference facilities (max 16 people incl up to 6 residential); early suppers for children ᵶ No wheelchair access ● No children under 11 in dining-room eves; dogs in 1 bedroom only; no smoking in dining-room and 1 bedroom; no cigars or pipes ▭ Access, Amex, Visa £ Single occupancy of twin/double £40 to £57, twin/double £80 to £88; deposit required. Set D £28.50. Special breaks available

---

AUCHTERARDER Perthshire & Kinross   map 11

Auchterarder House

Auchterarder PH3 1DZ
TEL: (01764) 663646 FAX: (01764) 662939

Superb baronial-style country-house hotel.

James Reid made his money in railways and spent it on this magnificent example of early Victoriana complete with turret, tower and crow-step gables. The man's portrait still gazes down on the grand reception hall, where he lavished his wealth on the intricately carved panelling: door-frames become Corinthian, pediments sprout fruit and the mantelpiece is defended by lions. The opulence extends to a mosaic-floored conservatory, where afternoon teas are served in summer, a clubby, book-lined library and an elegant dining-room with gilt and green ceiling. At the bottom of the stairs is a grand piano which owner Ian Brown occasionally plays after dinner – this is very much a home as well as a hotel. There are two dinner menus: the first allows a choice of three, four or five courses at increasing prices; the second, 'A Taste of Auchterarder', is a set three-course meal, offering plenty of Scottish fare like Aberdeen Angus steak and local trout or salmon. Desserts can be staunchly traditional like baked chocolate pudding or lighter affairs like iced pistachio and saffron ice-cream bombe. The best bedrooms are in the main wing of the house, and rooms Graham and Gordon get the full Victorian cabinetmaker's treatment: wonderful polished panels and fitted wardrobes throughout. Stuart has a superb original bathroom in chrome, marble and brass. Other rooms over in the turret wing are smaller and less stylish with more modern furnishings.

⊙ Open all year ⊉ On B8062, 2 miles north-west of Auchterarder. Private car park ⟞⟞ 12 twin/double, 3 suites; all with bathroom/WC; TV, room service, hair-dryer, trouser press, direct-dial telephone; tea/coffee on request ✅ Restaurant, 2 lounges, library, conservatory, garden; conference facilities (max 70 people incl up to 15 residential); croquet, pitch and putt; early suppers for children ⚹ No wheelchair access ⬤ No children under 12 ▭ Access, Amex, Delta, Diners, Switch, Visa £¦ Single occupancy of twin/double £80 to £125, twin/double £130 to £225, suite £135 to £160. Set L £15 to £18.50, D £27.50 to £50. Special breaks available

---

Gleneagles

Auchterarder PH3 1NF
TEL: (01764) 662231 FAX: (01764) 662134

Outstanding sport and leisure facilities with friendly, efficient service.

How about a round of golf, some aquarobics, a game of squash and a clay-pigeon shoot? Then breakfast: scrambled couch potatoes, perhaps. If you get out of breath just reading about all the possible activities at Gleneagles, then rest easy, for while this is indisputably a haven of athletic activities and the reception area positively buzzes with people planning to perspire, one member of staff let slip to us that most visitors just come, believe it or not, to relax. Gleneagles opened as a hotel in 1924, a solid unimaginative building that shows some very imaginative use of space by the modern interior designer. And there is a lot to fit in. Right beside reception is a decent slice of up-market retailing from Mappin & Webb to Harvey Nichols. The Country Club has a well-equipped children's play centre and a smart brasserie next to the indoor pool. The Strathearn Restaurant is the main place for dining, offering three set menus or an à la carte. Like the cocktail bar and conference rooms nearby this is a grandiose room – fluted columns, decorative drapes and high ceilings – but the friendly staff make sure the atmosphere is never pretentious. The bedrooms maintain the feel of a smart modern hotel with Edwardian touches. The best are those that look out towards the Glendevon Valley.

⊙ Open all year ⊉ On A823, just off A9 mid-way between Stirling and Perth. Private car park ⟞⟞ 27 single, 59 twin, 121 double, 9 four-poster, 18 suites; family rooms available; all with bathroom/WC; TV, room service, hair-dryer, mini-bar, trouser press, direct-dial telephone ✅ 3 restaurants, 3 bars, 2 lounges, library, conservatory, games room, garden; conference facilities (max 360 people incl up to 234 residential); fishing, golf, gym, sauna, solarium, heated indoor swimming-pool, tennis, clay-pigeon shooting, putting green, archery, falconry, croquet, horseriding, bowling; early suppers for children; babysitting, crèche ⚹ Wheelchair access to hotel (1 step), restaurants and WC (M,F), 12 ground-floor bedrooms, 2 specially equipped for disabled people ⬤ No dogs in public rooms ▭ Access, Amex, Delta, Diners, Switch, Visa £¦ Single £130, twin/double £205 to £335, family room from £225, suite £305 to £1,150; deposit required. Set D £39.50, Sun L £22.50; alc D £40; brasserie and light meals available. Special breaks available

AUCHTERHOUSE Angus

map 11

Old Mansion House

Auchterhouse, By Dundee DD3 0QN
TEL: (01382) 320366   FAX: (01382) 320400

A superb historical setting and friendly service are offered at this quiet country-house hotel.

The Old Mansion House's drive curls past the ivy-clad ruins of the Wallace Tower, where the eponymous Scottish hero reputedly stayed on the eve of the Battle of Falkirk. History is all-pervasive here: even the ladies' cloakroom dates back more than 500 years. With its huge, white walls, the house is an imposingly solid-looking building boasting some fine rooms, notably the book-lined bar and the restaurant, with its extravagant Jacobean ceiling – a wedding gift to the Countess of Buchan (although the effect is spoiled on cold days by an incongruous heater in the fireplace). As you'd expect in such a building, there's a ghost: in this case, Lady Matilda, who killed herself after her beloved lost a duel on the front lawn. If you're interested, a copy of the ballad that the tale inspired – *Sir James the Rose* – is kept behind the desk.

The bedrooms vary considerably in size, but all are comfortably furnished with a mix of reproduction and older pieces. While some are impressive – like Room 6, with its four-poster, and the old nursery, Room 4 – in comparison with the historical grandeur downstairs others can seem slightly disappointing. The restaurant offers à la carte or table d'hôte menus, and both are strong on using local ingredients in their dishes (for example, Cullen skink, a haddock and potato soup). Main-course selections can be described as country-house fare with a twist of the exotic, such as fillet of sole in breadcrumbs served with banana, mango chutney and a devilled sauce, or chicken in a curried-cream sauce, along with the more usual salmon, venison and beef dishes.

◑ Closed 24 Dec to 5 Jan   ⤢ 2 miles from Muirhead on B954. Private car park
⤶ 3 twin, 2 four-poster, 1 family room; all with bathroom/WC; TV, room service, hair-dryer, mini-bar, direct-dial telephone   ✣ Restaurant, 2 bars, library, garden; heated outdoor swimming-pool, tennis, croquet; early suppers for children
♿ No wheelchair access   ⦿ No dogs in public rooms; no smoking in restaurant
▭ Access, Amex, Diners, Switch, Visa   £ Single occupancy of twin £75, twin/four-poster £80 to £100, family room £95 to £125. Set L £17; alc D £27.50. Special breaks available

---

BALLACHULISH Highland

map 11

Ballachulish House

Ballachulish PA39 4JX
TEL: (01855) 811266   FAX: (01855) 811498

A fascinating history and friendly hosts can be found at this comfortable family home.

Looking out over Loch Linnhe, this simple, whitewashed house boasts more of a history than many stately piles: the orders for the Glencoe massacre were signed in the kitchen; the real-life version of *Kidnapped*'s Alan Breck Stewart suppos-edly stayed here; Cumberland's men set fire to the house; and (unsurprisingly) it is haunted. Liz and John Grey are more than a match for such a pedigree, however: John traded around the Hebrides in a 100-ton schooner before the vessel was lost; he then became a fisherman working off the coast of Mull. They keep a good-humoured house, which is smartly furnished with antiques, old prints and the occasional flourish such as the plaid carpet in the dining-room. The new chef, Breda McCarthy, serves four-course dinners, with an alternative choice for all but the soup. You might start with pancakes stuffed with mushrooms à la crème, follow with a curried parsnip soup, then savour roast leg of lamb, and round it all off with a Normandy apple tart. Although Ballachulish House is a Wolsey Lodge, guests are not expected to share tables.

The bedrooms are all of a good size; those on the first floor feature nice, old furniture, and their bookcases and ornaments maintain the family-home atmosphere that is a feature of the downstairs rooms. Those that are situated in the roof are more modern, and are decorated in co-ordinated colour schemes. Television is not really in keeping with the house's style, but all the rooms have television sockets, and sets are available on request.

◑ Closed Dec & Jan ⊿ At roundabout before Ballachulish Bridge, take A828 towards Oban. Hotel is 200 yards further on, on left. Private car park ⊨ 2 twin, 2 double, 2 family rooms; all with bathroom/WC; hair-dryer, direct-dial telephone; TV on request ⊘ Dining-room, lounge, TV room, drying-room, games room, garden; conference facilities (max 20 people incl up to 6 residential); croquet, billiards; early suppers for children ⅄ No wheelchair access ● No children under 3; dogs in bedrooms only, by arrangement; smoking in games room only ▭ Access, Delta, Switch, Visa ⟨£⟩ Single occupancy of twin/double £54, twin/double £72 to £80, family room from £87; deposit required. Set D £23.50

Balgonie Country House

Braemar Place, Ballater AB35 5RQ
TEL: (01339) 755482 (AND FAX)

Fine cooking and smart bedrooms feature in a family-run hotel.

Although it is approached along a suburban street, Balgonie is very much a country-house hotel in style. The trim, Edwardian building looks across a long lawn to the golf course and hills around Glen Muick. At breakfast time, guests can watch the red squirrels coming out on to the grass to feed. Owners Priscilla and John Finnie have opted for a bright, modern look inside the house: the dining-room is a smart, blue and white room decorated with Margaret Loxton prints, while the sitting-room and bar are also pleasant, airy places in which guests gather before dinner – John helping with the introductions when necessary. Chef David Hindmarch – once a senior cook at Buckingham Palace and Balmoral – has been greatly praised for his four-course dinners, which offer choices on all but the second course (usually a fish dish, such as sea bass with a tomato concassé and olives). The main courses demonstrate a strongly Scottish flavour, and might include local salmon with a horseradish crust or fillet of Aberdeen Angus.

The bedrooms are named after fishing pools on the Dee; those on the first floor are more traditional. Higher up, the rooms – which are furnished in light wood – are more modern and boast excellent elevated views south.

◑ Closed mid-Jan to mid-Feb 🔁 On the outskirts of Ballater, off A93. Private car park 🛏 3 twin, 6 double; 7 with bathroom/WC, 2 with shower/WC; TV, hair-dryer, direct-dial telephone, radio; tea/coffee-making facilities and trouser press on request ✅ Dining-room, bar, lounge, drying-room, garden; croquet; early suppers for children ♿ No wheelchair access ⬤ No children under 8 in dining-room eves; dogs in bedrooms only, by arrangement; no smoking in dining-room ▭ Access, Amex, Delta, Switch, Visa 💷 Single occupancy of twin/double £49 to £59, twin/double £77 to £97; deposit required. Set L £17.50, D £28.50. Special breaks available

Stakis Royal Deeside ☆

Braemar Road, Ballater AB35 5XA
TEL: (013397) 55858 FAX: (013397) 55447

Family-oriented facilities are offered at this country hotel on Deeside.

Originally built by the marmalade millions of the Keiller family as a country retreat, this late Victorian mansion was greatly extended and developed a decade ago, and has recently come under the ownership of Stakis. The older part of the building features polished panels and deers' heads, but the newer additions include a poolside disco, a squash court and a dry ski slope. The hotel's facilities are good, and an all-day crèche means that parents can get the chance to use them; the central feature is the pool, where a good-sized flume will keep the children happy. If all this activity gets a bit hectic, then you can retire to the peaceful study-bar – a convincing, nineteenth-century reproduction – or to the formal Oaks Restaurant, in which three- or four-course table d'hôte dinners are served, as well as an ambitious, à la carte alternative. A more informal option is the clubhouse restaurant beside the pool, where you can order light snacks or three-course meals.

The bedrooms in the older part of the house are smart and well equipped, and some boast decent views towards Lochnagar and Balmoral Forest. Families should opt for the suites: each consists of a double room and a lounge, in which two single beds fold away neatly during the day; a balcony offers views across the Dee valley.

◑ Open all year 🔁 1½ miles west of Ballater on A93. Private car park 🛏 13 twin, 18 double, 1 four-poster, 6 family rooms, 6 suites; all with bathroom/WC; TV, room service, hair-dryer, trouser press, direct-dial telephone ✅ 2 restaurants, 2 bars, lounge, study, games room; air-conditioning public rooms; conference facilities (max 100 people incl up to 44 residential); fishing, gym, sauna, solarium, heated indoor swimming-pool, tennis, dry ski slope, snooker, squash; early suppers for children; babysitting, crèche, outdoor games ♿ Wheelchair access to hotel (ramp), restaurants and WC (unisex), lift to bedrooms ⬤ No dogs; no smoking in restaurants ▭ Access, Amex, Delta, Diners, Switch, Visa 💷 Single occupancy of twin/double £99, twin/double £129, four-poster £184, family room £139, suite £199; deposit required. Continental B £7, cooked B £10.50; set D £24; light meals available. Special breaks available

Tullich Lodge

Ballater AB35 5SB
TEL: (01339) 755406   FAX: (01339) 755397

An individualistic commitment to excellence and wonderful antique furnishings.

This superb baronial belvedere commands the Pass of Ballater so well that it comes as a surprise to find the house is only a century old. The style is uncompromisingly individual and traditional; excerpts from the brochure give some idea: 'wireless in all bedrooms', 'jacket and tie for dinner' and 'children served high tea in the kitchen'. Owners Neil Bannister and Hector Macdonald have furnished their house with impeccable good taste and character – even the telephone in reception gets an antique mahogany and glass Time Machine to convey guests back to an era before mass production. The drawing-room is elegant with a baby-grand piano and views across the lawns. On the same floor is a chintzy sitting-room with panelled walls, rugs and plenty of books. Before dinner, guests gather in the bar with its odd collection of bric-à-brac, then move into the dining-room, which has magnificent mahogany panelling. The four-course dinners follow a set menu without choice, though special requests can be catered for with advance warning. The lack of choice means prices can be kept down and standards up: one menu gives dressed crab, spinach soup, lamb hot-pot and strawberries; the following night was smoked venison, watercress soup, seared scallops and strawberry ice-cream. Bedrooms maintain the period atmosphere with antique furnishings and some old-fashioned bathrooms. If you can handle the stairs, the Turret Room is a treat with its panelling, antiques and window seat view to the Glenshee range.

◑ Closed Nov to Mar   ⊿ 1½ miles east of Ballater on A93. Private car park   🅿 3 single, 4 twin, 3 double; all with bathroom/WC exc 2 with shower/WC; limited room service, hair-dryer, direct-dial telephone, radio; no tea/coffee-making facilities in rooms; TV on request; trouser press in some rooms   ✧ Dining-room, bar, lounge, drying-room, library, garden; early suppers for children; baby-listening   & No wheelchair access   ● No dogs in public rooms; no smoking in dining-room   ▭ Access, Amex, Diners, Switch, Visa   £ Single £100, single occupancy of twin/double £140, twin/double £200 (rates incl dinner). Set D £25; bar lunches available. Special breaks available

---

Delnashaugh Inn

Ballindalloch AB37 9AS
TEL: (01807) 500255   FAX: (01807) 500389

Comfortable, stylish inn close to the River Spey and whisky country.

The whitewashed walls of this former drover's inn catch the eye as you cross the River Avon (pronounced 'Arn') on the edge of the Ballindalloch estate. The river is fished for salmon, the number-one activity for many visitors, who can make use of the tackle room. Marion and David Ogden give a good welcome to non-anglers too, advising on local walks, golf or distillery visits (this is the heart of Speyside). Although the bar is open to the public it is very relaxed. In the elegant formal dining-room at the front of the inn, excellent four-course dinners are served. Our inspection meal was of grilled goat's cheese on red peppers, lentil and tomato soup, haddock florentine and blackcurrant sorbet – all good fresh ingredients, nicely cooked and served. Bedrooms show a light touch with pinks, floral prints and white fitted furniture. Housekeeping standards, as in the rest of the house, are immaculate.

◑ Closed Nov to early Mar ⤢ On A95, 13 miles from Grantown-on-Spey. Private car park ⤙ 8 twin, 1 double; all with bathroom/WC; TV, room service, hair-dryer, direct-dial telephone ✓ Dining-room, bar, lounge, drying-room; fishing, roe-buck stalking, shooting; early suppers for children; babysitting, baby-listening ♿ Wheelchair access to hotel (ramp), dining-room and WC (unisex), 5 ground-floor bedrooms ● No dogs ⊡ Access, Visa £ Single occupancy of twin/double £65 to £80, twin/double £110 to £130. Set D £22.50; bar lunches available

---

BALQUHIDDER Stirling　　　　　　　　　　　　　　　　　map 11

Monachyle Mhor

Balquhidder, Lochearnhead FK19 8PQ
TEL: (01877) 384622　FAX: (01877) 384305

A lively farmhouse, with good-natured hosts, situated in the heart of Rob Roy country.

The last 4 miles to Monachyle Mhor, alongside Loch Voil, have been busier than usual of late, thanks to Hollywood's penchant for turning those whom some might term cattle thieves into heroes. Rob Roy Macgregor is therefore responsible for the rebuilt road (and, indeed, for wearing out the old one), as visitors explore the area around his grave in Balquhidder (pronounced 'Bal-whidder') churchyard. It is certainly a journey worth making, and Jean, Rob and Tom Lewis' pink-harled farmhouse is a popular focus for visitors and locals alike; the public bar, with its crackling fire and good-humoured banter, is a particularly lively spot. Residents can also enjoy the quieter, smarter lounge, as well as the pine-clad conservatory restaurant, which boasts loch views. The cuisine is imaginative and competitively priced: a budget menu offers such traditional fare as roast pheasant or Cullen skink, while the superior, pricier, version might include entrecôte of venison, or roast quail. The bedrooms feature a fine blend of old and new furniture; those in the 'Byre' courtyard conversion are rather more stylish.

The 1998 Guide will be published in the autumn of 1997. Reports on hotels are welcome at any time of the year, but are extremely valuable in the spring. Send them to The Which? Hotel Guide, FREEPOST, 2 Marylebone Road, London NW1 1YN. No stamp is needed if reports are posted in the UK. Our e-mail address is: "guidereports@which.co.uk".

◑ Open all year ⊿ 11 miles north of Callander, on A84. Turn right at Kingshouse and continue for 6 miles along glen. Hotel is on right. Private car park ⟻ 2 twin, 8 double, 3 suites; some in annexe; all with bathroom/WC exc twins with shower/WC; room service, hair-dryer, direct-dial telephone, radio; TV in some rooms
♦ Restaurant/conservatory, dining-room, bar, lounge, TV room, drying-room, garden; conference facilities (max 20 people incl up to 13 residential); fishing, clay-pigeon and grouse-moor shooting, red-deer stalking; early suppers for children ↻ No wheelchair access ● No children under 10; no dogs; no smoking ⊟ Access, Visa £ Single occupancy of twin/double £29 to £37, twin/double £58 to £74, suite £74; deposit required. Set L £15, D £18/23; alc L, D £13.50

BANCHORY Aberdeenshire   map 11

Raemoir House

Banchory AB31 4ED
TEL: (01330) 824884   FAX: (01330) 822171

A characterful old house with friendly staff and management.

The grandeur of this mid-eighteenth-century mansion is apparent as soon as you turn into the drive and glimpse its façade through the trees. It's a grandeur that is mitigated by the friendly and delightfully unstuffy atmosphere that has been created by the Sabin family over the past half-century or so. After walking in through the main entrance, you'll find plenty of oil paintings, cases of fishing flies and dark, Victorian furnishings, but it is the idiosyncratic flourishes – such as the bar made from an ancient carved bed (broken by Tudor newlyweds, according to legend) – that bring it all to life. The other public rooms are equally interesting – particularly the oval ballroom, with its nineteenth-century velvet wall-coverings and family portraits. The bedrooms are more variable in style: one reader, who stayed in the separate, and older, 'Ha' Hoose', felt that his room did match up to that of his friend, who was in the Old English Room – which, with its vast four-poster bed (dated 1562), is undoubtedly the pick of them all.

The dining-room offers either an à la carte menu or a four-course table d'hôte, and typical dishes might include smoked salmon pâté, followed by cream of broccoli and basil soup, and then roast haunch of venison. The wine list has plenty of choices priced under £20. One source of irritation to some guests has been the 10 per cent service charge added to the bill, 'unless otherwise requested.'

◑ Open all year ⊿ 2 miles north of Banchory on A980. Private car park ⟻ 5 single, 14 twin/double, 8 double, 1 four-poster; family room and suites available; some in annexe; most with bathroom/WC, 2 with shower/WC; TV, room service, hair-dryer, trouser press, direct-dial telephone, clock radio ♦ Dining-room, bar, 2 lounges, TV room, drying-room, garden; conference facilities (max 60 people incl up to 28 residential); gym, sauna, solarium, tennis, croquet, pitch and putt, shooting; early suppers for children; toys, babysitting, baby-listening, outdoor games
↻ Wheelchair access to hotel, dining-room and WC (M,F), 7 ground-floor bedrooms
● No children under 10 in dining-room eves; dogs in some bedrooms only; no smoking in dining-room ⊟ Access, Amex, Delta, Diners, Visa £ Single £53, single occupancy of twin/double £68 to £79, twin/double £85 to £115, four-poster £125, family room £95 to £105, suite from £111; deposit required. Set D £25, Sun L £16; alc D from £15 (prices valid till Feb 1997); bar lunches available. Special breaks available

Kinloch House

By Blairgowrie PH10 6SG
TEL: (01250) 884237   FAX: (01250) 884333

A country-house hotel offering a fine setting and unobtrusive, but friendly, service.

A typical conversation in Kinloch House's grand lounge concerns the 18lb salmon caught that day and the prospects for the morrow. Sarah and David Shentall's country-house hotel could be a finishing school for salmon fishers (there is no formal tuition as such – just sit back and soak up the knowledge). The house is early Victorian, built for a jute baron who installed its magnificent oak-panelled hall and stairs, on which his portrait still hangs. Extended in 1911, the hotel maintains an Edwardian style throughout (even in the recently added wing, which boasts a tower). The bedrooms in this newer section tend to be larger, with more modern bathrooms; Clunie and Marlee feature stylish sitting-areas in the tower. Room 2, in the original part of the house, has the best view, which looks south across Marlee Loch to the Sidlaw Hills.

Dining is formal – jacket and tie for gentlemen – with the four-course dinners offering plenty of local fare and a good range of choices. Starters might include salmon marinated in herbs, honey and whisky, a chicken-liver pâté, or smoked eel; and while the main courses are strong on steaks, they also offer a fish choice – perhaps a suprême of halibut or sauté fillet of monkfish. A traditional sweets trolley rounds off the occasion.

◗ Closed 18 to 30 Dec   ⊠ On A923, 3 miles west of Blairgowrie. Private car park
🛏 5 single, 8 twin/double, 6 four-poster, 2 suites; most with bathroom/WC, some with shower/WC; TV, room service, hair-dryer, trouser press, direct-dial telephone
✧ Dining-room, bar, 2 lounges, TV room, drying-room, conservatory, garden; conference facilities (max 12 people residential/non-residential); fishing; early suppers for children; baby-listening, cot, high chair   ♿ Wheelchair access to hotel (1 ramp) and dining-room, 4 ground-floor bedrooms specially equipped for disabled people
● No children under 7 in dining-room eves; dogs in some bedrooms only; no smoking in dining-room   ▭ Access, Amex, Delta, Diners, Switch, Visa   £ Single £74, single occupancy of twin/double £110, twin/double/four-poster £173, suite £205 (rates incl dinner). Set L £16, D £29; light meals available

---

Busta House

Brae ZE2 9QN
TEL: (01806) 522506   FAX: (01806) 522588

Excellent views and comfortable rooms feature at this eighteenth-century laird's house.

Boasting a fine location looking across Busta Voe fjord, Busta House is said to be the oldest continuously inhabited building in the Shetland Islands. The white-painted house was built in 1714 by the Gifford family (the local lairds), and stands in 4 acres of grounds that slope down to a small sea harbour. In good weather, guests can use the hotel's boat for trips on the water. Inside the house, the atmosphere is friendly, and the careful and traditional décor mixes antique and reproduction furniture. The bedrooms are also tastefully decorated and well equipped.

The dining-room offers a table d'hôte four-course menu, and the cuisine concentrates on local fish: main courses might include baked whiting fillets, or grilled Shetland salmon served with a Stilton and grape sauce; the desserts are staunchly traditional crumbles, custards and cranachan. If you prefer a more informal setting, you can eat in the bar, where typical dishes might be breaded haddock, scampi or chicken curry.

◑ Closed 22 Dec to 3 Jan ⤢ 27 miles north of Lerwick and ferry terminal. Take A970 north; hotel is signposted after Brae. Private car park ⊨ 2 single, 6 twin, 10 double, 1 four-poster, 1 suite; family room available; most with bathroom/WC, some with shower/WC; TV, room service, hair-dryer, trouser press, direct-dial telephone
⊘ Dining-room, bar, lounge, drying-room, library, garden; fishing; early suppers for children; toys ⅙ No wheelchair access ⬤ No dogs in public rooms; no smoking in dining-room or library ▭ Access, Amex, Delta, Diners, Switch, Visa £ Single £63, twin/double £87, four-poster £95, family room from £84, suite £110; deposit required. Set D £22.50; bar meals available. Special breaks available

---

BUNESSAN Argyll & Bute   map 11

Ardfenaig House

By Bunessan, Isle of Mull PA67 6DX
TEL: (01681) 700210 (AND FAX)

A small, secluded hotel with friendly hosts.

Most of the visitors who come to this last, craggy finger of Mull are heading for the Iona ferry, but Jane and Malcolm Davidson's hotel makes a good stopping point. Set well away from the road, the Georgian house looks down along Loch Caol (pronounced 'cool'), and is an easy walking distance from its quiet sandy coves. Although once a hunting lodge, Ardfenaig House's décor steers clear of sporting souvenirs and settles for a simple, country-house style and an easy, sociable atmosphere. Plans are in hand to build a conservatory-style dining-room on to the front of the house, but at the time of our inspection the existing dining-room remained a smart, small room, featuring a pine dresser and a view over the gardens. The four-course dinners offer a choice of starters – perhaps smoked venison with rowanberry jelly, or a spinach, turmeric and lemon soup – and then a main-course dish such as halibut with scallops and prawns, followed by either profiteroles or iced Grand Marnier nougat. The bread is home-made, while a polytunnel nurtures seasonal vegetables. The bedrooms are comfortably furnished in a mix of antique and cottage-style pieces; those at the front enjoy a good view along the loch. 'A lovely setting, very friendly and relaxed welcome,' reported one reader.

● Closed 1 Nov to 31 Mar ⃟ Take A849 west through Bunessan; hotel is 3 miles beyond, on the right-hand side. Private car park ⌂→ 3 twin, 2 double; all with bathroom/WC; room service, hair-dryer ✓ Dining-room, bar, lounge, TV room, drying-room, garden; sailing, sea-fishing, croquet; early suppers for children ⅋ No wheelchair access ● No dogs; no smoking in bedrooms and discouraged in public rooms ⊟ Access, Visa £ Single occupancy of twin/double £73 to £87, twin/double £146 to £174 (rates incl dinner)

CALLANDER Stirling   map 11

Arran Lodge

Leny Road, Callander FK17 8AJ
TEL: (01877) 330976

An immaculately well-kept guesthouse, boasting a riverside location.

After you've driven out of Callander, a brisk turn off the busy main road and then a crisp stop on the short gravel drive in front of Pasqua Margarita and Robert Moore's small guesthouse is required. At first sight, Arran Lodge's frontage is pretty unremarkable, but a glance down the slope past the patio at the side (as well as what appears to be a small bungalow) suddenly reveals a Victorian, colonial-style house – complete with verandah – and expansive gardens leading down to the banks of the River Teith. Inside, the house is light, airy, and beautifully kept; the lounge features an Adams-style fireplace and white leather sofas. Robert likes to create a house-party atmosphere, and, as well as welcoming guests personally, chats with them after dinner – good traditional dishes served in the smart dining-room – which he also cooks.

The four bedrooms reflect the bright elegance of the public rooms; the two superior four-posters, Venacher and Achray, are the most popular, and are priced slightly higher than Lomond and Lubnaig.

● Closed 4 Nov to 6 Apr ⃟ On A84, on western outskirts of Callander. Private car park ⌂→ 1 double, 3 four-poster; twin and family rooms available; 2 with bathroom/WC, 2 with shower/WC; TV, hair-dryer ✓ Dining-room, lounge, drying-room, garden; fishing ⅋ No wheelchair access ● No children under 12; no dogs; no smoking ⊟ None accepted £ Single occupancy of twin/double £46 to £60, twin/double £58 to £70, four-poster £64 to £75, family room £86 to £103; deposit required. Set D £22. Special breaks available

---

Roman Camp

Callander FK17 8BG
TEL: (01877) 330003 FAX: (01877) 331533

Top-notch service in a fascinating, seventeenth-century house.

Once upon a time, the pink walls of the Roman Camp heralded safety for Jacobite vagabonds, and the hotel, which is tucked away behind Callander's bustling Main Street, still retains the atmosphere of a hideaway. The front entrance hall dates back to 1625 and, with its low ceilings and dark, gnarled beams, sets the tone for the rest of the building which, despite extensive

Victorian additions, is not pretentiously grand. The best of the older public rooms is the panelled, book-lined library, which includes a secret doorway leading to the chapel.

From the Art Deco lamps to the 'toppling' topiary in the walled garden, Marion and Eric Brown have added a light touch to the hotel's otherwise country-house style. The bedrooms in the older part of the house boast plush fabrics, canopied beds and gilt trimmings, while those in the more modern section, overlooking the garden, are decorated in bright pastel colours and plaids. Somewhere in between, in the Victorian part of the house, is the Barrie Suite, in which the creator of Peter Pan regularly stayed.

The formal restaurant offers a choice of à la carte or table d'hôte dinners. The latter could include an escalope of turbot with crayfish, followed by a consommé of pigeon, fillet of pork served with a confit of garlic and tomato, and a soft-fruit pudding.

◑ Open all year ☑ Heading north on A84 at the east end of Callander's Main Street, turn left between two pink cottages down a 300-yard drive. Private car park ⊨ 4 twin, 6 double, 1 four-poster, 3 suites; all with bathroom/WC exc 2 twins with shower/WC; TV, room service, hair-dryer, direct-dial telephone, radio ⊘ Restaurant, bar, lounge, drying-room, library, conservatory, garden; conference facilities (max 50 people incl up to 14 residential); fishing; early suppers for children; baby-listening ♿ Wheelchair access to hotel, restaurant and WC (M,F), 7 ground-floor bedrooms, 1 specially equipped for disabled people ● No children under 5 in restaurant after 7pm; no dogs in public rooms; no smoking in restaurant ▭ Access, Amex, Diners, Switch, Visa ⓔ Single occupancy of twin/double £69 to £85, twin/double £89 to £139, four-poster £89 to £109, suite £129 to £159; deposit required. Set L £19, D £34; alc L, D £45; light lunches available. Special breaks available

---

CONON BRIDGE Highland   map 11

Kinkell House

Easter Kinkell, Conon Bridge, By Dingwall IV7 8HY
TEL: (01349) 861270   FAX: (01349) 865902

A well-kept, small hotel, with friendly hosts.

Since its lofty position (overlooking the Cromarty Firth) is so handy for the Black Isle – or, indeed, for any other points to the north and west – Kinkell House makes a good base from which to explore the area. The original, mid-nineteenth-century house has experienced a few additions (most recently a new wing comprising four bedrooms) but all enjoy the panoramic view. There's a very pleasant conservatory, featuring a beechwood floor and dark, rattan easy chairs, along with three small, interlinking lounge areas that successfully create a warm, cosy atmosphere – an ambience that is also enhanced by Marsha and Steve Fraser's friendly welcome. A good supply of board games and magazines are on hand should the weather be bad.

The three-course dinners feature plenty of local ingredients, and a typical menu might include salmon and chive fishcakes, followed by pan-fried fillets of venison and pheasant, and finally a baked apple, rhubarb and almond pudding accompanied by vanilla ice-cream.

The newer bedrooms (which boast the finer views) will probably supplant the older ones as favourites, but all are comfortably furnished with a mixture of pine, antique and reproduction furniture, and the smart duvet covers add a splash of colour.

◑ Open all year ⊠ On B9169, 1 mile west of Duncanston. Private car park ⤙ 4 twin, 3 double; family rooms available; 3 with bathroom/WC, 4 with shower/WC; TV, room service, hair-dryer, direct-dial telephone ⌀ Restaurant, bar, lounge, drying-room, conservatory, garden; conference facilities (max 40 people incl up to 7 residential); early suppers for children ♿ Wheelchair access to hotel, restaurant and WC (unisex), 1 ground-floor bedroom specially equipped for disabled people ● No smoking in restaurant and bedrooms; dogs by arrangement ⊟ Access, Visa
£ Single occupancy of twin/double £39 to £44, twin/double £60 to £70, family room £78 to £88; deposit required. Alc L £12.50, D £19.50 (prices valid till Mar 1997). Special breaks available

---

CRINAN Argyll & Bute · map 11

Crinan Hotel

Crinan, By Lochgilphead PA31 8SR
TEL: (01546) 830261 FAX: (01546) 830292

Good food and fine views abound, but the rooms are somewhat overpriced at this seaside hotel popular with yachties.

Just far enough from the main tourist trails, Crinan is a delightful small village that marks the spot where the Crinan Canal meets the sea again, after a 9-mile journey across Kintyre. The white-fronted hotel looks out across the bay to Dunoon Castle – a marvellous view, and worth specifying when booking a room. Nick Ryan has owned Crinan Hotel for 26 years, and is conviviality and exuberance personified, whether he's demonstrating old restaurateur tricks to test for a prawn's freshness (hold them up by the tendrils, which should not break) or giving the precise time when they were landed (two-and-a-quarter hours earlier, at the pier). With its panelled, pub-style bar, comfortable lounge decorated in light, airy colours, and the monogrammed Crinan Hotel carpets, the building too has character. In places, there are signs of wear (all those thousands of yachty deck shoes have taken their toll on the carpet) and, considering that Crinan's pleasures do not come cheap, the bedrooms can be disappointing. Nevertheless, during our inspection visit the service was faultless and the dinner excellent. The emphasis is on freshly landed seafood that is cooked on that day (if you are visiting Crinan for that reason, it may be worth telephoning ahead to check that the boat is going out). Our meal consisted of a starter of apple and Stilton soup, followed by smoked salmon, and then the memorable Loch Crinan jumbo prawns, with a lemon tart to finish. Alternative choices might include Sound of Jura king clams, Loch Craignish mussels and Kintyre lamb; the Westward Restaurant downstairs offers a slightly wider choice than the totally seafood-oriented Lock 16.

◗ Open all year ⟶ Follow B841 from Cairnbaan, or A82/A83 along Loch Lomond, to Crinan at the north end of the Crinan Canal. Private car park ⟶ 2 single, 20 twin/double; family room available; all with bathroom/WC exc singles with shower/WC; TV, room service, hair-dryer, direct-dial telephone; no tea/coffee-making facilities in rooms ⌑ 2 restaurants, 3 bars, 2 lounges, garden; conference facilities (max 100 people incl up to 22 residential); early suppers for children ♿ Wheelchair access to hotel, restaurant, WC (M,F), lift to bedrooms, 1 specially equipped for disabled people ● No dogs or smoking in restaurants ⊟ Access, Amex, Switch, Visa £ Single £75 to £95, twin/double £130 to £230, family room from £150 to £250 (rates incl dinner); deposit required. Set D £30 to £40 (1996 prices). Special breaks available

---

CROMARTY Highland

map 11

Royal Hotel

Marine Terrace, Cromarty IV11 8YN
TEL: (01381) 600217 (AND FAX)

Exceptional value and friendly service can be found at this seafront inn.

Cromarty is an attractive little town, featuring whitewashed cottages and pink-stone Georgian houses. The pebble-dashed frontage of the Royal Hotel looks out to the sea which once gave the people herring fishing, but which now provides work on the oil platforms that can be seen on the horizon. Guests are given a good welcome, which – along with the fire in the lounge – was much appreciated by our inspector, who visited the hotel on a cold blustery day. Many hotel lounges seem to be rarely (if ever) used, but the Royal's is not of that type: books telling you about the area, stacks of games, comfy chairs, as well as easy access to the bar, ensure that guests spend time here. Dinners can be taken in the formal restaurant or in the bar. The cuisine is of a high standard – the grilled haddock smothered in lemon butter was a lesson to many far grander establishments – and the service is friendly and quick. The four-course set menu served in the restaurant offers a similar style of dishes to those that are chalked up on the blackboard in the bar, and represents tremendous value.

The bedrooms, featuring reproduction furniture and smart, floral bedspreads, are straightforward and comfortable; the electric blankets are a bonus on cold nights.

◗ Open all year ⟶ From A9, turn right 1 mile north of Inverness on to A832 to Cromarty. Private car park ⟶ 1 single, 2 twin, 5 double, 2 family rooms; suite available; all with bathroom/WC; TV; hair-dryer on request ⌑ Restaurant, 2 bars, lounge, drying-room, library, conservatory, garden; conference facilities (max 60 people incl up to 10 residential); early suppers for children ♿ No wheelchair access ● No dogs in public rooms ⊟ Access, Amex, Visa £ Single £30 to £32, twin/double £50 to £55, family room £63 to £70, suite £90 to £100. Set L £12.50, D £20; bar meals available. Special breaks available

---

The Guide *is totally independent, accepts no free hospitality, and survives on the number of copies sold each year.*

Druimard Country House

Dervaig, Isle of Mull PA75 6QW
TEL: (01688) 400345/400291FAX (01688) 400345

An informal country-house hotel serving excellent food.

Don't forget your binoculars if you're staying at Wendy and Haydn Hubbard's small hotel: the wildlife is pretty special. Otters can be observed from Room 1, there are hen harriers, golden eagles and sea eagles to be seen in the skies, as well as minke whales in the sea (a neighbour organises boat trips to see them). The wildlife finds its way into the house, too: a stoat bares its fangs in reception, while a peregrine protects its kill amid the usual antlers on the stairs. Druimard Country House stands above the River Beller, only a few hundred yards from the sea. The lounge and restaurant enjoy pleasant views; both are homely, comfortable rooms, and there is a small conservatory that is popular for pre-dinner drinks. Wendy is enthusiastically committed to good cooking (she had recently returned from a 'top-up' course when we called) and is steadily improving the standards. Her encouragement of the local market garden means that fresh vegetables and herbs are now more easily available, while fresh oysters and lobsters are landed nearby. Dinners usually offer a choice of at least three dishes for each of the three courses, and a typical meal might comprise a cream of cauliflower and Stilton soup to start, followed by a fillet of wild Mull salmon, and then a steamed chocolate pudding served with a café-crème anglaise. The bedrooms are bright and comfortable, with a cottagey atmosphere. During the summer season, the Mull Little Theatre next door (Britain's smallest professional company) provides entertainment in the evenings.

◑ Closed Nov to Mar ⬛ Approached from Tobermory, hotel is on right before the village. Private car park ⬅ 2 twin, 3 double, 1 suite; 1 with bathroom/WC, 3 with shower/WC; TV, direct-dial telephone ✅ Restaurant, lounge, conservatory; early suppers for children ♿ No wheelchair access ⬤ No dogs or smoking in public rooms ▭ Access, Visa £ Single occupancy of twin/double £45 to £50, twin/double £77 to £85, suite £110 to £120; deposit required. Set D £18.50 (1996 prices)

Polmaily House Hotel

Drumnadrochit IV3 6XT
TEL: (01456) 450343 FAX: (01456) 450813

A family-run and child-oriented hotel close to the shores of Loch Ness.

It's rare for children to be as well catered for as adults at a British hotel, but Sonia and John Whittington-Davis have four youngsters of their own, so they appreciate the fact that holidays should be for all the family. Their ten-bedroomed house and gardens offer both indoor and outdoor play areas, trampolining, a tree house, as well as a heated indoor swimming-pool. For the very small, there are also babysitting and -listening services – even the bikes for hire are equipped with baby seats. For older guests, the 18-acre grounds offer woodland walks, trout fishing in the pond or games of tennis. In the evening, you can plan the next day in the comfortable lounge with the help of the maps and guides available. Upstairs, more books feature in a small lounge. Children are served high tea ('proper food, too – not just burger and chips,' one happy parent reports), and are usually in bed before 8.30pm, allowing their parents to dine in peace in the two-section Urquhart Restaurant. The menus offer a reasonable choice of traditional dishes such as venison, Aberdeen Angus steaks and salmon. The smart and attractive bedrooms are generally spacious, and are furnished with a mix of old and new pieces. Families can make use of the connecting rooms.

◗ Open all year ⤢ At Drumnadrochit take A831 towards Cannich for 2 miles; hotel is on the right. Private car park ⌂ 2 single, 2 twin, 4 double, 1 four-poster, 1 suite; family rooms available; all with bathroom/WC exc singles with shower/WC; TV, room service, hair-dryer, direct-dial telephone ⌂ Restaurant, bar, lounge, drying-room, library, conservatory, garden; fishing, golf, heated indoor swimming-pool, tennis; early suppers for children; playroom, babysitting, baby-listening, outdoor games ♿ Wheelchair access to hotel, restaurant and WC (unisex), 1 ground-floor bedroom specially equipped for disabled people ● No dogs in public rooms; no smoking in bedrooms ▭ Access, Delta, Switch, Visa £ Single £35 to £54, single occupancy of twin/double £50 to £70, twin/double £70 to £108, four-poster/suite £88 to £126, family room from £77; deposit required. Set D £20; alc D £18; light lunches available. Special breaks available

---

DUNKELD Perthshire & Kinross map 11

Kinnaird

Kinnaird Estate, Dunkeld PH8 0LB
TEL: (01796) 482440   FAX: (01796) 482289

Premier country-house living on a Perthshire estate, offered at premier rates.

A leather-bound book on the desk in the drawing-room records one aspect of Kinnaird's previous incarnation: 'August 12, 1927 – 108 grouse'. The house has been owned by the Ward family since those halcyon days and, although it became a hotel in 1990, it still retains its country-house atmosphere: the shooting parties that head off on to the 9,000-acre estate, the afternoons in the billiard room with an audience of salmon in glass cases and the pre-dinner drinks in front of the log fire. The tone is set as soon as you enter the main door: no hotel signs or reception desk are visible; instead a long and elegant hall – decorated with a superb collection of ornithological prints – leads you down to the Cedar Room (named after its panelling), or to one of the dining-rooms, which boasts delicate, eighteenth-century décor and views across the Tay valley. Since Kinnaird was built a century before the Victorian taste for vast grandeur predominated, its rooms are not overbearingly huge. Like the public rooms, the nine bedrooms are classically furnished, with antique pieces featuring among the sofas and armchairs; Balmacneil has an excellent corner location, offering views down to the river. As you would expect, the superb cuisine is in grand style, with salmon fillets, beef steaks and breast of duck making main-course appearances. The starters might include smoked mussels and squat lobster, or a ravioli of rabbit and morels, while the puddings offer a wide choice, from traditional dishes such as apple and currant crumble to the lighter iced nougatine glacé or hot prune and Armagnac soufflé.

Guests at Kinnaird have praised the service: 'the most complete attention to detail without ever being obsequious. Even my walking boots were cleaned and polished.'

◑ Closed Mon to Wed from 6 Jan to 16 Mar ⤢ Travelling north on A9, after Dunkeld exit continue for 2 miles, then take B898 signed Kinnaird. Continue for 4½ miles. Private car park ⨽ 1 twin, 7 twin/double, 1 suite; all with bathroom/WC; TV, room service, hair-dryer, direct-dial telephone ✓ 2 dining-rooms, lounge, drying-room, study, games room, garden; conference facilities (max 25 people incl up to 9 residential); fishing, tennis, croquet, clay-pigeon shooting ♿ Wheelchair access to hotel (1 ramp) and dining-rooms, 1 ground-floor bedroom specially equipped for disabled people ● No children under 12; kennel for dogs; no smoking in dining-rooms ☐ Access, Amex, Delta, Switch, Visa £ Single occupancy of twin/double £190 to £265, twin/double £200 to £240, suite £275; deposit required. Set L £19.50/24, D £39.50. Special breaks available

---

DUNVEGAN Highland   map 11

Harlosh House

Dunvegan, Isle of Skye IV55 8ZG
TEL: (01470) 521367 (AND FAX)

A small hotel in remote position, boasting excellent views.

Situated in a quiet corner of Skye, Harlosh House, which offers a fine prospect across the bay to the Ullinish peninsula and the Cuillin hills, is superbly positioned for walks. The hotel itself is a small white-harled building, with a steep, slated roof and a storm porch at the front. The public rooms – a comfortable lounge featuring deep-pink décor and prints on the walls, and a cheerful restaurant – are quite small. Since Harlosh House is so close to the shore, a telescope is on hand to help to you to spot otters, eagles and seals. The bedrooms at the front of the house are clearly preferable on account of their views, but all are comfortably furnished. Space is at a premium, however, and one correspondent bemoaned the lack of anywhere to sit and read; another was more satisfied, remarking: 'very comfortable room – probably the cleanest hotel I have ever visited.' This year, the reports regarding the hotel's food have been mixed.

◑ Closed mid-Oct to Easter ⤢ 3 miles south of Dunvegan on A863, follow signs for Harlosh. Private car park ⨽ 3 twin, 3 double; family rooms available; 4 with bathroom/WC, 2 with shower/WC; room service, hair-dryer ✓ Restaurant, lounge; early suppers for children; toys, babysitting, baby-listening, cots, high chairs ♿ No wheelchair access ● No dogs; smoking in lounge only ☐ Access, Switch, Visa £ Single occupancy of twin/double £44 to £65, twin/double £90, family room £112; deposit required. Set D £24.50

Drummond House

17 Drummond Place, Edinburgh EH3 6PL
TEL: 0131-557 9189 (AND FAX)

A superbly renovated Georgian house within easy walking distance of Princes Street.

When Josephine and Alan Dougall were renovating their Georgian town house, they found an 1898 edition of *The Scotsman* newspaper under the hall floor. 'The sales were on,' says Alan, 'nothing changes.' Now fully restored, Drummond House displays all its original classical good looks, including the arched and columned hallway that leads to the smart public rooms, with their rug-covered polished-wood floors. The atmosphere is personal and friendly. The bedrooms usually remain unlocked and the modern, identikit gadgetry of the standardised hotel room will not be found here. The rooms boast canopied beds, rich fabrics and rugs, but there are no telephones, televisions or tea trays, unless someone specifically requests them.

The Blue Room is many visitors' favourite, but the two front rooms, with their views of the tree-filled Georgian square, are also popular. The beds are of an old-fashioned height, and there are many thoughtful touches, such as the electric blanket on each. Breakfasts are served around one table, at which guests often linger to chat. The only drawback to all this elegant town-house living is the lack of car-parking space, although Alan is always ready to help if you need to find a space or feed a meter.

◗ Closed Chr & some weeks in winter ⊿ ¼ mile north of St Andrew Square, at the east end of Great King Street. On-street parking (metered) ⊨ 1 twin, 2 double; all with bathroom/WC; hair-dryer; TV and tea/coffee-making facilities on request ✧ Dining-room, lounge ⅟ No wheelchair access ● No children under 12; no dogs; no smoking ⊟ Access, Delta, Visa £ Single occupancy of twin/double £60 to £85, twin/double £90; deposit required

Sibbet House

26 Northumberland Street, Edinburgh EH3 6LS
TEL: 0131-556 1078 FAX: 0131-557 9445

Smart, comfortable town house conveniently located in the New Town.

'We tend to get people who are refugees from hotels,' says Jim Sibbet of his guests and you can see why. The house offers an easy conviviality that suits anyone who likes to see a bedroom door without a number on it or prefers to linger over breakfast for the chance to chat to their host and meet other visitors. And then there's the entertainment: Jim giving bagpipe recitals after the cornflakes. Nevertheless, beneath the effortless charm, Jim and his wife Aurore run a seamlessly well-organised operation that brings people back year after year, particularly from the United States. Their Georgian town house is conveniently close to Princes Street, but away from traffic in a quiet side-road. In the hall a grandfather clock ticks gently among the various umbrellas, walking sticks and ornaments. On the first floor is the drawing-room, elegant and brightly decorated with pieces of china, cut-glass and family photographs. The television usually stays inside its polished cabinet, neglected as people get to know one another. The four bedrooms continue the style: bright, well equipped and comfortable with ornaments and pictures everywhere.

◑ Open all year ⬈ Northumberland Street runs parallel to Princes Street, four streets north. Private car park ⭲ 1 double, 1 four-poster, 2 family rooms; 2 with bathroom/WC, family rooms with shower/WC; TV, hair-dryer, trouser press, direct-dial telephone ⊘ Dining-room, lounge, TV room, library; early suppers for children; toys, cot, high chair 🚫 No wheelchair access ● No dogs; no smoking ▭ Access, Visa ⒠ Single occupancy of twin/double £55 to £65, twin/double/four-poster £70 to £80, family room from £70; deposit required. Set D £30

ERISKA Argyll & Bute   map 11

Isle of Eriska

Ledaig, By Oban PA37 1SD
TEL: (01631) 720371   FAX: (01631) 720531

A secluded country-house hotel offering good sports facilities.

It's only a short rattle across the old wrought-iron bridge to Eriska, but ever since the Norse invasions of the tenth century, the low, wooded island has been considered something of a sanctuary. These days, Eriska's visitors are more likely to be fugitives from office stress than warlords, and here they will find such modern methods of relaxation as golf, a swimming-pool and a gymnasium, along with the more traditional fresh air and long walks. The style of the house itself is Scots baronial, and it boasts a tower, turret and crenellations atop the bay windows. Inside, the décor is that of the classic country house: the oak-panelled reception area leads through to a plush drawing-room, with a grand piano and chintzy sofas, where guests take coffee after dinner. There's also a small library-bar featuring buttoned, leather chesterfields and an open fire. The bedrooms can be generous in size: Mull has a good view over the crenellations to the eponymous island; Skye, with its vaulted, wooden ceiling, is a good ground-floor option; while Iona (a single) has its own balcony.

Dining is done in style – jacket and tie are required for gentlemen – with roasts and salmon being carved at the table. The menus are refreshingly free of the heavy jargon that afflicts others, and poached eggs with a herb and mushroom sauce served on a crisp potato wheel might be followed by a cream of carrot and ginger soup, and then roast farmyard turkey, a steamed apple sponge pudding and custard, a savoury of Ayrshire bacon and, finally, cheese. Real trenchermen can also order pastries with their coffee. With the new chef, Ewan Clark, installed, reports on food would be welcome.

All entries in the Guide *are rewritten every year, not least because standards fluctuate. Don't trust an out-of-date* Guide.

◗ Closed Jan & Feb   ⤳ Cross Connel bridge and proceed to Benderloch; Isle of Eriska is signposted from there. Private car park ⤙⤙ 2 single, 15 twin/double; all with bathroom/WC; TV, room service, hair-dryer, trouser press, direct-dial telephone ⌁ Dining-room, bar, 3 lounges, library, games room, garden; conference facilities (max 30 people incl up to 17 residential); fishing, golf, gym, sauna, heated indoor swimming-pool, tennis, croquet, clay-pigeon shooting, putting green, water sports; early suppers for children; babysitting, baby-listening   ♿ Wheelchair access to hotel (1 ramp) and dining-room, 2 ground-floor bedrooms specially equipped for disabled people ● No children under 10 in dining-room eves; no dogs in public rooms ⊟ Access, Switch, Visa   £ Single £150, twin/double £185 to £215; deposit required. Set D £35. Special breaks available

---

FORT WILLIAM Highland   map 11

Inverlochy Castle

Torlundy, Fort William PH33 6SN
TEL: (01397) 702177   FAX: (01397) 702953

A castle that sets the standard for lesser country houses – but at a price.

'I never saw a lovelier or more romantic spot,' wrote one satisfied visitor in 1873 – and who could disagree with Queen Victoria about this splendid architectural extravagance? Inverlochy Castle's arched entrance brings you first into the Great Hall, which boasts a huge bay window, a frescoed ceiling and views towards Ben Nevis. A portrait of Bonnie Prince Charlie features among the oil paintings and a signed photograph of Queen Elizabeth II stands on the grand piano, but there's still a place for sets of dominoes, chess and Scrabble. The surroundings may be awesome, but the manager, Michael Leonard, encourages a good-humoured atmosphere: 'History and antiques can make a good room,' he says, 'but service and friendliness make a good stay.' From the formal elegance of the main dining-room to the audience of deers' heads in the billiards room, the other public rooms are equally grand. Some bedrooms are generously proportioned, with antique furniture to match; the luxuriously fitted bathrooms are more modern additions.

With their swagged windows, oil paintings and polished sideboards, the dining-rooms are unashamedly aristocratic. Dinners are four-course affairs, with a choice offered on all but the soup. You might start with gravad lax served with a dill and mustard sauce, follow with a cream of Jerusalem artichoke soup and pot-roasted guinea-fowl, and finish with a hot apple tart accompanied by cinnamon ice-cream.

◗ Closed Dec to Feb   ⤳ 3 miles north of Fort William on A82. Private car park ⤙⤙ 1 single, 15 twin/double, 1 suite; all with bathroom/WC; TV, room service, hair-dryer, trouser press, direct-dial telephone; no tea/coffee-making facilities in rooms ⌁ 3 dining-rooms, 2 lounges, drying-room, games room, garden; fishing, tennis; early suppers for children; toys, babysitting, baby-listening ♿ No wheelchair access ● No children under 12 in dining-rooms eves; no dogs; no smoking in bedrooms ⊟ Access, Amex, Delta, Switch, Visa   £ Single £160, twin/double £276, suite £330; deposit required. Set L £15/30, D £40/45. Special breaks available

GARVE **Highland** map 11

Inchbae Lodge

Garve IV23 2PH
TEL: (01997) 455269   FAX: (01997) 455207

A friendly roadside inn, with a cosy bar at its heart.

It would be easy to miss Judy and Pat Price's wayside lodge as you drive down the A835, which would be a shame as it is situated in a lovely, quiet spot. Built in 1840 as a hunting lodge for the Duke of Sutherland, Inchbae Lodge became a hotel just over a century later, catering mainly for anglers: the Blackwater River runs past the lawn at the back, and contains brown trout, although 'you have to work for them.' Pat is a keen fisherman, and is never at a loss when advising someone on a suitable spot for a good day's fishing; a record book in the lounge tells of one man catching 70 trout in a day. Other pastimes are also catered for with plenty of books and games. The dining-room is a pleasant and traditional room in which plenty of local game and fish is served. There's always an alternative choice offered for each of the four courses (except the soup).

Life in Inchbae Lodge definitely centres on the bar – somehow people seem to gravitate to its warmth and friendliness, as well as to the malt whiskies that Pat is happy to recommend. The bedrooms in the house are bright and comfortable, and feature neat stripe-dominated décor; those situated in the roof are the largest, and make good family rooms. There are also bedrooms in an annexe chalet, and these have been recently refurbished to the same standard as those in the house. Since the doors face directly towards the river, you'd do well to pack midge repellent during the summer months.

◑ Closed 25 to 29 Dec ☑ 6 miles north-west of Garve on A835 Inverness to Ullapool road. Private car park ⬅ 4 twin, 5 double, 3 family rooms; some in annexe; some with bathroom/WC, most with shower/WC; hair-dryer on request; clock radios in some rooms ⊘ Dining-room, bar, 2 lounges, drying-room, garden; fishing, clay-pigeon shooting; early suppers for children; toys, baby-listening, outdoor games, cots, high chair ⅘ No wheelchair access ● No smoking in bedrooms ☐ Visa £ Single occupancy of twin/double £37, twin/double/family room £64; deposit required. Set D £21; bar meals available (prices valid till mid-1997). Special breaks available

---

GIFFORD **East Lothian** map 11

Forbes Lodge

Gifford EH41 4JE
TEL: (01620) 810212

A gracious family home featuring fine rooms, antique furniture and lovely gardens.

If you have to stop in Gifford to ask for directions to Forbes Lodge, you will find that everyone knows the place – after all, it has been in Lady Marioth Hay's family for over 250 years. Inside you'll find all the history and heirlooms that such a grand family accumulates, from the full-length eighteenth-century portraits to the bound volumes in the library. Although elegant, the rooms are not overbearingly grandiose, and there's a homely touch to Forbes Lodge that extends to the straightforward, but tasty, evening meals – perhaps a starter of cold pea soup, followed by tarragon chicken and then orange mousse. The comfortable bedrooms boast some interesting features, such as a draught-proof box bath or a half-tester bed. The gardens are delightful and are worth exploring before dinner. Vegetables and fruit are grown here for the table, and there's a meandering stream too.

◑ Open all year ⏏ From Haddington follow signs to Gifford. In the village, turn towards Edinburgh; hotel is on the right. Private car park ⛵ 2 single, 1 twin, 1 double; 1 with bathroom/WC; hair-dryer ⚗ Dining-room, lounge, drying-room, library, garden; early suppers for children ⛟ No wheelchair access ● No children under 12; no dogs; no smoking in bedrooms ⊟ Access, Visa £ Single/single occupancy of twin/double £40, twin/double £80. Set D £18

GLASGOW Glasgow   map 11

Babbity Bowster

16-18 Blackfriars Street, Glasgow G1 1PB
TEL: 0141-552 5055   FAX: 0141-552 7774

A lively, multi-faceted venture, offering no-frills rooms.

Describing itself as a café/bar/restaurant/hotel, Fraser Laurie's Babbity Bowster is very much part of Glasgow's regeneration of its old commercial heart. Based in an eighteenth-century Robert Adam house, it contains a sparse, wooden-floored bar that is decorated with framed architectural prints and flower-painted beams. In addition to the usual evening crowd, the place can fill up at weekends with people who have come to listen to folk music or poetry recitals. The meals are straightforward and are based on home-made soups, fresh seafood and regular dishes such as beef collops in red-wine gravy. A tiled stairway leads up to the quieter Gallery Restaurant, where paintings by local artists are displayed, and where diners tuck into such dishes as smoked salmon, chicken stuffed with haggis, and clootie dumplings served with a sticky toffee sauce. The no-nonsense bedrooms are situated on the floor above the restaurant (which is licensed until midnight), and are simple places featuring pine furniture, plain bathrooms and direct-dial telephones.

◑ Closed 25 Dec & 1 Jan; restaurant closed Sun ⏏ In the city centre. Private car park ⛵ 2 single, 2 twin, 2 double, 1 suite; all with shower/WC; direct-dial telephone ⚗ Restaurant, bar/café ⛟ No wheelchair access ● No dogs ⊟ Access, Amex, Visa £ Single from £45, single occupancy of twin/double from £65, twin/double/suite from £65. Alc L £9.50, D £12.50

Report forms are at the back of the Guide; *write a letter or e-mail us if you prefer. Our e-mail address is: "guidereports@which.co.uk".*

Don't forget that other hotels worth considering are listed in our Visitors' Book.

Malmaison

278 West George Street, Glasgow G2 4LL
TEL: 0141-221 6400   FAX: 0141-221 6411

COUNTY
HOTEL
OF THE
YEAR

Stylish modernity is featured in this former church in the heart of Glasgow.

No frills, but bags of style: Ken McCulloch's hotel is founded on the simple ethos of providing good-quality rooms, without the fuss that results from extensive facilities and millions of minions. If you need to have your bag carried up from the smart reception atrium, a barman might be called. Continental breakfast is left on a tray outside the door. On the other hand, your bedroom will boast good bed linen, stylish soft furnishings upholstered in bold blue and burgundy, satellite TV, a CD player, a 'tuck shop' in the cupboard and a corkscrew by the bed. The building itself was once a church (although the grand, neo-classical entrance suggests Cecil B de Mille rather than the kirk) and, since the original Malmaison was the Parisian home of Josephine, there's a portrait of Napoleon on the gold-chequered wall behind reception, while his life story is related on the wrought-iron staircase. Stairs lead down to the trendy brasserie – formerly the crypt – with arched ceiling and columns. There's a *menu compris*, perhaps offering a spinach and blue-cheese salad, followed by polenta and mushrooms, or you could opt for à la carte dishes such as a Caesar salad, followed by slow-roasted chicken and then a lemon tart.

◑ Open all year   ⃤ In the city centre, just off Blythswood Square. On-street parking after 6pm   ⊫ 2 twin, 15 double, 4 suites; all with bathroom/WC; TV, hair-dryer, mini-bar, trouser press, direct-dial telephone, CD player   ✧ Restaurant, bar; early suppers for children; babysitting   ⅋ Wheelchair access to hotel (1 step), restaurant and WC (unisex), 10 ground-floor bedrooms   ● No dogs   ▭ Access, Amex, Diners, Visa   £ Single occupancy of twin/double £80, twin/double £80, suite £110; deposit required. Continental/cooked B £7.50; set D £7.50/10.50, set Sat, Sun L £7.50; alc L, D £17.50; bar meals available

---

One Devonshire Gardens

1 Devonshire Gardens, Glasgow G12 0UX
TEL: 0141-339 2001   FAX: 0141-337 1663

A Georgian hotel offering sumptuous luxury.

Although it occupies three large Georgian town houses situated close to the busy Great Western Road in Glasgow's West End, Ken McCulloch's hotel manages to cast a spell of peace and calm over you. The décor is stylish and modern, but always in keeping with the age of the building; deep-blue columns, gilt mirrors and extravagant flower displays lead to a lounge featuring plaid sofas, ornate plasterwork and classical music wafting from the CD player. Another entrance hall boasts a superb stained-glass window on the staircase, and there is a snug clubroom that leads to an unexpected patio garden. The bedroom furnishings reflect the same care for detail: CD players, TVs and mini-bars are tucked away in polished cabinets, stacks of cushions abound, as do vases full of orchids and acres of drapes. Even the bath oil has been praised – one visitor was so impressed that he ordered 10 litres from the manufacturer!

The menus stick to a three-course set lunch, with a soup added at dinner. 'Chef has a very light touch,' reported one reader, 'the scallops followed by cod were undoubtedly cooked by a master.' Other mouth-watering choices include oak-smoked Scottish salmon served with a simple horseradish, chive and radish cream, followed by poached corn-fed chicken, with a white-chocolate and coconut mousse to round it all off. A one-night stay led one correspondent to write, 'What a delightful experience: the friendliness and enthusiasm of the staff convey the joy they get from the place.'

◑ Open all year ⬗ In the West End of Glasgow, 10 minutes from the centre. On-street parking (metered) ⬅ 3 twin, 12 double, 10 four-poster, 2 suites; most with bathroom/WC, 3 with shower/WC; TV, room service, hair-dryer, mini-bar, trouser press, direct-dial telephone; CD player; no tea/coffee-making facilities in rooms ⬗ Dining-room, bar, 2 lounges, study, garden; conference facilities (max 32 people incl up to 27 residential); early suppers for children; babysitting, baby-listening ♿ No wheelchair access ⬤ No dogs in public rooms; no smoking in dining-room ▭ Access, Amex, Diners, Switch, Visa £ Single occupancy of twin/double from £135, twin/double from £160, four-poster £170, suite from £180; deposit required. Continental B £8.50, cooked B £13.50; set L £25, D £40. Special breaks available

---

Town House

4 Hughenden Terrace, Glasgow G12 9XR
TEL: 0141-357 0862 FAX: 0141-339 9605

A grand, Victorian terraced house with friendly, unassuming hosts.

Charlotte and Bill Thow's terraced Victorian town house must be one of the few small hotels in the world that is 'on the net' – a regular guest having set up its home page (http://www.cityscape.co.uk/users/cn56, for those also on-line). Located just off the Great West Road, the Town House is in a quiet backstreet and overlooks playing fields. Renovating the house was an enormous task: 14 layers of wallpaper had to be stripped off and a few loads of empty sherry bottles had to be removed from under the erstwhile Victorian governess's floorboards. The results include beautiful, airy and bright rooms, and fine period features such as the columned hallway and the broad, curling staircase on which potted plants reach up towards the glass cupola above. To all this Bill and Charlotte bring an easy, quiet manner, and you can relax on the sofa with a book or forsake the city restaurants in favour of a straightforward meal: prawn cocktail, sirloin steak and a fresh fruit salad, perhaps. The bedrooms are all of a good size, and are decorated in a pleasant, unfussy style.

◑ Closed Chr & New Year ⬗ In the West End of Glasgow, 10 minutes from the centre. On-street parking (metered) ⬅ 1 twin, 7 double, 2 family rooms; all with shower/WC; TV, limited room service, direct-dial telephone; hair-dryer and trouser press on request ⬗ Dining-room, lounge; conference facilities (max 20 people incl up to 10 residential); early suppers for children; baby-listening ♿ No wheelchair access ⬤ No dogs; no smoking in dining-room ▭ Access, Switch, Visa £ Single occupancy of twin/double £52, twin/double £62, family room from £65; deposit required. Alc D £20

GRANTOWN-ON-SPEY **Highland**   map 11

Culdearn House

Woodlands Terrace, Grantown-on-Spey PH26 3JU
TEL: (01479) 872106   FAX: (01479) 873641

A first-rate guesthouse, run with great efficiency and good humour.

When our inspector arrived, one guest was checking out; 'Don't believe a word
they say,' he laughed about the owners, and then confirmed a two-week
booking for later in the year. Isobel and Alasdair Little know many of their
visitors pretty well, and there is an atmosphere of easy conviviality about the
place – something that Alasdair works hard to encourage. Culdearn is a
late-Victorian family house on the wooded outskirts of Grantown-on-Spey.
Although the A95 passes the front drive, it is not busy enough to deter the red
squirrels and roe deer from crossing the road into the garden. Inside, the smart
décor – rich colours, marble fireplaces and chandeliers – is in keeping with the
age of the house. Guests gather in the lounge and get to know one another over
pre-dinner drinks, before moving across the hall into the dining-room. If people
have been chatting in the lounge, Alasdair takes the trouble to seat them
together, and also advises on the choice of wines. The three-course dinners offer
a choice of three dishes at each stage, and there is usually plenty of local interest
incorporated into the main courses: wild salmon, Aberdeen Angus, Highland
beef and Moray sole may be found on the menu.

  The bedrooms are decorated in feminine florals and pinks – all feature modern
bathrooms with shower units, while two have baths.

◗ Closed 1 Nov to 28 Feb   ⊿ Enter Grantown-on-Spey from the south-west on A95
and turn left at the 30mph sign. Private car park   ⊨ 1 single, 3 twin, 5 double; 2 with
bathroom/WC, 7 with shower/WC; TV, room service, hair-dryer   ⊘ Dining-room,
lounge, drying-room, garden; early suppers for children   ⅃ No wheelchair access
◖ No children under 10; no dogs; no smoking in dining-room and some bedrooms
⊟ Access, Amex, Delta, Diners, Switch, Visa   £ Single/single occupancy of
twin/double £55, twin/double £110 (rates incl dinner); deposit required. Special breaks
available

GULLANE **East Lothian**   map 11

Greywalls

Muirfield, Gullane EH31 2EG
TEL: (01620) 842144   FAX: (01620) 842241

A first-class country-house hotel in a splendid house with gardens.

Well-travelled visitors might find something familiar about the elegant curves
and classical proportions of Greywalls – distant New Delhi was also designed by
Edwin Lutyens, whose talents are well displayed here, both inside and out.
There's a particularly fine view from the magnificent library through a series of
arches and alcoves. Since 1924 the house has been in the Weaver family,
becoming a country-house hotel after the Second World War. Visitors have
remarked on the easy and welcoming atmosphere, backed up by an efficient

staff. The library is a focal point with its cosy fire, piano and book-lined walls. Enjoy a pre-dinner drink here and then head for the dining-room which overlooks the superb walled gardens designed by a Lutyens' contemporary, Gertrude Jekyll. The four-course dinner menu changes daily and offers a good selection, strong on fish and seafood: perhaps a main course of scallops marinated in lemon juice and sea salt with a tomato and shallot compote or a casserole of mixed fish under a puff pastry with a champagne and dill sauce. Puddings are generally traditional but not heavy. Bedrooms are smartly decorated and furnished with the occasional tapestry or painting to add colour. Golfers will want Room 18 for its links view (and because Nick Faldo stayed here when winning the Open in 1992).

◑ Closed Nov to Mar ⊿ Off A198 in Gullane village; signposted from A1 and Edinburgh by-pass. Private car park ⬐ 4 single, 11 twin, 6 double, 1 four-poster; some in annexe; all with bathroom/WC; TV, room service, hair-dryer, direct-dial telephone; no tea/coffee-making facilities in rooms ✇ 2 dining-rooms, bar, 2 lounges, drying-room, library, conservatory, garden; conference facilities (max 20 people residential/non-residential); tennis, croquet, putting green; early suppers for children; babysitting ⅚ No wheelchair access ● No dogs in public rooms; no smoking in dining-rooms ☐ Access, Amex, Diners, Switch, Visa £ Single £95, single occupancy of twin/double £120, twin/double £155 to £175, four-poster £175; deposit required. Set L £12.50, D £33; alc L £15. Special breaks available

---

HADDINGTON East Lothian   map 11

Brown's

1 West Road, Haddington EH41 3RD
TEL: (01620) 822254 (AND FAX)

A sumptuously decorated small hotel dedicated to good food.

As soon as you enter Colin Brown and Alex McCallum's hotel, you pick up a feeling of warmth and intimacy; this atmosphere is strengthened by the vibrant, Mediterranean colours of Scottish artist John Cunningham – whose canvases brighten the lounge – and continues throughout the flamboyant interiors. Everything is carefully considered, from the gilt picture frames and spotlights to the way in which the light falls from the cupola on a brass torso that stands at the head of the stairs. Featuring plenty of softened lighting and modern, patterned fabrics, the bedrooms reflect the same thoughtful touches.

With its mint-green walls, plaid drapes and, of course, artwork, the centrepiece has to be the dining-room. The four-course dinners offer a choice of main courses: roast goose stuffed with apple and pistachio, fillet of beef, or marinated pork with a soured-cream and Madeira sauce, perhaps. Typical starters might include steamed sea bass, followed by a fennel soup. The puddings, such as passion-fruit délices or orange-liqueur soufflé crêpes, steer well clear of heavy, traditional desserts.

Reports are welcome on any hotel, whether or not it is in the Guide.

◗ Open all year ⊠ On main road into Haddington off A1 from Edinburgh. Private car park ⟾ 1 single, 2 twin, 2 double; 3 with bathroom/WC, 2 with shower/WC; TV, room service, hair-dryer, direct-dial telephone; trouser press in some rooms
✓ Dining-room, bar, lounge, garden; early suppers for children; cot ♿ No wheelchair access ● No dogs; smoking in bar only ⊡ Access, Amex, Diners, Visa £ Single/single occupancy of twin/double £60, twin/double £78; deposit required. Set D £27.50, Sun L £18.50

INNERLEITHEN Borders map 11

The Ley

Innerleithen EH44 6NL
TEL: (01896) 830240 (AND FAX)

A top-notch country guesthouse in a peaceful rural location with friendly hosts.

The approach to Doreen and Willie McVicar's secluded country house is magnificent: you pass over a white bridge crossing the Leithen, and then follow a winding road through woodlands of beech and pine to the broad, creeper-clad façade. As the car engine dies, you hear only the noise of the tumbling stream, the birds and the breeze. Inside, the house is stylishly furnished with antiques, oil paintings and standard lamps. The long lounge swells out into the corner turret, making it a fine place in which to sink into a deep, comfortable sofa with a drink and one of the many magazines or books provided. Doreen's much-praised dinners are served by Willie in the smart, striped dining-room opposite; typically, Stilton pancakes with tomato sauce might be followed by a carrot and coriander soup, roast duck and then a pear tart. The seasonal vegetables are home grown.

The bedrooms are elegantly furnished with a mix of antiques and rattan, and thoughtful extras such as sherry, mineral water and fresh milk for tea are provided. Reports are totally positive: the atmosphere, reported one visitor, 'is cheerful, relaxed and helpful.' 'Cannot be praised too highly,' wrote another – 'top of any list.'

◗ Closed mid-Oct to mid-Feb ⊠ From Innerleithen take B709 for Heriot; continue for 2 miles through the golf course, then turn left over a white bridge for hotel. Private car park ⟾ 2 twin, 1 double; 2 with bathroom/WC, 1 twin with shower/WC; limited room service, hair-dryer, trouser press; TV on request ✓ Dining-room, lounge, TV room, drying-room, garden; croquet ♿ No wheelchair access ● No children under 12; no dogs; no smoking in bedrooms ⊡ None accepted £ Single occupancy of twin/double £46 to £49, twin/double £71 to £77. Set D £21.50

INVERNESS Highland map 11

Dunain Park

Inverness IV3 6JN
TEL: (01463) 230512 FAX: (01463) 224532

A relaxing and unstuffy country-house hotel with welcoming hosts.

A rhododendron-lined drive running through Dunain Park's gardens brings you to this Victorian mansion, which boasts an Italianate campanile tower and ivy-clad walls. The hotel's interior decoration – including deep carpeting, oil paintings and dark, leather chesterfields – lives up to the promise of the grand approach. But the many mementos, family photographs and curios also provide a homely feel and, indeed, this is a relaxing, down-to-earth place, run with thoughtful friendliness by former dairy farmers, Ann and Edward Nicoll. The dinners are cooked by Ann, and starters might include a curried carrot soup, followed by a mousseline of smoked haddock and whiting, then a beef Wellington, and finally fresh fruit or a cheeseboard. Coffee, which is served after dinner in the lounge, may be followed by a sampling of the hosts' malt-whisky collection (now numbering over 200). The bedrooms are situated in the older part of the house – where they have more character – or in the more modern wing, where the suites are huge. Two further suites are in cottages in the grounds.

◑ Closed 3 weeks Jan & Feb ◸ Off A82, 2 miles from Inverness. Private car park ⊨ 1 single, 2 twin, 2 double, 1 four-poster, 8 suites; some in annexe; all with bathroom/WC; TV, room service, hair-dryer, trouser press, direct-dial telephone, cassette player; tea/coffee-making facilities on request ⊘ Dining-room, 2 lounges, drying-room, garden; sauna, solarium, heated indoor swimming-pool; early suppers for children ⅙ Wheelchair access to hotel and dining-room, 3 ground-floor bedrooms, 1 specially equipped for disabled people ● No dogs in public rooms; no smoking in dining-room ▭ Access, Amex, Delta, Diners, Switch, Visa £ Single £55, single occupancy of twin/double £105, twin/double £138, four-poster £150, suite £138 to £158; deposit required. Set L £16.50; alc D £29. Special breaks available

---

INVERSNAID Stirling

map 11

Inversnaid Lodge

Inversnaid, By Aberfoyle, Stirling FK8 3TU
TEL: (01877) 386254

COUNTY
HOTEL
OF THE
YEAR

A hotel offering a friendly atmosphere and a tremendous lochside location for both photographers and walkers.

You cannot escape crime, even if you are 14 miles up a winding lane in the lonely depths of the Trossachs: while we were there, breakfast at Inversnaid Lodge was disrupted by the news that a fox had attacked the spring lambs, and so André Goulancourt was out moving the flock, leaving partner Linda Middleton to fry the bacon. Fortunately, such disturbances at this marvellously peaceful location on the eastern shore of Loch Lomond are rare, and not all the wildlife is so hostile: 'Bombproof', the badger, regularly comes to the kitchen door to be fed by hand.

The eighteenth-century hunting lodge is decorated with elegant simplicity, and the walls are hung with black and white photographs taken by André or by participants on his photography courses. The bedrooms have the same comfortable but uncluttered feel: there are no phones or TV, and no room numbers or keys to worry about. The lounge and dining-room share the same excellent view across the loch. The pre-dinner talk is usually of Hasselblads or blisters, as the visitors tend to be either photographers studying the intricacies of the zone system, or else walkers exploring the West Highland Way. Meals are served around one large dining table: straightforward three-course home-cooking is provided by Linda, who also waits on table and deftly nudges the conversation along when necessary. With enough advance warning, any particular likes or dislikes can be catered for.

◑ Closed Nov to Mar   🔁 From Aberfoyle take B829 for approximately 12 miles to a T-junction; turn left. Hotel is approximately 3 miles further down, on the right after the church. Private car park 🔑 4 single, 4 twin, 1 double; 1 in annexe; 1 twin with bathroom/WC, rest with shower/WC; hair-dryer on request ✤ Dining-room, lounge, drying-room, garden ♿ No wheelchair access ● No children under 16; no dogs; no smoking ▭ None accepted 💶 Single/single occupancy of twin/double £26, twin/double £52; deposit required. Set D £15

IONA Argyll & Bute   map 11

Argyll Hotel

Isle of Iona PA76 6SJ
TEL: (01681) 700334   FAX: (01681) 700510

A straightforward seafront hotel on a beautiful island.

Short though the ferry crossing from Mull's Fionnphort to Iona is, as you abandon the security of your car and venture across, you experience a real sense of adventure (wear stout footwear in bad weather because the waves can break over the ferry's ramp). In order to sample Iona's magic properly, you should certainly stay on the island and enjoy the long tranquil summer evenings, or experience the rigours of a Hebridean squall. The stone frontage of Fiona Menzies' seafront hotel extends into a warren of bedrooms at the back, which can disappoint if you were expecting to look out over the straits; all are comfortable and straightforward, however, and feature pine furniture and simple bathrooms. The two small lounges at the front boast a wealth of books (more than a few of which have religious themes), and there are some interesting paintings of the island dotted around the house. The dining-room is much larger, and extends into a conservatory which has a view of the sea – a nice place in which to enjoy after-dinner drinks or coffee. Unfortunately, our inspection meal was disappointing, although the service was attentive and brisk. 'Fabulous,' reported one reader, but our inspector's praise was more qualified.

◑ Closed 7 Oct to 27 Mar   🔁 200 yards from Iona's ferry jetty. Free parking at Fionnphort, Isle of Mull 🔑 8 single, 4 twin, 4 double, 1 family room; most with bathroom/WC, 3 with shower/WC ✤ Dining-room, 2 lounges, TV room, drying-room, conservatory, garden; conference facilities (max 17 residential); croquet; early suppers for children; toys, baby-listening ♿ No wheelchair access ● No dogs in public rooms; no smoking in some public rooms ▭ Access, Delta, Switch, Visa 💶 Single £50 to £58, twin/double £110 to £120, family room £135 to £140; deposit required. Set D £18.50; alc L £9

All rooms have tea/coffee-making facilities unless we specify to the contrary.

ISLE ORNSAY **Highland** map 11

Eilean Iarmain

Isle Ornsay, Sleat, Isle Of Skye IV43 8QR
TEL: (01471) 833332   FAX: (01471) 833275

A nineteenth-century inn boasting pretty rooms and excellent views.

If a trip to Skye has stimulated your desire to learn the local language, then Sir Iain Noble's hotel could be just the place for you: the staff and the menus are bilingual. In fact, since he is the chief of the company that recently built the graceful (although some dispute its attractiveness) Skye bridge, Sir Iain has helped more than a few visitors on to the island. Hotel Eilean Iarmain, however, looks out over the bridgeless Isle Ornsay, whose pretty little lighthouse was built by Robert Louis Stevenson's father. It's a traditional, snug sort of place and the hospitality from its friendly staff has been praised: 'Everyone was wonderful,' reported one visitor, 'and made it look so effortless to the guests.' The four-course dinners that are served in the panelled restaurant are strong on local seafood, including oysters from the estate's own beds, and scallops landed on the nearby jetty. More informal meals can be taken in the lively public bar.

The bedrooms are divided between the house and the Garden House; all are prettily decorated and feature solid, old furniture and beautiful views, as well as a complimentary dram.

◐ Open all year ⚋ From the ferry terminal in Broadford take A851 to Isle Ornsay. Private car park ⚋ 4 twin, 5 double, 1 four-poster, 2 family rooms; some in annexe; all with bathroom/WC exc 1 double with shower/WC; room service, hair-dryer, direct-dial telephone; TV and trouser press in some rooms ✓ Restaurant, bar, lounge, garden; conference facilities (max 90 people incl up to 12 residential); fishing; early suppers for children; baby-listening ⚋ No wheelchair access ● No dogs in public rooms; no smoking in restaurant and some bedrooms ▭ Access, Amex, Visa £ Single occupancy of twin/double £59 to £65, twin/double £78 to £86, four-poster £86 to £95, family room from £116; deposit required. Set L £16.50, D £26; bar meals available (prices valid till Apr 1997). Special breaks available

---

JEDBURGH **Borders** map 11

Hundalee House

Jedburgh TD8 6PA
TEL: (01835) 863011 (AND FAX)

A smart but competitively priced B&B in quiet, attractive location.

From Sheila Whittaker's house, you can see right across to the Cheviot Hills (which are often snowcapped late into the year), on the borders of Scotland and England. Hundalee House's steep gables, tall chimneypots and piles of chopped logs also give an indication of the climate, but when the sun is out, this is a very pretty spot. With its mullioned windows and imposing grey-stone façade, the Georgian house offers its guests country-house elegance, but at affordable prices. The reception hall, which is hung with antlers and foxes' heads, is agreeably dignified, while the smart lounge is decorated with dried grasses arranged in Chinese vases and also features a large, carved fireplace which is guarded by the figures of long-eared Egyptian dogs. The white china candelabra, silver-laden sideboard and stuffed animals make the dining-room similarly stylish. The breakfasts are reportedly huge, and eggs are provided by the house's own chickens – when the mood takes them.

The bedrooms boast bold, floral or striped décor, as well as the occasional fine piece of Art Nouveau furniture. Two are located over in the old servants' quarters and are slightly smaller than the four-postered double room in the house, whose private bathroom is across the landing.

◑ Closed Nov to Mar ⬈ 1 mile south of Jedburgh, off A68. Private car park ⛏ 2 twin, 1 double, 1 four-poster, 1 family room; some in annexe; 1 with bathroom/WC, 2 with shower/WC; TV, hair-dryer ⌘ Dining-room, lounge, garden ⅙ No wheelchair access ⊖ No dogs; no smoking ☐ None accepted £ Single occupancy of twin/double £20 to £35, twin/double £32 to £40, four-poster/family room £36 to £40; deposit required

---

The Spinney

℘

Jedburgh TD8 6PB
TEL: (01835) 863525 (AND FAX)

A small, good-value B&B, with a friendly hostess.

Sandra Fry's neat, whitewashed house lies just 2 miles south of the Borders town of Jedburgh, which features a ruined abbey. The Spinney's drive curls past well-tended lawns and rockeries around the back of the L-shaped house. Inside, the rooms are equally trim, with fresh flowers and plants adding a touch of colour; the comfortable lounge is furnished with red-leather chesterfields, and dolls abound in their display cases. Double-glazing minimises the traffic noise from the A68 (which runs past the house).

Pine furniture, dormer windows and lacy bed linen give a bright, cottagey atmosphere to the three bedrooms. There are shower units in two of the rooms, and guests staying in the one room which lacks *en suite* facilities have their own bathroom down the corridor – bathrobes are provided for the dash. The breakfasts offer a choice between a full fry-up, Scottish pancakes with maple syrup, croissants, kippers, or cheese and oatcakes.

◑ Closed Dec to Feb ⬈ 2 miles south of Jedburgh, on A68. Private car park ⛏ 1 twin, 2 double; 1 double with bathroom/WC, 2 with shower/WC; TV, hair-dryer ⌘ Dining-room, lounge, garden ⅙ No wheelchair access ⊖ No dogs; no smoking in bedrooms ☐ None accepted £ Single occupancy of twin/double £29, twin/double £40 to £44; deposit required

---

 This denotes that the hotel is in an exceptionally peaceful situation where you can be assured of a restful stay.

 This denotes that you can get a twin or double room for £60 or less per night inclusive of breakfast.

Ednam House

Bridge Street, Kelso TD5 7HT
TEL: (01573) 224168　FAX: (01573) 226319

*A genial and genteel atmosphere pervades at this traditional,
family-run hotel.*

One of Kelso's most prized possessions is pinned above the Ednam House bar in
a glass case. The 57lb salmon was caught almost a century ago and is the largest
ever pulled from the River Tweed. The hotel is big on fishing: rods, reels and
creels stand at the ready by the front door; men discuss catches by the lounge's
log fire; and the river itself is just an easy cast across the lawn. The Brooks family
have run the place for three generations on the successful philosophy that if it
works, don't fix it. Hence there are no new-fangled co-ordinated colour schemes
or suchlike, and things tick along quietly much as they have for the past 68 years.
The house itself is Georgian, built in 1761 by local prodigal son James Dixon,
who left under a cloud only to make his fortune from the Battle of Havana and
return sufficiently wealthy to command the finest riverfront position in the town
centre. His portrait is hung in the reception hall and the house retains many
original features with its marble fireplaces, carved woodwork, ornate plaster
cornices and cherubs cavorting across the lounge ceiling. Bedrooms are
traditional too with no-nonsense candlewick bedspreads, comfortable furniture
and good-sized bathrooms. The riverside restaurant serves food such as a pea
soup or deep-fried whitebait for starters, perhaps, followed by roast leg of lamb
and rhubarb crumble. The three-course set Sunday dinners are good value.

◐ Closed 23 Dec to 10 Jan　⬈ 100 yards from town square in Kelso. Private car
park 🅿 11 single, 21 twin; family room available; all with bathroom/WC; TV, room
service, hair-dryer, trouser press, direct-dial telephone　✓ Restaurant, 2 bars, 3
lounges, TV room, drying-room, garden; conference facilities (max 200 people incl up to
20 residential); early suppers for children; baby-listening　♿ No wheelchair access
◕ No dogs in restaurant　☐ Access, Switch, Visa　£ Single £48, twin £66 to £93;
deposit required. Set L £6, Sun L £10, D £9.50 to £18.50; bar lunches available (prices
valid till Nov 1996). Special breaks available

Sunlaws House

Kelso TD5 8JZ
TEL: (01573) 450331　FAX: (01573) 450611

A baronial-style country-house hotel set in splendid grounds.

Motoring down the long drive (and perhaps swerving to avoid a strutting
pheasant), you suddenly catch sight of this great baronial battleship of a
building across a wide expanse of lawn. Sunlaws House's dramatic historical
pedigree is impressive: long associated with doomed rebellions, and suitably
haunted, it was repeatedly burned to the ground, sacked and pillaged. Its recent
career as a hotel owned by the Duke of Roxburghe could therefore be regarded as
being a period of well-earned calm. The present house is largely Victorian and of

all the rooms, the reception and library/bar best capture the aristocratic promise of the façade. In the former you are confronted with a 13-pointed set of antlers and a vast crested fireplace, while the latter is a superb corner room in which you can mull over Napoleon's memoirs or the morocco-bound racing results for 1895, while trying one of the many available malt whiskies. Lunches are also served here, while the three-course country-house-style dinners are taken in the more formal main dining-room.

The bedrooms vary considerably in size and shape: Room 7 is a stylish four-poster offering peaceful views across the lawns, while Room 12 – a double – boasts the best views towards the River Teviot. The stable courtyard houses smaller rooms, which are popular with the anglers who come to hook the Tweed and Teviot salmon.

◑ Open all year 🚹 3 miles south of Kelso, on A698. Private car park 🅿 2 single, 8 twin, 6 double, 4 four-poster, 2 suites; family rooms available; some in annexe; all with bathroom/WC; TV, room service, hair-dryer, trouser press, direct-dial telephone; radio in some rooms ⍟ 2 dining-rooms, lounge, drying-room, library/bar, conservatory, garden; conference facilities (max 40 people incl up to 22 residential); fishing, golf, steam room, tennis, clay-pigeon shooting, croquet; early suppers for children; babysitting, baby-listening ♿ Wheelchair access to hotel (1 ramp), dining-rooms and WC (unisex), 3 ground-floor bedrooms, 1 specially equipped for disabled people ⦵ No smoking in dining-rooms ▭ Access, Amex, Diners, Switch, Visa £ Single £95, single occupancy of twin/double £105, twin/double £140, four-poster £180, family room from £165, suite £225; deposit required. Set L £12.50, D £30. Special breaks available

---

KENTALLEN Highland   map 11

Ardsheal House

Kentallen, By Appin PA38 4BX
TEL: (01631) 740227   FAX: (01631) 740342

COUNTY HOTEL OF THE YEAR

A beautifully situated country-house hotel with friendly staff.

The road cuts away from the shore of Loch Linnhe, south of Ballachulish, leaving a mysterious, isolated beak of craggy land that motorists rush by without noticing. Ardsheal House is situated here, on a 900-acre estate that was once part of the Stuart lands forfeited after Culloden. The architecture of the house itself dates from the eighteenth century, and various later additions have helped to create a pleasant – if slightly rambling – country house. A panelled and polished reception area leads into a lounge that features yellow chintzy sofas, and the country-house style continues in the smart dining-room, conservatory and snug little bar (once the butler's pantry). Only three of the bedrooms boast a view of the loch, and those at the back of the house can seem a bit dull in comparison, but all are carefully decorated and include some nice pieces of old furniture. Hotel manager Michelle Kelso promotes a friendly, convivial tone: 'People come here to relax, so they don't necessarily wear a tie for dinner.' The cuisine sticks to a straightforward style and has received good reports; a typical meal might include pan-fried local scallops served with a lemon and cucumber sauce, followed by roast saddle of venison, and then an apple and cinnamon crumble with toffee sauce.

◗ Closed 6 Jan to 6 Feb ☒ On A828, 5 miles south of Ballachulish Bridge, in village of Kentallen. Private car park ⟱ 1 single, 3 twin, 9 double; most with bathroom/WC, 3 with shower/WC; limited room service, hair-dryer, direct-dial telephone, radio
✅ Dining-room/conservatory, bar, 2 lounges, drying-room, study, games room, garden; conference facilities (max 25 people incl up to 13 residential); tennis, billiards; early suppers for children; baby-listening ⟨ No wheelchair access ● No smoking in dining-room; no pipes or cigars in bedrooms ☐ Access, Amex, Switch, Visa
£ Single £65 to £85, single occupancy of twin/double £65 to £100, twin/double £130 to £180 (rates incl dinner); deposit required. Set L £18, D £32.50; light lunches available. Special breaks available

---

Holly Tree

Kentallen, Glencoe PA38 4BY
TEL: (01631) 740292   FAX: (01631) 740345

An interesting converted building, enjoying a beautiful lochside position.

Situated right on the waterfront by Loch Linnhe, this former railway station was once a refreshment stop for visitors who were catching the steamer – for a long time the only means of access – to the Appin peninsula. The building's historical features have been carefully restored and developed. Although the old tea-room is now the present-day bar, its original polished-wood counter and the surrounding railway memorabilia recall the great days of steam (a scuba diver even fetched the old 'waiting room' sign from the bottom of the loch). This room opens into the restaurant – once the station's platform and track bed; big picture windows make the best of the magnificent view, and the décor and furniture echo the building's architectural style (Glasgow Art Nouveau). The menus offer a choice for each of the four courses, and the straightforward cooking makes the most of the hotel's lochside position – seafood is landed directly on the pier. All the bedrooms face the loch, and boast bright colour schemes and light-ash or cane furniture.

◗ Closed Nov ☒ 17 miles south of Fort William, on A828 to Oban. Private car park ⟱ 5 twin, 5 double; family rooms available; all with bathroom/WC; TV, room service, hair-dryer, direct-dial telephone ✅ Restaurant, bar, 2 lounges, drying-room, garden; conference facilities (max 60 people incl up to 10 residential); early suppers for children; baby-listening ⟨ Wheelchair access to hotel (1 ramp), restaurant and WC (unisex), 2 ground-floor bedrooms specially equipped for disabled people ● None
☐ Access, Amex, Switch, Visa £ Single occupancy of twin/double £65 to £75, twin/double £62 to £72, family room from £66; deposit required. Set D £25.50, Sun L £13; alc L £12, D £18. Special breaks available

---

The text of entries is based on unsolicited reports sent in by readers and backed up by inspections. The factual details are from questionnaires the Guide *sends to all hotels that feature in the book.*

Kildrummy Castle

Kildrummy, By Alford AB33 8RA
TEL: (01975) 571288   FAX: (01975) 571345

A smart country-house hotel in a superb setting.

Driving up through Kildrummy's beautiful gardens you pass the romantic ruins of the thirteenth-century castle where Robert the Bruce was betrayed to the English and then captured. The house itself, which was built by a soap tycoon in 1900, has a more prosaic past and – apart from a few half-hearted crenellations – makes no attempt to pretend to be a replacement for the original. Once inside, it is more impressive: running the whole length of the house is a long, panelled hall encrusted with antlers and oil paintings and heated by crackling log fires. The public rooms – a small library, a formal dining-room and an elegant drawing-room with delicate, pale-blue décor – all look across the terrace to the ruins. Dinner might feature a cream of game soup, fruits of the sea, roast pheasant and a lemon tart.

The bedrooms are decorated in a classic country-house style, mixing reproduction and antique furniture with the occasional original Victorian fireplace or four-poster; Stronnagaich is a good corner room, looking out towards the old castle and the gardens. The top-floor rooms are more contemporary in style, featuring pale-green décor and light-wood furniture.

◑ Closed Jan ⚡ Just off A97 Huntly to Ballater Road, 35 miles west of Aberdeen. Private car park ⬅ 1 single, 7 twin, 6 double, 2 four-posters; all with bathroom/WC exc 1 double with shower/WC; TV, room service, hair-dryer, trouser press, direct-dial telephone, radio ⌀ Dining-room, bar, lounge, drying-room, library, games room, garden; conference facilities (max 20 people incl up to 16 residential); fishing, billiards; early suppers for children; babysitting ♿ No wheelchair access ● No dogs in public rooms; no smoking in dining-room ⬒ Access, Amex, Delta, Switch, Visa £ Single £70, single occupancy of twin/double £100, twin/double £115 to £125, four-poster £135 to £145. Set L £14.50, D £28; alc L £30, D £35. Special breaks available

Killiecrankie Hotel

Killiecrankie, By Pitlochry PH16 5LG
TEL: (01796) 473220   FAX: (01796) 472451

A smart but unassuming country hotel with good food in a nice location.

'A superb example of true Scottish hospitality,' adjudged one satisfied visitor. Wildlife-lovers too will find plenty to please them around Carole and Colin Anderson's white-painted hotel: there's an RSPB reserve just across the River Garry, red squirrels in the garden and a wildcat in the vicinity. Amid the smart décor inside are photographs and pictures of the local flora and fauna. The dining-room extends into a conservatory, a nice place in which to take supper in summer and enjoy the view up the valley. Head chef John Ramsay serves unpretentious fare that has received good reports, particularly the fish dishes such as grilled halibut with peppers, orange and ginger. The four courses each offer some choice, and there are three or four main dishes such as braised game served with a chestnut, juniper and red-wine sauce; deep-fried goujons of monkfish and king prawns; or roast lamb. Desserts could include tiramisù or a bitter-chocolate praline mousse with home-made shortbread. Up-market pub food is served in the bench-seated bar across the hall; smoked-salmon pâté and oatcakes feature on the menu, along with beefburgers and ploughman's.

The bedrooms are neat and modern, with their stripped-pine furniture and white walls set off by floral bedspreads and curtains – 'quality furnishings and a lovely bed.' The better bathrooms have power-showers, which are worth asking for.

◑ Closed 10 days mid-Dec & Jan/Feb ⬀ Midway between Pitlochry and Blair Atholl on B8079. Private car park ⮌ 2 single, 2 twin, 5 double, 1 suite; family room available; all with bathroom/WC exc 1 single with shower/WC; TV, room service, hair-dryer, direct-dial telephone, radio ✅ Dining-room, bar, lounge, drying-room, conservatory, garden; early suppers for children; toys, baby-listening ♿ No wheelchair access ◆ No children under 5 in dining-room eves; no dogs or smoking in dining-room; smoking discouraged in bedrooms ▭ Access, Delta, Switch, Visa ₤ Single £70 to £79, twin/double £140 to £158, family room from £140, suite £140 to £158 (rates incl dinner); deposit required. Set D £29; bar lunches available. Special breaks available

---

KILMORE Argyll & Bute   map 11

Glenfeochan House

Kilmore, By Oban PA34 4QR
TEL: (01631) 770273   FAX: (01631) 770624

A fine baronial house with expansive gardens.

You gain entrance to Patricia and David Baber's Victorian mansion via the turret: there you find two identical doors, both following the curve of the wall, and neither of them labelled because this is not a hotel but a family home. Choose wrongly, and you are faced with a blank passageway; choose wisely, and the grand entrance hall, featuring one of Patricia's massive floral displays, is revealed. This is a house that hides its secrets: although you catch a glimpse of a lawn and some woods from the road, you see nothing that suggests 350 acres, which contain well over 100 species of rhododendrons alone. Neither does Patricia's simple comment, 'Oh, we use what we can from the garden,' do justice to Glenfeochan's wild strawberries, raspberries, currants, peaches, nectarines, various types of wild mushroom, as well as herbs and edible flowers – not to mention the salmon from the river, or the home-smoked foods and home-made cheeses. This is *The Good Life* on a very large scale.

The house itself shows touches of grandeur in the pine staircase, family portraits and ornate ceilings, but the atmosphere is that of a quiet family home. Bedrooms are furnished in keeping with the period of the house with antique furniture and plain, old-fashioned bathrooms.

551

Patricia once taught at the London Cordon Bleu school and makes inventive use of fresh, seasonal ingredients in such dishes as wild-strawberry soup, guinea fowl stuffed with herb-flavoured cream cheese, and rhubarb, ginger and orange sorbet. Guests dine around one large table in a room that faces west, thus catching the often magnificent sunsets.

◑ Closed 1 Nov to 1 Apr ⊿ 5 miles south of Oban on A816, at head of Loch Feochan. Private car park 🛏 1 twin, 2 double; all with bathroom/WC; TV, room service, hair-dryer, clock radio ✦ Dining-room, lounge, drying-room, garden; fishing, croquet ⅋ No wheelchair access ● No children under 10; no dogs; no smoking ▭ Access, Amex, Visa £ Single occupancy of twin/double £105, twin/double £140; deposit required. Set D £35; packed lunches available. Special breaks available

---

KINBUCK Stirling

map 11

Cromlix House

Kinbuck, By Dunblane FK15 9JT
TEL: (01786) 822125 FAX: (01786) 825450

A grand country-house hotel at the heart of a 3,000-acre estate.

You could not ask for a more convincing experience of true Scots baronial than a stay at Cromlix House: huge portraits on the grand staircase, stuffed animals galore, polished panelling and buttoned leather – one guest even raved about the wallpaper: 'So lucky for it to be preserved!' at which point owners Ailsa and David Assenti had to draw the line and point out that they had put the paper up only a few months before. Nevertheless, all is very much in keeping with the high-Victorian origins, from the rich red décor of the dining-rooms to the pictures on bedroom walls titled 'Sailor's Farewell' and 'Soldier's Return'. The rooms are often on a grand scale, but judicious use of coronet drapes and modern furnishings creates a warm, welcoming atmosphere among all the antiques. Some of the suites seem to have an entire wing to themselves, perhaps the best being Upper Turret, where there is a semi-circular chest of drawers that fits precisely into the turret. Lesser rooms may not quite match that but all show careful attention to detail. Dinners are five courses with two options at each stage, a main course of suprême of halibut with trout mousseline or medallion of beef with liver pâté could be followed by a warm lemon tarte or a brandy snap basket filled with cassis syllabub and strawberries.

◑ Closed Jan ⊿ 4 miles north of Dunblane leave A9 and take B8033; go through Kinbuck village and cross narrow bridge; hotel is 200 yards on left. Private car park 🛏 3 twin, 3 double, 8 suites; all with bathroom/WC; TV, room service, hair-dryer, direct-dial telephone ✦ 2 dining-rooms, 2 lounges, library, study, conservatory, garden, private chapel; conference facilities (max 40 people incl up to 14 residential); fishing, tennis, croquet; early suppers for children; baby-listening ⅋ No wheelchair access ● Children discouraged from dining-rooms eves; no dogs in public rooms; no smoking in dining-rooms ▭ Access, Amex, Diners, Switch, Visa £ Single occupancy of twin/double £80 to £140, twin/double £135 to £160, suite £175 to £215; deposit required. Set L £18.50, D £37. Special breaks available

---

Many hotels put up their tariffs in the spring. You are advised to confirm prices when you book.

KINLOCHBERVIE Highland map 11

Old School Restaurant

Inshegra, Kinlochbervie IV27 4RH
TEL: (01971) 521383 (AND FAX)

A friendly restaurant-with-rooms serving good seafood from the loch.

Englishman Tom Burt came to this spot planning to retire but, 16 years later, his retirement remains at the planning stage and his restaurant-with-rooms has taken over. The building looks out across Inshegra's folded inlets and racks of seaweed to a few lonely crofts, each with its own little green field and smoking chimney. Inside, the schoolroom has been converted into a simple restaurant, featuring plain, wooden tables, spoke-backed chairs and a small bar at one end. The happier memories of the building's past are recalled in photographs, maps and the blackboard menu; less pleasant memories are evoked, too, and ex-rebels will notice the menacing presence of the tawse hanging on the wall. The cuisine ranges from 'fill-ups', like sausage and chips, to such dishes as wild salmon and broccoli cooked in breadcrumbs. Seafood (from the local harbour) is well represented, with scallops, prawns, turbot, plaice and haddock – as well as lobster during the summer months – featuring on the menu. The puddings are traditional, and desserts such as apricot crumble and banana split hint at the school dining-hall in name only.

The bright and modern bedrooms are situated next to a tumbling brook, in a purpose-built annexe at the back, and are decorated in gentle colours and feature rattan armchairs. The 'lounge' is cupboard-sized, and hardly deserves the name.

◑ Closed 25 Dec & 1 Jan ⬚ From A838 at Rhiconich take B801 to Kinlochbervie. Private car park ⬚ 1 single, 3 twin, 2 double; family room available; all in annexe; doubles with bathroom/WC, 4 with shower/WC; TV, room service, hair-dryer, direct-dial telephone ⬚ Restaurant, bar, lounge, drying-room, garden; fishing; early suppers for children ⬚ No wheelchair access ⬚ No dogs or smoking in public rooms ⬚ Access, Visa ⬚ Single £27, single occupancy of twin/double £21 to £35, twin/double £42 to £54, family room from £64. Alc L, D £13; light lunches available

---

KINLOCH RANNOCH Perthshire & Kinross map 11

Cuilmore Cottage

Kinloch Rannoch PH16 5QB
TEL: (01882) 632218 (AND FAX)

Enjoy the good life in a tiny gem of a country crofter's cottage.

Raspberry canes by the gate, cats on the window ledges, a postman leaning on the stable door with geese clustering at his feet – to suburban escapees, Anita and Jens Steffen's cottage can seem like an adman's dream of rural life. The location is certainly idyllic: Cuilmore Cottage is set a few hundred yards from the shores of Loch Rannoch, with the brooding heights of Schiehallion peak looming above. The house, which was once a simple crofter's cottage, was extended in the 1930s, but still offers only two guest bedrooms. The front door opens directly into the kitchen, which leads to a small dining-room and sitting-room decorated with old crofters' tools and featuring a coffee table made from a cartwheel. The four-course dinners demonstrate a strong local flavour with a choice of main dishes such as poached fillet of salmon, pink-roasted pigeon breasts, or crusted lamb cutlets. Everything that can be home-made is, using the garden's organically grown fruits and vegetables. Guests' can sharpen their appetites by using the hotel's canoe to explore the nearby Dunnallister Water – home to many wildfowl.

The two bedrooms – a twin and a double – maintain the fine, country-cottage style with stripped-wood furniture, dried-flower arrangements and white muslin canopies over the beds.

◑ Closed Nov to Jan ◪ Take B846 from Aberfeldy to Kinloch Rannoch; hotel is 100 yards from the eastern corner of the loch. Private car park 🛏 1 twin, 1 double; both with bathroom/WC; hair-dryer ✓ Dining-room, lounge, garden; fishing ♿ No wheelchair access ● No children; no dogs in bedrooms; no smoking ▭ Access, Visa £ Single occupancy of twin/double £25, twin/double £50; deposit required. Set D £25. Special breaks available

KIRKCUDBRIGHT Dumfries & Galloway map 11

Gladstone House

£

48 High Street, Kirkcudbright DG6 4JX
TEL: (01557) 331734 (AND FAX)

Friendly hosts and comfortable modern rooms in this B&B.

Kirkcudbright – a small and pretty fishing town in which rows of smartly painted, sturdy cottages abound – is the sort of location that television scouts would drool over, and it is a popular base for artists – a sort of Scottish St Ives. Sue Westbrook originally came here to work in the food industry, and then stayed on to open her Georgian town house to visitors. Steps lead directly from the street up to the first floor, where there is a comfortable lounge furnished with some antique pieces, period pictures and a gas fire. Breakfasts are taken downstairs, in a bright, white-walled room, in which local artists display their work. The menu offers a reasonable selection, from a full fry-up to smoked salmon and scrambled eggs, or poached finnan haddock. In summer, there may also be home-grown strawberries, raspberries and gooseberries. Afternoon teas are served in the small garden at the back of the house – in fine weather, it is a nice little suntrap. The bedrooms are light and airy, with views from the tongue-and-groove dormer windows either across the town or to the River Dee. Impressionist prints add colour to the rooms, and plenty of thoughtful extras, such as electric blankets and mineral water, are included. The top room boasts a double aspect and a small sitting-area.

◑ Open all year ◪ On High Street, just behind Maclellans Castle and 200 yards from harbour. On-street parking 🛏 3 double; 2 with bathroom/WC, 1 with shower/WC; TV, room service, clock radio ✓ Dining-room, lounge, drying-room, garden ♿ No wheelchair access ● No children under 12; no dogs; no smoking ▭ Access, Delta, Visa £ Single occupancy of twin/double £25 to £34, twin/double £44 to £56; deposit required. Special breaks available

map 11

Foveran Hotel

St Ola, Kirkwall KW15 1SF
TEL: (01856) 872389   FAX: (01856) 876430

A comfortable modern hotel, suitable for business and tourist visitors.

Otter-watching between the soup and the main course is not something many restaurants can offer, but Ivy and Bobby Corsie's single-storey hotel has a magnificent view of Scapa Flow, and window tables are therefore equipped with binoculars. The hotel is surrounded by 34 acres of grounds, too, and so there's plenty of opportunity to build up an appetite by bird-watching or exploring some of the nearby beaches. Guests usually begin the evening with a drink by the open fire in the lounge, before moving through to the restaurant, which is furnished in Scandinavian-style light pine. Seafood is the menu's particular focus, and choices include scallops or Orkney bouillabaisse, as well as other local dishes such as smoked salmon, or wild mallard served with a morello-cherry sauce. Vegetarians also have a wide choice from a separate menu.

The eight bedrooms, which are decorated in bright contemporary fabrics, and feature white walls and pine furniture, are quite small, but are nevertheless comfortable and well equipped.

◐ Closed Jan   ⃗ From Kirkwall take A964 to Orphir for 2 miles; hotel is signposted on the left. Private car park   ⊨ 3 single, 3 twin, 2 double; family room available; 4 with bathroom/WC, 4 with shower/WC; TV, room service, hair-dryer, direct-dial telephone   ⌘ Restaurant, bar, lounge, drying-room, conservatory, garden; early suppers for children; baby-listening, outdoor games   ♿ Wheelchair access to hotel (1 ramp), restaurant and WC (M,F), 8 ground-floor bedrooms   ◐ No dogs in public rooms; no smoking in restaurant   ⊟ Access, Delta, Switch, Visa   £ Single £45, single occupancy of twin/double £50, twin/double £70, family room £80; deposit required. Alc D £22

---

 map 11

Enmore Hotel

Marine Parade, Kirn, By Dunoon PA23 8HH
TEL: (01369) 702230   FAX: (01369) 702148

A quiet family-run hotel, decorated in country-house style.

Visitors who cross the Clyde estuary and rush north to the Highlands often miss the pleasant coastal town of Dunoon and its neighbour, Kirn. Angela and David Wilson's whitewashed hotel was built for a rich cotton merchant, was extended during Victorian times and has more recently been given two squash courts. Featuring smart blue-and-gilt chairs in reception, and a comfortable sitting-room which includes a bar, Enmore Hotel's decorative style is that of a small-scale country house. David's five-course dinners offer alternatives for the first and main courses, and a typical menu might comprise a savoury-filled peach or smoked salmon to start, followed by vegetable soup, then either a honey-roast half-duckling or Loch Fyne scallops cooked in Pernod; after dessert there is Stilton accompanied by celery, with which to round it all off. The bedrooms vary in size, and are individually furnished with a mixture of antique and reproduction pieces. Room 8 enjoys a good sea view, a four-poster draped with lace, and an opulent bathroom, in which water gushes from a gilt swan into a corner bath. Room 2 boasts a water bed and whirlpool bath; the others rooms are not quite as flamboyant.

◗ Closed 22 to 29 Dec ⏋ On seafront at Kirn, 1 mile north of Dunoon on A815. Private car park ⤶ 2 single, 4 twin, 1 double, 3 four-poster, 1 family room; most with bathroom/WC, some with shower/WC; TV, room service, hair-dryer, direct-dial telephone ✦ Dining-room, bar, lounge, drying-room, games room, garden; conference facilities (max 36 people incl up to 11 residential); squash, table tennis; early suppers for children; toys, babysitting ♿ No wheelchair access ● No dogs or smoking in dining-room ▭ Access, Amex, Delta, Switch, Visa £ Single £35 to £39, single occupancy of twin/double £45 to £49, twin/double £50 to £75, four-poster £100 to £130, family room £50 to £80; deposit required. Set L £10, D £20; alc L £10, D £12.50. Special breaks available

---

LARGS North Ayrshire   map 11

Brisbane House

14 Greenock Road, Esplanade, Largs KA30 8NF
TEL: (01475) 687200   FAX: (01475) 676295

A smart seaside hotel featuring stylish interiors.

The Swiss and Scottish flags that flutter in the offshore breeze outside George Maltby and Jannick Bertschy's seafront hotel proclaim the nationalities of the owners. This internationality is also reflected in the dinner menu, in which you might find tournedos à la suisse appearing alongside malt-whisky-cured smoked salmon. The hotel is close to the new Vikingar Centre, a cultural and sports complex that emphasises Largs' background as the site of the Scots' last battle with the Viking invaders in 1263. Things are quieter now, and only the ferry to the Cumbraes occasionally disturbs the seagulls. The building's long façade extends from the bar into a stylish, modern conservatory in which lunches are served; there's also an elegant dining-room, whose big picture windows look out to the Isle of Bute. Guests can choose from the à la carte menu (in French), the table d'hôte menu (in English), or a seafood special; a bar menu offers simpler fare in less formal surroundings. The bedrooms are reached by means of a swish pair of curving staircases; all are well equipped and smartly furnished with rosewood pieces – the more expensive rooms boast coronet-crowned beds.

Report forms are at the back of the Guide; *write a letter or e-mail us if you prefer. Our e-mail address is: "guidereports@which.co.uk".*

🌙 Open all year 🅿 On the Clyde estuary, on A78 from Glasgow. Private car park
🛏 6 single, 5 twin, 12 double; family rooms available; all with bathroom/WC exc
singles with shower/WC; TV, room service, hair-dryer, trouser press, direct-dial
telephone ✅ Dining-room, bar/lounge, conservatory, garden; conference facilities
(max 100 people incl up to 23 residential); early suppers for children; baby-listening
♿ No wheelchair access ⊖ No dogs ▭ Access, Amex, Delta, Diners, Switch,
Visa 💷 Single £55, single occupancy of twin/double £70 to £80, twin/double £90 to
£100, family room £90; deposit required. Set D £20; alc D £22; bar meals available.
Special breaks available

LESLIE Aberdeenshire   map 11

Leslie Castle

Leslie, By Insch AB52 6NX
TEL: (01464) 820869   FAX: (01464) 821076

An imaginatively rebuilt castle, with friendly hosts.

From the outside, the pale-grey walls and slate-roofed turrets of Leslie Castle
make it look like a romantic vision of a Scottish clan's bastion – which is exactly
what it is. David Leslie's father used to bring him to see the castle's ruins when
he was a boy; then, in 1979, David heard that it was on the market and, just six
weeks later, was cutting stones in preparation for the rebuilding of the Leslie
stronghold. Inside, the castle is quite homely: no attempt has been made to
manufacture a false atmosphere with off-the-peg antiques; instead, David
designed the furniture in the spirit of the Scots Jacobean style. There are also
fitted carpets and plenty of other such modern creature comforts; somehow this
eclectic mixture works tremendously well. Leslie, David's wife, is the chef, and
produces a daily changing menu of four courses, offering two choices for each
course; a typical meal might start with smoked salmon or carrot soup, followed
by minted lamb or chicken tarragon, and finally a dessert such as sticky toffee
pudding or fresh fruit.

The winding staircase takes you up to the comfortable, white-walled
bedrooms – some include turreted corners, and you can peer through their gun
loops to see who is knocking at the front door. Earlier tenants would have
appreciated the Leslies' thoughtfulness: welcome touches include electric
blankets, decanters of sherry and scissors with which to open the sachets of
shampoo.

🌙 Open all year 🅿 From A96, 7 miles north of Inverurie, take B9002, signposted
Insch. After 2 miles, turn left to Auchleven/Clatt. At Auchleven crossroads, go straight
over and follow signposts to Leslie for 2 miles. Leslie Castle is on right, just before
hamlet of Leslie. Private car park 🛏 1 twin, 1 double, 2 four-poster; family rooms
available; all with bathroom/WC; TV, limited room service, hair-dryer, trouser press,
direct-dial telephone, clock radio ✅ 2 dining-rooms, bar, lounge, garden; early
suppers for children; toys, babysitting, baby-listening ♿ No wheelchair access
⊖ No dogs; smoking discouraged ▭ Access, Amex, Visa 💷 Single occupancy of
twin/double £87 to £89, twin/double £124 to £128, four-poster £136 to £140 family
room from £129; deposit required. Set D £30 (prices valid till Apr 1997). Special breaks
available

Two Waters

Lickisto, Isle of Harris HS3 3EL
TEL: (01859) 530246

A well-kept hospitable guesthouse that repeatedly entices visitors back.

Sea trout for breakfast, caught the night before by your host – sadly, this doesn't occur quite so often at Two Waters as once it did, since John Barber's fishing exploits have been curtailed by illness, but when it does, the fish is superb. And even without the freshly landed trout, there's a choice of at least nine different fish: some smoked, some fresh and all local. John and Jill came to this wild, remote spot 24 years ago and, after herculean building efforts, finally opened their modern bungalow to visitors; John holds court in the lounge in the evenings, and recalls every boulder that needed to be carted away in order to create the small garden. Jill cooks the four-course dinners – 'first-class' reported one visitor – and the ethos of her cuisine is based on self-sufficiency: you can enjoy home-made bread, biscuits and cakes, as well as home-smoked seafood – even the (free) wine served with dinner is fermented by the Barbers. While Jill cooks, John keeps the conversation bubbling along, providing expert tips on what to see and do locally. His pride and joy are the otters that live in the creek at the back of the house – so close that you can hear the satisfied chomp of the otters' jaws as a salmon is wolfed down.

The bedrooms are neat, well kept and thoughtfully equipped for every eventuality: you'll find, for example, fresh milk for your tea and coffee, shoe-cleaning brushes, cotton buds and a nail brush; only the synthetic duvet covers seem out of place.

◑ Closed 1 Oct to 30 Apr   ⬚ From Tarbert ferry point, travel south on A859 towards Rodel for 5 miles. Turn left on to C79 single-track road for 2 miles. Hotel is on left, after second bridge. Private car park   ⊨ 2 twin, 2 double; 1 twin with bathroom/WC, 3 with shower/WC; hair-dryer   ✦ Dining-room, lounge, drying-room, garden; fishing   ♿ No wheelchair access   ● No children under 12   ▭ None accepted   £ Single occupancy of twin/double £28, twin/double £56; deposit required. Set D £15

The Albannach ☆

Baddidarroch, Lochinver, Lairg IV27 4LP
TEL: (01571) 844407 (AND FAX)

A friendly, relaxed atmosphere is provided with some style at this small hotel.

Colin Craig is famed throughout Lochinver, as much for daring to wear a kilt while riding a Triumph motorbike as for steadily developing the Albannach with his partner, Lesley Crosfield. The three-storey white-walled hotel, featuring black window ledges and flying a flag with a Scottish lion, nestles in the craggy and boggy hillside on the north side of Loch Inver, looking across to the tremendous, domed peak of Suilven. Entry is via the new conservatory (recently built by Colin), which features a rug-covered flagstone floor and cane furniture. This leads to a smart little den of a lounge, which is furnished with plaid-covered comfortable pieces, and also to the restaurant – again, a snug room – in which both breakfasts and dinners are served. The menu has been considerably developed over the years, and emphasises locally caught fish and seafood. There's generally a choice of two dishes for the starter and pudding courses, while the soup and main courses are set – although 'we always discuss what people want.' You might find yourself faced with a choice of Lochinver oysters or smoked, wild venison, followed by a tomato and mint soup, local halibut and then a Scottish lemon tart or a chocolate, orange and brandy mousse accompanied by white-chocolate ice-cream.

The two older bedrooms feature low, wood-lined ceilings and plaid bedspreads; both offer a view to the loch through their small, cottage-style windows. The newer rooms are situated in the part of the house that was added in 1879 (when its erstwhile owner returned from Trinidad, having made good). The four-poster bedroom, which is decorated in deep-green colours and boasts plaid drapes and a Victorian fireplace, is particularly striking. None of the bedrooms has a TV or telephone, and guests tend to head for the conservatory or lounge after dinner when, in Colin's words, 'a lot of blethering goes on.'

◑ Closed Jan & Feb　↗ As you enter Lochinver, turn right over old stone bridge at foot of the hill, signposted Baddidarroch. After ½ mile, turn left after pottery. Private car park　🛏 2 twin, 1 double, 1 four-poster; all with bathroom/WC　✥ Restaurant, lounge, conservatory, garden　&. No wheelchair access　● No children under 6; no dogs; no smoking　▭ Access, Visa　£ Single occupancy of twin/double £34 to £60, twin/double £50 to £68, four-poster £62 to £68; deposit required. Set D £20/23; alc L £10. Special breaks available

---

Inver Lodge

Lochinver IV27 4LU
TEL: (01571) 844496　FAX: (01571) 844395

Friendly and attentive staff make this international-style hotel special.

As you drive along the shore through the bustling, small fishing settlement of Lochinver, you can see the rather dull and uninspiring-looking Inver Lodge Hotel on the skyline to the south. It's only when you climb up the hill to reach the hotel that you begin to appreciate some of its positive points, such as the dining-room, whose big picture windows reveal a view down to the silver sea as well as to the Isle of Harris way beyond. Furthermore, despite the fact that the hotel building itself lacks character, the attentive, friendly and good-humoured staff lift the place on to another plane entirely. The reception area and lounges – and even the little book shop, offering racks of bestsellers – are decorated in the smart, international style that is favoured by airport hotels the world over. The bedrooms also include everything that you might possibly need, from trouser presses to mini-bars; biscuits are provided alongside the kettle and tea bags, and stocks are replenished when the beds are turned down in the evening.

The dining-room is formal, but not stuffy. Our praise for the first-course plate of grilled Lochinver prawns drew the waiter's comment: 'Aye, they were caught by Andrew round at Inverkircaig.' A main-course dish of Aberdeen Angus beef was equally tasty, and was followed by the Scottish dessert cranachan. Most people head for a comfortable lounge for coffee and chocolates.

◑ Closed mid-Oct to mid-Apr ⤧ Take A837 to Lochinver. In village, travel towards harbour and take first left after village hall. Private car park ⛽ 11 twin, 9 double; all with bathroom/WC; TV, room service, hair-dryer, mini-bar, trouser press, direct-dial telephone, radio ✅ Dining-room, bar, 2 lounges, drying-room; fishing, sauna, solarium, snooker, stalking; early suppers for children ♿ Wheelchair access to hotel, dining-room and WC (unisex), 11 ground-floor bedrooms ● No children under 7 in dining-room eves; no dogs in public rooms ▭ Access, Amex, Delta, Diners, Switch, Visa £ Single occupancy of twin/double £80, twin/double £110 to £130; deposit required. Set D £27; alc L £12, D £27. Special breaks available

---

MARKINCH Fife   map 11

Balbirnie House

Balbirnie Park, Markinch, By Glenrothes KY7 6NE
TEL: (01592) 610066   FAX: (01592) 610529

A grand country-house hotel with a corporate emphasis, set in 420 acres of parkland.

The computer-designed shape and dimensions of the modern hotel room are so tediously familiar that any departure from the template creates a kind of temporary euphoria. When you find yourself somewhere more individual – as here – you are tempted to play tennis across the bed, water-ski down the bath, or go rambling in the wardrobes – there was certainly no lack of space in our inspection bedroom at Balbirnie House. The approach to the hotel gets you in the mood for your stay, as a long sweeping drive through the parkland delivers you to the foot of massive Ionic portals – as solid as the Balfour family money that built them back in 1815. Once inside, there is more grandeur – particularly in the elegant Long Gallery, in which *trompe-l'oeil* cherubs gambol. The dining-rooms and drawing-room are separated by the library, which is a good spot in which to warm up by the fire and study the menu. Our sample dinner was a chicken terrine, followed by onion soup, and then a main-course dish of cod in a mustard sauce – a dish rather overpowered by the mustard. The service was attentive, but a rather strange seating arrangement placed the two (single) diners facing each other at opposite ends of the room – rather like ghosts of some estranged aristocrats from a previous incarnation of the house.

Balbirnie House is well equipped for the corporate visitor, attracting much conference business and also weddings. Perhaps that was the reason why our inspector felt that the place lacked the personal touch. On leaving, as the rain sluiced down, no-one offered to help with a brolly or the bags.

Prices are quoted per room *rather than* per person.

◐ Open all year ⤴ Leave M90 at Junction 3, following the signs to the Tay Bridge. Turn right on B9130 to Markinch and Balbirnie Park. Private car park ⤶ 2 single, 15 twin, 10 double, 1 four-poster, 2 suites; all with bathroom/WC; TV, 24-hour room service, hair-dryer, trouser press, direct-dial telephone ⊗ 2 dining-rooms, bar, 2 lounges, drying-room, library, games room, garden; conference facilities (max 150 people incl up to 30 residential); golf, croquet, putting green; early suppers for children ♿ Wheelchair access to hotel (1 ramp), dining-rooms and WC (unisex), 1 ground-floor bedroom specially equipped for disabled people ● Dogs in bedrooms only, by arrangement ▭ Access, Amex, Diners, Visa £ Single £95, single occupancy of twin/double £110, twin/double £145 to £190, four-poster £198, suite £225; deposit required. Set D £27.50, Sun L £15; alc L £15. Special breaks available

---

MARNOCH Aberdeenshire   map 11

Old Manse of Marnoch

Bridge Of Marnoch, By Huntly AB54 7RS
TEL: (01466) 780873 (AND FAX)

**COUNTY
HOTEL
OF THE
YEAR**

An unpretentious up-market guesthouse with friendly hosts.

It's only when you get a really good welcome that you realise how much you missed it at all those lesser places. After negotiating a tricky driveway into the manse and an enthusiastic canine welcome, our late-arriving inspector was warmly greeted by Patrick Carter, whose unforced friendliness set the atmosphere for a relaxing stay.

The house has its back to the road and faces the River Deveron through some peaceful wooded gardens. Patrick and his wife, Keren, worked overseas for many years and built up an eclectic collection of artefacts and antiques: the comfortable lounge has some Middle Eastern souvenirs, the dining-room has a mercantile theme and there's even a ship's figurehead beached on the front step. Bedrooms have some good old pieces of furniture and plenty of space to sit if you don't want to socialise downstairs. The Carters are thoughtful hosts, providing fresh milk for tea and coffee in your room and a steady supply of home-made shortbread biscuits. Bathrooms have the same meticulous attention to detail down to a choice of bath salts or bubbles. Keren's meals are staunchly Scottish: breakfast porridge comes with a horn spoon and there's local salmon and venison along with traditional dishes like cock-a-leekie soup and a superb Scotch woodcock.

◐ Closed 2 weeks in Oct/Nov ⤴ On B9117, less than a mile from A97 between Huntly and Banff. Private car park ⤶ 2 twin, 3 double; 4 with bathroom/WC, 1 twin with shower/WC; TV, room service, hair-dryer ⊗ Dining-room, lounge, drying-room, garden ♿ No wheelchair access ● No children under 12; no dogs in public rooms; no smoking in dining-room ▭ Access, Visa £ Single occupancy of twin/double £54 to £60, twin/double £81 to £90; deposit required. Set D £25; packed lunches available. Special breaks available

---

It is always worth enquiring about the availability of special breaks or weekend prices. The prices we quote are the standard rates for one night – most hotels offer reduced rates for longer stays.

See the inside front cover for a brief explanation of how to use the Guide.

Maryculter House

South Deeside Road, Maryculter, Aberdeen AB1 0BB
TEL: (01224) 732124   FAX: (01224) 733510

A secluded business-style hotel, with an interesting history.

It is easy to see why the Knights Templar chose this spot on which to build a preceptory after King William had granted them the surrounding land in 1187. Half-hidden by woods and eastern ramparts, the site is folded into a protective curve of the River Dee. The huge old chimney bearing a Templar coat of arms, as well as the high, beamed ceiling of the bar, hint at its historical associations, but Maryculter House Hotel consists mainly of a series of more modern rooms, all pleasant, neatly painted in white and comfortably furnished. You can enjoy informal, pub-style food and views over the river in the Poacher's Pocket bar, while the stone-walled Priory Room offers a grander, four-course, table d'hôte menu, which might include a julienne of smoked mushrooms, followed by a sorbet, and then breast of pheasant stuffed with haggis, all rounded off with a chocolate and orange mousse served with chocolate sauce. The bedrooms have a standard, business-style layout, but also feature chintzy colour schemes and light-pine fittings.

◑ Open all year; restaurant closed Sun   ⊿ On B9077, beside River Dee in Maryculter. Private car park   ⊏⊐ 2 single, 12 twin, 9 double; suite available; all with bathroom/WC; TV, room service, hair-dryer, trouser press, direct-dial telephone   ⊘ Restaurant, bar, lounge, garden; conference facilities (max 200 people incl up to 23 residential); early suppers for children   ⎠ Wheelchair access to hotel (1 step), restaurant and WC (unisex), 7 ground-floor bedrooms   ● No dogs in public rooms   ▭ Access, Amex, Diners, Switch, Visa   £ Single/single occupancy of twin/double £85 to £105, twin/double £95 to £115, suite £95 to £115. Set D £27.50; bar lunches available. Special breaks available

---

Beechwood Country House

Harthope Place, Moffat DG10 9RS
TEL: (01683) 220210   FAX: (01683) 220889

Friendly, hospitable hosts and a quiet location at this small country-house hotel.

Situated close enough to Moffat's High Street to stroll into town, and backed by 12 acres of beech trees, Lynda and Jeff Rogers' small hotel enables you to forget about the car for a while. The solid, grey Victorian house has a conservatory extension in which lunches are served, while the lounge boasts good views across the Annan Valley. The friendly style is that of a country house (but on a low-key scale), and the guests typically chat about former visits, or swap news of other regulars. Jeff and Lynda work hard to ensure that everyone enjoys their stay: 'Very friendly,' reported one visitor, 'They come across as very genuine people.' The comfortable, light-coloured bedrooms feature sprigged wallpaper, and the bathrooms are well equipped, including such extras as bath salts and soap flakes. The restaurant has pleasant views across to the town's golf course (a major attraction for many visitors). The menus offer a choice on all four courses; you might select grilled-pork and apple sausages to start with, followed by a soup or sorbet, then baked halibut served with cream and dill, and finally a dessert of caramelised walnut tart with fresh cream.

◖ Closed 2 Jan to 16 Feb ⤢ At the north end of Moffat; turn right at the corner of St Mary's church into Harthope Place, and follow signs to the hotel. Private car park ⤶ 3 twin, 3 double, 1 family room; all with bathroom/WC exc 1 double with shower/WC; TV, room service, hair-dryer, direct-dial telephone ◈ Restaurant, bar, lounge, drying-room, library, conservatory, garden; conference facilities (max 12 people incl up to 7 residential); early suppers for children ♿ No wheelchair access ● No smoking in some public rooms ▭ Access, Amex, Visa £ Single occupancy of twin/double £49, twin/double £71, family room £85. Set L £14, D £22. Special breaks available

---

Well View

Ballplay Road, Moffat DG10 9JU
TEL: (01683) 220184 FAX: (01683) 220088

Good food and attentive hosts at this traditional small hotel.

Janet and John Schuckardt's house looks unremarkable on the outside: a three-storey Victorian family house in smart grey and brown stone overlooking the town. But correspondents have praised everything from the warm welcome to the rooms and cooking. 'Friendly, down-to-earth owners who treat their guests with courtesy as well,' wrote one. Rooms are light and airy, decorated with added colour from Impressionist prints in the lounge and flowers in the dining-room. Bedrooms vary in size but are nicely furnished and have plenty of extras like sherry, fruit and biscuits. Bathrooms are traditional in style and have bathrobes provided. Room 4 has a slightly more modern feel with its pine four-poster; Room 3 is a large twin with views over the town to the golf course. The four-course dinners offer a good selection, perhaps cauliflower and Stilton soup to start, fillet of salmon with vegetables, then an Ecclefechan butter tart and a selection of cheeses to finish.

◖ Open all year ⤢ Take A708 out of Moffat towards Selkirk; take first left turning past fire station; hotel is 300 yards down on right. Private car park ⤶ 2 twin, 2 double, 1 four-poster, 1 suite; 3 with bathroom/WC, 3 with shower/WC; TV, hair-dryer ◈ 2 restaurants, lounge, garden; conference facilities (max 12 people non-residential, 6 residential); early suppers for children ♿ No wheelchair access ● No children under 5 in restaurants eves; no dogs in public rooms; no smoking in restaurants ▭ Access, Amex, Visa £ Single occupancy of twin/double £36 to £44, twin/double £54 to £72, four-poster/suite £62 to £78; deposit required. Set L £13, D £26. Special breaks available

---

Where we know an establishment accepts credit cards, we list them. There may be a surcharge if you pay by credit card. It is always best to check when booking whether the card you want to use is acceptable.

MUIR OF ORD **Highland**   map 11

Dower House

Highfield, Muir of Ord IV6 7XN
TEL: (01463) 870090 (AND FAX)

Stylish comfort on a small scale at this nineteenth-century dower house.

There is something of the colonial hill-station bungalow about Mena and Robyn Aitchison's home: banks of rhododendrons lead you down the drive to the long low façade neatly painted in white and maroon. In fact, this was once a baronial home that was converted in 1800 into a dower house in the cottage-orné style. The front door leads directly into the lounge – a smart, chintzy room featuring bookshelves in the alcoves and a Victorian fireplace. Antiques, ornaments and floral drapes appear throughout the house, along with the occasional, idiosyncratic flourish such as the antler that conceals a knife, and the old pedal organ in the suite bedroom. 'It does work,' says Mena Aitchison of the latter: 'We sometimes hear guests use it.' The other bedrooms are decorated in similarly bold colours and include old-fashioned bedsteads, while the stripe-walled bathrooms are, in some cases, fitted with original Victorian pieces, like the claw-foot bath in Room 1.

Dinners follow a set four-course menu, but offer some interesting diversions from the usual country-house style; a typical meal might feature langoustines served with garlic mayonnaise, a broccoli and lemon-grass soup, fillet of venison with a rowan-jelly sauce, and finally a border tart accompanied by whisky cream.

◖ Closed 1 week Mar, 1 week Oct   ⬈ 1 mile north of Muir of Ord on A862 Dingwall road, turn left after double bend. Private car park   ⬳ 2 twin, 2 double, 1 suite; all with bathroom/WC exc 1 twin with shower/WC; TV, room service, hair-dryer, direct-dial telephone; no tea/coffee-making facilities in rooms   ⊘ Dining-room, lounge, drying-room, garden; conference facilities (max 5 people residential); croquet; early suppers for children; toys, babysitting   ♿ Wheelchair access to hotel (1 step), dining-room and WC (unisex), 5 ground-floor bedrooms   ⊖ No children under 5 in dining-room eves; no smoking in dining-room and 3 bedrooms; no dogs in public rooms   ▭ Access, Visa   £ Single occupancy of twin/double £45 to £100, twin/double/suite £70 to £110; deposit required. Set L £17.50, D £30 (1996 prices). Special breaks available

---

NAIRN **Highland**   map 11

Clifton House

Viewfield Street, Nairn IV12 4HW
TEL: (01667) 453119   FAX: (01667) 452836

A unique and wonderful hotel, full of exuberance and colour.

For 45 years, J Gordon Macintyre has been waging a one-man battle against the drab, the dispiriting and what he calls 'the grey sludge' of modern life. A visit to his hotel is rather like drinking a glass of vintage champagne after years of imbibing cheap Lambrusco. Everything about the house is colourful, enlivening and – most of all – theatrical (unsurprisingly, since the hotel is also a theatre: productions are staged in the deceptively large dining-room behind the black curtains at the rear of the sitting-room). Memories of past events feature in the drawing-room at the far end of the house, which is a deliciously decadent room, housing a log fire, oil paintings and photo albums. As you would expect, the library next door is the sort in which books are actually read.

The bedrooms continue the style set downstairs, and boast dark-wooden bedheads, painted red furniture hung with tassels, and top-quality linen ('people need good sheets, not UHT milk and television sets'). If you want to lock yourself away to write your magnum opus, then request the Top Room – you won't be the first. If you want a newspaper or tea, you can have it, but you'll need to ask for it in person, as there are no telephones in the bedrooms.

The handwritten dinner menus are in French (except for the puddings, which are described in English) and meals are served in the elegant dining-room or, if there is no theatrical production, in the performance room.

◑ Closed Dec & Jan   ⤳ Enter Nairn on A96, and then turn west down Marine Road at the only roundabout in town. Hotel is ½ mile further on, on the left. Private car park ⤶ 4 single, 4 twin, 2 double, 2 four-poster; family rooms available; all with bathroom/WC; room service, hair-dryer   ✧ 2 dining-rooms, 2 lounges, TV room, drying-room, library, garden; early suppers for children   ♿ No wheelchair access ● No dogs or smoking in dining-rooms   ▭ Access, Amex, Diners, Visa   £ Single £54, twin/double £90 to £96, four-poster £96, family room from £108; deposit required. Alc L £17.50, D £22.50. Special breaks available

---

Manor House

COUNTY HOTEL OF THE YEAR

Gallanach Road, Oban PA34 4LS
TEL: (01631) 562087   FAX: (01631) 563053

A hospitable and well-run small hotel with pleasant views across Oban Bay.

The Manor House may be located some way from the centre of Oban today, but its historical position is right at the heart of things. It was built for the Duke of Argyll in 1780 and went on to become the first bank in town; home to the late Fitzroy Maclean's family, it then became a base for the redoubtable Admiral Otter. He probably valued the place for its fine view north across the bay to the narrows, where the boats come in – these days, they are more likely to be ferries from Mull and Barra than fishing fleets. It's a view worth requesting when booking a room, although all the bedrooms are equally well decorated and furnished, with some old, polished pieces featuring among the reproduction furniture. With their warm colours and wood panelling, the two lounges and dining-room downstairs have the same cosy atmosphere as the bedrooms. The smart mosaic tiling in the reception area reflects the building's previous incarnation as a bank.

The competitively priced table d'hôte dinners offer five courses, with a choice of starter, main course and dessert; you might opt for poached asparagus, followed by cream of fennel soup, a sorbet, venison from Mull and then a wild-berry shortcake. The à la carte option places strong emphasis on local seafood.

◑ Closed 2 to 31 Jan and 23 Nov to 5 Dec ⊿ Follow signs to Oban ferry terminal; hotel is 200 yards past terminal on right-hand side. Private car park ⊫ 5 twin, 6 double; all with shower/WC; TV, room service, hair-dryer, direct-dial telephone ⊘ Dining-room, bar, 2 lounges, garden ⅋ No wheelchair access ● No children under 12; no dogs in public rooms; no smoking in dining-room ⊟ Access, Amex, Delta, Switch, Visa ⬲ Single occupancy of twin/double £59 to £79, twin/double £88 to £138; deposit required. Set D £22.50; alc D £24; bar lunches available. Special breaks available

---

Peat Inn

Peat Inn, Cupar KY15 5LH
TEL: (01334) 840206   FAX: (01334) 840530

Memorable food and luxurious rooms in a quiet location.

Head chef and owner, David Wilson, was juggling a batch of dough and a television crew when our inspector arrived. The dough took priority – food generally does at the Peat Inn. Once a simple (and lonely) overnight stop for stagecoaches, the inn gave its name to the village that grew up around it. The former stables are now the lounge, a cosy, thick-walled den in which guests gather in front of the fire for a pre-dinner drink – perhaps a dram of the restaurant's own, 12-year-old, malt whisky. 'A product of rigorous research and testing,' says David, with a laugh.

The restaurant is divided into three sections, all demonstrating an informal touch. Likewise, the food is unpretentious and gets enthusiastic reviews. The four-course set lunches are particularly good value, and the emphasis is on seafood: roasted scallops or langoustines, for example, appear in salads for starters, and may be followed by roast breast of guinea fowl or roast saddle of venison, and then a dessert of white-chocolate ice-cream.

Behind the inn stands the modern hotel building, which is generally used for overnight stops by visitors who want to sample David's cooking without facing a drive home afterwards. All but one are split-level suites, with a luxurious bedroom below that looks out on to the garden and a small lounge area above, where breakfasts are taken. One reader was peeved to find that breakfast was served in the room: 'an on-the-knee affair, no choice, and we had toast so well cooked we couldn't eat it.'

◑ Open all year; restaurants closed Sun & Mon ⊿ At the junction of B940 and B941, 6 miles south-west of St Andrews. Private car park ⊫ 8 suites; all in annexe; all with bathroom/WC; TV, room service, hair-dryer, direct-dial telephone, clock radio; no tea/coffee-making facilities in rooms ⊘ 3 restaurants, lounge, garden; ⅋ Wheelchair access to hotel, restaurants and WC (unisex), 8 ground-floor bedrooms, 1 specially equipped for disabled people ● No dogs or smoking in public rooms ⊟ Access, Amex, Diners, Switch, Visa ⬲ Single occupancy of suite £75 to £95, suite £120 to £140. Set L £18.50, D £28; alc D £34. Special breaks available

PORT APPIN

PEEBLES **Borders**	map 11

Cringletie House

Peebles EH45 8PL
TEL: (01721) 730233   FAX: (01721) 730244

A friendly, well-kept country-house hotel with excellent gardens.

As you motor up from Peebles, the sight of Cringletie's turrets and gables is every bit as impressive as the Victorian architect, David Bryce, intended. A rising sweep of drive brings you to the red sandstone walls, dreaming, perhaps, of pre-war splendours, 1920s flapper dresses and vintage Bentleys. Unfortunately, the house cannot hope to live up to the fantasy. You want wolfhounds and Waugh, but instead you get floral prints and fake log fires. Only the main lounge on the first floor, with its painted ceiling and walls hung with Murray family portraits, really captures the spirit of the exterior.

Cringletie does distinguish itself, however, with its service and welcoming atmosphere: 'Mrs Maguire and family are friendly, helpful and obviously concerned to make sure you enjoy your stay,' wrote one visitor. The food also gets good reports, and a 2-acre kitchen garden provides honey, fresh fruit and vegetables for the four-course dinner menu. Typically, this includes a beetroot and orange soup, followed by baked salmon with couscous and a saffron sauce, or roast duckling cooked with apples and calvados.

A recent addition to the hotel has been the conservatory, which is a pleasant place in which to relax over a drink and admire the 28 acres of gardens. The bedrooms are bright and cheerful, featuring simple, modern furniture and the occasional antique.

○ Closed 2 Jan to 7 Mar ☑ 2 miles north of Peebles, on A703 Peebles to Edinburgh road. Private car park ⊫ 1 single, 8 twin, 4 double; family rooms available; all with bathroom/WC; TV, room service, hair-dryer, trouser press, direct-dial telephone, clock radio; no tea/coffee-making facilities in rooms ⊘ 2 dining-rooms, bar, 2 lounges, drying-room, conservatory, garden; tennis, croquet, putting green; early suppers for children; baby-listening, cots, high chairs ⅙ No wheelchair access ⊜ No dogs in public rooms; no smoking in 1 lounge ▭ Access, Amex, Switch, Visa £· Single £55, single occupancy of twin/double £70, twin/double £110, family room from £123. Set D £25.50, Sun L £16; light lunches available. Special breaks available

---

PORT APPIN **Argyll & Bute**	map 11

Airds Hotel

Port Appin, Appin PA38 4DF
TEL: (01631) 730236   FAX: (01631) 730535

An up-market conversion of an old ferry inn into a smart country-house hotel.

Just across the narrow sea passage in front of this whitewashed inn (itself only a short stroll from the small ferry-boat landing) is the Island of Lismore, on which over 200 species of wild orchid grow. For Betty and Eric Allen, their family and many of their guests, this is reason enough to be here. You'll find flowers all over

567

the house too: big vases of beautifully arranged flowers abound, placed among the oil paintings and plush sofas in both the country-house-style drawing-room and the sitting-room. The elegant restaurant is a larger room, and boasts views across Loch Linnhe. Graeme Allen's food receives consistently good reports; his cuisine favours local ingredients, particularly Linnhe prawns and other types of seafood. There is usually plenty of choice for all but the soup course, and a typical meal might comprise a mousseline of scallops, then cream of swede and leek soup, followed by a fillet of monkfish accompanied by a ravioli of squat lobster and asparagus, and finally a chocolate ice-cream gâteau.

The comfortable and well-equipped bedrooms are decorated in the same style as the public rooms. 'Sparkling bathroom with constant change of towels and bathrobes,' reports one guest, 'but still no tea and coffee in the bedroom.'

◐ Open all year ⚡ 2½ miles off A828, midway between Ballachulish and Connel. Private car park ⮑ 1 single, 6 twin, 4 double, 1 suite; all with bathroom/WC exc 1 double with shower/WC; TV, hair-dryer, direct-dial telephone; no tea/coffee-making facilities in rooms ⌖ Restaurant, bar, 2 lounges, drying-room, conservatory, garden; early suppers for children; babysitting, baby-listening ♿ Wheelchair access to hotel and restaurant, 2 ground-floor bedrooms ⊖ No children under 8 in restaurant eves; dogs in bedrooms only, by arrangement; no smoking in restaurant ▭ Access, Amex, Switch, Visa £ Single £45 to £80, twin/double £100 to £160, suite £100 to £205; deposit required. Set D £35. Special breaks available

---

PORTPATRICK Dumfries & Galloway   map 11

The Crown

North Crescent, Portpatrick, Stranraer DG9 8SX
TEL: (01776) 810261   FAX: (01776) 810551

A traditional harbour-side pub, combining gritty local bars with a smart restaurant and bedrooms.

This smart seafront pub, with its white-harled walls and neat, blue lintels, is dedicated to the catching and eating of good seafood: the owner, Bernard Wilson, sometimes takes his boat across to Ireland to bring back the pick of the Hibernian fleet's catch, while the chef, Robert Campbell, catches the lobsters himself. The snug and smoky bars at the front of the Crown are the sort in which yarns are spun, and their window ledges are piled high with sou'westers and photographs of stormy seas breaking over the top of the hotel (thankfully, a rare occurrence). The back of the house contains a striking, bistro-style restaurant with tiled walls and dark-rattan furniture, which leads into a bright conservatory hung with Impressionist prints. The menus offer a good selection of seafood dishes, including baked monkfish tails, Portavogie breaded cod, or scallops cooked in white wine, as well as various steaks, salads and vegetarian dishes. There's a more reasonably priced bar menu, too, in which you might find scallops and tiger prawns, along with more usual pub fare such as sausage and chips. The bedrooms are neat and comfortable, and those at the front boast views to Ireland on a clear day.

◑ Open all year ⊿ On entering Portpatrick, keep left at war memorial. Continue to seafront and turn right; hotel is 100 yards further, on right. On-street parking ⊫ 4 twin, 8 double; family room available; all with bathroom/WC; TV, room service, direct-dial telephone ✅ Restaurant, 2 bars, conservatory, garden; conference facilities (max 50 people incl up to 12 residential); baby-listening, cots, high chairs ♿ No wheelchair access ● None ☐ Access, Switch, Visa £ Single occupancy of twin/double £38, twin/double £72, family room from £72; deposit required. Alc L, D £13; bar meals available. Special breaks available

Knockinaam Lodge

Portpatrick DG9 9AD
TEL: (01776) 810471   FAX: (01776) 810435

A sumptuous country house with enthusiastic owners and a marvellous location.

When Churchill met Eisenhower to plan the D-Day landings, he wanted to do so in a place of great peace and total seclusion; he chose Knockinaam Lodge. The room that he slept in is now named the Churchill Suite, and still contains the enormous, brass-tapped bath in which the great leader might have sailed his model landing craft. Appropriately, the hotel is now run by a North American and English team, Michael Bricker and Pauline Ashworth, who work hard to maintain a quiet, easy atmosphere, along country-house lines. A small club-style bar, featuring tartan-backed chairs and stags' heads, leads through to the smart morning-room, which boasts views to the seashore. The elegant dining-room, with its pink décor, china vases and colourful paintings by local artists, enjoys the same view. Dinners are four-course affairs offering a choice of desserts; a sample menu might include scallops served with pineapple, followed by a terrine of squab lobster and foie gras, and then fillet of cod, with a pear tart to finish. The bedrooms vary considerably in size, but all are tastefully furnished and have added features such as half-tester beds (Bay Room) and Delft fireplaces (Bawheler and Churchill); from its corner position, South offers the best views. There are plenty of little extras like video recorders (there is a film library downstairs), flowers and books.

◑ Open all year ⊿ Follow signs to Portpatrick on A77; 2 miles west of Lochans, turn left at the Knockinaam sign. Follow the signs to Knockinaam Lodge for 3 miles. Private car park ⊫ 1 single, 2 twin, 6 double, 1 four-poster; all with bathroom/WC exc single with shower/WC; TV, room service, hair-dryer, direct-dial telephone, VCR; no tea/coffee-making facilities ✅ Dining-room, bar, 2 lounges, drying-room, garden; conference facilities (max 20 people incl up to 10 residential); croquet, fishing, shooting; early suppers for children; babysitting, baby-listening ♿ No wheelchair access ● No children under 12 in dining-room eves; no dogs in public rooms; no smoking in dining-room ☐ Access, Amex, Diners, Switch, Visa £ Single £80, single occupancy of twin/double £100, twin/double £116 to £160, four-poster £160; deposit required. Set L £27, D £35. Special breaks available

The text of entries is based on unsolicited reports sent in by readers and backed up by inspections. The factual details are from questionnaires the Guide sends to all hotels that feature in the book.

PORTREE Highland   map 11

Viewfield House

Portree, Isle of Skye IV51 9EU
TEL: (01478) 612217   FAX: (01478) 613517

*An atmospheric, top-notch country-house hotel, situated
conveniently close to Portree.*

Any self-respecting Scots baronial house should provide a twin-barrelled
battery of grandeur on entry – usually expressed in the form of dead animals.
Hugh MacDonald's ancestral home lives up to these expectations with its gallery
of deer heads, horns and antlers – even the head of a man-eating Indian tiger that
a relative despatched during the last century – as well as weapons galore. There's
historical authenticity too: a rifle used in the '45 uprising can also be seen here.
The house itself is a Georgian mansion to which a Victorian addition has been
cleaved, demonstrating the sort of delightful disregard for architectural heritage
that would send modern-day purists up the creeper-clad wall. The MacDonalds
run Viewfield House as a family home rather than as a hotel, and guests tend to
fall into a convivial mood, chatting over pre-dinner drinks in the chintzy
drawing-room, and dining together under the eyes of the ancestral portraits that
hang in the dining-room. The five-course set dinners offer traditional
country-house fare: perhaps mushrooms cooked in port, followed by leek and
potato soup, then salmon steaks served with orange sauce, sherry trifle and a
selection of Scottish cheeses to round it all off. The bedrooms in the Victorian
wing have the edge over those in the Georgian part of the house and, for the best
views over the gardens and sea, try the tower room.

◗ Closed 15 Oct to 15 Apr ☑ On southern edge of Portree, just off A850. Driveway
is just before BP filling station. Private car park ⇦ 2 single, 3 twin, 5 double, 1 family
room; 9 with bathroom/WC; hair-dryer on request ✅ Dining-room, lounge, TV room,
drying-room; early suppers for children; baby-listening ♿ No wheelchair access
● No dogs in public rooms; no smoking in dining-room ☐ Access, Visa £ Single
£30 to £40, twin/double £60 to £80, family room from £80; deposit required. Set D £15.
Special breaks available

QUOTHQUAN South Lanarkshire   map 11

Shieldhill Hotel

Shieldhill Road, Quothquan, Biggar ML12 6NA
TEL: (01899) 220035   FAX: (01899) 221092

*The peaceful, secluded location of this classic country-house hotel
hides a turbulent past.*

One American guest at Joan and Neil Mackintosh's twelfth-century, fortified
house came downstairs to say, 'I thought your ghost was the Grey Lady, not two
children,' which was how they discovered that the Killiecrankie bedroom, as
well as Glencoe down the hall, was haunted. And Shieldhill is the perfect place
for ghosts to inhabit: set in remote countryside, with sweeping vistas of hills and

woods, the spot has been a busy one in Scottish history, with both Edward I and William Wallace marching their armies through it.

Inside the craggy grey walls, the style is that of the classic country house, with panelled walls (which, in the library, open to reveal a secret stairway leading down to reception), log fires and a smart mix of modern and antique furnishings. On the first floor is the California Lounge, a popular reception room for weekend wedding parties. The bedrooms vary in size and shape, and each has something to distinguish it: Chancellor has an enormous, pink whirlpool bath with views of the Tinto hills; Killiecrankie is an attractive four-poster with window seats; and Glencoe, in the oldest part of the building, has the Grey Lady, as well as an armchair that mysteriously moves itself in the night – or so one resident claimed when our inspector called.

◑ Open all year ◪ From Biggar, take B7016 towards Carnwath for 2 miles. Turn left into Shieldhill Road; hotel is 1½ miles further on. Private car park 🛏 1 single, 3 twin, 3 double, 4 four-poster; most with bathroom/WC, some with shower/WC; TV, room service, hair-dryer, direct-dial telephone; no tea/coffeee-making facilities; trouser press in some rooms ✓ Restaurant, bar, 2 lounges, drying-room, library, garden; conference facilities (max 40 people incl up to 11 residential); early suppers for children ♿ No wheelchair access ⊖ No children under 10; no dogs; no smoking in restaurant and bedrooms ▭ Access, Amex, Delta, Diners, Switch, Visa £ Single £68, single occupancy of twin/double £78, twin/double £104 to £114, four-poster £114 to £152; deposit required. Set L, £10 D £27. Special breaks available

---

The 1998 Guide *will be published in the autumn of 1997. Reports on hotels are welcome at any time of the year, but are extremely valuable in the spring. Send them to* The Which? Hotel Guide, FREEPOST, 2 Marylebone Road, London NW1 1YN. *No stamp is needed if reports are posted in the UK. Our e-mail address is: "guidereports@which.co.uk".*

If you have a small appetite, or just aren't feeling hungry, check if you can be given a reduction if you don't want the full menu. At some hotels you could easily end up paying £30 for one course and a coffee.

Use the index at the back of the book if you know the name of a hotel but are unsure about its precise location.

ST ANDREWS Fife

map 11

Old Course Hotel

St Andrews KY16 9SP
TEL: (01334) 474371   FAX: (01334) 477668

Sophisticated luxury on the spot where golf was born.

As you approach from from nearby St Andrews, the Old Course Hotel looms large; it is an unimaginative, dun-coloured building that reveals its advantages only once entered. Then you discover just how close the golf course is: take breakfast in the conservatory, and you might just get a golf ball, hit by some unlucky golfer on the seventeenth hole, in your orange juice. The bar, restaurant and many of the bedrooms boast spectacular views over the links and the sea. Make no mistake – this is a palace of golfing that aims to pamper both the players and those left behind. The public rooms are artfully lit and decorated with tapestries, paintings and bamboo blinds to evoke the atmosphere of past glories. There is also an elegant swimming-pool, a fiendishly well-equipped gym and, nestled under one wing, the Jigger pub – once the railway station, and now a cosy, down-to-earth watering hole. Bedrooms are smart and modern in subdued and tasteful tones. Some might consider that the impeccably uncontroversial interiors lack a personal touch; certainly, any books in the bedrooms were obviously bought by the crate. Who last read *Civil Estimates, 1937-38* in Room 226? And was it any good?

○ Open all year   ◪ As you enter St Andrews on A91, hotel is on the left. Private car park ⌁ 30 twin, 78 double, 17 suites; all with bathroom/WC; TV, room service, hair-dryer, mini-bar, trouser press, direct-dial telephone   ⌀ Restaurant, 2 bars, lounge, library, conservatory, garden; air-conditioning in all public rooms; conference facilities (max 300 people incl up to 125 residential); golf, gym, sauna, solarium, heated indoor swimming-pool; early suppers for children; toys, playroom, babysitting, baby-listening, outdoor games   ♿ Wheelchair access to hotel and restaurant, 2 ground-floor bedrooms specially equipped for disabled people   ● No dogs in public rooms   ☐ Access, Amex, Delta, Diners, Switch, Visa   £ Single occupancy of twin/double £165 to £185, twin/double £205 to £225, suite £305; deposit required. Set L £15, D £34.50; alc L £22, D £40 (prices valid till Oct 1996). Special breaks available

Rufflets

Strathkinness Low Road, St Andrews KY16 9TX
TEL: (01334) 472594   FAX: (01334) 478703

A family-run country-house hotel with fine gardens.

If you make a booking using a credit card and find after cancelling that the full amount has been charged to your card, raise the matter with your credit card company. It will ask the hotelier to confirm whether the room was re-let, and to justify the charge made.

The name comes from the rough pasture land that once surrounded this large house, which was built in the 1920s and was bought by the Russell family as a hotel in 1951. In the lounge, a framed advertisement from that year shows exactly what the Russells bought, and although they have developed and extended Rufflets considerably, the basic conception of a pre-war-style country house remains intact. The colour schemes are smart and sensible, and the large restaurant looks out over the beautifully kept gardens that slope down to a meandering stream. The elegant lounge features pale-pink rugs on a polished parquet floor, and the more informal bar is hung with paintings by local artist Sir William Russell Flint.

The bedrooms in the older part of the hotel, whose décor boasts floral fabrics and reproduction furniture, are staunchly traditional. The best of them survey the garden. Room 11 is Jack Nicklaus' favourite – he stayed in it when he won the British Open in 1970. More modern rooms, decorated in bolder colours and smart, plaid bedspreads, feature on the second floor.

The restaurant offers two- or three-course dinners, with a wide selection that changes daily. The menus usually have a strong Scottish flavour, with dishes such as haggis cooked with malt whisky, or a terrine of halibut for starters, and main courses of baked pheasant or venison seasoned with juniper.

○ Open all year ➋ On B939 Ceres/Kirkcaldy road, 1½ miles west of St Andrews. Private car park ⌁ 3 single, 9 twin, 6 double, 1 four-poster, 6 family rooms; some in annexe; all with bathroom/WC exc 1 twin with shower/WC; TV, room service, hair-dryer, trouser press, direct-dial telephone ✔ Restaurant, bar, lounge, drying-room, garden; conference facilities (max 50 people incl up to 25 residential); putting green; early suppers for children; babysitting, baby-listening, cots, high chairs ﬧ Wheelchair access to hotel (1 ramp), restaurant and WC (M,F), 3 ground-floor bedrooms, 1 specially equipped for disabled people ● No dogs; no smoking in some public rooms and some bedrooms ▭ Access, Amex, Diners, Switch, Visa £ Single/single occupancy of twin/double £53 to £79, twin/double/four-poster £106 to £158, family room from £158; deposit required. Set L £16, D £26.50; bar lunches available (prices valid till Oct 1996). Special breaks available

---

ST FILLANS Perthshire & Kinross   map 11

Four Seasons Hotel

St Fillans, By Crieff PH6 2NF
TEL: (01764) 685333 (AND FAX)

Straightforward family-run hotel well placed for touring.

The big front windows at the Four Seasons make the most of the view – a fine vista up Loch Earn towards the slopes of Ben Vorlich and Rob Roy country. This family-run hotel has a simple, friendly approach that is reflected in the décor: bright buttoned furnishings with pine panelling and watercolour paintings. At mealtimes choose between the airy, white-painted restaurant or the coffee shop for lunches and snacks. Both the three-course set menu and à la carte offer a good selection of local fare: smoked Loch Tay salmon or West Coast scallops for starters, Aberdeen Angus sirloin steak or halibut with oatmeal crust and Arran mustard to follow. Bedrooms are straightforward and simple. Owners Alan and Barbara Scott don't go in for fussy curtains or excessive design but use the occasional brass bedstead, canopy or colourful bedspread to add some individuality. For families an alternative is one of the A-frame chalets behind the hotel on the hillside. These stripped-pine two-room dens are in good condition despite their age and also have small terraces for sitting out on and enjoying that view.

○ Closed 25 Dec to Mar ⚡ On A85, 12 miles west of Crieff; hotel is situated at west end of village of St Fillans overlooking loch. Private car park ⚡ 11 twin, 7 double; family rooms available; some in annexe; all with bathroom/WC; TV, room service, hair-dryer, direct-dial telephone ✧ 2 restaurants, 2 bars, 2 lounges, drying-room, library; conference facilities (max 50 people incl up to 18 residential); fishing; early suppers for children; babysitting, baby-listening ⅙ Wheelchair access to hotel (1 step, 1 ramp) and restaurants, 3 ground-floor bedrooms ● No dogs in public rooms; no smoking in main restaurant ▭ Access, Amex, Diners, Switch, Visa £ Single occupancy of twin/double £39 to £59, twin/double £60 to £87, family room £70 to £85. Set L £14, D £23.50; alc L £11.50, D £20; light lunches available. Special breaks available

---

SCARISTA Western Isles   map 11

Scarista House

Scarista, Isle of Harris HS3 3HX
TEL: (01859) 550238   FAX: (01859) 550277

A splendid beach-front setting and sophisticated comfort at this Georgian manse.

The western coast of Harris is blessed with a clutch of superb white-sand beaches, dramatically poised between the mountains and the sea. And none is more impressive than that at Scarista, where a magnificent sweep of sand lies just a few hundred yards from Scarista House's doorstep. Jane and Ian Callaghan have made some changes at their white-walled manse since the arrival of their baby: the three bedrooms in the main house have now been reduced to one, the rest having been transferred to a separate building a short way up the hill. Inside the main house, the atmosphere is one of tranquillity and peace; you'll find plenty of antiques and fine furniture, but no television or radio; the lounge is warmed by a peat fire. There are plenty of books on wildlife in the library, in which you can check up on the day's sightings – corncrakes, eagles and otters are all found locally. Dinners are served either in the smart, dark-walled dining-room, or in a second, less formal, room. Jane's cooking receives good reports for her use of organic and free-range produce; all her cakes, bread and preserves are home-made, and farmed fish is not used.

The one Victorian-style bedroom in the main house is pleasant and spacious, and features a brass bedstead. The others are also nicely furnished with antiques and old pieces of furniture, and exude a country-house atmosphere. One rather minor irritation was that our inspector's attempt to book a room met with the reaction: 'We're too busy – can you phone back later?'. This may be a tribute to Scarista House's success, but is hardly the way in which to win new guests.

Don't expect to turn up at a small hotel assuming that a room will be available. It's always best to telephone in advance.

◗ Closed mid-Sept to mid-May ⚋ 15 miles south-west of Tarbert, on A859. Private car park ⟜ 3 twin, 2 double, 1 family room; suites available; some in annexe; all with bathroom/WC; room service, hair-dryer, direct-dial telephone ⊘ Dining-room, lounge, drying-room, library, garden; early suppers for children ⅙ No wheelchair access ⊖ No children under 8 exc babes in arms; no dogs or smoking in public rooms and some bedrooms ⬜ None accepted £ Single occupancy of twin/double £60 to £65, twin/double £90 to £100, family room £100 to £120, suite £100 to £110; deposit required. Set D £27

SCOURIE Highland

map 11

Scourie Hotel

Scourie, By Lairg IV27 4SX
TEL: (01971) 502396 FAX: (01971) 502423

A fisherman's favourite, and a good stopover if you're touring the far north-west of Scotland.

Seasoned anglers know when they've made it into the hall of fame at Scourie: their catches are mounted on the wall of the bar, which now features a gallery of mean-looking brown fish that were hooked in one or other of the 250 lochs to which the hotel has fishing rights. The hills that surround the Scourie Hotel were once higher than Everest – that is, until glacial erosion scoured them down to produce today's rounded hummocks full of peaty bogs and brooding tarns – perfect if you're a walker or a fisherman with an urge to discover new grounds. The hotel is built around an old keep, although the weatherboarded frontage gives no indication of this. Inside, the décor is well-maintained and chintzy; there are two interlinking lounges, as well as a plain dining-room that serves well-priced four-course dinners consisting of simple, filling food along the lines of roasts, fish pies, bakes and traditional crumbles and tarts. There's always a choice of three or four dishes, except for the second course (fish).

The bedrooms are straightforward, and feature candlewick bedspreads and old-fashioned bathrooms. The views are unexceptional, but Room 18 is a nice bright bedroom overlooking Scourie Bay's beach.

◗ Closed mid-Oct to 1 Apr ⚋ On A894, on the edge of Scourie Bay. Private car park ⟜ 5 single, 6 twin, 7 double, 2 family rooms; some in annexe; most with bathroom/WC; direct-dial telephone ⊘ Dining-room, 2 bars, 2 lounges, drying-room, garden; fishing; early suppers for children ⅙ No wheelchair access ⊖ No dogs in public rooms ⬜ Access, Amex, Delta, Diners, Switch, Visa £ Single £25 to £44, twin/double/family room £40 to £78. Set D £15; light lunches available

SHIELDAIG Highland

map 11

Tigh an Eilean

Shieldaig, Strathcarron IV54 8XN
TEL: (01520) 755251 FAX: (01520) 755321

COUNTY
HOTEL
OF THE
YEAR

Good food and service at this quiet hotel in a beautiful loch-side position.

One of the prettiest of the Highland coastal villages, Shieldaig is a ribbon of brightly painted cottages strung out along the shores of Loch Torridon. Tigh an Eilean itself stands opposite the small Isle of Pines nature reserve – hence its name, which means 'house of the island'. It's a country-house hotel on a low-key, intimate scale, and is tastefully decorated in blues and greens, with watercolours, maps and prints of modern art adding to the atmosphere. There's a small sitting-room furnished with cane chairs, a TV room and a self-service bar, as well as a larger, brightly decorated dining-room that looks across to the isle. A guest's report praises Callum and Elizabeth Stewart as being 'warm and welcoming hosts.' Callum's cooking makes good use of local ingredients, particularly of fresh fish and seafood, as can be seen in starters such as smoked-mackerel pâté or Torridon crab dijonnaise. Main-course selections might include roast loin of beef, grilled-salmon hollandaise, fillet of plaice condorcet, or breast of chicken. With just the slightest hint of national pride, one guest reported that it took a bit of persuasion to get Callum out of the kitchen to receive an accolade for his cuisine ('we Scots are usually reticent about receiving praise'). The bedrooms are straightforward and light; the single rooms are all located at the back of the house, while the doubles hog the view.

◐ Closed late Oct to Apr ⬀ In centre of Shieldaig village, off A896. On-street parking ⟻ 3 single, 4 twin, 3 double, 1 family room; all with bathroom/WC exc 1 single with shower/WC; hair-dryer on request ⬦ Dining-room, bar, lounge, TV room, drying-room; fishing; early suppers for children ⅙ No wheelchair access ● No dogs in public rooms; no smoking in dining-room and TV room ▭ Access, Delta, Switch, Visa £ Single £45, twin/double £95, family room from £95; deposit required. Set D £21; bar lunches available

---

SOUTH GALSON Western Isles   map 11

Galson Farm Guest House

South Galson, Isle of Lewis HS2 0SH
TEL: (01851) 850492 (AND FAX)

Hospitable, friendly atmosphere at this well-run guesthouse.

To see John Russell striding up the pasture with his sheepdog and a flock of lambs dashing ahead is to see a man content with his lot – although 61 lambs and three guest rooms do not give him much time to relax. He and his wife, Dorothy, saved the farmhouse from dereliction five years ago and have since turned it into a comfortable little guesthouse, offering bed and breakfast and dinner in a corner of the island where there is little other competition. Perhaps the nicest public room is the conservatory, with its leather chesterfields, books and potted plants – it catches the sun all day long (when it's shining). Guests often enjoy their pre-dinner drinks here or in the cosier lounge next door. Dinners are served around one table in the small dining-room, John helping the conversation along while Dorothy cooks. Orders are usually taken early in the day, and a much wider selection of traditional dishes is offered than you would expect, including lobster thermidor, beef Wellington and plenty of fish. The three bedrooms are all neatly fitted into the roof, and feature smart pine furniture and soft pastel colour schemes.

◑ Open all year ⚡ Take A857 from Stornoway to Port of Ness; hotel is 20 miles from Stornoway. Private car park 🛏 2 twin, 1 double; family room available; all with shower/WC; room service, hair-dryer; TV on request ✅ Dining-room, bar, lounge, drying-room, conservatory, garden; clay-pigeon shooting; early suppers for children; babysitting, baby-listening 🔥 No wheelchair access ● Dogs by arrangement; no smoking ▭ Access, Amex, Visa 💷 Single occupancy of twin/double £35, twin/double/family room £58; deposit required. Set D £16; alc D £18. Special breaks available

---

SPEAN BRIDGE Highland   map 11

Old Pines ☆

Spean Bridge, PH34 4EG
TEL: (01397) 712324   FAX: (01397) 712433

A delightfully informal child-friendly restaurant-with-rooms.

When turning in towards Sukie and Bill Barber's Old Pines, you might spot an old boat, a swing, various bikes and possibly also a smiling Joshua (aged 3), saying, 'Hello, I'm Joshua, and we've got a Land Rover' – which is quite true: Bill uses it to ferry hill-walkers back and forth. The hotel is a single-storey building that looks south through the trees to Ben Nevis and the Grampian mountain range. There's an open-plan sitting-room and restaurant with a flagstone floor, pine-lined walls and some cosy corners in which to tuck yourself away in a rattan chair with a book and a drink (bring your own, as the Barbers don't have a licence). Old Pines' cuisine is home-made: Bill bakes bread twice a day, and Sukie is responsible for the ice-creams and cakes – they even smoke their own salmon, mussels and cheeses. Dinner is served at 8pm, by which time children will probably be in bed (there's also a babysitter). Guests, who are introduced to each other by Sukie, usually gather in the sitting-room beforehand to chat – it's that sort of informal, sociable place. The five-course menu might feature fillet of Mallaig plaice, followed by carrot soup, venison Stroganov, raspberry meringue served with lemon-yoghurt ice-cream, and a selection of Scottish farmhouse cheeses accompanied by oatcakes to finish.

The pine-wood décor of the public rooms is repeated in the bedrooms, which are smartly decorated in pinks or plaid, and are spared television or phones. Families are easily catered for in the larger twin by means of bunk beds; children under 10 who share their parents' room are accommodated at no extra charge.

◑ Closed 2 weeks Nov ⚡ From A82, 1 mile north of Spean Bridge, take B8004 next to Commando Memorial. Hotel is 300 yards further, on right. Private car park 🛏 1 single, 2 twin, 3 double, 2 family rooms; suite available; all with shower/WC; room service, hair-dryer; tea/coffee-making facilities on request ✅ Restaurant, 3 lounges, TV room, drying-room, conservatory, garden; conference facilities (max 30 people incl up to 8 residential); early suppers for children; toys, playroom, cots, highchairs, babysitting, baby-listening, outdoor games 🔥 Wheelchair access to hotel (2 steps), restaurant and WC (unisex), 8 ground-floor bedrooms, 5 specially equipped for disabled people ● No dogs; no smoking ▭ Access, Amex, Delta, Switch, Visa 💷 Single £50 to £55, single occupancy of twin/double £55 to £65, twin/double £100 to £110, family room £110, suite £165 (rates incl dinner); deposit required. Set D £25; alc L £14. Special breaks available

Flodigarry Country House

Flodigarry, Staffin, Isle of Skye IV51 9HZ
TEL: (01470) 552203   FAX: (01470) 552301

A stylish and unstuffy country-house hotel in an excellent location.

When productions as diverse as *Highlander* and *Jackanory* are filmed in the same area, and the landscape has doubled as Easter Island in the Pacific, then the location must be something special. With its backdrop of spectacular, jagged peaks, and boasting a beach on which dinosaur footprints were recently discovered, Staffin is just such a place. Pamela and Andrew Butler's hotel manages to incorporate Flora Macdonald's cottage, as well as a Victorian military man's Moorish fantasy, and some pretty solid, period architecture. The cottage lies to one side of the main building (just by the terrace that recalls a Levantine crusader's castle), and threatens to outdo the popularity of the main house. Andrew took his inspiration from all the set designers that he's seen at work, and has created beautiful, cottage-style bedrooms that elegantly skate the fine line between tasteful and twee; even the kettles are made of copper, while the smart, plaid bedspreads and cushions contrast well with the white tongue-and-groove-clad walls. The bedrooms in the main house are less imaginative, but the authentically Victorian appearance of those on the second floor show a similar attention to detail, and modern comforts have not been sacrificed. Changes carried out over the past year have meant that the 16 rooms in the main house have now become 12 – those lost were the less expensive alternatives. Downstairs, you'll find a chic, country-house-style lounge, a Victorian conservatory restaurant and a dining-room which boasts lovely views through its picture window. The atmosphere is relaxed and informal, but if you really want a good knees-up, then the public bar is renowned for its spirited ceilidhs.

◑ Open all year   ⊅ From Portree, follow A855 north for 18 miles; hotel is 2 miles past Staffin, on right. Private car park   ⊨ 1 single, 5 twin, 8 double, 5 family rooms; suite available; some in annexe; most with bathroom/WC, 2 with shower/WC; room service, hair-dryer, direct-dial telephone; TV on request   ⌀ Restaurant/conservatory, dining-room, bar, lounge, drying-room, garden; conference facilities (max 40 people incl up to 20 residential); early suppers for children; toys, babysitting, baby-listening   ⌖ Wheelchair access to hotel, restaurant and WC (M,F), 4 ground-floor bedrooms, 1 specially equipped for disabled people   ⊖ No smoking in bedrooms   ⊓ Access, Delta, Switch, Visa   ⊞ Single £45, twin/double £90 to £110, family room from £110, suite £110; deposit required. Set D £25, Sun L £16; bar meals available. Special breaks available

---

All rooms have tea/coffee-making facilities unless we specify to the contrary.

The Guide *is totally independent, accepts no free hospitality, and survives on the number of copies sold each year.*

Chapeltoun House

Irvine Road, Stewarton KA3 3ED
TEL: (01560) 482696   FAX: (01560) 485100

An unstuffy country-house hotel with hospitable hosts.

Brothers Colin and Graeme McKenzie were brought up in the hotel trade –
Graeme can remember being given his first job, turning over records in the
dining-room, when he was just about tall enough to perform the task.
Nowadays, the two brothers run their own, Edwardian, country-house hotel,
conveniently positioned between Glasgow and the Ayrshire coast. When seen
from the gravel car park, the hotel appears rather unprepossessing, but once you
enter it, Chapeltoun House establishes its character: a panelled reception area
leads through to a smart bar area and a pleasant chintzy lounge. The bedrooms
continue the comfortable, Edwardian style with some antique pieces, wing
chairs and gentle colour schemes. The menus offer two or three courses, with
supplements available for most courses (calculating what your meal will cost
can require some mental gymnastics). There is a good choice, however, featuring
some local specialities, such as the starter dish of gâteau of Arbroath smokies in a
salmon case presented on a vermouth and chive cream sauce. To follow, you
might opt for roast loin of venison, and then a pudding of warm,
cinnamon-spiced pancakes served with calvados-soaked apples and Bailey's
ice-cream.

◐ Open all year   ⊿ 2 miles from Stewarton, on B769 towards Irvine. Private car
park   ⊫ 3 twin, 4 double, 1 four-poster; all with bathroom/WC exc 1 double with
shower/WC; TV, room service, hair-dryer, trouser press, direct-dial telephone; no tea/
coffee-making facilities in rooms   ✅ 2 dining-rooms, bar, lounge, garden; conference
facilities (max 80 people incl up to 8 residential); fishing; early suppers for children
   ♿ No wheelchair access   ● No children under 12; dogs in bedrooms only, by
arrangement   ▭ Access, Amex, Delta, Switch, Visa   £ Single occupancy of
twin/double £69 to £89, twin/double £80 to £139, four-poster £139; deposit required.
Set L £16, D £23.50. Special breaks available

Kilcamb Lodge

Strontian PH36 4HY
TEL: (01967) 402257   FAX: (01967) 402041

*A small country-house hotel with friendly hosts and a quiet
loch-side location.*

Peter Blakeway gave up a life of ocean-yacht racing to come to this idyllic spot to
manage his parents' hotel, and it's easy to understand why. The white-fronted
hotel stands beside the narrow Loch Sunart, looking across to the beautiful
Morvern Hills on the Ardnamurchan peninsula. Wild orchids grow in the 25
acres of grounds, sea otters can be spotted on the shoreline, salmon swim in the
river and a yacht bobs on the water.

Inside, the style is that of a smart country house, but the atmosphere is relaxed and unstuffy. Guests usually get to know one another, whether it is over the giant communal jigsaw puzzle which is slowly assembled over the summer months in the drawing-room or over a pre-dinner drink in the bar. The good-natured banter continues in the restaurant, which features polished sideboards, family silver and yachting trophies. The cuisine, which includes plenty of seafood from the loch, demonstrates a light touch (the soups are particularly recommended), and its presentation is sophisticated. A starter of smoked fish served with mushrooms in a creamy sauce might be followed by celery soup, then a breast of corn-fed chicken, and finally a baked lemon tart. All but the soup course offer a choice of two or three dishes.

Only three of the bedrooms enjoy the view over the loch, but all include a window seat and are carefully furnished and decorated in an up-market style with colourful plaids or floral fabrics. 'We were delighted with this hotel,' reported one visitor, 'service was both caring and courteous.'

◑ Closed early Nov to mid-Dec, and mid-Jan to early Mar ⌖ From A82 south of Fort William take Corran ferry, then A861 to Strontian. Private car park ⎆ 6 twin/double, 5 suites; all with bathroom/WC exc 1 twin/double with shower/WC; TV, hair-dryer
⌘ Restaurant, bar, 2 lounges, drying-room, garden; conference facilities (max 30 people incl up to 11 residential); fishing; early suppers for children; toys, babysitting, baby-listening, cot ♿ No wheelchair access ⬤ No children under 8 in restaurant eves; no dogs in public rooms and most bedrooms; smoking in bar and lounge only
▭ Access, Delta, Switch, Visa £ Single occupancy of twin/double £72, twin/double £144, suite £156 (rates incl dinner); deposit required. Set D £25; light lunches available (1996 prices). Special breaks available

---

Wheatsheaf Hotel ☆

Main Street, Swinton TD11 3JJ
TEL: (01890) 860257 (AND FAX)

Good food and simple, comfortable rooms at this village inn.

They know a thing or two about good food and drink at the Wheatsheaf: the landlord, Alan Reid, stalks red deer every autumn, and he'll tell you where to get an eel or a salmon smoked, and how the beer in the pump marked 'Wheatsheaf Ale' is brewed specially to the taste of his regulars. Canny fishermen book themselves into the hotel for a fortnight and, if they catch anything, Alan will know how best to cook it.

This restaurant-with-rooms stands on the main street of the village, right opposite the green; apart from houses, there is not a lot else, but Swinton is well placed for both Lothian and the Borders. Inside the hotel, there is a bar and two restaurants – one is a snug little place that is used on winter evenings, and the other is brightly furnished in rattan. The menus are dominated by fish, which is either hooked from the Tweed or brought up from Eyemouth. A typical starter could be marinated herring fillets cooked with dill and malt whisky, served with a potato and chive salad, followed by breasts of wood pigeon in a claret sauce, and then a steamed apple and bramble sponge pudding. There is always a good choice of both adventurous and conservative dishes chalked up on the blackboard menu.

The bedrooms are straightforward and comfortable, and feature smart, modern décor. It's a place that is well suited to those people who, tired after a day's fishing or walking, want a hot shower, a good dinner and a peaceful sleep.

◗ Closed last 2 weeks Feb and last week Oct; restaurant closed Sun eve Nov to Mar, and Mon ⤢ On B6461, Kelso to Berwick-upon-Tweed road. On-street parking
⤒ 1 twin, 3 double; family room available; 1 with bathroom/WC, 2 with shower/WC; TV, hair-dryer ✧ 2 restaurants, bar, lounge, drying-room, garden; conference facilities (max 20 people incl up to 4 residential); early suppers for children ♿ No wheelchair access ● No dogs or smoking in bedrooms ☐ Access, Visa £
Single occupancy of twin/double £30 to £45, twin/double £50 to £65, family room from £50; deposit required. Alc L £11.50, D £17.50; bar meals available. Special breaks available

---

THURSO Highland   map 11

Forss House

Thurso KW14 7XY
TEL: (01847) 861201   FAX: (01847) 861301

COUNTY HOTEL OF THE YEAR

A friendly family-run hotel popular with anglers.

Situated in the bleak, windswept landscape of Scotland's northern coast, Forss House is a welcome and congenial spot. The 20 acres of woodland that surround the grey-harled Georgian house run by James MacGregor are host to nesting sparrow hawks, buzzards and herons, while salmon can be spotted leaping up the Forss falls. One satisfied guest reported that 'there was much talk of fishing prospects and possibilities, and the most likely flies were provided.' Inside the house, the antique and modern soft furnishings complement each other in creating a light, pleasant atmosphere. A pine-panelled bar is decorated with angling souvenirs, and the fireplace is built from ship's timbers taken from Nelson's HMS *Briton*. Dinners follow a four-course table d'hôte menu, and plenty of reliable choices are offered for every course; a typical meal might include moules marinière or deep-fried whitebait to start, followed by soup of the day, then venison cooked in red wine, and finally an apple and blackberry pie accompanied by ice-cream. The bedrooms are smart, spacious and well equipped. Fully serviced lodges in the gardens offer five more rooms, and are a popular option with members of the fishing fraternity, who come here for the hotel's trout and salmon waters.

Prices are what you can expect to pay in 1997, except where specified to the contrary. Many hoteliers tell us that these prices can be regarded only as approximations.

Please let us know if an establishment has changed hands.

◗ Open all year 🅿 On A836, 4 miles west of Thurso. Private car park 🛏 8 twin, 2 double; family room and suite available; some in annexe; all with bathroom/WC exc 1 double with shower/WC; TV, room service, hair-dryer, trouser press, direct-dial telephone, clock radio ⚭ Dining-room, 2 bars, lounge, drying-room, conservatory, garden; conference facilities (max 35 people incl up to 10 residential); fishing; early suppers for children; toys, baby-listening, outdoor games ♿ Wheelchair access to hotel (note: 4 steps), restaurant and WC (M,F), 6 ground-floor bedrooms, 1 specially equipped for disabled people ● Dogs in bedrooms only, by arrangement; no smoking in dining-room or conservatory ▭ Access, Amex, Visa £ Single occupancy of twin/double £50, twin/double £80, family room from £80, suite £100. Set D £19.50; bar lunches available (prices valid till May 1997). Special breaks available

---

TONGUE Highland   map 11

Ben Loyal Hotel

Tongue, By Lairg IV27 4XE
TEL: (01847) 611216 FAX: (01847) 611212

A well-run small hotel in a little-visited part of Scotland.

You can see the most northerly palm tree in Britain from Pauline and Mel Cook's sitting-room; at midnight in midsummer, you could even go out and read under it. Although the whitewashed stone building appears unprepossessing from the outside, it boasts views both out to sea and up the valley to Ben Loyal; 'It's almost like an oasis,' says Mel of the valley, which is unexpectedly fertile compared to the barren, heather-carpeted hills above. The bar is an oasis, too, attracting tourists and locals alike with its food and comfortable furnishings. The blackboard menu gives details of such traditional pub-grub dishes as baked potatoes and burgers, as well as specialities like venison Macduff (local meat cooked in a casserole with spices and red wine). Guests also have the choice of the restaurant's set menu, which offers three or four choices for each of the three courses, and you might opt for fresh Tain mussels, chorizo salad, or leek and potato soup to start, followed by honey-roast duckling, Thurso Bay haddock, or stir-fried vegetables served with steamed rice.

The bedrooms are all furnished with stripped-pine pieces and feature brightly sprigged wallpaper and bedspreads. The bathrooms are simple and modern, and are designed for those who want a good, hot shower after a hard day's fly-fishing or walking.

◗ Closed Dec to Feb 🅿 Midway between Cape Wrath and John O'Groats, at junction of A838 and A836. Private car park 🛏 3 single, 8 twin, 6 double, 1 four-poster; some in annexe; most with bathroom/WC; TV in some rooms; hair-dryer on request ⚭ Restaurant, bar, lounge, drying-room, games room, garden; conference facilities (max 30 people incl up to 18 residential); fishing; early suppers for children ♿ No wheelchair access ● No dogs in public rooms; no smoking in restaurant ▭ Access, Delta, Switch, Visa £ Single £28 to £38, single occupancy of twin/double £41 to £53, twin/double £51 to £65, four-poster £70; deposit required. Set D £18.50; bar lunches available (prices valid till May 1997). Special breaks available

Lochgreen House ☆

12 Monktonhill Road, Southwood, Troon KA10 7EN
TEL: (01292) 313343   FAX: (01292) 318661

Good cooking and fine antiques distinguish this country-house hotel.

The meandering driveway that leads up to Catherine and Bill Costley's large, white-walled, red-roofed Edwardian house ensures that guests begin to slow down before their arrival – a process that the unhurried and meticulously well-kept house continues. The Costleys also run an antiques business and the profusion of fine, old furniture and ornaments would, if they weren't so neatly placed and arranged, make the reception area seem a little crowded. This leads into a smart and comfortable drawing-room, whose corner turret has been imaginatively converted into a malt-whisky parlour. There's a breakfast conservatory – featuring pine furniture and Austrian blinds – that looks out over the formal garden and woods, as well as an opulent library. Dinners are taken in the country-house-style dining-room; Bill's dedication to good food has resulted in the building of a demonstration kitchen, in which visiting chefs show off their skills. There is a wide choice offered for all of the three courses, and you might order a langoustine, avocado and citrus-fruit salad to start, followed by spiced monkfish served on a bed of fresh noodles, and then a bread-and-butter pudding to finish. The bedrooms are situated either in the main house or in the converted stables a short stroll away – all boast richly canopied beds and are decorated in a softly elegant style. Those in the stable conversion are slightly more modern, and have big bright bathrooms.

① Open all year   ② Take B746 to Troon; hotel is on left. Private car park   ⤶ 14 double, 1 suite; some in annexe; all with bathroom/WC; TV, room service, hair-dryer, trouser press, direct-dial telephone   ✓ Dining-room, bar, lounge, library, conservatory, garden; tennis   ♿ Wheelchair access to hotel, restaurant and WC (M,F), 7 ground-floor bedrooms, 1 specially equipped for disabled people   ● No dogs   ▭ Access, Amex, Switch, Visa   £ Single occupancy of twin/double £100, twin/double £130, suite £150; deposit required. Set L £18, D £28.50

Turnberry Hotel

Turnberry KA26 9LT
TEL: (01655) 331000   FAX: (01655) 331706

Swish service with health-and-fitness-oriented luxury.

Play a round of golf, enjoy a seaweed wrap and hydrotherapy, followed by a swim in the pool (to the accompaniment of underwater music), and then dry your costume in the gizmo that does it in ten seconds and set off for lunch. A typical morning programme at Turnberry can be determinedly health conscious – the staff will even arrange your jet-lag-recovery schedule, or provide a video analysis of that troublesome golf swing. This smart, Edwardian golf haven has come a long way since it opened over 90 years ago, but the main building, with its long, panelled hallway, marble columns and ornate plasterwork, still retains the charm and gentility of former times. Foodies are well catered for, and can choose from the main restaurant – a palace of plasterwork cornices and coving, boasting magnificent views across to Kintyre and Arran – or the more informal Bay Restaurant in the spa centre. This recent addition blends well with the architecture of the main house, with which it is linked by means of a hall under the drive. Apart from all the luxurious spa facilities, the bedrooms here are smart and well equipped (they even include a drinking fountain). Over in the main building, the rooms vary more in size, from the large, opulent suites to the standard twins and doubles, but all are comfortably furnished and feature the sort of personal touches that are not often found in such large establishments. And this is a big operation: there are 132 rooms in all, and the busy calendar of sporting activities keeps the place buzzing with activity.

Residents are allowed unrestricted access to the two golf courses and use of a new clubhouse that offers the ultimate in changing rooms, and may dine in a restaurant that overlooks both 18th holes.

◑ Open all year ⊠ On A77, south of Ayr. Private car park ⟕ 120 twin/double, 2 four-poster, 10 suites; all with bathroom/WC; TV, room service, hair-dryer, direct-dial telephone; mini-bar on request; no tea/coffee-making facilities in rooms ⌀ 3 restaurants (1 air-conditioned), 5 bars, 4 lounges, drying-room, library, conservatory, games room, garden; conference facilities (max 250 people incl up to 132 residential); golf, gym, sauna, solarium, heated indoor swimming-pool, tennis, health spa, snooker, putting green; early suppers for children; babysitting, baby-listening ⅊ Wheelchair access to hotel, restaurants and WC (M,F), 17 ground-floor bedrooms, 1 specially equipped for disabled people ● No dogs in public rooms ⊟ Access, Amex, Delta, Diners, Switch, Visa ⊡ Single occupancy of twin/double £150 to £190, twin/double £175 to £260, four-poster £205 to £260, suite £295 to £520. Set L £21.50, D £41.50; alc L £21.50, D £49.50 (prices valid till Apr 1997). Special breaks available

---

UIG **Western Isles**   map 11

Baile-na-Cille

Timsgarry, Uig, Isle of Lewis HS2 9JD
TEL: (01851) 672242   FAX: (01851) 672241

A fine, remote position and an unstuffy, sociable atmosphere.

Rabbits and sheep amble lazily off the road as you approach Joanna and Richard Gollin's white-painted manse; if you stop and listen, you may just hear the rattling welcome of the corncrake that lives in the graveyard. If the weather is good, it's almost impossible to resist the urge to drop your bags and rush out on to the stunning white sands of the bay. The house itself is attached to the converted stable block, and is surprisingly spacious inside. The three comfort-able, country-house-style public rooms – one containing a television, another providing games and table football, and a third offering music – allow guests to choose their own level of sociability, although most gravitate towards the third in order to indulge in conversation and admire the views over the bay. Dinners are taken at '7.30-ish' in the smart dining-room that overlooks the old graveyard and its Celtic crosses. Richard buzzes about, providing wisecracks, local gossip and heavily laden plates of food. This is a 'bring-your-own-wine' establishment

– that is, you bring a reasonably priced bottle from either the window ledge on the right or an even more reasonably priced bottle from the window ledge on the left. You are not required to sit with other people, but guests usually do. Our inspection meal was excellent, particularly the main-course dish of pork cooked with apple and served with a prune sauce, and the lemon-roulade pudding. 'Joanna is a very good cook,' wrote one guest, and concluded: 'We certainly commend the hotel very highly.' The bedrooms are located either in the old house or in the stable conversion; all are comfortably furnished and feature good beds and simple, straightforward décor.

◗ Closed 28 Sept to 22 Mar ⬚ Take B8011 to Timsgarry, then second right turning (signed Timsgarry), and second track on left. Private car park ⊨ 2 single, 2 twin, 8 double; family suites available; some in annexe; most with bathroom/WC; room service; hair-dryer on request ✔ Dining-room, lounge, TV room, drying-room, study, games room, garden; conference facilities (max 20 people incl up to 12 residential); fishing, tennis; early suppers for children; playroom ⚭ No wheelchair access ● Dogs by arrangement only; smoking in lounge only ⬚ Access, Visa £ Single/single occupancy of twin/double £31 to £35, twin/double £61 to £71, family suite from £92; deposit required. Set D £21; light lunches available

---

ULLAPOOL Highland   map 11

Altnaharrie Inn

Ullapool IV26 2SS
TEL: (01854) 633230   FAX: (01854) 633303

Outstanding food and service in this romantic hideaway.

'An unforgettable experience,' reported one visitor to Gunn Eriksen and Fred Brown's inn. It's an experience that begins in Ullapool, where you telephone ahead and receive instructions on where to meet your ferryman. Then, once safely aboard the launch, *Mother Goose*, you are sped over the sea loch to Altnaharrie, after which you wander up the beach to be greeted by Fred, 'a diligent host with a delightful, dry sense of humour,' according to reports. After such a dramatic build-up, the rooms provide a suitable second act: plain white walls, *objets d'art*, antiques, tasteful lighting and Gunn's own works of pottery produce a stylish series of interiors. The eight bedrooms vary in size (some are on the small side), but all are impeccably furnished; the torch by each bed is a reminder of the fact that the inn is remote enough to have to have its electricity supplied by its own generator.

Gunn's cooking receives consistently good reports, and Fred's attentiveness and good humour provide a nice balance of formality and friendliness. A sample menu might include a warm salad of scallops, soup of crab, fillet of lamb, and then a choice of cheeses, ice-creams, chocolate cake, or banana baked in pastry with orange, cream and Cointreau.

All entries in the Guide *are rewritten every year, not least because standards fluctuate. Don't trust an out-of-date* Guide.

● Closed mid-Nov to Easter ⨂ From Inverness take A835 to Ullapool, then phone hotel for details of the ferry. Private car park in Ullapool ⨅ 2 twin, 6 double; some in annexe; all with bathroom/WC; room service; no tea/coffee-making facilities in rooms ⊘ Dining-room, 2 lounges, garden ☍ No wheelchair access ● No children under 8; dogs in some bedrooms only, by arrangement; no smoking ⬚ Access, Delta, Switch, Visa £ Single occupancy of twin/double £145 to £185, twin/double £290 to £370 (rates incl dinner); deposit required. Set D £70

Ceilidh Place

14 West Argyle Street, Ullapool IV26 2TY
TEL: (01854) 612103 FAX: (01854) 612886

A lively mixture of a coffee shop, bookshop, restaurant and rooms.

From its humble beginnings as a coffee shop, the Ceilidh Place has grown into a central point in Ullapool, for both its accommodation and its support for the arts. Just a single week in summer can find the clubhouse across the road busy hosting comedy shows, folk-music recitals, plays and ceilidhs. With its pine tables and wide selection of snacks and light food that attract all types of visitors, from locals on shopping expeditions to tired walkers, the coffee shop remains at the heart of the operation. Behind it lies the conservatory-style restaurant, which offers a straightforward selection of seafood dishes, up-market pies, salads and puddings.

The residents' lounge is upstairs, and is a large but cosy room featuring a beamed roof, an honesty bar and small kitchen area in which you can make your own tea and coffee. Also provided are plenty of books to suit all ages, as well as baskets of toys. The bedrooms are simple and comfortable, and are furnished in a mix of old and new. In summer, budget travellers also have the option of staying in the Bunkhouse – featuring simple, red duvets and a sink in each room – which is popular with families.

● Open all year ⨂ In Ullapool, West Argyle Street is the first turning on the right after the pier. Private car park ⨅ 2 single, 4 twin, 5 double; 11 annexe rooms with bunk-beds; most with bathroom/WC; room service, hair-dryer, direct-dial telephone; TV on request; no tea/coffee-making facilities in rooms ⊘ 3 restaurants, 4 bars, lounge, drying-room, conservatory, games room, garden; conference facilities (max 70 people incl up to 22 residential); early suppers for children; baby-listening ☍ No wheelchair access ● No dogs in public rooms ⬚ Access, Amex, Switch, Visa £ Single/single occupancy of twin/double £40 to £55, twin/double £80 to £110, bunkhouse (room only, per person) £10 to £14; deposit required. Alc D £14; light lunches available (prices valid till mid-Oct 1996). Special breaks available

---

WALLS Shetland   map 11

Burrastow House

Walls ZE2 9PD
TEL: (01595) 809307 FAX: (01595) 809213

A friendly and informal small hotel serving good food.

Don't be alarmed if things go bump in the night at Burrastow House, it'll probably be murder weekend – an occasional special feature. Agatha Christie would have liked the idea of such events being held in this remote setting on Shetland's west coast, where you can observe otters and seals from the windows and enjoy the oak-panelled dining-room that is particularly atmospheric when the candles and peat fire are lit. The other rooms have an agreeable, lived-in feeling, and plenty of toys, books and videos are provided to keep all ages amused on rainy days. In better weather, you could hunt for orchids in the grounds, or take advantage of the sandy beach, the boat and the beautiful views across the sound to Vaila Island.

Bo Simmons' cooking receives consistently good reports, and the emphasis is on fresh, local ingredients and sound home cooking. There are usually three well-balanced choices offered for each course: possibly a sweet-potato, ginger and apple soup, followed by a mixed local-fish platter, and finally lemon cheesecake. The bedrooms are comfortably furnished with rugs and solid, old furniture in a mixture of styles.

◑ Closed Jan & Feb; dining-room closed Sun & Mon   ⤢ In Walls, drive up the hill over a cattle-grid and turn left. Private car park   ⇖ 2 twin, 2 double, 1 four-poster; family room available; 3 with bathroom/WC, twins with shower/WC; TV and hair-dryer on request; direct-dial telephone in 1 room   ⌀ 2 dining-rooms, lounge, drying-room, library, conservatory, garden; conference facilities (max 25 people incl up to 5 residential); fishing; early suppers for children; toys, babysitting, baby-listening, outdoor games, cots   ♿ Wheelchair access to hotel, dining-rooms and WC (unisex), 3 ground-floor bedrooms, 1 specially equipped for disabled people   ⊖ No dogs in dining-rooms and in bedrooms by arrangement only; no smoking in dining-rooms or bedrooms   ⊟ Access, Delta, Switch, Visa   £ Single occupancy of twin/double £78, twin/double/four-poster £146, family room from £181 (rates incl dinner); deposit required. Set D £28.50; alc L £13.50. Special breaks available

WALES

TŶ MAWR

BRECHFA

Penhelig Arms Hotel

Aberdovey LL35 0LT
TEL: (01654) 767215   FAX: (01654) 767690

Once a wayside inn on the Dovey estuary, now a smart, ever-improving hotel and restaurant.

The Penhelig Arms consists of several whitewashed cottages knocked together, and the intimate nature of the existing small front rooms has now been incorporated into an extremely well-turned-out hotel. Each of the public rooms along the front boasts views over the wide estuary, on which boats bob up and down almost within reach of the hotel. The focal point of the hotel is its restaurant, which offers a tempting menu with a good mix of fish dishes – including halibut, sole and cod – and meat. There is also an extensive wine list, which patriotically features a Welsh wine, Monnow Valley. The main bar is in a self-contained part of the hotel, and is a popular place with the locals as well as with the guests. While the bedrooms might well be small (as would be expected in eighteenth-century cottages), there have been some clever conversions. The standard of decoration is high, and there is a clean, fresh feel to the rooms. Each (except for Room 9) has a view of the estuary, and Room 1 is a nice-sized double. Keen to keep improving the hotel, the owners, Robert and Sally Hughes, now plan to build a terrace garden with even better views of the estuary. The one drawback for some might be the close proximity of the main road that passes outside the hotel.

◑ Closed 25 & 26 Dec   ⬈ On entering Aberdovey from Machynlleth on A493, pass under the railway bridge, and hotel is the first on the right. Private car park 🖛 1 single, 4 twin, 5 double; most with bathroom/WC, some with shower/WC; TV, room service, hair-dryer, direct-dial telephone   ⌀ Restaurant, 2 bars, lounge, drying-room, garden; fishing; early suppers for children   ♿ No wheelchair access   ● No smoking in restaurant or bedrooms   ▭ Access, Delta, Switch, Visa   £ Single/single occupancy of twin/double £39, twin/double £70 to £78; deposit required. Set D £19.50; Sun L £12.50; bar lunches available. Special breaks available

---

Plas Penhelig

Aberdovey LL35 0NA
TEL: (01654) 767676   FAX: (01654) 767783

A friendly and restful hotel, with superb views of the Dovey estuary and pretty grounds.

This Edwardian country house, set amid tall trees and well-kept gardens, enjoys a premier position high above the Dovey estuary, yet it is not too far from the town. Its shuttered bay windows and a stone terrace are also designed to capture as much of the view as possible. The public rooms may be grand, but their comfortably unfussy atmosphere makes them suitable places in which to sit and relax. The oak-panelled entrance hall is dominated by a large wooden fireplace and has a stained-glass window on one side. There's plenty of space here in which to sprawl out, or otherwise there is the lounge, which features an alcove area from where to catch glimpses of the view. The restaurant has a big picture window at one end, which means that it is popular both during the day and in the evening. When we stayed, the food on offer was good, straightforward and unshowy fare, while the service was attentive and friendly. There is no distinctive style to the bedrooms, and they lack the special touches that are shown in the public rooms.

◑ Closed 20 Dec to Mar 🚉 On entering Aberdovey from Machynlleth on A493, hotel drive is between 2 railway bridges on the right-hand side. Private car park 🛏 8 twin, 3 double; all with bathroom/WC exc 1 double with shower/WC; TV, room service, hair-dryer, direct-dial telephone ✧ Restaurant, bar, lounge; conference facilities (max 25 people incl up to 11 residential); croquet, putting green; early suppers for children ♿ No wheelchair access ● No children under 8 in restaurant eves; no dogs in public rooms 🗀 Access, Visa 💷 Single occupancy of twin/double £63, twin/double £116; deposit required. Set L £14.50, D £19.50. Special breaks available

---

ABERGAVENNY Monmouthshire   map 4

Llanwenarth House

Govilon, Abergavenny NP7 9SF
TEL: (01873) 830289   FAX: (01873) 832199

A tranquil house boasting a horsey tradition and a mixture of antiques.

The horses in the field in front of Llanwenarth House give a good indication of one of the proprietors' great loves, a passion confirmed by the many horsey pictures and photographs that adorn the interior walls. This impressive creeper-clad house is set in its own extensive grounds amid the beautiful mountainous Welsh countryside. The grand, sweeping wooden staircase is canopied with a wonderfully restored glass dome, and the decorative ceiling was painted by the proprietor, Bruce Weatherill. The furniture throughout comprises an interesting mix of antiques, and there is a lovely cottage-style eighteenth-century dresser in the formal dining-room, where tables are laid with gold and white crockery. Amanda Weatherill will provide dinner here by arrangement, and cooks with her own home-grown organic vegetables.

The bedrooms are individually designed, and the décor ranges from pink florals to plain cream tones, although one common feature is the antique fireplaces. The impressive front bedroom is light, thanks to the large windows that frame fabulous views of the estate and the surrounding mountains, and there is a grand double bed dating from 1850. A downstairs twin room boasts its own handy porch and entrance, but also a rather garish, modern, yellow shower-room, and it is the only room without a mountain view.

 This denotes that the hotel is in an exceptionally peaceful situation where you can be assured of a restful stay.

◐ Closed mid-Jan to late Feb ⤢ From A465 west of Abergavenny take exit to Govilon at roundabout; the drive to hotel is 150 yards further down on the right-hand side. Private car park 🛏 2 twin, 3 double; 3 with bathroom/WC, 2 with shower/WC; TV; hair-dryer on request ⚗ Dining-room, lounge, garden; croquet ♿ Wheelchair access to hotel (1 step), dining-room and WC (unisex), 1 ground-floor bedroom ● No children under 10; no dogs in public rooms; no smoking in dining-room and discouraged in bedrooms ▭ None accepted £ Single occupancy of twin/double £54 to £56, twin/double £74 to £76; deposit required. Set D £22.50. Special breaks available

---

Penyclawdd Court

Llanfihangel Crucorney, Abergavenny NP7 7LB
TEL: (01873) 890719   FAX: (01873) 890848

A wonderfully preserved historic Tudor manor, overlooked by the Brecon Beacons.

You could be stepping into a museum piece when you stay at Penyclawdd Court, which is surrounded by over 500 years of history. You might expect a ghostly figure in medieval costume to drift past you in the darkened corridors – and rumour has it that Penyclawdd Court has a few such mysterious inhabitants. With its low wood-beamed ceilings, crooked stairs, flagstone floors, wooden shutters, unfussy Tudor furniture and wood-panelled walls, this grey-stone manor house is full of antiquity. The bedrooms are extraordinary – the Granary Room features a large double and a single bed built from old, wooden church pews, while the Oak Room boasts a bathroom as big as the bedroom, which also offers views of the majestic Bryn Arw. To the rear of the house in the garden, sheep wander past the collection of manicured hedges that have been trimmed into the signs of the zodiac (although Cancer is missing!)

A medieval banquet is laid on by arrangement, cooked and served – Wolsey-Lodge style – on a long banqueting table by the obliging hosts, Julia Evans and Ken Peacock. The food is fresh and uses local ingredients, and is served by candle light; the large, open fire place brings images of roasting spits to mind. If you are curious as to what medieval dining comprises, it could mean supping on Welsh trout and laver bread (seaweed) for the first course, followed by stuffed quail with wild rice, salad and potatoes, with a delicious pudding of a crunchy and chewy home-made meringue nest accompanied by a zesty, lemon ice-cream – again, home-made – to round off.

A word of caution though: be careful of the underside of your car on the very rough track that approaches the house, which is better designed for a horse and cart than for delicate, modern automobile suspensions.

◐ Open all year ⤢ 4 miles north of Abergavenny turn left off A465 towards Llanfihangel Crucorney. Private car park 🛏 3 double; all with bathroom/WC; TV, limited room service; hair-dryer and iron on request ⚗ Dining-room, lounge, garden; croquet ♿ No wheelchair access ● No children under 15; no dogs; smoking allowed in public rooms if other guests consent ▭ Access, Visa £ Single occupancy of twin/double £50, twin/double £70; deposit required. Set D £20

ABERSOCH Caernarfonshire & Merionethshire

map 7

Porth Tocyn Hotel

Bwlch Tocyn, Abersoch LL53 7BU
TEL: (01758) 713303   FAX: (01758) 713538

Comfortable and well-established family hotel with superb views across the Lleyn peninsula back towards Snowdonia.

The Fletcher-Brewers have been running this smart seaside hotel for nearly 50 years and have built up an operation that can offer something for everyone. Though it is not solely a family hotel, they produce a handy leaflet of advice for parents, and from May to September there is an attractive shrub-surrounded heated swimming-pool that is ideal for children. Mindful of other guests, they welcome only children over 'maturity age seven' at dinner. Otherwise, children eat in a separate room, but can be assured that the quality of the food is as good as the grown-ups'. Porth Tocyn's food reputation is almost as old as the hotel itself and the aim is to appeal to all tastes – the atmosphere at dinner has also won praise. The main sitting-room offers plenty of space to stretch out, with plenty of large, plump, floral armchairs and an elegant grandfather clock in the corner. If you prefer something less relaxing, there's a TV room with games and a piano. The 17 bedrooms are divided between the old and new wings; all are of a comfortable standard with efforts made to make each room distinctive in some way.

○ Closed mid-Nov to week before Easter ⊞ Hotel is 2 miles south of Abersoch through hamlets of Sarn Bach and Bwlch Tocyn; follow signs marked 'Gwesty/Hotel'. Private car park ⬏ 3 single, 2 twin, 3 twin/double, 2 double, 7 family rooms; all with bathroom/WC; TV, limited room service, hair-dryer, direct-dial telephone; no tea/coffee-making facilities in rooms ✇ Restaurant, bar, 6 lounges, TV room, drying-room, garden; heated outdoor swimming-pool; tennis; early suppers for children; playroom, babysitting, baby-listening, cots, high chairs ♿ Wheelchair access to hotel (1 ramp) and restaurant, 3 ground-floor bedrooms ● No children under 7 in restaurant eves; no dogs in public rooms ⊟ Access, Delta, Switch, Visa £ Single £44 to £57, single occupancy of twin/double £67 to £92, twin/double £67 to £104, family room £103 to £125; deposit required. Cooked B £4; set D £20/27, Sun L £16 (1996 prices). Special breaks available

ABERYSTWYTH Cardiganshire

map 4

Conrah Country House

Chancery, Aberystwyth SY23 4DF
TEL: (01970) 617941   FAX: (01970) 624546

An unpretentious hotel close to the sea and hills, with an array of public rooms.

'This hotel is a treasure,' one reader told us after enjoying a winter break in this gleaming white mansion house at the end of a rhododendron-lined drive. Its position above the sea and proximity to the coastal paths as well as the rolling countryside, yet within sight of Aberystwyth, means that it has the best of both worlds. Many of the original fittings, such as the Victorian wood-panelled stairway, remain in place. The spacious public rooms, despite having been updated, have enough character to give them a homely feel. They also have wide windows from which to appreciate the view. We received compliments on the menu, too. The food – 'outstanding' according to one reader – is a combination of modern Welsh and English dishes, and offers plenty of choice, while the staff are 'friendly and ready to please.' The bedrooms are by no means lavish in design, but there are plenty of thoughtful touches which make each distinctive and comfortable.

◑ Closed 23 to 30 Dec　▰ In the village of Chancery, 3 miles south of Aberystwyth on A487. Private car park　▙⇥ 3 single, 5 twin, 11 double, 1 family room; some in annexe; most with bathroom/WC, some with shower/WC; TV, room service, hair-dryer, direct-dial telephone, clock radio　✓ Restaurant, bar, 2 lounges, study, garden; conference facilities (max 65 incl up to 20 residential); sauna, heated indoor swimming-pool, croquet　& No wheelchair access　● No children under 5; no dogs; no smoking in restaurant　▱ Access, Amex, Delta, Diners, Switch, Visa　£ Single £59, single occupancy of twin/double from £88, twin/double £88 to £108, family room £132; deposit required. Set D £25.50; alc L from £10; bar lunches available. Special breaks available

---

BEAUMARIS Anglesey　　　　　　　　　　　　　　　　　　　map 7

Ye Olde Bulls Head

Castle Street, Beaumaris LL58 8AP
TEL: (01248) 810329　FAX: (01248) 811294

An inviting historic inn with good food and cosy accommodation.

Situated in the main street, this medieval coaching-inn is close to the castle and the Menai Straits but sheltered from stiff sea breezes. The history of the building oozes out of every surface and through the years there have been numerous famous visitors, including in 1645 the Roundhead General Mytton, who commandeered the inn while his forces lay siege to the castle. The ground-floor area is divided between the convivial public bar and the impressive lounge – a sparse cavernous room with a roaring fire and plenty of character, but rather uncomfortable sofas – which is generally busy in the evenings with people drawn to the dining-room from a wide area. The menu concentrates on doing the simple things well and particularly tasty medallions of pork and chicken in a brandy, prune and walnut sauce were served on the night we visited. The bedrooms are mostly named after Dickensian characters (Dickens mentioned the inn in *The Uncommercial Traveller*), some have brass beds and there's a Victorian overtone to the quality decoration.

Hotels in our Visitors' Book *towards the end of the* Guide *are additional hotels that may be worth a visit. Reports on these hotels are welcome.*

◑ Open all year 🚗 In centre of Beaumaris. Private car park 🛏 1 single, 6 twin, 7 double, 1 four-poster; 1 in annexe; all with bathroom/WC; TV, limited room service, hair-dryer, direct-dial telephone ⚟ Dining-room, bar, lounge, drying-room; conference facilities (max 12 people residential/non-residential); early suppers for children; baby-listening ♿ No wheelchair access ⦵ No children under 7 in dining-room eves; no dogs; no smoking in dining-room and 4 bedrooms ▭ Access, Amex, Switch, Visa £ Single £45 to £47, single occupancy of twin/double £51, twin/double £75 to £77, four-poster £89; deposit required. Set D £20, Sun L £15; alc D £25; bar meals available. Special breaks available

---

BEDDGELERT Caernarfonshire & Merionethshire   map 7

Sygun Fawr

Beddgelert LL55 4NE
TEL: (01766) 890258

A straightforward hotel with enough comfort and peace to satisfy Snowdonian walkers.

This extensive rough-stone manor house lies just outside the picturesque village of Beddgelert, close to the confluence of the Colwyn and Glaslyn rivers. The surrounding woodland is breathtaking and Sygun Fawr has some beautifully tended gardens. The dining-room, the most striking room in the house, has exposed stone walls and ceiling beams with plates and brasses decorating the rafters, all dominated by the fireplace with seats set into the stone sides. The lounge is a good room for cold evenings, with dark-wood furniture and swagged curtains – there's even a cosy bar with wooden settles. The seven bedrooms are light, but on the small side, and offer gentle comfort – those upstairs have excellent views. It's an ideal base for an assault on Snowdon and tired walkers will appreciate the pine-panelled sauna which is available on request.

◑ Closed 31 Oct to 1 Feb, exc Chr 🚗 Approaching from Capel Curig on A498, take left-hand turn over first bridge; follow single-track road and hotel sign from bridge. Private car park 🛏 2 twin, 4 double, 1 family room; 3 with bathroom/WC, 4 with shower/WC; hair-dryer ⚟ Dining-room, bar, lounge, TV room, garden; sauna ♿ No wheelchair access ⦵ No dogs in public rooms; no smoking in dining-room ▭ Access, Delta, Switch, Visa £ Single occupancy of twin/double £39, twin/double £52, family room £78; deposit required. Set D £14; alc D £16 (1996 prices). Special breaks available

---

BENLLECH Anglesey   map 7

Bryn Meirion

Amlwch Road, Benllech, Anglesey LL74 8SR
TEL: (01248) 853118

A simple holiday guesthouse made exceptional by its friendly owners and good facilities for disabled people.

Tim and Chris Holland have used the skills they learned when working with disabled children to create a charming guesthouse that is equally suitable for disabled and able-bodied guests. They offer a variety of rooms that cater for everyone's requirements. Two bedrooms in the extension have been specially adapted, with plenty of rails in the bathrooms, a gantry for lowering a person into the bed or bath, drive-in showers and electric beds which can be adjusted in height. Other aids are also available on request. In the main house the emphasis is on simply designed rooms, with predominantly pine furniture, but there is no special equipment. Chris's cooking is traditional, though she will cater for any preferences or special diets. At dinner you can enjoy the expansive views across the Menai Straits towards Llandudno and the Great Orme, plus the carefully planned rock garden with its ponds, mini-conifers and fantasy castle which is lit at night. The Hollands are an up-beat couple who can offer plenty of help and suggestions for day trips. They also operate a converted Land Rover to take guests out into the wilds.

◗ Closed end of Oct to Easter exc Chr   ⬧ From A55, after crossing Britannia Bridge, follow A5025 for 9 miles; hotel is on right as you leave Benllech. Private car park
⊨ 2 twin, 1 four-poster, 4 family rooms; 3 with bathroom/WC, 2 with shower/WC; TV   ⬧ Dining-room, lounge, conservatory, garden; early suppers for children; babysitting   ⬧ Wheelchair access to hotel, dining-room and WC (M,F), 6 ground-floor bedrooms specially equipped for disabled people   ⬬ Dogs by arrangement only; no smoking in bedrooms   ☐ None accepted   £ Single occupancy of twin/double £26 to £28, twin/double/four-poster £52 to £56, family room from £52; deposit required. Set D £12; light lunches available

---

BERRIEW Powys   map 4

Lion Hotel

Berriew, Nr Welshpool SY21 8PQ
TEL: (01686) 640452   FAX: (01686) 640604

A traditional country inn in an attractive Welsh Marches village with comfortable rooms.

The Lion Hotel sits comfortably among the pristine half-timbered houses of this affluent-looking village. It's the sort of eye-catching place that would tempt in a thirsty traveller and indeed contains a popular bar that is reached through a separate entrance. Here you can get bistro-style meals, with the usual steaks and grills associated with a country pub. To the other side of the entrance there's a restaurant tucked neatly away among exposed beams, where the cooking is more adventurous, with lamb and venison, although steak is still a popular choice. Hotel guests may find their lounge uncomfortably small and strangely almost like an anteroom for the main restaurant. However, no expense has been spared on the seven bedrooms, with views either across the village or back towards the parish church across the graveyard. The efforts put into the decoration can be a little overwhelming at times, as there is a tendency to chintzy patterns, but all the rooms are of a uniformly high standard with good bathrooms. Room 5 is a small double with a nice feel and a subdued colour scheme. Room 4 is an attractive family room.

◑ Closed 25 & 26 Dec ⮧ In Berriew village next to church. Private car park ⮕ 6 double, 1 four-poster; family room available; all with bathroom/WC exc 2 doubles with shower/WC; TV, hair-dryer, direct-dial telephone; trouser press on request ⊘ 2 restaurants, bar, lounge; conference facilities (max 16 people incl up to 7 residential); fishing; early suppers for children; toys, babysitting, baby-listening ♿ No wheelchair access ⊖ No dogs; no smoking in bedrooms and some public rooms ▭ Access, Amex, Delta, Diners, Switch, Visa £ Single occupancy of twin/double £50, twin/double £70 to £80, four-poster £80 to £90, family room £85 to £95; deposit required. Set D £17; alc D £17; bar meals available. Special breaks available

---

BRECHFA Carmarthenshire   map 4

Tŷ Mawr

Brechfa, Nr Carmarthen SA32 7RA
TEL: (01267) 202332   FAX: (01267) 202437

A well-run small hotel in a fine old farmhouse building, with good views and plenty of walking country nearby.

Sitting proudly at the end of a stunning, snug valley, Tŷ Mawr is an immaculate Welsh stone farmhouse – perhaps slightly larger than most – with a hazelnut wash to its paintwork. As you pull up in the driveway, you will see tidy lawns and flower beds leading down to the babbling River Marlais. Beryl and Dick Tudhope have successfully retained the old qualities of the house, while furnishing it in a simple rural style. The thickness of the walls and the smallness of the windows make it feel cool in summer and give it a dark, cosy quality in winter. A musket hangs over the stone fireplace in the sitting-room, which also has plenty of comfortable sofas and chairs. With its solid, antique furniture and a sideboard groaning with silver teapots, the airy, split-level restaurant is the most attractive public room. Beryl has worked hard to create a menu filled with house specialities, such as Dominicans, a twice-baked cheese soufflé; local produce also figures strongly in such dishes as Welsh lamb cutlets served in a tomato and mixed-pepper sauce. In addition, Tŷ Mawr hosts a series of weekend courses on bread-making throughout the year. The five bedrooms are decorated in a smart modern style, and all have good-sized bathrooms, except for Marlais, whose bathroom is across the corridor. Cothi makes a comfortable family room.

◑ Closed 2 weeks in Nov-Dec, 25 & 26 Dec, 2 weeks in Jan ⮧ In the centre of Brechfa village. Private car park ⮕ 1 twin, 4 double; family room available; all with bathroom/WC; hair-dryer, trouser press ⊘ Restaurant, bar, lounge, drying-room, garden; conference facilities (max 20 people incl up to 5 residential); fishing; early suppers for children; baby-listening ♿ No wheelchair access ⊖ No dogs in public rooms; no smoking in bedrooms ▭ Access, Amex, Visa £ Single occupancy of twin/double £52, twin/double £84, family room £98; deposit required. Set D £22, Sun L £13. Special breaks available

---

Don't forget that other hotels worth considering are listed in our Visitors' Book.

☆ *A star next to the hotel's name indicates that the establishment is new to the* Guide *this year.*

BROAD HAVEN Pembrokeshire   map 4

The Druidstone

Druidstone Haven, Nr Broad Haven, Haverfordwest SA62 3NE
TEL: (01437) 781221   FAX: (01437) 781133

An eccentric holiday hotel perched on a rocky cliff top, with an emphasis on the arts, food and communal living.

In this remote and wild location, it's entirely appropriate to find such an unusual hotel. This was once the family home of Jane and Rod Bell, but now it is filled with holiday-makers and diners, and also plays open house to the curious visitors to the summer theatre and music shows. The grey solidity of the dark-stone Victorian house gives no indication of the continual innovations being carried out in the interior; the Druidstone now has a wedding licence and its own newspaper. There's a communal feel to the public rooms, which include a ramshackle sitting-room with rough carpets on the floor, and a breakfast area that is often strewn with papers relating to the Bells' other projects. Their food has a wide following, and is served at small tables on a stripped-pine floor in the basement, which has views of the bay. The nine bedrooms exude the bare, scrubbed feeling of a holiday house. These feature roughly painted white-board walls, and guests have to make do with three public bathrooms, strategically situated along the livid-green corridors. Some of the bedrooms are very large, and their ample space will accommodate the largest family. You can get a bit more privacy and comfort if you choose one of the four spacious, outlying (self-catering) cottages opposite the walled garden; two have access for wheelchair-users.

---

❶ Closed Mon to Wed 10 Nov to 18 Dec and 6 Jan to 6 Feb; dining-room closed Sun eve ⤢ From B4341 in Broad Haven turn right at the sea. After 1½ miles, turn left to Druidstone Haven; hotel is 1 mile further on, on the left. Private car park 🛏 2 single, 1 double, 6 family rooms ⤶ Dining-room, bar, lounge, TV room, drying-room, garden; conference facilities (max 40 people incl up to 9 residential); early suppers for children; baby-listening ♿ No wheelchair access ● No dogs or smoking in dining-room ⌸ Access, Amex, Delta, Switch, Visa £⌷ Single £27, single occupancy of twin/double from £32, twin/double £53 to £63, family room from £53; deposit required. Alc D £11; light lunches available (prices valid till Feb 1997). Special breaks available

---

CAERSWS Powys   map 4

Maesmawr Hall

Caersws SY17 5SF
TEL: (01686) 688255   FAX: (01686) 688410

A Tudor mansion with some modern additions, a friendly atmosphere and good service.

This fine half-timbered Elizabethan house makes an impressive sight as you approach it down a tree-lined avenue, made more striking by its isolated position in flat farming land. Since our report last year there has been some much-needed refurbishment to the bedrooms in the main house. This has met with approval from one reader who also commented favourably on the welcome, the food and the service. The Tudor character of the hotel is most prevalent at the front, where the lounge is full of solid wood panelling. The public areas are fairly limited; however, there is a bar and a restaurant, resplendent with red carpet and red tablecloths and large windows opening on to the garden. A function room at the rear has its own bar. The best bedrooms are those in the old building, where the rooms are characterful and a good size. The six bedrooms in the coach house are not quite up to the same standard.

◑ Closed 23 to 30 Dec ⬀ On A489, ½ mile from Caersws turning; 6 miles west of Newtown. Private car park ⬕ 1 single, 5 twin, 10 double, 1 four-poster; family rooms available; some in annexe; most with bathroom/WC, some with shower/WC; TV, room service, hair-dryer, direct-dial telephone ⬧ Restaurant, 2 bars, lounge, TV room, garden; conference facilities (max 50 people incl up to 17 residential); fishing, croquet; early suppers for children; baby-listening ⬕ No wheelchair access ⬤ No smoking in restaurant; no dogs or smoking in some bedrooms ⬚ Access, Amex, Delta, Switch, Visa £ Single occupancy of twin/double £45 to £50, twin/double £65 to £68, four-poster £70; deposit required. Set L £10, D £16/19 (prices valid till Apr 1997). Special breaks available

---

CAPEL COCH Anglesey   map 7

Tre-Ysgawen Hall

Capel Coch, Llangefni LL77 7UR
TEL: (01248) 750750 FAX: (01248) 750035

A large country hotel with spacious public rooms and distinctively decorated bedrooms.

The grand scale of this country pile, once owned by a Victorian copper magnate, is the most obvious feature of Tre-Ysgawen Hall. As you enter the hallway of this solid grey-stone building you will be struck by the fine oak staircase and the boldness of the green patterned carpet that washes down the stairs and into the lobby. Up above is a lofty ceiling and fine cornicing. Upstairs, the grand corridors and tall doors sustain the feeling of opulence. The 20 bedrooms are all individually decorated, with dark heavy fabrics in some rooms and paler colours and floral patterns in others. Room 1, a four-poster bedroom with a circular spa bath, is wonderfully proportioned and has good views of the landscaped gardens. Room 3, a smaller double, also has good views. All the bedrooms are a reasonable size. Public rooms have the same grand quality and contrasting decoration. There's a sitting-room to get lost in and two dining-rooms, one with a dark-wood and marble theme and another designed like a marquee with large picture windows. The food has won high accolades for its taste and adventure, seen in dishes such as ravioli filled with langoustines and lobster and flavoured with cardamom and ginger.

Many hotels offer special rates for stays of a few nights or more. It is worth enquiring when you book.

◑ Open all year ⊿ Take B5111 from Llangefni through village of Rhosmeirch to a house with green-painted windows; turn right and follow road for 1 mile; drive is on left. Private car park ⮐ 1 single, 7 twin, 9 double, 2 four-poster, 1 suite; family room available; all with bathroom/WC; TV, room service, hair-dryer, trouser press, direct-dial telephone; no tea/coffee-making facilities in rooms ⊘ 2 dining-rooms, bar, lounge, conservatory, garden; conference facilities (max 120 people incl up to 20 residential); early suppers for children; baby-listening ⎇ Wheelchair access to hotel, dining-rooms and WC (unisex), 3 ground-floor bedrooms ● No dogs or smoking in some public rooms ▭ Access, Amex, Delta, Switch, Visa £ Single £72, single occupancy of twin/double £94, twin/double £94, four-poster £138, family room from £104, suite £148; deposit required. Continental B £4, cooked B £8; set D £18, Sun L £14; alc D £24. Special breaks available

---

CAPEL GARMON Aberconwy & Colwyn   map 7

Tan-y-Foel

Capel Garmon, Nr Betws-y-coed LL26 0RE
TEL: (01690) 710507   FAX: (01690) 710681

A popular small hotel, where the presentation and quality of food, as well as of the bedrooms, have been praised.

Lots of compliments on Tan-y-Foel (which literally means 'the house under the hillside') have come this year from visitors who wrote to us about the food, the bedrooms and the service provided by Janet and Peter Pitman. It helps that this small hotel is set amid glorious scenery, and looks towards the mountains of Snowdonia. First, the bedrooms: the rich fabrics and colour of the décor were acclaimed, as were the small – but important – extras, such as bathrobes, toiletries, fresh flowers and chocolates. Of the bedrooms, our preference was for the two that are reached from outside the house. Janet's French-influenced cuisine, which has to be ordered after breakfast, also won plaudits for presentation as well as taste, while Peter 'serves the meal with much class and care.' Breakfast is also an event, and offers plenty of choice. It was impressive to hear that Janet can take special dietary requirements in her stride. 'I always feel pampered when I stay here,' concluded one of our reports.

◑ Closed mid-Dec to early Jan ⊿ Turn off A470 for Capel Garmon/Nebo and travel up the hill for 2 miles; hotel is on the left-hand side, before the village of Capel Garmon. Private car park ⮐ 3 twin, 2 double, 2 four-poster; some in annexe; most with bathroom/WC, 2 with shower/WC; TV, room service, hair-dryer, direct-dial telephone, iron; VCR in 1 room; no tea/coffee-making facilities in rooms ⊘ Restaurant, bar, 2 lounges, conservatory, garden; ⎇ No wheelchair access ● No children under 7; no dogs; no smoking ▭ Access, Amex, Delta, Diners, Switch, Visa £ Single occupancy of twin/double £53 to £76, twin/double £76 to £136, four-poster £136; deposit required. Alc D £28. Special breaks available

---

 Denotes somewhere you can rely on a good meal – either the hotel features in the 1997 edition of our sister publication, The Good Food Guide, *or our inspectors thought the cooking impressive, whether particularly competent home cooking or more lavish cuisine.*

CARDIFF Cardiff   map 4

The Angel

Castle Street, Cardiff CF1 2QZ
TEL: (01222) 232633   FAX: (01222) 396212

A traditional hotel brought bang up-to-date, in an enviable city-centre location.

The Angel is situated between two of Cardiff's most significant landmarks: the castle and the Arms Park, from which the roar of the rugby crowd could easily reach your ears in the hotel bar. The refurbishment programme that was started a few years ago has now been completed and has restored the hotel to its former Victorian pomp, although the sheen of newness is still evident in the public rooms. In our opinion, the cocktail bar – with its mirrors, spotlighting and curved marble bar – is more attractive than the lounge. Some might even prefer to linger in the splendid, cavernous reception hall, which has columns, cherubs, a crystal chandelier and a frescoed ceiling painted in a cloudy blue. The light, bright restaurant has a pleasing feel to it, and offers views of the castle. Up the grand staircase, the bedrooms and bathrooms have received a high order of decoration, and include all the features that the business person or weekend guest might require. Twelve of the rooms possess fax machines and irons, and the single-woman traveller will appreciate the safety feature of a chain on the door. Guests may also enjoy the downstairs gym, where a sauna, solarium and massage are on offer.

○ Open all year   ☑ Hotel is between the castle and Cardiff Arms Park. Private car park ⊨ 37 single, 32 twin, 16 double, 2 family rooms, 17 suites; all with bathroom/WC; TV, room service, hair-dryer, trouser press, direct-dial telephone ⌁ Restaurant, bar, lounge, games room; air-conditioning in function rooms and on 3rd floor; conference facilities (max 300 people incl up to 104 residential); gym, sauna, solarium; early suppers for children; babysitting, baby-listening   ⅙ No wheelchair access ● No dogs in public rooms ⊟ Access, Amex, Delta, Diners, Switch, Visa £ Single £62 to £78, single occupancy of twin/double £72 to £88, twin/double £75 to £92, family room £90 to £110, suite £90 to £130; deposit required. Continental B £7.50, cooked B £9.50; alc D £15. Special breaks available

CONWY Aberconwy & Colwyn   map 7

Berthlwyd Hall

Llechwedd, Conwy LL32 8DQ
TEL: (01492) 592409   FAX: (01492) 572290

A small Victorian country hotel with friendly service and good food.

Joanna and Brian Griffin have worked hard to recreate a country-house atmosphere at Berthlwyd Hall and their efforts appear to be paying dividends. One visitor has described the food and service as 'quite superior', yet at a reasonable price. One of the highlights is Truffles restaurant, which has an easy informality and plenty of attractive touches in addition to the food. An antique wine press, now overflowing with shrubs, was brought over from Bordeaux, where the Griffins used to live, and the French theme is reflected throughout the menu. For instance, there's magret de canard – breast of duckling grilled with fresh thyme and served with honey and wholegrain mustard sauce. Up the fine oak staircase, the best bedrooms are those with views across the tree tops towards Conwy Castle. However, other guests will also notice the caravan park in front of the hall. Two bedrooms attracted our attention, Room 3 with its free-standing claw-foot bath, from where it's possible to see the castle, and Room 5, another bedroom with a luxurious bath. Some of the bedrooms also have their original slate and tile Victorian fireplaces. An added treat for guests is the newly installed swimming-pool.

◑ Open all year　☑ Entering Conwy over bridge on A55, go into centre and turn left after Bangor Archway; proceed to T-junction and turn right into Sychnant Pass road; hotel is signposted on left after 1 mile. Private car park 🛏 1 twin, 6 double, 1 four-poster; family room available; all with shower/WC; TV, room service, hair-dryer, direct-dial telephone　✅ 2 restaurants, bar, lounge, garden; conference facilities (max 20 people incl up to 8 residential); heated outdoor swimming-pool; early suppers for children; babysitting, baby-listening　&. No wheelchair access　● No dogs in public rooms; no smoking in some bedrooms　▱ Access, Amex, Delta, Diners, Switch, Visa　[£] Single £53, single occupancy of twin/double £78, twin/double £78, four-poster £99, family room from £117; deposit required. Cooked B £4.50; set L £14.50, D £19.50; alc L, D £18. Special breaks available

---

CRICCIETH Caernarfonshire & Merionethshire　　　　map 7

Mynydd Ednyfed

Caernarfon Road, Criccieth LL52 0PH
TEL: (01766) 523269

A family hotel close to the coast with a gymnasium and solarium.

Just outside the tiny seaside resort of Criccieth, at the end of a private lane, lies this 400-year-old rough-stone farmhouse in peaceful countryside. From the hotel itself, looking back across the woods you get a lovely view of Tremadog Bay. There is a lack of fuss about the public rooms and they are practical and attractive. An airy bright conservatory with cane chairs and pink tablecloths is used as a breakfast-room in summer, and in a smaller yellow dining-room with a large bay window Maureen Edwards serves a sophisticated and varied menu. Husband Ian, a Welsh international and Wrexham footballer, concentrates on tending the 7 acres of gardens and providing guests with ways to keep fit. There's a tennis court, gymnasium and solarium, and shooting, fishing and golf can also be organised from the hotel. The bedrooms are simple, straightforward rooms decorated mostly with plain walls, floral borders and fabrics, and pine furniture, plus plenty of touches that make the guest feel welcome. Room 5 is a good family room with a double bed and a small adjoining room with bunk beds and toys. Room 1 and 4 have four-posters.

● Closed 24 to 31 Dec 🚗 From Criccieth take B4411 towards Caernarfon for 1 mile, then turn right and follow driveway. Private car park 🛏 1 single, 2 twin, 3 double, 2 four-poster, 1 family room; 4 with bathroom/WC, 5 with shower/WC; TV, room service, direct-dial telephone ✗ Dining-room, bar, lounge, drying-room, library, conservatory, games room, garden; conference facilities (max 60 people incl up to 9 residential); gym, solarium, tennis; early suppers for children; toys, baby-listening, outdoor games ⅙ No wheelchair access ● No dogs in public rooms; smoking in lounge and bedrooms only ☐ Access, Visa £ Single £27, single occupancy of twin/double £35, twin/double £60, four-poster £60, family room £66; deposit required. Alc D £16.50 (prices valid till Easter 1997). Special breaks available

CRICKHOWELL Powys   map 4

Gliffaes Country House

Crickhowell NP8 1RH
TEL: (01874) 730371 FAX: (01874) 730463

A large Victorian house with a fine terrace, original interior features and access to fishing on the Usk.

The grey stone of Gliffaes makes it unmistakably Welsh, despite the hint of Italian influence in the twin campanile that poke through the tree tops. It's been almost 50 years since the Brabner family began their association with the house and in that time they have carefully nurtured its mature Victorian garden. The house itself has many of its original features, such as the panelled sitting-room, which give it a lived-in, convivial feel matched by the friendly greeting. And in the bar you can browse through a large selection of fishing flies if you fancy taking a turn on one of the hotel's river beats. When we visited, guests were to be found relaxing in every nook and corner, especially on the stone terrace which runs along the Usk side of the house. Part of the terrace has now become an airy conservatory. The best rooms are 2, 3, 4, 6 and 17, all of which face out to the Usk and make great use of the view. These are not grand rooms, but their simple design, tiled fireplaces and occasional antique furnishings make them pleasing to the eye. Some of the other bedrooms don't quite compensate for the lack of a river view, but the beds, service and food have come in for some praise.

● Open all year 🚗 1 mile off A40, 2½ miles west of Crickhowell. Private car park 🛏 5 single, 14 twin, 7 double; family rooms available; some in annexe; most with bathroom/WC, some with shower/WC; TV, room service, hair-dryer, direct-dial telephone ✗ Restaurant, bar, 2 lounges, TV room, drying-room, conservatory, games room, garden; conference facilities (max 16 people residential/non-residential); fishing, tennis, putting green and golf practice net, croquet; early suppers for children; baby-listening ⅙ No wheelchair access ● No dogs in public rooms and most bedrooms ☐ Access, Amex, Delta, Diners, Switch, Visa £ Single £36, single occupancy of twin/double £69, twin/double £72 to £107, family room from £88; deposit required. Set D £21, Sun L £20; light lunches available. Special breaks available

If you make a booking using a credit card and find after cancelling that the full amount has been charged to your card, raise the matter with your credit card company. It will ask the hotelier to confirm whether the room was re-let, and to justify the charge made.

EGLWYSFACH **Cardiganshire**   map 4

Ynyshir Hall

Eglwysfach, Machynlleth SY20 8TA
TEL: (01654) 781209   FAX: (01654) 781366

*An exclusive Georgian country-house hotel with discerning and
tasteful design throughout.*

While many guests have praised Ynyshir Hall for its hospitality, owners Joan
and Rob Reen were particularly pleased with the comments made by one guest:
last year a visiting Royal praised Ynyshir Hall's beautiful landscaped grounds,
the delicious meal that he enjoyed while admiring the view, and said that he
'found it very easy to relax in the informal atmosphere in the hotel.' A typical
dish that you might savour here is sea bass smeared with tapénade, served on a
bed of grilled peppers with Thai butter. Food aside, it's easy to see what
impressed the Royal visitor. Rob Reen trained as an artist, and his bright, bold
paintings are on show around the house, setting the theme for its interior design;
Mediterranean colours such as terracotta, turquoise and lavender predominate.
The whole effect is eminently tasteful and relaxing, and guests should also look
out for the charming collection of Clarice Cliff pottery. The bedrooms are named
after artists, and no two are the same. Many feature distinctive antique beds –
one bedstead is made of brass and mother-of-pearl, while another is walnut and
dates from the 1860s. The Monet Garden Suite offers access to the gardens
through its own conservatory.

○ Open all year   ◪ Just west of A487, 6 miles south-west of Machynlleth. Private car
park   ⌂ 1 twin/double, 2 double, 1 four-poster, 4 suites; all with bathroom/WC exc 1
double with shower/WC; TV, room service, hair-dryer, direct-dial telephone; no tea/
coffee-making facilities in rooms   ⊘ 2 dining-rooms, bar, lounge, garden; conference
facilities (max 25 people incl up to 8 residential); pitch & putt   ♿ No wheelchair
access   ● No children under 9; dogs in 1 bedroom only, by arrangement; smoking in
bar and 3 bedrooms only   ▭ Access, Amex, Delta, Diners, Switch, Visa   £ Single
occupancy of twin/double £80 to £100, twin/double £110 to £150, four-poster/suite
£140 to £160; deposit required. Set L from £20, D from £30. Special breaks available

FISHGUARD **Pembrokeshire**   map 4

Manor House

11 Main Street, Fishguard SA65 9HG
TEL: (01348) 873260

*A tall town-centre house offering sea views and homely rooms with a
Victorian flavour.*

It's a bit of a misnomer to call this hotel a manor house – 'a pleasant, brown,
pebble-dashed, Georgian town house' is a more accurate description. Manor
House Hotel is situated close to the centre of Fishguard and, although the road
outside is fairly busy, as you enter the house a feeling of calm descends. This is
partly due to the room full of antiques and bric-à-brac to the right of the front
door that Beatrix and Ralph Davies have set up as a small shop for passers-by to

browse in. Some of their favourite pieces have clearly not made it into the shop, and can now be seen in the guest lounge on the other side of the doorway. A lot of work has been done on the bedrooms during the past year, and they are now all *en suite*. Room 5 has particularly benefited from this refurbishment, and has some nice, period furniture and a box seat in the window, affording views of a pretty sea inlet. The small restaurant is in the cellar, and is brightened up in the evening by the use of candle light. Typical dishes include monkfish, poached with vermouth, lemon and cream.

◑ Closed Chr ⮕ 200 yards past Fishguard's central roundabout, on the left-hand side of the road to Cardigan. On-street parking overnight ⮕ 1 single, 2 twin, 4 double; family room available; 2 with bathroom/WC, 4 with shower/WC; TV, hair-dryer ✓ Restaurant/bar, lounge, garden; early suppers for children ♿ No wheelchair access ● No dogs in restaurant; no smoking in some public rooms ▭ Access, Visa £ Single £25, single occupancy of twin/double £32, twin/double £46 to £50, family room £60; deposit required. Set D £15. Special breaks available

---

Plâs Glyn-y-Mêl ☆

Lower Town, Fishguard SA65 9LY
TEL: (01348) 872296 FAX: (01348) 874521

A large house in a picturesque valley, suitable for families.

Nestling in 20 acres of woods and paddocks along the Gwaun valley, this fine Georgian building once belonged to the local Victorian entrepreneur Richard Fenton. The house remains the family home of Jenny and Michael Moore and the atmosphere has been kept informal and conducive to relaxation. Certainly, given the access to a swimming-pool and to fishing in the river, just across from the house, the holiday atmosphere is ever-present. With tall windows at the front and a south-facing aspect, the spacious and elegant sitting-room, which has a generously stocked honesty bar, gets plenty of light. The breakfast-room on the other side is another fine room, but unfortunately dinner isn't on offer. Instead the Moores are happy to make reservations at local restaurants or, if you prefer, there is a sizeable kitchen for guests upstairs. The bedrooms have some nice pieces of furniture: the ones at the front are the most attractive. At the top of the house are two large self-contained family suites that can accommodate up to six people and have their own kitchens.

◑ Open all year ⮕ Take A487 out of centre of Fishguard towards Cardigan; go down steep hill to old harbour; turn sharp right at bottom. Private car park ⮕ 2 single, 2 twin, 4 double, 2 suites; all with bathroom/WC; TV, hair-dryer ✓ Dining-room, bar, lounge, drying-room, garden; fishing, heated indoor swimming-pool ♿ No wheelchair access ● No dogs in public rooms ▭ None accepted £ Single/single occupancy of twin/double £42, twin/double £70, suite £95; deposit required

---

Reports are welcome on any hotel, whether or not it is in the Guide.

We mention those hotels that don't accept dogs; guide dogs, however, are almost always an exception. Telephone ahead to make sure.

Three Main Street

3 Main Street, Fishguard SA65 9HG
TEL: (01348) 874275

A characterful and lively Georgian town house with some nice modern touches.

An eighteenth-century pale-grey-stone building, Three Main Street is close to the town square. If you arrive at lunchtime, you will immediately notice the buzz, as local shoppers come here between 10am and 2pm for coffee or lunch in the informal front room. The chatty atmosphere here is enhanced by the warm, coral walls and the fireplace, as well as by the tasteful paintings on the walls and the stripped and varnished floorboards. The combination of such modern styling and the original building's simple elegance is a real feature of Three Main Street. The three bedrooms are sparsely furnished, but are nevertheless attractive, and we particularly liked the hanging glass lightshades. Two bedrooms are situated at the front of the hotel, and the one at the back has a fine wooden bed; each has an *en-suite* shower. Dinner is served downstairs, in the smart and sedate back room. Food is taken seriously here, and you can expect to savour such dishes as mussel chowder served with bacon, vegetables, herbs and cream, followed by a breast of Barbary duck with passion fruit and Madeira.

◑ Closed Feb; restaurant closed Sun ⬛ From Fishguard's town square take the road to Cardigan. Hotel is second building on left, opposite the tourist information centre. Private car park ⬛ 1 twin, 2 double; family room available; all with shower/WC; hair-dryer and TV on request ✓ 2 restaurants, bar; conference facilities (max 12 people incl up to 3 residential); early suppers for children; toys ⬛ No wheelchair access ● No dogs; smoking in bar only ⬜ None accepted ⬜ Single occupancy of twin/double £30, twin/double £50, family room from £60; deposit required. Alc D £15.50; light lunches available. Special breaks available

---

Edderton Hall

Forden, Nr Welshpool SY21 8RZ
TEL: (01938) 580339   FAX: (01938) 580452

Superb views from this Georgian house that offers good food and plenty of local walks.

Offa's Dyke is just 400 yards from this eye-catching white Georgian house which guests are very much encouraged to treat as their home after a hard day's walking. Dogs are welcome and wellies can be left in the hallway. There is a pleasant disorder to the decoration at Edderton and the character of the present owners seeps through every room. Evelyn Hawksley's husband, Warren, is a Tory MP, so there is a parliamentary theme to prints and books in the sitting-room. The views from here and across the lawn towards the Severn Valley and Powys Castle are splendid. The dining-room boasts a similar view and here you can enjoy Evelyn's highly praised cooking. She believes it has improved since her eldest son, Cullum Giles-Gash, took over managing the hotel, leaving her free to concentrate on dishes like smoked halibut with hummus and fennelslaw salad, followed perhaps by brochettes of lamb with peppers, onion, mushroom, lambs kidney and devilled sauce. The bread is home-made and their own shoot provides the game. The eight bedrooms display a bit of a mish-mash of styles and decoration, but there are ongoing improvements. Room 2, a four-poster, has views of the valley and a free-standing bath which is rather fun.

◑ Open all year ▨ Off A490 between Welshpool and Montgomery. Private car park ⊨ 2 single, 1 twin, 3 double, 2 four-poster; 6 with bathroom/WC, 2 with shower/WC; TV, room service, direct-dial telephone; hair-dryer on request ✥ Restaurant, dining-room, bar, lounge, garden; conference facilities (max 60 people incl up to 8 residential); fishing; early suppers for children ⅙ No wheelchair access ● No dogs in public rooms ▭ Access, Amex, Diners, Visa £ Single £22 to £35, single occupancy of twin/double £30 to £35, twin/double £40 to £48, four-poster £50 to £80. Set L £13, D £18 to £22. Special breaks available

---

GANLLWYD Caernarfonshire & Merionethshire   map 7

Dolmelynllyn Hall

Ganllwyd, Nr Dolgellau LL40 2HP
TEL: (01341) 440273 (AND FAX)

A remote country hotel in Snowdonia, with a Victorian feel, reached up a steep wooded drive.

Although 'Dolly' has only a few acres of its own, it is surrounded by 1,200 acres of National Trust land, with the promise that one can walk all day without crossing a road. Parts of the house date back to the sixteenth century, but the subsequent mock-Tudor additions give it more of a Victorian look, enhanced by the attractive formal gardens at the back. This atmosphere is successfully transferred to the interior, where the hallway has a grandfather clock ticking ponderously. The lounge is an attractive, well-proportioned room that looks out to the garden and has friendly domestic touches, while the dining-room has some fine carving on its wood panelling. Owner Jon Barkwith does the front-of-house side of the operation while his daughter, Joanna Reddicliffe, does the cooking. Four-course dinners are available plus a smattering of daily specials. You might encounter Pencarreg and leek fritters on a three-pepper relish, followed by braised tenderloin of pork with roasted tarragon apples and a cider-vinegar sauce. After dinner the modest conservatory is a good place to relax in. The ten bedrooms vary considerably in size and have a range of decorative styles; some, such as Arram and Cadair, have corner baths.

Use the maps at the back of the Guide *to pinpoint hotels in a particular area.*

 This denotes that you can get a twin or double room for £60 or less per night inclusive of breakfast.

◐ Closed Dec to Feb ⬚ 5 miles north of Dolgellau on A470, at southern end of Ganllwyd. Private car park ⬚ 2 single, 3 twin, 2 twin/double, 1 double, 1 four-poster, 1 suite; all with bathroom/WC; TV, room service, hair-dryer, direct-dial telephone; trouser press available ⬚ Dining-room, bar, lounge, drying-room, library, conservatory, garden; fishing; early suppers for children ⬚ No wheelchair access ● No children under 8; dogs in 2 bedrooms only; no smoking ⬚ Access, Amex, Diners, Visa ⬚ Single £43 to £55, single occupancy of twin/double £55 to £60, twin/double £75 to £95, four-poster £95 to £105, suite £85 to £95; deposit required. Set D £23.50; light lunches available. Special breaks available

---

GLYNARTHEN Cardiganshire   map 4

Penbontbren Farm

Glynarthen, Cardigan SA44 6PE
TEL: (01239) 810248 FAX: (01239) 811129

A traditional Welsh farm atmosphere, but with plenty of modern comforts.

Although Barrie and Nan Humphreys are farmers by upbringing, the energy they channel into running this small hotel are considerable. The farmhouse itself is their home and two low converted out-buildings in the farmyard form the accommodation and the restaurant. All ten bedrooms have a comfortable feel, with pampering extras like a decanter of sherry and a bowl of fruit. Rooms 4 and 6 both have disabled access. It's a short walk across to the single-storey restaurant, which has roof-space stretching into the rafters. Non-Welsh speakers might at first be alarmed by the menu, but you will soon see the English translations. You could have *golwyth eog gyda saws hufen a pesto* (poached salmon with a cream and pesto sauce) followed by *melysion or troli* – sweets from the trolley. There is also plenty of choice for vegetarians as Nan is one herself. The Humphreys family have farmed Penbontbren for 120 years and Barrie and Nan have made efforts to bring its history to life with a fascinating museum of agricultural equipment, such as the farm's first tractor, delivered in 1943, and a Victorian grain winnower. Barrie has also devised a country trail walk with a helpful fact sheet explaining the flora and fauna and farm sights.

◐ Closed 23 to 29 Dec ⬚ Penbontbren is signposted off A487 between Tanygroes and Sarnau. Private car park ⬚ 2 twin, 2 double, 6 family rooms; all in annexe; all with bathroom/WC; TV, room service, direct-dial telephone ⬚ Restaurant, bar, 2 lounges, games room; conference facilities (max 30 people incl up to 10); early suppers for children; baby-listening ⬚ Wheelchair access to hotel and restaurant, 6 ground-floor bedrooms, 2 specially equipped for disabled people ● No children under 5 in restaurant eves; no dogs in public rooms; no smoking in restaurant ⬚ Access, Amex, Diners, Switch, Visa ⬚ Single occupancy of twin/double £38 to £43, twin/double/family room £68 to £74; deposit required. Alc D £16.50. Special breaks available

---

Many hotels put up their tariffs in the spring. You are advised to confirm prices when you book.

Castle Cottage

Pen Llech, Harlech LL46 2YL
TEL: (01766) 780479

A medieval cottage in a historic town, with fine food and cosy accommodation.

In the heart of Harlech, and only a cannon blast away from the mediaeval castle, sits this well-lived-in, snug and welcoming sixteenth-century cottage, which in previous times was a gin shop and a butcher's. The bar and lounge are small and cosy with low ceilings, but it is the restaurant that takes centre stage, and it's understandable once you tuck in. It's a surprisingly large room considering the size of the rest of the cottage and can seat up to 50. Owner Glyn Roberts, assisted by his wife, Jacqueline, is the chef and concentrates on providing light and healthy food made, whenever possible, with fresh produce. Rack of lamb comes garnished with pine-nut couscous and a red-wine, shallots and garlic sauce. If you don't find any pork on the menu then you will still find plenty around the rest of the cottage. Pig pictures and pottery crop up everywhere and the pastel and floral bedrooms are named after different species. British Lap on the top floor has a view of the sea and the castle, and a beamed bathroom. Berkshire has plenty of character and also has a castle view.

◗ Open all year ⤢ Just off High Street behind castle. On-street parking ⤒ 2 single, 1 twin, 3 double; all exc singles with bathroom/WC; TV, hair-dryer, trouser press on request ⟡ Restaurant, bar, lounge, garden; early suppers for children; toys ♿ No wheelchair access ● No dogs in public rooms; smoking in bar only ▭ Access, Amex, Delta, Switch, Visa £ Single/single occupancy of twin/double £25 to £35, twin/double £34 to £54; deposit required. Set D £17/19, Sun L £13. Special breaks available

Old Black Lion

26 Lion Street, Hay-on-Wye HR3 5AD
TEL: (01497) 820841

A well-established medieval inn with a restaurant in the heart of Hay-on-Wye.

Life centres around the candlelit bar and restaurant at one of Hay's best-known inns, where you will find the literati descending when the festival is in town. The low-beamed ceilings and dark medieval feel to the bar only help to concentrate the mind on the cuisine, which has been packing them in for years now. If you choose to eat in the restaurant you can let your mind wander from the convivial atmosphere to the eye-catching prints on the walls, a fishing net hanging from the ceiling and two unusual Chinese porcelain cats on the mantelpiece. Fish features a lot on the menu and you might start with salad of warm monkfish and pink grapefruit with a raspberry sauce, followed by baked

Cornish hake served on a squid provençal sauce. Alternatively, choose from the dazzling bar menu, or you can mix and match from both. John and Joan Collins are a couple devoted to their work, described respectively as 'God' and 'an outstanding landlady' by two very satisfied guests. 'They are friendly, outgoing and do all they can to make their guests feel at home.' As you would expect in a house that dates back to 1380 the bedrooms are not large, but they make up for it with their character. Room 6 is an outstanding example and has an upper gallery with twin beds on both levels. Room 9 is a good-size double in the annexe, suitable for disabled guests.

○ Open all year ⊿ In centre of Hay-on-Wye; 100 yards from junction of Lion Street and Oxford Road. Private car park ⇐ 1 single, 4 twin, 4 double, 1 family room; some in annexe; 4 with bathroom/WC, 5 with shower/WC; TV, direct-dial telephone, radio; hair-dryer on request ✓ Restaurant, bar, lounge, garden; fishing; early suppers for children ⅙ Wheelchair access to hotel and restaurant, 1 ground-floor bedroom ● No children under 5; dogs in bar and bedrooms only; smoking in bar, lounge and 6 bedrooms only ⊟ Access, Amex, Visa £ Single £20, single occupancy of twin/double £25, twin/double £46, family room from £56; deposit required. Set Sun L £10; alc L £9, D £16; bar meals available (prices valid till Easter 1997). Special breaks available

---

JEFFRESTON Pembrokeshire   map 4

Jeffreston Grange

Jeffreston, Nr Kilgetty SA68 0RE
TEL: (01646) 651291 (AND FAX)

A relaxed and friendly guesthouse in a traditional village setting.

At the heart of a typical Pembrokeshire village, opposite the Norman church, Jeffreston Grange is a traditional low whitewashed house made more jaunty by the fire-engine-red window frames and pretty potted plants around the garden path to the front door. June and Norman Williams are happy to describe their home as a restaurant-with-rooms, but their down-to-earth attitude and the attractive location mean a longer stay is warranted. The three bedrooms upstairs are neat and tidy: Skomer has good proportions and a view of the church (if you are a light sleeper the church bell might be a factor); Ramsey has rather a small bathroom with only a shower. The sitting-room is homely although a little dark. To the other side of the house the restaurant stretches to the back of the house and has a relaxed pubby feel to it, with a collection of jugs hanging from the roof beams, apparently less collected than accumulated. The menu is unpretentious; you'll perhaps find prawn cocktail to start, followed by Welsh Black beef steak with a red-wine and mushroom gravy.

○ Open all year ⊿ Take B4586 to Jeffreston; hotel is opposite church. Private car park ⇐ 1 twin, 2 double; doubles with bathroom/WC, twin with shower/WC; TV, hair-dryer ✓ Restaurant, bar, 2 lounges, garden ⅙ No wheelchair access
● No dogs in public rooms; smoking in 1 lounge only ⊟ Access, Visa £ Single occupancy of twin/double £26, twin/double £48; deposit required. Set D £15. Special breaks available

LAMPETER Cardiganshire   map 4

Falcondale Mansion

Lampeter SA48 7RX
TEL: (01570) 422910   FAX: (01570) 423559

---

*Unassuming family-run country hotel in Italianate mansion
surrounded by forest-fringed grounds.*

Close to the Cambrian foothills, Falcondale occupies a splendid position in 14
acres of rhododendron plantation and ornamental woodland. The Falcondale
estate first came into existence after a bigger estate was broken up following a
disastrous night of gambling in London by Sir Herbert Lloyd. Today's owners,
Stephen Smith and his family, are proving more careful proprietors. Efforts are
now being made to turn the clock back to the time when this coffee-and-cream
Italianate mansion was first built in 1859. In the post-war period, as with so
many big houses, it began a steady decline before finding new life as a country
hotel in 1980. However, there remains a conflict of styles in the decoration that
keeps the hotel from being in the luxury category. The bedrooms are all a good
size and many benefit from the rural views all around. All of them are
individually designed, principally with French reproduction furniture. Room
29 is an attractive double with more discreet colours than some other rooms.
More reports, please.

◑ Open all year; restaurant closed Sun eves Nov to Jan   ⊿ The main entrance is off
Lampeter High Street. Private car park   🛏 2 twin, 8 double, 2 four-poster, 9 family
rooms; most with bathroom/WC, 3 with shower/WC; TV, room service, hair-dryer,
direct-dial telephone   ✓ Restaurant, bar, 2 lounges, conservatory, garden;
conference facilities (max 60 people incl up to 21 residential); fishing, golf, tennis, pitch
& putt; early suppers for children; babysitting, baby-listening   ♿ No wheelchair
access   ● Dogs in bedrooms only, by arrangement; no smoking in some public
rooms and some bedrooms   ▭ Access, Amex, Delta, Visa   £ Single occupancy of
twin/double £45 to £50, twin/double £70 to £75, four-poster £75 to £85, family room
from £70; deposit required. Set D £17, Sun L £11; alc D £17.50

LAMPHEY Pembrokeshire   map 4

Court Hotel

Lamphey, Pembroke SA71 5NT
TEL: (01646) 672273   FAX: (01646) 672480

---

*A pleasant, large hotel, with good sports facilities and fine
surroundings.*

The Nash-style Court Hotel must be one of the grandest and most prominent
buildings in the area. The Ionic columns of the porticoed entrance gleam in the
sunshine, and look out over the sheep-filled countryside and a pretty, meandering stream; the ruins of the former Archbishop of St David's palace can be seen in
the grounds. Stressed travellers can make use of an extensive leisure complex
situated in outbuildings to one side of the house, as well as tennis courts.
Although none too personal, the public rooms are tidy and smart, and the large

conservatory, which offers splendid views of the countryside, acts as an elegant, informal restaurant. Sadly, the menu is disappointing: on our inspection we were served rather dull stir-fry prawns; followed by pork schnitzel with onion sauce and plentiful, but unexciting, vegetables; and finally a heavy jam roly-poly. The breakfast-room in the other corner of the house offers smart, green, upright chairs and plenty of light. The bedrooms, which are decorated in a browny-pink colour scheme, are comfortable and of an acceptable size.

◑ Open all year ⤢ In Milton village off A477 turn for Lamphey and watch for signpost to hotel. Private car park ⤢ 2 single, 11 twin, 13 double, 11 family rooms; some in annexe; all with bathroom/WC exc 1 single with shower/WC; TV, room service, hair-dryer, trouser press, direct-dial telephone ✓ Restaurant, bar, lounge, conservatory, garden; air-conditioning in conference suite; conference facilities (max 90 people incl up to 35 residential); gym, sauna, solarium, heated indoor swimming-pool, tennis, yacht; early suppers for children; babysitting, baby-listening ♿ Wheelchair access to hotel (3 steps), restaurant and WC (M,F), 5 ground-floor bedrooms ● Dogs in bedrooms only, by arrangement; smoking in bar only ▭ Access, Amex, Delta, Diners, Switch, Visa £ Single/single occupancy of twin/double £65, twin/double £85 to £99, family room £83 to £120; deposit required. Set D £17, Sun L £10; alc D from £20; light lunches available (1996 prices). Special breaks available

LITTLE MILL see Pontypool

LLANABER Caernarfonshire & Merionethshire   map 7

Llwyndu Farmhouse

Llanaber, Nr Barmouth LL42 1RR
TEL: (01341) 280144 FAX: (01341) 281236

A faithfully restored Elizabethan farmhouse close to the sea, with distinctive modern décor.

On a hillside above a stretch of wide sandy beach outside Barmouth, this solid cream-yellow farmhouse has been a home since the end of the sixteenth century. In fact, if you want to know more about its history, owner Peter Thompson, who has made an impressive study of Llwyndu and the land around, can fill you in. While respectful of the past he and his wife, Paula, have not been afraid to put their own stamp on the building and have come up with some bold and distinctive colours and designs for the interior. One notices this immediately on entering the lounge, which has stone walls painted dark red and a huge inglenook fireplace. In the restaurant opposite, the menu has a modern look and features stir-fried chicken with mushrooms and a tarragon sauce, followed by an enticing rhubarb and banana pie. Three of the bedrooms are in the house and four in the granary annexe; there is little to choose between them as each has exposed beams and bold colours. All the rooms are excellently turned out and Rooms 2 and 5 have four-posters, but the main difference is that the proportions of the granary rooms are more uniform than of those in the house.

◑ Closed 3 weeks in winter; restaurant closed Sun eve ⏎ 2 miles north of Barmouth on east side of A496. Private car park ⏎ 1 twin, 2 double, 2 four-poster, 2 family rooms; some in annexe; all with bathroom/WC exc 1 double with shower/WC; TV, hair-dryer ⍟ Restaurant, lounge, garden; early suppers for children; toys, babysitting, baby-listening ⑁ No wheelchair access ◒ No dogs; no smoking ⊟ None accepted £ Single occupancy of twin/double £36 to £40, twin/double £50 to £54, four-poster £60, family room from 53; deposit required. Set D £12.50/15.50

LLANARMON DYFFRYN CEIRIOG Wrexham   map 7

West Arms Hotel

Llanarmon Dyffryn Ceiriog, Nr Llangollen LL20 7LD
TEL: (01691) 600665   FAX: (01691) 600622

Character and unpretentious charm in this old country inn in a quiet Welsh village.

If you are looking for a typical Welsh country inn, perhaps with good walks in the nearby hills, look no further than the West Arms, a 400-year-old former farmhouse. Passing through the doorway of this whitewashed, slate-roofed house tucked into the sleepy Ceiriog Valley you are confronted with the trappings of Welsh life as it once was. Massive inglenook fireplaces, slate flagstones, dark grizzled exposed beams and brasses are all around. The deep-red walls around the inglenook in the front hall only add to the cosiness. The bedrooms all have something of interest about them, though it may be better to stick to the ones in the main house. Many have brass bedsteads and antique furnishings. Willow is huge, with a separate sitting-area and curious windows – over-large on one side and tiny on the other.

◑ Open all year ⏎ Take B4500 from Chirk (just off A5) to Llanarmon. Private car park ⏎ 11 twin/double, 2 suites; some in annexe; all with bathroom/WC; room service, hair-dryer, direct-dial telephone ⍟ Restaurant, 2 bars, lounge, TV room, drying-room, garden; conference facilities (max 29 people incl up to 13 residential); early suppers for children; baby-listening ⑁ Wheelchair access to hotel (1 step), restaurant and WC (unisex), 3 ground-floor bedrooms, 1 specially equipped for disabled people ◒ Dogs in bedrooms only, by arrangement; no smoking ⊟ Access, Amex, Delta, Diners, Switch, Visa £ Single occupancy of twin/double £55, twin/double £100, suite £110; deposit required. Set L £13.50, D £22.50. Special breaks available

---

LLANDDEINIOLEN Caernarfonshire & Merionethshire   map 7

Ty'n Rhos

Seion, Llanddeiniolen, Caernarfon LL55 3AE
TEL: (01248) 670489   FAX: (01248) 670079

A relaxing retreat with extremely comfortable bedrooms and mouth-watering food.

Until recently Ty'n Rhos was a full-time farm and that rustic feel still surrounds this pleasant cluster of buildings set in a vale between Snowdonia and the sea.

Nigel and Lynda Kettle have created an easy-going feel to the house, reflected in the bright lounge with its comfy armchairs, fresh flowers, tasteful decoration and fine views through the big picture windows. Lynda bakes her own bread rolls, buys all her meat and fish from small local producers and, in summer, uses vegetables and herbs straight from the garden. In addition to an à la carte menu, there is a set three-course dinner plus cheese and coffee. You could start with a spicy cod soup, followed by pan-fried fillet of pork with a pink peppercorn sauce, broccoli, fennel and château potatoes, then a steamed citrus pudding with lemon and mint sauce. If you have any problems with this you can ask, before 7pm, for an alternative. All bedrooms are handsomely furnished, mainly in pine, in a light, floral style.

◑ Closed 23 to 30 Dec 🚫 Off B4366 in hamlet of Seion, 1½ miles north-east of Bethel. Private car park 🛏 3 single, 3 twin, 8 double; some in annexe; all with shower/WC; TV, room service, direct-dial telephone ✓ 2 restaurants, bar, lounge, drying-room, garden; conference facilities (max 25 people incl up to 14 residential); croquet; early suppers for children ♿ Wheelchair access to hotel (1 step) and restaurants, 6 ground-floor bedrooms, 1 specially equipped for disabled people ● No children under 5; no dogs; smoking in lounge only ☐ Access, Amex, Switch, Visa 💷 Single £40 to £45, single occupancy of twin/double £55 to £65, twin/double £60 to £80; deposit required. Set D £19; alc D £23 (prices valid till Apr 1997). Special breaks available

---

LLANDEGLEY Powys   map 4

Ffaldau Country House

Llandegley, Llandrindod Wells LD1 5UD
TEL: (01597) 851421 (AND FAX)

 COUNTY HOTEL OF THE YEAR

A picture-postcard Welsh farmhouse set in hilly countryside, serving organic meat and vegetables.

Sylvia and Les Knott have transformed this derelict farmhouse in just over ten years. There are now baskets of flowers hanging from its cream stone walls and attractive flower beds in the garden. Inside, the ancient character of the low-beamed, stone-floored house has been retained. Dinner is served at a set time, and guests are summoned by means of a gong to the small, downstairs lounge, where they are served nibbles and drinks before they make their way into the dining-room. Sylvia's dinners are much praised, and guests sit down to such dishes as a Welsh three-cheese roulade rolled in roasted pine- and hazelnuts, followed by an organic, Llandegley-reared, guinea-fowl breast stuffed with herbs, apple and tomato. The accompanying vegetables will often have been organically grown in Les' plot. There are three bedrooms in the house itself: Rooms 1 and 2 are fairly small and feature tiny windows; Room 3, however, is more spacious, and has a charming bathroom that has been fitted into the eaves of the house. There's a small guest sitting-room on the landing, offering plenty of games and books for the evenings. Room 4 – a twin with a shower only – is in the annexe, and has more uniform proportions but less character.

● Open all year ⤢ Set back from the A44 in Llandegley, 2 miles south-east of Penybont. Private car park ⇌ 2 twin, 2 double; 1 in annexe; 2 with bathroom/WC, 2 with shower/WC; hair-dryer, trouser press; TV in some rooms ⌁ Dining-room, bar, lounge/bar, TV room, drying-room, garden; early suppers for children ⅋ No wheelchair access ● No children under 10; no dogs; smoking in lounge/bar only ▭ Access, Visa £ Single occupancy of twin/double £30, twin/double £40 to £48; deposit required. Set D £15 to £18

LLANDEILO **Carmarthenshire**   map 4

Cawdor Arms Hotel

Rhosmaen Street, Llandeilo SA19 6EN
TEL: (01558) 823500   FAX: (01558) 822399

A traditional Georgian coaching-inn that has benefited from a complete refurbishment.

This Grade-II listed, cream-faced inn with green trim situated in the High Street has known ups and downs during its 200 years. At the moment it is decidedly on the up, after loving refurbishment. The public rooms with their deep-pink mottled walls open out one into the other, leading to a spacious main lounge with polished floorboards, fresh flowers and attractive rugs. A sense of age has been added with choice pieces of antique furniture and oil portraits on the walls. The restaurant is a cooler room with a yellow theme and serves dishes such as roast fillet of lamb wrapped in cabbage with a rosemary and roast-garlic *jus*, or roast fillet of turbot on a nest of fried leeks and chive butter sauce. Much work has been done on the bedrooms in recent years to maintain the standards set downstairs. We liked the Rose Room with its fine four-poster, bay window and curved velvet settee; Aunt Maud's Room (named after the hotel's little old ghost) is a twin room with lavish wallpaper and a *chaise-longue*; the French Room is an attractive double with yellow walls and heavy red drapes, but it has only a shower.

● Open all year ⤢ In centre of Llandeilo on A40. Private car park ⇌ 2 single, 6 twin, 6 double, 2 four-poster; family rooms available; all with bathroom/WC exc 2 doubles with shower/WC; TV, room service, hair-dryer, direct-dial telephone ⌁ Restaurant, bar, lounge; conference facilities (max 80 people incl up to 16 residential); early suppers for children; baby-listening ⅋ No wheelchair access ● No dogs in public rooms; no smoking in restaurant and some bedrooms ▭ Access, Amex, Delta, Switch, Visa £ Single £55, single occupancy of twin/double £60, twin/double £65 to £75, four-poster/family room £85; deposit required. Set L £13, D £22.50

LLANDRILLO **Denbighshire**   map 7

Tyddyn Llan

Llandrillo, Nr Corwen LL21 0ST
TEL: (01490) 440264   FAX: (01490) 440414

A thoughtfully designed small country hotel with elegance and originality.

Close to the Berwyn Mountains and trout fishing on the River Dee, this small hotel is a fine place to enjoy the great outdoors and the luxurious indoors as well. Although from the outside it is a modest multi-chimneyed Georgian house, inside the distinctive style of Tyddyn Llan takes a grip. Peter Kindred has used his skills as a former BBC set designer (including *Fawlty Towers!*) to devise some elegant public rooms. There's the pale, restful sitting-room with its Ionic pediments and stately marble mantelpiece. Then there's the much-commented-on dining-room, with a small dome and french windows on three sides. The food is a mix of French and British, and a typical meal might include grilled goat's cheese with beetroot and a walnut crust, followed by navarin of Welsh lamb with red wine, olives and anchovies, finished off with creamed lemon rice with fresh fruits and a lime sauce. Breakfast is taken in an interesting cream-painted wood-panelled room, which gives no clue that it was originally a billiards room. The bedrooms are generally a good size, airy and light, and many have brass or wooden beds. Room 7 has been given a facelift with traditional furniture made especially to suit the size of the room.

◑ Open all year ⚡ From A5 at Corwen take B4401 through Cynwyd to Llandrillo; house is on right-hand side as you leave village. Private car park ⛳ 4 twin, 6 double; family rooms available; all with bathroom/WC exc 2 doubles with shower/WC; TV, room service, hair-dryer, direct-dial telephone ✅ 2 dining-rooms, bar, lounge, drying-room, garden; conference facilities (max 50 people incl up to 10 residential); fishing, croquet; early suppers for children; baby-listening, cots, high chairs 🔥 No wheelchair access ● No young children in dining-rooms eves; dogs in bedrooms only, by arrangement; no smoking in dining-rooms ☐ Access, Amex, Delta, Diners, Switch, Visa 💷 Single occupancy of twin/double £46 to £64, twin/double £92 to £102, family room £92 to £102; deposit required. Set L £11 to £13, D £23 to £25. Special breaks available

---

LLANDUDNO Aberconwy & Colwyn map 7

Bodysgallen Hall

Llandudno LL30 1RS
TEL: (01492) 584466   FAX: (01492) 582519

An exceptional historic stately home with extensive gardens and luxurious accommodation.

Staying at Bodysgallen Hall will give you the chance for a first-hand look at one of the great baronial houses of North Wales. From the Elizabethan age to this century, the hall was in the hands of the Mostyn family, who through the ages added layer upon layer to the original design. It now stands perched above 200 acres of fabulous parkland and formal gardens, including a rare seventeenth-century knot garden. You can gaze down on them through stone mullioned windows and turn round to savour the opulently decorated rooms with plump sofas, fine rugs and solid wooden sideboards and tables. In the main dining-room there are more leaded windows and a warm, comforting, egg-yolk-yellow colour to the walls. The three-course dinner in the evening can be supplemented by a gourmet option that adds a soup and a sorbet. From the main menu you might try loin of Anglesey pork on garlic potato purée with glazed apples, or from the gourmet section Dublin Bay prawn risotto served with a scallop tortellini and chive sauce. Bedrooms in the main house are well proportioned and don't have the problems of space associated with some medieval houses. There are also some stone cottages, grouped around a quiet courtyard which have sitting-rooms and kitchenettes – though they are not self-catering.

○ Open all year ⬓ Leave A55 on A470 towards Llandudno; hotel is 2 miles on right. Private car park ⬓ 2 single, 1 twin, 16 double, 1 four-poster, 16 suites; family rooms available; suites in annexe; all with bathroom/WC exc 2 suites with shower/WC; TV, room service, hair-dryer, trouser press, direct-dial telephone; tea/coffee-making facilities in annexe rooms only ✧ 2 dining-rooms, bar, 3 lounges, library, garden; conference facilities (max 50 people incl up to 28 residential); gym, sauna, solarium, heated indoor swimming-pool, tennis, beauty treatment rooms, steam room ⅙ No wheelchair access ● No children under 8; dogs in annexe rooms only ⊟ Access, Amex, Delta, Switch, Visa £ Single £79 to £85, single occupancy of twin/double £92 to £98, twin/double £115 to £130, four-poster £160 to £170, family room £135 to £150, suite £135 to £150. Continental B £7, cooked B £10; set L £13.50, D £27.50/36. Special breaks available

St Tudno

Promenade, Llandudno LL30 2LP
TEL: (01492) 874411 FAX: (01492) 860407

A smart hotel doing all the right things for the visitor who wants to enjoy the great British seaside.

In a Victorian seaside resort that considered itself suitable for the crowned heads of Europe, St Tudno comfortably sustains that superior image in the late twentieth century. It's ideally situated opposite the pier with a view along the sweeping Victorian promenade back towards the Little Orme headland. The dean of Christ Church, Oxford, brought his family here in 1861 and among them was his eight-year-old daughter Alice, soon to be immortalised by Lewis Carroll in *Alice's Adventures in Wonderland*. In the drawing-room, with its sedate armchairs, slate fireplace and ticking clock, you can enjoy the sea view and imagine Alice reading in the corner. The food at St Tudno is impeccable – perhaps aubergine pattie with a fresh tomato compote and a medley of vegetables, followed by quenelles of dark chocolate and nut fudge with a poached pear and a vanilla sauce – and is good from first course to last. The full breakfast was also perfectly cooked. Bedrooms are decorated to a high standard in smart modern colours and finishes and the bathrooms are all gleaming whiteness and metal.

It is always worth enquiring about the availability of special breaks or weekend prices. The prices we quote are the standard rates for one night – most hotels offer reduced rates for longer stays.

See the inside front cover for a brief explanation of how to use the Guide.

◑ Open all year ◪ On Llandudno's promenade, opposite pier entrance and ornamental garden. Private car park 🛏 2 single, 7 twin, 8 double, 1 four-poster, 3 family rooms; all with bathroom/WC exc 2 doubles with shower/WC; TV, room service, hair-dryer, mini-bar, direct-dial telephone ✓ Restaurant (air-conditioned), bar, 2 lounges, drying-room, garden; conference facilities (max 25 people incl up to 21 residential); heated indoor swimming-pool; early suppers for children; toys, babysitting, baby-listening, cots, high chairs ♿ No wheelchair access ⊖ No young children in restaurant eves; no dogs in public rooms; no smoking in restaurant or lounge ▭ Access, Amex, Delta, Diners, Switch, Visa £ Single/single occupancy of twin/double £73, twin/double £85, four-poster £145, family room £117; deposit required. Set L £15.50, D £22 to £29.50; bar meals available. Special breaks available

LLANFACHRETH Anglesey map 7

Tŷ Isaf

Llanfachreth, Nr Dolgellau LL40 2EA
TEL: (01341) 423261

A cosy Snowdonian retreat where guests are guaranteed good hospitality.

Diana and Graham Silverton are the jolliest hosts you could meet and they run their guesthouse with a chatty house-party atmosphere. Llanfachreth itself is as remote as you could wish for in Snowdonia, and this low longhouse occupies an attractive position opposite the formidable spired church of the village. Tŷ Isaf has a clean, fresh feel and the Silvertons have decorated to suit their own tastes with deep-blue sofas and a Chinese carpet in the inglenook lounge. You will have your complimentary drink either here or on the terrace before dinner and then enjoy a four-course meal, with dishes such as tomato and rosemary soup, lamb and cranberry pie, sherry and raspberry trifle finished off with cheese and coffee. Breakfast is also something of an occasion, with croissants, hash browns, kippers and haddock all available, plus milk from the herd of Golden Guernsey goats in the adjoining paddock. The three bedrooms are all tidy, with exposed beams and pine furniture. Straw Store and Stable have showers only, Hay Loft has a bath. Stable is suitable for those who don't want to attempt stairs.

◑ Open all year ◪ From Dolgellau go over town bridge and turn right on to Bala Road; take a left turn to Llanfachreth and follow road for 3 miles; hotel is opposite church in centre of village. Private car park 🛏 1 twin, 2 double; 1 double with bathroom/WC, 2 with shower/WC; hair-dryer, radio ✓ Dining-room, 2 lounges, TV room, garden ♿ No wheelchair access ⊖ No children under 13; no smoking in bedrooms and dining-room ▭ None accepted £ Single occupancy of twin/double £25 to £35, twin/double £50; deposit required. Set D £12

Denotes somewhere you can rely on a good meal – either the hotel features in the 1997 edition of our sister publication, The Good Food Guide, *or our inspectors thought the cooking impressive, whether particularly competent home cooking or more lavish cuisine.*

LLANGAMMARCH WELLS Powys　　　　　　　　　　　map 4

Lake Country House

Llangammarch Wells LD4 4BS
TEL: (01591) 620202　FAX: (01591) 620457

A large Victorian house that caters for country pursuits in its beautiful grounds.

This box-like mock-Tudor country retreat may not be an architectural gem, but it has all the ingredients necessary for a comfortable stay. There are 52 acres of grounds and the grassy banks that slope away from the house take you down to the babbling River Irfon and the eponymous lake, which cannot be seen from the house. Badgers roam the grounds and the lake is stocked with trout. Winston, the gillie, can give you advice, based on 40 years' experience, on the best stretches of river. If fishing is not your thing, then there's tennis, croquet or a six-hole golf course. Inside, the comforts of a large house have been successfully recreated, particularly in the enormous lounge with its oriental carpets, chandeliers and picture windows. The settings in the elegant restaurant have satisfyingly chunky cutlery and prim white tablecloths. On the menu there could be breast of duckling marinated in oriental spices and soy sauce on a sauté of sesame stir-fried cabbage, followed by caramelised rice pudding with orange, kiwi-fruit and a caramel orange sauce. Although the rooms are all of a similar size the best, such as Irfon and Badger, have a view towards the river. Each has a smattering of antique furniture and the beds are a generous size.

○ Open all year　⊿ Take B519 from Brecon across Mount Eppynt (6 miles); at foot of hill turn left at crossroads; hotel is 1 mile along road. Private car park　⊫ 2 twin, 4 double, 2 four-poster, 1 family room, 10 suites; all with bathroom/WC; TV, room service, hair-dryer, direct-dial telephone; no tea/coffee-making facilities in rooms
⊘ Restaurant, bar, 2 lounges, drying-room, games room, garden; conference facilities (max 80 people incl up to 19 residential); fishing, golf, pitch & putt, putting green, tennis, croquet, clay-pigeon shooting, billiards; early suppers for children; babysitting, baby-listening　& Wheelchair access to hotel (1 step), restaurant and WC (unisex), 2 ground-floor bedrooms　● No children under 7 in restaurant eves; no dogs in public rooms; no smoking in restaurant and some bedrooms　▭ Access, Amex, Delta, Diners, Switch, Visa　£ Single occupancy of twin/double £78, twin/double £120, four-poster £120, family room £150, suite £162; deposit required. Set L £15.50, D £27.50. Special breaks available

---

LLANGOLLEN Denbighshire　　　　　　　　　　　map 7

Bryn Howel

Llangollen LL20 7UW
TEL: (01978) 860331　FAX: (01978) 860119

A busy, large Victorian hotel with newly refurbished bedrooms, close to Llangollen Canal.

As you approach Bryn Howel it will come as no surprise to discover that its original Victorian owner was James Coster Edwards, the Welsh 'king of brick' himself. He owned the local Ruabon brick company and his house is a monument to its glory, interspersed with some mock-Tudor for good measure. Inside, the house has plenty of characterful late-nineteenth-century features, such as black and white tiled floors, dark oak panelling, thickly glazed tiles and leaded lights. The modern extension for bedrooms, on one side, is a bit soulless, but at least fits in with the overall design. Of the public rooms the intimate bar is noteworthy for its excellent intricate plasterwork on the ceiling and around the fireplace, which contrasts nicely with the Cedar Restaurant with its large picture windows with views over the Vale of Llangollen and the lawned garden. Menus might offer sorbet of honeydew melon served on a ginger jelly, followed by cannon of Welsh lamb marinated in herbs and spices, pan fried and served with asparagus couscous, then almond sponge filled with lemon mousse and served with an exotic fruit coulis to finish. An extensive refurbishment of the hotel's bedrooms has been carried out in recent years.

◑ Closed 25 to 27 Dec　🔁 2 miles east of Llangollen on A539. Private car park
⬅ 5 single, 18 twin, 12 double, 1 suite; family rooms available; all with bathroom/WC; TV, room service, hair-dryer, direct-dial telephone, radio; trouser press in some rooms
✧ Restaurant, 2 bars, lounge, conservatory, garden; conference facilities (max 300 people incl up to 36 residential); sauna, solarium; early suppers for children; babysitting, baby-listening　♿ Wheelchair access to hotel (1 ramp) and restaurant, 8 ground-floor bedrooms, 1 specially equipped for disabled people　◖ Dogs in bedrooms by arrangement only　▭ Access, Amex, Delta, Switch, Visa　£ Single £42 to £73, single occupancy of twin/double £73, twin/double £84 to £96, suite £140; deposit required. Alc L £14.50, D £24.50 (prices valid till Apr 1997). Special breaks available

---

Gales

18 Bridge Street, Llangollen LL20 8PF
TEL: (01978) 860089　FAX: (01978) 861313

A busy bistro-style wine bar featuring well-decorated bedrooms.

It is hard to give an exact definition of Gales. Is it a wine bar serving food, a restaurant-with-rooms, or a mixture of all these things? Certainly, in recent years Gillie and Richard Gale have been altering the balance, with the conversion of the former Butcher's Arms across the road into more bedrooms, including two executive suites with lounges. The wine bar is situated at the back of the main building – a solid-looking, old coaching-inn on the banks of the River Dee. It is the focal point of Gales and, with its walls lined with wine-related paraphernalia, such as prints of châteaux, framed labels and maps of wine regions, is also highly atmospheric. The food is served to guests seated on wooden chairs at scrubbed tables; on offer are robust meals that are full of flavour, ranging from soups and salads to curries and casseroles. The menu is also likely to include a selection of smoked meats from the local smoke house. Stripped-pine furnishings and antique beds characterise the bedrooms above the wine bar.

◑ Closed 24 Dec to 2 Jan; restaurant closed Sun 🔁 In Llangollen town centre. Private car park 🛏 4 twin, 9 double, 2 suites; some in annexe; some with bathroom/WC, most with shower/WC; TV, hair-dryer, direct-dial telephone ✅ Restaurant, bar; conference facilities (max 20 people incl up to 15 residential); early suppers for children ♿ Wheelchair access to hotel (1 step) and restaurant, 1 ground-floor bedroom ⬤ No dogs in bedrooms; no smoking in some bedrooms 💳 Access, Amex, Delta, Switch, Visa 💷 Single occupancy of twin/double £37, twin/double £48, suite £55; deposit required. Alc L £7, D £12

LLANSANFFRAID GLAN CONWY Aberconwy & Colwyn   map 7

Old Rectory

Llanrwst Road, Llansanffraid Glan Conwy, Colwyn Bay LL28 5LF
TEL: (01492) 580611   FAX: (01492) 584555

A classy Wolsey Lodge hotel with superior views and food.

The Vaughan family home perches above the Conwy estuary, with its romantic mix of soft wooded slopes and menacing mountains behind. This broad-fronted mustard-coloured Georgian house, run as a Wolsey Lodge, has a relaxed elegance that owes much to Michael and Wendy Vaughan's hands-on approach. The drawing-room is a delight – a wood-panelled room with a fine bookcase, antiques and Victorian watercolours. Meals are four courses, prepared by Wendy, and there is a strong Welsh identity to the food. Dinner might be fillet of arctic char (a fish found in Snowdonian lakes) on a bed of wild mushrooms with champagne sauce, followed by poached loin of Welsh mountain lamb wrapped in leeks with a tarragon *jus*. There's a sense of occasion to eating in the dining-room, which has oriental carpets on polished floorboards and a grand piano. The six bedrooms take their names from their most conspicuous piece of furniture, the bed. Mahogany Half-Tester has views towards Conwy Castle and a large corner bath; Walnut Twin has fancy walnut headboards with matching furniture and also has good views.

◑ Closed 20 Dec to 1 Feb 🔁 On A470, ½ mile south of junction with A55. Private car park 🛏 2 twin, 3 double, 1 four-poster; some in annexe; all with bathroom/WC exc 1 double with shower/WC; TV, room service, hair-dryer, direct-dial telephone, iron ✅ Dining-room, lounge, drying-room, garden; early suppers for children ♿ No wheelchair access ⬤ No children under 5; dogs and smoking in annexe bedrooms only 💳 Access, Amex, Diners, Switch, Visa 💷 Single occupancy of twin/double £80 to £90, twin/double £99 to £129, four-poster £129; deposit required. Set D £29.50. Special breaks available

---

LLANTHONY Monmouthshire   map 5

Abbey Hotel

Llanthony, Nr Abergavenny NP7 7NN
TEL: (01873) 890487

Settle down for the night in an atmospheric small hotel built into the ruins of a remote abbey.

This is not the sort of place to arrive at on a wild and windy night lit only by the full moon. The Abbey Hotel is actually part of the stark ruins of an Augustinian priory, built in the twelfth century, and is in part of the abbey that was converted in the eighteenth century into a hunting lodge. It's right on the Welsh border in an exposed location among pastures and in the shade of the heather-clad Black Mountains. Inside, the atmosphere is marvellously Gothic, with wooden tables in the refectory dining-room and rough-hewn walls and ceilings in the whitewashed vaulted bar. The five bedrooms are reached up a narrow stone spiral staircase – 62 stairs to the top room and no lift – and all have a suitably baronial feel to them. They are small, but they do have four-posters and half-testers, and great views across the abbey ruins. None is *en suite* and there's no central heating.

◑ Closed weekdays from Nov to end Mar ⊿ From A465 take road signposted Llanthony Priory. Public car park nearby ⌷➥ 2 twin, 1 double, 2 four-poster; family room available ✅ Dining-room, bar, garden; early suppers for children ♿ No wheelchair access ➂ No children under 10; dogs in bedrooms only, by arrangement 🗀 None accepted £ Twin/double/four-poster (Sun to Thur) £44 (Fri and Sat night package) £100; deposit required. Alc L £5, D £8.50

LLANWDDYN Powys
map 7

Lake Vyrnwy Hotel

Lake Vyrnwy, Llanddwyn SY10 0LY
TEL: (01691) 870692   FAX: (01691) 870259

A large up-market Victorian hotel with a sporting theme – but it caters for the sedentary guest just as well.

Lake Vyrnwy describes itself as a sporting country house, and certainly its pine-panelled entrance hall evokes the feel of a Victorian hunting lodge. While many guests will want to take advantage of the abundant trout-fishing or go bird-watching in the adjacent RSPB reserve, others will probably content themselves with some gentle walks or even just an armchair view across the magnificent lake. In the main body of the hotel the decoration metamorphosises into something less sporting and more plush and comfortable, with sharper modern designs. There are plenty of public areas to stretch out in, all with views, but pride of place in the viewing stakes goes to the restaurant, which is part conservatory, with large picture windows. For dinner you might have layered plaice and salmon terrine, followed by braise of Welsh spring lamb served with mushroom pâté and a cranberry and Cointreau sauce, finishing with a poppyseed and armagnac parfait with whipped cream and chocolate sauce. The kitchen at Vyrnwy must be a constant hive of activity, as they cure hams, make preserves and mustard, bake breads and pickle wild mushrooms. The bedrooms are possibly a notch up in style from the public rooms, with good bright fabrics, fresh flowers and good-size bathrooms. It would be a shame to come all this way and not have a lake view – it's a luxury well worth paying the extra for.

◑ Open all year ⚡ Hotel is at south-east end of Lake Vyrnwy, just off B4393. Private car park ⟻ 31 twin/double, 2 four-poster, 2 suites; family rooms available; all with bathroom/WC exc 1 twin/double with shower/WC; TV, room service, hair-dryer, direct-dial telephone ✓ Restaurant, 2 bars, 2 lounges, drying-room, conservatory, garden; conference facilities (max 120 people incl up to 35 residential); fishing, tennis, sailing, cycling, game/clay-pigeon shooting, canoeing, rafting; early suppers for children; babysitting, baby-listening, cots, high chairs ♿ No wheelchair access ● No dogs in public rooms; no smoking in restaurant ⊟ Access, Amex, Delta, Diners, Switch, Visa £ Single occupancy of twin/double £64 to £102, twin/double £82 to £133, four-poster £110, family room £82 to £133, suite £133; deposit required. Set L £14 to £15, D £22.50 (prices valid till Apr 1997). Special breaks available

---

LLANWRTYD WELLS Powys   map 4

Carlton House

Llanwrtyd Wells LD5 4RA
TEL: (01591) 610248   FAX: (01591) 610242

COUNTY
HOTEL
OF THE
YEAR

An attractively decorated Victorian house situated in a charming, out-of-the-way town in the Brecons.

Carlton House, which is situated close to the centre of LLanwrtyd Wells (the smallest town in either Wales or England), opposite the family butcher, has a jaunty yellow exterior which hides a busy and successful family-hotel operation. Mary Ann Gilchrist's cooking has once again come in for acclaim from appreciative guests, especially those who have attended her imaginative epicurean holiday breaks. At one of these, you might sit down to savour such dishes as pan-fried halloumi cheese served with a lime and caper vinaigrette, followed by seared fillet steak with a honey, ginger and soy sauce, and then a pudding and savoury. The number of twin and double bedrooms has been reduced from six to five since last year in order to accommodate a spacious new suite; further improvements are planned. Room 3 boasts a huge double bed, a bath reached by means of a stepped plinth, as well as a sofa bed for other family members, while the other rooms have tartan or oriental themes. There is a great sense of space throughout the hotel, which is compounded by the fine, wooden staircase that stretches to the top of the house, and also the restaurant that opens out into a lounge full of books, games and interesting furnishings and ornaments. The hotel has no grounds as such (although there is a rock garden at the front), but is very close to some bracing hill walks in the surrounding Brecon Beacons.

◑ Closed 18-30 Dec ⚡ In Llanwrtyd Wells town centre. On-street parking ⟻ 3 twin, 1 double, 1 suite; 3 with bathroom/WC, 2 with shower/WC; TV ✓ Restaurant, lounge; early suppers for children ♿ No wheelchair access ● No dogs in public rooms; no smoking in restaurant ⊟ Access, Visa £ Single occupancy of twin/double £35, twin/double £50, suite £59; deposit required. Set D £19.50; alc D £25. Special breaks available

---

The text of entries is based on unsolicited reports sent in by readers and backed up by inspections. The factual details are from questionnaires the Guide *sends to all hotels that feature in the book.*

Griffin Inn ☆

Llyswen, Brecon LD3 0UR
TEL: (01874) 754241   FAX: (01874) 754592

*A very comfortable inn with a sporting theme, good food and a
relaxed atmosphere.*

If Silver Wilkinson, Yellow Torrish, or Green Highlander mean anything to you,
then you will enjoy the Griffin Inn. Just a short stroll from the River Wye, on the
road between Hay-on-Wye and Builth Wells, this creeper-clad medieval inn is
now devoted to the pleasures of fishing and the countryside in general. For the
uninitiated, those strange names are various types of fishing fly and each
bedroom is named after one. There are also prints and pictures throughout on the
subject of birds, dogs, horses and of course fish. There's still an authentic
old-style bar at the Griffin, where locals and guests can relax close to a stone
fireplace with benches around the walls. In the comfortable lounge nearby you
can share some of the warmth and conviviality of the bar. There's a quieter
reading-room upstairs if you prefer. To the other side of the inn is the
dining-room, a light room with a low ceiling, which serves some excellent food.
We enjoyed perfectly cooked chargrilled salmon with fresh asparagus and a
butter sauce, with new potatoes, carrots and mange-tout. The five bedrooms, all
en suite, are smart and clean, with pine furniture and pleasant pastel colours.

◑ Closed 25 & 26 Dec; restaurant closed Sun eve   ⤴ On A470, 7 miles south-west
of Hay-on-Wye. Private car park   ⤶ 2 single, 2 twin, 2 double, 1 four-poster; all with
bathroom/WC exc 2 singles with shower/WC; limited room service, direct-dial
telephone, clock radio; TV and hair-dryer on request   ✅ Dining-room, bar, lounge, TV
room, drying-room, garden; conference facilities (max 10 people incl up to 7
residential); fishing, clay-pigeon shooting; early suppers for children; babysitting, baby-
listening, toys   ♿ No wheelchair access   ⊖ No dogs or smoking in dining-room
⊟ Access, Amex, Delta, Diners, Switch, Visa   £ Single £35, single occupancy of
twin/double £38, twin/double £60, four-poster £70; deposit required. Alc L £11.50,
D £17.50 (prices valid till Mar 1997). Special breaks available

Llangoed Hall

Llyswen, Brecon LD3 0YP
TEL: (01874) 754525   FAX: (01874) 754545

*Gracious living in an Edwardian retreat built by Sir Clough
Williams-Ellis in the Wye Valley.*

Llangoed Hall's elegant brochure is written by the owner, Sir Bernard Ashley,
husband of the late Laura Ashley, and it is his personal interest in the hotel that
sets it apart from its rivals in lavishness. Its aim is to create a turn-of-the-century
house party and that starts when you are greeted on the gravel drive by a
doorman who takes your bags inside. There are none of the obvious signs of a
hotel, no reception desk or bar; instead you enter a house of the

finest taste in art, antiques and decoration. Throughout the house is Sir Bernard's superb collection of Edwardian paintings, culminating in a series of Whistler prints in a small room. The Great Hall, with its baronial fireplace and stacks of wood, is the ideal place to admire the view of the lush valley with hills in the distance and has a satisfying number of deep sofas and armchairs – there's also a well-stocked drinks cabinet. The dining-room is pure Laura Ashley, with pale-blue chairs set against lemon walls. Here the cooking is modern classical in style, with dishes such as roast spring chicken served with linguine and asparagus, or Welsh lamb with a herb mousse and sun-dried tomato sauce. It would be hard to pick out one of the 23 bedrooms for special mention, as each is special and contrasting. Not all use Ashley fabrics; some have the stately formality of a country house while others are more daring.

◑ Open all year ⤢ 1½ miles north of Llyswen on A470 towards Builth Wells. Private car park ⬛ 1 single, 10 twin/double, 9 four-poster, 3 suites; all with bathroom/WC; TV, room service, hair-dryer, direct-dial telephone; no tea/coffee-making facilities in rooms ⌀ Dining-room, 2 lounges, games room, garden; conference facilities (max 50 people incl up to 23 residential); fishing, tennis, croquet, maze, clay-pigeon shooting, archery ♿ No wheelchair access ● No children under 8; dogs in kennels only ▭ Access, Amex, Diners, Switch, Visa £ Single/single occupancy of twin/double £95, twin/double/four-poster £155 to £195, suite £195 to £285; deposit required. Set L £16, D £29.50; alc L £30, D £35 (1996 prices). Special breaks available

---

MILEBROOK Powys   map 4

Milebrook House

Milebrook, Knighton LD7 1LT
TEL: (01547) 528632   FAX: (01547) 520509

A well-proportioned Victorian family house in the Teme Valley with a choice of bar and restaurant meals.

This large house was once the home of Wilfred Thesiger and has the distinction of having had an emperor as a house guest. Haile Selassie stayed here (Room 2) in the 1920s and must have found the lush rural surroundings very different from his Abyssinian homeland. Milebrook is a favourite stopover for shooting parties, and with this in mind an extension with four extra rooms is now being added. Despite the increase in size, the house still has a family feel, best illustrated in the sitting-room. Owner Beryl Marsden does the cooking and offers a choice between a formal sit-down meal or a bar meal, and both have their temptations. The bar is the place for simple dishes like steak or salmon; in the restaurant you might have duck breast in a cassis and blackcurrant sauce or steak with an armagnac and green peppercorn sauce. All the bedrooms are a good size. Our favourites are Rooms 2 and 6 – the latter is all airy pale pinks with solid wood furniture and a view of the lawns.

◑ Open all year; restaurant closed Mon eve   ⤺ 2 miles east of Knighton on A4113. Private car park ⤺ 4 twin, 6 double; family room available; all with bathroom/WC; TV, room service, direct-dial telephone   ✅ Restaurant, bar, lounge, drying-room, garden; conference facilities (max 30 people incl up to 10 residential); fishing, croquet, clay-pigeon shooting; early suppers for children   ♿ Wheelchair access to hotel (1 step) and restaurant, 2 ground-floor bedrooms, 1 specially equipped for disabled people   ● No children under 3; no dogs; no smoking in bedrooms and some public rooms   ⬜ Access, Amex, Switch, Visa   £ Single occupancy of twin/double £45, twin/double £66, family room £76; deposit required. Set L, D £15 to £20; bar meals available. Special breaks available

---

NANTGWYNANT Aberconwy & Colwyn   map 7

Pen-y-gwryd Hotel

Nantgwynant LL55 4NT
TEL: (01286) 870211

Characterful climbers' retreat, with good basic accommodation and traditional food.

This solid, square house is a hotel popular with climbers and has a rough-and-ready atmosphere that those who have been at the rock face all day will appreciate. The public bar has log-lined walls, an open fireplace, wooden bench seats and memorabilia that commemorate Everest climbers. It's a good place to relax and talk about the day's exertions. The residents' bar is wood panelled with an open fire, lots of books and a model of Snowdon to plan your ascent. And for after the assault, there's a games room and a sauna. The dining-room has a simple but warm atmosphere with a large grandfather clock, beautiful dark wood dresser and excellent views down to Pen-y-gwryd Lake. The food is traditional and you aren't likely to go away hungry after the five courses with good portions of soup and roast lamb, and a generous helping of spotted dick, bread-and-butter pudding or crumble to finish. The bedrooms are simple but comfortable and not without interest, with Welsh quilts thrown over sturdy wooden beds. Most share bathrooms.

◑ Closed Nov & Dec and midweek in Jan & Feb   ⤺ At Capel Curig turn on to A4086; inn is 4 miles further on at T-junction (note: plotting on map 7 is slightly inaccurate). Private car park ⤺ 1 single, 6 twin, 8 double, 1 four-poster; 1 in annexe; 4 with bathroom/WC, 1 with shower/WC; limited room service; no tea/coffee-making facilities in rooms   ✅ Dining-room, bar, lounge, drying-room, games room, garden; conference facilities (max 35 people incl up to 16 residential); fishing, sauna, snooker, table tennis, darts; early suppers for children   ♿ Wheelchair access to hotel (1 step), dining-room and WC (M,F), 1 ground-floor bedroom specially equipped for disabled people   ● No smoking in bedrooms; dogs in bedrooms at £1.50 per night   ⬜ None accepted   £ Single £20, single occupancy of twin/double £20 to £25, twin/double £40 to £50, four-poster £50; deposit required. Set D £15; light lunches available

---

Where we know an establishment accepts credit cards, we list them. There may be a surcharge if you pay by credit card. It is always best to check when booking whether the card you want to use is acceptable.

Cnapan

East Street, Newport SA42 0SY
TEL: (01239) 820575　FAX: (01239) 820878

*A small family-run hotel in a seaside village with a relaxed
atmosphere and a busy restaurant.*

This smart, but simple, pink-washed house next to Newport village's main
street is recommended by the locals for its food. For visitors from further afield, it
also offers accommodation in a typical Pembrokeshire seaside location, close to
some stunning coastal scenery. Judith and Michael Cooper try very hard to
maintain their home's family atmosphere, and the five bedrooms reflect that
spirit, featuring family photos on the walls, knick-knacks and plenty of
bookcases filled with holiday reading matter. Each has a small (but adequate)
en-suite shower. The rooms at the front, such as Room 2 – a twin – look up the hill
towards the church and the castle. The restaurant that runs through to the back of
the house is a no-nonsense double room, with whitewashed rough-stone walls,
solid, wooden tables and big linen tablecloths. The owners display a notice
verifying the quality of their locally produced beef, and you can enjoy it with
either garlic butter or a creamy mushroom sauce. To follow, you can perhaps
have a coffee-flavoured crème brûlée served with a rum topf of winter fruits.

◑ Closed Chr and Feb; restaurant closed Tue　🔟 In Newport town centre, on A487,
halfway between Fishguard and Cardigan. Private car park　🚗 3 twin, 1 double, 1
family room; all with shower/WC; TV, room service, hair-dryer　✅ Restaurant, bar,
lounge, garden; early suppers for children; toys, baby-listening　🚫 No wheelchair
access　🐕 No dogs; smoking in bar only　💳 Access, Visa　💷 Single occupancy of
twin/double £30, twin/double £50, family room £66; deposit required. Alc L £9.50,
D £17

Soughton Hall

Northop, Mold CH7 6AB
TEL: (01352) 840811　FAX: (01352) 840382

A striking hotel with touches of luxury and superb gardens.

This former bishops' palace built in 1714 is surrounded by some wonderful
formal gardens, including a fine tree-lined avenue. Much of the interior has been
restored by the Rodenhurst family and has a Victorian feel, enhanced by
judicious use of reproduction furniture. A previous owner was a great traveller
and his taste is certainly evident in the architecture: the styles range from Islamic
to Venetian and Gothic. The public rooms all have impressive proportions: the
drawing-room, for instance, has attractive walnut floorboards, a Chinese carpet,
tall drapes and light wood panelling. Each of the 14 bedrooms is individually
furnished, with luxurious touches. The restaurant in the main hotel is a simple
spacious room, again with walnut flooring, with views out to the formal
gardens, often busy with the chatter of a wedding party on summer weekends.

Main courses might be Welsh lamb with bubble and squeak, or baby chicken with tarragon. The Stables, a Grade-II listed building, has now been restored and opened. It has a bar downstairs; a restaurant, which offers a blackboard menu with an emphasis on plain food and fresh dishes, is upstairs in the hayloft.

◗ Open all year   ⊿   Off A5119, 3 miles north of Mold. Private car park   ⤞   4 twin, 9 double, 1 four-poster; family rooms available; 1 in annexe; all with bathroom/WC; TV, limited room service, hair-dryer, trouser press, direct-dial telephone   ⍁   2 restaurants, 2 bars, 3 lounges, library, garden; conference facilities (max 40 people incl up to 14 residential); golf, tennis, croquet   ♿   No wheelchair access   ●   No children under 12 in main hotel; no dogs; no smoking in bedrooms   ▭   Access, Amex, Visa   £   Single occupancy of twin/double £70 to £80, twin/double £99, four-poster £120, family room £130; deposit required. Alc L, D £27; light meals available. Special breaks available

---

PENALLY Pembrokeshire   map 4

Penally Abbey

Penally, Nr Tenby SA70 7PY

TEL: (01834) 843033   FAX: (01834) 844714

A country hotel that takes you effortlessly back to its Victorian origins.

Eileen and Steve Warren's creation is a lovingly restored stylish nineteenth-century country home close to the seaside. The views of the grassy dunes down to the sea and the picture-postcard village green are both glorious. At night you can sit by candle light at dinner while the chandeliers sparkle among the fine pieces of porcelain and furniture. Windows, doorways and even the cupboards have a graceful curve to them, often described as Strawberry Hill Gothic. This is best seen in the sitting-room, which has a piano, soft sofas and a *chaise-longue*. The bedrooms will not disappoint either: each has period touches and Room 5 includes a fine wooden wardrobe that came with the house. Most of the rooms have four-posters, and even without them Rooms 1 and 2 are appealingly cosy; the latter has a view of the church. Behind the house are 6 acres of woodland filled with bluebells in spring, and the tidy garden is ideal for afternoon tea. The bedrooms in the Coach House are less spacious but allow guests a bit more privacy. If you require recreation beyond enjoying the aesthetic charms of the house during your stay, head for the snooker room or the small swimming-pool.

◗ Open all year   ⊿   1½ miles south-west of Tenby, just off A4139 Pembroke coast road. Private car park   ⤞   1 twin, 4 double, 7 four-poster; family rooms available; some in annexe; all with bathroom/WC; TV, room service, hair-dryer, direct-dial telephone   ⍁   Restaurant, bar, lounge, drying-room, conservatory, games room, garden; conference facilities (max 16 people incl up to 12 residential); heated indoor swimming-pool, snooker; early suppers for children; toys, babysitting, baby-listening, outdoor games   ♿   Wheelchair access to hotel (1 step) and restaurant, 2 ground-floor bedrooms   ●   No children under 7 in restaurant eves; no dogs; no smoking in bedrooms or restaurant   ▭   Access, Amex, Switch, Visa   £   Single occupancy of twin/double £65, twin/double £94, four-poster/family room £106; deposit required. Set L £14.50, D £23.50; alc L £19.50, D £23.50. Special breaks available

George III Hotel

Penmaenpool, Dolgellau LL40 1YD
TEL: (01341) 422525   FAX: (01341) 423565

A friendly holiday hotel with two popular bars in a beautiful location.

Gerard Manley Hopkins is said to have written his poem 'Penmaenpool' in a copy of an old hotel guest book and certainly the George has been providing holidaymakers with a pleasant stay for more than 100 years. The hotel is divided between the main seventeenth-century building, which was once a pub and a ships' chandlers, and the Lodge, once the ticket office and waiting room of the pre-Beeching Cambrian Railways station. Tucked unobtrusively into the banks of the Mawddach, the peaceful position of the hotel cannot be faulted. Most bedrooms have a fine view, the best being Rooms 4 and 6, both tidy rooms with pale decoration. Downstairs is the cellar bar, a busy place for passing trade, with bench seats, stone walls and a place where you can hire bikes to travel along the disused railway. Upstairs are the main rooms of the hotel, all with river views. There's a light comfortable bar with a low ceiling, a plainly furnished restaurant and a fairly gloomy residents' lounge with an inglenook fireplace that might prove a little close to the bar area for some. All about are fascinating prints, photos and memorabilia of the railway, the countryside and boats.

○ Open all year ☑ 3 miles west of Dolgellau on A493. Private car park ⮠ 4 twin, 8 double; family rooms available; some in annexe; all with bathroom/WC; TV, room service, hair-dryer, trouser press, direct-dial telephone ✓ Restaurant, 2 bars, lounge, drying-room, garden; fishing, mountain bikes; early suppers for children
⅍ Wheelchair access to hotel (1 ramp), restaurant and WC (M,F), 5 ground-floor bedrooms ● No children in restaurant after 8pm; no smoking in restaurant and 1 bar ▭ Access, Switch, Visa £ Single occupancy of twin/double £50, twin/double £88, family room from £101; deposit required. Set Sun L £12; alc L, D £17.50. Special breaks available

---

Penmaenuchaf Hall

Penmaenpool, Dolgellau LL40 1YB
TEL: (01341) 422129 (AND FAX)

A country house furnished with care and attention overlooking the Mawddach estuary.

What this grey-stone Victorian mansion lacks in a lavish exterior it makes up for on the inside. The warm, welcoming feel of the entrance hall sums things up very well. Light streams in through stained-glass panels in the windows on to a fine display of dried flowers and an intricately carved wooden fireplace. Although this is a large house there is always a feel of intimacy. Mark Watson and Lorraine Fielding have created a hugely impressive country-house hotel that is improving all the time. Their assurance comes through in the pale furnishings of the morning-room, with various antique pieces dotted around, or the more sombre feel of the library, with its leather sofa and comfy armchairs. For dinner you could perhaps have steamed fillets of grey mullet flavoured with pickled ginger and set on a ratatouille, followed by an iced nougatine parfait on a blackcurrant coulis. Tasteful colour schemes, attractive bathrooms and ample beds mean that the bedrooms meet the same high standards. All except Williams have a panoramic view.

○ Open all year ◪ Off A493, 1 mile west of junction with A470. Private car park ⌷⌷ 5 twin, 8 double, 1 four-poster; all with bathroom/WC; TV, room service, hair-dryer, direct-dial telephone; mini-bar in some rooms ⬦ 3 restaurants, bar, 2 lounges, drying-room, library, conservatory, games room, garden; conference facilities (max 50 people incl up to 14 residential); fishing, croquet, snooker; early suppers for children; baby-listening ⅙ No wheelchair access ● No children under 8; dogs in entrance hall only; no smoking in most public rooms and 2 bedrooms ⊟ Access, Amex, Delta, Diners, Switch, Visa £ Single occupancy of twin/double £50 to £95, twin/double £95 to £140, four-poster £150; deposit required. Set L £12 to £14, D £23; alc L £14.50, D £24. Special breaks available

---

PONTFAEN Pembrokeshire   map 4

Tregynon Farmhouse

Pontfaen, Gwaun Valley, Nr Fishguard SA65 9TU
TEL: (01239) 820531   FAX: (01239) 820808

Simple rooms in an ancient rustic setting, ideal for walkers and vegetarians.

Tregynon dates back to the sixteenth century or a lot further if you include the Iron Age hill fort, dating back to 700 BC, that lurks in the undergrowth to one side of the house. The blue stones for Stonehenge came from around here, and it's not hard to understand why this spot has been inhabited for so long when one sees the superb view it gives of the entire broad Gwaun Valley and the rocky tip called Carn Ingli, Mountain of Angels. There are hints of the age of the house in the old stone walls in each room, and the impressive stone inglenook fireplace in the lounge, but the overall feel of Tregynon is thoroughly twentieth century. There are three small bedrooms in the house, each with a shower, and five more spacious rooms in the outlying buildings. There's nothing special about the outhouse rooms; the real advantage of staying here is the superb walking country and the tempting and original food prepared by June and Peter Heard. The emphasis is on wholefood and vegetarian cuisine – choose the vegetarian stuffed pancake with a tomato and muscatel sauce, or, if you are a carnivore, rack of Pembrokeshire lamb with elderberry and rosemary sauce. At breakfast there's home-made muesli and marmalade, or home-smoked bacon and kippers.

Don't expect to turn up at a small hotel assuming that a room will be available. It's always best to telephone in advance.

◑ Closed 2 weeks in winter 〆 At intersection of B4313 and B4329, take B4313 towards Fishguard; then take first right and right again. Private car park ⊨ 3 double, 1 four-poster, 4 family rooms; some in annexe; 5 with bathroom/WC, 3 with shower/WC; TV, limited room service, hair-dryer, direct-dial telephone ✣ 2 dining-rooms, bar, lounge, garden; early suppers for children; baby-listening �& No wheelchair access ● No young children in dining-rooms eves; no dogs; no smoking in bedrooms or dining-rooms ▭ Access, Delta, Switch, Visa £ Twin/double £48 to £64, four-poster £68, family room from £56; deposit required. Set D £16; alc D £20 (prices valid till Apr 1997). Special breaks available

---

PONTYPOOL Torfaen   plotted as Little Mill on map 4

Pentwyn Farm

Little Mill, Pontypool NP4 0HQ
TEL: (01495) 785249   FAX: (01495) 785247

Peacefully located and friendly farmhouse with communal dining.

Pentwyn Farm is a traditional Welsh two-storey longhouse made especially striking by its pale-pink-washed appearance. It's a small establishment and all the guests eat around a long wooden table in a wood-beamed dining-room, which has a fresh lemon décor that contrasts nicely with the dark furniture. The view from the window looks across at field upon field stretching away to the Brecon Beacons. A maximum of six guests can dine together, picking from a set menu with several choices of starter and main course. Dishes might include venison and redcurrant casserole or rabbit in Welsh mustard and thyme. Stuart and Ann Bradley have made their house particularly homely, best seen in the sitting-room with its large floral sofa and some bookcases to tempt the idle browser. There are four bedrooms in the house, two of which can be put together to form a family room, plus two single-storey stable cottages with fitted kitchens. During high season cottage-dwellers are welcome to join those in the house for dinner.

◑ Closed Chr & New Year; restaurant closed Sun eve 〆 Village of Little Mill is on A472, 3 miles from Usk. Private car park ⊨ 2 twin, 2 double; family room available; 2 with shower/WC ✣ Dining-room, lounge, drying-room, games room, garden; heated outdoor swimming-pool �& No wheelchair access ● No children under 4; no dogs; no smoking in bedrooms or dining-room ▭ None accepted £ Single occupancy of twin/double £20 to £25, twin/double £30 to £40. Set D £12

PORTHKERRY Vale of Glamorgan   map 4

Egerton Grey

Porthkerry, Nr Barry CF62 3BZ
TEL: (01446) 711666   FAX: (01446) 711690

A fine, small country house with good attention to detail, elegant furnishings and pretty surroundings.

This early-Victorian former rectory sits snugly in a discreet hollow close to the Bristol Channel, surrounded by tall mature trees. Although it is peaceful, the proximity of Cardiff Airport means that there is occasional overhead noise. Inside, the house exudes good taste, with period oil paintings dotted around and a relaxed charm to the decoration. The drawing-room is particularly lovely, with a bay window that lets in plenty of light and has acres of comfortable sofas and armchairs. The bedrooms are all attractively decorated and have good bathrooms, some with free-standing baths. Dinner is served in the former billiards room, which has a clerestory roof and cool dark-wood floors. The food has come in for praise and might include roast leg of Welsh lamb stuffed with leeks, apricots and hazelnuts on a rosemary-scented *jus*, followed by chilled toffee mousse served between layers of chocolate wafers on a mixed berry and cassis sauce. One visitor singled out the breakfasts for particular mention – the impressive menu includes home-made Glamorgan sausage made with cheese, potato and breadcrumbs.

◑ Open all year   ⊅ Leave M4 at Junction 33 and follow signs to airport past Barry; turn left at small roundabout at airport and left again after 500 yards. Private car park 🛏 1 single, 2 twin, 3 double, 1 four-poster, 2 family rooms, 1 suite; all with bathroom/WC exc single with shower/WC; TV, room service, hair-dryer, trouser press, direct-dial telephone   ⌘ Restaurant, lounge, library, conservatory, garden; conference facilities (max 40 people incl up to 10 residential); tennis; early suppers for children; babysitting, baby-listening   ⅗ No wheelchair access   ⊖ No children under 5 in restaurant eves; no dogs in public rooms and most bedrooms; no smoking in restaurant   ⊡ Access, Amex, Delta, Diners, Switch, Visa   £⋅ Single £55, single occupancy of twin/double £75, twin/double £95, four-poster £120, family room £95, suite £120; deposit required. Set L, D £18 to £25.50. Special breaks available

---

PORTMEIRION Caernarfonshire & Merionethshire   map 7

Hotel Portmeirion

Portmeirion LL48 6ET
TEL: (01766) 770228   FAX: (01766) 771331

A fabulous and unique luxury hotel that lives in its own little world on the wooded banks of Traeth Bach estuary.

This hotel has a spectacular setting on the banks of a sandy estuary and enough clever touches to make a stay here both memorable and soothing, despite the cost. Local architect Sir Clough Williams-Ellis started work on his grand design to build a fantasy village in the 1920s, but it was only in 1973, his ninetieth year, that it was completed. He created a whimsical and fascinating place, converting a Victorian house into a hotel and adding outlying cottages and grand buildings. The hotel resembles some tycoon's holiday mansion, with a gleaming white terrace and turquoise painting around the windows and roofs. There is a conspicuous effort inside to create dramatic and unusual effects, just like in the village itself. The public rooms mix and match styles from around the world: in one a huge stripy sofa covered with a rough ethnic fabric squats on a black and white tiled floor opposite a spectacular stone fireplace, above which are perched a curious row of black stone cats. The restaurant has a bold, cool, curvilinear sweep to it that absorbs a vast amount of the shoreline and foothills of Snowdonia beyond. It was good to see that service at dinner had improved since our last visit. The bedrooms continue the striking colour schemes of the house and most have views of the estuary; Room 9 wins the award for best views. Alternatively you can stay in a cottage, either as part of the hotel or self-catering.

◑ Closed 6 Jan to 7 Feb ⏏ In Portmeirion village. Private car park ⨃ 9 twin, 11 double, 2 four-poster, 3 family rooms, 12 suites; most in annexe; all with bathroom/WC; TV, room service, hair-dryer, direct-dial telephone ⬦ Restaurant, bar, lounge, drying-room, library, conservatory, garden; conference facilities (max 100 people incl up to 37 residential); heated outdoor swimming-pool, tennis; early suppers for children; babysitting ♿ No wheelchair access ● No young children in restaurant eves; no dogs; no smoking in public rooms and discouraged in bedrooms ▭ Access, Amex, Delta, Diners, Switch, Visa ⊡ Single occupancy of twin/double £55 to £65, twin/double £65 to £125, four-poster £115 to £125, family room £90 to £170, suite £85 to £160; deposit required. Continental B £6.50, cooked B £9; set L £14.50, D £27.50. Special breaks available

---

REYNOLDSTON Swansea map 4

Fairyhill

Reynoldston, Gower, Swansea SA3 1BS
TEL: (01792) 390139 FAX: (01792) 391358

A relaxing country hotel in the Gower, with a secluded rural setting and garden trails.

Fairyhill is discreetly placed behind the village of Reynoldston, between the moorland uplands and farmed lowlands of the Gower peninsula. Formerly a Georgian gentleman's house, it is grand for the area, though simple in design. It is seen at its best from one of the sides, where creepers grow up the wall and the lawn extends towards some 2 acres of spring-time daffodils. A dramatic refurbishment programme has been undertaken in recent years, so there is an odd mix of the older styles of decoration along with the better, newer style. This is most obvious in the bedrooms; Rooms 5, 6, 8 and 9 show a bold use of colours – strong yellows and greens in particular – and a sharp, modern design. Some of the other rooms are adequate, but lack any outstanding features. This determination to modernise is to be applauded, especially when it results in a CD player in every bedroom. Both restaurants have views over the gardens, and the one towards the back of the house is raised up with wooden floors which gives it a light, cabin-like atmosphere. Local produce features strongly on the menu, which might include a rich tart of crab with green chillies and lemon grass, followed, perhaps, by Brecon venison, served with an apple sauce made with coriander. More reports, please.

◑ Open all year ⏏ From Gowerton take B4295 and follow it for 9 miles; Fairyhill is signposted to the left. Private car park ⨃ 5 twin/double, 3 double; 6 with bathroom/WC, 2 with shower/WC; TV, room service, hair-dryer, direct-dial telephone, CD player; trouser press in some rooms ⬦ 2 restaurants, bar, lounge, conservatory, garden; conference facilities (max 24 people incl up to 8 residential); croquet ♿ No wheelchair access ● No children under 8; no dogs in public rooms and some bedrooms; no pipes or cigars in restaurants ▭ Access, Amex, Delta, Switch, Visa ⊡ Single occupancy of twin/double from £70, twin/double £85 to £150; deposit required. Set L £11.50/14.50, D £22/27. Special breaks available

RUTHIN **Denbighshire** map 7

Gorphwysfa

8A Castle Street, Ruthin LL15 1DP
TEL: (01824) 702748   FAX: (01824) 703320

A B&B in an ancient and characterful medieval town house.

Gorphwysfa is in an ideal central location in the oldest street in Ruthin. It is now seven years since Walter and Eleanor Jones started up their friendly B&B in this fifteenth-century half-timbered house. The wood-panelled entrance hall has a curious carved gallery and the breakfast-room is equally atmospheric with exposed stone walls and an inglenook fireplace. Not all the decoration is ancient: an eccentric collection of objects includes a piece of the Berlin Wall. In other parts of the house there is plenty of space to stretch out, with a capacious lounge and a small reading area. One of the three bedrooms runs the full length of the house and has a large bathroom; the other two are smaller and simpler and share a bathroom.

◑ Open all year ⬀ In centre of Ruthin. On-street parking 🛏 1 twin, 1 double, 1 family room; family room with bathroom/WC; hair-dryer on request ⊘ Dining-room, lounge, library ♿ No wheelchair access ⬤ None ▭ None accepted
£ Single occupancy of twin/double £17, twin/double £33, family room from £41

ST BRIDE'S WENTLLOOG **Newport** map 4

West Usk Lighthouse

Lighthouse Road, St Bride's Wentlloog, Newport NP1 9SF
TEL: (01633) 810126/815860   FAX: (01633) 815582

A Victorian lighthouse converted into an idiosyncratic B&B with a flotation tank.

To reach this former lighthouse you have to cross a small bridge with a sign by its side announcing 'Bridge Over Troubled Waters'. Such touches of humour are present throughout this quirky and eccentric place and also give a clue to the owner Frank Sheahan's previous life in the music business. The building is surprisingly low for a supposedly prominent landmark, but is helped by its position – flat pasture land – on the edge of the Severn estuary. Inside, the roundness of the building is less apparent – what is noticeable is Frank's eclectic collection of curios. There's a telephone box from a lifeboat station, a set of Buddhas and a Dalek tucked around the corner of the spiral iron staircase. Just off from here is the breakfast-room, a friendly jumble of furniture and nautical objects and an inviting coal fire. The bedrooms are not particularly spacious and have very small bathrooms, but they all have good views. Room 1 is probably the smallest and the least desirable, while Room 3 has a water bed. The water theme is continued in the flotation tank room – for those who want to get away from it all. After the dip in Epsom salts (£18 a session) you can shower down in the adjacent red telephone box. Frank claims to hold the world record for 'floating', at 24 hours.

○ Open all year ⚄ Take B4239 for St Bride's and turn at B&B sign into long private road. Private car park ⟶ 1 single, 1 twin, 2 double, 1 four-poster; family room available; 3 with shower/WC; TV, trouser press ✓ Dining-room, lounge, TV room, garden; conference facilities (max 20 people incl up to 5 residential); flotation tank; early suppers for children; toys, playroom ⅙ No wheelchair access ● No dogs; no smoking ⊟ Access, Amex, Delta, Switch, Visa £ Single occupancy of twin/double £27 to £45, twin/double £50 to £55, four-poster £65 to £70, family room from £63; deposit required. Set D £15. Special breaks available

SWANSEA Swansea   map 4

Hillcrest House

1 Higher Lane, Mumbles, Swansea SA3 4NS
TEL: (01792) 363700   FAX: (01792) 363768

A personable seaside hotel close to Swansea that has a thoughtful approach to its customers.

As its name suggests, this charming small hotel sits proudly on high ground with flags fluttering, just outside the centre of the Mumbles seaside resort, 4 miles from Swansea. While suburban in look and setting, it is extremely well maintained, with lots of personal touches that set it apart from the ordinary. The seven *en-suite* bedrooms are a delight and the decoration shows a lot of intelligence, combining the owner Yvonne Scott's love of travel with carefully chosen fabrics and colours. Botswana has leopard-skin chairs and African statues; Wales a huge daffodil lamp and curtains the colour of leeks. A nice touch is that fresh milk is served with tea and coffee in your room. Downstairs, the sitting-room has bookcases filled with holiday paperbacks, discreet lighting and smart chairs and sofas. The restaurant is a simpler room, but the food ventures beyond standard hotel fare with some success. Our inspector's starter of warmed Welsh goat's cheese with honey and a grapefruit vinaigrette was excellent and was followed by an equally tasty beef in filo pastry and a grain mustard sauce.

○ Closed 23 Dec to Jan; restaurant closed Sun eve ⚄ 4 miles south of city centre, just off Langland Road. Private car park ⟶ 1 single, 2 twin, 3 double, 1 four-poster; family room available; most with bathroom/WC, 2 with shower/WC; TV, room service, hair-dryer, direct-dial telephone ✓ Restaurant, bar, lounge, garden; conference facilities (max 15 people incl up to 7 residential); early suppers for children ⅙ No wheelchair access ● No dogs; no smoking in restaurant and some bedrooms ⊟ Access, Amex, Delta, Visa £ Single £45, single occupancy of twin/double £50, twin/double £60 to £65, four-poster £80, family room from £90; deposit required. Set D £15 to £18; alc D £18.50. Special breaks available

The 1998 Guide *will be published in the autumn of 1997. Reports on hotels are welcome at any time of the year, but are extremely valuable in the spring. Send them to* The Which? Hotel Guide, FREEPOST, 2 Marylebone Road, London NW1 1YN. *No stamp is needed if reports are posted in the UK. Our e-mail address is: "guidereports@which.co.uk".*

Maes-y-Neuadd

Talsarnau LL47 6YA
TEL: (01766) 780200   FAX: (01766) 780211

A manor house in beautiful grounds with attractively decorated rooms.

This Welsh slate and granite mansion has parts that date back to the fourteenth century. A thoughtful restoration has left plenty of exposed beams and rough stone yet given it a pleasant up-to-date feel. The house is set in beautiful Snowdonian countryside, with sloping lawns leading away to wooded hillsides and views of both the sea and the mountains. The long, narrow sitting-room with its large chintz sofas is a good place to sit to enjoy the scenery. In the Georgian dining-room the menu makes good use of the produce from the hotel's walled garden. The three- to five-course dinners might have a main dish of Trelough duck on a bed of bubble and squeak, or strips of beef with laverbread, celeriac and leeks. All the bedrooms are individually decorated with high-quality fabrics. Artro is noteworthy for its large bed and windows that let in plenty of light. The four coach-house rooms have a more rustic look and bright colour schemes.

◑ Open all year ⤤ 3 miles north-east of Harlech, signposted off B4573. Private car park ⤣ 1 single, 2 twin, 4 double, 8 twin/double, 1 four-poster; some in annexe; all with bathroom/WC exc single with shower/WC; TV, room service, hair-dryer, direct-dial telephone ⌘ Restaurant, bar, lounge, drying-room, conservatory, garden; conference facilities (max 40 people incl up to 16 residential); croquet; early suppers for children; baby-listening ⅙ Wheelchair access to hotel, restaurant and WC (M,F), 3 ground-floor bedrooms ⬤ Dogs in bedrooms only, by arrangement; no smoking in restaurant ▭ Access, Amex, Delta, Diners, Switch, Visa £ Single £56, single occupancy of twin/double £85, twin/double £122 to £165, four-poster £135, suite £148; deposit required. Set L £12.50, D £29. Special breaks available

---

Minffordd Hotel

Talyllyn, Tywyn LL36 9AJ
TEL: (01654) 761665   FAX: (01654) 761517

An immaculate small hotel in Snowdonia with a growing reputation for its food and hospitality.

Last year we asked for more reports about Minffordd, and the response was a resounding thumbs-up for the efforts of Mary McQuillan and Mark Warner. Situated close to Lake Talyllyn in a typically beautiful Snowdonian valley, this whitewashed former farmhouse huddles up to the side of the road. Considering the size of the house, the existing space has been utilised very well; the dining-room has received particularly ingenious treatment with the amalgamation of three or four small rooms – all on slightly different levels – while the old beams have been retained. Mark's cooking won more plaudits, and it was good to see that coffee and chocolates were *included* in the dinner price. Guests can opt for such dishes as loin of Welsh lamb served with a port and redcurrant sauce, or hake poached in lemon and bay with a lobster sauce, followed by steamed treacle sponge. This year a two-bedroom extension has been added, and the new rooms have tasteful, bright decoration and smart bathrooms. Of the older rooms, Room 4, which is tucked into the eaves of the house, is the most noteworthy. It's all summed up in the words of one guest: 'the warmth of the owners is well reflected in the running of this small, spotless hotel;' and the verdict from another is that 'we are definitely joining those who return to Minffordd time and time again.'

◑ Closed Jan & Feb ⤢ At the junction of A487 and B4405, midway between Dolgellau and Machynlleth. Private car park 🛏 2 twin, 4 double; all with bathroom/WC exc 1 double with shower/WC; room service, hair-dryer, direct-dial telephone ⊘ Dining-room, bar, lounge, drying-room, conservatory, garden; early suppers for children ⅃ No wheelchair access ⬤ No children under 5; no dogs; smoking in bar only ▱ Access, Delta, Visa £ Single occupancy of twin/double £52 to £62, twin/double £98 to £104 (rates incl dinner); deposit required. Set D £18.50. Special breaks available

---

THREE COCKS Powys   map 4

Three Cocks Hotel

Three Cocks, Brecon LD3 0SL
TEL: (01497) 847215 (AND FAX)

A medieval hostelry that is now an up-to-date small hotel offering food with a Belgian flavour.

There is a Cotswold look to this creeper-clad wayside inn, which despite its age and history has no pub on the premises. The public rooms have therefore been altered to suit the needs of hotel guests, which has resulted in a surprising sense of space inside and a pleasing mix of new furnishings and exposed stone walls and old fireplaces. The sitting-room is smart with light wood panelling and comfortable sofas and fresh flowers. The restaurant is a modern extension and has a cooler feel to it with exposed stone walls and french windows leading on to a pretty lawned garden. Owner Marie-Jeanne Winstone, whose flawless English belies her Belgian origins, is the cook. Her continental upbringing shows in the menu, with plenty of fish dishes and guinea-fowl Sambre et Meuse. There is also a selection of Belgian beers on offer. The bedrooms are all a good size and well maintained. Room 15 is a cosy double and Room 3 has great character as it nestles in the eaves of the house and has an oddly shaped wooden door. Although it is close to the main road one visitor said the hotel was a peaceful and homely place to stay.

All rooms have tea/coffee-making facilities unless we specify to the contrary.

◗ Closed Dec to mid-Feb; restaurant closed Tue eve 🖪 On A438, 11 miles from Brecon and 4½ miles from Hay-on-Wye. Private car park 🛏 3 twin, 4 double; family rooms available; all with bathroom/WC; hair-dryer on request ⌀ Restaurant, bar, lounge, TV room, drying-room, garden; conference facilities (max 20 people incl up to 7 residential); early suppers for children; toys, cots, high chairs ⅙ No wheelchair access ● No dogs ⌷ Access, Visa £ Single occupancy of twin/double £40 to £62, twin/double £62, family room from £62. Set L, D £25; alc L, D £29. Special breaks available

---

TINTERN Monmouthshire   map 2

Parva Farmhouse

Tintern NP6 6SQ
TEL: (01291) 689411   FAX: (01291) 689557

An up-to-date country guesthouse on the edge of the historic village of Tintern.

The oldest features of this seventeenth-century house are most obvious in the sitting-room, where there's a fine stone fireplace surrounded by dark leather chesterfields and a thick patterned carpet – a cosy place for winter evenings. Many of the bedrooms have views out over the tranquil narrow wooded valley of the Wye and the house itself looks back into Tintern and its ruined abbey. As the rooms are generally in the eaves of the house they all have an individual character and are clean, bright and fresh. Dereck and Vickie Stubbs also ensure a peaceful atmosphere in the house by having muted televisions in the bedrooms. It's Dereck who does the cooking and he has won praise from visitors in the past. The meals are wholesome and use the produce of the local area in dishes such as Welsh lamb cooked in honey and rosemary or baked fresh salmon with a light orange sauce.

◗ Open all year 🖪 On northern edge of Tintern village on A466. Private car park 🛏 3 double, 2 four-poster, 4 family rooms; all with bathroom/WC exc 2 doubles with shower/WC; TV, hair-dryer, direct-dial telephone ⌀ Restaurant, bar, lounge, drying-room, garden; conference facilities (max 18 people incl up to 9 residential); early suppers for children; baby-listening, cots, high chairs ⅙ No wheelchair access ● No dogs in restaurant ⌷ Access, Amex, Visa £ Single occupancy of twin/double £42 to £44, twin/double £60 to £64, four-poster £64 to £68, family room from £60; deposit required. Set D £17.50. Special breaks available

---

WELSH HOOK Pembrokeshire   map 4

Stone Hall

Welsh Hook, Wolf's Castle SA62 5NS
TEL: (01348) 840212   FAX: (01348) 840815

A small shuttered manor house with plain bedrooms and a reputation for its food.

Tucked away down winding country lanes, and shielded from the road by high shrubs and trees, Stone Hall is set in its own world. The six cats owned by Alan and Martine Watson give the house a lived-in feel, and it is a surprise to discover that some parts date back 600 years. The furnishings in the house have evolved and there has been no studious intention to add designer touches. The bar area is pure medieval, with big flagstones and rough wood beams. The restaurant is furnished in a similar vein – it has a huge inglenook fireplace and a fine Welsh dresser. Martine is French and the menu is bilingual, typically offering such things as Cardigan Bay scallops baked in tarragon. Breakfast is served in an airy bright room with a side table from which guests can take cereals and juice. This aspect of the house came in for severe criticism from one visitor who told us that the coffee was nasty, there was not enough milk and no brown bread, adding, 'I felt breakfast was an event to be got over rather than enjoyed.' We thought the five bedrooms were rather plain and drab, but they were a good size. More reports, please.

◑ Open all year; restaurant closed Mon eve in winter　🡒 Take A40 from Haverfordwest towards Fishguard; after 7 miles pass through village of Wolf's Castle and take first turning on left; Welsh Hook is 1 mile further. Private car park　🛏 2 single, 1 twin, 2 double; family room available; 3 with bathroom/WC, 2 with shower/WC; TV, room service, hair-dryer　✧ Restaurant, dining-room, bar, lounge, drying-room, garden; conference facilities (max 30 people incl up to 5 residential); early suppers for children; cot, high chair　&. No wheelchair access　● No dogs　⊟ Access, Amex, Diners, Visa　£ Single £46, single occupancy of twin/double £55, twin/double £65, family room £75; deposit required. Set D £16.50; alc D £19. Special breaks available

Hotels from our Visitors' Book

Here is a collection of hotels that are worth considering but which we think do not quite merit a full entry. They are marked on the maps at the back of the *Guide* with a hollow triangle. Please note that towns marked with a ◪ symbol contain one of our 'Visitors' Book' hotels as well as at least one full entry. Hotels marked with an asterisk are new to the *Guide* this year or have new owners and a new identity.

The price given for each hotel is the standard cost of a twin-bedded or double room with breakfast, and is the latest available as we go to press. Prices may go up sometime in 1997.

We would be particularly pleased to receive reports on these hotels.

LONDON

W8   **Abbey House**   11 Vicarage Gate   0171-727 2594
Good-value functional rooms in Victorian terrace near to Kensington High Street.   £58

SW1   **Alfa Hotel**   78-82 Warwick Way   0171-828 8603
Inexpensive but small rooms in busy Victorian terraced street not far from Victoria Station. Cheerful, if rather laid-back, service.   £55 to £77

WC2   **The Waldorf**   Aldwych   0171-836 2400
Large, grand hotel near to the City of London, with well-decorated rooms and helpful, amiable staff.   From £215

SW1   **Wilbraham Hotel**   Wilbraham Place   0171-730 8296
Basic rooms in an attractive Victorian building superbly located just off Sloane Square.   From £85

ENGLAND

Abberley (Hereford & Worcester)   **The Elms**   Stockton Road
(01299) 896666
Changes afoot at this grand Queen Anne manor as new broom Marcel Frichot (formerly of Knockinaam Lodge, Portpatrick) stamps his mark on the place. Reports welcome.   £110 to £135

Abbot's Salford (Warwickshire)   **Salford Hall**   (01386) 871300
Tudor manor with interesting period features, but bedrooms somewhat formulaic.   £105

Alston (Cumbria)   **Lovelady Shield**   (01434) 381203
Secluded moorland setting for this well-run country-house hotel close to the Scottish border.   £163 (rates incl dinner)

Ambleside (Cumbria)   **Three Shires Inn**   Little Langdale
(01539) 437215
*Grey slate Victorian country inn with plain but comfortable rooms and hearty
five-course evening meals.   £82 to £102*

Appleby (Cumbria)   **Appleby Manor**   Eden   (01768) 351571
*Red sandstone Victorian country house offering home cooking and a
comprehensive range of leisure activities.   £98*

Atherstone (Warwickshire)   **Chapel House**   Friars Gate
(01827) 718949
*Even the elegant furnishings in this town-centre Georgian house do not surpass
the sophistication of the food served in its popular restaurant.   £60 to £70*

Austwick (North Yorkshire)   **Traddock ***   nr Settle   (01524) 251224
*A homely, small hotel in a quiet village which would make a good base for
touring the Yorkshire Dales National Park. Bedrooms tend to be flowery and
many have extensive views.   £70*

Basingstoke (Hampshire)   **Audley's Wood Thistle Hotel**   Alton Road
(01256) 817555
*Impressive and elegant 'Gothic Renaissance' country house with grand rooms
and an airy restaurant, very close to the M3.   £96 to £124*

Bath (Bath & N.E. Somerset)   **Bath Spa Hotel**   Sydney Road
(01225) 444424
*Smart but not-too-formal luxury Forte hotel with 7 acres of peaceful grounds,
lots of leisure facilities, friendly service and a few quirky touches to add
character.   £178 to £198*

Bath (Bath & N.E. Somerset)   **Cliffe Hotel**   Crowe Hill, Limpley Stoke
(01225) 723226
*Hillside location with great valley views. Redecorated rooms in the main house
are superior to smaller annexe rooms.   £77 to £97*

Bath (Bath & N.E. Somerset)   **Leighton House**   139 Wells Rd
(01225) 314769
*Comfortable, well-kept B&B in large, late-Victorian house on main road
rising above city centre. Good-sized rooms and friendly hosts.   £62 to £68*

Belford (Northumberland)   **Blue Bell**   Market Place   (01668) 213543
*Old coaching-inn in a quiet village with friendly staff and convivial
atmosphere but rather uninspiring public areas and over-ambitious cooking.
£80 to £92*

Bellingham (Northumberland)   **Westfield House**   nr Hexham
(01434) 220340
*This homely Victorian house overlooks the village of Bellingham and has
pretty rooms with brass or four-poster beds and pine furniture.   £36 to £50*

Berkswell (Warwickshire)   **Nailcote Hall**   Nailcote Lane
(01203) 466174
*Country-house hotel with a handsome Tudor core and extensive conference and
leisure facilities that include a nine-hole golf course and lavish 'Roman-bath-
style' swimming-pool.   £120*

Berwick-upon-Tweed (Northumberland)   **The Old Vicarage**   Church Rd
(01289) 306909
*A well-kept guesthouse in a quiet suburb of Berwick, with lots of stripped pine,
stencilling effects and muted colour schemes.   £28 to £48*

Biggin by Hulland (Derbyshire)   **Biggin Mill House**   nr Ashbourne
(01335) 370414
*Home-made food and accommodation in just two fetching bedrooms amidst
lovely, wooded gardens, hidden away deep in the Derbyshire dales.   £75*

Bishop's Tawton (Devon)   **Downrew House**   Bishop's Tawton
(01271) 42497
*Rambling, partially seventeenth-century country-house hotel with big
swimming-pool and five-hole golf course. Remote rural setting.   £69 to £81*

Blackpool (Lancashire)   **Sunray Hotel**   42 Knowle Avenue
(01253) 351937
*Friendly and traditional seaside guesthouse on a side road close to the seafront,
beyond the north pier. Thoughtful touches.   £52*

Blandford Forum (Dorset)   **La Belle Alliance**   White Cliffe Mill St
(01258) 452842
*Pleasant rooms above an excellent restaurant near the centre of town.   £62
to £66*

Bodinnick (Cornwall)   **Old Ferry Inn**   (01726) 870237
*Pub/ hotel close to the ferry with splendid views of the Fowey estuary and one
big family room. Extensive pub food menu and additional, more formal,
restaurant with meals.   £40 to £70*

Bonchurch (Isle of Wight)   **Lake Hotel**   Shore Road   (01983) 852613
*Simple rooms in a nineteenth-century house nestling at the foot of the
undercliff.   £46*

Bracknell (Berkshire)   **Coppid Beech Hotel**   John Nike Way
(01344) 303333
Large, bustling business hotel close to the M4.   £73 to £140

Branscombe (Devon)   **Masons Arms**   (01297) 680300
*Atmospheric pub/ hotel with good food. The converted thatched cottages
opposite have quieter rooms.   £54 to £74*

Broadway (Hereford &Worcester)   **Leasow House**   Laverton Meadows
(01386) 584526
*Imaginatively restored seventeenth-century farmhouse in peaceful location
with thoughtful owners. Furnishings in some of the rooms are incongruously
modern.   £52 to £60*

Brockenhurst (Hampshire)   **Whitley Ridge**   Beaulieu Road
(01590) 622354
*A fine Georgian country house under family management in the heart of the
New Forest. Rolling grounds, but rather unexceptional rooms.   £82 to £96*

Bryher (Isles of Scilly)   **Hell Bay Hotel**   (01720) 422947
*Low-rise, cottagey and comfortable base on an unspoilt island.   £106 to
£148 (rates incl dinner)*

Buxton (Derbyshire)   **Coningsby Guesthouse**   6 Macclesfield Rd
(01298) 26735
*Three unfussy but good-quality bedrooms in a no-smoking Victorian house
close to town centre. Dinners available.   £45 to £50*

Cambridge (Cambridgeshire)   **Regent Hotel**   41 Regent Street
(01223) 351470
*Friendly staff in this well-located, business-oriented hotel, although the rooms
are on the small side.   £80*

Canterbury (Kent)   **County Hotel** *   High Street   (01227) 766266
*Conveniently located city-centre hotel with good restaurant and comfortable
though conventional rooms.   From £84*

Canterbury (Kent)   **Thanington Hotel**   140 Wincheap
(01227) 453227
*Grade II-listed Georgian town house with comfortable rooms, indoor
swimming-pool and games room. Very convenient for city centre.   £63 to
£65*

Cawston (Norfolk)   **Grey Gables**   Norwich Road   (01603) 871259
*Peacefully located restaurant-with-rooms offering extensive wine list and
simple accommodation.   £54 to £60*

Chale (Isle of Wight)   **Clarendon Hotel & Wight Mouse Inn**
(01983) 730431
*Comfortable bedrooms at a bustling pub – noise disturbance is likely until
closing time.   £70*

Chartham Hatch (Kent)   **Howfield Manor**   (01227) 738294
*Manor-house-style hotel with comfortable but unremarkable rooms, close to
Canterbury.   £87.50*

Cheltenham (Gloucestershire)   **Abbey Hotel**   16 Bath Parade
(01242) 516053
*Welcoming and friendly proprietors at this town house with simple bedrooms,
conveniently located for the city centre.   £50 to £55*

Claverdon (Warwickshire)   **Ardencote Manor**   Lye Green Road
(01926) 843111
*Hotel and country club incorporating a much-extended Victorian manor, 40
acres of parkland and impressive leisure facilities.   £135*

Clawton (Devon)   **Court Barn**   (01409) 271219
*Pleasant, largely Victorian, country-house hotel in park-like grounds, with
elegant but cluttered rooms.   £58 to £78*

Copthorne (West Sussex)   **Copthorne Hotel**   (01342) 714971
*Surprisingly pleasant hotel which combines old beams with modern brickwork.
Good facilities, excellent restaurants, lovely gardens and perfectly situated for
Gatwick.   From £95*

Crantock (Cornwall)   **Crantock Bay Hotel**   (01637) 830229
*Family-run hotel on headland with wonderful views. Excellent swimming-pool
amongst other leisure facilities.   £77 to £82*

Crathorne (North Yorkshire)   **Crathorne Hall**   nr Yarm
(01642) 700398
*The last great Edwardian house built in England is now an up-market
country-house hotel run by the Virgin group. The staff are friendly and
professional but the sheer scale of the place can make it seem impersonal.*
£145

Croyde (Devon)   **Croyde Bay House**   Moore Lane   (01271) 890270
*Relaxing family-holiday hotel overlooking beautiful Croyde Bay, with views
of distant Lundy Island.*   £62 to £78

Crudwell (Wiltshire)   **Mayfield House**   (01666) 577409
*Friendly and relaxing hotel with good-value breaks and pleasant walled
gardens. Ask for a newly redecorated bedroom.*   £62

Cullompton (Devon)   **Manor House**   2–4 Fore St   (01884) 32281
*Striking half-timbered town-centre hotel with restaurant and bar meals,
midway between Exeter and Taunton.*   £54

Dartmouth (Devon)   **Royal Castle**   The Quay   (01803) 833033
*Interesting 300-year-old hotel overlooking harbour, with restaurant and well-
furnished rooms. Favourable reports of service received recently.*   £89

Donnington (Berkshire)   **Donnington Valley Hotel**   Old Oxford Road
(01635) 551199
Large, modern golfing hotel with good-sized, well-equipped rooms.   £90 to
£103

Dorking (Surrey)   **Burford Bridge**   Box Hill   (01306) 884561
*A good-quality Forte hotel, parts of which date back to the sixteenth century,
with business-class bedrooms and pretty gardens set under beautiful Box Hill.*
£84 to £109

Drewsteignton (Devon)   **Hunts Tor**   (01647) 281228
*Small, partially seventeenth-century hotel with pleasing décor just off village
square; advance notice required for popular no-choice dinners.*   £60 to £70

Dunster (Somerset)   **Exmoor House Hotel**   12 West Street
(01643) 821268
*Cosy, small hotel with modern, feminine bedrooms created out of much older
building; conveniently positioned for Dunster Castle and forays to Minehead.*
£55

Durham (Co Durham)   **Three Tuns Hotel**   New Elvet
0191-386 4326
*Open-plan bars and a panelled dining-room in an old coaching-inn near the
centre of town. Part of the Swallow group.*   £109

Elterwater (Cumbria)   **Britannia Inn**   (01539) 437210
*Traditional whitewashed inn with oak-beamed bar and restaurant, and simple,
cottage-style rooms.*   £46 to £60

Exeter (Devon)   **St Olaves Court Hotel**   Mary Arches St
(01392) 217736
*Highly rated restaurant and convenient city-centre location, but drab rooms
don't live up to expectations and lounge sometimes requisitioned for outside
parties.*   £60 to £80

Fareham (Hampshire)   **Solent Hotel**   Rookery Avenue
(01489) 880000
Surprisingly characterful public rooms and well-equipped bedrooms in a new, business-oriented hotel with excellent leisure facilities.   £108 to £120

Gamlingay (Bedfordshire)   **The Emplins**   Church Street
(01767) 650581
Family home that happens to be a fifteenth-century house – bags of character and very friendly hosts.   £50

Gittisham (Devon)   **Combe House Hotel**   nr Honiton
(01404) 42756/43560/41938
Slightly faded but otherwise splendid Elizabethan mansion in extensive grounds; optional riding and fishing.   £100 to £131

Great Hucklow (Derbyshire)   **Hucklow Hall**   Lye Green Road
(01298) 871175
Good food and friendly hosts in this 300-year-old stone farmhouse with beautiful gardens, surrounded by stunning scenery.   £39 to £48

Great Langdale (Cumbria)   **New Dungeon Ghyll**   (01539) 437213
Stunning views and an excellent location for walkers based at this Lakeland stone guesthouse.   £59

Greenham (Somerset)   **Greenham Hall**   nr Wellington
(01823) 672603
Nineteenth-century castle with grand exterior, pleasant views and spacious rooms offering B&B. Rather old-fashioned furnishings.   £35

Hardwicke (Hereford & Worcester)   **The Haven**   (01497) 831254
Friendly hosts offer a warm welcome and civilised accommodation in a bookish, old-fashioned house close to the bibliophile's Mecca of Hay-on-Wye.   £44 to £53

Headlam (Co Durham)   **Headlam Hall**   nr Gainford   (01325) 730238
This grand Jacobean manor house is often used for weddings at weekends, something solitary travellers or couples may find intrusive. There are some unusual dining areas, like the glass-topped Edwardian room.   £70 to £95

Henley-on-Thames (Oxfordshire)   **Hernes**   (01491) 573245
Beautifully furnished ancestral home with just three guest rooms and impressive grounds.   £60 to £75

Herstmonceux (East Sussex)   **Cleaver's Lyng**   Church Road
(01323) 833131
A pretty sixteenth-century red-brick cottage with modern extension. Beautiful views and a peaceful setting off the beaten track.   £45

Holford (Somerset)   **Combe House Hotel**   (01278) 741382
Beguiling hotel on edge of the Quantocks created out of seventeenth-century tannery, with intact waterwheel. The indoor heated swimming-pool can't quite make interior live up to promise of exterior.   £75

Holne (Devon)   **Church House Inn**   (01364) 631208
Pretty village pub/hotel dating back to fourteenth century, with an unusual half-timbered porch but less interesting bedrooms. B&B only.   £39 to £50

Hopton Wafers (Shropshire) **Crown at Hopton** (01299) 270372
Traditional inn with cosy rustic bar and restaurant. Some niggles over the plumbing and friendly but patchy service. More reports, please. £68

Horley (Surrey) **Vulcan Lodge** 27 Massetts Road (01293) 771522
Good-value, friendly and chintzy B&B close to Gatwick Airport. £42

Hunmanby (North Yorkshire) **Wrangham House Hotel** Stonegate (01723) 891333
Restful former vicarage with low-key public areas and quiet, unostentatious bedrooms. £69

Kington (Hereford & Worcester) **Penrhos Court *** (01544) 230720
Striking combination of medieval and Elizabethan character, glitzy modern bedrooms and seriously accomplished food. £70 to £90

Kirkbymoorside (North Yorkshire) **The Lion Inn *** (01751) 417320
Ancient, rustic pub in a gloriously isolated moorland setting. Comfortable rooms but solid, rather unimaginative pub grub. £33 to £59

Knowstone (Devon) **Masons Arms** (01398) 341231/341582
Picture-postcard thatched pub/hotel in tiny village; good food but not one for early-nighters. £55

Land's End (Cornwall) **Land's End Hotel *** (01736) 871844
One to avoid on principle if you abhor mass tourism. But if you're after a stylish, modern place within easy reach of plentiful children's entertainment, where you can appreciate the setting when crowds are gone, then this should fit the bill surprisingly well. £79 to £144

Leamington Spa (Warwickshire) **Flowerdale House** 58 Warwick New Rd (01926) 426002
Inexpensive old-fashioned B&B in a Victorian house on the edge of town. £40

Leicester (Leicestershire) **Spindle Lodge** 2 West Walk 0116-233 8801
A Victorian guesthouse with simple bedrooms (some with en-suite facilities) in a peaceful part of the city near Leicester University. £49 to £62

Leusdon (Devon) **Leusdon Lodge** (01364) 631304/631573
Small country-house hotel overlooking the Dart Valley in Dartmoor National Park; ideal for golf and fishing holidays. £60 to £88

Lew (Oxfordshire) **Farmhouse Hotel** University Farm (01993) 850297
Historic farmhouse with light, modern furnishings and lovely gardens, part of working dairy farm. £55

Lichfield (Staffordshire) **Swinfen Hall Hotel** Swinfen (01543) 481494
Fine eighteenth-century manor-house hotel with memorably ornate public rooms but less noteworthy bedrooms. £85

Linton (West Yorkshire) **Wood Hall** Trip Lane (01937) 587271
Country-house hotel on a grand scale with sweeping staircases, oak panelling and lovely wood carvings. Top-notch leisure facilities mostly free to hotel guests and over a mile of fishing rights on the River Wharfe. £109 to £155

Longframlington (Northumberland)   **Embleton Hall**   Longframlington
(01665) 570249
*Unpretentious country-house hotel with an elegant dining-room, spacious,
restful bedrooms and cheerful staff.   £70*

Long Melford (Suffolk)   **The Bull**   Hall Street   (01787) 378494
*Splendid old chain-hotel with suitably antique public rooms but rather bland,
standard bedrooms.   From £100*

Lower Slaughter (Gloucestershire)   **Washbourne Court**
(01451) 822143
*Recently approved expansion plans should provide this pleasant country-
house-style-hotel, in a prime site in this picture-postcard village, with much-
needed public areas to complement its smart bedrooms.   £88 to £98*

Lowick (Cumbria)   **Lowick House**   (01229) 885227
*Elegant family house in landscaped grounds offering Wolsey Lodge
accommodation.   £66*

Lydford (Devon)   **Moor View House**   Vale Down   (01822) 820220
*Pleasant, small Victorian house on the western fringes of Dartmoor, offering
traditional English cooking.   £55*

Lynton (Devon)   **Combe Park Hotel**   Hillsford Bridges
(01598) 752356
*Small country-house hotel in National Trust grounds, with Hoar Oak Water
running past. Traditional English table d'hôte menu for single-sitting dinners.
£68*

Lynton (Devon)   **Woodlands Hotel ***   Lynbridge Rd
(01598) 752324
*Spectacularly sited small hotel overlooking the Lyn Valley. It boasts seven
comfortable rooms and many souvenirs of proprietors' Far Eastern travels, also
reflected in some dinner menus.   £32 to £39*

Macclesfield (Cheshire)   **Chadwick House**   55 Beech Lane
(01625) 615558
Neat and attractive town-centre hotel with welcoming hosts.   £44 to £55

Middleham (North Yorkshire)   **Castle Keep ***   Castle Hill
(01969) 623665
*Two pretty Victorian-style bedrooms above a busy teashop in a seventeenth-
century Grade II-listed building. Cheerful proprietor.   £42 to £46*

Much Wenlock (Shropshire)   **Raven Hotel**   (01952) 727251
*Old coaching-inn with smart bedrooms and attractive restaurant. The lounge
and bar lack the same degree of style.   £85*

Newcastle upon Tyne (Tyne & Wear)   **Vermont Hotel**   Castle Garth
0191-233 1010
*Ex-council building close to the Tyne Bridge and castle, now housing luxury
hotel with an impressive dining-room and well-equipped bedrooms.   £89 to
£142*

Newlyn (Cornwall)   **Higher Faughan**   (01736) 62076 (number to be
prefixed by 3 from Jan 1997)
*Comfortable Edwardian hotel in 10 acres of grounds, with heated outdoor
swimming-pool, tennis court and inviting bedrooms.   £76 to £98*

Norwich (Norfolk)   **Maids Head Hotel**   Tombland   (01603) 209955
*The bar and restaurant, and bedrooms in the old wing have the most character
in this city-centre hotel.   £82 to £108*

Over Haddon (Derbyshire)   **Lathkil ***   (01629) 812501
*Splendid views from this courteously run, few-frills pub overlooking Lathkil
Dale. Only four bedrooms, smart and well-equipped but small.   £70*

Painswick (Gloucestershire)   **Painswick Hotel**   Kemps Lane
(01452) 812160
*Restrained Palladian mansion whose grand but austere public rooms run to a
private chapel. Superior rooms are worth the supplement they command.
£98 to £130*

Pluckley (Kent)   **Elvey Farm Country Hotel**   nr Ashford
(01233) 840442
*Comfortable rooms in rose-clad converted stable and oast house on working
farm in beautiful setting. Breakfast served in converted barn filled with
farming antiques. Friendly and welcoming hosts.   £50 to £56*

Porlock Weir (Somerset)   **Anchor Hotel and Ship Inn**
(01643) 862753
*Fifteenth-century oak beams alongside nineteenth-century elegance in a
marvellous harbourside location.   £74 to £100*

Port Isaac (Cornwall)   **Port Gaverne Hotel**   (01208) 880244
*Pretty seventeenth-century pub/ hotel dominating Port Gaverne Bay. A
variety of rooms, some in eighteenth-century cottages across the road.   £94*

Powerstock (Dorset)   **Three Horseshoes Inn**   (01308) 485328
*A good range of imaginative food at this traditional Victorian village inn.
Simple, old-fashioned bedrooms.   £60*

Reading (Berkshire)   **Holiday Inn**   Caversham Bridge   (01189) 259988
*This modern business hotel with an indoor swimming-pool and large public
rooms is right on the river.   £62 to £125*

Rickling Green (Essex)   **Cricketers' Arms ***   (01799) 543210
*A pleasant pub with welcoming service. Modern bedrooms have lots of facilities
but are a little bland.   £60*

Ripon (North Yorkshire)   **The Old Deanery ***   Minster Road
(01765) 603518
*Restaurant-with-rooms located directly opposite the cathedral, where the first-
class cooking (and dreamy desserts) are more likely to stay in the memory than
the two plain, spacious bedrooms.   £130 (rates incl dinner)*

Rochford (Essex)   **Hotel Renouf**   Bradley Way   (01702) 541334
*Business hotel with character and restaurant specialising in duck.   £68 to
£78*

Ross-on-Wye (Hereford & Worcester)   **Chase Hotel**   (01989) 763161
*Elegant country house with friendly staff on the outskirts of Ross-on-Wye, let
down on our inspection by patchy service and poor room maintenance.   £80*

Rotherwick (Hampshire)   **Tylney Hall**   nr Hook   (01256) 764881
*A vast and stately red-brick manor house with grand spacious public rooms, 66
acres of parkland, enormous bedrooms and modern leisure facilities. Luxury at
a price.   £124*

Rowsley (Derbyshire)   **Peacock Hotel**   (01629) 733518
Jacobean hotel-cum-inn with plenty of antiques and a high level of comfort.
However, it is part of a chain and is located on a main road.   £99

Rye (East Sussex)   **Mermaid Inn**   Mermaid Street   (01797) 223065
An ancient, wistaria-clad smugglers' inn with authentic medieval atmosphere.
£112 to £128

St Ives (Cornwall)   **Garrack Hotel**   Burthallan Lane   (01736) 796199
Small hotel with fine swimming-pool in quiet position overlooking the sea.
Convenient for the Tate Gallery.   £102

St Keyne (Cornwall)   **The Old Rectory**   Duloe Rd   (01579) 342617
Graceful early-nineteenth-century house in pretty gardens with country views,
undergoing refurbishment by new owners. More reports, please.   £50 to £70

St Mawes (Cornwall)   **Hotel Tresanton**   27 Lower Castle Rd
(01326) 270544
Pretty white and blue hotel straggling up hillside, with fine estuary views.
Reports welcome.   £60 to £100

St Mawes (Cornwall)   **Rising Sun**   (01326) 270233
Just yards from St Mawes harbour, this pub/ hotel was undergoing complete
refurbishment at time of writing. Reports, please, on new arrangements.
£59

Salcombe (Devon)   **Marine Hotel**   Cliff Rd   (01548) 844444
Large hotel with equally generous-sized indoor swimming-pool and fine views
over the Salcombe estuary.   £162

Salisbury (Wiltshire)   **The Old Mill**   Town Path, West Harham
(01722) 327517
Converted paper mill in peaceful riverside location, across the meadows from
city centre. Comfortable pub bedrooms, reached via a steep staircase, with river
views.   £65

Sawbridgeworth (Hertfordshire)   **Manor of Groves**   High Wych
(01279) 600777
Georgian house with good sport and leisure facilities in beautiful grounds.
From £112

Scole (Norfolk)   **Scole Inn**   Ipswich Road   (01379) 740481
Attractive, historic building – select a bedroom in the main part of the hotel.
£66

Sherborne (Dorset)   **Almshouse Farm**   Heritage   (01963) 210296
Friendly, relaxing B&B far from the madding crowd in working dairy farm,
once a sixteenth-century monastery.   £38

Shipton-under-Wychwood (Oxfordshire)   **Shaven Crown**   High Street
(01993) 830330
Fourteenth-century hospice with characterful public bar and basic, old-
fashioned rooms.   £75

Slinfold (West Sussex)   **Random Hall**   Stane Street   (01403) 790558
A wistaria-covered sixteenth-century farmhouse with a large, modern
extension at the rear. Public areas have authentic feel thanks to dark beams,
stone floors and nooks and crannies, but bedrooms lack character in spite of
exposed timbers.   £68

Sourton (Devon)   **Collaven Manor Hotel**   nr Okehampton
(01837) 861522
This small, creeper-covered, fifteenth-century stone manor house offers B&B only but possesses quaintly beamed bedrooms.   £45

Southwold (Suffolk)   **Westbury House ***   5 South Green
(01502) 725117
B&B crammed with Victoriana by very friendly owners. Bedrooms are small – go for those on the second floor, which have separate bathrooms.   £45

Stoke-on-Trent (Staffordshire)   **Haydon House**   Haydon Street
(01782) 711311
A decent family-run hotel occupying a peaceful terrace of Victorian buildings. Atmospheric public areas and good-quality executive bedrooms, but dowdy standard bedrooms.   £65

Stourbridge (West Midlands)   **Talbot Hotel**   High Street
(01384) 394350
Appealing and substantial old coaching-inn in the town centre. Popular with locals.   From £56

Stow-on-the-Wold (Gloucestershire)   **Wyck Hill House**
(01451) 831936
Eighteenth-century manor house a short drive from the village. Spacious bedrooms, but slightly formal atmosphere.   £105

Studland (Dorset)   **The Knoll House**   (01929) 450251
Child-friendly country-house hotel with extensive leisure facilities, just above a National Trust beach.   £146 (rates incl dinner)

Sutton (Cheshire)   **Sutton Hall**   Bullocks Lane   (01260) 253211
Friendly and historic old inn in a secluded spot.   £85 to £90

Tewkesbury (Gloucestershire)   **Puckrup Hall**   Puckrup
(01684) 296200
Regency house, expanded to contain glamorous leisure facilities. Big in the corporate-entertainment market.   £124

Thame (Oxfordshire)   **Thatchers Inn**   29–30 Lower High Street
(01844) 212146
Thatched Elizabethan building in the centre of a busy market town. Mix of ancient and modern bedrooms – those in the main building have more character.   £70 to £80

Thornton-Cleveleys (Lancashire)   **Victorian House**   Trunnah Road
(01253) 860619
Two large, characterful rooms in a Victorian house where the main business is food – in either the bright bistro or the more traditional French-influenced restaurant.   £50

Thundridge (Hertfordshire)   **Hanbury Manor**   (01920) 487722
Excellent leisure facilities in this lovely Jacobean-style mansion with rather grand, well-equipped rooms.   £214 to £224

Tintagel (Cornwall)   **Old Millfloor**   Trebarwith Strand
(01840) 770234
Simple B&B accommodation in converted mill by stream in exquisite setting. Just ten minutes' walk to fine beach. No en-suite facilities.   £36

Torquay (Devon)　**Orestone Manor Hotel**　Rockhouse Lane
(01803) 328098
*Comfortable, welcoming country-house hotel on outskirts of town, with lovely
garden and fine sea views. A variety of bedrooms but rather old-fashioned
décor.*　£120 to £170 (rates incl dinner)

Totnes (Devon)　**Old Forge**　Seymour Place　(01803) 862174
*Six-hundred-year-old smithy with original prison cell, now serving up
excellent bed and breakfast. The lavishly decorated rooms are very
comfortable, but may be too fussy for some tastes.*　£52 to £64

Tring (Hertfordshire)　**Pendley Manor**　Cow Lane　(01442) 891891
*Much-extended Victorian manor house in large grounds with well-equipped
rooms.*　£98 to £120

Tring (Hertfordshire)　**Rose and Crown**　High Street　(01442) 824071
*Tudor-style country house with relaxed atmosphere and plain but well-
equipped rooms.*　£60 to £79

Trispen (Cornwall)　**Laniley House**　Newquay Rd　(01872) 75201
*B&B in a large, unconventional Victorian house, with only three bedrooms,
on outskirts of Truro.*　£32 to £36

Tuckenhay (Devon)　**Maltster's Arms ***　(01803) 732350
*Beautifully situated pub/hotel backing on to Bow Creek in small village.
Three bedrooms, whose furnishings are astonishingly over the top for the
location. Recently taken over by new management. Reports please.*　£70 to
£90

Tunbridge Wells (Kent)　**Spa Hotel**　Mount Ephraim　(01892) 520331
*Built in 1776 as a country mansion, this grand building now houses a privately
owned hotel with excellent leisure facilities. Rooms are comfortable but rather
characterless.*　From £97

Uppingham (Leicestershire)　**Rutland House**　61 High Street
(01572) 822497
*B&B with ample, well-equipped bedrooms in a Victorian town house at the
end of the high street.*　£39

Walkington (East Riding of Yorkshire)　**Manor House**　Northlands
(01482) 881645
*A late nineteenth-century manor house in 3 acres of peaceful grounds. In
summer the conservatory, with its view over the terrace and lawns, is the stage
for the ex-Dorchester chef's culinary creations.*　From £89

Warkworth (Northumberland)　**Warkworth House Hotel**　16 Bridge St
(01665) 711276
*Cheerful, informal service and a friendly lounge bar are the plusses, over-loud
piped background music and unimaginative décor the minuses. Dinner comes
somewhere in the middle.*　£75

Westerham (Kent)　**King's Arms Hotel**　(01959) 562990
*Georgian coaching-inn set on a busy main road in the centre of a lively market
town. The good-sized rooms are named after historical figures – one of the best
is the Henry VIII room with its impressive four-poster bed.*　From £90

Willersey (Hereford & Worcester)   **The Old Rectory**   Church Street
(01386) 853729
*In a picturesque setting with lovely gardens, this charming B&B continues to
benefit from further renovations.   £60 to £95*

Wilmington (Kent)   **Rowhill Grange Country House Hotel** *
(01322) 615136
*A comfortable hotel with really excellent leisure facilities – all very new.
Reports welcome.   From £115*

Windermere (Cumbria)   **Beaumont Hotel**   Holly Road
(01539) 447075
*Good-value B&B hotel on a quiet side street in the centre of the town. Fresh
and homely bedrooms.   £52 to £56*

Windermere (Cumbria)   **Hawksmoor Guesthouse**   Lake Road
(01539) 442110
*Small hotel on the main road between Bowness and Windermere, offering
modest-sized but comfortable rooms, traditional English food and a friendly
atmosphere.   £48 to £53*

Windsor (Berkshire)   **Sir Christopher Wren's House**   Thames St
(01753) 861354
*Smart, elegantly furnished, Georgian house overlooking the river in busy
tourist town. Premier bedrooms are more lavish and worth the extra.   £79 to
£137*

Woburn (Bedfordshire)   **Bell Inn**   34/35 Bedford Street
(01525) 290280
*Red-brick town house with smart frontage, less than a mile from Woburn
Abbey. Bedrooms are plain but comfortably furnished and have well-equipped
bathrooms.   £69*

Woodstock (Oxfordshire)   **The Laurels**   Hensington Road
(01993) 812583
*Immaculate B&B in Victorian house near the centre of busy tourist town,
with pretty rooms and easy-going hosts.   £46*

Woodstock (Oxfordshire)   **Star Inn**   22 Market Place   (01993) 811373
*Seventeenth-century town house on the main street at the centre of tourist
bustle, with plain, old-fashioned rooms.   £50*

Woody Bay (Devon)   **Woody Bay Hotel**   (01598) 763264
*Secluded Victorian hotel a steep hike above Woody Bay itself, offering special
interest breaks for ornithologists, painters and photographers among others.
£50 to £66*

York (North Yorkshire)   **Grange Hotel**   Clifton   (01904) 644744
*Country-house living in a Regency town house just outside the old city walls.
Atmospheric vaulted cellar brasserie or the more formal Ivy Restaurant are the
choices for dinner.   £105 to £135*

Zeals (Wiltshire)   **Stag Cottage**   Fantley Lane   (01747) 840458
*Three spruce, thatched cottages combined into cosy, crafts-oriented tearooms
with very friendly hosts. Pretty bedrooms with low-ceilings, not all en suite.
£30 to £36*

SCOTLAND

Aberdeen (Aberdeen) **The Marcliffe at Pitfodels** North Deeside Road
(01224) 861000
*Swanky city hotel combining country-house ambience with business-style
accommodation.* £95 to £125

Appin (Highland) **Stewart Hotel** Glen Duror (01631) 740268
*Bedrooms in a motel-like extension to a nineteenth-century hunting lodge with
peaceful gardens.* £87

Ardvasar (Highland) **Ardvasar Hotel** Sleat, Isle of Skye
(01471) 844223
*Unpretentious eighteenth-century coaching-inn with comfortable rooms and
good views. Reports commend the cooking.* £65 to £70

Ballater (Aberdeenshire) **Darroch Learg** Braemar Road
(01339) 755443
*Good-value old-fashioned country hotel – the best rooms are in the older part
of the house.* £85 to £100

Banchory (Aberdeenshire) **Banchory Lodge** (01330) 822625
Traditional, waterfront hotel popular with fishermen. £110 to £130

Beattock (Dumfries & Galloway) **Auchen Castle** (01683) 300407
*Grand Victorian house with attractive grounds. Rooms in the main house are
preferable.* £78 to £86

Dunkeld (Perthshire & Kinross) **Stakis Dunkeld House**
(01350) 727771
Business-style, riverside chain hotel with comfortable rooms. £112

Edinburgh (Edinburgh) **Malmaison** 1 Tower Place, Leith
0131-555 6868
Excellent waterfront position for this stylish modern hotel. £95

Elgin (Moray) **Mansion House** The Haugh (01343) 548811
Country-house style hotel with up-market leisure facilities. £120 to £150

Fort William (Highland) **Ashburn House** Achintore Road
(01397) 706000
A good-value, homely B&B on the A82 south of Fort William. £60 to
£70

Fort William (Highland) **Factor's House** (01397) 702177
*Good previous reports of this hotel, sister to the grander Inverlochy Castle.
Under refurbishment at time of inspection.* £120

Galashiels (Borders) **Woodlands Country House** Windyknowe Rd
(01896) 754722
A fine baronial-style house with comfortable rooms. £68 to £74

Girvan (South Ayrshire) **Glen Tachur Hotel** Barrhill
(01465) 821223
*Friendly owners and simple rooms at this pleasant, small hotel with decent
food. Handy for golf on the Ayrshire coast.* £64

Glamis (Angus) **Castleton House** by Forfar (01307) 840340
Good food at this small country-house-type hotel. £100

Glasgow (Glasgow)   **The Devonshire**   5 Devonshire Gardens
0141-339 7878
Smart, bright West-End hotel, a neighbour of One Devonshire Gardens (see entry).   £150

Glasgow (Glasgow)   **Glasgow Hilton**   1 William Street
0141-204 5555
Business hotel with stylish themed bars and restaurants.   £130 to £155

Glasgow (Glasgow)   **Stakis City Hotel** *   Hill Street   0141- 333 1515
Straightforward, business-style hotel with efficient service and good breakfasts.
£68

Isle of Arran (North Ayrshire)   **Auchrannie Country House**   Brodick
(01770) 302234
Peaceful location for this friendly, modernised country hotel.   £84 to £105

Isle of Colonsay (Argyll & Bute)   **The Hotel**   (01951) 200316
Isolated nineteenth-century inn offering a friendly welcome and good food.
£118

Kilchrenan (Argyll & Bute)   **Ardanaiseig Hotel**   by Taynuilt
(01866) 833333
Lovely gardens and loch views at this quiet country house.   £96 to £160

Kinclaven (Perthshire)   **Ballathie House**   (01250) 883268
Peaceful Tayside location, popular with anglers.   £150 to £200

Kingussie (Highland)   **Homewood Lodge Guest House**   Newtonmore Rd
(01540) 661507
Under new owners but offering the same good-value home-cooking and accommodation. Reports welcome.   £34

Lochcarnan (Western Isles)   **Orasay Inn**   South Uist   (01870) 610298
Comfortable rooms in an area popular with birdwatchers. Friendly hosts in a close-knit community.   £58

Melrose (Borders)   **Burt's Hotel**   Market Square   (01896) 822285
Good bar food at this traditional town-centre hotel with friendly staff.   £78

Oban (Argyll & Bute)   **Knipoch Hotel**   Knipoch   (01852) 316251
Convivial hotel with rather plain bedrooms, overlooking Loch Feochan.
£138

Port Appin (Argyll & Bute)   **Pierhouse Hotel** *   (01631) 730302
Friendly seafood restaurant with rooms, handy for the Lismore ferry.   £79

Salen (Argyll & Bute)   **Glenforsa Hotel**   Salen by Aros, Isle of Mull
(01680) 300377
Pine-built, chalet-style hotel with approachable owners and popular with light-aeroplane enthusiasts. Rooms are plain but cosy.   £73

Stirling (Stirling)   **Heritage Hotel**   16 Allan Park   (01786) 473660
Restaurant-with-rooms with good traditional food and interesting public rooms.   £70

Stirling (Stirling)   **Stirling Highland Hotel**   Spittal Street
(01786) 475444
Business-oriented hotel near the castle. Rooms are well equipped but bland.
£118

Stornoway (Western Isles)   **Ardlonan**   Francis Street
(01851) 703482
Cosy and comfortable B&B conveniently located for ferries.   £38

Strathyre (Stirling)   **Creagan House**   (01877) 384638
Good reports on the food and hospitality at this family-run restaurant-with-rooms.   £65

Tain (Highland)   **Morangie House**   Morangie Road   (01862) 892281
Extended Edwardian house with comfortable rooms and pleasant restaurant.
£65 to £70

Talladale (Highland)   **Loch Maree Hotel**   by Achnasheen
(01445) 760288
Smart bedrooms at this friendly hotel on shores of the loch.   £80

Torridon (Highland)   **Loch Torridon Hotel**   by Achnasheen
(01445) 791242
Large, baronial-style country-house hotel – a good base for exploring the remote Applecross peninsula.   £100 to £220

Troon (South Ayrshire)   **Highgrove House ***   Old Loans Road
(01292) 312511
Edwardian hotel on hill with good views west and smart, comfortable rooms.
Reports regarding food are good.   £80

Walkerburn (Borders)   **Tweed Valley Hotel**   (01896) 870636
Unpretentious country hotel, popular with anglers.   £74 to £94

Wick (Highland)   **Bilbster House**   (01955) 621212
Good-value B&B with theatrical overtones and a homely style.   £28 to £30

WALES

Bontddu (Caernarfonshire & Merionethshire)   **Bontddu Hall**
(01341) 430661
Attractive Victorian mansion in its own grounds with superb views of the Mawddach estuary.   £80 to £150

Cardiff (Cardiff)   **Jury's ***   Mary Ann Street   (01222) 341441
Modern, functional hotel close to the conference centre.   £59 to £104

Llandudno (Aberconwy & Colwyn)   **Belmont Hotel**   21 North Parade
(01492) 877770
Neat small hotel with views of the promenade and completely adapted for blind and visually impaired guests.   Weekly bookings only, £75 to £205 full board

Nantgaredig (Carmarthenshire)   **Cwmtwrch Hotel ***   (01267) 290238
Converted Georgian farmhouse and outbuildings adjoining the family-run restaurant. Facilities include a swimming-pool, gym and par-three golf course.
£50

Newport (Pembrokeshire)   **Celtic Manor Hotel**   Coldra Woods
(01633) 413000
A business hotel whose Victorian origins give it a touch of style.   £80 to
£118

Pontyclun (Rhondda Cynon Taff)   **Miskin Manor ***   (01443) 224204
*Large, stone-walled manor dating back to 1092 set amid picturesque scenery,
with good leisure facilities. A few antique pieces in the bedrooms amidst much
standard hotel furniture.*   £100 to £120

Pumpsaint (Carmarthenshire)   **Glanrannell Park**   (01558) 685230
Large Victorian house set in woods and overlooking a small lake.   £64

Rossett (Wrexham)   **Llyndir Hall**   Llyndir Lane   (01244) 571648
A comfortable business hotel with some style, close to Chester.   £110

Swansea (Swansea)   **Windsor Lodge Hotel**   Mount Pleasant
(01792) 642158
*A fine Georgian building with comfortable en-suite rooms close to the city
centre.*   £50 to £56

Talyllyn (Caernarfonshire & Merionethshire)   **Tynycornel Hotel**
Tywyn   (01654) 782282
*A modern, low-rise building on the edge of a stunning Snowdonian lake. All
the bedrooms have been recently refurbished.*   £93

Trecastle (Powys)   **Castle Coaching Inn**   (01874) 636354
Simple rooms in a friendly village inn. Handy for the Brecon Beacons.   £40

Tresaith (Cardiganshire)   **Glandawr Manor**   (01239) 810197
*A secluded Georgian house, close to the coast, with good straightforward
cooking and simply decorated rooms.*   £57

Tywyn (Caernarfonshire & Merionethshire)   **Ty Mawr**   (01654) 710507
*A small guesthouse in a modern barn conversion in an exceptionally peaceful
setting.*   £40

Whitebrook (Monmouthshire)   **The Crown at Whitebrook**
(01600) 860254
*Splendid restaurant, with a dozen rooms, in a hidden valley close to the River
Wye.*   £80

Wrexham (Wrexham)   **Llwyn Onn Hall**   Cefn Road   (01978) 261225
*An attractive Georgian house with pleasantly decorated bedrooms and a
popular restaurant.*   £74

Writing reports

Help us to keep this *Guide* as up-to-date, as vivid and as useful to others as possible by telling us about any hotels you stay at in Britain, whether or not they appear in this *Guide*. Write a letter if you would prefer, and send brochures or other material too. Or send your reports by e-mail to: "guidereports@which.co.uk".

Reports need not be long: just a few pithy sentences will help us sort out the best from the rest. Please comment on any of the following: the welcome, the quality of your room and of the housekeeping, points of interest about public rooms and the garden as well as any special facilities, aspects of service throughout your stay, and details of meals eaten.

In order to guard our independence we ask that reports be unsolicited by the hotelier and that you have no personal connection with the hotel.

Access for disabled visitors

Below we list hotels in the main section which we believe have access for guests in wheelchairs. To help hoteliers reply to our questionnaire we pointed out that the hotel entrance must be at least 80cm wide and passages at least 120cm wide (in accordance with RADAR recommendations) in order to be suitable. Nevertheless, we strongly advise you to confirm before booking that the hotel can supply your particular requirements.

Those hotels which told us that they have bedrooms specially adapted for wheelchair users are marked with a ‡ symbol.

London

Bryanston Court
Cannizaro House
The Capital
Concorde Hotel
The Connaught
Covent Garden Hotel
Durrants Hotel
The Goring
L'Hotel
The Leonard‡
Park Lane Hotel‡
The Savoy‡

England

Aldeburgh, Uplands Hotel‡
Alderminster, Ettington Park‡
Alton, Alton Towers Hotel‡
Ambleside, Drunken Duck Inn
Ambleside, Rothay Manor‡
Apuldram, Crouchers Bottom‡
Arrathorne, Elmfield Country House‡
Ashbourne, Callow Hall‡
Ashburton, Holne Chase‡
Aspley Guise, Moore Place Hotel
Aston Clinton, Bell Inn
Aylesbury, Hartwell House‡
Balsall Common, Haigs Hotel
Bassenthwaite Lake, Pheasant Inn
Bathford, Old School House
Battle, Powdermills‡
Bepton, Park House‡
Bibury, The Swan
Birch Vale, Waltzing Weasel
Blackwell, Blackwell Grange‡
Bolton Abbey, Devonshire Arms‡
Bosham, The Millstream

Boughton Lees, Eastwell Manor
Bournemouth, Langtry Manor
Bovey Tracey, Edgemoor‡
Bowness-on-Windermere, Lindeth Fell‡
Bowness-on-Windermere, Linthwaite
    House
Bradford, Victoria Hotel‡
Brampton, Farlam Hall
Broadway, Lygon Arms
Broxted, Whitehall
Burnham Market, Hoste Arms‡
Bury St Edmunds, Ravenwood Hall
Carbis Bay, Boskerris Hotel
Castle Ashby, Falcon Hotel‡
Castle Combe, Manor House Hotel
Chagford, Easton Court
Chilgrove, Forge Cottage‡
Chipperfield, Two Brewers
Colerne, Lucknam Park
Coreley, Corndene‡
Corse Lawn, Corse Lawn Hotel
Cranford, Dairy Farm
Crookham, Coach House at Crookham‡
Dorchester, Casterbridge Hotel
Dulverton, Carnarvon Arms
Easton Grey, Whatley Manor
East Portlemouth, Gara Rock
Edith Weston, Normanton Park
Eversholt, Summer Lodge‡
Exeter, Southgate Hotel‡
Falmouth, Penmere Manor
Farnham, Museum Hotel
Ford, White Hart
Gateshead, Eslington Villa
Gillingham, Stock Hill House
Goathland, Mallyan Spout

Grange-in-Borrowdale, Borrowdale Gates
Grange-over-Sands, Graythwaite Manor
Great Longstone, Croft Country House‡
Guildford, Angel Hotel‡
Hadley Wood, West Lodge Park‡
Halifax, Holdsworth House‡
Hambleton, Hambleton Hall
Harome, Pheasant Hotel‡
Hassop, Hassop Hall
Hawkridge, Tarr Steps
Hawkshead, Queen's Head
Haytor, Bel Alp House
Hilltop, Wenlock Edge Inn
Hinton Charterhouse, Homewood Park‡
Horley, Langshott Manor‡
Horton, Northill House‡
Ipswich, Belstead Brook Hotel‡
Isley Walton, Park Farmhouse‡
Kemerton, Upper Court‡
Kettlewell, Langcliffe Country
    Guesthouse‡
Kingham, Mill House
Lacock, At the Sign of the Angel
Langho, Northcote Manor‡
Lavenham, Angel Hotel
Leeds, 42 The Calls‡
Lewdown, Lewtrenchard Manor
Longhorsley, Linden Hall‡
Lower Beeding, South Lodge‡
Lowestoft, Ivy House Farm‡
Lyme Regis, Alexandra Hotel
Madeley, Madeley Court Hotel‡
Malmesbury, Old Bell
Malvern Wells, The Old Vicarage
Manchester, Holiday Inn Crowne Plaza‡
Manchester, Victoria & Albert Hotel‡
Martinhoe, Old Rectory
Meldreth, Chiswick House
Meriden, Forest of Arden‡
Midhurst, Angel Hotel‡
Minehead, Periton Park Hotel‡
Mithian, Rose-in-Vale‡
Mollington, Crabwall Manor
Mosedale, Mosedale House‡
Motcombe, Coppleridge Inn‡
Moulsford, Beetle & Wedge
Mullion, Polurrian Hotel‡
Needham Market, Pipps Ford‡
Newcastle upon Tyne, The Copthorne‡
New Milton, Chewton Glen‡

Newquay, Headland Hotel
Nidd, Nidd Hall
Northampton, Swallow Hotel‡
Nottingham, Rutland Square Hotel‡
Nunnington, Ryedale Lodge‡
Oakham, Barnsdale Lodge‡
Oxford, Randolph Hotel‡
Parracombe, Heddon's Gate Hotel
Penrith, North Lakes Hotel‡
Peterstow, Peterstow Country House
Prestbury, White Horse Manor
Quorn, Quorn Country Hotel‡
Ravenstonedale, Black Swan‡
Ravenstonedale, The Fat Lamb‡
Redmile, Peacock Farm‡
Rhydycroesau, Pen-y-Dyffryn Hall‡
Ripley, Boar's Head‡
Romaldkirk, Rose and Crown
Ruan High Lanes, Hundred House Hotel
Sandiway, Nunsmere Hall
Sandringham, Park House‡
Seaton Burn, Horton Grange
Sedbusk, Stone House
Shrewsbury, Albright Hussey‡
Shurdington, The Greenway‡
Sidmouth, Hotel Riviera‡
Southwold, The Swan‡
Sparsholt, Lainston House
Stapleford, Stapleford Park
Stonor, Stonor Arms‡
Sturminster Newton, Plumber Manor
Sutton Coldfield, New Hall‡
Taunton, Castle Hotel
Tavistock, Horn of Plenty
Tenterden, Little Silver‡
Tetbury, Calcot Manor
Titchwell, Titchwell Manor‡
Towersey, Upper Green Farm‡
Tresco, Island Hotel
Trowbridge, Old Manor
Truro, Alverton Manor‡
Uckfield, Horsted Place
Uffington, The Craven‡
Veryan, Nare Hotel‡
Wansford, Haycock Hotel‡
Wareham, Priory Hotel
Weedon, Crossroads‡
Wells, Swan Hotel
Welwyn Garden City, Tewin Bury
    Farmhouse‡

Widegates, Coombe Farm
Wimborne Minster, Beechleas
Winchester, Hotel du Vin & Bistro‡
Windermere, Gilpin Lodge‡
Woolstone, Old Rectory
Woolton Hill, Hollington House
Worfield, Old Vicarage‡
Wye, Wife of Bath

Scotland
Aberfeldy, Farleyer House Hotel‡
Aberfeldy, Guinach House
Arduaine, Loch Melfort Hotel
Auchterarder, Gleneagles‡
Ballater, Stakis Royal Deeside
Ballindalloch, Delnashaugh Inn
Banchory, Raemoir House
Blairgowrie, Kinloch House‡
Callander, Roman Camp‡
Conon Bridge, Kinkell House‡
Crinan, Crinan Hotel‡
Drumnadrochit, Polmaily House‡
Dunkeld, Kinnaird‡
Eriska, Isle of Eriska‡
Glasgow, Malmaison
Inverness, Dunain Park‡
Kelso, Sunlaws House‡
Kentallen, Holly Tree‡
Kirkwall, Foveran Hotel
Lochinver, Inver Lodge
Markinch, Balbirnie House‡
Maryculter, Maryculter House
Muir of Ord, Dower House

Peat Inn, Peat Inn‡
Port Appin, Airds Hotel
St Andrews, Old Course Hotel‡
St Andrews, Rufflets‡
St Fillans, Four Seasons Hotel
Spean Bridge, Old Pines‡
Staffin, Flodigarry Country House‡
Thurso, Forss House‡
Troon, Lochgreen House‡
Turnberry, Turnberry Hotel‡
Walls, Burrastow House‡

Wales
Abergavenny, Llanwenarth House
Abersoch, Porth Tocyn Hotel
Benllech, Bryn Meirion‡
Capel Coch, Tre-Ysgawen Hall
Glynarthen, Penbontbren Farm‡
Hay-on-Wye, Old Black Lion
Lamphey, Court Hotel
Llanarmon Dyffryn Ceiriog, West Arms
    Hotel‡
Llanddeiniolen, Ty'n Rhos‡
Llangammarch Wells, Lake Country
    House
Llangollen, Bryn Howell‡
Llangollen, Gales
Milebrook, Milebrook House‡
Nantgwynant, Pen-y-gwryd Hotel‡
Penally, Penally Abbey
Penmaenpool, George III Hotel
Talsarnau, Maes-y-Neuadd

Index

All entries are indexed below, including those in the Visitors' Book. An asterisk indicates a new entry.

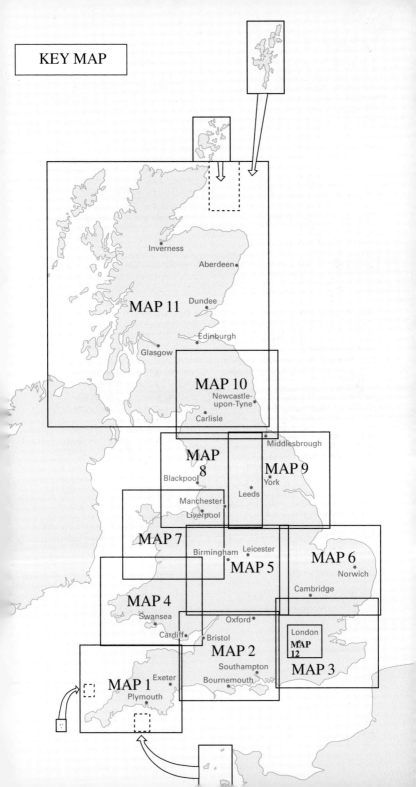

KEY MAP

MAP 11

Inverness

Aberdeen

Dundee

Edinburgh

Glasgow

MAP 10

Newcastle-upon-Tyne

Carlisle

Middlesbrough

MAP
8

MAP 9

Blackpool

York

Manchester

Leeds

Liverpool

MAP 7

Birmingham

Leicester

MAP 6

MAP 5

Norwich

Cambridge

MAP 4

Swansea

Oxford

Cardiff

Bristol

London

MAP 12

MAP 2

MAP 3

Southampton

Bournemouth

MAP 1

Exeter

Plymouth

MAP 1

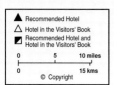

- ▲ Recommended Hotel
- △ Hotel in the Visitors' Book
- ◪ Recommended Hotel and Hotel in the Visitors' Book

0 — 5 — 10 miles
0 — 15 kms
© Copyright

Isles of Scilly
28 miles WSW of Land's End

Bryher △   ▲ St Martin's
▲ Tresco
Hugh Town ●   ▲ St Mary's

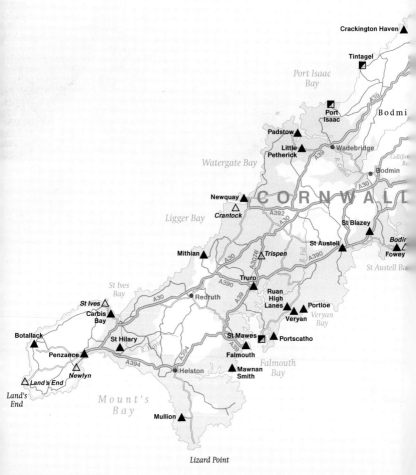

Lundy Island

Bude Bay

Crackington Haven ▲

Tintagel ◪

Port Isaac Bay

Port Isaac ◪

Bodmi

Padstow ▲

Little Petherick ▲

Wadebridge ●

Watergate Bay

R. Camel

Collifor
Ra

Bodmin ●

Newquay ▲

Crantock △

CORNWALL

Ligger Bay

St Blazey ▲

Bodir

St Austell ▲

Fowey △

Mithian ▲

Trispen △

St Austell Ba

Truro ▲

Ruan High Lanes ▲   Portloe ▲

St Ives Bay

St Ives △

Veryan ▲   *Veryan Bay*

Carbis Bay ▲

Redruth ●

St Hilary ▲

St Mawes ▲   ◪ Portscatho

Botallack ▲

Penzance ▲

Newlyn △

Falmouth ▲

Falmouth Bay

△ Land's End

Mawnan Smith ▲

Land's End

Mount's Bay

Helston ●

Mullion ▲

Lizard Point

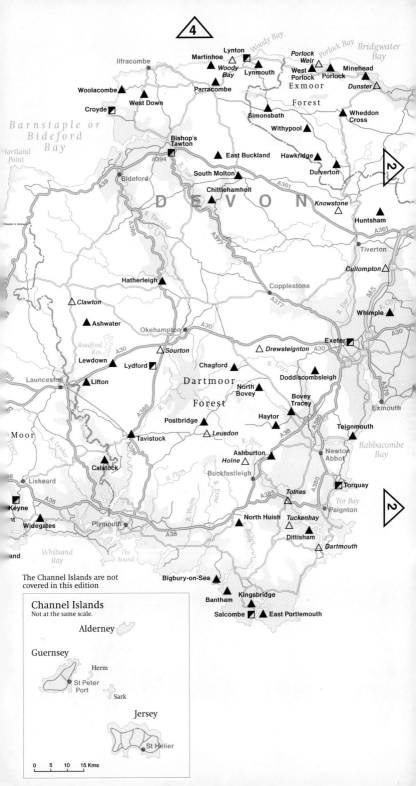

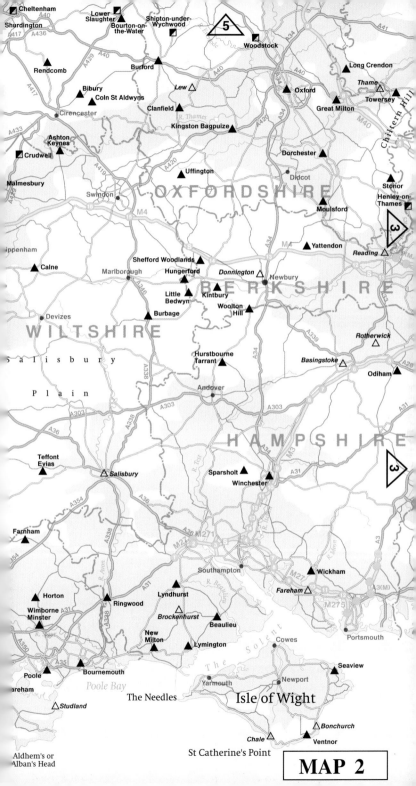

MAP 2

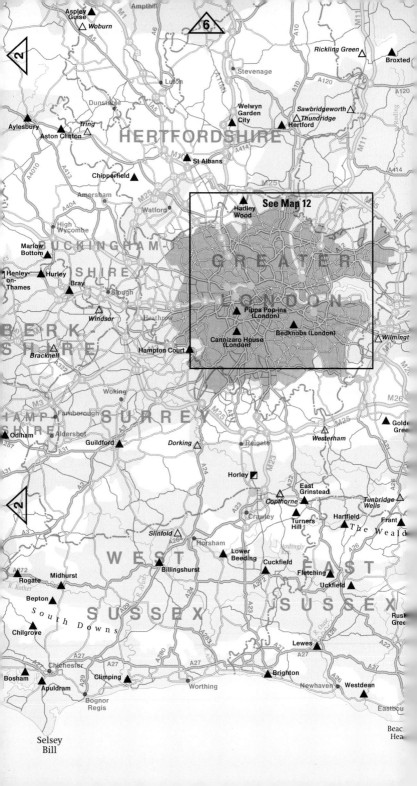

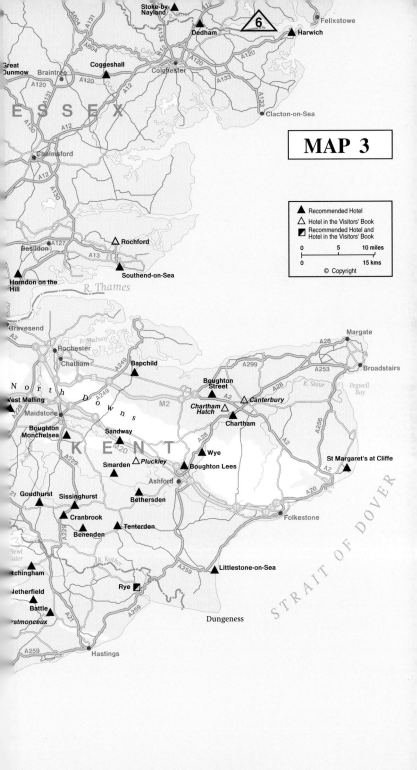

MAP 3

▲ Recommended Hotel
△ Hotel in the Visitors' Book
◪ Recommended Hotel and
  Hotel in the Visitors' Book

| 0 | | 5 | | 10 miles |
| 0 | | | 15 kms |

© Copyright

MAP 4

▲ Recommended Hotel
△ Hotel in the Visitors' Book
◨ Recommended Hotel and
   Hotel in the Visitors' Book

0   5   10 miles
0   15 kms
© Copyright

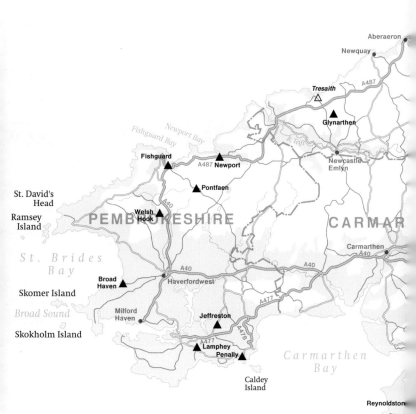

CARDIGAN

BAY

Aberaeron

Newquay

Tresaith △

▲ Glynarthen

Newport Bay

Fishguard Bay

▲ Fishguard   A487 ▲ Newport

R Teifi

Newcastle
Emlyn

▲ Pontfaen

St. David's
Head

▲ Welsh
Hook

PEMBROKESHIRE   **CARMAR**

Ramsey
Island

Carmarthen
A40

*St. Brides
Bay*

A40   Haverfordwest   A40

Skomer Island

▲ Broad
Haven

Broad Sound

Milford
Haven

A477

Skokholm Island

▲ Jeffreston

A477

▲ Lamphey
Penally ▲

*Carmarthen
Bay*

Caldey
Island

Reynoldston

BRISTOL

MAP 5

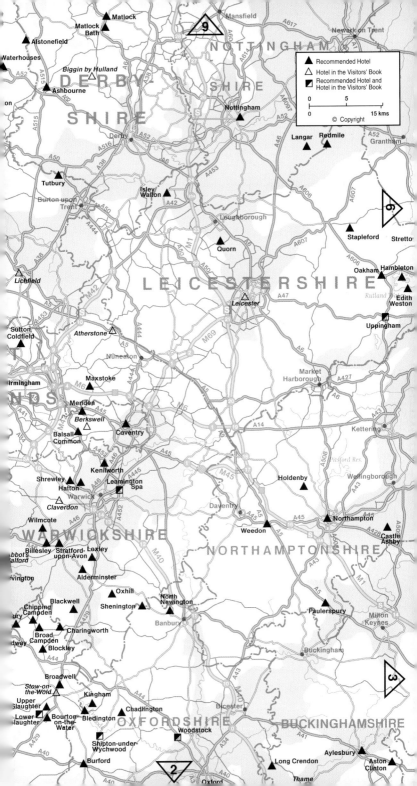

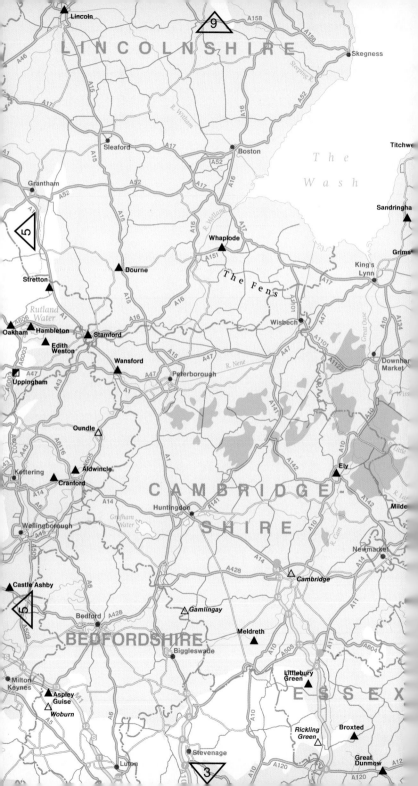

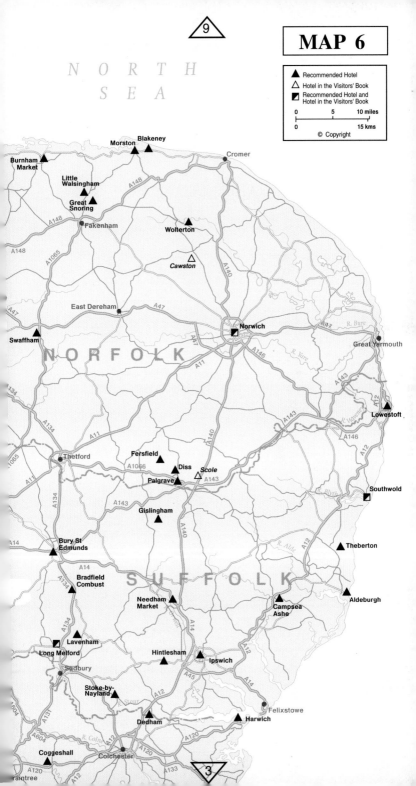

MAP 7

Legend:
- ▲ Recommended Hotel
- △ Hotel in the Visitors' Book
- ◨ Recommended Hotel and Hotel in the Visitors' Book

0 — 5 — 10 miles
0 — 15 kms
© Copyright

IRISH

SEA

Holyhead Bay

Llyn Alaw

Anglesey

▲ Benllech

Red Wharf Bay

Conwy Bay

Holyhead

Holy Island

▲ Capel Coch

ANGLESEY

▲ Beaumaris

A5

Bangor

A55

▲ Llandudno
Colwyn B.
▲ Conwy
▲ Llansanffraid Glan Conwy

Menai Strait

A487

Fell Fras
942

ABERC
CO

Caernarfon

▲ Llanddeiniolen

Carnedd Llywelyn
1044

A5

Glyder Fawr
999

Caernarfon Bay

1085
Snowdon

872
Carnedd Moel-siabod

A470

▲ Ca
Gar

▲ Beddgelert
▲ Nantgwynant

CAERNARFONSHIRE

A487

Porthmadog

Lleyn Peninsula

▲ Criccieth

▲ Portmeirion
▲ Talsarnau

MERIONETHS

Tremadog Bay

▲ Harlech

A470

▲ Abersoch

Bardsey Sound

Bardsey Island

▲ Ganllwyd
▲ Llanfachreth

Aran Be
884
Aran Faw

Bontddu
△

▲ Llanaber

▲ Penmaenpool
Dolgellau

Barmouth

Cader Idris
893 ▲

A494

◨ Talyllyn

△ *Tywyn*

Macynlleth

▲ Aberdovey
▲ Eglwysfach

A48

CARDIGAN

BAY

A487

▲ Aberystwyth

A44

CARDIGANSHIRE

A487

▽ 4

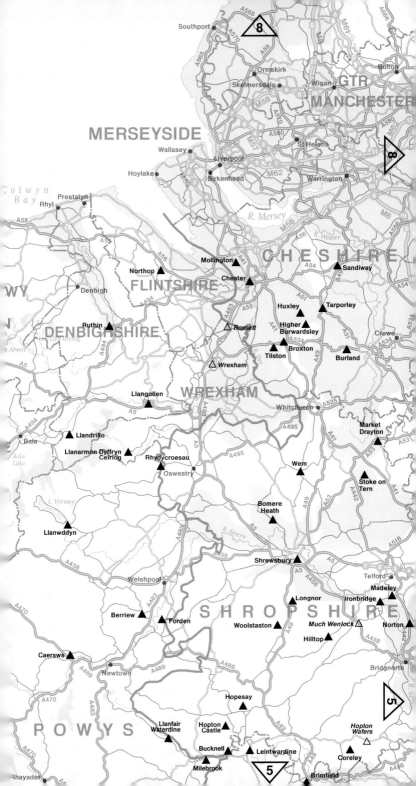

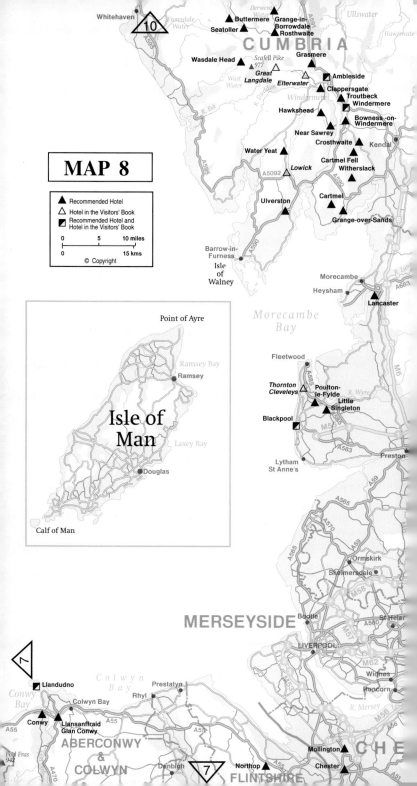

MAP 8

▲ Recommended Hotel
△ Hotel in the Visitors' Book
◩ Recommended Hotel and
Hotel in the Visitors' Book

| 0 | 5 | 10 miles |
| 0 | | 15 kms |

© Copyright

Whitehaven

⑩

Ennerdale Water
Derwent Water

▲ Buttermere
Grange-in-
Borrowdale
Rosthwaite
▲ Seatoller

CUMBRIA

Ullswater

Hawyswater

▲ Wasdale Head

Scafell Pike
977
△
Great
Langdale

West Water

R. Duddon

R. Esk

Grasmere ▲

◩ Ambleside
▲ Clappersgate
Elterwater ▲
Troutbeck ▲
◩ Windermere
Windermere

▲ Hawkshead

Bowness-on-
Windermere ◩

▲ Near Sawrey
Crosthwaite ▲
Kendal

▲ Water Yeat
Cartmel Fell ▲
Witherslack ▲

A5092
△ *Lowick*

A595

Ulverston ▲

Cartmel ▲
Grange-over-Sands ▲

Barrow-in-
Furness
Isle
of
Walney

A590

Morecambe
Heysham

Morecambe
Bay

R. Lune
M6

Lancaster ▲
A683

Fleetwood

Thornton
Cleveleys △
Poulton-
le-Fylde ▲
Little
Singleton
R. Wyre

Blackpool ◩

M55
A585
A583
Preston

Point of Ayre

Ramsey Bay
Ramsey

Isle of
Man

Laxey Bay

Douglas

Calf of Man

Lytham
St Anne's

A59

A565

Ormskirk

Skelmersdale

M58

MERSEYSIDE
Bootle
St Helens
A580

LIVERPOOL
M62
Widnes
M57
Runcorn
R. Mersey
M56

⑦

Colwyn
Bay
Llandudno ◩
Colwyn Bay
Prestatyn
Rhyl

Conwy
Bay

Conwy ▲
Llansanffraid
Glan Conwy ▲

A55

ABERCONWY
&
COLWYN

A470

A55

Denbigh

⑦

Northop ▲

FLINTSHIRE

Mollington ▲

Chester ▲

CHE

A51

A41

Foel Fras
942

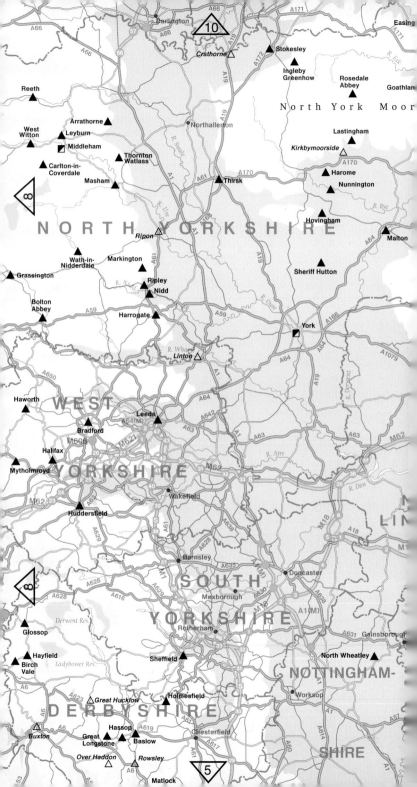

MAP 9

▲ Recommended Hotel
△ Hotel in the Visitors' Book
◩ Recommended Hotel and
   Hotel in the Visitors' Book

0   5   10 miles
0   15 kms
© Copyright

Whitby

A171

▲ Scarborough

A170

A64

▲ Filey

△
Hunmanby

A65

Flamborough ▲
           Flamborough Head

Bridlington

*B r i d l i n g t o n
      B a y*

A166

A165

Y o r k s h i r e   W o l d s

A63

**EAST RIDING
OF YORKSHIRE**

A1035

A1079   A165

△
Walkington

A63

**KINGSTON
UPON HULL**

● Kingston
  upon Hull

R. Humber

Barton-upon-Humber

▲ nteringham

A15

A160

H

NSHIRE

cunthorpe

M180

A18

● Grimsby   Spurn Head

A173   A46   **N.E.
           LINCOLNSHIRE**

A18

A46

▲ Swinhope

A1103

● Louth

A631

A15

A46   *T h e   W o l d s*

A16

A158

A158

▲ Lincoln   **L I N C O L N S H I R E**

A158

● Skegness

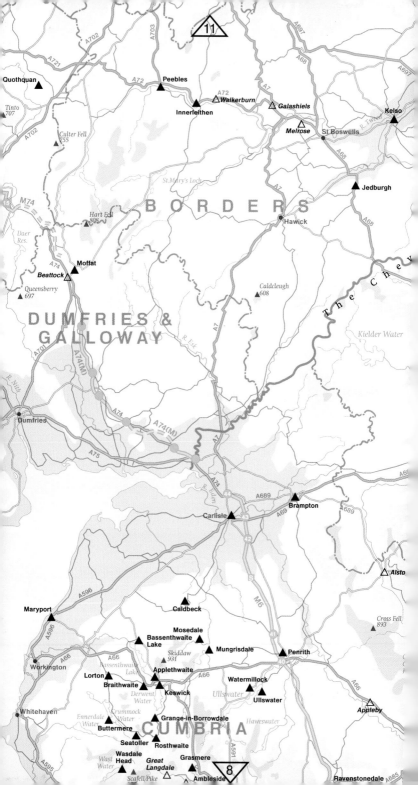

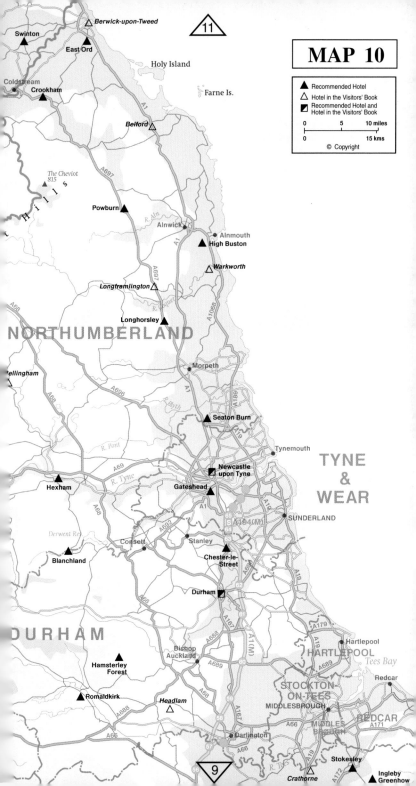

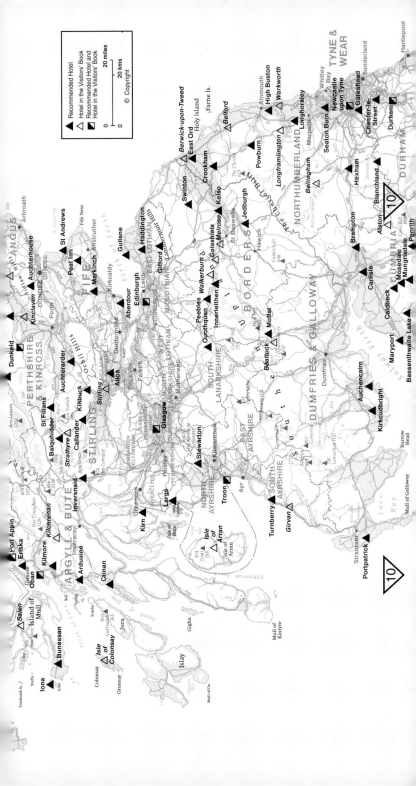

Central London

MAP 12

▲ Recommended Hotel
△ Hotel in the Visitors' Book

| 0 | 440 | 880 yds |
| 0 | | 800m |

© Copyright

To: The Editor, *The Which? Hotel Guide*, FREEPOST,
2 Marylebone Road, London NW1 1YN

Name of hotel

Address

I visited this hotel on:

My report is:

(Continued overleaf)

Reports received up to May 1997 will be used in the research of the 1998 edition.

I am not connected in any way with the management or proprietor of this hotel.

_____

My name is:
_____

Address:
_____

Report form

To: The Editor, *The Which? Hotel Guide*, FREEPOST,
2 Marylebone Road, London NW1 1YN

Name of hotel
_____

Address
_____

I visited this hotel on:
_____

My report is:

(Continued overleaf)

Reports received up to May 1997 will be used in the
research of the 1998 edition.
  I am not connected in any way with the management
or proprietor of this hotel.

_____

My name is:

_____

Address:

_____

Report form

To: The Editor, *The Which? Hotel Guide*, FREEPOST,
2 Marylebone Road, London NW1 1YN

Name of hotel

Address

I visited this hotel on:

My report is:

(Continued overleaf)

Reports received up to May 1997 will be used in the research of the 1998 edition.

I am not connected in any way with the management or proprietor of this hotel.

My name is:

Address: